Intellectual Property Law for Engineers, Scientists, and Entrepreneurs

Intellectual Property Law for Engineers, Scientists, and Entrepreneurs

SECOND EDITION

Howard B. Rockman

Adjunct Professor of Engineering
University of Illinois at Chicago, USA

Adjunct Professor of Engineering
Northwestern University, Illinois, USA

Patent Clinic Faculty Supervisor
John Marshall Law School, Chicago, USA

Intellectual Property Attorney
Rockman, Videbeck & O'Connor
Oakbrook Terrace, Illinois, USA

A UIC/Novellus Systems Endeavor

IEEE PRESS

WILEY

Published by John Wiley & Sons, Inc., Hoboken, New Jersey.
Published simultaneously in Canada

Library of Congress Cataloging-in-Publication Data is available.

Hardback: 9781119381976

Printed in the United States of America

10 9 8 7 6 5 4 3 2 1

“Ingenuity should receive a liberal encouragement.”

Thomas Jefferson
(*V Writings of Thomas Jefferson*, pp. 75–76)

“The first thing we do, let’s kill all the lawyers.”

William Shakespeare
(2 Henry VI, Act IV, Scene II)

Contents

Foreword

The first edition of the book *Intellectual Property Law for Engineers and Scientists* by Howard B. Rockman was adopted as a textbook for an online graduate-level course that Mr. Rockman has taught for almost two decades in the College of Engineering of the University of Illinois at Chicago. That book proved to be very popular among professionals interested in intellectual property law at the international level.

Mr. Rockman has now updated the material in his book to incorporate changes in patent law that have occurred during the past 15 years. I am sure that this second edition will be as well received as the first one.

Piegiorgio L. E. Uslenghi, Ph.D.
Distinguished Professor Emeritus
College of Engineering
University of Illinois at Chicago

Foreword to the First Edition

A few years ago, I contacted Mr. Howard B. Rockman, a patent attorney, and asked him to develop a graduate-level course in Engineering Law to be offered on the Internet to all students enrolled in our Master of Engineering web-based degree program, as well as to senior undergraduates in all fields of engineering. That course was very successful, and a follow-up course in Intellectual Property Law quickly followed. It soon became clear that no satisfactory textbook existed for this second course, hence I convinced Mr. Rockman to write such a textbook and put him in touch with the publications office of the Institute of Electrical and Electronics Engineers, Inc. (IEEE).

The IEEE Press and John Wiley & Sons decided to publish Mr. Rockman's manuscript, whose first edition is here presented to all practicing and student engineers and scientists who have an interest in intellectual property. I am convinced that this timely book will be very well received and will be very useful to both technical and legal personnel not only in the United States, but worldwide.

Piergiorgio L. E. Uslenghi, Ph.D.
Professor and Associate Dean
College of Engineering
University of Illinois at Chicago

Preface

THE PROPER PERSPECTIVE—A FABLE

After a long and productive life on earth, an engineer arrived at the gates of heaven. The gatekeeper scanned through the book of expected arrivals, and then advised the engineer that there was a mistake and that he was supposed to go to the "other place." The engineer was directed by the gatekeeper to a long escalator, and told to take the escalator all the way down, where he would be greeted by someone in a red suit. The engineer did what he was told, and ended up in Hades.

After being in Hades for a short while, the engineer noticed that it was uncomfortably hot. Being that he had been a heating, ventilating, and air conditioning (HVAC) engineer on earth, he began assembling various parts of scrap materials lying around, and, in a matter of 3 weeks, had constructed and was operating an air conditioning system throughout Hades. A week later, he had completed a cold water delivery system. Shortly thereafter, God and the devil were on the phone for their monthly status conference call, and the devil stated: "You wouldn't believe! We have an engineer down here, of all people. He's installed air conditioning and cold water down here; he's done great things. It's almost livable down here now." God replied: "You have an engineer down there? That's a horrible mistake! You have to send him up here right away!"

"No!" said the devil. "He's doing wonderful things down here, and I love him a lot!"

God said: "You send him up here right away!"

"No!" retorted the devil.

"You send him up here immediately, or I'll sue you," responded God.

The devil said: "You're bluffing."

"What do you mean, I'm bluffing!" said God.

The devil replied: "Where are you going to get a lawyer?"

OVERTURE

Having thus established the appropriate relationship between technology and the law, the material in this second edition pertains to the protection afforded by the law to the ideas, creations, and inventions of engineers, scientists, entrepreneurs, and others covered by the umbrella term "technology professionals." With technological advancements moving forward today at what appears to be an exponential rate, the need to transform intangible novel ideas into tangible, protectable assets has increased. Where, in the past, the words "patent" or "copyright" only rarely appeared in the daily newspapers, today the popular press is repeatedly reporting news items regarding the effect of intellectual property protection in our everyday lives. For example, pharmaceuticals and patents have become a global issue. Also, each time you install a new program on your computer, or open the shrink wrap on a package containing software, you must "agree" to respect the intellectual property rights of the creator of the software.

The fields of science and engineering have, and always have had, a direct correlation to the work of intellectual property attorneys and agents throughout the world. In case you are wondering, the term "intellectual property attorney" encompasses all of us who toil in the areas of patent, copyright, trade secret, trademark, and unfair competition law, and their related fields, as included in this text. For example, I have been counseling and working with engineers, scientists, and other creative types for over 50 years, and, throughout this period, I have constantly tread along the interface between technology and the law that, for the most part, defines "intellectual property creation and protection."

The one thing that has been evident to me throughout my practice is that the engineers and scientists I have worked with have high levels of education and experience in the technology field. However, practically, each time I have advised an inventor or creator of the steps to be taken to protect their new invention or novel creation, I have found myself describing the relevant law to them from the beginning. Since an inventor or creator may actually lose rights in their intellectual property before deciding whether to obtain protection or not, I came to an understanding that technology professionals should at least have a handy resource available to obtain general knowledge about intellectual property law before they complete their inventions and creations, so as to avoid taking steps that would cause the loss of all or mostly all intellectual property rights before they have the opportunity to reap the rewards of their creative work.

As an adjunct faculty professor at the College of Engineering of the University of Illinois at Chicago (UIC), I prepared a course in 2002 entitled "Intellectual Property Law for Engineers and Scientists," which was, and still is, taught as part of the Master of Engineering degree program offered totally over the Internet. The course comprises 15 weekly lectures of 1–1.5-hour duration. The lectures are delivered orally to students who enroll in the course as a voiceover to a slide presentation depicting highlights of each lecture. In addition, the entirety of each lecture is posted on our web site, on a week-by-week basis, and can be downloaded, printed, and used to follow the audio presentation. My ad libs, some anecdotes, and poor attempts at humor forming the audio broadcast are not included in the written text. From the assignment answers submitted by the students, I can perceive a keen interest in the subjects covered in our course, and enrollment in the course keeps increasing.

Professor George Uslenghi, Associate Dean of the College of Engineering at UIC, suggested that the series of lectures that I prepared, with augmentation, be prepared as a draft manuscript and submitted for publication. Professor Uslenghi determined that a proper background in intellectual property modalities was becoming increasingly important for an engineer and scientist to have an awareness of. To make a long story into a saga, the result of the professor's suggestion was the first edition of this text, published in 2004.

The publisher of this text asked me recently to prepare a second edition to update the information in the first edition, as necessary, to bring newly developed information about intellectual property law to you, the reader. For example, since 2004, U.S. Patent Law has been significantly amended by passage of the American Invents Act (AIA) in 2011, most importantly to grant patent rights to the first to file a patent application, and not the first to invent, when two or more inventors or groups of inventors have nearly simultaneously filed patent applications covering the same or similar inventions.

In addition, the applicable law governing the patent eligibility of computer-related and life science inventions has been modified radically in recent years as a result of court decisions. Several other recent nuances in patent law are also updated and explained in this second edition, such as new procedures allowing others to challenge the issuance of a patent before the U.S. Patent and Trademark Office (USPTO), and thus avoiding litigation in the federal courts.

In addition, the U.S. Congress, in 2016, enacted the Federal Defend Trade Secrets Act, which provides additional remedies for those whose trade secrets or confidential information have been misappropriated by someone else, such as a former employee. This new federal law now runs parallel to the various state statutory and common law trade secret laws protecting trade secrets. Also, this second edition includes expanded materials regarding the commercialization and management of intellectual property assets, technology transfer, and enforcement of intellectual property rights.

This text was not written to be read from cover to cover in one sitting. The table of contents and index have been carefully crafted to allow you, the reader, to go directly to the information you need regarding a specific project in which you are involved. For example, I expect electrical and mechanical engineers to avoid the chapter on biotechnology.

A major purpose of this text is to enable you, as an inventor or creator, to efficiently interface with an intellectual property attorney, for example, and provide him or her with information enabling you to obtain the maximum protection for your invention or creation. On the other side of the coin, the text material will aid you and your intellectual property attorney to take steps to ensure that your invention or creation does not infringe upon the intellectual property rights of others. The last thing in the world you want is to invite a lawsuit when you introduce your new product or process to the world.

Included in this text are patent, copyright, trade secret, mask work, trademark, and cybersquatting legal and procedural principles, as well as how to properly use the new vehicles of intellectual property protection for novel software, biotech, and business method inventions. Also, this text covers trademark protection for domain names, and other ancillary matters that fall within the genre of intellectual property protection.

The material in the pages that follow also provides you with information regarding employment contracts as they relate to an assignment of intellectual property rights to an employer, the concepts of confidentiality of proprietary information, and covenants not to compete following a change in employment. With increasing movement between employment positions, typical covenants not to compete in employment contracts are receiving closer scrutiny by the courts, and by state legislatures.

By no means is this text intended to transform you into an intellectual property attorney, or to do the work of one. The purpose is to provide you with knowledge of a very arcane, but important, adjunct to the technology professions, that of the protection of the technology you develop, and the steps necessary to prevent stepping on the intellectual property "toes" of others.

Between each of the chapters of this second edition, I have placed essays on famous and noteworthy inventors and their inventions, followed by a copy of the first page of patents resulting from these inventors' efforts. A complete copy of each patent may be obtained from the USPTO website (http://patft.uspto.gov/netahtml/srchnum.htm). The feedback I received from the first edition included comments that students who used the text for the course work enjoyed the inventor and invention essays interspersed between the chapters of the book. Taking these comments to heart, this second edition includes several additional essays of inventors and inventions I considered interesting. I hope you find these essays both interesting and informative. I found the research devoted to these historical incidents to be fascinating, particularly the differences between those who developed their inventions through diligent periods of trial and error, and others whose inventions resulted from acts of serendipity.

The content of this text does not provide everything there is to know about intellectual property protection. Such a text would be too thick to be mobile. In covering each of the subjects, I have taken you, the reader, to the point where your next step will be to consult with a competent intellectual property law professional to provide you with the detailed information necessary to protect the results of your intellectual endeavors. Keep in mind that neither I nor the publishers of this text are offering or rendering legal advice, or other professional services, to the reader. Also, since the law on any given subject changes constantly, it is important that you seek the advice of a competent intellectual property lawyer or agent to ensure that you receive the most updated advice available.

This text was not prepared to be completely read at one sitting. My purpose is to provide selected information on the several subjects addressed in the following pages that are of interest at any given moment in time, by consulting the index. Most importantly, the information in this text does not constitute legal advice. It is highly recommended that if you need advice as to a specific problem or question that you are facing, a qualified intellectual property law professional should be contacted.

Howard B. Rockman
rockman@rvoiplaw.com

Acknowledgments

I am greatly indebted to many people and organizations that assisted me in the preparation and production of this second edition. My thanks go out to each, and the order in which their names appear is not indicative of the degree of my appreciation. You were all awesome.

The publishers—IEEE Press and John Wiley & Sons—are to be commended for allowing me to present the intellectual property information in this work to the engineering, scientific, and entrepreneurial community. It is my fervent desire that, by bringing this material to those who generate inventions and creative works, a greater awareness will be created on how the worldwide intellectual property laws work to advance technology, science, and the creative arts, leading to more developments reaching the light of day. To Mary Hatcher, Sarah Keegan, Nicole Hanley, and Peter Mitchell of IEEE Press and John Wiley & Sons, thank you for your guidance throughout the publication process.

A large measure of my appreciation goes to George Uslenghi, PhD, Professor and Associate Dean, College of Engineering, University of Illinois at Chicago (UIC), for creating the online Master of Engineering program at UIC, where my two courses, "Engineering Law" and "Intellectual Property Law for Engineers and Scientists," are taught to students worldwide over the Internet. It is the latter of these two courses that provided the foundation for the first and second editions of this work, and it was Prof. Uslenghi who initially shepherded this project through the IEEE Publications Committee. My thanks also extend to Carolyn C. Williams, the administrator of the Masters of Engineering program at UIC, who has been of extraordinary assistance in my interface with academia, and who seeks only chocolates as a reward.

My thanks also go out to two fine attorneys who assisted me in the preparation of the biotechnology patent and cybersquatting chapters of this text, Krista Vink Vinegas (krista.vinegas@morganlewis.com) and Peter Berk (pberk@fvldlaw.com). In addition, U.K. patent attorney James Leach (james.leach@mewburn.com), a member of the Mewburn Ellis firm, contributed mightily to the portion of this text on the patent eligibility of computer-related inventions in Europe. Credit is also due to Richard Gruner (7gruner@jmls.edu), former director, Center for Intellectual Property, John Marshall Law School, Chicago, Illinois, for his contributions to the coverage of international intellectual property creation, protection, and enforcement. My law partner, Mercedes V. O'Connor, deserves the highest accolades for getting me through the computer-related material included in this text. My having gone through engineering school with only a slide rule, since computers were not available then, her assistance was invaluable.

My thanks also go out to William T. McGrath, an excellent copyright law attorney with the Chicago law firm of Davis and McGrath, who provided guidance to me on the intricacies of copyright law, including the Digital Millennium Copyright Act (DMCA). Bill has taught copyright law at John Marshall Law School for many years, and I have the utmost respect for his wisdom in the mysterious ways of copyright law.

This text could not have been produced without the able assistance of Sharen Lahti and Susan Kilburg. Without them, the pages of this work may have been chiseled on stone tablets.

Hearty thanks also are due to the National Inventors Hall of Fame, whose website provided the starting point for my idea to include brief biographies of inventors and inventions between the chapters of both the first and second editions of this text. I also want to thank all of the authors of the many research materials given attribution in my bibliographies. The hardest part of preparing the inventors and inventions essays was deciding which fascinating facts about these enlightened individuals had to be omitted for the sake of brevity. My thanks also extend to Anthony Loder, son of famed actress/inventor Hedy Lamarr, for furnishing me with first-hand knowledge about his mother's invention of what is known today as *spread spectrum technology*.

For assistance in researching the history of the Wright Brothers, my appreciation is extended to Ronald C. Young, a local historian from Blue Island, Illinois. My essay on Nikola Tesla would not have been possible without the kind cooperation of the wonderful people at the Nikola Tesla Museum, Belgrade, Serbia, and the Antique Wireless Association of the United States. Also, my hand is extended to Paul Schatzkin for furnishing me with invaluable documentation on the Farnsworth–Zworykin patent battle.

Maxwell Rockman deserves a well-earned thank you for conducting the preliminary research for the inventors and inventions essays in the first edition, while I struggled to keep up with my daytime vocation as an intellectual property attorney. Maxwell, your service was well above and beyond the call of duty.

Debbie Greenberg researched and prepared several of the inventors and inventions essays included in this second edition, and my warmest appreciation extends to her.

JoAnn Rockman, my wife of 34 years, deserves more expressions of appreciation than I am capable of giving. First, she had to tolerate my "lack of attention" while the underlying UIC course materials were developed. Then, she had to stand by and watch while her spouse pored over the papers and research material to prepare 36 chapters of text and the numerous inventors and inventions essays. As a consolation, I now have turned control of the dining room table back to her and the family.

Howard B. Rockman
rockman@rvoiplaw.com

Top Ten List of Intellectual Property Protection

There are several important points regarding the potential loss of intellectual property rights by the actions of an inventor or creator, and other matters, that warrant special and advanced mention. Adherence to these points will help you avoid the unintended loss of rights to your novel technology. Each of these matters is discussed in detail in this text, but I want to prevent the potential loss of intellectual property rights until you get to the appropriate page.

1. Do not publicly disclose your patentable invention to anyone outside your development team until either a provisional or non-provisional patent application covering your invention has been filed with the USPTO, or your respective home patent office. In the United States, in broad terms, an inventor has 1 year following the public disclosure of an invention to file a patent application. However, public knowledge of your invention anywhere will destroy all patent rights in most countries outside the United States. These countries adhere to the "absolute novelty" rule that requires a patent application to be filed covering an invention in the inventor's home country before *any* public disclosure of the invention. Thus, by filing your patent application in your home country before any public disclosure of the invention, you have saved all of your international patent rights. If you must disclose your invention to another before a patent application can be filed, have the recipient of the disclosure sign a confidential non-disclosure agreement before receiving the information. This makes the disclosure "non-public," and saves your patent rights.
2. Even though you obtain a patent on your invention, products or processes incorporating your invention may still infringe the patent rights of someone else. Therefore, my advice is to have a freedom-to-use search conducted before you bring your new, and patentable, product to market.
3. Be sure you advise your patent attorney of all prior art relating to your invention that you are aware of before the patent application covering your invention is filed, and during the pendency of your application. It is a strict requirement that all material prior art publications and activities of which you are aware be submitted to the U.S. patent examiner.
4. Since the United States has adopted the "first-to-file" system, if you are working in a highly competitive industry, your patent application, provisional or non-provisional, should be prepared and filed at the earliest practical time.
5. When beginning a new employment, carefully read and fully understand the agreements you sign, particularly the language regarding ownership of inventions made prior to your employment, and those inventions made during your employment. Also make sure you understand any language that may affect your ability to work for a competitor if and when your new employment terminates.

6. If you are adopting a name, trademark, logo, etc., for use in your business, have a search conducted to ensure that someone else in the same or a similar line of business is not already using a confusingly similar name or symbol.
7. When asking a vendor or supplier to provide input to a development project, have the vendor first sign an agreement that any contribution they make toward the development of protectable intellectual property will belong to you or your company, and not to the vendor.
8. If you intend to maintain certain information as trade secrets, fully inform yourself of the steps you legally have to take to prove later that you have in place a strict policy and safeguards for maintaining the secrecy of all confidential information.
9. The copyright law prevents copying. You may set forth a previously written-about concept or development in your own words, but do not copy the same expression of that concept as used by someone else.
10. Consider initially that any new development you produce may be patentable, or may be covered by one or more of the other intellectual property vehicles. Just as science and technology changes, intellectual property laws also change to protect new forms of innovation.

SECTION I

The Intellectual Property Universe

◆ INVENTORS AND INVENTIONS ◆

Eli Whitney

THE COTTON GIN

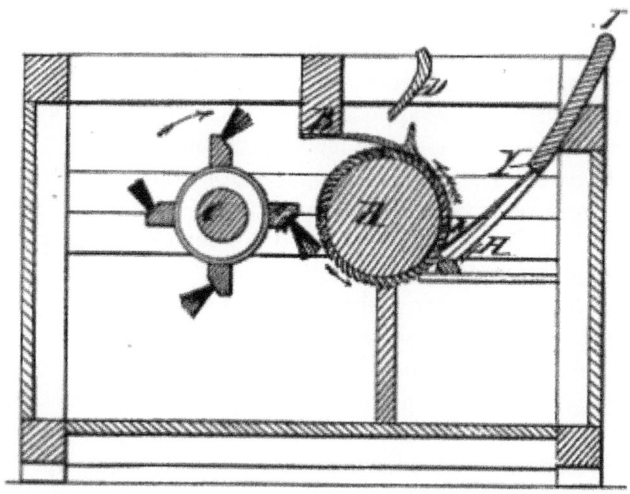

The first patent of major importance to be issued by the U.S. government after it was formed was Eli Whitney's patent for the cotton gin ("gin" is short for "engine"), which was issued on March 14, 1794. The patent description is in longhand, for reasons I cannot explain.

Upon graduating Yale as an engineer in 1792, Whitney, like many college graduates of today, found himself in debt and in need of a job. He left his home in Massachusetts and took a job as a teacher in South Carolina. That job fell through, and Katherine Greene, the war widow of General Nathanial Greene, invited Whitney to stay at her Georgia cotton plantation in early 1793. He noticed that long-staple cotton, which was readily separated from its seed, could only be grown along the coast. The inland-grown variety of cotton had sticky green seeds that were difficult to cull from the fluffy white cotton bolls, and thus was less profitable to grow and harvest. It took 10 hours of hand labor to sift out a single point of cotton lint from its seeds.

Whitney, after observing the manual process being used for separating the sticky seeds from the cotton bolls, built his first machine, which did not work. The bulk cotton was pushed against a wire mesh screen, which held back the seeds while wooden

Intellectual Property Law for Engineers, Scientists, and Entrepreneurs, Second Edition. Howard B. Rockman.

Published 2020 by John Wiley & Sons, Inc.

teeth extending from a rotating drum pulled the cotton fibers through the mesh screen. However, this machine jammed. His next version incorporated thin wire hooks to replace the wooden teeth, and the collected fibers were cleared away by a moving brush. This second machine was successful.

According to some accounts, a question remains to this day whether Whitney or his employer, Mrs. Greene, was the "inventor" of the key element of the successful cotton gin—the wire hooks. Some say the plantation foreman suggested to Greene that the wooden teeth be replaced by wires, and that Greene then told Whitney. Whitney's supporters, on the other hand, cite a letter to the editor of *Southern Agriculturist* magazine, admittedly based on shaky sources, that Whitney specifically asked Mrs. Greene for a pin to use at the start of his experimentation. A factor tending to swing the pendulum toward Whitney was that, before he left Massachusetts, he was the new country's only hatpin manufacturer.

In 1794, Whitney filed a patent application for his (or Greene's) cotton gin. He also gave a demonstration of his model to a few friends, producing in 1 hour a full day's output of several workers. The witnesses to this demonstration immediately had whole fields planted in green seed cotton. Word spread, and the farmers grew excited and impatient. Whitney's shop was broken into, and examinations made of his new cotton gin. Then, more fields were planted with cotton.

Before Whitney had a chance to prepare a patent model of his invention (required in those days), or to secure patent protection, the cotton crops were ready for harvest, and the planters did not have time to work within ethical or legal parameters. Whitney's cotton gin was simply pirated. Whitney and his partner, Phineas Miller, decided to build cotton gins and lease, not sell, them to the planters in exchange for 1 pound of every 3 pounds of cotton put through their machines. The planters revolted at this arrangement, as a virtual flood of white cotton was erupting from the Southern soil.

The partners, heavily in debt, were forced to approach the Southern courts to enforce their patent rights, which resulted in disaster. In 1801, they opted for grants from several Southern states, and, in return, the cotton gin would become public property. One state, South Carolina, accepted, offered $50,000, made a down payment of $20,000, and never paid the remainder. Eventually, Whitney and Miller received about $90,000 from the states, which was used up immediately to pay legal costs and other expenses. In 1803, the states repudiated their agreements, and sued Whitney for the return of the money paid previously. In 1804, Whitney petitioned the U.S. Congress for relief, and by one vote avoided financial ruin. At that point, he felt the past 10 years were wasted. Whitney became discouraged with cotton, and left the South forever.

Upon returning to New Haven, Connecticut, he started manufacturing goods and developing mass production techniques and factories. In time, his manufacturing process developments changed the industrial capabilities of the North, just as his cotton gin had changed the face of the South.

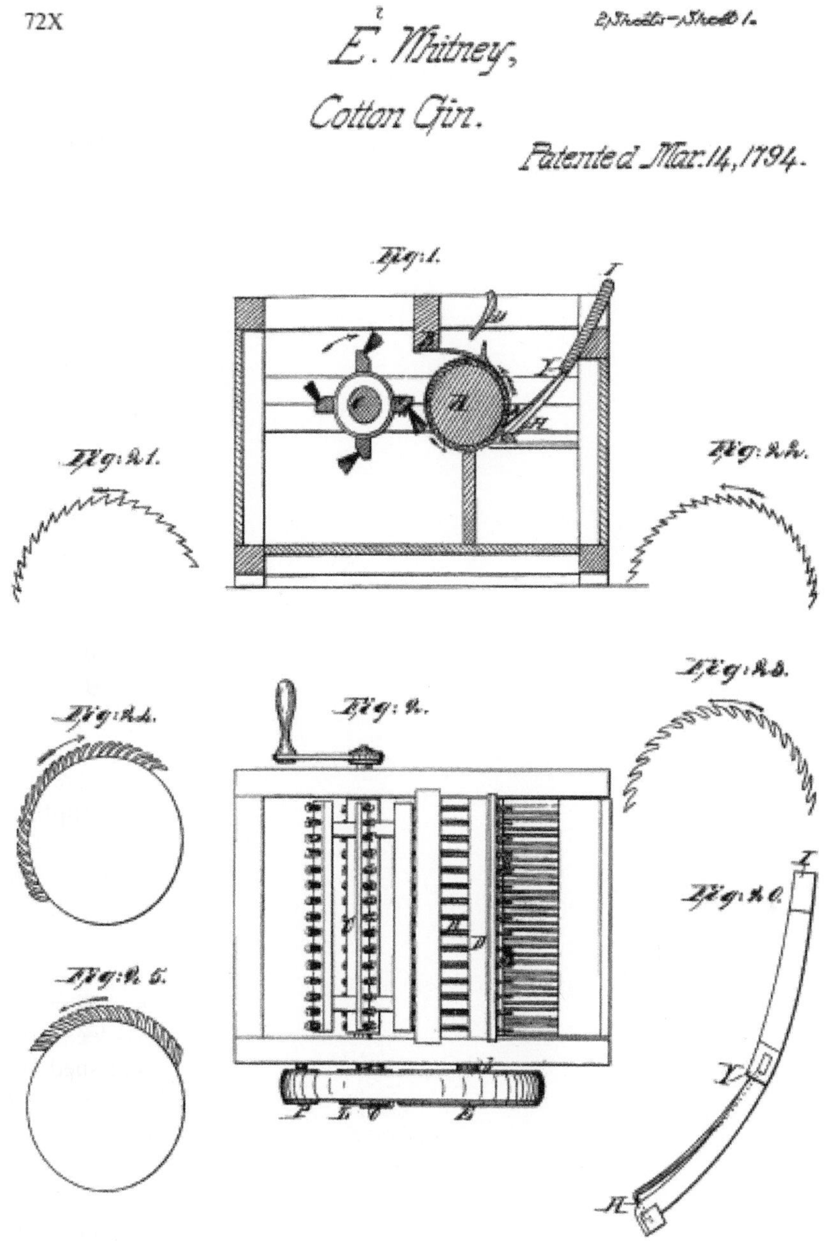
72X
2 Sheets—Sheet 1.
E. Whitney,
Cotton Gin.
Patented Mar. 14, 1794.
Fig: 1.
Fig: 2.

◆ INVENTORS AND INVENTIONS ◆

Charles Babbage

THE DIFFERENCE ENGINE

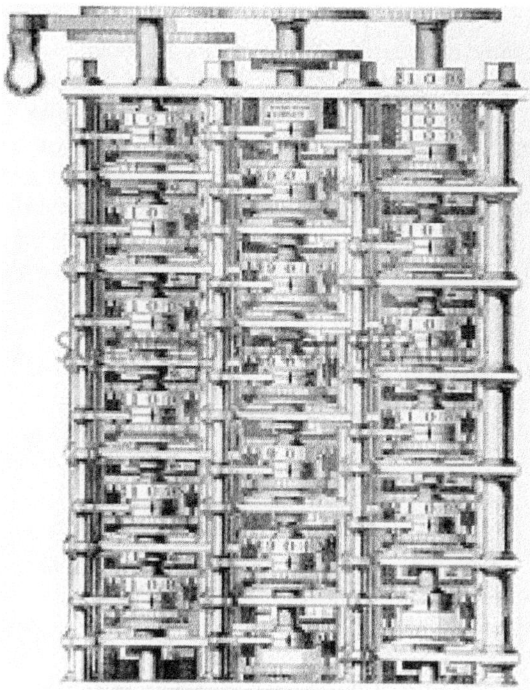

Charles Babbage was a man of many talents. However, completing projects he started was not one of them. This essay will skip over many of the accomplishments of Mr. Babbage in his lifetime, and go straight to the point where he became known as a computing pioneer. Babbage, an Englishman, is credited with developing the first mechanical computers. However, his models were never completed, largely because of economic problems, and possibly clashes of personality, particularly with the Astronomer Royal of England.

Babbage directed the construction of early steam-powered calculating machines that achieved modest success, but those machines also suggested that the calculations could be mechanized. He received British government funding for his calculation

Intellectual Property Law for Engineers, Scientists, and Entrepreneurs, Second Edition. Howard B. Rockman.

Published 2020 by John Wiley & Sons, Inc.

mechanism project for over 10 years, but eventually the treasury in England lost faith in him, and stopped funding his project. The machines that Babbage did manage to prototype were mechanical, and their basic architecture was similar to a modern computer. For example, the program memory and the data memory were separated, operation was based on instructions, the control unit could make conditional jumps, and his devices had a separate input/output unit.

In Babbage's time, printed mathematical tables were calculated by humans. As you might expect, errors were constantly known to occur in the transcription of such calculations. Babbage at one time prepared his own account of how he began thinking about mechanical mathematical computations to replace those that were made by hand. In his own words, he stated that, in 1812, he was in his room in the Analytical Society, reviewing a table of logarithms, which he concluded was full of mistakes. He then had the thought of computing all tabular functions by machinery. He knew that the French government had previously produced several tables by a new method, where several French mathematicians decided how to compute the tables, six more divided the operations into simple stages, and the work itself, which was merely addition and subtraction, was performed by 80 human "computers" who knew only those two arithmetical processes. Babbage considered that this was mass production applied to arithmetic, and became enthralled by the concept that the labors of unskilled human computers could be taken over completely by faster and more reliable machinery.

In about 1819, Babbage's interests were turning to astronomical instruments, and his ideas became more precise. He conceived of a plan to construct tables using the method of differences by mechanical means. He began to construct a small prototype "difference engine" in 1819, which he completed by 1822. He described his invention in a paper published on June 14, 1822, by the Royal Astronomical Society of England, titled "Note on the Application of Machinery to the Computation of Astronomical and Mathematical Tables." At the time the paper was written, Babbage had also thought about a machine that could print the results of the difference engine, but this printer was not completed at the time his paper was written. An assistant of Babbage's was required to write down the results obtained by the difference engine by calculating successive terms of the sequence n^2+n+41. Babbage urged that a larger difference engine could do the work undertaken by many people, saving costs and being totally accurate. However, such a larger machine was never built during his lifetime.

Babbage's difference engine was designed to compute values of polynomial functions. The calculations were supposed to be done automatically by using the method of finite differences, which made it possible to avoid the need for multiplication and division. In his 1822 paper, he described a machine using the decimal number system that was powered by cranking a handle. Babbage worked with Joseph Clement on the prototype of his design for a difference engine in 1823. In 1831, the collaboration between Babbage and Clement ended over arguments involving money. The prototype that Babbage and Clement did construct evolved into the first difference engine, but remained unfinished. This prototype was approximately one-seventh of the calculating section of the difference engine that Babbage initially envisioned. Even though Babbage's design was feasible, the metalworking techniques of the early 1800s could not economically produce the needed parts in the quantity and to the precision required. The design of the first difference engine would have included, had it been completed, around 25,000 parts, weighed 15 tons, and would have been 8 feet tall.

Babbage received ample initial government funding for the project; however, the device was never completed.

A *difference engine* can be defined as an automatic mechanical calculator designed to tabulate polynomial functions. The name derives from the method of divided differences, a way to interpolate or tabulate functions by using a small set of polynomial coefficients. Most mathematical functions commonly used by engineers, including logarithmic and trigonometric functions, can be approximated by polynomials, allowing a difference engine to compute several useful tables of numbers. The difficulty in producing an error-free table by teams of mathematicians or human computers was the driving force behind Charles Babbage's desire to build a mechanical device to automate the calculating process.

In 1827, the costs of constructing Difference Engine No. 1 were becoming astronomical, and work stopped on the project in 1834. Up to that time, the British government had invested £17,000 into the project, and Babbage had invested £6,000 of his own funds. From 1834 to 1842, the British government did not make a decision on whether to continue to support Babbage in his projects, but the decision not to proceed was taken in 1842 by Robert Peel's government.

Between 1847 and 1849, Babbage produced detailed drawings for an improved version, which he called Difference Engine No. 2, but he failed to receive funding for this project from the British government.

After failing at his efforts to complete Difference Engine No. 1, Babbage worked on a design for a more complex machine, which he called the "Analytical Engine." He and C. G. Jarvis, who had previously worked for Clement, worked on the analytical engine, which was a transition from mechanized arithmetic to full-fledged general-purpose computation. It is largely on his development work on the analytical engine that Babbage's reputation as a computer pioneer was established, although the analytical engine was never completed in Babbage's lifetime.

The analytical engine was to be programmed with punch cards that would control a mechanical calculator, which would use the results of preceding computations as input. The device was also intended to employ several features subsequently used in modern computers, including sequential control, and looping and branching. It would have been the first mechanical device to be considered a complete computer. The analytical engine was not a single physical machine, but rather a succession of designs that Babbage continued working on until he died in 1871.

By 1834, Babbage had completed the first drawings of the analytical engine, which is now considered by some as the forerunner of the modern electronic computer. The analytic engine never progressed beyond detailed drawings; however, it is quite similar in logic components to present-day computers. Babbage's writings described five logic components of his computer: the store, the mill, the control, the input, and the output. The store contains all the variables to be operated upon, as well as all quantities that had arisen from the results of other operations. The mill, which is similar to the CPU in a modern computer, is a locale into which the quantities about to be operated upon are always brought. The control was carried out by a Jacquard loom–type device, operated by punch cards. The punch cards comprised a program for the particular task, where every set of cards made for any formula would at any future time recalculate the formula with whatever constants would be required. Thus, Babbage envisioned that his analytical engine would possess a library of its own—with every set of cards, having once been made, reproducing at any time the calculations for which it was first configured. Babbage designed the analytic engine to effectively have infinite storage by outputting data to punch cards, which could be read into the system again at a later stage when necessary. As the difference engine, the analytical engine was never completed by Babbage.

Babbage visited Luigi Federico Menabrea in Turin, Italy, in 1840. During this visit, Menabrea collected all the material needed to describe Babbage's analytical engine, which Menabrea published in October 1842. Ada Lovelace, also known as Lady Byron, the daughter of Lord Byron, translated Menabrea's article into English, adding considerably more extensive notes than the original memoir. Lovelace's work was published in 1843.

Ada Lovelace described seeing Babbage's working prototype in 1833: "We both went to see the thinking machine (or so it seems) last Monday. It raised several numbers to the 2nd and 3rd powers and extracted the root of a quadratic equation."

Ada Lovelace was credited with developing an algorithm that would enable the analytical engine to calculate a sequence of Bernoulli numbers. Therefore, Ada Lovelace is often considered the first computer programmer, although no programming language had yet been invented during her time.

When Babbage turned his attention to developing the analytical engine, he further undermined the British government's support of his difference engine, and this was one reason government financial support was withdrawn. By improving the concept as an analytical engine, Babbage had obsoleted his earlier difference engine.

Believe it or not, Babbage's design was finally constructed between 1989 and 1991 using his plans and nineteenth-century manufacturing tolerances. Lo and behold, this machine performed its first calculation in the Science Museum in London, returning results to 31 digits. During the 1980s, Allan G. Bromley, assistant professor at the University of Sydney, Australia, looked at Babbage's original drawings for both the difference engine and the analytical engine that were located at the Science Museum Library in London. Ultimately, the Science Museum was persuaded to construct a working Difference Engine No. 2, which was built between 1980 and 1991 to tolerances achievable with nineteenth-century technology. In 2000, the printer that Babbage had originally designed for the difference engine was also completed. Construction revealed some minor errors in Babbage's design, which some commentators surmise had been purposefully introduced as protection in case his designs were stolen. These errors were corrected, and once completed both the difference engine and his printer worked flawlessly, and still work to the present day. This resolved the long-standing debate as to whether Babbage's design would have actually worked.

Babbage's printer's primary purpose was to produce stereotype plates for use in printing presses, by pressing type into soft plaster to create a flong. Babbage's plans show that the engine's results would be conveyed directly to mass printing, having recognized that many errors in previous tables were not the result of human calculating mistakes, but resulted from errors in the manual typesetting process. Therefore, the printer's paper output is a means of checking the difference engine's performance.

There are many articles and books written about Babbage's work and how his difference engine operates. Those of you who are interested in delving into this subject matter further are encouraged to review the literature and gain more information about the earliest computer ever made from these sources, several of which are named in the Bibliography section of this text.

1 Overview of Intellectual Property Law

1.1 DEFINING "INTELLECTUAL PROPERTY"

First, we need to define the core term of our subject: *intellectual property*. The term "intellectual property" generically describes those "intangible" property rights—those you usually cannot see or touch—which are initially created by one's intellectual creative efforts. The results of those intellectual efforts, in most cases, are then anointed with these intangible property rights that give their creator or owner the "exclusive" ability to control, and profit from, the results of this creativity. "Intellectual Property Law" is that field of law which defines those intellectual creations that are entitled to protection as intellectual property, how to obtain (or lose) those intellectual property rights, how to properly use and benefit from those rights, and how to obtain enforcement and compensation when those intellectual property rights are infringed upon by a competitor or other evil person. Intellectual Property Law also provides guidance to a competitor who desires to produce a new product or use a new process, by designing around, and thus avoiding, the proprietary territory defined by your intellectual property rights.

Winning or losing out in business and financial opportunities many times heavily depends upon whether your creative output, inventions, products and business ideas and services are protected by patents, trademarks, copyrights, trade secret rights, mask work rights, and others. Commercially new and useful ideas, inventions, products, and business services are the foundation of practically every highly successful business. As a result, successful business owners and entrepreneurs typically place a high value on the exclusive rights granted to intellectual property developed by their employees.

Businesses have succeeded or failed because of their owner's efforts to protect their intellectual property, or their failure to do so. The value of many publicly traded companies has taken huge swings based principally upon whether the company has been successful in obtaining and enforcing its patent rights, for example. There are many common myths and misunderstandings surrounding the need for and the difficulty in obtaining patent, trademark or copyright protection. Understanding the protection rules and processes and appreciating the valuable rights which can be acquired ensures that your intellectual property is protected, as well as that of your employer.

"Tangible" property includes things such as land, houses, jewelry, communication system terminals and networks, and even animals—things you can see and feel and physically possess. Intellectual property rights, on the other hand, are "intangible"

Intellectual Property Law for Engineers, Scientists, and Entrepreneurs, Second Edition. Howard B. Rockman.

Published 2020 by John Wiley & Sons, Inc.

rights which cannot be seen or touched, but they still exist, or can exist, if the rules laid down by centuries of Intellectual Property Law are understood and followed. Intangible property, to be protectable, must ultimately be described or depicted in some tangible form, such as a description in a patent grant, or a work of art or manuscript of a book covered by a copyright certificate. In each of these two examples, the law describes the intangible exclusive rights possessed by the owner and/or creator of a patentable or copyrightable work.

The building blocks of intellectual property law are patents, copyrights, trademarks and service marks, as well as anti-cybersquatting laws, unfair competition laws, trade secret protection laws, and mask work protection laws. These are all concepts that were created by legal systems in most of the countries of the world, and, although they are merely legal devices, they provide powerful instruments of protection for your intellectual creations. These systems of rights were developed to document the existence of intellectual property rights and how they can be protected, and to give the creators the right to exclusively use, own, transfer ownership, or license their exclusive intellectual property rights.

In general terms, each Intellectual Property Law system throughout the world is devised to document enforceable protection for specific types of creative and innovative output, and to allow people and business entities to own and transfer ownership in the exclusive rights in their intellectual property. For example, patents cover novel, useful, and non-obvious machines; articles of manufacture; compositions of matter; ornamental designs; plants; manufacturing, electrical, and chemical processes; and other methods, including software algorithms and methods of doing business. Patents also cover any improvement made to an article or process falling in any of the preceding categories. Copyrights cover the creative works of authors, composers, software developers, artists and the like. Trademark and service mark registration laws, as well as the common law, which I shall explain, protect the source identity of a product or service, such as the name and/or logo, and sometimes product configuration, under which goods or services are advertised and marketed to the trade or public, and that differentiates such goods and services from those of others. Trade secret protection laws prevent a competitor or another from misappropriation of valuable and confidential information that is not generally known or available to a competitor or to the public, such as a secret chemical formula or a secret process. Mask work protection is a recent intellectual property structural block that provides exclusive rights in creative mask works used in the manufacture of semiconductors. In all, the specific nature and content of the results of your creative endeavors determines which vehicle or vehicles of the various intellectual property laws are best suited to protect the ultimate output of your efforts.

1.2 SPECIFIC INTELLECTUAL PROPERTY VEHICLES

1.2.1 Patents

A U.S. patent grant covering your invention can only be obtained from the U.S. government, namely, the United States Patent and Trademark Office (USPTO), currently located across the river from Washington, D.C. in Alexandria, Virginia. Most of the business of the USPTO is conducted electronically, and patent and trademark applications can be filed, examined, and prosecuted online. In foreign nations too, patents are granted only by the nation's government. Each country's patents are enforceable only in the issuing country and its territories. There are also a few regional patent systems—such as the one controlled by the European Patent Office (EPO), which issues patents enforceable in each country of the European Union. In the United States, the Patent Law is found at Title 35 of the United States Code, a body of laws periodically enacted and amended from 1790 to the present by the U.S. Congress, as mandated by Article 1, Section 8, of the U.S. Constitution. These U.S. laws define what can and cannot be patented, the conditions and requirements for obtaining a patent grant on patentable subject matter, the rights granted by a patent, the ability of a patent owner to enforce the exclusive rights embedded in the patent grant, and the ability of a patent owner to license or transfer ownership of the intangible rights embedded in the invention and patent grant for monetary consideration.

As mentioned briefly in the preceding text, patents are granted on "new and useful processes, machines, manufactures or compositions of matter, or any new and useful improvement thereof" (35 U.S.C. §101). Designs of utilitarian articles of manufacture may also be protected by a Design Patent. Recent court decisions have held that anything "new" made by man or woman falling within the definition of 35 U.S.C. §101, quoted earlier, can be the subject of a patent. This includes new forms of animal life, for example, the Harvard Mouse, which is particularly susceptible to cancer and therefore valuable in research, and the modified *E. coli* bacterium, which produces insulin. Also, more recently, novel and unobvious methods of conducting business have also been pronounced to be the subject of patents, as well as software under certain circumstances, as discussed in detail later in this text. By way of comparison, any material that appears naturally in nature cannot be the subject of a patent, since it was not "invented" by the alleged inventor. Also, pure abstract ideas and concepts that have no "physical" embodiment are not protectable under the patent laws. However, as discussed later, a novel concept embodied in a new and useful device or procedure may come close to being fully protected by effective and creative patent application and claim drafting.

An issued patent grant describes and illustrates the covered invention, and its advantages over the "prior art," and also includes specifically worded "claims" that define the metes and bounds of the protection afforded by the patent grant. If a competing device or process falls within the definition set forth in a patent's claim or claims, or comprises equivalent structure, the competing device infringes the patent. However, I am getting ahead of myself—the topic of patent infringement will be covered later.

1.2.2 Trademarks and Service Marks

Trademarks, services marks, collective membership marks, trade dress or product configuration, trade names and the like are indicia of origin of one's products or services. These indicia are directed toward the protection of the reputation and goodwill of the manufacturer of a product or a provider of services, who uses a mark or symbol distinguishing the source of origin of its products or services from those of another manufacturer or service provider. These marks may comprise a name, logo, symbol, product shape, container shape, or other distinctive and non-functional feature of a product or service which indicates that a certain supplier or group is the sole source for that particular brand of product or service, and the supplier or group stands behind the quality and reputation of the particular product or service. Rights in the exclusive use of the mark are protected to avoid the likelihood of consumer confusion in the marketplace as to the source of the goods or services they purchase, thereby protecting the public against fraud by the second user of a confusingly similar mark.

A trademark or service mark registration application must be submitted to the government (the USPTO in the United States) to obtain federal registration, and sets forth both the identifying mark and those goods or services with which the mark is, or is intended to be, used. A trademark never stands alone. A trademark or service mark is always considered as an adjective, modifying the goods or services to which it pertains. Thus, "Scotch tape" is proper usage, as long as the "Scotch" is followed by the identifying word "tape." When used, a trademark or service mark should always be followed by the descriptive term of the associated goods or services.

Trademarks and service marks may also be protected in the United States and certain other common law countries without registration, if long usage and advertising of the mark has advised the public that the name or symbol has been adopted as a distinctive mark by its owner. As discussed later, each state of the United States has a trademark/service mark registration system directed to marks for goods and services that do not travel across state lines, such as a dental office, for example.

1.2.3 Copyrights

A copyright is a form of intellectual property that protects the expression of authorship or artistic rendition of the author or creator, but does not protect the idea or concept upon which the expression is based. A concept for doing something cannot be protected by copyright, but the fixation, or expression of that concept, can be protected. For example, the concept of writing a book about tornado hunters is not protectable. However, a book or film about tornado hunters is a "fixation" of the author's expression, and the expression, but not the concept, is protectable under the copyright statutes.

Copyright protection is normally easier and less expensive to obtain than either patent or trademark protection. Under existing law, the creator of a copyrightable work obtains an intangible copyright in the work immediately upon the fixation of the work in a tangible medium of expression. To obtain a U.S. registration of that copyright, which provides tangible evidence of the existence of the copyright, an application setting forth, among other things, the author's name, the identity of the work to be protected, and its date of creation are submitted on an appropriate form to the Register of Copyrights, along with a deposit sample of the work. The Register of Copyrights works under the aegis of the U.S. Library of Congress. The application is subjected to an examination procedure, which is much quicker than the examination of patent or trademark applications, because there is no examination for novelty or likelihood of confusion as compared to existing copyrighted works. The copyright application must indicate which portions of the work are original and which are not. This permits the public to ascertain which portions are protected and which remain in the public domain. Copyrights are used to protect books, films, videos, works of art, sculptures, and, more recently, choreography and software.

It is possible to overlap protection between the copyright and patent laws. For example, a novel, useful and non-obvious computer program may be protectable under both patent laws and the copyright laws. The expression of an algorithm or formula can be protected as a literary work under the copyright law. In addition, a novel method for controlling a machine by use of an algorithm may qualify for patent protection.

1.2.4 Trade Secrets

As discussed later in this text, patents and copyrights expire after a term of years, while trade secret protection does not. As long as the information covered by a trade secret umbrella remains secret, that information is protected from improper discovery or use by others, unless the secret is independently discovered, as by reverse engineering, or otherwise lawfully made public by someone else. Where the secret is very difficult to discover and the owner is willing to maintain security to ensure its secrecy, trade secret protection is a valuable option and has no endpoint.

However, once the trade secret becomes known, there is no way to restore secret status. If the secret is discoverable upon reviewing the articles in which the secret is used, trade secret protection is useless. In such cases, patent or copyright protection should be considered instead. Unlike patents and copyrights and trademarks, until recently, there was no federal law regulating trade secret protection in the United States. However, in 2016, the U.S. Congress enacted a federal law to protect trade secrets, which is discussed in Chapter 27 of this text. Each state has its own trade secret protection law, and if it is determined that the best way to protect your intellectual property is through the trade secret law, an attorney familiar with this area of your state law should be consulted in the state or states in which you are operating. In the State of Illinois, where I practice, the state legislature has enacted the Illinois Trade Secrets Act, which is currently in effect. This Act sets forth what types of subject matter are considered as trade secrets, such as secret processes, formulas, customer lists, confidential future business plans, etc., and how they are protected. Even if a particular state has not enacted a statute granting trade secret protection, the common law may be available in that state to enforce trade secret rights against misappropriation once the secret is created.

1.2.5 Mask Works for Semiconductors

In 1984, the U.S. Congress enacted a law to protect mask works used in creating semiconductor microprocessor chips. This law became part of the Federal Copyright Statute. Chapter 26 of this text describes in detail how mask work protection can be obtained for semiconductor chips.

1.3 WHICH FORM OF INTELLECTUAL PROPERTY PROTECTION TO USE?

Depending on the nature of the technological project you are engaged in, one or several of the vehicles of intellectual property may be advisable to use. In some situations, you may not have any choice. If the subject matter of protection is a book or manuscript, patent or trademark protection cannot be obtained. For example, book titles other than periodical titles cannot be the subject of trademark registration, since each book title is descriptive of the precise book sold under that title. In some situations, multiple forms of protection will be available. In the case of a novel form of packaging, both article and design patent protection may be available, covering a novel construction embedded in the packaging, as well as the aesthetic outward design of the package. Also, the name of the product on the packaging would be susceptible to trademark protection, while the graphics used on the packaging label could be protected under copyright laws.

Which protection to be used is a business decision that must be arrived at by the owner of the invention or originator of the creative work. This decision should be made with the assistance of an attorney with experience in the intellectual property law field, and after the creator or owner has a full understanding as to the best vehicle or vehicles to be used for protection.

◆ INVENTORS AND INVENTIONS ◆

Frank J. Sprague

THE ELECTRIC STREETCAR

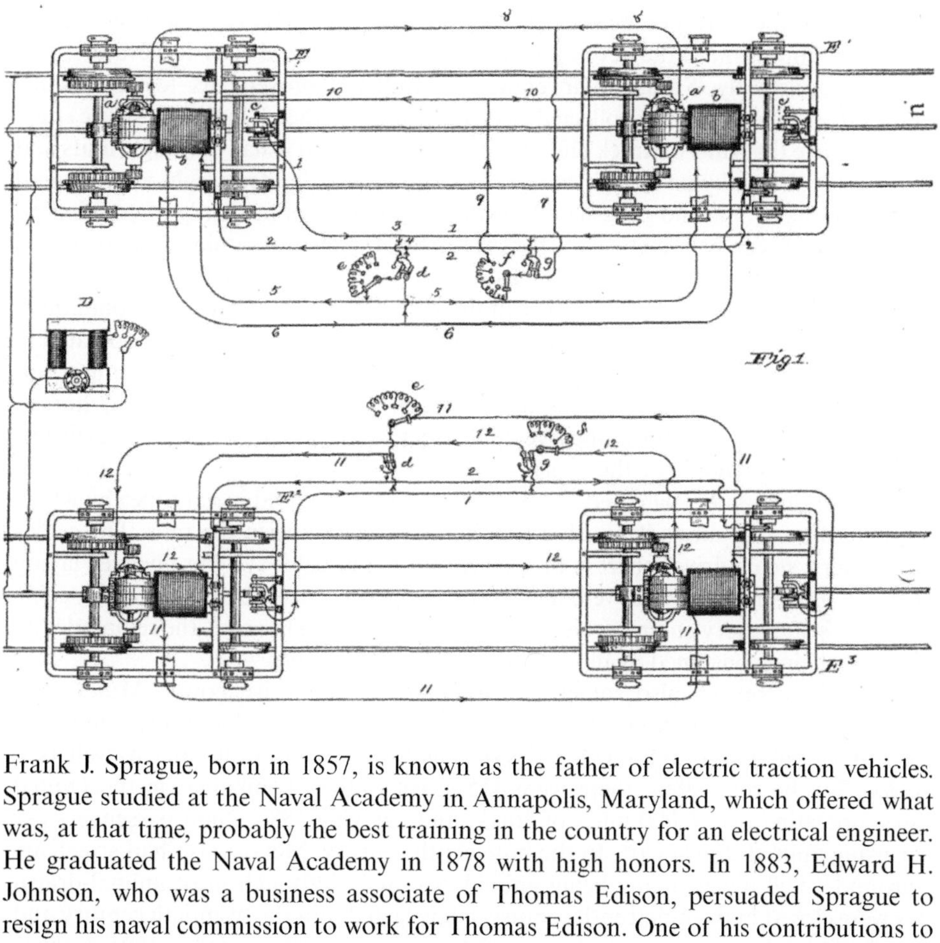

Frank J. Sprague, born in 1857, is known as the father of electric traction vehicles. Sprague studied at the Naval Academy in Annapolis, Maryland, which offered what was, at that time, probably the best training in the country for an electrical engineer. He graduated the Naval Academy in 1878 with high honors. In 1883, Edward H. Johnson, who was a business associate of Thomas Edison, persuaded Sprague to resign his naval commission to work for Thomas Edison. One of his contributions to the Menlo Park Edison laboratory in New Jersey was the introduction of mathematical methods in the work performed at the laboratory. Before he arrived, Edison's team conducted several costly trial-and-error experiments. Sprague's approach was to use

Intellectual Property Law for Engineers, Scientists, and Entrepreneurs, Second Edition. Howard B. Rockman.

Published 2020 by John Wiley & Sons, Inc.

mathematics to calculate the optimum parameters, thus saving much needless tinkering. Sprague also developed a mathematical determination of electrical distribution useful in planning and balancing the distribution circuits of Edison's central electricity plants. However, in 1884, Sprague decided that his interests in the exploitation of electricity should be directed more towards power generation elsewhere, and he left Edison to found the Sprague Electric Railway and Motor Company. By 1886, Sprague's company perfected two important inventions. The first was a constant-speed non-sparking motor with fixed brushes. The second was a regenerative braking system that uses the drive motor to return power to the main supply system. His motor was the first to maintain constant speed under varying load, and was ultimately endorsed by Edison as the only practical electric motor available. His regenerative braking system was important in the development of electric trains and electric elevators.

Most importantly, Sprague's inventions included improvements to designs for electric streetcar systems that collected electricity from overhead lines. An electric street car is a vehicle that runs on track laid in the streets, operated usually in single units and most usually driven by an electric motor. A streetcar is of lighter weight as compared to conventional trains and is designed for the transportation primarily of passengers, but occasionally can be used to carry freight. Streetcars operate within, close to, or between nearby towns and/or cities on tracks running primarily on the streets.

The first mass transportation vehicle in the United States was called an "omnibus." Pulled by horses, it had the appearance of a stagecoach. The first omnibus operated in America up and down Broadway in New York City in 1827. The first important improvement over the omnibus was the streetcar, which was also pulled by horses. However, instead of running along a regular street, streetcars rolled along special steel rails placed in the middle of the street. On January 17, 1871, a San Francisco citizen, Andrew Smith Hallidie, patented the first cable car, which used metal ropes by which cars were drawn by an endless cable running in a slot between the rails. The cables passed over a steam driven shaft in the power house. The cable systems involved laying expensive infrastructure, and were inefficient to operate because only 18% of a cable car system's stationary engine power was applied to moving the cars, the remainder of the energy being consumed by moving the weight of the cable.

The early streetcars also sometimes used mules for motive power. Mules were thought to provide more hours per day of useful transit service than horses, and were especially popular in southern U.S. cities such as New Orleans, Louisiana, as well as in Mexico. By the mid-1880s, there were 415 street railway companies in the United States, operating over 6,000 miles of track, and carrying 188 million passengers per year using animal-drawn cars. In the nineteenth century, Mexico also had streetcars in around 1,000 towns, many being animal powered. Although most animal-drawn lines were closed in the nineteenth century, a few lasted into the twentieth century and later. Toronto's horse-drawn streetcar operations, for example, ended in 1891. In New York City, the regular horse-powered service lasted until 1917, and in Pittsburgh, Pennsylvania, until 1923. The last regular mule-drawn cars in the United States operated in Sulphur Rock, Arkansas, until 1926.

The obvious advantages of a system that eliminated animal drive power included doing away with the need to feed the animals, and, more importantly, cleaning up their waste after they ate. In Chicago, for example, there were an estimated 6,600 horses owned by the street railways in the 1880s, dumping a considerable amount of manure and urine on the streets. Further, many horses were killed in the Chicago Fire of 1871, and then an influenza-like equine epizootic decimated the surviving horses the following year. In 1867, some street railway systems tried to replace horses with small steam locomotives, but the public objected to the smoke, noise and sparks that they generated.

Some early streetcars also depended on power supplied by storage batteries; however, these proved to be very expensive and inefficient. Invention of the dynamo or generator led to the application of electric power by means of overhead electrified wires, and to streetcar lines which subsequently proliferated in the United States, Europe, and the rest of the world. Prior to Sprague, there had been early experimental electric railways. Most of these were erected as electrical exhibitions at fairs and expositions as tourist attractions, and were usually dismantled after the exhibitions closed.

In 1888, Sprague developed streetcars that collected DC electricity from overhead wires, using a spring-loaded trolley pole that had been invented in 1880. The trolley pole comprised a bent piece called a "bow," or a collapsible and adjustable frame called a "pantograph," which was used in foreign countries as compared to the single-trolley pole in the United States. The ground return was through the iron street rails. Sprague's trolley pole traveled along the wire above the streetcar. The Sprague system motors were mounted beneath the cars, and centered on the axles, with both motors operated by a single control switch inside the car. Variable speed of the motors was obtained by varying the resistance of the field winding of the motors traversed by the current. Power was supplied through the overhead wire and the trolley pole. Many of these features were also used on subsequent light railways. General Electric and Westinghouse adopted many streetcar features on their railroad equipment.

After testing his trolley system in 1887 and 1888, Sprague installed the first electric street railway system in Richmond, Virginia. This was the first large-scale and successful use of electricity to operate an entire system of city streetcars. Overhead wires were installed over the Richmond city streets, and a spring-loaded streetcar pole would contact the electric wire. Back at the power house, steam engines turned huge generators to produce the electricity required to operate the streetcars. The name "trolley cars" was soon developed for the streetcars powered by electricity. The Richmond electric streetcar system, 12 miles long and with 40 cars, was in operation by February 2, 1888, and had a significant impact upon the burgeoning electric trolley industry in the United States. Sprague's use of a trolley pole for DC current pick-up from a single line, with ground return via the street rails, was the pattern that was eventually adopted in many other cities. The hills of Richmond, Virginia, which included grades of over 10%, provided an excellent proving ground for acceptance of Sprague's new technology. The Richmond electric streetcar system remained in service until November 25, 1949.

By January 1889, Boston had the first electric streetcars in the United States, which would be the first to operate underground 8 years later. Boston's last carriage-drawing horse was retired in 1987. Within a year of the Richmond system, electric power began to replace the more costly horse-drawn cars in many cities. By 1890, over 200 electric street railways, half incorporating Sprague's equipment and 90% based on his patents, had begun operation or were planned on several continents. In 1890, the General Electric Company, which manufactured most of Sprague's equipment, bought Sprague's electric streetcar business. Sprague left to establish the Sprague Electric Elevator company, and developed and installed electric elevators in several New York buildings before selling that business to Otis Elevator Company.

By the 1920s, most United States municipalities had abandoned horse-drawn cars for electrically powered streetcars. The rapid growth of streetcar systems resulted in the ability of people to live outside of a city and to commute into the city for work on a daily basis. The success of streetcars also gave rise to inter-urban lines, which were basically streetcars that operated between cities, and also served in remote rural areas.

The electric streetcar continued to be improved. Tiny, four-wheeled cars were replaced by heavy, eight-wheeled cars, providing a much greater carrying capacity. Wooden car bodies were replaced by steel ones. In time, the electric streetcar became the primary means of urban transit.

Sprague's later experience with elevator controls led him to develop a multiple unit system of electric railway operation, which accelerated the development of electric streetcar operation. In a multiple unit system, each car of the train carried electric traction motors. Using relays energized by train-line wires, the engineer or the motorman commanded all of the traction motors in the train to act together. For lighter streetcars, there is no need for a locomotive, so each car in the train can generate revenue. Sprague's first multiple unit order was from the Southside Elevated Railroad, the first of several elevated railways locally known as the "L" in Chicago. This success was followed by substantial multiple unit contracts in Brooklyn (New York) and Boston (Massachusetts).

Sprague's electric traction inventions allowed a significant expansion in the size of cities, while his elevator developments later on permitted greater concentration of workers in commercial sections of urban areas, and increased the profitability of commercial buildings. Over a hundred years later, his inventions also resulted in the development of light rail and rapid transit systems that still function on the same principles today.

Today, only Toronto still operates a streetcar network essentially unchanged in layout and mode of operation as originally constructed. St. Charles streetcar line in New Orleans is generally viewed as the world's oldest continuously operating streetcar line.

Between 1895 and 1929, almost every major American city had at least one streetcar labor strike. Sometimes they lasted only a few days; however, more often, the strikes were marked by almost continuous and sometimes violent conflict. At times, the strikes amounted to prolonged riots and civil insurrection. The 1929 New Orleans streetcar strike was one of the last of its kind. The rise of private automobile ownership took the edge off the impact of the strikes.

Here is where the history of streetcars gets interesting, at least to me. As the twentieth century moved forward, the heavy expense of track construction and maintenance ultimately rendered streetcars uneconomical. In the United States, streetcars began to be supplanted by automobiles and buses in the 1930s, which trend accelerated during the 1940s and 1950s. Readers who are aged 70 years or older may wonder what happened to all the trolley cars that they rode when they were younger.

There is no question that the rail trolley car systems of the early twentieth century have been almost entirely supplanted by the operation of buses and a few light rail train systems these days. Many commentators write that the Great Depression of the 1930s resulted in the closure of many streetcar lines in North America, but the onset of WWII delayed the closure of some streetcar lines as civilians used them to commute to war-related factory jobs during a time when rubber tires and gasoline were rationed. After WWII, automobile use continued to increase, and was assisted in the 1940s and 1950s by the passage of the Trans-Canada Highway Act of 1948. Also, the Federal Aid Highway Act of 1956 in the United States was enacted. Some commentators have stated that declining ridership and traffic jams caused on city streets by streetcars are often cited as reasons to shut down the remaining streetcar lines in various cities. However, while these facts may or may not be true, the demise of city streetcars systems was aided by several companies in the United States who took unlawful measures to increase the sales of their products.

The abandonment of city streetcar systems in the mid-twentieth century led to accusations of a conspiracy that a combination of automobile, oil, and tire manufacturers purposefully shut down streetcar systems to further the use of buses, gasoline, and rubber tires, which products the alleged conspirators were selling.

On April 9, 1947, nine corporations, including National City Lines, Pacific City Lines, General Motors, Firestone Tire Company, Mack Manufacturing Corporation, Phillips Petroleum, Standard Oil of California, and Federal Engineering Corporation, along with seven individuals, were indicted by the U.S. Justice Department, criminally charging them with, among other things, conspiring to monopolize certain portions of interstate commerce in the public transit sector, in violation of Section 2 of the United States Sherman Anti-Trust Act. The defendants were charged, more specifically, with having conspired to monopolize the portion of interstate commerce in the United States consisting of the sale of buses, petroleum products, tires, and tubes used by local transportation systems in those cities in which two of the defendants, National and Pacific, owned, controlled, or had a substantial financial interest in the streetcar systems. The indictment stated that the supplier defendants, which were Firestone, Standard Oil, Phillips, General Motors, and Mack, would furnish capital to defendants, National and Pacific, and these two latter companies would purchase city streetcar companies, dismantle the streetcar systems, and then cause their operating companies to purchase from the supplier companies substantially all their requirements of tires, tubes, and petroleum products. Or the city transit systems were converted from trolleys to buses. It was also alleged that the money made available by the supplier defendants would be utilized by National and Pacific to purchase control of, or a financial interest in, local public transportation systems in various states. It was also alleged that National and Pacific and their operating companies would not renew or enter into any new contracts for the purchase or use of products, such as tires, tubes, oil, and buses, other than from the supplier defendants once the conversion was completed.

The facts upon which these allegations in the indictment were based are that, as of April 1, 1939, one of the defendants, National City Lines, Inc., had risen from a humble beginning in 1920, operating two second-hand buses in Minnesota, to ownership or control of 29 operating transportation companies located in 27 cities in 10 states across the United States. When the indictment was returned in 1947, defendants Pacific and National had expanded their ownership or control to 46 transportation systems located in 45 cities in 16 U.S. states. The supplier defendants were manufacturers and marketers of buses, tires, tubes, and petroleum products, necessarily used by the local operating bus companies of National and Pacific City Lines.

National and Pacific City Lines and their suppliers entered into various oral and written agreements where the operating companies for the transit systems, National and Pacific, purchased preferred stock from the supplier defendants at prices in excess of the prevailing market prices, amounting to over US$9 million. The money received from the sale by National and Pacific of such stock was used to acquire control of, or a substantial financial interest in, various local transportation companies throughout the entire United States. The respective supplier defendants then entered into separate 10-year contracts with National and Pacific, under which all of the buses, tires, tubes, and petroleum product requirements of the National and Pacific operating companies were purchased from the supplier defendants, with an agreement not to buy any of these products from any party competing with the supplier defendants. Existing purchase contracts of all the operating companies with competitive suppliers were terminated at their earliest possible time, and the operating companies began equipping all their units with defendant supplier products, including buses, to the exclusion of any products competitive with them. National and Pacific also agreed that they would not renew or enter into any new contracts with other competitors of such products, or change any then existing equipment or purchase any new equipment using any fuel or means of propulsion other than gasoline.

National City Lines had been organized in 1936 as a holding company to acquire and operate local transit companies. Pacific City Lines was organized to acquire local transit companies on the Pacific coast, and began business in January 1938. There was another company, American City Lines, that was organized to acquire local transportation systems in the larger metropolitan areas in various parts of the United States in 1943, and American merged with National in 1946.

In a decision rendered by the Seventh Circuit Court of Appeals on January 31, 1951, upholding the previous District Court's and jury's conviction of the defendants on charges of monopolization, the Appellate Court found that, in 1938, National City Lines conceived the idea of purchasing transportation systems in cities where streetcars were deemed to be no longer practical, possibly due to the Depression and a trend at supplanting streetcar systems with passenger buses. National City Lines' capital was limited, and its earlier experience in public financing showed that it could not successfully finance the purchase of an increasing number of operating companies in various parts of the United States by normal financing means. As a result, National City Lines devised the plan of procuring funds from manufacturing companies whose products National City's operating companies were using constantly in their bus operating business.

National approached General Motors, which manufactured and delivered buses to the various sections of the United States. National also approached Firestone, whose business of manufacturing and supplying tires also extended throughout the United States. In the Midwest, where a large part of its operating subsidiaries were to be located, National City Lines solicited investment of funds from Phillips Petroleum, which operates throughout the Midwest but not on the east or west coast. Pacific City Lines undertook the procurement of funds from General Motors and Firestone, as well as from Standard Oil of California. Mack Truck Company was also solicited for funds. The Court of Appeals held that evidence was clear that, when any one of these manufacturing suppliers was approached, they appeared interested in helping finance National and Pacific under the condition that it should receive a contract for the exclusive use of its products in all of the operating companies of National and Pacific, so far as buses and tires were concerned, and, as to the oil companies, in the territory served by the respective petroleum companies.

It appears from the Appellate Court opinion that the District Court jury was justified in inferring that the proposal for financing came from National City Lines, but that the proposal of exclusive contracting was created by the suppling companies. Eventually, each supplier entered into a written contract of long duration, whereby National and Pacific City Lines, in consideration of the supplier's help in providing financing, agreed that all of National's and Pacific's operating subsidiaries should use only the supplier's products.

Based on these facts, the Court of Appeals of the Seventh Circuit upheld the conviction of the defendants on charges of monopolization. Another factor in the case was that, after National City Lines and Pacific City Lines purchased the various streetcar operating companies, they ripped up the rails in the different cities, tore down the electric lines, and dismantled and even sometimes burned the streetcars. Usually, the systems would be converted to buses within 90 days of National or Pacific's financial involvement. The first electrified surface transportation system that was demolished and replaced by buses was in New York City.

Strangely enough, however, even though the federal government won the lawsuit against these defendants, no meaningful penalty was imposed on anyone other than small symbolic fines, such as a US$5,000 fine levied on the companies, and a US$1 fine on the individuals. Commentators have noted that it is possible that, at this time, the Truman administration decided it required the undivided assistance of General Motors in fighting the ongoing Korean War and also in pursuing the Cold War against the former Soviet Union. Maybe the government at that time, decided that the support of large corporations was a higher priority than having electric mass transit systems operating in major population areas. Thus, it appears that there may have been economic reasons for the demise of electric streetcar systems; however, in the opinion of this writer, this natural progression was greatly assisted by the "conspiracy" discussed earlier.

In the 1920s, many American cities and towns were connected by a network of electric railroads and interurban electrified trolley cars. Within the cities, electric street railways, trolleys, and elevated trains moved large numbers of people easily and inexpensively. Between 1920 and 1955, General Motors, through National City Lines and Pacific City Lines, bought up more than 100 electric mass transit systems in 45 cities, allowing them to deteriorate and then replace them with rubber-tired, diesel-powered buses, which some writers say are more expensive, less efficient, and much filthier than electric rail systems.

Cities where electric rail systems were eliminated and replaced through this conspiracy to monopolize included New York, Philadelphia, Baltimore, St. Louis, Oakland, Salt Lake City, and Los Angeles. The only large city in California where National or Pacific did not take over the transit company was San Francisco, whose transit system was owned by the city.

(No Model.) 2 Sheets—Sheet 1.

F. J. SPRAGUE.

ELECTRIC RAILWAY SYSTEM.

No. 321,149. Patented June 30, 1885.

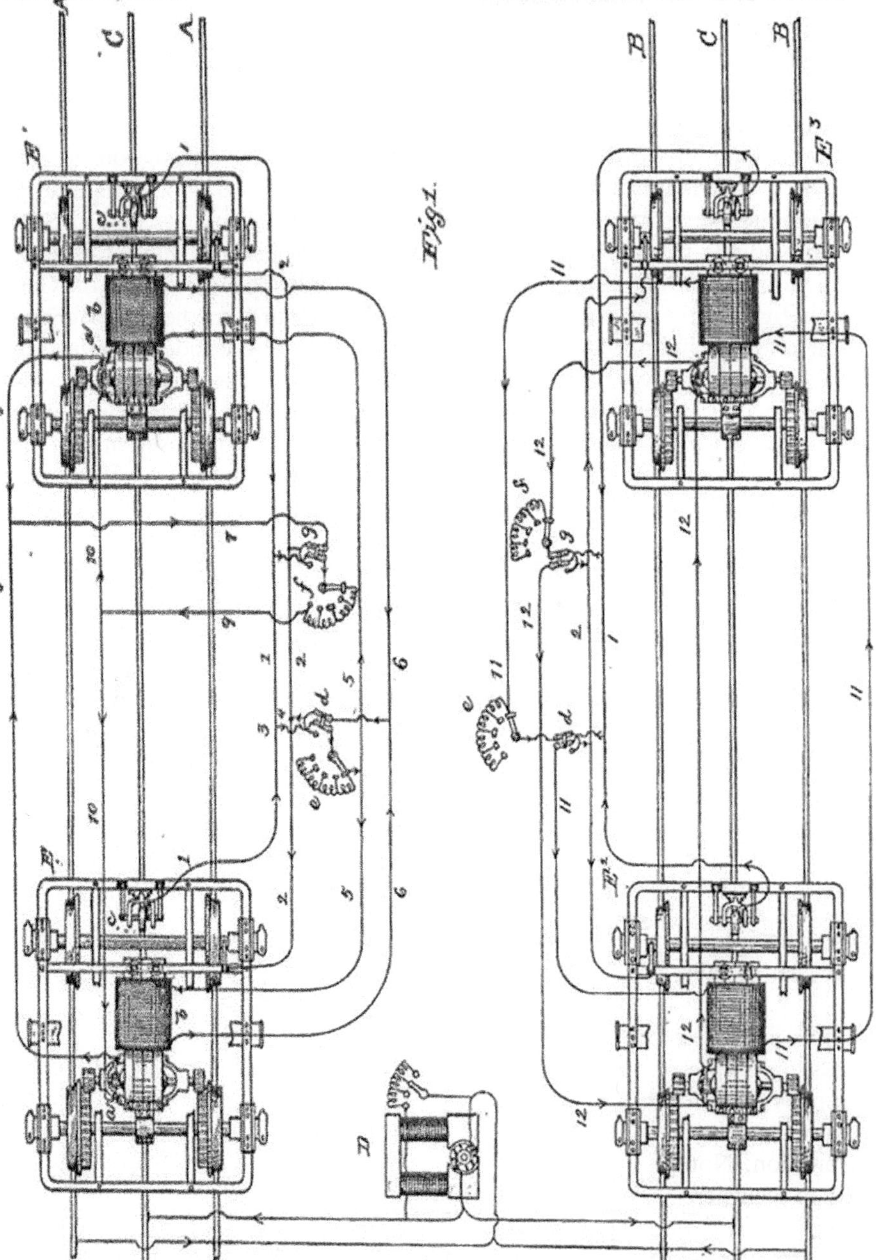

ATTEST:

E. C. Rowland

A. W. Kiddle

INVENTOR:

Frank J. Sprague

By Dyer & Seely

Attys

◆ INVENTORS AND INVENTIONS ◆

Mary Anderson

WINDSHIELD WIPER BLADE

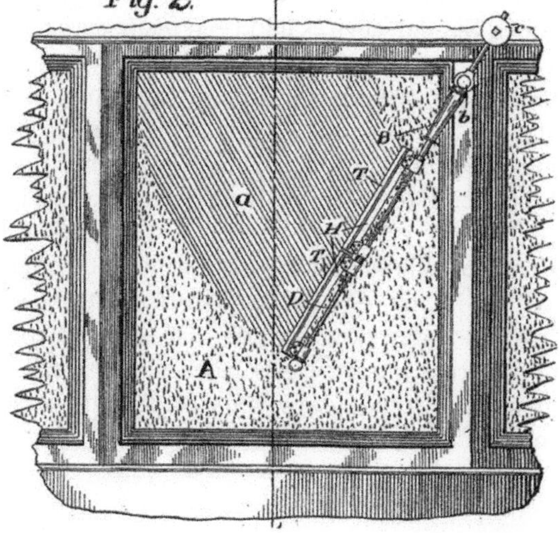

Mary Anderson was a real estate developer, rancher, and inventor of the windshield wiper blade. She received her first patent, No. 743,801, in November 1903 for an automatic car window cleaning device that was controlled from inside the vehicle.

Mary was visiting New York City in the winter of 1902, and, while riding in a trolley car on a particularly icy day, she noticed that the motorman drove with both panes of the double-front window open because of the difficulty in keeping the windshield clear of falling sleet. She also observed that the trolley driver often had to stop the trolley, and go outside to clear the window. The trolley's front-split, two-panel window was designed for bad-weather visibility, allowing the driver to move the panel comprising the snow or rain-covered section out of his line of vision. However, the multi-pane windshield system worked very poorly by exposing the driver's uncovered face (not to mention all the passengers sitting in the front of the trolley) to the falling precipitation. Notably, the multi-pane construction did not improve the operator's ability to see where he or she was going.

Mary Anderson began to sketch her wiper device right there on the trolley car. She then returned to Alabama, and hired a designer to sketch a manually operated device

Intellectual Property Law for Engineers, Scientists, and Entrepreneurs, Second Edition. Howard B. Rockman.

Published 2020 by John Wiley & Sons, Inc.

to keep a windshield clear. She then had a local company produce a working prototype, consisting of a set of wiper arms made of rubber and wood that could be controlled and operated by a lever within the trolley operator's reach. She applied for, and in 1903 was granted, a patent for the windshield wiper, which was directed to a lever inside the vehicle, which controlled the rubber blade on the outside of the windshield. The lever was accessible to the operator, and, when the lever was pivoted, the spring-loaded arm and the wiper blade moved reciprocally across the outside of the windshield, clearing rain, ice, sleet, mist, snow, and other unwanted materials from the windshield surface while the operator remained wholly inside the trolley. A counterweight maintained contact between the wiper blade and the windshield surface. Mary Anderson's patented device also included a feature where the wiper assembly was removable in fair weather. Similar devices had been made earlier, but Anderson's was the first to work effectively.

Detractors argued that her wiper would be a dangerous distraction to vehicle operators. Also, during the first decade of the twentieth century, many cars did not go fast enough to require windshields. Even though windshield wipers became standard equipment by 1916, her patent expired before she obtained any royalties for her invention.

In 1905, Anderson tried to sell the rights to her invention through a noted Canadian firm, but they rejected her, saying "We do not consider it to be of such commercial value as would warrant our undertaking its sale." Her patent expired in 1920, just as the automobile manufacturing industry was beginning to grow. In 1922, Cadillac became the first car manufacturer to adopt Mary Anderson's windshield wiper blade as standard equipment.

No. 743,801. PATENTED NOV. 10, 1903.

M. ANDERSON.

WINDOW CLEANING DEVICE.

APPLICATION FILED JUNE 18, 1903.

NO MODEL.

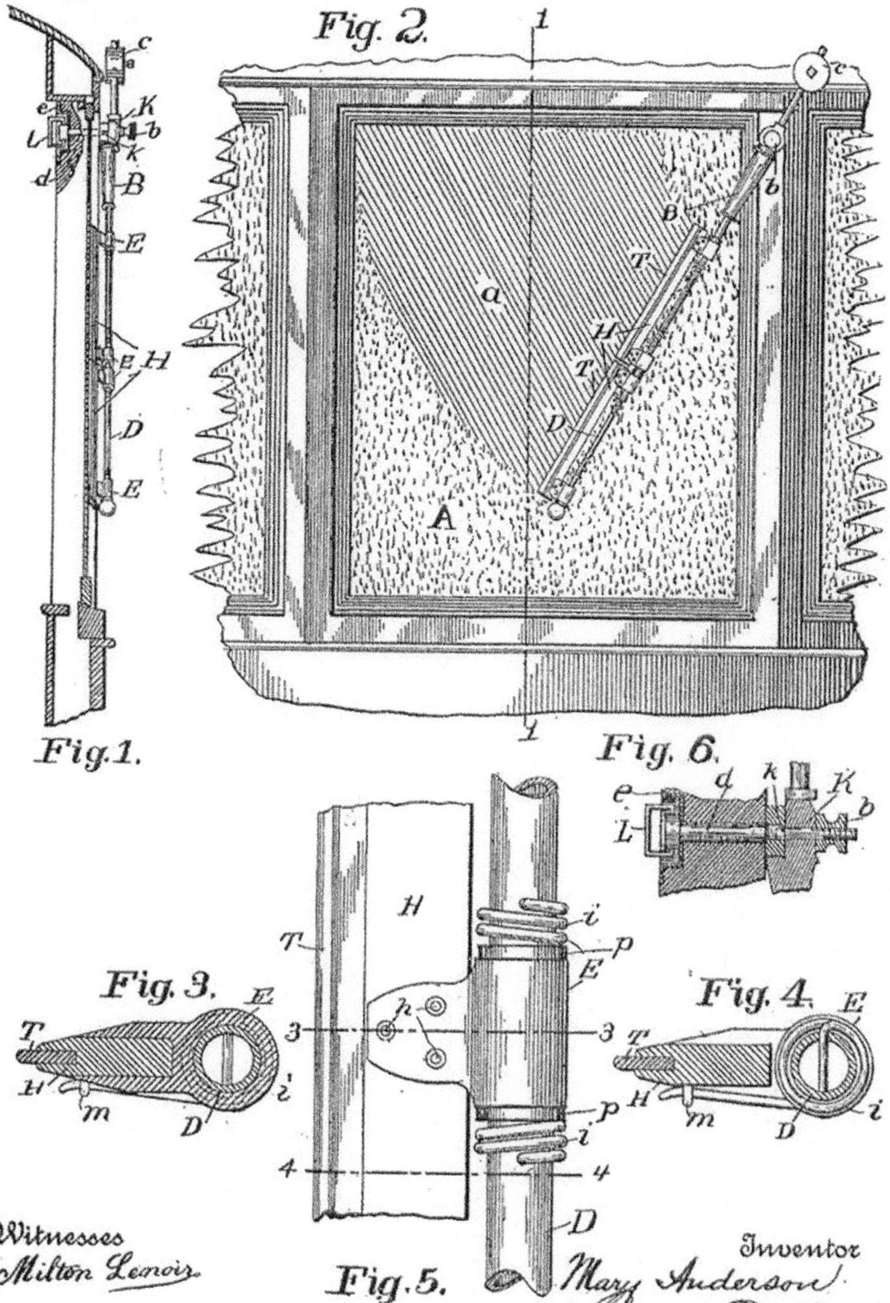

Witnesses

Milton Lenoir

Watts T. Estabrook

Inventor

Mary Anderson

by [illegible]

his Attorneys

THE NORRIS PETERS CO., PHOTO-LITHO., WASHINGTON, D. C.

2 Brief Overview of the Law

2.1 INTRODUCTION

Throughout the rest of this text, we will be discussing how intellectual property rights are created and enforced under various statutes passed by legislative bodies, and how these rights are interpreted and enforced by the various courts of the United States and other judicial systems. Hence, before we delve into these topics, I thought it helpful if a brief overview was provided of how the systems of law emerged, and how the U.S. legal system, by way of example, is structured. This should make it easier to comprehend how the statutory laws and judge-made laws are woven together to provide the tapestry that we know as Intellectual Property Law.

2.2 DEVELOPMENT OF THE LAW AND LEGAL PRINCIPLES

The laws of nature, or the natural laws such as the law of gravity, are universal laws, and cannot be changed by human-made laws. Such laws would exist even if legislative acts were passed against them. A state legislature once tried to set the value of Pi as 3.000 to make calculations involving the diameter and circumference of a circle more convenient. Obviously, this did not work.

The study of law concerns human-made laws governing relationships between people. The *law* refers to a set of rules and principles set up by society to restrict the conduct, and protect the rights, of its members. Each individual must control his or her behavior in such a manner that the rights of others are protected. As the urban societies of the globe grow, people interact with and depend on others to a higher degree, which requires more laws and restrictions of greater complexity to govern our behavior in a civil manner.

Laws began centuries ago as social customs and norms where it was proper for each member of the society to behave in a certain manner under particular circumstances. Tribal chiefs and, later, priests developed and enforced the laws, the latter based on laws of Divine origin.

Intellectual Property Law for Engineers, Scientists, and Entrepreneurs, Second Edition. Howard B. Rockman.

Published 2020 by John Wiley & Sons, Inc.

2.3 DIVINE LAWS

Two codes of Divine laws are worthy of note.

The first is the Code of Hammurabi, created around 1750 BC, and it was based on the principle of an eye-for-an-eye and a tooth-for-a-tooth, based on one's position in society. The early U.S. justice system was sometimes not far removed from this concept.

The Code of Hammurabi is one of several codifications of laws during ancient times. Hammurabi, the sixth Babylonian king, enacted the code, partial copies of which are engraved on a 7.5-foot stone stele, as well as on various clay tablets discovered by modern archaeologists in 1901. The code consists of 282 laws, with variable punishments based on one's position in society, and free man versus slave. The subjects covered in this early code include matters of contract, the terms of a transaction, the liability of a builder when a house collapses, damage to the property of another, inheritance, divorce, paternity, sexual behavior, and military service.

The preamble of the code states its purpose as:

> "… to bring about the rule of righteousness in the land, to destroy the wicked and the evil-doers; so that the strong should not harm the weak; so that I should … enlighten the land, to further the well-being of mankind."

The code has been cast as an early fundamental law, regulating a government in the manner of an early constitution. For example, it is one of the earliest statements of the presumption of innocence, and of the rule allowing both the accused and the accuser the opportunity to present evidence on their behalves. The most repeated law from Hammurabi's Code is the "eye-for-an-eye" provision, which states as follows:

> "Ex. Law No. 196. If a man destroy the eye of another man, they shall destroy his eye. If one break a man's bone, they shall break his bone. If one destroy the eye of a freeman or break the bone of a freeman, he shall pay one gold mina. If one destroy the eye of a man's slave or break a bone of a man's slave he shall pay one-half his price."

The second noteworthy set of Divine laws are the Ten Commandments, which are short and simple, and presumed to be known by every person. Knowledge of law is a presumption that has to be made. If not, anyone can plead ignorance of law and thereby avoid the operation of law. Today, most people can recall the Ten Commandments, or most of them; however, it would be impossible to know all of the laws which govern our lives today. However, there is a presumption under American law that every citizen is held to the knowledge of every law. Ignorance of the law is no defense to unlawful behavior in a nation which is governed by the rule of law.

2.4 THE FOUR TYPES OF LAW

2.4.1 Constitutional Law

Constitutional Law, or Basic Law, creates the operation of a government, defining its powers, and also establishes the limits on the government's exercise of its powers over its people. A constitution sets forth the fundamental principles and the relationships between the state and the citizens of that state. In the United States, citizens have rights both under individual state and federal Constitutions. A purpose of the U.S. Constitution is to protect the rights of minorities against the fiats of the majority.

2.4.2 Statutory Law

A statute is a law enacted by a legislative body, stating the express declarations of the will of the legislature on a given subject. A state law prohibiting gambling is an example of statutory law. Federal laws such as the Interstate Commerce Act, and municipal laws or ordinances regulating traffic, are also examples of statutes. Treaties and administrative regulations also have the same force and effect as statutes passed by the legislatures.

A primary reason for passing a statute is general dissatisfaction among the public with a present law situation in a particular field. The passage of a statute voids the common law covering the same point when the legislature's jurisdiction is invoked. However, there are limitations on the statutes passed by the legislature. For example, a statute cannot conflict with the U.S. Constitution or with the state Constitution involved. If a case arises involving a statutory issue, the courts may find that the statute conflicts with the Constitution, and the statute may be held invalid. Thus, the Constitutions are the supreme laws of their respective jurisdictions.

Legislatures also pass laws to develop a comprehensive set of rules to deal with specific problems and situations. Under the common law system, on a case-by-case basis, many years and several complex decisions may evolve before the law in a certain area changes. A legislature has the ability to cut through that time and enact legislation immediately to establish new laws.

2.4.3 Common Law

The U.S. common law was brought over from England by the colonists, and remains the basis of the legal system today in all but one state (Louisiana) of the United States. The common law is used by a court to decide issues between parties when no statute or constitutional law covers the particular legal problem involved. The common law arose with the practice of judges writing their opinions, giving the general principles and reasoning they followed in deciding cases. When the facts were similar in later cases, judges tended to follow the earlier opinions of other judges. These decisions eventually were followed by the courts throughout a particular jurisdiction in cases with similar or near-similar facts. This gave rise to the term "common law" to describe these judge-made decisions.

A primary principle of American law involves abiding by previous decisions—a doctrine known in Latin as *stare decisis*. This is the embodiment of the main feature of the common law wherein the law itself is built on prior case decisions. Thus, a judge uses earlier cases with similar facts as the foundation for that judge's decision in a particular case. Case law today is reported, and readily available to lawyers, parties, and the judges for precedent purposes. This body of precedential law in the United States forms the body of common law used by both the state and federal governments, except for the state of Louisiana, which still uses the French Civil Code system.

The common law is defined in Kent's Commentaries (an early legal treatise) as "those principles, usages, and rules of action applicable to the government and security of persons and property which do not rest for their authority upon any express or positive declaration of the will of the Legislature." This sets forth the principle that the common law is extracted from recorded decisions of courts. As new factual situations arise before the courts, new interpretations of law are made by the courts, and the common law is continuously amplified and modernized.

2.4.4 Business Custom

Courts will often make use of a relevant established and widely used business custom. For example, silence on the part of one to whom an offer is made usually cannot constitute acceptance of that offer. However, if there has been a history of dealings between persons, or if there is a practice in a particular business or trade, such that silence constitutes acceptance, the court will consider this and decide accordingly. Also, terminology particular to a trade is given its common trade usage in interpretation in a court of law. Business customs also involve something called the "law merchant." Merchants often need certainty about the rules that would be applied to any dispute by courts in various locations. Thus, a body of law that developed beginning in the Middle Ages continues until today out of business customs, and this set of laws is used by various courts in deciding commercial cases between merchants.

2.5 CIVIL LAW SYSTEMS

Two great systems of law are used in Western civilization.

1. The common law is used in most English-speaking countries.
2. The code or civil law is used in the remainder of Western societies.

The code or civil law, also known as the "continental system," originated around 450 BC as the Law of the Twelve Tables in the Roman Empire. This system expanded and contracted during the next ten centuries, and statutes were passed during that time and meanings clarified in court decisions. This civil law spread to other countries and became the foundation of the legal systems used in continental Europe today, and in other "civil law" countries.

Civil or code law is predicated on the establishment of comprehensive and complete written codes or statutes, the court's task being to apply the correct statute to the particular set of facts in each case.

Common law is built on the use of prior court decisions determining the outcome of subsequent cases presenting similar factual situations. Most of the law brought to the United States by its earlier settlers was the English common law. However, in certain areas of the United States settled by the French and Spanish, remains of civil law systems may be found, such as in Louisiana, Texas, and California.

The term "civil law" has two meanings. First, it means the code of law based on the Roman codes, and second, it is the system of private law as distinguished from criminal law, the latter regulating the conduct of individuals vis-a-vis the state.

2.6 ENFORCEMENT OF LAWS

The enforcement of laws takes one of three forms:

1. Punishment such as fines or imprisonment, usually for a crime, but also used in civil contempt situations, such as disobeying a court order.
2. Relief in actions involving private rights. This amounts to monetary damages awarded to the person who has been harmed, or a court order such as an injunction preventing future harm.
3. Social censure, which is the fear of public opinion, and, although not a recognized legal means of enforcement, its existence, strength, and importance as a deterrent to bad behavior cannot be overlooked.

Most of the people in a civil society comply with most of the laws unconsciously. The laws have been a part of our lives since early childhood.

2.7 CHANGES IN THE LAW

It is common knowledge that the law is slow to change. However, the law does change to reflect changes in society and changes in technology. For example, several years ago, the patent laws did not cover software algorithms. Today, the law has been changed by the courts, and software and algorithms, to an extent, can be patented. Thus, the laws can be changed in one of two ways: either by the decisions of courts being overruled by higher courts, or by the enactment of statutes by the legislatures. In addition, certain government agencies have the authority to make changes by executing rules and orders, such as interest rate changes by the Federal Reserve System.

The courts do have the ability to overrule or not follow prior decisions; however, in the interest of retaining stability, consistency, and predictability in the law, courts are quite reluctant to overrule or not follow prior decisions. However, at the same time, courts recognize that nothing is as permanent in this world as change itself, and, based on slightly different facts, a court may or may not follow an earlier decision, or may completely overrule an earlier decision as being outdated. For example, in 1904, the U.S. Supreme Court decided that separate but equal schools divided on racial lines was not a violation of the Constitution. In 1954, however, the Warren Court, based on additional evidence showing actual unfairness of such separate but equal schools, reversed the earlier court and decided that separate but equal schools along racial lines was a violation of the Constitutional right of equal protection of the law.

2.8 EQUITY

During the first two or three centuries following the inception of Kings Courts in England, English law underwent a hardening process where the remedies that were offered by the courts became standardized and quite limited. As a result of these limited remedies, courts of equity were created.

Consider this example. A contractor is hired to build a structure for Able. During the excavation, Baker, the next-door neighbor, notes an impending separation of her house from its foundation. Baker's walls start to crack and the ceiling begins to bulge. At this point, under common law, Baker has no remedy against Able since no real injury has occurred yet. Under common law, Baker would have to await whatever damages might be forthcoming, such as destruction of the house, and then sue Able to recover compensation for such damages.

However, under equity, Baker can do something now without waiting until her home is destroyed, by seeking a temporary injunction or restraining order to halt the excavation next door until something more appropriate can be done to prevent damage to her house.

The common law courts would not do any of the following: (a) prevent a wrong from taking place; (b) order persons to perform their obligations; or (c) correct mistakes. These gaps in the law were filled by the equity courts, known today as the Courts of Chancery in some jurisdictions. This was because, in the early days, the kings delegated their chancellors with the responsibility of deciding "equity" cases involving these "unusual" remedies. In most states today and in the U.S. federal court system, law and equity have been completely combined, whereby you can seek monetary damages and injunctive relief in a single litigation, such as seeking an injunction and monetary damages for infringement of your intellectual property rights.

The remedies in a common law court act "*in rem*," or upon an object. Equity courts, however, operate "*in personam*" in crafting remedies, which are directed to ordering a person. The common equity remedies of injunction and specific performance are directed to prevent or to compel a person to do, or not to do, something. Divorces, mortgage foreclosures, accountings, reformation of contracts, and injunctions against patent and copyright infringement are examples of equity remedies. The word "equity" itself defines a system where the court can act in any way necessary to secure a right or remedy for a wrong. Also, if a remedy must be invented to serve a particular purpose, that can be accomplished by a court of equity.

Injunctive relief can be either permanent or temporary, and it is an act in contempt of court for anyone who has knowledge of the order, and who is subject to it, to fail to obey the order. Such contempt can be punished by monetary fine or imprisonment. Specific performance arises in connection with contracts involving land, and celebrity contracts such as concert performances. In land deals, if a seller refuses to deed land to a buyer after a lawful contract has been signed by all parties, the seller may be forced to part with the land by an order for specific performance. Likewise, a performer who tries to back out of a concert performance could be forced by a court of equity to proceed with the performance if undue hardship would occur were that celebrity not to perform.

Specific performance could also apply to contracts for sale of an antique or a rare painting or other one-of-a-kind item. The courts of equity have substantial power, and also have the ability to issue a remedy both by way of injunction or specific performance, and the award of monetary damages. Patent infringement and trade secret cases are examples of such equity matters where the plaintiff seeks monetary damages for past infringement by the defendant, and an injunction prohibiting the defendant from any further acts of infringement.

To obtain preliminary injunctive relief, one must prove all of the following to the court's satisfaction:

a. A substantial likelihood of ultimate success on the merits at the termination of the litigation.
b. Irreparable injury that cannot be compensated by monetary consideration.

c. That the harm, if the relief requested is denied, outweighs the harm if the relief is granted.
d. That public interest is not disserved by granting the injunction.

A situation of dumping toxic materials, operating unsafe machinery, or having continual smoke in a workplace would be a basis for seeking equity jurisdiction. These types of injuries are irreparable if allowed to continue. A Court of Equity may permit the granting of a temporary injunction, lasting for the remainder of the litigation, if you can establish the preceding four requisites for granting a temporary injunction. In equity cases, there is no jury.

Keep in mind that a Court of Equity can enjoin situations before they get to the point of damages, such as unlawful waste disposal, even though no one has yet been injured by such disposal.

2.9 U.S. COURTS, STATE AND FEDERAL

One of the hallmarks of the beginning of civilized behavior was creating a system for best determining the truth of an accusation. Court trials with a judge, jury, and attorneys representing the plaintiff and defendant have not always been used. We have seen enough movies and television shows that indicate that the earliest form of trial was usually by battle. The accused and accuser, or their representatives, faced each other in battle, with the outcome determining the justice of the accusation. The shortcomings of justice and equity being based on such a system are obvious.

In many early civilizations, trial by battle was replaced by trial by ordeal or trial by jury. The Code of Hammurabi required trial by ordeal, such as throwing the accused into the divine river. If the river held the defendant, for example, if he could not swim, the guilty verdict and punishment were delivered simultaneously. However, more realistically, trial by a jury of your peers in one form or another existed in many ancient civilizations. Our present jury trial system developed with the common law, and is now guaranteed in the Sixth and Seventh Amendments of the U.S. Constitution in both criminal and civil cases.

Keep in mind that a jury must usually determine the facts of a particular occurrence *after* that occurrence has happened. The jury bases its decision upon the evidence that the court allows it to hear, and on the instructions in the law given to the jury by the judge. Keep in mind that, once an event has happened, and all witnesses to that event are unavailable, there is no way of knowing exactly what happened, and the facts may never truly be known. The jury system, although possibly flawed, is still the best system known for determining the truth. As Churchill once remarked about democracy, it is a bad form of government—however, it is better than all the rest. In my judgment, the same principle can be applied to the jury system.

In the United States, a court system exists for each state, as well as a system of federal courts. Both the federal and state systems provide an ultimate tribunal, the federal Supreme Court and the state's highest courts, respectively. Beneath the supreme court and highest state court in each system are the appellate courts. The appellate courts handle appeals from the lower courts. The lower courts are designated as district courts in the federal system, and usually as county courts in the state systems. One anomaly is that the lowest court in the State of New York is designated the Supreme Court, the highest court is the New York Court of Appeals.

2.10 THE FEDERAL COURT SYSTEM

2.10.1 The Supreme Court

The U.S. Supreme Court is the highest tribunal in the United States. The final court of appeal, the Supreme Court is established under Article III of the U.S. Constitution, which provides for a Supreme Court and whatever inferior federal courts that Congress may from time to time require. Since the Constitution mentions "a" Supreme Court, all nine justices sit at one time on all cases, and the court is not divided into smaller panels, although this procedure would at least triple the ability of the Supreme Court to hear cases.

There are certain situations in which the Supreme Court has direct jurisdiction to handle cases. These are the ones involving ambassadors, public ministers, counsels, cases in which a state is a party, and a few others. In all other cases, matters reach the Supreme Court by appeal, and the Supreme Court has the ability to accept or not accept an appeal. Cases are appealed to the Supreme Court from either U.S. appellate courts or from the state's highest courts in the normal course of events. An appeal from an appellate court in the federal system is usually made to the Supreme Court by seeking a "writ of certiorari." If the writ is accepted by the Supreme Court, the Supreme Court will hear the case and render a decision. Only a very small number of such writs of certiorari are accepted by the Supreme Court, presently in the range of 1–20. In those cases where the Supreme Court does not accept certiorari, it may be understood that the Supreme Court agrees that the appellate court decision being appealed from is correct and should be allowed to stand.

The nine Supreme Court justices have the final say about what our law shall be in many important respects. They are not the legislative branch of the government; however they have a highly significant function to interpret what is meant by the wording of the Constitution or of a particular statute passed by Congress. The court also determines the lawful interpretation to be used in future cases of lower courts. If the Supreme Court gives an interpretation to a particular statute of Congress, and Congress disagrees with that interpretation, Congress can then enact legislation that would overcome the Supreme Court's interpretation of the language of the statute.

2.10.2 Courts of Appeals

The Courts of Appeals of the federal judicial system normally consist of three-judge panels, which were first established by Congress in 1891 because of the burden of appeals on the U.S. Supreme Court. The appellate courts do not conduct trials, and disputes between parties are appealed only on the basis of a conflict in the interpretation of the law. The facts decided previously in a lower court are not changed by the Court of Appeals. As a general rule, an appellate court does not have the ability to make an adverse decision regarding a fact established in a lower court.

The Court of Appeals for the Federal Circuit ("CAFC") is a U.S. Court of Appeals with a primary facility in Washington, D.C. The CAFC was created by Congress in 1982, which merged the then-existing U.S. Court of Customs and Patent Appeals and the appellate division of the U.S. Court of Claims. Of particular importance, the CAFC is the only appellate-level U.S. court with the jurisdiction to hear and decide appeals in patent lawsuits originating in any one of the U.S. district courts.

A unique feature of the CAFC is that it is the only appeals court in the federal judicial system whose jurisdiction is based wholly upon subject matter, rather than on geographic location.

The CAFC has exclusive appellant jurisdiction over appeals from:

a. U.S. district court cases relating to patents.
b. The U.S. Patent Trial and Appeal Board.
c. The U.S. Trademark Trial and Appeal Board.
d. Appeals arising from an action against the Commissioner of Patents and Trademarks where the USPTO has refused to issue a patent.
e. The U.S. Court of International Trade, which hears cases involving the importation of foreign goods that have been alleged to infringe one or more U.S. patents, trademarks, or copyrights.
f. Appeals from several government tribunals that do not involve intellectual property.

Decisions by the CAFC in patent cases are binding precedent in other patent cases heard in all of the district dourts throughout the United States. Only the U.S. Supreme Court, or Congress, can reverse or change a decision by the CAFC in a patent case.

2.10.3 District Courts

In the federal system, the trial courts, those in front of whom witnesses appear and juries decide cases as well as judges, are known as "district courts." There are approximately 100 or so in the United States, such that no state is without a Federal District Court, and larger states have several. The number of presiding judges in a U.S. district court is determined by statute and is usually based on the number of federal cases arising in the district.

For a case to be tried in a federal court, it must meet at least one of several criteria:

a. The issue must arise from the U.S. Constitution, federal laws, or treaties of the United States.
b. It must arise in admiralty.
c. It must involve two or more states as parties.
d. It must involve the United States as a party.
e. It must be between citizens of different states, with the amount in controversy greater than $75,000.
f. It must be between a U.S. citizen and a foreign country or its citizens.

Most of the controversies handled involve federal statutes or the U.S. Constitution, better known as federal question cases, or diversity cases, which are those between citizens of different states. Patent, copyright, trademark, restraint of trade, federal tax, and infringement of personal rights alleged to violate the Constitution are typical of cases tried in the U.S. district courts.

2.11 STATE COURTS

The 50 state court systems in the United States are far from uniform throughout the country. The systems as well as the names of the courts differ. Also, the law applied in similar-fact situations may also vary among the states.

Each state has a final court of appeal, normally the supreme court or the court of appeals of that particular state. The highest court practically always confines its work to appeals of cases tried in lower courts. In several states, to ease the workload of the higher court, courts of intermediate appellate jurisdiction are interposed between the higher courts and the lower trial courts.

Below the appellate courts in a state system are the trial courts in a general jurisdiction known either as circuit courts, courts of common pleas, county courts, superior courts, or, as stated previously in New York, the supreme court. Other courts such as probate courts or surrogate courts handle cases involving wills, trusts, and estates. Such courts are usually limited in geographical jurisdiction to a particular county, district, or other major political subdivision of the state.

At the lower end of the chain involving state courts are various municipal courts, police courts, justices of the peace, small claims courts, juvenile courts, and recorders courts who handle cases of very limited jurisdiction.

2.12 JURISDICTION

The *jurisdiction* of a court is defined as its scope of authority to hear and determine the causes of action presented to the court, given either by a legislature or U.S. or state Constitution. The jurisdiction of a court is dependent upon the geographical region in which the injury or activity occurred, where the individuals reside or do business, to types of cases, and possibly to the amount of money or type of relief concerned. The courts not only have jurisdiction over the people in front of them, they have jurisdiction over those individuals' property, both real and personal, located within their assigned geographical limits. The courts have the authority under the law to take property of one party in satisfaction of a judgment in favor of another party, where the latter was damaged by the conduct of the one party. However, a court has no authority in a state over property lying outside its territorial limits. For example, a court in Illinois could force a defendant to sell the defendant's property in Illinois to satisfy a judgment against the prevailing plaintiff; however, the court would have no authority to force the defendant to sell property located in another state.

Regarding personal jurisdiction, the court has jurisdiction over persons who have had sufficient contacts with the state, as long as the exercise of jurisdiction does not offend traditional notions of fair play and substantial justice, whether the persons are residents or not. For example, assume a company or individual is doing business on the Internet offering items for sale worldwide. Even though the Internet-using company is lodged in one building in one state, the mere fact of offering goods over the Internet throughout the country will give a court in another state jurisdiction over that person or company and that business, even though that person or company has never been in the state in which the action is brought.

The courts initiate their jurisdiction by serving the accused person with a summons, or other legal process. A witness is served with a subpoena to compel the appearance of that witness before a court. Summonses and subpoenas can be served in person or by mail.

Jurisdiction of courts may also be limited as to the type of cases they have authority to adjudicate. For example, under many state systems, criminal courts do not handle civil matters. In the federal system, federal district courts handle civil, equity, and criminal matters. For example, in one state court case in which I was participating, our civil matter was interrupted by the return of a jury in a criminal matter, and momentarily I had two gentlemen standing next to me in prison clothes, their feet and hands shackled, while the judge was answering a question posed by the jury in their case. When these gentlemen returned from whence they came, I asked someone who they were, and I was advised that they had killed a rather elderly lady by stabbing her several times and stuffing her body into a freezer. I felt momentarily uncomfortable, to say the least!

SECTION II

Patents

◆ INVENTORS AND INVENTIONS ◆

Charles Goodyear

VULCANIZATION OF RUBBER

Charles Goodyear was born in New Haven, Connecticut, in December 1800, and eventually entered the hardware business with his father. However, their hardware business failed in 1830, forcing father and son into bankruptcy. At that time, natural or "India" rubber had little usefulness to industry. Rubber products melted in hot weather, froze and cracked after becoming brittle in cold weather, and stuck to virtually everything they came in contact with.

After the failure of the hardware business, Goodyear tried selling a valve for rubber life preservers, but the rubber market was going down because of rubber's aforementioned drawbacks. Hence, Goodyear decided he should try to revive the failing market. He began his research in jail, where he was serving time because of debt. In jail, Goodyear worked with rubber and a rolling pin for hours at a time.

Rubber, being a natural adhesive, was very sticky, so after being freed from jail, Goodyear decided to use a powder to dry out the rubber. He started with magnesia powder that he purchased at drugstores. The added magnesia made the rubber less sticky, and, armed with this improvement, he received some backing from a friend to make rubber overshoes. Before he could market them, however, summer arrived, and the shoes melted.

Goodyear started adding quicklime to his mix, and, at a trade show in New York, he was awarded a medal for his work.

One day in 1836, while working with rubber, he began to run low on samples, so he decided to melt down and reuse old rubber. By this time, Goodyear had started painting his samples, so he used nitric acid to remove the old paint, but the rubber turned black and he decided he could not use it. A day or so later, Goodyear noticed that the sample was smooth and dry, so he retrieved it from trash and started working with this new improved smooth rubber. He obtained more money based on this new rubber, but, after a vacation with his family, he returned to his nitric acid–treated rubber and found it was still the soft glue that it always was. By 1839, Goodyear was still experimenting, now using sulfur. One day, while showing off his new rubber formulation and getting nothing but laughs, he became furious, and the rubber slipped out of his hands, landing on a sizzling-hot potbellied stove. Instead of melting the rubber, it charred into a leather-like substance and around the burnt area was a springy brown part or "gum elastic." Goodyear observed that heat was required to cure or

Intellectual Property Law for Engineers, Scientists, and Entrepreneurs, Second Edition. Howard B. Rockman.

Published 2020 by John Wiley & Sons, Inc.

strengthen a rubber–sulfur compound. This changed the rubber into an almost completely new substance. Goodyear had invented waterproof rubber, through what he called the "vulcanization" process.

Goodyear still needed to know how long to cook his rubber. This was the hardest time for Goodyear and his family as he spent even more time trying out heating techniques. He was forced to sell most of his family's possessions, but then he finally found that steam, under pressure, applied for 4–6 hours at approximately 270°F, gave him the most uniform results. In 1844, Goodyear obtained a patent on his vulcanization process after spending 5 years developing the process. Vulcanization is a process in which sulfur reacts with carbon–carbon double bonds in the rubber to form "bridges" of sulfur atoms that cross-link the molecules.

As you might expect, the principal use of Goodyear's process is in the manufacture of tires, hoses, and footwear. Goodyear's unique process strengthened rubber, made it resistant to heat and cold, and ultimately revolutionized the rubber industry. However, Goodyear was unable to profit financially from his discovery, although he did license his process. His numerous patents were continually infringed upon, and he spent large sums of money on unsuccessful businesses, costly experiments, and attempts to promote his process. The company that bears his name today was founded many years after Charles Goodyear's death. He was able to establish his rights legally, but died in 1860 a poor man.

UNITED STATES PATENT OFFICE.

CHARLES GOODYEAR, OF NEW YORK, N.Y.

IMPROVEMENT IN INDIA-RUBBER FABRICS.

Specification forming part of Letters Patent No. 3,633, dated June 15, 1844.

To all whom it may concern:

Be it known that I, CHARLES GOODYEAR, of the city of New York, in the State of New York, have invented certain new and useful Improvements in the Manner of Preparing Fabrics of Caoutchouc or India-Rubber; and I do hereby declare that the following is a full and exact description thereof.

My principal improvement consists in the combining of sulphur and white lead with the india-rubber, and in the submitting of the compound thus formed to the action of heat at a regulated temperature, by which combination and exposure to heat it will be so far altered in its qualities as not to become softened by the action of the solar ray or of artificial heat at a temperature below that to which it was submitted in its preparation—say to a heat of 270° of Fahrenheit's scale—nor will it be injuriously affected by exposure to cold. It will also resist the action of the expressed oils, and that likewise of spirits of turpentine, or of the other essential oils at common temperatures, which oils are its usual solvents.

The articles which I combine with the india-rubber in forming my improved fabric are sulphur and white lead, which materials may be employed in varying proportions; but that which I have found to answer best, and to which it is desirable to approximate in forming the compound, is the following: I take twenty-five parts of india-rubber, five parts of sulphur, and seven parts of white lead. The india-rubber I usually dissolve in spirits of turpentine or other essential oil, and the white lead and sulphur also I grind in spirits of turpentine in the ordinary way of grinding paint. These three articles thus prepared may, when it is intended to form a sheet by itself, be evenly spread upon any smooth surface or upon glazed cloth, from which it may be readily separated; but I prefer to use for this purpose the cloth made according to the present specification, as the compound spread upon this article separates therefrom more cleanly than from any other.

Instead of dissolving the india-rubber in the manner above set forth, the sulphur and white lead, prepared by grinding as above directed, may be incorporated with the substance of the india-rubber by the aid of heated cylinders or calender-rollers, by which it may be brought into sheets of any required thickness; or it may be applied so as to adhere to the surface of cloth or of leather of various kinds. This mode of producing and of applying the sheet caoutchouc by means of rollers is well known to manufacturers. To destroy the odor of the sulphur in fabrics thus prepared, I wash the surface with a solution of potash, or with vinegar, or with a small portion of essential oil or other solvent of sulphur.

When the india-rubber is spread upon the firmer kinds of cloth or of leather it is subject to peel therefrom by a moderate degree of force, the gum letting go the fiber by which the two are held together. I have therefore devised another improvement in this manufacture by which this tendency is in a great measure corrected, and by which, also, the sheet-gum, when not attached to cloth or leather, is better adapted to a variety of purposes than when not prepared by this improved mode, which is as follows: After laying a coat of the gum, compounded as above set forth, on any suitable fabric I cover it with a bat of cotton-wool as it is delivered from the doffer of a carding-machine, and this bat I cover with another coat of the gum—a process which may be repeated two or three times, according to the required thickness of the goods. A very thin and strong fabric may be thus produced, which may be used in lieu of paper for the covering of boxes, books, or other articles.

When this compound of india-rubber, sulphur, and white lead, whether to be used alone in the state of sheets or applied to the surface of any other fabric has been fully dried, either in a heated room or by exposure to the sun and air, the goods are to be subjected to the action of a high degree of temperature, which will admit of considerable variation—say from 212° to 350° of Fahrenheit's thermometer, but for the best effect approaching as nearly as may be to 270°. This heating may be effected by running the fabrics over a heated cylinder; but I prefer to expose them to an atmosphere of the proper temperature, which may be best done by the aid of an oven properly constructed with openings through which the sheet or web may be passed by means of suitable rollers. When this process is performed upon a fabric consisting of the above-named compound it must be allowed to remain upon the cloth on which it is made, in order to sustain it, as it is so far softened during the operation as not to be capable of supporting its own weight without such aid. If the exposure be to a temperature exceeding 270°, it must continue for a very brief period.

Having thus fully described the nature of the process by which I prepare my improved india-rubber fabric, I do hereby declare that I do not now claim the combining of sulphur with caoutchouc, either in the proportion named or in any other, this combination having been the subject of a patent granted to me on the 24th of February, 1839; but

I do claim—

1. The combining of the said gum with sulphur and with white lead, so as to form a triple compound, either in the proportions herein named or in any other within such limits as will produce a like result; and I will here remark that although I have obtained the best results from the carbonate of lead, other salts of lead or the oxides of that metal may be substituted therefor, and will produce a good effect. I therefore under this head claim the employment of either of the oxides or salts of lead in the place of the white lead in the above-named compound.

2. The formation of a fabric of the india-rubber by interposing layers of cotton-batting between those of the gum, in the manner and for the purpose above described.

3. In combination with the foregoing, the process of exposing the india-rubber fabric to the action of a high degree of heat, such as is herein specified, by means of which my improved compound is effectually changed in its properties so as to protect it from decomposition or deterioration by the action of those agents which have heretofore been found to produce that effect upon india-rubber goods.

CHARLES GOODYEAR.

Witnesses:

Thos. P. Jones,
B. R. Morsell.

◆ INVENTORS AND INVENTIONS ◆

John Boyd Dunlop

PNEUMATIC VEHICLE TIRES

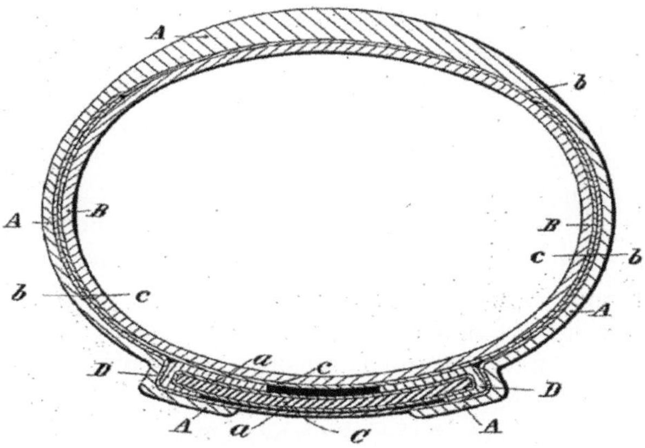

The wheel was invented around 3500 BC. Thousands of years later, the wheel is no longer made of wood, and the ride is much smoother. This is because of the pneumatic tire, developed by John Boyd Dunlop from Scotland.

Charles Goodyear invented vulcanized rubber in 1839 when he developed the vulcanization process, which made rubber more pliable and increased its rigidity and durability, allowing rubber to be used for a much wider array of purposes. Soon after the discovery of vulcanization, vehicle tires began to be made of solid rubber, and they were strong, absorbed shocks, and resisted cuts and abrasions. However, these solid tires were very heavy and failed to provide a smooth ride over the rough roads of the day.

In October 1887, John Boyd Dunlop developed the first practical pneumatic or inflatable tire. He put an experimental tire he built on his son's tricycle in the yard of his home in Belfast, Northern Ireland, after fitting the tire to a wooden disc 96 cm across. He made his first tires by wrapping the solid rubber tires on his son's tricycle with glued rubber sheets, and filled the cavity with air.

He took this wheel and a metal wheel from his son's tricycle, and rolled both of them across the yard together. The metal wheel stopped rolling, but the pneumatic wheel continued until it hit a gatepost and rebounded off the post. Dunlop then placed

Intellectual Property Law for Engineers, Scientists, and Entrepreneurs, Second Edition. Howard B. Rockman.

Published 2020 by John Wiley & Sons, Inc.

pneumatic tires on both rear wheels of his son's tricycle, and the tricycle's rolling improved. He then constructed larger tires for bicycles with even more startling results.

He began testing his pneumatic tires at a sports ground in Belfast, and obtained a patent on his pneumatic tires on December 7, 1888. However, completely unknown to Dunlop, another Scotsman, Robert William Thompson from Stonehaven, had patented a pneumatic tire in 1847. Thompson had earlier placed his tires on horse-drawn carriages in London, but they never caught on, because at the time they were too expensive to manufacture. Frustrated with this result, Thompson turned to solid rubber tires for his future inventions. Hence, it might be said that John Dunlop "reinvented" the pneumatic tire.

In 1889, William Hume won a bicycle race in Ireland using Dunlop tires for the first time, and he subsequently won more races in England. Hume was the first member of the public to purchase a bicycle fitted with pneumatic tires, after Dunlop suggested that Hume use them in a race. On May 18, 1889, Hume won all four cycling events at the Queen's College Sports Event in Belfast. A short time later, in Liverpool, he won all but one of the cycling events, lifting inflatable tires into the spotlight, and making them the standard for bicycles. Losers in the Liverpool event included the sons of the head of the Irish Cyclist Association, Harvey Du Cros. Du Cros saw an opportunity, and proceeded to build a personal relationship with Dunlop. Together, they formed a company, which acquired the rights to Dunlop's patent.

Two years after Dunlop was awarded his patent, he was officially informed in 1891 that his patent was invalid, based on Thompson's earlier patent, which issued in France in 1846 and in the United States in 1847. However, Dunlop and Du Cros continued to capitalize on pneumatic tires for bicycles, and they acquired a Dublin company and renamed it Pneumatic Tyre and Booth's Cycle Agency. Dunlop retired in 1895, and Du Cros sold the entire bicycle tire business in 1896 to a British financier, Terah Hooley, for £3 million. Hooley then made improvements, and resold the company to the public for £5 million. Du Cros remained head of the business until he died. Early in the twentieth century, the company was renamed Dunlop Rubber.

The production of automobile tires did not begin until 1900, well after Dunlop's retirement. As a result, Dunlop did not acquire any considerable remuneration from his invention.

Inflatable tires provide a smoother ride and increased traction since the wheel deforms slightly when it meets the road, creating a friction bond between the vehicle and the road as the tire deforms and casts a wider and longer footprint. This is in contrast with solid rubber tires, which do not deform. For reasons that do not appear as clear as they should, solid rubber tires remain the material of choice for tricycle wheels, while today inflatable tires are the choice for bicycles and most other vehicles worldwide. At the time Dunlop came up with his invention, bicycles were becoming extremely popular, and the lighter, air-filled tire resulted in a better ride with less vibration.

For 50 years after Dunlop's invention, vehicle tires were made using an inner tube containing compressed air and an outer casing. The casing protected the inner tube and provided the tire with traction. The tire casing was reinforced with layers comprising rubberized fabric cords embedded in the rubber, and these were known as "bias ply tires," since the cords in the single ply ran diagonally from the bead of one inner rim to the bead on another rim. The orientation of the cords is reversed from ply to ply, so the cords crisscross each other. Today, you can still find bias ply tires as equipment for antique and collector cars, and for various types of off-road tractor tires.

In 1948, steel-belted radial tires appeared in Europe, and are so named because the ply cords radiate at a 90° angle from the wheel rim, such that the casing is strengthened by a belt of steel fabric extending around the circumference of the tire. Radial tire ply cords are composed of nylon, rayon, or polyester. The advantages of radial tires include longer tread life, improved steering, and less rolling resistance, which results in increased gas mileage. On the negative side, radial tires have a harder riding quality, and are also about twice as expensive to make as previous pneumatic tires.

(No Model.)

J. B. DUNLOP.

WHEEL TIRE FOR CYCLES.

No. 435,995. Patented Sept. 9, 1890.

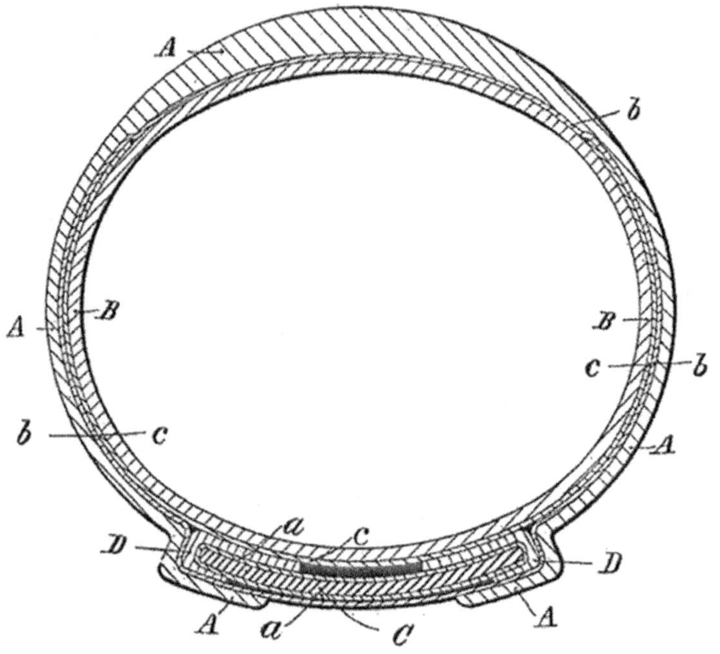

Witnesses.

Benjamin King

Charles Ennis

Inventor.

John Boyd Dunlop

per James Stevenson

Attorney.

3 Introduction to Patents

3.1 BRIEF HISTORY OF PATENT PROTECTION

3.1.1 Early European Patent Custom

It is commonly recognized that the history of patents is wrapped in obscurity and uncertainty. Prior to any patent system, there was a "patent custom" in many countries throughout Europe. Before the creation of the U.S. Constitution, the governments of several European countries granted exclusive rights in patentable and sometimes unpatentable subject matter as a "privilege" of the crown, rather than a property right available to all inventors. At the time the United States transitioned to a federal form of government under its Constitution, the patenting of inventions had been known and practiced in several countries for centuries. The "patent custom" that was known to the framers of the U.S. Constitution, simply put, was the practice of the state granting some form of limited-term exclusive right to engage in a new trade or craft, sometimes denominated an industry, to the person or persons responsible for introducing that industry into the state, either by creation or importation. The privilege consisted of a temporary and exclusive right to commercialize the new subject matter, covered by the grant, whether it be called a patent, letters patent, or something else.

The early patent custom involved grants of privileges rather than property rights. The distinction between a patent privilege and a patent property right is an important one and not always recognized in the early literature of the patent law. Nonetheless, inventors, who had the most practical interest in obtaining exclusive rights to commercialize their inventions, were increasingly aware of the distinction, and, by the eighteenth century, they began to argue that they had a natural, inherent property right in their inventions, which it was the obligation of the state to protect, thus arguing that the state had no right to refuse granting them an exclusive position in their inventions for a limited time.

In an effort to encourage individuals who contributed to the advance of a culture, earlier governments recognized the "natural" right of a person to his or her own ideas and inventions, and strengthened that right by granting governmental proclamations and regulations restraining others from exercising the opposing "natural" right to copy. For the most part, this protection was limited in terms of time by those early governments. Since these early forms of government were of an authoritarian nature,

Intellectual Property Law for Engineers, Scientists, and Entrepreneurs, Second Edition. Howard B. Rockman.

Published 2020 by John Wiley & Sons, Inc.

ruled by monarchs, sovereigns, kings, and emperors, the practice that was most prevalent then was to grant royal favors to certain individuals, giving exclusive rights to sell certain commodities which had previously been available to be sold by anyone. Needless to say, this type of monopoly did not find favor with the general public. These so-called city or state monopolies were outlawed in the Roman Empire in a proclamation by Emperor Zeno in 480 AD. His proclamation read:

> "We order that no one will dare exercise a monopoly upon any garment or fish or … any kind of thing in that respect, or any material, whether it is already ascertained in a sacred way, or by a later rescript which ascertains it, or by empirical decree, or by a sacred notation of a kindness…"

Similar state or royal monopolies were outlawed in medieval Europe and Great Britain at much later dates. Despite this general prohibition on state monopolies, various practices developed to reward individuals for certain unique ideas. The archives of Venice indicate that protection was granted from about the year 1200 AD to dredges, wells, flour mills, and other water-controlling or water-utilizing facilities. The Guilds of Venice, unlike those of most medieval Europe, encouraged the granting of protection to new devices and arts. Thus, between 1400 and 1432 AD, the Senate of Venice enacted a statute providing a 10-year exclusive privilege to use any machine or process that a person invents to speed up silk-making or to improve the process. This grant was given by the Guild Welfare Board of the Republic, and was soon extended to other devices and arts such as flour mills, cook stoves for die shops, a device for raising water, the art of printing, and mills for grinding grain products. All this protection was granted in the fifteenth century. Such exclusive grants were made not only to encourage the citizens of Venice to invent unique materials and methods, but also to attract ingenious persons into the republic.

Before granting a patent, the Guild Welfare Board of Venice usually examined the invention to be certain it was new and, indeed, useful. The disclosure of the invention was made by public use, not by filing a written document such as a patent application, and examination of the invention took place by interview, observation, and the explanations of experts. The grant of exclusivity was often based on a showing that the invention had to be truly useful and could achieve the advantages asserted by the inventor. What is believed to be the world's first general patent statutes evolved from these practices, and, in 1474 AD, the Senate of the Republic of Venice reorganized its patent system by enacting a statute with the clear intent of encouraging both native ingenuity and the importation of new ideas. The preamble to the statute is noteworthy, and is dated March 19, 1474:

> "We have among us men of great genius, apt to invent and discover ingenious devices; and in view of the grandeur and virtue of our city, more such men come to us every day from diverse parts. Now, if provision were made for the works and devices discovered by such persons, so that others who may see them could not build them and take the inventor's honor away, more men would then apply their genius, will discover, and will build devices of great utility and benefit to our commonwealth."

This was followed in the Venice law by the grant of a 10-year exclusive right to anyone who constructed any new and ingenious device in Venice, which was not previously made. Notice had to be given of the invention to the Guild Welfare Board of Venice.

The penalty for infringement was 100 ducats, and the infringing device would be destroyed immediately. It should be noted, from the vantage point of modern patent statutes, that this act by the fathers of Venice included concepts that the device be actually constructed, that it be useful, and that it be novel. Also, the further test of innovation apparently is referred to by the term "ingenious devices" in the Venice statute. It is interesting to note that most of these concepts are presently embedded in modern patent laws worldwide. Today, you may obtain a patent on a new, useful, and unobvious device, but you need not construct your invention to obtain an enforceable patent.

Modern patent law systems developed out of a realization by the state that there was indeed a societal need to both recognize and protect a "property right" with respect to inventions, as opposed to making such grants a privilege, although for reasons having very little to do with any perceived "natural law" right. At the time of the creation of the United States, this "property right" theory and its realization was beginning to come into full flower in England. As Great Britain was the mother country, its laws were most familiar to those in the new nation. Thus, the United States embodied a property right in inventions as part of the Constitution in 1787.

The term "exclusive property right" involves the limited-term exclusive right with regard to the invention, as opposed to a property right in ownership of the invention itself, or in the physical device embodying the invention. This distinction is important because it is almost embarrassing how often the controversial idea of a property right in a physical invention is confused with the non-controversial idea of exclusive property rights in a patent. You must have the patent to acquire the exclusive property right.

While most of the history of the U.S. patent system relies upon English law, it is now clearly established that the custom of granting limited-term exclusive privileges to inventors or importers for introducing new trade or industry into a state began in the Italian city-states, and particularly in Venice late in the fourteenth and early in the fifteenth centuries. From there, the patent custom spread to Germany, France, the Netherlands, England, and to the United States.

The term "patent custom" describes the practice in each country of granting inventors limited exclusive rights in inventions, but without a fully developed uniform system or administrative practice, nor consistent legal principles applicable under rules of law which properly define a true patent system. The first attempts to develop such a patent system occurred in England, and subsequently the United States, both of which will be discussed shortly in detail. Prior to the U.S. Constitution, some of the post-colony states were granting patents, while other states had in their Constitutions provisions declaring that the granting of monopolies was abhorrent. Certain states were enacting individual private laws granting exclusive patent rights. Under the English patent custom, as it had been in Europe for almost four centuries at the time of the creation of the American republic, patents were granted not only to those who made new inventions, but also to those who brought inventions known or used elsewhere and introduced them into the country. The patent custom had developed and spread throughout Europe primarily as a means of encouraging importation of new trade or industry, and only secondarily as a means of encouraging the creation of new inventions. The U.S. Congress, in its deliberation of the Patent Act of 1790, the first U.S. patent law, specifically removed provisions that would have expressly authorized patents of importation.

At the time the U.S. Constitution was ratified, a patent custom existed in a number of states which granted exclusive rights in inventions by private legislative enactment. There was nothing in the Constitution which precluded states from continuing to issue patents, but the advent of a federal patent system was viewed by almost everyone as removing any need for state patents. A few states, most notably New York, would continue to issue state patents for several decades after the Constitution came into effect.

3.1.2 The British Patent System

The transition from a patent custom to a patent system came about in Great Britain through the recognition of patents as a form of property right to be granted to inventors, rather than merely a privilege. As was typical in Venice, Great Britain had a long history of royal grants prior to the first formal statute establishing patents.

As an island nation, the importation of skills from abroad was encouraged by the British in an effort to compete with the progress of other European countries. In the fourteenth century, the arts of weaving, ship making, glass making, and iron making were stimulated in England by special grants to foreign artisans. During the reign of Queen Elizabeth I, which began in the year 1558, the first elements of a modern patent system appeared. Patents for a dredging machine, and for the making of soap, alum, and saltpeter, were granted. However, in England as well as in other countries, there was abuse of the royal prerogative in granting patents, and public opinion in opposition was reflected in complaints to the House of Commons, and in the ultimate enactment of legislation to halt the practice of royal patent grants. In the year 1602, the case of *Darcy v. Allin*, 11 Coke 846 (King's Bench 1602), came before the court of England, called the "King's Bench," challenging the right of the Crown to grant monopolies to items, in this case, playing cards, which the citizens of London claimed a free right to trade in. Apparently, in this case, it was decided that the monopoly was not valid.

In another case before the English courts in 1614 which involved the weaving art, entitled *The Cloth Workers of Ipswich*, Godbolt, tit. 351, p. 252, 254 (1614), it was held that the king could not create a monopoly that would take away free trade, which is the birthright of every subject. However, the court held that, if one brings a new invention or a new trade into the kingdom, or has made "a new discovery, in such cases, the king, of his grace and favor, may grant by charter that only he the inventor shall use such a trade or traffic for a certain time, because at first the people of the kingdom are ignorant and do not have the knowledge or use of the new invention or trade." The court went on to hold that, when the patent right is expired, the king cannot make a new grant, for when the trade has become common and others have bound apprentices to the same trade, there is no reason that such use should be forbidden.

About 10 years after the *Cloth Workers* decision, the English Statute of Monopolies was passed in 1623 during the reign of James I. This law invalidated the prior grants of patent rights given by the Crown, and declared that "any patent granted shall be maintained for a fourteen-year period or under, if the patents were directed to new manufactures within the realm, to the true and first inventor and inventors of such manufactures, which others, at the time of making such Letters Patent and grant, shall not use so as also they be not contrary to the law." The key point of this statute was that the granting of an exclusive right by way of Letters Patent was taken away as a prerogative of the Crown, and given as an inherent right to any inventor, and at that time, one who brought new inventions into the realm, as a right that could not be deprived by the Crown. This subtle but important difference is embodied in all of the patent laws of the world today. Note also that the Statue of Monopolies, as did the early Venetian statute, referred to "new" manufactures within the realm, setting up the universally accepted requirement of novelty as a prerequisite to the grant of patent protection.

Although the patent custom originated in other European countries prior to adoption in Britain, the patent custom began to flourish in Britain during the reign of Elizabeth I. But it was not until the Statute of Monopolies was enacted in 1623 that the custom was given a statutory foothold in England. This law arose from a particular exemption to the general ban on monopolies, and Letters Patent were granted for a limited term of 14 years. This statutory language, together with the few common law judicial opinions that interpreted patent law in England, provided the legal basis for the English patent law that existed in 1787 when the American Constitution was being drafted.

However, there was a virtual dearth of reported common law cases in England relating to patents. For example, during the seventeenth century, there were only three reported common law cases on patents, and two of those had occurred prior to 1623. By the time of the American Constitution, there was considerable uncertainty in England as to the nature of what the patent law was because of the lack of court decisions interpreting the statutory provision. That uncertainty was compounded in the United States.

The framers of the U.S. Constitution also based their provision regarding patents and copyrights on the patent custom that was practiced during the colonial period, and later by the states right after the Revolutionary War.

The early English patent custom arose out of a desire to create new industry in the realm, primarily by importation and only secondarily by what would now be termed invention by entrepreneurs. As a consequence, novelty, which is the *sine qua non* for patentability throughout the world today, was predicated on whether the subject matter of the grant was presently being worked in England. It mattered not whether the art or manufacture was known and practiced elsewhere or even whether it had previously been practiced or worked in England. Originality was only peripherally involved, and the inventive subject matter was considered new if it had not been worked in England within recent memory. The seminal belief was that the Statute of Monopolies of 1623 did not change this.

3.1.3 The U.S. Constitution and the Development of the Present U.S. Patent Examination System

3.1.3.1 Origin and Early Development of Patent Law in the United States

The development of the U.S. patent law extends from 1787 at the Constitutional Convention, to the enactment of the Patent Act of 1836, which is the foundation for the modern patent system in use today. During this time frame, the U.S. system changed from a patent custom to an established patent system.

Prior to the Constitutional Convention of 1787, many of the American colonies and states of the Confederation preceding the U.S. Constitution had enacted legislation forbidding monopolies, except as for such new inventions that were profitable to the colony, and those grants would only be for a short time. Massachusetts had such a law in 1641, and Connecticut in 1672. By the time of the Declaration of Independence in 1776, many colonies had been issuing patents, and they continued to do so between the time of the Declaration of Independence and the Constitutional Convention in

1787. The granting of patents by individual states even continued to some degree after the adoption of the Federal Constitution in 1789 and the passage of the first patent act of 1790. However, the granting of individual state patents eventually ceased.

The members of the Constitutional Convention were aware of the activities of inventors and authors, and of the efforts to aid them in the individual state legislatures and in the Continental Congress that preceded the Constitutional Convention. James Madison and Charles Pinckney, the latter from South Carolina, each submitted proposed clauses to the Constitutional Convention in August of 1787, which stated as follows:

> "The Congress shall have power ... to promote the progress of science and useful arts, by securing for limited times to authors and inventors the exclusive right to their respective writings and discoveries."

The Constitutional Convention, which gave rise to the U.S. Constitution in effect today, took place in hot and humid Philadelphia from May until September 1787. Little is written on how the patent and copyright clause was placed into the Constitution. What is known is that, after discussing and debating the more important issues in the Constitution, on August 31, 1787, the delegates to the convention agreed to refer portions of the Constitution that had been postponed up to that time to a committee made up of a member from each state. Since Rhode Island had never been asked to attend the constitutional convention, and the New York delegation had left the convention in the middle to go back to their farming, this became the Committee of Eleven. On September 5, 1787, the Committee of Eleven reported out five unresolved matters pertaining to the powers to be granted to Congress, and the fifth of these became the Intellectual Property Clause of the U.S. Constitution, "to promote the progress of science and useful arts, by securing for limited times to authors and inventors the exclusive right to their respective writings and discoveries." On September 12, 1787, a committee of the convention reported a draft of the entire Constitution that left the Intellectual Property Clause intact. The final draft of the Constitution was approved on September 17, 1787, including the Intellectual Property Clause.

Apparently, the provision was uncontroversial, as there is no record of any debate on this matter. James Madison, writing in *Federalist* No. 43, stated that an author's copyright has long been adjudged in Great Britain to be a right held by the author at common law. The right to useful inventions seems with equal reason to belong to inventors. Thus, this statement, by one of the leading founders of our nation, supports the right of inventors to exclusive rights in their inventions, as distinguished from prerogative writs granted at will and fiat by the government.

It should be noted that an inventor does not have an exclusive right to his invention at common law, as that statement is strictly read. In 1850, the U.S. Supreme Court, in the case of *Gayler et al. v. Wilder*, 51 U.S. (10 How.) 477 (1850), held that the inventor of a new and useful improvement has no exclusive right to the invention until he obtains a patent grant. This right is created by the patent, and no action can be maintained by the inventor against an infringer before the patent is issued. The Court went on to hold that this exclusive right did not exist at common law, but was created by the Act of Congress in enacting the patent statutes. Again, in 1913, the U.S. Supreme Court, in the case of *Bawer & Cie. v. O'Donnell*, 229 U.S. 1 (1913), stated that the right to make, use, and sell an invented article is not derived from the patent law. The patent law secures to the inventor the exclusive right to make, use, and sell the patented item, and to prevent others from exercising like privileges without the consent of the patentee. The Court stated that the patent law was passed for the purpose of encouraging useful inventions and promoting new and useful improvements by the stimulation of exclusive rights awarded to inventive genius, and was intended to secure to the public, after the lapse of the exclusive privileges granted, the full benefit of such inventions and improvements.

3.1.3.2 Initial U.S. Patent Laws

The first patent law established by the Congress of the United States was the Patent Act of 1790, which created an examination system that was way ahead of its time. This examination system and law lasted only 3 years, and was repealed by the Patent Act of 1793, which, in turn, established a registration system rather than the prior short-lived examination system, which registration system was somewhat similar to the English system at that time. Apparently, the time and expense of running a patent examination system in 1790 was too much for the young government, and delays and frustration eventually occurred. In the next 43 years, five additional patent acts were passed, but all for the purpose of correcting some perceived deficiency in the existing legislation.

Under the Act of 1793, inventors would be required merely to submit written statements describing their invention, and the government would register those statements. The flaw in this system was that the courts were left to interpret what exactly was covered by the statements submitted by inventors and developers in view of infringements that may or may not have exactly corresponded to the material submitted and covered by the letters patent. It was also difficult to determine from the inventor's statement what was new about an invention in comparison to what was previously known and in the public domain.

After many years of having courts wrestle with trying to determine what the actual invention was, based upon the inventor's description of the invention covered by the certificate of registration, with no examination by the government to define the limits of the grant, the modern Patent Act was enacted in 1836, which set up a Patent Office charged with responsibility for the examination of the novelty, utility, and importance of an invention, and established the office of the Commissioner of Patents to oversee the new examination system. This law also embodied the prior court-established rules for submitting specifications setting forth the invention, stating precisely what it was that the inventor saw as the "novelty" or "invention" covered by the patent grant. The requirements of a written specification, and a statement or statements defining the scope of the invention, and its novel features, were created from the previous court decisions and enacted in the Patent Act of 1836. In a subsequently enacted patent statute, a patent application was required to specifically "claim" or state the subject matter of the invention in separate claims forming part of the patent application. The difference between the former registration system and the new examination system of 1836 was that, under the registration system, the courts developed the entire body of patent law in the United States, without any assistance or guidance from Congress. Beginning in 1836, with the enactment of a comprehensive legislative act, Congress set forth the standards of patentability and patentable subject matter to guide the courts, as well as inventors. It is this examination system, with the established law guiding the courts, that is in existence today and comprises the U.S. patent system with various amendments over the years.

3.1.3.3 Inventions, Not Discoveries

It is important to note that, although the Constitutional mandate uses the word "discoveries," there is a strong distinction in patent law as to whether patents can be obtained on "inventions" and "discoveries." An invention, or creation of a work of art or authorship under the copyright law, is a creation by a human being of something new, and something that is not found before, either manmade or in nature. This is the substance of what can be covered under the Intellectual Property Laws. To the contrary, if someone "discovers" something that already exists in nature, or exists because of someone else's creation, such "discovery" is not rewarded by exclusive rights under the Intellectual Property Laws. It is possible that early use of the term "discovery" referred to inventions or novel things that were novel to a particular country, and, when someone discovered them overseas and then brought them into the realm, they were awarded exclusive rights under the patent laws. However, that provision has been written out of every patent law in the world, and today, universally, a patent can only be granted on something developed by an inventor or inventors. You cannot obtain exclusive rights on something found overseas and then brought into your home country.

This, in my mind, raises interesting issues involving the patenting of genomes and DNA strains, where most of the public is of the understanding that scientists are discovering something that is in all of our bodies. And, therefore, how can someone obtain a patent on something that already exists? The quick answer is that patents today may be granted on new living organisms, such as recombinant DNA, which is modified from its form found in nature. For a more thorough discussion of recombinant DNA patent protection, see Chapter 14.

3.1.3.4 Importance of Disclosure of the Invention

Disclosure of one's invention to the public is the primary object of patent systems everywhere, with exclusive rights granted to those inventors to commercialize the invention for a limited period being their reward for publicly disclosing their invention. Prior to the existence of patent laws, inventors were operating their inventions in secret, trying to maintain such secrecy as long as possible so as not to have their invention stolen from them. As early as 1623 in England, it was decided that, to urge these inventors to disclose their inventions to the public and make such inventions available for the public good, a limited exclusive right should be granted to those inventors for the commercialization of their inventions. In exchange for that limited exclusive right, the law required that the inventors make full disclosure of their inventions to the public, so that once the patent grant expired, the public would have the full benefit of using that particular invention. Today's patent law requires, for example, that the specification in a patent contain a full, clear, exact, and concise description of the invention so as to enable one skilled in the art to practice the invention upon the expiration of the patent without undue experimentation. The U.S. patent law also requires that the inventor must place in the specification the "best mode" of practicing the invention as of the date of filing the patent application. This prevents an inventor from setting forth in any patent specification a less than perfect embodiment of the invention, while exploiting a more perfect version of the invention.

Therefore, the laws of the United States and many countries are quite specific as to the depth of description that must be placed in the patent application, including drawings where necessary to inform one skilled in the related art of the structure and operation of the invention. In the case of software inventions, some inventors place the source code in the patent specification. Others do not, and use flow diagrams to fully describe the invention. I have been looking for court decisions that may indicate that, if a patent issues without a source code on software, the invention has not been fully disclosed. So far, I have not seen such a decision. It is my understanding, being a mechanical engineer, that possibly one can duplicate an algorithm or a computer program without information supplied from the source code. See Chapter 13 for the existing law regarding obtaining patent protection for computer-related inventions.

3.1.3.5 Present Patent Law, Rules, and Guides

In 1952, the Patent Act, as it primarily exists today, was enacted by Congress as part of 35 U.S. Code (35 U.S.C. §100 et. seq.), the federal statutory scheme. The 1952 Patent Act has been modified frequently over the past 60+ years to bring some of its requirements into harmonization with international patent laws and treaties, and to clarify or change details in the U.S. law. The latest major revision to the U.S. Patent Law was the America Invents Act (AIA), enacted by Congress in 2011, and which is discussed in more detail in Chapter 18.

The Patent Act authorizes the U.S. Patent and Trademark Office (USPTO) to issue its own Rules of Practice, which set forth in further detail the particulars of how the USPTO operates, procedurally, substantially, and financially. These rules, which are found in Volume 37 of the U.S. Code of Federal Regulations (37 C.F.R.), have been enacted under the Administrative Procedures Act, and have the authority of law.

The USPTO has also issued a rather lengthy tome entitled "The Manual of Patent Examining Procedure" (MPEP), which comprises the set of guidelines the patent examiners and other personnel of the USPTO adhere to when examining or otherwise processing U.S. patent applications. Those of us, patent attorneys and agents alike, also refer to the MPEP as a reference in preparing, amending, and prosecuting U.S. patent applications. The MPEP is a set of guidelines issued by the USPTO, and does not have the effect of law, as compared to the Patent Act (35 U.S.C.) and the Rules of Practice (37 C.F.R.), which both have the effect of law.

The Patent Act, the Rules of Practice, and the MPEP are all available on the website of the USPTO (www.uspto.gov), as well as a wealth of other information relating to patents.

3.2 TYPES OF PATENT COVERAGE

3.2.1 What Is a Patent?

A *patent* is far more than simply a legal document. It is a technical publication, a sales brochure, and a precise definition of the fence around the technology protected by the exclusive right encompassed by the patent grant. As a technical document, the patent contains a written description of the patented invention sufficient to permit anyone interested in the field of technology to which the patent relates to make and use the invention after expiration of the patent, by reading the information in the patent. It follows, therefore, that the USPTO provides a wealth of technical information available to the public that may be unavailable elsewhere. As a sales brochure, the patent describes the prior art that was known before the invention set forth in the patent, and then describes how the invention improves, advances, and provides advantages over the known state of the art. As a complete description of the invention, along with claims setting forth the metes and bounds of the inventor's exclusive rights, the patent also acts as an advisory to those who would be infringers as to the limits of the inventor's exclusive technological territory.

Original issued patents comprise a set of printed pages, and drawings where required, bound together with a red ribbon under a gold seal. Duplicate copies of each patent are available from the USPTO, or from the Internet at www.uspto.gov. In the USPTO, patents are arranged electronically by subject matter, in excruciating detail, by class and sub-class for ease of searching, which will be discussed in Chapter 8.

As a bottom line, a patent is a grant by the government of intellectual property rights that permits the patent owner to stop others from making, using, selling, offering for sale, or importing the patented invention covered by the claims, and supported by the specification, of the patent. The components of a patent are the drawings, where required, the specification which describes and explains the patented invention, and the claims which define that which the patent right covers. These documents are called "patents" because the word means "open, exposed, or evident." Letters patent have always been open to public inspection once granted, setting forth the knowledge contained in the grants. Under existing U.S. law, U.S. pending patent applications are published electronically 18 months after filing, unless the applicant states that he or she will not file corresponding patent applications in countries outside the United States and files a non-publication request.

"Letters patent" and "patent" mean the same thing. The USPTO issues several types of patents, namely: utility patents, including article or apparatus patents; method or process patents; design patents; and plant patents. Upon expiration of a patent, it cannot be renewed, and its subject matter enters the public domain. If an improvement is made to an originally covered invention by either the original inventor, or someone totally different, an entirely new patent on that improvement can be obtained. However, it is important to remember that, once a patent reaches its expiration date, its contents fall into the public domain, and there is no renewal provision.

3.2.2 Article or Apparatus Patents

Article, or apparatus, patents protect new machines, articles of manufacture, and compositions of matter. Article patents can also be written to cover improvements in any of these categories. These patents are granted for a term beginning on the date the patent issues, and normally ending 20 years from the date the application for the patent was first filed in the United States. If the patent claims priority from an earlier-filed U.S. patent application directed to the same invention, other than a provisional application, 20 years from the date of the earliest such U.S. application would be the date of expiration. The term of patenting in the United States previously was 17 years from the date of issue; however, that was changed by the U.S. Congress in 1994.

3.2.3 Method or Process Patents

Method, or process, patents cover the novel process or steps that transform material from one state to another. They can also cover a novel process or method of manufacturing or using a machine to perform an operation on an article of manufacture or a composition of matter. In method or process patents (the names are synonymous), it is the process used, and not the end result, that must be novel and non-obvious to support patentability. The enforcement term of method or process patents is the same as the article or apparatus patents described earlier.

3.2.4 Design Patents

Design patents are granted for any new, original, ornamental, and non-functional design of, or such design placed on, an article of manufacture. Design patents are granted for a term of 15 years from the date of issue and cannot be renewed. These patents cover the esthetic features of the article shown in the patent illustrations; however, functional features of the design are specifically excluded from protection under the design patent. If a functional feature of the article is novel, that particular feature should be covered by an article patent. Design patents are covered in more detail in Chapter 12.

3.2.5 Plant Patents

Plant patents are granted to one who invents or asexually reproduces any distinct and new variety of plant, including cultivated spores, mutants, hybrids, and newly found seedlings, other than a tuber-propagated plant or a plant found in an uncultivated state.

Asexually propagated plants are those that are reproduced by means other than from seeds, such as by the rooting of cuttings, by layering, budding, grafting, inarching, etc. With reference to tuber-propagated plants, for which a plant patent cannot be obtained, the term "tuber" is used in its narrow horticultural sense as meaning a short, thickened portion of an underground branch. Examples of plants covered by the term "tuber-propagated" are the Irish potato and the Jerusalem artichoke.

An application for a plant patent consists of the same parts as other applications: specification, claim, and illustration. The term of a plant patent is 20 years from the date on which the application for the patent was filed in the United States, or, if the application contains a specific reference to an earlier-filed application, 20 years from the date the earliest application was filed.

The specification of a plant application should include a complete, detailed description of the plant and its characteristics that distinguish the new plant over related known varieties, and its antecedents, expressed in botanical terms in the general form followed in standard botanical textbooks or publications dealing with the varieties of the kind of plant involved (evergreen tree, dahlia plant, rose plant, apple tree, etc.), rather than a mere broad, non-botanical characterization such as commonly found in nursery or seed catalogs. The specification should also include the origin or parentage of the plant variety sought to be patented, and must particularly point out where and in what manner the variety of plant has been asexually reproduced. The Latin name of the genus and species of the plant should be stated. Where color is a distinctive feature of the plant, the color should be positively identified in the specification by reference to a designated color as given by a recognized color dictionary. Where the plant variety originated as a newly found seedling, the specification must fully describe the conditions (cultivation, environment, etc.) under which the seedling was found growing, to establish that it was not found in an uncultivated state.

A plant patent is granted on the entire plant. It therefore follows that only one claim is necessary, and only one is permitted.

The oath or declaration required of the applicant for a plant patent, in addition to the statements required for other patent applications, must include the statement that the applicant has asexually reproduced the new plant variety. If the plant is a newly found plant, the oath or declaration must also state that the plant was found in a cultivated area.

Plant patent drawings are not mechanical drawings and should be artistically and competently executed, disclosing all the distinctive characteristics of the plant capable of visual representation. When color is a distinguishing characteristic of the new variety, the drawing must be in color. Two duplicate copies of color drawings must be submitted.

Specimens of the plant variety, its flower or fruit, are not submitted, unless specifically requested by the examiner. Plant patent applications may be published pursuant to Title 35, U.S. Code, Section 122(b). A plant patent application is the only type of patent application filed with the USPTO that is not permitted to be filed electronically.

The Plant Variety Protection Act (Public Law 91577), approved December 24, 1970, provides for a system of protection for sexually reproduced varieties, for which protection was not previously provided, under the administration of a Plant Variety Protection Office within the U.S. Department of Agriculture.

Plant patents are quite important to the agricultural industry in the United States, as well as the flower industry. For example, there has been controversy between the manufacturers of patented seed corn and the farmers who raise seed corn using the patented seeds, who then take the results of that crop and plant the seeds themselves for their new crop. The courts have held that the patent was enforceable, and that the farmers could not use the patented seed to plant their next years crop without obtaining a license. See: *Bowman v. Monsanto*, 569 U.S. 278(2013).

3.2.6 New Technologies

As touched on previously, process patents have been extended recently to cover methods of doing business, which were not considered as protected under the patent laws until a court decision in 1998. Also, computer-related inventions are now subject to patent protection under certain conditions, as well as biotechnology creations, such as genomes and DNA strains. See Chapters 13 and 14 for more on these. As science progresses and creates totally new categories of subject matter, the patent law is initially seen as a bulwark against the protection of such new technology. However, once the importance of such new technology to the economy and to the welfare of society as a whole is realized, then the patent laws are generally interpreted by the courts to allow patent protection for such new technologies.

3.3 HOW TO DETERMINE WHAT TO PATENT AND WHAT NOT TO PATENT

3.3.1 Broadly, What Can and Cannot Be Patented Under the Law

To be eligible for a patent, an invention must fall within one of the categories of patentable subject matter. Thus, not all inventions are patentable. Normally, the USPTO is somewhat liberal in applying the limitations of the invention categories, providing that an invention is presented for examination in a suitable fashion.

To understand what may be patentable, it is helpful to first discuss items that are not patentable. Unpatentable subject matter includes business forms, perpetual motion machines (because they are not useful under the Constitutional mandate), promotional advertising schemes, intended results of desired goals, functions without any apparatus to perform those functions, nebulous or abstract concepts or ideas, items appearing in nature, and laws of nature. However, the useful and novel application of a law of nature or abstract idea could be subject to patentability. Therefore, while desired functions are not patentable, the product or method that provides that function can be patented, while not the mere result.

In general terms, to be patentable, an invention must be useful, novel, and unobvious. This presumes, of course, that the invention first falls into one of the patentable categories mentioned earlier. "New" and "useful" are requirements that are easy to ascertain and understand. The unobviousness requirement has provided more difficulty over the years, as discussed in Chapter 6.

A process or method patent can be obtained to cover a new use for a known apparatus or composition—for example, a known pharmaceutical or an existing machine. Using a known asthma drug to suppress pre-term labor contractions would be a new use for a known composition, and would be patentable subject matter as a new method.

3.3.2 From a Business Standpoint, What Should Be Patented

There are many reasons that go into deciding whether a patent should be obtained for a particular invention. The first criterion, of course, is whether or not the invention is patentable, based on the previously mentioned criteria. Another consideration is the importance the invention has to the profitability of the company for whom the inventor works. Also, an independent inventor can determine what importance the invention will have to that inventor's future economic situation. A further consideration is whether or not there exists a market for the product or process which will include the invention, or whether a market could be created from scratch for the particular product or process where there is no other item on the market quite like the subject invention.

After an invention is made, consider the importance of protecting the invention against competition by others when you create your market introduction plans for the invention. Is there a large competitor that can copy your product and put you out of business if your product is not covered by a patent? Consideration must also be given to the potential for foreign markets for the product or process, and whether foreign patent protection should be sought for your invention. Also, consider whether a competitor would have the capability of manufacturing a product in a foreign country to compete with you on a global scale, and whether or not you should obtain patent protection in that foreign country to deny the competitor the ability to manufacture in that country, thereby choking off potential infringement at the source.

There are additional factors that impact the decision whether or not to spend resources to obtain a patent, and these additional factors pertain to the individual characteristics of the given company and the industry in which the company operates. When decisions of a business nature have to be made, it is important to seek the advice of a competent patent professional, so that all of the options regarding intellectual property protection for your intellectual assets may be provided to those responsible for making business decisions. Obtaining worldwide patent protection on an important invention is an expensive proposition, and careful consideration should be given to making such decisions.

Careful study should likewise be given to the required investment for creating a new product, and bringing that product to market. Consideration should be given to the possibility of making necessary changes in existing production facilities to produce and launch a new product. Consideration of the extensive advertising budget required to convince the public of the reasons they should buy a new product, and to change their buying habits to accept the new product, is important. The size of the market for the new product and profitability studies are also important factors.

While the commercial importance of an invention is probably the most important consideration as to whether to obtain a patent, the credibility granted to the inventor(s) associated with an invention is a primary factor in assisting the inventor to convince his/her employer to commercialize the invention. A successful inventor requires credibility in the same way that a successful artist or author does. If the inventor has no prior successes to advertise, the inventor must establish credibility by proving that the product embodying the invention is worthy of the investment of resources. A favorable sales history for a patented product also builds credibility. All of these factors make it easier for the inventor to span the gap between a conceived idea and actual commercialization of the embodiment of that idea.

The inventor must also determine whether the public is ready for the invention. For example, a variety of economic, production, and management factors may come into play to shift the period of patent protection away from the period when the invention is commercially important. Several of my clients have attempted to interest companies in licensing their inventions, and a frequent response was that the company had no further funds available that year to introduce new products. This can be disappointing to the inventor, and not because the invention did not have a high profitability forecast. An example is heavy industries, where actual production methods may lag behind current available technology by a period that is much longer than the life of a patent. Thus, the value of a patent can be greatly influenced by the patterns for change that exist for specific products in given industries. Anecdotal information reveals that many inventors often underestimate the cost and difficulty of commercializing their inventions, and overestimate the market size and expectations of purchaser acceptance. The inventor must be prepared to face and overcome numerous difficulties before an invention returns a monetary award, and the inventor must be willing to work hard and not be dissuaded in the face of negative responses to move the invention to market before he/she realizes any reward. In other words, keep pushing your idea, and—above all—be patient!

3.4 BROADLY, WHAT DATA GOES INTO A PATENT

3.4.1 Describing the Background and Essential Elements of the Invention

An article or process patent begins with a title generally describing the invention, followed by a short paragraph comprising a broad statement of the field of technology to which the invention relates. This is immediately followed by a more specific statement as to the subject matter of the invention.

The specification next sets forth a statement of the background of the invention, including an explanation of the problems in the existing art to which the invention is directed towards solving, and the known relevant prior art that can be shown to have failed to specifically solve these problems. The prior art is that which the inventor is aware of, or has obtained from a pre-examination novelty search (see Chapter 8 for searches). The patent at this point may also state briefly what the various prior art reference patents disclose, followed by one or two statements indicating what the reference patents lack, compared to the details of the subject invention.

The background of the invention section may also include a statement of the objects of the invention. These are usually broad statements setting forth the results achieved by the invention that are different from and superior to the results obtained by using the devices or methods disclosed in the prior art, without setting forth the details concerning the structure and functioning of the invention's elements to achieve those results. This latter information appears later in the patent document.

Next, the patent includes a summary of the covered invention, which is a short statement of the elements of the invention, how they relate to each other, and a statement of the functions of those elements. Also included is a statement setting forth how the invention will meet the objects or results set forth in the previous paragraph.

The background of the invention is followed by a brief description of the drawings or illustrations, where present, describing the view depicted of the device in each figure.

After the brief description of the drawings is the all-important detailed description of the illustrated embodiment of the invention, which sets forth a complete explanation of the invention's structure, the relationships between all structural elements, and the operation/function of the structural elements of the invention shown in the drawings. This description includes only the essential features of the invention, eliminating descriptions of features that are non-essential. In this portion of the patent specification, each essential element of the inventive structure is named, numbered, and the numbers coordinated with the illustrations in the drawings. The accuracy of this particular section of the application is important, since it must enable a person skilled in the art to replicate the invention once the patent expires without undue experimentation. The description must be a full, clear, concise, and exact description of the invention. Common terminology in the industry or trade is used to describe the invention, with the patent attorney having some latitude in using broader language than that normally used to describe an element or function of the invention. Where a process or method is described and no illustration is necessary to understand the invention, a detailed description of the process used, including examples, is set forth.

3.4.2 Claiming the Invention

The patent concludes with one or more numbered single-sentence statements, or "claims," which particularly point out and distinctly claim the subject matter that the applicant regards as the invention. These claims form the "heart" of the patent, and are normally written in "non-prose" terms that the average reader may find cumbersome to read. The claims define a specific point or points of novelty embodied in the invention. The claims must also recite the specific non-novel structure necessary to properly "locate" or support the elements of novel structure of the invention. As will be discussed in Chapter 10, the objective of a patent's claims is to define the elements of the invention in terms such that the claims cover any related or competitive device or method developed in the future falling within the same product or process category, and at the same time each claim must not cover or "read on" the vast body of relevant prior art, or prior technology, that preceded the invention. Therefore, the claims set forth the narrow point of "invention" that is fenced off to define the exclusive rights of the inventor.

3.5 WHAT A PATENT IS NOT

As discussed previously, a patent is not a trademark or copyright or trade secret, these being distinct additional elements of intellectual property protection ostensibly having little to do with one another. Whether goods are patented or not has nothing to do with the rights afforded by trademark law, and the same can be said of the interface between copyright and patent law.

A copyright permits the copyright owner to exclude others from copying the copyrighted material, such as books, plays, music, sculptures, motion pictures, television programs, computer programs, etc. Copyright protection does not extend to an underlying invention which, for example, might be described in the copyrighted material. Thus, a copyright could be used to prevent others from copying a book describing an invention, but the copyright cannot be used to prevent someone from using the knowledge set forth in the book and then making, using, or selling the invention. That restriction would have to be found in a patent.

It is also very important to understand that owning a patent on an invention does not confer the right to make, use, sell, offer to sell, or import the invention. What is granted is strictly the legal right to exclude others from doing so. For example, a patent may be obtained on an invention, the manufacture and sale of which can infringe a different patent owned by someone else. This is an important concept. You may obtain a patent on your invention—however, your invention may also infringe a broader patent of a prior inventor. The classic illustration I use is where you have a patent on a chair, without arms, and I decide to improve your chair by adding arms to the chair. You have your patent on your chair; I now have a patent on the chair plus the arms. However, every time I manufacture a chair with arms under my patent, I am infringing your patent on the chair per se. Another example of a patent not assuring the inventor that the invention can be introduced is a new drug that is patented, since the U.S. Food and Drug Administration requires approval before any drug is marketed to the public.

A patent is not self-enforcing. The government issues the patent, but will not take any positive action on behalf of the patent owner to enforce the inventor's rights established by the patent. The government simply grants the owner of the patent the right to exclude others from practicing the invention, and leaves it to the patent owner to enforce the patent in the courts. The Constitution of the United States provides the Federal Judicial System, through which patent enforcement can be obtained.

Since a patent simply grants the intangible right to exclude, its value rests entirely upon the utility and importance of the invention, and the desire of others to use it or to be in possession of the right to exclude. For example, someone may desire to buy the patent from its owner. The patent is simply a document, and not an invention. The invention is that which is described and claimed in the patent.

A patent, and the information that it discloses, cannot be kept secret. An essential aspect of obtaining a patent is that a full and complete disclosure of the invention needs to be made, so that others may practice the invention upon expiration of the patent without having to go through undue experimentation. U.S. patent applications are published 18 months after filing, unless no foreign corresponding patent applications will be filed. Patent applications, if published, are held secret in the USPTO until the date of publication, and, if not published, until the patent is issued after the examination process. However, issued patents and published patent applications are freely available to the public, with certain limited exceptions where national security is involved. The patent grant does give the right to the inventor to not commercialize the invention, or to refuse to allow others to commercialize the invention by a refusal to grant licenses. However, the patent itself issues as a public document available to all. Thus, inventions themselves may be suppressed by keeping the technology out of the public eye, but patents can neither be kept secret nor suppressed.

A U.S. patent is limited in enforcement to the 50 states of the United States and its territories and possessions. A U.S. patent cannot be enforced in Canada, Japan, Europe, or any other foreign country. However, a U.S. patent may be used to stop the importation of products that infringe the patent from abroad into the United States. Also, if a U.S.-patented method is used to manufacture a product overseas, the product made by that method may be stopped from entering the United States by enforcement of the U.S. method patent against the importer of the product, even though the infringing method was not used in the United States.

The United States has ratified several treaties that provide significant advantages for those seeking foreign patent protection, based on a patent application initially filed in the United States. Remember, at present, there is no such thing as an international patent; patents must be obtained in each of the countries or regions in which patent protection is sought. At present, there is a single European patent.

3.6 INVENTIONS RELATING TO ATOMIC WEAPONS

As part of the Atomic Energy Act of 1954, the U.S. Congress enacted a separate law covering inventions that have utility solely relating to nuclear material or atomic weapons. This statue appears at 42 U.S.C. §2181, and is entitled "Inventions Relating to Atomic Weapons." Section 2181(a) states: "No patent shall hereafter be granted for any invention or discovery which is useful solely in the utilization of special nuclear material or atomic energy in an atomic weapon. Any patent granted for any such invention or discovery is revoked, and just compensation shall be made therefore." Section (b) of the statute states that: "No patent hereafter granted shall confer any rights with respect to any invention or discovery to the extent that such invention or discovery is used in the utilization of special nuclear material or atomic energy in atomic weapons. Any rights conferred by any patent heretofore granted for any invention or discovery are revoked to the extent that such invention or discovery is so used, and just compensation shall be made therefore."

The statute also provides a definition of an "atomic weapon." Note that if an invention can be used in an atomic weapon, but it also has non-weapon utility, a patent may issue. However, the patent may be held up in the secrecy division of the USPTO, preventing the inventor from commercializing the invention.

3.7 THE U.S. GOVERNMENT'S RIGHT TO PRACTICE YOUR PATENTED INVENTION

During World War I, the U.S. government mobilized the nation's industries to provide munitions and other materials to support the war effort. This program ran into several barriers when patent owners filed patent infringement lawsuits against government contractors, and obtained injunctions stopping the production of needed weaponry, among other military necessities. To correct this situation, the Congress, circa 1918, passed a law that is now codified at 28 U.S.C. §1498. This law provides that, whenever a manufacturer is using or manufacturing an invention described in a U.S. patent for the government and with the authorization and consent of the government, the patent owner cannot bring a patent infringement suit against the infringing user or manufacturer. The patent owner's only remedy is to file a patent infringement action against the government in the Court of Federal Claims, and the patent owner can only recover "reasonable and entire compensation for such use and manufacture" (28 U.S.C. §1498(a)). The patent owner cannot obtain an injunction stopping the use or production of the patented invention when the government is the ultimate customer.

Under this law, which is still in effect today, the government, by authorizing and consenting to have a patented process used, or a product manufactured, on its behalf, is effectively taking a license under the patent under the powers of eminent domain, whether or not the patent owner wants to grant the government a license. This procedure is akin to the government's ability to condemn and take private property to construct a highway, for example. When such "taking" occurs, the one whose property, or patent right, has been taken is entitled to be reasonably and entirely compensated, with money, for such taking.

If you discover that the U.S. government has awarded a contract to a competitor who underbid you, and you hold a patent on the subject of the contract, you cannot sue your competitor for patent infringement. You must file your lawsuit against the government in the Court of Federal Claims, and the government lawyers of the U.S. Department of Justice will respond to your lawsuit, usually raising defenses of non-infringement, patent invalidity, unenforceability of the patent, plus any other of the many defenses to patent infringement that are available. If your competitor, who is the selected government contractor, has agreed in the contract to indemnify or hold the government harmless from patent infringement, the Justice Department attorneys may be accompanied by your competitor's attorneys in defending against your lawsuit. At the end of the lawsuit, if you prevail, you are awarded your "reasonable and entire compensation" as determined by the Court, which usually is based on a reasonable royalty payment for the infringing sales. However, you will not be awarded an injunction stopping the government from obtaining infringing products from your competitor.

If you discover that the U.S. government has awarded your competitor a contract for the use or manufacture of an invention on which you hold a U.S. patent, my advice is that you contact your patent professional to make a determination regarding the viability of asserting your patent against the government. Remember that, since the U.S. government can obtain a license under any U.S. patent, the contract award can be made to the lowest bidder, regardless of who owns the patent on the subject invention.

Additionally, the same or similar provisions apply to the U.S. government taking a copyrighted work (28 U.S.C. §1498(b)), a patented plant variety (28 U.S.C. §1498(d)), or a mask work or vessel hull design (28 U.S.C. §1498(e)).

◆ INVENTORS AND INVENTIONS ◆

George Westinghouse

STEAM-POWER BRAKE DEVICES AND ALTERNATING CURRENT

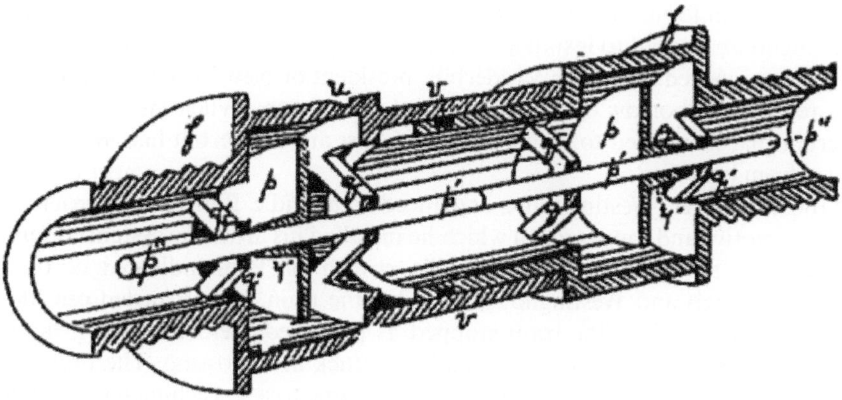

George Westinghouse is considered by some as one of the most productive inventors of his era, who helped perpetuate the Industrial Revolution through his ambition to resolve technical, commercial, and social obstacles. For example, in 1871, his employees were given a half-day off on Saturday, the initial step toward the five-day work week. He created an employee pension fund in 1908, and his workers were given paid vacations in 1913. The first radio station in the world was Westinghouse KDKA in Pittsburgh.

George Westinghouse was born in Central Bridge, New York, on October 6, 1846. He worked in his father's farm machinery shop in Schenectady, New York, until the age of 15, when he joined the Union Army as a cavalry scout, and then the Union Navy as a naval engineer where he served throughout the Civil War. He briefly attended Union College, and, upon returning to his father's shop in 1865, he developed and patented a rotary steam engine, a device for replacing derailed freight cars, and a railroad frog.

In 1866, after the war was over, Westinghouse, while working for his father, was a passenger in a train that stopped suddenly to avoid colliding with a wrecked train ahead. He got out, looked over the site, talked to the trainmen, and determined that there must be a better way to brake a heavy train. At that time, the railroads were heavily prone to accidents because each railroad car had its own brakes that were applied separately and manually by brakemen, leaping from car to car upon a signal from the engineer. The danger inherent in this system is obvious.

Intellectual Property Law for Engineers, Scientists, and Entrepreneurs, Second Edition. Howard B. Rockman.

Published 2020 by John Wiley & Sons, Inc.

Meanwhile, in 1867, Westinghouse married Margaret Erskine Walker and moved to Pittsburgh, where he had met others who shared his interest in inventing and manufacturing products for the railroad industry. Westinghouse continued to seek a solution to the train braking problem. He first considered using a chain to couple all of the train's brake controls, but this did not work. His next idea of using the steam generated by the locomotive to operate steam brakes on each car became impractical when the steam condensed to water and froze in cold weather before reaching the brake systems.

He then learned that engineers drilling dynamite holes in an Alpine tunnel had used a steam engine to produce compressed air that was piped 3000 feet into the tunnel to run the air drills. He applied this technology to an air brake system for trains, and obtained a patent for his air brake on April 13, 1869.

Westinghouse wanted to install a test air brake system on a full-sized steam-driven train and approached Cornelius Vanderbilt, president of New York Central Railroad, with a request to "borrow" a locomotive and several cars. When Westinghouse told Vanderbilt that he wanted to stop a train with just air, Vanderbilt had Westinghouse removed from his office.

In 1869, however, Westinghouse convinced Panhandle Railroad to provide him with a locomotive and four cars, on which he installed his air brake system. A test was arranged over the Pittsburgh–Steubenville stretch of Panhandle's right of way. Panhandle officials and Westinghouse boarded the train, and it started out. At the first and second stations, the train stopped as promised. Before reaching the third station, the engineer saw a horse and carriage stuck at a crossing. The brakes were applied by the engineer hard and fast. The train came to a screeching halt, with most passengers being hurled to the floor. This convinced the Panhandle officials, and Westinghouse, that the engineer-operated air brake was a vast improvement over the prior manual braking system.

As Westinghouse Air Brake Company, which was organized in July 1869, began to receive orders, Westinghouse built his first factory in Pittsburgh. His brake system gave railroad passengers greater confidence in the safety of their ride, and provided increased efficiency to the owners of the railroads. The Railroad Safety Appliance Act of 1893 made air brakes required equipment on all U.S. trains. The use of air brakes also took hold in Europe, and is today the industry standard.

Business expanded, and Westinghouse bought land east of the city where he erected a larger plant, and in 1890 built a town around the plant. The town was named "Wilmerding," the name of the family from whom he had bought the land. Unlike other U.S. factory towns of the late nineteenth century, the stores were privately operated, and not by Westinghouse Company. Workers were not bound by a scrip system, and houses were either rented from the company or could be purchased at a modest cost. In addition to the benefits mentioned in the first paragraph of this essay, Westinghouse Company also provided pensions covering the wives and orphans of retirees, sickness and accident benefits, student training courses in the company's shop, employee incentive plans, and the basic principles of collective bargaining.

In 1879, Westinghouse invented a pneumatic interlocking railroad signal system to control the increased speed and flexibility that railroads gained by the invention of the air brake. In 1881, he organized the Union Switch and Signal Company to develop and sell his railroad safety and traffic control inventions.

In the mid-1880s, Westinghouse became interested in electricity and, in particular, the disadvantages of the DC power systems fostered by Thomas Edison. He pursued

AC power–generating technology, bought the U.S. rights to Gaulard and Gibbs' AC distribution system in 1885, and hired William Stanley to improve on the Gaulard–Gibbs "transformer." In 1886, Westinghouse organized the Westinghouse Electric Company to advance the introduction and use of AC power systems in direct competition with Edison's DC power systems, as described in more detail in the essay titled "Current Events" following Chapter 36, supra. In 1887–1888, Westinghouse also acquired rights under Nikola Tesla's AC polyphase system patents, and hired Tesla to work for Westinghouse Electric and develop the AC motor with the rotating magnetic field that Tesla had conceived and had been working on. In 1892, Westinghouse, using Tesla's AC polyphase system, was awarded the contract to light the "White City," the 1893 Columbian Exposition in Chicago. Westinghouse's company also installed the electrical generators to turn the kinetic energy of Niagara Falls into hydroelectric energy. Commercial service of these huge generators began in the fall of 1896. Due to financial problems, Westinghouse lost control of his electric company in 1907, but retained control of his other companies.

George Westinghouse was issued 361 patents in all, and died on March 12, 1914, in New York City. He and his wife are buried in Arlington National Cemetery. In my judgment, George Westinghouse appears to be a successful industrialist who was driven more by the desire that his efforts would benefit mankind than by the drive for money for money's sake.

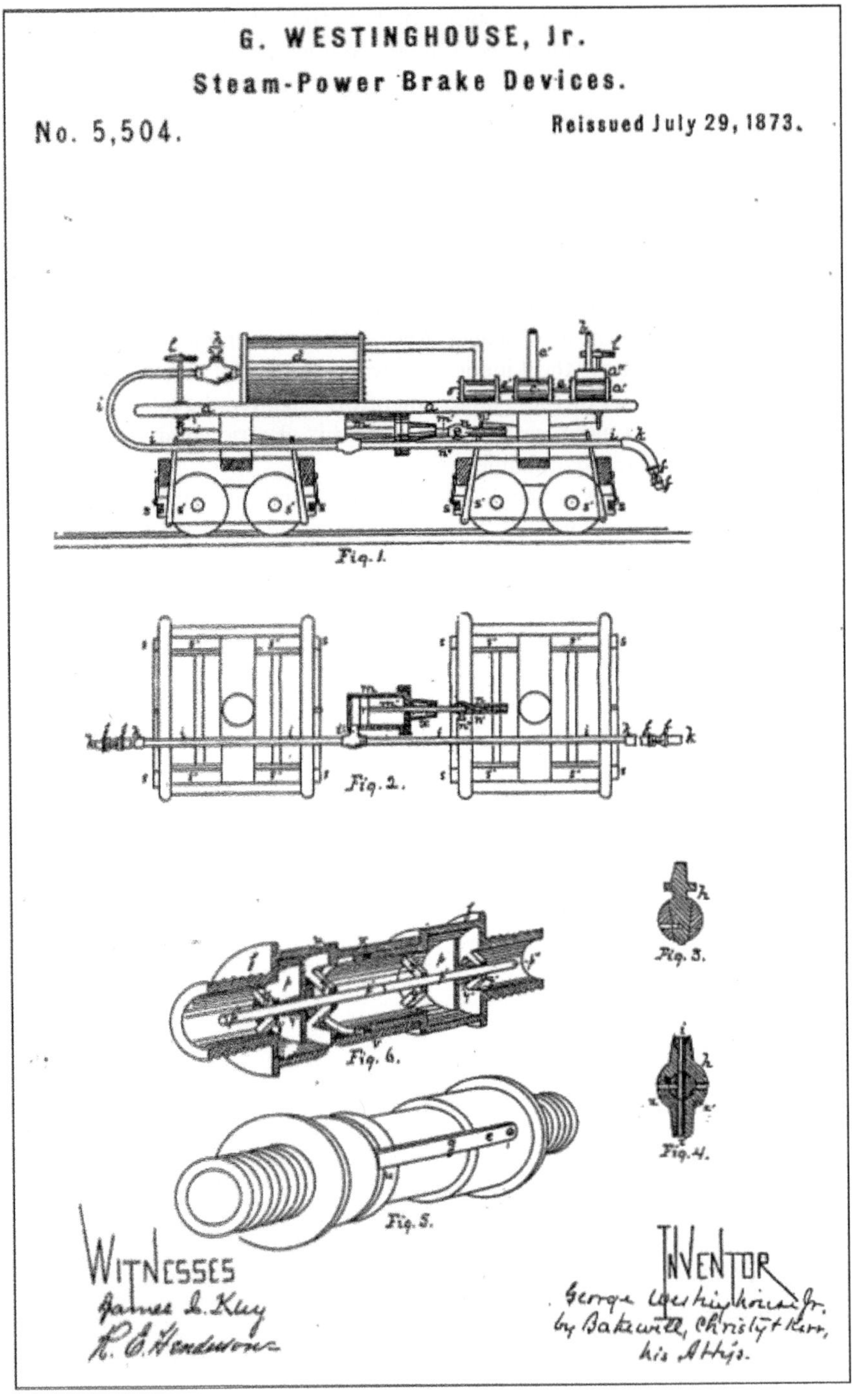
G. WESTINGHOUSE, Jr.
Steam-Power Brake Devices.
No. 5,504.
Reissued July 29, 1873.
Fig. 1.
Fig. 2.
Fig. 3.
Fig. 6.
Fig. 4.
Fig. 5.
WITNESSES
INVENTOR
George Westinghouse Jr.
by Bakewell, Christy & Kerr,
his Attys.

◆ INVENTORS AND INVENTIONS ◆

Gideon Sundback

ZIPPER

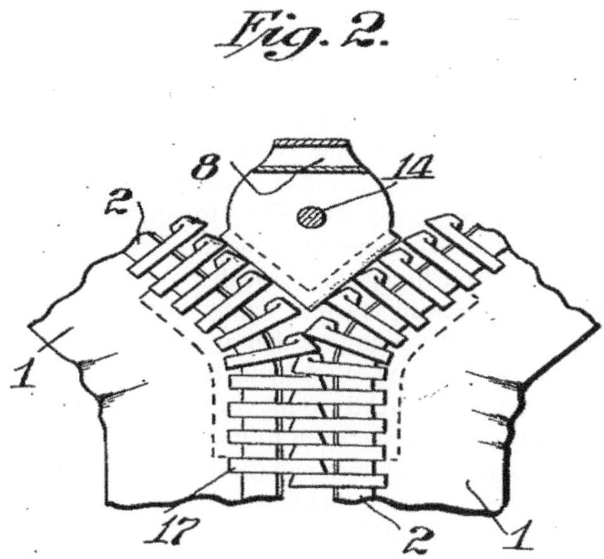

Elias Howe is recognized as the inventor of the sewing machine, but he also received a patent in 1851 for an "Automatic Continuous Clothing Closure." However, because his sewing machine was very successful, Howe opted not to pursue his clothing closure invention. Forty-four years, later Mr. Whitcomb Judson, who also invented a pneumatic street railway, marketed a "clasp locker," a device that was similar to the 1851 Howe closure. The clasp locker was a complicated hook and eye shoe fastener. Universal Fastener Company was created by Judson to manufacture the new fastener that had its public debut at the 1893 Chicago Columbian Exposition. However, the Judson device met with limited commercial success, because it kept snapping open.

Gideon Sundback was born in Sweden, and, after his electrical engineering studies in Sweden, he moved to Germany, where he studied at the Polytechnic School in Bingen am Rhein. In 1903, he took his engineering exam, and, in 1905, he immigrated to the United States, where he was hired by Universal Fastener Company. He possessed

Intellectual Property Law for Engineers, Scientists, and Entrepreneurs, Second Edition. Howard B. Rockman.

Published 2020 by John Wiley & Sons, Inc.

excellent design skills, and, full disclosure, he was married to the plant manager's daughter. Sundback eventually rose to the position of head designer at Universal Fastener.

Between 1906 and 1914, Sundback produced several improvements on the fasteners previously designed by Howe and Judson. Judson's fastener was based on hooks and eyes, and Sundback eventually developed an improved version of that product, called the Plako. However, the Plako fastener had a tendency to pull apart, and was no more successful than previous fasteners. Sundback solved the pulling apart problem in 1913 when he invented the first fastener version not based on the hook and eye principle of previous fasteners. Known as "Hookless Fastener No. 1," he increased the number of fastening elements used in previous fasteners from four per inch to 10–11 per inch. His invention also comprised two facing rows of teeth that were pulled into a single connected piece by a slider. Sundback also increased the opening for the teeth guided by the slider.

In 1914, Sundback developed "Hookless No. 2," a version of his fastener based on interlocking teeth, which was the same as the modern metal zipper of today. In this fastener, each tooth was punched to have a recessed dimple on its bottom, and a nib or conical projection on its top. The nib on top of one tooth mated with the matching dimple in the bottom of the tooth that follows it on the other side as the two strips of teeth are brought together through the two Y-channels of the slider. The teeth are ultimately crimped together tightly to form a strong fabric cord defining the selvage edge of the cloth tape that attaches the fastener length to the garment. The teeth on one side are offset by half a tooth's height from those on the other side. The teeth are held tightly to the cord and tape so that, once meshed, there is insufficient play to allow the teeth to pull apart. A tooth cannot rise up enough on the nib below it to break free, and the top nib cannot become dislodged from the dimple in the tooth above it. Sundback's U.S. Patent No. 1,219,881 for his Separable Fastener was issued in 1917.

Sundback also created a manufacturing machine for his new fastening device. The machine took a special Y-shaped wire and cut scoops from the wire, then punched the scoop dimple and nib, and clamped each scoop on a cloth tape to produce a continuous fastener chain. Within the first year of operation, Sundback's machine was producing several hundred feet, about 100 meters, of fastener per day.

During World War I, Sundback's separable fasteners were reportedly used in U.S. Navy flight suit prototypes. However, the aviator garments apparently did not work well initially, but the flight suit prototypes created initial interest in these new fasteners in the garment industry.

In 1923, B.F. Goodrich Company developed the name "zipper," and used the device on their new galoshes that were designed to be worn over dress shoes to keep the shoes dry in wet weather. The term "zipper" became short for "zipper up," which is a manifestation of the "zzziiip" sound a zipper makes when it is being zipped up. At that time, boots, gloves, and tobacco pouches were the primary use for zippers. It took another 20 years before zippers were commercially noticed by the fashion industry. By World War II, the zipper had achieved wide acceptance for the flies of trousers and the plackets of skirts and dresses.

In the 1930s, a sales campaign began for children's clothing featuring zippers, with the theme that young children would become self-reliant by allowing them to dress themselves in self-help clothing. In 1937, French fashion designers raved over the use of zippers in men's trousers. *Esquire* magazine at one time stated that the zipper was the newest tailoring idea for men, and a virtue of zipper flies was that they would prevent "the possibility of unintentional and embarrassing disarray."

A boost for the zipper arrived when zippers could open on both ends, such as on jackets. Thousands of zipper miles are presently produced daily. You may see the letters "YKK" printed on some metal zipper pull-up tabs. This stands for "Yoshida Kogyo Kabushikikaisha," a Japanese manufacturer that produces approximately 50% of all zippers sold throughout the world.

G. SUNDBACK.

SEPARABLE FASTENER.

APPLICATION FILED AUG. 27, 1914.

1,219,881. Patented Mar. 20, 1917.

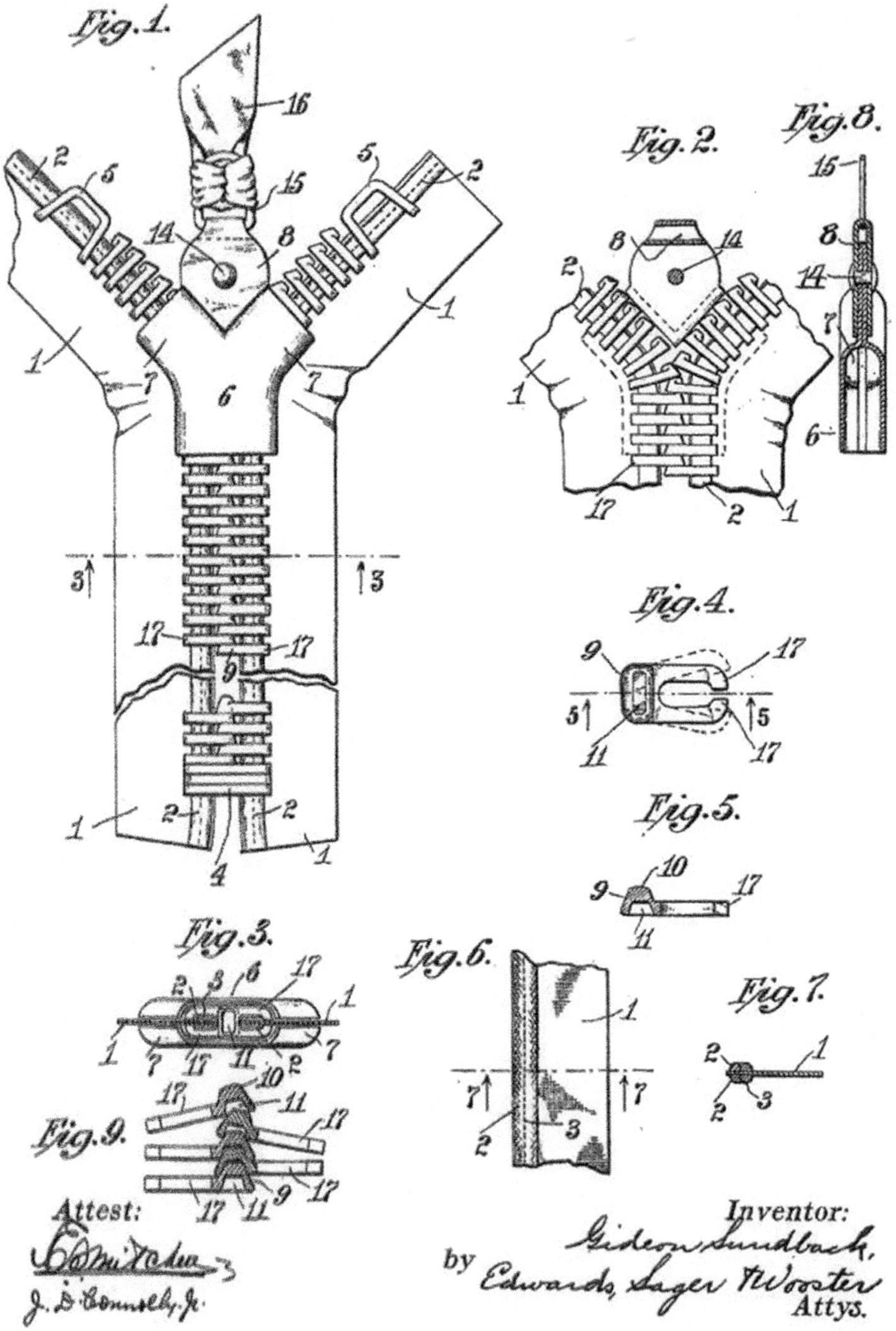

Attest:

J. D. Connolly, Jr.

Inventor:

Gideon Sundback,

by Edwards, Sager & Wooster

Attys.

4 Introductory Comments on Patentable Subject Matter and Utility

4.1 WHAT CONSTITUTES PATENTABLE SUBJECT MATTER?

4.1.1 Categories of Patentable Subject Matter

The first threshold that must be reached in determining whether your invention constitutes patentable subject matter is to establish that the invention itself is in the form of an embodiment, such as a prototype, or has been described or illustrated in terms sufficiently tangible and concrete, and not merely conceptual, to qualify for patent protection. Once this tangible or illustrated embodiment of your invention has been created, it must be determined whether the invention falls within one of the statutory classes of patentable inventions covered by 35 U.S.C. Section 101, which means that the invention must be a process, a machine, an article of manufacture, or a composition of matter, or any new and useful improvement thereof. At this point, it must also be determined whether an article patent, method (process) patent, design patent, or a combination of any of these would best serve the interests of protecting the technology embedded in the invention. More recently, algorithms embodied in software and tied to a machine, biotech strains, and business methods are patentable subject matter, but only under certain conditions. These three types of inventions and the present rules regarding their patent eligibility will be discussed in the ensuing chapters owing to the somewhat complex nature of the legal analyses applicable to these categories of inventions.

More specifically, a *process* or *method* may involve treating a material to produce a particular result or product, or may involve manipulating tangible matter to produce a desired end result. One example would be a process to temper glass to make it break resistant. Processes can also comprise a new use for a known composition, such as a new use for a known chemical compound.

A *machine* is a device that performs a useful operation, usually having mechanical or electrical components, such as, for example, springs, hinges, transistors, resistors, sensors, controls, etc. A *composition of matter* is a combination of two or more substances, and includes chemical elements or compositions, such as a soft drink formulation or a drug compound.

A *manufacture* is a catch-all category for the remaining statutory subject matter which comprises anything not a process, machine, or composition of matter. A manufacture may be a human-made genetically engineered bacterium, for example, which is

Intellectual Property Law for Engineers, Scientists, and Entrepreneurs, Second Edition. Howard B. Rockman.

Published 2020 by John Wiley & Sons, Inc.

capable of breaking down crude oil. Included among "things" that are not patentable subject matter are purely mental processes, naturally occurring articles, scientific principles, and abstract ideas.

4.1.2 The Invention Must Be Useful and Work for Its Intended Purpose

To be patentable, an invention must be shown to work for its intended purpose. Under the Constitutional mandate of Article 1, Section 8, patents can only be granted for advances in the "useful" arts. A patent cannot be granted for an inoperative device or method, and is subject to post-grant cancellation if the covered device is proven to be inoperative. This is the reason why patents on perpetual motion machines are not granted—they do not work. See Section 4.2 ahead.

4.1.3 The Invention Must Be Novel Compared to the Prior Art

Throughout the globe, patents are granted only on inventions that are novel, as measured against the vast body of relevant prior art existing in the world. For example, a public disclosure, use, or sale of, or an offer to sell, a product anywhere in the world by you or someone else, which product embodies your "new" technology prior to the home country filing date of your patent application, is considered prior art in many industrialized countries and would bar you from obtaining a patent. In the United States, an inventor has a 1-year grace period to file a patent application after a public disclosure of the invention. These and other limitations on novelty will be covered in more detail in Chapter 5.

4.1.4 The Invention Must Be Non-Obvious as Compared to the Prior Art

The U.S. patent statutes, and most patent statutes throughout the world, state that, even though there are differences between the invention attempted to be patented and the prior art, if those differences would be mere obvious manifestations of the technology by one skilled in the art to which the subject matter of the patent relates, patent protection may not be obtained. The determination of obviousness is rather difficult to those uninitiated in dealing with patents, and Chapter 6 is dedicated solely to the history, and technical and legal determinations, involved in showing how the standard of unobviousness plays an important role in the granting and enforcement of patents.

4.1.5 The True Inventors Must Be Named

In the United States, patent applications must be originally filed setting forth the names of the inventor, or inventors if there are more than one, or in the name of a business entity to which the inventor or inventors are obligated to assign their invention, possibly pursuant to an employment contract or other agreement. The application, upon filing, can be immediately filed in the name of the company for whom the inventors work. Also, if the inventors have decided prior to filing the application that they desire to assign the rights either equitably among each inventor, or to other individuals, the application may be filed in the name of each inventor or such other individuals or company. However, it is important to know that, in the United States, the true inventors must initially be identified in a patent application data sheet that accompanies filing of the patent application. These inventors must be the true inventors of the subject matter claimed to be novel and non-obvious in the patent application. A signed assignment document may be filed for recording in the USPTO along with the initial patent application, or later, in which document the inventors assign their rights over to their employers or others.

Regardless of assignment, it is imperative in the United States that the actual inventor or inventors be named in the application documents. The patent laws do not allow those to be named as inventors who did not contribute to the conception or reduction practice of the invention. In several instances during my years of practice, politics within a business environment have resulted in inventors being named who had nothing to do with the actual conception or reduction to practice of the invention. This should be avoided. After the patent issues, and the owner attempts to enforce the patent against an infringer, the acts of invention by the named inventors will be part of the discovery and trial testimony in the case. If it is ultimately determined that the individuals who are named are not the inventors, the patent's validity and/or enforceability could be jeopardized. Therefore, when working with a patent attorney, the inventors must ensure that all of the proper inventors be named, and also be sure that those who are not inventors do not appear on the application as inventors.

To determine the identity of actual inventors on a project that involves several people, I have applied a simple test, which you may also find useful. The addition of technical features to an invention usually does not qualify as contributing to the "invention." Thus, one who can take a sketch appearing on a piece of paper, and create a workable and valuable product, composition, or other item from the sketch, is normally not named as an inventor. By contrast, an inventor starts with a blank piece of paper and places the sketch on the sheet, which the technician eventually works from. Therefore, in determining who are to be named as inventors in a patent application, it is important to determine who started with the blank sheet of paper, and who acted only in a purely technical capacity and carried out the invention that was actually conceived and reduced to practice by others. In complying with this requirement of the patent law, management should understand that there is no room for politics in the naming of inventors in patent applications.

4.1.6 Brief Commentary on Notable Recent Developments Attempting to Determine Patentable Subject Matter

Several years ago, upon the development of mathematical algorithms for use in computer software, the USPTO refused to grant patent applications on such algorithms, since they were considered to be merely abstract mathematical expressions that existed before. However, as protection for such embedded software became important to business and society, the interpretations of Patent Laws were changed by the courts and the USPTO to include some such algorithms, and the machines that use these algorithms, within the scope of patentable subject matter under certain conditions. Due to the complexity of this issue, Chapter 13 explains the present status of the patentability of computer-related inventions in deeper detail.

Additionally, courts have previously held that living organisms could not be the subject of a patent. However, at present, *modified* living organisms that are the product of genetic engineering, e.g., human intervention, can be patented, except that people cannot be patented. The products of genetic engineering that are patentable must satisfy all the other conditions for patentability, including usefulness, novelty, and non-obviousness. Two examples are: the Harvard Mouse, which has been genetically engineered to be more susceptible to certain strains of cancer for purposes of medical research (see U.S. Patent No. 4,736,866); and, second, certain genetically modified organisms which can absorb oil to clean up oil spills that occur when a tanker or pipeline accidentally splits open (see U.S. Patent No. 4,259,444).

Today, the whole subject of genetics falls within the scope of patentable subject matter, and discussions are continually ongoing about the patentability of the results of the Genome Project, which was recently completed. It is my prediction that, in the future, additional patent laws or court decisions will be required to determine which newly developed subject matter may be patented, and which may be available for public use without restraint, as medical procedures are today. The subject matter of biotechnology patents is discussed in detail in Chapter 14.

Prior to 1998, methods of doing business did not fall within any of the categories of patentable subject matter. However, the *State Street* decision in 1998 (*State Street Bank & Trust v. Signature Financial Group*, 149 F.3d 1368 (Fed.Cir. 1998)), by the U.S. Court of Appeals of the Federal Court, held that methods of doing business, whether or not implemented using a computer or software, may also be patented, provided all of the other conditions for patentability are met. One such example of a patent that embodies a business method and which has been litigated in court is a patent covering the method of ordering a product online using a single click of the mouse rather than a double click. The patentability of business methods is discussed in Chapter 15.

The law relating to patentability of inventions in each of the three genres—computer-related inventions, life science inventions, and business methods subject matter—has been vacillating sinusoidally recently. Therefore, you and your patent professional may find it worthwhile to file a patent application covering an invention that does not, or may only marginally, meet the current criteria for patentable subject matter, with an eye toward the future that your patent claims may be found to cover a new, not-yet-determined category of patentable subject matter. As of this writing, certain stakeholders in the U.S. patent system, such as the American Bar Association Intellectual Property Law Section and the American Intellectual Property Law Association, among others, have proposed specific legislation to Congress to clarify what is and is not patent eligible in these three areas. Your patent professional will keep you updated as to any relevant changes enacted by Congress.

4.2 UTILITY – THE INVENTION MUST BE USEFUL

As briefly touched upon previously, under the Constitutional mandate of Article 1, Section 8, patents can only be granted for advances in the "useful" arts. Following this directive, the USPTO and the courts have determined that a patent cannot be granted for an inoperative device or method, and that a patent is even subject to post-grant cancellation if the covered device is proven to be inoperative.

Also required is that the disclosure in the patent application specification must define an invention and a device that will work for its intended purpose. If the device will not work for the purpose set forth in the specification, the patent, if granted, will become unenforceable and invalid.

The requirement of usefulness also holds that a patent cannot be granted to inventions that have not been developed to the point where a working embodiment can be disclosed in the patent application. This requirement that the invention must be useful is especially significant for new chemical compounds (including pharmaceuticals), because there may be no known use for a new compound. Often, much work must be conducted to experimentally verify the utility of a new compound before a patent application can be filed.

Upon development of any invention, the inventors should ask themselves the question: "What is my idea useful for, and why?" Once this question has been answered, the patent application can be drafted around it, showing that the invention will solve problems in the area in which your idea has been determined by you to be useful.

By way of anecdotal information, many years ago when I was a patent examiner, some of the other examiners in the chemical arts, over lunch, would tell stories about patent applications that were filed on chemical compounds, and that the usefulness for these chemical compounds was described as "for filling sandbags." These were patent applications that were filed before the applicant corporation really knew what the chemical could be useful for. Today, the requirement is that the invention must have some stated use before the patent application is filed. I do not think filling sandbags today will carry much weight!

◆ INVENTORS AND INVENTIONS ◆

John Deere

HORSE-DRAWN PLOW

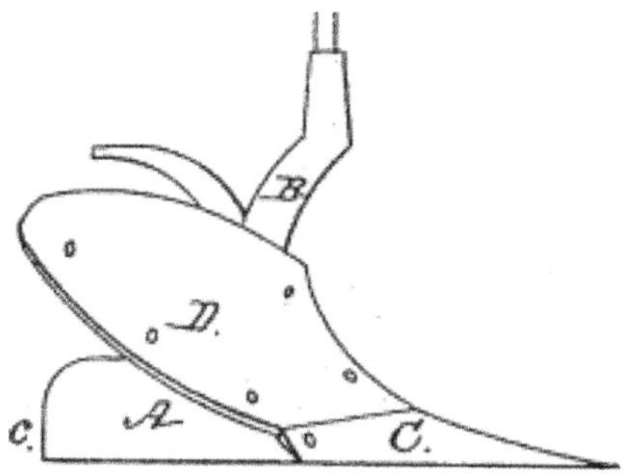

If you have ever been to the country, you have undoubtedly either seen a hat with his name on it or been stuck driving behind one of the behemoth tractors named after him. John Deere is his name, and the self-polishing cast steel plow is his invention.

John Deere was born in Rutland, Vermont, on February 7, 1804. He lived in Middlebury, Vermont, for a good portion of his life. In 1825, after serving a four-year apprenticeship, Deere started working as a blacksmith, producing hay forks and shovels, among other implements. He was so good that he soon gained significant fame in the area for his careful workmanship and ingenuity. During the Great Depression of the 1830s, things were not good for Deere or the people of Vermont. Many people decided to move out west, and they sent back stories of "golden opportunities." After hearing these stories, Deere decided to abandon his business in Vermont and he moved to Grand Detour, Illinois, which was settled by other natives of Vermont. He brought with him a small amount of cash and his tools, which was fortunate because the town needed a blacksmith. Two days after his arrival he had already set up a shop, built a forge, and was busy working. His family then followed him to Grand Detour.

Deere became busy working in his new shop shoeing horses and oxen, and making and repairing farm equipment. From repairing farm equipment, Deere discovered that the rich, fertile soil of the Midwest prairie would stick to the plow bottoms. Plows designed for the light, sandy New England soil could not handle cutting and turning the Midwest soil. Farming in the Midwest became a slow, labor-intensive task, and many farmers considered moving further west or back east.

Deere thought about this problem, and decided if he made a plow that was highly polished and shaped in the right way, it would scour itself and the prairie soil would

Intellectual Property Law for Engineers, Scientists, and Entrepreneurs, Second Edition. Howard B. Rockman.

Published 2020 by John Wiley & Sons, Inc.

not stick to the plow. Deere, with help from his partner, Major Leonard Andrus, made a plow to these specifications in 1837. The cutting part of this plow was constructed of steel, cut from an old sawmill blade and shaped by bending the blade over a log. The moldboard, used for lifting and turning the soil, was made of wrought iron and polished on the upper surface to prevent clogging. The plows were successfully tested on a farm near Grand Detour.

His new plow was very successful, and Deere, instead of making them as they were ordered, would produce a supply of plows and go out into the country and sell them. This approach was completely different from previous farm implement sales methods, and word quickly spread of Deere's "self-polishers."

Deere encountered a few problems, however. Living in the frontier, there were few banks, poor transportation, and a scarcity of steel. Deere's first plows were made from any steel he could find. In 1843, Deere ordered a shipment of specially rolled steel from England. This shipment had to cross the Atlantic Ocean, go up the Mississippi and Illinois Rivers, and go forty miles in a wagon to reach Deere's shop in Grand Detour. In 1846, cast steel plows rolled in Pittsburgh and shipped to Moline, Illinois, solved this problem.

The Deere plow was so successful that by 1846, Deere and his partner were selling one thousand plows a year. Deere decided to sell his interest in the Grand Detour business to his partner, Leonard Andrus. He then organized a plow company in Moline, Illinois, in 1848, taking advantage of the water energy and transportation provided by the Mississippi River. He began experimenting with imported English steel, and had a cast steel plow made for him in Pittsburgh. By 1855, he was selling more than 13,000 such plows a year. He obtained his first patent for a walk-behind, horse-drawn plow in 1865, Patent No. 46,454.

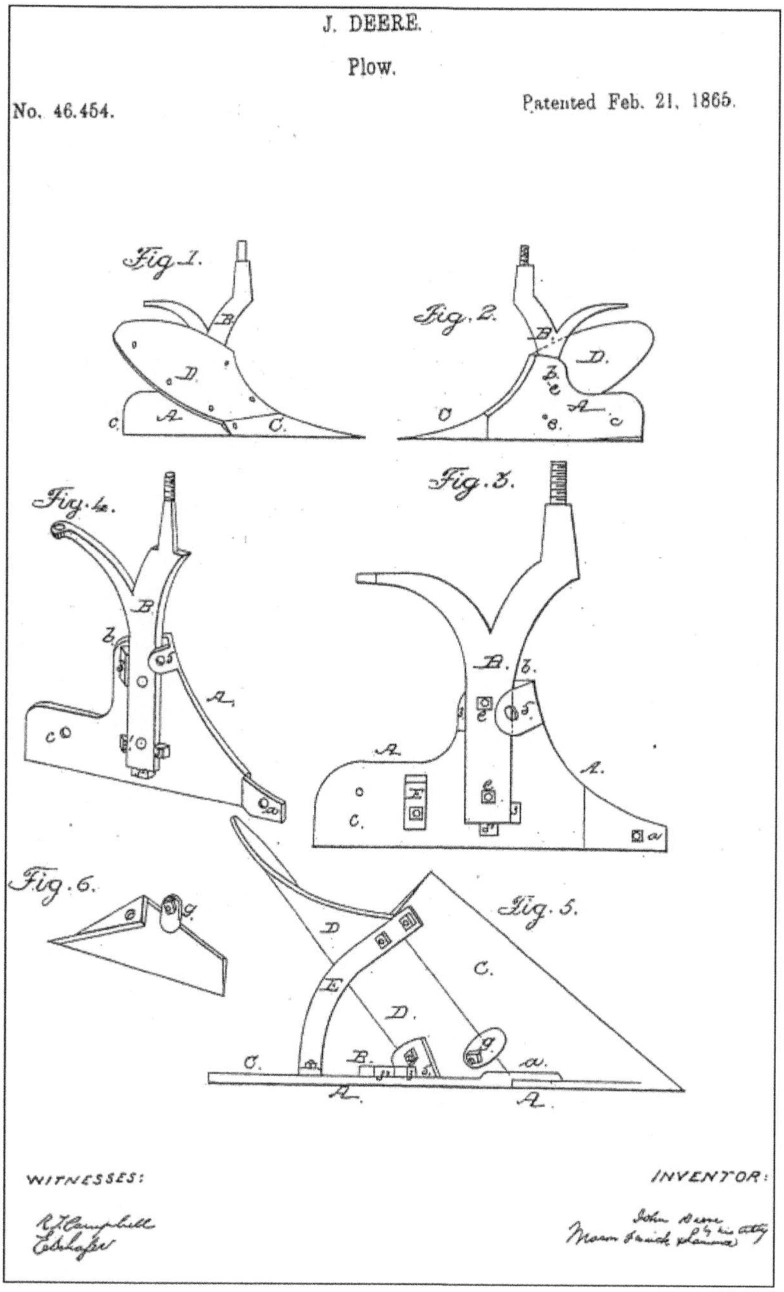
J. DEERE.
Plow.
No. 46.454.
Patented Feb. 21, 1865.
Fig. 1.
Fig. 2.
Fig. 3.
Fig. 4.
Fig. 5.
Fig. 6.
WITNESSES:
INVENTOR:

◆ INVENTORS AND INVENTIONS ◆

Erastus Brigham Bigelow

POWERED CARPET-MAKING LOOMS

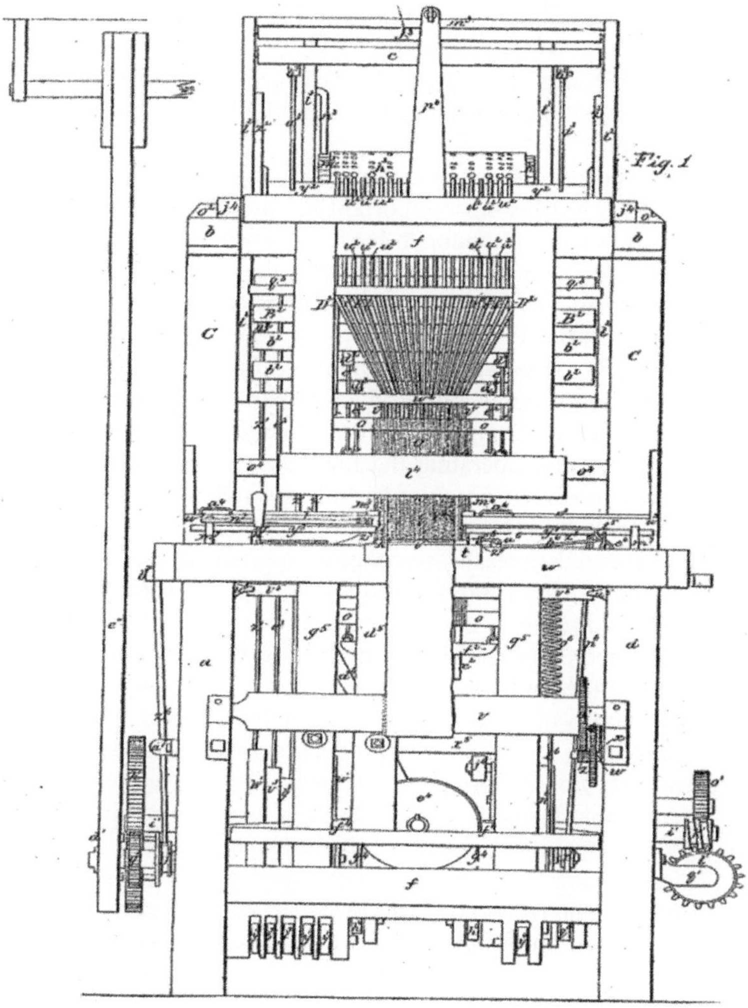

Intellectual Property Law for Engineers, Scientists, and Entrepreneurs, Second Edition. Howard B. Rockman.
© 2020 by The Institute of Electrical and Electronics Engineers, Inc.
Published 2020 by John Wiley & Sons, Inc.

Erastus Brigham Bigelow was born in 1814, the son of a cotton weaver. Early in his life, he worked in his father's business, which was not very successful. He then turned his attention to inventing, and before reaching the age of 18, had invented a hand loom for weaving webbing used in suspenders. Bigelow, at one time, was studying medicine at the Leicester Academy, intending to go to Harvard University. However, his financial situation deteriorated, and he left school to devote his time to inventing. In 1837, he developed a power loom for weaving lace used in coach lights. Bigelow then saw that the ideas behind his power loom could be modified to manufacture other fabrics, such as gingham. In 1839, he contracted to produce a power loom capable of weaving two-ply ingrain carpets, which had previously been woven only by a handloom producing 8 yards of material a day. With his first power loom, Bigelow succeeded in obtaining 10 or 12 yards daily, which constantly increased through improvements until 25 yards per day was regularly achieved. However, the manufacturer of Bigelow's first power loom failed, which resulted in Bigelow earning no profit from his first invention.

Later in 1841, he invented a power loom for weaving pictorial tapestry and velvet tapestry carpets, which was his most important invention and drew vast amounts of attention at the World's Fair in London in 1851. The town of Clinton, Massachusetts, owed its growth in manufacturing importance to Bigelow, as the town was home to the Coach Lights Works and The Lancaster Quilt Company, which companies used the direct results of his inventions.

Bigelow, his brother, and other investors founded the Clinton Company in about 1838, to operate Bigelow's looms and produce carpets. The Clinton Company later became the Bigelow Carpet Company. Central Massachusetts had abundant waterpower, which was perfect for operating Bigelow's power looms. The factory jobs his loom created attracted a diverse group of Irish, English, Scottish, and German immigrants, as well as women from New Hampshire and Vermont.

Over a span of several decades, Erastus Bigelow created and developed increasingly faster and more capable power looms, resulting in rugs and carpets becoming more affordable. He obtained patents on approximately 35 looms used in the manufacture of carpets in the United States and England. Prior to Bigelow, fine rugs and carpets were accessible only to the wealthy, but Bigelow's inventions enabled ordinary consumers to enjoy the luxury of heavily textured rugs in their homes. Within a year of the introduction of Bigelow's powered loom, production of carpets in the United States doubled. He was recognized during his lifetime as the inventor of all the basic machinery for carpet and tapestry weaving. Bigelow was also nominated at one time, but not elected, for the position of Senator from the Commonwealth of Massachusetts.

In 1861, Bigelow was one of the 21-member committee that created the Massachusetts Institute of Technology. Bigelow's first automatic powered carpet loom is on display today in the Smithsonian Institution in Washington, D.C.

Sheet 1 - 3 Sheets.

E. B. Bigelow.
Loom.

No. 169. Patented Apr. 20, 1837.

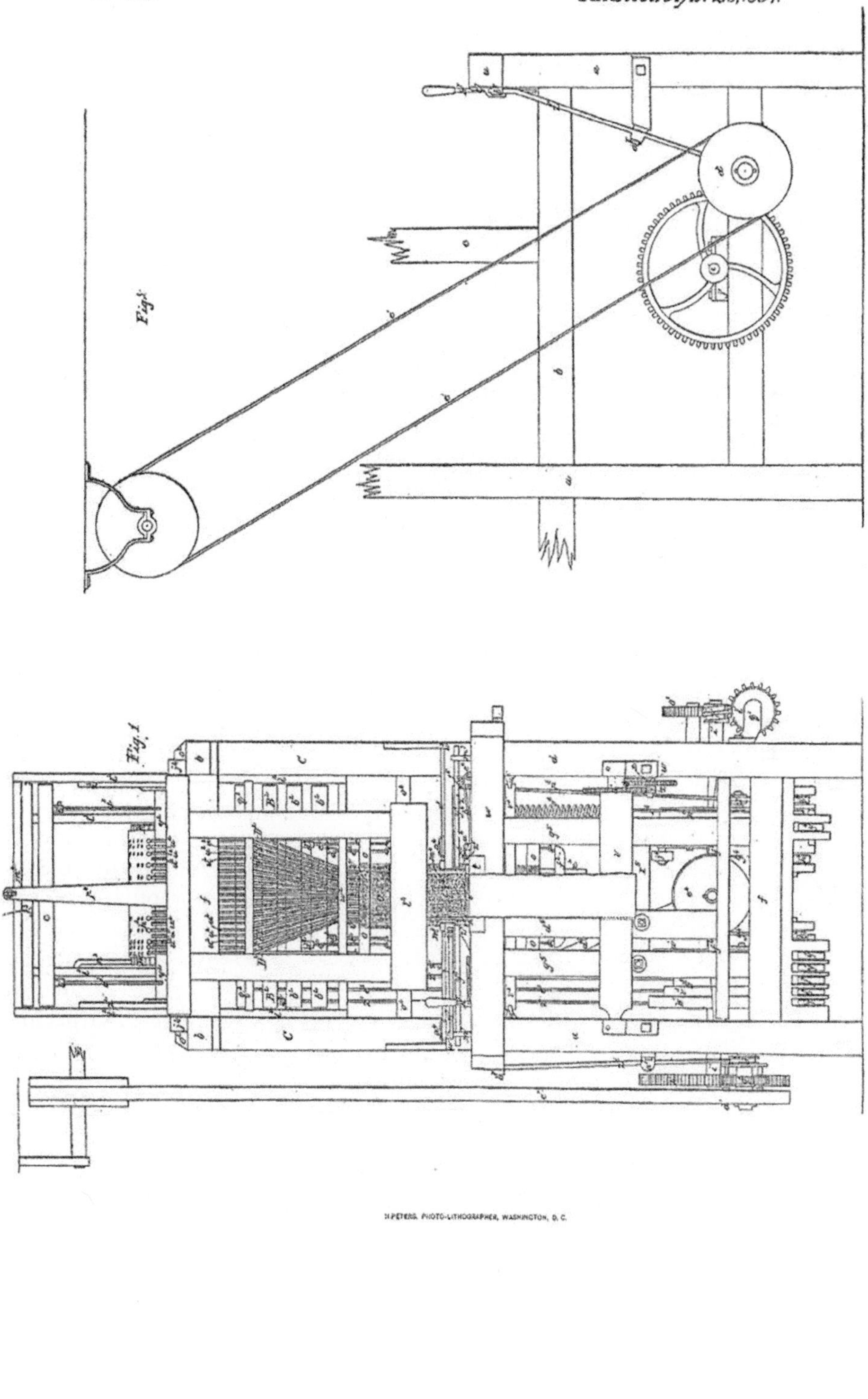

N. PETERS, PHOTO-LITHOGRAPHER, WASHINGTON, D. C.

5 Novelty—The Invention Must Be New

5.1 STATUTORY REQUIREMENTS

Starting a development project, the engineer or scientist has at hand the full wealth of known prior technology related to the goals of the project. This is what is defined as the "prior art." The developer knows, however, that the amassed knowledge of the prior art cannot solve the current problem; the prior art must be advanced to reach the current goals of this new development project. Thus, the inventor toils until an advance over the prior art allows the new goal to be reached. At project's end, the inventor's advanced structure, and its function or method are measured against the state of the prior art to establish the novelty of the advance, and to ensure that such an advance would not be obvious, given the teachings of the prior art. When the advance satisfies these criteria, patentable invention is made out, and a meaningful patent can be obtained to provide exclusive rights to the owner of the invention, as long as the other criteria for patentability are satisfied.

5.1.1 Time Limits for Filing a Patent Application

The time at which a patent application is initially filed is important as it provides a benchmark applicable to the activities of the inventor and to the inventions of others. By way of example, consider a modified version of history regarding the discovery of the wheel as a way of explaining some of the time limits for patentability.

Suppose the first inventor of the wheel merely recognized the problems associated with moving large loads on rolling logs, which comprises the prior art. At this point, the inventor has only recognized the need for a better structure, and a patent application would not yet be timely since a patentable invention has not yet been fully thought through. A patent application is not proper until a working form of an invention has been fully conceived. At the time when a complete invention is mentally pictured, and is conceived in operating form, such as by prototype or illustration, the inventor may properly pursue patent protection.

In continuing with the example, quite independently of the effort to obtain patent protection on the wheel, the same inventor might have published a description of his or her wheel, or may have built a wagon and gone into the moving business prior to seeking patent protection. Such activities raise another question of timing under the Patent Laws. In the U.S., a patent application must be filed within one year after the

Intellectual Property Law for Engineers, Scientists, and Entrepreneurs, Second Edition. Howard B. Rockman.

Published 2020 by John Wiley & Sons, Inc.

invention is first described in any publication anywhere in the world, or placed on sale, sold, used, or known publicly anywhere in the world. This is known as the one-year "grace period," and is based on the philosophy that the inventor abandons his or her patent rights if a proper patent application is not filed in the inventor's home country within one year from public disclosure or commercial activity with respect to the invention. As explained below, most other major industrial countries do not have an equivalent one-year grace period in their patent laws.

A major exception to the rule that public disclosure of the invention by the inventor more than a year before filing for a patent may destroy patent rights is the case of the public disclosure during a period of legitimate "experimental use" to perfect or develop the invention. The U.S. one-year grace period does not start until experimentation is completed. Thus, if you conducted further R&D and made changes to the invention after the public disclosure, you may be able to establish that the public disclosure was only an experimental version of the invention.

For example, in a famous case dating back to the late 1800s, an inventor filed a patent application directed to asphalt paving material that was used for six years on a public highway before the patent application was filed. The U.S. Supreme Court held that the patent was still valid since six years of experimentation were required to determine whether the highway material would hold up under long and continued use.

Present patent case law dated back to 1946 holds that an inventor cannot publicly offer, use, or sell a product that embodies a trade secret, and then after one year file a patent application directed to patenting that trade secret. The inventor has been given a choice—apply for a patent and disclose your trade secret to the public for use after your patent expires, or maintain the invention as a trade secret that only benefits you and not the public at large. You cannot have it both ways.

However, there is language in Section 102 of the AIA enacted in 2011 that some patent law scholars have interpreted as allowing one to keep technology a secret, although selling products embodying the trade secret, and later (after one year) obtain a patent on the trade secret. As of this writing, the courts have not handed down a decision on this point, so if this issue is important in your technology development and marketing processes, I suggest you consult with your intellectual property professional for the latest information on this point. Trade secrets per se are discussed in further detail in Chapter 27.

The law of novelty of inventions also covers situations where an inventor places a product in public use, but the invention is not discernible to the user upon observation. One such case involved the invention of an improved golf ball cover that was marketed by the inventor, which cover comprised a "secret ingredient" that the inventor did not disclose to the public. In other words, the public use of the improved golf balls was a "non-informing use" of the secret ingredient. The Court held that had the inventor filed a patent application on his invention more than one year after the "non-informing" use of the new golf balls, his application would have been barred, notwithstanding the fact that the user could not ascertain the "secret ingredient." The invention was held to be in "public use" for more than one year.

In this non-informing use case, the Court offered three reasons for its conclusion. First, even the non-informing use gives the public the benefit of the invention, and the invention has had an impact in the marketplace. Second, even though the complete formulation of the golf ball cover was not available to the user, when the article itself is freely available to the public, it is fair to presume that the secret will be uncovered by potential competitors, such as by reverse engineering, long before a patent would have expired based upon a timely filed patent application.

Third, the inventor is under no duty to apply for a patent, and is free to elect to contribute the invention to the public. For these reasons, the Court held that the inventor's non-informing use of the golf balls with the inventive cover was a "public use" that qualified as prior art in a lawsuit involving someone else's patent covering a similarly covered golf ball.

It is also important to remember is that it is highly recommended to keep careful records of the conception of inventions and their development, which also should be signed by a witness. This is to assist later in corroborating the dates that the invention was conceived and reduced to practice, if it becomes necessary to prove that someone else derived, or "stole" your invention from you, as discussed in Chapter 18. A good suggestion is to file a patent application at the earliest practical time, and most importantly before any public description or disclosure or commercial development of the invention has been made.

A further timing consideration involves the protection of foreign patent rights. It is important to know that any publication, public knowledge, or public use of an invention that takes place anywhere before the filing date of a patent application in the United States may prevent the inventor from obtaining valid patents in many foreign countries that rely upon the "absolute novelty" standard, which are those countries that do not allow the one-year grace period. In those countries, a patent application must be on file in the inventor's home country prior to any public use or disclosure of the invention anywhere in the world. Chapter 16 covers in more detail how to adequately protect your foreign patent rights.

Keep in mind also that a long delay in applying for a patent may result in the loss of all patent rights, which may end up going to a second independent inventor of the same subject matter who acts more promptly to file a patent application. The highly recommended route to follow is to file a patent application at the earliest practical time, and most importantly before any public description or disclosure or commercial development of the invention has been made.

5.1.2 Prior Art Activities of the Inventor and Others That Can Defeat Patent Rights

The U.S. Patent Law, at 35 U.S.C. §102, as amended by the AIA, states that an inventor shall be entitled to a patent unless the invention (1) was known or used by others, or (2) patented or described in a printed publication, or (3) placed on sale or sold, anywhere in the world, before the patent application filing date. Therefore, if the same invention was made public by someone else prior to your filing date, you cannot obtain a patent.

This provision of the Patent Law also prevents a person who merely recognizes the commercial merits of an existing product, or who discovers the product in an ancient document, in the U.S. or a foreign country, or from another pre-existing source, from properly obtaining a U.S. patent, since patents in the United States are granted only to "an inventor." The activities of others who may have publicly disclosed the same invention as yours, without necessarily obtaining any patent protection for that invention, may defeat your right to a patent if those activities occurred prior to your patent application filing date.

A further provision of the Patent Law, which was touched upon previously, prohibits an inventor from obtaining a patent if the invention (1) was patented or described in a printed publication in this or a foreign country by the inventor, or (2) was in public use, on sale, offered for sale, or publicly available anywhere more than one year prior to the date of the filing of the application for patent in the United States as a result of actions of the inventor. This is a very important provision, and controls the time in which patent protection must be applied for, or patent protection is lost. This is the provision that includes the U.S. "grace period" requiring that a patent application be filed within one year from the date of first public disclosure or publication anywhere of the invention. The purpose of this provision is to require inventors to make a prompt decision regarding filing a patent application, so that the public will obtain the benefit of the inventor's work upon expiration of the patent that much earlier. One who suppresses, abandons, or conceals their invention is not entitled to patent protection.

Under this provision of the Patent Law, the activities of the inventor or inventors themselves, as well as the activities of others, may defeat rights to patents. For example, if one completes an invention, and then publishes a paper or delivers a speech that is later furnished to members of the audience in paper or electronic form, such as a paper or speech delivered to a professional or a trade group, that inventor then has one year from the time of that publication or disclosure to file a U.S. patent application. Therefore, it is imperative that inventors consider the patentability of their inventions during that first year period, or face the loss of all patent protection.

It is also important to note what was briefly discussed previously about avoiding the loss of foreign patent rights. If at all possible, it is highly recommended to seek the advice of a patent professional prior to any public disclosure of any invention, so that foreign patent rights will not be lost. In today's global economy, I cannot think of one invention that would have use solely in the United States, and not be potentially marketable in other countries throughout the world in one form or another.

If during the development of your invention, it becomes necessary to disclose the invention outside your company, or outside the group of inventors working on the invention, such disclosure should be made only after a confidential non-disclosure agreement has been signed by the recipient party to whom the disclosure is being made. The non-disclosure agreement should state, among other things, that the recipient party will not use the disclosed information for its own benefit, nor disclose the subject matter of your invention to anyone else, without your prior written consent. In addition, all information and physical devices given to the recipient party relating to the invention should be clearly and boldly marked CONFIDENTIAL. This will establish later, if necessary, that the disclosure of the invention to the recipient party was confidential, and was not a "public" disclosure under the Patent Laws. Taking these steps, therefore, allows you to privately disclose your invention to another, without starting the one-year clock from running under the U.S. Patent Law, and will also simultaneously save a majority of your foreign patent rights from extinction.

For more information on the provisions in a typical Confidential Non-Disclosure Agreement, see Chapter 21 of this text.

Public use of an invention that can be proven to be an experimental use is not considered a prior public use when applying the requirement that an application must be filed within one year from public use. However, it is important to realize that in litigation against an adversary party, any disclosure which you may have considered experimental may ultimately be held by a court or a jury to be proven as a public use. In one instance I can recall, a conversation on a bus traveling between a hotel and a convention center during a trade show, where the inventor disclosed some of the ideas of his invention to someone on the bus, constituted a public disclosure. Therefore, it is important to note that if any public comments or disclosures are made about an invention, the inventor should be aware of what can and what cannot be done with regard to protecting patent rights in the United States and throughout the world. Appropriate non-disclosure agreements should be used to cloak invention disclosures, at all times when possible, to prevent a disclosure from being "public."

5.1.3 Prior Publications, U.S. and Foreign, as Prior Art

In the U.S. Patent and Trademark Office, and in the courts, the novelty of an invention and thus the validity of a patent application or of an issued patent is tested against the body of prior patents, public inventions, and published material known as "prior art," which basically encompasses everything known throughout the world that took place prior to the filing date of your patent application. Under the U.S. patent examination and legal system, (1) any publication that shows all or part of your invention prior to your patent application filing date is prior art, and (2) any prior publication or patent that was made public or issued more than one year before your patent application filing date is also prior art. In addition, any foreign patents, foreign publications, information in text books or databases, and any other publicly available knowledge about work that was performed relating to your invention becomes prior art for use by the Patent Examiner and the courts in determining the novelty of your invention, and thus the validity of your patent application or patent.

An inventor is charged with "constructive knowledge" of all public prior art that was generated from the beginning of time up until the date of his or her patent application filing date, regarding the subject matter of his or her invention. Although it is impossible for any single inventor to know all of this subject matter, without such constructive knowledge the patent system would not work. As will be explained in Chapter 8, it is possible to obtain a search of literature, patents, and other materials prior to filing a patent application to substantially determine the state of the prior art regarding the subject matter of any invention. Thus, it is possible before the filing of a patent application for an inventor and the inventor's attorney to obtain a fairly large and detailed amount of information regarding the state of the prior art to which an invention pertains, upon which to base a decision regarding the novelty of your invention.

Upon examination by a Patent Examiner, and later in litigation before the courts, such prior publications, uses, and knowledge are used to limit the scope of the claims of a patent application or issued patent to define only that which is novel, and to eliminate those claims which cover the prior art. The claims of a patent are drafted to potentially encompass everything related to the invention which may be devised by others in the future, and yet the same claims, read as a whole, cannot cover any material that has been shown or disclosed in the prior art. Thus, determining the content of the prior art is of the utmost importance in the patenting process. The claims of a patent are its most important content, and are discussed in detail in Chapter 10.

5.2 PRELIMINARY COMMENTS ON PROTECTING FOREIGN PATENT RIGHTS

As alluded to previously, a significant number of foreign countries throughout the world utilize what is called the "absolute novelty" rule, which requires that a patent application be on file in that country before any public disclosure of the invention. In other words, there is no one-year grace period as offered by U.S. law. However, based upon a series of treaties adhered to by the United States and most countries, procedures have been established to protect the patentability of inventions throughout the world.

Pursuant to these treaties, if an inventor files a patent application in the inventor's home country, and a corresponding patent application is filed in a foreign country within one year of the date of the home country application filing date, the constructive filing date of the foreign patent application is the home country application filing date, or the "priority date," under the provisions of the Paris Convention of 1883 (discussed in further detail in Chapter 16). By way of example as to how this system works, if you were to file an application for a patent on an invention on January 1 in the USPTO, and then publicly disclose that invention at a trade show, sales meeting, or otherwise on January 2, and then file patent applications in the European Patent Office, Japan, India, South Korea, and Australia on December 1 of the same year, the effective filing date of all of your foreign patent applications would be the same as your United States filing date, and therefore your patent application in those foreign countries would not be barred based upon your public exposure of the invention on January 2. There is a further treaty called the Patent Cooperation Treaty (PCT) which allows you to file a document within that one-year period with the USPTO, that extends the time that you have to file foreign patent applications for a total of up to 30 or 31 months from your initial U.S. patent application filing date. PCT applications are also covered in Chapter 16.

Therefore, if you determine that your invention has potential worldwide acceptance and value, it is extremely important to ensure that there is no public disclosure of your invention before your U.S. or home country patent application filing date. After filing, you are free to publicly show and commercialize your invention. There are provisions in the United States Patent Law, such as Provisional Patent Application filings, which allow the patent attorney to make a rapid and proper application filing in the USPTO, and obtain an official filing date before you make any public disclosure of your invention. If necessary, the patent attorney can work to one or two day requirements in preparing a Provisional Patent Application. However, it is not recommended that you wait until such a late date to inform your patent attorney about the subject matter of your invention, and your desire to obtain protection in several countries.

5.3 ADDITIONAL COMMENTS ON EXPERIMENTAL USE VERSUS ACTUAL USE OF THE INVENTION

If for reasons that are beyond your control, such as a lack of financing, or the fact that a budget for introduction for new products for a given year has already been expended, you find yourself in a situation where your invention, or certain aspects of your invention, may have been exposed to third parties more than a year before your patent application filing date without being covered by a Confidential Non-Disclosure Agreement, consideration must be given to inquiring whether such use can be established as experimental use and not public use by revisiting the facts surrounding such disclosure. One major consideration is whether or not the disclosure to third parties involved a disclosure of a complete, workable invention, or whether or not development work was still being conducted on the invention, and additional work on the invention took place after such disclosure. A disclosure that will defeat the validity of a patent must be a disclosure of the complete invention. Disclosures to third parties such as vendors or potential marketing partners more than a year before the patent application was filed may be held to be "experimental uses" if it can be shown that development work continued from the point of that disclosure forward to perfect and modify the invention, and the invention was not technically complete and should not be considered an "invention" upon the date of disclosure. Any significant changes to your invention made after such disclosure tend to prove that the disclosure was made only of the experimental model, and not the completed invention. Also, public uses of the invention for technical test purposes are usually considered as experimental uses, while on the other hand, market testing of the complete or near-complete invention are considered as public uses, and not experimental uses.

To avoid any possibility of creating "public information" that may affect the validity of the patent adversely, I suggest that as soon as you have determined that the project you are working on may lead to a patentable invention, and before there is any public disclosure of the invention outside the realm of the inventors or the company for or with whom you may be working, consideration be given to patenting your invention, and that you gain information from a patent professional as to what disclosure of the invention can or cannot be made, and how "confidential" disclosures can be made that will not affect patent rights. This will avoid issues adverse to patentability from arising in the first place.

◆ INVENTORS AND INVENTIONS ◆

Alfred Nobel

DYNAMITE

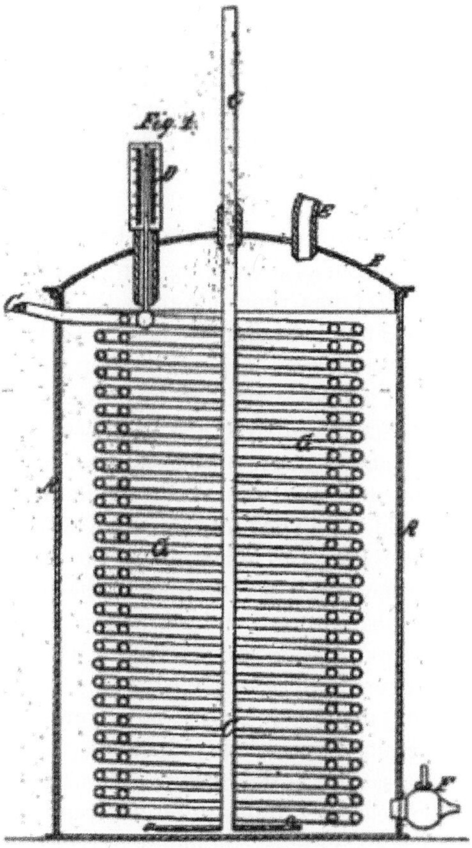

Recall all those cartoons from your childhood where the bad guy would always think of an elaborate plot to beat the good guy, and time after time the bad guy would pick up a box of Acme TNT and get blown up. If it were not for Alfred Nobel and his invention, we probably would not have those wonderful memories of dynamite blowing up the bad guy.

Intellectual Property Law for Engineers, Scientists, and Entrepreneurs, Second Edition. Howard B. Rockman.

Published 2020 by John Wiley & Sons, Inc.

Alfred B. Nobel was born in Stockholm, Sweden, on October 21, 1833. His father left his family in Sweden in 1837 and moved to St. Petersburg, Russia, to start a new business, producing submarine mines and torpedoes that he designed for the Russian government. In 1842, the family, including Alfred, his mother, and three brothers, moved to St. Petersburg. The mines made by Alfred's father were submerged wooden caches filled with gunpowder, and were successfully used in the Crimean War (1853–1856).

Alfred Nobel and his brothers were all educated by private teachers, and they also traveled extensively. At the age of 17, Alfred was fluent in five languages, and had taken an early interest in chemistry, as well as physics, English literature, and poetry. During his travels, he visited Paris, where he met Ascanio Sobrero, an Italian chemist who had previously invented nitroglycerine, a highly explosive liquid. Nitroglycerine was a powerfully explosive but unstable mixture of glycerin and sulfuric and nitric acids. It would explode unpredictably when subjected to heat and pressure, and was considered too dangerous for practical use. Alfred Nobel became interested in solving the safety problems inherent with nitroglycerine and finding a method for its controlled detonation.

In 1852, Alfred Nobel returned to St. Petersburg to work in the family business, where he and his father experimented in reducing nitroglycerine to a useful explosive for construction purposes. After the Crimean War, in 1863, Alfred's parents and one of his brothers, Emil, returned to Stockholm, where they worked on developing a useful form of nitroglycerine. Several explosions in their shop, including one in 1864 that killed Emil and several others, led the Stockholm city government to forbid nitroglycerine experiments within city limits. Alfred moved his experiments to a barge on Lake Mälaren, where he began to mass-produce nitroglycerine.

Through further experimentation, he found that mixing nitroglycerine with silica would form a paste that could be molded into rods that would fit into construction drilling holes and which did not react to minor changes in temperature and pressure. He obtained a patent on this invention in 1867 (1868 in the United States), and called his product "dynamite." He also invented and patented a detonator, or blasting cap, for the dynamite rods. Fortuitously, at the same time, the diamond drilling crown and the pneumatic drill began being used in the construction and excavating industries. The market for dynamite and detonating caps rapidly grew. His factories also developed a gelatin form of dynamite that was safe to handle.

Alfred Nobel also was a skillful entrepreneur and businessman, and eventually established factories and research facilities in 90 different locations in more than 20 countries. He made his home in Paris, though he traveled constantly. At the age of 43, he advertised for a woman to take employment as secretary and supervisor of his bachelor household. An Austrian woman, Countess Bertha Kinsky, was hired, but worked for Nobel for a very short time; she returned to Austria to marry Count Arthur von Suttner. Alfred and Bertha remained friends, and corresponded for many years. Bertha von Suttner became a leader of the anti-armament race proliferating throughout Europe at that time, and authored a famous book, *Lay Down Your Arms*. Sources indicate that she influenced Alfred Nobel when he included prizes for persons or organizations promoting peace in his final will, which was signed on November 27, 1895.

In point of fact, the 1905 Nobel Peace Prize was awarded to Bertha von Suttner by the Norwegian Parliament.

Alfred Nobel died at his home in San Remo, Italy, on December 10, 1896, but that was not the end of his influence on humanity. When his will was opened, those who knew him, and particularly his relatives, were surprised to learn he had left the bulk of his sizeable fortune to establish an invested fund. The interest of the fund was to be distributed in the form of prizes in the categories of physics, chemistry, physiology or medicine, literature, and peace "to those who, during the preceding year, shall have conferred the greatest benefit on mankind." The paragraph from his will establishing the Nobel Prizes is reprinted on page 102.

The executors of his will, two young engineers, Rudolf Lilljequist and Rognar Sohlman, formed the Nobel Foundation to accomplish Nobel's lofty purposes. These young men successfully battled Alfred Nobel's relatives and the authorities in several countries who challenged and questioned the will. Upon successfully battling the opposition, the first Nobel Prizes were awarded in 1901.

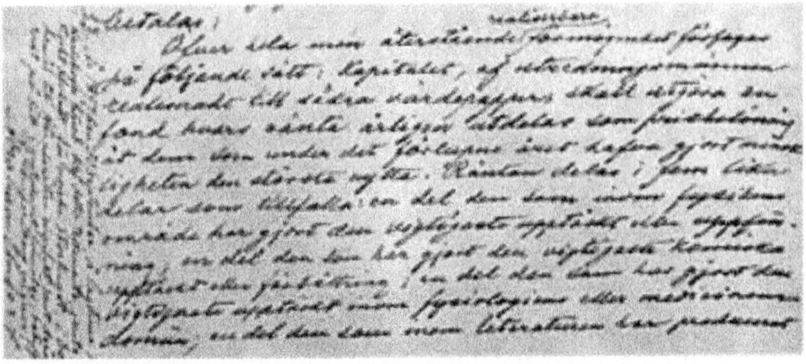

"The whole of my remaining realizable estate shall be dealt with in the following way: the capital, invested in safe securities by my executors, shall constitute a fund, the interest on which shall be annually distributed in the form of prizes to those who, during the preceding year, shall have conferred the greatest benefit on mankind. The said interest shall be divided into five equal parts, which shall be apportioned as follows: one part to the person who shall have made the most important discovery or invention within the field of physics; one part to the person who shall have made the most important chemical discovery or improvement; one part to the person who shall have made the most important discovery within the domain of physiology or medicine; one part to the person who shall have produced in the field of literature the most outstanding work in an ideal direction; and one part to the person who shall have done the most or the best work for fraternity between nations, for the abolition or reduction of standing armies and for the holding and promotion of peace congresses. The prizes for physics and chemistry shall be awarded by the Swedish Academy of Sciences; that for physiology or medical works by the Karolinska Institute in Stockholm; that for literature by the Academy in Stockholm, and that for champions of peace by a committee of five persons to be elected by the Norwegian Storting. It is my express wish that in awarding the prizes no consideration be given to the nationality of the candidates, but that the most worthy shall receive the prize, whether he be Scandinavian or not."

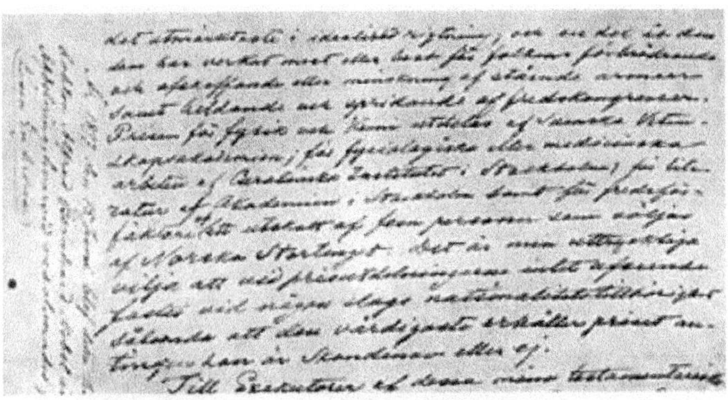

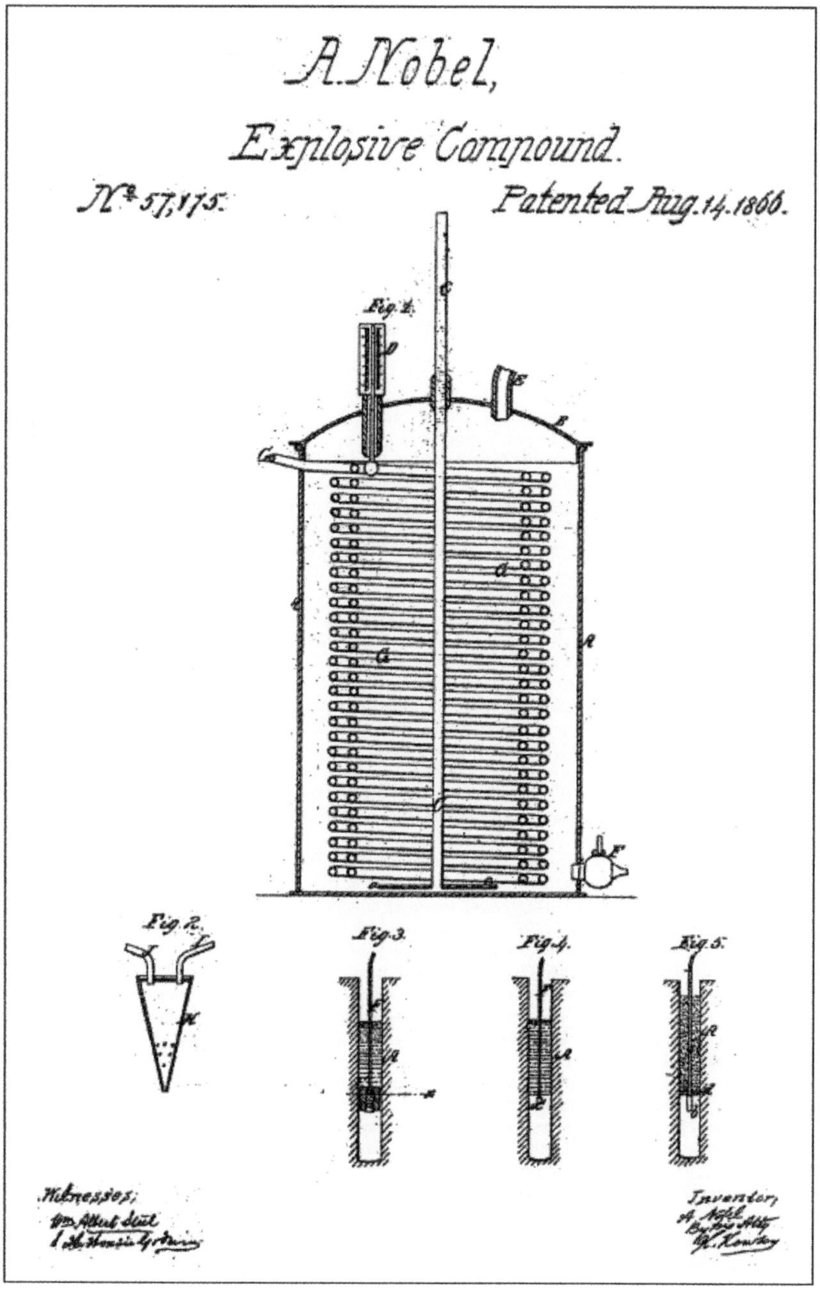
A. Nobel,
Explosive Compound.
No 57,175.
Patented Aug. 14. 1866.
Fig. 1.
Fig. 2.
Fig. 3.
Fig. 4.
Fig. 5.
Witnesses;
Inventor,
A. Nobel

United States Patent Office.

ALFRED NOBEL, OF HAMBURG, GERMANY, ASSIGNOR TO JULIUS BANDMANN, OF SAN FRANCISCO, CALIFORNIA.

Letters Patent No. 78,317, dated May 26, 1868.

IMPROVED EXPLOSIVE COMPOUND.

The Schedule referred to in these Letters Patent and making part of the same.

TO ALL WHOM IT MAY CONCERN:

Be it known that I, ALFRED NOBEL, of the city of Hamburg, Germany, have invented a new and useful Composition of Matter, to wit, an Explosive Powder.

The nature of the invention consists in forming out of two ingredients long known, viz, the explosive substance nitro-glycerine, and an inexplosive porous substance, hereafter specified, a composition which, without losing the great explosive power of nitro-glycerine, is very much altered as to its explosive and other properties, being far more safe and convenient for transportation, storage, and use, than nitro-glycerine.

In general terms, my invention consists in mixing with nitro-glycerine a substance which possesses a very great absorbent capacity, and which, at the same time, is free from any quality which will decompose, destroy, or injure the nitro-glycerine, or its explosiveness.

It is undoubtedly true, as a general rule, that nitro-glycerine, when mixed with another substance, possesses less concentration of power than when used alone; but while the safety of the miner (to prevent leakage into seams in the rock) prohibits the use of nitro-glycerine without cartridges, which latter must of course be somewhat less in diameter than the bore-holes which are to contain them, the powder herein described can be made to form a semi-pasty mass, which yields to the slightest pressure, and thus can be made to fill up the bore-hole entirely. Practically, therefore, the miner will have as much nitro-glycerine in the same height of bore-hole with this powder as with nitro-glycerine in its pure state.

This is the real character and purpose of my invention; and in order to enable others skilled in the art to which it appertains (or with which it is most nearly connected) to make, compound, and use the same, I will proceed to describe the same, and also the manner and process of making, compounding, and using it, in full, clear, and exact terms.

The substance which most fully meets the requirements above mentioned, so far as I know or have been able to ascertain from numerous experiments, is a certain kind of silicious earth or silicic acid, found in various parts of the globe, and known under the several names of silicious marl, tripoli, rotten-stone, &c. The particular variety of this material which is best for my compound is homogeneous, has a low specific gravity, great absorbent capacity, and is generally composed of the remains of *infusoria*.

So great is the absorbent capacity of this earth, that it will take up about three times its own weight of nitro-glycerine and still retain its powder-form, thus leaving the nitro-glycerine so compact and concentrated as to have very nearly its original explosive power; whereas, if another substance, having a less absorbent capacity, is used, a correspondingly less proportion of nitro-glycerine will be absorbed, and the powder be correspondingly weak or wholly inexplosive.

For example, most chalk will take but about fifteen per cent. of nitro-glycerine and retain its powder-form. Twenty per cent. will reduce it to a paste.

Porous charcoal has also a considerable absorbent capacity, but it has the defect of being itself a combustible material, and also of less elasticity of its particles, which renders it easy to squeeze out a part of its nitro-glycerine.

The two materials are combined in the following manner:

The earth, thoroughly dried and pulverized, is placed in a wooden vessel. To it is introduced the nitro-glycerine in a steady stream so small that the two ingredients can be kept thoroughly mixed.

The mixing may be effected by the naked hand, or by any proper wooden instrument used in the hand, or by wooden machinery

Sufficient of nitro-glycerine should be used to render the compound explosive, but not so much as to change its form of powder to a liquid or pasty consistency.

Practically, about sixty parts, by weight, of nitro-glycerine to forty of earth, forms the useful minimum,

16,317

and seventy-eight parts, by weight, of nitro-glycerine to twenty-two of earth, the useful maximum of explosive power. The former has a perfectly dry appearance, the latter is pasty.

Between these two extremes the composition will be explosive powder, and it will be more easily exploded, and its explosive power greater, as the relative proportion of the nitro-glycerine is greater.

The proportions, by weight, of seventy-five of nitro-glycerine to twenty-five of earth, gives a powder as well adapted to ordinary practical purposes as that from any proportions I am now able to name, and can be easily compressed to a specific gravity nearly equal to that of pure nitro-glycerine.

When the mass has been intimately mixed and thoroughly incorporated by stirring and kneading, it is rubbed through a hair, silk, or brass-wire sieve, (iron corrodes,) and any lumps which may remain are rubbed with a stiff-bristle brush till they are reduced and made to pass through the sieve.

The powder is then finished and ready for use.

The fineness desired for the powder will determine the fineness of the sieve to be used.

The chief characteristic of this powder is its nearly perfect exemption from liability to accidental or involuntary explosion.

It is far less sensitive than nitro-glycerine to concussion or percussion, and contained in its usual packing, (a wooden cask or box,) the latter may be smashed completely to pieces without any danger of an explosion.

Unlike gunpowder, in the open air or in ordinary packing, (a wooden cask or box,) it burns up, when set fire to, without exploding. It can, therefore, be handled, stored, and transported with less danger than ordinary gunpowder.

When confined in a tight and strong enclosure it explodes by heat applied in any form when above the temperature of 360° Fahrenheit. Under all other circumstances it may be exploded by some other explosion in it or into it.

The most simple and certain method known to me of exploding it is as follows:

The end of a common blasting-fuse is inserted into a percussion-cap, and the rim of the cap crimped tightly and firmly about the fuse by nippers, or other means, so as to leave the fulminating-powder of the cap and the end of the fuse tightly and firmly enclosed together. The end of the fuse, with the cap attached, is then embedded in the powder—the more firmly, the more certain the explosion.

In blasting, the powder is pressed tightly about the cap and fuse, and tamping, of sand or other proper material, added, and pressed but not pounded in. A tamping firmly pressed is as good as if rammed in the most solid manner.

The fuse explodes the cap, and this explosion explodes the powder.

I will add here that by carefully packing the end of a good fuse amidst the powder of a charge enclosed, like a blasting charge, in a tight place, the fuse alone will explode the powder, especially if the powder is strongly charged with nitro-glycerine. But this method of explosion requires too much care, and is too uncertain to be depended upon or generally used.

As before stated, the more strongly the powder is charged with nitro-glycerine the more easily it explodes. If, therefore, the powder contains a low proportion of nitro-glycerine, it is necessary to employ in its explosion a correspondingly long, strong, and heavily-charged percussion-cap, made especially for the purpose. For the sake of certainty of explosion it is better to use such a cap in all cases.

If the fire from the fuse comes in contact with the powder before the cap is exploded, which is liable to occur if the fuse is leaky and the cap extends too far into the powder, a portion of the powder will be burned before the explosion takes place. To guard against this, the cap should only be fairly inserted into the powder, and poor fuses wound next to the cap firmly with strong glued paper or hemp, or otherwise secured.

The bore-holes, as a practical but not absolute rule, should be about one-half the size, and the charge should be from one-fifth to one-tenth the quantity ordinarily used in gunpowder-blasting.

A very convenient form in which to use the powder is to pack it firmly in cartridges of strong paper.

Having thus described my invention, what I claim as new, and desire to secure by Letters Patent, is—

The composition of matter, made substantially of the ingredients and in the manner and for the purposes set forth.

ALFRED NOBEL.

Witnesses:

Fr. T. Frohme,
Heinr. Barteltssen

6 Requirement of Non-Obviousness for Patentability

6.1 DEVELOPMENT OF THE STANDARD OF NON-OBVIOUSNESS

The preceding chapters were, in part, directed toward the requirement that an invention must be "novel" in order to be patentable, and must be a "patent-eligible" invention. These represent threshold hurdles to overcome—however, establishing novelty alone does not automatically establish that your invention is patentable relative to the prior art. Thus, after it is established that the claimed invention differs structurally or functionally, or both, from the prior art, which means that the patent claim does not read literally on a single item of prior art, Section 103 of the U.S. Patent Statute (35 U.S.C. §103) becomes applicable. Section 103 requires that the claimed invention as a whole also be *non-obvious* at the time of the effective filing date of the patent application claiming the invention to a hypothetical "person having ordinary skill in the art to which the subject matter of the patented invention pertains." This condition deals with the level or degree of "invention," or "inventive step," required to obtain a patent. Thus, the non-obviousness requirement comes into play only when the claimed invention is not identically disclosed or described in the prior art as set forth in Section 102 of the patent statute, the latter which determines novelty. If the claimed invention is not novel, it is identically described in the prior art, falling under one of the subsections of Section 102. If this occurs, no valid patent is possible, and the question of patentability is ended.

However, where the claimed invention is not identically described in any single prior art disclosure, there is then the hurdle of non-obviousness that must be overcome to obtain a patent. The question becomes: does the invention for which you seek to obtain a patent represent sufficient innovation, or non-obviousness, over the prior art to support the grant of a patent?

6.2 HISTORICAL BACKGROUND

The first U.S. Patent Act in 1790 provided for the issuance of patents by the Secretaries of State, the Department of War, or the Attorney General, or any two of them, who should deem the invention or discovery sufficiently useful or important. After 3 years, the Patent Act of 1793 eliminated altogether the examination procedure in the grant of patents. However, the language regarding "useful" and "important" as to patents

Intellectual Property Law for Engineers, Scientists, and Entrepreneurs, Second Edition. Howard B. Rockman.

Published 2020 by John Wiley & Sons, Inc.

did reappear in the patent statute of 1836, which also reinstituted the patent examination process. This language was also included in all patent acts preceding the 1952 Patent Act, which is primarily the law in operation today, with periodic amendments. The latest major amendment was the AIA enacted in 2011.

Apparently, the fact that an invention had to be both useful and important was universally ignored by the U.S. courts prior to 1952. However, in dealing with patents, the courts did institute certain criteria for innovation above and beyond the test of novelty. Thus, case law began to develop around this test of "importance" of the invention. The various cases decided by the several courts set forth a great variety of definitions relating to the requirement for innovation, in addition to novelty, to support patentability. The question always has been, and still is, to determine whether a novel invention is a sufficient advance in the art that its disclosure to the public warrants granting the right to exclude others from use of the invention for a limited time period. This is the statement of the law as it exists today, and the answer to this question lies in the analysis of the technological advance of the particular invention over the content of the prior art.

The requirement that the subject matter of a patent grant be non-obvious was first embodied in statutory form in the 1952 Patent Act in Section 103, which stated:

> Conditions for Patentability: Non-Obvious Subject Matter
> "A patent may not be obtained though the invention is not identically disclosed or described as set forth in Section 102 of this title (novelty requirements), if the differences between the subject matter sought to be patented and the prior art are such that the subject matter as a whole would have been obvious at the time the invention was made to a person having ordinary skill in the art to which said subject matter pertains. The patentability shall not be negatived by the manner in which the invention was made...."

The AIA made a change to Section 103 as follows:

> "A patent for a claimed invention may not be obtained, notwithstanding that the claimed invention is not identically disclosed as set forth in Section 102, if the differences between the claimed invention and the prior art are such that the claimed invention as a whole would have been obvious before the effective filing date of the claimed invention to a person having ordinary skill in the art to which the claimed invention pertains. Patentability shall not be negated by the manner in which the invention was made."

The key change made by the AIA was in making the non-obviousness test applicable at the time the patent application for the claimed invention was filed, and not as of the invention date as in pre-AIA §103. This conforms the definition of prior art in Section 103 with the definition of prior art in Section 102. The only other material change in the obviousness section relates to situations where (1) the prior art under consideration ("subject matter developed by another" in the statute) was commonly owned with the claimed invention, or (2) if the subject matter sought to be patented was subject to an obligation of assignment to the same person on the filing date of the application under examination. In either situation, patentability will not be precluded. In other words, the common ownership, obligation to assign, or a joint research agreement must exist on or before the effective patent application filing date of the claimed invention. Under the previous law before the AIA, these conditions had to be in existence before the date the invention was made. If any one of these conditions are met, a disclosure is not prior art at all, and cannot be used to reject a patent claim for lack of novelty or obviousness.

The legislative history of the 1952 Patent Act indicates that there was no provision in prior patent acts that corresponds to rejecting patents on the grounds of obviousness. However, U.S. courts had been holding patents invalid on the grounds of lack of invention since at least as early as 1850. The statement about non-obviousness was purposely left broad in the statute, with no definition of "obvious" offered by Congress. Congress hoped that the courts would later develop a more explicit statement of criteria that may be worked out to determine whether inventions are obvious or not in view of the prior art. Also, the legislative history indicates that the second sentence, relating to how the invention is made, states that patentability is not to be negated by the manner in which the invention is made. That is, it is immaterial whether or not the invention resulted from long toil and experimentation, or from a "flash of genius." This specific provision overruled a series of prior Supreme Court and other court cases, which held that, to meet the requirement of inventiveness, or non-obviousness, the invention had to be the result of a flash of genius, rather than something resulting from long efforts and constant empirical experimentation, as is the case with most modern innovation. For example, it took Thomas Edison and his team of 20 or so engineers 2 years of steady work and experimentation to develop the first practical incandescent lightbulb.

6.3 SUPREME COURT CASES PREDATING THE 1952 PATENT LAW SECTION 103 NON-OBVIOUSNESS TEST

There were five Supreme Court decisions handed down between 1850 and 1950 that form the background to the introduction of the non-obviousness test for patentability into the U.S. patent system. My purpose is to give you a brief discussion of each of these cases, and to advise you of the types of criteria that were used by the courts to determine whether or not an invention rises to the level of patentability, or is merely an obvious manifestation of the prior art. By understanding the thought processes expounded by these Supreme Court justices, you should be in a good position to think about the non-obviousness of your invention.

6.3.1 *Hotchkiss v. Greenwood,* Supreme Court, 1850

In this case, the U.S. Patent Office had issued a patent on a mode of fastening a rod or shank to a knob, such as a doorknob. In this case, the knob was made of clay; however, the method of fastening the shank to the knob had been known and used by others in the prior art, and had been applied by others previously for the fastening of shanks to metallic knobs, but not to clay knobs. Apparently, clay knobs had been known and used before, and the shank and spindle by which the shank was attached to the knob were known before. However, this known means of attachment had never before been used to attach a shank to a knob made of potter's clay. It was shown that, prior to this invention, metallic knobs had been attached to shanks by means of a cavity in the form of a dovetail and infusion of melted metal, which is the same mode claimed in the invention before the Court considering the clay doorknob. The Supreme Court ultimately held in this case that substituting a knob of clay was simply the substitution of one known material for another, and therefore obvious.

The Supreme Court stated that the improvement, if any, consisted in the superiority of the material, clay versus metal, and this was not considered new over materials previously employed in making knobs. The difference between the patented invention and the prior art was merely formal, and destitute of ingenuity or invention. The Court also stated that the invention gave evidence of judgment and skill in the selection and adaptation of the materials used in the manufacture of the instrument for the purposes intended, but nothing more. In other words, the Court felt that a skilled technician could merely substitute clay for metal knobs, and that would constitute the subject matter of the alleged invention. The Court went on to say that, "unless more ingenuity and skill in applying the old method of fastening the shank and the knob were required in the application of it to the clay or porcelain knob than were possessed by an ordinary mechanic acquainted with the business, there was an absence of that degree of skill and ingenuity which constitutes an essential element of every invention." In other words, the improvement here was the work of a skillful mechanic, not that of an inventor.

This was the first case in which the Supreme Court added the requirement of "invention or non-obviousness" to the requirements for patentability. Remember that such non-obviousness requirement was not in the patent statute of 1836, under which the case of *Hotchkiss v. Greenwood* was decided.

6.3.2 *Atlantic Works v. Brady,* Supreme Court, 1882

The patent in question in this case involved dredge boat construction, the invention consisting mainly of attaching a screw to the forward end of a propeller dredge boat, the boat being provided with tanks for settling it in the water. The dredge is operated by sinking the boat until the screw comes in contact with mud and sand, which, by the rotation of the screw, is thrown up and mingled and carried away with the current. The use of tanks for the purpose of keeping the vessel level while she settled was already old in the art, having been used in dry docks previously. It was also shown that the same tanks for leveling craft were used in many light-draft monitors during the "late war." I would like to quote directly from this case to show what the Supreme Court in 1882 felt was the difference between patentable invention and merely the exercise of technical skill:

> "The process of development in manufactures creates a constant demand for new appliances, which the skill of ordinary head-workmen and engineers is generally adequate to devise, and which, indeed, are the natural and proper outgrowth of such development. Each step forward prepares the way for the next, and each is usually taken by spontaneous trials and attempts in a hundred places. To grant to a single party a monopoly of every slight advance made, except where the exercise of invention, somewhat above ordinary mechanical or engineering skill, is distinctly shown, is unjust in principle and injurious in its consequence."
>
> "The design of the patent laws is to reward those who make some substantial discovery or invention, which adds to our knowledge or makes a step in the useful arts. Such inventors are worthy of all favor. It was never the object of those laws (patent laws) to grant a monopoly for every trifling device, every shadow of a shade of an idea, which would naturally and spontaneously occur to any skilled mechanic or operator in the ordinary progress of manufactures. Such an indiscriminate creation of exclusive privileges tends rather to obstruct than to stimulate invention. It creates a class of speculative schemers who make it

their business to watch the advancing wave of improvement, and gather its foam in the form of patented monopolies, which enable them to lay a heavy tax upon the industry of the country, without contributing anything to the real advancement of the arts."

As you can see, the justices of the Supreme Court sometimes wax poetic when describing their ideas of what should be patentable and what should be not.

6.3.3 *Goodyear Rubber and Tire Company v. Ray-O-Vac Company,* Supreme Court, 1944

The patent in suit here was for a very narrow advance in a crowded art, and covered a leak-proof dry cell battery, where insulating material was placed around the conventional cylindrical zinc cup of a flashlight battery, and this was covered by an outside protective metal sheath that would enclose the insulated sidewalls of the zinc cup and tightly embrace both the upper and lower closures to prevent leakage of the electrolyte and depolarizing mix constituting the internal portions of the battery.

The Supreme Court held that, viewed after the event with hindsight, the invention covered by this patent may seem simple. However, the Court noted that, during the prior period of 50 years in which flashlight batteries were used, no one devised a method of curing the defect of leakage. Once the method of the patent in suit was used, it became publicly and commercially successful. The Court held that the fact of commercial success was entitled to weight in determining whether the improvement amounted to an "invention" and should, in a close case, tip the scales in favor of patentability. In this case, the leak proof battery patent was upheld as not "obvious."

6.3.4 *Cuno Engineering Corporation v. Automatic Devices Corporation,* Supreme Court, 1941

This case involved a patent on the cigarette lighter commonly found in automobiles. The prior art against which the obviousness of this cigarette lighter was tested comprised two patents, one covering a wireless or cordless cigarette lighter for a car, and another covering an electric lighter for cigars and cigarettes with a thermostatic control. The device of the patent in question added to the so-called wireless or cordless lighter a thermostatic control responsive to the temperature of the heating coil, which automatically returned the plug to its off position after the heating coil had reached a predetermined maximum temperature. The plug was then manually removed from the dashboard of the car to light the smoking material. When replaced in the socket after use, the cigarette lighter was held in an open circuit position until next needed.

The Court held that the thermostatic controls of a heating unit operating to cut off an electric current energizing the unit when its temperature had reached its desired point were well known when the patentee made his invention. The Court held that the advance of the inventor over the thermostatically controlled electric lighter was the use of the removable plug bearing the heating unit, which plug was shown in the other prior art patent to establish the automatic control circuit. The Court said the question was whether it was invention (or non-obvious) to apply the automatic circuit of one patent to the removable heating unit in substitution for a circuit manually controlled as shown by another patent. The Court in this case held that, if an "improvement" is to obtain the privileged position of a patent, more ingenuity must be involved than the work of a mechanic skilled in the art.

The Court recognized that the principles set forth in the *Hotchkiss v. Greenwood* case applied to the adaptation or combination of old or well-known devices for new uses. However, the Court went on to say that "the new device, however useful it may be, must reveal the flash of creative genius, not merely the skill of the calling." In this case, the court went on to say that the patent in question did not reach this level of inventive flash of genius. The so-called inventor merely incorporated the well-known thermostat into the old wireless lighter to produce a more efficient, useful, and convenient article. A new application of an old device may not be patented if the result claimed as new is the same in character as the original result. The use of a thermostat to break a circuit in a "wireless" cigar lighter is analogous to, or the same in character as, the use of such a device in electric heaters, toasters, or irons, whatever may be the difference in detail of design. Ingenuity was required to effect the adaptation, but no more than that to be expected of a mechanic skilled in the art. Then, the Court went on to say, rather poetically: "Strict application of that test is necessary lest in the constant demand for new appliances the heavy hand of tribute be laid on each slight technical logical advance in an art."

6.3.5 *The Great Atlantic and Pacific Tea Company v. Supermarket Equipment Corporation,* Supreme Court, 1950

The claims of the patent before the Supreme Court in this case asserted the invention of a cashiers' counter (such as the check-out counter in a grocery store) equipped with a three-sided, horizontally disposed, U-shaped frame or rack, with no top or bottom. When pushed or pulled along the top of the checkout counter, the frame moved the groceries deposited within it by a customer to the checking clerk, and left them there when pushed back to repeat the operation. I recall these devices being used in grocery stores when I was young—they have now been replaced by moving conveyor belts.

The Supreme Court noted that this device had been widely adopted and successfully used, but did it only bring old elements together? The Court held that the mere aggregation of a number of old parts or elements, which in the aggregation perform or produce no new or different function or operation than they performed individually before, is not patentable invention. The Court noted that there was no finding that the old elements that made up this device performed any additional or different function in the combination than they performed out of it. The Court stated that the three-sided rack would draw or push goods put within it from one place to another—just what any such rack would do on any smooth surface—and the guide rails keep it from falling. The Court held that a patent for a combination that only unites old elements with no new change in their respective functions, such as presented here, obviously withdraws what technology is already known to others into the field of its monopoly and diminishes the resources available to skillful men. The Court held that the patentee had added nothing to the total stock of knowledge, but had merely brought together segments of prior art in an attempt to claim them in congregation as a monopoly.

The Court continued by saying that the framers of the Constitution plainly did not want to grant exclusive rights freely. To justify a patent, the invention had to serve the ends of science—to push back the frontiers of chemistry, physics, and the like; to make a distinctive contribution to scientific knowledge. The court went on to reaffirm the "inventive genius" test for patentability as set forth in the previously mentioned Cuno Engineering case. The Supreme Court in the present case stated:

> "The Constitution never sanctioned the patenting of gadgets. Patents serve a higher end—the advancement of science. An invention need not be as startling as an atomic bomb to be patentable. But it has to be of such quality and distinction that masters of the scientific field in which it falls will recognize it as an advance."

Thus, the Supreme Court in 1950 reinforced the "flash of genius test" as a test for patentability, thereby begging the question whether inventions that had taken a long time to develop would qualify as patentable inventions. Fortunately, this issue was directly taken up by the U.S. Congress, which passed a new patent statute in 1952, specifically overruling the Cuno Engineering case "flash of genius" test by stating that the patentability of an invention will not be negated by the manner in which the invention is made. Therefore, the "flash of genius" test is no longer applicable to determine patentability, and those inventions that resulted from dogged determination and perseverance over a period of time qualify as non-obvious and patentable, upon meeting the other criteria of patentability—falling into a category of patentable subject matter; utility for a stated purpose; and novelty over the prior art.

6.4 THE 1952 PATENT STATUTE AND THE CASE OF *GRAHAM V. JOHN DEERE COMPANY* (1966)

Previously, I discussed the U.S. Patent Law of 1836, which was the basis for the existing modern patent law. In the 1836 law, the requirement of novelty was set forth in great detail; however, there was no standard of non-obviousness written into the statute. The concept of an invention not only being novel, but also being non-obvious to one skilled in the art, was created 170 years ago in the Supreme Court case of *Hotchkiss v. Greenwood*. This was the first case in which a court held that more than just novelty was required for patentability, even though the 1836 statute had specified nothing but novelty as a requirement for distinguishing over the prior art. Subsequent to the *Hotchkiss* case, thousands of cases were decided dealing with the subject of obviousness of inventions, without any apparent consistency or common thread through all these decisions. Thus, until only within the last 55 years or so, there was great confusion by the courts in applying the standard of what would be obvious to one skilled in the art differentiating an invention from the genre of the prior art.

When the 1952 patent statute was enacted, the drafters of the law included Section 103, which required that, to be patentable, the invention be non-obvious, as well as novel and useful. However, the law did not state any single, generic, bold print rule as to how the law should be applied to enable an inventor or the courts to easily determine whether an invention was non-obvious as compared to what had gone before.

The object of the non-obviousness clause introduced in the 1952 patent statute was to indicate to the creative world that, while everyone who does something different or new has created an "invention," unless the subject matter had been published, publicly used, or patented by someone else, a determination still had to be made whether the invention was non-obvious and therefore meritorious enough to support the grant of exclusive rights. Even though you make an invention, because it is new to you, someone else unbeknownst to you may have come up with the same or a similar idea years before and obtained a patent on it or published it. These prior events may render your invention unpatentable, as not novel or non-obvious under the patent statute—however, you have still created an "invention."

Thus, the drafters of the law in 1952 set forth no exact test to be used to determine obviousness, and indicated that the determination of what is obvious is still one of judgment to be determined case by case, invention by invention.

During my career in patent law, which began in 1959, most of the inventors and engineers that I have spoken to tend to tell me, at the onset, that the invention they have just developed would actually be obvious to anyone. Of course, with hindsight, anything is obvious. Once the invention or the improvement has been shown, then everybody can say "Oh, I could have thought of that." However, this is not true. During your engineering and science careers, before you make a decision as to whether or not the project you are working on and the results of that project meet the standards of patentability, ask yourselves these five questions:

1. How long did a need exist for the improvement you came up with?
2. How many inventors before you tried to find a solution, but could not?
3. Did the surrounding and analogous arts disclose the means or steps to make your improvement?
4. How immediately was your invention recognized as an answer to a problem by those who use your new variant?
5. Has your invention met with commercial success?

It was not until 1966, in a trilogy of cases, now referred to as the *Graham v. John Deere Company,* 383 U.S. 1 (1966) cases, that the Supreme Court set forth guidelines that now assist engineers, scientists, and their attorneys to determine whether or not an invention will meet the requirement of non-obviousness necessary to secure a patent. The Supreme Court in the *Graham* case established the following test for determining obviousness:

1. Determine the scope and content of the prior art. This determination is made from an analysis of all prior art known by the inventor, and from additional prior art that may also be uncovered by a patentability search conducted prior to filing a patent application.
2. Next, determine the differences between the invention under consideration and the content of the prior art. Remember, if there are no differences, your invention is not novel and does not pass the first test for patentability—that is, novelty.
3. Next, determine the level of ordinary skill in the art. Imagine a hypothetical person, skilled in the art such as you are, and what that person would know and not know.
4. Keeping in mind the differences between the prior art and the invention you have just made, decide what modifications to the prior art would be necessary to make the prior art correspond to, or rise up to, your invention.

5. Determine whether the prior art materials you are aware of, or even common knowledge that would be available to one skilled in the art, taken in combination, suggest the "necessary" modifications to the prior art you have determined from Step 4. If the answer to this question is "yes," the invention is obvious and not patentable. If the answer is "no," the invention is patentable.
6. Keep in mind the so-called secondary considerations bearing on the question of non-obviousness:
   a. What is the commercial success, if any, of the invention you are analyzing in comparison with the prior art? If your invention has achieved commercial success, it would therefore not have been obvious to modify the prior art to derive your invention.
   b. Does the invention fill a long-felt, but as-yet-unresolved, need in the relevant industry?
   c. The failure of others to solve the problem to which the invention is directed.
   d. The invention provides a new or different function as well as an unexpected result.
   e. A synergistic result is produced, wherein one plus one equals three.
   f. The invention you have just derived directs one contrary to the teachings of the prior art.

In determining the test of obviousness, I refer to the terms "prior art" or "references" that are used to make this comparison to your invention. This prior art is the same as defined under Section 102 of the patent statute, providing for novelty as a requirement of patentability. If a patent publication, prior use or sale, or publicly available knowledge of the product does not fall within the definition of "prior art" under Section 102, it is not "prior art" that can be used in combination with other prior art to determine non-obviousness under Section 103.

In applying the test to determine non-obviousness, the relevant time period is the time when the patent application, covering the subject invention, was filed. Also, when considering whether your invention can meet the standard of non-obviousness, please consider a few other points that may help you in making this decision:

1. Does the combination of the devices or processes shown in the prior art lead to a device or process that produces the same or a different result as your invention?
2. Does the device or process derived from combining the prior art function the same as your invention?
3. Is the combined device or process derived from the prior art as efficient as your invention?
4. Is the combined device or process derived from the prior art operative—that is, will it work to produce the intended function and result of your invention?
5. Would the combined device or process from the prior art be more expensive to produce or operate as compared to your invention?

Answers to these questions will help determine whether or not the hurdle of non-obviousness has been overcome.

The following are a few additional factors taken from cases decided in the field of patent law regarding the question of non-obviousness over the past several years. For example, if the only difference between your invention and the prior art involves the selection or substitution of a known material due to its known suitability for its intended function or purpose, your invention may not be patentable. See, for example, the *Hotchkiss* Supreme Court case mentioned previously. Keep in mind, however, the common knowledge that a vast majority of all patentable inventions are combinations of known elements that are formed in a different and novel array to provide a new and unexpected result. Therefore, when determining whether the solution to the problem you have been working on is non-obvious over the "known elements," consider whether the result you have obtained is predictable or not from the known elements. As recently described to me by a sage colleague, the standard of meeting the requirement of non-obviousness is not "Eureka!" It's more along the lines of "That's cool."

If your invention involves the application of optimum ranges within ranges set forth in the prior art, or you merely provide the mechanical or automatic means to replace a manual operation, without any further contribution to the art, you also may not be able to obtain a patent. Additionally, changes in the size, degree, proportion, and sequence of adding ingredients do not lend patentability, unless some new and unexpected result or function can be derived from such changes. For example, making a catalytic converter smaller to fit smaller-sized cars is not a patentable advance in the art, unless some new structure or function evolves from the change of size.

Conversely, a combination of elements in your invention that produces an improved and unexpected result will lead to patentability, since the invention would be non-obvious. Also, if your invention omits one or more of the elements that are shown in the prior art devices, but still retains the function of those missing elements in the resulting combination, you may have a patentable invention.

6.5 THE 2007 U.S. SUPREME COURT CASE OF *KSR V. TELEFLEX*

In 2007, the U.S. Supreme Court had before it a patent case decided previously by the Court of Appeals of the Federal Circuit (CAFC), involving criteria for determining whether a claimed invention was non-obvious in view of the prior art. The CAFC had applied the single test it had been using in previous non-obviousness cases:

> "Is there some teaching, suggestion, or motivation in the prior art that would have led one of ordinary skill to modify the prior art reference, or to combine a plurality of prior art reference teachings, to arrive at the claimed invention?"

The Supreme Court held that, while this "teaching, suggestion, or motivation" test could be used to determine the obviousness or non-obviousness of an invention in view of the prior art, this was not the only test to be applied. The Supreme Court then set out six additional rationales that an inventor, a Patent Examiner, or a court or jury, could apply to support a conclusion that a claimed invention is "obvious," or "lacks an inventive step." These six additional rationales are listed below, and any one or more could be applied in an obviousness analysis:

1. Combining prior art elements according to known methods to yield predictable results.
2. Simple substitution of one known element for another to obtain predictable results.
3. Use of known techniques to improve similar devices, methods, or products in the same way.
4. Applying a known technique to a known device, method, or product ready for improvement to yield predictable results.
5. "Obvious to try"—Selecting from a finite number of previously identified, predictable solutions, with a reasonable expectation of success.
6. Known work in one field of endeavors may prompt variations of the known work for use in either the same field or a different field, based on design incentives or other market forces, if the variations would have been predictable to one of ordinary skill in the art.

6.6 ILLUSTRATIVE NON-OBVIOUSNESS ANALYSIS

It is apparent from the preceding comments that a determination of whether your novel and useful invention would ultimately be declared as non-obvious over the prior art, and therefore worthy of a patent, is one that is not easily arrived at. Therefore, one of the services that you should solicit when engaging a patent attorney is that the patent attorney carefully look at all of the related prior art and provide you with an opinion about whether your invention is both novel and unobvious. You should ensure that any report on patentability that your attorney submits to you includes an analysis of the question of non-obviousness as well as novelty. It would not be wise to spend the time and money to prepare a patent application where there is a high risk that the USPTO will reject the application on grounds of obviousness. Do not try this at home—leave it to the professionals!

Having said all of this regarding the fitful test of non-obviousness, I feel it prudent to provide you at this point with a hypothetical example illustrating how a determination of non-obviousness works through one's thought processes. Assume that someone invents a general-purpose, programmable, digital computer, and that this computer is colored green. The inventor files a patent application claiming a green digital computer. Assume also that the physical structure of the computer is old in the art, but never had a computer been colored green before, and that there is not a single prior art reference or patent showing a green computer. Consider also that dozens of other colors and shades in the visible spectrum were used as colors for the same kind of computer.

The first question is whether the claimed green computer is novel over the prior art. This determination must be made first, because the question of unobviousness becomes moot if there is no novelty. In this particular situation, the green computer is novel, since it is not identically described in any single item of prior art. For purposes of our analysis, a green computer must be considered structurally different from a computer of any other color. Therefore, it is now appropriate to examine the "green" technology embodied in this computer to determine whether it is an unobvious advance over the prior art.

At first glance, you may determine that using the color green surely would be obvious as compared to computers using all the other colors of the visible spectrum. However, further analysis in my hypothetical may show that this answer is not correct. For example, given the same set of facts assume that, when the computer is green, the frequency band of the green color serves to absorb and concentrate ambient cosmic and ultraviolet rays that, in combination, change the static electrical charge in all of the components of the computer, including the conductive and semi-conductive elements in the computer. As a consequence, all the electrical and electronic operations are speeded up by a factor of 1.2, wherein the computer literally operates 1.2 times as fast, and also is possibly 1.2 times more valuable than a computer that is not colored green. Given all of these new and unexpected results of using a green computer, the subject invention also passes the test of non-obviousness, since no one else has ever used the color green to obtain these results in a computer.

The preceding example points out the fact that no structural or functional difference between your invention and the prior art may be ignored in determining questions of novelty and unobviousness. The differences may be slim; however, the subject matter as a whole may still be unobvious over the prior art to a person of ordinary skill in the relevant technology.

◆ INVENTORS AND INVENTIONS ◆

Louis Pasteur

PASTEURIZATION PROCESS

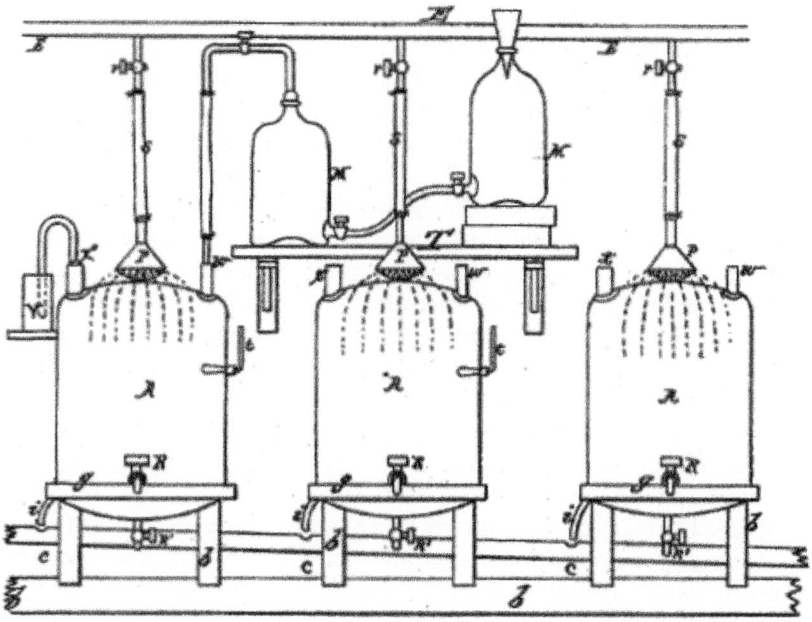

Throughout human history, physicians have struggled with the problem of determining what cause diseases. In the mid-19th century, many people believed in Miasma, the concept that disease was caused by polluted air. However, the milestone work leading to understanding the causes of diseases was not made by a doctor, but by a chemist, Louis Pasteur. Pasteur destroyed the widely held myth of spontaneous generation as the cause of diseases, thus setting the direction for modern biochemistry and biology.

Louis Pasteur was born on December 27, 1822, in Dole, Jura, France, and grew up in the nearby town of Arbois. As a child, Pasteur showed an interest in chemistry, and the headmaster of the local college convinced Louis and his father that Louis should try to enter the École Normale Suprieure in Paris, a highly regarded French university specifically created to train students for university careers in science and the arts. Pasteur began his successful journey as a scientist in the École Normale.

Intellectual Property Law for Engineers, Scientists, and Entrepreneurs, Second Edition. Howard B. Rockman.

Published 2020 by John Wiley & Sons, Inc.

When Pasteur was 26 years old, crystallography was a new branch of chemistry. One of his first projects while working at the École Normale was attempting the crystallization of tartaric acid, an organic acid that exists in the sediments of fermenting wine. A second acid, paratartaric acid or racemic acid, was also found in the sediment in wine barrels. At the time of the beginning of his studies, science had already determined that tartaric and paratartaric acids had identical chemical compositions; however, tartaric acid rotated a beam of polarized light passing through it to the right, and paratartaric acid did not rotate the light at all. Pasteur was determined to find out what caused this difference. Upon microscopic examination, Pasteur discovered that the paratartrate crystals comprised two types of optically asymmetric crystals, one being the mirror image of the other.

Pasteur then performed one of the more elegant procedures in the annals of chemistry experimentation. He separated the left and right paratartrate crystal shapes from each other with a dissecting needle to form two collections of crystals. When placed in solution, one form of the crystal rotated light to the left, the other to the right. This showed that organic molecules having the same chemical composition can have two different stereospecific forms. He concluded that this molecular asymmetry was one of the mechanisms of life, in that living organisms only produce molecules of one specific orientation, and these molecules are always optically active. He also found that fermenting solutions contained optically active compounds, which led him to surmise that fermentation was a biological process performed by microorganisms, or germs. This hypothesis, designated the germ theory, was used by Pasteur as a foundation for his experiments that positively demonstrated the existence of microorganisms and their effect in the fermentation process. The germ theory was the basis of his work in the large-scale brewing of beer and wine, the pasteurization of milk, antiseptic operations on humans, and in curing contagious diseases since he also discovered that the blood of diseased humans contained increased amounts of germs. He, and later other scientists, discovered that manipulation of infection agents in test tubes could be used to immunize humans and animals against diseases caused by germs.

Pasteur later began teaching at Strasbourg University, where his studies on molecular asymmetry continued. While at Strasbourg, Pasteur married the university rector's daughter, Marie Laurent, with whom he spent the rest of his life. In 1854, Pasteur became Dean and Professor of Chemistry at the Faculty of Sciences in Lille, France. This was a blue-collar town, with numerous factories and distilleries. The Minister of Public Instruction of Lille encouraged the university faculty to conduct work and studies that would assist the industries of the surrounding countryside.

Pasteur took this advice to heart, taking his students on tours of the local factories and advising managers of his availability to help solve their problems. Thus, in 1856, M. Bigot, the father of one of his chemistry students, called upon Pasteur to help overcome problems in the manufacture of alcohol by fermentation of beetroot. Bigot's problem was that his fermentations, instead of producing alcohol, yielded lactic acid.

At that point in time, chemistry was just starting to take root as a true scientific discipline, wrenching itself from the work of the alchemist. The chemical processes involved in living animals were slowly being discovered, and the chemist Lavoisier had showed, among other things, that sugar, the initial product of the fermentation process, could be broken down into alcohol, CO_2, and H_2O by placing a sugar solution on a heated plate of platinum. In addition, Wöhler had amazed the scientific community by synthesizing urea, demonstrating for the first time that organic compounds, previously believed only to be synthesized by living animals, could be produced in a test tube. Pasteur's previous work on crystals also led to the routine discovery of the internal structure and analysis of complex organic compounds.

Given this environment in 1856, fermentation, which was used in the production of wine, beer, and vinegar, was thought to be a process involving the chemical breakdown of sugar into the desired molecules based upon the existence of destabilizing vibrations in the molecules. It was known at the time that yeast cells existed in the fermenting vats of wine, and had been recognized as living organisms, but they were believed to be a product of fermentation or catalytic agents that infuse the ingredients that allow fermentation to take place. Ridicule befell those few biologists who had concluded that yeast was the cause of, and not the result of, fermentation. Also, at that time, the scientists of the community were not providing much assistance to the wine, beer, and vinegar producers, who were facing serious economic downturns directly related to the fermentation processes. Yields of alcohol fell off, wine grew sour or turned to vinegar, and vinegar, when desired, ended up as lactic acid instead. Most importantly, the quality and taste of beer was prone to change from vat to vat, making quality control impossible.

Into this world came Louis Pasteur, entering Mr. Bigot's factory with his microscope. Pasteur found that when alcohol was produced normally, the yeast cells were plump. However, when lactic acid would form instead of alcohol, rod-like microbes were mixed with the yeast cells. He also found that amyl alcohol and other complex organic compounds were formed during the fermentation process, which could not be explained by the simple catalytic breakdown of sugar shown by Lavoisier. Pasteur concluded that some additional processes must be involved. Also, based on his earlier work on crystallography, he found that some of the compounds rotated light, and were, therefore, asymmetric. His early work had shown that only living cells produced asymmetrical compounds, and thus he extrapolated his findings to determine that living cells—yeast—were forming the alcohol from sugar, and that other microorganisms contaminated the fermentation, and turned the fermentation sour.

Over the next several years, Pasteur isolated and then identified specific microorganisms that led to both abnormal and normal fermentations in wine, beer, and vinegar production. He determined that if wine, beer, or milk were heated to moderately high temperatures for a short period of time and then cooled, living microorganisms could be killed, thereby sterilizing (later known as pasteurizing) the fermentation batches and preventing their degradation. Thus, if microbes and yeasts in pure cultures were added to sterile fermentation masses and air was prevented from entering the vats by sealing them, predictable fermentation would follow.

Pasteur's earlier work on crystallography, chemistry, and optics led him to formulate the theory that asymmetric molecules are the result of living forces, and his work developed the new science of stereochemistry. In his work on fermentation, he demonstrated that each type of fermentation is caused by the existence of a specific microorganism or ferment, which is a living organism that can be studied through cultivation in a sterile medium. This is the basis of microbiology today.

Following his work in fermentation, and his discovery that the living microorganisms could be controlled to prevent the spoliation of products, Pasteur went on to a successful career as a chemist, with several major discoveries to his name. For example, he debunked the theory of spontaneous generation, which held at that time that microbes could be generated spontaneously from spoiling matter. Through his work on fermentation, he proved that microorganisms found during fermentation and putrefaction came from the outside, such as from dust in the air, and destroyed every theory that supported the spontaneous generation argument. He also concluded that microscopic beings are generated from parents similar to themselves.

Pasteur went on to research and cure a devastating disease among silkworms that was destroying the French silk industry. He also discovered the germ theory of disease and the use of vaccines in humans to prevent those diseases. It was only through the teachings of Pasteur, Lister, and others that antiseptic medicine and surgery began saving many lives. Pasteur also made major advances in dealing with anthrax, rabies, and the use of vaccines in humans.

While experimenting with biochemical agents for use against an increasing rabies infection epidemic in France, Pasteur discovered that contagions were the cause of disease. He also identified different germs that were present in the human body during illness. With this information, he found the causes of several diseases, and also discovered how to protect uninfected people through the use of vaccines that he ultimately developed. Pasteur made successful vaccines for diphtheria, tetanus, anthrax, chicken cholera, silk worm disease, tuberculosis, and the plague. In 1858, he proved garlic could be used as an antibacterial agent, which he ultimately gave to people who were seriously ill or had developed plague. His work on sterilization in medical procedures was slow to be adopted by many hospitals, but during his lifetime he spent much of his time working in hospitals with doctors trying to find ways to sterilize the equipment and the rooms in which operations were performed.

In 1885, Pasteur was working on experiments with rabies vaccines involving dogs, but had not used the vaccine on humans because he was afraid of unanticipated results and his inability to isolate the substance causing rabies. However, as in the development of all significant scientific discoveries and inventions, fate played its hand. A 9-year-old, Joseph Meister, appeared in Pasteur's laboratory on July 6, 1886, with his mother. The young boy had been bitten by a rabid dog, and he could hardly walk. Pasteur, up to that time, had successfully treated 40 dogs, but had never used his vaccine on a human. Pasteur then consulted with many of his physician colleagues, and with much hesitation and reluctance treated the youth with his vaccine. Joseph Meister recovered, and lived a long and healthy life. Following this, people bitten by rabid dogs in many countries, including Russia and the United States, came to Pasteur for treatment. Newspapers reported these treatments and cures with overwhelming interest, making Pasteur a legend. Funded by public and governmental funds, the Pasteur Institute was created in Paris, initially to treat victims of rabies. Eventually, other Pasteur Institutes were built, including three in the United States, to treat rabies and other diseases.

The treatment of rabies was the last major project of Louis Pasteur. At the age of 46, he suffered a serious stroke, and his general health began failing. After suffering additional strokes, he died in 1895.

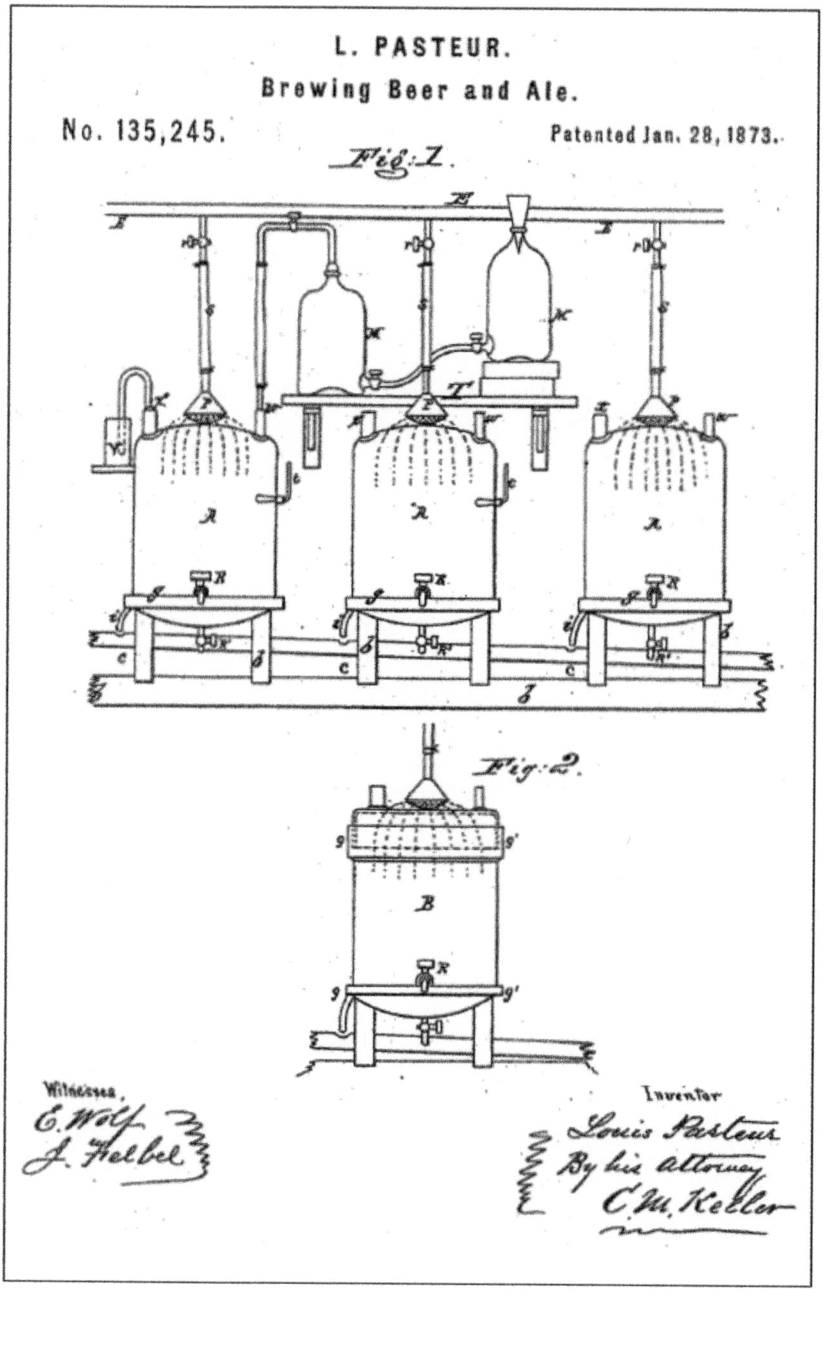
L. PASTEUR.
Brewing Beer and Ale.
No. 135,245.
Patented Jan. 28, 1873.
Fig: 1.
Fig: 2.
Witnesses.
E. Wolf
J. Helbel
Inventor
Louis Pasteur
By his attorney
C. M. Keller

◆ INVENTORS AND INVENTIONS ◆

Elisha Otis

SAFETY ELEVATOR

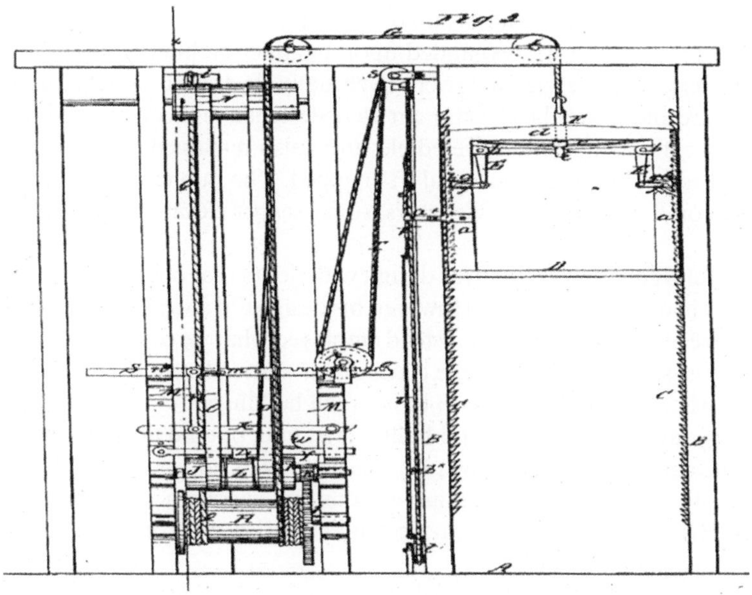

Elisha Graves Otis was an American industrialist and founder of The Otis Elevator Company. Practically everyone reading this essay has been on an elevator and seen the name Otis; however, Mr. Otis did not invent the elevator. He is famous for inventing a safety device that prevents elevators from falling if the hoisting cable fails.

Throughout the centuries, humans have employed many, many ingenious forms of elevating people, animals, and a variety of loads. The earlier lifts used man, animal, and water power to raise loads. In ancient Greece, Archimedes developed an improved lifting device operated by ropes and pulleys, where the hoisting ropes were coiled around a winding drum operated by a capstan and levers. By C.E. 80, gladiators and wild animals rode crude elevators up to the arena level of the Roman Coliseum.

Early elevators were open cars comprising a platform using hoists that were difficult to move vertically. The hoists were typically worked manually by people or animals. Where available, water wheels and water power were employed for the hoisting.

Intellectual Property Law for Engineers, Scientists, and Entrepreneurs, Second Edition. Howard B. Rockman.

Published 2020 by John Wiley & Sons, Inc.

The first elevator designed for a human passenger was built in 1743 for King Louis XV of France. His elevator went up only one floor from the first to the second, and was known as the "flying chair." It was outside of the building, and was entered by the King from his balcony off his apartments. The mechanism comprised a carefully balanced arrangement of weights and pulleys deployed inside a chimney. Men stationed inside the chimney raised or lowered the flying chair at the King's command, who used it primarily to visit his lady friend's apartment on the second floor, as some literature has indicated.

In the 1800s elevator technology began to move forward, and they no longer had to be worked manually. For example, in 1823, two British architects built a "steam powered ascending room" to take tourists up on a platform for a view of London. Several years later, their invention was expanded upon by other architects, who added a belt and counterweight to the steam tower. Eventually, hydraulic systems using water pressure to raise and lower the elevator car were designed and constructed. Hydraulic elevators were safer, but steam-powered elevators also remained. Accidents occurred when the cables holding the elevator aloft snapped. The public was not enthusiastic about getting on these dangerous elevators, so passenger elevators were basically just a novelty.

One Otis Tufts patented an elevator design with doors that opened and closed automatically, and had bed seats inside. However, his design did away with the typical cable system because of safety issues, and instead employed what we consider an impractical and expensive system of threading the elevator car vertically upon a giant screw. Can you imagine what the cost would be in today's tall buildings?

In his early days, Otis designed and built a grist mill, but did not earn enough from the mill, so he converted it into a sawmill, which also was not successful. By that time, he had a family, and he started building wagons and carriages, which was within his capabilities. His wife then passed away, leaving him with two sons, one eight and the other still in diapers.

He then remarried, and moved to Albany, New York, working as a doll maker. He tired of taking all day to make only a dozen toys, and later invented and patented a robot wood turner that could produce bedsteads four times faster than could be done manually. His boss gave him a $500 bonus, and Otis then started his own business making bedsteads. He also started designing a safety brake that could stop trains instantly, and an automatic bread baking oven. As luck would have it, his business failed when the stream he was using as a water power supply was diverted by the city of Albany to be used as a fresh water supply.

Becoming disillusioned with Albany, Otis relocated to Yonkers, New York, in 1852 as the manager of an abandoned saw mill which was to be converted into a bedstead factory.

While cleaning up the factory, Otis wondered how he could lift all the trash, as well as heavy equipment and machinery to the upper levels of the factory. He knew that cables lifting hoisting platforms of the day often broke, and he and his workers were unwilling to risk their lives. So he and his two sons designed a safety elevator and tested it successfully. In the beginning, he thought so little of this invention that he neither patented it nor requested a bonus from his superiors. Ultimately, Otis did file for and obtained U.S. Patent No. 31,128 on January 15, 1861.

His safety device consisted of a used wagon spring attached to both the top of the hoist platform and the overhead lifting cable. Under ordinary circumstances, the spring was kept in place by the downward pull of the platform's weight on the lifting cable. However, if the cable broke, the pressure on the spring was suddenly released, and the spring caused laterally extending ratchets to spring open in a jaw-like motion. When this occurred, both of the ratchets moved laterally outward and engaged saw-tooth ratchet-receiving bar beams that Otis had installed on either side of the elevator shaft, bringing the falling elevator to a complete halt.

After the bedstead factory declined, Otis took the opportunity to make an elevator company out of his work, and he first named his company the Union Elevator Works. Later, the name was changed to Otis Brothers and Company. His new elevator business did not start out well, but the 1854 New York World's Fair appeared to offer him a chance at gaining publicity. At the New York Crystal Palace, Otis constructed an elevator according to his designs, and ordered the only rope holding the platform on which he was standing to be cut. The rope was cut by a man handling an ax, and the platform fell only a few inches and then halted. His ratcheted safety locking mechanism had worked, and the public gained a greater willingness to ride in traction elevators, which then came into common usage and helped make present-day skyscrapers accessible. After the World's Fair, Otis continuously received orders, and he also developed different types of engines, such as a three-way steam valve engine that could transition the elevators between up to down and stop rapidly.

Before Otis' invention of the elevator brake, buildings only reached seven stories high, because elevators were considered too dangerous to ride in. The first elevator shaft actually was built in 1853, four years ahead of the first safety elevator built by Otis. Architect Peter Cooper was confident that a safe elevator would soon be invented, and designed New York's Union Foundation Building with an internal cylindrical shaft, thinking that being the most efficient shape. Cooper opined that somehow somebody later on would develop an elevator to fit in the shaft. Otis later did design an elevator just for that building.

In 1857, the first Otis passenger elevator was installed at 488 Broadway in New York, following which the Otis elevator appeared in the Eiffel Tower in Paris and the Empire State Building in New York.

In 1890, an elevator was installed in the Washington Monument in Washington, D.C. In 1913, an elevator was installed by Otis Company in the 60-story Woolworth Building in New York City, which at the time was the world's tallest building.

In these modern days, it is virtually impossible for an elevator to plummet and kill passengers. Multiple steel cables hold the elevator's weight, plus a multitude of different braking systems are installed to stop an elevator from falling if any of the cables do happen to snap. If the elevator does fall, there are shock absorbers at the bottom of the shaft, making it unlikely that death will result.

Here is an interesting note. We previously described Otis' daring elevator safety demonstration at the World's Fair in 1854. His demonstration was hyped by Phineas T. Barnum of circus fame.

E. G. OTIS.

HOISTING APPARATUS.

No. 31,128. Patented Jan. 15, 1861.

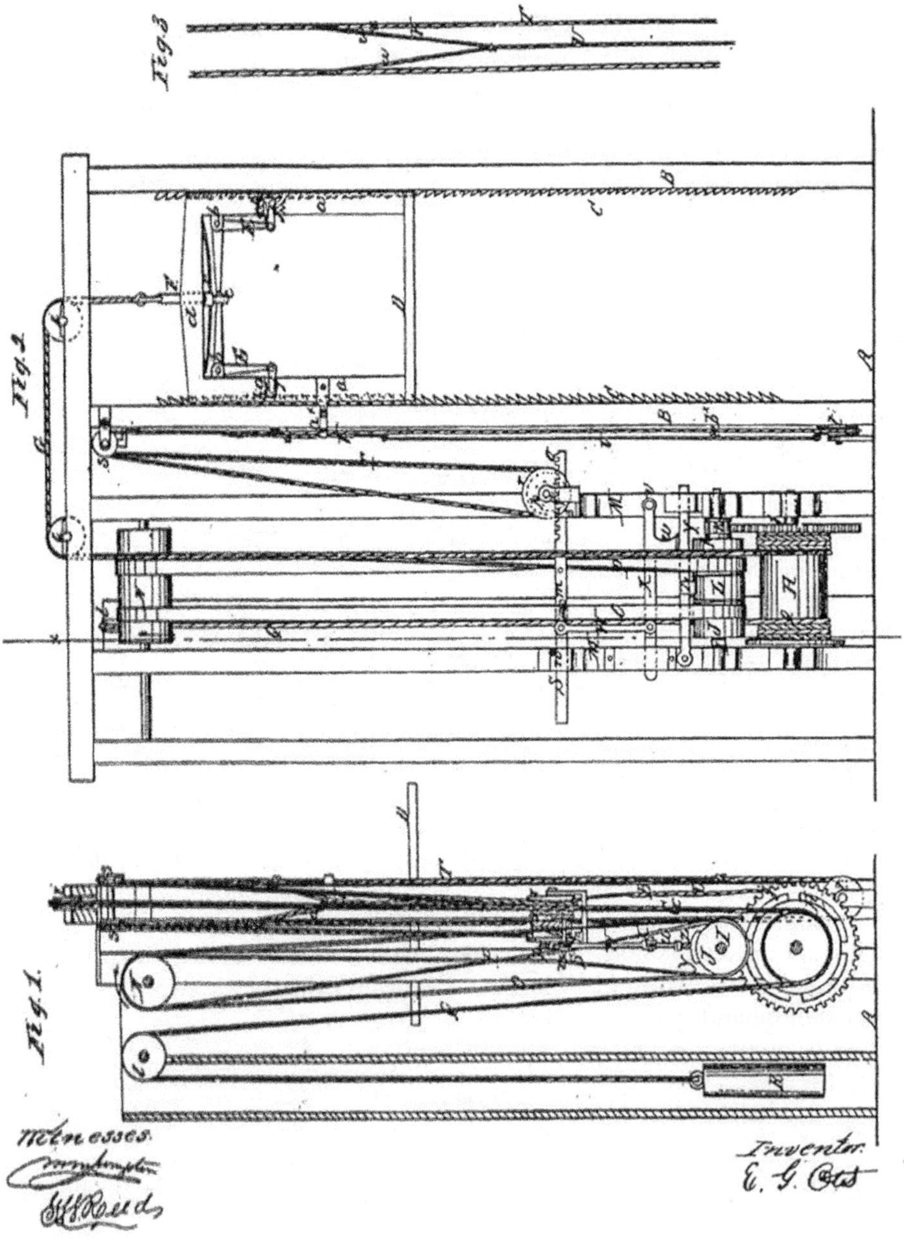

THE N. PETERS CO., WASHINGTON, D. C.

7 The Patenting Process

7.1 WHO MAY OBTAIN A PATENT: INVENTORSHIP AND OWNERSHIP OF PATENT RIGHTS

In the United States, patents are granted only to the first and original inventor or joint inventors who are first to file a patent application describing and claiming the subject invention, or anyone asserting rights obtained from the inventor, such as an employer to whom the inventor(s) are obligated to assign their inventions, such as commonly found in employment agreements. It must be understood that one who merely recognizes the commercial merits of an existing product or idea, or who discovers technology in a previously written document, may not properly be awarded a patent. The invention must have been invented by the person or persons applying for the patent. In the United States, a corporation or business entity can pursue patent protection on a development independently of the inventor, if, as stated earlier, the inventors have agreed to assign patent rights to their employer, usually as a condition of employment. The patent assignment document is usually signed by the employee on the first day of employment, along with tax documents and confidentiality agreements.

An invention can be made by one, two, or any number of persons. Thus, many patent applications frequently name joint inventors. However, the following important rule must be kept in mind among the joint inventors. Unless there is an agreement or an obligation to assign the patent to one or a few of the inventors, or to a certain third party, such as the employer or a company set up by the inventors, each inventor will end up with the independent right to commercialize the invention, with no duty to account to the other inventor or inventors for his/her actions, or his/her royalties or revenues. This would be true regardless of the percentage of the patent any one joint inventor owns. Also, none of the joint inventors has the right to exclude any of the other joint inventors from practicing the invention, nor to prevent any joint inventor from granting licenses to others under the patent rights.

Normally, the question of ownership of an invention, and of the patent rights covering that invention, are handled in a corporate or large entity environment by obligating all of the inventors to transfer all of the rights in the patents to the employer by way of assignment from the individual inventors. However, if several inventors combine to produce an invention on their own, outside of a corporate structure, for example, it is extremely important that the rights, obligations, and limitations of the joint inventors vis-à-vis the invention be defined in a written joint development

Intellectual Property Law for Engineers, Scientists, and Entrepreneurs, Second Edition. Howard B. Rockman.

Published 2020 by John Wiley & Sons, Inc.

agreement before the patent application is even filed or ultimately issued to prevent problems in the future. In such cases, the number of inventors may form a separate new entity, such as their own corporation, LLC, or partnership, to which the patent rights are assigned. Then, it becomes the duty of the management of the new corporation or partnership to decide the direction of and limitations on commercialization of the invention, and the distribution of the rewards from that commercialization through prudent corporate management principles. If you find yourself in this situation, I strongly suggest discussing a joint development agreement with your patent professional.

It is not uncommon for several inventors, working independently of each other, to develop a same or similar invention at the same time, and for each to file for patent protection covering their invention. This is sometimes true, for example, in the pharmaceutical field, where several different companies are seeking a cure or treatment for a certain disease, and have all started with the same known "prior art" treatments. Each of these inventors or groups of inventors may arrive at the same end point independently. In this situation, who gets the patent? Under the recently enacted AIA, the patent is awarded to the first to file a patent application, unless one inventor or group of inventors derived the invention from the second to file, as discussed in section 7.2.1 of this chapter.

7.2 PROPER DOCUMENTATION OF THE INVENTION

7.2.1 Conception

The AIA eliminated the previous interference procedure by awarding a patent to the first to file a patent application when two or more inventors or inventor groups have developed the same invention at approximately the same time. However, the AIA now includes a new section 35 U.S.C. §135, which provides a second-to-file inventor the ability to have the USPTO correct the inventorship in the first filed application if it can be established that the first-to-file inventor derived the invention from the second-to-file inventor. Due to the possibility that this scenario can occur, it is important for all inventors to keep adequate records, witnessed preferably, to establish the dates of conception and reduction to practice of the invention before it was "stolen."

The act of conception relates to the first concept, idea, or informal description of a working example of the invention. Usually, the first conception of an invention takes place either on a computer screen, on small scraps of paper where the idea was initially set down, or possibly on other media of recording the inventive idea, such as a dictating machine. It is important to record the earliest date of conception because conception followed by diligence in reducing the invention to practice, in a working model or a complete illustration of a working model, would determine the date of invention that the inventor can rely upon in a derivation proceeding. My experience has shown that the initial act of conception can also be proven by presenting evidence of comments made to others in the project control group that they recall, sketches on restaurant or tavern napkins, or stained lab notebook papers.

One comment made earlier is worthy of repetition. Most inventors today work by themselves, in cells or in cubicles, in developing an invention. It is important, however, that early work on inventions be somehow witnessed by others and documented, so that, at a later time, a second party or a document can corroborate your first date of invention. Working alone on your idea without disclosing the same to other people within your working group and not having them witness and sign off on your invention is not recommended practice. Certain corporations with which I have been involved require their inventors to keep notes in lab or log books, and to have each page of the lab or log book dated and witnessed by another person in the group at the end of each day.

The reason for this exercise is that, whenever an inventor is required to testify in court or any other judicial proceeding that his or her invention has been derived by another, the inventor's testimony must be corroborated by other documentation or the testimony of live witnesses that the inventor actually did conceive the invention at the time that he or she reported. It is obvious that anyone can sit on a witness stand and testify that they had invented a certain device before someone else, but unless they have proof of such conception, such oral evidence alone will not be accepted by the court. Therefore, keep in mind as you develop inventions throughout your careers that each step you take may have to be ultimately corroborated by someone else or by your documentation, electronic or otherwise, to prove the veracity of your statements regarding conception.

7.2.2 Reduction to Practice

The act of conception followed by diligently reducing the invention to practice are the two components that equal the act of invention, which was more important in the interference proceedings that have been eliminated by the enactment of the AIA. However, for derivation proceedings, reduction to practice may still be important. Remember, however, that the reduction to practice need not culminate in a working embodiment or model of the invention. Illustrations, drawings, screen shots, CAD files, and sketches of a workable concept also constitute a constructive and acceptable reduction to practice. Thus, you need not have a working model to file a patent application, or to prove derivation. In many instances, the filing of the patent application itself constitutes the constructive reduction to practice of the invention. Even though you do not have a working model of your invention, drawings and/or sketches that show how your invention will work and is constructed are enough to start the patenting process on its way.

The reduction to practice, however, must be of the complete invention that you ultimately are going to be claiming as the invention to be covered by your patent. The subject of claiming your invention will be covered in detail in Chapter 10. Thus, it is important to conclude from your conception, diligent efforts, and reduction to practice that the invention will work for its intended purposes, and will work the way you will ultimately describe the invention in your patent application.

Using drawings corresponding to your invention, and a written description of the structure and operation of your invention, a patent application will be prepared and filed with the U.S. Patent and Trademark Office. Therefore, it is important that, prior to meeting with a patent attorney or agent, you have a complete invention to submit for patenting, which includes the complete reduction to practice of the invention, either on paper or on a computer screen, or with the help of a working model. Again, it is not necessary or recommended to have a working model of the invention before you proceed to discuss the patenting process with your patent professional. An "actual reduction to practice" consists of the production and operation of a working model of your invention. A "constructive reduction to practice," which is more common, consists of an expression of the invention in a written or electronic medium, such that one skilled in the art could read that expression of your invention and understand its structure and operation. Again, the constructive reduction to practice must be a description of a complete and operable invention.

7.2.3 Witnesses

In a derivation proceeding, it is important that the inventor establish the acts of conception and reduction to practice that support the patentability of the invention. Documentary pieces of paper, electronic fixations on media, and scraps of other materials are usually challenged by the defense lawyer as lacking authenticity. By having your relevant documents signed and witnessed by other parties, and dated, these other parties can then testify at trial that they signed those documents when dated, thus proving their authenticity. Also, if you tell somebody within your project control group about your invention, they can testify that they discussed the invention with you at that time. However, it is important to remember that the invention should not be discussed with anybody working outside of the project control group involved in the development and/or production of the invention. Public disclosure of the invention during its development stage and reduction to practice stage, absent a signed nondisclosure agreement (NDA), should be avoided.

7.3 THE INVENTION DISCLOSURE, AND THE INVENTION DISCLOSURE MEETING

7.3.1 Preparation of a Complete Description of the Structure and Function of the Invention, How the Invention Operates, and What Advantageous Results Are Obtained by the Invention

The patent application ultimately prepared covering the invention must contain sketches or illustrations showing the important elements of the invention, where the invention comprises an article of manufacture, machinery, an electronic circuit, electrical circuit or the like, as well as a specification comprising a complete description of the structure of the invention, followed by a description of one cycle of operation of the described structure. The description of the structure and operation of your invention are keyed to the drawings through the use of reference numerals and lead lines identifying parts in the drawing that are described in the patent specification, somewhat similar to technical drawings. Therefore, it is important that the inventor or inventors prepare an adequate disclosure of the invention, with sketches and a description of the structure and function of the operation, prior to meeting with the patent professional at an initial invention disclosure meeting. It is no secret that patent agents and lawyers charge for their time, and an inventor can save substantial time, and thus money, by shortening the time the patent lawyer or agent has to spend preparing the patent application. By preparing detailed sketches and descriptions of the invention for presentation to the patent professional, hundreds and possibly thousands of dollars can be saved in the cost of obtaining and prosecuting the patent application.

There are additional materials and information that the inventor or inventors should bring to the invention disclosure meeting with the patent professional, which will be covered in more detail as this chapter proceeds.

Your initial invention disclosure must be clear, although it is not necessary that it be typewritten. Also, a good disclosure is not necessarily long, but the important features of the invention and their operation and advantages must be adequately disclosed. When submitting your invention disclosure, always give the benefit of the doubt to including more in your disclosure rather than omitting information. The patent attorney can help decide what information you provide should be made part of the patent application, and which should not. Any drawings or sketches you prepare to submit to the patent attorney should be clear and sufficiently detailed, and coordinated with your written description. This is accomplished by numbering the various parts of the invention on the drawing and keying the numbers with the written disclosure. If you submit alternative embodiments, also submit the drawings or illustrations directed to those alternatives. If a model of the invention has been prepared, submit the model to the patent attorney with the other descriptive materials. Photographs of your model can also be used as the basis for the drawings initially filed with the patent application.

The key factor in preparing the initial disclosure of the invention and its different embodiments is to remember to present all information you know about your invention, and the environment in which it functions, to the patent attorney, leaving nothing out. The more information about your invention in the patent application, the more difficult it is for a potential infringer to design around your patent coverage. As will be explained in Chapter 10, the claims in your patent application will be drawn to cover all embodiments of your invention, and hopefully these claims will later be interpreted to cover those competing devices marketed in the future that are directed toward solving the same problems that your invention is directed toward solving.

7.3.2 Disclosing the Best Mode of the Invention

The U.S. Patent Law, for many years, has required that the ones seeking patent protection disclose the "best mode" of practicing the subject invention in the patent application. This requirement is retained in the AIA, which ensures that their invention that goes into the public domain is the best version of the invention conceived and reduced to practice from the inventor(s), rather than some inferior version.

However, the AIA removes any penalty for failing to disclose the best mode of the invention in a patent application by stating that "the failure to disclose the best mode shall not be a basis on which any claim of a patent may be cancelled or held invalid or otherwise unenforceable…" (35 U.S.C. §282(b)(3)(A)). Despite this, 35 U.S.C. §112(a) of the new AIA Patent Law, in mandating the contents of a patent application specification, states that the applicant "shall set forth the best mode contemplated by the inventor or joint inventor of carrying out the invention." The new law also provides that a patent application filed first in a foreign country and then filed in the United States does not have to disclose the best mode of the invention.

The consensus is that this removal of the defense of the failure to disclose the best mode in a patent application was enacted to accommodate global patent harmonization efforts, since, generally, foreign patent statutes do not have a best mode requirement.

In addition, in the way the AIA has changed this element of the Patent Law, it appears that, even though a patent applicant is required to disclose the best mode of practicing the invention in the patent application, the lack of best mode cannot be raised by third parties in post-grant reviews of patents newly authorized by the AIA.

Theoretically, a Patent Examiner could still reject a patent application on the grounds of failing to disclose the best mode of the invention. However, since the USPTO rules do not allow a Patent Examiner to obtain information from the applicant through a "discovery" process as used in litigation in the United States, the examiner has practically no way of determining whether or not the inventor has disclosed the best mode.

In my opinion, this is one of the conundrums that may be understood further as time goes by, and as future court decisions consider this point.

In my judgment, best practices dictate that the disclosure of the invention in the patent application must be of the best mode of practicing the invention known to the inventor at the time of the invention disclosure meeting. Since there is a time lag between the first meeting with the patent attorney and the actual completion of the patent application, if the invention has been improved during that time period, the later developments must be described to the patent attorney, so that the latest, best mode of the invention can be included in the patent application upon filing. Also, if the inventors have developed alternative embodiments of the invention during this time period, these should be described so that the patent attorney can determine which of the alternative embodiments should also be described in the patent application. Each and every remote possible embodiment does not need to be described, but the presentation of alternate embodiments helps the lawyer draft the description and claims in the patent application to provide broad enough protection to cover any manifestation of the invention that a potential infringer could later develop.

7.3.3 Dates of First Public Disclosure, If Any, and What Was Disclosed

As we have already discussed, if an invention was in public use or on sale, or offered for sale anywhere more than a year before the date that the invention is initially disclosed to the patent attorney, patent protection cannot be obtained for that particular invention. In those cases, I have usually advised inventors to develop an improvement to their invention, and then a patent application can be filed covering the improvement. However, the prior public activities of the inventor more than a year before the filing of the patent application may have destroyed any patent rights the inventor might have obtained in the original invention.

Also, determine whether or not there has been a public disclosure or public knowledge of the invention less than a year before the date of the invention disclosure meeting, since it is important to know whether foreign patent rights have been affected by such disclosure. It is also important to know when the 1-year U.S. "statutory bar" will be effective due to a public disclosure of the invention, to enable a patent application to be filed before the 1 year bar date.

In making your disclosure to the patent attorney, it is important to indicate what acts took place and what facts surround the circumstances relating to any prior disclosure of your invention that was made to others, either prior to a year or within a year of the invention disclosure meeting. It's possible that the public disclosures you made were only of an experimental version of your invention, and therefore did not comprise disclosure of a complete invention such as will destroy patent rights. If there has been no prior public disclosure of the invention, the patent attorney will most assuredly advise you to refrain from disclosing, publicly using, selling, or offering to sell the invention prior to the date the patent application is actually lodged with the U.S. Patent & Trademark Office. The potential adverse effects of such public disclosures on patent rights need not be repeated.

You must also disclose to the patent attorney how you gained knowledge of the concept of your invention. Obviously, if you derived the invention from a showing of the same invention from another source, you are not the first inventor and cannot obtain a patent. Also, an applicant cannot discover an invention in another country and apply for a patent in the United States, since the applicant cannot comply with that portion of the statute requiring that the inventor certify that he or she is the original and first inventor.

Since "experimental use" is not a public use of a complete invention and therefore is not a bar to obtaining a U.S. patent, when meeting with the patent attorney for the first time, the inventor should, in describing all outside uses and showings of the invention to others, present sufficient facts to enable the patent attorney to determine whether or not such use could be classified as "experimental" or not. Thus, even though you may have previously exposed a portion of the subject of the invention to third parties, the attorney may advise you that this is not necessarily a bar to patentability. Also, it is important to advise the attorney of any prior publication(s) by the inventor or inventors to determine when and which features of the invention were disclosed, and which were not disclosed in such prior publications. Non-disclosed features can still form the subject matter of a patent application. Keep in mind also that disclosures to others made under the aegis of a signed NDA are not "public" disclosures, and are not a bar to obtaining a patent.

7.3.4 Advantages of the Invention Over Known Devices/Processes

After disclosing to the patent professional your information about the structure, operation/function, and results achieved by your invention, it is important to disclose to the patent professional the advantages of your invention, and how those advantages are realized from the structure of the invention, the operation or function of that structure, and the results achieved by the operation and/or function of that structure. In other words, what structure and/or function of the invention produces the advantages over the prior art. The advantages should be expressed both in broad terms and in more limited terms. These advantages provide the "selling points" for persuading the Patent Examiner that the invention is indeed a step forward in the useful arts. Such advantages also may assist in defining the "contribution" to the advance in the art that this particular invention offers to the public. More importantly, I have personally noticed that the courts tend to rely upon the advantages of the invention and the contribution of the inventor to an advance in the art to support their decisions upholding patentability. If the patent attorney at the initial meeting does not ask you what advantages are provided by the invention, tell him or her anyway. In my view, this is most important.

7.3.5 What Prior Art the Inventor is Aware of for Disclosure to the Patent Examiner

During the first meeting with your patent professional regarding an invention, the patent professional will prudently ask you to disclose to her or him all information you are aware of regarding the state of the prior art relating to the subject matter of your invention. This involves disclosure to the patent attorney of your knowledge of printed or electronic publications, similar devices already existing in the market, issued patents, and any other prior acts or materials of either the inventor(s) themselves or others that may relate to the subject matter of the invention. The reason is that Rule 56 of the USPTO Rules (37 C.F.R. §1.56) *requires* that an inventor *and* the inventor's attorney or agent disclose "information they are aware of which is material to the examination of the application" to the Patent Examiner prior to the commencement of examination, and during the entire time of the examination process. The determination of whether such prior art would be material to examination depends upon whether that prior art would be considered by the Examiner as information which is material to patentability in deciding whether or not to issue the patent. Normally, an Information Disclosure Statement is submitted to the Patent Examiner at the time of filing the application, setting forth all prior art that the inventor and the attorney are aware of that is material to examination of the application. This would include all prior art that was uncovered by a pre-filing patentability search.

In my judgment, the purpose of the prior art disclosure rule is twofold. First, the applicant and the attorney are legally held to a strict duty of candor in making a showing before the USPTO of the reasons they believe the inventor is the first inventor. It is no longer possible to attempt to hide prior art that you are aware of from the Examiner, and obtain issuance of a patent upon the theory that the Examiner will never find that information. In this regard, the disclosure to the Examiner must also include any activities of the inventors themselves which are material to consideration as possible statutory bars for granting a patent, such as public uses, offers for sale or sales, or public knowledge prior to your patent application filing date, as explained previously. By way of example, an explanation of the inventor's activities relating to the invention that transpired more than 1 year prior to the filing date, which activities could or could not be considered as public disclosures, should be presented to the Examiner, along with an explanation as to why such activities were only experimental or test activities and do not give rise to a disabling "public use," "on sale," or "publicly available" situation.

The second reason for submitting this prior art to the USPTO is that the patent application is prepared with a view toward ultimately being enforced, if necessary, before a federal court, explaining to the court every step taken in developing the invention and obtaining patent protection. In patent litigation, the lawyer representing the alleged infringer will introduce into evidence all prior art believed to be relevant in an effort to invalidate your patent by showing that your patent should not have issued in the first place. However, under existing law governing patent litigation, the court can give short shrift or completely ignore prior art that was previously considered by the Patent Examiner during the examination process, if such prior art is presented as part of an invalidity defense in court by the alleged infringer. In simple terms, the court is asking defense counsel to present prior art that was not previously considered by the Patent Examiner. Therefore, the more prior art you present to the Examiner and introduce into the history of the examination of the patent application, the more difficult it becomes for a lawyer representing an infringer to obtain additional prior art material in an effort to invalidate the patent. Thus, in my opinion, it is definitely to the inventor's advantage to have as much prior art as possible presented in the USPTO examination and prosecution history and reviewed by the Examiner, as a way of strengthening the patent if and when that patent faces enforcement in a court proceeding.

7.4 ADDITIONAL MATTERS DISCUSSED DURING THE INVENTION DISCLOSURE MEETING BETWEEN THE INVENTOR AND THE PATENT PROFESSIONAL

7.4.1 Confidentiality of the Meeting

The meeting at which the inventor discloses the invention to the patent attorney is held in strict confidence, and the confidentiality of the invention is protected by the attorney/client privilege. This ensures that the client need not fear that the attorney will "steal" the invention. If the inventor is not satisfied with this explanation, the attorney can sign an NDA binding the attorney to secrecy regarding the invention. However, the cannons of ethics which bind an attorney to confidentiality regarding information passing between the client and the attorney are sufficient to re-assure the inventor of the confidentiality of his/her invention disclosure. In view of the fact that an attorney may lose his or her license to practice law, and therefore the ability to earn a living, upon violating the cannons of ethics of the profession, it is extremely rare, and I have never known it to happen, that an attorney would attempt to misappropriate the invention of one of his/her clients.

7.4.2 Does the Invention Qualify for Patent Protection

Once the disclosure of the invention has been provided to the patent attorney, the attorney must decide and discuss with the inventor whether the subject matter is sufficiently concrete, and not merely conceptual, to qualify for patent protection. Next, it must be determined whether the invention falls within one of the statutory classes covered under Patent Law—that is, if the invention is a process, machine, manufacture, or a composition of matter, and/or any new and useful improvement thereof. The patent attorney must also determine whether an article patent, method patent, design patent, or a combination of several of these would best serve your purposes. Also, the possibility of using trade secret, trademark, and copyright protection must also be discussed, depending upon the nature of the invention.

7.4.3 Preliminary Novelty Inquiry

The inventor must disclose to the attorney at the patent disclosure meeting all material information known to the inventor which is relevant to related prior technology, either of the inventor or of others. For example, any information or activities the inventor has knowledge of regarding the use or disclosure of a similar device or process, or whether there are any third-party publications, articles, or prior patents which disclose the invention of which the inventor is aware, should be discussed. These articles, patents, and other materials should also be produced to the patent attorney. All of such printed and electronic information in books, articles, brochures, and patent publications, as well as general knowledge and items that are available to the public, are all included within the definition of "prior art" against which the novelty of the invention is measured, and which the claims of the patent application must avoid covering.

Chapter 8 discusses the pre-examination patentability search that is sometimes conducted to discover prior art that may bear on the patentability of your invention. This search will ultimately disclose whether or not there is a single prior art publication or event that would destroy novelty under 35 U.S.C. §102(a) or (b), or whether the invention is rendered obvious through a combination of prior art materials under 35 U.S.C. §103.

7.4.4 Determining the Date of Invention

The inventor should also disclose to the patent attorney the events and the dates of those events relating to the conception, diligence, and reduction to practice of the invention. This includes the initial activities of the inventor in conceiving the invention, and the sketches and rough drawings, usually on scrap paper, cocktail napkins, or lab notebooks, as discussed previously. This information is important if it becomes necessary to initiate a derivation proceeding against a first-to-file applicant who misappropriated your invention.

7.4.5 Will the Invention Work as Claimed by the Inventor?

Sufficient information must be given to the patent attorney by the inventor to establish that the invention will work for its intended purposes. The Constitutional mandate states that patents can only be granted for advances in the "useful" arts. A patent cannot be granted for an inoperative device or method, such as a perpetual motion machine, and a patent is subject to post-grant cancellation if the device is proven to be inoperative. Thus, the inventor should be prepared at the initial invention disclosure meeting to provide sufficient information establishing the workability of the invention. A model need not be presented to the patent attorney since the patent attorney has a technical background.

7.4.6 A Brief Comment Regarding Foreign Patent Rights

The inventor should ask the patent attorney to explain the ability to obtain foreign patent rights covering the invention, considering the possibility of any prior public disclosure by the inventor that may have adversely affected such foreign patent rights. The attorney should explain to the inventor whether or not there has been any affect on foreign patent rights due to the prior activities of the inventor before the initial invention disclosure meeting. The subject of foreign patent rights is covered in more detail in Chapter 16.

7.4.7 What the Prior Art Lacks

The inventor should disclose to the patent attorney those problems which exist in the art, and how the proposed invention is designed to solve such problems. Also, the inventor should describe what prior art devices or process he or she is aware of that have attempted to solve the same problems, and how the prior art devices have failed to solve such problems. The inventor should explain in full detail how his/her invention, which is being considered for patentability, particularly solves those problems in the prior art that no one else has been able to solve. This information is important for the preparation of a persuasive patent application.

7.4.8 Inventor's Initial Concept of Novel Features

The inventor next describes his or her understanding of what is believed to be novel about the invention for which a patent is being sought. There may be one or more points of novelty. Remember, no patentability search has yet been conducted to determine what actually may be novel about the invention, so the only reference point at this meeting is the inventor's knowledge.

Although the inventor will explain what he/she believes the novelty to be, it is always prudent to conduct a patentability search of prior art patents and literature to determine more precisely what the point of novelty is, and upon what features of the invention it can be expected that valid patent claims can be obtained. This patentability search, and indeed the examination process itself, may indicate to the inventor that his or her initial thoughts regarding novelty were not exactly correct, but that other novel features do reside in the invention for which patentability can be claimed. This process is known as "shifting the point of novelty," and is quite common in the prosecution and development of patents.

To prepare a patent application that will support all points of novelty, all of the structure, operation, and advantages of the invention, as well as the results of the invention, should be clearly disclosed to the patent professional by the inventor. Thus, the patent application will be drafted with all necessary elements included, so that, if the point of novelty shifts during the examination process, the new novel elements relied upon will be included in the application. Thus, it is important to present a full disclosure of the invention to the patent professional. Once a patent application is filed, no new matter can be added to the application.

7.4.9 Non-Obviousness

As mentioned in Chapter 6, the inventor cannot obtain a patent if the differences between the subject matter sought to be patented and the prior art are such that, at the time a patent application is filed, the subject matter as a whole would have been obvious to a person having ordinary skill in the art to which the subject matter pertains. Thus, you must furnish sufficient information to the patent attorney as to the relevant prior art and prior activities that you are aware of to allow the patent attorney to determine whether or not any differences between your invention and the prior art could be considered obvious. This is a cost benefit consideration, since it is folly to file a patent application where you are advised that a patent may never be obtained because the differences between the invention and the prior art would be obvious to one skilled in the art.

7.4.10 Enablement

A patent application must be drafted so that one skilled in the art can read the issuing patent 20 years from its date of filing and reconstruct the invention, without undue experimentation, from the information contained in the patent. If such complete information is not presented, the patent itself may be declared invalid by a court of law when attempted to be enforced against an infringer, on the basis that the patent itself eliminates certain essential material that is necessary to enable one to practice the invention. Therefore, it is not wise to hold back secret information from the patent attorney which would be required to furnish a complete operating working paper on how to reconstruct and operate the invention in the patent application. The enablement requirement has been very strictly construed by the courts in recent decisions, and a lack of an enabling disclosure has been the basis for invalidating several patents. Therefore, it is important to remember the enablement requirement when providing descriptive information that goes into the patent application. Keep in mind also that technical details such as dimensions, sizes, angles, materials and the like need not be set forth in the patent application, unless these details are relevant to the operation, novelty, or non-obviousness of the invention.

7.4.11 The Best Mode Requirement

Since the patent statutes require that the "best mode" of the invention contemplated by the inventor at the time of filing the patent application be described in the application as filed, you, as the inventor, must describe to the patent attorney the best mode of carrying out the invention as of the date of your invention disclosure meeting. You must also keep your patent attorney advised of further significant activities in the progress of developing the invention while the patent application is being prepared, so that, on the filing date, the application will contain the best mode of the invention. This may require that you, the inventor, take a day off work to allow the patent professional to complete and file the application before you make any further improvements.

7.5 INVENTION DISCLOSURE FORM

At the end of this chapter is a sample invention disclosure form (Fig. 7.1) that I use quite often in my practice, which should be completed by the inventor prior to the first invention disclosure meeting, and then brought to the meeting for discussion. Better yet, the disclosure form and materials should be forwarded to the patent attorney prior to the meeting. This will shorten the meeting, and provide the patent attorney with most of the information for review prior to the meeting. Also, the inventor should come to this meeting with all prints, drawings, sketches, photos, and written and electronic material that describe the structure, operation, and advantages of the invention.

Howard B. Rockman
(630) 627-4552
rockman@rvoiplaw.com

INVENTION DISCLOSURE FORM
(CONFIDENTIAL)

This form is used to identify and screen inventions submitted by clients for patentability evaluations, the preparation of an application for patent, and for considering other appropriate types of proprietary protection. For purposes of completing this form, an "invention" may be just about anything. The typical subjects regarded as an invention include a useful idea, concept, method, process, machine, algorithm, device, article of manufacture, composition of matter, apparatus, improvement, or development.

This form is three pages long. Your signature and the date should be on the last page.

Answer all questions. Attach additional pages, copies of your notes, sketches, blueprints, computer-generated drawings, or other materials to explain your responses and provide full details of your disclosure.

****

1. Client name: ______________________ Client matter: ____________________
2. Date of submission of this disclosure: ____
3. (a) This submission is by (person's name): ____________________________________
   (b) Address: ____
4. Title of invention: ____
5. Using drawings, sketches, computer-generated drawings, photos, and/or text material, attach a complete description of the structure, function, operation, and advantages of the invention.
6. Using text, and drawings, if appropriate, answer the following questions, separately and specifically, as each relates to the invention. Additional pages may be necessary for completion of this section.

   (a) What is the purpose of the invention?
   ____
   ____
   ____

   (b) What were the prior methods, techniques, or devices known to you used to accomplish the purpose or comparable aim of the invention? ______________________________
   ____
   ____

   (c) What were the disadvantages of these methods, techniques, or devices? ____________
   ____
   ____

   (d) Practically, where will the invention be useful, and to what extent will it be used?
   ____
   ____

7. State the earliest date and place the invention was conceived, and include a brief description of circumstances:
   Date: _________________ Place: _________________________
   Circumstances: ____
   ____
   ____

Figure 7.1 Sample invention disclosure form.

8. State the date and present location of:

   (a) First sketch or drawing of invention: ____________________

   (b) First written description: ____________________

9. If a test has been made or an operating mode, breadboard, or prototype constructed:

   (a) For any test, state the date and place; describe any general rules; and identify witnesses to the tests.

   Date: ____________

   Place: ____________________

   Results: ____

   Witnesses: ____

   (b)For any model, breadboard, or prototype, state the date of completion; fabricator of the model or prototype; and present location of the model or prototype:

   Date: ____________

   Fabricator: ____________________

   Present location: ____

10. State the names and dates of any disclosure of the invention to other persons, and whether the disclosure was made pursuant to a signed non-disclosure agreement (NDA).

    (a) To employees of the client:

    Names: ____

    Date: ____

    (b) Other persons and dates of disclosure:

    Names: ____

    Company: ____________________ Date: ____________________

11. Has any publication, submission for publication, or written report of the invention been made?

    ____________ Yes ____________ No

    If "Yes," provide contract or job: ____

    ____

12. Was the invention made in performance of work for a customer?

    ____________ Yes ____________ No

    If "Yes," provide contract or job: ____

    ____

13. If an embodiment of the invention has left your possession or custody, or control of your employer, or has otherwise been shipped from you or your employer's premises, state the date and circumstances of shipment:

    Date: ____________ Circumstances: ____________________

    ____

Figure 7.1 (*Continued*)

14. If the invention was made for internal use (rather than for use by third-party customers), state the first date on which use of the invention was made in commercial production. Identify whether such use was a test. Briefly describe circumstances and results:

    Date: ____________________ Test? ________ Yes __________ No

    ____

    ____

15. List commercial products, publications, or patents related to the invention, or prior art related to the invention, if you know of any:

    ____

    ____

    ____

16. Who do you consider to be the inventor(s)? More than one person may be named.

    Name: ________________________

    Address: ____________________________

    ____

    Name: ________________________

    Address: ____________________________

    ____

17. Your signature: __________________________

    Date: __________________

Figure 7.1 (*Continued*)

◆ INVENTORS AND INVENTIONS ◆

Alexander Graham Bell

TELEPHONE

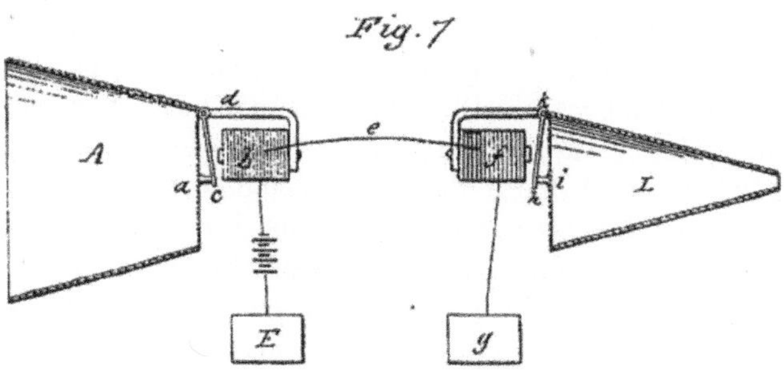

Alexander Graham Bell is credited with inventing the practical telephone, which can be defined as a device for transmitting human speech by electricity. The history of the development of the telephone shows that there were several others working on similar projects at the same time, such as Elisha Gray and Thomas Edison. For example, in the United Kingdom, some consider Gray as the telephone's inventor. As a result, the U.S. patent that was ultimately issued on Bell's telephone, and his ensuing telephone patents, were the subject of 600 patent infringement lawsuits, all won by Bell, and all upholding his patents.

Alexander Graham Bell was born in Edinburgh, Scotland, on March 3, 1847. His father, Alexander Melville Bell, was a teacher who taught deaf and mute students how to speak. Bell's father also created a code of symbols, indicating positions of the lips, tongue, and throat in making sounds, helping the deaf learn to speak. This was known as "visible speech."

Alexander's mother, Eliza Bell, was practically totally deaf, and by pressing his lips against his mother's forehead, Bell discovered that he could make the bones in her head resonate to his voice. Bell was also a talented pianist who learned early on to define and discriminate pitch. He noticed that a chord struck on one piano would be echoed by a piano in another room, and that entire chords could be transmitted through the air, vibrating at the receiving end at the same pitch as transmitted. This observation eventually was involved in the development of the telephone.

After Bell's oldest and youngest brothers died of tuberculosis in Scotland, the family moved to Tutelo Heights, near Brantford, Ontario, Canada. Bell's father subsequently took a position in Boston, Massachusetts, teaching deaf children to speak,

Intellectual Property Law for Engineers, Scientists, and Entrepreneurs, Second Edition. Howard B. Rockman.

Published 2020 by John Wiley & Sons, Inc.

and his son began a successful teaching career in Boston. His students included George Sanders, the son of a successful leather merchant, and Mabel Hubbard, the daughter of a successful lawyer. Later in life, Mr. Hubbard and Mr. Sanders were to become Bell's chief financial backers, and Mabel Hubbard became his wife.

The early experiments of Bell that eventually led to the invention of the telephone did not even involve thinking about a telephone. Bell was trying to develop a multiple telegraph, one that could be used to convey several messages simultaneously, each at a different pitch. Telegraphy at that time involved transmission of an electrical current that was interrupted in a pattern known as the Morse Code. In the 1870s, Bell, Edison, and Elishia Gray were all seeking a telegraph device that could send upward of four messages simultaneously. Bell's work on his multiple telegraph stemmed from Helmholtz's device, which used a single tuning fork that continually interrupted the circuit and a resonator that kept the other tuning forks in the system in constant vibration. The Helmholtz device was used to produce vowel sounds using electromechanical means, and Bell assumed that if the vowels could be transmitted over wires, so could other sounds, including the consonants and musical tones.

Bell found it difficult to determine how to make and break the current at the precise pitch required as the pitch was conveyed along a telegraph wire. While on vacation in 1874, he constructed an "ear phonoautograph" using a hay reed and the ear bones from a dead man mounted on a wooden frame. Sounds delivered to the ear bones caused the hay reed to trace the shape of the sound waves on a smoked glass. Using his previous knowledge of electricity, speaking machines, and pitch, Bell was inspired to conclude that the smoked glass could be rolled back and forth beneath the hay reed. This also led Bell to conclude that sound could be translated into visible waves, from which he theorized that vibrations of a reed could be transformed into an undulating electrical current and reproduced as sound. The undulating current concept was crucial to his later development of the telephone.

Bell initially conceived of a device made of a plurality of reeds extending over a magnet. As the reeds responded to one's voice, they would ultimately vibrate in the direction of and then away from the magnet, creating the undulating current. This "harp apparatus," as Bell himself called it, did not resemble the telephone that he ultimately developed.

In 1874, Bell sketched, but never built, his "harp apparatus," showing how undulating sound waves could be translated into electric currents of the same form. This sketched apparatus included two permanent horseshoe magnets with two steel reeds on each. Bell conceived that this would serve as a transceiver for two separate signals, the signals corresponding to each of the reeds. Bell used permanent magnets in his harp apparatus rather than the electromagnets he had previously used in his multiple telegraph experiments. He reasoned that if a magnet is moving away from a coil half of the time and moving toward the coil the other half of the time, the induced current should imitate the vibrating magnet, since the flux would be increasing half of the time when the magnet moves toward the coil, and decreasing the remaining half of the time when the magnet moves away from the coil. This periodic increasing and decreasing of the flux at discrete intervals would produce the same periodic induced current in the coil.

Bell postulated a device with a first steel reed having a specific harmonic mounted on a horseshoe-shaped permanent magnet, and a second reed having a different harmonic on the same magnet (a transceiver). He then thought of placing a third reed having the same harmonic as the first reed, and a fourth reed having the same harmonic as the second reed on a duplicate transceiver. When the first reed was vibrated, the third reed on the transceiver would also vibrate. Likewise, when the second reed was vibrated, the fourth reed on the transceiver also vibrated.

When the first reed vibrated toward the coil, the current became more positive or negative, depending upon which pole of the magnet the first reed was on and the winding pattern of the underlying coil. When the first reed vibrated away from the coil, an opposite current was induced. The signal was sent across as a sinusoidal wave, which was precisely the same waveform produced by the phonautograph on smoked glass.

This is what Bell referred to as his "undulating current," which became the primary feature of his first telephone patent, issued in 1876. This wave expressed in a graphical manner the vibratory movement of the air while the reeds were producing their musical tones, and the vibrations of the individual reeds attached to the permanent magnet resulted in a single undulating current waveform. Bell determined that if the waves from the two reeds could be combined to produce a more intricate wave, the proper combination of waves could be used to produce all sounds.

Bell used this mental model to develop the postulate that undulating waves traced into the smoked glass in his phonautograph could be transformed into undulating electric current, and then be reproduced as sound. This use of undulating current was different from the intermittent current used in telegraphy to produce dots and dashes. Bell also discovered that by combining undulating currents, the result would be a different sine curve produced for every combination of sounds, allowing discrimination among different messages. His future father-in-law, Gardiner Hubbard, who was his primary backer, urged Bell to direct his efforts toward the multiple telegraph, and forget trying to produce a "speaking" telegraph.

Bell's initial multiple transmitter and receiver (transceiver) made and broke contact with a dish of mercury that ultimately completed an interrupted circuit. At the receiving end, electromagnets attracted the tuning fork each time the circuit was completed, thus causing the fork to vibrate. Bell had thought through a complete system for his multiple telegraphy device, and had succeeded in patenting different parts of it by the spring of 1875. A key part of his thinking was that the multiple telegraphy system would transmit an undulatory current, as opposed to the intermittent or make-or-break current used in single-transmission telegraphy.

By June 2, 1875, Bell had constructed three multiple telegraph stations, each with three tuned relays. When Bell caused one of the reeds at the first station to vibrate, the corresponding reed at the second station also vibrated. His assistant, Mr. Watson, who was in another room with the third corresponding reed, advised Bell that the reed was stuck. To release the stuck reed, Watson vibrated it with his finger, and Bell noticed that the corresponding reed at Station II vibrated violently. Bell then placed his ear next to each of the other reeds at the second station in succession, and heard both the overtones and the pitch of the tuned reeds. He concluded from this incident that magneto-electric undulating currents generated by the vibration of an armature in front of an electromagnet could produce audible effects that could be utilized for multiple telegraphy and speech transmission. Later, Mr. Watson was to comment that the speaking telephone was born as a result of this experiment.

However, extensive work did remain before a workable electric telephone was developed. As a result of the stuck reed, Bell learned that a single reed, when dampened or stuck, could also induce a current that was capable of transmitting complex vibrations or sounds over a distance, and the multiple reeds of the harp structure were not necessary. Bell then asked Mr. Watson to construct a device in which a reed relay was attached to a membrane or diaphragm having a speaking cavity. As one spoke into the cavity, the membrane vibrated, and these vibrations were translated into electric current by the dampened reed. The current thus generated was received by a similar device at the end of an electrical wire. The receiving device produced mumbling, rather than intelligible speech. However, Bell and Watson considered that they were heading in the right direction.

On January 20, 1876, Bell signed a patent application directed to his use of electrical undulations induced by the vibration of a body capable of inductive action to transmit sound. This was before speech had been transmitted electrically. Bell's patent application was submitted to the United States Patent Office on February 14, 1876, four days after his 29th birthday, and merely a few hours before Elisha Gray submitted a caveat for a speaking telegraph. (A caveat was a document submitted by a potential inventor with the U.S. Patent Office, setting forth a broad outline of an invention they intended to make, but which was not complete. The use of caveats in the United States terminated circa 1909.)

When the Bell patent application was filed, he and Watson had still not developed a working device. On March 10, 1876, Bell removed the electromagnet from the device he and Watson had constructed that produced the mumbling transmission, and substituted a dish of water that was used as a spark arrester; i.e., the water acted as a resistance that prevented sparks in the telegraph relay. These liquid experiments led to the famous quote, "Watson, come here. I want you," which occurred on March 10, 1876. Thus, when Bell obtained his U.S. Patent No. 174,465 on March 7, 1876, it was three days before he finally achieved a working telephone.

Claim 5 of Bell's patent was rather broad, and reads as follows:

> 5. The method of, and apparatus for, transmitting vocal or other sounds telegraphically, as herein described, by causing electrical undulations, similar in form to the vibrations of the air accompanying the said vocal or other sound, substantially as set forth.

Subsequently, the basic Bell telephone patent was subject to 600 lawsuits of various kinds, mainly suits filed by Bell to prevent others from infringing on his patent.

The first lawsuit filed under the Bell patents was the so-called Dowd case, in which Western Union was the alleged primary infringing defendant. This lawsuit was filed on September 12, 1878, in the Circuit Court of the United States for the District of Massachusetts, and there is no published court decision because the case was settled after trial while the judge had the case under advisement. This first lawsuit turned out to be the heart of the ensuing litigation that took place over the next 20 years.

Bell had very little in the way of documents, correspondence, sketches, or drawings to help his memory regarding his work in developing the telephone. In his search for such documentation, Bell even asked his wife, Mabel, for the keys to a bureau where she kept his love letters written to her before they were married, in an attempt to find any statement that he might have made in those letters that would help fix the dates of his telephone experiments. Bell told Mabel that he did not have the remotest intention of publishing any of his love letters.

In the litigation against Western Union, Bell's attorney did not base his strategy on the concept of undulatory current as something that was new, but on the use of electricity in general for transmitting speech, as exemplified by the instruments described in the Bell patents. This strategy worked, because the Western Union lawyers had built their case around showing that undulatory currents were not new with Bell. Bell's case, however was predicated on the *application* of undulatory currents. This led to the Bell Company winning control, with their patents, of the basic principle of telephony, not merely the particular devices used in telephony.

However, Bell still needed to present documentary evidence showing that he had worked on the telephone. During the spring and summer of 1879, Mabel Bell, his wife, and her cousin Mary Bletchford, went through all the old correspondence between Bell and his then fiancé, and also the notebooks that Bell was able to maintain, and found nothing. In the movie *The Story of Alexander Graham Bell* (1939), the Hollywood version of the story shows that the entire lawsuit depended upon one love letter submitted to the court by Mabel Bell. Thus, Hollywood used poetic license to turn a patent litigation matter into an interesting love story.

The lawsuit against Western Union was eventually settled before decision, when Western Union assigned its telephone patents to the Bell Company in exchange for Western Union being awarded 20% of rental receipts by Bell for the next 17 years. The Edison carbon transmitter patent, along with additional improvement patents, were obtained by the Bell Company as a result of the settlement, along with the network of agencies and customers of Western Union. Thus, after the settlement, the stock of American Bell Telephone Company nearly doubled in a few days.

The Bell Company's decision to settle the case was predicated not on the theory that there was any weakness in Bell's patents, but upon the fact that Western Union had brought other lawsuits against the Bell Company for infringement of later improvement patents, such as the Edison transmitter. As in any litigation, the parties considered that victory by either side is not a certainty, but distraction and the expense of resources are certain. Therefore, Bell and his advisors felt that the settlement was the best business choice.

Two other Bell patent-related lawsuits are worthy of mention in this treatise. The first is the case of *American Bell Telephone Company v. Globe Telephone Company, Antonio Meucci, and others,* 31 Fed. 728 (SDNY, 1887). In this case, the defendants were attempting to invalidate broad Claim 5 of the basic telephone patent No. 174,465 obtained by Bell on March 7, 1876. The primary evidence offered in the defendant's attempt to invalidate the Bell patent was Meucci's allegation that he had developed a speaking telephone for domestic use as early as 1871, and since he was too poor to obtain a patent, his invention was made public by being published in *Eco D'Italia,* a local newspaper for Italian immigrants in New York in the latter half of the 19th century. Meucci had filed a caveat in the United States Patent Office on December 28, 1871, describing his device. The Globe Company, at the time of the suit, had never constructed any telephones, but was obtaining money from investors, after telling the investors that Globe had acquired patents that would be used to defeat the Bell patents, and that Globe's patents would protect the purchasers or licensees against the Bell Company patents. The Globe Company realized that its own patents were worthless unless the Bell patent could be invalidated, and thus did not manufacture any telephones, so that the Bell Company could not accuse them of infringement. At the time of the trial, Mr. Meucci did not have any of his original devices to offer in evidence to show what it was he had developed, since his wife had sold them at a "garage sale" to raise money. The Meucci caveat was originally filed in 1871; it was renewed in December 1882, and again in December 1883. During that time, Mr. Meucci did not make any improvements on the device that was disclosed in his 1871 caveat.

Upon reviewing the evidence, the court in the Globe case held that the Meucci device resulted in nothing beyond conveying speech mechanically by means of a wire telephone. His caveat disclosed a metallic conductor as a sound conveying medium, and he merely supposed that by electrifying the apparatus or the operator, he could obtain a better result. He did not communicate his invention to anyone else who could appreciate it or assist him in perfecting and introducing his invention to the public, but between 1859 and 1871, he did file several patent applications for other inventions. Meucci was also in close association with one William E. Rider, who paid the expenses of his experiments. Therefore, the court in the *Bell v. Globe* case disregarded Mr. Meucci's claims of poverty. The relation with Rider continued until 1867, when Mr. Rider became convinced that Meucci's inventions were not sufficiently practical or profitable.

The court further held that the caveat of Meucci did not describe any elements of an electric speaking telephone, but that Meucci employed the then well-known physical conducting effect of metallic conductors to convey sound, and enhanced the results by electrically insulating both the conductor and the communicating parties. The caveat filed by Meucci consisted of isolating two persons by placing them upon glass insulators, and putting them in communication by means of a telegraph wire. He then amended this statement by stating that the person sending the message was insulated, with the person receiving the signal in free electrical communication with the ground. These conditions could also be reversed.

The court held that Meucci's device consisted of a mechanical telephone comprising a mouthpiece and an earpiece connected by a wire, and that beyond this the invention of Meucci was only imagination. The patent attorney who prepared the caveat for Mr. Meucci told Meucci that his idea gave promises of usefulness, but would require many experiments to prove the reality of his concept. This case, as were all of the other cases in which the validity of the original Bell telephone patent was in dispute, was resolved by upholding the validity of the Bell patent.

Despite this court decision, over 100 years later, on June 11, 2002, the United States House of Representatives in Washington, D.C. passed a resolution honoring the achievements of Antonio Meucci. This resolution briefly sets forth the fact that Meucci developed his speaking device in 1871 so he could communicate with his ailing wife on a different floor of his house, that he published a description of his invention in New York's Italian language newspaper at the time, and that he was too poor to obtain patent protection or commercialization of his invention. The resolution also implies that Meucci submitted his earlier models to Western Union, who then lost them, but that before they were lost, Alexander Graham Bell conducted experiments in the same laboratory at Western Union where Meucci's earlier materials were stored. The resolution also refers to a lawsuit filed by the United States Government on January 13, 1887, to annul the Bell patent on the grounds of fraud, which lawsuit is discussed a few paragraphs below. The resolution concludes that if Meucci had been able to pay the $10 fee to maintain his caveat after 1874, no patent on the telephone would have been issued to Alexander Graham Bell.

My continuing research led me to the rebuttal comments of Edwin S. Grosvenor, published at http://www.alecbell.org/meuccimemo.html. In his memo, Mr. Grosvenor refers back to the case of *American Bell Telephone Company v. Globe and Meucci,* and points to those facts in the court's decision that would completely repudiate the grounds set forth in the 2002 resolution of the U.S. House of Representatives. The Grosvenor article points out that the Meucci caveat disclosed a mouthpiece and an earpiece connected by a taut wire that transmitted vibrations of sounds mechanically (not electrically) over the wire. The Grosvenor article also states that Meucci had financial help and he was not destitute, and could have commercialized his invention had it been worth anything. Grosvenor thus concludes that the Meucci caveat, and indeed his "invention," does not describe or suggest any of the elements of electrical communication of voice, or the principle of undulating current that is set forth in the broadest claim of the Bell patent.

Upon my review of the *American Bell Telephone Company v. Globe and Meucci* court decision of July 19, 1887, I conclude that the comments of Mr. Grosvenor are more likely correct in comparison to the statements by the United States House of Representatives. I draw this conclusion knowing full well that Mr. Grosvenor is the great-grandson of Alexander Graham Bell.

Another incident that is of interest is the lawsuit filed by the United States Government, referred to in the House of Representatives resolution discussed above, attempting to invalidate the Bell telephone patents on the grounds that they were obtained by fraud. One Dr. James Rogers of Tennessee conceived that a legal challenge to the Bell patents, having merit or not, would protect infringers for a period of time, even if the challenge was not legitimate. The purpose was to delay the American Bell Telephone Company from successfully suing infringers until the Bell patents expired. Rogers' son, an electrician, came up with a series of inventions, which apparently were primarily a figment of his imagination. Casey Young, a former member of the U.S. Congress from Tennessee, and several associates incorporated the Pan-Electric Company, and 10% of the stock was given to Augustus H. Garland, a former governor of Arkansas, and at that time a Senator from Arkansas. Garland was also appointed as the attorney for Pan-Electric Company. Garland assured investors that the Rogers patents covered devices that did not infringe on the Bell patents, and thus was able to raise substantial investment capital for Pan-Electric.

In 1884, the Pan-Electric organizers convinced the United States House of Representatives to enact a bill granting authorization to the federal government to file lawsuits to invalidate patents under a listing of potential circumstances. The Senate failed to pass the act, but Grover Cleveland was elected President later that year, and he appointed none other than Augustus H. Garland, attorney for Pan-Electric, as United States Attorney General. The Pan-Electric principals asked Garland to file a lawsuit in the name of the United States seeking annulment of Bell's patents on the grounds that Bell had obtained his patents by fraud, and that Bell was not the first inventor of the telephone. Garland then left on a hunting trip in Arkansas, and the Solicitor General, one of the Attorney General's staff members, hastily granted the request while the Attorney General was away. The Secretary of the Interior upheld the decision to file the lawsuit, applying the reason that charges of fraud were being made against federal officials in the Patent Office, and the truth of these charges should be tested by the filing of a lawsuit at government expense against the American Bell Telephone Company.

The government lawsuit was filed in January 1887, and the initial government effort in the litigation to enjoin Bell from filing further lawsuits against infringers did not succeed. Previously, in 1885, the New York newspapers had exposed the intricate stock holdings of Pan-Electric by the United States Attorney General, members of Congress, and past and present members of the Federal Executive Branch. A congressional committee investigated the matter and concluded that Garland was not guilty of any misdeeds. Grover Cleveland retained Garland as Attorney General.

The government case lumbered through the litigation process, without ever reaching a result. The lawyer in charge of the government's case passed away in 1896, and the government let the case drop. During 1892, Bell spent a total of nine weeks, at intervals, testifying in the government lawsuit and providing a complete account of the development work that led to the invention of the telephone. In 1908, the American Bell Telephone Company printed the complete testimony of Alexander Graham Bell, both direct and cross-examination, in a 445-page document.

The government case at an interim point reached the United States Supreme Court on Bell's motion to dismiss the lawsuit. The government case against Bell was decided by the Supreme Court on November 12, 1888, which remanded the case to the lower court for further litigation. See *United States v. The American Bell Telephone Company,* 128 U.S. 315 (1888). The Court held that *if* Bell was aware when he filed his patent applications that the same subject matter had been previously discovered and put in operation by other persons, he was guilty of a fraud upon the public, and that the monopoly that the patents granted to him ought to be revoked and annulled. The Supreme Court held that the federal courts do have the power to grant such relief when it is proven that patents were obtained by fraud. The rationale of the Court's decision is that to obtain a patent, the inventor must know that he or she was the original inventor. However, the case never reached the point where the fraud allegations in the complaint were proven to be true or false.

The United States House of Representatives in its resolution of June 11, 2002, states merely that the government of the United States filed the lawsuit, and that the Supreme Court found the complaint viable and remanded the case for trial. The House of Representatives resolution, in my opinion, leaves out many of the salient details, and presents a disjointed and incorrect view of the invention of the telephone.

Bell subsequently worked on transmitting sounds on a beam of light, a precursor of today's fiber optic systems. He also did work on techniques for teaching speech to the deaf, and was instrumental in 1888 in founding the National Geographic Society. The entire story of Alexander Graham Bell, including his involvement in other inventions such as aircraft, would unduly lengthen this chapter. Therefore, the reader is directed to the resources listed in the Bibliography to gain a further understanding of the genius and works of Alexander Graham Bell.

Bell eventually obtained 18 patents in his own name, and 12 additional patents in which he was a joint inventor. Alexander Graham Bell died on August 2, 1922, near his home in Nova Scotia, Canada.

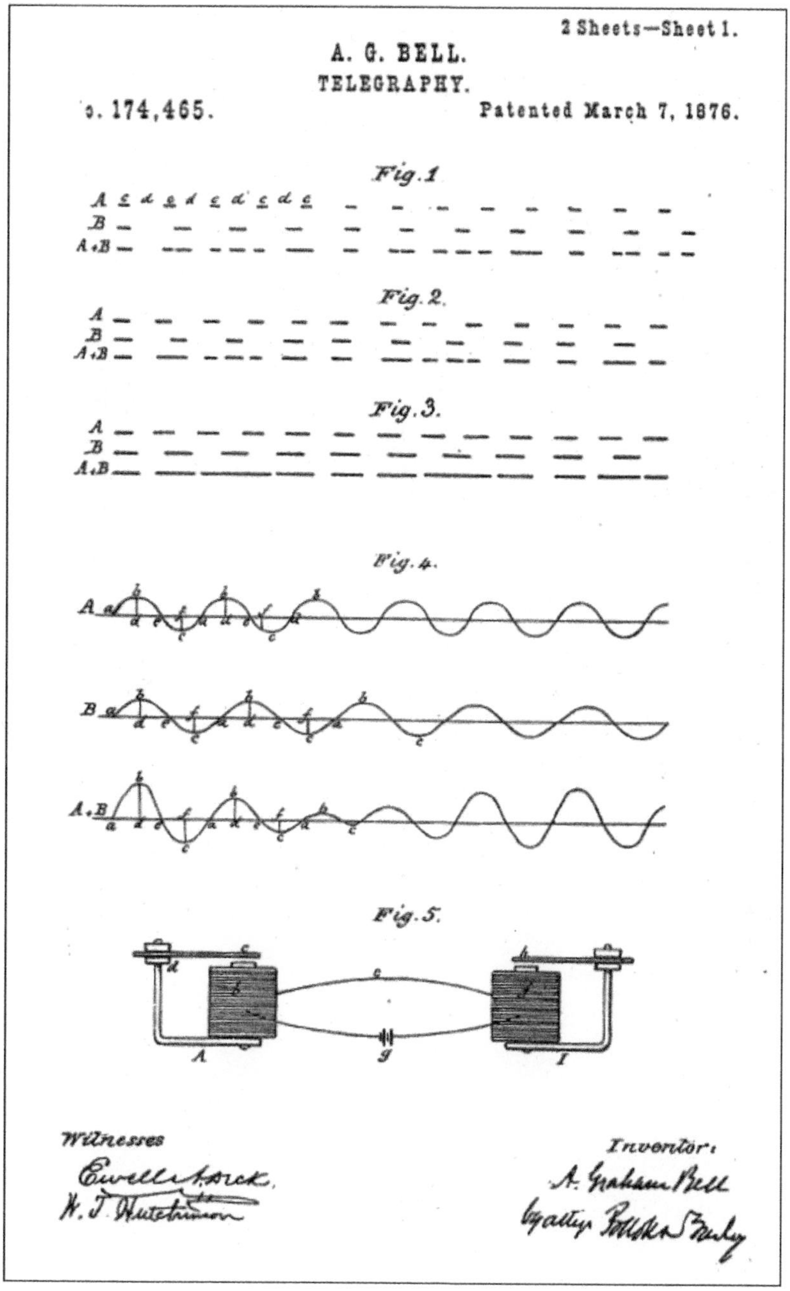
2 Sheets—Sheet 1.
A. G. BELL.
TELEGRAPHY.
o. 174,465.
Patented March 7, 1876.
Fig. 1
Fig. 2.
Fig. 3.
Fig. 4.
Fig. 5.
Witnesses
Inventor:
A. Graham Bell

8 The Patentability Search, Freedom-To-Use Search, and Other Searches

8.1 SEARCHING THE CONTENT OF THE PRIOR ART TO DETERMINE PATENTABILITY OF THE INVENTION

Since one of the most important aspects of obtaining a patent on your invention is the comparison of your invention to the state of the prior art, the best way to gain an understanding of the content of the prior art before committing to the expense of filing a patent application is to conduct a patentability search prior to the preparation of a patent application. The search occurs after the patent attorney gains a full understanding of your invention from the disclosure meeting, and after you have described to him or her all the prior art materials with which you are familiar. Since the patentability search expands the scope of knowledge available to the inventor and the patent attorney regarding technology related to the invention, the patentability search provides the first real opportunity to explore the prior art surrounding your invention in significant detail. This search is optional and is not a requirement for obtaining a patent, but it is very helpful.

The most complete and accessible library of prior art is housed in the electronic patent and published patent application files of the U.S. Patent and Trademark Office. U.S. patents issued since the year 1790 can be searched on the U.S. Patent & Trademark Office website (www.uspto.gov), and further prior art can be accessed on other available websites. It is possible for an inventor to make his or her own preliminary patentability search; however, it is usually wise, and cost-effective, to have an experienced professional conduct the search.

The patent searcher will normally provide the patent attorney with copies of or links to relevant patents, literature, and other materials uncovered during the search, but the searcher normally does not provide her or his patentability review or evaluation of the patents. Nor does the searcher usually provide a legal patentability opinion. The results of the search are commonly forwarded to your patent attorney, who conducts an evaluation of the content of the prior art and provides you with a legal opinion as to whether or not your invention is sufficiently novel and non-obvious over the prior art to support the granting of a patent. The report you receive from your patent attorney should (a) set forth an evaluation of each relevant prior art reference uncovered by the search, commenting on what each reference does and does not

Intellectual Property Law for Engineers, Scientists, and Entrepreneurs, Second Edition. Howard B. Rockman.

Published 2020 by John Wiley & Sons, Inc.

disclose about your invention, and (b) comment on whether any combination of the uncovered references might be used by a Patent Examiner to support an argument that your invention is obvious in view of the teachings of these combined references.

It is important to keep in mind that in certain circumstances, it may be practical to forego a search before filing a patent application. Thus, if the subject matter is too difficult to search, or the product has been scheduled for production before a search can be conducted, or where the inventor has years of experience and a keen knowledge of the prior art, you may decide that it is not cost beneficial to conduct a search and that it would be better to file the patent application as soon as possible.

If the search reveals that the invention is not patentable, this will save the inventor the cost of filing the patent application. On the other hand, if the search reveals that the invention is potentially patentable, the search provides an additional valuable function in furnishing useful background information and advice to the patent attorney as to the scope of the prior art, enabling the patent attorney to draft more effective patent claims covering your invention over the prior art. Further, as stated previously, the patentability search produces a library of technical information the inventor can use in further development of the invention to which the search was directed, or improvements to his or her invention. This, of course, must be done without infringing any of the unexpired patents uncovered by the search. The subject of patent infringement will be covered in Chapter 17.

8.2 PATENTABILTY SEARCH PARAMETERS

The patent attorney you have contacted normally will not perform the search himself or herself, and will solicit the services of an experienced patent searcher. Therefore, the patent attorney must be able to furnish the searcher sufficiently accurate information regarding the description of the invention, its function, its advantages, objectives, and purpose; so that the searcher's direction will be focused on the important features of the invention the inventor has determined provide novelty and non-obviousness. Note also that the information about your invention furnished to the search associate by your patent attorney constitutes a confidential disclosure, and the confidentiality of that disclosure is protected by the searcher as the search is conducted. Thus, the disclosure of the invention to the search associate does not jeopardize any U.S. or foreign patent rights.

Since the subject matter of any search of the prior art is finite in quantity, no such search can be complete, in view of all the publicly available or generally known information relating to your invention which bears upon the questions of novelty and non-obviousness. To conduct a search of all publicly known prior art worldwide would be cost prohibitive, if at all possible. Thus, do not be surprised if the Patent Examiner, or an accused infringer, uncovers prior art not uncovered by your search.

Any later-appearing relevant prior art materials you become aware of during the examination of your patent application after the application is filed with the U.S. Patent & Trademark Office must be submitted to the Patent Examiner for consideration under Rule 56. Any relevant prior art you become aware of after your patent has issued may be submitted to the Patent Examiner for consideration in a reexamination proceeding or other post-grant proceeding established by the AIA. These procedures are discussed at Sections 11.11 and 18.10, respectively. The advantage of a reexamination or post-grant proceeding is to have the Patent Examiner consider the later-found prior art, and to decide that the claims of your patent define novelty over the later-found prior art.

Besides the material lodged in the U.S. Patent and Trademark Office database, other sources of information that constitute the prior art comprise foreign patents and published foreign patent applications, information in scientific journals, technical bulletins, product literature and brochures, safety data sheets, trade publications, press releases, product or service catalogs, and the myriad of information posted on the Internet. In the best of all possible worlds, it would be desirable to be able to evaluate patentability with reference to all existing relevant prior art; however, to amass this amount of information is a practical impossibility. Thus, the patent searcher usually looks only to U.S. patents and published U.S. patent applications, relevant scientific or technical published literature that is available, such as on the Internet, and foreign patents and published patent applications as available.

Where the invention is of significant importance to the inventor or the inventor's employer, a search of foreign patents can be obtained on the websites of several foreign patent offices, such as https://worldwide.espacenet.com, http://www.wipo.int/patentscope/en, and https://patents.google.com. Espacenet is the online search website of the European Patent Office (EPO) with free access to over 100 million patent documents. Also, you or your patent attorney could contact search associates in Japan, China, Taiwan, Hong Kong, India, South Korea, and other areas of technical innovation throughout the world to conduct searches at their national patent offices. However, the extent of each search, as anything else, must be weighed against its cost and expected benefit. It is normally concluded that the patent search conducted on the database of the U.S. Patent & Trademark Office, plus an Internet search, provides prior art material that reliably may be extrapolated to the full content of the prior art to a certain degree and at a reasonable cost.

8.3 ADDITIONAL TYPES OF SEARCHES

In addition to the patentability search, there are other searches for existing patents and published technology that can be conducted. Keep in mind that the patentability search discussed above is directed to answering the question "Is the invention sufficiently novel and non-obvious to be patentable?" Or to put it in a more practical way, "Should the inventor proceed to spend his or her resources to obtain a patent?"

8.3.1 The Freedom-to-Use Search

Since others normally have obtained patents in the field related to your invention, a freedom-to-use search should be conducted upon completion of the development of the product or process embodying your invention, which asks the question "Will my new invention, as embodied in a marketable product or process, infringe another unexpired patent of which we are currently unaware?" By way of a hypothetical example, suppose your new invention relates to a pencil having an eraser on one end. It would be important to find out whether anyone holds a patent on a pencil alone, because the manufacture and sale of your pencil plus eraser will infringe the earlier patent owner's right to exclusively make, use or sell pencils. Thus, the purpose of a freedom-to-use search is to uncover prior active unexpired patents to determine whether your invention, or any subset of your invention, would be covered by claims of another unexpired patent.

In conducting a freedom-to-use search, each claim of the unexpired patents uncovered by the search must be examined to determine whether your invention may be covered by any of these claims. If only a single claim in a patent reads on your product or process, that patent is infringed. If it is found that there is a possibility of an infringement issue arising upon the marketing of your new product or process, a right-to-use search may be appropriate (see Section 8.3.3). Alternatively, it may be possible to create a modification of your invention or device which "designs around" the patent claims that potentially cause infringement problems. In so doing, you are attempting to avoid infringement.

8.3.2 State-of-the-Art Search

Another type of search that can be conducted is the state-of-the-art search, which asks the question "What is the general state of the art or technology concerning the area of my invention?" The results of this search are broader in scope than a patentability search, but the search is still limited to the technology related to your invention. This type of search normally results in a collection of patents, published patent applications, and literature that yield valuable technical data and knowledge concerning the area of related technology, and may be useful to an inventor in further development of the invention, so long as potential infringement problems are avoided.

8.3.3 Right-to-Use Search

A further type of search, alluded to above, is the right-to-use search. This is also commonly called a validity search. This search attempts to answer the question "Even if it appears that the invention or device under analysis infringes another unexpired issued patent, is there a basis for determining that the potentially infringed patent is invalid or otherwise cannot or should not be enforced with respect to my invention?" Prior to initiating this type of search, the patent attorney normally analyzes how the potentially infringed issued patent was obtained by reviewing the prosecution history or "file wrapper" of the subject patent before the U.S. Patent & Trademark Office. This analysis includes an evaluation of the prior art applied by the Patent Examiner against the claims of the potentially infringed patent. Very often, in obtaining a patent and avoiding the prior art, the patent attorney, during prosecution of that patent and amending the claims, will represent to the Patent Examiner that the language and scope of the patent claims are somehow limited to specific structure or process steps not shown in the applied prior art. Such admissions by the patentee's attorney in the prosecution history can be used to show that an accused device falls outside a particular claim limitation. The prosecution history analysis attempts to find these limitations, or loopholes, in the scope of protection of the potentially infringed patent. From the relevant communications and changes to the claims made by the attorney to the Patent Examiner in the prosecution of the potentially infringed patent, your attorney can determine whether or not your invention falls inside or outside the issued patent's scope of protection.

Following such an analysis, if it is determined that your invention may still potentially infringe one or more claims of the issued patent in question, a right-to-use search is requested from a searcher in an effort to obtain prior art not considered previously by the Patent Examiner which would render the claims in question anticipated or obvious, and therefore invalid.

8.4 DATABASE SEARCHES

The searches conducted up to a few years ago were conducted by the searcher manually leafing through the collections of paper patents in the public search facilities of the U.S. Patent & Trademark Office. However, most, if not all, search associates today use a computer database in conducting their searches.

The website of the U.S. Patent & Trademark Office (www.uspto.gov) provides one with the ability to search all patents issued in the United States since the year 1976 using key word search techniques. Patents issued between 1790 and 1975 are available in image format only if you know the patent number. Thus, today both manual and computer database searching are combined to conduct a complete search of issued patents and published patent applications. Assuming that the inventor and patent attorney have provided the searcher with the identity of the inventor's largest competitors in the area of technology covered by the search, the searcher can also use the U.S. Patent & Trademark Office database to obtain a list of all patents and the titles of these patents owned by each competitor subsequent to 1976. This will enable the searcher to pinpoint particular patents, and furnish the patent attorney and the inventor with a precise list of relevant patents owned by such competitors. The same key word techniques are used to conduct an Internet literature search.

The U.S. Patent & Trademark Office database allows searching by subject matter back to 1976, through the incorporation of key words into the search. Thus, if you are looking at a combination of electrical heating elements particularly useful for heating engine blocks, by typing the key words "heater" and "engine block" into the computer search engine, you will obtain the numbers of referenced patents issued since 1976 that correspond to that key word search. The same applies to searching published patent applications. Thus, it is important to provide your patent attorney with as much information as possible regarding the terms used in defining the technology to be searched so that these terms may be keyed into the database search.

8.5 U.S. PATENT AND TRADEMARK OFFICE PATENT CLASSIFICATION SYSTEM

Because of the vast number of patents that are filed and cross-referenced in its database, the U.S. Patent & Trademark Office employs a numerical classification system to identify each of the many areas of technology. Class and subclass numerical designators pinpoint the specific technology and art to be searched. By examining the first page of a patent, the numbers of the classification system appear as "Field of Search." All of these classifications are listed in a rather extensive classification manual. The entire manual is posted on the U.S. Patent & Trademark Office website (www.uspto.gov).

The manual classifies all patents according to subject matter by classes and subclasses. There are well over 400 classes and 20 000 subclasses that cover practically every category of technology and type of invention known. The patent classification manual is basically an index to issued patents and published applications, and the searcher uses the manual to determine which classes and subclasses relate to your technology.

The patent classification system does more than divide patents into manageable related groups. The system divides the Patent Examiners into their own art groups, or areas of expertise. Thus, when directing a search, the attorney can particularly relate the scope of that search to the potential Patent Examiner's specific area of knowledge. For example, when I was a member of the United States Patent Office examining corps in the early days of my career, I examined patent applications directed to automatic transmissions, automatic transmission fluid control systems, differential drive mechanisms for vehicles, and locking devices to override the differential action upon slippage of one of the wheels. By examining patent applications in these areas of technology on a daily basis, I gained a degree of expertise in each these particular technology areas. Thus, as new patent applications were filed that related to my area of technological expertise, it was easy for me to understand the technology, and the alleged advance in the technology. The work of the Patent Examiner will be covered in Chapter 11.

◆ INVENTORS AND INVENTIONS ◆

Thomas Alva Edison

THE LIGHT BULB

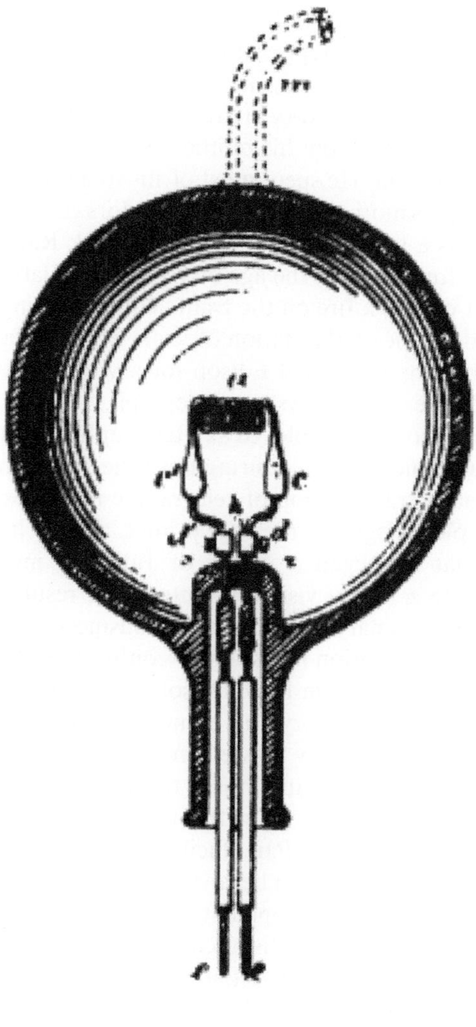

Intellectual Property Law for Engineers, Scientists, and Entrepreneurs, Second Edition. Howard B. Rockman.

Published 2020 by John Wiley & Sons, Inc.

The icon of an American inventor is probably Thomas Alva Edison, who invented the phonograph, the first practical electric light bulb, an automatic timer for a telegraph, an electric voting machine, improvements in the telegraph and telephone, and electrical systems to power his light bulb. Besides being an inventor, Edison was also a shrewd businessman, and the methods he used to carry his inventions to the public, to his profit, involved many activities that might be deemed questionable given today's business ethics and laws. This essay is limited to Edison's life and his invention of the light bulb. The battle between DC and AC current involving Edison, Telsa, and Westinghouse will be discussed in the essay "Current Events" following Chapter 36.

Thomas A. Edison was born on February 11, 1847, in Milan, Ohio, the youngest child of Samuel and Nancy Edison. At the age of seven, Edison and his family moved to Port Huron, Michigan. Edison reportedly had hearing problems as a child, and although he had difficulty with his lessons in school, he became an avid reader, and by the age of 10 had established a laboratory in the basement of his house. Edison learned reading, writing, and arithmetic from his mother, who had taken him out of school because of his hearing problem. He spent most of his free time reading technical and scientific journals. When his mother got tired of the odors coming from the basement, Edison obtained a job as a train boy on the Grand Trunk Railway, and built a new laboratory in an empty freight car at the age of 12. Edison's laboratory in the boxcar was shut down when it caused a fire on the train. While working for the railroad, he saved the life of a child of one of the station officials who had fallen on the tracks in front of an oncoming train. To reward Edison for saving his son, the father began teaching Edison how to use the train system's telegraph.

From 1862 to 1868, Edison was employed as a telegrapher throughout the Midwest, New England, the South, and Canada. During this time, he invented a repeating telegraph, allowing automatic transmission of telegraphic messages. In 1869, his inventions, including the duplex telegraph, message printer, and an improved stock ticker, were doing so well that he began a career of full-time inventing and business development. He became a highly visible inventor as a result of his inventions in telegraphy, which was the primary system used by business and finance concerns in those days to obtain the information necessary to control their businesses.

Edison moved to New York City in 1869. He sold his inventions for $40 000, allowing him to establish his first laboratory and manufacturing facility in Newark, New Jersey, in 1871. He also married Mary Stilwell and began his family. In 1876, Edison sold his Newark, New Jersey, facility and moved to Menlo Park, New Jersey, 25 miles away from New York City. Edison, along with two assistants, Charles Batchelor and John Kruesi, moved into the Menlo Park facility in March 1876. This laboratory employed highly skilled technicians, and became the prototype for later modern facilities devoted to only research and development, such as Bell Laboratories.

In 1877, urged by Western Union, Edison created a carbon-button transmitter for use in telephone speakers and microphones that is still in use today. While experimenting with devices for recording telegraph signals, Edison developed the phonograph, which moved him to the top of the charts as an inventor in the late 19th century. However, it took 10 years for the phonograph to be available as a commercial product. Edison also invented the first talking moving pictures in 1913. He held 1,093 patents, leading all other American inventors in that category.

Edison was not the first to develop an electric light bulb. In the latter half of the 19th century, gas lights, oil lamps, and candles were used to light homes and offices.

Electric arc lights, which used high-voltage electricity to create a spark between two pieces of carbon, could only be used outdoors, such as in street lamps, lighthouses, and other public areas. The carbon arc created a blindingly bright light, which could not be "subdivided" to make small electric lights, which were unknown at the time. An arc light produced a light of approximately 4000 candle power, compared to the 10 or 20 candle power light produced by gas in the home. Arc lights were also operated by inefficient generators. When Edison began his experiments with light, it was known that an incandescent light could be made moderate enough for indoor use if the device could be constructed so that it would not extinguish itself rapidly. Prior to Edison's work, all of the filament elements used in incandescent light experiments either burned up in the heat or melted. These experiments had preceded Edison by approximately 20 years, without any meaningful advances.

An English inventor, Sir Joseph Wilson Swan, is credited with inventing the first electric light bulb, which he demonstrated in 1878. However, the filament had a short life, and the bulb was not practical. The Swan invention, which used high current and low voltage, is still used in flashlights and in automobiles. One of the approaches used prior to Edison to obtain a practical electric light was to use filament materials composed of platinum that had a relatively high melting point and did not oxidize. The platinum material always reached its melting point despite efforts to prevent this from happening. A second pre-Edison approach was to use a filament material such as carbon, whose melting point was so high that melting would not be a problem. However, the use of carbon in the lamp usually resulted in combustion of the carbon, despite the use of vacuum pumps to evacuate air from the bulb.

In mid-1878, Edison was described as ill and very tired from the burdens of maintaining his position as the premier inventor in the United States. In the summer of 1878, he took a vacation to Wyoming with other scientists to view a solar eclipse. The other scientists on the trip discussed the fact that their compatriots were not able to come up with an electric light to replace the gas, oil, and carbon lights presently in use. Upon his return from vacation, Edison visited the workshop of William Wallace in Connecticut, where Mr. Wallace had on display an electric arc lighting system comprised of eight electric lights that were all lit at the same time by an electric generator, each arc light being equal to 4000 candles. Again, the subdivision of this light into smaller light units was then unknown. Edison realized that he had a window of opportunity to develop a subdivided electric light, since the demonstration by Mr. Wallace showed him that science had not yet reached the point of making a practical, subdivided electric light suitable for home use.

When he returned to Menlo Park, Edison, with the help of Charles Batchelor, started experimenting to produce a practical subdivided electric light. They began by constructing lamps using spirals of platinum wire as the filaments or "burners." They controlled these lamps with regulating devices designed to halt the current to the bulb if the platinum reached its melting point. Edison was so confident that he had solved the problem that he publicly announced that in "a few weeks" he would have a practical light bulb available. As a result of his announcement in 1878 that he was nearing completion of a practical light bulb, the stock exchanges witnessed a vast drop in gas company stocks, while others sought to invest in the new technology. Thus, Edison started the Edison Electric Light Company, whose backers were J. P. Morgan and the Vanderbilt family. Following his announcement, Edison and his workers continued their experiments, including testing generators to power the system and to prepare patent applications. Besides working on the light bulb, Edison felt it was important to construct and market an electric generating system that could be used to power the light bulbs he would sell to the public.

After the "few weeks" went by, his light bulb still did not work. The lamps using the platinum filaments flickered out of control, the filaments either broke or melted, and any light that was produced was too low. Edison, up to this time, was working on his own mental juices, and had not investigated prior work on incandescent lights to see what had been done by others, nor did he derive the details of the distribution and generation systems necessary to provide electricity to light his bulbs.

In November, 1878, Edison did two things. First, he hired a young physicist, Francis Upton, impressing upon his investors that he was ready to use the latest in modern science to assist in developing his inventions. Second, he began reviewing the state of the art as to every lighting system extant at that time. He reviewed the work of his competitors, studied prior patents, and, in effect, began all over again, looking for the proper filament for his light bulb.

Edison's team saw that the amount of electrical current required to operate previously devised electric lighting systems was large. Edison was attempting to develop a light bulb that would provide the same convenience of gas light, and make it possible to turn one light on or off without affecting other lights. This led him to conclude that the lights would have to be in a parallel circuit, not a series circuit, since electric current would have to be delivered independently to each lamp. Although generally known, Edison's team also noted that a system required to light a plurality of lamps would require either a high voltage or a large current. Large currents required thicker conducting wires, and copper was an expensive commodity in the late 19th century. If a system were developed using small currents and large voltages, each lamp would require a high resistance, which is the solution that Edison settled upon.

At that time, Edison was using platinum as the filament in his light bulb experiments. However, small lengths of platinum provided a low resistance, so Edison began using long spirals of thin platinum wire as filaments. These broke easily upon being heated to an incandescent temperature. For an extended period of time in 1879, Edison's team failed in their attempts to create spiral filaments sufficient for a long-lasting light bulb. What he did discover was that when efficient vacuum pumps were used to evacuate the air in the light bulb, the life of the platinum burner was extended, though not long enough for practicality.

During the early part of 1879, Edison and his team continued their light bulb experiments, and they also devoted a portion of their efforts to creating a generator that would create a high-voltage system to light their bulbs. By the middle of 1879, Edison and his team still could not make the platinum filament lamp operate properly. In approximately October 1879, Edison and his team gave up on platinum and looked for other materials from which their filaments could be made. As a result of their intensive research efforts, the fact that carbon would provide the desired results was determined in a matter of a few weeks. Carbon had been used previously in the electric lamps of other inventors, but in those experiments the carbon either disintegrated or burned up. However, carbon appeared to be workable in the high vacuum created in Edison's bulbs. Edison had been familiar with carbon, which he had used in his telephone receiver invention.

The records of Edison's laboratory indicate that in the middle of October 1879, Batchelor and Upton were making notes of their measurements of carbon's resistance and how to shape the carbon strands into spiral configurations. However, the carbon spirals always seemed to break. Batchelor's notes indicate that by October 22, the team had performed experiments using several inches of carbonized cotton thread, which had a resistance of 100 ohms, significantly larger than the resistance of platinum. This lamp appeared to be as bright as a gas lamp, and did not flicker out. In the end, and after all the time, money, and experimentation, the result, using hindsight, was simply a glass globe with the air evacuated, in which a short strand of carbonized thread was mounted between two electrodes.

On New Year's Eve of 1879, a public demonstration of the light bulb was made in Edison's Menlo Park laboratory. The event was heavily attended by the press, shooting Edison's popularity way up in the ratings. Edison filed for a patent on his invention on November 4, 1879, and the patent on the first practical light bulb was issued on January 27, 1880. Also, by the first demonstration, Edison's workers had discovered that Bristol board made more reliable filaments than cotton thread.

Edison and his team not only invented the practical electric bulb, but an entire electric lighting system with all of the equipment required to make the incandescent light economical, operable, safe, and practical. For example, to make his system work, Edison also had to develop, create, and invent light sockets with on/off switches, safety fuses and insulating materials, constant-voltage delivery systems, an underground conductor network, improved electrical generating dynamos, a durable long-lasting light bulb, and parallel electric circuits. The Edison Electric Company established its first commercial central power station on Pearl Street in Lower Manhattan in New York City in 1882, furnishing electric power to a small area of the city. Other buildings set up dynamos in the basement to provide electricity for the building.

By the end of the 1880s, central electric power producing stations were established in many U.S. cities, each being limited to a few blocks in area due to the ineffective transmission of direct current (DC) electricity, to which Edison was wedded until his fight with the creators of alternating current, circuits, and systems was resolved many years later. Edison created several electric companies, and on April 24, 1889, they were all brought together to form the Edison General Electric Company. In 1892, Edison General Electric merged with Thompson-Hudson, its leading competitor, the name Edison was dropped from the company name, and the company became General Electric Company. After the turn of the century, and facing financial difficulty, Edison sold his stock in the General Electric Company. To this day, the General Electric Company is a leading producer of electrical and electronic systems and equipment, including light bulbs. Edison never controlled the Edison General Electric Company, since the amount of capital required to develop the electrical and lighting industry necessitated the involvement of investment bankers, such as J. P. Morgan, and financiers such as Vanderbilt.

In November 1887, Edison moved his research and development team to a new facility in West Orange, New Jersey. He began working on the phonograph, which project he had set aside when developing the electric light bulb in the late 1870s. By 1890, Edison was manufacturing phonographs for both home and business. He also developed the entire system to make the phonograph work, including the records, equipment to record sound on the records, and equipment to manufacture both the records and the phonographs. Edison used cylindrical paraffin records to produce sound, but in later years the circular recording disk was developed, putting Edison out of the record business. Regarding movies, Edison also developed the complete system needed to both make movies and to show motion pictures, and in 1913 introduced the first talking movies. By 1918, the motion picture industry, which he was instrumental in creating, became so competitive that Edison got out of this business altogether.

On June 8, 1903, Thomas Alva Edison signed an agreement with his son, Thomas A. Edison, Jr., whereby Edison's son agreed not to use his own name in a business enterprise in exchange for a weekly allowance of $35.

One of the commentators relied upon during my research noted that the public, in the latter part of the 19th century, looked upon the developments of scientific technology as a source of hope, not with distrust. This commentator felt that the positive public attitude garnered toward the power of science and technology as a result of Edison's work, among others, is one of the most important legacies to emanate from the technological developments of that era.

In 1884, Edison's first wife Mary passed away, leaving him with three small children. He married Mina Miller in 1886. Thomas Alva Edison died in West Orange, New Jersey, on October 18, 1931. Today, he has truly attained folk hero status thanks to his inventions.

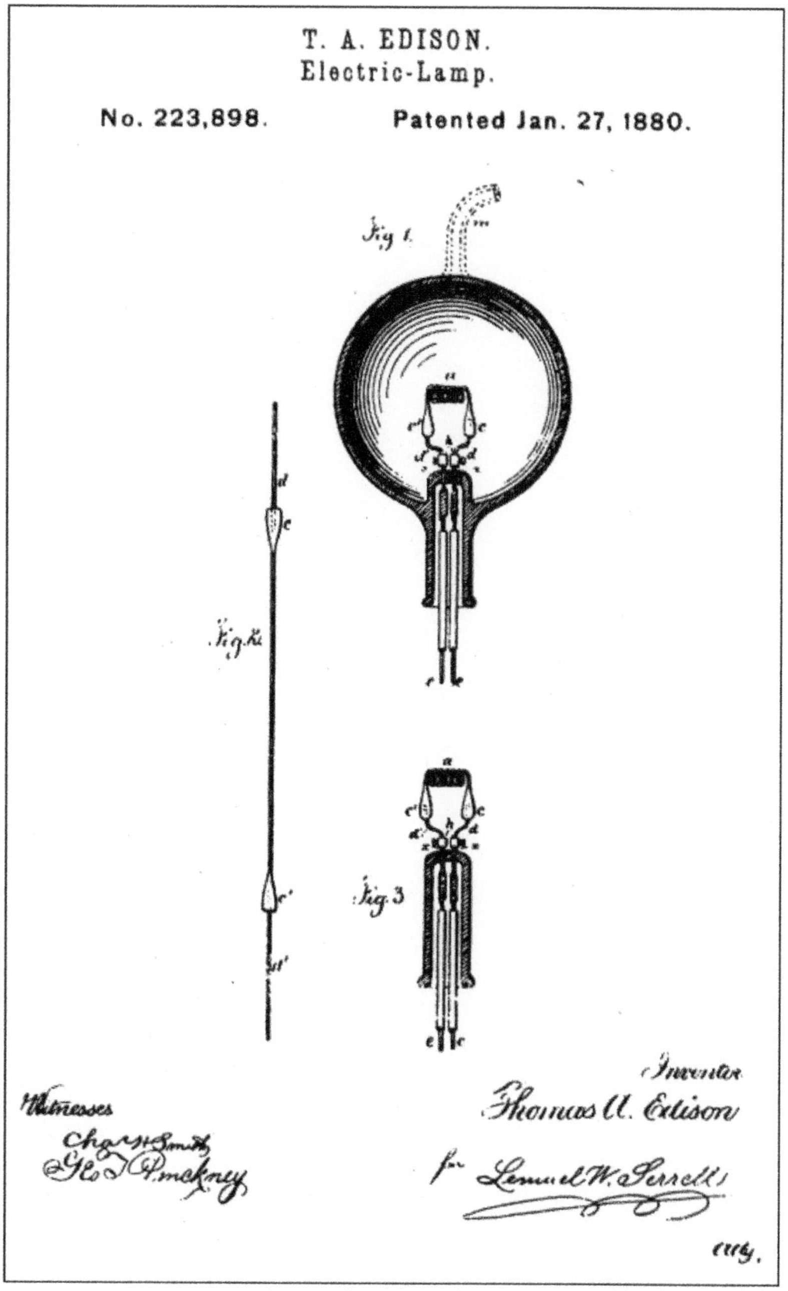
T. A. EDISON.
Electric-Lamp.
No. 223,898.
Patented Jan. 27, 1880.
Fig. 1
Fig. 3
Witnesses
Inventor
Thomas A. Edison

9 The Patent Application

9.1 INTRODUCTION

This chapter discusses the information that goes into a properly prepared patent application, enabling you to adequately review an application covering your invention when it is presented for your review and comments prior to filing the application. One of the important aspects of the Patent Law is that an inventor should carefully review his or her patent application for correctness and completeness before it is filed with the U.S. Patent and Trademark Office. This chapter also briefly summarizes the history of patent application content leading to the present system and its requirements for a properly filed application. Also discussed are the goals intended to be met in the preparation of a properly prepared application, the use of provisional patent applications, and how to conduct a rigid review of a patent application covering your invention.

9.2 REGISTRATION SYSTEM EVOLVING INTO AN EXAMINATION SYSTEM

You will recall from earlier chapters that from the year 1793 until 1836, there was no patent examination system in the United States, and inventors were merely required to furnish the government with a description of their invention, and the government would then register that explanation. This procedure caused immense difficulty when infringers were brought to court, and the court had the burden of determining just what the inventor was claiming as his or her invention, without any direct statement in the registration certificate that defined the novel point or points of the invention. Thus, the courts had no knowledge of the prior art against which the novelty of the "invention" could be measured.

This system changed in 1836, owing to the efforts primarily of Senator John Ruggles of Maine. Congress created a Patent Office and an examination system, and inventors were required not only to describe their invention in their applications for a patent, they had to specifically set forth what it was they were urging as novel over the prior art. The requirements of the system today are basically the same as established in 1836, even as the level of technology has increased approximately one hundred fold. One of my favorite tests to measure advances in technology between 1836 and the

Intellectual Property Law for Engineers, Scientists, and Entrepreneurs, Second Edition. Howard B. Rockman.

Published 2020 by John Wiley & Sons, Inc.

present is to determine how fast a human being could possibly travel in 1836 using any means possible, for example, a horse, and how fast a human being can travel today using any means possible, for example, an orbiting space shuttle. The answer may stagger your imagination.

9.3 GOAL OF A PROPERLY PREPARED PATENT APPLICATION

On the basis of historical development, the patent application today must clearly and completely include a specification that sets forth a complete and proper description of the invention, and claims that specifically define the scope of patent protection sought by the inventor. The patent application also must result in an issued patent that will advise and inform the public of the strict definitions of the metes and bounds of the technology protection you have obtained from the government. Competitors must be able to easily ascertain what they can produce and what they cannot produce in view of the patent fence that has been erected through your patent. The patent application specification must also describe each important detail of the structure and at least one cycle of operation of your invention. The claims must also define your invention beyond the state of the prior art. Your patent is ultimately a technical paper advising posterity of the advance in technology embodied in your invention. Remember, the history of the patent laws stresses that the 20-year exclusive position in your invention is granted as consideration for the full and complete disclosure of your invention to the public for use after your patent rights expire.

In my law school course, where I teach students on track to become patent attorneys, I begin my lecture on patent application preparation by indicating that the application is basically a sales document, where you are selling the concept to the Patent Examiner that the application defines an invention, without question, and that the only issue for examination is to ensure that the invention has been adequately defined over the prior art in the claims.

The patent application itself, in general terms, consists initially of a statement of the field or art to which the invention pertains. This is followed by setting forth the problem which the invention is directed toward solving and a statement of how others have attempted to solve the same problem and failed. This is followed by stating that your invention will achieve certain advantages and results that are not achieved by the technology shown in the prior art, and this is followed by a statement, in summary form, of the specific structure, elements, and/or function of your invention which provide these advantages, objectives, and results.

Following the above in a patent application is a brief description of the various drawing views, where applicable, followed by a complete description of the invention, which sets forth in concise detail a description of the complete interrelated structure of the invention, referring only to important elements of the invention, followed by a description of at least one cycle of operation. This is followed by the all-important claims, which will be discussed separately in Chapter 10.

The above general "outline" for a patent application usually varies among some patent attorneys. For example, some patent applications are drafted without reference to advantages, results, or objectives. Whatever preparation technique was used to prepare your application, satisfy yourself upon your review that all aspects of your invention are clearly covered in the patent application.

9.4 PROVISIONAL PATENT APPLICATIONS

The U.S. Patent Laws were amended several years ago to allow the filing of provisional, or partially complete, patent applications to secure to the inventor a filing date prior to the time a complete patent application could be prepared, and requiring that the complete application be filed within one year from filing the provisional patent application. The purpose of the change in the law was to allow an inventor to establish a priority date as to his or her invention, without depending upon the workload, or the speed of preparation, of a patent attorney.

A provisional patent application can be filed without any claims, without any declaration of inventorship by the inventor or inventors, and without a disclosure of prior art know by the inventor. The provisional application is basically a "shorthand" way of filing your novel technical information with the USPTO, indicating that within one year you expect to file a regular, non-provisional patent application covering the same technology. The purpose of the provisional application is to "save the date." However, the provisional patent application cannot be too threadbare, since 35 U.S.C. §112 requires that the completeness of the invention described in a provisional application must also meet the standard of completeness of a regular, non-provisional application.

To place a provisional patent application on file with the USPTO, the inventor and/or his or her attorney file, among other things, a cover sheet that identifies the application as a provisional application, the identity of all the inventors usually in the form of an unsigned declaration setting forth the names and addresses of the inventors, and materials, usually furnished by the inventor, consisting of a description and drawings of the invention, which need not necessarily be in the form of a normal patent application. The description and the drawings must be sufficient to allow the Patent Examiner and the public to fully understand the invention, since within one year a regular patent application will be filed, and the provisional application will become part of the prosecution history available to the public upon issuance of the patent from the regular patent application. The provisional application material must include all of the technology you include in the claims of your regular, non-provisional patent application when the latter is filed.

I challenge the definition of a provisional patent application as being an "application," because the rules clearly state that no provisional application will be examined for patentability, nor will it ever be issued as a U.S. patent. It is more of a "statement" that provides an early priority date if a regular, non-provisional patent application is subsequently filed within one year. Also, the priority period provided by the provisional application is not included in the 20 year term of enforceability of the patent counting from the date of filing the regular application. Note further that provisional patent applications cannot be filed for design inventions.

The term "Patent Pending" may be used in connection with inventions that are the subject of provisional patent applications. Since 12 months after the filing of the provisional application the application and your priority date automatically lapse if a non-provisional application is not filed, it is important to file the regular non-provisional patent application within that 12-month period or you will lose your priority filing date. It is possible to file a second provisional patent application describing the same invention as the first one, but the second provisional application cannot claim the priority date of the first provisional patent application.

9.5 REGULAR, NON-PROVISIONAL PATENT APPLICATION; NO NEW MATTER

As you probably have discerned by now, a patent application is a series of documents filed with the USPTO with the objective of ensuring that the application proceeds successfully through an examination process and ultimately is issued as a patent. The most important thing to keep in mind when reviewing your application prior to filing, and in furnishing your patent attorney with information about your invention, is that once the application is filed with the USPTO, amendments can be made to the application during the examination process only within the framework of the material in the application as originally filed. There is a very strict rule that prohibits the introduction of "new matter" into any pending patent application. New matter is defined as any subject matter that is not described, shown, or suggested in the four corners of the patent application as first filed. Thus, by way of example, if the inventor develops a new embodiment or an additional improvement to the invention covered by the filed patent application, that new material covering the new embodiment or additional improvement cannot be placed in the pending patent application. A new patent application, designated a "continuation-in-part application," which will be described in Chapter 11, can be filed to cover the new material related to the invention. As such, the inventor will ultimately end up with two or possibly more patents. Therefore, it is important when assisting the patent attorney preparing your patent application, that all of the subject matter relating to your invention, including all new material, improvements, and new advantages, be disclosed to him or her for inclusion in the originally filed application, to the extent possible.

It is also important that you provide the patent attorney with full knowledge of a completely conceived invention, the best mode contemplated for practicing the invention, and sufficient information to enable one skilled in the art to practice the invention without undue experimentation upon expiration of the patent. As stated previously, it is also important to provide your patent attorney with all prior art of which you are aware. The attorney may introduce some of the prior art in the body of the patent application itself in describing prior attempts at solutions to the same problem which your invention is directed toward solving.

9.6 CONTENT OF A REGULAR NON-PROVISIONAL PATENT APPLICATION

When working with your patent attorney, you will be asked to assist in the preparation of the application by initially furnishing all information relating to the structure, operation, and advantages of your invention. There are many ways of describing an invention; however, over the years and aided by court decisions as to what the content of a patent application should be, and having the USPTO codify rules as to what they expect in a patent application, a somewhat definitive content of a patent application has developed over the last 225 years or so of the U.S. Patent System. As a result, most patent attorneys today use a similar "format" in preparing their patent applications. While this format may vary from case to case, the following sets forth the most acceptable way of presenting your material to the Patent Examiner in the judgment of the author.

9.6.1 Title of the Invention

The title of the invention should broadly describe the purpose of the invention, or the structure of the invention. Thus, the title could be "Apparatus for Preheating Engine Blocks" or "Process for Detasseling Corn," or something similar. Note that the USPTO website lists patents owned by inventors, corporations, and other entities by their title and patent number, which enables easier searching for relevant patents if the title is descriptive of the disclosed invention to a certain degree.

9.6.2 Cross-Reference to Other Applications

In many instances, your patent application will be a continuation, continuation-in-part, or division of a previously filed related patent application, discussed in Chapter 11, or claiming priority to previously filed provisional patent application. To properly establish the chain of the parent patent application(s) in your present application, it is necessary to place a statement in your current patent application referring to these earlier applications of which the present application is a family member. This sets forth the continuity of these patent applications, and allows later filed patent applications to rely upon the earlier filing date of the parent application as a priority filing date for commonly disclosed subject matter.

It is important to note that patent applications that have not issued as patents are maintained in secrecy for 18 months after filing. After 18 months from filing of the earliest application, such as a provisional, for example, the patent application, as originally filed is published on the USPTO website. If the applicant does not want the application published, they must advise the USPTO that they will not be filing foreign patent applications directed to the same invention, and the application is not published. If the applicant changes its mind about filing corresponding foreign patent applications, the USPTO is so notified, and the patent application is published on the USPTO website shortly thereafter. When a patent does issue, any abandoned or previously identified patent application mentioned in the specification of that issued patent becomes available for public scrutiny.

9.6.3 Background of the Invention

9.6.3.1 Definition of the Field of the Invention

This portion of the specification comprises a very brief statement of the area of technology of the invention in general terms. Usually, a broad statement of the related art, followed by a specific statement identifying a particular branch or subdivision of the art to which the invention relates, is set forth. A statement as to the utility of the invention is usually also included.

9.6.3.2 Brief Description of the Problems That Exist in the Prior Art That the Invention is Directed Toward Solving

This portion of the patent application describes the problems which your invention is directed toward solving, followed by statements describing the content of a few closely related known prior art references that represent attempts by others to solve the same or similar problems in the past. The prior art is described, in brief terms, as what is disclosed in the reference patents or literature, followed by brief statements as to specific limitations or disadvantages of the prior art in terms of your invention, that is, what the prior art does *not* disclose. This indicates to the reader of the patent the specific problems in the related prior art that were not solved, and which your invention is directed toward solving.

The discussion of prior art in this portion of the application is in addition to any prior art statement (Information Disclosure Statement or IDS) that is submitted to the USPTO pursuant to Rule 56 (37 C.F.R. 1.56). The IDS lists prior art that the Patent Examiner is required to consider during examination, and should not be substituted for the portion of the patent application specification setting forth the content and shortcomings of specific prior art references. The language chosen in this portion of the patent application should emphasize the *advantages* of your invention over the prior art, and set forth the problems that remain unsolved by the prior art and which problems your invention solves.

9.6.3.3 The Results, Objectives, and Advantages of the Invention Not Achieved by the Prior Art

The next portion of the patent specification sets forth the results, advantages, and objectives sought to be obtained by your invention. At this stage of the application, these objectives, advantages, and results are stated without describing the structure or elements of the invention by which these results are obtained, or the function of the invention. As discussed in Chapter 10, the claims of the patent application are directed to defining the structure, steps, or elements of your invention, and the function of these elements; the portion of the specification referred to now sets forth the objectives, advantages, and results of using the elements, steps, and functions set forth in the claims. Conversely, the claims do not recite results. While the claims are intended to describe what the invention is, your statement of objects, advantages, and results is intended to describe what the invention accomplishes. These are statements of the broad aims to be achieved by the invention that are not achieved by the prior art.

The entire background portion of the specification is what I refer to as "the sales pitch" of the patent application. This is where you explain the differences between your invention's objectives and the prior art, set forth the advantages of your invention over the prior art, and inform the reader of the problems your invention solves. This is the portion of the patent specification that will be referred to during the examination stage to convince the Patent Examiner that the only issue is the scope of the claims, not whether or not the application sets forth inventive subject matter. Well-thought-out statements of objectives and results help the examiner reach this intended result.

9.6.4 Brief Summary of the Important Elements of the Invention

This section of the patent application specification includes a brief summary of the invention, setting forth its elements and function, and immediately precedes the description of the drawings and the illustrated embodiments of the invention. The summary should set out the exact nature, operation, and purpose of the invention, and usually paraphrases the subject matter of the broadest claim. The summary of the invention is normally concise and reasonably general, and usually contains references to structure to enable the reader to understand the nature of the invention from the summary.

9.6.5 Brief Description of the Drawings That Illustrate the Invention

When drawings are submitted with the patent application, this portion of the specification sets forth a brief series of indented subparagraphs comprising descriptions for each figure shown. These subparagraphs are extremely brief, and specify information allowing the reader to determine what view of the invention they are looking at. The drawings are usually described in terms of perspective, plan, elevation, section, fragmentary, schematic, or exploded views. As stated before, in many chemical patent applications, no drawings are submitted with the application.

9.6.6 Detailed Description of the Illustrated Embodiment of the Invention

This is the longest section of the specification of the patent application, and comprises a detailed description of the invention's structure and interrelated functions of the structural elements, followed normally by a description of one cycle of operation of the structure, where there is a cycle of operation. For example, compositions of matter do not have an operation to describe, except probably the method of making the composition. The description of the invention in this portion of the specification also describes the interrelationship between each of the elements of the invention, and their cooperation with each other. The description of the invention, as mentioned previously, must be set forth with such particularity to enable any person skilled in the art to make and use the claimed invention without undue experimentation once the patent expires. Since the extent of the knowledge of those skilled in the art varies from art to art, the level of detail varies from patent application to patent application. However, any doubt as to the amount of detail which should be included in the description of the invention should be resolved by adding detail. Remember that once the patent application is filed, no new matter can be added to the specification. Therefore, it is important to include all material elements and functions in the patent specification as initially written.

Normally, in describing a mechanical or electrical invention, the structure is defined in a logical way, usually from an input to an output, or from a base upward as in describing the construction of the invention. In the chemical field, detailed descriptions include a wide range of specific examples or embodiments of the invention, as well as all known equivalents of the specific elements of the invention. In non-chemical cases, the detailed description need only cover one specific embodiment of the invention; however, it is preferable that alternative embodiments of the invention be set forth in the specification to advise the reader of the issued patent that several embodiments of the invention are covered by the issued patent's claims.

Since there is a requirement, even after the AIA, that the detailed description of the patent application set forth the "best mode" of the invention contemplated by the inventor at the time the application is filed, you must ensure yourself that the best mode is set forth in the application. This requires that if you have performed additional work on the invention while the patent attorney was preparing the patent specification, you must add the additional material to the application after the application has been drafted and furnished to you for review and comment. Keep in mind that a "best mode" of the invention discovered one day after or at any time subsequent to the filing of the application is of no consequence. That "mode" can be covered in a subsequently filed continuation-in-part patent application.

The patent specification also points out features of the subject invention that produce the previously described advantages, and which comprise improvements over the prior art. This again is part of the "sales" presentation advising the Patent Examiner how the invention differs from past technology. The specification can also point out how your invention solves a long-standing problem or need in the prior art. This will reinforce the argument that the invention was not obvious to one skilled in the art.

Upon reviewing the patent application once it is completed by the patent attorney, satisfy yourself that the description of your invention is correct, complete, and is set forth in a logical, flowing manner. The description of the structure should be in an easy-to-understand format, and the statement of operation or function should also be logical, starting, for example, from an input and working through to the output, or from the beginning of the operation to the end.

Also, when reviewing the patent application submitted to you by the patent attorney, determine whether you believe that the Patent Examiner, when he or she reads the application, will determine instantaneously that there is an invention described in the patent application. Also, ensure that the patent attorney has adequately defined all of the novel features of your invention.

To obtain a filing date for the patent application, it must be filed with the USPTO with at least one claim, all the pages of the specification, and all the drawings. If any one of these elements is omitted, no filing date will be assigned to the application.

If you determine from reading the prior art obtained through a pre-filing patentability search that the Patent Examiner may make an argument of lack of novelty, or obviousness based on the prior art, the patent application specification should anticipate these arguments and furnish rebuttal information in the specification itself. Therefore, when reviewing the patent application, be sure that you understand the differences between your invention and the disclosures of the prior art of which you are aware.

In the patent specification, technical details such as dimensions, angles, materials of construction, circuit components, values, and the like may be omitted, unless they are critical to the novelty or understanding of the invention. However, all details critical to the practice of the invention must be set forth. Again, my recommendation is to err on the side of inclusion if you cannot determine the essentiality of all details. Also, remember that if your issued patent is ultimately subjected to enforcement in a court of law, the ultimate reader of the patent may be a federal judge and/or jury who have no technical knowledge whatsoever. Therefore, when reviewing the patent application, review it from the standpoint that some day a nontechnical person may have to determine the scope and content of the invention described in the issued patent.

The specification must also include sufficient information to enable a person skilled in the art to make and use the invention. If it is found that the specification is not complete, or describes an inoperable invention, the issued patent ultimately could be held to be unenforceable. It has been my experience that a properly prepared patent application is a finite merger of proper technical disclosure and description, and excellent and artful use of the English language, all applied to technology.

The description portion of the patent specification concludes with a general statement of intent not to restrict the invention to the precise embodiments described, but to have the patent cover any device or process that falls within the scope of the claims that are ultimately allowed by the Patent Examiner.

9.6.7 Claims Distinctly and Precisely Pointing Out the Definition of the Invention

As a preface to Chapter 10, which discusses patent claims in detail, it suffices to say that the claims of a patent application should be written broadly enough to cover any competing device or process that may be marketed in the future, and at the same time narrowly enough so they do not cover, or "read on," the prior art. The construction of the claims usually turns on the combined efforts of the inventor and the patent attorney, working in conjunction to ensure that the fine line of invention over the prior art is adequately and precisely defined.

9.6.8 The Abstract

The USPTO rules require that the patent application include an "Abstract of the Invention" of not more than 150 words, briefly describing the novel features of the invention. The Abstract is reprinted on the first page of the issued patent, which is normally called the Information Page. The purpose of the Abstract is to provide the reader with the "heart" of your invention in a few concise sentences. Usually, the patent attorney will divide the broadest claim of the patent application into a series of short sentences, which eliminate the "legalese" of the broad claim. By reading the Abstract, one reviewing the issued patent should be able to decide if they desire to read further.

It is important that the Abstract be worded with the same degree of care as the rest of the patent application. In at least one reported decision, the Court of Appeals of the Federal Circuit (CAFC) has referred to the Abstract in deciding to limit the scope of claim coverage of a patent.

9.7 YOUR REVIEW OF THE PATENT APPLICATION

Once the patent application is prepared by the patent attorney, the application is forwarded to the inventor for the inventor's review and comment. Once the application is correct in all details, the inventor signs a Declaration or Oath, wherein the inventor declares that he or she believes himself or herself to be the first original and sole or joint inventors of the subject matter of the application.

Upon reviewing your completed patent application, you must ensure that the invention has been adequately and broadly described, and that the claims adequately cover the invention to the extent permitted by the content of the prior art. If, upon your review, you determine that a competitor can "design around" your broad claims, advise your patent attorney, who will suggest adding even broader claims to the application to cover your "design around" embodiment. I refer to this analysis as having the inventor assume the role of "devil's advocate" vis-à-vis the claims of the patent application.

I advise my clients that we, as patent attorneys, have no pride of authorship, and therefore the inventor can make any and all additions, changes, or comments they deem necessary. If the patent attorney concludes that certain of these recommended changes by the inventor may add limitations to the patent application rather than broadening the scope, he or she will then discuss these proposed changes with the inventor.

Ultimately, once the patent application is approved by both the inventor and the patent attorney, the formal documents supporting the application are signed, and the application is filed with the USPTO to await examination.

9.8 EXECUTION OF THE DECLARATION, POWER OF ATTORNEY, AND ASSIGNMENT UPON COMPLETION OF THE PATENT APPLICATION

Upon completion of the review of your patent application, including the claims, which are covered in detail in Chapter 10, documents commonly known as the "formal papers" are completed and furnished to the USPTO along with the application. These papers constitute a Declaration (or Oath) that the inventor or inventor(s) sign, as described in Section 9.7.

Where the patent application has been prepared by a patent attorney or agent who will be responsible for the continued prosecution of the application through examination by the USPTO, a Power of Attorney form is executed by the inventor(s), providing the attorney or agent with the power to prosecute the application further on behalf of the inventor(s) or the applicant, such as the inventor's employer.

If the invention is to be owned by a corporation or other entity or group of entities other than the inventor or inventors, an Assignment document is also signed by the inventors, granting all rights, title and interest, or portions thereof, of the invention and patent application to the assignee. The Assignment document, the formal papers, and the patent application are then submitted to the USPTO with the appropriate government filing fee. The Assignment document is recorded by the USPTO, and returned to your attorney.

An Application Data Sheet (ADS) is also filed with the application, identifying the title of the invention, the names and mailing address and country of residence of each inventor, correspondence information of the attorney or agent representing the inventor(s), prior patent applications related to the application being filed or upon which priority is based, foreign priority information, if applicable, and other information regarding the application. In addition, under the AIA and 37 CFR §1.605, it is now possible to designate as the applicant in the ADS the employer or other entity to whom the inventor(s) have assigned the invention, or to whom the inventor(s) are obligated to assign the invention pursuant to a contract or an employment agreement (the employment agreement is considered as a contract) or to a person who otherwise shows sufficient proprietary interest in the invention. The ADS is signed by the patent attorney or agent when completed.

In addition, to comply with the provision of the USPTO rules that the inventor and the inventor's attorney must submit all material prior art that they are aware of to the Patent Examiner, it is normal practice for the patent attorney to prepare and file with the patent application, or shortly thereafter, an IDS, which lists all prior art known by the applicant and the attorney, for consideration by the Patent Examiner. The IDS consists of:

1. A list of all relevant U.S. patents and U.S. patent application publications known by the applicant and attorney for consideration by the Patent Examiner.

2. A legible copy of each foreign patent or patent application publication or portions thereof, and a legible copy of other literature information identified in the IDS.
3. An explanation of the relevance of any patent publication or other information not in the English language, and a copy of any translation of same if in the inventor(s) or attorney's possession.

All the above formal documents are submitted to the USPTO along with the completed patent application to initiate the examination process. The IDS can also be submitted to the Patent Examiner at any time prior to the initial examination, without monetary penalty. Also, the inventor and the inventor's attorney have a continuing obligation to submit material prior art they become aware of to the Patent Examiner up to the date the patent issues. This is an important point to remember, and cannot be stressed enough.

Your patent attorney will advise you that certain applicants may qualify for reduced government filing fees as "small entities" or "micro entities," and what the criteria are for qualifying for the reduced fees. If the applicant(s) so qualify, the status of the applicant is provided with the initial information furnished to the USPTO when the patent application is filed.

◆ INVENTORS AND INVENTIONS ◆

George Eastman

PRACTICAL PHOTOGRAPHY

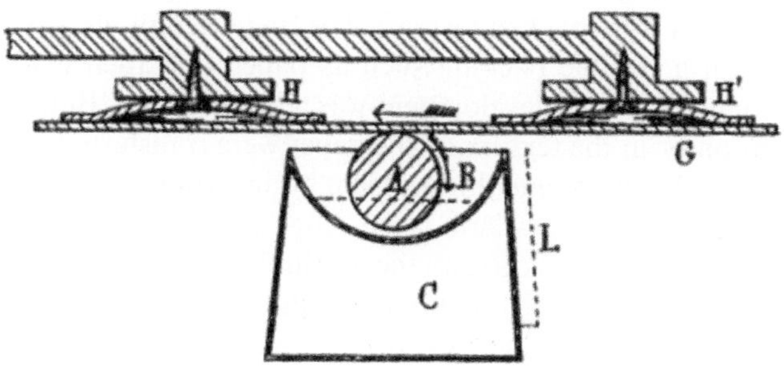

George Eastman is responsible for making photography practical, widely available, and more convenient, since his invention made it possible to take a camera anywhere. He was born on July 12, 1854, in the same house in which his father was born in the village of Waterville, New York. When George was five, his family moved to Rochester, New York, where his oldest sibling established the Eastman Commercial College. When the college failed and George's father died, the family became financially unstable.

George quit school at the age of fourteen to start working to support the family. He had several jobs working at insurance firms and the Rochester Savings Bank, and his pay ranged from three to fifteen dollars per week. When Eastman was twenty-four, he made plans to take a trip to Santo Domingo. Following a suggestion from a coworker at the bank, Eastman bought a photographic outfit equipped with all the supplies needed for wet-plate photography. His camera was as big as a sewing machine and required a heavy tripod as a support. He also purchased plate holders, chemicals, tanks, and a tent, all of which were necessary to be able to apply photosensitive emulsion on glass plates, expose the emulsion, and then develop the images before the emulsion dried. This amounted to approximately 50 pounds of equipment. Eastman said that the equipment "was a packhorse load."

After all this, Eastman did not make the trip, but he was enticed to find an easier way to take pictures. In 1877, after reading in British journals about photographers creating their own dry gelatin emulsions, which meant that even after the plates became dry they were still sensitive to light, Eastman decided he would do the same. Beginning with a formula he obtained from one of the British journals, he worked on creating his

Intellectual Property Law for Engineers, Scientists, and Entrepreneurs, Second Edition. Howard B. Rockman.

Published 2020 by John Wiley & Sons, Inc.

own gelatin emulsions almost nonstop. After three years of working in the bank during the day, and experimenting in his mother's kitchen at night, he came up with a formula for dry plates that worked, and by 1880 he had obtained patents covering both his formula and a machine that prepared large numbers of plates.

Eastman leased a floor of a building in Rochester in April 1880 to begin manufacturing his dry plates for sale. His company prospered and grew, but faced a downturn at least once when plates went bad in the hands of dealers and Eastman recalled them and replaced the faulty plates with good ones. This recall was costly, but it greatly enhanced Eastman's reputation.

In 1884, Eastman started working on ways to make a photographic film lighter than the dry plates that were backed by glass. His first attempt was to put the photographic emulsion on a flexible backing such as paper, and then load it into a roll holder. Despite some flaws, this development was a huge success. But, Eastman found that imperfections on or in the texture of the paper were transferred to the developed image. He then decided to eliminate this problem by applying a soluble layer of gelatin over the insoluble light-sensitive gelatin layer. After development, the soluble gelatin layer bearing the image was lifted off, and the insoluble layer was transferred to a sheet of clear gelatin and varnished with collodion, a cellulose mixture that hardened into a rigid, transparent film. His development of transparent roll film and a roll holder resulted in the introduction of the Kodak® Camera in 1888, the first camera built to hold roll film. Film rolls capable of holding 100 pictures were loaded in the camera. After exposure, the entire camera and film were sent back to Eastman's company, where the film was developed, the camera was reloaded and returned to the customer, all for $25.00.

A year later, Eastman created flexible transparent film, which proved vital to the development of the motion picture industry. In 1892, he established the Eastman Kodak Company at Rochester, New York. In 1900, the Kodak Brownie became the first roll-film, hand-held camera.

George Eastman was also very generous with the fortune he earned, donating in excess of $75 million to a multitude of projects. He endowed the Eastman School of Music in 1918 and the University of Rochester School of Medicine and Dentistry in 1921. He also gave $20 million to the Massachusetts Institute of Technology.

On one day in 1924, George Eastman donated $30 million to the University of Rochester, M.I.T., Hampton Institute, and Tuskegee Institute. The latter two were schools for African-American students, whose education was a particular concern of George Eastman.

Near the end of his life, Eastman became quite ill and became progressively disabled as a result of hardening of the cells in his lower spinal cord. He died at age 77 of his own hand on March 14, 1932.

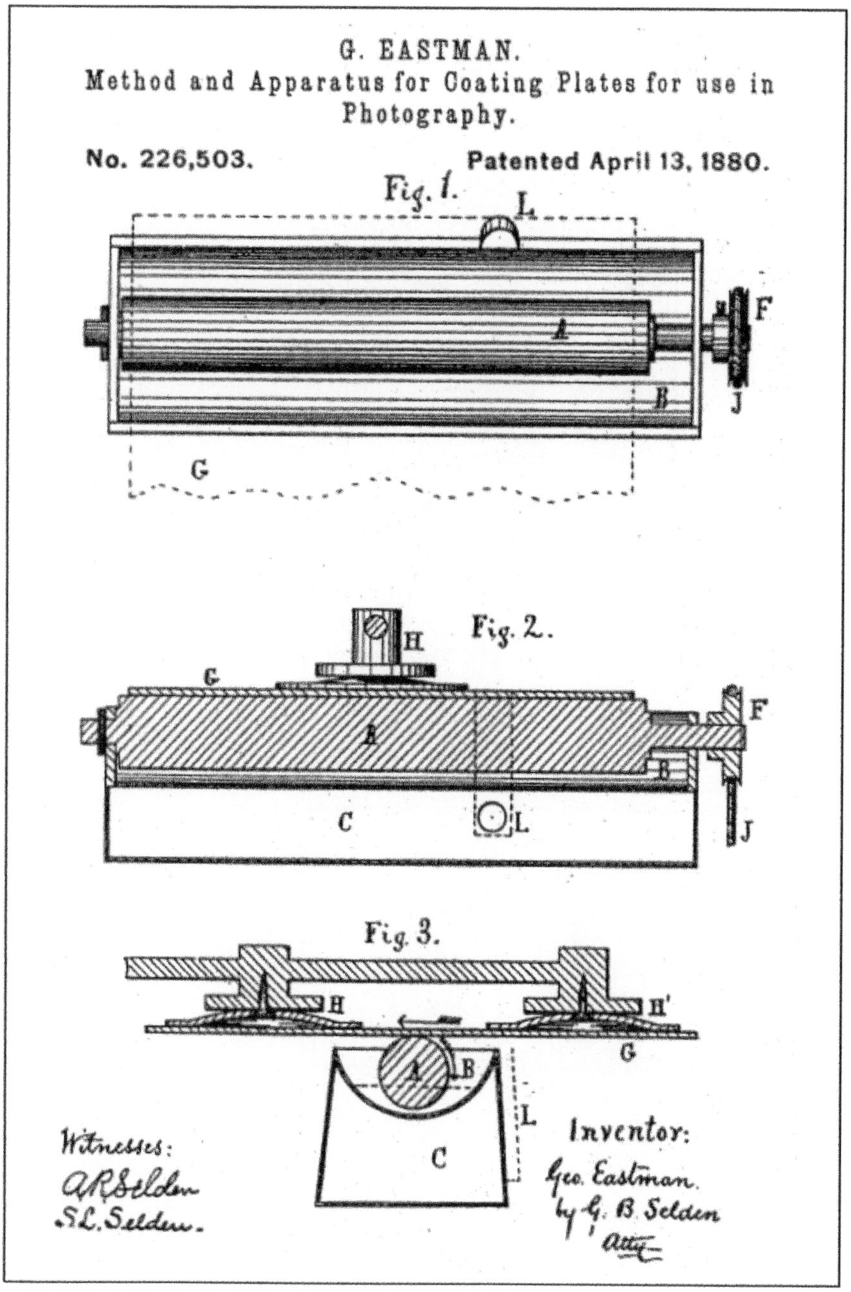
G. EASTMAN.
Method and Apparatus for Coating Plates for use in Photography.
No. 226,503.
Patented April 13, 1880.
Fig. 1.
L
F
A
B
J
G
Fig. 2.
H
G
A
F
B
C
L
J
Fig. 3.
H
H'
G
A
B
L
C
Witnesses:
A R Selden
S.L. Selden
Inventor:
Geo. Eastman
by G. B. Selden
Atty

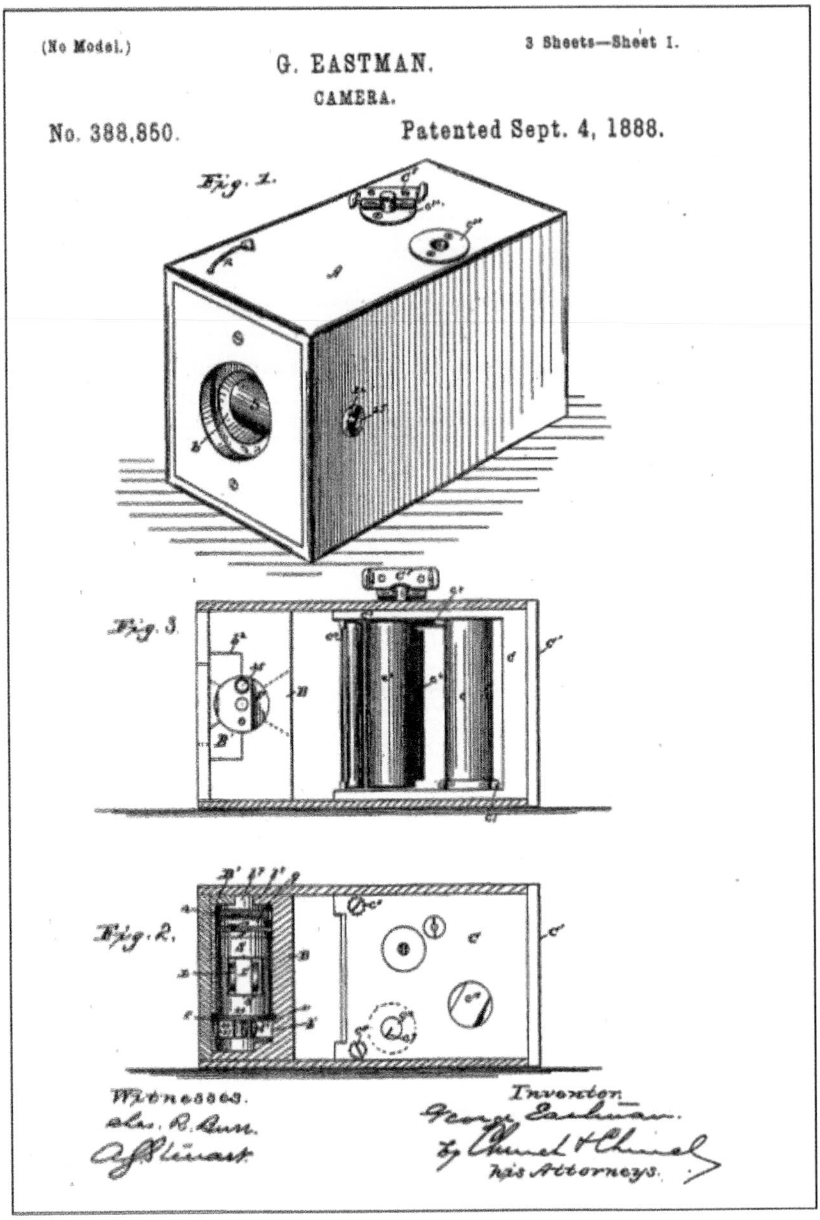

(No Model.)
3 Sheets—Sheet 1.
G. EASTMAN.
CAMERA.
No. 388,850.
Patented Sept. 4, 1888.
Fig. 1.
Fig. 3.
Fig. 2.
Witnesses.
Inventor.
his Attorneys.

◆ INVENTORS AND INVENTIONS ◆

Emile Berliner

DISC SOUND RECORDING

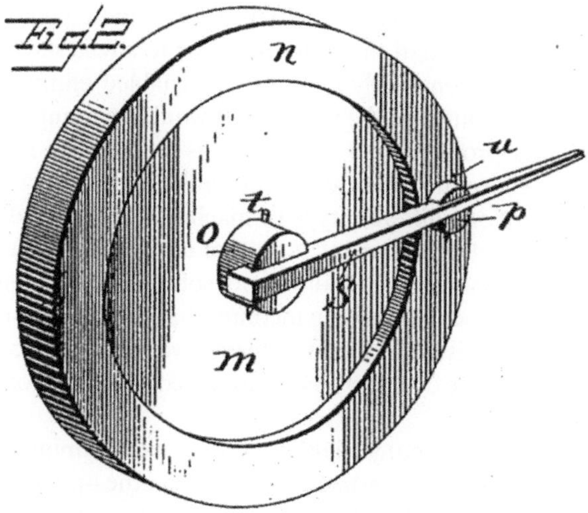

During the 1880s a contest developed between Thomas Edison and Volta Laboratory, a research laboratory founded by Alexander Graham Bell, where Bell's cousin, Chichester A. Bell, and Charles Sumner Tainter worked on improving the phonograph that Edison had developed in 1877. The contest was directed toward transforming Edison's 1877 tin foil phonograph, or talking machine, into a device capable of taking its place alongside the typewriter as a business correspondence device. The contest involved, among other things, finding a substance to replace tin foil as a recording medium.

By the beginning of 1887, both sides in the contest announced the invention of a machine using a wax cylinder that would be incised vertically to match the sound vibrations. The same machine used to make the recording would be used for playback. Edison defined his wax cylinder apparatus a "phonograph." C.A. Bell and Tainter named their apparatus a "graphophone." Neither machine was much of a success. The phonograph did not succeed as a dictating device, so Edison's company began to market pre-recorded wax cylinders of popular music that could be played in the office or home, or even in coin slot machines in arcades, saloons, and elsewhere.

Intellectual Property Law for Engineers, Scientists, and Entrepreneurs, Second Edition. Howard B. Rockman.

Published 2020 by John Wiley & Sons, Inc.

Tainter made improvements to the Volta graphophone, and his team also entered the entertainment field. Both sides of the contest had applied for a patent on the vertical cutting or incising of sound vibrations into a wax cylinder, and both sides made recordings on phonograph cylinders that could be played on the graphophone and phonograph.

Meanwhile, Emile Berliner in Washington D.C. began examining in detail both the phonograph and the graphophone to learn the advantages and disadvantages of each. He soon came to the conclusion that the wax recording cylinder was too soft and fragile to last as a permanent recording. A wax cylinder would wear out rapidly, so he sought a more durable substance. Also, the vertical cut, or hill and dale cut and grooves, were not deep enough to keep the stylus from skidding across the surface of the cylinder. The graphophone had the stylus attached to a feed screw that carried the stylus over the cylinder. A constantly deep groove enabled elimination of the feed screw, but something different from the vertical cut would be required. Soft wax cylinders could not be mass produced, so if recordings were to be widely distributed, another method of mass production of exact facsimiles was necessary.

Thus, there was a need for a different type of machine in the recording industry, one that did not use soft wax cylinders, one that did not use vertical cut grooves that were alternately deep with loud sounds and shallow with soft sounds, and one that employed a relatively hard and permanent recording medium that could be easily reproduced in large quantities. Both the Edison and Tainter teams eventually overcame many of the cylinder's defects; however, the cylinder record appeared already doomed to extinction by the flat disc record.

Emile Berliner went through many trials and errors in developing what he called the "gramophone." Early in his work, Berliner decided upon the disc format using the lateral vibration developed by Leon Scott in Scott's phonautograph. Scott had developed his machine in the 1850s for the sole purpose of visually recording vibrations of the voice so they could be studied by those involved in analyzing human speech. Scott's vibrations were made by speaking into the large end of a megaphone whose small end included a thin diaphragm that could freely vibrate. A thin brush attached to the diaphragm would make tiny tracks on blackened glass. These lateral vibrations could then be photographed and studied. Apparently, it never occurred to Scott or anyone else at the time that if these tiny tracks could be fixed, and the stylus passed through the tracks, the reverse process would take place and sounds would be reproduced through the large end of the megaphone.

Starting with Scott's phonautograph, Berliner first tried to replicate the thin tracing Scott made on blackened glass on a sturdier substance through a photoengraving process. Berliner was unaware that this was a practice that had been previously advanced by a Frenchman, Charles Cros, in a paper written in April 1877 and deposited with the French Academy. In this paper, Cros for the very first time, stated a theory for recording and reproducing sound. However, Cros never acted upon his theory. Had he done so, he would have been the inventor of the talking machine and not Thomas Edison. Edison was never aware of Cros or his paper, and Edison's tin foil machine owed nothing to Cros' theory. Meanwhile, Berliner found that trying to photoengrave the surface of a glass disc led to problems, so he then turned to an etching process.

After attempting many different substances, Berliner turned to zinc. After many failed attempts, he developed a process for coating a zinc disc made from regular stone maker's zinc, with a beeswax and cold gasoline mixture. The coating was then cleared away with fine lines made by a stylus attached to a mica diaphragm so that it would vibrate. After coating the blank reverse side of the disc with varnish, the disc was immersed in an acid bath. After a certain time, the acid etched the fine lines into grooves on the zinc, leaving the remaining parts of the disc untouched. With the vibrations fixed into the zinc, the disc was able to be placed on a turntable, and the sound reproduced with a steel stylus.

Early disc records were made using this process. Berliner's method, however, required two machines, one for each process. As a name for the whole operation, the inventor coined the word "gramophone." His earlier patents on this device were No. 372,786 dated November 8, 1887, and No. 382,790 dated May 15, 1888. Berliner then faced the problem of finding a process to reproduce the master zinc record. First, the master had to be electroplated resulting in a metal reverse, or negative record, with grooves projecting outward instead of inward. The negative could then be used to stamp positive copies of a substance that would hold the impression exactly.

Berliner tried numerous substances, including Plaster of Paris and sealing wax, with unsatisfactory results. It then occurred to him that a new substance on the market called celluloid might provide the answer. Berliner contacted J.W. Hyatt, the inventor of celluloid, and Mr. Hyatt felt certain he could provide exact duplicates of Berliner's records. However, it soon became clear that the material could not withstand the pressure of repeated playings using big, hard steel needles under the full weight of tone arm and horn. Therefore, Berliner abandoned the celluloid process. If you locate an early celluloid disc today, you probably have a very rare and valuable item in your hands.

Berliner next began contacting manufacturers of hard rubber items. He found that warming the rubber made it possible to stamp copies of a zinc negative.

Berliner began marketing his gramophone in the early 1890s. The first samples of laterally cut disc records were issued in Germany, and not in the United States. In 1887, Berliner had obtained patents in both Germany and England for the gramophone. In 1889, he went to Germany to demonstrate his invention to German scientists. While visiting his native Hanover, he was approached by members of the firm of Kammerer and Reinhardt, a toy manufacturer in the town of Waltershausen, who offered to place small discs and small hand-turned machines on the toy market, and Berliner agreed. For several years, five inch Berliner Gramophone records were manufactured in Germany, and several were exported to England. Some of the first discs were made of celluloid, while the later discs were made in part of rubber. However, this was a very small operation.

Subsequently, Berliner returned to the United States and entered into an agreement with several New York investors, and they formed the American Gramophone Company. The company never got off the ground, and then Berliner organized the United States Gramophone Company in Washington, D.C. He stated that he formed the new company at the same time that he switched from celluloid to rubber discs. A patent application for the hard rubber discs was submitted to the U.S. Patent Office in 1893, and the rubber discs entered the market in 1894, the year following the application for the rubber records patent. Today, many consider that that creation of the United States Gramophone Company in Washington, D.C. in 1894 was the true beginning of the American record industry. Gramophone discs and machines reached rapid popularity. Until 1894, all available records were wax cylinders designed to be played on cylinder machines. These wax cylinders were easily broken and did not last long. Also, they could not be mass produced and could be copied only in limited numbers. Moreover, cylinders employed a vertical or hill and dale cut, and the machines had to have a feed screw attachment to prevent the reproducer stylus from jumping out of the grooves, and the feed screw easily came out of adjustment.

Berliner's disc record was made of hard rubber that was difficult to break and could be mass produced so that the discs could be widely marketed. His discs had a constant deep groove with sound vibrations on the walls; thus, the stylus could be lodged down into the groove, and the groove itself would pull the stylus with its attached tone arm and horn across the face of the disc. One other advantage was that the discs had a blank center area where the title, performer, and disc number could be etched, or a permanent paper label could be attached. The fact that the gramophone machine could not be used for making home recordings as a cylinder machine could does not seem to have had much effect on Berliner's invention's popularity with the public.

Soon after the beginning of the United States Gramophone Company, Berliner lost faith in rubber pressings. He then turned to the Duranoid Company, which made shellacked electrical parts. In 1895, Berliner sent Duranoid a nickel-plated stamper, and the company returned to him a shellac pressing that was in every way superior to the hard rubber pressings. By the middle of 1895, all Berliner discs were being made by Duranoid using the shellac process.

In 1896, Berliner licensed a group of businessmen to market and distribute his products. They formed the Berliner Gramophone Company of Philadelphia and hired Frank Seaman to organize the National Gramophone Company in New York to handle the distribution of the discs and machines. Recordings were made in Washington and Philadelphia and the stampers were made in the Washington laboratory, and pressings were made by Duranoid.

The major problem Berliner faced at this time was with the playback machines. Originally, these were hand turned. Spring motors were attached to some, but the springs were rather weak and required a high degree of power to rotate the gramophone with its heavy tone arm and horn, compared to a cylinder machine and its floating stylus. Berliner then began working with a machine shop owned by Eldridge Johnson in Camden, New Jersey, to manufacture machines with spring motors. Johnson eventually designed a gramophone using a spring driven turntable of his own design. The Johnson machine, while not entirely satisfactory, was the best that could be produced at the time.

On September 29, 1897, a tragedy occurred when the Washington Traction Company, where the laboratory of the Gramophone Company was located, burned to the ground. The Gramophone Company lost at least 100 zinc masters that had not been pressed, as well as all of its equipment. Everything had to be replaced.

During the late 1890s, the market for Berliner's discs began to expand into foreign countries. Berliner had obtained patents in Germany and England, and in the following years, patents were obtained in Italy, France, Belgium, and Austria. In April 1898, he formed the Berliner Gramophone Company of London. Two gentlemen were sent to Germany to form a German branch with the main office in Hanover. Eventually, there were gramophone companies in all the major countries of Europe including Russia. Berliner's sons, Herbert and Edgar, opened the Berliner Gramophone Company of Montreal, Canada, in 1899. Subsequently, after Berliner lost his fight against illegal competitors, the Berliner name was gradually dropped from each corporation so that, for instance, the London branch became simply the Gramophone Company.

In 1898, the first of illegal recordings generated by the financial success of Berliner's invention hit the market. Records made by the Standard Talking Machine Company were simply copies of Berliner records, but with the number "1" added to the disc number. This obvious infringement of Berliner's patents was soon halted. In 1899, a more serious challenge arose when advertisements appeared for the Vitaphone Disc and Machine made by the American Talking Machine under rights from the Graphophone Company. However, the lawyers for the Berliner Gramophone Company pointed out that the graphophone patents covered vertical cuts, while the Vitaphone's lateral cuts were an infringement of Berliner's patents. The Vitaphone operation was subsequently shut down, but not until a large number of records were sold.

Finally came the Zonophone made by Universal Talking Machine Company. It was disclosed that Universal's president was O.D. LaDelow, who was at the same time secretary and general manager of the National Gramophone Company, and that Frank Seaman, president of National, was also an executive of Universal. This was perceived by Berliner as a betrayal of the Gramophone Company's interests, and the Philadelphia organization refused to send Seaman and LaDelow any more records or machines. Seaman's lawyer brought suit claiming that by its 1896 contract, the Philadelphia organization was legally obliged to continue to supply National with discs and machines. Despite Seaman's and LaDelow's extra-legal methods, which included issuing original Berliner discs with all identifying information except the title erased and exchanging the Gramophone Company label pasted onto Johnson's machines for one reading "the Zonophone," in June 1900 a court miraculously issued an injunction that shut down the Berliner Gramophone Company of Philadelphia and left Emile Berliner with no way to operate his company. Attempts were made by Berliner over several years to overturn the injunction, but without success.

Berliner ultimately transferred his patent rights to the maker of the machine, Eldridge Johnson, who in 1900 formed the entirely new Consolidated Talking Machine Company at the same address as the defunct Berliner Gramophone Company of Philadelphia. Subsequently, Johnson changed the name of the company to "Manufactured by Eldridge Johnson" and then in 1901 he made a final name change to the Victor Talking Machine Company (RCA). He built a large plant in his native Camden, New Jersey, and Victor, a direct descendant of the Berliner Gramophone Company, became the largest and best-known record company in the world.

The word gramophone, like the word graphophone, was subsequently dropped in the United States in favor of the generic term phonograph. Until World War II, citizens of Great Britain and other countries continued to use the word gramophone for a disc record or disc machine. In the United States, the term gramophone is the basis of the term "Grammy," the annual music award presentation by the members of the Recording Academy.

Berliner's disc recordings were not superseded for almost 60 years, when manufacturing techniques were improved. Zinc masters were replaced by wax masters, the speed of disc revolution that varied in the early years finally settled down to approximately 78 rotations per minute, and in 1925 the electric recording process was developed. But until the development of stereo LP records, which employed Berliner's lateral cut combined with the cylinder's vertical cut, there was no basic change to what Berliner had begun to produce in 1894.

Berliner left one other legacy to the recording industry. In 1899, he visited the offices of the London branch of his company where he noticed a painting hanging on the wall, of a small dog with cocked head posed in front of the horn of Johnson's gramophone machine. The little terrier was listening to "his master's voice" coming from the horn. The painting had been created by English artist Francis Barraud, using his own dog Nipper as the model for the terrier. Berliner than contacted Barraud and asked him to make a copy of the painting. Berliner brought the copy back to the United States and immediately applied for a trademark registration for the painting. The trademark was granted by the U.S. Patent Office on July 10, 1900. It was too late for Berliner to use the mark; however, Berliner allowed the Montreal office to use the trademark, and he passed the mark on to Eldridge Johnson, who began to apply the mark on his Victor record catalogs and then on his paper labels on the disks. Then the Gramophone branches overseas adopted the mark, and shortly, "His master's voice" became one of the best-known trademarks and logos in the world. Therefore, if you are ever in a trivia contest, and the question is asked: "What is the name of the dog on the RCA record labels?" the answer is "Nipper."

(No Model.)

E. BERLINER.

GRAMOPHONE.

No. 372,786. Patented Nov. 8, 1887.

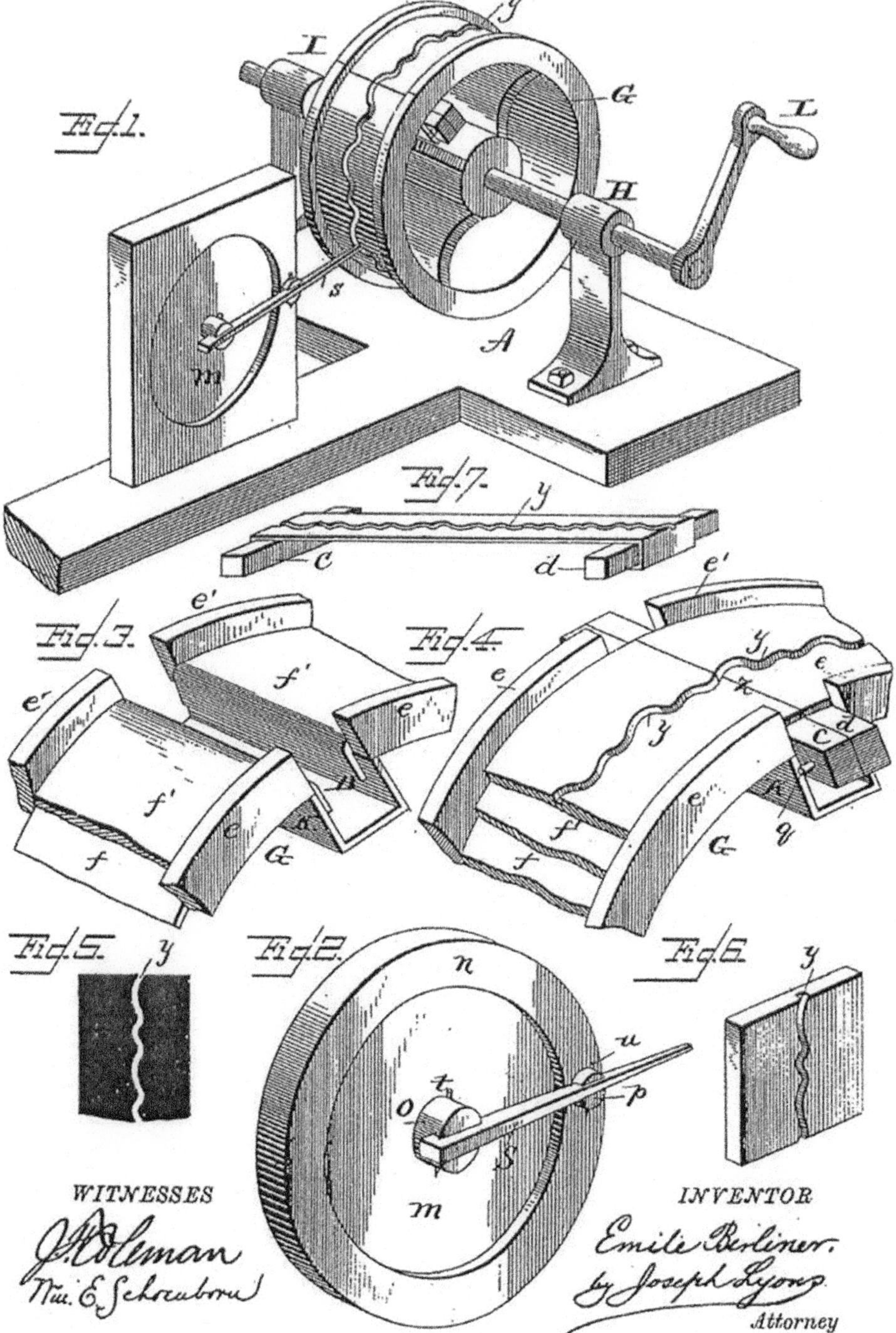

WITNESSES

J. K. Coleman

Wm. E. Schoenborn

INVENTOR

Emile Berliner,

by Joseph Lyons

Attorney

10 Claims of a Patent Application

10.1 INTRODUCTION TO PATENT CLAIMS

Upon completion of your patent application and prior to its filing with the U.S. Patent & Trademark Office (USPTO), your patent attorney will furnish you with a copy of the application for your review, comments, additions, and corrections. As you read the application, all goes well until you reach a series of numbered "paragraphs" at the end of the application. All of a sudden, you are reading English language statements that appear to be written by a patent attorney from a different planet. These numbered "paragraphs" are the "claims" of your patent application; they serve many purposes, the two primary among them being to define the limits where your invention transcends the prior art, and to provide notice to competitors and potential infringers of the exclusive territory you have fenced in by your patent grant upon issuance of your patent. In this chapter, we shall discuss the historical origin of these somewhat arcane claims, an explanation of what patent claims are, different types of claims, and most importantly, a short guide on how to read and understand the claims your patent attorney has drafted to cover your invention.

10.2 HISTORICAL DEVELOPMENT OF PATENT CLAIMS

The requirement of claims in patents and patent applications evolved from problems courts were having when trying to understand the novel features of the early patent "registration certificates" that resulted in a grant of exclusivity. Congress ultimately recognized the existence of this problem, and took steps to remedy the situation.

10.2.1 Court Decisions

As mentioned in Chapter 3, in 1790 the United States enacted its first Patent Law, which called for an examination procedure by two out of three high government officials. Well, apparently they got tired of this practice in a hurry, because three years later the second Patent Act of 1793 was enacted, which did away with the examination procedure altogether. From 1793 to 1836, all an inventor was required to do was submit a statement of his or her invention to the government, and the government

Intellectual Property Law for Engineers, Scientists, and Entrepreneurs, Second Edition. Howard B. Rockman.

Published 2020 by John Wiley & Sons, Inc.

would register that statement as a patent without any examination, granting exclusive rights to an invention described in the registration certificate.

Once an inventor obtained a registration certificate, and an infringer appeared on the horizon, the inventor filed a lawsuit in the federal courts accusing the interloper with patent infringement. It was then up to the courts to determine whether or not the infringer had actually adopted the novel features of the patented invention in the alleged infringing device or method. However, in the majority of those cases the alleged infringer had not exactly duplicated the protected invention, as is the case in most infringement controversies even to the present time, and it was each court's burden to define what the invention was from reading the inventor's description, to determine what was novel about the invention covered by the certificate, and then to determine whether or not the infringer had embodied the novelty of the invention in the alleged infringing device or process. The court's analysis was complicated by the fact that there was nothing in the patent registration certificate that indicated what the inventor claimed was novel, and conversely, what was common throughout the prior art. This caused frustration among the courts, and difficulty in determining acts of infringement.

Consider the time also. This was a period when the United States was largely agrarian, but was also moving into the Industrial Age. Industry and even farming depended to a large degree on mechanical devices that would increase the power and leverage that could be applied to an object beyond that of human strength. The steam engine was still years in the future, electricity had still to be evolved as a medium for controlling mechanical movements, and the term "physics" had not even entered common parlance. However, by 1836, at least one U.S. senator, Senator John Ruggles of Maine, saw a need to assist the courts by recommending the enactment of a patent examination system, the establishment of a Patent Office that would examine patent applications for novelty of submitted inventions, require that the novelty of the invention be defined, and take the burden of determining what is novel in an invention from the courts. The proposed new system provided a government determination whereby patents would not be issued until the inventor was able to prove to a Patent Office Examiner that the invention did incorporate novel features.

10.2.2 1836 Patent Law

The U.S. Patent Law of 1836 was enacted in response to continuing public and judicial complaints with regard to the state of the Patent Law, which then substantially relied upon the Patent Act of 1793. Senator Ruggles, newly appointed from Maine in 1835, had long practiced law in his state, was a justice of the state's Supreme Court before being appointed to the Senate, had a strong interest in mechanics and engineering, and had a desire to become a patentee in his own right. Senator Ruggles set out to determine what was causing the inadequacies in the operation of the Patent Law, and in 1835 expressed to the Senate the complaints he had heard from the courts. He asked the Senate to appoint a committee to consider the situation and, as is common in all political and societal situations, he himself was appointed chairman of the committee to conduct the investigation. He discovered that the heart of the matter was that the then constituted Patent Office was obligated to issue a patent if technical and filing requirements were satisfied, regardless of novelty. After the patent issued, it was up to the courts to decide what exclusive rights, if any, existed with respect to the issued patent, and whether the patent was infringed.

The head of the Patent Office at that time also urged upon Senator Ruggles that the Patent Office should be able to prevent the issuance of a patent for an invention which was not novel, or which claimed invention in technology disclosed in an earlier patent. This could be performed by an examination system for novelty. Although England at that time had a system that allowed patents for imported inventions, it was felt that the United States system should be confined to patents relating only to new inventions. It became clear to Senator Ruggles that patents should be allowed only for such inventions as are in fact new, and entitled by the merit of originality and utility to be protected by law. Note that the question of non-obviousness of an invention was not a factor in 1836. As stated previously, the concept of non-obviousness did not arise in the United States until 1850 in the courts, and in 1952 in the legislature.

The law enacted in 1836 required that each patent contain a specification comprising a description of the invention in full, clear, and exact terms, and that the specification "particularly specify and point out the part, improvement, or combination claimed to be the invention." The exact language of the Patent Act of 1836 defining the specification and claims is as follows:

> "But before any inventor shall receive a patent for any such new invention or discovery, he shall deliver a written description of his invention or discovery, and the manner and process of making, constructing, using, and compounding the same, in such full, clear and exact terms, avoiding unnecessary prolixity, as to enable any person skilled in the art or science to which it appertains, or with which it is most nearly connected, to make, construct, compound, and use the same; and in case of any machine he shall fully explain the principle, and the several modes in which he has contemplated the application of that principle, whereby which it may be distinguished from other inventions; and shall particularly specify and point out the part, improvement or combination which he claims as his own invention or discovery."

Thus, for the first time in the United States, an inventor was obligated to set forth a written statement in the patent application defining what was novel in his or her invention, as compared to the prior art. Since the inventor was therefore "claiming" that portion of his or her invention that was novel, these statements in the patents became known as claims, and in a later Patent Statute, the claims were required to be separate "paragraphs" at the end of the specification, as they are in any modern patent document. At present, the requirements of a patent application are the same.

10.3 WHAT CLAIMS ARE

The present U.S. Patent Law defines the claims of a patent application in quite the same manner as described in the Patent Law of 1836, set forth above. The patent application claims set forth in words the content and scope of the exclusive property rights the inventor is attempting to secure through the patent grant. Each claim defines a separate and distinct property right. Thus, the claims of a patent define the subject matter of the invention and serve as the metes and bounds of the legal rights conferred by the patent. The claims also serve to provide notice to the public of the precise area of technology that is "fenced in" by the exclusive rights of your patent grant, so that competitors and would-be infringers know where not to tread.

A patent claim recites the structural and/or functional elements of the invention, or the method steps of a process, or the constituent parts of a composition of matter. Language defining the structural and/or functional relationships between elements or method steps is usually included in patent claims to clarify how the device or the method operates, and how the combination of elements "fit together" to place your invention in its proper environment. As is true with any definition, the language in a patent claim can be broad, or it can be specific. Most patents contain several claims written in broad, intermediate, and specific terms to define the invention. The broader the language allowed in a patent claim, the broader the scope of protection of the patent grant. The breadth of a patent claim, however, is limited in that the claim cannot "read on" the prior art. Stated another way, each patent claim must define over the prior art.

Thus, your patent attorney's objective in drafting patent claims is to initially submit to the Patent Examiner the broadest claims that you deem possible, to cover your invention in the broadest possible scope. The examiner will then apply prior art to the claims, and if necessary, will require that the claims be limited to the novelty of the invention in more specific or limited terms, such that the claims do not also encompass what is previously in the prior art, or in the public domain. This balancing of the description of the invention is the primary "art" of the patent attorney. In my humble estimation, without proper training and experience, it would be practically impossible for an individual to draft a valuable patent claim that is sufficiently broad to cover the invention, and yet not read on the prior art.

A patent application normally contains more than one claim, varying in degree of scope or breadth. Thus, if one or more claims of an issued patent are held invalid as reading on prior art not applied by the Patent Examiner, as may result in a court proceeding during an infringement lawsuit in an effort by an accused infringer to invalidate the patent, or in a post-grant proceeding in the USPTO, certain other claims of the patent of less breadth are still held valid and possibly infringed. Note that while a tract of land can only be described by one definition, inventions can be described by many claims, varying in scope and breadth from broad to narrow. Prudence dictates including several claims of varying scope in your patent application so that the patent survives if one or more claims are ultimately held invalid.

One of the key concepts in preparing patent claims is to draft claims that do not read on the prior art, and yet define your invention in such terms that any competitor in the future who tries to compete with you cannot produce a duplicate or near-duplicate of your invention without falling within the scope of your patent's claims. A great deal of foresight is required to prepare patent claims that will encompass any future competing device or process within the claim language. This requires looking beyond the precise physical structure embodied in the invention, and visualizing how the same results, objectives, and/or advantages of the invention may be obtained by more or less obvious modifications or substitutions of elements or steps. Thus, the patent attorney or agent, while drafting the claim, at the same time considers how to avoid or "design around" the claim he or she is drafting, as if they were a competitor. The patent attorney, with input from the inventor, then adjusts the claim language to close the loophole that has just been created in his or her own mind. Since most patent attorneys and inventors do not have access to working crystal balls, the requirement of drafting valuable patent claims calls into play a significant amount of imagination applied to the technological field related to the invention. This, in my opinion, is one of those great junction points between science and art, bonded together by the adhesive of imagination.

When one first reads a patent claim—and indeed the same has been true for my students at the law school where I have taught patent claim drafting—the claims appear awkward and difficult to read. However, properly drafted patent claims do make sense, and further in this chapter at Section 10.10, I will provide you with additional information on how to read and understand patent claims. When drafting a patent application, including the claims, the patent attorney realizes that the ultimate audience for the patent application, and the patent issuing therefrom, is first the inventor, second the Patent Examiner, third the competitors of the inventor, and fourth, if infringement ensues, a judge and/or jury. Thus, the claims ultimately have to be explained to, understood, and interpreted by those with little or no technical knowledge, for example, the judge and/or jury.

Existing Patent Law (35 U.S.C. §112) requires that the patent application comprise claims that particularly point out and distinctly claim the subject matter that the applicant regards as his or her invention. This brief statement encompasses the only comments regarding the subject of patent claim scope and content that Congress included in the Patent Law. No other guidelines are set forth in the Patent Law regarding the procedure for properly drafting a patent claim.

In determining whether or not a patent is infringed, it is the patent claims that are measured against the alleged infringing device, not the detailed description of the invention in the specification of the patent. If the alleged infringing device falls within the scope of only one of the claims of your patent, infringement is made out. In addition, multiple claims in a patent may legally form the basis for parceling out several different licenses for different embodiments of the invention, each claim supporting a separate license. Since the claims are always preceded by the patent specification, the claims use language which is supported by the language and description of the invention in the specification. The patent claims are also supported by the drawings that appear with the patent application, when necessary. Thus, the patent document itself is taken as a whole to determine the scope and content of the invention set forth in the claims.

Another major function of patent claims is that they ultimately advise a potential infringer of the metes and bounds of the invention that falls within the scope of the issued patent's protection. Therefore, the potential infringer is duly advised to work around the patent claims in attempting to develop a competing device. This type of "hopscotching" around patent claims has led to the advancement of the arts to which the patent laws are directed. Believe it or not, in my experience, this process works to constantly move technology forward.

10.4 YOUR REVIEW OF THE CLAIMS OF YOUR PATENT APPLICATION

As potential or actual inventors, you should remember that once a patent application directed to your invention is initially drafted, it is next submitted to you for review. When conducting your review, pay careful attention to the claims to ensure yourself that the claims (1) adequately and correctly describe your invention and (2) are broad enough to prevent a competing device from being made with minor alterations, and therefore get around your patent claims while accomplishing the same purposes, advantages, and results as your invention. Therefore, when reviewing patent applications over your career, review the claims carefully to ensure that your invention will be adequately protected.

I also recommend that you discuss the scope of the claims at each stage of the patent application preparation and prosecution stages with your patent attorney to ensure that you have achieved the broadest possible protection. While claims are placed last in the patent application, their importance is decidedly first, since the claims must properly cover the invention, or the rights covered by the patent grant issuing from your patent application diminish in value. Indeed, the examination and prosecution of a patent application largely involves comments back and forth between the inventor, the patent attorney, and the Patent Examiner, ensuring that the claims are written in acceptable form, and that the claims clearly define the invention over the prior art.

The most effective patent application is the result of a joint effort between the inventor and the patent attorney. Thus, there should always be total communication between the two, and the lawyer should always be given all the relevant information relating to preparing the patent application. Nothing should be held back by the inventor. Basically, a patent application, including the claims, is a complex document, and the inventor usually provides the information, with the patent attorney drafting the application. The review of the application, however, is a joint effort between the inventor and the patent attorney. I always advise my clients that I have no pride of authorship, and that each inventor is to review the entire application carefully to determine if there are any corrections or additions to be made to finalize the application. If you as the inventor suggest adding certain elements to the claims, be prepared to have the patent attorney advise you that adding elements to patent application claims may unnecessarily limit the scope of the claims, and therefore the language initially prepared and inserted by the patent attorney may be the broadest way to go. For example, what you define as a "spring" may be recited in a patent claim as a "resilient force element."

10.5 DISTINGUISHING DIFFERENT TYPES OF CLAIMS

Upon reviewing your patent application, you may encounter different types of claims, including those known as apparatus claims, means-plus-function claims, and method or process claims. The first two are used to define machines, articles of manufacture, and compositions of matter, while method claims define a series of novel and nonobvious steps of a process of doing something, such as transforming a piece of matter from one state to another, or the operation of a piece of machinery, or the steps of a computer program. Apparatus claims set forth the elements of the covered machine, article of manufacture, or composition of matter, the physical relationship between the elements comprising the invention, and the functional relationship between those elements. These features of apparatus claims are set forth in more detail in Section 10.10.3 of this chapter.

Means-plus-function claims also cover machines and articles of manufacture, but in a format that defines each, or some, of the claimed elements in terms of the function they perform, rather than their physical structure. For example, you are now reading a "book." In means-plus-function terminology, this "book" would be defined as a "means for conveying information." This type of terminology is used to provide a broad scope of claim coverage to your patent. Consider, for example, that the term "book" narrowly defines a physical structure with information set forth on pages. On the other hand, a "means for conveying information" has a broader scope, encompassing a computer, an audio book system, a billboard, or any other information conveying medium. However, there is a limit. Means-plus-function claims are limited to covering only the corresponding structure described in your patent specification, or equivalent structure (the latter being determined on a case-by-case basis). Therefore, whenever you see an element of your invention described in your patent application claims in terms of "means-plus-function," be sure that all known substitutions and equivalents for that structure are also defined in the specification of your patent application.

Samples of apparatus, means-plus-function and method claims are set forth below, describing a simple electrically driven clock.

- Apparatus Claim:
  An electrically operated timepiece, comprising:
  a. a cylindrical housing;
  b. an electric motor mounted in the housing;
  c. a clock face mounted on the cylindrical housing, the clock face having a centrally disposed aperture;
  d. a pair of rotatable shafts driven by the electric motor, the shafts extending through the aperture and one shaft coaxially disposed around the other shaft;
  e. a first minute hand attached to and rotated by the one shaft at a rotational speed of one rotation per hour; and
  f. a second hour hand attached to and rotated by the other shaft at a rotational speed of one rotation every twelve hours.
- Means Plus Function Claim:
  An electrically operated timepiece, comprising:
  a. a cylindrical housing;
  b. means indicating hours and minutes mounted on an opening of the housing;
  c. means mounted in the housing for providing rotational movement to a pair of shafts, one shaft coaxially mounted around the other shaft;
  d. means mounted to each of said shafts to designate hours and minutes on the hour and minute indicating means;
  e. the means for providing rotational movement to the shafts driving one shaft at a rotational speed of one rotation per hour and driving the other shaft at a rotational speed of one rotation every twelve hours.
- Method Claim:
  A method of indicating time on a clockface using a pair of rotating hands comprising the steps of:
  a. placing both of said hands adjacent the clock face;
  b. rotating one of the hands at a first rotational speed of one rotation every hour; and
  c. rotating the other hand at a rotational speed of one rotation every twelve hours.

10.6 MORE ON METHOD OR PROCESS CLAIMS

If the invention is a new method, or a new use for an old product which is expressed as a method (see below), the patent claims recite the steps of the method or process of doing something which is considered novel. These claims normally do not require reciting the mechanical relationship between parts, but merely require the recitation of the steps of the novel and non-obvious process, something like writing a recipe in a cookbook. The ideal method patent claim recites as little structure as possible in carrying out the method. For example, if the process uses a heating or cooling step, you do not recite the heater or the cooling compressor. You merely recite the step of heating or cooling. However, where structure is necessary for an understanding of the process, the method claim will include such structure.

In mechanical or electrical inventions, the operation of the patented structure may also involve a novel method or process. If you determine that this is so, advise the patent attorney that novelty not only resides in the structure and function of the device itself, but also in the method implemented by the device. Thus, the patent attorney should include method claims drawn to the novel process used by the machinery or electrical or electronic circuit, in addition to claims directed to the apparatus.

In Patent Law, the terms “process” and “method” are used interchangeably. The term process also includes “a new use of a known process, machine, manufacture, composition of matter, or material.” Thus, if you have a new way of using a device or apparatus that has been on the market for years, or even centuries, you may obtain a patent on the method of using that old device to accomplish the new process. Consider, for example, drafting a claim for a method of using beer to prevent baldness. No, I have not figured that one out yet; I just pose it as a hypothetical.

As in apparatus claims, method claims may be broad, intermediate, or narrow. The steps in a method claim must be recited in a logical order; however, a process can infringe a method claim even though the accused process does not accomplish the steps in the same order as recited in the claims. But, if the claims of the method patent recite that the steps must be performed in a specific order, then there is no infringement unless the steps are carried out by the accused infringing process in the same order set forth in the claims. Thus, if sequence numbers or letters, or any indication of sequence or order are set forth in a method claim, more than likely that claim will be limited to cover only the sequence of steps in the order recited in the claim. The rule is, therefore, that the novel steps of the method claim may be recited in any order, unless a particular order is crucial for the operation of the method, or for the novelty or non-obviousness of the method.

Among the elements of method claims are acts, manipulative steps, or even thought processes which are in some cases performed upon an article. The essence of a method claim and the key to patentability in these situations involves the change of the item being worked upon to an altered condition by the new method. Steps such as “determining,” “establishing,” etc., are used as steps in method claims. Method claims are also required to particularly point out and distinctly claim the steps of the method the inventor considers as novel to support patentability.

When submitting your invention disclosures to a patent attorney in the future, if at all possible recommend that method claims be included where practicable, even with regard to mechanical and electrical inventions. The reason lies in a piece of legislation called the U.S. Process Patent Act of 1988. This law was created to allow U.S. courts to enforce method claims in U.S. patents against articles imported into the United States, where the articles were manufactured overseas using the method or methods encompassed by a United States patent. Prior to 1988, any article imported into the United States which did not infringe a U.S. apparatus patent did not constitute infringement of a method patent where the patented method was not performed in the United States. This 1988 legislation changed the law, and it is important to note that method claims now have a broader applicability to stop the importation of goods where an infringing process covered by a U.S. patent has been utilized overseas.

10.7 COMPOSITION OF MATTER CLAIMS

Very briefly, inventions and patents can be directed to new compositions of matter which are novel combinations of chemical substances. These patent claims usually are drafted in single lines setting forth the new chemical composition. Thus, these types of patents do not describe moving parts, electrical circuits, or processes of performing an act on another article. They are patents and claims directed to new compounds, using a new combination of chemical substances.

10.8 DESIGN PATENT CLAIM

A design patent includes drawings comprising several views of a novel design of the nonfunctional features of an article of manufacture, and has a single claim which merely recites:

> "The ornamental design for a (product) substantially as shown and described."

A design patent, as discussed in detail in Chapter 12, consists of a series of illustrations that show all the views of the particular item for which design protection is sought. The claim of the design patent will cover only the nonfunctional esthetic features of the product disclosed. Any functional features, of course, have to be covered by article patents to obtain protection.

10.9 DEPENDENT CLAIMS

In looking at a patent, you will oftentimes note that certain claims depend from other claims previously recited in the patent. Any claim that depends from a previous claim is known as a "dependent claim," and is merely a shorthand way of incorporating by reference each and every element of the previous or base claim or claims into the new claim. Thus, if claim 2 depends upon claim 1 in a patent, claim 2 incorporates by reference all of the elements of claim 1, and adds the elements recited in claim 2. You will find, for example, that a dependent claim repeats the major elements of the preamble of the base claim, followed by words such as "as recited in claim 1."

Dependent claims are used to modify the parent claim by:

1. Adding an element not included in the parent claim; and/or
2. Qualifying an existing element of the parent claim; and/or
3. Qualifying a relationship between previously recited elements in the parent claim.

A dependent claim can also depend from a prior dependent claim. Such a claim will incorporate by reference the elements of both the base claim and the intermediate claim or claims. Thus, to infringe such claim, the infringing device must incorporate all of the subject matter from the first claim and each intervening dependent claim. Care must be taken in drafting dependent claims so that the latter claims are not excessively limited by having too many elements incorporated by reference. The more elements set forth in the claim, the easier it is for a competitor to avoid infringement by eliminating or modifying one or more of the claimed elements.

10.10 HOW TO READ AND UNDERSTAND PATENT CLAIMS DRAFTED BY YOUR PATENT ATTORNEY

To comprehend how to read and understand patent claims, in my judgment furnishing you with a brief summary of how claims are drafted by a patent attorney is the best way to demonstrate how these arcane forms of the English language are derived. Consider, for example, a simple computer and screen combination. Patent claims directed to the computer as an apparatus may read as follows:

1. An apparatus for storing, manipulating, and displaying data upon the command of an operator, comprising:
   a. a central processing unit including data storage drives and access elements that provide selective access to and manipulation of data stored on the drives;
   b. a keyboard electronically connected to the access elements in the central processing unit, the keyboard having a plurality of keys which, when actuated, access and manipulate selected data stored on the drives; and
   c. a display device electronically connected to the central processing unit, the display device displaying selectively accessed data upon actuation of the keys of the keyboard.
2. The apparatus for storing, manipulating, and displaying data of claim 1 wherein the display device is a plasma display screen.
3. The apparatus for storing, manipulating and displaying data of claim 1 wherein the display device is a cathode-ray tube.

The following is a description of how these claims are structured, as a patent attorney would draft and view the claims.

10.10.1 Preamble

The initial portion of claim 1, which reads "An apparatus for storing, manipulating, and displaying data upon the command of an operator," is referred to as the "preamble" of the claim. In claims 2 and 3 the statement "The apparatus for storing, manipulating, and displaying data of claim 1" comprises the preamble of the dependent claims.

The preamble sets forth the category of the patentable invention that is ultimately claimed, and includes (optionally) a recitation of the purpose or object of the device in terms of results. Thus, the preamble sets forth information about the environment in which the invention operates.

The preamble of my example indicates that the invention lies in an apparatus for storing, manipulating, and displaying data upon the command of an operator. This lets you know, for example, that the invention is not directed to an agricultural combine, or to a chemical process. The environment of the invention is clearly set forth in the preamble.

By way of another example, where the invention sets forth a machine to perform work upon an object or a work piece, and the invention is in the combination of machine elements, the specific operation to be performed upon the work piece by the machine is clearly set out in the preamble. For example, "A machine for making paper" would be a proper preamble for a claim directed to a paper making machine. Likewise, a sample claim preamble would be: "A connector for the transmission of high voltage electricity," or "A composition for fertilizing the soil." Thus, the preamble may also set forth the intended purpose of the inventive structure.

Another example of a method claim preamble would be "A method of treating a liquid mixture containing partial oxidation products of different molecular weights in the range of aldehyde fatty acids." Yet another example is "An improvement in methods for manufacturing rubber tires from molten rubber, in which the molten rubber is formed at high temperatures and subject to the application of high pressure."

10.10.2 Transition Phrase

The transition phrase of a patent claim leads from the preamble to the recitation of the specifically related elements of the claim, and uses the participle form of a verb: "comprising," "consisting of," "including," or "consisting essentially of." In the above example, in Claim 1, the transition phrase is "comprising:" in line 2. With reference to the ultimate of details, the transition phrase is separated from the preamble by a comma, and followed by a colon in accepted patent parlance. And believe it or not, the transition phrase, even though possibly one word, substantially affects the scope of coverage of the claim.

The term "comprising" used as a transition phrase in a patent claim means the same as "including." When the transition phrase "comprising" is used, the scope of the invention set forth in the claim is "open ended" and may contain other elements besides the enumerated elements. In other words, when the word "comprising" is used as the transition phrase, it literally means "including the following elements, but not excluding other elements." Therefore, prior art having your recited elements, plus others, still invalidates your claim. Likewise, an infringing device having each of the recited elements, plus others, still infringes your claim.

On the contrary, the terms "consisting of" or "consisting essentially of" are restrictive or "closed-end" transition forms, and define an embodiment of the claimed invention that is made up *only* of the recited elements. The sole exception is that if trace amounts or impurities of non-recited ingredients are found in a composition of matter alleged to infringe a patent claim, the trace amounts are not taken into account for the infringement analysis. These restrictive transition word forms are normally found in chemical patent claims to cover a product which can be constructed by eliminating certain previously used components, or eliminating certain steps shown in the prior art.

Therefore, it is important to ensure that your patent attorney has properly used the words "comprising" or "consisting of" in patent claims to make sure that the patent claims are not unduly restrictive.

10.10.3 The Body of the Claim

10.10.3.1 Elements

The body of the claim, which constitutes sub-paragraphs (a), (b), and (c) in the example claim above, recites the main and necessary elements of the invention, while setting forth only those minimum number of elements required to define the operable inventive combination in its workable environment. The elements are the structural parts of a machine or article, the steps of a process, or the ingredients of a composition of matter. The definition of the elements in a claim also includes a description of the structural relationship between the elements, that is, how the elements are combined, connected, operatively connected, or otherwise physically or functionally associated with each other.

10.10.3.2 Functional Relationship of the Elements

The body of a patent claim also sets forth a statement of the functional relationship between each of the elements recited, describing how the elements function and cooperate in their structural relationship to form the inventive combination and to accomplish the result set forth in the preamble. Each claim should also recite a statement of those elements and features, and/or characteristics of those elements or features, which produce the beneficial results and define the novelty and non-obviousness of the inventive combination.

10.10.3.3 Results Should Not Be Included in the Body of a Claim

As stated above, the elements and functional relationship of the elements are recited in the body portion of the claim to define the novel features of the invention which accomplish the beneficial results set forth in the preamble. However, results and objectives of the subject invention are not recited in the body portion of the claims. Only structure, structural relationships, functions, and functional relationships of the elements are recited in the body of the claims. Results should be omitted, and left to the claim's preamble and to the specification portion of the patent application that appears before the claims.

10.10.3.4 The Two Dependent Claims of the Example

Claims 2 and 3 of the above example are each dependent claims, which qualify an existing element of the parent claim, that is, the display device, or screen as it is commonly known. Claim 2 specifies that the display device of Claim 1 is a plasma display screen, while Claim 3 recites that the display device of claim 1 is a cathode-ray tube. Note that Claims 2 and 3 are each more limited in scope than Claim 1, and that each dependent claim incorporates by reference each of the elements and functions of parent claim 1.

◆ INVENTORS AND INVENTIONS ◆

Ottmar Mergenthaler

THE LINOTYPE® HOT-TYPE COMPOSING MACHINE

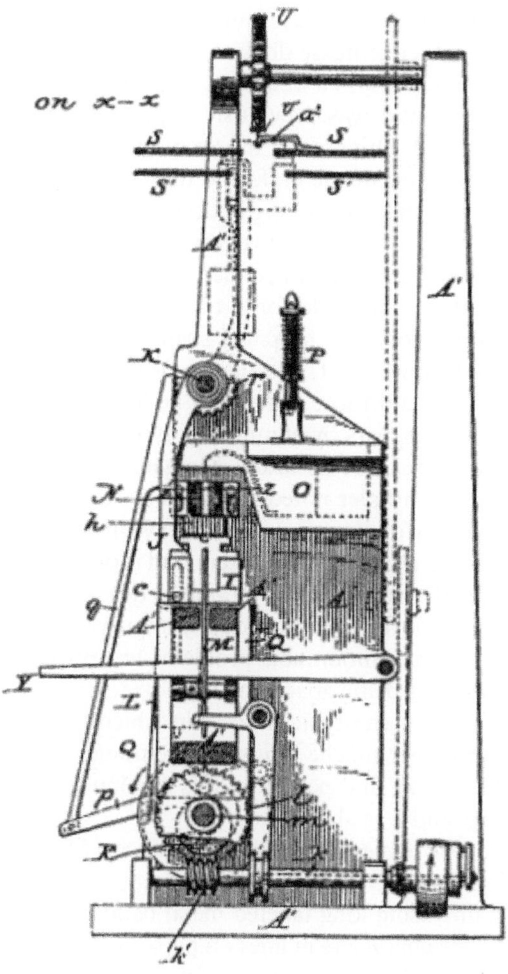

Ottmar Mergenthaler's contribution to the state of the printing art in 1886 is today considered by many as the most important advance in printing since Guttenburg's invention of movable type approximately 400 years previously.

Intellectual Property Law for Engineers, Scientists, and Entrepreneurs, Second Edition. Howard B. Rockman.

Published 2020 by John Wiley & Sons, Inc.

Ottmar Mergenthaler was born on May 11, 1854, in Hachtel, Baden Wuerttemberg, in what is now Germany. His mechanical ability surfaced early. The clock in the Lutheran church bell tower in his family's hometown had stopped for many years. No one had been able to repair it, not even skilled clock repairers. One evening, the bell suddenly rang because 14-year-old Ottmar Mergenthaler had fixed the clock. As a matter of fact, his ambition at that time was to become a watchmaker, and he spent four years as an apprentice to a relative of his family learning the watch- and clock-making trade.

In 1872, Mergenthaler noticed that soldiers were returning from the Franco-Prussian Wars, and he thought that his opportunities for advancement would be better in the United States. On October 26, 1872, a ship carrying the 18-year-old Mergenthaler in steerage with only a wooden suitcase docked in Baltimore, Maryland. He immediately went to Washington to work in a knife and tool shop operated by the son of the relative to whom Mergenthaler was previously apprenticed in Germany. However, business was rather poor in Washington at the time, and in 1874 Mergenthaler moved to Baltimore along with the rest of the knife and tool shop in which he was working.

The shop that Mergenthaler was working in designed and constructed clocks, bells, weather devices, and patent models for inventors who were seeking to patent their inventions. One day in 1876, an inventor named Charles Moore came into the shop looking to have a patent model made for a typing machine he had designed that printed characters in lithographic ink on paper strips. The impressions of the characters were mounted on a backing sheet, and the words were ultimately transferred to a lithographic stone for printing. Moore stated that he held a patent on a transfer typewriter used for making newspapers by eliminating typesetting by hand. However, his prior invention did not work, and he asked Mergenthaler whether a better model could be constructed. Mergenthaler noted that Moore's design was problematic, and Mergenthaler started working on improvements. Two years later, in 1878, Mergenthaler had constructed a machine that stamped letters and words on cardboard; however, this was not what Mergenthaler ultimately wanted to develop.

Mergenthaler continued working and eventually improved the reliability of Moore's typing machine. However, insurmountable problems in transferring the lithographic images resulted in this process being abandoned. In 1878, one of Moore's backers proposed the development of a stereotypic process in which the typing machine would impress characters onto papier-maché strips. Mergenthaler devised a rotary impression machine and obtained his first patent on this machine, but, eventually, this process was not satisfactory, and was abandoned.

In 1883, this backer, one James O. Clephane, financed Mergenthaler's attempts to develop a new machine that Mergenthaler had first conceived in 1879. Mergenthaler developed a band machine using long tapered metal bands with raised characters that created impressions of type characters in lines on papier-maché strips. Difficulties arose using this machine and in making satisfactory castings. In 1884, Mergenthaler developed a second machine using bands of indented characters that were located in the machine in such a way that lines of type could be cast from molten lead. This became Mergenthaler's initial Linotype machine. Mergenthaler's backers then formed the National Typographic Company, and named Mergenthaler as manager of its Baltimore factory. The name of the company was changed to Mergenthaler Printing Company in 1885.

However, Mergenthaler realized that the second band machine that he had developed would still not produce type of the quality of hand-set type. He then proposed a third machine, using matrices, or molds, of single characters that would immediately cast the characters in molten metal in the same machine. This principle of circulating single matrices became the foundation of all subsequent Linotype machines. When a Linotype operator pressed a key, that stroke identified which letter molds were to be retrieved from the magazines in the machine. The machine then assembled a row of metal molds of characters, called matrices. Molten lead was then poured into the matrices, producing a line of type, but in reverse. Thus, the type would read properly when ink was applied to it and the image was transferred to the printed page. The matrices were automatically restored by the machine to the magazines after the lead was poured. It has been reported that Mergenthaler got the idea for his brass matrices from the wooden molds used to make Christmas cookies in Germany.

The first commercial machine using this structure was completed in 1886 and installed at the plant of the *New York Tribune* to set both newspaper type and a 500-page book. Whitelaw Reid, the publisher of the *Tribune*, saw the potential of this machine and provided additional money to the Mergenthaler Printing Company.

By 1888, the usefulness and reliability of the Mergenthaler Linotype machine was noticed by Mr. Reid, and he wanted machines produced quickly for sale, but Mergenthaler still wanted a perfect machine. At that time, unable to resolve his differences with the company, Mergenthaler resigned as factory manager. Reid ultimately moved the factory to Brooklyn, New York. Mergenthaler responded by opening his own shop in Baltimore, where he developed improved Linotype machines that were built in both the Brooklyn and Baltimore shops.

In 1891, Mergenthaler perfected his newer Model I Linotype machine, overcoming the difficulties faced by newspaper publishers with the earlier machine. In 1895, as many as 2,608 Model I machines were installed at 385 locations in the United States. It was in this year that the Linotype machine was recognized by the printing industry as the first revolutionary advance over the hand typesetting procedures invented by Johann Guttenberg circa 1450.

Prior to Mergenthaler's death in 1899, the Mergenthaler Company was compelled to defend its patent rights in patent interference proceedings, and sued infringers who were manufacturing competing machines. In 1895, the Mergenthaler Company also acquired a competitor, and along with it the patent rights for the double-wedge spaceband, which justified the lines of type. In 1913, Mergenthaler's principal patents expired and competing hot-metal typesetting machines immediately entered the market.

It was not until after World War II that the use of Mergenthaler's hot-type systems began declining in use. The development of offset printing, cold-type, and photocomposition, and, ultimately, computers compelled the Mergenthaler Company to stop production of Linotype machines in 1971, but by that time the company had built approximately 90,000 Linotype machines. Several thousands of these machines are probably still in use in the United States and elsewhere.

Mergenthaler's contribution to the printing industry cannot be overlooked. The use of the Linotype machines geometrically increased the dissemination of ideas, concepts, and information throughout the literate world. The Guttenberg system allowed printers to set type by hand one letter at a time. The Linotype machine could set a complete line of type using a 90-character keyboard. Mergenthaler's machine allowed newspapers to compose pages five times faster than using hand-set type, and one Linotype operator could perform the work of six hand-setting typographers.

Mergenthaler died on October 28, 1899, in his home in Baltimore, Maryland. The church in which his funeral services were held, the Old Zion Lutheran Church, to this day has a stained glass window featuring Mergenthaler's first Linotype machine.

(No Model.)

3 Sheets—Sheet 1.

O. MERGENTHALER.

MACHINE FOR PRODUCING PRINTING BARS.

No. 317,828. Patented May 12, 1885.

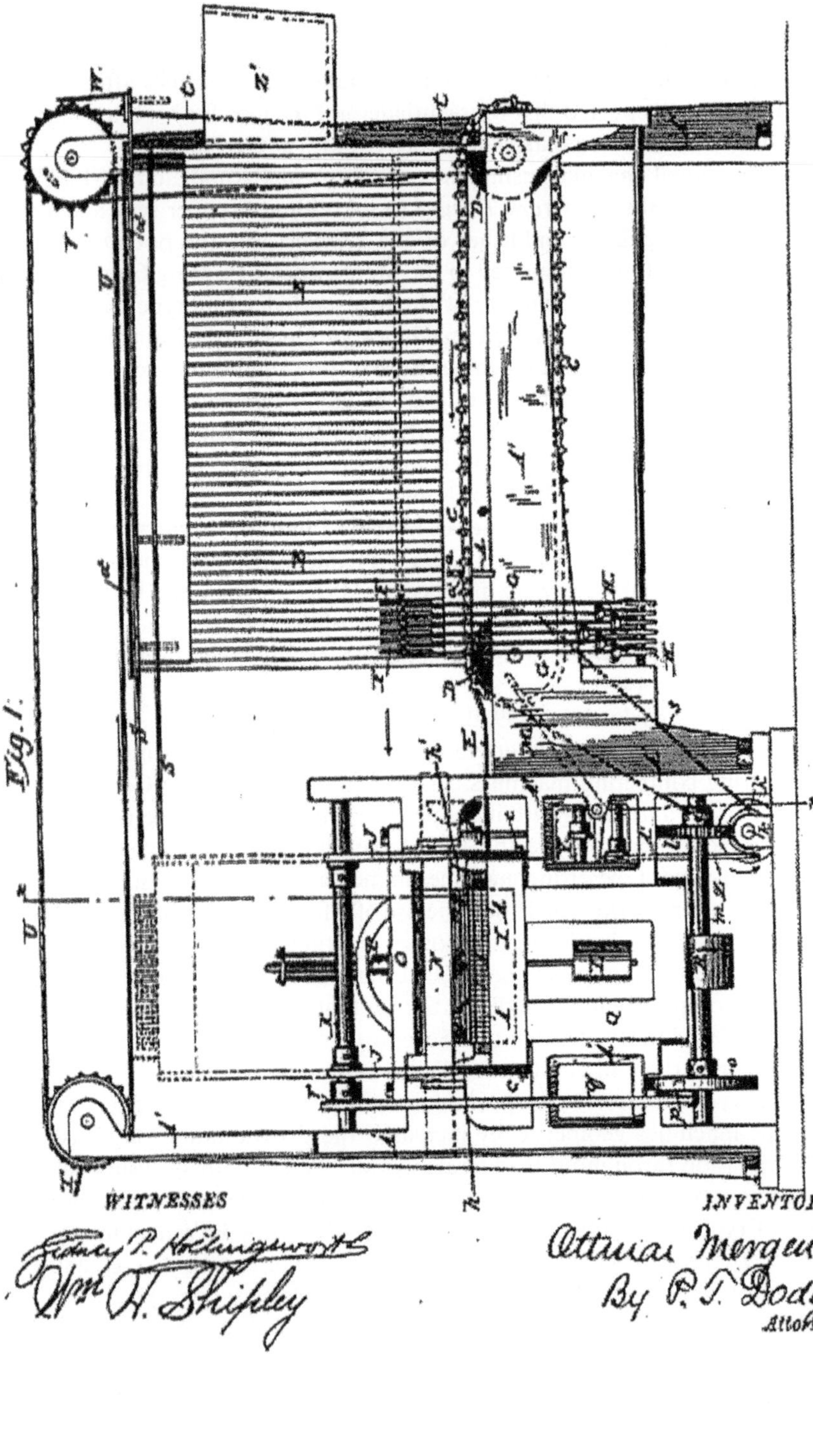

WITNESSES

Sidney P. Hollingsworth
Wm H. Shipley

INVENTOR

Ottmar Mergenthaler
By P. T. Dodge
Attorney

◆ INVENTORS AND INVENTIONS ◆

Theodore Maiman and Gordon Gould

LIGHT AMPLIFICATION BY STIMULATED EMISSION OF RADIATION (LASER)

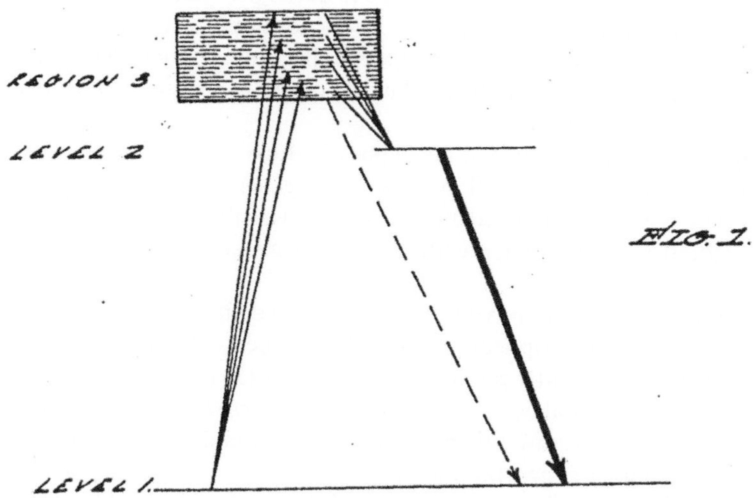

Our ancestors believed, but could not establish, that light rays carried mysterious powers. At the start of the 20th century, X-rays, radio waves, and radioactivity were discovered, as scientists delved into the entire radiation spectrum, looking at wavelengths longer and shorter than light waves (the visible spectrum). The scientific community at that time thought of light rays as electromagnetic waves, such as radio waves, but with significantly shorter wavelengths. Now it is known that rays with shorter wavelengths carry more information and more energy than rays of longer wavelengths.

The development of the laser began in about 1900, when Max Planck, a German theoretical physicist, published a work in which he deduced that energy could be emitted or absorbed only in discrete particles, which he labeled "quanta." Later, in 1905, Albert Einstein published a paper directed to the "photoelectric effect," hypothesizing that light also delivers energy in bundles, such as discrete quantum bundles, which are now defined as photons.

Intellectual Property Law for Engineers, Scientists, and Entrepreneurs, Second Edition. Howard B. Rockman.

Published 2020 by John Wiley & Sons, Inc.

In 1917, Einstein theorized the “simulated emissions” process underlying the eventual development of lasers. Einstein deduced that in addition to absorbing and emitting light spontaneously, the stimulation of electrons in a substance could emit light of a particular wavelength.

The history of the invention of the laser now jumps forward about 30 years to 1951, when Charles Townes of Columbia University, while sitting on a park bench in Washington D.C., conceived of a “maser” (microwave amplification by stimulated emission of radiation) as a way of harnessing energy through the principle of stimulated emission.

In 1950, it was known that microwaves, which were short-wavelength radio waves, were capable of vibrating a group of atoms. Surplus radar equipment from World War II was modified to provide the radiation. During the war, the U.S. Office of Naval Research pushed Townes and other physicists to develop a system to produce powerful beams of radiation at shorter wavelengths. It was not until 1951 that Townes came up with a solution when he thought that a proper collection of molecules could generate radiation on its own. Townes predicted that the output generated from such a device would be at a single frequency.

In 1954, Townes, Herbert Zeiger, and James Gordon, a graduate student, demonstrated an ammonia maser to obtain the first generation and amplification of electromagnetic waves by simulated emissions. This was the first experiment based on Einstein’s theoretical works. In September 1957, Townes sketched an optical maser (or laser) in his lab notebook.

In 1958, Bell Labs, for whom A.L. Schawlow worked and Townes consulted, filed a patent application for the “optical maser,” which issued in 1960 as U.S. Patent No. 2,929,922. The two also jointly published a paper in 1958 in *Physical Review Letters*, describing how masers could be configured to operate in the optical and infrared spectrum, and they proposed how this could be done. Notably, Townes and Schawlow never constructed a device incorporating their ideas.

In 1955, in Moscow, Nikolai G. Basov and Alexander M. Prokhorov were also explaining the application of maser concepts in the optical region of the spectrum, and they proposed a method to produce a negative absorption they called the “pumping” method.

For years, scientists were trying to control even shorter wavelengths, leading to work with far-infrared waves and considering how to make a maser using infrared waves. Townes, in 1957, while studying amplification radiation equations, conceived of a maser using very short waves rather than far-infrared waves. By 1957, scientists were attempting to develop maser-like amplification of visible light. Townes mentioned his ideas to Arthur Schawlow, Townes’ colleague and brother-in-law. Schawlow then came up with a concept to incorporate Townes’ thoughts for an “optical maser,” or laser, by placing the atoms to be stimulated in a narrow, long crystal or other medium with mirrors at each end.

A flashing or “pumping” light tube introduces intermittent light energy in the form of photons to the crystal. Atoms in the crystal absorb the light energy resulting in electrons of the atoms jumping to a higher energy level. Milliseconds later, the electrons go back to their original energy level, and by doing so give off photons of light. The photons travel the length of the crystal while inside the crystal, and at the speed of light.

Frequently, a traveling photon stimulates a previously excited atom, which emits a photon, and the original photon is recovered also. This is known as “stimulated emission." Since one light photon has now produced two, the light has been amplified and made stronger. Thus, "light amplification" is caused by "stimulated emission of radiation."

A mirror at each end of the crystal maintains the constant reciprocal movement of photons in the crystal. One of the mirrors has a small aperture allowing some of the reciprocating photons to escape, creating a very powerful and concentrated collimated beam of light at a single or monochromatic frequency at a long distance. Compared to the mixed-up light waves in a common flashlight beam, laser light waves are "in step." The crest of all the waves align with one another, presenting a coherent light.

In the fall of 1957, Gordon Gould, a Columbia University graduate student, had discussed amplification of light by stimulation with Townes. Gould had previously been working on "pumping" atoms to a higher energy state to emit light as part of his doctoral thesis. Gould thought about what he and Townes had discussed, and wrote his own ideas on his analysis and suggested application of lasers in his notebook on November 13, 1957, describing the essential elements for light amplification by a stimulation device, and using the term LASER in his description. Gould had the foresight to have his notebook page notarized at a Bronx candy store. This notarized document became the focus of Gould's 30 year fight (described ahead) to obtain patent rights to his embodiment of the laser.

A few months after his notebook entry, Gould left Columbia before completing his doctoral studies to join a private research entity, Technical Research Group (TRG). Gould convinced TRG to support his research, and TRG obtained U.S. Defense Department funding to develop Gould's laser concepts, which project was classified "secret." However, in 1945, Gould had worked on the Manhattan Project, but was dismissed as a result of his participation in the Communist Political Association. After joining TRG in 1957, Gould found out that he could not obtain a "secret" security clearance due to his previous communist affiliation. Gould stayed at TRG, but could not work on the project, even though the project was dedicated to develop his ideas. Some commenters have postulated that perhaps as a result of Gould's inability to work on the project, Theodore Maiman at Hughes Research Laboratories (discussed ahead) built the first working laser.

Beginning in April 1959, TRG and Gould began filing many patent applications directed to lasers based on Fabry-Perot optical resonators, optical pumping, optical amplifiers, and several other laser-related inventions. When the Townes/Schawlow Bell Labs Patent No. 2,929,922 issued on March 22, 1960, TRG and Gould began a legal challenge asserting that Gould's 1957 notebook entry showed he had invented the laser before Townes/Schawlow. At that time, the U.S. Patent Law awarded patents to the first to invent, not the first to file, and interference proceedings were then used by the U.S. Patent Office to determine who was the first inventor.

During the long time that this battle was fought in the U.S. Patent Office and the courts, Bell Labs, Hughes Research Laboratories, Westinghouse, IBM, and others including TRG were developing specific laser technologies, and filing patent applications directed to these technologies. By the end of 1960, at least three different types of lasers had been exhibited by several research organizations.

At this point in our narrative, I am compelled to interrupt the Gould patent saga and direct your attention to another important figure relevant to the invention of the laser. Theodore Harold Maiman is credited with the actual construction of the first working laser. Maiman, an engineer and PhD physicist, directed his doctoral thesis at Stanford University to microwave-optical measurements of fine structural splitting in excited helium atoms. In 1956, Maiman joined the Atomic Physics Department of Hughes Aircraft Company (later Hughes Research Laboratories), as head of the ruby maser redesign project for the U.S. Army Signal Corps. His team was successful in reducing the size of the cryogenic device from 2.5 tons to 4 pounds, while enhancing its performance.

In 1959, Maiman convinced Hughes to financially support his laser project. The project was based on Maiman's previous conception of a solid-state laser design including advancing the microwave frequency of masers 50,000 times up to the frequency of light in the electromagnetic spectrum. This required determining a workable lasing medium and an excitation source before designing the system. Maiman and his team were aware of the 1958 *Physical Review Letters* publication by Townes and Schawlow, which provided a theoretical proposal for a gaseous system using potassium vapor excited by a potassium lamp. However, Maiman pursued his own solid-state design instead. His team ultimately successfully developed synthetic pink ruby crystal cylinders with reflective silver-coated ends as the lasing medium, and a helical xenon pulsed light source lasting only a few milliseconds to excite, or pump, the solid ruby rod. The resulting laser was a short flash of light rather than a continuous wave.

On May 16, 1960, Maiman's solid-state pink ruby laser emitted the first intense, narrow, coherent light beam, where all of the rays were the same wavelength, and totally in phase.

Maiman submitted a short description of this laser to the *Physical Review Letters* journal, which was refused publication by the editor. One editor at the time has stated that this was because in June 1960, Maiman had published an article on the excitation of ruby with light flashes, with an examination of the relaxation times between quantum states, and that this new article seemed to cover the same subject. Maiman then submitted his material to *Nature*, considered a more selective journal, which published his article on August 6, 1960.

Hughes also filed patent applications on Maiman's invention, resulting in the issuance of U.S. Patent No. 3,353,115 directed to the first operating laser. Thus, in May 1960, Maiman and Hughes won the race against Gould and TRG to construct the world's first working laser, probably due in part to Gould being disqualified from working on TRG's project.

One of the unexpected results of Maiman's work, in addition to the use of a pulsed light source, was that he emptied the lowest-energy state (ground state) of ruby to a point where stimulated emission could occur from an excited to a ground state. Maiman concluded that the ground state could be sufficiently emptied by a pulsed light source to provide the laser action, and it turned out he was correct.

Shifting our story back to the patent aspects, consider that when Bell Labs' U.S. Patent No. 2,929,922 issued on March 22, 1960, no one had yet demonstrated a workable laser. That did not occur until Maiman's May 16, 1960 showing. Patent applications can be filed before the invention described in the application has been proven to be workable. If the invention is ultimately found to be inoperable, the patent will be invalid.

Upon issuance of the Bell Labs patent on March 22, 1960, and while the Gould/TRG first patent application that was filed in April 1959 was still pending before the U.S. Patent Office, Gould and TRG took legal action in the Patent Office, alleging he was the first to conceive of the laser. That legal battle lasted many years, with Gould's first patent issuing in 1968 covering an obscure use of lasers. This patent, however, included the full description of his laser invention from this 1959 application, which then became "prior art" used by Patent Examiners to reject later filed patent applications submitted by others that were substantially parallel to Gould's other pending patent applications.

Gould and TRG ultimately lost the fight to obtain the original laser patent, basically because his 1957 notarized notebook did not sufficiently state that the sidewalls of the laser medium were to be transparent, even though he considered optically pumping the gain medium through the sidewalls, and he considered the possible loss of light by diffraction through the sidewalls.

Another issue raised in these battles was whether Gould's notebook provided sufficient information to enable a laser to be actually constructed, since Gould and TRG were unable to do so before Theodore Maiman demonstrated his workable laser in 1960.

Gould and TRG were able to obtain patents in foreign countries, while they continued their fight to obtain patents in the United States. The question of just who should be acknowledged as the first to invent the laser remains unsolved by technology historians to this day. I suggest that with the information provided above, you can come to a conclusion that cannot be rebutted by those having a different opinion.

As a postscript to the laser patent situation, in 1970, TRG was purchased by Control Data Corporation, which had no interest in lasers. Gould purchased back his patent rights for $1000 plus a diminutive share of future profits. In about 1973, after losing court battles on the laser itself, Gould and his attorneys decided to focus their efforts on patenting the optical amplifier, a necessary part of any laser. On October 11, 1977, Gould was awarded U.S. Patent No. 4,053,845, directed to optically pumped laser amplifiers. This patent was based on, and included the description of one of his earlier patent applications filed on April 6, 1959, eighteen years earlier. One of the prior art references applied by the Patent Examiner was the Schawlow/Townes 2,929,922 patent, which application was filed nine months before Gould filed his first patent application.

If Gould's 1977 patent could be upheld as valid in court, the laser industry which had grown significantly from 1961 to annual sales of about $400 million, would owe Gould and his inventors substantial royalties. As could be expected, the laser industry fought back in an effort to avoid paying Gould. Legal battles ensued for years, with Gould obtaining U.S. Patent 4,161,436 in 1979, directed to a long list of laser applications, including heating and vaporizing materials, communication systems, television, and photocopiers, to name just a few. This patent resulted in the laser industry responding with more lawsuits to avoid paying royalties on this patent also. In 1979, Gould and his backers formed Patlex, a company to hold the patent rights and to license and enforce Gould's patents. The laser industry fought Gould in the courts, and also in the U.S. Patent Office with review proceedings to prevent any of Gould's still pending applications from being issued, and to invalidate his two issued patents.

In 1985, the Court of Appeals of the Federal Circuit ordered the U.S. Patent and Trademark Office to issue Gould's then pending patent application covering collisionally pumped laser amplifiers. The Patent Office appealed, but lost, and Gould was issued U.S. Patent No. 4,704,583. The Patent Office was also ordered by the Court to stop its efforts to invalidate Gould's prior issued patents. Gould's Brewster's angle patent was subsequently issued as U.S. Patent No. 4,746,201.

With the Patent Office actions ended by the Court, Patlex patent infringement lawsuits proceeded, and in 1987 Patlex won a major victory against Control Laser Corp., a producer of lasers. As a result, the ownership of Control Laser Corp. was turned over to Patlex as part of a settlement arrangement. Other laser producers and users then agreed to settle their respective lawsuits and enter into license agreements with Patlex, mostly on Patlex's terms.

Ultimately, Gould obtained 48 patents, the most valuable being directed to optical pumping and collisional pumping, and patents covering applications of laser technology. As is evident, the delay in the issuance of Gould's patents meant that his patents became enforceable, and much more valuable than had his patents been enforced when the laser industry was in its infancy. Gould had assigned 80% of his royalties to finance his court and Patent Office battles; however, he still made several million dollars at the end.

It is worth noting that under today's U.S. Patent laws, some of Gould's battles would have had vastly different outcomes. Certain of his patents were issued on applications filed many years prior to being issued. For patent applications filed on or after June 8, 1985, the patent enforcement term is 20 years from the filing date of the earliest U.S. or international (PCT) application to which priority is claimed (excluding provisional patent applications). See 35 U.S.C. §154. For example, Gould's U.S. Patent No. 4,053,845, the cover page which is among those following this essay, issued in 1977, based on a patent application filed on April 6, 1959. Under the Patent Law in effect in 1977, Gould and Patlex were able to collect royalties for 17 years after the patent issued. However, if today's Patent Law were in effect in 1977, Gould's patent would have expired on April 6, 1979, twenty years from the initial priority filing date, or about one and a half years after the patent issued. Thus, the expected royalties to be collected from infringers would have been substantially less.

Following this essay are the cover pages of each of the important patents referenced in this essay. I could find no reference in the literature of enforcement actions taken regarding Theodore Maiman's U.S. Patent No. 3,353,115.

For more concise information about the invention of the laser and the approximately 30-year long patent fight that followed, your attention is directed to the book *LASER: The Invention, the Nobel Laureate, and the Thirty Year Patent War,* published by Simon & Schuster, 2000, ISBN 0-684-83515-0.

March 22, 1960 A. L. SCHAWLOW ET AL 2,929,922

MASERS AND MASER COMMUNICATIONS SYSTEM

Filed July 30, 1958

FIG. 1

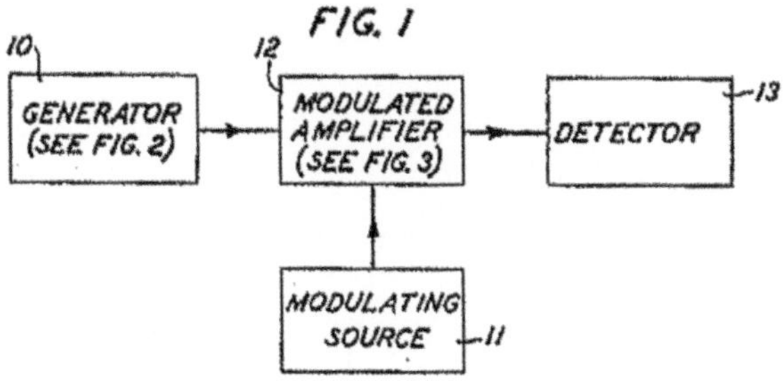

FIG. 2

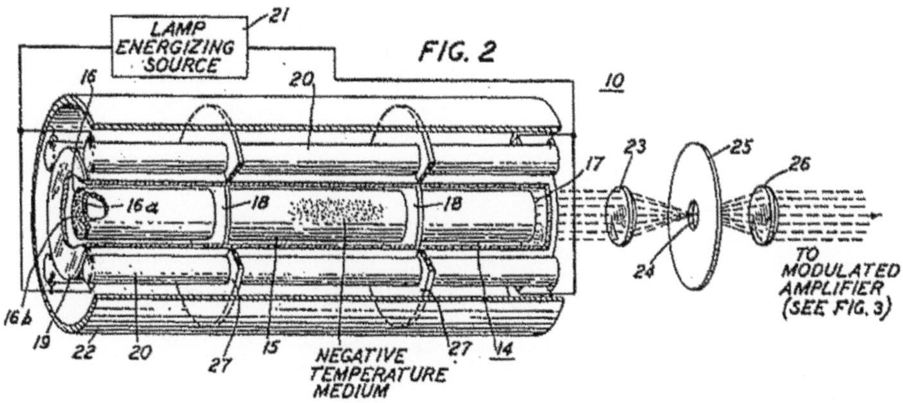

FIG. 3

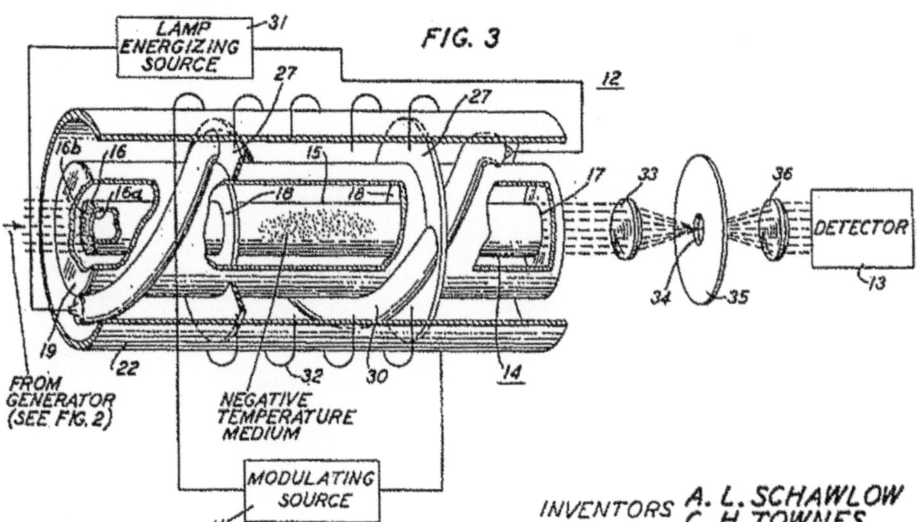

INVENTORS A. L. SCHAWLOW
C. H. TOWNES
BY Lucian C. Canepa
ATTORNEY

Nov. 14, 1967 T. H. MAIMAN 3,353,115

RUBY LASER SYSTEMS

Original Filed April 13, 1961 5 Sheets-Sheet 1

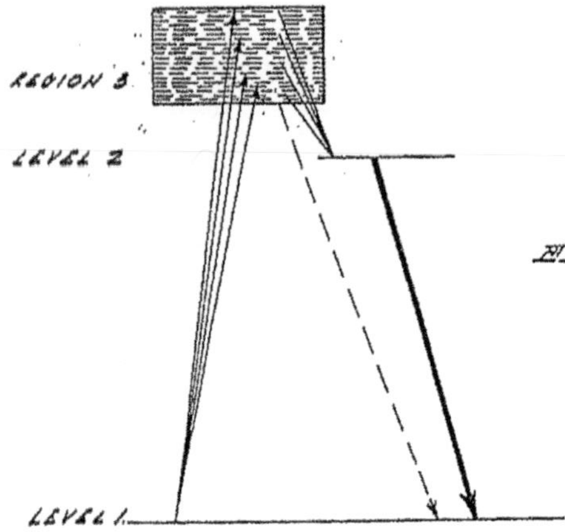

FIG. 1.

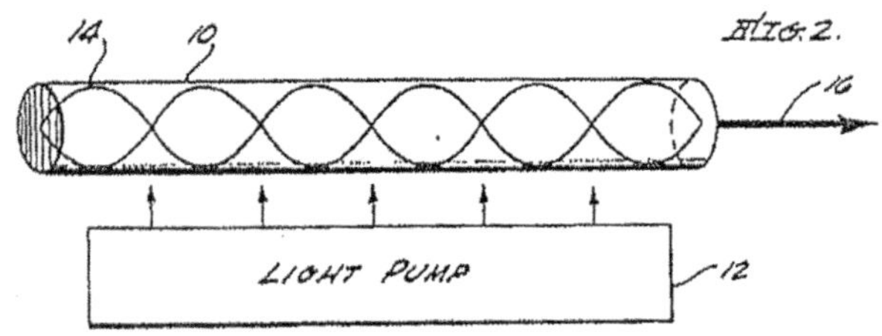

FIG. 2.

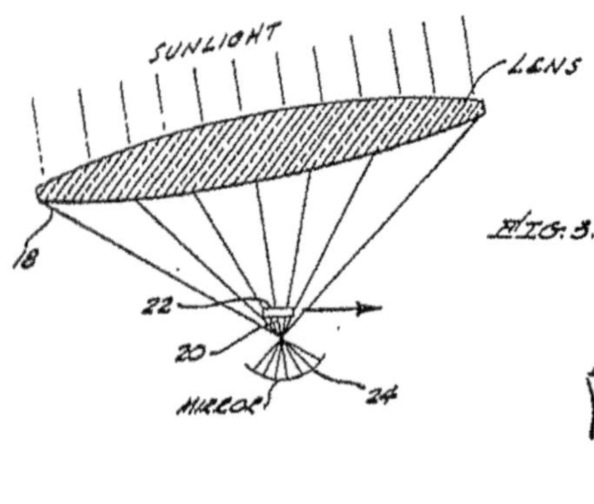

FIG. 3.

INVENTOR
BY THEODORE H. MAIMAN,
Daniel T. Anderson
ATTORNEY

United States Patent [19] [11] **4,053,845**
Gould [45] **Oct. 11, 1977**

[54] **OPTICALLY PUMPED LASER AMPLIFIERS**

[76] Inventor: **Gordon Gould**, 329 E. 82 St., New York, N.Y. 10028

[21] Appl. No.: **498,065**

[22] Filed: **Aug. 16, 1974**

Related U.S. Application Data

[60] Continuation of Ser. No. 644,035, March 6, 1967, abandoned, and Ser. No. 804,540, April 6, 1959, abandoned, said Ser. No. 644,035, is a division of Ser. No. 804,540, , and a continuation-in-part of Ser. No. 804,539, April 6, 1959.

[51] **Int. Cl.**[2] **H01S 3/091; H01S 3/22**
[52] **U.S. Cl.** .... **330/4.3**; 331/94.5 G; 331/94.5 P
[58] **Field of Search** .... 330/4.3; 331/94.5 G, 331/94.5 P, 94.5 D; 324/15 F

[56] **References Cited**

U.S. PATENT DOCUMENTS

2,929,922 3/1960 Schawlow et al. 330/4.3

FOREIGN PATENT DOCUMENTS

148,441 1959 U.S.S.R. 330/4.3
123,209 1959 U.S.S.R. 330/4.3

OTHER PUBLICATIONS

Fabrickart, "Electronic and Ionic Devices (Translation)", Trudy, vol. 41, 1940, pp. 236–296.
Butaeva et al., "Investigations in Experimental and Theoretical Physics", 1959, pp. 62–70, Studies in Experimental and Theoretical Physics.
Levgyel, "Evolution of Masers and Lasers", Amer. Jour. of Physics, vol. 34, No. 10, 10/66, pp. 903–913.

Primary Examiner—Nelson Moskowitz
Attorney, Agent, or Firm—Lerner, David, Littenberg & Samuel

[57] **ABSTRACT**

Optically pumped laser amplifiers are disclosed. One type of such amplifier utilizes an excitable medium, the atoms, ions or molecules of said medium having well defined energy states including a lowest state, a lower state above said lowest state, and a higher state above said lower state, and a bright pumping light source composed of a radiative substance different from such medium which radiative substance emits energy in a spectral range which can be absorbed by such medium, and wherein the major portion of the energy absorbed by such medium causes transitions of the atoms, ions, or molecules thereof to populate the higher state. Another type of such amplifier utilizes a medium of atoms, ions, or molecules, some of which have broad bands of energy levels corresponding to a broad band of absorption transitions and energy levels corresponding to at least one fluorescent emission transition, the upper energy levels of said broad bands being above the upper level of said fluorescent emission transition, and wherein some of the upper energy levels above the upper level of said fluorescent emission transition are rapidly quenched via non-radiating transitions to the upper level of said fluorescent emission transition. In a preferred embodiment of the latter amplifier, the lower energy level corresponding to the fluorescent emission transition is relaxed by non-radiating transitions.

12 Claims, 7 Drawing Figures

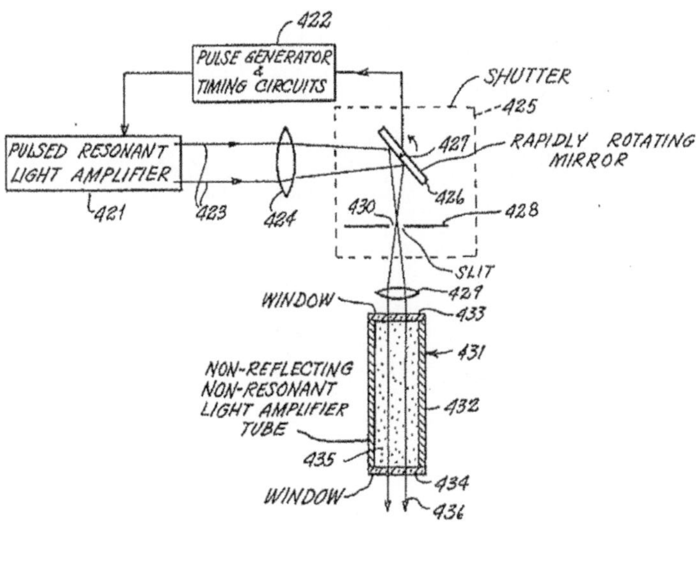

United States Patent [19] [11] **4,161,436**

Gould [45] **Jul. 17, 1979**

[54] **METHOD OF ENERGIZING A MATERIAL**

[76] Inventor: **Gordon Gould,** 1200 N. Nash Ave., Arlington, Va. 22209

[21] Appl. No.: **840,050**

[22] Filed: **Oct. 6, 1977**

Related U.S. Application Data

[60] Division of Ser. No. 498,065, Aug. 16, 1974, Pat. No. 4,053,845, which is a continuation of Ser. No. 644,035, Mar. 6, 1967, abandoned, and Ser. No. 804,540, Apr. 6, 1959, abandoned, said Ser. No. 644,035, which is a division of said Ser. No. 804,540, and a continuation-in-part of Ser. No. 804,539 Apr. 6, 1959, abandoned.

[51] **Int. Cl.²** **B01J 1/10**
[52] **U.S. Cl.** .... **204/157.1 R;** 250/527
[58] **Field of Search** .... 204/157.1 R, DIG. 11

[56] **References Cited**

U.S. PATENT DOCUMENTS

2,929,922 3/1960 Schawlow et al. 250/7

Primary Examiner—Howard S. Williams
Attorney, Agent, or Firm—Lerner, David, Littenberg & Samuel

[57] **ABSTRACT**

This application discloses light amplifier apparatus and uses for the same. A light amplifier apparatus is disclosed in which population inversion is created by optical pumping. Another light amplifier apparatus is disclosed in which population inversion is produced by collisions with other particles. Uses for light amplifiers are taught including heating of material which includes evaporation of the same, distance measuring, communication systems, television, and certain industrial applications. This application also teaches the use of optical elements at Brewster's angle for the purpose of polarization and reducing losses in passing a light beam along a path.

3 Claims, 19 Drawing Figures

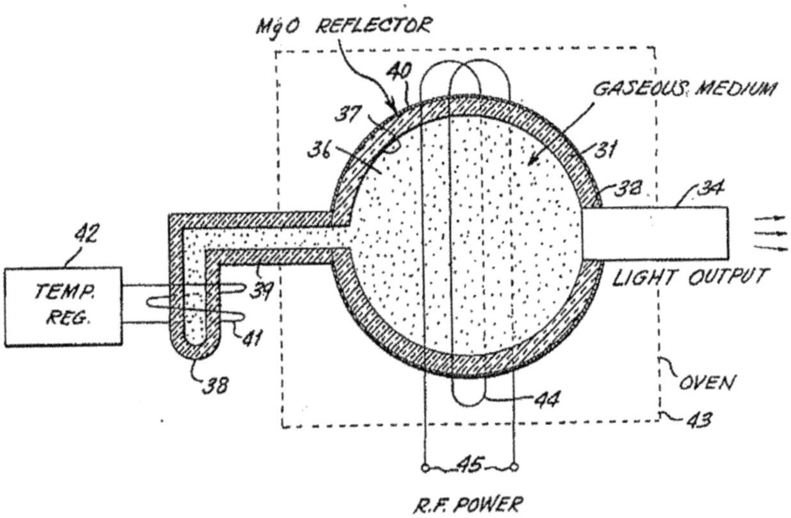

United States Patent [19]
Gould

[11] **Patent Number:** **4,704,583**
[45] **Date of Patent:** **Nov. 3, 1987**

[54] **LIGHT AMPLIFIERS EMPLOYING COLLISIONS TO PRODUCE A POPULATION INVERSION**

[76] Inventor: **Gordon Gould**, 1200 N. Nash Ave., Arlington, Va. 22209

[21] Appl. No.: **823,611**

[22] Filed: **Aug. 11, 1977**

Related U.S. Application Data

[60] Division of Ser. No. 498,065, Aug. 16, 1974, Pat. No. 4,053,845, which is a continuation of Ser. No. 644,035, Mar. 6, 1967, abandoned, and Ser. No. 804,540, Apr. 6, 1959, abandoned, said Ser. No. 644,035, is a division of Ser. No. 804,540, Apr. 6, 1959, abandoned, and a continuation-in-part of Ser. No. 804,539, Apr. 6, 1959, abandoned.

[51] **Int. Cl.**[4] **H01S 3/00; H01S 3/22; H01S 30/097**

[52] **U.S. Cl.** **330/4.3; 372/34; 372/55; 372/85; 372/100**

[58] **Field of Search** .... 331/94.5 G, 94.5 P; 330/4.3; 372/55, 85

[56] **References Cited**

U.S. PATENT DOCUMENTS

2,929,922 3/1960 Schawlow et al. 330/4.3

OTHER PUBLICATIONS

Fabrikant, "Trudy Vsesoiuznoe Eleckttotekhniiheskii Institut, 41, 254, pp. 273–274.
Headrick et al., "Collisions of the Second Kind etc. . . ", 3/15/31, pp. 736–755, Physical Review, vol. 37.
Mitchell et al., "Resonance Radiation and Excited Atoms", 1934, pp. 57–89 and 154–255, MacMillan Co.
Schawlow et al., "Infrared and Optical Movers", 12/58, pp. 1940–1949, Physical Review, vol. 112.
Biberman, "V. A. Fabrikant", 5–6/68, pp. 798–799, Soviet Physics Uspekhi, vol. 10, #6.

Primary Examiner—Nelson Moskowitz
Attorney, Agent, or Firm—Lerner, David, Littenberg, Krumholz & Mentlik

[57] **ABSTRACT**

This application discloses light amplification apparatus in which population inversion is created in which energized particles collide with a lasing medium to create a population inversion. In the preferred embodiment the energized particles are atoms, ions, or molecules different than the lasing medium which are excited to a long-lived state above the ground state. Various materials usable in such light amplification apparatus are disclosed as well as means for passing light through an amplification region.

15 Claims, 6 Drawing Figures

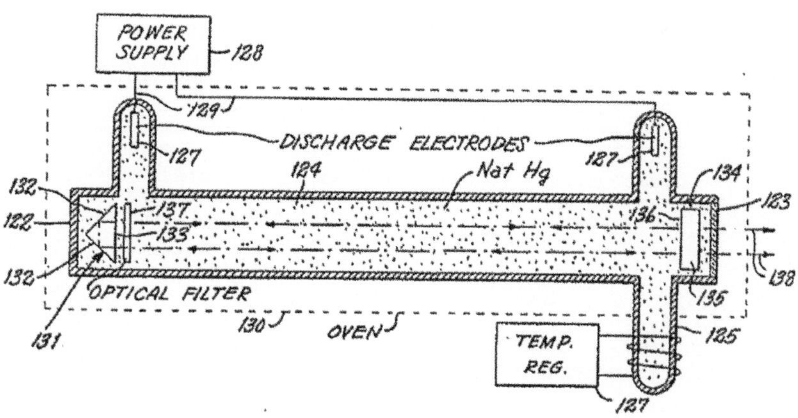

United States Patent [19]
Gould

[11] **Patent Number:** **4,746,201**
[45] **Date of Patent:** **May 24, 1988**

[54] **POLARIZING APPARATUS EMPLOYING AN OPTICAL ELEMENT INCLINED AT BREWSTER'S ANGLE**

[76] Inventor: **Gordon Gould**, 1200 N. Nash Ave., Arlington, Va. 22209

[21] Appl. No.: **869,831**

[22] Filed: **Jan. 16, 1978**

Related U.S. Application Data

[60] Division of Ser. No. 823,665, Aug. 11, 1977, which is a division of Ser. No. 498,065, Aug. 16, 1974, Pat. No. 4,053,845, which is a continuation of Ser. No. 644,035, Mar. 6, 1967, abandoned, and Ser. No. 804,540, Apr. 6, 1959, abandoned, said Ser. No. 644,035, is a division of Ser. No. 804,540, , and a continuation-in-part of Ser. No. 804,539, Apr. 6, 1959, abandoned.

[51] **Int. Cl.**^{4} **G02B 27/28**; G02B 5/30
[52] **U.S. Cl.** **350/394**
[58] **Field of Search** .... 350/147, 152, 286, 370, 350/394, 399, 379–383; 356/112, 90–92, 351, 352, 364, 28.5, 152, 359; 330/4.3; 331/94.5 C; 362/19

[56] **References Cited**

U.S. PATENT DOCUMENTS

1,610,423	12/1926	Cawley	350/394
1,783,031	11/1930	Alexanderson et al.	350/152
2,309,268	1/1943	Noske	350/286
2,660,916	12/1953	Zobel et al.	356/359
2,703,505	3/1955	Senn	356/152
2,726,173	12/1955	Martin	250/225
2,851,652	9/1958	Dicke	250/225
2,870,671	1/1959	Falconi	356/152
2,929,922	3/1960	Schawlow et al.	331/94.5 C
2,998,746	9/1961	Gievers	356/152
3,073,168	1/1963	Adams et al.	356/28.5

FOREIGN PATENT DOCUMENTS

319869	10/1929	United Kingdom	350/152
460666	1/1937	United Kingdom	350/399
953721	4/1964	United Kingdom .	
953722	4/1964	United Kingdom .	
953723	4/1964	United Kingdom .	
953726	4/1964	United Kingdom .	
953727	4/1964	United Kingdom .	
953724	9/1964	United Kingdom .	
953725	9/1964	United Kingdom .	

OTHER PUBLICATIONS

Jenkins & White, "Fundamentals of Optics", McGraw Hill, 1950, pp. 225–228, 264–275, 444–448, & 494–498.
Bird et al., "Pile-of-Plates Polarizers for Infrared; Improvement in Analysis & Design", Jr. Opt. Soc. Am., 3-1959, pp. 235–237.
Lengyel, "Evolution of Masers and Lasers", American J. Physics, vol. 34, No. 10, pp. 903–913, (1966).
Maiman, "Stimulated Optical Radiation in Ruby", Nature, vol. 187, pp. 493–494, (1960).
Rabinowitz et al., "Continuous Optically Pumped Cs Laser", J. Applied Optics, vol. 1, No. 4, pp. 513–516, (1962).
Javan et al., Physical Review Letters, vol. 6, No. 3, pp. 106–110, (1961).
Schawlow et al (II), Physical Review, vol. 112, No. 6, 12/15/58, pp. 1940–1949.
TR6 Report, AD-278053, vol. 1, 1962, pp. (3–49)-(-3–52).
TR6 Report, AD-292165, 1962, pp. (5–6)-(5–12).
Makas et al., "New Arrangement of Silver Chloride Polarizer for the Infrared", Jr. Optical Soc. America, vol. 45, 1955, pp. 998–999.
Jenkins et al., "Fundamentals of Optics", McGraw-Hill, 1950, pp. 486–492.
Partington, J. R., "An Advanced Treatise on Physical Chemistry", Longmans Green & Co., 1953, pp. 104–107.

Primary Examiner—Harvey E. Behrewd
Attorney, Agent, or Firm—Lerner, David, Littenberg, Krumholz & Mentlik

[57] **ABSTRACT**

This application disclosed light polarizing apparatus in which light traverses a light path more than once. The light path passes through an amplification region caused by a population inversion. An optical element is mounted to intersect the light path at Brewster's angle polarizing the light passing therethrough.

3 Claims, 8 Drawing Sheets

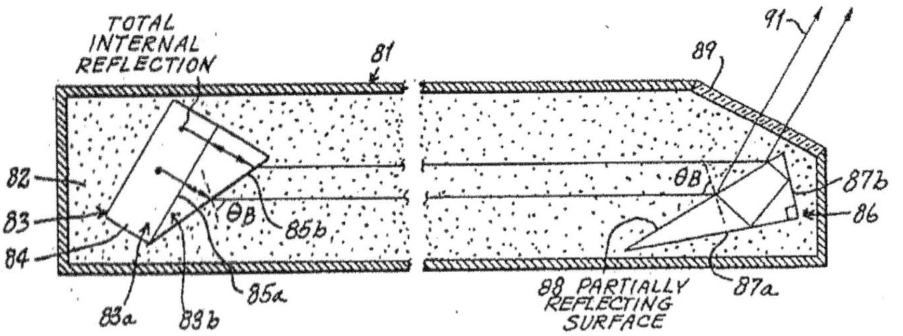

11 Examination and Prosecution of a Patent Application

11.1 U.S. PATENT EXAMINATION PROCESS

Once your patent application is filed with the U.S. Patent & Trademark Office (USPTO), it is examined for compliance with technical filing requirements, novelty, non-obviousness, patent eligible subject matter, and utility. A Patent Examiner will report the results of the examination to your patent attorney, or directly to you if you have filed your application on your own. In most cases, the application will not be allowed after this first report, and you and your attorney will be required to confer to review the Patent Examiner's action, and to file a response that overcomes the examiner's objections and/or rejections. This back-and-forth process may continue over several exchanges between your attorney and the examiner. The purpose of this chapter is to provide you with information regarding the patent examination process, which in turn will enable you to understand the content of the report from the examiner, and how to assist your attorney in preparing a persuasive response, and obtain issuance of your patent.

11.2 THE PATENT EXAMINATION SYSTEM—A LITTLE MORE HISTORY

This chapter starts after your patent application was completed and reviewed, you signed the formal papers, and the application was forwarded to the USPTO for examination by a Patent Examiner, who is an employee of the USPTO, a federal agency. The patent examination process that takes place today is, in substance, the same as the procedure established by Senator Ruggles' Patent Act of 1836—except for the short time in the late 1800s that the Commissioner of Patents reportedly closed the Patent Office, since he believed that nothing further of any use could be invented. Also recall that prior to 1952; Patent Examiners only examined a claimed invention for novelty. It was not until the 1952 Patent Act that non-obviousness was made a statutory requirement for the issuance of a patent by the U.S. Patent Office, as it was called then.

Intellectual Property Law for Engineers, Scientists, and Entrepreneurs, Second Edition. Howard B. Rockman.

Published 2020 by John Wiley & Sons, Inc.

11.3 FILING THE PATENT APPLICATION WITH THE USPTO

Upon arriving at the USPTO, your patent application receives a filing date and is assigned an application serial number. When the application issues as a patent, it receives a patent number, which is different from, and unrelated to, the application serial number. The filing date is the date on which your application was electronically filed, or remitted by express courier, such as the Express Mail service of the U.S. Postal Service, to the USPTO, not the date the application was actually received. Thus, using electronic filing or express courier service to file your application allows you to obtain an earlier filing date than if other means of transmittal are used.

The assigned filing date establishes the effective filing date of the application, which also establishes the date for defining prior art, as previously explained, and is also important in perfecting foreign patent rights. Also, once the application receives a filing date, the running of any statutory bar period stops, and commercialization and public disclosure of the invention can begin without fear of losing U.S. or foreign patent rights as a result of the statutory bar or public disclosure restraints discussed previously. There is no need to wait until the patent issues to begin commercializing your invention. The serial number and filing date also serve to identify and provide access to the patent application by the Patent Examiner and by your patent attorney during the examination and prosecution of the application. Note also that sole inventors, small groups of inventors, and those inventors not under any obligation to assign their invention and patents to a company or entity having more than 500 employees are entitled to reduced government filing, issue, and other fees charged by the USPTO for examining and issuing patents.

After your patent application is granted a serial number and filing date, the application is assigned to an art unit of the USPTO, which comprises a group of Patent Examiners who handle patent applications in the technology area to which your application is directed. Once in the appropriate art unit, the application is placed on the docket of (assigned to) an individual Patent Examiner who has a technical degree and expertise in the technology area of your invention, and who has examined many other patent applications in the same genre of technology. Due to the backlog of patent applications awaiting examination by the corps of Patent Examiners, it may take from approximately 8 months to 2 years, and sometimes more, for your application to reach its initial examination. After reviewing your application, the Patent Examiner conducts a search of the prior art, prepares a written report of the examination results, and forwards the report to your attorney. Your attorney will notify you of the content of the report, and you and your attorney will discuss an appropriate response to the examination report. Both the examination process and the response process are discussed later in this chapter at Sections 11.4 to 11.6 in more detail.

Patent applications filed prior to November 29, 2000, remain in secrecy until they issue as a patent. Those patent applications filed after November 29, 2000, are published prior to issuance 18 months after their effective filing date, unless the applicant or his or her attorney states in writing upon filing the application that there is no present intention of filing foreign counterpart patent applications, and that the applicant desires that the application not be published. If the applicant later changes his/her mind, the USPTO is so notified, and the U.S. patent application is then published at the 18th month date, or thereafter if that point in time has passed. Currently, the USPTO is electronically publishing patent applications 18 months after filing, and not on paper. If a provisional patent application has been filed, the non-provisional application is published 18 months after the *provisional* application filing date.

Keep in mind, therefore, that the patentability search conducted prior to filing your patent application will not uncover pending patent applications that are maintained in secrecy by the USPTO until they issue or are published. By logging on to the USPTO website (www.uspto.gov), you and/or your patent attorney or searcher can access those patent applications published upon reaching 18 months of pendency, where no intent to forego foreign patent application filings has been noted in the record of the patent application. A published pending patent application filed before your patent application filing or priority date can be used as prior art during the examination of your application.

11.4 EXAMINATION OF THE PATENT APPLICATION

Upon reaching a new (not previously examined) patent application, the Patent Examiner reviews the application to ensure that three primary criteria are met. First, the Patent Examiner verifies that all technical filing requirements have been met. For example, is there a complete specification with at least one claim? Are drawings present, if drawings are described in the specification? Is a signed Declaration or Oath in the file? Has the fee been paid? Has the patent application been assigned to the proper Art Unit? Is one invention or more than one distinct invention claimed in the application? Is the specification in understandable English, and are the claims clearly worded and in proper form, for example, proper multiple dependency? Discrepancies sometimes occur in patent applications initially drafted abroad to be filed first in a foreign country, which applications are then translated and filed in the USPTO in the format of the first filed country. These discrepancies are normally corrected in the response of your patent attorney to the first communication from the Patent Examiner, as will be explained further in Section 11.6.

Second, the Patent Examiner ensures that the claimed invention falls into one of the categories of patentable subject matter set forth in 35 U.S.C. §101. For example, if the invention is set forth in the claims in purely conceptual terms, with no structure or function to embody or define the invention, the application will be rejected. An example would be a claim which reads: “A fibrous cloth having a tendency to wear rough rather than smooth.” This “claim” is improper since it describes only the result achieved by the fibrous cloth, without defining any structure to accomplish that result. In addition, if the Patent Examiner, based upon his or her expertise in the related technical field, deems that the claimed or described invention will not work for its intended use, or if the invention has no use at all, the application will be rejected. Additional non-statutory, and thus non-patentable subject matter includes:

1. Printed matter.
2. Naturally occurring articles, such as a shrimp with the head and digestive tract removed.

3. Scientific principles; natural phenomena; laws of nature; purely abstract concepts.
4. Inventions concerned with atomic energy, which are dealt with in the U.S. Atomic Energy Act.

Several years ago, methods of doing business and software algorithms were on the above list. However, these two categories are now defined as patentable subject matter under certain conditions. The same is true for genetically modified living creatures.

Third, the Patent Examiner conducts a search of the prior art, and based on his or her search results, determines whether the claims of the application define an invention that is novel and non-obvious compared to the prior art. Recall that filed with your patent application is the Information Disclosure Statement, listing all prior art you and your attorney are aware of that could be material at this stage of examination of your claimed invention. Upon reading your specification and claims to the point of understanding what the claims define as novel about your invention, the Patent Examiner determines the appropriate class and subclass of the prior art that should be searched to uncover issued patents and published articles related to your claimed invention. The relevant prior art is stored and classified in a search area on electronic document retrieval systems within the confines of the Patent Examiner's art unit.

The Examiner then searches the relevant classes and subclasses to determine the closest related prior art, using the state-of-the-art electronic search databases to assist in conducting the search. If deemed necessary, the Patent Examiner also searches analogous prior art classes and subclasses to possibly find prior art references relating to portions or details of your claimed invention to be combined with references found in the initial search. For example, during my experience as a Patent Examiner, the automatic vehicle transmissions in my area of technology responsibility incorporated parallel systems of planetary gear sets, with brakes and clutches controlling the braking or movement of single or multiple elements of the gear sets. On numerous occasions, I consulted with examiners in the brake art and in the clutch art to determine the novelty, or lack thereof, of brake and clutch elements embodied in the transmission claimed in a patent application I was examining. When deemed necessary, I extended my search to the analogous brake and/or clutch classes and subclasses.

The search by the Patent Examiner is conducted to determine whether the submitted claims in your application define an invention that is totally shown or taught in a single prior art reference under 35 U.S.C. §102, or whether your claimed invention would be obvious to one of ordinary skill in the related art, as concluded from the content of a combination of two or more prior art references under 35 U.S.C. §103.

11.5 RESULTS OF THE EXAMINATION—THE "OFFICE ACTION"

Upon completing the examination of your patent application, the Patent Examiner is required by the Patent Statute to prepare a written report of the results of the examination, including identifying all prior art references cited in the examination report and explaining how the prior art reads on the claims in the application. This examination report is commonly known as an "Office Action," and is forwarded to your patent attorney, or to the applicant in the rare case where the inventor is not represented by an attorney. If your patent application has been prepared and filed by your patent attorney, and you have executed a Power of Attorney, the Patent Examiner will communicate only with your attorney, who reviews the Office Action upon receiving same. The examiner will not communicate directly with you.

The Office Action must set forth in detail the Patent Examiner's position on all of the claims in your application regarding patentable subject matter, utility, novelty, and/or obviousness issues, and present comments on other technical matters that must be corrected to place the patent application in proper form. The USPTO rules require that the Office Action be complete, and that it clearly set forth all reasons supporting the examiner's decisions. The purpose of this clarity requirement is that upon receipt of the Office Action, the applicant and his or her attorney must decide, based upon the examiner's comments, whether it is worthwhile to continue with the expenditure of resources to further the prosecution of the patent application. In many instances, the examiner will suggest language changes in the claims that in the examiner's opinion may assist in defining your invention over the prior art, or which may overcome some technical objection to a portion of the application.

Since a patent application is normally written with claims that attempt to define the invention in the broadest possible terms to elicit citation by the Patent Examiner of the most relevant prior art, most patent applications do not result in allowance of the claims or issued patents upon the first examination. Therefore, expect the first Office Action to normally be a "rejection" of some or all of the claims. That is no reason to worry, however. Read on to find out how such rejections are responded to and overcome!

11.6 YOU AND YOUR ATTORNEY'S RESPONSE TO THE OFFICE ACTION

Upon your attorney's receipt of the Office Action from the Patent Examiner, the attorney can be expected to quickly review the claims, the Office Action, and the prior art cited and applied by the Patent Examiner. The purpose of this review is to determine whether or not the cited prior art can be overcome by proper amendment and/or argument back to the Patent Examiner, or whether the prior art so closely resembles the claimed invention that in the patent attorney's opinion, patent protection may not obtainable.

A copy of the Office Action and all cited and applied prior art, as well as the attorney's comments, are then forwarded to the inventor for review, and to determine if the inventor continues to be interested in going forward with protecting the invention. The first inquiry is whether the client desires to pursue the patenting process, since it is quite possible that in the 8 to 12 months it took the USPTO to act upon the patent application, the invention may no longer be of importance to the applicant, and thus the expenditure of further resources on patent prosecution should be ended. Note also that since the enforceable term of a patent dates from its filing date, and not its issue date, and enforcement of the patent cannot begin until the issue date, it is important that you receive from your patent attorney the Office Action and any relevant comments at the earliest possible time so that no delay is encountered in ultimate issuance of the patent.

The letter to you accompanying the Office Action and prior art furnished by your attorney should also request your input as to whether or not the prior art can be overcome based upon your review. You will be requested to examine the prior art in detail, and to furnish your patent attorney with your comments regarding all differences between the prior art and your invention in structure, function, advantages, and/or results obtained. In most instances, you as the inventor can observe several specific differences between your invention and the prior art that escaped the eyes of your patent attorney. If necessary, you can confer with the patent attorney directly to obtain a further understanding of the content of the prior art cited and applied by the Patent Examiner in examining the claims of your patent application.

If you and your employer have decided that it is advantageous to continue with the examination and prosecution of the application, a response must be furnished to the Patent Examiner within three months. An additional three months to respond can be "purchased" from the USPTO in one-month increments; however, it is the normal practice of the patent attorney to respond to the Patent Examiner within the initial three months to avoid unnecessary costs. Delaying beyond the three-month period only increases the expense of prosecution. Note also that an extension of time up to six months is the maximum response time allowed. If the Patent Examiner has not received a response within that six-month period, the patent application is abandoned, and further difficulty and expense may be incurred in trying to revive the abandoned application.

In the Office Action, the Patent Examiner may have determined that the invention itself, compared to the prior art, is just not patentable. Or, the examiner may have recognized that the patent specification does describe a patentable invention, and the only argument is over the form and scope of the claims, which the examiner may determine in their present state read on the prior art based upon the examiner's interpretation of that prior art. Ultimately, it is the purpose of your response to have the Patent Examiner recognize both the existence of a patentable invention, and confirm that the form and scope of the claims adequately define that patentable invention over the content of the prior art. Keep in mind also that if the Patent Examiner is not ultimately satisfied about the patentability of your claimed invention, an appeal process in the USPTO is also available.

Upon receipt of the Office Action and prior art from your patent attorney, you should immediately review these materials to determine what type of response will be necessary to overcome the examiner's position. For example, you may have personal knowledge of one of the devices disclosed in the prior art, and also have personal knowledge that the disclosed device is inoperative, or functions poorly. To submit that information to the Patent Examiner, a Declaration or Affidavit from you may be necessary. Since it will take time to prepare such a Declaration or Affidavit, your patent attorney should be notified shortly after your review of the prior art that you have noticed this discrepancy in the prior art, and that a Declaration or Affidavit should be prepared. Also, if there are any other comments that you desire to place in the record of the patent application in support of patentability, a Declaration or Affidavit setting forth your comments should also be prepared.

After reviewing the Office Action, discuss with your patent attorney the possible benefits of an interview with the examiner, in person or by phone, to limit or clarify the rejections and/or objections lodged against your application. This may lead to a clearer understanding of how the examiner reads the prior art, and may prevent the incorporation of unnecessary limiting amendments to your claims or the inclusion of written comments in response to the Office Action that later may limit the scope of your claim language.

In responding to the Patent Examiner's position, it may be advisable to amend the claims to limit their scope to overcome the prior art. This can be accomplished so long as the amendments do not introduce any new matter or new material into the patent application. Conversely, it may be the position of you and your attorney that the Patent Examiner has completely misinterpreted the prior art, and that the prior art references cited by the examiner do not in any way anticipate or render obvious your claimed invention. In such a case, the response to the Patent Examiner may not be an amendment to the claims, but may instead consist of strenuous arguments showing the technical reasoning supporting your opinion that the Patent Examiner's interpretation of the prior art is incorrect. In a section headed REMARKS in the response to the Office Action, comments and arguments are made in support of your position of allowability of the claims in the application, whether they have been amended or whether they remain the same. In addition, amendments may be made to the claims to eliminate any discerned ambiguity or indefiniteness noticed by the Patent Examiner.

It is important to use the minimum number of arguments in supporting amendments to your claims, since the old expression that anything you say may be held against you is particularly true in patent prosecution. For example, if you strenuously argue that your application claims that a coil spring is a resilient element to define your claims around a showing in a prior art reference, and a potential infringer later uses a spongy material as a resilient element, your patent claims may be limited to the coil spring and not be construed to encompass the spongy material. Therefore, the patent attorney and the inventor should be careful in the language they choose in responding to the Patent Examiner so as not to add unintentional limitations to the scope of the claims.

It is also important to ensure that the arguments made in your response to the Patent Examiner relate to the subject matter that is recited in the claims of your patent application. It is the claims that define the invention, not the patent specification, and the differences between the prior art and your invention must be recited in those claims, and those differences should be clearly pointed out to the examiner in your response to the Office Action.

You, as the inventor, should assure yourself that when the claims of your patent application are amended, the patent attorney has not unduly limited the scope of the definition of your invention. Therefore, I recommend that you instruct your patent attorney to furnish you with a copy of the amendments to the claims that he or she suggests sending back to the Patent Examiner in response to the Office Action, so that you may determine whether you, or anyone else can "design around" the claims as amended. If you can easily get around these claims, then changes will have to be made again to the claims so that your invention is not unduly limited by the amended claims.

The response to the Office Action also corrects any technical errors in the filing requirements that the examiner notes, as well as any typographical errors or other errors that are encompassed within the four corners of the patent application.

Keep in mind that the patent examination process should not be deemed an adversarial process. The examiners adhere to the policy of wanting to issue claims. You and your patent attorney or agent just have to convince the examiner that you are not asking for more claim coverage than you deserve in view of the prior art.

11.7 FURTHER PATENT PROSECUTION

Following you and your attorney's response to the initial Office Action of the Patent Examiner, the Examiner may issue a second Office Action rejecting the same claims, or finding that some previously rejected claims still fail to define novelty or non-obviousness over the prior art, while other claims have been found allowable. Or, the examiner may issue a Notice of Allowance indicating that the examiner has found that all claims in the application, including those that have been amended, define a patentable invention over the prior art. In this latter case, the application will subsequently issue as a patent after the "Issue Fee" has been submitted to the USPTO.

In those cases where the second Office Action reports that certain of the claims still fail to define your invention over the prior art, this Office Action may be designated a "final" rejection, which is not really final. You and your attorney have one more chance to respond to the final rejection, either amending the claims or furnishing arguments in response to the comments of the Patent Examiner in the Final Office Action, or both. If you and your attorney are persuasive in this "Amendment After Final," the application will be allowed by the examiner by withdrawing his or her objection and rejection of the claims, and ultimately your patent will issue.

If you and your attorney's response to the Final Office Action is not persuasive, you may (1) pay an additional filing fee and continue the prosecution of the patent application by submitting further arguments and amendments to the claims in an attempt to change the examiner's position, or (2) abandon the application. A third option, where you conclude that the Patent Examiner is in error, such as in his or her interpretation of the content of one or more of the prior art references, is to file an appeal before the USPTO Patent Trial and Appeal Board (PTAB). This board has the authority to overturn the Patent Examiner's decision based upon the persuasive arguments of your patent attorney, which you played a major role in preparing. If the Patent Examiner's decision is overturned by the PTAB, ultimately your patent will issue.

Upon the initial filing of the patent application, the applicant has the option of requesting the USPTO to expedite the process of examination of the application by submitting a Request for Prioritized Examination, and paying an additional fee set by the USPTO. If the request is granted, the application is acted upon by the examiner within three months of filing, and an effort is made to have the patent issue within one year of filing. However, if the examination process reaches the point of a "final rejection," and the applicant decides to file a "Request for Continuing Examination," an additional prioritized examination fee must be submitted to keep the examination process on the fast track.

11.8 GRANTING THE PATENT

After all of the claims remaining in the patent application have been allowed by the Patent Examiner, and all technical matters in the application have been taken care of, such as the correction of typographical errors, a Notice of Allowance and Issue Fee Due is transmitted by the examiner to your attorney, along with a notification that the Issue Fee must be paid within a certain time period. Also, the Notice of Allowance may require that formal drawings of your invention be submitted, if the application was originally filed with informal drawings that did not comply with the USPTO requirements for illustrating the invention.

Upon compliance with the requirements noted in the Notice of Allowance, the patent application is advanced to be printed, sealed, and issued as a U.S. Patent. At this point, your patent application stands in line behind other previously issued patents also waiting to be printed. Your application waits in this line for a few weeks before issuing as a patent.

The Patent Statute, at 35 U.S.C. §282, decrees that once a U.S. Patent issues following the examination process, the issued patent is presumed by law to be a valid patent. Further, the law states that each claim of the issued patent shall be presumed valid independently of the validity of the other claims, whether they are dependent claims or not. Also, a dependent claim shall be presumed valid even though it may depend upon an invalid claim. The law is strict that the burden of establishing invalidity of an issued patent or any claim of an issued patent shall rest on the party asserting invalidity in a court of law, or before the Patent Trial and Appeal Board.

The presumption of validity of a patent means that an accused infringer has the burden of establishing by "competent evidence" that the patent is not valid, usually as a defense to a charge of infringement in a lawsuit. As mentioned previously, this "competent evidence" presented by the alleged infringer must be prior art material that has not previously been considered by the Patent Examiner during the examination of the asserted patent. Again, this highlights the importance of having the Patent Examiner review all of the prior art that you can present to the examiner, so that the presumption of validity of the patent is ultimately strengthened.

Note also that, under the law, a "presumption" is a fact that stands only until it is successfully rebutted. Therefore, even though the issued patent is presumed valid, an alleged infringer in a lawsuit is permitted to present evidence of prior art not previously considered by the Patent Examiner in an attempt to overcome the presumption of validity. If the alleged infringer is successful, the patent will ultimately be held invalid, and the infringer will not be held liable for any acts of infringement of the invalid patent.

11.9 INFRINGEMENT DURING EXAMINATION OF THE PATENT APPLICATION

A patent cannot be enforced against an alleged infringer until the patent has issued from the USPTO. However, a procedure has been established within the USPTO to advance examination of your patent application where an alleged potential infringement has been discovered on the horizon. Therefore, where you and/or your company discover that someone is producing and marketing a product that is potentially infringing the claims of your pending patent application, it is important for you to advise your patent attorney immediately. At that point, your attorney will examine the potentially infringing product, determine whether the claims of your pending application cover that particular product, and if the answer is yes, a "Petition to Make Special" will be prepared and filed with the USPTO requesting the authorities there to instruct the examiner to expedite examination and issuance of your patent application.

Note also that your patent application at this point in time may not contain claims that read on the potentially infringing device, but the specification of your application may include a sufficiently complete description of your invention that claims can be amended or added that would cover the infringing device, without adding "new matter" to your patent application. Your attorney then will prepare new or amended claims to cover the infringing device, assuming such new claims (1) will not read on the prior art and (2) are supported by the disclosure of the originally filed patent application.

If the USPTO first determines that the evidence submitted in your Petition to Make Special warrants expedited examination of the application, the examiner will be so advised. The examiner will then act on your application out of order, and provide you with an immediate examination and Office Action. This examination may result in a further rejection of your claims, and it will then be incumbent upon you and your attorney to respond to the Patent Examiner as quickly as possible to maintain the expedited examination process.

Although you have created an expedited examination process, it will take some time to issue the patent, since the patent examination process cannot be completed immediately. For example, one of my clients had a patent application pending several years ago, and noticed an infringement—as a matter of fact, several infringements—in the market. We filed our Petition to Make Special, and it still took three years of arguing with the Patent Examiner and ultimately having the examiner overturned by the Board of Appeals and Interferences as the PTAB was known at that time, before the patent issued. When the patent issued, the infringers agreed to stop manufacturing the product covered by the patent, after a free ride on my client's technology for three years.

Note also that once the issue fee is paid and the patent application is set in line to be printed as a patent, that printing process takes a few weeks, and nothing can change that. Ultimately, however, your patent will issue, and all alleged infringements that can be proven will have to stop if an injunction is warranted by the facts.

11.10 ADDITIONAL PROBABLE PATENT PROSECUTION EVENTS

11.10.1 Continuation Patent Applications and the Request for Continuing Examination

As stated previously, you and your attorney may not obtain allowance of all the claims following the second action upon your application by the Patent Examiner. A continuation application is a procedural vehicle that is used to continue the examination of the patent application after the final rejection, and the refusal of the examiner to allow the application after the response to the final rejection. Also, a continuation application can be filed at any other time during pendency of your application; however, this is normally unnecessary until after a final rejection. The rationale behind filing a continuation application is, in my opinion, that for the fee you pay initially, you are entitled to two Office Actions and consideration of one amendment after the Final Office Action. At this point, if the examiner decides that the application is not yet in condition for allowance, you must file a continuation application, and pay a new filing fee to be entitled to further examination. In other words, for your initial filing fee, you get two bites at the apple. For an additional fee, you obtain more bites.

The filing of a continuing application in response to a Final Office Action is normally handled by filing a "Request for Continuing Examination" and submitting an additional application filing fee. After filing a request for continuing examination, the application retains the same serial number, and examination proceeds. If a continuation application is filed separately, it is given a new serial number.

Technically, a continuation application, or a request for continuing prosecution, is defined as the second patent application for the same invention claimed and disclosed in the first or parent application, where the continuation application is placed on file before the first, or parent, patent application becomes abandoned, or has issued as a patent, or has otherwise had proceedings terminated. The continuation application is afforded the benefit of the earlier filing date, or priority date, of the parent application. This is important, since by the time a continuation application has been filed, the invention may have been placed in public use by the inventor. Therefore, if the continuation application were not granted the benefit of the earlier filing date, the continuation application may not meet the requirement that the application be filed within one year of public use or sale of the disclosed invention. Note also that no new matter may be inserted into the continuation application that is not included in the original application.

Another reason for ensuring that the continuation application retains the filing date of the original application is that under the AIA, the earlier filing date defines what prior art the examiner can use during the examination process. The earlier your priority date, the less prior art is applicable.

One other point bears mentioning. As a result of the examination process of your patent application, certain broad claims may still be facing rejection, while more limited claims may have been allowed. If you have a reasonable basis for concluding that your broad claims do define patentable subject matter over the prior art, and that these claims define important technology, it may be advisable to file a continuation patent application containing only those yet non-allowed claims, and to have the first, or parent application, issue with the allowed but more limited claims. You can then continue to persuade the examiner that the non-allowed claims in your continuation application are allowable over the prior art applied by the examiner, and that your second application with the broader claims should also issue as a patent. In this case, it is permissible to have two patents covering the same invention: one with broad claims, and the other with narrower claims. Both of these patents will expire on the same day, for example, 20 years from the filing date of the original, or parent, patent application.

11.10.2 Continuation-in-Part Patent Applications

A continuation-in-part patent application is one filed during the pendency of any earlier filed patent application, and that includes new subject matter which is not disclosed in the earlier application, and which would constitute new matter if attempted to be added to the earlier or parent application. The continuation-in-part application substantially repeats most of the parent application, and adds drawings, descriptive material, and claims regarding the new subject matter in the application. A continuation-in-part application effectively ends up with two application filing dates: one for the originally disclosed subject matter that dates back to the original parent application, and a new filing date pertaining to the added material.

11.10.3 Divisional Patent Applications

The Patent Statutes and USPTO policy require that one patent is issued for one invention. If more than one invention is disclosed in a patent application upon filing, the examiner uses a form of objection designated a Restriction Requirement to compel the inventor and the attorney to comply with this policy. Thus, if two or more independent and distinct inventions are claimed in one patent application, the examiner may require the application to be restricted to one of the inventions for examination. You will receive this action from the Patent Examiner when there is no disclosed relationship between two or more claimed inventions in an application, or when the inventions are related but are capable of separate use and are patentably distinguishable.

Although one invention may be claimed in a single patent application, a reasonable number of species or varying embodiments of the single invention may also be described and claimed in the application if there is an allowable generic claim covering all of the species or embodiments.

In response to a Restriction Requirement by the examiner, the inventor's attorney selects one of the inventions for continued examination in the parent application. The claims to non-elected inventions are withdrawn from further consideration. Ultimately, before the originally filed application issues as a patent on the elected invention, a second or divisional patent application is filed including the non-elected claims to the separate and distinctive invention or inventions. The divisional application then proceeds through the examination process, ultimately toward issue or abandonment. If the divisional application issues, the inventor then has two patents covering each of the inventions. In certain instances, more than two inventions can be filed in an initial application, and several restriction requirements are requested by the examiner. In that case, it is possible that a multitude of patents may issue from the single originally filed patent application.

It is a common practice among the patent profession to file a patent application knowing ahead of time that there may be several inventions set forth and claimed in the application, and that ultimately divisional patent applications will be required. It is more expeditious and usually less expensive to group the inventions in a single application initially, obtain an early filing date, and deal with the separate invention issue and divisional applications as examination of the application proceeds.

Consider the following example: You are a member of the R&D department of a manufacturer of steam irons. You have developed a new hand-operated steam iron for ironing clothing with a novel switch mechanism that automatically turns the steam iron off when in the vertical position, and then turns the steam iron on when moved to the horizontal position for use. You have also determined that the novel switch mechanism may have use in products other than steam irons where it is desired to turn the product on and off depending upon movement between vertical and horizontal orientation. Your patent attorney files a patent application with a first set of claims directed to the combination of the steam iron and novel orientation-responsive switch, and a second set of claims directed to the novel switch per se. As your attorney and you anticipated, the first Office Action from the examiner states that your patent application is directed to two distinct inventions, i.e., the combination of iron and switch, and the switch alone, and only one of those sets of claims can be moved forward for examination in this application. Your attorney can select either set of claims, but since the combination claims are more important to your company, the combination claims are selected. The claims to the switch per se are withdrawn from the examination process in this application, and at any time before the application with the combination claims is issued, or abandoned, a second "divisional" patent application is filed. This divisional application consists of the same specification and drawings as the originally filed patent application, but only the claims to the novel switch by itself are included in the newly filed divisional patent application. The divisional application then proceeds on its own examination track, separate from the parent application.

11.11 RE-EXAMINATION OF AN ISSUED PATENT BY THE APPLICANT, THE INFRINGER, OR THE COMMISSIONER OF PATENTS

Any person, either the applicant or anyone else, at any time during the period of enforceability of an issued patent, may file a request with the USPTO for re-examination of any or all of the claims of the issued patent. Such request must be based upon pertinent and applicable prior art patents or other printed publications that were not previously reviewed by the Patent Examiner during the examination of the patent in question. The USPTO will initially determine whether or not the newly submitted prior art raises new questions of materiality and patentability, and then decide whether or not a re-examination should be conducted. If it is determined that no re-examination is to be conducted, the USPTO will then so notify the person seeking the re-examination. If the USPTO decides that the new prior art submitted is material to certain or all of the claims of the issued patent, a re-examination procedure will be established, and the request will be sent to the original Patent Examiner for handling.

Re-examination proceedings can arise in several different ways. First, if a lawsuit is filed against an alleged infringer, and the alleged infringer introduces prior art during the lawsuit that was not considered by the examiner during examination of the patent, the patent owner during the pendency of the lawsuit has the right to go back to the USPTO, submit this new prior art to the Patent Examiner for re-examination, and hopefully obtain a decision that the new prior art is no more pertinent to the issued patent than the prior art previously applied by the examiner during prosecution of the patent. In that case, the owner of the patent in the litigation has thus eliminated that patent as prior art for consideration by the judge or jury.

Also, the defendant or potential infringer in a patent lawsuit may submit new prior art to the USPTO in an attempt to have the examiner determine that the patent is invalid, rather than to cast the lot of invalidity before a judge or jury. Further, the Commissioner of Patents, on his or her own volition, may seek re-examination of a patent on a myriad of grounds.

Note that during a re-examination proceeding, the patent owner can amend the claims to possibly avoid the new prior art, and then emerge with a re-examined patent that may be stronger and may still cover a potentially infringing device. This amendment process during a re-examination allows the claims to be narrowed in coverage, but not to be broadened.

The recently enacted AIA provisions and rules regarding Inter Parties Re-examination are discussed in Chapter 18.

11.12 RE-ISSUE PATENTS

A re-issue patent application is filed, when necessary, after a patent has issued and review of the issued patent indicates that an "error" has occurred. One such "error" can be that the scope of claim coverage in the patent is too limited, without any deceptive intent. Therefore, it is possible to file for re-issuance of a patent within the first two years of its enforceable life to obtain broader claim coverage. After two years from the date of issue of the patent, a broadening re-issue is not allowed. Note that the re-issue patent has the same life as the patent from which it has been re-issued, that is, 20 years from the date of filing of the original patent application.

Narrowing re-issue patent applications may be filed at any time during the enforceable life of the issued parent patent. Some reasons to consider when thinking of filing a re-issue patent application are the following: (1) to present claims of modified scope for evaluation over additional prior art, (2) to correct a misjoinder of inventors, (3) to claim the benefit of an earlier filing date, (4) to obtain broader claim coverage within the first two years, and (5) to obtain enhanced validity of the patent. The problem with re-issues is that once a request to re-issue a patent has been filed, the patent undergoes a new examination process, and the possibility exists that the examiner may uncover additional prior art that was overlooked before and reject the claims. This is a risk that has to be evaluated before submitting a patent for re-issue, and the risk can be minimized by conducting a search of the prior art before submitting the patent for re-issue.

◆ INVENTORS AND INVENTIONS ◆

Nicolaus Otto

THE INTERNAL COMBUSTION ENGINE

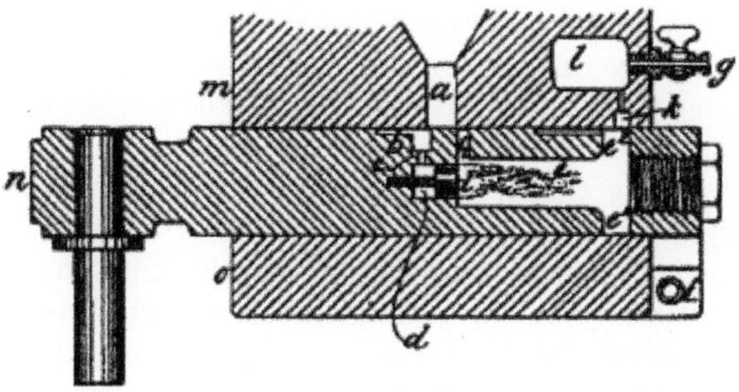

The most universal method of producing power today in both moving vehicles and in stationary factories and other facilities is the internal combustion engine. Today's internal combustion engines operate in practically the same way as the ones that were developed during the latter part of the 19th century.

The first self-propelled, over-the-road vehicles were powered by steam engines. The earliest of such vehicles was built by Nicolas J. Cugnot of France in 1769. However, steam-propelled vehicles were fueled by coal and were inefficient, and those with an interest in mechanics in the 19th century endeavored to provide more efficient power for both moving vehicles and stationary power sources. It was the invention of the four-stroke internal combustion engine, operating on liquid fuel, that provided the means for developing and producing the millions of motor vehicles in operation today.

The development of the internal combustion engine dates back, believe it or not, to the year 1680 when a Dutch physicist, Christian Huygens, designed an internal combustion engine fueled with gun powder. However, Huygens never built his engine. More than a century later, in 1807, Francois Isaac de Rivas, of Switzerland, designed an unsuccessful vehicle using an internal combustion engine powered by a blend of oxygen and hydrogen as fuel.

In 1858, a Belgian engineer, Jean Joseph Étienne Lenoir, developed and in 1860 obtained a patent on a two-stroke, coal-gas-fueled internal combustion engine using electric spark ignition. In 1863, Lenoir improved his engine, using petroleum and a carburetor, which he attached to a wagon that completed a 50-mile overland tour. This was the first workable internal combustion engine.

Intellectual Property Law for Engineers, Scientists, and Entrepreneurs, Second Edition. Howard B. Rockman.

Published 2020 by John Wiley & Sons, Inc.

In 1862, Alphonse Beau de Rochas of France obtained French patent number 52,593 for a four-stroke engine. However, de Rochas never constructed this engine. In 1864, an Austrian, Siegfried Marcus, constructed a single-cylinder internal combustion engine, which he attached to a cart that completed a 50-foot tour. The modern four-cycle gasoline powered internal combustion engine that is used practically universally today is primarily the creation of Nicolaus Otto. His Otto cycle engine, which was named after him, was conceived in 1861, and later constructed, successfully tested, and used in 1876.

Nicolaus August Otto was born on June 14, 1832, in Holzhausen, Germany. At the age of 16, Otto dropped out of high school and worked successfully as a clerk in a grocery store and as a traveling salesman, marketing sugar, kitchenware, and tea to grocery stores. According to his biographers, Otto took these positions to make enough money to marry the love of his life, Ann, who he met at a carnival in Cologne in 1858 when he was 26.

Throughout his selling career, Otto maintained a keen interest in mechanical devices, particularly the technology of engines related to horse-drawn carriages and small factories. Kurt Rathke, in his biography of Otto, indicates that Otto was inspired in his technology dreams by watching smoke rise from a chimney while sitting on a park bench. Like all inventors and discoverers, Otto was effectively drawn into his development work by his intense characteristics of curiosity, fascination, and wonder. According to Rathke, Otto made the decision that the explosion in a gas engine, which he compared to the chimney, should receive a rich fuel mixture. Otto's idea was to allow fresh air to enter the engine first and mix with unburned gases from the previous working stroke. After that, the fuel mixture would be inducted.

In approximately 1860, Otto learned about Lenoir's successful experiments with two-stroke internal combustion engines. However, the Lenoir engine did not achieve popular success. Not only did the engine have a less than reliable electrical ignition system, but it consumed expensive gas, almost 100 cubic feet of gas per horsepower per hour. In addition, the Lenoir engine required massive amounts of cooling water, and the heat generated usually ruined the bearings unless they were inordinately oiled; when not oiled, the engine seized. Otto concluded that the Lenoir engine would be improved if operated with a liquid, rather than gas, fuel.

While employed as a salesman in 1861, Otto had been sharing his ideas on internal combustion technology with Ugen Langen, the proprietor of a sugar factory, who was also a technician. Otto confided his ideas to Langen during his trips to Langen's shop to buy and sell sugar. In 1864–1865, Langen and Otto established N.A. Otto & Cie., the first company in the world to manufacture engines. Gottlieb Daimlar and Wilhelm Maybach later joined N.A. Otto & Cie. The company still exists today under the name Deutz AG, Köln, which remains one of the largest engine-producing companies in the world. In 1867, two years after the company was formed, Langen and Otto were awarded a gold medal at the Paris World Exhibition for their development and construction of a two-stroke atmospheric gas engine. The award was given for the development of the most economical power for small businesses.

Otto, however, continued in his attempts to develop and perfect his idea of a four-stroke internal combustion, high-compression engine that would use all types of fuels and be suitable for all types of applications. In May 1876, Otto realized his ambition when he built the first practical high-compression, four-stroke liquid-fuel-powered engine with an ignition device. The engine's first stroke drew in a combustible mixture of air and fuel. The second stroke of the piston compressed the mixture, and the compressed air–fuel mixture was exploded by the ignition system. The expansion of the exploded air–fuel mixture drove the piston downward for its third stroke. The fourth stroke of the piston, moving upward, exhausted the burnt fuel, and evacuated the cylinder to begin the cycle again. Otto patented his four-cycle internal combustion engine in 1887. Due to its relative quietness, efficiency, and reliability, more than 30,000 of Otto's engines were sold during the 10 years following its development in 1876. Gottlieb Daimlar attached Otto's engine to a bicycle to make what is considered to be the first motorcycle. Karl Benz built his first three-wheeled automobile incorporating an Otto engine. Otto never became involved directly in automobile production, but it is unquestioned that his four-stroke engine, which was the first practical alternative to the steam engine, began the era of modern automobile and heavy vehicle production.

After developing his four-stroke engine in 1876, Otto developed the first magneto engine ignition system using low voltage in 1884. In 1882, Otto, along with Alexander Graham Bell, was awarded an honorary doctorate degree by the University of Wurzburg. Ultimately, Otto's Patent No. 365,701 on his original liquid fuel engine of 1877 was invalidated based upon the previous de Rochas patent for the four-stroke engine that Rochas never built. Thus, although Rochas put his ideas on paper, Otto was the first to build a working engine based upon the four-cycle combustion process principle.

Nicolaus Otto died at age 59 on January 26, 1891, in Cologne. His engine was the prototype of internal combustion engines built from 1876 to today.

Oh, and by the way, he ultimately did make enough money to marry his sweetheart, Ann.

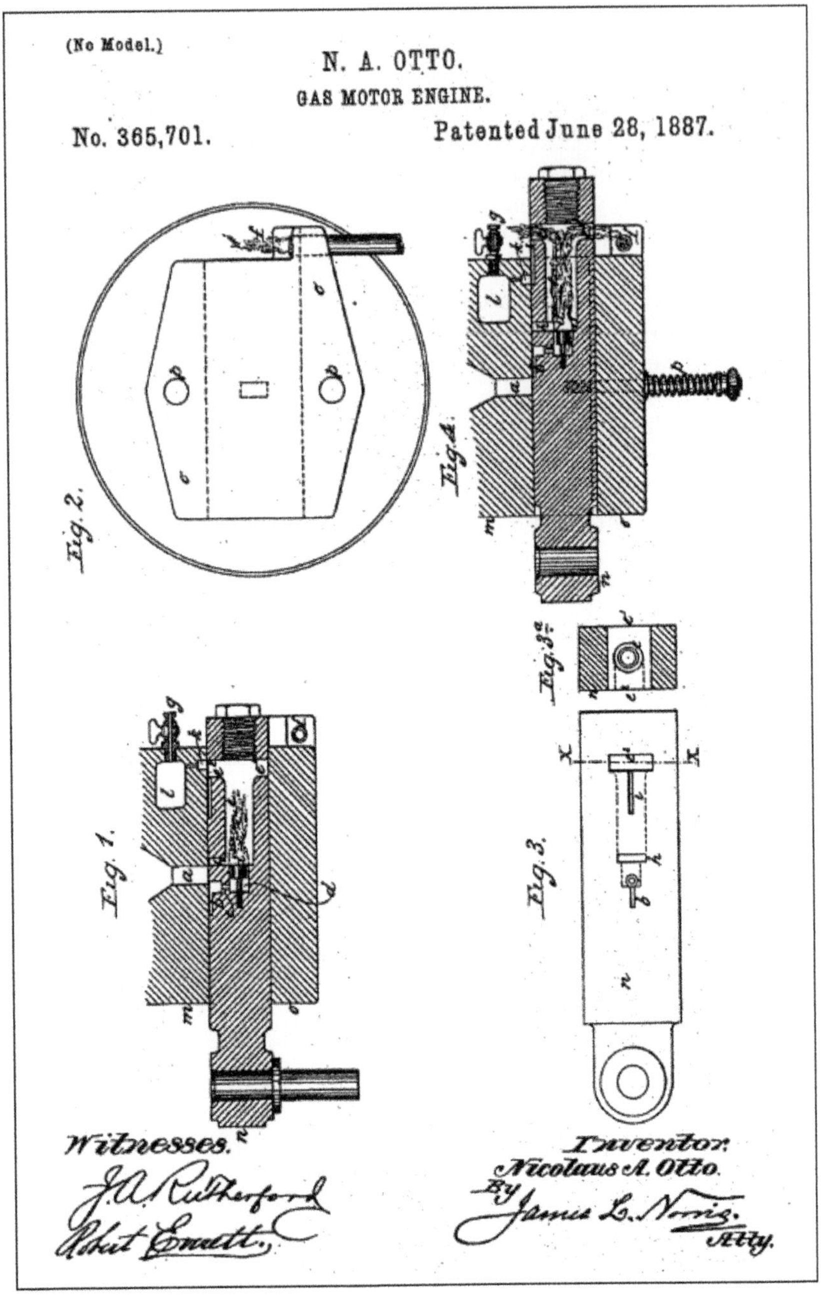
(No Model.)
N. A. OTTO.
GAS MOTOR ENGINE.
No. 365,701.
Patented June 28, 1887.
Fig. 1.
Fig. 2.
Fig. 3.
Fig. 4.
Witnesses.
Inventor.
Nicolaus A. Otto.
By James L. Norris,
Atty.

◆ INVENTORS AND INVENTIONS ◆

Rudolf Diesel

THE INTERNAL COMBUSTION ENGINE

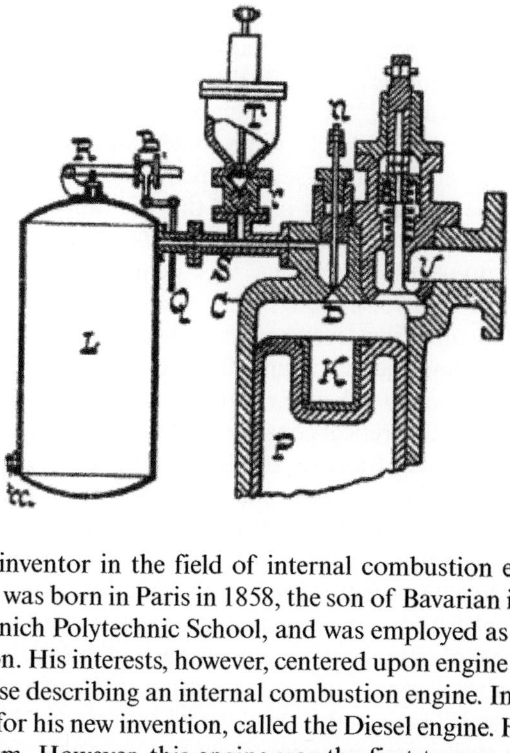

The second major inventor in the field of internal combustion engines is definitely Rudolf Diesel, who was born in Paris in 1858, the son of Bavarian immigrants. He was educated at the Munich Polytechnic School, and was employed as a refrigerator engineer after graduation. His interests, however, centered upon engine design, and in 1893 he authored a treatise describing an internal combustion engine. In 1894, he filed for a patent in Germany for his new invention, called the Diesel engine. His engine exploded and nearly killed him. However, this engine was the first to prove that fuel could be ignited without an ignition spark. His first successful engine was operated in 1897. In 1898, he obtained U.S. Patent No. 608,845 for his diesel internal combustion engine.

During his studies at the Munich Polytechnic, Diesel was inspired by a thermodynamics lecture in 1878 by Carl Linde, in which Linde espoused on the relatively poor efficiency of steam engines, and made comparisons to the theory by the French physicist Sadi Carnot, whose cyclic pressure and volume process foresaw higher energy efficiencies in power production. It is reported that Diesel made a lecture note to study whether it was possible to fully realize the Carnot cycle. The result of his lifetime of studies was to be the diesel engine, which even today is the internal combustion engine having the highest degree of efficiency.

Intellectual Property Law for Engineers, Scientists, and Entrepreneurs, Second Edition. Howard B. Rockman.

Published 2020 by John Wiley & Sons, Inc.

After completing his studies, Diesel returned to Paris, where for about 10 years he was the manager of the French branch of the German Linde Ice Machine Company. In 1890, he returned to Berlin where he took over management of Linde's technical office. One day, Diesel noticed a pneumatic cigarette lighter in which small pieces of tinder were held in a small glass tube. A piston was used to compress the air in the tube, and the tinder glowed. This vision started him on the path to developing the diesel engine.

During this time, Diesel's obsession with creating an efficient internal combustion engine led him to file a patent application, which issued on February 23, 1983: German Patent No. 67207, entitled "Working Method and Design for Combustion Engines." This patent application was based upon Diesel's theoretical ideas, and he realized that to reduce these theories to practical use required substantial resources. He sought support from several companies, one of them being Machinenfabrik Augsburg-Nurenberg (MAN) of Germany. With funding from MAN and others, Diesel began his own business and used the MAN facilities to develop his engine. As early as July 1893, he completed a test engine in Augsburg, which could not run on its own. He then built a second prototype in the summer of 1894 that did function and was 16.6% efficient, but was not suitable for Diesel's intended uses. On New Year's Eve of 1896, the third Augsburg prototype of his engine was demonstrated, with a theoretical mechanical efficiency of over 75%.

Diesel's work leading up to the development of these engines began with the second law of thermodynamics and the maximum efficiency espoused for the Carnot cycle. Thus, Diesel began his work to enhance existing internal combustion engines of the day on the basis of purely theoretical considerations, using natural physical processes to provide the necessary heat transfer. In 1893, he wrote a famous thesis entitled "Theory for the Construction of a Rational Thermal Engine to Replace the Steam Engine and Other Internal Combustion Engines Currently in Use." Diesel's hypothesis embodied raising the temperature of pure air to an extremely high degree through aggressive adiabatic compression in a piston/cylinder engine. As the pistons started to descend, fuel would enter the cylinder in exact quantities at the proper time and self-ignite. The heat of combustion at any time would replace the heat lost through expansion. Thus, the total energy in the fuel during the expansion phase would be converted to mechanical energy, and no heat would be wasted. This theory was based on the closed Carnot cycle implementation, including the compression phase, to determine the efficiency of the engine.

Diesel's self-ignition principle was considered to be embedded in thermodynamic considerations. Self-ignition occurred during the compression phase when maximum pressure was realized at the beginning of isothermal expansion, leading to higher temperatures in the cylinder. Thus, the injected fuel spontaneously ignited at these high temperatures. Diesel considered using pulverized coal as fuel, in addition to other elements such as gas, petroleum, peanut oil, and even hemp.

Over his years of development, Diesel ran into many problems with his engine, one of which was fuel injection. For example, the air compression and injection system in the diesel engine meant the injection of heavy, space-consuming aggregate.

In 1893, the diesel engine was not considered suitable as a motor vehicle propulsion system. The Otto internal combustion engine, which required a spark to ignite the air–fuel mixture, used an externally supplied ignition system. Meanwhile, the diesel engine ignited on its own when the air in the cylinder was compressed and heated, so that the fuel introduced just before the compression stroke ignited in the hot air. This fundamental difference between Otto's engine and the diesel engine resulted in greater weight and dimension requirements for the diesel engine. Thus, the initial diesel engines were only suitable for static power sources when they were first successfully developed. The main reason for the size and weight differential was that the introduction of the fuel into the cylinder in a diesel engine under high pressure required that the fuel be induced using pressurized air, which was possible only with pumps or pressure inducers that were not only heavy, but also part of the engine.

Diesel originally thought that the efficient small engine that he would develop would enable independent artisans and craftsmen to compete effectively against competition from large industries that monopolized the power source industry, which at that time was powered by the oversized and expensive fuel-wasting steam engine. Diesel never realized his goal of using his engine to assist small businessmen. Instead, large industries quickly adopted his engine, and Diesel became wealthy from his royalties.

Diesel's work in developing his engine was not without controversy. He had persuaded professors at a number of universities that his ideas, although theoretical, were valid. However, many of these professors were more practice-oriented than their counterparts at the newer, theoretically oriented technical universities. A chasm erupted between those who favored fundamental theory and those who favored technical applications.

Diesel worked from 1893 to 1897 developing his engine at MAN. After 1897, Diesel figured that he had completed his engine, and turned to marketing it. However, it was not ready for the market and needed 11 more years of improvement through the help of additional engineers. During this process, he apparently was not very respectful to other engine designers, and derided their work.

Diesel ran into problems not only in the interface between thermodynamics and mechanical engineering but because, in the late 19th century, practical material applications lacked a sound materials science basis. The diesel engine required materials that could withstand heavy stresses caused by high pressures attained during the combustion stages. Thus, one of Diesel's research projects led him to read an entire book on the materials science of machine elements by Carl Bach. This analysis took almost a year, and delayed his development of the diesel engine by an equal amount of time. Diesel did use the information from the Bach text to achieve the calculations and dimensioning of the different components of his engine.

Even now, due to the weight and noise of diesel engines, their use is primarily limited to stationary power-developing machines and in ships, trucks, submarines, and larger utility vehicles. It was not until 1920 that the diesel engine, with an injection pump delivering a metered amount of fuel into the combustion chambers, gained acceptance in vehicle manufacture, and it was not until 1936 that Daimler-Benz unveiled the first real diesel engine passenger car. Because of its low fuel consumption and sturdiness, the diesel engine made an ideal taxicab engine. Long after the Second World War, the heaviness, low performance, and low driving comfort of diesel-equipped automobiles made them the second choice for consumers compared to the engine that Otto developed. During the first oil crisis of 1973–1974, the diesel engine gained a greater share of the automobile market. However, as long as relatively low gasoline prices prevail, it appears that the Otto cycle engine will outsell the diesel cycle engine in the passenger automotive field.

The criticisms that were aimed at Diesel seemed to have had an effect on him. Many felt that it was the development work following his early theoretical efforts that actually achieved the successful working of a diesel engine. Diesel himself felt that the diesel engine was his idea and that he was the one who gave it its start. Apparently, Diesel failed to see that his engine was made viable by the addition of inventive thinking by many other bright engineers. In September 1913, Rudolf Diesel boarded the mail ship *Dresden* sailing from Antwerp to Harwich, England, across the English Channel. He was not seen departing from the boat when it landed, and he was never seen again after that. His disappearance is one of the great mysteries of the modern era. There have been many stories told about plots against Diesel; however, the majority opinion of those who have investigated the subject matter concludes that he committed suicide.

During my research, I came across what I consider to be an interesting footnote. Diesel expected that his engine would be powered by vegetable oils, including hemp, as well as seed oils. It appears that at the 1900 World Fair, Diesel ran his engines on peanut oil and that Henry Ford at one time demonstrated that automobiles equipped with diesel engines could run on hemp. Pollution abatement was important to Diesel, and he saw his engine as reducing the pollution formed by the petroleum engines of his time. The report that I read indicated that influential moneyed interests who were invested in timber and petroleum resources saw hemp-operated engines as a threat to their investments.

As most of you know, hemp, or *Cannabis sativa,* is the same plant that produces the controlled substance, psychoactive marijuana. Hemp has been used from the dawn of history for food, clothing, building materials, medicine, and, of importance to this discussion, fuel. In the 1920s and 1930s in the United States, reformers heated up the movement to ban the possession and use of marijuana, and the hemp plant from which it originated. Also, the petrochemical and pulp paper industries of that time would have faced stiff competition if hemp's commercial potential were fully developed. For example, major chemical companies had developed and patented fuel additives such as tetraethyl lead and the sulfite and sulfate methods for producing pulp paper and many synthetic products.

Meanwhile, potential competitors were developing synthetic products from renewable biomass origins, including hemp. The hemp decorticator patented by George W. Schlichten in 1919, U.S. Patent No. 1,308,376, potentially could eliminate a large portion of the need for wood pulp paper. Consider that drafts of the United States Declaration of Independence and Constitution were written on hemp paper. At least one car manufacturer announced its aim to replace products made from petroleum hydrocarbons with products produced from cannabis carbohydrates. To counter this prospective competition, those who had a vested interest in the petrochemical and pulp paper processing industries lobbied the United States Treasury Department for the prohibition of cannabis, or hemp.

Since hemp was a local crop, the United States Congress could control only interstate or international shipments of hemp. Efforts to have each state pass a uniform law banning the production of hemp failed in all but 10 states by 1935. However, with continued pressure by "reformers" and certain moneyed interests, with less than three month's deliberation, the United States Congress ultimately passed the Marijuana Tax Act, which imposed a prohibitive transfer tax and an excise tax upon certain dealings in marijuana, including hemp seed and hemp oil. The legislation was signed by President Roosevelt on August 2, 1937.

For more excellently enumerated details on why there is no present movement to adopt hemp oil as a fuel for diesel engines, I refer you to *The Great Book of Hemp* by Rowan Robinson (Park Street Press, Rochester, VT, 1996). However, at present, the move to legalize the recreational use of marijuana in the U.S. is gaining speed. Possibly, this could also lead to the development of hemp oil as a fuel for diesel engines. Time will tell.

Diesel was looking for an engine to approach the thermodynamic limit established by Carnot in 1824. His object was to expand the fuel in the cylinder at constant pressure. He patented this concept in 1892 while working for Linde in Berlin. This meant that his engines had to run at low speeds, with limited power. Diesel insisted that they be run this way, which delayed their successful development. Although Rudolf Diesel was not able to realize the theoretical Carnot cycle in his engine, which was his idea from the very beginning, he did create the most efficient internal combustion machine that, to date, remains the internal combustion engine that operates most economically compared to all others.

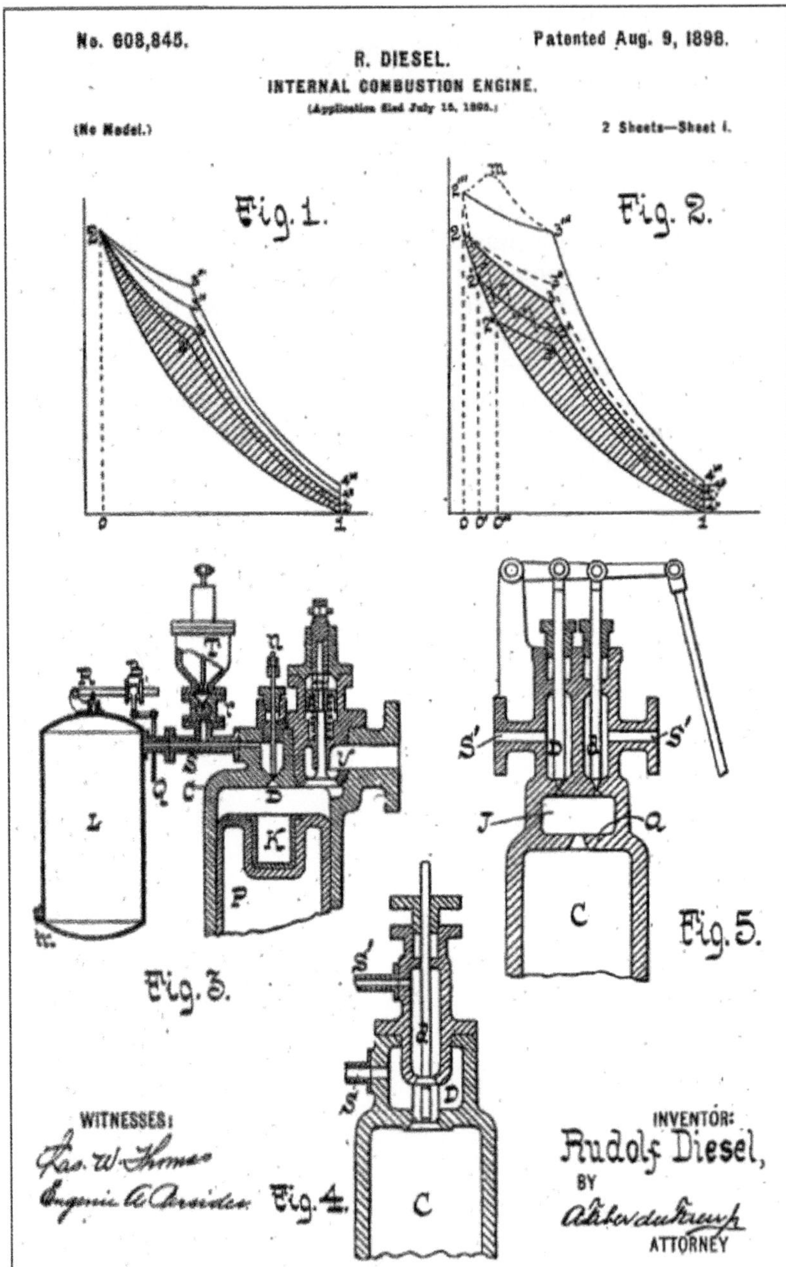
No. 608,845.
Patented Aug. 9, 1898.
R. DIESEL.
INTERNAL COMBUSTION ENGINE.
(No Model.)
2 Sheets—Sheet 1.
Fig. 1.
Fig. 2.
Fig. 3.
Fig. 4.
Fig. 5.
WITNESSES:
INVENTOR:
Rudolf Diesel,
BY
ATTORNEY

12 Design Patents

12.1 COVERAGE OF DESIGN PATENTS

In recent years, the coverage afforded by design patents has increased in importance from the standpoint of protecting product designs from slavish copying. When introducing a new product, a business will often chose to protect both its structure and function, as well as the overall design of the product, to prevent competitors from producing an identical, or knock-off copy. The granting of design patents covering original, unique, visual, ornamental, and non-functional aesthetic designs of an "article of manufacture" is authorized by the U.S. Patent Law at 35 U.S.C. §171-173. "Ornamentability" of the article of manufacture is a requirement for design patents, as distinguished from the requirement for "utility" in article patents. To establish the patentability of a design, its novel features must not be found in the prior art, and the design features must be non-obvious over the prior art in the view of a designer with ordinary skill in the related art. The spirit of the design patent statute is to encourage development of the decorative arts.

Design patents in the United States are enforceable for a period of 15 years from their date of issue, and they are not renewable. Under the previous law, design patents issuing on applications filed before May 13, 2015, are enforceable for 14 years from date of issue. This was changed on December 18, 2012, when the Patent Law Treaties Implementation Act of 2012 (PLTIA) was signed into law. Among other things, the PLTIA adopted the 1999 Geneva Act of the Hague Agreement Concerning the International Registration of Industrial Designs (the "Hague Agreement"), which took effect in the United States on May 13, 2015. The term of a U.S. design patent was changed from 14 to 15 years to conform to the Hague Agreement. As a result, U.S. design patents issuing from applications filed after May 13, 2015, are enforceable for a 15-year term from the date of grant. For more details on the Hague Agreement, see Section 12.9 ahead.

Importantly, functional features of the article of manufacture covered by a design patent are excluded from protection by the design patent. Such functional features should properly be protected by an article patent, if novel and non-obvious. Design patent protection covers the design features of the article shown in the patent illustrations.

Intellectual Property Law for Engineers, Scientists, and Entrepreneurs, Second Edition. Howard B. Rockman.

Published 2020 by John Wiley & Sons, Inc.

However, all illustrated features that are dictated solely by function cannot be protected by the design patent. In other words, a design patent protects how an article looks, and not the way it functions.

A new and non-obvious ornamental design that incorporates a mixture of design and function is protectable by a design patent, which will be interpreted as protecting only the design features. However, if the shape of every part of the article is dictated by the utility to be performed by the article, design patent protection is not allowed. Thus, even though an article illustrated in a design patent may embody a mechanical function, the design patent is acceptable and valid provided that the design is also pleasing, attractive, novel, useful, and the result of invention. See *R.E. Dietz Co. v. Burr and Starkweather Co.*, 243 Fed. 592, 594 (2 Cir. 1917).

A design of an article of manufacture is embodied in the outward visual appearance of the article. Therefore, the subject design covered by a design patent may be directed to the shape or configuration of an article, or to the surface ornamentation of the article, or to the combined appearance of both the configuration and surface ornamentations.

An issued utility patent prevents others from making, using, offering to sell, or importing a product or device that is structurally and/or functionally covered by the claims of the patent, without any regard to how the patented or allegedly infringing product or device looks. A design patent directed to the same article or device protects *only* the configuration and/or surface non-functional ornamentation of the patented product or device. Consider also that having a design patent or application on file gives you the ability to mark your product "Patented" or "Patent Pending," whichever is applicable.

Both utility and design patent applications and patents can cover the same product or article of manufacture. The utility patent covers the structure and function of a useful invention; the design patent protects only the novel, non-obvious, non-functional ornamental aesthetic features of the design of the product.

A design is a unitary entity, and all of its portions are material in that they contribute to the appearance that constitutes the design. See *Ex. parte Daniels,* 40 U.S.P.Q. 2nd 1394 (Bd. of Pat. App. & Int'f. 1996). However, a design patent may be utilized to cover a design embodied in only a portion or part of an entire article of manufacture.

It is interesting to note that the first U.S. design patent statute enacted in 1842 originally referred to protection of "useful" designs. This was changed in the 1902 statute to "ornamental" designs.

12.2 THE DESIGN PATENT APPLICATION

The purpose of a design patent application is to illustrate the visible appearance of the new and unique ornamental characteristics, or elements, embodied in or applied to an article, device, or product, as reflected in its outward appearance, and excluding any ornamental features dictated by its function.

A design patent application illustrates only the specific design to be covered by the issued patent document, with minor variations, and therefore may be quite limited in scope of coverage. The patent application includes no written text description of what the patent covers, and normally all six views (front, back, two sides, top, and bottom) of the article to be covered by the design patent are illustrated. Occasionally, it is helpful to include one or more perspective drawings of the design in the patent application.

A properly drawn design patent application should illustrate only the design features of the article it covers in solid lines. Functional and non-aesthetic features should be illustrated by the use of phantom or dotted lines. This illustrating technique will define only the ornamental features of the article as being covered by the patent. Thus, if an infringer copies the protected ornamental elements of your product, but alters the design of the functional features of its competing product, your design patent can be used to prevent adoption of the ornamental design by the infringer, regardless of the shape of the remainder of the infringing device.

A design patent application includes a general description of each view of the covered design, such as "perspective view," "front view," "side view," etc. There is only a single "claim" in a design patent which reads as follows:

"The ornamental design for (generic name of article), substantially as shown (or substantially as shown and described.)"

Upon examination, the illustrated design is compared to the relevant prior art to determine if the ornamental design in the drawings satisfies the novelty and non-obviousness criteria required for the granting of all patents. To satisfy the novelty test, all that must be shown is that there is no single prior art reference that shows the identical design.

The non-obviousness test is applied by the examiner where there is no single prior art reference that shows the identical design for which patent protection is sought. The question is whether the claimed design would have been obvious to a designer of ordinary skill who designs articles of the type involved. Initially, the examiner looks for a primary reference, the design characteristics of which are basically the same (but not exactly the same) as the design claimed in the patent application. If such a primary reference, or references are located, two questions then must be answered: (1) what is the correct visual impression created by the illustrated design as a whole in the application, then (2) finding a secondary reference or references that are applied to modify the primary reference to create a combined or modified design that has the same overall visual impression or appearance as the claimed design illustrated in the patent application. In this non-obviousness analysis, the secondary references may only be used to modify, or may be combined with the primary reference(s) if the secondary references are so related to the primary reference(s) that the appearance of certain ornamental features in one would suggest the application of those design features to the other design.

12.3 INFRINGEMENT OF A DESIGN PATENT

To determine whether a design of an article of manufacture falls within the scope of coverage of an existing design patent, the Supreme Court established a test in the 1871 case of *Gorham Manufacturing Company v. White,* 81 U.S. 511 (U.S. Supreme Court 1871). Over 140 years later, the Gorham test is still the standard for design patent infringement in the United States. The Gorham test, which is also commonly known as the "Ordinary Observer" test, states that:

> "If in the eye of an ordinary observer, giving such attention as a purchaser usually gives, two designs are substantially the same, if the resemblance is such as to deceive such an observer, inducing him to purchase one supposing it to be the other, the first one patented is infringed by the other."

Thus, a second design does not have to be exactly identical to the illustration in a design patent to constitute infringement of that patent. All that needs to be proven is that the two designs are substantially similar, so that an ordinary purchaser would be deceived by the second design into thinking it was the first design. Terms such as "sameness of effect upon the eye" and "same general effect" were described in the *Gorham* case to define infringement.

The Ordinary Observer test for design patent infringement has undergone a slight turn in recent years, which I shall attempt to set forth here, without being too legalistic. Also, the comments in this and the next few paragraphs are a short lesson on how the law on a specific point can ebb and flow, and even add uncertainty to a legal principle that many considered settled long ago.

In 1984, over 100 years after the *Gorham* decision, the Court of Appeals for the Federal Circuit (CAFC) appended an additional set of facts a design patent owner needed to establish in asserting infringement of a design patent. In the case of *Litton Systems, Inc. v. Whirlpool Corp.*, 728 F. 2d 1423, 1444 (Fed. Cir. 1984), the CAFC held that, as a separate test for proving design patent infringement, the accused [allegedly infringing] device must appropriate the novelty in the patented device which distinguishes it from the prior art. In other words, the CAFC held in *Litton* that a design patent infringement comparison must look for similarities to "the novelty which distinguishes the patented device from the prior art." By example, even though the patented and accused microwave ovens in the *Litton* case looked similar in the eyes of the casual buyer, the similarity was due to a feature commonly used by several microwave manufacturers with products then on the market. Under the rule of the *Litton* case, a determination first had to be made during the lawsuit of the novel features of the patented design over the prior art. Second, the judge or jury must then compare this point of novelty against the alleged infringing design, and decide whether the alleged infringing design incorporated this or these novel design feature or features.

Moving forward to 2007, in an en Banc decision (all 13 of the CAFC judges participating) in the case of *Egyptian Goddess, Inc. v. Swisa, Inc.*, 543 F.3d 665 (Fed. Cir. 2008), the CAFC held that using a separate point of novelty test was inconsistent with *Gorham*'s Ordinary Observer test, and eliminated the use of the point of novelty comparison as a separate test of design patent infringement.

However, in pronouncing an analytical process for determining infringement of design patents in future situations, the CAFC said the following in its *Egyptian Goddess* decision in reaffirming *Gorham*'s Ordinary Observer test:

> When the differences between the claimed and accused design are viewed in light of the prior art, the attention of the hypothetical ordinary observer will be drawn to those aspects of the claimed design that differ from the prior art. And when the claimed design is close to the prior art designs, small differences between the accused design and the claimed design are likely to be important to the eye of the hypothetical ordinary observer. (543 F.3d at 676).

The CAFC, in simpler terms, held that *Gorham's* Ordinary Observer test was the only test to be applied in determining design patent infringement, *but* the judge or jury could look to prior art designs as a factor in applying the Ordinary Observer test, i.e., how an ordinary observer would view the overall aesthetic impression of the product.

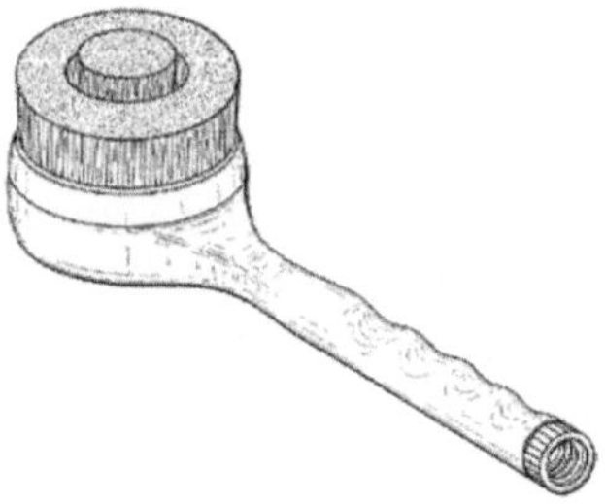

Figure 12.1 D'990

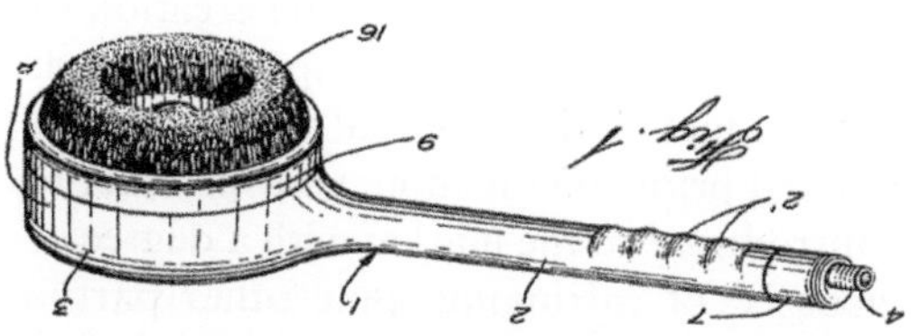

Prior Art '826 Patent

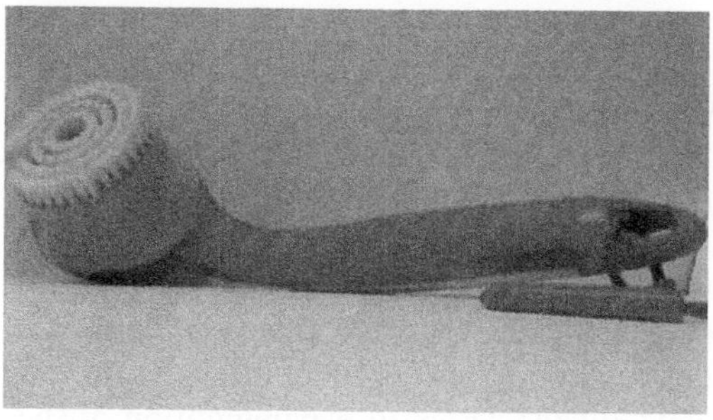

Ideavillage's Accused Product

The case of *Wallace v. Ideavillage Products Corp.*, 640 F. App'x 970 (Fed. Cir. 2016) is regarded as a good example of how a design patent infringement analysis should be conducted. The design patent D'990, covered a body washing brush and Ideavillage's alleged infringing product was a handheld bath brush, as shown in Figure 12.1. The prior art brush is illustrated upside-down for comparison purposes.

The District Court first compared the patented design and the accused design to determine if they visually appear "substantially the same," or would an ordinary observer confuse one product for the other. If the first step leads to a conclusion that the designs are "plainly dissimilar," the second step is applied. The second step of the analysis compares both the patented design and alleged infringing product design with the relevant prior art to allow the fact finder to "attach importance to differences between the claimed design [of the patent] and the prior [art] depending on the overall effect of those differences on the designs," as directed by the *Egyptian Goddess* decision.

The District Court in this case found six differences in the overall appearances of the patented and accused designs, concluding that the two brush designs were "sufficiently distinct" and not the same in appearance. The district court also held that significant similarities were found between the design of the plaintiff's patent, and the designs of the brush shown in the D'826 prior art patent, illustrated in

Figure 12.1. The court found that the similarities between the plaintiff's patented design and the prior art D'826 patent were differences between the plaintiff's patented design and the accused product design. By making a comparison of the patented designs to the prior art design, the district court was able to attach significance to differences between the patented and accused designs that might not be noticeable without including the prior art-patented design comparison in the analysis. In this case, the CAFC affirmed the analysis of the District Court.

The *Wallace* case, therefore, is a good example of how the two steps of the Ordinary Observer test for design patent infringement should be applied, and how they are intertwined in the analysis. For those who are engaged in the creation of new product designs, particularly for consumer products where sales appeal depends on a favorable first visual impression of the product by the potential purchaser, it is suggested that the above analysis be conducted prior to launching your product to ensure that the new product can be freely introduced to the market with a degree of certainty that the product will not be accused of infringing some other party's design patent.

12.4 IMPORTANCE OF DESIGN PATENTS

When a new product being introduced to the market comprises novel ornamentation, either in its product configuration or in its surface design, a design patent should be obtained to protect the marketing, advertising, and promotional value of that design. There have been many instances where copiers will substitute the inner workings of a product with subpar components to make the "knock-off" product inferior and less costly to produce, but still copy the complete outside design or ornamentation of the product. Next, the copied product is offered to your customers at a price you cannot match. Those of you who have purchased "fine" watches at ridiculously low prices from street vendors may have an idea of what I mean. Design patent protection gives the producer of the "original" the means to prevent such copies from reaching the marketplace.

More importantly, many products today comprising articles of manufacture are copied in their totality, both mechanically and/or electronically, in overall product design, packaging, and even accompanying literature such as instruction booklets. If a knock-off product looks like a widely sold and advertised product, the copy of the product could be marketed at a significantly lower price, since the copier has no research and development costs, design development costs, or advertising costs. In my experience, this type of product design knock-off copying is quite prevalent, and obtaining design patent protection covering your product's appearance that is viewable by the consumer has taken on new importance with the advent of the increased globalization of marketing and sales. Thus, it is the author's recommendation that when you consider obtaining article patent coverage for your invention, you should also consider whether the design of your product is novel enough and unobvious enough to support a design patent. Design patents are normally considerably less expensive to obtain than article patents, and in the judgment of this patent warrior, are well worth the minimal expense. Therefore, do not overlook the possibility of obtaining design patent protection when you discuss intellectual property protection for your new product configuration or ornamentation.

12.5 EXAMPLES OF DESIGN PATENTS

Appended at the end of this chapter is a U.S. design patent, No. D291,645, to Pasquale Bruno covering an oiling can design. This is an example of a design patent covering a product configuration.

Interestingly, in 1967, the U.S. Court of Customs and Patent Appeals (the predecessor to today's CAFC) decided that the continuous flow or spray of water in motion in a particular pattern produced by a water fountain constituted patentable design subject matter, as an article of manufacture defined by the patent statute. The case is *In re Hruby,* 153 U.S.P.Q. 61 (CCPA 1967). An illustration of the design submitted for protection and covered by that design patent is shown in Figure 12.2.

The court held that even though the water sprays cannot exist by themselves, and are dependent on the existence of the nozzles and water under pressure, the spray itself is a three-dimensional design. The existence of the design was seen by the court as dependent on something outside of itself, such as the nozzles and water pressure, similar to the design of hosiery not being apparent until placed on one's leg. Thus, the water spray design was held to be an "article of manufacture" and the design of the spray was patentable.

12.6 DESIGN PATENTS ON COMPUTER SCREEN ICONS

Both the U.S. Patent and Trademark Office (USPTO) and the courts have traditionally held that a picture, such as a photograph, standing alone is not proper subject matter for a design patent. The design must be part of an "article of manufacture." See *In Re Schnell,* 46 Fed. 2nd 203 (CCPA 1931). However, the USPTO has, in the last

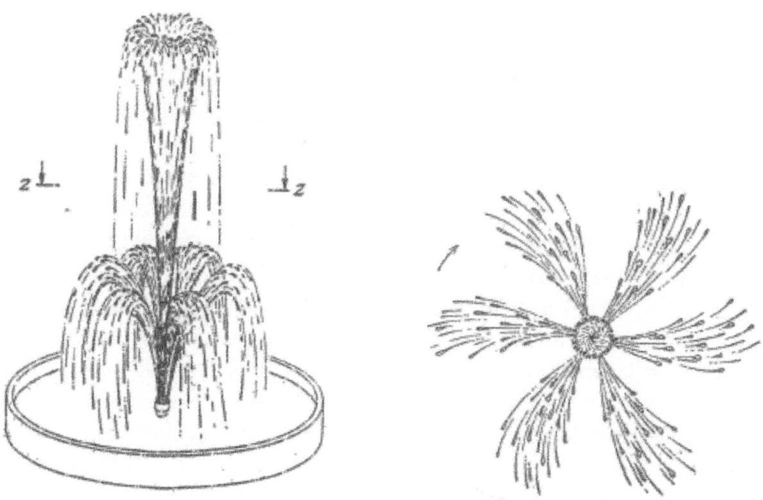

Figure 12.2 Illustration from design patent application in the *In re Hruby* case.

several years, instructed its design Patent Examiners to accept design patent applications directed to novel and non-obvious computer-displayed icons. In the application, the patent applicant must claim, and illustrate, the icon in association with a computer screen, monitor, or other visual display device. See *USPTO Manual of Patent Examining Procedure*, Section 1504.01(a) (9th Edition, January 2018, U.S. Patent & Trademark Office, pp. 1500-13 to 15).

12.7 DESIGN PATENTS CONTRASTED WITH COPYRIGHTS

The Design Patent Law and the Copyright Law are closely related, yet there are material differences between them. A design patent, according to 35 U.S.C. §171, may be obtained on any new, original non-functional and ornamental design for an article of manufacture. The article must provide an aesthetically pleasing appearance to the eye of the beholder, and the design must be primarily ornamental and not solely dictated by the function or performance of the article. Non-utilitarian features of a product are included only for their visual appearance, and not for any usefulness. To obtain design patent protection, the remaining provisions of the Patent Law must also be complied with. Therefore, the design must be novel and non-obvious.

In contrast, the Copyright Law covers original works of authorship, such as a work of art, or a label used for an article of merchandise, or technical drawings. However, there is a certain degree of overlap, since both design patents and copyrights protect the aesthetic features of products. Consider, for example, a decorative column used as a support for a balcony. Copyright protection would be available for the original artistic features of the column. In addition, design patent protection would be obtainable if the decorative column design was new and non-obvious.

Copyrightable works are endowed with exclusive rights as soon as the works are in a sufficiently stable form, such as fixed in any tangible medium of expression as set forth in 17 U.S.C. §102(a) of the U.S. Copyright Law. However, to obtain design patent protection, an application must be filed with the USPTO, and the application must survive an examination process for novelty and non-obviousness.

The examination process for a U.S. copyright application is much less stringent than the examination of a design patent application. The requirement of originality for copyright protection is a relatively lenient standard, mandating only that the named author must have actually created or originated the work, and that the work was not copied from another source. In addition, only a minimal amount of creative authorship is required for a work to fall under one of the categories of copyrightable subject matter. Copyrightable subject matter need not be strikingly unique or novel. In other words, the originality required to support a copyright is independent creation, and not novelty. As a result, the search for prior art that is normally conducted by an infringer to challenge the validity of a design patent has no bearing in copyright cases.

Regarding infringement criteria, any product design that is "substantially similar" to a patented design infringes the design patent, whether the infringer copied or even knew about the design patent or the product covered by the design patent. In contrast, one is liable for copyright infringement only if they are proven to have "copied" the work protected by copyright. Also, unlike design patent infringement, copyright infringement could possibly lead to criminal liability.

12.8 DAMAGES FOR DESIGN PATENT INFRINGEMENT

Damages in design patent infringement lawsuits are normally based on the same rules applied to article patent cases, involving an award of a reasonable royalty to a successful plaintiff, or the infringer's profits if certain criteria can be established.

A major, but inconclusive design patent damages decision was handed down by the U.S. Supreme Court in 2016 in the *Apple v. Samsung* ongoing litigation saga (*Samsung Electronics Co., Ltd. V. Apple Inc.*, 15–777, 137 S. Ct. 429 (Dec. 6, 2016)). The patent infringement litigation between these tech behemoths began in 2012 in a Federal District Court in California. A jury found that 26 Samsung products infringed three Apple utility patents and three Apple design patents, and the jury awarded Apple $399 million in damages, the entirety of Samsung's profits on smartphone sales. Keep in mind that this was only 1 of over 50 lawsuits filed by one party against the other in nine separate countries. A full history of these lawsuits, and their current status, can be found on the Internet and is not germane to the remainder of this discussion on design patent infringement damages.

The design patents asserted by Apple in the California Federal lawsuit covered several embodiments of smartphones and tablets having a large rectangular display surface on the front face, rounded corners, a rectangular speaker slot, a grid of icons on the screen face, and very little, if any, ornamentation. Samsung's smartphones were found to have infringed Apple's IPhone patented design, but Samsung's tablets were found not to infringe Apple's IPad design patent.

On appeal, the CAFC held that Samsung's entire smartphone was an "article of manufacture" upon which damages for design patent infringement should be calculated under 35 U.S.C.§289. (A person who makes or sells any article of manufacture to which a patented design or colorable imitation has been applied shall be liable to the patent owner to the extent of his total profit (paraphrased)). The issue before the Supreme Court in *Samsung v. Apple* was whether the award of damages should be based upon Samsung's profits for smartphone sales considered as a whole "article of manufacture," or whether profits could be narrowed to profits associated with only separate or individual components, even though those components are not sold to consumers apart from the entire smartphone.

The Supreme Court sided with Samsung on this issue, and held that the term "article of manufacture" in 35 U.S.C. §289 is broad enough to encompass both a whole product sold to a consumer *and* a component of that product. The case was remanded back to the CAFC to determine whether, for each of the subject design patents, the relevant "article of manufacture" upon which damages should be calculated is the entire smartphone, or a particular smartphone component. The Supreme Court did not offer any suggestions how a judge or jury was to decide whether damages for design patent infringement should be applied to the whole product or to its components, because, said the Court, this question was not briefed by either Apple or Samsung.

The case went back to the CAFC, which on February 7, 2017, remanded the *Samsung v. Apple* case back to the District Court for the Northern District of California for further proceedings, including a retrial on the damages issue if deemed necessary, to work out a test to identify the "article of manufacture" to which damages should be calculated. On May 24, 2018, a jury awarded Apple $533.3 million for Samsung's infringement of three design patents, plus $5.3 million for infringement of two utility patents, for a total of $538.6 million.

§289 of the Patent Law is a special law enacted to provide that profits of the infringer may be awarded to one successfully asserting design patent infringement. However, a design patent owner can also seek traditional patent infringement damages under 35 U.S.C. §284, usually on a reasonable royalty basis, which damages can be increased by the court up to three times.

12.9 THE HAGUE AGREEMENT CONCERNING THE INTERNATIONAL DEPOSIT OF INDUSTRIAL DESIGNS (THE HAGUE SYSTEM)

The Hague Agreement, or Hague System as it is frequently called, is an international agreement that provides for registration of an industrial design in several countries by filing a single application in one language and one set of fees with the World Intellectual Property Organization (WIPO). At present, 66 countries, including the United States and most other major industrial nations of the world, are signatory members. In some countries, industrial designs are protected under the nation's patent laws, as in the United States. In other countries, designs are protected under separate industrial design laws.

The owner of a registered industrial design or a design patent has the right to prevent others from making, selling, offering, or importing products incorporating or embodying an ornamental design that is identical, or substantially identical, to the protected design when the alleged infringing product is commercially marketed. Packaging for products, as well as the products themselves, can be protected as industrial designs. Graphic icons and graphic user interfaces may also fall under the sphere of protection of registered industrial designs. In some countries, unregistered designs may also be protected for a more limited time and more limited scope. The industrial design laws of a selected country must be reviewed to determine if unregistered industrial design protection is available. For example, such unregistered protection is not available in the United States.

Applicants qualify to file applications under the Hague Agreement if they are a national or are domiciled in one of the member countries, if they have a real and effective industrial or commercial establishment in a member country, or if the applicant has its habitual residence in a member country. A single application can include up to 100 different designs, so long as the designs are in the same product classification established by WIPO.

Upon filing, the application is examined by the International Bureau of WIPO for satisfaction of formal requirements. Once all formal requirements have been satisfied, the design application is recorded in the International Register, and published in the International Designs Bulletin on the WIPO website. The design must be novel to constitute a valid registration. Unless a member country notifies WIPO that the registered design does not meet its domestic rules for registrability, such as lack of novelty, the international registration becomes enforceable in each member country.

A Hague Agreement registration is enforceable for five years, extendable in further five-year periods up to the maximum total period allowed by each member country upon the payment of a renewal fee.

Additional information regarding the Hague Agreement and the steps required to file an application to obtain design patent, or industrial design, protection in the present 66 signatory countries can be found on the WIPO website (www.wipo.int) and the USPTO website (www.uspto.gov). Use the key words Hague Agreement or Hague System. It is also highly recommended that your obtain advice on the benefits of filing a Hague Agreement application from your patent professional.

United States Patent [19]

Bruno

[11] **Patent Number: Des. 291,645**

[45] **Date of Patent: ** Sep. 1, 1987**

[54] **COOKING OIL CAN**

[75] Inventor: **Pasquale Bruno**, Chicago, Ill.

[73] Assignee: **Amco Corporation**, Chicago, Ill.

[**] Term: **14 Years**

[21] Appl. No.: **882,693**

[22] Filed: **Jul. 7, 1986**

[52] **U.S. Cl.** D7/321; D7/58; D9/374; D9/376; D23/11

[58] **Field of Search** D7/300, 312, 321, 322, D7/58; D9/376, 374, 373, 375; D23/5, 11

[56] **References Cited**

U.S. PATENT DOCUMENTS

D. 2,504	11/1866	Hauck	D9/374
D. 2,681	6/1867	Jones	D7/321
D. 2,862	1/1868	Hauck	D9/374
3,031	4/1843	Cornelius .	
D. 85,355	10/1931	Voisine .	
95,948	10/1869	Staples .	
D. 170,639	10/1953	Hoffman, Jr.	D9/375
D. 193,120	6/1962	Gerber .	
D. 196,146	8/1963	Lello .	
D. 241,248	8/1976	Burke et al.	D23/11
D. 251,129	2/1979	Behling	D23/11
D. 259,767	7/1981	MacFarlane	D9/374
D. 267,473	1/1983	Telzrow	D9/374
D. 267,630	1/1983	MacFarlane	D9/374
D. 278,799	5/1985	Maynard	D9/376
1,641,051	8/1927	Rheney .	
1,849,950	3/1932	Murdock .	
4,030,664	6/1977	Tisbo et al.	D23/11 X

OTHER PUBLICATIONS

HFD-*Retailing Home Furnishings*, Jul. 13, 1981, Sec. D, p. 8, bottom r. panel "Cooking With Oil" Stainless Steel Oil Can, Mark Louis Co.

Primary Examiner—Winifred E. Herrmann

Attorney, Agent, or Firm—Laff, Whitesel, Conte & Saret

[57] **CLAIM**

The ornamental design for a cooking oil can, substantially as shown.

DESCRIPTION

FIG. 1 is a left side elevational view of a cooking oil can showing my new design;

FIG. 2 is a front elevational view thereof;

FIG. 3 is a top plan view thereof;

FIG. 4 is a right side elevational view thereof;

FIG. 5 is a rear elevational view thereof; and

FIG. 6 is a bottom plan view thereof.

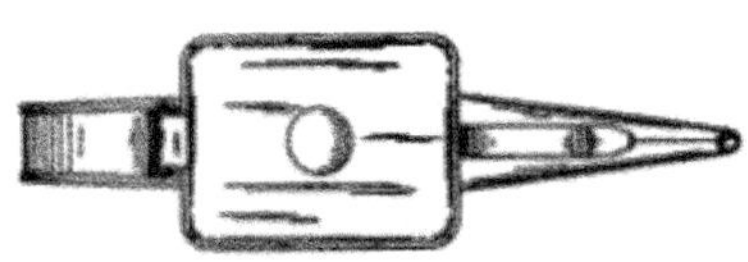

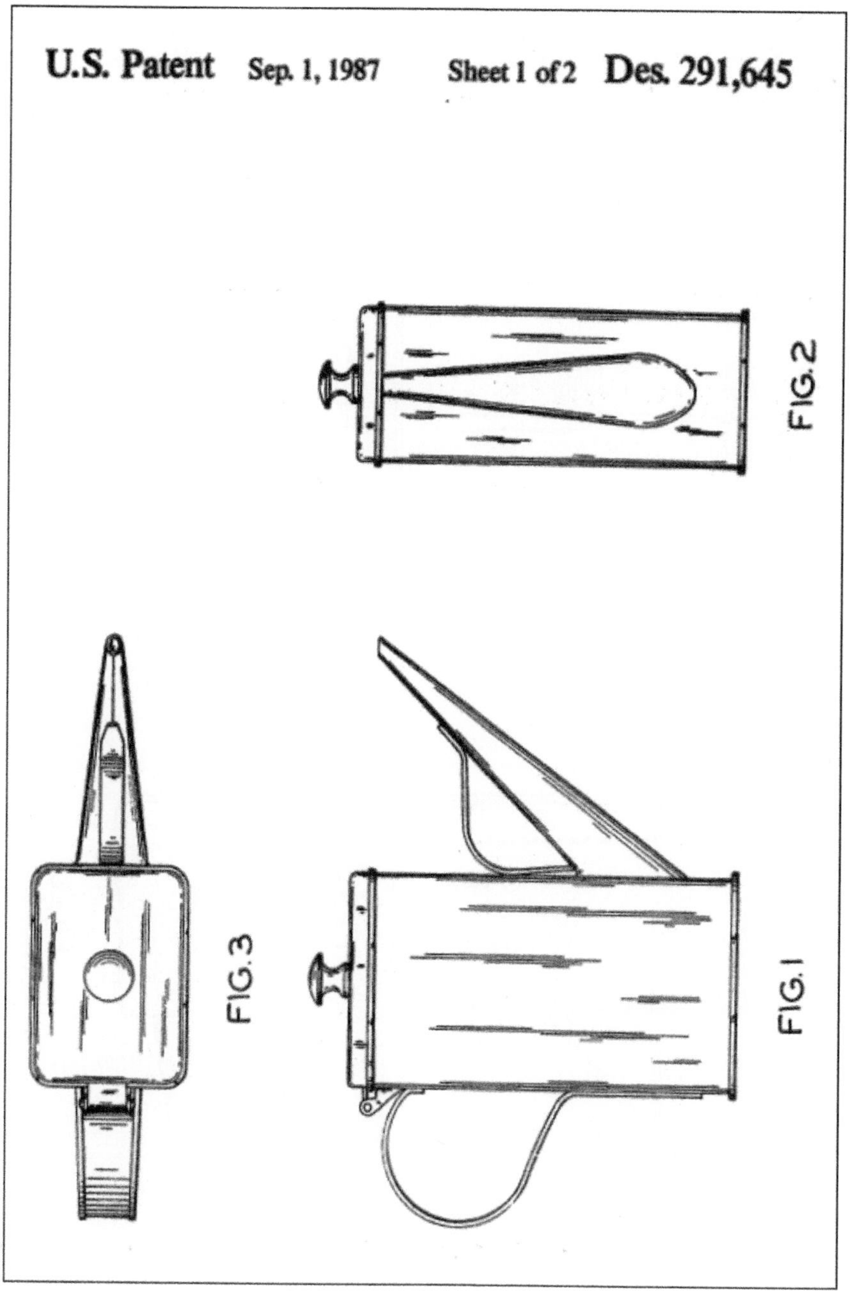
U.S. Patent Sep. 1, 1987 Sheet 1 of 2 Des. 291,645
FIG.2
FIG.3
FIG.1

U.S. Patent Sep. 1, 1987 Sheet 2 of 2 **Des. 291,645**

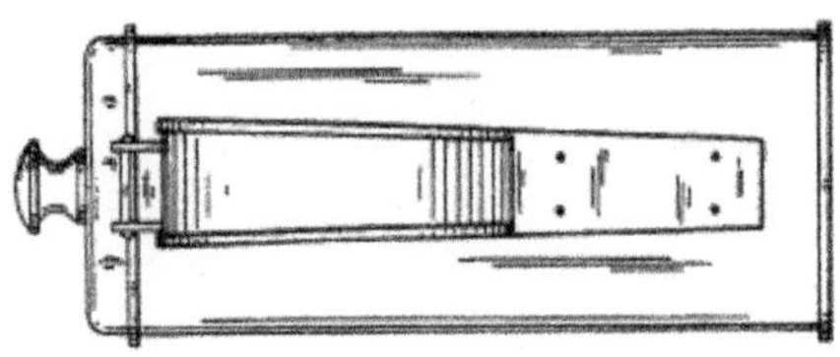

FIG.5

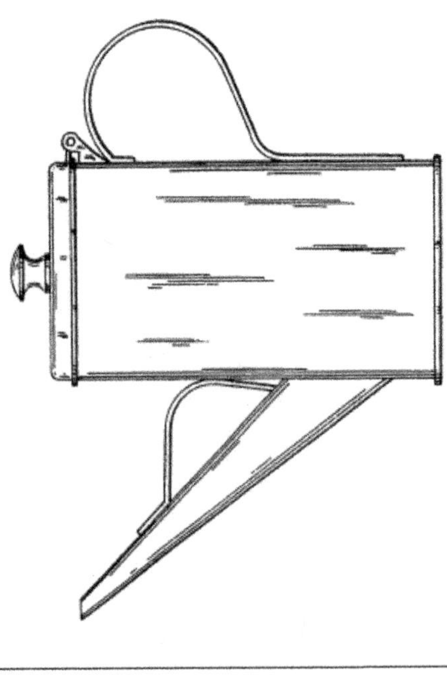

FIG.4

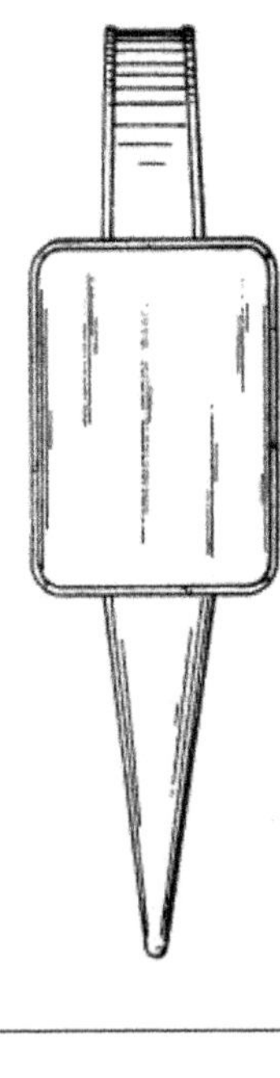

FIG.6

◆ INVENTORS AND INVENTIONS ◆

Nikola Tesla

AC INDUCTION MOTOR AND RADIO

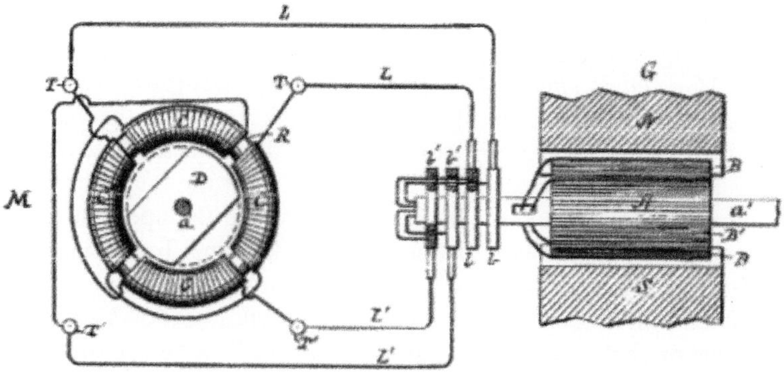

Some consider Nikola Tesla to embody the essence of genius, and to be one of the world's greatest inventors. His name is connected with innovations such as the Tesla coil transformer, the induction motor, the rotating magnetic field principle, polyphase alternating current systems, radio and wireless communication, fluorescent lights, and other technologies. He is named as an inventor in over 700 patents.

Nikola Tesla, who was to become the master of alternating current electricity at the turn of the 19th century, was born at the stroke of midnight between July 9th and 10th, 1856, in Smiljan, Croatia, a province of Lika, which was then part of the Austro-Hungarian Empire. Though born in Croatia, he was the son of a Serbian Orthodox priest and a Serbian mother, from whom he inherited a photographic memory. Just as Mozart could visualize completely scored and orchestrated music in his head, Nikola Tesla had the ability to visualize completely structured and operating technology and inventions in his mind, without resorting to experiments, drawings, or prototype models. In his high school math classes, he would shout out answers to complicated problems without the use of pencil or paper. Alas, he therefore needed no sketches, models, or experiments to "complete" his inventions, and, as a result, he left little in the way of records or evidence of many of his innovative uses of electricity. His practice was to make a working model of his inventions after he had worked out all of the details and made the necessary modifications in his imagination.

Tesla began his electrical engineering education in 1875 at the Polytechnic College of Graz, Austria. In 1881, he took a position in the Central Telegraph Office of the Hungarian government in Budapest, which was also associated with Thomas Edison's

Intellectual Property Law for Engineers, Scientists, and Entrepreneurs, Second Edition. Howard B. Rockman.

Published 2020 by John Wiley & Sons, Inc.

telegraph subsidiary. While an undergraduate student, Tesla first noticed the problems with the induction motors of that time. He noticed that a direct-current Gramme dynamo being operated in a classroom demonstration as a motor was creating sparks between the brushes and the commutator. His professor did not think much of Tesla's suggestion that motors without commutators could be developed by switching to alternating current. At that time, Tesla had no idea how to accomplish his idea, but he was intrigued. He came to the United States in 1884 to work with Thomas Edison. Later, he was to form his own company, and he continued to experiment and invent for the rest of his life. He died on January 7, 1943, of heart failure at the age of 86.

I have purposely skipped over many important facets of the life of Nikola Tesla, as I am compelled to do for the sake of brevity. For those of you who desire to learn more about one of the most amazing technical intellects of his, or any, time, I recommend reading *Tesla, Man Out of Time* by Margaret Cheney (Dorset Press, New York, 1989), as well as other works referenced in Ms. Cheney's book. However, there are two facets of the life and work of Tesla that are worthy of remark in this treatise.

First, after leaving the Polytechnic at Graz, Tesla kept the image of the sparking dynamo in his mind. In about 1881–1882, while he was in Budapest, after recovering from what doctors had diagnosed as a "nervous breakdown," Tesla was walking with a friend, Anital Szigety, in the city park, and was reciting poetry—Goethe's *Faust* as the story is told. Then, as the seed of an idea came to him, he took a stick and drew a sketch in the dust on the ground of the park. He sketched a motor in the dirt, and said to his friend, "Watch me reverse it." That same diagram was displayed 6 years later at an appearance Tesla made before the American Institute of Electrical Engineers. His demonstration was considered to be a new scientific principle, and it later transformed the world of power system technology.

Tesla had conceived, in the dust, not only a new motor, but the principle of the rotating magnetic field created by two or more alternating currents that were out of phase with each other. He had eliminated the requirement for a commutator (which reverses the direction of direct electric current), and the brushes necessary for providing a path for the current used in prior DC motors.

Alternating current had been employed prior to Tesla by Elihu Thomson to power arc lights, and in transformers for modifying power transmission voltages. The first AC transformer was developed and patented by Europeans Gaulard and Gibbs, and the U.S. rights to their invention were bought by George Westinghouse, an early advocate of AC electrification. However, there was no successful, practical AC motor until later when Tesla invented his induction motor.

In 1882, Tesla took a position with the Edison telephone subsidiary in Paris, where he learned of Edison's revulsion at the mere mention of alternating current. Tesla's responsibilities included investigating and curing the shortcomings of Edison power facilities in Germany and France. While in Strasbourg, Alsace, on company business, he built his first AC induction motor, which used a rotating magnetic field and an armature that rotated without commutation. By the end of the summer of 1883, Tesla had twice repeated his experiments, and became convinced that AC was the power of the future.

Tesla was next asked to repair a railroad station lighting facility that lost a wall portion caused as a result of a DC short circuit during the grand opening of the station. Tesla was promised a bonus if he could solve the problem, but after successfully getting the system operational, he was denied his bonus, and he resigned. However,

Charles Batchelor, the manager of the Paris plant and a close assistant to Edison over the years, saw Tesla's talents, and recommended Tesla for a position at Edison's Menlo Park research center in the United States. Batchelor wrote a glowing letter of recommendation to Edison, that in the words of Margaret Cheney (Id. p. 26) involved "introducing the one egocentric genius to the other." Everyone agreed, and at age 28, Nikola Tesla landed in the United States in 1884. Edison was then 32 years of age.

While working for Edison, Tesla at the beginning impressed Edison with his skills, and was awarded broad freedom in tackling the operation and design problems of Edison's electric power systems. Tesla devised a way in which the outdated Edison dynamos could become more efficient, and was promised (again) a $50,000 bonus if he could succeed. Tesla then redesigned and improved over twenty dynamos, and installed automatic controls.

Edison's sometimes faulty dynamos powered all of the new-fangled electrical devices in New York City. The electrically operated trolley cars frightened nearby pedestrians as well as the riders. The citizens of Brooklyn, who felt particularly victimized by malicious electric trolleys, became known as "Trolley Dodgers." When the borough of Brooklyn was endowed with a baseball franchise, the team was naturally anointed the Brooklyn Dodgers.

Edison's and Tesla's different approaches to problem solving soon drove a wedge between the two geniuses. Edison used the empirical approach, trying out solutions and employing a process of elimination until one worked. Tesla, meanwhile, was analytical, using theory and calculation to solve difficult situations. On top of this, Edison saw Tesla's interest in AC as a threat to his myopic and total devotion to DC, partly because Edison thought (incorrectly) that only DC could light his incandescent bulbs.

After Tesla's redesign of the Edison dynamos was complete, he asked for his $50,000 bonus. Tesla's supporters report that Edison merely replied that Tesla simply misunderstood America's (and Edison's) sense of humor. Tesla, feeling cheated by another Edison company, resigned. He was then approached by investors, who helped him create the Tesla Electric Light Company, with the aim of producing better electric arc lights for street and factory lighting. Tesla developed an arc lamp that was simple, safe, and cost less than available gas lights. However, even though successful, Tesla was forced out of his own company with little compensation. The years 1886–1887 saw slow economic times, and Tesla barely survived, working as a street laborer. Meanwhile, his arc-lighting inventions resulted in the award of seven patents, plus other patents related to light.

Lady Luck came to Tesla's rescue. The foreman of Tesla's street labor crew knew of his induction motor, and introduced Tesla to A. K. Brown, the manager of Western Union, who happened to have an interest in alternating current. Brown assisted Tesla in forming the Tesla Electric Company, with the goal of developing and building the AC induction motor and system that Tesla sketched in the Budapest dust in 1882, and had successfully built in Alsace in 1883.

In 1888, Tesla was awarded U.S. Patent No. 381,968, titled "Electric Magnetic Motor." He also obtained U.S. Patents Nos. 381,969, 381,970, 382,279, 382,280, 382,281, and 382,282 for a complete AC system, including his single and polyphase motors, split-phase induction motors, a distributor system, and polyphase transformers for producing, transmitting, and using electricity. Only his first induction motor patent is reprinted here; the remaining patents can be found at the U.S. Patent & Trademark Office website, www.uspto.gov.

At the Chicago Columbian Exposition of 1893, Westinghouse, using Tesla's AC power system, lit up the entire City of Tomorrow, started fountains and machinery, and raised banners and flags. AC was a hit and was here to stay. The Tesla polyphase system is used today practically everywhere. Compared to DC, higher voltages could be generated through Tesla's AC systems, and the transmission of electricity became possible over hundreds of miles and more, compared to DC requiring electrical substations every few miles. Edison's light bulb could be switched on using either AC or DC. For more on this aspect of Tesla's life, see the essay "Current Events," following Chapter 36.

The second Tesla saga involves the radio, whose invention is popularly credited to Guglielmo Marconi. However, the Teslaites dispute this conclusion. They argue that as a child, Tesla had a fascination with rain and lightning, observing that "the electrical energy enclosed in the precipitation of the water was inconsiderable, the function of the lightning being much like that of a sensitive trigger." Tesla's vision was to control lightning, and with it enhance the world's water supply. He considered the technology needed to develop electric forces of the magnitude of those found in nature similar to that required to successfully transmit energy without wires (see N. Tesla, "Inventions," p. 62.)

In February 1892, Sir William Crookes published an article suggesting the use of Hertzian waves for wireless telegraphy by the then-known means of generating electromagnetic waves of any desired wavelength, and transmitting the waves through the air to a receiver. The sending and receiving devices would be attuned to a definite wavelength. Crooke's hypothesis confirmed Tesla's thoughts on using the air to transmit electrical signals and energy.

One year later, in speeches in 1893 before the Franklin Institute in Philadelphia and the National Electric Light Association in St. Louis, Tesla presented, in detail, the principles of the transmission of electrical signals through the air. His supporters point to the fact that during the St. Louis speech in 1893, Tesla presented the first public demonstration of adjustable high-frequency oscillations for transmission of wireless messages. Marconi made his "first" radio transmission in 1895.

Figures 1 and 2 from Tesla's speeches delivered in Philadelphia and St. Louis in February and March 1893 are shown below. Figure 1 diagrams the laboratory setup Tesla used to produce high-frequency currents from either continuous or low-frequency alternating currents utilizing then-known dynamos. In conjunction with the portion of his presentation relating to Figure 2, Tesla proposed that the high-frequency currents could be used to produce electric waves for the transmission of wireless telegraph messages. Tesla, referring to Figure 2, described in his speeches a system of creating electromagnetic waves from a source of high-frequency currents, with an elevated conducting surface connected to a terminal of the source, and the other source terminal connected to underground pipes, or to earth. These figures have been relied upon by Tesla supporters and the Supreme Court to support the conclusion that Tesla was the first to demonstrate the transmission of wireless signals.

Tesla's St. Louis transmitter circuit assembly consisted of a high-voltage (5 kilovolts) pole-type, oil-filled transformer connected to a condenser consisting of a bank of Leyden jars, a coil, a spark gap, and a wire extending to the top of the room. His receiver circuit assembly, 30 feet away, included a similar wire suspended from the ceiling and an identical coil and bank of condenser Leyden jars. However,

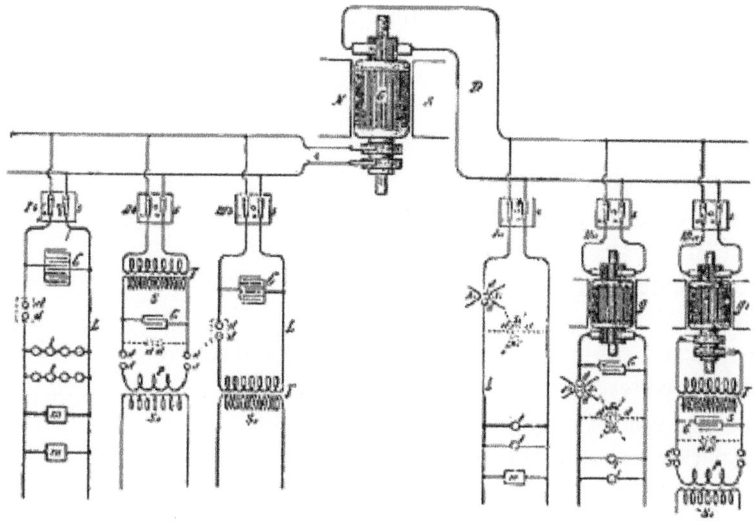

Figure 1

Figure 2

instead of the spark gap used in the transmitter, the receiver included a Geissler tube that would glow upon the application of voltage. No wires connected the receiver and transmitter.

When Tesla powered up the transmitter circuit assembly, corona appeared at the foil edges of the Leyden jars. The spark gap made a noisy discharge, and electromagnetic waves radiated from the transmitter antenna (although these waves were invisible).

At the receiver assembly, the Geissler tube became excited by the electromagnetic waves, and lit up.

This demonstration by Tesla, his supporters argue, displayed all of the fundamental principles of radio:

1. An arrangement of four circuits.
2. An open antenna circuit coupled through a transformer to a closed charging circuit.
3. An open antenna circuit at the receiver similarly coupled to a closed detector circuit.
4. The open and closed circuits in the transmitting and receiving circuits in electrical synchronized resonance with each other.
5. Achieving synchronized resonance by adjusting the length of wire in the secondary winding of the oscillation transformer in the transmitter, and similarly in the receiver, such that the antenna circuit is resonant with the frequency developed in the charging circuit of the transmitter.
6. The primary coil and the secondary coil of the receiver are preferably carefully adjusted to vibrate synchronously with the transmitting coil.

As a prologue to the subsequent patent battles between Tesla and Marconi, it must be mentioned that Sir Oliver Lodge, in 1894, built a system that transmitted wireless telegraph signals using Hertzian waves over a 150 yard distance. Lodge adjusted the tuning of his device by varying the self-inductance of the antenna circuits. Lodge demonstrated that the adjustment of wavelengths, and thus frequency, in the circuits was accomplished by varying either or both the inductance and capacitance, which are the factors controlling wavelength, and hence frequency, in the antenna circuits. Tuning the radio circuit by varying inductance was not demonstrated by Tesla in 1893.

In 1896, Marconi demonstrated in London a wireless radio transmitter and receiver. Margaret Cheney, in her book *Tesla, Man Out of Time* on page 69 reports that the Marconi wireless device was identical to Lodge's, and exactly what Tesla had discussed in his widely published and circulated 1893 lectures, which had been translated into several languages.

Tesla's first U.S. radio patent application for a remote-controlled device was filed on July 1, 1898, and granted on November 8, 1898, as No. 613,809. Tesla's second radio patent application (for wireless signal and power transmission) was filed on September 2, 1897, and was granted on March 20, 1900, as No. 645,576. Marconi's first U.S. patent application was granted on July 13, 1897, as U.S. Patent No. 586,193 and reissued on June 4, 1901, as Re. No. 11,913.

Marconi's second patent was filed on November 10, 1900, and was initially rejected as lacking novelty over the Lodge prior art. Marconi's attorneys then submitted a new specification and claims, canceling the initially filed material. The Patent Examiner consistently rejected Marconi's second set of claims in view of the Tesla, Lodge, and Braun prior art, and refused to believe Marconi's assertion that he had no knowledge of the "Tesla Oscillator," which had been widely described in the technical press. After the application was abandoned, and after a first refusal by the Commissioner of Patents to revive the Marconi application,

Marconi's attorneys requested reconsideration of the Commissioner's decision. Reconsideration was granted, and the Marconi application was given to a different Patent Examiner, who allowed the application. Marconi's U.S. Patent No. 763,772 was granted on June 28, 1904.

The second Patent Examiner decided that Marconi's claims directed to the use of variable inductance to tune the antenna circuits were distinguishable from prior art of Stone that showed adjusting the length of the antenna conductor to tune the antenna circuits. However, this conclusion overlooked Lodge's prior U.S. Patent No. 609,154, which disclosed a variable inductance in the aerial circuit.

Marconi, however, was an excellent marketer, and his Marconi Worldwide Wireless Company gained the lead in developing and commercializing radio. Eventually, on August 4, 1915, Tesla sued Marconi for infringing Tesla's wireless patent. However, Tesla lacked the financial resources to pursue his case.

Then, on July 29, 1916, the Marconi Wireless Telegraph Company of America filed a lawsuit against the U.S. Government charging infringement during the First World War of Marconi's U.S. Patent No. 763,772 and three other patents. The lower court held claim 16 of the Marconi patent valid and infringed, and awarded Marconi's company $42,894.93 in damages. The lower court also held that Marconi's reissue patent, No. 11,913, was not infringed, and Marconi did not appeal this ruling. On November 20, 1919, all of the assets, including the patents, of Marconi's company were assigned to the Radio Corporation of America, but the Marconi Company retained the right to prosecute the lawsuit against the U.S. Government. Marconi's case lumbered through the federal court system for the next 27 years, culminating in a decision by the United States Supreme Court on June 21, 1943, holding claim 16 of Marconi's Patent No. 763,772 invalid in view of the prior public disclosures and patents of Nikola Tesla, Lodge, and others, thus awarding priority of invention of the radio to Tesla and his 1893 presentation in St. Louis. See *Marconi Wireless Telegraph Co. of America v. United States,* 320 U.S.1 (1943).

The Supreme Court defined the "invention" in the Marconi Patent No. 763,772 as:

> … [T]he use of two high frequency circuits in the transmitter and two in the receiver, all four so adjusted as to be resonant to the same frequency or multiples of it. The circuits are so constructed that the electrical impulses in the antenna circuit of the transmitter vibrate longer with the application to the transmitter of a given amount of electrical energy than has been the case in the previous structures known to the art, and the selectivity and sensitivity of the receiver is likewise enhanced. Thus increased efficiency in the transmission and reception of signals is obtained.

This definition is not specifically directed to the transmission of voice and music, which was made possible subsequently by de Forest, whose Audion provided variable frequency modulation.

In its 80-page opinion, the Supreme Court found that the Tesla '576 patent, which was issued before Marconi's '772 patent was even applied for, disclosed a four-circuit system, two each at the receiver and transmitter, and suggested that all four circuits be tuned to the same frequency. Although Tesla's device was designed primarily for the transmission of energy to any form of energy-consuming device, Tesla also recognized that his system could be used, without change, for wireless communication of intelligible messages. Tesla's' 576 patent disclosed the following features of the Marconi' 772 patent:

A charging circuit in the transmitter for causing oscillations of the desired frequency, coupled, through a transformer, with the open antenna circuit, and the synchronization of the two circuits by the proper disposition of the inductance in either the closed or the antenna circuit or both. By this and the added disclosure of the two-circuit arrangement in the receiver with similar adjustment, he [Tesla] anticipated the four-circuit tuned combination of Marconi. (80 U.S. at pp. 15, 16).

The Court also held that a feature of Marconi's patented device not shown by Tesla's patent for the use of a variable inductance to adjust the tuning of the antenna circuit of both transmitter and receiver was developed by Lodge (U.S. Patent No. 609,154) after Tesla's patent but before Marconi's patent.

Thus, among his other acts of inventive genius, the Tesla supporters point to this 1943 U.S. Supreme Court decision, and the facts referred to by the Court, as defining Nikola Tesla as the true inventor of radio.

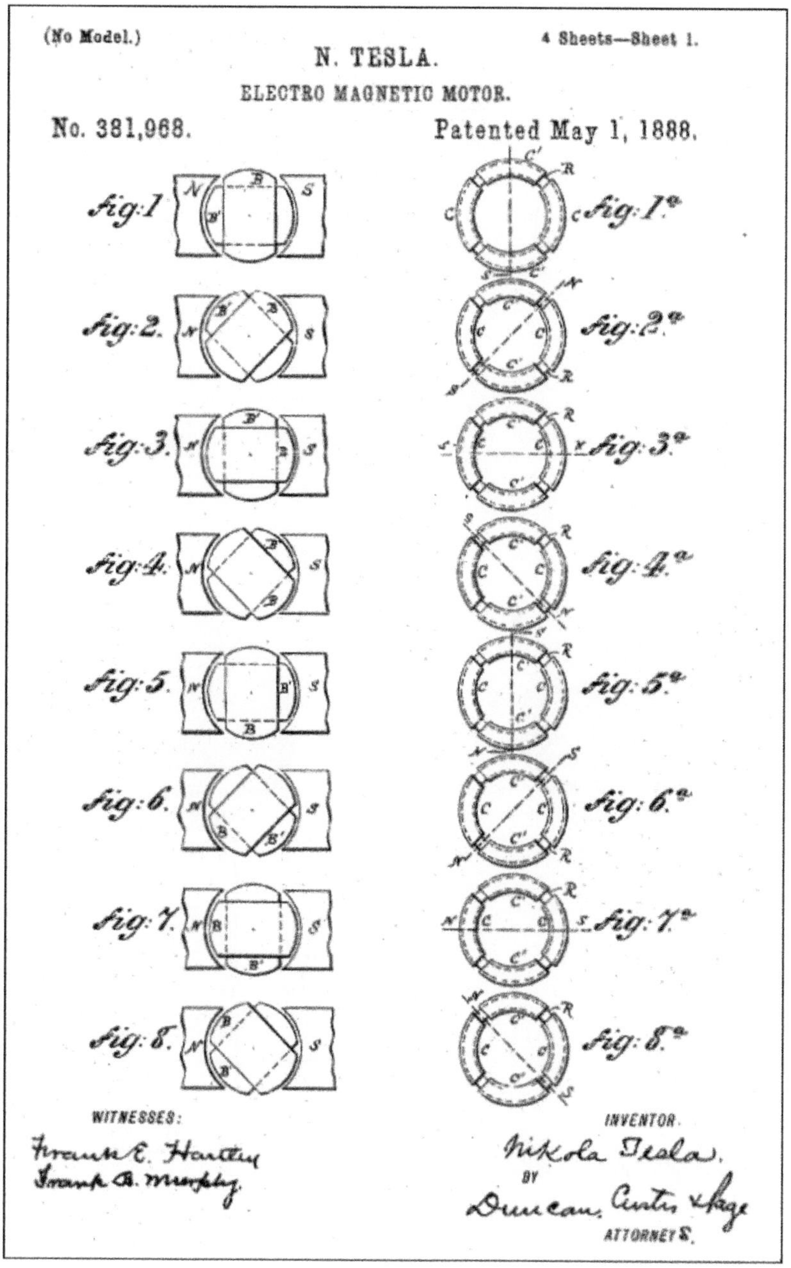
(No Model.)
4 Sheets—Sheet 1.
N. TESLA.
ELECTRO MAGNETIC MOTOR.
No. 381,968.
Patented May 1, 1888.
Fig:1
Fig:1a
Fig:2.
Fig:2a
Fig:3.
Fig:3a
Fig:4.
Fig:4a
Fig:5.
Fig:5a
Fig:6.
Fig:6a
Fig:7.
Fig:7a
Fig:8.
Fig:8a
WITNESSES:
INVENTOR
Nikola Tesla.
BY
ATTORNEYS.

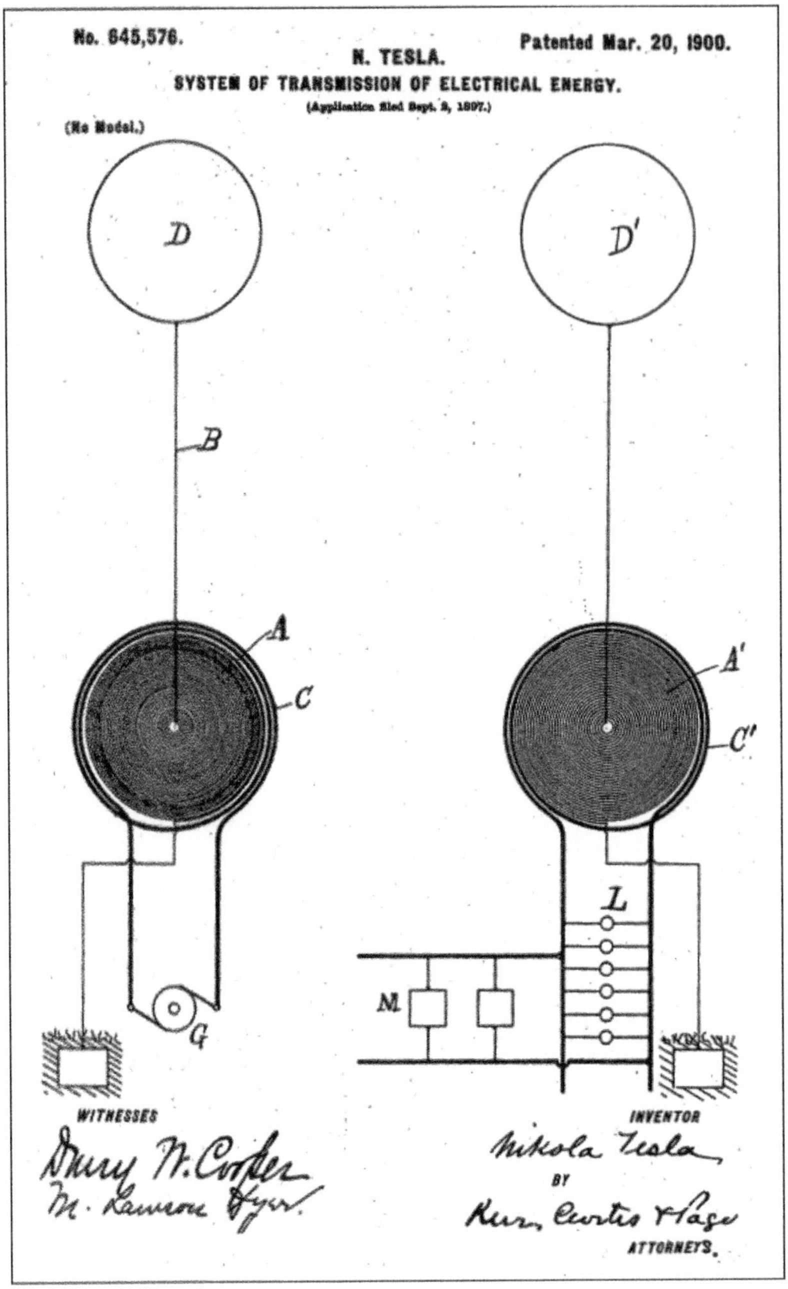
No. 645,576.
Patented Mar. 20, 1900.
N. TESLA.
SYSTEM OF TRANSMISSION OF ELECTRICAL ENERGY.
(Application filed Sept. 2, 1897.)
(No Model.)
D
D'
B
A
C
A'
C'
L
M
G
WITNESSES
INVENTOR
Nikola Tesla
BY
ATTORNEYS.

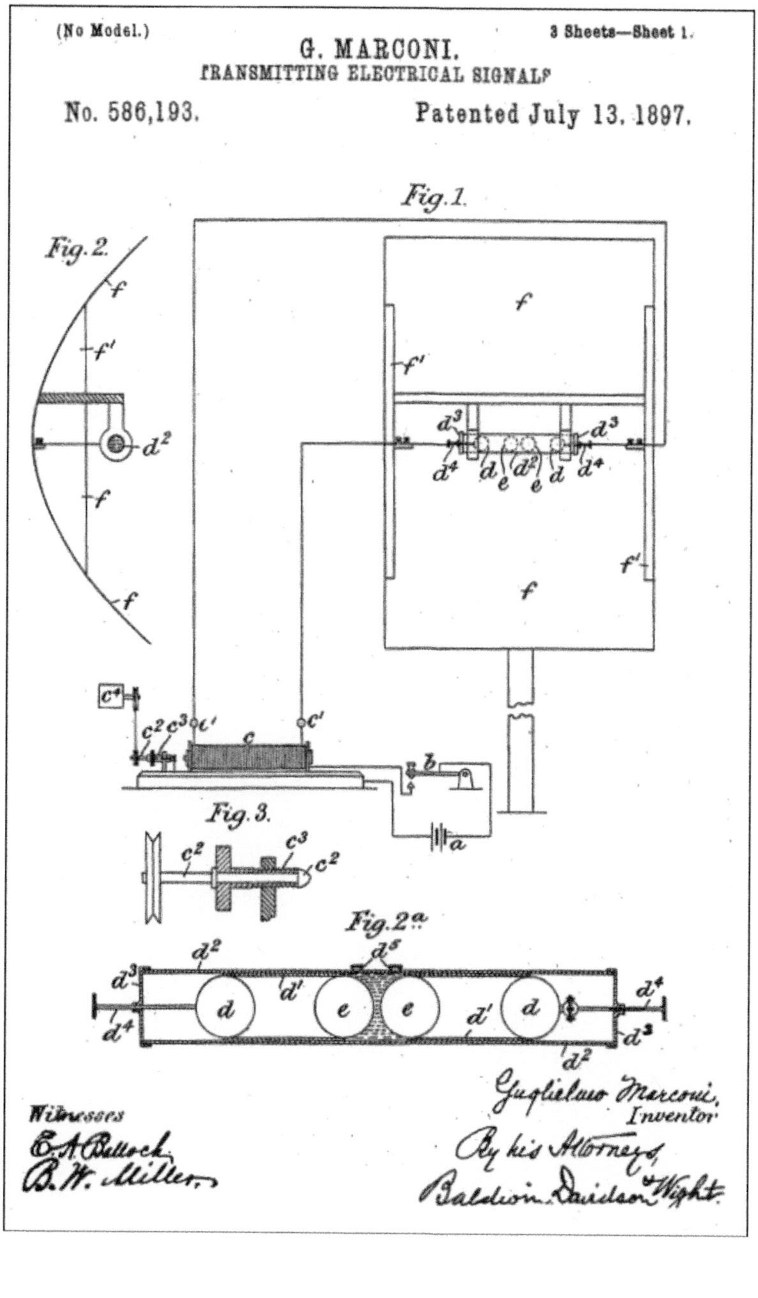
(No Model.)
3 Sheets—Sheet 1.
G. MARCONI.
TRANSMITTING ELECTRICAL SIGNALS
No. 586,193.
Patented July 13, 1897.
Fig. 1.
Fig. 2.
Fig. 3.
Fig. 2a.
Witnesses
Inventor
By his Attorneys

◆ INVENTORS AND INVENTIONS ◆

Clarence Birdseye

FROZEN FOOD

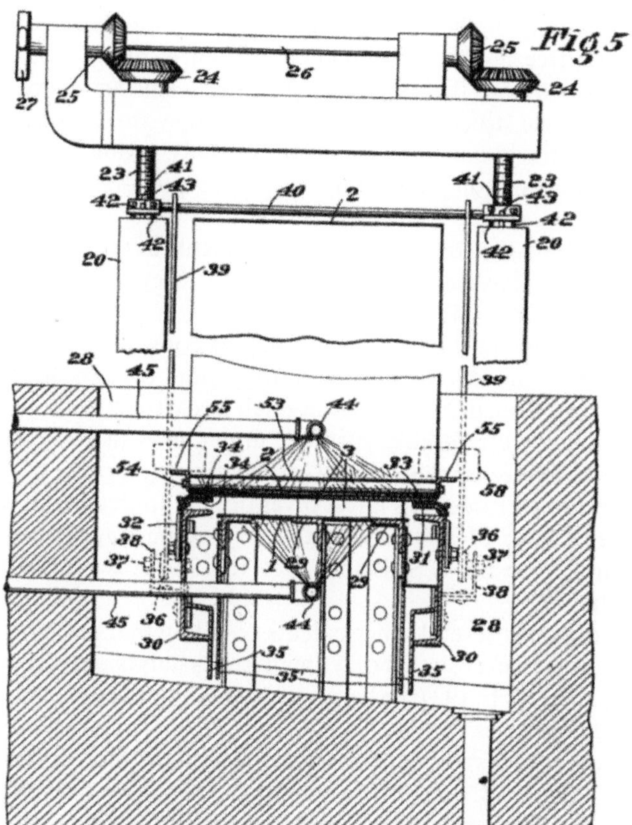

Clarence Birdseye is credited with improving the world's diet and creating a new industry based on his food preservation processes. During an expedition to Labrador, Canada, in the early 1900s, Birdseye observed native fisherman freezing their catch by throwing the fish on surface ice. The fish were frozen almost immediately in the frigid air, and Birdseye recognized that the speed of freezing prevented frost damage. He

Intellectual Property Law for Engineers, Scientists, and Entrepreneurs, Second Edition. Howard B. Rockman.

Published 2020 by John Wiley & Sons, Inc.

later observed that large ice crystals that damaged the fish tissue resulted from slow-freezing the food, whereas rapid freezing almost retained the original flavor and texture of the fish.

Birdseye had an early career as a taxidermist. While in Labrador between 1912 and 1915, he became interested in food preservation by freezing, especially fast freezing, when he was taught by the Inuit how to ice fish under very thick ice. In −40°C weather, he discovered that the fish he caught froze almost instantly, and then when thawed and cooked tasted fresh. He recognized immediately that the frozen seafood sold in New York was of lower quality than the frozen fish of Labrador, and saw that applying this knowledge could be profitable.

Conventional freezing methods of the time were commonly performed at higher temperatures. Thus, freezing occurred much more slowly, allowing ice crystals more time to grow. It is now known that fast freezing produces smaller ice crystals that cause less damage to the tissue structure of the fish. When slow-frozen foods thaw, cellular fluids leak from the tissue damaged by the ice crystals, giving the resulting food a mushy or dry consistency upon preparation. Birdseye's quick-frozen process overcame this problem.

In 1922, Birdseye conducted fish freezing experiments at the Clothel Refrigerating Company, and then established his own company, Birdseye Seafoods Inc., to freeze fish fillets with chilled air at −43°C (−45°F).

In 1924, his company went bankrupt for lack of consumer interest in his products. That same year he developed an entirely new process for commercially viable quick freezing, consisting of packing fish in cartons, and then freezing the contents between two refrigerated surfaces under pressure. He then created a new company in 1926, General Seafood Corporation, to utilize this method. His new company employed Birdseye's latest invention: a double belt freezer in which cold brine chilled a pair of stainless belts carrying packaged fish, freezing the fish quickly. This led to his U.S. Patent No. 1,773,079, which inaugurated the frozen foods industry.

Birdseye later obtained several other patents on additional machinery that cooled the food product even quicker so that only small ice crystals could form and cell membranes were not damaged. In 1927, he began to extend his process beyond fish to meat, poultry, fruit, and vegetables.

In 1929, Birdseye sold his company and patents for 22 million dollars to Goldman Sachs and the Postum Company, which eventually became General Foods Corporation, which then founded the Birdseye Frozen Food Company. Clarence Birdseye continued working with the company developing additional frozen food technology. In 1930, the company began sales experiments in retail stores around Springfield, Massachusetts, to test consumer acceptance of quick-frozen foods. The initial product line featured 26 items, including 18 cuts of frozen meat, spinach and peas, a variety of fruits and berries, blue point oysters, and fish fillets. Consumers approved of the new products, and today this is considered the beginning of retail frozen foods.

The Birdseye name remains a leading frozen food brand. Today, Clarence Birdseye is credited with increasing the quality of the American diet by providing high-quality foods for long-time preservation without drying, pickling, or canning.

Aug. 12, 1930. C. BIRDSEYE 1,773,079

METHOD OF PREPARING FOOD PRODUCTS

Filed June 18, 1927 5 Sheets-Sheet 1

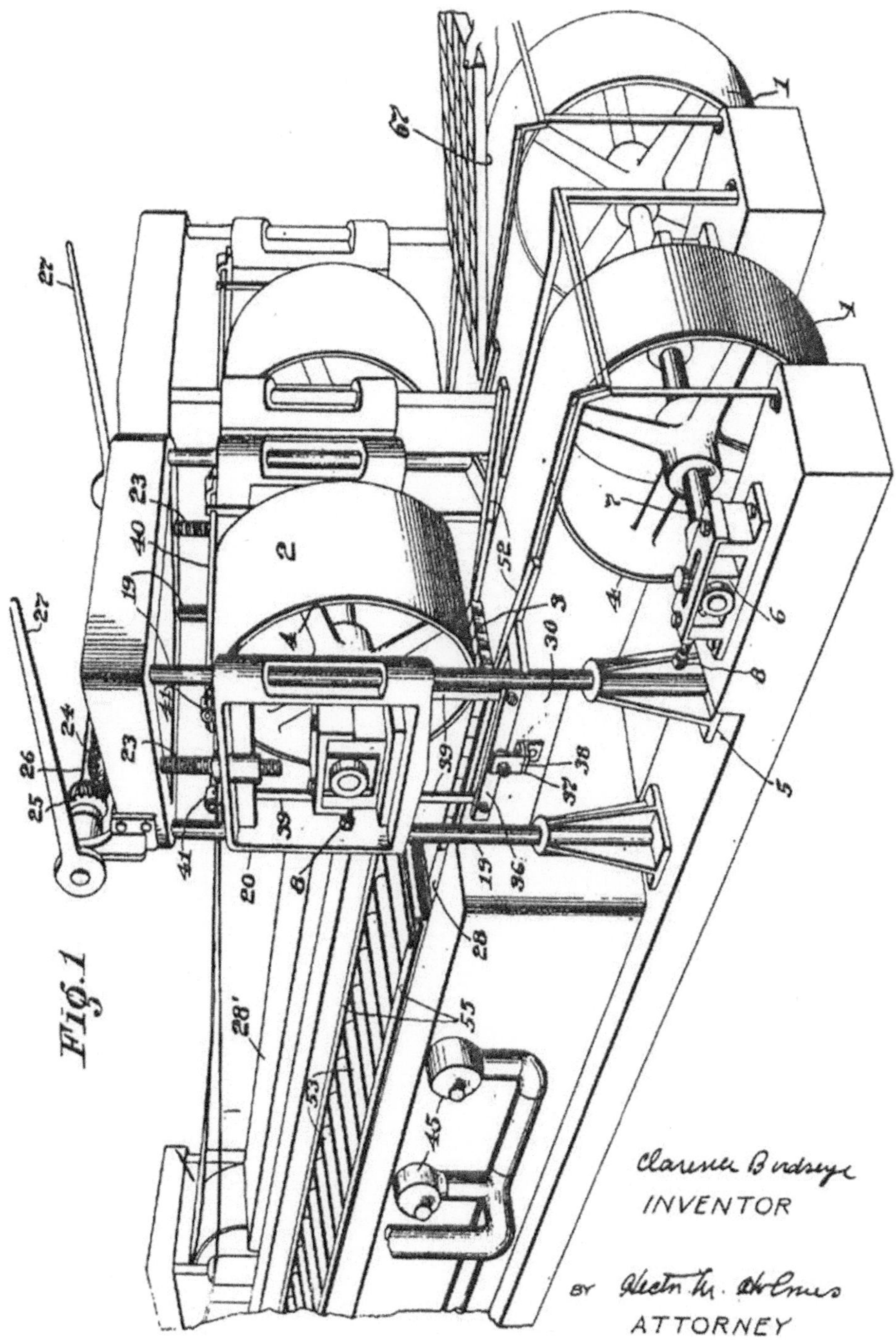

13 Protection of Computer-Related Inventions

13.1 INTRODUCTION

One of the questions asked most frequently of patent attorneys during the past 40 years or more has been: "Is computer software or a computer-related invention eligible to be patented?" The answer has progressed over time from a flat "no," through the stage of a "definite maybe," to the current "yes, if specific criteria are met." The purpose of this chapter is to provide you, the computer-related and software-developing engineer or scientist, with sufficient information to: (1) determine whether the computer-related technology you develop constitutes patent-eligible subject matter; and (2) if it does, how to ensure that the patent application prepared to cover your invention is sufficiently crafted to obtain ultimate issuance of a patent. The pertinent rules in this area of Patent Law established by the courts and the U.S. Patent and Trademark Office (USPTO) are not for the faint-hearted, and the devil is definitely in the details. The following sections include many examples in an attempt to clarify the present state of the applicable law, rather than just reciting a single standard to be applied—because there is none.

Over the past several years, court decisions regarding the patent eligibility of computer-related inventions have taken many twists and turns. At present, the status of the law on this point is fluid, and I have attempted to be clear in the following paragraphs and sections, which, I admit, may not be readily understandable at first reading. But I shall make every effort to guide you through the murky waters.

As stated earlier in Chapter 4, the patent statutes dictate that patents be granted on new and non-obvious processes, machines, articles of manufacture, compositions of matter, or any new and useful improvement of such inventions. Some examples of claimed subject matter that do *not* fall within one of these categories, and do *not* define patentable subject matter are:

1. Transitory forms of electronic signal transmission, such as a propagating electrical or electromagnetic signal per se (carrier waves).
2. A human per se, or part of a human.

Intellectual Property Law for Engineers, Scientists, and Entrepreneurs, Second Edition. Howard B. Rockman.

Published 2020 by John Wiley & Sons, Inc.

3. A legal contractual agreement between two parties.
4. A mere arrangement of printed matter.
5. Data per se.

After it has been determined that an invention *does* fall within one of the statutory categories of patentable subject matter, it must be found whether the claimed invention wholly embraces a "judicially recognized exception" (rules created by court decisions, not by the legislature) to the patent-eligible invention categories listed in the statute. These exceptions, which do *not* comprise patentable subject matter, include:

1. Laws of nature.
2. Natural phenomena.
3. Abstract ideas, such as pure mathematical algorithms and scientific principles.

Each of these exceptions are characterized by the fact that they were not created by human intervention.

13.2 THE TORTUROUS PATH THROUGH THE COURTS

The discipline of computer science began when general-purpose computers reached the capacity to run a large variety of programs. At this point, designers of programs (software) began to distinguish themselves from the designers of the machines on which the software ran (hardware). Other than the programmers themselves, and the hardware engineers, not many people understood the nature of software at this time. In the 1950s and early 1960s, patent applications were filed covering software inventions, and the USPTO rejected them all, stating that software was definitely not patentable subject matter. Those programmers who were able to obtain patents did not obtain the patent on the software itself, but on combinations of hardware and software, since the hardware was a "machine." Through a long and torturous path, the U.S. Supreme Court and the Court of Appeals for the Federal Circuit (CAFC) began to understand computer programming and its value to business and society in general. The pendulum swung, and rules and guidelines now exist to enable patent protection for computer-related inventions, even those embedded in software, *if* the combination of program and machine meets certain criteria.

13.2.1 *Gottschalk v. Benson*, 1972

The first relevant Supreme Court case regarding computer-related inventions is *Gottschalk v. Benson*, 409 U.S. 63 (1972). The patent application in the *Benson* case was directed "to the processing of data by program, and more particularly to the programmed conversion of numerical information" in a general-purpose digital computer. The claimed invention was a method for converting binary-coded decimal (BCD) numerals into pure binary numerals. The claims in the patent application were not limited to any particular art or technology or to any particular apparatus or machinery, or to any particular end use. The USPTO rejected the application as not defining statutory patentable subject matter. However, the claims were held to constitute patentable subject matter on appeal to the Court of Customs and Patent Appeals (the predecessor of the CAFC). The Supreme Court agreed to hear the case, which was appealed by the USPTO.

The question before the Supreme Court was whether the method described and claimed in the *Benson* patent application was a "process" within the meaning of patentable subject matter under the patent statutes. The Supreme Court determined that the conversion of BCD numerals into pure binary numerals can be performed mentally through use of a table showing how decimal numbers are expressed as binary symbols using only a zero and a one. The method sought to be patented varies the ordinary arithmetic steps a human would use by changing the order of the steps, changing the symbolism for writing the multiplier used in some steps, and by taking subtotals after each successive operation. The mathematical procedures claimed in the patent application could be carried out in existing computers long in use, with no new machinery being necessary, and the procedures could also be performed in one's mind without a computer.

The Supreme Court held that one may not patent an idea, and in practical effect that would be the result if the formula in this case for converting BCD numerals to pure binary numerals were patented. The *Benson* mathematical formula, the Court said, has no substantial practical application except in connection with a digital computer, which means if the appellate court judgment allowing the patent to be issued were confirmed, the patent would wholly preempt others from using the mathematical formula, and in practical effect would be a patent on the algorithm itself. The Court went on to say that it may be that Patent Law should be extended to cover these programs; however, the extant President's Commission on the Patent System rejected the proposal that these programs constitute patentable subject matter.

The decision of the Supreme Court in the *Benson* case appears to have been founded on the principle that a patent should not be allowed for inventions that are basic and fundamental to future advances in technology, since these patents would unduly burden future inventors by patenting fundamental tools or building blocks of science and decreasing the incentives for improvements in technology. One possible rationale for deciding that algorithms are not patentable subject matter, as the Court did in the *Benson* case, is "the underlying notion is that a scientific principle, such as that expressed in the patent applicant's algorithm, reveals a relationship that has always existed."

13.2.2 *Parker v. Flook*, 1978

Following *Benson*, the Supreme Court held in *Parker v. Flook*, 437 U.S. 584 (1978) that a claimed invention for a method of adjusting alarm limits in response to changes occurring during normal operation of a catalytic converter that removes pollutants through the conversion of hydrocarbons during the process of refining oil defined patent-ineligible subject matter. The limits, representing numbers between which a catalytic converter normally operates, are derived using a time-weighted average of a relevant operating parameter in accordance with a smoothing algorithm. The patent application claimed the numbers representing the alarm limits.

The patent claims in the *Parker* case differed from *Benson* by claiming a specific application for the formula as a limitation in the claim (a "field of use" limitation). The Supreme Court held that the *Flook* patent claim did not meet the criteria of a patent-eligible process, since the patent application claim was directed to a "principle" or "law of nature." The Court stated:

> "Even though a phenomenon of nature or mathematical formula may be well known, an inventive application of the principles may be patented. Conversely, the discovery of such a phenomenon cannot support a patent unless there is some other inventive concept in its application."

The Supreme Court also decided that, even though the patent claims included the application of the formula for use in the catalytic conversion of hydrocarbons (the "field of use"), the claim was still patent ineligible, since: "A competent [patent] draftsman could attach some form of post-solution activity to almost any mathematical formula..." The Court did agree, however, that patents involving the application of formulas, laws of nature, or abstract principles are eligible for patenting, but only if the application of the principle is both novel and unobvious. In the *Parker* case, it was conceded that there was no other inventive concept in the *Flook* patent application, and that the process claimed in the *Flook* application was applied only in a conventional, known way.

One lesson to be drawn from *Parker v. Flook* is to ensure that the patent application filed covering your computer-related invention includes language that makes it clear that the application or implementation of the algorithm or formula is new, and not merely conventional or trivial, as was conceded in the *Parker v. Flook* case. The patent application specification should state that the application of the algorithm or formula has a novel, non-obvious and inventive quality, and explain how. Simply applying an abstract idea embedded in an algorithm on a generic computer will not lead to an allowable patent claim.

13.2.3 *Diamond v. Diehr*, 1981

The next case on computer-related inventions decided by the Supreme Court was *Diamond v. Diehr*, 450 U.S. 175 (1981). The patent before the Court claimed a process for curing synthetic rubber, including several steps utilizing a mathematical formula and a programmed digital computer. The Court held that the claimed physical and chemical process for molding precision synthetic rubber products was patentable subject matter, since the patent application claims covered the step-by-step transformation of an article, in this case, raw, uncured, synthetic rubber, into a different state or thing. The claims described a method, beginning with the loading of a mold with raw, uncured rubber, and ending with the eventual opening of the press at the conclusion of the curing process. The Court's conclusion was not altered by the fact that several, but not all, of the steps of the process involved a mathematical equation and a programmed digital computer.

The Court, in the *Diehr* case, differentiated its decision from the *Benson* case, the latter involving an algorithm used to convert binary code decimal numbers to equivalent pure binary numbers, which was held to constitute non-patent-eligible subject matter. The sole practical application of the *Benson* algorithm was in connection with the programming of a general-purpose digital computer. In the *Benson* case, the Court defined an "algorithm" as "a procedure for solving a given type of mathematical problem," and concluded that such an algorithm, or mathematical formula, is comparable to a law of nature, which cannot be the subject of a patent grant.

In the *Diehr* case, however, the patent claims were not directed to a mathematical formula. Instead, they were directed to a process of curing synthetic rubber. The *Diehr* process admittedly employed a mathematical equation, but the patent applicants did not seek to preempt the use of that equation. They only sought to foreclose others from using that equation in conjunction with all of the other steps in their claimed process, including the physical and chemical steps of processing the rubber. The Court held that one does not need a computer to cure natural or synthetic rubber, but if the use of the computer incorporated in the claimed process lessens the possibility of over-curing or under-curing, the process as a whole amounts to patentable subject matter.

The Court in the *Diehr* case concluded that a patent claim drawn to subject matter otherwise protectable by a patent does not become unpatentable simply because it uses a mathematical formula, computer program, or a digital computer. The court also held that the application of a law of nature or mathematical formula to a known structure or process may well be deserving of patent protection. Thus, while a scientific truth, or the mathematical expression of that truth, is not patentable, a novel and useful structure or process created with the aid of that knowledge and scientific truth is patentable subject matter, once the criteria of novelty and unobviousness are also satisfied.

13.2.4 *Arrhythmia v. Corazonix*, 1992

In the 1992 CAFC case of *Arrhythmia Research Technology, Inc. v. Corazonix Corp.* 958 Fed. 2d 1053 (Fed. Cir. 1992), the patent claims in question related to a method of detecting those heart attack victims who were more at risk of suffering later complications. The claimed technique involved measuring and then processing electrocardiograph signals. In sustaining the claims as being directed to patentable subject matter, the CAFC reasoned that, although the claims recited a mathematical algorithm, the number obtained from the algorithm is not just an abstraction, but a measure in microvolts of a specified heart activity. In this case, the apparatus claims of the patent application called for a "means" for converting electrocardiograph signals from analog form to digital form. The patent application specification described this "means" as a conventional analog-to-digital converter. Calculations performed on a microcomputer were stored in the form of electrical signals. The computer-performed operations transformed a particular input signal to a different output signal. The CAFC reasoned that "The claimed invention … converts one physical thing into another physical thing just as any other electrical circuitry would do," relying on a prior 1980 decision finding that patent claims directed to an apparatus for analyzing seismic signals, including mathematically described means for "sonogramming," "dividing," and "plotting," described patentable subject matter.

Therefore, the CAFC determined that data or signals in this invention were not abstractions; they were related to the patient's heart functions. It is clear from this decision that an electronic apparatus or device for transforming electrical signals constitutes patentable subject matter.

13.2.5 *In re: Alappat*, 1994

In the 1994 CAFC case of *In re Alappat*, 33 Fed. 3d 1526 (Fed. Cir. 1994), the invention under consideration was an improved technique for reducing apparent discontinuities or jaggedness in the display of wave forms on an oscilloscope. Specific mathematical formulae were used to interpolate between data points to display a continuous line on the oscilloscope rather than discrete points. The patent application claims recited features representing circuitry elements that performed mathematical calculations. The CAFC held that the claimed invention, as a whole, constituted patentable subject matter directed to a combination of interrelated elements that combine to form a machine for converting discrete wave form data samples into anti-aliased pixel illumination intensity data to be displayed on a display device. This is not a disembodied mathematical concept that may be characterized as an abstract idea, but rather a specific machine to produce a "useful, concrete, and tangible result."

Although the Alappat invention was only directed to a new process that could be implemented on existing hardware, the majority of the court felt that the patentable invention was still in a "new machine." The court said that "such programming creates a new machine, because the general-purpose computer in effect becomes a special-purpose computer once it is programmed to perform particular functions pursuant to instructions from program software." Thus, the court appears to be holding that a standard computer, when programmed to do a certain function, becomes a "new machine," and new machines constitute patentable subject matter. Under this analysis, the court looked at the software, and the hardware that it operates, as a single unit, and each time a new piece of software is added to the hardware, a new machine totality is created.

13.2.6 The 1996 USPTO Guidelines

In early 1996, the USPTO issued new examination procedures for software patent applications, titled "Examination Guidelines for Computer-Related Inventions," which can be found at 61 Fed. Reg. 7478 (1996) (the "1996 guidelines"). The 1996 guidelines recognized that abstract ideas, natural phenomenon, and laws of nature are non-statutory and non-patentable subject matter under patent laws. These three important exclusions recognize that subject matter that is not a practical application or use of an idea, a law of nature, or a natural phenomenon is not patentable. Thus, the 1996 guidelines base the patentability of software upon its utility, and rely on the patent applicant's total invention disclosure in the patent application to establish that the patent application is directed to patentable subject matter.

Where a use or uses for specific hardware or specific software are adequately described in the patent application specification to support a claim, the claim will probably be found to define patentable subject matter. However, patent application disclosures set forth in generalities without establishing a tangible, concrete use for the invention will probably not lead to the grant of a patent. While the guidelines do not have the force of law, many courts rely upon these guidelines in reaching their decisions on the patentability of software-related inventions. Courts have, on more than one occasion, given weight to views of the experts of the USPTO.

13.2.7 The 1998 *State Street* Case

Of major importance is the 1998 CAFC case of *State Street Bank and Trust Company v. Signature Financial Group, Inc.*, 149 Fed. 3d 1368 (Fed. Cir. 1998). Signature owned a patent entitled "Data Processing System for Hub and Spoke Financial Services Configuration," which was generally directed to a data processing system for implementing a financial investment structure developed for use in Signature's business as an administrator and accounting agent for mutual funds. The program facilitates a structure whereby mutual funds (spokes) pool their assets in an investment portfolio (hub) organized as a partnership. This investment configuration provides an administrator of a mutual fund with the advantageous combination of economies of scale in administrating investments, coupled with the tax advantages of a partnership. State Street Bank, after unsuccessfully trying to negotiate a license under the Signature patent, brought a declaratory judgment court action, alleging, among other things, that the Signature patent did not claim statutory subject matter under Patent Law.

The patented system provided a way for daily allocation of assets for two or more spokes that are invested in the same hub, and determined the percentage share that each spoke maintained in the hub, while taking into consideration daily changes both in the value of the hub's investment securities and in the concomitant amount of each spoke's assets. The system ultimately enables the determination of the true asset value of each spoke and an accurate calculation of allocation ratios between or among spokes.

A mutual fund administrator is required to calculate the value of the shares in the fund to the nearest penny within as little as an hour and a half after the stock market closes each day. Given the complexity of these calculations, a computer or equivalent device is a virtual necessity. The patent claims in question were in "means plus function" format. The CAFC held that the patent claims were properly construed as being directed toward a machine which included "means" as the structural elements.

The decision of the CAFC in the *State Street* case is reprinted in pertinent part at the end of this chapter. In that decision, note that the court paraphrases the seven elements of the Signature patent claim, and shows how the term "means" defines a particular physical structure, such as a personal computer, a data disc, etc. Claim 1 of the subject patent was construed as being directed to a machine, namely, a data processing system for managing a financial services configuration. The machine is made up, at the very least, of the specific structures disclosed in the written description in the patent, and those structures correspond to the "means plus function" elements recited in the claim. The court went on to state that a machine is proper patentable subject matter.

The *State Street* decision includes a very important analysis indicating that the lower court erred in concluding that the subject matter fell into two exceptions to the patentable subject matter classification, these being mathematical algorithms and business methods. Prior to the *State Street* case, mathematical algorithms and business methods were not considered patentable subject matter. However, the *State Street* case substantially changed all that. The court repeated a previous comment by the Supreme Court that Congress intended Section 101 of the Patent Statute, which defines patentable subject matter, to extend to "anything under the sun that is made by man."

An analysis of the "Mathematical Algorithm" portion of the *State Street* decision follows. The "Business Method" portion of *State Street* is discussed at Chapter 15, Section 15.2.

13.2.8 The "Mathematical Algorithm" Exception Analysis of *State Street*

Prior to the *State Street* decision, the Supreme Court in the *Diehr* case had identified three categories of subject matter that are unpatentable, namely laws of nature, natural phenomenon, and abstract ideas. This is still the law today. In the *Diehr* case, the

Court also held that mathematical algorithms are not patentable subject matter to the extent that, standing alone, they are merely abstract ideas, and did not reach the level of patentability until reduced to some type of practical application providing a "useful, concrete, and tangible result."

Unpatentable mathematical algorithms are identifiable by showing that they are merely abstract ideas constituting disembodied concepts or truths that are not "useful." Thus, to be patentable, a mathematical algorithm must be applied in a "useful" way. For example, in the *Alappat* case, it was held that data transformed by a machine through a series of mathematical calculations to produce a smooth wave form display on a rasterizer monitor constituted a practical application of an abstract idea, because it produced a useful, concrete, and tangible result—that is, a smooth wave form display.

In the *State Street* case, the court held that the transformation of data, representing discrete dollar amounts, by a machine through a series of mathematical calculations into a final share price constituted a patentable practical allocation of a mathematical algorithm, formula, or calculation, because it produced a useful, concrete, and tangible result. That result is a final share price momentarily fixed for recording and reporting purposes, and even accepted and relied upon by regulatory authorities and in subsequent trades.

The question of whether a computer-related invention encompasses patentable subject matter should focus on the central characteristics of the subject matter, and particularly its practical utility. In *State Street*, the machine programmed with the hub and spoke software produced a useful, concrete, and tangible result, defining statutory and patentable subject matter. This is true even though the useful result is expressed in numbers, such as price, profit, percentage, cost, or loss.

Based on the *State Street* case, inventors applying for patents covering software inventions should describe and claim their inventions in terms of a process having a stated utility. These applicants do not have to rely solely on claiming the software in association with a machine, such as a computer system or CPU.

13.3 RECENT COURT DECISIONS AND USPTO GUIDELINES ATTEMPTING TO DEFINE PATENT-ELIGIBLE SUBJECT MATTER REGARDING COMPUTER-RELATED INVENTIONS

13.3.1 *Bilski v. Kappos*

In its decision in *Bilski v. Kappos*, 561 U.S. 593 (2010), the Supreme Court held that the patent applicant's claims directed to how buyers and sellers of commodities in the energy market can manage, protect, or "hedge" against the risk of price changes were directed to an "abstract idea," and thus were not patent eligible, in part because the claimed method was long in use before the use of computers. The Court, however, did not "provide a satisfying amount [definition] of what constitutes an unpatentable abstract idea," as noted by Justice Stevens in a concurring opinion.

Prior to the *Bilski* decision, the CAFC had relied on the "machine-or-transformation" test to determine the patentability of a process or method. This test required that, to be patent eligible, a process must either (1) be associated with or performed by a machine, or (2) involve a transformation of an article into a different state or a different "thing." The Supreme Court in *Bilski* decided that, while the machine-or-transformation test was one useful clue for determining the patent eligibility of processes, it was not the only test for making that determination. However, the Court did not iterate what these additional tests might be.

The Supreme Court in *Bilski*, in rationalizing that the claim at issue defined only an "abstract idea," cited three of its prior decisions. In *Gottschalk v. Benson*, 409 U.S. 63 (1972), and in *Parker v. Flook*, 437 U.S. 584 (1978), the Court had held that software was not patentable subject matter because software was analogous to the laws of nature and existing mathematical formulae, and therefore abstract ideas. In *Diamond v. Diehr*, 450 U.S. 175 (1981), the Court backpedaled somewhat, holding that patentability would not be denied just because the invention utilized computer software in a practical application. Other than commenting on these three cases, the *Bilski* decision did not offer further guidance toward defining an "abstract idea."

The *Bilski* decision also confirmed that business methods remained patentable subject matter if other requirements for patentability were satisfied. See Chapter 15.

13.3.2 *Alice Corp. Pty. Ltd. v. CLS Bank*

The most recent Supreme Court case on this point is *Alice Corp. Pty. Ltd. v. CLS Bank Int'l.*, 573 U.S. 208, 217–218, 134 S. Ct 2347, 2354 (2014) (the "*Alice*" case). The *Alice* case involved the question of whether patents that disclose and claim a computer-based method and system for mitigating "settlement risk" constituted patentable subject matter. The risk was that only one party to an agreed-upon financial exchange would satisfy its obligation. Particularly, the patent claims were designed to facilitate the exchange of financial obligations between two parties by using the computer system as a third-party intermediary. The patents-in-suit claimed: (1) a method for exchanging financial obligations, (2) a computer system configured to carry out the method for exchanging obligations, and (3) a computer-readable medium containing program code for performing the method of exchanging obligations. Both the District Court and the CAFC held that the patent claims were directed to an abstract idea and, therefore, the claims were not directed to patent-eligible subject matter.

The Supreme Court confirmed the opinions of both lower courts. In deciding the case, the Supreme Court stated that the Court has long held that Section 101 of the patent statute, which defines the subject matter eligibility for patent protection, contains an implicit exception for laws of nature, natural phenomena, and abstract ideas, which are not patentable subject matter. The Supreme Court stated that, in making its decisions, the Court must distinguish patents that claim the building blocks of human ingenuity, which are ineligible for patent protection, from those that integrate the building blocks into "something more," thereby transforming these building blocks into a patent-eligible invention.

The Court decided that a two-step test must be applied. First, it must be determined whether the claims at issue are directed to a patent-ineligible concept, such as an abstract idea. If so, the Court then goes to step two and asks whether the claims include additional elements, considered both individually and as an ordered combination, that are sufficient to ensure that the claimed subject matter, in practice, amounts to "significantly more" than defining the abstract idea itself.

In applying this analysis, the Court first stated that the claims at issue in the *Alice* case were directed to a patent-ineligible concept—the abstract idea of an intermediated financial settlement. The Court went on to say that, under its long-standing rule that an idea in and of itself is not patentable, it has found ineligible patent claims in previous cases involving (1) an algorithm for converting binary-coded decimal numerals into pure binary form, (2) a mathematical formula for computing alarm limits in a catalytic conversion process, and (3) in the *Bilski* case, a method for hedging against the financial risk of price fluctuations. The Court stated that it follows from these cases, and *Bilski* in particular, that the claims in the *Alice* case were directed to an abstract idea. On their face, the claims were drawn to the concept of an intermediated settlement, which is the use of a third party to mitigate settlement risk. Like the risk hedging in *Bilski*, the concept of an intermediated settlement is a fundamental economic practice long prevalent in our system of commerce, and the use of a third-party intermediary or clearing house is a building block of the modern economy. Thus, an intermediated settlement, as is hedging, is an abstract idea beyond Section 101's scope of patentable subject matter.

The Court then applied the second step of its test, holding that the method claims in the *Alice* case, which merely required generic computer implementation, failed to transform that abstract idea into a patent-eligible invention. Simply appending conventional steps, specified at a high level of generality to a method already well known in the art, is not "enough" to supply the "inventive concept" needed to make the transformation to patent eligibility. The introduction of a computer into the claimed process or system does not alone alter the analysis. Wholly generic computer implementation is not generally the sort of "additional feature" that provides any "practical assurance" that the process is more than a drafting effort designed to monopolize the abstract idea itself. The representative method claim in the *Alice* case was held to be no more than to simply instruct the practitioner to implement the abstract idea of intermediated settlement on a generic computer. The function performed by the computer at each step—creating and maintaining shadow accounts, obtaining data, adjusting account balances, and issuing automated instructions—is purely conventional in the related art. The Court went on to state that, as an ordered combination, these computer components added nothing that is not already present when the steps are considered separately. Also, viewed as a whole, these method claim steps simply recite the concept of an intermediated settlement as performed by a generic computer. They do not purport to improve the functioning of the computer itself or effect an improvement in any other technology. An instruction to apply the abstract idea of intermediated settlement using some unspecified generic computer is not enough to transform the abstract idea into a patent-eligible invention.

The Court continued by stating that the patent owner's system claims and media claims added nothing of substance to the underlying abstract idea. The method claims recited the abstract idea implemented on the generic computer, and the system claims recited a handful of generic computer components configured to implement the same idea. Also, the media claims were the same as the method claims, and the decision by the Court regarding the method claims was also directly applicable to the media claims.

Other terms used by courts to describe non-patentable subject matter include "physical phenomena," "scientific principles," "systems that depend on human intelligence alone," "disembodied concepts," "mental processes," and "disembodied mathematical algorithms and formulas," for example. The *Alice* decision reflects the Supreme Court's view that the basic tools of scientific and technological work and research are not patentable, and that such fundamental principles and truths cannot be given to one as an exclusive right.

However, while laws of nature, natural phenomena, and abstract ideas are not patent eligible, methods and products employing applications and implementations of abstract ideas, natural phenomena, and laws of nature that perform a real-world function may be patentable. Thus, if the individual or combined elements of the claimed invention amount to "significantly more" than the judicial exception, patentability may be established. If the claimed invention comprises a particular novel application of an abstract idea, natural phenomena, or law of nature, patent protection may be available.

13.3.3 CAFC Decisions Subsequent to *Alice v. CLS Bank*

Following the *Alice* decision, the CAFC decided several cases in which patents covering computer-related inventions were held invalid as being directed to "abstract ideas," and several other cases where the patents in the same genre were held valid. However, trying to accurately define the dividing line between these series of cases has been elusive, so please bear with me as I try to explain the current status of this important concept of Patent Law.

After the Supreme Court decision in the *Alice* case, one of the first cases decided by the CAFC where the CAFC held claims valid directed to a computer-related invention was *Enfish LLC. v. Microsoft Corporation*, 822 F.3d 1327 (Fed. Cir. 2016), decided on May 12, 2016, where the invention was directed to software and a database. The CAFC in *Enfish* advised that an analysis should be conducted to compare the invention to other inventions found to be abstract ideas in previous cases, and those *not* found to define abstract ideas. Also, the CAFC held that claims to the invention should be interpreted in view of the definitions of the elements or steps of the invention set forth in the patent's specification. The court went on to hold that a claim is not abstract if the claimed invention provides improvements in computer-related technology, such as chip architecture or an LED display, which are not abstract ideas. Further, the CAFC in this case held that, since software can make non-abstract improvements to computer technology, just as hardware can, software is *not inherently* abstract. The Court held that claims directed to an improvement to computer-related technology, such as computer functionality, may not be directed to abstract ideas. In the *Enfish* case, the claims were held valid.

Closely following *Enfish*, the CAFC decided *TLI Communications, LLC v. AV Automotive LLC*, Case No. 15-1372 (Fed. Cir. 2016), on May 17, 2016, which provides a contrast between non-abstract claims directed to an improvement to computer functionality and abstract claims directed, for example, to generalized steps to be performed on a computer using conventional computer activity. In the *TLI* case, the claims of the patent described steps of recording, administration, and archiving of digital images, and the CAFC found them to be directed to the abstract idea of classifying and storing digital images in an organized manner. The CAFC then found that the additional elements of performing these functions using a telephone unit and a server did not add significantly more to the abstract idea because they were all well understood, routine, conventional activities. In this case, therefore, following *Enfish*, the CAFC held the claims invalid. The takeout of this case is that, if the patent claim recites a concept that is similar to concepts previously found abstract by the courts, the claim will be held invalid as covering an abstract idea. However, the fact that a claim is directed to an improvement in computer-related technology, such as operation of the computer itself, can demonstrate that the claim does not recite a concept similar to previously identified unpatentable abstract ideas, and may support patentability.

An important, yet complex decision from the CAFC came down on November 1, 2016, in *Amdocs v. Openet Telecom, Inc.*, Case No. 15-1180 (Fed. Cir. 2016), which, by some analyst's opinions, gave a boost to software patentability. The Plaintiff in this case accused the Defendant of infringing four patents, each related to parts of a computer-based system designed to solve an accounting and billing problem faced by network service providers. In a nutshell, these patents describe components that were arrayed in a distributed architecture that minimized the impact on network and system resources by collecting and processing data close to the source of the data, thereby reducing congestion in network bottlenecks that had made it previously difficult to keep up with the mass of record flows from the network devices, and which therefore required huge databases. In this particular case, the term "enhanced" was used in the patent's claims and was interpreted by the CAFC to mean to apply a number of field enhancements in a distributed fashion. Importantly, in reading the specification, the CAFC approved the terms "in a distributed fashion" and "close to the source" of network information requirements as being part of the claim coverage because of the word "enhance" in the claims.

The CAFC's analysis went like this: Patent Law states that whoever invents or discovers any new and useful process, machine, manufacture, or composition of matter or any new and useful improvement thereof may obtain a patent. Court decisions have placed limitations on that definition, holding that certain fundamental principles are not included within patentable subject matter, which are called the "judicial exceptions" to patentable subject matter. These judicial exceptions are laws of nature, natural phenomenon, and abstract ideas. The Supreme Court, in the *Alice* case, set out a two-step analysis to determine whether particular inventions meet the requirements of patentability. First, it must be determined whether the patent claims are directed to one of those patent-ineligible concepts, such as an abstract idea. If the claims are so directed, a second step in the analysis considers the elements of each claim, both individually and as defining a combination, to determine whether the additional elements of the claim transform the nature of the claim into a patent-eligible application. The second step requires searching for an element or combination of elements in the claim that are sufficient to ensure that the patent would amount to "significantly more" than a patent upon the ineligible concept, or abstract idea, itself. In the life sciences area, the ineligible concept may rely upon natural phenomenon or a law of nature, while, in the computer-related invention field, emphasis is placed on the "abstract idea" of the judicial exceptions.

If the first step is applied and the claim is found not to be directed to an abstract idea or any other exception, the claim is held patent-eligible without going into the second step.

The second step of the analysis determines whether or not an invention is eligible for patenting based on the generally accepted and understood definition of what an abstract idea encompasses when dealing with computer-related inventions. However—and this is important—at present, there is no single succinct useable definition or test stated by any court defining what an abstract idea is! As stated by the CAFC in the *Amdocs* decision, this vagueness may be preferable because it is difficult to fashion a workable definition to be applied to as yet unknown cases with as yet unknown claimed inventions. Therefore, the CAFC decided that, instead of relying on a "bright line definition" of an abstract idea, the courts should now apply a test that examines earlier patent cases and decisions in which a similar or parallel descriptive nature in the claim language can be seen—that is, what prior computer-related invention cases were about, and which way they were decided. In other words, what the CAFC is suggesting is that, when determining whether a computer-related invention is patent-eligible, the claims in the case at hand should be compared to claims held either eligible or ineligible in previous cases, of which there are well over 100 at present.

The CAFC determined in *Amdocs* that this is the classic common law methodology for creating law when a single governing definition is not available. Therefore, the problem facing inventors and their patent attorneys going forward is that the claims covering their inventions must not be directed to abstract ideas in the face of the fact that the courts have admitted that there is no single definition for what is or is not an abstract idea. One point, however, is to determine whether or not the invention meets the requirement of an inventive concept as actually applied in the real world, and to scour previous CAFC decisions for guidance on how the claims defining your computer-related invention should be written.

In the *Amdocs* case, in an effort at further guidance, the CAFC made a somewhat extensive analysis of several previous decisions regarding claims that were held patent ineligible, and then several where the claims were held to be patent eligible. With its analysis of decisions that held patent claims ineligible, the CAFC first examined the case of *Digitech Image Techs., LLC v. Elecs. For Imaging, Inc.*, 758 F.3d 1344, 1350 (Fed. Cir. 2014). The patent claim in question in *Digitech* was directed to an ineligible abstract process of gathering and combining data that does not require input from a physical device. The two data sets and the resulting device profile were held to be patent-ineligible subject matter. The CAFC observed that, without additional limitations, a process that employs mathematical algorithms to manipulate existing information to generate additional information is not patent eligible, and is an abstract idea.

The second case the CAFC commented upon was *Content Extraction and Transmission, LLC v. Wells Fargo Bank*, 776 F.3d 1343, 1345 (Fed. Cir. 2014). Under step one, the CAFC held that the patent claims at issue were directed to an abstract idea of (1) collecting data, (2) recognizing certain data within the collected data set, and (3) storing the recognized data in a memory. The CAFC recognized that data collection recognition and storage were undisputedly well known in the prior art, and went on to observe that the role of the computer in a computer-implemented invention would only be meaningful under Patent Law if the invention involved more than the performance of well-understood, routine, and conventional activities previously known to the industry. The claims in this case fell short of this criterion and were patent ineligible.

The third case reviewed by the CAFC in this section of its opinion was *TLI Commc'ns LLC Patent Litigation*, 823 Fed.3d 607, 610 (Fed. Cir. 2016). Under step one, the CAFC found the claims were directed to the abstract idea of classifying and storing digital images in an organized manner. Also under step one, the CAFC found that the claims were not directed to a specific improvement in computer functionality, but instead were directed to the use of a conventional or generic technology in a nascent but well-known environment, without any claim that the invention reflected an inventive solution to any problem presented by combining the two. Instead, the recited components and functions were well-understood, routine, conventional activities previously known in the industry.

The CAFC in *Amdocs* next switched to a discussion of patent-eligible claims in previous decisions of the CAFC, beginning with the case of *DDR Holdings v. Hotels.com, L.P. et al*, 773 Fed.3d at 1257 (December 5, 2014), where the court had found that the asserted claims did not recite a step or function performed by a computerized mathematical algorithm, but were instead focused on a challenge particular to the Internet. The CAFC observed that the claimed solution to the problem in this case was necessarily rooted in computer technology to overcome a problem specifically arising in the realm of computer networks, and that the claim in this patent was not merely directed to a routine or conventional use of the Internet. On this basis, the claim in this case was held to be patent eligible.

The second patent-eligible claims case cited by the CAFC in its *Amdocs* decision was *Bascom Global Internet Servers v. AT&T Mobility*, 827 Fed.3d 1341, 1345 (June 27, 2016), where the court first held that the claims were directed to an abstract idea under step one. However, under step two, the CAFC found that the ordered combination of the limitations in the claim provided the requisite inventive concept, that is, the installation of a filtering tool at a specific location remote from the end users, with customizable filtering features specific to each end user. This was held not to be a conventional or generic process, and the claims did not preempt all ways of filtering content on the Internet. The CAFC thus distinguished ineligible abstract idea–based solutions implemented with generic technical components in a conventional way from the patent-eligible claim in this case that described a technology-based solution *and* a software-based invention that improved the performance of the computer system itself.

Keep in mind that these are only five of the CAFC cases out of more than 100 other decisions that could have been analyzed in the same way. Obviously for brevity, these cases were not discussed in the *Amdocs* case, nor in this treatise. A listing of court decisions of patent eligibility issues is available on the USPTO website (www.uspto.gov), under the heading "Subject Matter Eligibility Court Decisions (Formerly Appendix 3)."

In the *Amdocs* case, after reciting the aforementioned background of previous cases, the CAFC turned to an examination of the claims of the patents that were involved in the case at hand, with the added caveat that the Judges interpreted the claims in view of the written description or specification of the patent. This is often done by courts when a patent claim term may be a broad term, and the broad term has to be defined more particularly by referring to the patent specification.

In the *Amdocs* case, four separate patents were being reviewed, and each of the patents was held to comprise patent-eligible claims. In analyzing the first of the four patents, the CAFC first cited the *Enfish* case, discussed previously, where the court found that the patent claims did not define an abstract idea because the patent claims in *Enfish* solved a technology-based problem with conventional generic components combined in an unconventional manner. In *Amdocs*, the CAFC held that the claims in the first patent were much closer to those in *Bascom* and *DDR Holdings* than they were to the claims in *Digitech* and *In re TLI*, and that even if claim 1 was directed to an ineligible abstract idea under step one, the claim is eligible under step two because it contains a sufficient inventive concept. The Court noted that claim 1 required computer code for using the accounting information with which a first network accounting record is correlated to enhance the first network accounting record. In other words, the CAFC stated that this claim entails an unconventional technological solution (enhancing data in a distributed fashion) to a technological problem (massive record flows which previously required massive databases). The claim's "enhancing" limitation required that these generic components operate in an unconventional manner to achieve an improvement in computer functionality. Contrasting this particular patent claim to the *Digitech* case, the CAFC held that the claim under analysis in *Digitech* was not tied to any particular structure that broadly preempted related technologies, and merely involved combining data in an ordinary manner without any inventive step. The CAFC distinguished the present *Amdocs* claims by stating that the *Amdocs* claims constituted an architecture providing a technological solution to a technological problem, providing the requisite "something more" than the performance of well-understood, routine, and conventional activities previously known in the computer industry.

The CAFC also held that claim 1 of the first patent solved a technological problem (massive data flows requiring huge databases) akin to the problem in *DDR Holdings* (conventional hyperlink protocol preventing websites from retaining visitors). The court also commented about the *Bascom* case, which permitted the system to have a filtering tool with the benefits of the filter on a local computer and the benefits of a filter on an ISP server. The benefits in *Bascom* were realized because of customizable filter features at specific locations remote from the user due to the distributed remote enhancement that produced an unconventional result—reduced data flows and the possibility of smaller databases. The arrangement in this particular *Amdocs* claim is not so broadly described as to cause preemptive concerns; instead, it is narrowly circumscribed to cover the particular system outlined. Therefore, this claim was held to be a patent-eligible application of a generic concept.

The second patent examined in the *Amdocs* case related to a network usage system where information is collected in real time from a plurality of networked devices at a plurality of layers, and is filtered and aggregated before being completed into a plurality of data records. The collection, filtering, aggregating, and completing steps all depend upon the invention's unique and unconventional distributed architecture. The specification of the patent explained that the distributed architecture allows the system to efficiently and accurately collect network usage information in a manner designed for efficiency to minimize impact on network and system resources, enabling load distribution, making it easier to keep up with record flows, and allowing for smaller databases. The CAFC also stated that, while some individual limitations arguably may be generic, others are unconventional, and the ordered combination of these limitations yields an inventive concept sufficient to confer eligibility without undue preemption of a generic concept.

The third patent under analysis in the *Amdocs* decision included claims directed to reporting on the collection of network usage information from a plurality of network devices, requiring the completion of a plurality of data records in a manner that depends upon enhancement—which depends upon the system's distributed architecture. The CAFC also held these claims to be patent eligible for the same reasons it decided the first two *Amdocs* patents to be eligible.

The fourth patent in the *Amdocs* case involved one record that included customer usage data for each of the plurality of services used by the customer and allowed the inclusion of a plurality of services by aggregation. The CAFC held that this aggregation depends upon the invention's distributed architecture, and held this patent's claims also to be patent eligible based upon the analyses regarding the previous patent claims in the *Amdocs* decision.

Two instructive decisions were recently decided by the CAFC on two consecutive days. On August 15, 2017, the Court rendered a 2 to 1 decision in *Visual Memory LLC v. Nvidia Corp.*, 867 F.3d 1253 (Fed. Cir. 2017), holding that a Visual Memory patent directed to an improved computer memory system, and not to the abstract idea of categorical data storage, covered patent-eligible subject matter. The patent claims recited a memory system having one or more programmable operational characteristics, the characteristics being defined through configuration by the computer based on the type of processor, and determining a type of data stored by the cache.

Importantly, the court relied on the specification of the Visual Memory patent to support its conclusion that the claims defined something more than an abstract idea of categorical data storage, which would not be patent eligible. The specification explained that the improved memory system provided multiple benefits as compared to the prior art. These benefits included, as specifically enumerated in the specification: (1) different types of processors to be installed with the improved memory system without significantly compromising their individual performance, (2) obviating the need to design a separate memory system for each type of processor, which was costly and inefficient, (3) avoiding the performance problems of prior art memory systems, (4) enabling interoperability with multiple processors, and (5) the selective definition of the functions of the cache memory based on processor type results in a memory system that can outperform a prior art memory system that is armed with a cache many times larger than the cumulative size of the caches described and claimed in the Visual Memory patent.

The important takeout from this case is that, in preparing a patent application directed to a computer-related invention, the specification should clearly describe all of the features, functions, and results of the invention that define a technological improvement, such as the enhanced computer memory system in this lawsuit. Here, the specification of the patent clearly defined the programmable computer operational characteristics that were configurable based on the type of processor to be a technological improvement in computer functionality, and not a patent-ineligible process that qualified as an abstract idea for which computers are invoked merely as a tool.

Thus, when reviewing the patent application drafted by your patent professional, be sure that the specification fully defines the technological improvements and enhancements provided by your invention over the prior art. In the *Visual Memory* case, the court relied upon the fact that the patent's specification made clear that the inventors viewed their innovation as the creation of a memory system that was efficiently operable with different types of host processors, and how that new memory system should be implemented. Similar types of clear descriptions should be included in your computer-related invention patent application.

On the following day, August 16, 2017, the CAFC upheld without opinion a district court decision, holding that patent claims directed only to the abstract idea of a method of preparing a video for sharing in streaming video, online format for sharing over a computer network, did not define patent-eligible subject matter. In *VideoShare, LLC v. Google, Inc. and YouTube, LLC*, C.A. No. 13-cv-990 (GMS) (D.C. Del. 2016), the district court defined the claimed subject matter as preparing a video in streaming video format for sharing over a computer network, relying on language in the patent's specification to distill the thrust of the claims into a short statement.

The *VideoShare* district court found that the claims of the asserted patents were directed to an abstract idea because the claimed invention was not directed to an improvement in computer functionality, and the physical components recited in the claims merely provided a generic environment for carrying out the abstract idea. The court also noted that the specifications of the asserted patents disclosed only generic software built upon third-party technologies that provide file format conversions, which are generally algorithmic in nature. The court also noted that the patent specifications did not disclose any specific algorithms or specific software code that carries out the file format conversion. Again, the content of the specification of the patent was important in informing the court of the true nature of the invention.

The *VideoShare* district court found that the patented claims described a method that merely automated a sequence of known steps using conventional technology so that a human is not burdened with various manual steps, and that did not provide any discernable benefits to computer functionality. Also, the court held that the physical elements in the claims (receiving computer, first computer, web page) merely provided a generic environment for carrying out the abstract idea of preparing a video in streaming video format for sharing over a computer network.

The *Visual Memory* and *VideoShare* decisions, in my judgment, show the importance of describing the elements, functionality, and advantageous results of a computer-related invention in the specification. This allows a court to read the patent's claims and specification together and come to the conclusion either that the invention is not merely an abstract idea, or, if the claimed subject matter is an abstract idea, that the invention comprises an element or combination of elements sufficient to ensure that the patented invention, in practice, amounts to significantly more than the ineligible abstract idea itself when the elements of the patent's claims are considered both individually and as an ordered combination. Your patent professional's advice will be important in determining if and how a valid patent can be obtained covering your computer-related invention.

13.3.4 Additional Exemplary Comments Regarding Patent-Eligible Subject Matter and Computer-Related Inventions

As discussed in the previous sections of this chapter, computer-related inventions are patentable in some instances and not in others. There are many issued patents today covering machines operated and controlled by software, and electronic devices that incorporate software. On the other side of the coin, there are some software inventions that cannot be patented.

In one case, the invention was a method for seismic exploration used for oil prospecting. In that invention, seismic waves reflected from subsurface formations were summed to simulate substantially plane or cylindrical waves. A computer summed the reflection signals and processed them to obtain meaningful subsurface information. The court said the invention was patent eligible. It was not a mere solution to a mathematical algorithm (summing), but defined the process of taking substantially spherical seismic signals and converting them into another form, that is, a form representative of a plane or a cylindrical wave. This case established that signals are physical, and a process that involves physically transforming signals into different states can be patentable. Here, the plane or cylindrical wave could be viewed on a computer display.

A mathematical formula or abstract idea alone cannot be protected through patents. In another case, the invention was a method and apparatus for controlling the motion of objects such as robotic machines to avoid collisions with other objects, either fixed or moving. The invention used a "bubble hierarchy" technique, in which the object to be avoided is encircled by theoretical spheres. This bubble hierarchy technique was previously known, and the invention was in placing these bubbles along a particular "medial axis" of the object. The claim broadly recited a method for generating a data structure that represents the shape of the physical object by first locating the medial axis of the object and then creating a hierarchy of bubbles on the medial axis. The CAFC held that the steps of "locating a medial axis" and "creating a bubble hierarchy" were nothing more than the manipulation of basic mathematical constructs, or an abstract idea. The "data structure" was not considered a useful, tangible result.

We see here that the way in which a patent claim is drafted and the way the specification is written are critical in determining whether the claims define patentable subject matter. Merely locating the medial axis and creating the bubble hierarchy to generate a data structure does not produce a useful, tangible result. If the claims had defined a method of preventing the collision of objects that included the steps of locating the medial axis and creating the hierarchy of bubbles on the medial axis, the claim might have been patentable. In other words, the discovery of locating the medial axis from the object and using it to create the hierarchy of bubbles was not patentable, but the application of that algorithm or idea to prevent collisions might have been patentable, if so defined in the specification and claims of the subject patent.

We learn from all these cases that, even if a mathematical formula or program implemented with software is involved, there still might be a patentable invention, even though the mathematical formula is not patentable by itself. We also learn, however, that the manner in which the claim is drafted makes a difference. A good test of whether a claim defines patentable subject matter is whether a step or a component in the claim describes a tangible, concrete, and useful result.

13.4 THE USPTO EXAMINATION PROCESS TO DETERMINE SUBJECT MATTER ELIGIBILITY OF A COMPUTER-RELATED INVENTION

Pursuant to guidelines issued by the USPTO in 2014 after the Supreme Court's *Alice* decision, and further guidelines issued in 2015, a memorandum issued to the Patent Examining Corps on May 4, 2016, and revised patent subject matter eligibility guidance issued January 7, 2019 (all available on www.uspto.gov), Patent Examiners are instructed to apply a two-step analysis to determine the subject matter eligibility of a computer-related claim in a patent application.

Under the USPTO Guidance rules, the first step applied by an Examiner is to determine that a patent claim falls within one of the four statutory categories of patentable subject matter: process, machine, article of manufacture, or composition of matter. The 2019 Guidelines do not alter this step.

The 2019 Guidelines have a revised Step 2A, which is a two-pronged analysis.

Under Prong One of Revised Step 2A, Examiners determine whether the patent claim recites a judicial exception, such as an abstract idea, applying the broadest reasonable interpretation of the claimed invention. If the patent claim does not recite a judicial exception, the patent claim is eligible under Prong One and no further analysis is necessary. If the patent claim recites a judicial exception, the patent claim is not dead in the water, but requires further analysis under Prong Two of Revised Step 2A.

Under Prong Two of Revised Step 2A, Examiners determine whether the patent claim recites additional elements that integrate the exception into a practical application of that exception. To determine if the judicial exception is integrated into a practical application, Examiners determine whether there are any additional elements recited in the patent claim beyond the judicial exception. Those additional elements are evaluated individually or in combination to determine whether they integrate the judicial exception into a practical application, giving consideration to both the element and how it is used or arranged in the claim as a whole. Prong Two of Revised Step 2A does not evaluate whether an additional element is well-understood, routine, conventional activity. Therefore a patent claim that includes conventional elements may still integrate the judicial exception into a practical application. If the patent claim integrates the judicial exception into a practical application of that judicial exception, the patent claim is eligible under Prong Two and no further analysis is necessary. If the patent claim does not integrate the judicial exception into a practical application of that judicial exception, the patent claim requires further analysis under Step 2B of the USPTO 2019 Guidance.

Under Step 2B, Examiners evaluate the additional elements individually and in combination to determine whether the additional elements provide an inventive concept and amount to significantly more than the judicial exception itself. For example, an inventive concept may be present if the additional elements add a specific limitation or combination of limitations that are not well-understood, routine, conventional activity in the field. If the patent claim includes additional elements that provide an inventive concept, the patent claim is eligible.

The 2019 Guidelines also identify specific categories of concepts defined by the USPTO as abstract under Prong 1 of Step 2A, and which are subject to further analysis under Prong 2 of Step 2, and Step 2B. These categories include:

Mathematical Concepts – mathematical relationships, formulas or equations: mathematical calculations.

Methods of Organizing Human Activity – fundamental economic principles or practices, commercial or legal interactions, managing personal behavior or relationships or interactions between people, the latter including such as teaching, social activities and following rules or instructions.

Mental Processes – concepts formed in the human mind, including observation, evaluation, judgment, opinion.

Note that mental processes can be included as part of a method claim. See Chapter 10, Sections 10.5 and 10.6

The above 2019 Guidance has been used by Patent Examiners since January 2019. However, at some time, the CAFC will probably have the opportunity to comment on whether the Court agrees or disagrees with the USPTO 2019 Guidelines. At the time of this writing, the CAFC had not yet rendered a decision in a case where the 2019 Guidelines were applied. In at least one case, a panel of CAFC Judges criticized the USPTO's May 4, 2016 Guidance on Patent legibility, stating: "While we greatly respect the PTO's expertise on all matters relating to patentability, including patent eligibility, we are not bound by its guidance. And, especially regarding the issue of patent eligibility and the efforts of the courts…, we are mindful of the need for consistent application of our case law." *Cleveland Clinic Foundation et al v. True Health Diagnostics, LLC*, No. 2018-1218 (Fed. Cir. April 1. 2019).

The reason I have included the preceding information in this treatise is to allow you to converse meaningfully with your patent professional when determining whether, and how, to obtain patent protection on your computer-related invention. You should explain to your patent professional what elements or steps of your computer-related invention go significantly beyond defining just an abstract idea, and that the totality of the invention, including the additional steps, involve more than merely well-understood, routine, conventional activity. You should explain to your patent professional all of the new, non-obvious, and advantageous results of the various steps of your computer-related invention, which will be included in the patent application to convince the Patent Examiner that the invention goes well beyond an abstract idea.

Due to the fluid nature of the law related to patent protection for computer-related inventions, I strongly advise that you seek advice from your patent professional when you are in the development stages of your invention. This advice is particularly relevant where the computer-related invention will be the heart and soul of a new business venture you are excited about, and you are directing all of your efforts and resources toward launching a successful enterprise.

13.5 RECOMMENDED STEPS TO OBTAIN PROPER PROTECTION OF COMPUTER-RELATED INVENTIONS

After the CAFC decided that computer-related inventions, including software and hardware, constituted patentable subject matter under certain criteria, the USPTO issued new guidelines at several times to assist Patent Examiners in the examination of patent applications directed to such inventions. These guidelines do not have the force of law; however, courts (sometimes) and the USPTO have been relying upon these guidelines in the examination, allowance, and interpretation of computer-related patents. In addition to these guidelines, the "Manual of Patent Examining Procedure" (MPEP) published by the USPTO incorporates significant useful information to not only assist the examiner, but to guide the inventor of a computer-related invention in ensuring that his/her patent application properly defines patent-eligible subject matter.

"Computer-related inventions," according to the MPEP, include inventions implemented in a computer, and inventions employing computer-readable media. The following discussion is equally applicable to claimed inventions implemented in either hardware or software.

13.5.1 How to Prepare a Proper Patent Application Covering a Computer-Related Invention

13.5.1.1 Specification

Your patent application covering a computer-related invention should set forth precisely what you, the inventor, have invented and are seeking to patent. The specification of the application should pointedly state how the claims relate to and define the specific point or points of novelty of your invention.

Before the recent changes in the law of patenting computer-related inventions, discussed previously, Patent Examiners rejected applications that merely recited a "mathematical algorithm." Today, however, the examiners are advised to review the complete specification, including the detailed description of the invention, any embodiments that are described, the claims, and, most importantly, specific, substantial, and credible practical utility or usefulness asserted for the invention.

After the *State Street* case, the USPTO followed the rule that the invention as claimed, as a whole, must accomplish a practical application; that is, the invention must produce a useful, concrete, and tangible result. Thus, your patent application should set forth a "real-world" value, as opposed to subject matter that represents nothing more than an idea or concept, or simply a starting point for future investigation or research. Thus, it is important that the complete disclosure in your patent application contain an indication of all practical applications for the claimed invention, along with a description of the significant functionality of your computer-related invention for which a patent is sought.

The USPTO takes the position that merely claiming non-functional descriptive materials stored in a computer-readable medium does not make the invention eligible for a patent. For example, a patent application claim directed to a word processing file stored on a disc or CD may satisfy the "utility" requirement, since it has real-world value. However, the mere fact that the claim may satisfy the "utility" requirement does not mean that a useful result is achieved under the "practical application" requirement. The claimed invention, as a whole, must produce a useful, concrete, and tangible result to have practical application.

In its guidelines, the USPTO has set forth certain examples of computer-related inventions that have been determined to have a practical application, and as producing a useful, concrete, and tangible result:

a. A long-distance telephone billing process containing mathematical algorithms, since the claimed process applies the Boolean principle to produce a useful, concrete, and tangible result without preempting other uses of the mathematical principle.
b. The transformation of data, representing discrete dollar amounts, by a machine through a series of mathematical calculations into a final share price. This constitutes a practical application of a mathematical algorithm, formula, or calculation, since it produces a useful, concrete, and tangible result—namely, a final share price momentarily fixed for recording and reporting purposes.
c. Patent claims drawn to a rasterizer for converting discrete wave form data samples into anti-aliased pixel illumination intensity data to be displayed on the display means (monitor), since these claims define a specific machine to produce a useful, concrete, and tangible result.

The important thing to remember is that the inventor and the patent application provide sufficient information to set forth concrete evidence regarding why the invention is useful. Patent Examiners will focus their efforts on statements made in the patent specification that identify all practical applications for the invention. The patent applicant may assert more than one practical application. However, at least one such practical application asserted in the application is necessary to satisfy the utility requirement. The examiners will also review the application specification to ensure the presence of a description of that structure and/or those functional elements that are necessary to accomplish at least one asserted practical application of the invention. Therefore, a word to the wise. Be sure when reviewing your patent application directed to a computer-related invention that utility is clearly and emphatically set forth in the specification.

It is also important that the patent application explicitly explain the relative significance of the various features of the invention. It is strongly suggested that the application include the following detailed information:

a. What the programmed computer does when it performs the processes dictated by the software—that is, the functionality of the programmed computer. For example, it is true that a modern digital computer manipulates data, usually in binary form, by performing mathematical operations, such as addition, subtraction, multiplication, division, or bit shifting. However, this is only how the computer does what it does. Of importance is the significance of the data and their manipulation in the real world—that is, what the computer is doing.
b. How the computer is to be configured to provide the functionality set forth in the patent application specification. For example, describe those elements which constitute the programmed computer, and how those elements are configured and interrelated to provide the specified functionality.
c. Where applicable, the specification should set forth the relationship of the programmed computer to other subject matter outside the computer that constitutes the invention. This would include machines, devices, materials, or process steps other than those that are part of or performed by the programmed computer. The specification should also adequately explain the role of the programmed computer in the overall process performed by the machine, and how the programmed computer is to be integrated with the other elements of the apparatus used in the process.
d. Where software constitutes a part of the best mode of carrying out the invention, be sure to include a description of this best mode, including a disclosure of the functions of the software, such as with a flow diagram. Source code listings are not a requirement for adequately disclosing the functions of the software.

The disclosure of a software program per se is not necessary to satisfy the "best mode" requirement where the functions of the software program are readily apparent from the patent application specification, and one skilled in the art could generate the necessary software program to implement the disclosed functions from the flow diagram.

13.5.1.1.1 Adequate Written Description

All patent applications must contain an adequate written description of the invention intended to be covered by the patent issuing from the application. For the written description requirement to be satisfied, a patent applicant's specification must reasonably convey to those skilled in the art that the inventor was in possession of the claimed invention as of the date of the invention. The claimed invention subject matter need not be described literally, that is, using the same terms, in order for the disclosure to satisfy the description requirements. Software aspects of inventions may be described functionally.

13.5.1.1.2 Enabling Disclosure

A computer or software inventor's patent application must contain a specification that will enable a person skilled in the art to make and use the claimed invention without undue experimentation. Obviously, in computer-related inventions, the type of experimentation necessary may be rather complex. However, the fact that experimentation is complex will not make it "undue" if a person skilled in the art typically engages in such complex experimentation.

The disclosure in a patent application for a computer-related invention must enable a skilled artisan to configure the computer to possess the requisite functionality, and where applicable, to readily interrelate the computer with other elements to yield the claimed invention. It is important that the patent specification for a computer-related invention disclose how to configure a computer to possess the requisite functionality, or how to integrate the program's computer with other elements of the invention, unless a skilled artisan would know how to do so without such disclosure. A proper disclosure of computer-related inventions has been found in the following situations:

1. Where a programmer of reasonable skill could write a satisfactory program with ordinary effort based on the disclosure in the patent application.
2. The invention was adequately disclosed for purposes of enablement even though all of the circuitry of a word processor was not disclosed, since the undisclosed circuitry was deemed inconsequential, because it did not pertain to the claimed circuit in the patent application.
3. A computerized method of generating printed architectural specifications dependent on the use of a glossary of predefined standard phrases and an error-checking feature was enabled by an overall disclosure generally defining errors.
4. The enablement requirement was satisfied by the employment of block diagrams and descriptions of their functions, since the represented structure was conventional and could be determined without undue experimentation.
5. A software invention that does not require a detailed description of all the circuitry in the complete hardware system.

Many computer-related patent applications describe inventions that involve more than one field of technology. For such applications, the disclosure set forth in the patent application specification must satisfy the enablement standard for each aspect of the invention. Thus, when an invention, in its different aspects, involves separate and distinct arts, that specification is adequate which enables those skilled in each art, since they have the best chance of being enabled from the invention disclosure and to carry out the aspect proper to their specialty. For example, if the invention in question relates to a computer-controlled fuel injection system, the patent application must enable a person skilled in the electronic computer art, in cooperation with a person skilled in the fuel injection art, to make and use the disclosed invention. Likewise, for example, a proper specification describing an invention for a programmed computer that determines and displays the three-dimensional structure of a chemical compound must:

1. Enable the invention to a person skilled in the art of molecular modelling to understand and practice the underlying molecular modelling processes.
2. Enable a person skilled in the art of computer programming to create a program that directs a computer to create and display an image representing the three-dimensional structure of the compound.

Many patent applications directed to computer-related inventions comprise a disclosure that describes a programmed computer by outlining the significant elements of the programmed computer using a functional block diagram. To avoid an adverse examination result, the application specification should include, along with the functional block diagram, a disclosure that provides information that adequately describes each "element" in the hardware, or the hardware and its associated software, and how such elements are interrelated. In other words, the patent specification must itself inform those skilled in the art about the invention, and not merely direct those skilled in the art to seek out relevant information for themselves. Thus, the application disclosure must constitute more than a sketchy explanation of flow diagrams or a bare group of program listings together with a reference to a proprietary computer on which they must be run, to satisfy the requirement that the patent specification must enable one skilled in the art to perform the invention without undue experimentation.

13.5.1.2 Claims

The claims identify the boundaries of the protection sought by a patent applicant, and the claims are looked at to understand and define what the inventor has indicated is the invention to be patented. In computer-related patent applications, the physical structure or material in a patent claim may consist of hardware or a combination of hardware and software. The elements in a patent claim must relate to those same elements that describe the particular limitation in the specification. When a Patent Examiner reviews the application, this relationship of claim elements to the description in the specification ensures that the Patent Examiner correctly interprets each claim limitation.

Language in patent claims that merely suggests or makes optional, but does not require steps to be performed, or does not limit a patent claim to a particular structure, does not adequately limit the scope of the claim to a particular structure, and does not adequately limit the scope of the claim for patent eligibility. Examples of language in a patent claim for a computer-related invention that may cause problems are:

a. Statements of intended use or field of use.
b. "Adapted to" or "adapted for" statements.
c. "Wherein" or "whereby" clauses.

If the patent application claims define a means or a step, followed by a functional limitation, the specification must include the corresponding structure, material, or acts for performing the stated function. If the patent application specification defines what is meant by the claim language, the claim limitation will be interpreted as having that meaning and its equivalents. This should avoid any problems in determining the scope of the claimed limitation. With computer-related inventions, conventional programming need not be described in the application. The recommended procedure is to use flow diagrams to illustrate and describe the process.

The claims of a computer-related patent application need not explicitly recite every feature of the invention. For example, if the invention is a particular computer, the claims of the application do not have to recite every element or feature of the computer. The claims should be prepared in a form that emphasizes what the inventor has invented, that is, what is new in the combination rather than old.

Computer-related patent claims may often be drafted in terms of a "means" to perform a particular "function," or the "means plus function" format, as it is known among patent professionals. Means plus function language in a patent claim must be preceded by the description of the invention in the specification, which makes it clear that the "means" corresponds to a well-defined structure of a computer or computer component implemented in either hardware, or software and its associated hardware platform. Examples of defining such elements in claims are as follows:

1. A programmed computer with a particular functionality implemented in hardware or hardware and software.
2. A logic circuit or other component of a programmed computer that performs a series of specifically identified operations dictated by a computer program.
3. A computer memory encoded with executable instructions representing a computer program that can cause a computer to function in a particular manner.

The scope of a "means" limitation in a patent claim is defined as the corresponding structure or material, for example, a specific logic circuit, as set forth in the written specification that precedes and supports the claim, and equivalents of that corresponding structure. For example, if the patent application discloses only functions to be performed and provides no express, implied, or inherent disclosure of hardware, or a combination of hardware and software that performs the functions, the patent application will be faulted as having not disclosed any "structure" which corresponds to the "means" in the claims.

Therefore, it is important that the computer-related invention covered in your patent application be described as including at least one specific structure or material that corresponds to the "means" used in the claim. If the corresponding structure is disclosed as a memory or logic circuit that has been configured in some manner to perform the particular claimed function, for example, using a defined computer program, the application has then disclosed "structure" properly which corresponds to the claimed "means".

When a claim or part of a claim in a patent application is defined in computer program code, whether in source or object code format, a person skilled in the art must be able to ascertain the metes and bounds of the invention from the language in the claim. In certain circumstances, as where self-documenting program code is employed, the use of programming language in a patent application claim would be permissible, because such program source code presents a sufficiently high-level language and descriptive identifiers to make it universally understood to others in the programming art without the programmer having to insert any comments. The MPEP recommends that patent applicants in their application be encouraged to functionally define the steps that the computer would perform, rather than simply reciting source or object code instructions. This is a matter you should surely bring to the attention of the patent professional preparing your computer-related patent application, where applicable.

In reviewing the claims of your computer-related patent application, ensure that each claim includes all of the elements which you consider essential and critical to the structure and functioning of the invention. If the desired patentability is based on specific ranges, the specification must show that these ranges are critical.

13.5.1.3 Determination of Whether a Computer-Related Invention Defines Patent-Eligible Subject Matter Under Patent Laws

A patent application directed to a computer-related invention that is found to claim non-patent-eligible subject matter falls into the same general category as non-statutory subject matter in other arts, namely, natural phenomena such as magnetism, and abstract ideas or laws of nature that constitute "descriptive material."

"Descriptive material" that falls outside the realm of patent eligibility can be characterized as either "functional descriptive material" or "non-functional descriptive material." In this context, "functional descriptive material" consists of data structures and computer programs which impart functionality when employed as a computer component. "Data structure" is defined as the physical or logical relationship among data elements, designed to support specific data manipulation functions. This definition is derived from the *IEEE Standard Dictionary of Electrical and Electronics Terms, 5e* (1993, page 308). "Non-functional descriptive material" includes, but is not limited to, music, literary works, and a compilation or mere arrangement of data.

Both functional and non-functional descriptive material are not patent-eligible subject matter when claimed in a patent application as descriptive material by themselves. When functional descriptive materials are recorded on a computer-readable medium, the descriptive material becomes structurally and functionally interrelated to the medium, and may be considered as patent-eligible subject matter, since the use of technology permits the function of the descriptive material to be realized. For example, a patent directed to data structure stored on a computer-readable medium that increases computer efficiency was held to constitute patent-eligible subject matter. Also, a patent claim to a computer having a specific data structure stored in memory was held to be patent-eligible product-by-process subject matter. Similarly, a patent claim directed to a data structure standing alone was held to be non-patent-eligible subject matter.

Where non-functional descriptive material is recorded on a computer-readable medium, it does not define patentable subject matter, since no requisite functionality is present to satisfy the practical application requirement of the patent statutes. Thus, music per se is not a computer component, and does not become patent eligible by merely placing it on a compact disc. Protection for this type of work is provided under the Copyright Law, which is discussed in Chapter 24.

Some patent applications have been filed claiming an invention in processes that do nothing more than solve mathematical problems or manipulate abstract ideas or concepts. Such patent applications are more complex in determining whether the subject matter can be patented. If the "acts" of a process manipulate only numbers, abstract concepts or ideas, or signals representing any of the foregoing, the acts are not being applied to appropriate patentable subject matter. Thus, a process consisting solely of mathematical operations, such as converting one set of numbers into another set of numbers, does not manipulate appropriate subject matter, and thus cannot constitute a patent-eligible process.

Non-patent-eligible processes can be defined as:

a. Claimed subject matter that consists solely of mathematical operations without some claimed practical application, such as executing a mathematical algorithm.
b. Or, claims which define subject matter that simply manipulates abstract ideas, such as a bid or a bubble hierarchy, without some claimed practical application.

To complicate matters, the Supreme Court, in its decisions regarding computer-related inventions, has not been clear to state exactly what kind of mathematical subject matter may or may not be patent eligible. The Supreme Court has used terms such as "mathematical algorithm," "mathematical formula," and "mathematical equation" in describing types of mathematical subject matter that, standing alone, are not entitled to patent protection.

Certain mathematical algorithms are not patentable subject matter because they represent a mathematical definition of a law of nature or a natural phenomenon. By way of example, an algorithm representing the formula $E=mc^2$ is a "law of nature"— it defines a "fundamental scientific truth," that being the relationship between energy and mass. Someone claiming an invention in a process which consists solely of the steps that one must follow to solve the mathematical representation of $E=mc^2$ would find his or her application rejected as being indistinguishable from the law of nature. Thus, if a patent application such as this were granted, the patent would not allow others to solve the mathematical representation of $E=mc^2$. A patent cannot be granted on such a process. However, although $E=mc^2$ is not patentable, that does not preclude the equation from being included in a patent claim.

13.5.1.4 Functional Descriptive Material: "Data Structures" Representing Descriptive Material per se or Computer Programs Representing Computer Listings per se

Data structures not described or claimed in a patent application as embodied in a computer-readable medium constitute descriptive material per se, and are not patent eligible, because they are not capable of causing functional change in the computer. Such data structures do not define any structural and functional interrelationships between the data structure and other claimed aspects of the invention which permit the functionality of the data structure to be realized. Such claimed structures are distinguishable from a computer-readable medium encoded with a data structure defining structural and functional interrelationships between the data structure and the computer software and hardware components which permit the data structure's functionality to be realized.

Similarly, computer programs set forth as computer listings per se, that is, the descriptions or expressions of the programs, are not physical "things." They are neither computer components nor processes, as they are not "acts" being performed. Such computer programs also do not define any structural or functional interrelationships between the computer program and other claimed elements of the computer which permit the computer program's functionality to be obtained. Again, such computer listings per se must be distinguished from a claimed computer-readable medium encoded with a computer program, which is a computer element that defines structural and functional interrelationships between the computer program and the rest of the computer. This latter computer-readable medium is patent eligible. Thus, it is important to ensure that your patent application clearly distinguishes between descriptive material per se and language that defines structural and functional interrelationships between the elements of the computer program and/or the computer.

Where the computer program is set forth in a patent claim as part of an otherwise patent-eligible article of manufacture or machine, the patent claim remains patentable irrespective of the fact that the computer program is included in the claim. The same result occurs when a computer program is used in a computerized process where the computer executes the instructions set forth in the computer program. However, where the claimed invention, taken as a whole, is directed to a mere program listing, that is, to only its description or expression, such claim constitutes descriptive material per se and hence is not patent eligible.

It must be remembered that a computer program is merely a set of instructions capable of being executed by a computer, and the computer program itself is not a process. Thus, a patent claim on a computer program, without the computer-readable medium needed to realize the computer program's functionality, is not patent eligible, since it constitutes functional descriptive material. When a computer program is claimed as an invention in a process where the computer is executing the computer program's instructions, that claim will be treated as a process claim. When a computer program is recited in conjunction with a physical structure such as a computer memory, Patent Examiners will treat that claim as a product or system claim.

13.5.1.5 Non-Functional Descriptive Material

Descriptive material that cannot exhibit any functional interrelationship with the way in which computing processes are performed does not constitute patent-eligible subject matter. Where certain types of descriptive material, such as music, literature, art, photographs, and minor arrangements and compilations of facts or data, are merely stored so as to be read or outputted by a computer without creating any functional interrelationship, either as part of the stored data or as part of the computing process performed by the computer, such descriptive material alone does not impart functionality either to the data so structured or to the computer. Such descriptive material does not fall within the category of patent-eligible subject matter. Data consists of facts, which become information when the data is seen in context and conveys meaning to people. Computers process data without any understanding of what that data represents.

Music is commonly sold to consumers in the format of a compact disc, and the known compact disc acts as nothing more than a carrier for non-functional descriptive material. This purely non-functional descriptive material cannot alone provide the practical application, which constitutes the physical disc.

Non-functional descriptive material may be claimed as inventive in combination with other functional descriptive multi-medium material on a computer-readable medium to provide the necessary functional and structural interrelationship to satisfy the requirements for patent-eligible subject matter. By way of example, a computer that recognizes a particular grouping of musical notes read from memory, and which, upon recognizing that particular sequence, causes another defined series of notes to be played, defines a functional interrelationship between that data and the computing process performed when utilizing that data. Thus, this latter example provides patent-eligible subject matter because it implements a process as defined under Patent Law.

13.5.1.6 Natural Phenomena Such as Electricity and Magnetism

Patent claims directed to nothing but the physical characteristics of a form of energy, such as a frequency, voltage, or the strength of a magnetic field, or a defined energy or magnetism per se, do not qualify as being directed toward patent-eligible subject matter. However, a single claim directed to a practical application of electromagnetic energy is defined as covering patent-eligible subject matter, regardless of its transitory nature.

13.6 STATUTORY SUBJECT MATTER

13.6.1 Types of Claimed Subject Matter

The legal principles are the same in defining whether a patent application is directed to a machine or a process when determining whether patent-eligible subject matter is presented.

a. *Statutory Product Claims.* "Products" in patent law are defined as either machines, manufactures, or compositions of matter.
   - A "machine" is defined as "a concrete thing, consisting of parts, or of certain devices and combinations of devices."
   - A "manufacture" is defined as "the production of articles for use from raw or prepared materials by giving to these materials new forms, qualities, properties, or combinations, whether by hand labor or by machinery."
   - A composition of matter is "a composition of two or more substances or a composite article, whether it be the result of chemical union, or of mechanical mixture, or whether it be a gas, fluid, powder, or solid."

If a patent application is directed to a machine or manufacture, and identifies the physical structure of the machine, or manufacture, in terms of its hardware or its hardware and software combination, the application is directed to patent-eligible subject matter. A claim submitted in a patent application limited to a machine or manufacture using software which has a practical application in the technological arts also defines patent-eligible subject matter. In the *Alappat* case, 33 Fed.3rd at 1544, the CAFC stated that "the claimed invention as a whole is directed to a combination of interrelated elements which combine to form a machine for converting discrete waveform data samples into anti-aliased pixel illumination intensity data to be displayed on a display means (such as a computer screen). This is not a disembodied mathematical concept which may be characterized as an 'abstract idea' but rather a specific machine to produce a useful, concrete, and tangible result."

b. *Statutory Process Claims.* If your patent-eligible invention is one that requires several acts or steps to be performed, your invention is defined as a "process" or "method." To constitute patent-eligible subject matter, a claimed computer-related process must either:

1. Result in a physical transformation outside the computer for which a practical application in the technical arts is either disclosed in the patent application specification, or would have been known to a person skilled in the art.
2. Or, be limited to a practical application within the technological arts. For example, in the case of *Diamond v. Diehr*, 450 US at 183-184, the CAFC stated that "a [patent-eligible] process is a mode of treatment of certain materials to produce a given result. It is an act, or a series of acts, performed upon the subject matter to be transformed and reduced to a different state or thing .... The process requires that certain things should be done with certain substances and in a certain order; but the tools to be used in doing this may be of secondary sequence."

Even though a scientific principle per se may be unpatentable, the practical application of that principle may be patentable. If a physical transformation occurs outside of the computer, the patent application disclosing that invention must permit a skilled artisan to practice the claimed invention—that is, to put it to a practical use. It is necessary for the claimed invention to be read as a whole to produce a practical result if there is only a transformation of signals or data inside a computer, or if a claimed process merely manipulates concepts or converts one set of numbers into another.

13.6.2 Independent Physical Acts, or Post-Computer-Process Activity

A process defines patent-eligible subject matter if it requires physical acts to be performed outside the computer, independent of and following the steps to be performed by a programmed computer, where those acts involve the manipulation of tangible physical objects that result in the object having a different physical attribute or structure. Thus, a process claim is patent eligible if it includes one or more post-computer process steps that result in a physical transformation outside the computer, beyond merely conveying the direct result of the computer operation.

Examples of this type of process which constitute patent-eligible subject matter include the following:

1. A method of curing rubber in a mold which relies on updating process parameters, using a computer processor to determine a time period for curing rubber, using the computer processor to determine when the time period has been reached in the curing process, and then opening the mold at that stage.
2. A method of controlling a mechanical robot which relies on storing data in a computer that represents various types of mechanical movements of the robot, using a computer processor to calculate the positioning of the robot in relation to the given tasks to be performed by the robot, and controlling the robot's movement and position based on the calculated position.

In contrast, the following are examples of computer-related processes that do not achieve a practical application and are not patent eligible:

1. The step of "updating alarm limits" that constitutes merely changing the number value of a variable to represent the result of the calculation.
2. The final step of "equating" the process outputs to the values of the last set of process inputs, since the process merely stores the result of calculations.
3. The step of "transmitting electrical signals representing" the result of calculations. The computer was instructed to transmit electrical signals representing the results of its calculations, and did not constitute the type of "post-solution activity" found patent eligible in previous cases. The final transmitting step was held to constitute nothing more than reading out the result of the calculations.
4. The step of displaying a calculation as a grayscale code.

13.6.3 Manipulation of Data Representing Physical Objects or Activities; Pre-Computer-Process Activity

Another process incorporating patent-eligible subject matter is one that requires the measurements of physical objects or activities to be transformed outside of the computer into computer data, where the data comprises signals corresponding to physical objects or activities external to the computer system, and where the process causes a physical transformation of the signals which are intangible representations of the physical objects or activities.

Examples of this type of patent-eligible processes include:

1. A method of using a computer processor to analyze electrical signals and data representative of human cardiac activity by converting the signals to time segments, applying the time segments in reverse order to a high-pass filter, using the computer processor to determine the amplitude of the high-pass filter's output, and using the computer processor to compare the value to a predetermined value. In this example, the data is an intangible representation of physical activity—that is, human cardiac activity. The transformation occurs when heart activity is measured and an electrical signal is produced. This process has real-world value in predicting vulnerability to ventricular tachycardia immediately after a heart attack.
2. A method of using a computer processor to receive data representing computerized axial tomography (CAT) scan images of a patient, performing a calculation to determine the difference between a local value at a data point and an average value of the data in a region surrounding the point, displaying the difference as a grayscale code for each point in the image, and displaying the resultant image. In this example, the data is an intangible representation of a physical object—that is, the portions of the anatomy of the patient. The transformation occurs when the condition of the human body is measured with x-rays and the x-rays are converted into electrical digital signals that represent the condition of the human body. The real-world value of the invention lies in creating a new CAT scan image of body tissue without the presence of bones.

3. A method of using a computer processor to conduct seismic exploration by imparting spherical seismic energy waves into the earth from a seismic source, generating a plurality of reflected signals in response to the seismic energy waves at a set of receiver positions in an array, and sending the reflection signals to produce a signal simulating the reflection response of the earth to the seismic energy. In this example, the electrical signals processed by the computer represent reflected seismic energy. The transformation occurs by converting the spherical seismic energy waves into electrical signals which provide a geophysical representation of formations below the earth's surface. Geophysical exploration of formations below the surface of the earth has real-world value.
4. A method of displaying x-ray attenuation data as a signed grayscale code signal in a "field" using a particular algorithm, where the antecedent steps require generating the data using a particular machine, such as a computer tomography scanner.

The following are examples of processes relating to precomputing that do not meet the requirements for patent-eligible subject matter:

- "Perturbing" the values of a set of processed inputs, where the subject matter "perturbed" was a number and the act of "perturbing" consists of substituting the numerical values of variables. The step of perturbing the values of a set of process inputs, in addition to being a mathematical operation, appears to be a data-gathering step of the type that is insufficient to change a non-patent-eligible method of calculation into a patentable process. In this instance, the perturbed process inputs were not even measured values of physical phenomena, but were instead derived by numerically changing the values in the previous set of processed inputs.
- Selecting a set of arbitrary measurement point values.

13.6.4 Computer-Related Processes Limited to a Practical Application in the Technological Arts

If a claim in a patent application does not clearly fall into one or both of the categories mentioned in Section 13.5.1.4 or 13.5.1.5, the patent claim and invention may still constitute patent-eligible subject matter if the claimed subject matter is limited to a practical application in the technological arts.

There is always some form of physical transformation within a computer because a computer acts on signals and transforms them during its operation, and changes the state of its components during the execution of the process. Even though this physical transformation occurs within a computer, such activity is not determinative of whether the process qualifies as patent-eligible subject matter under Patent Law. What is determinative of patent-eligible subject matter is not how the computer performs a process, but *what* the computer does to achieve a practical application.

A process that merely manipulates an abstract idea or performs a purely mathematical algorithm constitutes non-patent-eligible subject matter despite the fact that it might inherently have some usefulness. To qualify such subject matter as patent eligible, the process must be described as having a practical application of the abstract idea or mathematical algorithm in one of the technological arts. An inventive process is limited to a practical application when the process, as claimed in the patent application, produces a concrete, tangible, and useful result. Likewise, an invention to a machine constitutes patentable subject matter when the machine, as claimed in the patent application, produces a concrete, tangible, and useful result. For example, a computer process that simply calculates a mathematical algorithm that models noise does not constitute patent-eligible subject matter. However, a claimed process for digitally filtering noise employing the mathematical algorithm is patent-eligible subject matter.

Additional examples of claimed processes that have been found to constitute useful patentable subject matter are as follows:

1. A computerized method of optimally controlling transfer, storage, or general retrieval of data between cache and hard disk storage devices, such that the most frequently used data is readily available.
2. A method of controlling parallel processors to accomplish the multi-tasking of several computing tasks to maximize computing efficiency.
3. A method of making a word processor by storing an executable word processing application program in a general purpose digital computer's memory, and executing the stored program to impart word processing functionality to the general purpose digital computer by changing the state of the computer's arithmetic logic unit when program instructions of the word processing program are executed.
4. A digital filtering process for removing noise from a digital signal comprising the steps of calculating a mathematical algorithm to produce a correction signal and subtracting the correction signal from the digital signal to remove the noise.

13.7 THE COMPUTER-RELATED INVENTION MUST STILL BE NOVEL AND NON-OBVIOUS

Once your patent specification establishes that the computer-related invention covered in your application constitutes "patent-eligible subject matter," as discussed in the previous sections of this chapter, the claimed invention must still meet the requirements of novelty and non-obviousness. All of the factors considered previously to establish novelty and non-obviousness apply without any modification to computer-related inventions. Moreover, merely using a computer to automate a known process does not by itself impart novelty or non-obviousness to the process.

If the difference between the relevant prior art and the invention you are claiming as patentable in your patent application is limited to descriptive material stored on or employed by a computer, it must be determined whether the descriptive material is functional descriptive material or non-functional descriptive material, as described previously in Sections 13.5.1.3 to 13.5.1.5 of this chapter. If the functional descriptive material stored on or employed by the computer would not have been suggested by the prior art, then your invention is patentable over the prior art. However, non-functional descriptive material cannot render non-obvious an invention that would otherwise be obvious. Situations involving non-novel and obvious non-functional descriptive material are set forth in the following examples:

1. A computer-readable storage medium that differs from the prior art solely with respect to non-functional descriptive material, such as music or a literary work, encoded on the medium.
2. A computer that differs from the prior art solely with respect to non-functional descriptive material that cannot alter how the machine functions—that is, the descriptive material does not reconfigure the computer.
3. A process that differs from the prior art only with respect to non-functional descriptive material that cannot alter how the process steps are to be performed to achieve the utility of the invention.

Thus, if the prior art suggests storing a song on a disk, merely choosing a particular song to store on the disc would be presumed to be well within the level of ordinary skill in the art. In this case, the difference between the prior art and the claimed invention would only be a non-patentable rearrangement of non-functional descriptive material on the known disc.

13.8 COMPUTER PROGRAMMING AND A SUFFICIENT DISCLOSURE

In patent applications directed to all inventions that are sought to be patented, the requirements for sufficient disclosure of the invention is the same, and thus applies to those patent applications involving computer programming. As stated previously, the application specification must sufficiently enable someone to make and use the invention set forth in the claims of the patent application.

In applications involving computer programs, software, firmware, or block diagram illustrations, where one or more of the block diagram elements are at least partially comprised of a computer software component, the USPTO guidelines set forth certain requirements to ensure that the disclosure sufficiently describes the invention. The sufficiency of disclosure in computer-related patent applications necessarily requires an inquiry into both the sufficiency of the disclosed hardware as well as the disclosed software, due to the interrelationship and interdependence of computer hardware and software. Thus, this writer suggests that the patent specification, when filed, contain a complete disclosure of the invention recited in the claims, and that the inventor review the patent application carefully before filing to ensure that this is the case.

As discussed previously in Chapter 9, Section 9.6.6, the inventor is required to submit to the USPTO the best mode of carrying out and practicing the invention known to the inventor on the date of filing the application. As a general rule, where software constitutes part of a best mode of carrying out an invention, a description of such best mode is satisfied by disclosure of the functions of the software. Normally, writing code for such software is within the skill of the art, and does not require undue experimentation once its functions have been disclosed. A source code listing is not a requirement for adequately disclosing the functions of software. This is a very important point, and avoids the necessity of having to divulge source codes to support a patent application. Customarily, flow charts are used to convey the proper functionality.

13.8.1 What Constitutes an Adequate Disclosure in Computer Programming Patent Applications

In a typical computer-related patent application, system components are often represented by a "block diagram" representing the elements of the system, functionally labeled and interconnected by straight lines. The USPTO, during examination, categorizes such block diagram disclosures into (a) systems that include, but are more comprehensive than, a computer, and (b) systems wherein the block elements are totally within the confines of the computer.

13.8.1.1 Block Elements More Comprehensive Than a Computer

In this first category, your block diagram includes a representation of a computer as well as other system hardware and/or software components. The diverse functions attributed to each block element should be particularly set forth in the specification, including how each component could be implemented. If more than routine experimentation would be required by one of ordinary skill in the art to implement such a component or components, the specification will most likely be challenged by the examiner as inadequate. Additionally, the specification should set forth whether certain of the hardware or software components depicted as block diagrams are themselves complex assemblies which have widely different characteristics, and which must be precisely explained as to their coordination with other complex assemblies.

It is proper in a patent application to refer to prior art patents or publications to demonstrate that particular block diagram hardware or software components are old in the art. However, it may not always be self-evident to the Patent Examiner how such components are to be interconnected to function in the disclosed complex manner in your invention. The higher the complexity of the invention described and claimed in your computer-related patent application, the more explanation is necessary to avoid an adverse comment by the Examiner that the invention is not adequately described.

In addition, in complex systems including a digital computer, a microprocessor, and/or a complex control system as one of many block diagram elements, the timing between various system elements may be of extreme importance. In such cases, I recommend that a timing chart relating the timed sequences for each element be included. If this is omitted, an unreasonable amount of work, time, and effort may be required to decipher the detailed relationships that the inventor in the application states that he or she has solved.

Consider, for example, a block diagram disclosure in a patent application of a complex system which includes a microprocessor and other system components controlled by the microprocessor. A mere reference to prior art that is commercially available covering the microprocessor, without any description of the precise operations to be performed by the microprocessor, will most likely be determined as failing to disclose how such microprocessor could be properly programmed to either perform any required calculation or to coordinate the other system components in the proper timed sequence to perform the functions disclosed. If, in such a system, a particular program is disclosed, you should ensure that the patent specification teaches that the scope of the disclosure is commensurate with the scope of the functions contributed to the program in the claims of the patent application. If the disclosure fails to disclose any program, and if more than routine experimentation would be required by one skilled in the art to generate such a program, the patent application will be challenged by the examiner.

The amount of experimentation that is considered "routine" by one skilled in the art will vary, depending on the facts and circumstances of individual inventions. The amount of required experimentation must, however, be reasonable. For example, one court found that the amount of experimentation involved by one skilled in the art was reasonable where a skilled programmer could write a general computer program directed to one of the embodiments of the invention shown in the patent application within 4 hours. In another case, where the opposite result was reached, it was shown that those skilled in the art would take 1–2 man-years to develop a particular program from the disclosure in the patent application. This latter situation would be clearly unreasonable.

13.8.1.2 Block Elements Within a Computer

The second category of block diagram patent application cases occurs most frequently with regard to pure data processing inventions, where the combination of block elements is totally within the confines of a computer, there being no interface with an external apparatus other than normal input/output devices. To provide an enabling disclosure for such inventions, it is recommended that the disclosure contain (1) a reference to and a teaching of reliance upon an identified prior art computer system, and (2) an operative computer program for the referenced prior art computer system. The specification should show that the individual program's steps are specifically interrelated with the operative structure of elements in the referenced prior art computer system. The application should not merely set forth a sketchy explanation of flow diagrams or a bare bones group of program listings together with reference to a proprietary computer in which they might be run. The disclosure should provide considerable detail in explaining the interrelationships between the disclosed hardware and software elements. Because of the significance of the program listing and the reference to and reliance on an identified prior art computer system, absent either of the items, a block element disclosure within the confines of a computer must present ample disclosure in the same manner as the first category of block diagram cases discussed in the immediately preceding section.

Regardless of whether a patent specification discloses block elements more comprehensive than a computer, or block elements totally within the confines of a computer, the specification must be adequate to teach how to practice the claimed invention. If such practice of the invention requires a particular apparatus, the application must therefore provide a sufficient disclosure of that apparatus.

There is no universally applicable rule that exists for determining whether a patent application specification involving computer programs is sufficiently or insufficiently disclosed. However, disclosures which fail to include either the computer program itself, or a reasonably detailed flow chart which delineates the sequence of operations the program must perform, will most likely be rejected by the Patent Examiner in the first instance. In programming patent applications, software disclosure only includes a flow chart. As the complexity of functions and the generality of the individual components of the flow chart increase, the chance of the application being held to constitute an insufficient disclosure based on such a minimalist flow chart increases, since the likelihood increases of more than routine experimentation being required to generate a working program from the flow chart.

It is imperative that the inventor in a computer program patent application show that his or her specification would enable one of ordinary skill in the art to make and use the claimed invention without resorting to undue experimentation. In certain instances, efforts to meet this burden involve submitting affidavits or declarations from the inventor, or others on the inventor's development team, referencing prior art patents or technical publications, arguments of the patent professional or attorney prosecuting the application, or combinations of these approaches, to establish that one of ordinary skill in the computer arts could practice the invention.

13.8.2 Affidavit or Declaration Practice

When submitting evidence in a patent application to support the degree of skill necessary to practice the invention from the disclosure, affidavits or declarations from inventors or others may be submitted to the Patent Examiner, setting forth facts necessary to establish what the level of ordinary skill is in the art. One must be careful when submitting such information that the person making the declaration or affidavit is not established as having a level of skill higher than that required by a "routineer," or one of ordinary skill in the related art.

Such affidavits and declarations should not merely set forth conclusions or opinions, without facts to support or bolster these conclusions. As one bad example, in one case, the patent application included broadly worded block diagrams of the inventive structure, but no flow charts or program listings of the programs of the controller to control a message switching system. No evidence was submitted in the affidavits as to the number of programmers and the number of hours required to develop the program, or the level of skill of programmers needed to produce the program required to practice the invention, starting with the patent application disclosure. Thus, affidavits and declarations submitted to establish the skill of one of ordinary skill in the art should present factual evidence directed to the amount of time, effort, and level of knowledge required for the practice of the invention from the disclosure alone.

13.8.3 Referencing Prior Art Documents

In computer programming patent applications, it is necessary to identify a prior art computer system for purposes of enabling the computer program in question. However, merely citing extracts from technical publications in an affidavit or declaration is not sufficient, if it is not made clear that a person skilled in the art would know which, or what parts, of the cited circuits in the prior art could be used to construct the invention described in the patent specification, or how they could be interconnected to act in combination to produce the required results. Such a submittal is less critical where the circuits comprising the inventive system are essentially standard components comprising an identified prior art computer system and a standard device attached to the system.

Also, it is important that such prior art patents used as a basis for enablement have an issue date earlier than the effective filing date of your patent application. Also, do not rely only on arguments of your patent attorney or agent in the prosecution of the patent application to support the adequacy of the disclosure. Factual affidavits or declarations should be supplied to support the enablement requirement.

13.9 THE PROTECTION OF SOFTWARE THROUGH CONTRACTS

Software can be protected in many ways through contracts when both parties negotiate the contract at arm's length. The problem is more difficult when software is mass marketed. In that situation, many software publishers sell or license their software through a "shrink-wrap" license or a "click" license. A typical shrink-wrap license or click license provides that, by opening the shrink-wrap cellophane around the program, or clicking on the downloaded program, the customer accepts the terms of a license written on or in the package, or displayed on the "Terms of Agreement" on the display screen.

Another consideration in software licensing is warranties. A contract may provide for express warranties, but there may be implied warranties (unwritten warranties) as well. While some implied warranties can be disclaimed, there is the question as to whether the disclaimers are permissible when applied to consumer products.

13.10 PATENT ELIGIBILITY OF SOFTWARE AND COMPUTER-RELATED INVENTIONS IN EUROPE

13.10.1 Introduction

Patent law in Europe is governed primarily by the European Patent Convention (EPC), an agency completely separate from the European Union (EU). The EPC includes written provisions (Articles 52(2)(c) and (3)) that explicitly exclude computer programs from patent protection "as such." However, these exclusions are applied in a complex manner such that it is still possible, under certain circumstances, to obtain patent protection in Europe for software and computer-related inventions. The EPC covers EU countries and some that are not a part of the EU.

In simple terms, in order for software and computer-related inventions to be viewed as patentable by the European Patent Office (EPO), the patent application describing the invention must claim "technical" features which solve a "technical problem" in a non-obvious manner. The EPO accepts the fact that a computer program can, in principle, have "technical" features that solve a "technical problem

13.10.2 The EPO Examination Approach to Computer-Related Inventions

The EPO in practice combines its patent eligibility subject matter test with an analysis of whether the claimed invention is obvious. To achieve this, the EPO first separates the patent claim into "technical" features and "non-technical" features, depending on the examiner's point of view. Claimed features which appear to relate to subject matter excluded from patentability, including software features, are likely to be viewed as "non-technical" by the EPO, unless it is shown that these "non-technical" features do have a "technical" character" through either (1) being capable of causing a change in the physical nature or technical functioning of clearly technical features recited in the claim, or (2) reflecting technical considerations required to carry out the disclosed invention.

Next, in determining whether the claimed invention is obvious or not, the EPO patent examiner removes the non-technical features from the claimed invention, and formulates a technical problem solved by the remaining technical features in relation to the prior art. Then, the EPO examiner determines whether the technical features of the claimed invention would have been obvious to a person having ordinary skill in the art, starting from this technical problem and the prior art.

In accordance with this analysis, the EPO examiner considers the "non-technical" features of the claimed invention to form part of the prior art, even if there is no evidence to suggest that this is actually true. It follows that, in order to successfully obtain a European patent on an invention that is devised in software, it is necessary to establish to the examiner's satisfaction that the claimed invention contains "technical" features that would have been non-obvious to a person skilled in the art who is armed not only with the prior art but also with knowledge of any non-technical features of the claimed invention.

The result is that, when arguing patent eligibility of an invention in software or computer-related devices at the EPO, the arguments must focus on whether or not the claimed features thought to be novel and non-obvious have "technical character." If this argument is lost, that is, if the claimed features thought to be novel and non-obvious are viewed by the examiner as "non-technical," the EPO is more than likely to reject the claimed invention as being obvious even if there is no evidence in the record to suggest that the non-technical features of the claimed invention are actually disclosed or suggested in the prior art.

Under the European Patent Rules, the term "software" is considered by itself to be ambiguous, because it may refer to a program listing written in a programming language to implement an algorithm, but also may refer to binary code loaded in a computer-based apparatus, and may also encompass the accompanying documentation. The EPO prefers to use the term "computer implemented invention" in place of software. A computer-related invention can be understood as an invention involving the computer, the computer network, or other programmable apparatus where one or more features are realized fully or partly by means of a computer program. Under the EPO procedure, a computer program claimed as such is not a patent-eligible invention. For a patent to be granted for a computer implemented invention in the EPO, as stated earlier, a technical problem has to solved in a novel and non-obvious manner.

For example, software comprising or including a new algorithm for controlling the operation of a steel mill to produce higher-quality steel should, in principle, be patentable at the EPO. Similarly, software comprising new code that allows a computer processor to process data more efficiently or more rapidly should also be patentable at the EPO. In each of these examples, it is straightforward to argue that a "technical problem" has been solved (e.g., how to produce better-quality steel or how to process data more efficiently), since the technical effects produced clearly go beyond the normal physical effects produced by an ordinary piece of software.

Similarly, a computer-implemented method of encoding audio information in a communication system to reduce distortion induced by channel noise would likely be viewed as "technical" by the EPO. This is the case even though the idea underlying this method may be a mathematical method that, on its own, would likely be viewed as non-patentable by the EPO. An important point here is that the encoding method as implemented by a computer is not a mathematical method ("as such") and seeks to solve a "technical problem," and can thus be considered "technical" by the EPO.

Similarly, a new method of encrypting or digitally signing electronic communications to provide improved security may be regarded as "technical" by the EPO, even if the method is based on a new mathematical scheme.

In order for a software feature to be viewed by the EPO as "technical," it is usually necessary for the software, when executed, to produce a technical effect that goes beyond the normal physical effects produced when an ordinary piece of software is executed on computer hardware (such as the graphical display of data on a monitor or the movement of data from one location to another).

By way of a contrasting example, business methods, such as complex financial systems, may use computers and software to monitor the movement of large numbers of stocks, such as to recommend buying or selling activity according to predetermined criteria. Generally, software implementing such business or financial methods will not be patent eligible at the EPO, even if the underlying financial methods are new and unobvious. The difference from the examples given in the previous paragraphs is that the beneficial effects produced by software implementing financial methods are highly unlikely to be viewed as "technical" by the EPO examiner, because these effects are primarily financial. However, a new method devised in the context of an administrative or financial environment could in principle be viewed as patentable by the EPO, if it can be shown that a "technical problem" has been solved—for example, a computer-implemented method that helps reduce the latency at which financial transactions are performed could potentially be viewed as patentable by the EPO.

Often, it will not be clear whether patent protection will be available at the EPO for an invention relating to software. Accordingly, the determination as to whether or not patent protection will be available in the EPO for such inventions must be determined on a case-by-case basis, in consultation between you, the inventor, and your patent professional.

13.10.3 Acceptable Claims for Software Inventions at the EPO

Once the EPO has determined that a claimed software invention comprises patentable subject matter, that is, that the claim defines technical features which solve a "technical" problem in a non-obvious manner, the EPO is quite liberal in the formulation of claims it will allow.

In November 2016, the EPO issued guidelines providing example claim formulations relating to computer-related and software inventions. These guidelines can be found at the EPO website; however, this author strongly suggests that you contact your patent professional to obtain advice before making a determination on your own as to your ability to obtain European patent protection for your computer-related invention, and before spending your resources on trying to obtain patents on inventions that, from the outset, would be very difficult to acquire from the EPO.

The EPO guidelines set forth many examples of claim formulations that are considered patent eligible, and those that are deemed non-patent-eligible. These guidelines are not definitive in all situations, but they may provide a useful reference that will assist the inventor and the inventor's patent professional in preparing a viable European patent application.

13.10.4 Software and Computer-Related Inventions and Patent Eligibility in the UK

Statutory law in the UK regarding patent eligibility of software inventions is primarily the same as it is in the EPO. However, unlike the EPO, the United Kingdom Intellectual Property Office (UKIPO) applies the law, in practice, by assessing whether a claimed invention relates to non-patent-eligible subject matter independently from its assessment of whether the claimed invention is obvious. To obtain patent protection on computer-related inventions and software in the UK, it is necessary to show that the claimed invention provides a "relevant technical effect." Keep in mind that neither the English courts, nor the statutes, nor the UKIPO have set forth a formal definition of what constitutes a relevant technical effect, and it is unlikely that such definition will be forthcoming. However, the UK High Court has established the following factors as being "useful signposts" for determining whether a claimed technical effect is a relevant technical effect in obtaining patents on computer-related and software inventions:

1. Whether the claimed technical effect operates on a process that is carried on outside the computer.
2. Whether the claimed technical effect operates at the level of the architecture of the computer—that is, whether the effect is produced irrespective of the data being processed or the applications being run.
3. Whether the claimed technical effect results in the computer being made to operate in a new way.
4. Whether the computer is made a better computer in the sense of running more efficiently and effectively as a computer.
5. Whether the perceived problem is overcome by the claimed invention as opposed to merely being circumvented.

Courts in the UK have indicated that the approaches used by the UKIPO and the EPO should produce the same results. However, it seems in practice that the UKIPO appears to take a much narrower view of what can be considered "technical" as compared to the EPO. Unfortunately, as a result of this approach, the prospects of obtaining granted patents for software inventions at the UKIPO appear to be considerably limited than at the EPO.

At the time of writing this text, the UK was in the process of seeking withdrawal from the EU ("Brexit"). However, even if the UK withdraws from the EU, the UK will remain a member state of the European Patent Organisation as well as the European Patent Convention (EPC), and EPC patents will continue to apply to the UK because the EPO is not an EU institution. Therefore, regardless of the outcome of "Brexit" negotiations, European patents granted by the EPO will still be able to take effect in the UK, and be enforced through UK courts, as at present. This is not the same for trademarks or designs.

Information on obtaining patent protection on software and computer-related inventions in Europe was kindly furnished to the author by James Leach (European patent attorney and Chartered patent attorney), who is a partner of the European intellectual property firm Mewburn Ellis LLP (www.mewburn.com).

149 F.3d 1368 (1998)

STATE STREET BANK & TRUST CO., Plaintiff-Appellee,

v.

SIGNATURE FINANCIAL GROUP, INC. Defendant-Appellant.

No. 96-1327.

United States Court of Appeals, Federal Circuit.

July 23, 1998.

1369 *1369 William L. Patton, Ropes & Gray, Boston, Massachusetts, argued for plaintiff-appellee. With him on the brief were James L. Sigel and James S. DeGraw. Also on the brief was Maurice E. Gauthier, Samuels, Gauthier, Stevens & Reppert.

Steven L. Friedman, Dilworth, Paxson, Kalish & Kauffman LLP, Philadelphia, Pennsylvania, argued for defendant-appellant. With him on the brief were Steven J. Henry, Wolf, Greenfield & Sacks, P.C., Boston, Massachusetts; and Philip G. Koenig, Pittas //Koenig, Winchester, Massachusetts.

William T. Ellis, Foley & Lardner, Washington, D.C., for amicus curiae Information Technology
1370 Industry Council. With him on the brief were Harold C. Wegner, Richard L. *1370 Schwaab, and Mary Michelle Kile. Of counsel was John F. Cooney, Venable, Baetjer, Howard & Civiletti, LLP.

Robert C. Scheinfeld, Baker & Botts, L.L.P., New York, New York, for amicus curiae Mastercard International Service. With him on the brief was Lawrence T. Kass. Of counsel on the brief for amicus curiae VISA International Service Association were Laurie S. Hane, Donald S. Chisum, and Alan L. Durham, Morrison & Foerster LLP, Palo Alto, California.

Before RICH, PLAGER, and BRYSON, Circuit Judges.

RICH, Circuit Judge.

Signature Financial Group, Inc. (Signature) appeals from the decision of the United States District Court for the District of Massachusetts granting a motion for summary judgment in favor of State Street Bank & Trust Co. (State Street), finding U.S. Patent No. 5,193,056 (the '056 patent) invalid on the ground that the claimed subject matter is not encompassed by 35 U.S.C. § 101 (1994). *See* *State Street Bank & Trust Co. v. Signature Financial Group, Inc.*, 927 F.Supp. 502, 38 USPQ2d 1530 (D.Mass.1996). We reverse and remand because we conclude that the patent claims are directed to statutory subject matter.

BACKGROUND

Signature is the assignee of the '056 patent which is entitled "Data Processing System for Hub and Spoke Financial Services Configuration." The '056 patent issued to Signature on 9 March 1993, naming R. Todd Boes as the inventor. The '056 patent is generally directed to a data processing system (the system) for implementing an investment structure which was developed for use in Signature's business as an administrator and accounting agent for mutual funds. In essence, the system, identified by the proprietary name Hub and Spoke®, facilitates a structure whereby mutual funds (Spokes) pool their assets in an investment portfolio (Hub) organized as a partnership. This investment configuration provides the administrator of a mutual fund with the advantageous combination of economies of scale in administering investments coupled with the tax advantages of a partnership.

State Street and Signature are both in the business of acting as custodians and accounting agents for multi-tiered partnership fund financial services. State Street negotiated with Signature for a license to use its patented data processing system described and claimed in the '056 patent. When negotiations broke down, State Street brought a declaratory judgment action asserting invalidity, unenforceability, and noninfringement in Massachusetts district court, and then filed a motion for partial summary judgment of patent invalidity for failure to claim statutory subject matter under § 101. The motion was granted and this appeal followed.

DISCUSSION

On appeal, we are not bound to give deference to the district court's grant of summary judgment, but must make an independent determination that the standards for summary judgment have been met. *Vas-Cath, Inc. v. Mahurkar,* 935 F.2d 1555, 1560, 19 USPQ2d 1111, 1114 (Fed.Cir.1991). Summary judgment is properly granted where there are no genuine issues of material fact and the moving party is entitled to judgment as a matter of law. Fed.R.Civ.P. 56(c). The substantive issue at hand, whether the '056 patent is invalid for failure to claim statutory subject matter under § 101, is a matter of both claim construction and statutory construction. "[W]e review claim construction *de novo* including any allegedly fact-based questions relating to claim construction." *Cybor Corp. v. FAS Techs.,* 138 F.3d 1448, 1451, 46 USPQ2d 1169, 1174 (Fed.Cir.1998) (*in banc*). We also review statutory construction *de novo. See Romero v. United States,* 38 F.3d 1204, 1207 (Fed.Cir.1994). We hold that declaratory judgment plaintiff State Street was not entitled to the grant of summary judgment of invalidity of the '056 patent under § 101 as a matter of law, because the patent claims are directed to statutory subject matter.

The following facts pertinent to the statutory subject matter issue are either undisputed or represent
1371 the version alleged by the nonmovant. *See Anderson v. Liberty Lobby,* *1371 *Inc.,* 477 U.S. 242, 255, 106 S.Ct. 2505, 91 L.Ed.2d 202 (1986). The patented invention relates generally to a system that allows an administrator to monitor and record the financial information flow and make all calculations necessary for maintaining a partner fund financial services configuration. As previously mentioned, a partner fund financial services configuration essentially allows several mutual funds, or "Spokes," to pool their investment funds into a single portfolio, or "Hub," allowing for consolidation of, inter alia, the costs of administering the fund combined with the tax advantages of a partnership. In particular, this system provides means for a daily allocation of assets for two or more Spokes that are invested in the same Hub. The system determines the percentage share that each Spoke maintains in the Hub, while taking into consideration daily changes both in the value of

the Hub's investment securities and in the concomitant amount of each Spoke's assets.

In determining daily changes, the system also allows for the allocation among the Spokes of the Hub's daily income, expenses, and net realized and unrealized gain or loss, calculating each day's total investments based on the concept of a book capital account. This enables the determination of a true asset value of each Spoke and accurate calculation of allocation ratios between or among the Spokes. The system additionally tracks all the relevant data determined on a daily basis for the Hub and each Spoke, so that aggregate year end income, expenses, and capital gain or loss can be determined for accounting and for tax purposes for the Hub and, as a result, for each publicly traded Spoke.

It is essential that these calculations are quickly and accurately performed. In large part this is required because each Spoke sells shares to the public and the price of those shares is substantially based on the Spoke's percentage interest in the portfolio. In some instances, a mutual fund administrator is required to calculate the value of the shares to the nearest penny within as little as an hour and a half after the market closes. Given the complexity of the calculations, a computer or equivalent device is a virtual necessity to perform the task.

The '056 patent application was filed 11 March 1991. It initially contained six "machine" claims, which incorporated meansplus-function clauses, and six method claims. According to Signature, during prosecution the examiner contemplated a § 101 rejection for failure to claim statutory subject matter. However, upon cancellation of the six method claims, the examiner issued a notice of allowance for the remaining present six claims on appeal. Only claim 1 is an independent claim.

The district court began its analysis by construing the claims to be directed to a process, with each "means" clause merely representing a step in that process. However, "machine" claims having "means" clauses may only be reasonably viewed as process claims if there is no supporting structure in the written description that corresponds to the claimed "means" elements. *See In re Alappat*, 33 F.3d 1526, 1540-41, 31 USPQ2d 1545, 1554 (Fed.Cir.1994) (*in banc*). This is not the case now before us.

When independent claim 1 is properly construed in accordance with § 112, ¶ 6, it is directed to a machine, as demonstrated below, where representative claim 1 is set forth, the subject matter in brackets stating the structure the written description discloses as corresponding to the respective "means" recited in the claims.

> 1. A data processing system for managing a financial services configuration of a portfolio established as a partnership, each partner being one of a plurality of funds, comprising:
>
> (a) computer processor means [a personal computer including a CPU] for processing data;
>
> (b) storage means [a data disk] for storing data on a storage medium;
>
> (c) first means [an arithmetic logic circuit configured to prepare the data disk to magnetically store selected data] for initializing the storage medium;

(d) second means [an arithmetic logic circuit configured to retrieve information from a specific file, calculate incremental increases or decreases based on specific input,
1372 allocate the results on a percentage basis, and store the output in a *1372 separate file] for processing data regarding assets in the portfolio and each of the funds from a previous day and data regarding increases or decreases in each of the funds, [sic, funds'] assets and for allocating the percentage share that each fund holds in the portfolio;

(e) third means [an arithmetic logic circuit configured to retrieve information from a specific file, calculate incremental increases and decreases based on specific input, allocate the results on a percentage basis and store the output in a separate file] for processing data regarding daily incremental income, expenses, and net realized gain or loss for the portfolio and for allocating such data among each fund;

(f) fourth means [an arithmetic logic circuit configured to retrieve information from a specific file, calculate incremental increases and decreases based on specific input, allocate the results on a percentage basis and store the output in a separate file] for processing data regarding daily net unrealized gain or loss for the portfolio and for allocating such data among each fund; and

(g) fifth means [an arithmetic logic circuit configured to retrieve information from specific files, calculate that information on an aggregate basis and store the output in a separate file] for processing data regarding aggregate year-end income, expenses, and capital gain or loss for the portfolio and each of the funds.

Each claim component, recited as a "means" plus its function, is to be read, of course, pursuant to § 112, ¶ 6, as inclusive of the "equivalents" of the structures disclosed in the written description portion of the specification. Thus, claim 1, properly construed, claims a machine, namely, a data processing system for managing a financial services configuration of a portfolio established as a partnership, which machine is made up of, at the very least, the specific structures disclosed in the written description and corresponding to the means-plus-function elements (a)-(g) recited in the claim. A "machine" is proper statutory subject matter under § 101. We note that, for the purposes of a § 101 analysis, it is of little relevance whether claim 1 is directed to a "machine" or a "process," as long as it falls within at least one of the four enumerated categories of patentable subject matter, "machine" and "process" being such categories.

This does not end our analysis, however, because the court concluded that the claimed subject matter fell into one of two alternative judicially-created exceptions to statutory subject matter.[1] The court refers to the first exception as the "mathematical algorithm" exception and the second exception as the "business method" exception. Section 101 reads:

> Whoever invents or discovers any new and useful process, machine, manufacture, or composition of matter, or any new and useful improvement thereof, may obtain a patent therefor, subject to the conditions and requirements of this title.

The plain and unambiguous meaning of § 101 is that any invention falling within one of the four stated categories of statutory subject matter may be patented, provided it meets the other requirements for patentability set forth in Title 35, i.e., those found in §§ 102, 103, and 112, ¶ 2.[2]

1373 *1373 The repetitive use of the expansive term "any" in § 101 shows Congress's intent not to place any restrictions on the subject matter for which a patent may be obtained beyond those specifically recited in § 101. Indeed, the Supreme Court has acknowledged that Congress intended § 101 to extend to "anything under the sun that is made by man." *Diamond v. Chakrabarty*, 447 U.S. 303, 309, 100 S.Ct. 2204, 65 L.Ed.2d 144 (1980); *see also Diamond v. Diehr*, 450 U.S. 175, 182, 101 S.Ct. 1048, 67 L.Ed.2d 155 (1981).[3] Thus, it is improper to read limitations into § 101 on the subject matter that may be patented where the legislative history indicates that Congress clearly did not intend such limitations. *See Chakrabarty*, 447 U.S. at 308, 100 S.Ct. 2204 ("We have also cautioned that courts 'should not read into the patent laws limitations and conditions which the legislature has not expressed.'" (citations omitted)).

The "Mathematical Algorithm" Exception

The Supreme Court has identified three categories of subject matter that are unpatentable, namely "laws of nature, natural phenomena, and abstract ideas." *Diehr*, 450 U.S. at 185, 101 S.Ct. 1048. Of particular relevance to this case, the Court has held that mathematical algorithms are not patentable subject matter to the extent that they are merely abstract ideas. *See Diehr*, 450 U.S. 175, 101 S.Ct. 1048, *passim; Parker v. Flook*, 437 U.S. 584, 98 S.Ct. 2522, 57 L.Ed.2d 451 (1978); *Gottschalk v. Benson*, 409 U.S. 63, 93 S.Ct. 253, 34 L.Ed.2d 273 (1972). In *Diehr*, the Court explained that certain types of mathematical subject matter, standing alone, represent nothing more than abstract ideas until reduced to some type of practical application, i.e., "a useful, concrete and tangible result." *Alappat*, 33 F.3d at 1544, 31 USPQ2d at 1557.[4]

Unpatentable mathematical algorithms are identifiable by showing they are merely abstract ideas constituting disembodied concepts or truths that are not "useful." From a practical standpoint, this means that to be patentable an algorithm must be applied in a "useful" way. In *Alappat*, we held that data, transformed by a machine through a series of mathematical calculations to produce a smooth waveform display on a rasterizer monitor, constituted a practical application of an abstract idea (a mathematical algorithm, formula, or calculation), because it produced "a useful, concrete and tangible result" — the smooth waveform.

Similarly, in *Arrhythmia Research Technology Inc. v. Corazonix Corp.*, 958 F.2d 1053, 22 USPQ2d 1033 (Fed.Cir.1992), we held that the transformation of electrocardiograph signals from a patient's heartbeat by a machine through a series of mathematical calculations constituted a practical application of an abstract idea (a mathematical algorithm, formula, or calculation), because it corresponded to a useful, concrete or tangible thing — the condition of a patient's heart.

Today, we hold that the transformation of data, representing discrete dollar amounts, by a machine through a series of mathematical calculations into a final share price, constitutes a practical application of a mathematical algorithm, formula, or calculation, because t produces "a useful, concrete and tangible result" — a final share price momentarily fixed for recording and reporting purposes and even accepted and relied upon by regulatory authorities and in subsequent trades.

The district court erred by applying the Freeman-Walter-Abele test to determine whether the claimed subject matter was an unpatentable abstract idea. The Freeman-Walter-Abele test was
1374 designed by the Court *1374 of Customs and Patent Appeals, and subsequently adopted by this court, to extract and identify unpatentable mathematical algorithms in the aftermath of *Benson* and *Flook*. See In re Freeman, 573 F.2d 1237, 197 USPQ 464 (CCPA 1978) as modified by In re Walter, 618 F.2d 758, 205 USPQ 397 (CCPA 1980). The test has been thus articulated:

> First, the claim is analyzed to determine whether a mathematical algorithm is directly or indirectly recited. Next, if a mathematical algorithm is found, the claim as a whole is further analyzed to determine whether the algorithm is "applied in any manner to physical elements or process steps," and, if it is, it "passes muster under § 101."

In re Pardo, 684 F.2d 912, 915, 214 USPQ 673, 675-76 (CCPA 1982) (citing In re Abele, 684 F.2d 902, 214 USPQ 682 (CCPA 1982)).[5]

After *Diehr* and *Chakrabarty*, the Freeman-Walter-Abele test has little, if any, applicability to determining the presence of statutory subject matter. As we pointed out in Alappat, 33 F.3d at 1543, 31 USPQ2d at 1557, application of the test could be misleading, because a process, machine, manufacture, or composition of matter employing a law of nature, natural phenomenon, or abstract idea is patentable subject matter even though a law of nature, natural phenomenon, or abstract idea would not, by itself, be entitled to such protection.[6] The test determines the presence of, for example, an algorithm. Under *Benson*, this may have been a sufficient indicium of nonstatutory subject matter. However, after *Diehr* and *Alappat*, the mere fact that a claimed invention involves inputting numbers, calculating numbers, outputting numbers, and storing numbers, in and of itself, would not render it nonstatutory subject matter, unless, of course, its operation does not produce a "useful, concrete and tangible result." Alappat, 33 F.3d at 1544, 31 USPQ2d at 1557.[7] After all, as we have repeatedly stated,

> every step-by-step process, be it electronic or chemical or mechanical, involves an algorithm in the broad sense of the term. Since § 101 expressly includes processes as a category of inventions which may be patented and § 100(b) further defines the word
> 1375 "process" as meaning "process, art or *1375 method, and includes a new use of a known process, machine, manufacture, composition of matter, or material," it follows that it is no ground for holding a claim is directed to nonstatutory subject matter to say it includes or is directed to an algorithm. This is why the proscription against patenting has been limited to *mathematical* algorithms....

In re Iwahashi, 888 F.2d 1370, 1374, 12 USPQ2d 1908, 1911 (Fed.Cir.1989) (emphasis in the original).[8]

The question of whether a claim encompasses statutory subject matter should not focus on *which* of the four categories of subject matter a claim is directed to[9] — process, machine, manufacture, or composition of matter — but rather on the essential characteristics of the subject matter, in particular, its practical utility. Section 101 specifies that statutory subject matter must also satisfy the other "conditions and requirements" of Title 35, including novelty, nonobviousness, and adequacy of disclosure and notice. *See* In re Warmerdam, 33 F.3d 1354, 1359, 31 USPQ2d 1754, 1757-58 (Fed.Cir.1994). For purpose of our analysis, as noted above, claim 1 is directed to a machine programmed with the Hub and Spoke software and admittedly produces a "useful, concrete, and tangible result." *Alappat*, 33 F.3d at 1544, 31 USPQ2d at 1557. This renders it statutory subject matter, even if the useful result is expressed in numbers, such as price, profit, percentage, cost, or loss.

[1] Indeed, although we do not make this determination here, the judicially created exceptions, i.e., abstract ideas, laws of nature, etc., should be applicable to all categories of statutory subject matter, as our own precedent suggests. *See Alappat*, 33 F.3d at 1542, 31 USPQ2d at 1556; *see also In re Johnston*, 502 F.2d 765, 183 USPQ 172 (CCPA 1974) (Rich, J., dissenting).

[2] As explained in *In re Bergy*, 596 F.2d 952, 960, 201 USPQ 352, 360 (CCPA 1979) (emphases and footnote omitted):

The first door which must be opened on the difficult path to patentability is § 101 .... The person approaching that door is an inventor, whether his invention is patentable or not .... Being an inventor or having an invention, however, is no guarantee of opening even the first door. What kind of an invention or discovery is it? In dealing with the question of kind, as distinguished from the qualitative conditions which make the invention patentable, § 101 is broad and general; its language is: "any * * * process, machine, manufacture, or composition of matter, or any * * * improvement thereof." Section 100(b) further expands "process" to include "art or method, and * * * a new use of a known process, machine, manufacture, composition of matter, or material." If the invention, as the inventor defines it in his claims (pursuant to § 112, second paragraph), falls into any one of the named categories, he is allowed to pass through to the second door, which is § 102; "novelty and loss of right to patent" is the sign on it. Notwithstanding the words "new and useful" in § 101, the invention is not examined under that statute for novelty because that is not the statutory scheme of things or the long-established administrative practice.

[3] The Committee Reports accompanying the 1952 Act inform us that Congress intended statutory subject matter to "include anything under the sun that is made by man." S.Rep. No. 82-1979 at 5 (1952); H.R.Rep. No. 82-1923 at 6 (1952).

[4] This has come to be known as the mathematical algorithm exception. This designation has led to some confusion, especially given the Freeman-Walter-Abele analysis. By keeping in mind that the mathematical algorithm is unpatentable only to the extent that it represents an abstract idea, this confusion may be ameliorated.

[5] The test has been the source of much confusion. In *In re Abele*, 684 F.2d 902, 214 USPQ 682 (CCPA 1982), the CCPA upheld claims applying "a mathematical formula within the context of a process which encompasses significantly more than the algorithm alone." *Id.* at 909. Thus, the CCPA apparently inserted an additional consideration — the significance of additions to the algorithm. The CCPA appeared to abandon the application of the test in *In re Taner*, 681 F.2d 787, 214 USPQ 678 (CCPA 1982), only to subsequently "clarify" that the Freeman-Walter-Abele test was simply not the exclusive test for detecting unpatentable subject matter. *In re Meyer*, 688 F.2d 789, 796, 215 USPQ 193, 199 (CCPA 1982).

[6] *See e.g. Parker v. Flook*, 437 U.S. 584, 590, 98 S.Ct. 2522, 57 L.Ed.2d 451 (1978) ("[A] process is not unpatentable simply because it contains a law of nature or a mathematical algorithm."); *Funk Bros. Seed Co. v. Kalo Inoculant Co.*, 333 U.S. 127, 130, 68 S.Ct. 440, 92 L.Ed. 588 (1948) ("He who discovers a hitherto unknown phenomenon of nature has no claim to a monopoly of it which the law recognizes. If there is to be invention from such a discovery, it must come from the application of the law to a new and useful end."); *Mackay Radio & Tel. Co. v. Radio Corp. of Am.*, 306 U.S. 86, 94, 59 S.Ct. 427, 83 L.Ed. 506 (1939) ("While a scientific truth, or the mathematical expression of it, is not a patentable invention, a novel and useful structure created with the aid of knowledge of scientific truth may be.").

[W]hen a claim containing a mathematical formula implements or applies that formula in a structure or process which, when considered as a whole, is performing a function which the patent laws were designed to protect (e.g., transforming or reducing an article to a different state or thing), then the claim satisfies the requirements of § 101.

Diehr, 450 U.S. at 192, 101 S.Ct. 1048; *see also In re Iwahashi*, 888 F.2d 1370, 1375, 12 USPQ2d 1908, 1911 (Fed.Cir.1989); *Taner*, 681 F.2d at 789, 214 USPQ at 680. The dispositive inquiry is whether the claim as a whole is directed to statutory subject matter. It is irrelevant that a claim may contain, as part of the whole, subject matter which would not be patentable by itself. "A claim drawn to subject matter otherwise statutory does not become nonstatutory simply because it uses a mathematical formula, computer program or digital computer." *Diehr*, 450 U.S. at 187, 101 S.Ct. 1048.

[7] As the Supreme Court expressly stated in *Diehr*, its own holdings in *Benson* and *Flook* "stand for no more than these long-established principles" that abstract ideas and natural phenomena are not patentable. *Diehr*, 450 U.S. at 185, 101 S.Ct. 1048 (citing *Chakrabarty*, 447 U.S. at 309, 100 S.Ct. 2204 and *Funk Bros.*, 333 U.S. at 130, 68 S.Ct. 440.).

[8] In *In re Pardo*, 684 F.2d 912 (CCPA 1982), the CCPA narrowly limited "mathematical algorithm" to the execution of formulas with given data. In the same year, in *In re Meyer*, 688 F.2d 789, 215 USPQ 193 (CCPA 1982), the CCPA interpreted the same term to include any mental process that can be represented by a mathematical algorithm. This is also the position taken by the PTO in its Examination Guidelines, 61 Fed. Reg. 7478, 7483 (1996).

[9] Of course, the subject matter must fall into at least one category of statutory subject matter.

◆ INVENTORS AND INVENTIONS ◆

Hedy Lamarr

SPREAD SPECTRUM TECHNOLOGY

Once upon a time (in 1913 to be precise), a lady named Hedwig Eva Maria Kiesler was born in Vienna, Austria. At a young age, she dropped out of school in 1930 and studied acting under theater director Max Reinhardt in Berlin. When she was only 19-years-old, she made worldwide cinema history because of a ten-minute appearance in a few nude swimming scenes in the Czech film *Ecstasy* in 1932. Needless to say, this brought fame to Ms. Kiesler. Why is this story here? Read on.

At age 19, Hedwig Kiesler's parents accepted her marriage to a wealthy Austrian munitions dealer, Fritz Mandl. They lived in a luxurious apartment in the heart of Vienna. As Mandl's wife, she accompanied him on many trips to meet high ranking officers of Hitler's German and Mussolini's Italian armies, where Mandl engaged in selling munitions, even if such sales were in violation of the Versailles Treaty. To assist him in the success of his arms deals, Mandl often took Hedwig with him to help impress his prospective customers with her dazzling beauty and charm. She also attended meetings between Mandl and his munitions engineers. Having a curious

Intellectual Property Law for Engineers, Scientists, and Entrepreneurs, Second Edition. Howard B. Rockman.

Published 2020 by John Wiley & Sons, Inc.

mind, she did not just idly stand by and smile at these meetings. She learned a great deal by listening carefully to the conversations about weaponry and weapons systems. She also learned of problems Mandl and his engineers were trying to solve with radio-controlled torpedoes.

Hedwig felt herself cast more in a role as a trophy wife to Mandl, who was a very possessive control freak. He even attempted to buy back all of the prints of *Ecstacy* he could find. Mussolini had a copy, but would not sell it to Mandl. Prints are still out there today. At about the same time, she became disenchanted with the Nazis. After four years of marriage to Mandl, she made the decision to leave him.

In 1937, she made it to London, where she worked in several stage productions. She was introduced to MGM's Louis B. Mayer, who signed her to a contract in 1939, but with mixed emotions because of *Ecstasy*. Her nude performance had brought about an international scandal of sorts (it *was* 1932 and the U.S. Government operated a film censorship office in those days), but her notoriety and fame added up to dollars. Mayer said her name had to be changed, and she would make only wholesome movies from then on. While traveling together to New York on the Normandy, Mrs. Mayer came up with the name Lamarr, as in Barbara Lamarr. The name means "the ocean," which Hedwig thought appropriate. "Kiesler" was changed to "Lamarr" and her former name "Hedwig" was shortened to "Hedy," which she had been called by her family and friends in Austria.

She immediately became one of the sultry glamour stars in the MGM world, making her American debut in the 1939 film, *Algiers,* and appearing in many films such as *White Cargo* (1942) and *Samson and Delilah* (1949). Are you still asking why this matters? Read on.

Prior to the U.S. entry into World War II, Ms. Lamarr became involved with a composer named George Antheil. As the story is told, she was listening to a concert where Antheil used 16 player pianos. At the same time she was thinking of how to make an anti-jamming radio control for naval torpedoes. I will bet you always wondered what movie stars think of in their spare time.

The constantly varying notes on the piano gave Ms. Lamarr an idea. Rather than transmitting radio control signals to a torpedo over a single transmit and receive frequency, which can be readily jammed or intercepted, the signals could be sent over continually changing frequencies in a pre-established pattern, similar to the continually changing notes of a piano composition. By synchronizing the transmitter and the receiver to the same pattern of frequency changes, the transmitter and receiver could communicate, and an enemy who was unaware of the frequency change pattern could not locate or jam the signal.

This was 1941, and Mr. Antheil designed a device using many player piano mechanisms that would create the frequency change pattern ("frequency hopping") for the transmitter and the receiver. On June 10, 1941, Ms. Lamarr and Mr. Antheil filed a patent application covering their device and system, which issued as U.S. Patent No. 2,292,387, and is titled "Secret Communication System." A copy of the cover page of the this patent follows. In filing the patent application, Ms. Lamarr used her married name at that time, Hedy Kiesler Markey. The navy scoffed at the idea of player piano rolls in torpedoes and shelved the idea, to Hedy's disappointment. However, she gave the patent to the U.S. government as gratitude for being in America. It was subsequently held in secrecy by the wartime government and not made public until 1981.

Their "frequency hopping" idea involved two paper player piano rolls perforated with identical patterns, one roll in the airplane overhead to guide the torpedo to its target, and the other in the torpedo receiver. Signals emitted by the transmitter, over rapidly changing frequencies, are recognized by the receiver in the torpedo. The objective was to prevent an enemy from deflecting the torpedo by false transmissions, or by jamming a single frequency.

Due to the size of the device George Antheil designed to embody the invention, the navy never adopted the system, which was 20 years ahead of its time. Lamarr helped the war effort in another front—she sold war bonds. During one promotion, a purchase of $25,000 worth of bonds earned a kiss from Hedy Lamarr. In one night, she sold $7 million worth of bonds.

After the war, the idea behind the Lamarr–Antheil invention virtually disappeared. However, in 1957, engineers at Sylvania Electronics Systems Division resurrected the "frequency hopping" idea and used a transistor circuit to make the concept work. Ships deployed to quarantine Cuba in 1962 were the first to use the Lamarr–Antheil system. The patent had expired by then.

Today, the concept disclosed in Hedy Lamarr's 1942 patent is known as "spread spectrum" technology. Systems that presently use this technology include Qualcomm's code-division multiple access (CDMA) cell phone technology, high-speed 802.11 wireless Internet access systems, videoconferencing, and the U.S. military's Milstar satellite communications network, wireless heart monitoring in hospitals, wireless PDAs and Internet, high-end cordless phones, and Bluetooth, to name a few. In excess of 1000 issued U.S. patents directed to spread spectrum technology have the Lamarr–Antheil patent cited as a prior art reference.

Hedy Lamarr's idea is considered by many as the foundation for the modern wireless technologies used today, allowing a large number of signal transmitter and receiver devices to operate in the same radio spectrum, with no interference among each other's signals. Thus, a multiplicity of cell phones can operate simultaneously in a similar radio spectrum without bumping into one another, because each signal is broadcast over differing patterns of microsecond frequency changes. Today, interlocking cells of radio signal coverage and spread spectrum technology often work together in wireless communication systems.

Hedy Lamarr passed away in 2000, having never made a dime on her patent or invention. However, she was pleased that her idea led to a massive change in the way people throughout the world communicate. In 1997, Hedy Lamarr and George Antheil received a special award by the Electronic Frontier Foundation for their development of the technology that became a key component of wireless data systems. In 2002, IEEE honored women who "distinguished themselves as engineers." Hedy Lamarr was one of them—and now you know why her story appears here.

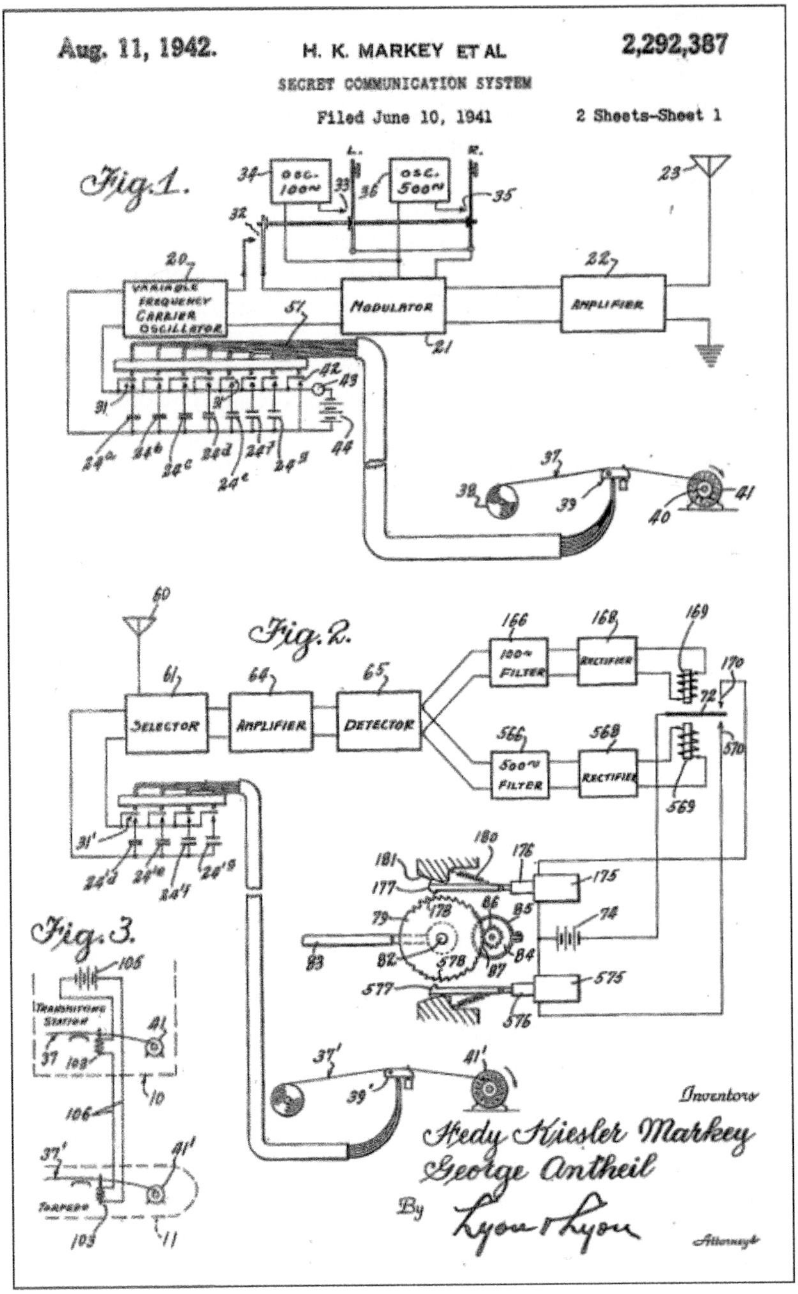
Aug. 11, 1942.
H. K. MARKEY ET AL
2,292,387
SECRET COMMUNICATION SYSTEM
Filed June 10, 1941
2 Sheets-Sheet 1
Fig. 1.
OSC. 100~
OSC. 500~
VARIABLE FREQUENCY CARRIER OSCILLATOR
MODULATOR
AMPLIFIER
Fig. 2.
SELECTOR
AMPLIFIER
DETECTOR
100~ FILTER
RECTIFIER
500~ FILTER
RECTIFIER
Fig. 3.
TRANSMITTING STATION
TORPEDO
Inventors
Hedy Kiesler Markey
George Antheil
By Lyon & Lyon
Attorneys

◆ INVENTORS AND INVENTIONS ◆

Herman Hollerith

TABULATING MACHINE

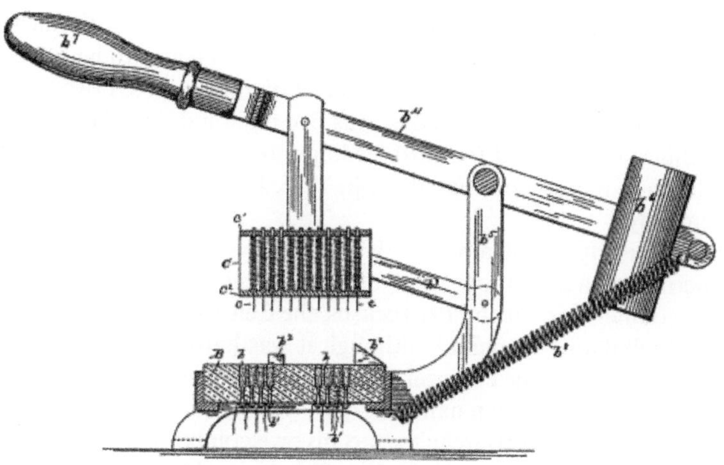

Herman Hollerith was the man who initially made it easy for the government to determine how many people live in the United States. Beginning in 1890, the U.S. Census was tabulated with the help of Hollerith's statistics tabulating machine.

Hollerith was the son of German immigrants who came to the United States in 1848. Although never particularly good in public school because of spelling problems, with the help of the family's Lutheran minister as a tutor, he was able to enroll in the City College of New York and also receive an engineering degree with distinction from the Columbia School of Mines (now part of Columbia University) in 1879. One of Hollerith's teachers, W. P. Trowbridge, was impressed with him and made him his assistant. Hollerith accepted and started working at Columbia University and later the Census Bureau when Professor Trowbridge was appointed as Chief Special Agent to the Census Bureau. While working for the Census Bureau, Hollerith appreciated that there was a need to find a better, faster way to mechanically manipulate large amounts of statistical and other data. During his time at the Census Bureau, Hollerith met Dr. John Shaw Billings, from whom the idea for a tabulating machine first came. Dr. Billings suggested "something on the principal of the Jacquard loom, whereby holes in a card regulate the pattern to be woven."

In 1882, Hollerith began teaching mechanical engineering at the Massachusetts Institute of Technology. During this time, he began working with Dr. Billings' idea,

Intellectual Property Law for Engineers, Scientists, and Entrepreneurs, Second Edition. Howard B. Rockman.

Published 2020 by John Wiley & Sons, Inc.

examining how the Jacquard loom worked, and if its principles could be used for his intended tabulating purposes. Although the loom idea would not work for the census, the idea of punch cards seemed to provide a very efficient way to store information. Another idea came to Hollerith on a train ride as he watched the conductor punch tickets, which led to an easier way to punch information on cardboard cards.

Hollerith then began working on a tabulating system, first using a perforated paper tape, and later cards, and he filed for his first of over 30 patents in 1884. He developed a hand-fed "press" that sensed the holes in punched cards. A wire would pass through the holes into a cup of mercury beneath the card, closing an electrical circuit and creating an electrical impulse. This process triggered mechanical counters and sorter bins and tabulated the appropriate data. His system, including keyboard punch tabulator and sorter elements, allowed the official 1890 population count to be tallied between September 1890 and December 12, 1890, instead of the budgeted two years if tabulating were done manually. The total cost was five million dollars below the forecast. His later machines mechanized the card feeding process, added numbers, and sorted cards, in addition to merely counting data. In 1896, Hollerith founded the Tabulating Machine Company.

The U.S. Census Bureau again used Hollerith's system for the 1900 census, but because Hollerith had a monopoly on tabulating machines, he set the price at a rather steep level. To counter this, for the 1910 census, the Census Bureau developed its own, more advanced tabulating machines, although it was hard to get around Hollerith's patents. But James Powers, the engineer who developed the new machine, was allowed to obtain patent rights in his own name.

Powers then left the Census Bureau to start his own company, the Powers Tabulating Machine Company, which rivaled Hollerith's Tabulating Machine Company. After a merger in 1911 with another company, Hollerith's company became the Computer Tabulating Recording Company, for which Hollerith acted as a consultant until he retired in 1921. In 1924, Arthur Watson, president of Computer Tabulating Recording Company, changed the company's name to International Business Machines Corporation (IBM). Herman Hollerith died in 1929.

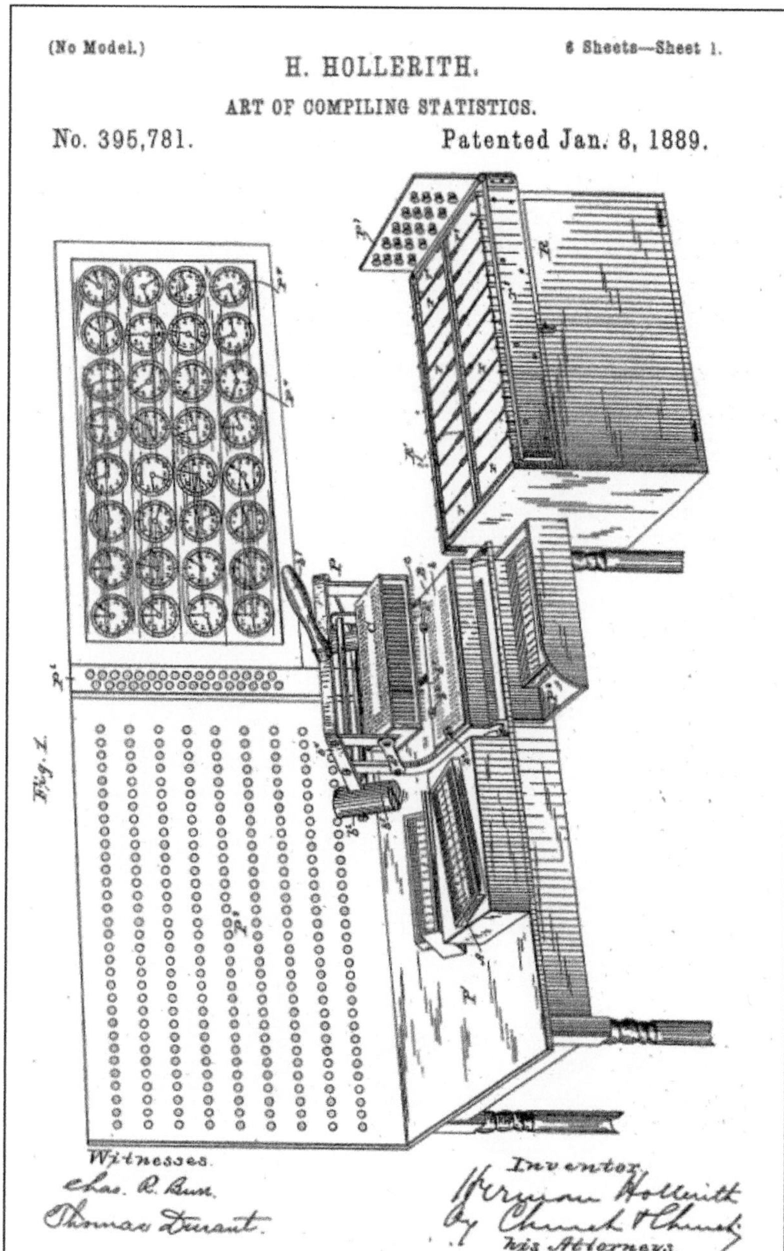
(No Model.)
6 Sheets—Sheet 1.
H. HOLLERITH.
ART OF COMPILING STATISTICS.
No. 395,781.
Patented Jan. 8, 1889.
Fig. 1.
Witnesses.
Inventor.
his Attorneys.

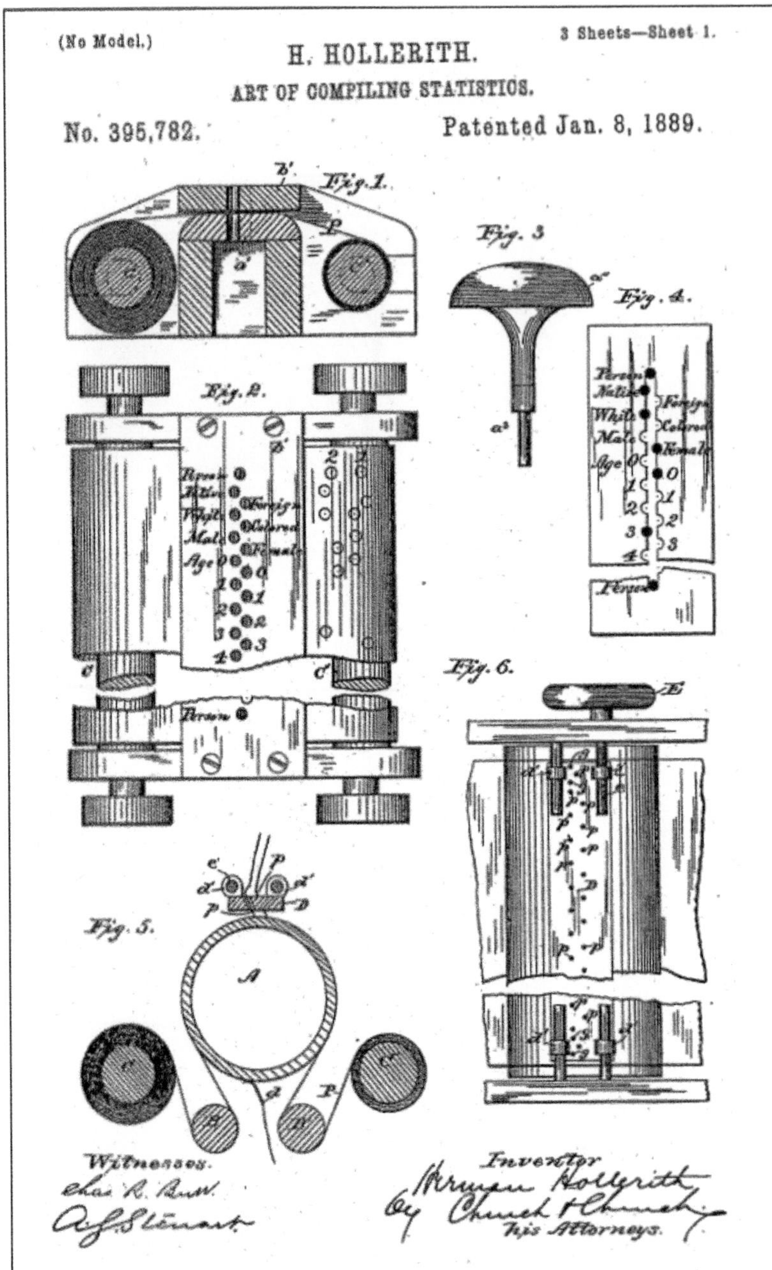
(No Model.)
3 Sheets—Sheet 1.
H. HOLLERITH.
ART OF COMPILING STATISTICS.
No. 395,782.
Patented Jan. 8, 1889.
Fig. 1.
Fig. 2.
Fig. 3
Fig. 4.
Fig. 5.
Fig. 6.
Witnesses.
Inventor
his Attorneys.

14* Biotechnology Inventions

14.1 INTRODUCTION TO BIOTECHNOLOGY

Biotechnology is a broad field that encompasses a range of different scientific processes. At its most basic, biotechnology is any process or technique that involves the use of living organisms or cell processes to make useful products. In fact, the UN Convention on Biological Diversity provides a relatively straightforward definition of biotechnology: "any technical application that uses biological systems, living organisms, or derivatives thereof, to make or modify products or processes for specific use." This definition encompasses ancient and well-known processes, including the use of yeast to make beer (developed by the ancient Sumerians and Babylonians around 6000 BCE) and thousands of years of agriculture and animal breeding.

Over time, the definition of biotechnology has evolved, as advancements were made in various fields, including drug development, human and animal nutrition, agricultural improvements, and environmental protection. Modern biotechnology usually relates to the genetic engineering technology developed in part by Stanley Cohen and Herbert Boyer in their Stanford University lab in 1973. From Cohen and Boyer's first experiments demonstrating the cloning of DNA, similar genetic engineering techniques have been developed that allow scientists to create engineered biological molecules, design genetically specific microorganisms and cells, and find new genes and figure out how they work.

As part of this biotechnical revolution, commercial applications for biotechnology exploded. Today, biotechnology can be separated into three main market segments: medical, agricultural, and chemical. The medical industry uses biotechnology to help research genes and proteins associated with a specific disease that can be used as drug targets or diagnostic markers. Then, chemical or biological compounds are screened to find potential drugs that affect the target. All told—with more than 250 biotechnology

---

* The information in this chapter was prepared by Krista L. Vink Venegas, a partner of the Morgan Lewis law firm, krista.venegas@morganlewis.com.

Intellectual Property Law for Engineers, Scientists, and Entrepreneurs, Second Edition. Howard B. Rockman.

Published 2020 by John Wiley & Sons, Inc.

health care products and vaccines currently available to patients—medical biotech has revenues exceeding U.S. $150 billion annually.

Agricultural biotechnology involves the use of genetic engineering to improve crop insect and herbicide resistance and facilitate the use of environmentally sustainable farming practices. More than 18 million farmers in 28 countries around the world now use agricultural biotechnology to improve crop yields. And while genetically modified organisms (GMOs) continue to generate controversy, the International Service for the Acquisition of Agri-biotech Applications reported that 179.7 million hectares of GMO crops were planted in 2015.

Biotechnology is applied to the production of chemicals—using fermentation and biocatalysts to discover newer and greener processes for making organic chemicals and fuels. The U.S. Office of Energy Efficiency & Renewable Energy reports that approximately 30 integrated biorefineries are completed or currently under construction in the United States. These biorefineries use diverse biomass feedstocks to produce biofuels and chemicals from renewable materials, which can help reduce greenhouse gas emissions.

With the increased development of biotechnological devices and procedures, inventors have increasingly sought patent protection for their research. Due to biotech's integration with living organisms, obtaining patent protection for biotech applications involves some specific issues that are not often seen in other technologies. This chapter will explore some of the specific pitfalls and strategies that arise when seeking patent protection for biotechnological inventions.

14.2 HISTORY OF BIOTECHNOLOGY PATENT PROTECTION

Biotechnology, by definition, uses living organisms to make useful products and processes. Due to its connection with already existing organisms, courts have historically struggled to find a balance between rewarding inventors and researchers for their biotechnological developments while also realizing that a biological material that is a product of nature cannot be patented.

The legal debate surrounding the prohibition against patenting a "product of nature" typically starts with the 1911 case *Parke-Davis & Co. v. HK Mulford Co.*, 189 F. 95 (SDNY 1911). The opinion in *Parke-Davis* was written by the famous judge, Learned Hand, and continues to be cited in court cases related to the patentability of a product of nature to this day. At issue in the case was a patent that covered a purified form of adrenaline, owned by Parke-Davis and marketed to the public as "Adrenalin." Back in the early 1900s, adrenaline was processed directly from the adrenal glands of cows and sheep, and sold as an unpurified mixture with the other glandular tissue that could not be separated during manufacturing. Then, a chemist named Jokichi Takamine, working with Parke-Davis, came up with a process for removing and purifying adrenaline from adrenal glands—allowing Parke-Davis to sell only the purified hormone. But was this hormone itself—which was naturally occurring—patentable? According to Learned Hand, yes:

> [E]ven if [Adrenalin] were merely an extracted product without change, there is no rule that such products are not patentable. Takamine was the first to make it available for any use by removing it from the other gland-tissue in which it was found, and, while it is of

> course possible logically to call this a purification of the principle, it became for every practical purpose a new thing commercially and therapeutically. That was a good ground for a patent.

This passage set forth the original grounds of what made a "product of nature" patentable. As long as a product of nature has been isolated or purified into a form which is *not* found in nature, it could be appropriate grounds for a patent. This concept of isolation and purification would continue to develop over the years.

The next key development in the patentability of biotechnological inventions is the 1948 U.S. Supreme Court case *Funk Brothers Seed Co. v. Kalo Inoculant Co.*, 333 U.S. 127 (1948). The technology behind this case is related to farming and crop rotation—key areas in biotechnology. Crop rotation often involves planting legumes (kidney beans, chickpeas, alfalfa, clover, etc.), because legumes have the ability to turn nitrogen from the atmosphere into ammonia or other molecules which are useful to other crops. In order to convert nitrogen, the legume roots must be exposed to certain strains of bacteria. So farmers would often purchase bundles of these bacteria to spread among their crops. However, these strains of bacteria are plant specific, and often negatively interact with one another—so each crop required purchasing a separate individual bundle of bacteria.

Kalo came along and discovered that by mixing only certain strains of bacteria, it could find a group of bacteria that covered multiple crops and did not negatively interact. It then patented and sold a combination of six strains of bacteria. Unfortunately for Kalo, the Supreme Court ruled that its combination of bacteria was not patentable:

> Discovery of the fact that certain strains of each species of these bacteria can be mixed without harmful effect to the properties of either is a discovery of their qualities of noninhibition. It is no more than the discovery of some of the handiwork of nature, and hence is not patentable. The aggregation of select strains of the several species into one product is an application of that newly discovered natural principle. But however ingenious the discovery of that natural principle may have been, the application of it is hardly more than an advance in the packaging of the inoculants. Each of the species of root nodule bacteria contained in the package infects the same group of leguminous plants which it always infected. No species acquires a different use. The combination of species produces no new bacteria, no change in the six species of bacteria, and no enlargement of the range of their utility. Each species has the same effect it always had.

The Supreme Court premised its rejection of the Kalo patent on the idea that a law of nature, just like a product of nature, was simply not patentable by itself:

> The qualities of these bacteria, like the heat of the sun, electricity, or the qualities of metals, are part of the storehouse of knowledge of all men. They are manifestations of laws of nature, free to all men and reserved exclusively to none. He who discovers a hitherto unknown phenomenon of nature has no claim to a monopoly of it which the law recognizes. If there is to be invention from such a discovery, it must come from the application of the law of nature to a new and useful end.

Thus, *Funk Brothers* added an important aspect to the patentability of biotechnology research—a patent cannot claim only a simple application of a law of nature.

Against this historical backdrop, the Supreme Court made a critical ruling in 1980 that allowed biotechnological patenting to explode. With the 1930 Plant Protection Act and the 1970 Plant Variety Protection Act, Congress first extended patent protection to living organisms. But the USPTO was reluctant to allow patents for living things that were not specifically approved under the Congressional Acts. Thus, before 1980, the USPTO generally understood 35 U.S.C. Section 101 as prohibiting the patenting of living things. Enter genetic engineer Ananda Mohan Chakrabarty—who created a genetically modified bacterium that could break down multiple components of crude oil. Chakrabarty inserted multiple plasmids (small circular DNA molecules) that could each break down different components of crude oil into a single bacterium. Chakrabarty and his employer, General Electric, proposed that this bacterium could be used to treat oil spills. Chakrabarty filed for patent protection related to both the process for creating the bacteria and, more importantly, the engineered bacteria itself. But, the USPTO rejected these claims based on the fact that the bacterium was a living organism that could be found in nature.

The dispute went all the way to the Supreme Court. In *Diamond v. Chakrabarty*, 447 U.S. 303 (1980), the Supreme Court ruled once and for all, that living organisms were patentable subject matter under 35 U.S.C. § 101—relying on the terms "manufacture" and "composition of matter" found in the statute:

> In choosing such expansive terms as "manufacture" and "composition of matter" modified by the comprehensive "any", Congress plainly contemplated that the patent laws would be given wide scope... Judged in this light, respondent's micro-organism plainly qualifies as patentable subject matter. His claim is... to a non-naturally occurring manufacture or composition of matter—a product of human ingenuity.

After the *Chakrabarty* decision, biotechnology patenting exploded, allowing biotech researchers to file for patent protection for their genetically engineered bacteria, plants, and animals. But what is the limit of the *Chakrabarty* decision? Can you really get a patent for "anything under the sun that is made by man" as suggested by the Supreme Court? For a while, the answer was yes, but in recent years, the courts and USPTO have reined in and better defined patent-eligible subject matter in the biotechnology field.

14.3 PATENT-ELIGIBLE SUBJECT MATTER AND BIOTECHNOLOGY

As mentioned above, biotechnology patents frequently run into patent-eligible subject matter issues under Section 101. However, unlike computer programming patents, which are often rejected because they are directed to abstract ideas—biotechnology patents deal more with the prohibition against patenting laws of nature or products of nature. In recent years, the Supreme Court and Federal Circuit have looked more closely at patents related to DNA and diagnostic tools to determine when and to what extent such technologies can be patented.

In 2012, the Supreme Court decided *Mayo v. Prometheus*, 132 S. Ct. 1289 (2012), and ruled that Prometheus' patents were not directed to eligible subject matter. Prometheus sold diagnostic testing kits related to the use of thiopurine drugs to treat autoimmune diseases. While the use of thiopurine drugs was well known, there was often difficulty in determining the correct dosage for these drugs. The Prometheus kits relied on a previously unknown relationship between the level of a metabolite in a patient's system after taking the thiopurine drugs and the effectiveness of the drugs. Prometheus' patents claimed a method for utilizing that relationship, including the steps of giving the drug to the patient, measuring the metabolite, and then altering the dosage to improve the effectiveness based on the level of the metabolite.

The Supreme Court determined that these claims were not eligible for patent protection because they simply identified a previously unknown natural law and used routine and well-known activity to apply the natural law. Thus, *Prometheus* left two relatively straightforward conclusions related to biotechnology patenting: (1) a newly discovered law of nature is not patentable, and (2) the application of the newly discovered law is not patentable if the application relies on elements already known in the scientific community.

The Supreme Court then revisited the issue of patent-eligible subject matter, this time in the context of DNA, in *Association for Molecular Pathology v. Myriad Genetics*, 569 U.S. ___ (June 13, 2013). In the mid-to-late 1990s, Myriad worked with researchers at the University of Utah to isolate and sequence the BRCA1 and BRCA2 genes, which are associated with an increased risk for breast cancer. Myriad then began to sell breast cancer screening kits, which detected certain mutations in the BRCA1 and BRCA2 genes that put women at a high risk for breast cancer.

The Myriad patents were directed to two different types of DNA sequences: (1) isolated DNA sequences, which are identical to the DNA sequences found in a human cell, but separated from the remaining DNA and (2) cDNA sequences, which are synthesized from mRNA found in a cell. Importantly, cDNA is not actually found in a human cell in the same sequence as it is claimed in the Myriad patents—but cDNA in general, is often used to clone genes.

The Supreme Court ruled that "[a] naturally occurring DNA segment is a product of nature and not patent eligible merely because it has been isolated, but cDNA is patent eligible because it is not naturally occurring." This ruling threw a major wrench in biotechnology patent protection. Before *Myriad*, it was the USPTO's general practice to allow claims related to isolated DNA sequences. In fact, about 2000 isolated human genes had been patented in the United States before the case started. The *Myriad* decision puts all of those patents into question.

Since the *Prometheus* and *Myriad* decisions, the Federal Circuit has applied the Supreme Court guidance on patent-eligible subject matter in biotechnology applications on several occasions. These decisions provide some guidance on what biotechnological inventions will be patentable going forward. In *Univ. of Utah Research Found. v. Ambry Genetics Corp.*, 774 F.3d 755 (Fed. Cir. 2014), the Federal Circuit reviewed additional claims on the BRCA genes and found these claims patent ineligible. There were two types of claims: (1) claims directed to DNA primers ("short, synthetic, single-stranded DNA molecule[s] that bind[] specifically to…intended target nucleotide sequence[s]") and (2) claims directed to methods of comparing patient BRCA sequences to wild-type BRCA sequences. Against the *Myriad* framework, the Federal Circuit found that the claimed primers "are not distinguishable from the isolated DNA found patent ineligible in Myriad," and that they "necessarily contain the identical sequence of the BRCA sequence directly opposite to the strand to which they are designed to bind." Thus, because the primers were identical to naturally occurring DNA, they were not patent eligible. In addition, the method claims were ineligible in light of *Prometheus* because they used well-known techniques to compare "the patient's gene with the wild-type [genes] and identify[] any differences that arise."

Then, in *Ariosa Diagnostics, Inc. v. Sequenom, Inc.*, 788 F.3d 1371 (Fed. Cir. 2015), the Federal Circuit again applied *Prometheus* to rule that a diagnostic method for detecting Down Syndrome was not patent eligible. Sequenom's patent took advantage of the fact that fetal DNA is present in the mother's bloodstream along with the mother's own DNA. The patent then described a method to detect that fetal DNA by amplifying only DNA fragments containing paternally inherited DNA—which would necessarily be the fetal DNA and not the mother's DNA. The fetal DNA could then be used to screen and diagnose genetic conditions in the child. The claim itself only had two steps: amplifying and then detecting the paternally inherited DNA from the plasma sample. The Federal Circuit ruled that the claims "are directed to a patent-ineligible concept" because the "method begins and ends with a natural phenomenon" (i.e., the fetal DNA). Since the claimed method used only well-known techniques to detect and amplify the DNA, it did not "'transform' the claimed naturally occurring phenomenon into a patent-eligible application" of the phenomenon.

Finally, in *Genetic Technologies Limited v. Merial LLC*, 818 F. 3d 1369 (Fed. Cir. 2016), the Federal Circuit rejected a claimed method of detecting coding regions of DNA as being patent ineligible. Genetic Technologies owned a patent that capitalized on a newly discovered linkage between noncoding DNA regions (DNA that does not code for proteins) and coding DNA regions (DNA that is eventually expressed into a protein). The patent claimed a method of identifying the coding regions by using the noncoding regions. The Federal Circuit rejected the claims as being directed to a law of nature because the relationship between the regions was a consequence of the "body's natural processes," analogous to the claims in *Prometheus*. The Federal Circuit then ruled that the additional claimed steps of amplifying DNA and analyzing the DNA were well-known techniques and thus were not a patentable application of the natural law.

In light of this precedent, it is clear that biotechnology patents—especially those related to DNA or gene sequences—are much more difficult to obtain. No longer can an inventor or researcher obtain patent protection for simply discovering a new connection between a gene and a specific disease. Instead, patents going forward will need to be more narrowly tailored—directed to a novel technical application related to the gene or to a new method of identifying the gene.

14.4 BIOTECHNOLOGY AND THE WRITTEN DESCRIPTION REQUIREMENT

Another interesting intersection between biotechnology and patent law involves the written description requirement—especially when it comes to biotechnology in the medical industry. As discussed in earlier chapters, a patent specification must convey to those skilled in the art that the inventor was in possession of the claimed invention. This can create a problem in biotechnology research, because initial research—and that disclosed in a patent specification—is usually related to animal research. However, the ultimate claim is directed to either using the technology on humans or on mammals in general. This question is, does describing the animal testing in the specification meet the written description for other species—like humans—or for the entire genus—mammals?

This question was first addressed by the Federal Circuit in *Regents of the University of California v. Eli Lilly Co.*, 119 F.3d 1559 (Fed. Cir. 1997). University of California scientists isolated cDNA from rats that was used to create insulin. Their patent specification included the sequence for the rat cDNA and described methods for isolating cDNA in other species. But the claims themselves were directed to the cDNA coding for insulin in (1) all vertebrates, (2) all mammals, and (3) humans. The Federal Circuit found that there was no adequate written description for these claims in the specification. Since the specification did not identify any other examples of specific insulin cDNA, nor did it describe any common structural features of the cDNA that would be present in other species, one skilled in the art could not visualize or recognize the claimed cDNA of other species. The description of the function of the insulin cDNA alone was not enough to satisfy the written description requirement.

But the Federal Circuit did not stop there. In *Amgen, Inc. v. Hoechst Marion Roussel, Inc.*, 314 F. 3d 1313 (Fed. Cir. 2003), it distinguished its decision in *Regents of the University of California*, and found in favor of the patent owner. Amgen's patents were related to making a non-naturally occurring protein—EPO—for treating patients who lack normal levels of naturally occurring EPO. The process involved transplanting DNA that coded for EPO into other cells to use those cells to make EPO in significant amounts. The patent specification included two examples of using the process to transplant the DNA into one species of vertebrate cells and one species of mammalian cells. The claims, on the other hand, were directed to the entire genus of both vertebrates and mammals—which would both include humans. The Federal Circuit found that the specification provided an adequate written description for the claims because other types of vertebrate and mammalian cells were known in the art and the description of one example in each category allowed one with ordinary skill in the art to "visualize or recognize" the remaining members of each category. The Federal Circuit thought this was different from *Regents of the University of California*, because Amgen was not claiming an unknown and unidentified cDNA sequence—but simply the EPO producing cells, which were better known in the art.

There are a couple of key takeaways from these sets of cases. First, the detail that must be provided in order to satisfy the written description requirement often changes based on the type of technology at issue. The more unpredictable the technology, the more information and examples required for the disclosure of the invention in the specification. This is particularly true for patents that seek to gain broad protection for new discoveries. If your technology is new and not well known, it is necessary to do a significant amount of research and provide a significant number of examples. Second, you can adequately describe a group of compounds or DNA sequences by explaining the function—but only as long as the specification also identifies a correlation between the function and the common structures of the compounds or describes a correlation that is otherwise known by other people in the field. In addition, enough examples must be provided in order for a person in the field to "visualize or recognize" the members of the group of compounds. Thus, for less predictable technologies like biotechnological or pharmaceutical applications, the patent specification should provide a sufficient number of examples. This means more than two—especially when seeking claims that include functional language or are directed to a large genus of compounds.

14.5 BIOTECHNOLOGY AND PATENT EXHAUSTION

The doctrine of patent exhaustion prevents a patent owner from suing someone for patent infringement for using or selling a patented article that the patent owner originally sold. Once you purchase a patented product from a legitimate source, you can then use that product however you want—including reselling it to someone else. However, patent exhaustion does not permit a legitimate purchaser to make copies of the patented article—you can only use the product you purchased, not make new products.

This doctrine has some interesting implications in biotechnology applications. Many biotechnology products involve a living organism that is self-replicating—genetically engineered bacteria, animals, or plants. In fact, the purpose of many of these products is to make copies of itself—for example, when a farmer buys genetically modified seed to plant, he is expecting that the seed will produce many copies of itself by turning into a fully grown crop. This creates a unique situation with the doctrine of patent exhaustion because the farmer's use of the patented article (which is typically protected by the doctrine and not subject to an infringement lawsuit) actually produces new copies of the patented article (which is prohibited under the doctrine, and amounts to patent infringement). So how have the courts and agriculture companies navigated this issue? The Supreme Court answered that question in *Bowman v. Monsanto Co.*, 569 U.S. 278 (2013).

Monsanto—a multinational agricultural biotechnology company and leading producer of genetically engineered seed—developed and patented engineered soybeans that were resistant to some herbicides. These seeds allowed farmers to spray herbicides over the entire crop—killing the weeds but keeping the crop alive. Typically, Monsanto sells seeds to farmers with an express license allowing farmers to plant and grow those seeds, but preventing them from saving seeds from the resulting crop. In *Bowman v. Monsanto*, Bowman grew multiple generations of Monsanto seeds without a license to do so. The Supreme Court found that these activities constituted patent infringement, and that by planting and harvesting additional crops from Monsanto seeds without a license to do so, Bowman had impermissibly made copies of the patented product. This ruling solidified patent protection for genetically engineered seeds. If the Supreme Court had found that the doctrine of patent exhaustion applied to allow purchasers to make and grow additional generations of seeds from a legitimately purchased group of seeds, patents on genetically engineered seeds would be almost worthless.

However, as a result of the *Bowman v. Monsanto* ruling, some farmers became concerned that they would be sued by Monsanto for unknowingly growing genetically engineered crops. For example, what would happen if seeds from a neighboring field of genetically engineered soybeans blew over into a field of non-Monsanto soybeans? Would those farmers—who had purposefully planted non-Monsanto seeds—be liable for patent infringement because they had accidentally grown patented Monsanto crops? In *Organic Seed Growers & Trade Assoc. v. Monsanto Co.*, 718 F. 3d 1350 (Fed. Cir. 2013), a coalition of organic farmers, seed distributors, and anti-GMO organizations sued Monsanto in an attempt to invalidate several seed patents. Now, in order for this case to go to court, the organic farmers had to demonstrate a substantial risk that Monsanto might sue the farmers for patent infringement in the future. The farmers argued that this risk was present because their fields had been accidentally contaminated with Monsanto seeds, opening the farmers up to lawsuits. To counter this, Monsanto pointed to a statement on its website where it had promised not to bring an infringement lawsuit against farmers who only grew Monsanto crops because of accidental contamination. In light of this statement, the Federal Circuit found that there was no risk of future patent litigation by Monsanto, and dismissed the case.

Unfortunately, this does not answer the underlying infringement question. Could another company who makes and patents genetically engineered seeds—one who has not made a similar promise—sue for accidental contamination? The answer is probably yes. Remember, patent infringement does not require intent—if you make a product that infringes a patent you are liable for infringement, even if you don't even know that the patent exists. This sheds some light on why the issue of patent exhaustion for self-replicating products is of critical importance. Typically, when someone makes a physical product—a machine part, for example—there is significant effort involved in obtaining and shaping the metal or plastic pieces. With a self-replicating product like a crop, you can make a patented product without really doing anything. Genetically engineered seed could blow onto your land and grow—potentially making you liable for patent infringement. Of course, it would not make much financial sense to sue someone for accidentally growing a genetically engineered crop. But it could be done.

14.6 BIOTECHNOLOGY AND GOVERNMENT REGULATION

Many of the inventions in biotechnology are related to health care and treatment—including pharmaceutical drug products, biologic drug products, and medical devices. However, each of these industries is regulated by the U.S. government and typically requires government approval before a product can be launched and marketed in the United States. These regulations and the government approval process are intertwined with biotechnology patents.

The Hatch-Waxman Act, formally known as the Drug Price Competition and Patent Term Restoration Act of 1984, provides the legislative backdrop for approval of small molecule drugs. The Hatch-Waxman Act improved the approval process for pharmaceutical products in four main ways. First, it provided a faster approval process for generic drugs. Instead of requiring generics to perform the same clinical testing showing that the generic was safe and effective in large patient populations, a generic drug can be approved if it is shown to be "bioequivalent" to an already approved branded drug—meaning that it performs the same way as the already approved drug in a patient's body. This approval process cut down the number of clinical studies necessary for generic drugs.

Second, the Hatch-Waxman Act provides for time periods of exclusivity—when a new generic cannot enter the market—after a product is approved. Some of this exclusivity is completely separate from patents. For example, when a new active ingredient is approved as a drug for the first time, or when new clinical studies are performed in a new patient population, a generic product cannot be approved for the new active ingredient or new patient population for a certain number of years. In addition, owners of brand-name-approved drugs identify the patents that cover their drugs to the FDA—which publishes the list and makes it available to the public in what is called the "Orange Book."

Third, the Hatch-Waxman Act allows for extensions of a patent's expiration date. Often, approval for brand name drugs takes a number of years—but patents covering those drugs are usually applied for and granted before the approval process starts. So during the lengthy approval process—before the patented drug can be sold—the patent is getting closer and closer to expiring. The Hatch-Waxman Act helps solve this issue by allowing for an extension of a patent's expiration date due to delays in FDA approval.

Finally, and most importantly, the Hatch-Waxman Act set forth a process for suing a generic manufacturer for patent infringement. Any time a manufacturer seeks generic approval, it must evaluate the patents listed in the "Orange Book" for the brand name drug. If the generic manufacturer wants to launch before expiration of the listed patents, it must certify to the FDA that either the patents are invalid or that its generic product would not infringe the patents. The manufacturer must also send detailed grounds for its invalidity or non-infringement positions to the owner of the brand name drug and the patent owner. The Hatch-Waxman Act made such certification an artificial act of patent infringement—meaning that as soon as it receives the detailed grounds for invalidity or non-infringement, the patent owner can sue the generic manufacturer for infringement of the Orange Book-listed patents. Such a lawsuit delays approval of the generic for at least two-and-a-half years. This allows the patent landscape to be settled before a product is launched.

Partly due to the success of the Hatch-Waxman Act, Congress enacted the Biologics Price Competition and Innovation Act of 2009 (BPCIA) to regulate approval of biological drugs (biologics)—or drugs that are isolated from living organisms. These biologics are often created using biotechnological methods utilizing the cutting edge of genetic engineering research. The BPCIA performed many of the same functions as the Hatch-Waxman Act—introducing an approval process for generic biologics (or biosimilars), providing non-patent exclusivity for approved biologics, forming a mechanism for patent term extensions for approval delays, and creating a patent litigation process for brand name biologic and biosimilar manufacturers to resolve patent disputes. The BPCIA is still in its infancy, and courts are still determining how the language of the BPCIA should be interpreted. For example, to kick off the litigation process in the BPCIA, the biosimilar manufacturer provides manufacturing information to the brand name biologic owner—allowing the owner to identify patents that may cover the biosimilar manufacturing process. But in *Sandoz Inc. v. Amgen Inc.*, 582 U.S. ___, 137 S. Ct. 1664 (2017) the Supreme Court ruled that the biosimilar manufacturer is not actually required to provide the manufacturing information—allowing them to skip out on the pre-launch BPCIA litigation process altogether. In the coming years, as more biosimilar applications are filed and courts make further rulings regarding the scope of the BPCIA, we can expect further developments in this area.

Finally, the FDA has a separate approval process for medical devices. Unlike generic small molecule drugs and biosimilars, there is no expedited approval for generic medical devices—and no statutory scheme for patent litigation. However, patent term extensions are also available due to delays in the approval process for medical devices—allowing patent owners to regain some lost periods of potential exclusivity.

14.7 PHARMACEUTICAL PATENT STRATEGIES

The frequent interplay between biotechnology patents and pharmaceutical inventions also merits an exploration of the types of strategies pharmaceutical companies frequently use to protect their inventions by taking advantage of nuances in patent law.

The first type of patent—and the type that is most favored by pharmaceutical companies—is a patent that covers the active ingredient itself. These product claims to a chemical formula provide broad protection and are difficult to design around or invalidate. However, new pharmaceutical products are often based on old chemicals that are already well known but were too expensive to manufacture or impossible to keep stable. These types of products can often be protected by patents covering the process for making a stable version of the compound. Process patents can have method claims that cover the steps of the process itself, or claims can instead be directed to intermediates used in the manufacture of the product. These claims are relatively strong, but a competitor can design around the claims by devising a new process to produce the same active ingredient.

Another option for patent protection is to direct claims to ancillary parts of the drug—typically by including the inactive ingredients in the claim. A patent claim that includes a composition of the active ingredient along with other inactive ingredients is called a formulation patent. These types of patents often describe the different ratios of ingredients. Thus, they can be designed around by using a different ratio or composition without changing the active ingredient.

Finally, pharmaceutical companies often identify new ways to deliver an old drug or find that old drugs can be used to treat new diseases. In those cases, the old drugs are typically protected with method of treatment claims. These types of claims can be written to claim a method of treating a new disease using an already known drug. Or alternatively, the patent can claim a new way of administering the drug. In either case, the protection is limited. Method of treatment claims are hard to enforce unless a competing company is advertising the new use of the drug. If a generic is already on the market for a different disorder, physicians can prescribe it for the new indication even if it is not advertised for that use—and the manufacturer is not liable for infringement. With method of delivery claims, the alternative delivery mechanisms are always available.

Thus, pharmaceutical companies prefer to obtain patents that cover the active ingredient of a drug whenever possible. This is due not only to the difficulty in designing around such claims, but also because it is very difficult to prove that a chemical compound is obvious. With formulation patents, obviousness is a much more straightforward approach: (1) what formulations that include the active ingredient are already known in the art, and (2) would it be obvious to replace the inactive ingredients in the known formulation with those in the patented formulation? But how do you determine whether a molecule is obvious? The key determination is identifying the molecule that can serve as the starting point—the lead compound as it is known in the art. Courts have taken two different approaches to identifying a lead compound. Historically, the Federal Circuit outlined the requirements for a lead compound in *In re Dillon*, 919 F.2d 688, 692 (Fed. Cir. 1990). Under the *Dillon* approach, a prior art compound qualified as a starting point if it was structurally similar to the claimed compound and had *any* utility—even if the utility was unrelated to the utility of the claimed compound.

This approach has now taken a back seat to the Lead Compound Analysis (LCA) first described in *Yamanouchi Pharm. Co., Ltd. v. Danbury Pharmacal, Inc.*, 231 F.3d 1339 (Fed. Cir. 2000). Under the LCA, a prior art compound must have sufficiently attractive properties to motivate a chemist to select that compound out of the prior art. There is no longer any presumption that any structurally similar compound with useful properties is a valid starting point. After identification of the lead compound, the patent is only invalid if the prior art described reasons to modify the lead compound, and the necessary modifications could be made by routine and predictable steps. The LCA is a much more difficult method of proving obviousness—reinforced by the fact that the Federal Circuit has only once found a compound invalid using LCA: *Bristol-Myers Squibb Co. v. Teva Pharm. USA, Inc.*, 752 F.3d 967 (Fed. Cir. 2014).

Due to the strength of compound patents, they are clearly favored by pharmaceutical companies. However, pharmaceutical companies take advantage of other types of patents as well, often using a controversial technique referred to as "evergreening." Evergreening is a technique in which patent owners try to extend the life of their brand name drugs by making modifications to the formulation, dosing strength, delivery mechanism, or other aspect of a brand name drug—thus releasing a slightly changed "new version" of the drug. While doctors are still quite able to prescribe the generic version of the older product, the brand name companies put an incredible amount of money into marketing the newer version. This newer version is protected by newly issued patents, and the marketing efforts are designed to encourage doctors and patients to purchase the new brand name version rather than the older generic version. By using evergreening, brand name manufacturers can obtain patent protection for the same family of drugs for much longer than the 20 years originally provided by a patent.

14.8 MEDICAL PROCEDURES

The "Trade-Related Aspects of Intellectual Property" (TRIPS), part of the GATT Agreement, was ratified by the United States several years ago. This is the treaty that established the World Trade Organization (WTO). Article 27(3)(a) of TRIPS allows member nations to exclude from patentable subject matter "diagnostic, therapeutic and surgical methods for the treatment of humans or animals." The TRIPS Agreement does not compel a member nation to enact such legislation; however, the European Patent Office does forbid patents to be granted on such diagnostic, therapeutic, and surgical methods, on the grounds that exclusive rights should not prevent patients from having access to the finest medical treatment available. For the same reasons, for many years, the patenting of pharmaceutical products in many countries was forbidden. Today, the TRIPS Agreement allows countries to issue patents on pharmaceutical products.

In 1996, the United States Congress enacted legislation that, while allowing the granting of patents covering medical procedures and techniques, severely limited the remedies an inventor or owner of such patents could recover for infringement. In January 1992, a Dr. Pallin obtained U.S. Patent No. 5,080,111, entitled "Method of Making Self-Sealing Episcleral Incision," directed to a method of making incisions during surgery on the eye. An infringement suit was filed, *Pallin v. Singer,* 36 U.S.P.Q.

2d 1050 (D. Vt 1995), where the District Court denied summary judgment without deciding whether or not the surgical method was patentable or not. The lawsuit was terminated when each party agreed to the patent's invalidity based upon prior art. The litigation, however, was the subject of much controversy in the medical profession, primarily because it raised awareness of the fact that the USPTO had a practice of granting patents on surgical procedures.

As a result, Section 287(c) was added to the U.S. Patent Act in 1996, the primary provision which states:

> "(c)(1) With respect to a medical practitioner's performance of a medical activity that constitutes an infringement under Section 271(a) or (b) of this title, the provisions of Sections 281, 283, 284 and 285 of this title shall not apply against the medical practitioner or against a related healthcare entity with respect to such medical activity."

The statute defines "medical activity" as "the performance of a medical or surgical procedure on a body." The statute also expressly states that the use of patented machines, compositions of matter, the practice of a patented use of a composition of matter, and the practice of a patented biotechnology process do not comprise "medical activity." The exemption for processes covered under a "biotechnology patent" was inserted into the legislation at the behest of the biotechnology industry. However, the term "biotechnology patent" is not defined in the statute.

The effect of the statute is that the performance of a surgical procedure may still constitute an infringement of a patent. However, the medical professionals, and the organizations for which they work, are not liable for monetary damages or attorney's fees, and no injunctive relief may be obtained by a patent owner against the use of the method by a medical professional or a related healthcare entity. The statute defines "related healthcare entities" as clinics, HMOs, hospitals, and any entity "with which a medical practitioner has a professional affiliation." Note that the statute does not exempt the patient who receives the procedure. Subparagraph (3) of Section 287(c) sets forth an "anti-research" exemption. Researchers "engaged in the commercial development ... of a machine, manufacture or composition of matter" are not afforded protection under the statute. This may be considered an anomaly, since this provision specifically works against encouraging research and development by failing to protect researchers against patent infringement.

It is interesting to note that this statute only covers "medical practitioners," and not a lay person who offers medical help in an emergency. It is doubtful whether a case will actually arise regarding enforcement of a medical procedure patent against a citizen offering emergency medical help to someone in need. However, these are the kinds of issues that ultimately end up providing fodder for discussion and debate between doctors and attorneys. Therefore, when a patent is sought on a method constituting a medical procedure, you will probably be advised by your patent professional that claims should be directed to the apparatus, machine, or device by which the procedure is carried out, and possibly eliminate claims in the patent application directed to the steps of the medical procedure itself. Note that the European Patent Office does not even allow method claims directed to a surgical procedure to remain in a patent application.

Therefore, it is important that if your medical device and procedure patent application is to be filed in several countries, including Europe, claims be included in the patent application that your patent professional knows will be accepted in those foreign countries.

A short word on pharmaceutical patents. Before the TRIPS Agreement was concluded, a large group of developing nations excluded from their patent laws the ability not only to obtain patents on medical therapies and devices, but also pharmaceutical products. Several major nations did not grant pharmaceutical patents until recently. For example, such patents were authorized in Japan only as of 1976, Switzerland in 1977, and Italy in 1978. Other countries such as Greece, Norway, Portugal, and Spain did not allow the issuance of pharmaceutical patents until 1988. One of the goals of the TRIPS Agreement is to end such exclusions, and to forbid developing and other countries from excluding pharmaceuticals from the realm of patent protection. Article 27 of the TRIPS Agreement requires nations to provide patents for pharmaceuticals, although "developing" countries had until January 2005 to pass legislation to grant such patents, if such patent grants had been previously excluded.

◆ INVENTORS AND INVENTIONS ◆

Rosalind Franklin, James Watson, Francis Crick, and Maurice Wilkins

DISCOVERY OF THE MOLECULAR STRUCTURE OF DNA

The discovery of the molecular structure of deoxyribonucleic acid (DNA), which makes up the chromosomes in every human cell, is a story of intense competition, intrigue, questions of betrayal and duplicity and of professional and scientific ethics, the Nobel Prize for Medicine and Physiology, charges of sexism, and, above all, continued debate after almost 70 years as to who should receive proper credit for the discovery. I will present the facts according to my research, and let you be the judge and jury regarding the propriety of the conduct of the participants in this story.

DNA was originally discovered in 1869, but scientists considered that it only had a small part to play in genetics. At that time, scientists were convinced that proteins, which perform most of the essential tasks in the human body, were probably responsible for passing on hereditary traits. The DNA molecule that was discovered in 1869 seemed too simple a molecule to perform this function.

DNA contains the patterns for constructing proteins in the body, including the various enzymes. For years, scientists tried to uncover the structure of the DNA molecule that led to heredity and to hereditary disease. As is known today, DNA consists of two chains twisted around each other in the form of a double helix of alternating phosphate and sugar groups on the outside of the helix "ladder." The two chains are held together by hydrogen bonds between pairs of organic bases. These bases are adenine (A) with thymine (T), and guanine (G) with cytosine (C). The discovery of the structure of DNA created the science of modern biotechnology, which includes the ability to modify the DNA of host cells that will then produce a desired product, for example, insulin.

In 1950, biologists were still concerned whether protein or DNA held the secret to genetic inheritance. Even after 80 years, most researchers felt that proteins were the answer, and only a few scientists were involved with DNA research. One of these handful of scientists pushing DNA was Linus Pauling of the California Institute of Technology, who preferred constructing Tinkertoy-like models of molecules, and rearranging the pieces until they fit together. In approximately 1950, Pauling used this procedure to discover that certain proteins had a corkscrew, or helical, shape. This led

Intellectual Property Law for Engineers, Scientists, and Entrepreneurs, Second Edition. Howard B. Rockman.

Published 2020 by John Wiley & Sons, Inc.

other scientists to speculate that possibly DNA might also be helix shaped. In the fall of 1951, it was known that Pauling was looking for good photographs of DNA to confirm the structure of his DNA molecule. However, Pauling's model yielded a fundamentally flawed three-chained helix with its backbone in the center, as was later determined.

The groundwork that was a precursor leading to an understanding of the DNA molecule structure and its appearance comprised several benchmark events:

1. DNA was already known for its exclusive role as genetic material—the only molecule that stored all of the information required to naturally create a living being.
2. The advances in X-ray crystallography in studying macromolecules.
3. Increasing evidence from geneticists that heredity stemmed from DNA, not protein, in chromosomes.
4. Erwin Chargaff's discovery that DNA includes equal numbers of A and T bases and of G and C bases.
5. Pauling's discovery of the helical shape of some proteins.

Before continuing the story, a brief biography of the four individuals mentioned at the top of this essay is in order. Rosalind Franklin was a British scientist who was born in England in 1920, decided to become a scientist at the age of 15, and enrolled in the Newnham College at Cambridge, England, in 1938, studying chemistry and physics and graduating in 1941. In 1942, in the middle of the war, she took a position at the British Coal Utilization Research Association, making fundamental studies of carbon and graphite microstructures, and earning a doctorate degree based on her studies from Cambridge in 1945.

She spent 1947 to 1950 in Paris at the Laboratoire Central des Services Chimiques de l'Etat, where she became highly regarded as an expert in X-ray diffraction photographic techniques. While in Paris, Rosalind Franklin was introduced to the technique of X-ray crystallography, which was used in studying organic macromolecules. She became a respected authority in industrial physicochemistry. In 1951, Rosalind Franklin returned to England as a biophysics research associate in John Randall's laboratory at King's College, London. Her responsibility there was to upgrade the X-ray crystallographic laboratory at King's College for work on DNA, and to investigate the crystal structure of DNA. Her work was guided by her feelings that science, as was life, was based upon fact, experience, and experiment.

Maurice Wilkins was already working for Randall at King's College London, and it was his idea to study DNA by biophysical and biochemical molecular analysis, which he had already begun to implement when Franklin was appointed to the laboratory by Randall. However, the relationship between Wilkins and Franklin was, unfortunately, very bad, and the two hardly ever talked to each other. This is due to the fact that when Rosalind Franklin was appointed by Randall, it was her understanding that she was to head her own project on DNA research. This occurred while Wilkins was on vacation, and when he returned, it was his understanding that Rosalind Franklin was only a research assistant, and was subject to his authority. As a result, during the entire time they worked "together," they hardly spoke, and did not enjoy the comaraderie, cooperation, and exchange of ideas that is the hallmark of quality scientific research.

Crystallography in 1950 was a new process for studying biological molecules. It involved shining X-rays on a molecule, and as the beams ricocheted off the atoms, the result was captured on film. This was found to be an excellent tool to comprehend the structure of complex molecules such as DNA. Using this technique, the location of atoms in any crystal can be mapped by viewing the image of a crystal under an X-ray beam. Many of the photographs were fuzzy and difficult to interpret. However, at King's College Laboratory in London, Wilkins and Franklin were taking the world's finest portraits of DNA.

Notwithstanding the friction with Wilkins, Rosalind Franklin applied her substantial talents to the DNA molecule. After making a complicated analysis, she discovered, and was the first to propose, that the sugar–phosphate pairs of the bases of DNA were on the outside of the molecules. She also photographed the basic helical construction of the DNA molecule. She discovered the B form of DNA, recognized that there were two states of the DNA molecule, and defined the conditions for the transition. Her work was the foundation for the quantitative analysis of diffraction patterns.

Meanwhile, in 1951, James Watson, from Chicago in the United States, arrived at the Cavendish Laboratory in Cambridge, England, with a degree in zoology and a doctorate from the University of Indiana, also in zoology, where he became interested in genetics. At the Cavendish Laboratory, there were several important X-ray crystallographic projects in progress under W. L. Bragg's leadership, including Max Perutz's investigation of hemoglobin. Working under Perutz was Francis Crick, who was a physicist from University College, London. When Watson arrived at the Cavendish Laboratory, he recruited Crick to assist him in working with molecular models. The two rapidly put together several models of DNA using all the information they could obtain at the time.

In November of 1951, Watson was invited by Wilkins to hear Franklin speak in London, and Watson expected that Franklin would show him her DNA photographs, which did not happen. Watson did not take notes at that lecture, but tried to memorize most of Franklin's comments. Franklin, in her comments, stated that DNA was probably a helix with the sugar–phosphate backbone on the outside. Upon returning to Cambridge, Crick and Watson built a model based on Watson's recollection of Franklin's seminar talk. This model consisted of a three-stranded helix with the A, T, G, and C bases poking inward.

Watson and Crick subsequently invited Franklin and Wilkins to observe the model they had constructed. Franklin and Wilkins advised them that the model was wrong, stating that it contained several errors of basic chemistry, a subject which neither Cambridge scientist was familiar with. For example, the three-chain model of DNA was wrong, and the phosphates were likely hydrated and on the outside of the molecule. Following this, Sir Lawrence Bragg, leader of the Cavendish Laboratory, ordered Crick and Watson to forget about DNA, and to work on other projects. Bragg felt that it would not be fair to compete with King's College's scientists who had previously begun working on the DNA molecule.

In May 1952, while keeping up her pace of generating X-ray photos of DNA, Franklin took a photo that she labeled Photograph 51. In December that year, Watson found that Pauling had figured out DNA's structure and would soon publish an article on the structure of the DNA molecule. Watson and Crick obtained an early draft of Pauling's article, and were happy to note that Pauling's DNA model was built of three strands, and was therefore wrong, just as they had been advised by Franklin and Wilkins that their own model was wrong.

On January 28, 1953, Watson went to London again, to hear Franklin present a seminar on the unpublished results of her latest DNA experiments. Wilkins, who at that time was not on speaking terms with Franklin, quietly pulled Watson aside and showed Watson Franklin's unpublished Photograph 51. The disclosure of Photograph 51 to Watson by Wilkins was without the knowledge of Franklin, and Franklin was never told that Wilkins had surreptitiously shown the information to Watson. Watson stated in a later publication that the instant he saw the picture, his mouth fell open and his heart began to race. When he saw Franklin's crisp, high-resolution photograph of DNA, he immediately recognized the black cross of reflections could only arise from a helix structure, and it provided him with several of the vital helical parameters. Watson then asked Wilkins for information on the measurements from the photographs, such as the distance between each corkscrew turn of the helix and the density of the atoms in the pack. Wilkins divulged the details.

On his way back to Cambridge, Watson sketched the DNA molecule with the corkscrew-like helical strands, and a few days later he and Crick secretly started building a new model of the DNA molecule. In an effort to gain more information, Wilkins was invited to lunch by Crick, and during the lunch Wilkins stated that Franklin had prepared a report on her latest measurements of the DNA molecule for the British Medical Research Council, a government agency. Franklin's unpublished report was not confidential nor was it in wide circulation. Crick later obtained a copy of the report from a member of the Council, Max Perutz. Upon seeing Franklin's information, Crick concluded that the DNA molecule was indeed made of two strands—a double helix—and that the strands ran in opposite directions. Commentators have proposed that Watson and Crick were model builders who required the collaboration of the experimentalists Franklin and Wilkins, since only the latter were capable of providing the necessary X-ray evidence of the helical configuration of DNA.

Watson was the one who put the final piece into the puzzle. He pondered the cardboard replicas he and Crick had constructed of the four bases that constitute DNA's alphabet: adenine, thymine, guanine, and cytosine, or A, T, G, and C. He realized that an adenine–thymine (A–T) pair held together by two hydrogen bonds was identical in shape to a guanine–cytosine (G–C) pair. These pairs of bases could then serve as the rungs on the twisting ladder of the DNA molecule. The "complementarity" between A and T and between C and G was the key to replication. In the double helix, a single strand of genetic alphabet, say, CAT, is paired, rung by rung, with its complimentary strand, GTA. Upon the unzipping of the helix, the complimentary strand becomes a template; its G, T, and A bases naturally attract bases that amount to a precise copy of the original strand, CAT. In this way, a new double helix is constructed. On the night of February 28, 1953, Crick walked into the Eagle Pub in Cambridge, England, and announced that "we had found the secret of life." Thus, this date is now recognized as the discovery of the structure of the DNA molecule.

Rosalind Franklin died of ovarian cancer in 1958 at the age of 37. Up to the time she died, she was never advised that Watson had viewed her Photograph 51, shown to him by Wilkins. In 1962, Watson, Crick, and Wilkins were jointly awarded the Nobel Prize in Medicine and Physiology. Rosalind Franklin was not mentioned, because the Nobel Prize is not given posthumously. Crick later stated that in his view, if Franklin had lived, "it would have been impossible to give the prize to

Wilkins and not to her, because she did the key experimental work." Franklin's supporters urge that her involvement in the development work that resulted in Watson, Crick, and Wilkins receiving the Nobel Prize, and in advising Watson and Crick that their earlier three-helix model was wrong, which sent them back to the drawing board, and her notebook entries, all show that she was working toward the solution until Watson saw her Photograph 51 and figured out the rest. Her notebook showed that she had narrowed the DNA molecule structure down to a sort of double helix, but she did not use the type of three-dimensional molecular models that Watson and Crick were building at Cambridge. John Bernal, the eminent physics professor at Birkbeck College, who worked with Rosalind Franklin during the last five years of her life, was quoted in the *London Times* as stating that Rosalind Franklin's ingenious experimental and mathematical techniques of X-ray analysis enabled her to verify the hypothesis of Watson and Crick regarding the double spiral structure of DNA. She positively established that the main sugar–phosphate chain of nucleic acid lay on the outside, and demonstrated that a double helix structure was compatible with the X-ray patterns of both the A and B forms of DNA. She also contributed the technique of preparing X-ray photographs of the two hydrated forms of DNA, and applied Patterson function analysis to demonstrate that the structure was best accounted for by a double spiral of nucleotides, in which the phosphorus atoms lay on the outside.

As stated above, the relationship between Franklin and Wilkins was such that the two scientists rarely spoke to each other, and, therefore, did not share their findings. Meanwhile, Crick and Watson worked famously together, and shared information between them that probably led them to win the race for the discovery of the structure of the DNA molecule. For example, it was Crick who had knowledge of a theoretical hunch of a natural attraction between A and T, and C and G. He then urged that Watson accept the complementarity hypothesis as a possible explanation of "Chargaff's rules," which hold that DNA contains like amounts of adenine and thymine, and of guanine and cytosine. It was later stated by authorities that it was this type of synergy that Rosalind Franklin lacked in her work with Wilkins. Also, working in a largely male scientific field at a time when women were not even allowed in the faculty dining room, Franklin had no one to bond with; she lacked the support of someone like Crick, whose knowledge matched her gaps or whose gaps her knowledge matched.

Crick and Watson wrote up their findings and had them published in the journal *Nature* on April 25, 1953, in an article titled "A Structure for Deoxyribose Nucleic Acid." Wilkins and Franklin also prepared accompanying corroborating articles that were printed simultaneously in *Nature*. Franklin was pleased, not bitter, that her work was used in the discovery of the DNA molecule structure.

Today, it is clear that the DNA molecule appears as a spiral staircase, having a twisted double strand of alternating phosphate and sugar molecules on the outer rails, while hydrogen bonds between pairs of groupings of the four "bases" (A, C, T, and G) form the steps of the staircase and hold the two twisted strands together. It is also clear that the base pairing is critical to the hereditary function of DNA. The discovery by Franklin, Wilkins, Watson, and Crick led future scientists to learn not only how the DNA molecule duplicated itself, but also how it stored information and turned it into a usable form. Many have stated the view that Rosalind Franklin's contribution to the discovery of the structure of the DNA molecule was equal to those who were awarded the Nobel Prize. One historian noted that although Franklin was a bold experimentalist, she was critical of speculation and leaned toward inductive reasoning, which worked to her benefit in her work with coal, but which allowed others to pass her on DNA.

At the request of the Royal Society (London), Franklin prepared an exhibit at the 1958 Brussels World's Fair on the structure of DNA and the structure of small viruses. In 2002, the British Trade and Industry Secretary created a Franklin Medal in honor of Rosalind Franklin, to raise the profile of other women scientists, carrying a £30 000 annual prize awarded by the Royal Society for exceptional innovation by men and women scientists.

◆ INVENTORS AND INVENTIONS ◆

Stanley N. Cohen and Herbert W. Boyer

RECOMBINANT-DNA (rDNA)*

Recombinant-DNA (rDNA) technology, which is the way genetic material from one organism is artificially introduced into the genome of another organism and then replicated and expressed by that other organism, was invented largely through the work of Herbert W. Boyer and Stanley N. Cohen, although many other scientists made important contributions to the new technology as well.

After Paul Berg's 1971 landmark gene-splicing experiment, the next modern biotechnology groundbreaking development was the insertion of rDNA into bacteria such that the foreign DNA would replicate naturally. This step was taken by Herbert W. Boyer at the University of California, San Francisco (UCSF), in collaboration with Stanley N. Cohen of Stanford University.

In 1972, researchers, including Boyer, realized that the enzyme *EcoRI*, which had actually been discovered in Boyer's UCSF lab, cut DNA such that the ends were staggered, not blunt, so that no molecular additions were needed to make one severed piece latch on to another piece possessing complementary cuts. Boyer and a colleague, Robert Helling, began their effort to create rDNA to insert in the bacteria *Escherichia coli* by trying to use *EcoRI* to open up the DNA of the bacterial virus lambda. They became frustrated, however, when the enzyme cut the DNA in five places instead of one, as desired.

November 1972 found both Boyer and Cohen in Hawaii presenting papers at a U.S.-Japan joint meeting on plasmids. A plasmid is DNA, found especially in bacteria, that is physically separate from and can replicate independently of the bacterium's chromosomal DNA. While Boyer's presentation was describing his data showing the nature of the DNA ends generated by *EcoRI* cleavage, Cohen was reporting on a procedure recently discovered in his Stanford laboratory that enabled bacteria to take up plasmid DNA and produce offspring that contained self-replicating plasmids identical to the original implant: clones. Over sandwiches late one night at the conference, the two men laid plans for a collaborative project to discover what genes are present on plasmids and how they are arranged.

The collaboration between Boyer and Cohen was very close. Plasmids isolated at Stanford were transported to Boyer's lab at UCSF for cutting by *EcoRI* and for analysis

* Reprinted with permission: Science History Institute; sciencehistory.org.

Intellectual Property Law for Engineers, Scientists, and Entrepreneurs, Second Edition. Howard B. Rockman.

Published 2020 by John Wiley & Sons, Inc.

of the DNA fragments. These were transported back to Stanford, where they were joined and introduced into *E. coli*, where they multiplied. Then the new recombinant plasmids were isolated and analyzed in each laboratory.

The first success of the Boyer–Cohen collaboration occurred in the spring of 1973 and involved one of Cohen's plasmids, pSC101. Plasmids were already known to transfer drug resistance among bacteria, and this one could make *E. coli* resistant to the antibiotic tetracycline. The plasmid pSC101 was cleaved by *EcoRI* at only one site, leaving intact the plasmid's ability to replicate. When the linearized pSC101 DNA was mixed with other DNA that had been cleaved by the same enzyme, the complementary ends of fragments from both sources of DNA joined together into new loops. Treatment with another enzyme closed the still-visible nicks in the DNA loops, which were then introduced into calcium chloride-treated bacteria. The bacteria were spread on a culture containing tetracycline, and only the bacteria with the rDNA plasmids survived.

Boyer and Cohen soon moved on to more complicated cloning experiments. They joined tetracycline-resistant plasmids with kanamycin-resistant plasmids (kanamycin being another antibiotic) and inserted them in *E. coli*. Next they showed that genetic materials could indeed be transferred between species, thereby disproving a long-held myth. They snipped a piece of *Staphylococcus* plasmid (*Staphylococcus* is the bacteria responsible for staph infections), spliced it with one of the many *E. coli* plasmids, and inserted the whole in *E. coli*. An even greater triumph of interspecies cloning was the insertion into *E. coli* of genes taken from the South African clawed frog.

Commercial ventures quickly started up and are operating today with the objective of capitalizing on Boyer and Cohen's new rDNA technology, despite ongoing controversy over the technology and public fear of cloning.

Reprinted with permission: Science History Institute; sciencehistory.org.

United States Patent [19] [11] **4,237,224**

Cohen et al. [45] **Dec. 2, 1980**

[54] **PROCESS FOR PRODUCING BIOLOGICALLY FUNCTIONAL MOLECULAR CHIMERAS**

[75] Inventors: **Stanley N. Cohen**, Portola Valley; **Herbert W. Boyer**, Mill Valley, both of Calif.

[73] Assignee: **Board of Trustees of the Leland Stanford Jr. University**, Stanford, Calif.

[21] Appl. No.: **1,021**

[22] Filed: **Jan. 4, 1979**

Related U.S. Application Data

[63] Continuation-in-part of Ser. No. 959,288, Nov. 9, 1978, which is a continuation-in-part of Ser. No. 687,430, May 17, 1976, abandoned, which is a continuation-in-part of Ser. No. 520,691, Nov. 4, 1974.

[51] **Int. Cl.**[3] **C12P 21/00**

[52] **U.S. Cl.** .... **435/68**; 435/172; 435/231; 435/183; 435/317; 435/849; 435/820; 435/91; 435/207; 260/112.5 S; 260/27R; 435/212

[58] **Field of Search** .... 195/1, 28 N, 28 R, 112, 195/78, 79; 435/68, 172, 231, 183

[56] **References Cited**

U.S. PATENT DOCUMENTS

3,813,316 5/1974 Chakrabarty .... 195/28 R

OTHER PUBLICATIONS

Morrow et al., Proc. Nat. Acad. Sci. USA, vol. 69, pp. 3365–3369, Nov. 1972.
Morrow et al., Proc. Nat. Acad. Sci. USA, vol. 71, pp. 1743–1747, May 1974.
Hershfield et al., Proc. Nat. Acad. Sci. USA, vol. 71, pp. 3455 et seq. (1974).
Jackson et al., Proc. Nat. Acad. Sci. USA, vol. 69, pp. 2904–2909, Oct. 1972.
Mertz et al., Proc. Nat. Acad. Sci. USA, vol. 69, pp. 3370–3374, Nov. 1972.
Cohen, et al., Proc. Nat. Acad. Sci. USA, vol. 70, pp. 1293–1297, May 1973.
Cohen et al., Proc. Nat. Acad. Sci. USA, vol. 70, pp. 3240–3244, Nov. 1973.
Chang et al., Proc. Nat. Acad. Sci, USA, vol. 71, pp. 1030–1034, Apr. 1974.
Ullrich et al., Science vol. 196, pp. 1313–1319, Jun. 1977.
Singer et al., Science vol. 181, p. 1114 (1973).
Itakura et al., Science vol. 198, pp. 1056–1063 Dec. 1977.
Komaroff et al., Proc. Nat. Acad. Sci. USA, vol. 75, pp. 3727–3731, Aug. 1978.
Chemical and Engineering News, p. 4, May 30, 1977.
Chemical and Engineering News, p. 6, Sep. 11, 1978.

Primary Examiner—Alvin E. Tanenholtz
Attorney, Agent, or Firm—Bertram I. Rowland

[57] **ABSTRACT**

Method and compositions are provided for replication and expression of exogenous genes in microorganisms. Plasmids or virus DNA are cleaved to provide linear DNA having ligatable termini to which is inserted a gene having complementary termini, to provide a biologically functional replicon with a desired phenotypical property. The replicon is inserted into a microorganism cell by transformation. Isolation of the transformants provides cells for replication and expression of the DNA molecules present in the modified plasmid. The method provides a convenient and efficient way to introduce genetic capability into microorganisms for the production of nucleic acids and proteins, such as medically or commercially useful enzymes, which may have direct usefulness, or may find expression in the production of drugs, such as hormones, antibiotics, or the like, fixation of nitrogen, fermentation, utilization of specific feedstocks, or the like.

14 Claims, No Drawings

15 The Patenting of Business Methods

15.1 THE EVOLUTION OF PATENTS FOR METHODS OF DOING BUSINESS

In Chapter 13, we discussed the present state of the law regarding the patent eligibility of computer-related inventions, most of which involve steps carried out, or partially carried out, on a computer. Many of these inventions also fall under the definition of a "business method." Conversely, there are inventions that comprise business methods that are not computer related, such as a financial method that does not use a computer, and these inventions may also be patent eligible. Thus, if you are interested in the patent eligibility of a computer-related invention, Chapter 13 is for you. If your invention is a business method sans the computer, Chapter 15 is where you should be. One caveat: in discussing the patent eligibility of business methods, the information emanating from the U.S. Patent and Trademark Office (USPTO), the courts, and other learned sources often melds business method patent eligibility with computer-related invention patent eligibility. As a result, the information in this chapter overlaps the two disciplines to some degree, and many business method patent concepts are explained in the context of a business method invention carried out using computers.

On January 8, 1889, the era of automated financial/management business data processing method patents was born. U.S. Patents Nos. 395,781, 395,782, and 395,783 were granted to inventor Herman Hollerith. Mr. Hollerith's method and apparatus patents automated the tabulating and compiling of statistical information for businesses and enterprises. The protection afforded by his patents allowed his fledgling Tabulating Machine Company to succeed. In 1924, Thomas J. Watson, Sr. changed the company name to International Business Machine Corporation (IBM). Hollerith's manual punch cards (IBM punch cards) and his methods for processing business data were still being used up until the birth of the personal computer.

Many additional automatic business data processing methods were invented over the ensuing 100 plus years; however, the bulk of that time was spent perfecting the automated business data processing machines upon which the methods were run. Only

Intellectual Property Law for Engineers, Scientists, and Entrepreneurs, Second Edition. Howard B. Rockman.

Published 2020 by John Wiley & Sons, Inc.

recently have data processing systems become sufficiently developed to allow the economy to begin to fully tap the ingenuity and value in the business method itself.

The arrival of electricity as a component in business data processing systems was a major historical watershed event. Electrical-mechanical devices included switches that were ultimately replaced by individual transistors. Individual transistors were ultimately replaced by small-scale integrated circuits, which, in turn, were replaced by large-scale integrated circuits. Each new generation of technology resulted in increased business data processing power and new inventions. However, one key element was not significantly improved by these advances. Each data processing system had to be individually designed at the transistor level and hard-wired to perform the correct business data functions. The replacement of specific-function large-scale integrated circuits by software-controlled microprocessors became the latest evolutionary step that led the economy to the use of business data processing systems and the methods they incorporate throughout industry and business today.

Prior to the 1998 *State Street* decision, the pertinent portion of which is reprinted at the end of this chapter, many court decisions assumed, and held, that methods or processes of doing business did not qualify as patentable subject matter under the patent laws. However, these prior cases also found the method claimed in the patents before the courts at that time unpatentable for other reasons, such as lack of novelty of the claimed process, the claims merely presenting an abstract idea in the form of a mathematical algorithm, or the claims being too broad to be patentable.

Prior to the *State Street* decision, several courts tackled the question of whether borderline "business method" patents should be allowed. In the case of *Paine Webber, Jackson and Curtis, Inc. v. Merrill Lynch, Pierce, Fenner and Smith, Inc.*, 564 F. Supp. 1358 (Del. 1983), the patent claims involved an innovative cash management system developed by Merrill Lynch. The District Court refused to invalidate the claims as constituting a "business method." The Court stated that the patent claims described a highly useful business method that would be unpatentable if done by hand; however, the Court did uphold the patent stating:

> The CCPA, however, has made clear that if no Benson algorithm exists, the product of the computer program is irrelevant, and the focus of analysis should be on the operation of the program on the computer. The Court finds that the '442 patent claims statutory (patentable) subject matter because the claims allegedly teach a method of operation on a computer to effectuate a business activity. Accordingly, the '442 patent passes the threshold requirement of Section 101.

It is apparent that the USPTO and the courts began to recognize that new technology was bringing software and new business methods to the point of having enhanced value in the world economy. Most new business techniques, particularly in the financial industry, were implemented by computer software, and could be characterized as computer-related inventions. Prior to *State Street,* the USPTO was issuing patents on computer-related financial and business inventions, where these patents appear to rely upon their computer dependence for their validity. However, the *State Street* case expanded the trend of the USPTO to the granting of patents on computer software, on computer-related business techniques, and to all business methods, whether computer-related or not.

15.2 THE *STATE STREET* CASE

For years, patent attorneys, the courts, and the USPTO held, counseled, and thought that business methods could not be patented because they were not patentable subject matter. Today, it is clear that novel business methods can be patented if the other requirements of patentability are satisfied. While many business method patents involve software, even novel business methods that do not use software or computers may be patentable.

Adhering to the long tradition of denying patent protection to computer software inventions, the U.S. Supreme Court held in *Gottschalk v. Benson*, 409 U.S. 63 (1972) and *Parker v. Flook,* 4370 U.S. 584 (1978) that software was not patentable subject matter because software was analogous to laws of nature and mathematical formulae, and therefore constituted an abstract idea. However, the U.S. Supreme Court subsequently ruled, in *Diamond v. Diehr*, 450 U.S. 175 (1981) that patentability would not be denied just because the invention utilized computer software.

The patentability of business methods was first established in *State Street Bank & Trust v. Signature Financial Group*, 149 F.3d 1368 (Fed. Cir. 1998) and in *AT&T Corp. v. Excel Communications, Inc*., 172 F.3d 1352 (Fed. Cir. 1999). *The State Street* case involved a computerized accounting system for managing a mutual fund investment structure. In the patented system, a "hub and spoke" arrangement was used, in which separate mutual funds ("the spokes") are pooled in an investment portfolio ("the hub"). The patent described and claimed a computer system for making the necessary daily calculations required to administer this structure.

In the State Street decision, the CAFC cleared the air and firmly held that method or process claims in a patent directed to a method of doing business, whether or not implemented in a computer-related system, were to be treated as any other process claims, and not turned down on the sole grounds of being directed to a business method. Such patent application claims may still be rejected as defining an old and/or obvious method, or as being too broad or too vague, but not for the singular reason that the patent is directed to a business method.

The patent in the *AT&T* case described a process for taking advantage of introducing additional data into a message record of a telephone system to provide appropriate billing for subscribers based on whether the subscriber and the person called subscribed to the same long-distance carrier. The patent claims covered a system that takes data representing discrete dollar amounts through a series of mathematical calculations to determine if a discounted rate should be applied. However, in the Supreme Court case of *Bilski v. Kappos* (see Section 15.3), Justice Breyer mentioned in a concurring opinion that the Court was of the unanimous opinion that the "mathematical formula" claim of the *AT&T* case was *not* patent eligible in view of the *Bilski* decision. The *Alice and Mayo* decisions also support this conclusion. The *Alice* decision is discussed in Chapter 13, and the *Mayo* decision is discussed in Chapter 14. Thus, the *AT&T* case stands for the proposition that business methods may be patentable, but that the specific "mathematical formula" claim in the *AT&T* patent was *not* patent eligible.

The State Street and *AT&T* cases held that patent protection extended to methods of doing business just as well as it extended to other inventions. Soon after these decisions, the USPTO adopted the position that business method inventions were proper subject matter for patents, and abandoned its general opposition to granting patents on software and to business methods, if the other requirements for patentability were also satisfied. Prior to these decisions, the USPTO Manual of Patent Examining Procedure (MPEP) instructed examiners to reject claims in patent applications directed to methods of doing business. Such guidelines, however, were not based on any legal decisions, and thus the CAFC in the *State Street* and *AT&T* cases broke the barrier established by tradition, and decided that methods of doing business were, in certain cases, susceptible to patent protection.

In 1999, a year after the *State Street* decision was decided by the CAFC, the U.S. Patent Act was amended by adding a new Section 273, which provided "prior user rights." Section 273 establishes an absolute defense available to an accused infringer of a "business method" patent if the accused infringer had, acting in good faith, actually reduced the patented subject matter to practice at least one year before the effective filing date of the allegedly infringed patent, and the accused infringer had commercially used the subject matter before the effective filing date of the patent. Note that this defense is limited solely to patent claims directed to "a method of doing or conducting business." The purpose of this statute was to protect individuals or businesses who achieved the relevant invention before the patent owner did, but who did not apply for, or may not have been entitled to, a patent on the invention.

Under Section 273, it would be possible for a person who "invents" the business method after the invention date of the patent holder to successfully assert a defense, if that person had used the invention commercially one year before the effective filing date of the patent. Therefore, if you are contemplating the filing of a business method patent, it would be prudent to file the application at the earliest possible time, before the business method is made public, to prevent a subsequent user of the business method from asserting this defense. Also, under Section 273, courts in the future will be faced with the problem of defining whether a method is a method of "doing business" or whether the patent defines the means or elements of carrying out the method of doing business.

The bottom line is that if you have developed a new method of doing business, it would be prudent to discuss your method with your patent attorney, and let him or her investigate to determine whether the method constitutes patentable subject matter. Based upon the present trend of the law, if properly claimed, your new method may be patentable.

As you can imagine, as the use of e-commerce and software has become more pervasive over the past many years, the number of patent applications filed with the USPTO relating to business methods has vastly increased.

15.3 THE *BILSKI* CASE

In 2010, the Supreme Court decided the case of *Bilski v. Kappos*, 561 U.S. 593 (2010) by holding that a business method claim to be patentable as claiming patentable subject matter under 35 U.S.C. §101 must define a method that defines a "useful, concrete, and tangible result," and accomplishes some practical, real-world application. The *Bilski* case also decided that even though a business method claim was directed to an abstract idea, there were other factors to be considered that may establish the patentability of a business method claim.

In *Bilski*, the claims at issue were directed to a method of managing consumption risk costs of a commodity (hedging), which the members of the Court agreed was an abstract idea and not patentable subject matter. The Court also attempted to lay down guidelines as to how courts, the USPTO, inventors, and their attorneys could determine, in the future, whether claims directed to a business method constituted patentable subject matter under 35 USC §101. For example, method claims that recite the operation of a machine, or a process that transforms an object from one state to another, may comprise patentable subject matter. This test for patentability was applied prior to the *Bilski* case. The Supreme Court decided that the machine or transformation test was still a proper test for patentability, but was not the only test.

15.4 WHAT IS A BUSINESS METHOD INVENTION?

Neither the previous U.S. Patent Law, the AIA, the CAFC, nor the USPTO have set forth a black letter definition of a "business method invention." So today, a multitude of processes relating to "business" may be patentable, provided the criteria of patentable subject matter (not an abstract idea, for example), novelty, non-obviousness, and usefulness are satisfied. Most, but not all, patent applications filed today directed to business methods relate to e-commerce and computer-related automated business methods, and much of the discussion about business method patents relates to subject matter that is computer related in one form or another.

The USPTO has established a class and several sub-classes of business method subject matter for examination purposes in Class 705 (www.uspto.gov/web/patents/classification/USPC705/defs705.htm). The formal definition of subject matter falling in Class 705 is "machines and their corresponding methods for performing data processing or calculation operations, where the machine or method is utilized in the (1) practice, administration, or management of an enterprise, or (2) processing of financial data, or (3) determination of the charge for goods and services."

Under this definition, Class 705 encompasses subject matter in more than 20 financial and management data processing areas, such as:

Insurance
Stock/Bond Trading
Healthcare Management

Reservation Systems
Computerized Postage Meter Systems

Electronic Shopping
Business Cryptography
Operations Research/Market Analysis

Incentive/Rewards Programs
Credit and Loan Processing
Billing/Banking/Funds Transfer
Tax Processing
Investment/Financial Planning
Accounting
Inventory Management

15.5 THE USPTO GUIDELINES

Following the *Bilski* decision, the USPTO established guidelines its examiners are to apply in conducting an analysis of patentable subject matter regarding business method claims. The factors set forth by the USPTO to be considered in determining whether a method claim comprises an abstract idea, for example, are:

a. Whether the method involves or is executed by a particular machine or apparatus. If so, the claims are less likely to be drawn to a non-patent eligible abstract idea. If not, they are more likely to be drawn to an abstract idea.

   When a machine or apparatus is recited or inherent in a method claim, the following factors are also relevant:

   1. The particularity or generality of the elements or parts of the machine recited in the claim. For example, the degree to which the machine in the claim can be specifically identified.
   2. Whether the machine implements the steps of the method. Integral use of the machine or apparatus to achieve performance of the method weighs toward eligibility, compared to where the machine or apparatus is merely an object on which the method operates, which weighs against eligibility.
   3. Whether the involvement of the machine or apparatus is extra-solution activity or a field of use. For example, the extent to which or how the machine or apparatus imposes meaningful limits on the execution of the claimed method steps is a factor. A machine that contributes only nominally or insignificantly to the execution of the claimed method, for example, a data-gathering step or a field-of-use limitation, leads toward non-eligibility.

b. Whether performance of the claimed method results in or involves a transformation of a particular article. If such a transformation exists, then the claims are less likely to be drawn to an abstract idea.

c. Whether performance of the claimed method involves an application of a law of nature even in the absence of a particular machine, apparatus, or transformation. If such application exists, the claims are less likely to be drawn to an abstract idea.

d. Whether a general concept such as a principle, theory, plan, or scheme is involved in executing the steps of the method. The presence of a general concept can be a clue that the claim is drawn to an abstract idea. Where a general concept is present, the following factors are relevant:

   1. The extent to which use of the concept would preempt its use in other fields. In other words, would the claim effectively grant a monopoly over the concept itself, which cannot be awarded a patent?
   2. The extent to which the claim is so abstract and sweeping as to cover both known and unknown uses of the concept, and could be performed through any existing or future machinery or device, or even without any apparatus.
   3. The extent to which the claim would effectively cover all possible solutions to a particular problem, for example, that the claim is a statement of the problem versus a description of the particular solution to the problem.

4. Whether the concept is disembodied or whether it is instantiated, that is, implemented in some tangible way.
5. The mechanisms by which the steps are implemented, such that performance of the process is observable and verifiable, rather than subjective or imperceptible. Steps that are observable and verifiable weigh in favor of eligibility.
6. Examples of non-eligible general concepts include basic economic practices and theories, basic legal theories, mathematical concepts, mental activity, interpersonal interactions or relationships, teaching concepts, human behavior, and instructing how business should be conducted.

In making a determination of patent eligibility, it should first be determined whether the claim as a whole is drawn to an abstract idea such that the claim would effectively grant exclusive rights over the whole abstract idea. If the factors indicate that the method claim does not merely cover an abstract idea, it is eligible for patentability as long as all of the other statutory requirements such as novelty, usefulness, and non-obviousness are met. If the claim is directed toward a practical application of an abstract idea, this leads toward holding the patent claim eligible. However, the claim must be more than a mere statement of a concept and describe a particular solution to a problem to be solved. The claim must also implement the concept in some tangible way, and the performance of the steps must be observable and verifiable.

With business method inventions, one patentability question involves a determination of how technology is used to facilitate processing the claimed steps. Where the business method is claimed in association with software, it is apparent that it is important to thoroughly describe the system and processes from a technological level. As was explained in the case of *DDR Holdings v. Hotels.com L.P.*, 773 F.3d 1245 (Fed. Cir. 2014), for software patent claims to be patent eligible, they must not "merely recite the performance of some business practice known from the pre-Internet world along with the requirement to perform it on the Internet." To be patent eligible, claims for software must be rooted in computer technology in order to overcome a problem specifically arising in the realm of computer networks. This analogy is extremely relevant to business methods because a naked business method is no longer patent eligible. To be patentable, a computer-related business method must be tied to a particular computer technology in a meaningful and substantial way in the performance of the process by the computer.

The business method to be patentable really needs to be performed by and through a concrete and tangible system, where the system and processes are fully described. To be patentable, the business method claim must define the method in a concrete and tangible manner so that your written description in the specification of the patent satisfactorily conveys the description of a real invention, and not merely a concept or abstract idea. It is important that the description of the business method be as complete as possible in the specification of the patent application that you first filed, which could be a provisional or non-provisional application. This is true particularly to properly provide priority, because a provisional or a non-provisional patent application must completely articulate the invention with enough detail to satisfy the requirements of 35 U.S.C. §112, which dictates that the invention must be described in full, clear, concise, and exact terms. In other words, the requirements for defining the invention in the specification of a provisional patent application are no different from those required for describing an invention in a regular non-provisional patent application.

15.6 RECOMMENDATIONS

The following recommendations are made to adequately identify a business method invention that is linked to some kind of computer implementation:

1. The business method should be described in the specification in a way that *clearly identifies* the practical and real-world values of the business method. Describe the result the business method accomplishes, and *how* it accomplishes the tasks leading to that result. This is usually accomplished by the use of flowcharts that depict the steps associated with the overall business method. The system should be described from the user perspective, from the perspective of the central computer, *and* also by identifying the business method from all possible viewpoints in addition to those mentioned.
2. The patent claims should also identify what the central computer does when it performs the process required by the business method. This could be encompassed in the detailed description of the functionality of the central computer. This description should be complete and with as much technical information as possible, including setting forth how the central computer is to be configured to provide the required functionality.
3. It is also recommended that an overview be provided of the system used to implement the business method. This requires a description of the relationship of the central computer tò other subject matter outside the computer, which together represent the system for carrying out the business method. In other words, explain how the central computer is to be integrated with other elements that are part of the invention, and further explain how these other elements work to facilitate the business method.
4. If you are describing specialized software in the claim, provide a description of the best way to carry out the invention using the software by disclosure of the functions of the software. This can be accomplished by using flowcharts. Flowcharts are usually fundamental to conveying the function of software. If flowcharts are used, it may also be satisfactory to disclose the algorithms, but being careful not to disclose trade secrets.
5. Disclosure of the software code is not necessary because one skilled in the art could generate a different, but necessary, software code to implement the disclosed function from a properly described flow diagram. However, where trade secrets are not involved, the disclosure of some of the code may be a good idea particularly when filing a provisional application. The code provides an effective way to convey aspects relating to the core functionality of the computer operated method. When a computer programmer reads code, the code conveys the pinpoint accuracy of the requirements and any number of alternatives that could be employed to achieve the same functionality.

It is recommended to those of you who are thinking about or filing patent applications relating to computer-related and other business method inventions that you present the above material to your patent attorney during the preparation of the patent application.

For additional information regarding the above discussion on business method patents, particularly those relating to computer-enhanced inventions, I suggest reading an article by Gene Quinn, dated August 29, 2015 appearing in IP Watchdog, which can be found at www.ipwatchdog.com/2015/08/29/patenting-business-methods-and-software/id=54576. In addition, there are many other relevant aspects and suggestions promulgated by the USPTO on preparing and filing patentable business method claims that can be researched by you and your patent attorney when considering filing a patent application relating to the subject matter of business method claims.

15.7 UNDERSTANDING A SAMPLE BUSINESS METHOD PATENT CLAIM

Perhaps the best way to understand the invention in the *State Street Bank* case is to look at Claim 1 of the patent, reproduced below. The patent claim used "means plus function" language, where the term "means" covers the corresponding structure disclosed in the specification and equivalents of that structure. To understand means plus function language better, the structure that performs the functions defined in the means plus function language has been inserted in the claim in brackets.

1. A data processing system for managing a financial services configuration of a portfolio established as a partnership, each partner being one of a plurality of funds, comprising:
   a. computer processor means [a personal computer including a CPU] for processing data;
   b. storage means [a data disc] for storing data on a storage medium;
   c. first means [an arithmetic logic circuit configured to prepare the data disc to magnetically store selected data] for initializing the storage medium;
   d. second means [an arithmetic logic circuit configured to retrieve information from a specific file, calculate incremental increases or decreases based on specific input, allocate the results on a percentage basis, and store the output in a separate file] for processing data regarding assets in the portfolio and each of the funds from a previous day and data regarding increases or decreases in each of the funds, [sic; fund's] assets and for allocating the percentage share that each fund holds in the portfolio;
   e. third means [an arithmetic logic circuit configured to retrieve information from a specific file, calculate incremental increases and decreases based on specific input, allocate the results on a percentage basis and store the output in a separate file] for processing data regarding daily incremental income, expenses, and net realized gain or loss for the portfolio and for allocating such data among each fund;
   f. fourth means [an arithmetic logic circuit configured to retrieve information from a specific file, calculate incremental increases and decreases based on specific input, allocate the results on a percentage basis and store the output in a separate file] for processing data regarding daily net unrealized gain or loss for the portfolio and for allocating such data among each fund; and
   g. fifth means [an arithmetic logic circuit configured to retrieve information from specific files, calculate that information on an aggregate basis and store the output in a separate file] for processing data regarding aggregate year-end income, expenses, and capital gain or loss for the portfolio and each of the funds.

The Court rejected the argument that the claim merely recited a mathematical algorithm:

> Today, we hold that the transformation of data, representing discrete dollar amounts, by a machine through a series of mathematical calculations into a final share price, constitutes a practical application of a mathematical algorithm, formula, or calculation, because it produces "a useful, concrete and tangible result" - a final share price momentarily fixed for recording and reporting purposes and even accepted and relied upon by regulatory authorities and in subsequent trades.

The Court also rejected the argument that the claim was unpatentable because it defined a business method:

> Whether the claims are directed to subject matter within Section 101 [the statute that defines patentable subject matter] should not turn on whether the claimed subject matter does 'business' instead of something else." 47 USPQ2d at 1604.

However, the conclusion of many patent scholars is that while the CAFC found this claim to be patent eligible in 1998, the same claim would *not* be patentable today under the Supreme Court's later *Bilski*, *Alice* and *Mayo* decisions, with which conclusion I agree.

15.8 THE COVERED BUSINESS METHOD REVIEW

Responding to criticism that overly broad business method patents were being issued by the USPTO, partly due to the lack of prior art information available to Patent Examiners in a category of inventions dating back only to 1989, Congress in the AIA created an important program and procedure in the USPTO to reconsider the validity of business method patents after they have issued. This program is known as the Covered Business Method Review (CBMR), and granted patents that claim "a method or corresponding apparatus for performing data processing *or other operations* used in the practice, administration or management of a financial product or service" are covered by this program. A defendant accused of infringing a business method patent falling within the scope of CBMR, such as by the patent holder filing a lawsuit or sending a cease and desist letter, can take action to challenge the validity of the patent by initiating a proceeding before the Patent Trial and Appeal Board (PTAB) of the USPTO, a tribunal composed of patent-knowledgeable administrative law judges. The CBMR procedure is markedly less expensive than litigating in court, and the PTAB is obligated to hand down its decision in one year or less—also significantly shorter than district court litigation.

I suggest that if you find yourself or your company on the receiving end of a charge of infringement of a covered business method patent, as for example one asserted by a "patent troll," contact your patent professional for further details of the CBMR program.

149 F.3d 1368 (1998)

STATE STREET BANK & TRUST CO., Plaintiff-Appellee,
v.
SIGNATURE FINANCIAL GROUP, INC. Defendant-Appellant.

No. 96-1327.

United States Court of Appeals, Federal Circuit.

July 23, 1998.

The Business Method Exception

As an alternative ground for invalidating the '056 patent under § 101, the court relied on the judicially-created, so-called "business method" exception to statutory subject matter. We take this opportunity to lay this ill-conceived exception to rest. Since its inception, the "business method" exception has merely represented the application of some general, but no longer applicable legal principle, perhaps arising out of the "requirement for invention" — which was eliminated by § 103. Since the 1952 Patent Act, business methods have been, and should have been, subject to the same legal requirements for patentability as applied to any other process or method.[10]

The business method exception has never been invoked by this court, or the CCPA, to deem an invention unpatentable.[11] Application of this particular exception has always been preceded by a ruling based on some clearer concept of Title 35 or, more commonly, application of the abstract idea exception based on finding a mathematical algorithm. Illustrative is the CCPA's analysis in *In re Howard,* 55 C.C.P.A. 1121, 394 F.2d 869, 157 USPQ 615 (CCPA 1968), wherein the court affirmed the Board of Appeals' rejection of the claims for lack of novelty and found it unnecessary to reach the Board's section 101 ground that a method of doing business is "inherently unpatentable." *Id.* at 872, 55 C.C.P.A. 1121, 394 F.2d 869, 157 USPQ at 617.[12]

1376 *1376 Similarly, *In re Schrader,* 22 F.3d 290, 30 USPQ2d 1455 (Fed.Cir.1994), while making reference to the business method exception, turned on the fact that the claims implicitly recited an abstract idea in the form of a mathematical algorithm and there was no "transformation or conversion of subject matter representative of or constituting physical activity or objects." 22 F.3d at 294, 30 USPQ2d at 1459 (emphasis omitted).[13]

State Street argues that we acknowledged the validity of the business method exception in *Alappat* when we discussed *Maucorps* and *Meyer:*

> *Maucorps* dealt with a business methodology for deciding how salesmen should best handle respective customers and *Meyer* involved a "system" for aiding a neurologist in diagnosing patients. Clearly, neither of the alleged "inventions" in those cases falls within any § 101 category.

Alappat, 33 F.3d at 1541, 31 USPQ2d at 1555. However, closer scrutiny of these cases reveals that the claimed inventions in both *Maucorps* and *Meyer* were rejected as abstract ideas under the mathematical algorithm exception, not the business method exception. *See In re Maucorps,* 609 F.2d 481, 484, 203 USPQ 812, 816 (CCPA 1979); *In re Meyer,* 688 F.2d 789, 796, 215 USPQ 193,

199 (CCPA 1982).[14]

Even the case frequently cited as establishing the business method exception to statutory subject matter, *Hotel Security Checking Co. v. Lorraine Co.*, 160 F. 467 (2d Cir.1908), did not rely on the exception to strike the patent.[15] In that case, the patent was found invalid for lack of novelty and "invention," not because it was improper subject matter for a patent. The court stated "the fundamental principle of the system is as old as the art of bookkeeping, i.e., charging the goods of the employer to the agent who takes them." *Id.* at 469. "If at the time of [the patent] application, there had been no system of bookkeeping of any kind in restaurants, we would be confronted with the question whether a new and useful system of cash registering and account checking is such an art as is patentable under the statute." *Id.* at 472.

This case is no exception. The district court announced the precepts of the business method exception as set forth in several treatises, but noted as its primary reason for finding the patent invalid under the business method exception as follows:

> If Signature's invention were patentable, any financial institution desirous of implementing a multi-tiered funding complex modelled (sic) on a Hub and Spoke
> 1377 configuration would be required to seek Signature's permission before embarking on *1377 such a project. *This is so because the '056 Patent is claimed [sic] sufficiently broadly to foreclose virtually any computer-implemented accounting method necessary to manage this type of financial structure.*

927 F.Supp. 502, 516, 38 USPQ2d 1530, 1542 (emphasis added). Whether the patent's claims are too broad to be patentable is not to be judged under § 101, but rather under §§ 102, 103 and 112. Assuming the above statement to be correct, it has nothing to do with whether what is claimed is statutory subject matter.

In view of this background, it comes as no surprise that in the most recent edition of the Manual of Patent Examining Procedures (MPEP) (1996), a paragraph of § 706.03(a) was deleted. In past editions it read:

> Though seemingly within the category of process or method, a method of doing business can be rejected as not being within the statutory classes. *See* Hotel Security Checking Co. v. Lorraine Co., 160 F. 467 (2nd Cir.1908) and *In re Wait*, 24 USPQ 88, 22 C.C.P.A. 822, 73 F.2d 982 (1934).

MPEP § 706.03(a) (1994). This acknowledgment is buttressed by the U.S. Patent and Trademark 1996 Examination Guidelines for Computer Related Inventions which now read:

> Office personnel have had difficulty in properly treating claims directed to methods of doing business. Claims should not be categorized as methods of doing business. Instead such claims should be treated like any other process claims.

Examination Guidelines, 61 Fed.Reg. 7478, 7479 (1996). We agree that this is precisely the manner in which this type of claim should be treated. Whether the claims are directed to subject matter within § 101 should not turn on whether the claimed subject matter does "business" instead of something else.

CONCLUSION

The appealed decision is reversed and the case is remanded to the district court for further proceedings consistent with this opinion.

REVERSED and *REMANDED.*

[10] As Judge Newman has previously stated,

[The business method exception] is ... an unwarranted encumbrance to the definition of statutory subject matter in section 101, that [should] be discarded as error-prone, redundant, and obsolete. It merits retirement from the glossary of section 101.... All of the "doing business" cases could have been decided using the clearer concepts of Title 35. Patentability does not turn on whether the claimed method does "business" instead of something else, but on whether the method, viewed as a whole, meets the requirements of patentability as set forth in Sections 102, 103, and 112 of the Patent Act.

In re Schrader, 22 F.3d 290, 298, 30 USPQ2d 1455, 1462 (Fed.Cir.1994) (Newman, J., dissenting).

[11] *See* Rinaldo Del Gallo, III, *Are "Methods of Doing Business" Finally out of Business as a Statutory Rejection?,* 38 IDEA 403, 435 (1998).

[12] *See also* Dann v. Johnston, 425 U.S. 219, 96 S.Ct. 1393, 47 L.Ed.2d 692 (1976) (the Supreme Court declined to discuss the section 101 argument concerning the computerized financial record-keeping system, in view of the Court's holding of patent invalidity under section 103); *In re Chatfield,* 545 F.2d 152, 157, 191 USPQ 730, 735 (CCPA 1976); *Ex parte Murray,* 9 USPQ2d 1819, 1820 (Bd.Pat.App & Interf. 1988) ("[T]he claimed accounting method [requires] no more than the entering, sorting, debiting and totaling of expenditures as necessary preliminary steps to issuing an expense analysis statement ....") states grounds of obviousness or lack of novelty, not of non-statutory subject matter.

[13] Any historical distinctions between a method of "doing" business and the means of carrying it out blur in the complexity of modern business systems. *See* *Paine, Webber, Jackson & Curtis v. Merrill Lynch,* 564 F.Supp. 1358, 218 USPQ 212 (D.Del.1983), (holding a computerized system of cash management was held to be statutory subject matter.)

[14] Moreover, these cases were subject to the *Benson* era Freeman-Walter-Abele test — in other words, analysis as it existed before *Diehr* and *Alappat.*

[15] *See also* *Loew's Drive-in Theatres v. Park-in Theatres,* 174 F.2d 547, 552 (1st Cir.1949) (holding that the means for carrying out the system of transacting business lacked "an exercise of the faculty of invention"); *In re Patton,* 29 C.C.P.A. 982, 127 F.2d 324, 327-28 (CCPA 1942) (finding claims invalid as failing to define patentable subject matter over the references of record.); *Berardini v. Tocci,* 190 F. 329, 332 (C.C.S.D.N.Y. 1911); *In re Wait,* 22 C.C.P.A. 822, 73 F.2d 982, 983 (CCPA 1934) ("[S]urely these are, and always have been, essential steps in all dealings of this nature, and even conceding, without holding, that some methods of doing business might present patentable novelty, we think such novelty is lacking here."); *In re Howard,* 55 C.C.P.A. 1121, 394 F.2d 869, 157 USPQ 615, 617 (CCPA 1968) ("[W]e therefore affirm the decision of the Board of Appeals on the ground that the claims do not define a novel process [so we find it] unnecessary to consider the issue of whether a method of doing business is inherently unpatentable."). Although a clearer statement was made in *In re Patton,* 29 C.C.P.A. 982, 127 F.2d 324, 327, 53 USPQ 376, 379 (CCPA 1942) that a system for transacting business, separate from the means for carrying out the system, is not patentable subject matter, the jurisprudence does not require the creation of a distinct business class of unpatentable subject matter.

◆ INVENTORS AND INVENTIONS ◆

Yvonne Brill

SATELLITE PROPULSION SYSTEM

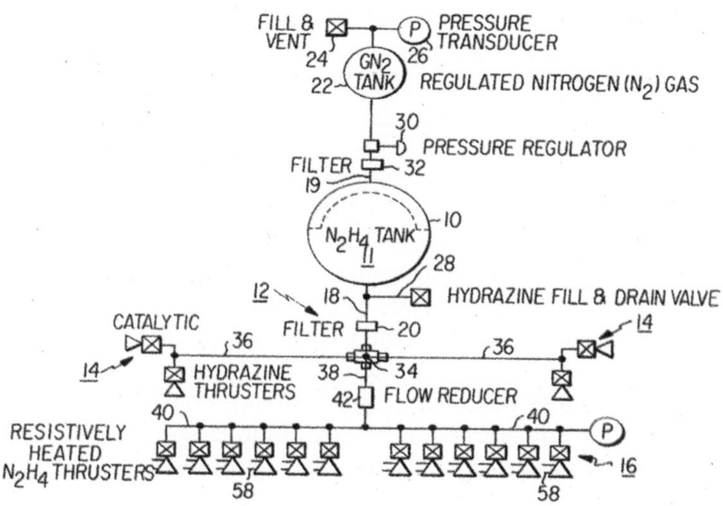

Yvonne Brill was a Canadian-American propulsion engineer who is known for her development of rocket and jet propulsion technologies. She is considered a pioneering rocket scientist, who after taking an eight-year break to raise her family, then proceeded to develop a propulsion system that is used to prevent satellites from slipping out of their orbits. Her invention was developed in the early 1970s, and today remains the industry standard for unmanned space craft. She was awarded the National Medal of Technology and Innovation from President Obama in 2011. At that time, he commented that satellites using her invention formed the backbone of the worldwide communication network.

Yvonne Brill was considered a trailblazer at a time when women were very rarely or not encouraged to go into the science and technology fields. She succeeded in her endeavors even without an official engineering degree. Well into her 80s, she was encouraging women to become engineers and scientists.

Early on, Brill applied to study engineering at the University of Manitoba, Canada; however, they refused to let her major in engineering because there were no accommodations for women at an outdoor engineering camp, which all students were required to attend. Instead, she studied mathematics and chemistry and graduated first in her

Intellectual Property Law for Engineers, Scientists, and Entrepreneurs, Second Edition. Howard B. Rockman.

Published 2020 by John Wiley & Sons, Inc.

class in 1945. Upon graduation without an engineering degree but with a chemistry degree, she began working for Douglas Aircraft Company in California and was working in the area of propellant chemistry. She later said that she did not have an engineering degree, but the engineers did not have a chemistry and math degree. She ultimately also earned her master's degree in chemistry from the University of Southern California.

While at a chemistry lecture presided over by Nobel Prize winner Linus Pauling, she met her future husband, Bill Brill, who had a PhD in chemistry. They were married in 1951. His job opportunities were in the east and hers were in the west. But she made a decision to follow his career, stating at one point that "good jobs are easier to find than good husbands." Due to the post-war advances in rocket technology and her expertise, she was rarely out of work. She was employed at the RAND Corporation, a Douglas spin-off, and then Wright Aeronautical New Jersey until she left full-time work to raise her family.

After engaging in some consultancy work during this period, in 1966 she returned full time to RCA's rocket subsidiary, Astro Electronics, where she developed her satellite propulsion system. Her system is known as the electro-thermal hydrazine thruster. This allowed engineers to move efficiently to alter and monitor the positions of satellites in a geosynchronous orbit around the earth. Her system was patented in 1974, and the first communication satellite using her technology was launched in 1983. Her invention also allowed satellites to carry less fuel and more scientific equipment, and to remain in space for a longer period of time. Her thrusters have the task of maneuvering a weightless satellite that weighs 2.5 tons on earth.

From 1981 to 1983 Brill worked at NASA headquarters in Washington as the director of the space shuttle solid rocket motor program. Anecdotally, she was inducted into the National Inventors Hall of Fame in 2010 at the same time as the inventors of Post-It Notes. She commented at the time it took two men to come with adhesive stationery, but only one woman to discover how to keep satellites aloft in space. In 1980, *Harper's Bazaar* Magazine and the DeBeers Corporation presented her with their Diamond Superwoman Award for returning to a successful career after starting a family.

Yvonne Brill was believed to have been the only woman in the United States actually engaged in rocket science in the mid-1940s when she worked on the first designs for an American satellite. From 1981 to 1983, she worked at NASA developing the rocket motor for the space shuttle.

When she went to work for Douglas, the satellite project became the foundation of the RAND Corporation, which was an early research center. It was at RAND that she worked on the first American satellite designs. In 1966, when she went back to work after raising her family, she worked at RCA's rocket subsidiary. As of a few years ago, her technology was still being used by satellites that handled worldwide phone service, long range television broadcasts, and many other tasks.

The hydrazine resistive jet that she developed used a single propellant because of the simplicity and value that a single propellant would provide. This resulted in higher engine performance and increased the reliability of the propulsion system. Also greater payload capability and extended mission life resulted. Her invention has translated into many millions of dollars of revenue for communication satellite owners today.

United States Patent [19]

Brill

[11] **3,807,657**

[45] **Apr. 30, 1974**

[54] **DUAL THRUST LEVEL MONOPROPELLANT SPACECRAFT PROPULSION SYSTEM**

[75] Inventor: **Yvonne Claeys Brill,** Skillman, N.J.

[73] Assignee: **RCA Corporation,** New York, N.Y.

[22] Filed: **Jan. 31, 1972**

[21] Appl. No.: **221,955**

[52] **U.S. Cl.** .... **244/1 SB**
[51] **Int. Cl.** **B64d 3/00**
[58] **Field of Search** 244/1; 60/200–204, 206–207, 218–220, 224–225, 229, 242

[56] **References Cited**

UNITED STATES PATENTS

2,968,919	1/1961	Hughes et al.	60/242
3,011,309	12/1961	Carter	60/242
3,015,210	1/1962	Williamson et al.	60/229
3,054,252	9/1962	Beckett et al.	60/203
3,231,223	1/1966	Upper	244/1 SA
3,303,651	2/1967	Grant, Jr. et al.	60/203
3,535,879	10/1970	Kuntz	60/200 R
3,673,801	7/1972	Goldberger	60/218
3,165,382	1/1965	Forte	60/218
3,583,161	6/1971	Simms	60/203

Primary Examiner—Duane A. Reger
Assistant Examiner—Jesus D. Sotelo
Attorney, Agent, or Firm—Edward J. Norton; Joseph D. Lazar

[57] **ABSTRACT**

A flight auxiliary propulsion system for velocity trim, station keeping, momentum adjustment for a spacecraft comprising rocket or reaction motors, also designated thrusters, utilizing thermally decomposable monopropellants such as hydrazine and other derivatives, thereof hydrogen peroxide, and isopropyl nitrate. The thrusters are arranged in a distribution or manifold system so that one set of thrusters provides for relatively large thrusts of force in the order of 1 to 5 pounds and another set of thrusters develop low thrusts in the millipound range. The large thrusts are developed by the catalytic decomposition of the monopropellant into a thrust chamber and through a throat and expansion nozzle to the ambient externally of the spacecraft. The low level thrusts are developed by heating catalytically or thermally decomposed monopropellant by electrical heating elements more commonly known as resisto-jet elements. Dual thrust levels may also be achieved by a common motor with a controllable resisto-jet and variable throat-area control.

10 Claims, 5 Drawing Figures

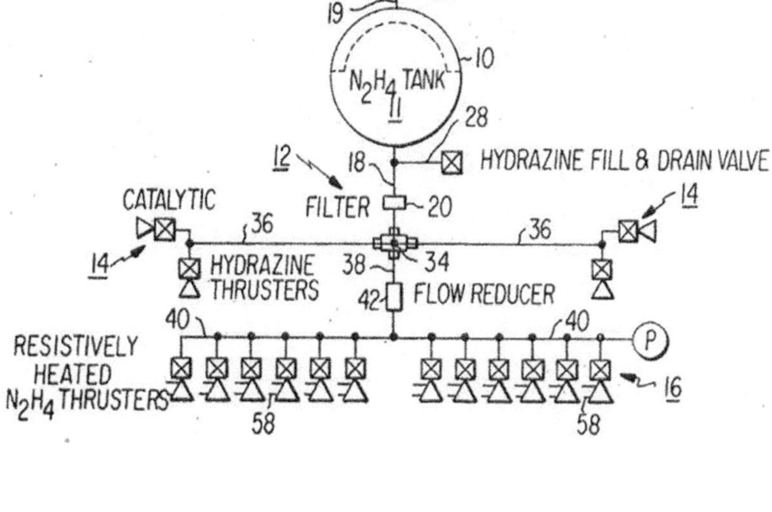

◆ INVENTORS AND INVENTIONS ◆

Luther Burbank

PLANT BREEDING

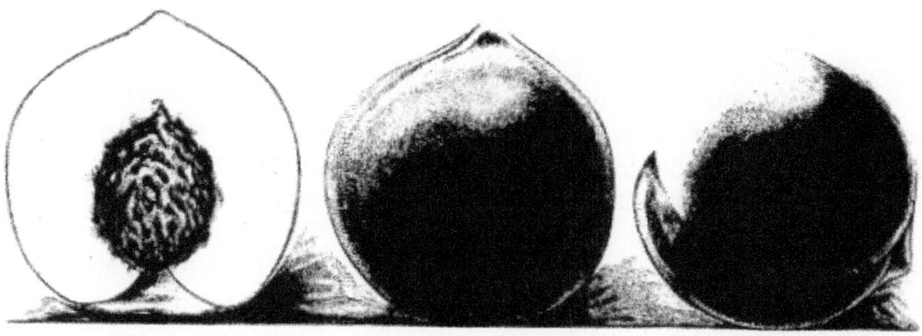

Luther Burbank was a horticulturist who devoted his life to breeding plants. He is credited with developing over 800 strains or varieties of plants, including 113 varieties of plums and prunes, 10 varieties of berries, 50 varieties of lilies, the freestone peach, and the Idaho potato.

Luther Burbank was born on March 7, 1849, on a farm near Lancaster, Massachusetts. He showed interest in nature and mechanics at an early age, although he received little more than a high school education. He obtained much of his encouragement and enthusiasm for nature from his uncle, who was a department head at a Boston museum, and his uncle's friend, the Swiss/American naturalist, Louis Agassiz.

Upon his father's death, Burbank and his family moved to a small farm in Groten, Connecticut. At the age of 21, he purchased 17 acres of land close to Lunenburg, Massachusetts, and began a career of plant breeding and growing that lasted the remaining 55 years of his life. Drawing inspiration from Charles Darwin's *Variations of Animals and Plants Under Domestication,* Burbank decided that better plants could be developed through natural selection, and new plant varieties could be created through cross-breeding or hybridization. In 1871, he planted 23 seeds from a potato seed ball in a special plot, which yielded many large firm potatoes. He then replanted these and reaped the small harvest of fine potatoes called the Burbank potato, which was ultimately introduced into Ireland to help combat the potato famine. He then sold the rights to his potato for $150, which money he used to travel to California, where he established a nursery garden, greenhouse, and experimental farms in Santa Rosa.

The Santa Rosa Farm became famous throughout the world. Burbank worked primarily by obtaining multiple crosses of foreign and native strains of fruits, vegetables,

Intellectual Property Law for Engineers, Scientists, and Entrepreneurs, Second Edition. Howard B. Rockman.

Published 2020 by John Wiley & Sons, Inc.

and flowers to obtain seedlings. He grafted those seedlings onto fully developed plants and was able to rapidly assess their hybrid characteristics. His work at natural selection and hybridization techniques in developing new plants was by no means small. At any one time, he was working on three experiments at the same time, involving millions of plants on his farm. Regarding plums alone, he tested about 30,000 new varieties. Much of his experimental data is not available, but he did write several books. In 1914–1915, his 12-volume work, *Luther Burbank, His Methods and Discoveries and Their Practical Applications,* was published. Burbank is credited with developing many of California's plums and prunes, the Shasta daisy, and novelty fruits such as plum cots, furless blackberries, and the spineless cactus.

In 1930, the Congress of the United Sates passed the "Plant Patent Act of 1930," providing protection for new and distinct varieties of asexually reproduced plants, except for tuber-propagated plants. This law resulted from the fact that plant breeders were aware that they had no financial incentive to breed plants because they could not exercise control over their discoveries. Although Luther Burbank died four years before the enactment of the Plant Patent Act, 16 plant patents were issued to Burbank posthumously.

Just before his death at the age of 77 in 1926, Luther Burbank found himself compelled to voice his opinions supporting his philosophy as a naturalist, in both the scientific and philosophical arenas. Up until 1926, Burbank was not known for expressing his thoughts on the universal contest between science and religion. However, the Scopes "monkey trial" of 1925 had pushed the concepts of Darwin's evolution onto the national stage, and Henry Ford, Luther Burbank's close friend, had published his own views in favor of reincarnation. A reporter for the *San Francisco Bulletin,* Edgar Waite, conducted an interview with Burbank and obtained his reaction to Ford's ideas. The resulting article which appeared on January 22, 1926, ran the headline "I am an infidel," declares Burbank, casting doubt on the soul immortality theory. During the interview, Burbank doubted that there was an afterlife, and later repeated and reinforced his comments that he was an infidel. Burbank considered himself a scientist, who believed in the truth as developed by science, and felt that religions were on a tottering foundation. In 1926, this story created shockwaves around the world, and Burbank was the object of hatred within 24 hours. He was inundated with thousands of letters, and he assumed the obligation to respond to as many as possible. This controversy proved to be Burbank's last battle. Because of the physical task in responding to the volume of letters he received, using mild but fearless comments in response to those who were attacking him, and amplifying his original statements for those who supported him, he fell ill in attempting to keep up with the task. Luther Burbank died in April 11, 1926. Ten thousand people attended his funeral.

April 5, 1932. L. BURBANK Plant Pat. 15

PEACH

Filed Dec. 23, 1930

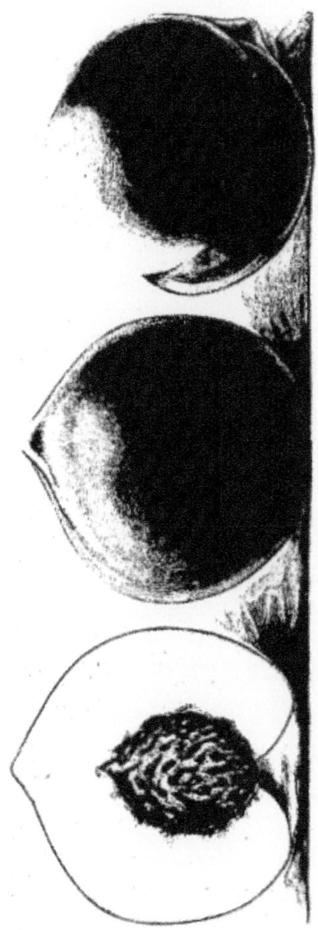

E. W. BURBANK
Executrix of
LUTHER BURBANK, Deceased
By Robb & Robb
ATTORNEYS

16 Foreign Patent Protection

16.1 INTRODUCTION

Up to now, we have covered how a patent is obtained and enforced in the United States and its possessions. Keep in mind, however, that with the advent of market "globalization," your inventions will most likely be valuable in many countries outside the United States. Obtaining a U.S. patent does not provide patent protection in any other country, and unlike copyright protection, which we delve into in Chapter 24, there is no "world patent." A patent right is enforceable against an infringer only in the country which issues the patent. Thus, patents must be obtained from the patent office, or equivalent government agency, in each of the countries where protection is sought. If a product or process is being marketed or used in a foreign country, you must have obtained a patent in that country to stop such infringement, and to collect damages resulting from the infringement.

Although the substantive standards for obtaining patent protection in most countries are generally the same, there are several important differences. For example, we have previously discussed briefly the different rules defining "novelty" in the United States and most of the other industrialized nations of the world. Under U.S. Patent Law, an inventor has one year in which to file a patent application following a "public disclosure" or "public availability" of the invention. "Public disclosure" is a flexibly defined term, and a public disclosure of an experimental version or prototype does not always result in invalidating a patent in the United States. However, in many foreign countries where you may be seeking patent protection, there is no one-year "grace period" between public disclosure and filing a patent application. In those countries that adhere to the "absolute novelty" rule in their patent statutes, the patent application must be filed with the patent office of that country before there is any public disclosure, public knowledge, or public availability of the invention anywhere. There are limited exceptions to this rule in some countries, such as a public disclosure prior to filing the patent application at a "recognized trade show" in the country in point, which may allow the inventor three months or so from the date of the trade show to file a patent application without losing patent rights.

Intellectual Property Law for Engineers, Scientists, and Entrepreneurs, Second Edition. Howard B. Rockman.

Published 2020 by John Wiley & Sons, Inc.

In an effort to prevent a public disclosure from having an adverse effect on patent rights anywhere on the globe, I encourage my inventor clients to refrain from any public showing of their invention before we can prepare and file a patent application, provisional or non-provisional. For reasons I shall explain, this one step, if adhered to, will protect the inventor's ability to obtain foreign patent rights in the invention, while doing the opposite will most likely destroy the possibility of obtaining patent rights in many important countries.

Remember, however, that refraining from disclosing your invention may not be easy. Most inventors I have met consider their invention as their own "babies" which they conceived and gave birth to. How many mothers will agree to hold back showing off their newborn child? But, if you desire to gain maximum advantage from the intellectual effort that went into creating your invention, you will have to keep the cover over the baby buggy until your patent attorney gives you the OK to lift it.

Over 100 years ago, the nations of the world recognized problems in protecting foreign patent rights in what was fast becoming an industrialized world with interconnected markets, and enacted a treaty that would assist inventors in their efforts against losing foreign patent rights in the invention conceived and reduced to practice in their home countries. Subsequent to that time, two other additional important treaties have come into effect that also dovetail with the earlier treaty to protect the loss of foreign patent rights. These three treaties are the Paris Union Convention of 1883; the Patent Cooperation Treaty (PCT), which became operational in 1978; and the European Patent Convention (EPC), which also became operational in 1978. All of these three treaties are compatible, and work with each other. The Paris Union Convention and the PCT are worldwide patent treaties, while the EPC is a regional treaty that applies to most European countries only.

16.2 THE TRADITIONAL SYSTEM OF OBTAINING FOREIGN PATENTS

Until 1978, obtaining patents in foreign countries was controlled by the Paris Union Convention of 1883, which is commonly known among patent attorneys as the Paris Convention. This treaty remains in force today for most of the major industrialized countries of the world, covering approximately 177 countries as of January 2019. Prior to enactment and enforcement of the PCT in 1978, obtaining patent protection under the Paris Convention involved the filing of a first patent application in the inventor's country of origin, and within one year of filing the home or first patent application, directly filing a separate patent application corresponding to the first patent application in each country where patent protection was sought. Note that the original patent application, which in most cases for United States inventors is drafted in English, is merely sent to a patent attorney or agent in the foreign country, where the application is filed without translation if the foreign country is English speaking, or the patent application is translated before or after filing in non-English-speaking countries, depending on the specific country. Therefore, it is important to note at this juncture that the patent application originally crafted by your patent attorney and filed in the United States is not rewritten for foreign filing. But, under the provisions of the Paris Convention, the separate patent applications must be drafted or translated into the language of each selected country and filed according to the applicable laws and rules of the patent office of each selected country.

The important feature of the Paris Convention is that patent applications filed in the foreign countries within the prescribed 12 month period provided under the treaty, and which claim priority to the home country application, are considered as though they had been filed in the foreign country on the previous filing date in the home country. This is defined as a "right of priority." As a result of the Paris Convention, the effective filing date of your foreign patent application is the same as the U.S. filing date. It follows that if the U.S. filing date is prior to any public disclosure, public knowledge, or publication of the invention, then your rights in foreign countries are protected vis-a-vis the rules of absolute novelty of those foreign countries. Thus, it is important to remember that obtaining a U.S., or home country filing date before any public disclosure of the invention saves your foreign patent rights. As a corollary, a public disclosure of your invention one day after the U.S. or home country filing date will not destroy foreign patent rights in most countries, as long as the Paris Convention rules are adhered to and foreign patent applications are filed within the 12-month period from the initial U.S. or home country filing date. It is extremely important to remember this provision, since most of the inventions that you will work on during your career, I am sure, will have potential use in countries outside your home country.

16.3 THE PATENT COOPERATION TREATY (PCT)

In 1978, the PCT went into effect, which dovetails with the Paris Convention of 1883. Thus, subsequent to 1978, applicants for foreign patents can also claim the benefit of the right of priority (their U.S. or home country filing date) under the PCT. Under the Patent Cooperation Treaty, the priority period for filing a PCT application is 12 months from the home country filing date, the same as with the Paris Convention. Also, claiming the right of priority is available under the PCT to applications filed in any member country of the Paris Union.

The PCT came into effect in 1978 to cure one of the major drawbacks of the Paris Convention. Under the Paris Convention, several separate patent applications in various different countries in a one-year period have to be filed, which involves considerable duplication and multiple filings and searches in each of the countries, and in the languages of each of those countries. Under the Paris Convention, the several global patents that are granted based upon your first filed home country patent application typically have different claims resulting from the different and separate examination procedures of different countries. Additionally, annuity fees must also be paid in the currency of each country in which your patent application was filed under the Paris Convention.

Therefore, one of the major goals of the PCT was to reduce the time and expense involved in obtaining international patent protection under the Paris Convention. Another factor was to provide additional time beyond the 12-month period of the Paris Convention in which an inventor, or the inventor's employer, could decide whether significant sums of money should be spent to obtain foreign patent protection. The period for filing international patent applications has been increased to up to 30 or 31 months from the original priority date, depending on the country.

Keep in mind, however, that none of the treaties that I have mentioned so far provide that single "world patent" that would be enforceable in every country. That result may be achieved someday, but not now. Every so often various countries of the world try to get together to harmonize their patent statutes, but each country recommends that all the other countries adopt their procedures. On that issue, the most recent harmonization efforts are getting closer. One of the major drawbacks in the past was the provision that is standard in many foreign countries that the first inventor to file a patent application will ultimately be granted the patent on the same or similar invention, and not necessarily the first inventor. The U.S. law, in an effort to move toward harmonization, now has been changed to include the first to file provision.

16.3.1 The Broad Provisions of the PCT

The PCT is an international treaty with 152 contracting states. The PCT makes it possible to reserve the right to seek patent protection for an invention simultaneously in a large number of countries by filing a single "international" patent application instead of initially filing several separate national or regional patent applications. The ultimate granting of patents remains under the control of national or regional patent offices in what is called the "national phase."

The first economic simplification provided by the PCT is that the form and content of an international patent application filed under the PCT is the same for all signatory countries. Thus, an application that complies with the PCT rules also meets the requirements of the U.S. Patent and Trademark Office (USPTO), and all other signatory national patent offices.

The PCT procedure begins by filing an international application with a national or regional patent office designated as a central receiving office, such as the USPTO or WIPO (World Intellectual Property Organization). The PCT application must be filed within 12 months of the home country priority date, complying with PCT formality requirements, in one language, and with payment of only one set of fees. If you have previously filed a home country provisional patent application, and are now filing the regular, non-provisional patent application 12 months after the provisional application filing date, the one-year date for filing the PCT application is on or about the same date the non-provisional application must be filed. The PCT application can be filed in the name of the inventor(s), or the applicant can be designated as the employer or other entity to whom the patent rights have been assigned, or to whom the inventor(s) are obligated to assign the invention or patent rights, such as pursuant to an employment agreement provision.

The form to be submitted with the application automatically designates all signatory countries, giving the applicant the opportunity to later select those signatory countries in which patent protection is desired, or may be desired. You are not compelled later to actually seek patent protection in all of those countries. Again, to obtain the benefits of the Paris Convention, the PCT application must be filed on or before the first year anniversary of the original home filing date, which is now known as the "priority date."

An international searching authority or ISA, which is one of the world's major patent offices, automatically conducts a search and identifies the published patent documents and technical literature comprising prior art that may influence whether or not your invention is patentable, and the ISA furnishes you with a written opinion on your invention's potential patentability. If your U.S. patent application is still pending before the USPTO when the ISA search report is received, any prior art identified in the ISA search report that has not previously been identified to the USPTO *must* be submitted to the U.S. examiner under Rule 56 as discussed previously by way of a supplemental Information Disclosure Statement (IDS).

As soon as possible after the expiration of 18 months from the earliest filing or priority date, the content of your international application is published by WIPO and disclosed to the world.

A supplementary international search is optional at the inventor's or application owner's request. This supplementary search is made by another ISA and identifies published documents that may not have been found by the first ISA that conducted the first search, because of the diversity of prior art in different languages and in different technical fields. In other words, the supplementary international search will be deeper and is directed to possibly uncovering additional prior art.

Further, an international preliminary examination is also optional. One of the ISAs, and only at your request, carries out an additional patentability analysis, usually on an amended version of your application.

After the end of the PCT procedure, usually at 30 or 31 months from the earliest filing or priority date of your initial application, depending upon which countries you are interested in, you start to pursue the grant of your patent directly before the national or regional patent offices of the countries in which you have chosen to obtain patent protection.

16.3.2 Options for Obtaining Foreign Patent Protection

Patents are territorially limited. To protect your invention in multiple countries, you have a few options.

a. The Direct or Paris Convention Route. You can directly file separate patent applications at the same time in all of the countries in which you desire to protect your invention, and for some countries regional patents such as the European Patent Office may be available. Or, having filed a patent application in a Paris Convention country, which would be one of the member states of the Paris Convention for the Protection of Industrial Property, discussed above, you next file a separate patent application in other Paris Convention countries within 12 months from the filing date of the first or home country patent application. This gives you the benefit in all of those countries of claiming priority based on the filing date of the first application you filed in your home country.
b. The PCT Route. You can file an application under the PCT with WIPO or a designated PCT receiving office directly on or before the 12 month period provided for by the Paris Convention from the filing date of the first application. The PCT application is valid in all contracting states of the PCT and is therefore simpler, easier, and more cost-effective than both direct or Paris route filings. The effect of filing an international application under the PCT is that subsequent adaptation to varying national or regional formal requirements and the cost associated therewith will not be necessary.

16.3.3 The PCT, or International, Patent Application

An international patent application can be filed directly with a national patent office, or directly with WIPO. WIPO maintains several major patent offices throughout the world as "receiving offices" in which PCT applications can be filed. The USPTO is a receiving office. In a majority of cases, applications pursuant to the PCT are filed electronically, and PCT applicants generally pay three types of fees when they file their international applications under the PCT. These include an international filing fee, a search fee, and a transmittal fee. Not incurred at this stage of the procedure are the costs that would arise if you prepared and filed separate applications in national and regional offices.

In most cases, you have an additional 18 or 19 months to file national patent applications from the time you file your international patent application under the PCT. This usually works out to 30 or 31 months from the filing date of the initial patent application from which you claimed priority, before you have to begin the national phase procedures within the individual patent offices, and fulfill the national patent office requirements. This additional time is useful for evaluating the chances of obtaining patents, and also the favorable commercialization of your invention, in the countries in which you plan to pursue patent protection. You can also assess both the technical value of your invention and the continued need for protection in those countries during this time period. If desired, you could always request an early entry into any national phase. In the national phase, each patent office is responsible for examining your application in accordance with national or regional patent laws regulations and practices. As a result, the time required for the examination and grant of a patent varies across patent offices.

Referring to the expression "claiming priority," generally patent applicants who desire to protect their invention in more than one country first file a national or regional patent application with their own national or regional patent office, and within 12 months from the filing date of the first application, which is the time limit set in the Paris Convention, the applicant files an international application under the PCT. The effect of claiming priority of the earlier patent application is that a patent shall not be invalidated by reason of any acts in the interval such as another filing, or the publication or sale of the invention. Therefore, your patent rights are protected against you or someone else making a public disclosure of the invention.

Note also that the international application is filed in any language that the receiving office accepts. Therefore, for U.S. inventors, the original application is filed in English, and the international application is also filed in English.

Basically, a PCT international search is a high-quality search of the relevant patent documents and other technical literature in those languages in which most patent applications are filed. The results of this search are published in an International Search Report, and a written opinion of the ISA on the potential patentability of your invention is furnished to you or your attorney.

16.3.4 The International Search Report and Opinion

The International Search Report consists primarily of a listing of references to published patent documents, technical journal articles, and other publicly available information that pertain to the patentability of the invention disclosed in the international or PCT application. The report contains indications for each of the documents listed as to their possible relevance to the critical patentability questions of patent eligibility, novelty, and non-obviousness, with non-obviousness sometimes called the inventive step. The International Search Report and the written opinion are sent to you by the ISA in response to your filing of the PCT application. The search report enables you to evaluate your chances of obtaining patents in PCT contracting states. Further, as mentioned above, under U.S. rules, the prior art cited in the PCT search and opinion must be furnished to the U.S. Patent Examiner if your U.S. patent application is still pending, under Rule 56 of the USPTO.

If you receive a search report or opinion that unfavorably identifies documents that may challenge the novelty and/or obviousness of your invention, you do have the opportunity to amend the claims in your PCT international application so as to distinguish your invention from the disclosures of those documents.

At or about the same time you are furnished with the International Search Report, comments are also made in the preliminary and non-binding opinion on whether the invention appears to meet the patentability criteria in light of the search results. The written opinion, which is sent to you along with or shortly after the International Search Report, helps you understand and interpret the results of the search report with specific reference to the text of your international application. The written opinion may be made available to the public at the same time as the application.

The Supplementary International Search mentioned previously permits the applicant to request one or more supplementary international searches in addition to the automatic international search, each to be carried out by an ISA other than the ISA that carried out the first or main international search. The additional search has the potential of reducing the risk of new patent documents and other technical literature being discovered in the national phase of examination of your application. By requesting the supplementary search, the applicant can enlarge the linguistic and/or technical scope of the search. The optional Supplementary International Search Report comments on documents discovered during the supplementary international search. This report may contain a more detailed explanation than that of the first or automatic search report. This is due to the fact that unlike the main international search, no written opinion is established with the Supplementary International Search Report unless the applicant asks for one.

WIPO publishes the international application shortly after the expiration of 18 months from the priority date, unless the patent application has been withdrawn previously. Also, at the same time the International Search Report is also published. Until the 18-month period from the priority date has elapsed, no third party is allowed access to the international application. When international publication occurs, certain documents in the international application file are made available on the website of WIPO.

The Supplementary International Search Report, when requested by the applicant, also provides a second evaluation of the potential patentability of the invention. If you desire to make amendments to your international application to overcome documents identified in the International Search Report and conclusions stated in the written opinion of the ISA, this process provides the only possibility to actively participate in the examination process and potentially influence the findings of the examiner during the international phase before entering the national phase. You can also submit amendments and arguments, and are entitled to an interview with the examiner if an International Supplementary Search Report on patentability is requested.

What is the value of an international preliminary or supplementary report on patentability? These reports consist of an opinion in compliance with the international patentability criteria of each of the claims that have been searched, such as novelty and non-obviousness. It provides a stronger basis on which to evaluate the chances of obtaining patents in foreign countries, in most cases at this point on an amended application. Consider that your U.S. patent application may have advanced through examination, and claims amended, before you receive the preliminary or supplementary report on patentability from an ISA. It may be prudent at this time to amend the claims in the international application to conform to the amended claims in the U.S. application. If the preliminary or supplementary report on patentability is favorable, a stronger basis on which to continue with your application before the national and regional patent offices has been created. The decision on the granting of the patent remains the responsibility of each of the national or regional offices in which you enter the national phase. The reports on patentability that we were discussing are usually considered by the regional and national offices, but are not binding on these offices.

16.3.5 The National Phase of the PCT

After you have selected those countries in which you wish to obtain patent protection, you must fulfill the requirements for entry into each of the countries in the national phase. These requirements include paying national fees, and in some cases filing translations of the applications. Steps must be taken before the end of the 30th or 31st month period from the priority date. The PCT maintains a list of those countries that are 30-month countries and 31-month countries. For example, the United States is a 30-month country, and the European Union is a 31-month regional area. Further, you may be required to appoint local patent agents or attorneys in each of the countries where you file your national phase applications.

Once you have entered the national phase, the national or regional patent offices concerned begin the process of determining whether they will grant you a patent in their country. Any examination that these offices may undertake should be made easier by the PCT International Search Report and written opinion that you received and, therefore lower the expense of responding to the Patent Examiners in the national and regional stages. The national/regional patent offices are not bound by the PCT's International Search Report and written opinion, and in most cases the Patent Examiners conduct their own searches.

There are also procedures available to fast-track the examination procedures in the national phase and contracting states that have PCT-Patent Prosecution Highway agreements with other countries, as detailed on the USPTO website, www.uspto.gov. Further, the WIPO website may also provide an effective means of advertising the fact that you are willing to license your invention, and attract potential licensees.

16.4 NATIONAL PATENT LAWS AND THE PCT: DIFFERENCES AND ALTERATIONS

Under the PCT, patent applications are published 18 months after their priority, or home country filing date. This provision has been matched in the United States, where U.S. patent applications filed today are published within 18 months after filing, unless the U.S. applicant notifies the USPTO that the applicant has no desire to file a foreign patent application. One advantage of publication of the patent is that of providing notice to potential infringers in the U.S. and abroad of the existence of your patent application.

The single most important advantage provided by the PCT is the ability to obtain at the outset, with a single standardized application, the equivalent of preserving the right to file patent applications in a larger number of foreign countries. Translation costs and application filing costs are deferred to a later stage of the proceedings, usually after the inventor or the inventor's company has determined that the invention has commercial possibilities and that such expenses are now warranted. Since the single application that complies with the PCT requirement also complies with the national requirements of all contracting members of the PCT, no, or minimal, alterations to the application to meet national requirements are necessary. Thus, it can be expected that fewer objections will arise, if any, from the foreign Patent Examiners, and a quicker and more sustained resolution of the patent granting procedure in the foreign countries can be expected.

16.5 THE EPC

The EPC established a regional patent system that became operational in 1978, and the European Patent Office (EPO) began operation in Munich. Most, but not all, European nations are signatory to the EPC. Norway, for example, is not a member. Each member state has a patent office to receive patent applications, and only one set of documents is required at the initial stage of filing in one of three official languages: English, French, and German.

Following the award of a filing date of your patent application with the EPC, a preliminary search of the invention claimed in the patent application is performed and the results published. The application is then examined by the EPO, and if found patentable, is again published for possible opposition by third parties. Some nations, if designated, may require the entire application to be translated into their native language before a patent is issued in those countries.

The EPO grants a single patent and publishes only one patent specification that acts as a national patent in each country designated by the applicant, and where specifically registered by the applicant. Therefore, once the EPO allows your patent application, you must then designate the countries under the EPC in which you desire to obtain patent protection. A fee, which is not insubstantial, must be paid to each of the country's patent offices in which registration of your European patent is effected. Therefore, it is not necessary to designate your patent to be enforceable in all of the countries of the EPC. In addition, annual annuities must be paid during the life of the patent application and patent in each separate country under the EPC.

Here is an additional important fact to remember. It is quite possible that your U.S. patent application may still be pending before the USPTO at the time when your foreign national stage patent application is undergoing search and examination by a national or regional patent office. Additional prior art developed in those national phase examinations will be furnished to your patent attorney. Under United States Patent Office Rule 56, all prior art that you and your attorney are aware of must be brought to the attention of the U.S. Patent Examiner, if the U.S. patent application is still pending. Therefore, it is important to remember that any new prior art developed during the foreign patent examination process must be forwarded to the United States Patent Examiner at any time up to issuance of the U.S. patent application. Failure to do so could invalidate your patent if an action is brought in the United States to enforce your patent against an infringer.

16.6 THE EUROPEAN UNITARY PATENT AND UNIFIED PATENT COURT

The EPO, at this writing, is in the process of introducing the Unitary Patent and the Unified Patent Court (UPCA). The aim is to provide a single patent right and a single patent litigation forum throughout Europe. European countries that have ratified the Unitary Patent Court Agreement will become contracting member states of both the Unitary Patent and the Unitary Patent Court. The countries of the European Union were in the process of ratifying these treaties at the time of publication of this text.

Under the Unitary Patent system, upon the granting of a European patent, the applicant for the European patent will have the option to request a Unitary Patent. This will provide a single patent right covering the ratifying member states and is effective at the time the patent is granted. Other EPC countries can be covered by the normal validation process of the European patent. The aim of this system is to provide a simple alternative to the existing patent system in Europe and provide a more cost-effective path to patent protection and dispute resolution.

Those preferring to seek protection in individual EPC contracting states may still file patent applications with those states' national patent offices. It will also remain possible to validate a European patent in one or more EPC contracting states. A Unitary Patent is an additional option for patent protection in Europe that will become available in tandem with the two existing options, namely, the national route, or a classic European patent.

A Unitary Patent will cover the territories of those participating member states in which the UPCA has taken effect at the date of registration of unitary effect of the EPO. Twenty-six EU member states are presently participating in the Unitary Patent ratification process. Unitary Patents registered in the beginning will not cover all 26 of the territories because some of these territories may not have ratified the UPCA. Your European patent professional can provide you with information on the extent of protection a Unitary Patent would provide.

After requirements are met, the EPO will register a Unitary Patent for the European Patent country(s) as requested by the applicant. The Unitary Patent will provide uniform protection and has equal effect in all of the participating member states. It may only be limited, transferred or revoked, or lapse in respect of all of the participating member states. However, the Unitary Patent may be licensed in respect to the whole or part of the territories participating in the Unitary Patent procedure.

The Unified Patent Court (UPC), when created, will provide a single court for patent litigation across those European countries that are signatories to the UPC. This will allow one litigation action to have effect in several jurisdictions instead of conducting litigation in several national courts at the same time.

Existing granted European patents will automatically fall under the jurisdiction of the UPC when it comes into force, unless the patent proprietor opts out of such jurisdiction.

The United Kingdom is expected to continue to participate in the Unitary Patent and the Unitary Patent Court after its withdrawal from the European Union. The protection of acquired rights and the preservation of legal certainty are general principles of law respected throughout Europe.

The pre-grant phase for obtaining a Unitary Patent is the same as for European patents today. Applicants will file a European patent application seeking the grant of a European patent for some or all the EPC contracting states with the EPO. The EPO will examine the application in accordance with the law, and when the formal and substantive requirements for patentability are met, the European patent will be granted. Once a European patent has been granted, a separate post-grant procedure can be initiated at the EPO with a view toward obtaining a Unitary Patent. This procedure is expected to be less complex and significantly less expensive than the existing system of national validation, and thus offers an attractive alternative for an applicant's European patents.

16.7 PRIVILEGED COMMUNICATIONS BETWEEN A U.S. PATENT ATTORNEY AND A FOREIGN NON-ATTORNEY PATENT AGENT

In the United States, the practice of patent law and prosecution of patents before the USPTO is primarily performed by licensed patent attorneys, who are lawyers as well as members of the separate bar of the USPTO. However, in most foreign countries, the practice of patent prosecution is conducted by registered patent agents, who are not legally trained, and who are not lawyers. As you are probably aware, any communication in the United States between a lawyer and that lawyer's client is privileged, and cannot be disclosed by the lawyer to a third party. The question arises whether or not the communication between your patent attorney and a non-lawyer foreign patent agent is also privileged. This becomes important in litigation, where your patent attorney in the United States may have discussed several negative aspects of examination of your invention in a foreign country with the foreign patent agent. If litigation ensues, it is not prudent to have such negative statements entered into the record of your litigation. Thus, there is a universal rule that if the communication between a non-attorney patent agent and his or her client in a foreign country is subject to a privilege against disclosure in that country, that same privilege will apply to communications between your U.S. patent attorney and the non-attorney patent agent in that country. This is a point that I recommend you clarify with your patent attorney when it comes time for you to consider and file patent applications in foreign countries.

◆ INVENTORS AND INVENTIONS ◆

Wilbur and Orville Wright

CONTROLLED POWERED FLIGHT

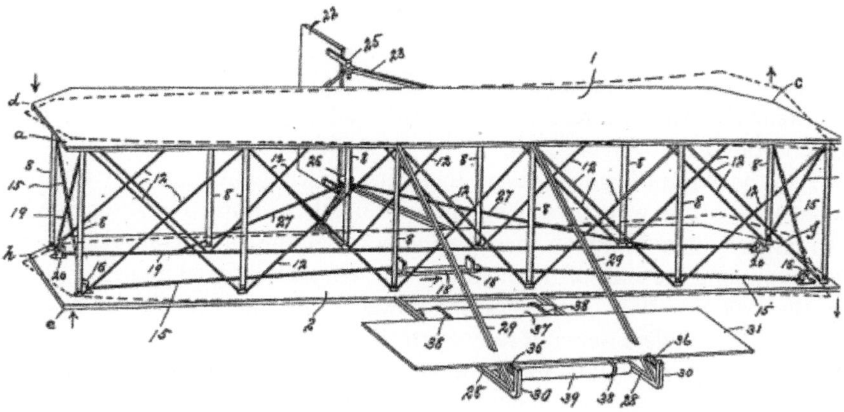

For those of us who are beyond middle age, it is practically impossible to listen to Rossini's *William Tell Overture* without thinking of our Western hero, The Lone Ranger. Likewise, most of the world today cannot hear the word "inventor" or "flight" without immediately thinking of the Wright brothers. The Wright brothers are credited with achieving the first powered, sustained, and controlled flight of a heavier-than-air airplane.

Wilbur and Orville Wright were the sons of Milton Wright, a bishop in the United Brethren Church. Wilbur was born on April 16, 1867, on a farm near New Castle, Indiana. Orville Wright was born in Dayton, Ohio, on August 19, 1871. Both went through high school in Dayton, but never received their diplomas. After Orville initiated a printing business, the brothers later launched a weekly newspaper, the *West Side News,* edited by Wilbur. They then began to sell and lease bicycles, and by 1896 migrated to manufacturing and assembling bicycles in a room above their shop.

The Wright brothers reportedly became interested in flight after reading about the death in 1896 of Otto Lilienthal who was a glider pioneer. They began studying the construction of gliders and, based upon the Weather Bureau's recommendation, picked Kill Devil Hills, a small strip of sand near Kitty Hawk, North Carolina, to conduct their experiments. Kitty Hawk provided the high-velocity winds necessary to launch the gliders off the ground, and the soft sand to cushion the impact when a glider flight was not successful.

Intellectual Property Law for Engineers, Scientists, and Entrepreneurs, Second Edition. Howard B. Rockman.

Published 2020 by John Wiley & Sons, Inc.

The Wright brothers observed that all of the newspaper accounts of earlier aircraft reported that such aircraft lacked controls. They felt that a pilot in an aircraft should be able to balance the aircraft in the air, somewhat as bicyclists balance their bicycles while riding them, banking or leaning into their turns. Wilbur also saw that buzzards, when turning, twisted one wing tip up while the other twisted down. Then, Wilbur was playing with a narrow, long cardboard box, which he twisted over and over again—one edge up, one edge down. The box retained its rigidity and did not break. The brothers then installed a series of pulleys and wire ropes that allowed them to "warp" the glider wings up and down. They first tested this theory in a biplane kite constructed in 1899 in their Dayton shop, with a wing that mechanically twisted (warping). They continued these tests in two additional gliders they constructed.

The Wrights constructed their glider wings on the basis of an idea of Octave Chanute, an American aviation pioneer of French origin, which was to use biplane wings stiffened with a Pratt truss. The Pratt truss had been patented in 1844 by Thomas and Caleb Pratt, not for flying craft, but for an earthbound railroad bridge.

In 1900, the Wright brothers tested their first glider that could carry a person; it measured 16 feet from wing tip to wing tip. In 1901, they returned to Kitty Hawk with an even larger glider. Although these two gliders demonstrated control of sideways balance by tipping the ends of the right and left wings at different angles to the wind, neither the 1900 nor 1901 gliders had the power to produce the lift they had anticipated. Also, these gliders were not fully controllable.

During the winter of 1901–1902, the Wright brothers constructed a 6-foot wind tunnel in their shop to conduct an analysis of the optimum wing shape for an airplane. They reportedly tested more than 200 wing models in the tunnel. As a result of these tests, the Wright brothers produced the first reliable tables of air pressures on curved surfaces. They also found that the air pressure tables produced previously by Otto Lilienthal were wrong. By using their own analytical tables, the Wright brothers designed a wing surface and controls for the wing surface that ultimately led to successful flight. By the end of the 1902 flying season, the third Wright glider is credited with being the first fully controllable aircraft, with roll, pitch, and yaw controls.

With their 1902 glider, the Wright brothers made almost 100 glides covering distances of more than 600 feet on some of the flights. In 1903, the Wright brothers applied for a U.S. patent with the help of an experienced patent attorney; the patent discloses the 1902 glider. Note that the patent, which is reprinted following this essay, does not mention power or an engine.

During the winter of 1902–1903, the Wright brothers' mechanic, Charles Taylor, assisted the Wrights in constructing a light gasoline combustion engine that was powerful enough to drive a propeller for an aircraft. They also used the time to design the first true airplane propellers, and constructed a new powered aircraft. This became known as the 1903 Wright Flyer I. Their new aircraft, which cost less than $1000 to build, had a wing span of 40.5 feet, and weighed approximately 750 pounds, including the weight of the pilot.

In the summer of 1903, the Wright brothers found themselves under severe pressure. Samuel P. Langley, the secretary of the Smithsonian Institution in Washington, had also constructed a powered aircraft, modeled after his previous unmanned "Aerodrome," which had flown successfully in 1896. The Wright brothers were also encountering problems with their propeller shafts and the weather, which gave Langley time to test his aircraft two times in late 1903. However, both attempts by Langley failed, and on December 17, 1903, Wilbur and Orville Wright prepared to test their powered aircraft at Kill Devil Hills in North Carolina.

The Wright brother's theoretical work predicated on their wind tunnel experience is credited with allowing them to create the first successful controllable powered aircraft. The Wright brother's gliders were typically unstable, and the success of the Wright brothers is largely due to their ability to balance their craft in the air. For example, Octave Chanute was in Europe in 1902 and, while passing through France, addressed a group of aeronautical engineers, experimenters, and enthusiasts who had been concentrating their efforts on lighter-than-air aircraft, such as balloons and dirigibles. He described to the French his own work in heavier-than-air aircraft and the gliding experience of the Wright brothers that successfully took place in 1902. Although the French aeronautical enthusiasts constructed many variations of the Wright glider design over the next three years, none paid attention to the theoretical and analytical work of the Wright brothers. The French concentrated on creating an inherently stable aircraft, one that would remain pointed in a single direction with the right side up, with little input from the pilot. The French failed to understand the importance of control, which was the Wright brothers' ultimate reason for success. Much later than the Wright brothers, the French finally came around to understanding that the Wright brothers' theory of control is the most important aspect in successful controlled powered flight.

December 17, 1903, is the day that marks the beginning of controlled powered flight. Considering all of the different types of aircraft flying today, it is hard to believe that this event happened only a little over 100 years ago. The Wright brothers arrived in Kitty Hawk in September 1903 to test out their new powered and controlled aircraft. However, defects and storms on the coast prevented them from conducting their experiments until December 17.

The Wright brothers had a certain modicum of anticipation that their flights at Kill Devil Hills in December 1903 would be successful. Their previous glider flights in 1902 had proven the reliability of their aircraft's control system. The brothers had also become skilled pilots, and their research work with the wind tunnel had given them a sense of aerodynamics that allowed them to use technical analysis to arrive at the design of their aircraft.

On the evening of December 16, 1903, a northeast storm hit the Wright brothers' camp at Kitty Hawk. By morning, the rain had stopped, but the winds continued to blow in from the ocean, gusting at approximately 30 miles an hour. The wind chill factor was 4°F. However, the Wright brothers decided to go ahead and attempt their flight, and it is reported that one of the main reasons was that if they were unable to leave Kitty Hawk shortly, they would not be back in Dayton, Ohio, in time for Christmas.

Shortly past 10:00 AM, the Wright brothers hoisted a red blanket on the side of their hanger, which was a signal advising the Kitty Hawk Lifesaving Crew that they needed additional manpower to prepare their aircraft for flight. The Wright brothers began preparing the wooden track extending 200 feet from the hanger while waiting for the lifesaving crew to arrive.

Then, five men—John Daniels, Adam Etheridge, Will Dough, W. C. Brinkley, and John Moore—arrived and helped the Wright brothers drag their 600-pound-plus aircraft across the frozen sands of Kill Devil Hills. These gentlemen offered their services out of the warmth of their own hearts, and were not compensated by the Wright brothers.

By 10:30, the Wright brothers' crew had the Wright Flyer I on its launching rail, the brothers cranked the propellers, and the engine groaned into operation. It was Orville's turn to fly in their rotation, and he mounted the flyer in the middle of the lower wing. He warped the wings, rotated the rudder, operated the elevators, and checked the controls. At that point, history was rewarded when Wilbur asked John Daniels of the lifesaving crew to take a photograph just as the Wright Flyer I reached the end of its launching rail. Wilbur also asked the rest of the crew to clap, be joyful, and make a lot of noise to cheer Orville on his way.

At 10:35, Orville Wright released the wire restraining the aircraft, and the craft moved along the rail into a 27 mile an hour headwind. Wilbur ran alongside the aircraft, something that you probably could not do today during takeoff. Approximately two-thirds along the length of the rail, the Wright Flyer I lifted into the air. Orville had not accurately predicted the elevators' effectiveness, and the craft rose rather quickly. To compensate, Orville moved the elevator down and the aircraft dived. For 12 seconds, the aircraft went up and down, up and down, and then landed, both the pilot and the airplane in one piece except for a cracked skid. The plane had traveled 120 feet from the end of the launching rail. But, for the first time in history, a flying aircraft under power had taken off from level ground, flown through the air under the control of its pilot, and also landed under the control of its pilot. The trip was a nerve-wracking one, the controls were unsteady, and the craft wavered during flight, but it was under control.

Not satisfied with just a single flight that day, at approximately 11:30, the Wright brothers made a second flight, this time with Wilbur acting as pilot, and flew 175 feet. Shortly thereafter, Orville took the controls and the craft flew for a third time, arriving approximately 200 feet from its starting point. And then, at approximately noon, Wilbur returned to the controls for the fourth flight. The beginning of this flight was as rocky as the first three flights, with the aircraft pitching in the wind as Wilbur struggled to control the elevator. It is reported that approximately 100 feet out, the aircraft was moving up and down like a bull at a rodeo. The bucking got worse at 200 feet, but after approximately 300 feet, Wilbur obtained a feel for the elevator and the craft's path smoothed out. Wilbur flew past the 800 foot mark, when a gust of wind caused the airplane to begin its wild, bumpy ride again. Wilbur tried to regain control, but the Flyer suddenly darted for the ground, as Orville later described it. The plane finally landed approximately 850 feet from its starting point and 59 seconds later. Other than damaging the support for the elevator, the pilot and the craft were both in one piece.

However, as the crew was in the process of carrying the craft back to the launching point for a possible fifth flight, a sudden gust of wind picked up one wing. Daniels, the photographer, grabbed one of the wing struts and ended up being caught in the bracing wires while the machine was rolled over several times by the wind. When the craft stopped rolling with Daniels attached to it, nothing was left but shards of wood, ripped cloth fabric, and an unharmed Daniels. Due to this damage, the world's first true powered and practical airplane would never fly again.

Almost a hundred years later, analysts and aeronautical engineers used computers to reconstruct the flight characteristics of the Wright Flyer I. They discovered that the elevator was extremely sensitive, making the craft nearly uncontrollable. According to the computer simulation, the pilot needed the strength of a professional athlete to control the plane while in the air.

Following their fourth flight on December 17, the Wright brothers sent a telegram back to their father, Bishop Milton Wright in Dayton, Ohio, marking their success. Milton Wright immediately telegraphed the news to Octave Chanute, who was Orville's high school chum and who had been collaborating with the Wright brothers. From this time on, man was not limited to two-dimensional travel along the earth's surface. Human life from that time on became three dimensional.

Prior to their December 1903 flights, the Wright brothers decided to obtain additional resources to continue their aeronautical experiments. To accomplish this purpose, they concluded that they needed a patent to protect their invention. The brothers had previously filed a patent application themselves, which had been rejected by the United States Patent Office. This time, they made a decision to hire an accredited patent attorney, Henry A. Toulmin, of Springfield, Ohio, who initially advised the brothers to continue their work on a practical flying machine, but not to publicly disclose their invention until the patent was granted. Thus, the Wright brothers continued their experimentation in secret, making no public flights, including the flights in December 1903. They even went to the extent of attempting to sell aircraft to the United States and other governments, under the condition that the purchase contracts be signed before any demonstration flight was made to the prospective purchaser. As a result of that proviso, and the fact that the Wright brothers had difficulty making additional long, sustained flights during the next two years, the various governments refused to enter into contracts with them for the construction of powered aircraft. For example, in 1904, 40 efforts at flight were made by the Wright brothers, the longest being only 600 feet. The problem, they later discovered, was that the aircraft itself had to move at 27 to 28 miles per hour relative to the wind for a successful takeoff. If the wind was moving slower, the airplane had to go down the launch rail at a much faster speed. For example, the winds at Kitty Hawk on December 17 were so high that forward motion of the aircraft of only three miles per hour was required to lift the Wright Flyer I off the launching rail that day.

The Wright brothers filed their patent application through Mr. Toulmin on March 23, 1903, almost nine months prior to their first successful flight. This patent application, one of many filed by the Wright brothers, disclosed the control structure and mechanisms of the 1902 glider, and makes no mention of, nor any disclosure of, an engine or any means for powered flight.

The Wright brother's patent application issued as U.S. Patent No. 821,393 on May 22, 1906. Once the patent was noted as allowed, the Wright brothers decided to make public flights of their aircraft. The first public flight by the Wright brothers was in France on August 8, 1908, and was followed by others. These public flights finally resulted in the Wright brothers obtaining fame for their aeronautical feats. They set up a factory to manufacture aircraft and opened flight schools in both the United States and Europe.

Once their aircraft had flown in public, it was easy for others to copy the Wright brothers' designs, which resulted in the Wright brothers being involved in lengthy and expensive patent law suits in both America and Europe. The most bitter of these, and one that had a profound and lasting effect on both of the brothers, was the patent fight with Glenn Curtiss. In the patent litigation instituted by the Wright brothers, Curtiss, in an effort to prove his defense of patent invalidity, borrowed Langley's previously unsuccessful aircraft from the Smithsonian Institution and rebuilt and modified it in an effort to prove that the Aerodrome could have flown before the Wright Flyer I.

Curtiss had to make extensive alterations to the Aerodrome to get Langley's aircraft in the air, and the court ruled in favor of the Wright brothers. However, the actions by the Smithsonian in supporting Curtiss' argument resulted in a long-lasting antagonism of the Wright brothers toward the Smithsonian Institution.

Additionally, money in the aircraft business in those days was to be made in exhibition flying, where audiences were looking for death-defying feats of aeronautical daredevilry. The Wright brothers employed pilots who were compelled to fly increasingly more recklessly to satisfy their audiences. As pilots began to die in accidents, the stress of this plus the legal battles distracted the brothers from their work of invention and innovation. Thus, by 1911, aircraft manufactured by others were considered better than the Wright brothers' flying machines.

In 1912, Wilbur Wright became exhausted from both the legal and business problems, and died from typhoid. In 1916, Orville Wright sold the Wright Company and began working on other projects that interested him.

One of Wilbur's projects was a long, continuing battle with the Smithsonian Institution, that continued after the First World War, when the Smithsonian promoted Langley's contributions to the history of flight, while seeming to make little of the Wright brothers' contribution. The battle to rewrite history continued over many years. As retaliation, in 1928 Orville sent the repaired 1903 Wright Flyer I, in which he and Orville had made the first powered flights, to the Science Museum of London in England. In the 1930s, even Charles Lindbergh attempted to arbitrate the battle between the two, but to no avail. In 1942, Orville Wright's biographer, Fred Kelly, encouraged the Smithsonian to back down from its statements and provide the public with the truth. When this was done, Orville instructed the Science Museum to return the Wright Flyer I to America. However, the Second World War intervened, and the Wright Flyer I was finally returned to the Smithsonian in 1948, where it is displayed to this day.

Orville Wright died on January 30, 1948, of a heart attack. The invention and innovation of the Wright brothers lives on in modern society. The basic principles of their aircraft, on display at the Smithsonian, are used in every airplane manufactured today.

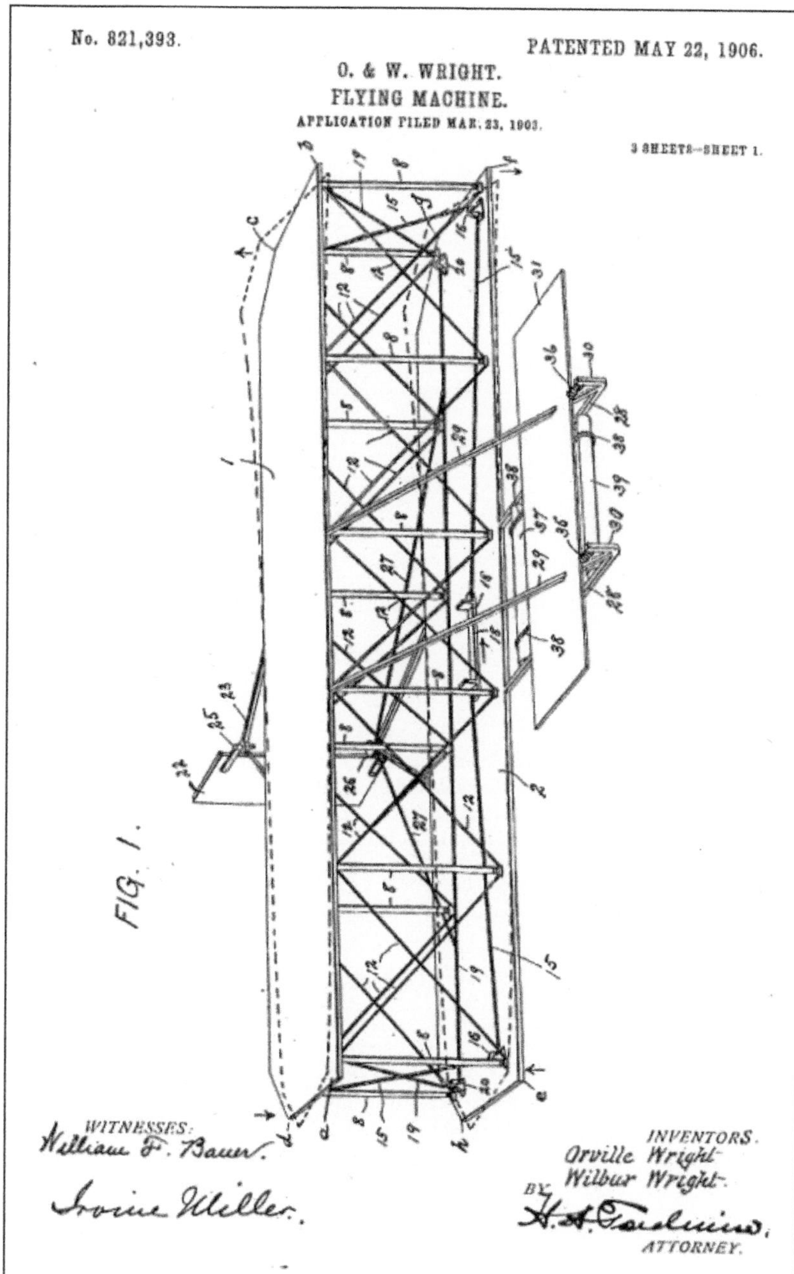
No. 821,393.
PATENTED MAY 22, 1906.
O. & W. WRIGHT.
FLYING MACHINE.
APPLICATION FILED MAR. 23, 1903.
3 SHEETS—SHEET 1.
FIG. 1.
WITNESSES:
William F. Bauer.
Irvine Miller.
INVENTORS.
Orville Wright
Wilbur Wright
BY
H. A. Toulmin.
ATTORNEY.

17 Enforcement of the Patent Right

17.1 THE PATENT CLEARANCE PROCESS

Previously in this text, we have reviewed the procedures for obtaining a patent covering your invention. Now the patent has issued with all claims found allowable, and the issued patent is available to the public, including your competitors. A savvy competitor will obtain a copy of your patent to determine the scope of coverage (metes and bounds) of your patent claims for the purposes of:

1. Ensuring that no present product of the competitor infringes the patent.
2. Ensuring that development projects in progress do not lead to products that potentially infringe your patent.

At this point, the focus of this chapter may shift from time to time away from you as the inventor, and placing you in the shoes of a competitor. What steps do you take to avoid infringing someone else's patent? The following recommended procedures apply even to a product or process for which you may have obtained a patent, because your patented item or method may still infringe an earlier patent. Avoiding patent infringement is important because defending your product in a patent infringement lawsuit is very expensive in terms of cost and expenditure of time of personnel who could well be working on more productive matters.

17.1.1 The Freedom-to-Use Search and the Non-Infringement Opinion Letter

In my intellectual property law practice, when a client presents me with his or her invention of a new product or process for patenting, we initially conduct a patentability search, as discussed in Chapter 8. In many instances, I recommend that the search also include a "preliminary infringement search." This authorizes the searcher not only to be aware of prior art bearing on the issues of novelty and non-obviousness, but also to be on the lookout for issued, non-expired patents that potentially may cause infringement problems if the development project for the new product continues in its present design direction. Normally, patentability searches are conducted at the beginning of product development, and the finished product is still months, or even years away. It is not practical to conduct a full patent infringement or freedom-to-use

Intellectual Property Law for Engineers, Scientists, and Entrepreneurs, Second Edition. Howard B. Rockman.

Published 2020 by John Wiley & Sons, Inc.

search until the final design has been signed off, since most, if not all, products and processes change radically throughout the development process. From the results of this "preliminary infringement search," I have been able to advise clients to make "mid-course corrections" during the product development stage to avoid potential infringement problems when deemed prudent.

Once the patent attorney receives the results of the patentability and "preliminary infringement" search, he or she will advise you, as part of his or her confidential opinion letter, which unexpired patents uncovered by the search may raise potential infringement problems. Of course, an expired patent cannot be infringed. You may then find it practical to meet with your patent attorney to discuss potential patent infringement problems and how to avoid these problems at an early stage of your development program.

Certain companies, and inventors take an additional step in ensuring they are aware of potentially infringed patents as such patents issue, and establish a patent "watch" procedure. As mentioned previously, U.S. patents issue every Tuesday of the year, holiday or not, and are accessible on the USPTO website on the date of issue. The issued patents are organized in order of class and subclass of issuance and thus by accessible technology categories. Prudent product development managers have their patent attorney or someone in-house review the particular classes and subclasses of inventions that relate to their business each week on the USPTO website, and furnish the product manager and patent attorney with information about those newly issued patents that should be reviewed for potential infringement issues. Since the issued patents are organized by subject matter, a review of the claims of relevant issued patents by the patent attorney can be accomplished relatively quickly and inexpensively on a weekly basis.

Near completion of the development project, after the final design has been approved, a full infringement or freedom-to-use search should be conducted to determine what unexpired patents there are that would lead their owners to think about charging you with patent infringement. This search is also best conducted by a professional searcher, who has access to electronic copies of relevant patents, as well as other electronic searching tools. The infringement analysis is slightly more expensive than the patentability analysis, since the claims of those patents which appear relevant from the drawings and abstract must be read and interpreted. Upon completion of the infringement search, the results comprising those patents of some relevance to your device or process are forwarded to your patent attorney for analysis of the claim coverage of each. Note also that expired patents may also be included in the search results. If the expired patents disclose that some elements or features of your invention are in the public domain, those features are available to include in your development project.

Your patent attorney reviews each of the claims of the unexpired patents uncovered by the search, since infringement of one claim constitutes infringement to the same degree as infringing several claims of the same patent. It is also possible that your new development may potentially infringe claims in more than one patent. All claims that recite an element that your development product or process does not include are cast aside as not infringed, unless your product or process includes an equivalent to the missing element or step. Under the legal doctrine known as the "Doctrine of Equivalents," if your development product or process does not include all of the elements or steps of an article or method claim, respectively, of a patent, there still may be infringement. Application of the Doctrine of Equivalents is discussed in Section 17.4 of this chapter. If a patent appears to give rise to potential infringement problems, your patent attorney will probably read the history of that patent during examination and prosecution before the USPTO to determine if the claims have been limited in interpretation and scope by the application of prior art by the Patent Examiner, and by responsive limiting amendments by the inventor's patent attorney.

The results of the infringement search are set forth in a carefully crafted opinion letter directed to you or your company's legal counsel. However, prior to furnishing the infringement opinion letter, do not be surprised if your attorney calls you or meets with you face to face to discuss potential infringement problems uncovered by the search, and ways to alter your design direction to avoid infringement. I have spent considerable hours working with inventors assisting them in making changes to their designs so that a path toward infringement is avoided. The patent attorney will most likely not put in writing that your design infringes another's patent. As I will explain in a moment, the infringement opinion letter may in some instances be admitted as evidence in future patent litigation, and a document stating that your device or process infringes the asserted patent is not helpful to your defense of non-infringement. After you and your patent attorney have modified the design to avoid all apparent potential infringement problems, the patent attorney prepares the non-infringement opinion. If infringement cannot be avoided, alternative actions are to change the design parameters completely, or begin negotiations with the owner of the potentially infringed patent to obtain a license at a reasonable royalty, or possibly acquire ownership of the patent. Licensing and assignment of patent rights are covered in Chapter 19.

The attorney's non-infringement opinion letter that you receive is very valuable if and when the owner of one of the patents discussed in the opinion decides to charge you and/or your company with patent infringement. Here's why. Normally, a charge of patent infringement is initiated by one party sending a letter to the potential infringing party, notifying the latter of the existence of the patent, demanding that the infringing activities cease and desist immediately. A copy of the asserted patent is usually attached to the letter. The recipient of that letter, and patent, is henceforth "on notice" of the existence of the patent, and any infringing activities carried out after the day of receipt of the letter may be characterized as "willful and wanton." In patent litigation, if you are found to have "willfully and wantonly" infringed a patent, the Judge has the discretion to penalize you by increasing, by up to three times, the damages you are required to pay to the patent owner.

In defending a charge of "willful and wanton" infringement alleged by a patent holder/plaintiff in a patent infringement lawsuit, the accused infringer/defendant may contend that its continued activities after notice of the patent are not "willful and wanton" because they were acting upon "advice of counsel" that the patent in question was not infringed, was not valid, and/or was not enforceable. The "advice of counsel" is set forth in the non-infringement opinion letter received from the defendant's patent attorney. When this defense is raised, the opinion letter, and any exhibits and/or attachments, may be entered as evidence in the litigation. The patent attorney who authored the opinion is then subject to having his or her deposition taken, while the plaintiff's attorney attempts to uncover flaws in the opinion and show that the opinion is erroneous. The author of the opinion, i.e., your patent attorney, may also be compelled to testify at the trial about the thoroughness and accuracy of the opinion letter.

Where does this lead us? Back to the infringement (freedom-to-use) search and preparation of the non-infringement opinion letter. Whenever I prepare a non-infringement opinion, I ensure that the information in the letter is sufficiently detailed in technical comparisons and legal support to defy attack by another lawyer. I prepare these opinions knowing that someday I may have to defend each step of my analysis while undergoing rigorous cross-examination by an opposing lawyer. I highly recommend that you, as the producer of a potentially infringing product, carefully review the technical conclusions reached by your patent attorney in a non-infringement opinion letter to ensure that all technical conclusions about your product and about the patent claims are correct. Better you than a patent owner's attorney find mistakes in the opinion. If you do find flaws, your patent attorney can prepare a supplemental opinion letter stating why the first opinion was in error, but still concluding there is no infringement, when such is the case. However, if you do discern technical errors in your patent attorney's opinion letter, and the revised conclusion is that the potential risk of infringement is high, go to "plan B," which is discussed immediately in the next section.

17.1.2 The "Right-to-Use" or "Knock-Out" Search

If your infringement search and the patent attorney's analysis conclude that there is one, or more than one, patent claim that is potentially infringed and (a) you cannot work around the patent claim(s) and (b) your chances of obtaining a license from the patent owner are slim to none, a "right-to-use" or "knock-out" search is commissioned. This search is directed to seeking out relevant prior art not previously cited or considered by the Patent Examiner during examination of the potentially infringed patent before the USPTO. If such prior art is found, your patent attorney will advise you whether the newly found prior art is strong enough in its technical disclosures to support a defense that the patent in question is invalid in view of the newly discovered prior art. Even though the patent in question, and for that matter any issued patent, has undergone rigorous examination by the Patent Examiner, a U.S. federal court has the power to declare the patent invalid and unenforceable based on prior art not considered by the Patent Examiner during examination of the patent. Other challenges to the validity of the potentially infringed patent may be raised before the USPTO under new provisions of the AIA. These new provisions are discussed in Chapter 18.

17.2 THE ATTEMPT TO DESIGN AROUND THE CLAIMS OF A PATENT: MOST INFRINGERS DO NOT SLAVISHLY COPY THE PATENTED INVENTION

The purpose of printing and publishing issued patents, and pending patent applications 18 months after filing, is to make them available to potential competitors so that competing non-infringing products may be developed outside of the fence of exclusivity awarded to the inventor by the patent grant. The grand scheme is that by designing around another's patent claims, the competitor will develop a new and even better product, and advance technology and the "progress of the useful arts" as our Founding Fathers mandated in the U.S. Constitution.

Upon being made aware of the scope of claim coverage in relevant unexpired patents uncovered by your search, and as advised by your patent attorney, you begin to develop or modify your proposed competing product or process by using a combination of elements, functions, or steps that are not covered by the claims of any patent. You are also careful to avoid substituting elements, functions, or steps which may be deemed "equivalent" to an element of the patent claim(s) you are trying to avoid.

The prior art comes in handy during this process. If the novel feature of a patent claim under analysis is, say, element A, and you find that you can replace element A and its function with element B and its function, and element B and its function are both shown in the prior art in existence before the filing date of the patent under analysis, you may take the position that infringement has been avoided because your competing product follows the disclosure of the prior art, and not the unexpired patent claim. Put another way, if the patent claim under analysis is interpreted to read on your newly developed competing product, that patent claim also will read on the prior art which you incorporated, since your competing device follows the prior art. However, such an interpretation of the claim under analysis cannot be made. Each issued patent is presumed by statute (35 U.S.C. §282) to be valid, and by law, a patent claim cannot be given an interpretation that would cause the claim to read on the prior art and become invalid.

Remember also that if you see a competing product on the market that you feel may infringe a patent of yours, the chances are that the competing product was designed with input from the competitor's patent attorney, who advised the competitor that its product does not infringe your patent. However, your patent attorney may compare the competing product to your patent claims, and conclude that there is infringement. How can two competent patent attorneys come to divergent opinions on patent infringement regarding the same patent and same product? Don't get me started, but believe me, it happens. This is the nature of the law, and the practice of the law. Sometimes these different opinions are what lead to the filing of lawsuits to expensively determine who is right. Where millions of dollars are at stake in product sales, the expense may be worth it.

17.3 LITERAL INFRINGEMENT OF A PATENT CLAIM

This next section goes into the details of how a determination is made whether or not a patent claim is being infringed by a device or process. This analysis applies both to those situations where your patent is being compared to the potentially infringing device of a competitor to determine whether infringement exists, and to the situation where your product or process is being compared to a competitor's patent to determine whether or not your product or process is free of patent infringement. The same principles will apply to both types of analyses.

Thus, an infringement analysis normally begins in one of two ways. The first is when you are the owner of an issued patent, or you have a pending patent application going through prosecution, and you determine that a competitive product has appeared on the market that may fall within the scope of protection of the claims of your patent or pending patent application. In such situations, you will require the opinion of a patent attorney to determine whether or not infringement exists. If your patent application is still pending, it may be possible to amend your application during prosecution to add broader claims to more clearly cover the potentially infringing device. Second, you may be part of an organization that desires to bring a new product to market, and the question becomes whether your new product would infringe someone else's patent, such as a competitor's. Again, a detailed study must be made of any patents that may possibly be infringed, and comparison of those patents to the potentially infringing product you intend to bring to market.

It is important to remember that in a patent infringement analysis, it is the claims of the patent or the patent application you have under consideration that are compared to the structure or process of the accused or prospectively accused device. Keep in mind that this is unlike the patentability investigation we discussed previously, where the invention for which you are attempting to obtain patent protection is compared to the entire disclosure of a prior art reference patent publication or public disclosure, or publicly sold device.

The initial step in conducting an infringement or freedom-to-use analysis is to determine whether or not the patent contains a claim or several claims which literally read on the accused device. This means that each of the elements of the patent claim are found in the accused device. Literal patent infringement occurs where the device or process under investigation incorporates each and every one of the claimed elements literally set forth in the patent claim. If the device or process does not incorporate all of the elements of the claim, there still may be infringement under the Doctrine of Equivalents, discussed shortly, where the only difference between the patent claim and the device or process under analysis constitutes a substitution of equivalent elements or steps.

In certain patents, the claims are written in "means plus function language" wherein the element of the claim is described as a means for accomplishing a certain function. For example, your computer screen can be described as a plasma display screen. However, a patent attorney might describe the same screen as a "means for displaying electronically formed images," which language would not only cover a cathode ray or plasma type of screen, it would also cover a billboard made of light bulbs or any other electronic display device, if the billboard or other device were mentioned in the specification of the patent. As another example, a table can also be described as a means for keeping documents from falling on the floor. Of course, a hammock full of papers would also meet that requirement, while the hammock would not qualify as a table or desk. For many years, means plus function language has been used by patent attorneys in patent claims in an effort to broaden the scope of protection afforded by the patent. However, today means plus function language in patent claims is limited to those specific elements described in the patent specification, and any equivalents to such elements described in the specification that perform that function. Therefore, if the claim under interpretation does contain means plus function language, it would be prudent to obtain the services of a qualified patent attorney to understand the true scope of the claim.

If it is determined that viable questions of literal infringement exist after comparing the patent claims to your device or process, it is next advisable to have your patent attorney review the examination history of the competitor's patent application before the USPTO to determine if the scope of any element in the patent claims has been limited by amendments and/or comments in the prosecution of the patent. This rule applies whether you are comparing a competitor's device to your patent or comparing your device to a competitor's patent.

17.4 THE "DOCTRINE OF EQUIVALENTS" WHERE THE CLAIM IS NOT LITERALLY INFRINGED

17.4.1 How the Doctrine of Equivalents Works

In applying the test above to determine whether literal infringement of a patent claim exists, it may be determined that one or more of the elements in the patent claim are not found in the potentially infringing device. However, the test for patent infringement does not end at this point, since the Supreme Court has established the "Doctrine of Equivalents." Infringement of a patent under the Doctrine of Equivalents occurs where the accused device or process, although not literally the same as the elements of the patent claims, accomplishes substantially the same result in substantially the same way and with substantially the same elements as are recited in the patent claim or claims, and the differences between the elements in the patent claim and the elements in the accused device or process are "insubstantial." Thus, where the patent claim differs from the accused device or process in only small or equivalent ways, patent infringement is still a possibility. The purpose of this doctrine established by the Supreme Court was to prevent an infringer from getting away with patent infringement by merely substituting known equivalent elements for the elements in the patent claims. Thus, if my patent claim calls for a coil spring as one of the elements, and you have substituted a torsion spring to accomplish the same purpose in the same way, and the torsion spring is determined to be substantially the same element as the coil spring, patent infringement still exists. A key pronouncement by the Supreme Court regarding the Doctrine of Equivalents can be found in the case of *Warner-Jenkinson, Co. v. Hilton-Davis Chemical Company*, 117 S. Ct. 1040, 41 USPQ 2nd 1865 (1997).

In making an infringement determination under the Doctrine of Equivalents, look for the element that is missing from the literal infringement analysis, and determine if there is any feature in the device or process under analysis that is technically equivalent to the missing element. Then apply the previously stated analysis. Your patent attorney will be of significant assistance in applying this highly complex test.

17.4.2 Limits on the Doctrine of Equivalents

When applying the Doctrine of Equivalents, you are essentially determining whether or not an element set forth in a patent claim can be given an interpretation beyond its literal meaning to cover potentially equivalent structure or steps in the device or process under analysis. However, the examination process of the patent before the USPTO may have placed certain limitations on the application of the Doctrine of Equivalents. In the example above, regarding the coil spring and the torsion bar, assume there was a prior art patent reference applied by the Patent Examiner during the prosecution of the patent in question, which reference showed a torsion bar, and to obtain allowance of the patent claim the patentee and his or her attorney had to amend the claim to particularly distinguish the coil spring from the torsion bar. Under this situation, there is no infringement under the Doctrine of Equivalents, because during the prosecution of that patent, a sharp distinction was made between a coil spring and the torsion bar to obtain allowance of the claim. In such instances, the patent claim would be limited to the coil spring, and the torsion bar would not constitute an equivalent element. Thus, when applying the Doctrine of Equivalents, it is important to have your patent attorney review the prosecution history of the patent before the USPTO, and determine what amendments were made to the claims, and what remarks the patent attorney prosecuting that patent made to the Patent Examiner by way of arguments and changes to the claims to obtain allowance over the prior art. Comments and/or amendments may have been made that limit the scope of the claims such that they cannot be applied to the device or process being reviewed under the Doctrine of Equivalents.

Also, it is important to have the patent attorney review the prior art cited and applied by the Patent Examiner to determine whether the potentially infringing device or process does or does not follow the structure and function of the prior art, thereby precluding the application of the claims of the patent to the accused device or process under the Doctrine of Equivalents. As stated previously, a common precept of patent law is that the accused infringer never slavishly copies the patented product. Therefore, the application of the Doctrine of Equivalents is very important in determining if infringement exists, whether it is your device or process, or that of a competitor that is under analysis.

Also remember that under the Doctrine of Equivalents, the claim cannot be construed to have a meaning such that the claim will then read on the prior art. This would give the claim an invalid meaning, and this cannot be done due to the statutory presumption of validity of a patent claim. Also, you cannot stretch the meaning of an element in the claim to read on, or apply to, an element that has been excluded or distinguished in responding to the Patent Examiner. This latter rule is known as the "Doctrine of Prosecution History Estoppel."

In sum and substance, the point to remember from this portion of the text is that even though a patent claim does not literally read on a device or process under comparative review, the application of the Doctrine of Equivalents may result in a holding of infringement. Therefore, it is highly recommended that a complete and thorough analysis of infringement be conducted prior to bringing a product to market so that all possible avenues of infringement allegations are closed off. Also, ensure that your patent attorney provides you with a competent and thorough non-infringement or freedom-to-use opinion.

17.5 DEFENSES TO A CHARGE OF INFRINGEMENT

17.5.1 Non-Infringement

Let us move to the situation where your product is accused of infringing someone else's patent. We use this scenario for purposes of analysis; however, remember that the same analysis would apply if you accused a competitor's device or process of infringing your patent, and the competitor set about to determine defenses to that charge.

One of the primary defenses against the charge of patent infringement is, of course, that the device or process in question does not infringe the claims of the patent, either literally or under the Doctrine of Equivalents. When asserting this potential defense, the owner or producer of the accused device will most likely set forth arguments and provide charts and other technical data showing why the potentially accused device does not fall within the scope of the patent claims. This analysis involves interpretation of the claims, and a review of the specification and the patent's examination history before the USPTO to determine the precise meaning of the claims. Prior to litigation being started, it is normal that a letter be sent to an accused infringer, and the accused infringer also responds by letter, and quite possibly several additional letters of infringement accusations and denial will go back and forth between the two parties. Ultimately, if no agreement or license or assignment can be reached on the issue of infringement, it is quite possible that the owner of the patent may file a lawsuit in a federal court to obtain an injunction and damages for infringement.

17.5.2 Patent Invalidity

Another defense normally asserted on behalf of the potential infringer of a patent is that for one of several possible reasons, the patent may be invalid, and should never have been issued by the USPTO in the first place. Since an invalid patent cannot be infringed, the invalidity defense is raised in most, if not all, patent litigation. There are several grounds that are normally asserted by an accused infringer in asserting that the patent is invalid. These include, among others:

1. The subject matter of the patent claims is shown in prior art not previously considered by the Patent Examiner.
2. The patent owner and/or inventor and/or the inventor's attorney were guilty of "inequitable conduct" in that they were aware of material prior art that was not disclosed to the Patent Examiner during the prosecution of the patent application before the USPTO.
3. The inventors named in the patent are not the true inventors of the patented subject matter.
4. The description of the invention in the specification is insufficient to enable one skilled in the art to practice the invention once the patent expires.
5. The device shown and claimed in the asserted patent is inoperative for its intended purpose.
6. The inventor publicly disclosed the invention to another more than one year before filing the patent application.
7. The claimed subject matter was invented and publically disclosed by another inventor prior to the application filing date of the asserted patent.

Any one of these defenses when proven by competent evidence could result in the patent being held invalid and unenforceable. During a recent conversation with a federal judge during a break in settlement discussions of a patent infringement lawsuit, the judge, who is a particularly congenial individual, asked me why patent attorneys in litigation always attack the work of other patent attorneys. He thought that was rather unusual. I thought for a moment and responded that the statute provides defenses to one who is charged with patent infringement that require the "beating up" of the inventor and the patent attorney who obtained the patent in order to establish a defense of patent invalidity. He thought this was rather strange, and so did I; however, at present, this is way the patent laws are written, and how the system works.

17.5.3 Unenforceability of the Patent

Aside from the other defenses named above, a patent can be held unenforceable against a particular defendant for several reasons. One of these defenses is called the "Doctrine of Laches," which means that the patent owner knew about the infringing activity, but waited too long to file its lawsuit. In other words, the patent owner sat on his or her rights while the infringing activity continued. During the long wait, the defendant/potential infringer forms the opinion due to the inaction of the patent owner that the patent owner was not going to charge his or her device with infringement, and therefore continued to produce and sell the product in question.

Another grounds for holding a patent to be unenforceable is known as the Doctrine of Equitable Estoppel, wherein the patent owner has taken some positive steps, including silence where a response was due, that led the potential infringer to understand that no charge of patent infringement would be lodged. Relying upon this action or silence, the potential infringer continued to produce and sell the product. The two Doctrines of Laches and Equitable Estoppel are somewhat related, and their differences lie in the application of legal principles, which it is not necessary for me to bore you with at the moment.

Another grounds for holding a patent to be unenforceable against the potential infringer is that the potential infringer has obtained a license or an implied license from the patent owner, which allows the patent infringer to continue manufacturing the product. As an example of an implied license situation, I recall a patent lawsuit that I was involved in many years ago while an attorney in of the Patent Litigation Section of the United States Department of Justice in Washington. A patent owner company had licensed the supplier of a particular crimping tool to the government under a first patent owned by the patent owner. The patent owner then purchased a second broader patent that also covered the same crimping tool. The company, now holding both patents, then sued the U.S. Government for infringing the second, broader patent. I raised the argument that this was unfair since the government was licensed under the more limited patent, and the government should also be considered to have a license under any other patent, broader or otherwise, that the same company owned, so that the government was able to practice the license granted under the more limited patent. The court accepted my argument, and held that the license granted under the more limited patent also "implied" that the government would have a license under any other dominating patent owned by that same company. This was another situation where the good guys won.

17.6 PENALTIES AND DAMAGES FOR PATENT INFRINGEMENT

The patent laws provide to a prevailing plaintiff in a patent infringement action the ability to obtain an injunction against any further infringement of the patent, when the patent owner establishes that an injunction is warranted. Thus, the losing defendant in a patent infringement case may be ordered by the court to stop the manufacture, sale, marketing, advertising, use, etc., of the alleged infringing device. This may include a recall by a manufacturer of infringing devices previously sold to its customers.

The patent owner, when prevailing in a patent infringement case, is also entitled to monetary damages, such as a reasonable royalty covering all past infringement involved in the litigation. One of the rules of patent infringement litigation, however, is that the patent owner cannot collect royalties moving backward beyond six years from the date of filing the Complaint. A reasonable royalty is usually established by the prevailing royalty standard in the industry, and/or other licenses that may have been granted by the Plaintiff and/or the Defendant, or other competitors in the same industry. Royalties apply to the past sales of the infringing product by the Defendant. If the infringer takes a license covering future production, the royalty rate applies to future sales. In those cases where the infringing device is a small part of a larger machine, the royalty percentage is applied only to the value of the small part, and not to the whole machine. Therefore, if the infringing device is a lug nut on a wheel assembly of an automobile, the reasonable royalty rate is not applied to the cost of the entire automobile.

Where a patent owner can show that no one else is active in the industry and that the infringing Defendant and the patent-owning Plaintiff are the only ones producing, selling, or using the patented product or process, the patent owner may convince the court that it is entitled to its lost profits rather than a reasonable royalty, which profits are usually higher. The reasoning is that had the Defendant not infringed the Plaintiff's patent, the patent owner would have made the sales and profits of the infringer. Thus, if you are in a situation where your product infringes the patent of another, investigate to determine whether or not the patent owner and you are the only ones in the market. If so, you face the potential loss of additional damages in the form of lost profits to the patent owner.

As stated previously, if infringement can be shown to be willful, where the infringer knew of the existence of the patent and continued its infringing conduct, the court may increase damages by multiplying them by up to three times to compensate the patent owner and punish the Defendant for such willful infringement. Therefore, as we discussed earlier in this chapter, it is important to have a competent opinion from your patent attorney prior to engaging in potentially infringing activities that there is no viable charge of willful infringement that can be lodged against you and/or your company.

17.7 MARKING THE PATENTED PRODUCT WITH THE PATENT NUMBER

Section 287 of the U.S. Patent Law (35 U.S.C. §287) states that patentees and persons making, offering for sale, or selling a patented article or importing an article may give notice to the public that the same is patented by placing the patent number on the product, or where the character of the article prohibits this, by fixing the patent number to the package or a label. When the patented product is so marked, damages for all infringement by the patentee may be recovered, dating back six years from the date of filing a lawsuit. In the event of a failure to mark the product with the patent number, no damages for patent infringement shall be recovered by the patentee except from the date that the infringer was actually notified of the patent and its infringement, where the one on notice continued to infringe thereafter. Thus, infringement damages may be recovered only for infringement occurring after actual notice if the product is not marked with the patent number. Under the provisions of the AIA, posting the patent number on the website featuring the product or process also provides adequate notice to the public.

Therefore, it is good advice to mark each patented product, or its container, label, point of purchase literature, or related website with the patent number to ensure that if an infringer appears on the horizon, the full measure of damages can be recovered from that infringer.

◆ INVENTORS AND INVENTIONS ◆

Robert Goddard

ROCKET PROPULSION AND CONTROL

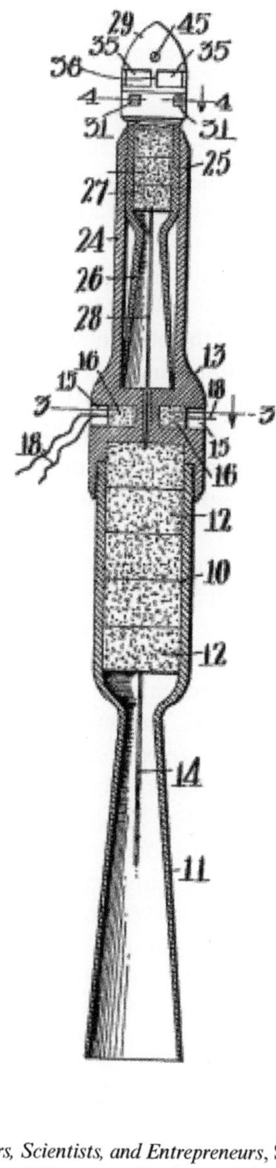

Intellectual Property Law for Engineers, Scientists, and Entrepreneurs, Second Edition. Howard B. Rockman.

Published 2020 by John Wiley & Sons, Inc.

His name is synonymous with rocketry, and his work enabled people to be sent into space. Robert H. Goddard is recognized as the father of modern rocket propulsion, and he held 214 patents related to rocketry.

Goddard was born on October 5, 1882, in Worcester, Massachusetts. Even as a young boy, Goddard was interested in rocketry. At the age of 5, he watched electricity being produced from a Leclanché battery in his uncle's workshop. He also observed that he could make sparks by scuffing his feet along the carpet. He decided that if he combined the two, he could create a large enough spark to propel him to the moon. So he took a zinc rod, rubbed it on his shoes, and scuffed his feet on the sidewalk in front of his house. During his experiment, his mother came out and told him to be careful and that it might work and send him sailing away with no way to bring him back. Because of this, he hid the zinc rod and decided to give up on the study of space flight for the time being.

Goddard attended Worcester Polytechnic Institute from 1904 to 1908. In 1907, he first attracted public attention. This was the result of a large cloud of smoke created by a powder rocket he "launched" in the basement of the physics building at Worcester Polytechnic Institute. Instead of expelling Goddard, the school took interest in its student's work.

In 1912, Goddard first mathematically investigated the use of rocket power to reach a high altitude and escape gravity. In July 1914, he received two U.S. patents. One was for a gun rocket using liquid fuel, and the other covered a two- or three-stage solid-fuel rocket. These patents are reprinted following this biography.

In 1918, Goddard developed and demonstrated several types of solid-fuel rockets that could be fired from a tripod or hand-held launching tubes. His launching platform was a music stand. This, of course, was the basis of the American "bazooka."

At his own expense, Goddard conducted studies of the propulsion force produced by various types of gunpowder. In 1916, he documented his studies in a request for funds to continue his research from the Smithsonian Institution. This study was published, along with additional research he and the Navy conducted, in the *Smithsonian Miscellaneous Publication* No. 2540, in January 1920. The study was entitled "A Method of Reaching Extreme Altitudes." Near the end of his treatise, Goddard referred to the possibility of a rocket reaching the moon and exploding a quantity of flash powder to visibly prove its arrival. This was too much for the *New York Times,* which, on January 13, 1920, published an editorial pronouncing that space travel was impossible, since the lack of an atmosphere in space would not provide a resistance that a rocket force could push against. The *Times* commented that Professor Goddard (of Clark University) lacked "the knowledge ladled out daily in high schools." Goddard, from that time on, had a cool, and sometimes nonexistent, relationship with the press. After Apollo II blasted off in 1969 to land the first human on the moon, almost 25 years after Goddard's death, the *New York Times* looked back at its 1920 editorial. The paper, in 1969, commented that: "Further investigation and experimentation have confirmed the findings of Isaac Newton in the 17th century, and it is now definitely established that a rocket can function in a vacuum as well as in an atmosphere. The *Times* regrets the error."

The derision he received from the press did not stop Goddard's experiments. In 1923, he tested the very first liquid-fuel rockets, and on March 16, 1926, he launched the first liquid-fuel rocket at Auburn, Massachusetts. The fuel was made of gasoline and liquid oxygen. The rocket, called Nell, was 10 feet long, flew 41 feet up, and reached a speed of 60 miles per hour, landing 2½ seconds later, 184 feet away in a frozen cabbage patch. The Smithsonian Institution, which had given Goddard a subsidy, was not too impressed with the report of the flight. They wanted larger rockets that could perform as well as smaller ones.

Goddard's Nell rockets became increasingly large and harder to hide from his critics. In 1929, an 11 foot missile launch resulted in an intervention by the Worcester police, followed by the press. The local headline the next day laughingly touted: "Moon Rocket Misses Target by 238,799½ Miles." Soon after, on July 17, 1929, Goddard sent up a rocket carrying scientific instruments, a barometer, thermometer, and a small camera. He continued theses studies from 1930 to 1942 in Roswell, New Mexico, with the aid of a Guggenheim Foundation grant. His research was greatly expanded, and his new rockets could reach heights of one-and-a-half miles and speeds of up to 550 miles per hour.

NASA named a space flight center in Greenbelt, Maryland, after him on May 1, 1959. On September 16, 1959, the 86th Congress authorized the issuance of a gold medal in honor of Professor Robert H. Goddard.

Goddard made most of his engineering advances in rocketry in the 1920s and 1930s. He calculated the energy-to-weight ratio of several potential fuels; he discovered that a rocket could fly in a vacuum (see Newton's laws of action and reaction); he did away with powder fuels by using liquid propulsives, such as kerosene or liquid hydrogen mixed with liquid oxygen, to allow combustion to occur in airless space. He also developed rockets that climbed to 9000 feet, exceeded the sound barrier, and incorporated fin-stabilized steering. He also obtained patents covering gyroscopic guidance systems, multistage rockets, and a multitude of other inventions.

Goddard's 1920 Smithsonian report was distributed in Europe, where the German Rocket Society was founded in 1927, and the German Army initiated a rocket program in 1931. German scientists began contacting Goddard with technical questions on rocketry, and he would informally send responses. In 1939, the inquiries from Germany abruptly stopped. Being disturbed by this, Goddard approached the U.S. Army in Washington, and showed films of his various Nell rocket launches. The Army thanked him for the information, and dismissed him and his ideas. Five years later, the first German V-2 rocket headed for London, and by 1945, Germany had launched over 1100 V-2's. At the end of World War II, Goddard inspected a German V-2 and determined that it appeared to utilize his technology. An anecdote holds that when a captured German scientist was debriefed about the V-2 rocket development, he was heard to respond: "Why don't you ask Dr. Goddard? He knows better than any of us." U.S. scientists then worked alongside "imported" German scientists after the war to incorporate Goddard's improvements into the Redstone rocket, which launched the first Americans into space, and was the precursor of almost every other rocket used by the United States.

Robert Goddard died on August 10, 1945. During his long career dedicated to rocket propulsion theories and the practicalities needed to enable the rocket to begin the "space age," he was a creative scientist who also had the engineering skills to bring his theories to fruition. Although his work in rocketry was mostly disregarded in the United States during his lifetime, the dawn of the space age has caused the scientific, engineering, and government communities to recognize all that this man accomplished.

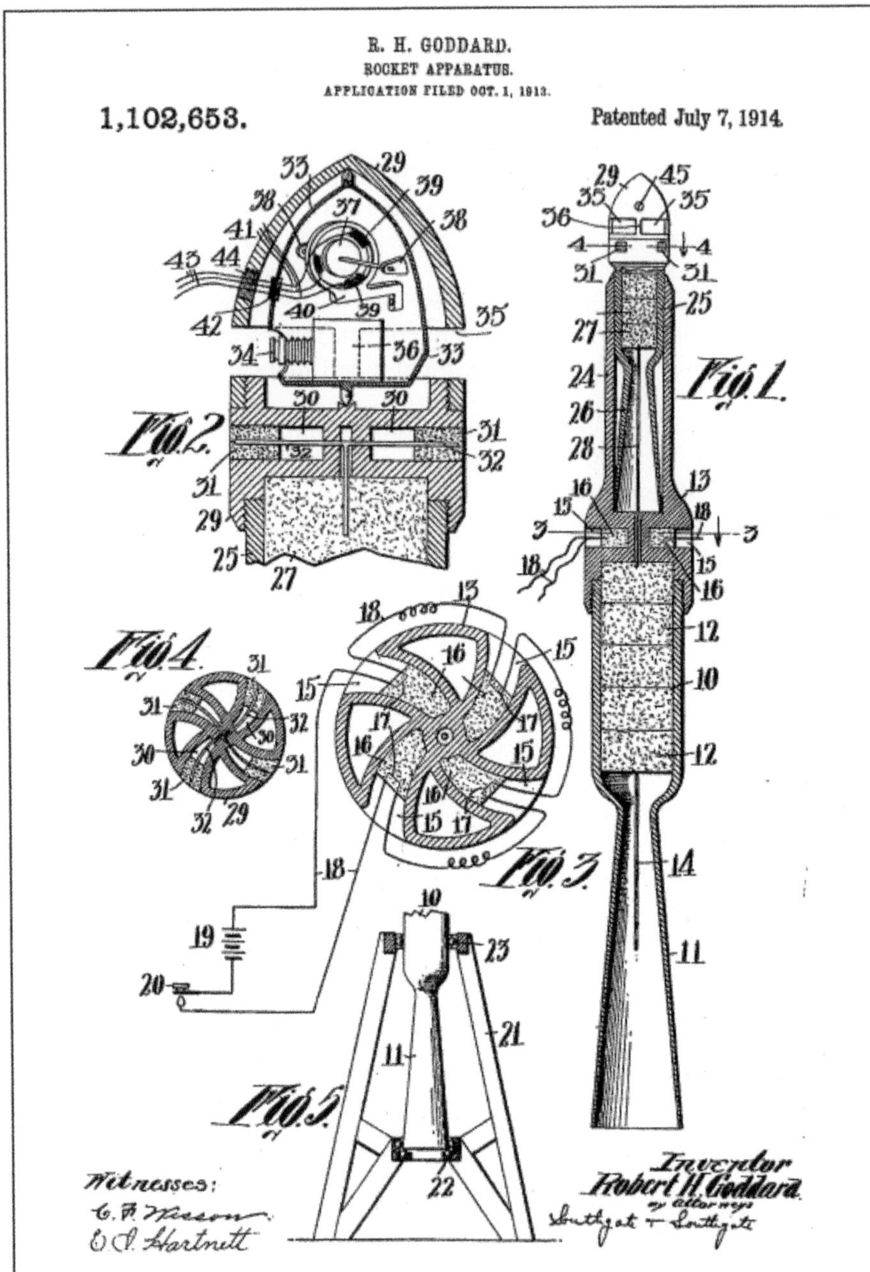
R. H. GODDARD.
ROCKET APPARATUS.
APPLICATION FILED OCT. 1, 1913.
1,102,653.
Patented July 7, 1914.
Fig. 1.
Fig. 2.
Fig. 3.
Fig. 4.
Fig. 5.
Witnesses:
Inventor
Robert H. Goddard
by attorneys

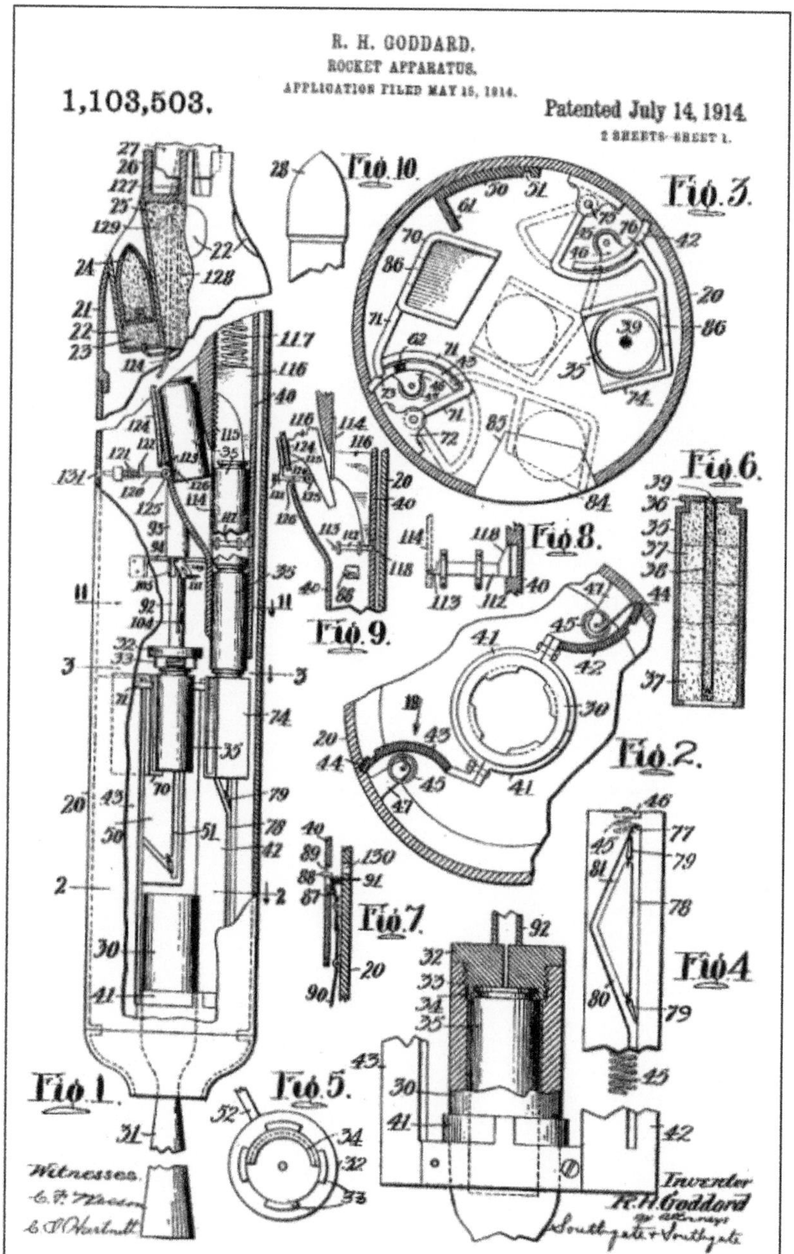
R. H. GODDARD.
ROCKET APPARATUS.
APPLICATION FILED MAY 15, 1914.
1,103,503.
Patented July 14, 1914.
2 SHEETS-SHEET 1.
Fig.1.
Fig.2.
Fig.3.
Fig.4
Fig.5.
Fig.6.
Fig.7.
Fig.8.
Fig.9.
Fig.10.
Witnesses.
Inventor
R. H. Goddard
by Attorneys
Southgate & Southgate

◆ INVENTORS AND INVENTIONS ◆

C. Donald Bateman

GROUND PROXIMITY WARNING SYSTEM

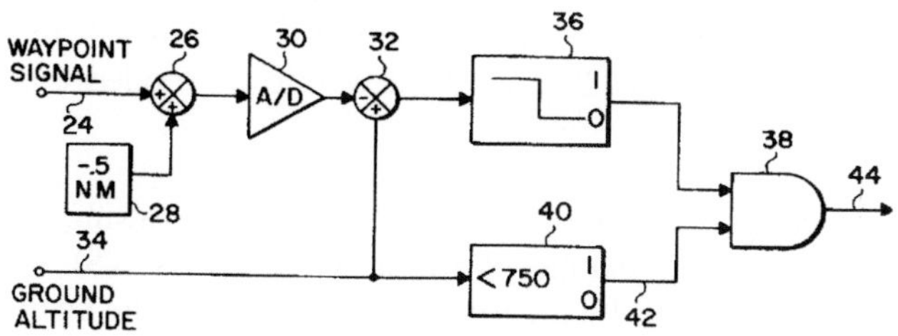

It has been said in the aircraft industry that Donald Bateman has probably saved more lives than any other single person in the history of aviation. Following numerous aircraft accidents that resulted from controlled flight impacting terrain (CFIT), Bateman created a solution to these accidents. CFIT is defined as where a pilot has the aircraft under control but unknowingly flies into terrain, usually in poor visibility. Bateman felt it was within his capabilities to design and construct a system that would detect hazardous terrain in the aircraft's anticipated path.

Tragic airplane crashes during the 1960s compelled airline owners to seek ways to improve a pilot's ability to know if he or she is flying too low or approaching a mountain or other terrain feature. The ground proximity warning system (GPWS) that Bateman developed used a computer to analyze data from a radio altimeter that alerted a pilot with a voice warning that the aircraft was in danger of flying into hazardous terrain or into the ground. Bateman figured that the weight point signal of an area navigation system (ANS) could be used in combination with an altitude above ground signal to compute a minimum terrain altitude for each point along the aircraft's approach to a runway. The minimum altitude is compared with the aircraft's actual altitude, and if the actual altitude is below the minimum, an alarm is activated. The abstract from Bateman's U.S. Patent No. 3,922,637 covering the GPWS describes a radar altimeter system to keep track of the aircraft's height above ground, with the system sounding an alarm if the aircraft is at an unsafe altitude.

Intellectual Property Law for Engineers, Scientists, and Entrepreneurs, Second Edition. Howard B. Rockman.

Published 2020 by John Wiley & Sons, Inc.

The GPWS technology improved flight safety; however, it was still imperfect because of two problems:

1. *No warning*. The primary cause of CFIT occurrences with no GPWS warning is landing short of the runway, when the landing gear is down and landing flaps are deployed. The GPWS expects the airplane to land and therefore issues no warning.
2. *Late warning or improper response*. This is primarily caused by blind spots within the terrain, or a sudden change in altitude. A steep slope, for example, would receive a late warning, and the pilot would be unable to avoid the obstacle. This problem was implicated in the Garuda Indonesia Flight 152 accident in 1992, when an Airbus A300B4-220 aircraft flew into a wooded mountain on an approach to the airport.

Bateman continued his work, and, by going back to the drawing board, he developed the Enhanced Ground Proximity Warning System (EGPWS), which corrected the shortcomings of the GPWS by incorporating a GPS into the analysis of the terrain, and incorporating terrain elevations from a terrain data base. This made it possible for EGPWS to predict the path of the aircraft and the terrain ahead of the aircraft for several miles, and to provide the pilot with digital terrain maps featuring hazardous obstacles and features that warn the pilot when to pull up the aircraft even in poor weather. Also, with EGPWS, landing does not inhibit the performance of the system, and landing and departure are safer, since these are the most dangerous aspects of flight.

EGPWS automatically warns pilots that their aircraft is approaching the ground or water. Although the U.S. Federal Aviation Administration began requiring GPWS in aircraft in 1973, Bateman and his team continued to develop advanced technology that made their warning systems more effective and reliable. They added sophisticated ways of determining the distance from the aircraft to threatening terrain, provided wind shear warnings, integrated other avionic systems, and included computerized color pictures of topographical data. EGPWS is now mandatory for turbine aircraft with at least six passenger seats, and similar laws are in effect in most countries in the world.

Before the development of GPWS and EGPWS, there were 10 aircraft crashes due to CFIT. For the last several years, the annual CFIT accident rate in the United States has been nearly zero.

United States Patent [19]
Bateman

[11] **3,922,637**
[45] **Nov. 25, 1975**

[54] **AIRCRAFT LANDING APPROACH GROUND PROXIMITY WARNING SYSTEM**

[75] Inventor: **Charles Donald Bateman,** Bellevue, Wash.

[73] Assignee: **Sundstrand Data Control, Inc.,** Redmond, Wash.

[22] Filed: **Oct. 3, 1974**

[21] Appl. No.: **511,757**

[52] **U.S. Cl.** .... **340/27 R;** 244/77 A
[51] **Int. Cl.²** **G08G 5/00;** B64C 13/50
[58] **Field of Search** .... 340/27 R; 244/77 A, 77 V

[56] **References Cited**

UNITED STATES PATENTS

3,381,295 4/1968 Blackledge .... 244/77 A;77 V

Primary Examiner—Thomas B. Habecker
Attorney, Agent, or Firm—Michael B. McMurry; Ted E. Killingsworth

[57] **ABSTRACT**

In order to provide for the additional effectiveness of a ground proximity warning system during a landing approach, the waypoint signal of an Area Navigation System is used in combination with an altitude above-ground-signal to compute a minimum terrain altitude for each point along the aircraft's approach to the runway. The minimum altitude is compared with the aircraft's actual altitude and if it is below the minimum an alarm is activated.

11 Claims, 2 Drawing Figures

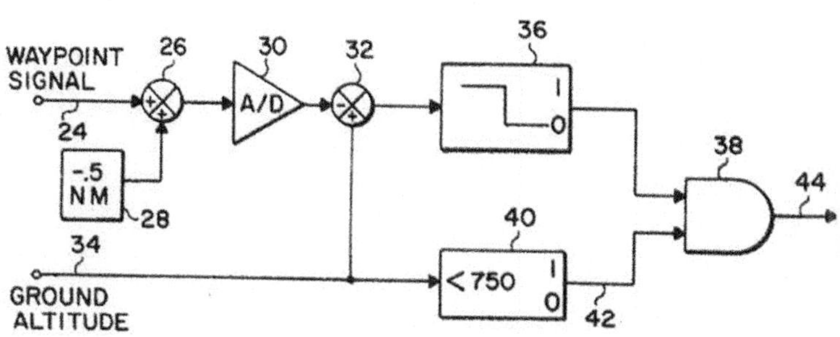

18 The America Invents Act of 2011

18.1 FIRST TO FILE AND THE DEFINITION OF "PRIOR ART"

The America Invents Act of 2011 ("AIA") legislated several important changes in U.S. patent laws, some substantive, but mostly procedural. Two important changes are (1) the first to file a patent application is awarded the patent rights over a second inventor who subsequently filed a patent application directed to the same or similar invention, where previously it was the first to invent who was awarded the patent rights after a complicated interference proceeding; and (2) "prior art" is now defined as information that was publicly available prior to the filing date of a U.S. patent application, regardless of the date of invention of the subject matter claimed in the patent application.

The first-to-file standard is easy to apply when conflicting patent applications are filed. However, the prevalent takeaway from this change in the law is that it is now important to file your patent application at the earliest possible time (provisional or non-provisional), particularly where you are working in a crowded research and development genre, and there is a likelihood that someone else may file a patent application on similar technology before you do. As explained previously, the first-to-file rule does not apply where you can establish that the inventor of the first filed patent application derived the invention from you, and you were the second-to-file inventor.

Under Section 102(a) (35 USC §102(a)) of the AIA, a person is entitled to a patent, *unless*:

1. The claimed invention was patented, described in a printed publication, or in public use, on sale, or otherwise available to the public before the effective filing date of the claimed invention, or
2. The claimed invention is described in an issued U.S. patent or in a published U.S. application, which names another inventor, and was effectively filed before the effective filing date of the claimed invention.

Thus, the effective filing date of patents and published applications under the AIA determines whether such is prior art. For the present, also consider materials displayed on the Internet as published materials for purposes of reviewing the prior art related to your invention. Issued patents and published patent applications are publicly available on the USPTO website.

Intellectual Property Law for Engineers, Scientists, and Entrepreneurs, Second Edition. Howard B. Rockman.

Published 2020 by John Wiley & Sons, Inc.

The "public use" and "on sale" bars to patentability that are publicly accessible now apply to any publicly accessible activities worldwide, whereas, prior to the AIA, only public uses and on sale activities occurring in the United States barred patentability. As under the prior law, published and publicly accessible material anywhere in the world as of the filing date of a patent application is "prior art."

The prior art category of "otherwise available to the public" is new, and may expand the definition and amount of prior art in future cases. Moving forward, the courts will apply this provision to applicable situations. I suggest that, to ensure that your patent rights are secure, no public disclosures of your invention be made prior to filing a provisional or non-provisional patent application, and any necessary public disclosure only be made under the aegis of a signed non-disclosure agreement. It may become necessary to establish that you made a deliberate attempt to keep the invention a secret before your patent application was filed.

18.2 THE NARROWED GRACE PERIOD

The AIA retains the grace period of the prior law, providing an inventor 1 year after a public disclosure of the invention to file a U.S. patent application. This grace period applies only after the inventor has made the invention publicly accessible less than 1 year prior to the application filing date, which disclosure, of course, will destroy the ability to obtain significant foreign patent rights. See Chapter 16. Under the previous law, the inventor had some modicum of protection by relying on the earlier date of invention, but that has been eliminated by the AIA.

It remains to be seen how the courts interpret the meaning of the terms "disclosure," "publicly disclosed," and "otherwise available to the public" in forthcoming cases. However, to be safe in maintaining your ability to secure patent protection, either refrain altogether from making public any information about your invention before filing at least a provisional patent application, or, if disclosure of the invention is necessary before an application can be filed, talk to your patent professional before making the disclosure for advice as to what steps can be taken to avoid the loss of patent rights, such as the use of confidentiality agreements.

18.3 DISCLOSING THE BEST MODE OF THE INVENTION

The U.S. Patent Law for many years has required that one seeking patent protection disclose the "best mode" of practicing the subject invention in the patent application. This requirement is retained in the AIA, which ensures that the invention that goes into the public domain is the best version of the invention conceived and reduced to practice by the inventor(s), rather than some inferior version of the invention.

However, the AIA removes any penalty for failing to disclose the best mode of the invention in a patent application by stating that "the failure to disclose the best mode shall not be a basis on which any claim of a patent may be cancelled or held invalid or otherwise unenforceable…" (35 U.S.C. §282(b)(3)(A). Despite this, 35 U.S.C. §112(a) of the new Patent Law, in mandating the contents of a patent application specification, states that the applicant "shall set forth the best mode contemplated by the inventor or joint inventor of carrying out the invention." The new law also provides that a patent application filed first in a foreign country, and then filed in the United States, does not have to disclose the best mode of the invention.

The consensus is that this removal of the defense of failure to disclose the best mode in a patent application was to accommodate global patent harmonization efforts, since, generally, foreign patent statutes do not have a best mode requirement.

In addition, in the way the AIA has changed this element of U.S. Patent Law, it appears that, even though a patent applicant is required to disclose the best mode of practicing the invention in the patent application, the lack of best mode will not be able to be raised by third parties in post-grant reviews of issued patents newly authorized by the AIA.

Theoretically, a Patent Examiner could still reject a patent application on the grounds of failing to disclose the best mode of the invention. However, since the USPTO rules do not allow a Patent Examiner to obtain information from the applicant through a "discovery" process as used in litigation in the United States, the examiner has really no way of determining whether or not the inventor has disclosed the best mode.

In my opinion, this is one of the conundrums that may be understood further as time goes by, and future court decisions consider this point.

18.4 PRIOR USER DEFENSE IN ENFORCEMENT PROCEEDINGS

The "Prior User Defense" relates to cases where an alleged infringer in patent litigation developed the patented invention before the inventor named in the issued patent, but used the invention secretly and commercially. In 1999, the First Inventor Defense Act included a personal defense only for prior users of business method patents who commercially used the subject invention before the effective filing date of the asserted patent.

The AIA expands the availability of the prior user defense to challenge patents directed to machines, articles of manufacture, and compositions of matter used in manufacturing or other commercial processes. The prior use must have taken place in the United States and in good faith by the person against whom the issued patent is being asserted. The provision also requires that the prior commercial use have taken place more than 1 year prior to the effective filing date of the asserted issued patent.

The prior user defense under the AIA is not available where the asserted patent is owned by a university, or subject to an obligation to assign the invention to a university. The prior user defense is available, however, where the R&D necessary to reduce the invention to practice by the university could not have been undertaken using funds provided by the federal government.

18.5 PATENT MARKING

The Patent Law has long encouraged patent holders to give notice to the public of their patent rights by marking the patented product, or container of fungible goods, with the corresponding patent number(s). The AIA extends this patent notice by providing that an Internet posting including the patent number gives adequate notice to the public. Under both the prior law and the AIA, if the product, container, or Internet site does not include the patent marking(s), the patent holder in a lawsuit cannot collect damages for infringement for the period of infringing activity that took place before the infringer had actual knowledge of the subject patent and continued to infringe. Thus, it is important to mark products, containers, and Internet sites with the patent numbers pertaining to your products.

Some courts have held that patent marking is not required for method patents. However, if a product is produced by a patented method, the patent number of the resulting product and the number of the process patent should be displayed on the product.

18.6 FILING A PATENT APPLICATION IN THE NAME OF THE ASSIGNEE

An important procedural change brought about by the AIA allows company-assignees to apply for a patent directly in the name of the assignee-company. An "assignee-company" is defined in the statute as a person, including legal entities such as corporations, LLCs, and the like, to whom the inventor has assigned the invention, or is under an obligation to assign the invention. Under these circumstances, the corporation, etc., may file the patent application in its own name. However, the actual and true inventors must still be named in the documents filed with the USPTO.

In addition, a person (individual, corporation, etc.) who otherwise shows sufficient proprietary interest in the invention may file a patent application on behalf of and as agent for the inventor, where such action is appropriate to preserve the rights of the parties. If a patent issues under this provision of the AIA, the patent is issued to the real party in interest and upon notice to the inventor(s).

18.7 PRIORITY EXAMINATION FOR IMPORTANT TECHNOLOGIES

The AIA allows the Director of Patents to prioritize or expedite the prosecution of some patent applications for "products, processes, or technologies that are important to the national economy or national competitiveness" without the payment of any additional fees. See 35 U.S.C. §2(b)(2)(G). This is in addition to existing rules that allow for expedited examination of a patent application with a required fee. For example, expedited examination can be granted, by petition and without payment of an extra fee, based on the applicant's age or health, if the products, processes, or technologies aid in the advancement of the environment, development or conservation of energy, or countering terrorism. A fee-based petition for expedited examination can be based on the appearance of an infringing product or process on the market, or inventions relating to recombinant DNA.

18.8 THIRD-PARTY CHALLENGES TO PATENT RIGHTS

The AIA includes three provisions that allow someone other than the patent applicant, known in legal jargon as a "third party," to challenge the granting of a patent by the USPTO to the patent applicant. These provisions encompass:

1. Pre-grant submissions;
2. Post-grant submissions; and
3. Post-grant review.

18.8.1 Pre-Grant Submissions

This provision allows a third party to submit supposedly relevant prior art patents, published patent applications, or any other printed published material to the USPTO during the examination process of a pending patent application. Such material must have potential relevance to the examination of the application. Keep in mind that most pending patent applications are published on the USPTO website 18 months after filing, and are available to competitors or others who may be aware of publicly available prior art. The submittal of prior art under this provision must be accompanied by a concise description of the asserted relevance of each submitted document. The submittal may be made without identifying the real party in interest making the submittal. The Patent Examiner is then free to consider the submittal and determine if the material is more relevant to examination than the prior art uncovered by the examiner's own search.

18.8.2 Post-Grant Submissions

35 U.S.C. §301 of the Patent Law prior to the AIA provided that any person at any time could submit to the USPTO printed published prior art material which that person believed to have a bearing on the patentability of any claim of a particular issued patent. This submittal, if accompanied by a written statement explaining the pertinence and manner of applying the prior art, would become a part of the official file of the patent.

The AIA expanded the type of written material that could also be submitted under this provision to include statements of the patent owner filed in a federal court or USPTO proceeding in which the patent owner took a position on the scope of any claim of a particular issued patent. If the person making the submittal under this provision also submits a statement as to the pertinence and manner of applying the prior art to any claim of the patent, the submittal becomes part of the official USPTO file of the subject issued patent. At the request of the submitter of prior art to the USPTO, the name of the submitter will be excluded from the patent file and kept confidential.

18.8.3 Post-Grant Reviews

The AIA includes new provisions for a third party who is not the owner of the subject issued patent to initiate a post-grant review of the patent by a petition filed no later than 9 months after the patent issues. Once initiated, a post-grant review is conducted by the Patent Trial and Appeal Board, in a proceeding similar to a court proceeding, including discovery of the other party's evidence and an oral hearing. The patent owner has one opportunity to amend the patent claims during the proceeding if deemed prudent to avoid the challenge raised against the patent. Declarations, other factual supporting evidence, and expert opinions may be submitted with the petition seeking review.

The patent owner has the right to file a response stating reasons why the petition should not be granted. The Director of Patents then determines whether the post-grant review procedure should or should not go forward. Upon the conclusion of the post-grant review process, the Director issues a certificate either confirming the validity of any challenged claim, or cancelling one or more of the challenged claims.

18.9 INTER-PARTES REVIEW OF AN ISSUED PATENT

The prior Patent Law provided for "Inter Partes Reexamination." This title has been replaced by "Inter Partes Review," with several enhancements. This procedure is used when someone who is not the owner of an issued patent desires to challenge the validity of the patent in view of prior art patents and printed publications. Prior public uses, offers for sale, and other non-published public disclosures cannot be submitted in an Inter Partes Review proceeding.

A petition to the Director of Patents to initiate an Inter Partes Review may be filed only after 9 months have elapsed from the issuance of the subject patent. The first 9 months are available for the "Post-Grant Review" process, described in Section 18.8.3. Thus, the Inter Partes Review cannot be filed until a post-grant review is completed, or the 9-month time period for instituting a post-grant review has passed.

A petition requesting an Inter Partes Review identifies the claims of the patent under challenge, the reasons for the challenge, and is accompanied by copies of patents and printed publications that are relevant to the challenge, which alleges lack of novelty and obviousness of the subject invention. The statements and arguments of the petitioner must convince the Director of Patents, or his or her designated USPTO officer, that "there is a reasonable likelihood that the petitioner would prevail with respect to at least one of the (patent) claims challenged in the petition." This is a higher standard than previously required to initiate a reexamination proceeding under the earlier Patent Law, in that the new law requires a showing of at least a modicum likelihood of success in the challenge.

Under the AIA, the burden of proof applicable to the petitioner is that, once the Inter Partes Review has been initiated by the Director of Patents, the petitioner must prove its case by a "preponderance of the evidence" directed toward establishing the non-patentability of the invention. This, among patent practitioners, is considered a relatively low standard of proof. As a result, the Inter Partes Review proceeding may be the choice of a prospective patent challenger as compared to federal court litigation, particularly when time, allocation of resources, personnel, and costs are compared.

The patent owner is furnished with a copy of the petition when filed, and is allowed a preliminary response to be considered before the petition by the challenger is granted or denied. This new rule was promulgated to speed up the process to give the patent owner a chance to speak his or her piece early in the proceeding. The new rules also allow the patent owner to file one motion to amend, cancel, or substitute claims in an effort to derail the challenger's attack. In addition, the AIA states that the final determination must be made by the USPTO no later than 1 year after an Inter Partes Review petition has been granted.

During an Inter Partes Review proceeding, discovery is allowed, but is limited to the deposition of witnesses who have submitted sworn declarations and/or affidavits. Protective orders are permitted that protect the disclosure of confidential information. Further, these proceedings are conducted by the Patent Trial and Appeal Board staffed by Administrative Law Judges, rather than by patent examiners who determined previous reexamination proceedings. Oral arguments are also permissible.

18.10 SUPPLEMENTAL EXAMINATION

This proceeding has been added to the Patent Law by the AIA at the end of the section dealing with Amendments and Correction of Patents, directed in part to the patent reissue process. The reissue process is directed to reissuing a patent where errors appear in the specification, claims, or drawings, but does not apply regarding the patentability of the subject invention, such as issues relating to the patent owner's obligation to disclose to the Patent Examiner, during the examination process under Rule 56, all information known to the applicant that is material to the examination process.

The AIA supplemental examination provision allows patent owners to ask the USPTO to consider, reconsider, or correct information relevant to the patentability of the invention in the patent owner's judgment. This procedure follows the reexamination procedure, but allows the patent owner to submit for consideration possible evidence of public disclosures, public uses, and/or offers for sale that may have a bearing on the validity of the subject patent. This procedure gives the owner of a patent time to head off issues he or she becomes aware of by a competitor, potential licensee, or infringer regarding compliance with the known prior art disclosure rule by submitting this issue, or any others, bearing on patentability in an effort to have the USPTO "clear out" these issues, so that a potential challenger cannot raise such matters later. Recall that a patent issued by the USPTO is presumed valid, and, to challenge a patent, the challenger must rely on evidence not considered previously by the USPTO examiner. One caveat: this proceeding does not prevent an infringer from arguing in a litigation setting that the findings of the USPTO upon supplemental examination were erroneous.

In summary, the supplemental examination provisions of the AIA allow a patent owner to pre-empt failure-to-disclose-prior-art arguments, or other lack of patentability arguments, raised by a potential challenger, and provide the patent owner with the opportunity to have these issues vetted by the USPTO. This new procedure allows the patent owner to have the USPTO look at these issues prior to, or instead of, expensive litigation.

There are many other procedural matters introduced into Patent Law by the AIA. As a good source for researching these matters, and for a more in-depth discussion of the AIA, I recommend reference to the following text: "Patent Reform 2011," Edward D. Manzo et al., Thomson Reuters, publisher (2011).

◆ INVENTORS AND INVENTIONS ◆

Charles Kettering

AUTOMOTIVE SELF-STARTER

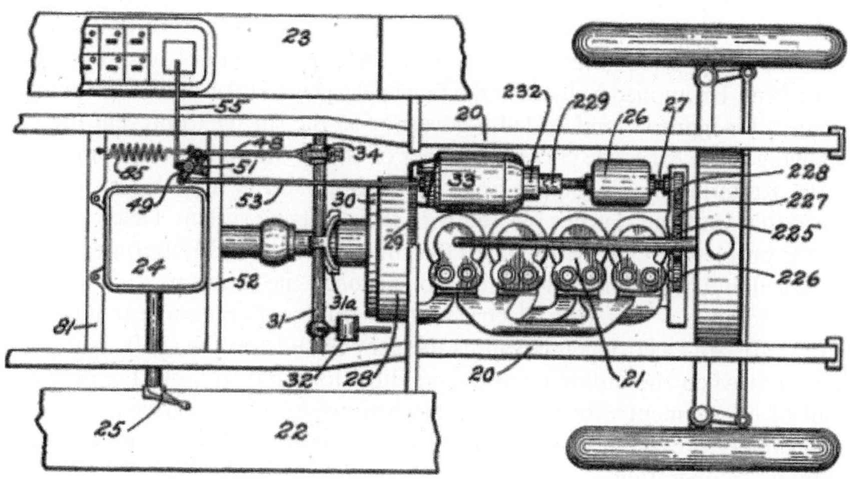

If you are over the age of 16, and not a total environmentalist, you have probably used his invention. No, not the car but the electrical ignition system. The inventor's name is Charles Franklin Kettering.

Charles Kettering invented the first electrical ignition system, the self-starter for automobile engines, and the first practical engine-driven generator. He was born on a farm near Loudonville, Ohio, on August 29, 1876. He earned an engineering degree from Ohio State University in 1904, and joined the engineering staff of National Cash Register Company (NCR). At NCR, he oversaw the development of several products, including the electrically operated cash register and accounting machines. One source states that he invented the automobile ignition system while moonlighting in Edward Deeds' barn in Dayton, Ohio.

In 1909, Kettering left NCR, and he and Deeds formed the Dayton Engineering Laboratories Company, now known as Delco. Before Delco was acquired by General Motors in 1916, Kettering invented his most significant engine devices, including the Delco engine-driven generator that furnished electricity to millions of people in rural areas.

By 1910, automobiles had developed enough to be considered practical. They had speedometers, lights, almost workable brakes, and a rudimentary suspension system.

Intellectual Property Law for Engineers, Scientists, and Entrepreneurs, Second Edition. Howard B. Rockman.

Published 2020 by John Wiley & Sons, Inc.

One problem stood out—each car had a handle, or crank, at the front that was attached to the engine crankshaft. Using both hands, and sufficient muscle on the crank, the engine could be turned through several revolutions. By retarding the ignition, advancing the throttle, and enriching the air/fuel mixture, the engine could start. If not, the driver cranked until the engine started, or his arms gave out. Most women at the time did not have the upper body strength to operate the crank. At times, an engine would backfire and kick the crank back with excessive force, causing injury to a driver who was still holding on. At least one driver of a Cadillac was killed in 1910 when a crank hit him in the face.

The first attempt at building a self-starter for automobiles was patented by Clyde Coleman in 1903, as U.S. Patent No. 745,157, reprinted following this biography. Coleman's solution failed to satisfactorily meet the requirements of torque and starter disengagement. He applied a clutch in the flywheel to try to take care of the disengagement issue after ignition, and added a governor to the starter to prevent the starter from drawing down excessive current. Neither of these solutions proved practical.

Charles Kettering developed the first practical self-starter at Delco in 1911, when he learned that Cadillac was not pleased with their starting system. Delco was invited to solve the problem. Delco then licensed Coleman's patent, and Kettering drew on his own electrical and mechanical knowledge to approach the problem.

A starter today is a "fattened" electric motor with a small pinion gear at the end of the drive shaft. An electromagnet causes the gear to slide on the shaft to engage the flywheel teeth when the motor turns in one direction, and to move the gear on the shaft out of engagement with the flywheel when power to the starter is cut off. The starter has thick wires connected to a solenoid since it draws several hundred amperes of current when operating.

Kettering, in 1911, did not solve the disengagement problem. His electric motor was permanently engaged with the flywheel. When the engine started, the engine flywheel rotated the starter shaft, and the starter was transformed into a generator, charging the battery. This was a practical solution, since the rpm's of automobile engines in 1911 were relatively low. Torque requirements were met by engaging the pinion gear with a flywheel having 25 times the number of teeth on the pinion gear. Consider the problem this would cause in today's automobiles operating at 3000 rpm. Kettering's early starter shaft, if directly driven by the flywheel, would rotate at 75,000 rpm, leading to the real possibility that pieces of starter motor would be scattered throughout the parking lot.

Two years after Kettering developed his self-starter in 1911, Victor Bendix created a starter design that disconnected the starter gear from the flywheel after ignition. However, Kettering's starter was tested and accepted in 1911 by Cadillac, and Delco was given an order for several thousand starters, which were installed in 1912 Cadillacs. Delco licensed its starter technology to other manufacturers, and practically all cars offered an optional electric starter by 1920. Consider also that Kettering's self-starter invention allowed motoring to be accepted by women, which doubled the size of the potential automobile purchasing market.

Kettering went on to have an illustrious and rewarding technology career, with over 140 patents to his name.

When Kettering and Deeds sold Delco to General Motors for nine million dollars in 1916, they started a factory to produce Kettering's farm lighting system. Kettering also helped establish the Dayton Airplane Company, which enlisted the skill of Orville

Wright as a consulting engineer. One of the company's main goals was to perfect Orville's automatic flight system, and produce planes for private use.

After the United States entered World War I, the Dayton Airplane Company received a contract to produce 5000 DeHavilland warplanes with the new "Liberty" engine and a new, more reliable ignition system for the "Liberty" engine. During the war, Kettering developed the first synthetic aviation fuel and was asked to produce a "flying bomb" that would carry explosives to their target 50 miles away. Kettering selected Dayton Wright as the contractor and Orville Wright as the aeronautical consultant. World War I ended before the flying bomb, or "Kettering Bug" as it was commonly called, could be put to use. The bug was patented, however, and kept as a military secret until World War II when the Germans produced the V-1 rocket, employing the same concept.

In 1920, General Motors took over many other business interests of Kettering's and created the General Motors Research Corporation with Kettering appointed as president. Soon after that, he was made vice-president of General Motors and named to its board of directors.

Kettering proceeded to find a practical gasoline additive to eliminate engine "knock." With the help of Tom Midgley, he discovered that tetraethyl lead was the most effective substance. Kettering's ethyl gasoline added more horsepower, greater safety, reliability, and speed not only to cars but to airplanes. Today, leaded gasolines are banned in the United States as environmentally dangerous.

Charles Kettering is probably best known for the Sloan-Kettering Institute for Cancer Research in New York City. He and Alfred Sloan, president of General Motors, created the institute with an endowment in 1945. Charles Kettering died on November 25, 1958.

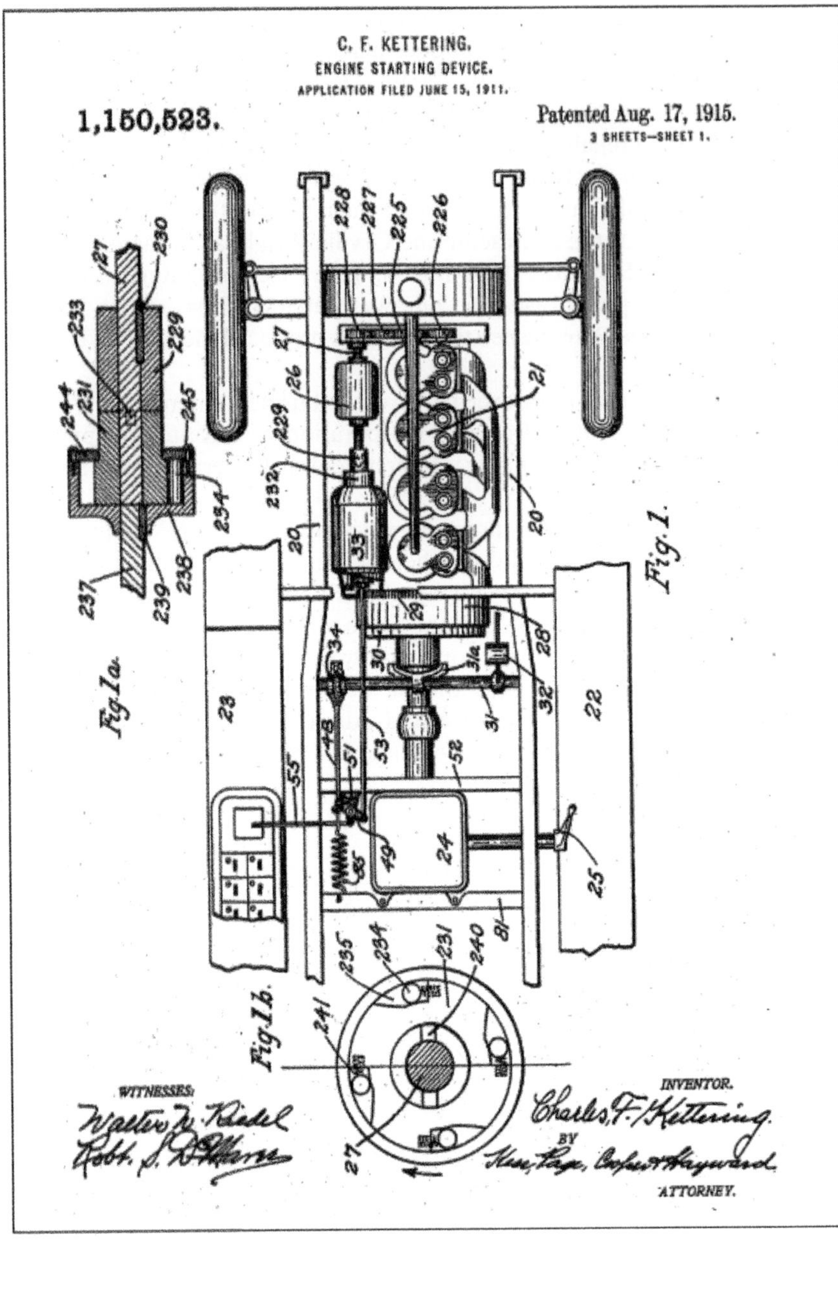
C. F. KETTERING.
ENGINE STARTING DEVICE.
APPLICATION FILED JUNE 15, 1911.
1,150,523.
Patented Aug. 17, 1915.
3 SHEETS—SHEET 1.
Fig. 1.
Fig. 1a.
Fig. 1b.
WITNESSES:
INVENTOR.
Charles F. Kettering
BY
ATTORNEY.

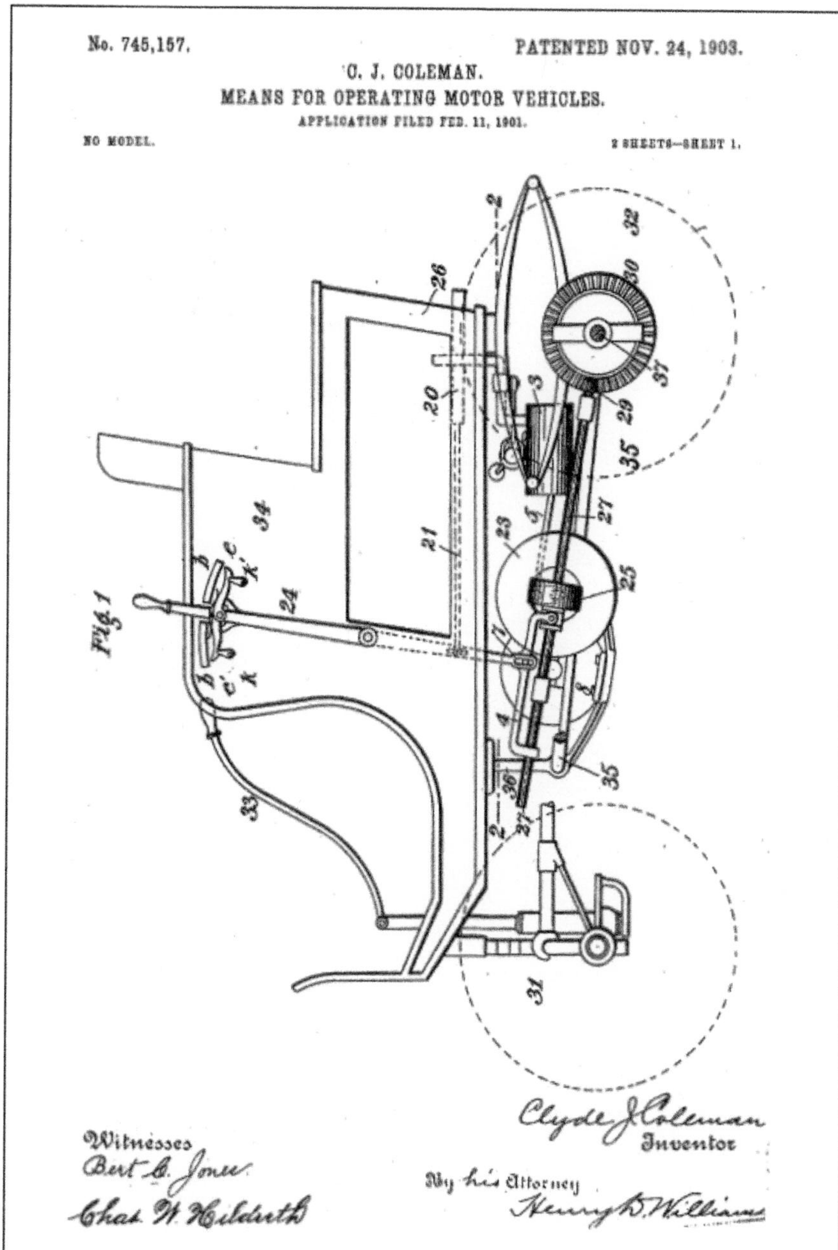
No. 745,157.
PATENTED NOV. 24, 1903.
C. J. COLEMAN.
MEANS FOR OPERATING MOTOR VEHICLES.
APPLICATION FILED FEB. 11, 1901.
NO MODEL.
2 SHEETS—SHEET 1.
Fig. 1
Witnesses
Bert C. Jones
Chas. W. Hildreth
Clyde J. Coleman
Inventor
By his Attorney
Henry D. Williams

◆ INVENTORS AND INVENTIONS ◆

Calvin Souther Fuller, Gerald Pearson and Daryl Chapin

EFFICIENT SOLAR CELLS

The three inventors named above worked for Bell Laboratories and are credited with producing the first high-efficiency solar cells.

The invention of the first efficient solar cells actually begins in the 1860s, when Willoughby Smith, an electrical engineer, used selenium bars in a device for detecting possible breaks in the transatlantic cable before submersion. He noted that the selenium bars worked well enough at night; however, they performed much better in sunlight. Smith then placed the bars in a box with a sliding cover, and when the box was closed to prevent light from shining on the bars, the bar's electrical resistance was at its highest and remained constant. When the cover of the box was removed and light reached the bars, the conductivity of the bars immediately increased in accordance with the intensity of the light. Smith conducted a series of further experiments and concluded that the resistance of the selenium bars changed in response to the intensity of the light. It was clear that a current could be started in the selenium by the action of the light alone, as found by a later scientist, and it was determined that light caused a flow of electricity through a solid material, and the current produced by light was called "photoelectric current."

Moving forward to the 20th century, Albert Einstein, in a paper published in 1905, showed that light possesses an attribute that earlier scientists had not recognized: light contains packets of energy, then called "light quanta," and now called "photons." Einstein argued that the amount of power that the light quanta carries varies according to the wavelength of the light, where the shorter the wavelength, the higher the power. He determined that the shortest wavelength includes photons that are about four times as powerful as those of the longest. By the 1920s, scientists referred to this phenomenon as the "photovoltaic effect."

Around 1953 or 1954, two scientists, Calvin Fuller and Gerald Pearson of Bell Labs, led an effort to take the silicon transistor from theory to practice. Pearson was an experimentalist and Fuller was a chemist, the latter learning how to control the introduction of the impurities necessary to form silicon to the point of being the preeminent conductor of electricity. At one point, Fuller gave Pearson a silicon rod containing a small concentration of gallium. The gallium positively charged the silicon. Pearson then dipped the rod into hot lithium according to Fuller's formula,

Intellectual Property Law for Engineers, Scientists, and Entrepreneurs, Second Edition. Howard B. Rockman.

Published 2020 by John Wiley & Sons, Inc.

and the portion of the silicon immersed in the lithium became negatively charged. Where the positive and negative silicon met, a permanent electrical field developed. This is a p-n junction (positive negative junction), the heart of the transistor and the solar cell where all electronic activity occurs. Silicon so produced requires outside energy for activation, which was provided by lamplight in one of Pearson's experiments. The specially prepared silicon was connected by wires to an ammeter, which recorded a significant electrical current.

At the same time that Fuller and Pearson were busy improving transistors, another Bell scientist, Daryl Chapin, was working on a project aimed at providing small amounts of intermittent electrical power in remote humid locations. Under normal humidity, traditional dry cell batteries would work, but in the tropics the batteries had a short life due to humidity-induced degradation. Bell Labs asked Chapin to look into the feasibility of employing alternative sources of free-standing power, including wind machines, thermo-electric generators, and small steam engines that could be used in tropical climes. Chapin suggested to Bell Labs that he also include solar cells in his investigation, and his supervisors agreed.

In February 1953, Chapin began his photovoltaic research. He placed a commercial selenium cell in sunlight and recorded that the cell produced 4.9 watts per square meter, giving an efficiency, measured as a percentage of sunlight converted into electricity, of less than 0.5%. Pearson heard of the results of Chapin's work, and advised Chapin to stop working with selenium. Pearson then gave Chapin the silicon solar cell that he had constructed. The silicon solar cell had an efficiency of 2.3%, five times greater than the selenium cells. Chapin then dedicated all of his time to improving the silicon solar cell, and calculated that an ideal solar cell made of silicon could use 23% of the incoming solar energy to produce electricity. However, he set a modest goal of obtaining an efficiency of nearly 6%, which at that time was a threshold that engineers thought was necessary to establish that photovoltaic cells were a serious and reliable source of electric power.

Chapin then did most of the engineering work, trying new materials, testing various configurations, and he went through a period where it seemed that nothing would work. A breakthrough came from his knowledge of Einstein's light quanta (photon) work. Chapin determined that it appeared necessary to place the p-n junction very close to the surface of the cell so that the more powerful photons belonging to light of shorter wavelengths could effectively move electrons to where they could be harvested as electricity. This required collaboration with Fuller. Chapin also observed that silicon's shiny surface reflected a good deal of sunlight that could and should be absorbed and used. He then replaced the coating on the surface of the silicon with a dull transparent plastic. He also added boron to the top of the cell, which permitted better photon harvesting by allowing improved electrical contact on the silicon strips while keeping the p-n junction close to the surface. Chapin ultimately reached his 6% goal, and the three inventors ultimately constructed a number of solar batteries and demonstrated them at a press conference, and at an annual meeting of the National Academy of Sciences.

The three inventors also created an array of several strips of silicon, each one about the size of a razor blade, and placed the strips in sunlight. This captured free electrons from the sun and turned them into electrical current. Therefore, these scientists had also created the first solar panel.

Bell executives introduced the Bell solar battery to the press on April 25, 1954, demonstrating a cell panel using solely light power to operate a 21 inch Ferris wheel. The following day, they demonstrated a solar-panel-powered radio transmitter, broadcasting voice and music to America's top scientists meeting in Washington, D.C. The *New York Times* reported that the work of Chapin, Fuller, and Pearson resulted in the first solar cell capable of generating useful amounts of power.

Robert W. Fuller, Calvin's son, has related the following story:

> I was home during vacation from college in 1954 to visit my parents, and my father came home with something that looked like a quarter with wires sticking out of it. He connected this device to a small electric windmill that stood on the table and shined a bright flashlight on the quarter-like object, which was actually a silicon solar cell. The blades of the windmill started turning, so actually the world's first silicon solar battery that became known as a silicon solar cell operated a small windmill.

The first public service installation of the Bell solar battery was with a telephone system in 1955 in Americus, Georgia. In 1958, the Department of Defense used solar cell batteries in deploying self-positioned vehicles and satellites in space that received their power from the sun.

Feb. 5, 1957 D. M. CHAPIN ET AL 2,780,765

SOLAR ENERGY CONVERTING APPARATUS

Filed March 5, 1954

FIG. 1

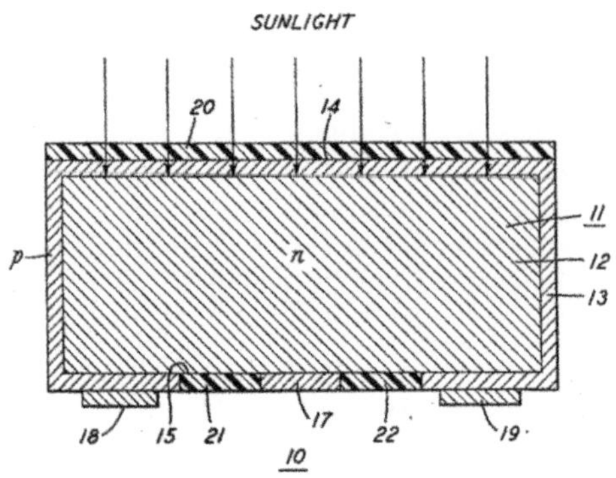

FIG. 2

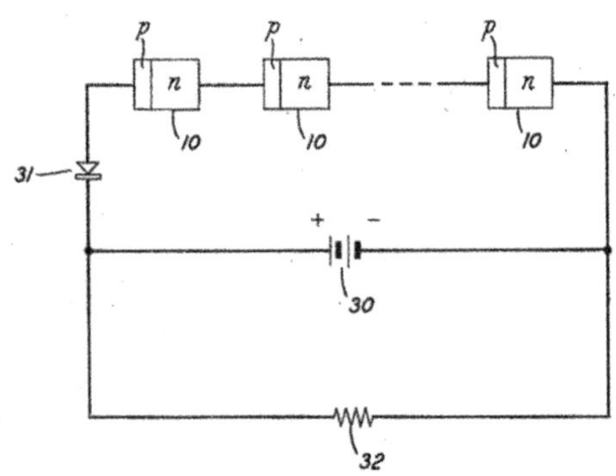

INVENTORS: D. M. CHAPIN
C. S. FULLER
G. L. PEARSON

BY Arthur J. Torsiglieri
ATTORNEY

19 Ownership and Transfer of Patent Rights

19.1 INVENTORSHIP, OWNERSHIP, AND ASSIGNMENT OF PATENT RIGHTS

Once a patent on your invention is granted, you may treat the exclusive rights provided by the grant as an asset, just like money, stocks, property, etc. Your exclusive rights may be sold to, or licensed to another party. Under certain circumstances, your employer may obtain a legal, non-exclusive right to use your invention, even though you did not intend to grant this right to your employer. Assignments and licenses are effected by written contracts, in most cases after you have decided to have someone else commercialize your invention on your behalf. Thought must be given to whether (1) you are going to manufacture, market, sell, and distribute your invention yourself, (2) you are going to sell all rights in your invention to someone else for a sum of money, or (3) you will license someone else to produce and bring your product to market under specified terms that must be met for the licensee to keep the license. If you decide on the license route, terms satisfactory to you and your licensee must be mutually agreed upon and placed in a license agreement. This chapter discusses how you, either as the inventor or as one seeking to obtain rights under another's invention, can achieve your goals.

19.1.1 The Patent Right as an Asset

As discussed previously, the rights given to an inventor or inventors under the Patent Law are intangible rights. You cannot see or touch them, such as cash, a stock certificate, or a bank account statement. However, once the inventor has shown the U.S. Patent and Trademark Office (USPTO) that a novel and un-obvious invention has been created, a certificate of Letters Patent is awarded, and those intangible rights are now memorialized in a tangible, readable written document, bearing a U.S. Government seal. The Letters Patent precisely define the extent and limitations of the awarded patent rights. By reading the Letters Patent, the rest of the world is made aware of, and is on notice of, the exclusive rights secured to the inventor, as well as the limitations on those rights.

The intangible patent rights defined by the tangible Letters Patent, which can be seen and understood, have also now been transmogrified into an "asset" of their owner. This asset can now be dealt with by the owner in the same manner as any other

Intellectual Property Law for Engineers, Scientists, and Entrepreneurs, Second Edition. Howard B. Rockman.

Published 2020 by John Wiley & Sons, Inc.

asset. The "patent asset" may be transferred by assignment, license, or any other applicable legal vehicle, in whole or in part.

The term "Assignment" defines a sale of the patent rights to another, where the inventor relinquishes all ownership of the patent rights. A "License" grants another party the right to make, use, import, offer for sale, and/or sell the patented article or method under the authority of the patent owner, and the patent owner retains the ownership of the patent. When a patent is assigned, the prior owner primarily bows out of the picture. However, when a patent right is licensed, the owner of the patent normally includes provisions in the license agreement that give the patent owner considerable say in the commercialization of the patented product or process by the licensee.

The owner of the Letters Patent is entitled to receive a negotiated compensation for the transfer of the patent rights to someone else, just as a seller of any asset receives value in return for the transfer of the asset. Thus, the patent system has changed what once was merely an intellectual image in the mind of an inventor, or group of inventors, into a tangible "thing," i.e., intellectual property, that can be sold or otherwise transferred, sometimes for large sums of money, similar to any other valuable asset, such as your house, car, or boat. Compensation for assigning patent rights can be in the form of a one-time payment, or a royalty based on future sales of the patented invention, or a combination of both.

19.1.2 Initial Ownership of the Patent Right

The role and definition of the "inventor(s)" in the creation of the invention, and ultimately the patent rights in that invention were described previously. Recall that in the United States, patent applications can be filed with the USPTO in the name(s) of the true inventor(s), or in the name of a company or other entity that owns, or will own the patent rights. At that moment, the inventor(s) own all of the patent rights applied for, except where they have previously agreed, in writing, to assign the invention and the patent rights in that invention to another, such as an employer.

If you are hired by a company, firm, partnership, or other business entity to develop new products or processes, you will probably be required as a condition of your employment to agree on the first day of your employment to transfer ownership of any of your inventions or proprietary developments to the employer that relate to the employer's business that you come up with while in the company's employ. This agreement normally covers even those inventions or ideas you derive while at home, on your own time and with your own tools and materials, that may have value to your employer's business. However, I have seen several situations where an inventor developed a novel device at home and on his own time, which had no relation to his employer's business. According to the employment agreements these inventors signed, there was no obligation to assign these inventions to their employers, since the agreement to assign only pertained to inventions related to the company's business. Therefore, when you are entering a new employment situation, or are asked to sign an "invention rights" contract, read the document carefully to determine whether you have an obligation to assign "all" inventions you come up with while an employee, or only those inventions which relate to the business of the employer. It could make a difference as to how you spend your spare time.

Also, even though your invention may relate to the company's business, management may state that it has no interest in using your invention. Your next step is to ask management to sign a release of their invention assignment right, and grant you the right to commercialize the invention on your own, so long as your commercialization activities do not conflict with the employer's business interests.

If you have not signed an invention rights assignment agreement, and a patent application is filed covering your invention, you as the inventor own all rights to the invention, the patent application, and any patent that issues from the application. You may assign your patent rights to anyone at any time during this period and up to the time the issued patent expires. You may also assign your patent rights to one of your co-inventors, or assign a portion of your patent rights to someone else while retaining a portion of the rights yourself. Remember, though, that any person or company that owns even a small fraction of a patent right can commercialize that patent right without accounting to the other owners as to the financial or other benefits received for such commercialization. However, the default position that no accounting is owed to the other patent owners can be modified by a written contract between the inventors or co-owners of the patent rights, such as a Joint Development Agreement.

19.1.3 Shop Rights

Some inventors conceive of an invention that has nothing to do with their employer's business, or under other situations where there is no obligation to assign the invention to the employer. However, to reduce the concept to a concrete form, let us say the inventor used his employer's time and/or materials and/or equipment and/or personnel, as a matter of necessity or not. This factual circumstance gives rise to a "shop right" in the employer, who automatically and under the operation of law, obtains a royalty-free, non-exclusive license to use or otherwise exploit the invention as the employer sees fit, and whether or not the inventor desires to give his or her employer such rights. Therefore, before you develop an invention at work, using your employer's material, time, personnel, and/or machinery, consider whether you would be better off doing your development work at home, using your own or borrowed equipment.

The shop rights obtained by an employer, however, may have certain limitations. For example, the shop right generally does not give the employer the right to grant sub-licenses under the patent. Some states have laws preventing the employer from using the invention beyond the employer's normal course of business.

19.2 PATENT LICENSING

A patent license allows the licensor, usually the inventor or owner of the patent rights, to grant permission to someone else to commercialize the patented invention (the licensee). A decision to grant a license is normally weighed against the advantages, or disadvantages, of producing and marketing the product embodying the invention yourself, or assigning your patent rights outright to another party, such as an established manufacturing company. If your ultimate decision is to grant a license, an acceptable licensee must first be sought. Once an acceptable "license partner" is found, the license agreement must be negotiated and set forth in a written document. While patent attorneys normally are not involved in your search for an appropriate licensee, the attorney is normally involved in negotiating and preparing the license agreement. The same is normally true of assignment agreements.

19.2.1 The Difference Between a Patent Assignment and License

When an inventor, or subsequent owner of a patent, assigns or sells the intangible rights embodied in the Letters Patent, the inventor or owner divests themselves of all rights they had in the patent prior to the sale. The former owner has no right to control who may make, use, or sell the patented invention, cannot sue infringers of the patent, and cannot collect royalties for another's use of the invention. Just like the sale of a house, you cannot move back in without repurchasing the house.

In most well drafted, astute patent assignment agreements, the former owner, also described as the seller or assignor, receives a one-time payment, or time-scheduled payments, of a fixed amount as consideration for relinquishing the patent rights. Alternatively, the assignor may receive a royalty-based payment for the assignment, where compensation is based on a royalty or percentage of the sale price of each product sold, or process used, which includes the invention covered by the patent. In this latter situation, the inventor or assignor can anchor his or her compensation to the success of the product.

One other point is worth mentioning. In most patent assignment agreements I have been responsible for preparing, the inventor agrees that if an infringement lawsuit is brought by the new owner, or if other litigation flares up questioning the validity of the patent, the inventor will assist the assignee in defending the patent against attacks on the patent. These defensive attacks, mentioned in Chapter 17, are normally asserted by an alleged infringing defendant in patent lawsuits. The inventor also agrees to provide deposition and trial testimony, if necessary and if requested to do so by the new owner of the patent rights.

A patent license is, for our purposes, a completely different creature compared to an assignment. Assume the following: You are the inventor of a new form of hybrid internal combustion/electrical powered automobile power system that showed enormous potential during two years of testing. You are an automotive power expert working on this project for a major engineering institution of higher learning in the United States. You and your school have an agreement to share in any income obtained from commercializing your invention. You recognize that (1) your invention could have considerable importance in the near future, particularly during the 20 years of exclusive rights afforded by a patent grant, and (2) there are several truck, automobile, boat, and engine manufacturing companies that are interested in further developing and commercializing your invention. You and your school decide that for an invention of such potential importance, you want several, if not all, of these companies to adopt and work with your invention, and not provide any single company with an exclusive right to make, use, and sell your invention. You also decide that you and your school should retain control over the future development and commercialization of your invention.

Therefore, instead of assigning your invention to a single company, which would relieve you entirely of your patent rights, your patent attorney suggests that you initiate a program offering non-exclusive licenses under the patent to those interested companies. If your invention is as important as expected, this procedure will result in several licensees paying royalties to you and your school, rather than just a single source of income were the patent assigned to a sole entity.

A license, as distinguished from an assignment, provides many benefits. When granting a license, you maintain ownership and control over the patent rights, but are giving someone else the right to make, use, and/or sell the patented invention pursuant to mutually agreed upon terms which are set forth, normally, in a written license agreement, which is a legally binding contract between the licensor (owner of the patent right) and the licensee (the party desiring to make, use and/or sell the invention). Thus, the licensee can use the inventive technology without infringing the patent.

19.2.2 When To Think "License"

In the movie *The Candidate*, after successfully being elected a U.S. Senator as an "outsider" reformist against the "entrenched" established candidate in a bitter campaign, Robert Redford utters the famous last lines of the movie: "What do we do now?" No one answers as his campaign staff walks out of the room, and the story ends. As an inventor, you ultimately reach the point in the development of your invention where the patent application has been filed with the USPTO, and you ask the question: "What do we do now?" Unlike the Robert Redford movie, I will attempt to answer that question.

Once your patent application has been filed, you are free to begin commercializing your invention to obtain the benefit of all of your hard work in bringing the invention to fruition. Under U.S. Patent Law, you could have begun publicly commercializing your invention no earlier than one year before your patent application filing date. However, as mentioned previously, such activities would lead to adverse effects on obtaining patent protection in many other major industrialized nations. So, for purposes of explanation, we shall consider that you did not make your invention publicly known prior to the filing date of your U.S. patent application.

By filing your provisional or non-provisional patent application, you have now perfected an "official filing date" for your patent application. When the rules of the international treaties governing patents are followed by your patent attorney, your U.S. filing date, or "priority date," is the effective filing date in those countries that are part of the treaties, which is almost every country. Therefore, you can now publicly disclose your invention without fear of losing foreign patent rights. In addition, since your invention is now of record as a filed patent application with a U.S. government office, no one else can steal your invention and file a patent application on that invention prior to your filing date. As a result, it is now safe to make your invention publicly known, and take steps leading toward the entry of a product or products, or process, into the marketplace so that the world will have the benefit of your invention, and you will reap the rewards for the advancement of technology embodied in your invention.

It is highly recommended, however, that even after your patent application has been filed, the invention should be disclosed to others only after a confidential, non-disclosure agreement has been signed by the recipient. This should continue at least until a public disclosure of your invention occurs, such as a public sale, offer for sale, or public use of the invention, or the patent is published or issued. This affords added protection for the invention, since the interaction between patents and trade secrets in the early stages of patent application filing complement one another, and are not mutually exclusive.

Consider the following true example: Company A filed a patent application covering its invention, and also had disclosed the invention to Company B under a non-disclosure agreement. A patent issued on the invention, and Company A eventually claimed that Company B infringed the patent and that the non-disclosure agreement was breached. Damages of over $50 million were awarded to Company A. On appeal, the appeals court held the patent invalid, but let the damages award stand because of the breach of the non-disclosure agreement. Therefore, had Company A not had the non-disclosure agreement in place, it would have recovered nothing.

We are now also considering the situation where you, as the inventor, are under no obligation to assign your invention to another, such as your employer. The invention and the patent rights you have applied for are yours to deal with as you please. If you have access to manufacturing, marketing, distribution, sales, financial, accounting, and advertising capabilities, you may be able to place your invention on the market yourself. However, all of the inventors I have dealt with, who have not previously assigned their patent rights to their employers, were not in a position to successfully bring a product to market without considerable financial and other help. Consider my client the bank manager who developed a new automotive accessory product, or the college student who developed a technical advance in in-line skates. The list goes on. It is these inventors who should "think license" as a way to make their invention publicly available.

I have represented several inventors who have attempted to form a business, such as a company, partnership, LLC, or other entity, to produce and sell their inventions. These inventors usually have no prior experience in the market for their invention, or have not previously attempted to start a business from the ground up. The initial problem each of these inventors face is raising enough money, usually in the one-half million to several-million-dollar range, to finance a new company's ability to get started. Most of these efforts take either a long time to produce results, or fail altogether. The proper way to raise financial backing for a new venture is beyond the scope of this treatise, so I shall immediately fast forward to the subject of licensing, which I perceive as the more expedient, less stressful way to gain the benefits of the work you put into your invention, and to place your invention in the hands of the waiting public.

Efforts toward licensing your patent rights can, and should, begin as soon as possible after the patent application has been filed. There is no need to wait until the patent issues. Most license agreements are written granting license rights under a pending patent application, covering any patent or patents that ultimately issue from the application. Since the search conducted prior to preparation and filing of your patent application indicated that your invention, or elements of your invention, were novel and non-obvious in view of the prior art, you operate under the assumption that ultimately a patent will be granted covering your invention. Therefore, your efforts at obtaining someone to license your invention can justifiably proceed on a positive note regarding obtaining an issued patent.

19.2.3 Developing an Initial Relationship with a Licensee

In some technology areas and industries, a trade association or other industry source may have a list of established businesses that are looking for new inventions and products to add to their existing product lines, or to improve their present products. If you can locate such a list, your first step should be to contact those on the list that meet your criteria for a successful licensing partner. These criteria will be covered shortly. This is accomplished by sending a letter to the prospective licensee, broadly defining your invention and what your invention accomplishes, and inquire if they have any interest. Of course, if you obtained the name of the prospective licensee from a list defining the technology they were interested in, you highlight the advantages of your invention from the standpoint of the technology the prospective licensee is looking for. Also, you state in your letter that you have a patent application pending covering your invention.

In most instances, you will receive a response letter indicating that the recipient has a policy of not considering unsolicited or outside ideas, unless the inventor agrees that the invention is being submitted on a non-confidential basis, and that if the inventor ever makes an accusation that the prospective licensee acted unlawfully with respect to the invention, the inventor will only resort to its patent or copyright rights, and will not accuse the prospective licensee of misappropriation of trade secrets. This form of agreement protects the recipient of your letter in the event, for example, they reply that they have examined your invention and have no interest in it, and several years later, you discover they are selling your invention without your approval. It is much more difficult to defend against a theft of trade secret case, so the prospective licensee protects itself against a possible lawsuit in the future. However, the prospective licensee is agreeing to honor your patent rights.

When you receive a non-confidential disclosure letter such as described above, my advice is to have your patent attorney review the letter to ensure it does not include any additional adverse provisions. If the letter is approved by your attorney, sign it and send it back. Why? You already have a patent application pending covering your invention, which in all probability will ultimately issue as a patent. If the prospective licensee does unlawfully adopt your invention, you will be able to use your patent to stop such conduct.

19.2.4 The Selection of an Appropriate Licensee

Assume you desire to have someone else develop and introduce your invention to the market, and to pay you handsomely for the right to do so. Besides looking for someone interested in your invention from among those seeking new technology, another avenue is to seek out prospective licensees who may not necessarily be looking for new technology, but may be interested in your invention once they see it.

The first step is to determine who manufactures products, or uses processes, in the area of technology of your invention. If your patent professional conducted a patentability search prior to the preparation of your patent application, most if not all of the patents uncovered by the search will (1) disclose other inventions closely related to yours, and (2) provide information as to the owners of those prior art patents. Since your invention is an improvement over the prior art inventions, the owners of these patents, if they are manufacturers of the prior art inventions, may be interested in adopting your new technology to improve their existing products. Thus, the manufacturer owners of the prior art inventions uncovered by your search should be on your list of potential licensees.

Also, if your invention falls within a technology area represented by a substantial trade or professional association, the membership list of that association will provide you with a source of potential licensees. A further way to seek out potential licensees is to ask a retail store manager to give you the name of a distributor of a related product. You then can ask the distributor for the names of those who manufacture products that would be enhanced by your invention.

Once you have the names of several manufacturers in hand, contact the marketing department of one or more of those companies, not the engineering or technical departments. Why? It is called the NIH syndrome—"not invented here." The postulate goes that when you present your invention to other engineers, they may initially conclude that if your idea were a good one, they would have thought of it. Since the idea came from an outside source, these internal engineers may decide that your idea is not very good. However, by approaching the marketing department first, you are talking to business- and project-oriented personnel, not technicians. If you can convince the marketing department that your invention would be a profit making addition, extension, or improvement to their existing product line, those marketing types will provide an opening for serious consideration of your invention by the target company.

A word on selecting your target companies. Your invention most probably requires further development work to engineer its most expedient production, and to bring the manufacturing cost down to a minimum. Then the product incorporating the invention has to be manufactured by your target company, which can most economically be accomplished by using existing production machinery and electronics of your target, without major new capital outlays. Therefore, you should investigate to determine if one or more target companies satisfy, or come close to satisfying, these criteria.

After manufacture, the product embodying your invention will have to enter a distribution channel that moves the products to distributors, wholesalers, and the like, each of whom have marketing, advertising, and sales capability to place your product in the hands of the type of retail store where your inventive product can be purchased by a consumer. It follows that your investigation should lead you to conclude that your target companies have distribution, sales, marketing, and advertising capability, as well as manufacturing potential. For example, if your invention is a new hardware item, a company with distribution to appliance stores will not do you any good. Your target company should have a distribution network already in place that sends its salespeople to every hardware store or buying consortium in the country, and in other countries as well.

Once you select one or more target companies, contact each of them with a letter explaining your invention, stating that you have initiated the process for obtaining patent protection, and where possible, include a prototype of your invention in an attractive form or display to appeal to the recipient's aesthetic senses. The better your product looks, the easier it is to interest someone else. If you receive a non-confidential invention submittal form, have your patent attorney review it, and if approved, sign the form and send it back. If your target is interested, negotiations toward a license agreement come next.

License negotiations most effectively begin with one of the parties preparing a Letter of Intent, and forwarding same to the other party. The Letter of Intent follows an initial discussion between you and your potential licensee of the broader terms and objectives of the desired licensing arrangement. The Letter of Intent, which is not a binding agreement, sets forth those general terms that the parties desire to include in the final agreement after successful negotiations. For example, the Letter of Intent is merely an expression of understanding between you and your target, which generally indicates whether an exclusive or non-exclusive license under the patent rights is contemplated; the identification of the parties to the agreement; the extent of the technology licensed; whether the license is for certain countries, parts of countries, or worldwide; and a brief statement of the financial arrangement contemplated by the parties, e.g., royalty payments, lump sum payment, and advance against royalties.

You have most likely selected your target company without assistance from your patent attorney, because it is not wise to pay legal fees for such a non-legal function.

However, after you have selected and initially discussed interest in your invention by the target company, I recommend that you seek assistance from your patent attorney in preparing the Letter of Intent, and in negotiating the terms of the license agreement.

19.2.5 Primary License Negotiation and Agreement Considerations

After the Letter of Intent has exchanged hands and has been signed by all parties, and the parties agree to move forward and execute a formal license agreement, the patent attorney for one of the parties is requested to prepare the first draft of the license agreement, which is forwarded to that lawyer's client for approval before it is sent to the lawyer for the other party.

To give you an idea of the principal terms that are usually placed in a Patent License Agreement, I have listed and discussed some of these points below. Remember, however, these points are not all inclusive, and where special conditions apply, such as receipt of FDA approval before the term of the license begins in a medical device Patent License Agreement, these matters will be added to the agreement.

19.2.5.1 Exclusivity Or Non-Exclusivity In The Covered Territory

In all probability, your licensee will request an exclusive license under your patent rights, which means that you will not be able to grant any other licenses. This is to enable the licensee to gain a foothold in the market with your new product without the fear of competition eroding its position. This is contrasted to the previous example, where you granted non-exclusive licenses to many manufacturers in a given industry. Here, in order to get your invention off the ground, the licensee is requiring exclusivity in the territory covered by your patent rights. If you have only filed a patent application in the United States, your territory is limited to the United States and its possessions. However, if you have protected your ability to file foreign patent applications, the license that you grant may be worldwide, or cover only those segments of the world in which your exclusive licensee has marketing capability. Therefore, in negotiating a license, make sure you do not grant worldwide rights to a manufacturer or licensee that does not have the capability to sell your invention worldwide.

Most license arrangements are conducted and finalized during that time period in which the inventor still has the choice in which countries he or she will file foreign patent applications. Since your licensee is obtaining an exclusive license, and you are substantially locked into the arrangement, certain other provisions that I will discuss shortly are inserted in the license agreement to ensure performance by your licensee. If certain requirements are not met, either the license agreement is cancelled, or it reverts to a non-exclusive license.

19.2.5.2 Advance Against Royalties at Signing

By the time you begin negotiations with the licensee concerning your patent rights, you have expended time and your own resources to bring the invention and the patent rights to the point at which they now exist. One of the theories of patent licensing is that the licensor, or the inventor, receive an advance against royalties at the signing of the license agreement that will at least repay the inventor for expenditures relating to development work and obtaining the patent up to the time of signing the license agreement. Besides determining your out-of-pocket expenses, it is prudent to calculate the amount of hours spent in bringing the invention and patent rights to the present point, and to assign an hourly rate to your work. This amount should be added to your out-of-pocket expenses, such as sums paid to your patent attorney and payment for materials and other costs you incurred in developing and perfecting your invention. The advance against royalties amount negotiated in the contract should be equal to or more than the calculated amount spent by the inventor prior to entering into the licensing agreement. Another reason supporting the advance royalty amount is that this is the cost the licensee would have incurred had the licensee developed the same invention, secured patent rights, and advanced the invention to the point where it could be commercialized. Thus, the licensee is merely paying you back for your work on their behalf up to the time the license agreement is signed.

19.2.5.3 Royalty Rate As Quid Pro Quo for the Grant of the License

Your license agreement could provide that you receive a one-time lump sum payment for the grant of the license. However, most license agreements tie the inventor's compensation to the success of the licensed product. The normal procedure is to provide that the inventor is compensated by an applied royalty rate to the net sale amount of products sold. The calculation of the royalty rate, in theory, is based upon dividing the profits from the sale of the invention, or the products containing the invention. For example, if you determine that the licensee will earn a 10% profit on the sale of goods comprising your invention, a reasonable royalty rate may be 5%. Thus, you and your licensee are equally splitting the profit gained from sales of the invention. Of course, this theory is not quite precise, since the licensee will incorporate the cost of your royalty payments into the cost of manufacturing, and then predicate profit from that point. However, it is usually considered good practice to compensate an inventor at approximately half of the net profit from sales of the invention, although this is a matter for negotiation.

If necessary, the royalty rate can be negotiated between the parties based upon other royalty rates that the licensee is paying on licenses under other patents. Also, a given industry may have a standard recognized royalty rate that is paid among its members, and the royalty rate you negotiate can be one or two points above or below that particular figure, as arrived at during an arm's length negotiation. If, however, your invention is a pioneer invention that will create a totally new industry or new series of product lines, the negotiated royalty rate can be higher. Further, if the licensee indicates that because of the newness of the product and the industry, massive advertising expenditures must take place to introduce the public to the new product, the licensee may ask for a lower royalty rate to take into account the additional early advertising expenses.

Also, there are license agreements where the royalty rate is reduced after certain increased levels of sales are made of the product, to provide an incentive for the licensee to aggressively market the product.

19.2.5.4 To What Is the Royalty Rate Applied

The negotiated royalty rate is usually a percentage of "net sales" of the product embodying the invention. Net sales is normally defined as the price charged by the licensee to its customers, less pass-through items such as taxes, insurance, advertising, and shipping costs. Most license agreements contain a formula for the determination of net sales to which the royalty rate is applied. The licensee is usually required to provide the licensor with quarterly reports of net sales, and to submit this report along with a royalty check payable to the inventor.

When the license relates to a process rather than a product, the royalty rate may be applied to a certain quantitative value, such as tons or square feet of product produced by the licensed process. If the process relates to the production of a gaseous material, the total cubic feet of production, for example, could be used as a basis for applying the royalty.

19.2.5.5 Minimum Royalty Payments

As stated previously, you are willing to grant your licensee an exclusive license under your patent rights. Since you are prevented from granting other licenses, additional provisions must be put in the agreement to keep the licensee's feet to the fire in terms of aggressively promoting sales of your invention. One provision to accomplish this purpose is to require the licensee to make minimum annual royalty payments to maintain the exclusivity of the license. This minimum royalty payment requirement may increase each year into the term of the license agreement, which reflects the fact that you expect your licensee to continually increase its sales from year to year. The minimum royalty payment is a negotiated amount that the licensee must meet each year to retain exclusivity under the agreement. If the minimum royalty payments are not met, the license reverts to a non-exclusive agreement, giving you the right to seek additional licensees.

In those instances where the actual royalty rate to be paid by your licensee over a year period falls slightly short, the licensee has the option of making up the difference by paying the additional amount to meet the minimum royalty payment requirement, and thus retaining the exclusive license. However, if this practice continues during the term of the license, you as the inventor lose your advantage of maximizing the full economic potential of your patent rights. You did not enter into the agreement to have your licensee sell only enough licensed products to meet the minimum royalty requirements of the agreement. The pre-agreement negotiations to establish the minimum royalty payments are based upon expected reasonable sales of products over the term of the license agreement. As the inventor, you naturally expect those sales and royalty payments to increase.

19.2.5.6 Sales Goals or Minimum Production Goals

In addition to the requirement of minimum royalty payments, the license agreements I negotiate include sales goals the licensee must meet each year, failing which the licensor, which is you the inventor, has the right to terminate the agreement and seek a new licensee. When a process is involved, minimum production goals are established that if not met also give the inventor the right to terminate the agreement. Therefore, the combination of minimum royalty payments and sales goals or minimum production goals is effective in giving the licensee the incentive to aggressively market the product embodying your invention, or lose exclusivity, or lose the license agreement altogether. Negotiated sales goals are arrived at by determining the level of reasonably expected sales per year during the term of the agreement.

19.2.5.7 Territorial Extent of The License

Most license agreements are negotiated at that point in time where the inventor/licensor has filed PCT and/or Foreign National Phase Patent applications that have not issued and are still pending, where the examination process is moving forward to protect your invention in many foreign countries. Thus, you have the ability to grant your exclusive licensee, or a non-exclusive licensee, rights under any one or more of your international patent rights. It is important, therefore, to investigate the marketing extent of your potential licensee, and determine those countries in which your licensee has marketing and sales organizations. If there are certain parts of the world where your licensee does not have sufficient sales capability, you do not want to grant your licensee an exclusive right in those countries. Therefore, the license agreement should state that your licensee has exclusive rights under your patent rights in only certain countries. This will enable you with the ability to establish other exclusive licenses with additional licensees in those countries not covered by your original license.

Also, if necessary, you may grant an exclusive license for only portions or regions of one country, such as the United States. For example, you may give one party an exclusive license to sell your product east of the Mississippi, while another party has an exclusive right to sell your product west of the Mississippi. You may also grant one party the exclusive right to sell your invention to one trade or industry, and grant another licensee the exclusive right to sell your invention to another trade or industry. For example, if your invention relates to internal combustion engines, you could grant one licensee the right to manufacture and sell the inventive product in the automotive field, while giving someone else the right to license the product for use in small internal combustion engines, such as lawn mower engines. Yet another exclusive license could be granted to manufacture the product for use in engines for driving electrical generators.

19.2.6 Additional License Considerations

In addition to those recommended license provisions discussed previously, there are additional matters to be considered to properly construct a license arrangement with your potential licensee.

19.2.6.1 The Time and Form of Payment

The license agreement should indicate when the licensee is to tender payment to the licensor. This provision should, if practical, be tied into the existing accounting practices of the licensee. Normally, the licensee is required to perform an accounting after every three-month period of sales of the licensed product, prepare a report of total amounts of licensed products sold, the net sales in dollars of the licensed products sold, and a calculation of the amount due to the licensor when the royalty rate is applied to the total net sales. This report is furnished to the inventor/licensor, along with a check for the amount of the royalty payment due as shown by the accounting. The inventor/licensor is normally given the right to have an independent accountant inspect the books of the licensee at least once a year to determine that the reports and royalty payments are correct.

While the quarterly payment program is used in many industries, it may be more prudent for your licensee to pay you either monthly or yearly, or any other term. Also, if the licensee is in another country, it may be prudent to indicate that the payment is to be made in U.S. dollars, euros, or some other convenient currency. There are certain countries that deduct taxes before your licensee in that country remits payment under your license agreement. In such cases, provisions for handling and deducting of tax amounts and how they affect the amount you receive should be negotiated into the contract.

19.2.6.2 Who Enforces the Patent Against Infringers

The license agreement should take into consideration the prospect that infringers of your patent rights may try to enter the market in competition with your licensee. Taking action to halt such infringing conduct is an expensive proposition, and the decision regarding who will be responsible for enforcing the patent rights must be carefully negotiated. For example, you, as the inventor, may not have the immediate financial resources to support a patent infringement action against a potential infringer at the time the license is being negotiated. Therefore, the license agreement could prudently state that the licensee, who may be a major corporation, would be responsible for enforcing the patent against potential infringers. The agreement may also lower the amount of royalty payments you receive during the pendency of the infringement action to enable the licensee to expend its resources toward successfully enforcing the patent.

On the other hand, if you as the inventor are sufficiently reimbursed from the royalty payments under the agreement, you may agree to enforce the patent rights when requested to do so by the licensee. The patent rights enforcement provision must be carefully negotiated to ensure that the combination of the inventor and the licensee have the ability to successfully enforce the patent. In some cases, both the licensee and the licensor share equally in the expense and responsibility for enforcing the patent against infringers, and share in any damages awarded against the infringer.

19.2.6.3 Defense of the Licensed Product Against a Charge of Infringement of a Third Party Patent

As discussed previously, the fact that you have a patent on your product does not necessarily mean that the licensed product manufactured under your patent rights will <u>not</u> infringe a patent of a third party. The Patent License Agreement takes this into consideration by including a clause that gives one party or the other, or both of them, the responsibility for defending the licensed product against charges of infringement of another patent. A prudent measure prior to entering into the license agreement and bringing the product to market is to conduct a full infringement (freedom-to-use) search to ensure, as best you can, that there are no unexpired patents that may be infringed by sale of the licensed product. However, there may be issued patents that were pending and unpublished when your freedom-to-use search was conducted, and were not revealed by your search, and issued after your licensed product hit the market.

If a patent lawsuit is filed against your licensed product, it is prudent to insert a clause in the agreement that both parties will share in the cost of defending the licensed product against the charge of infringement. Alternatively, the licensee alone may take on the laboring oar of defending the infringement suit brought by the third party, with a reduction in royalty payments during the pendency of such litigation. Again, these provisions are subject to negotiation between you the licensor, and your licensee.

19.2.6.4 Term of the License

The term of the license agreement may extend to the time of expiration of the last of the patents licensed under the license agreement. If there is only one patent being licensed, the license agreement would end at the expiration of that licensed patent. It is unlawful for a license to extend beyond the expiration of the licensed patent. Where you grant a license for the life of the patent, it is important to include the minimum royalty payment and minimum sales goal or production goal default provisions discussed previously in your agreement. It would not be in your best interests to exclusively tie up your patent rights for the life of the patent with a licensee that does not aggressively market the product and maximize your royalty payments.

Many license agreements are written for a term of 5 or 10 years, where the licensee has a right to renew the contract on equal terms, or lesser terms, on a year-to-year basis. This allows the licensee to continue the license agreement as long as sales of licensed products is profitable, and to terminate the agreement if the product becomes non-profitable. In the same vein, most license agreements do not provide the licensor with the right to yank the license from the licensee after the licensee has invested its resources in tooling up, creating a production capability, and advertising and marketing the invention embodied in the licensed products. The one thing I have always strived to accomplish when I represent a licensee in a patent license negotiation is to prevent the licensor from having the ability to terminate the license if a competitor offers a higher percentage royalty to the licensor if the licensor would terminate the agreement with my licensee client.

The term of the license could also reflect the expected life of the licensed product. For example, if your invention lies in an industry where normally a product is successful for three or four years, and then is overcome by new advances in technology, establishing the first term of the license for three years, with renewal rights after that, may be the way to go.

19.2.6.5 Indemnification

A license agreement, by itself, does not protect the licensee from the possibility that another's intellectual property rights will be infringed, or from the possibility that the patented product will injure someone, giving rise to tort liability on both the patent owner and the licensee. Indemnification clauses are inserted in license agreements to enable the patent owner and the licensee to balance the risks and rewards of the business venture embodied in the license agreement. As an example, the extent of the patent owner's indemnification may be capped at a sum equal to royalty payments received under the agreement.

In many negotiations, failure to agree on indemnification leads to a failure to conclude a contract. Patent owners should be particularly aware of this issue, since many patent owners mistakenly conclude that if they indemnify the licensee, their total liability cannot exceed the royalties they receive. This is incorrect, and an ill-considered indemnity clause can potentially cost the patent owner an excessive amount of money, and possible bankruptcy.

Agreement on indemnification should take into consideration who will profit more from the deal, and which party is in the best financial position to bear the risk. Consider also that tort liability is normally the subject of insurance coverage, and coverage against liability for patent infringement may be obtained.

19.2.6.6 Acts Causing Termination of the License

Breach of Contract. Most license agreements, and as a matter of fact most legal agreements, contain a provision that the contract can be terminated by either party where the other party has breached any of the material terms of the agreement. The contract will then set forth what type of conduct may be considered a material breach, giving the other party the option to terminate the contract immediately. The agreement may also define less important breaches, which will give the breaching party 30 days to cure or correct the breach and keep the agreement in force. Normally, the failure to make a royalty payment within 30 days or so of its due date constitutes a material breach of the contract, giving the inventor/licensor the right to terminate the contract immediately. Other breaches, which may not be that serious, give rise to the right of the breaching party to cure or overcome the breach and continue the agreement.

Insolvency. Many license agreements include a provision that if the licensee becomes insolvent or files for bankruptcy, the license agreement is terminated. However, the bankruptcy courts are now ignoring that clause, and holding that the license agreement is an asset of the bankrupt licensee that can be sold to someone else for revenue that would bring money into the bankruptcy estate, which can be distributed to the bankrupt's creditors. Therefore, the situation exists where if your licensee declares bankruptcy, the license agreement instead of being terminated, can be sold to one of your major competitors, and your competitor now has a license under your patents. This may not be in your best interests, since the competitor may be one that you would not want to license your patent rights to in the first place. This matter should be discussed with your patent attorney negotiating your license, who will need assurances of the strong financial status of your prospective licensee.

19.2.6.7 Confidentiality

A well-crafted license agreement will also include a provision stating that any information of a confidential nature that you furnish to the licensee that enables them to perform efficiently under the agreement will be held in confidence by the licensee, will not be used on other products that the licensee may be manufacturing without your permission, and will not be disclosed to any other party. The confidential information should be returned to you upon termination of the license.

19.2.6.8 Grant Back Clauses

A grant back clause covers the situation where the licensee, during the development and production of your licensed product, makes patentable improvements to the product.

A grant back clause states that any such improvement to the licensed product made by the licensee shall be owned by you, the original inventor and licensor, and any patent rights arising from such improvement inventions will be owned by you, the licensor. The grant back clause also grants the licensee a license under such improvement patents without any additional cost. The clause also usually indicates that any confidential information regarding the improvement given by the licensee to the licensor shall be held in confidence by the licensor.

19.3 CONCLUSIONS

As is apparent from the above discussion, a license agreement contains many paragraphs that are intertwined and dependent upon each other. My recommendation is that when the time arrives when it is prudent for you to begin license negotiations with a potential licensee relating to your patent rights, you should engage the services of a competent patent attorney to negotiate the terms of the agreement on your behalf. In addition to the types of terms that go into a typical agreement that I have mentioned above, there are additional terms that may be peculiar to your particular industry or particular product. For example, if you are licensing a telecommunications transmitting product that must be compatible with receiving equipment, the license agreement should include provisions requiring the licensee to inform you of its quality control measures to ensure the compatibility of the licensed product with receiving devices already in the market.

Remember that your license agreements are consensual, and call for mutual agreement by both parties to enter into a final, executed agreement. During the negotiations you may be asked to give up certain provisions you want in exchange for the other party giving up certain provisions that it wants. Also, remember that a license agreement is drafted at a time when you and your licensee are working toward a common goal. However, the license is also crafted to take care of situations that arise in the future where the licensee and you may have major disagreements over one or several aspects of the manufacturing, marketing, or sales of the licensed product. The license agreement should include provisions that enable both parties to mutually discuss any foreseeable problems that may arise, and to attempt to work out a satisfactory conclusion. Once signed by both parties, the license agreement becomes a legal contract, binding both sides, and which may be enforced in a court of law. Also, please remember not to sign the agreement until you understand and agree with *all* of the terms in the agreement.

◆ INVENTORS AND INVENTIONS ◆

Philo Farnsworth

THE INVENTION OF TELEVISION

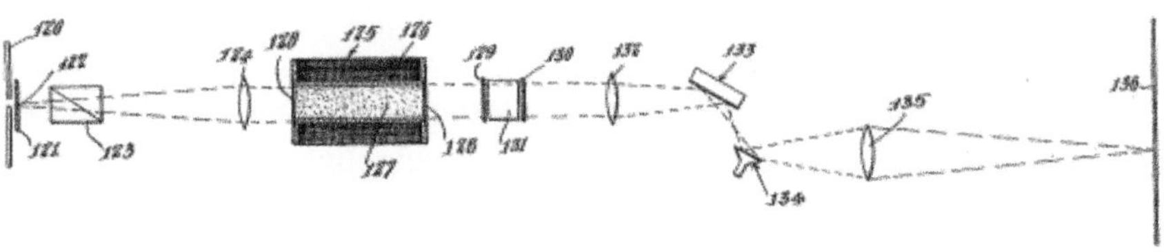

The story of the invention of television is still shrouded in controversy, characterized by many as the classic battle between the sole inventor and the large corporation, between individual creativity and corporate strength. Although the Radio Corporation of America (RCA) is usually given credit for bringing television to the forefront, the name of Philo Taylor Farnsworth has been relegated to the background. However, researchers of late have dug into the details of the stories and have begun to promote Farnsworth as the true father of television. As usual, in contests over inventorship between inventors, the United States Patent Office became involved and, in this case, produced decisions that gave solace to the Farnsworth supporters.

The story of Philo T. Farnsworth and his development of television begins as he was plowing a field while attending Rigby High School, Idaho, in 1921. As he himself related during subsequent lawsuits regarding the inventorship of television, at that time he had a dream to send pictures over the air, as sound was sent over the radio. At age 14, he was plowing a field with his horse-drawn disc harrow and visualized that the tracks in the field would be the same as tiny electrons creating a beam that could scan an image line by line. Beginning with this inspiration, Farnsworth eventually developed the first working electronic television, in contrast to the mechanical televisions that predated it. Believe it or not, in his later years, Farnsworth stated that he felt he had created some kind of monstrous device that provided people with a means to waste their time. He complained about the programming. Does this sound familiar?

Philo Taylor Farnsworth was born in a log cabin in Indian Creek, Utah, in 1906, and lived his early life in rather remote areas that were devoid of modern technological facilities. When he was 12 years old, the family moved to a ranch home in Snake River Valley, Idaho, where Farnsworth found hidden in the attic of the house a large quantity of magazines devoted to science and radio. In the magazines, Farnsworth read about a favorite topic of science and science fiction writers at the time: television, the concept

Intellectual Property Law for Engineers, Scientists, and Entrepreneurs, Second Edition. Howard B. Rockman.

Published 2020 by John Wiley & Sons, Inc.

of transmitting pictures through the air. Farnsworth also read about the almost fictional particle that was invisible to the eye, the electron. He considered that the electron, with its relative freedom from inertia, satisfied all the necessary requirements for his considerations of a workable all-electronic television transmitter and receiver system. The ranch in Idaho was the first place he had lived where there was electricity, and he began creating devices that he attached to the power generator. For example, since he had the household chore of operating the crank handle for his mother's hand-operated washing machine, he created a motor by rewinding an armature, and attached the motor to his mother's washing machine.

In the early 1900s, transmitting messages along wires via telegraph and transmitting sound across wires or the airwaves by telephone and radio were already in an advanced stage of development and were generally known to most people. Farnsworth, however, thought about the next advance in technology, changing images into electric impulses or signals and transmitting them to a receiving unit where they would produce a viewable image. At that time, other partly electrical, partly mechanical television devices had been created, most employing rotating disks. However, he strove for the use of electrons in television transmission to produce improved images without moving or mechanical parts.

Farnsworth was fascinated with electricity and electron movement, and persuaded his high school chemistry teacher, Justin Tolman, to provide him with special instruction and also allow him to audit a senior course in electronics. One day in 1921, Farnsworth decided to present his "television" idea to Justin Tolman. Going to the blackboard, Farnsworth drew a series of diagrams that were rough sketches of a vacuum tube containing a cathode and an anode with an external lens and a static machine, according to Tolman's recollection. Farnsworth also indicated to Mr. Tolman that he had been reading about mechanical television systems then being developed on the East Coast, and that electron systems would eventually replace spinning-wheel systems.

According to young Farnsworth's concept, light from an optical image would be projected upon a photosensitive cathode where each elementary area of the cathode emitted electrons at a rate proportional to the intensity of light falling upon that area. The electrons would flow to the anode and return to the cathode by means of external circuits and a battery that Farnsworth developed, thus creating a current flow between the cathode and anode, and through the external circuits. Electrons emitted from the elementary areas of the cathode would travel toward the anode plates in substantially parallel lines due to the high potential between the cathode and the anode. The electron flow would create an electron beam and the various elementary areas of any transverse cross section of the beam would produce an electron or current density proportional to the intensity of light falling on the corresponding elementary area of the cathode at the instant of emission of the electrons in the cross section. Therefore, the cross section of the electron beam constituted a current pattern corresponding to the light pattern of the optical image that originated the current flow. This defined the "electrical image" as described in Farnsworth's United States Patent No. 1,773,980, which he obtained on his television system on August 26, 1930, upon an application filed on January 7, 1927.

Only the electrons directly in line with an aperture and a plate passed through the aperture and impinged on the target anode in Farnsworth's device. Thus, the current from only a single elementary area of the electron beam or "electrical image" passed through a resistance. Sawtooth voltages, however, applied to deflecting plates caused the electron beam to continually move across the face of each plate such that each of the elementary areas of the beam were successively directed toward the aperture, and the electrons in the areas impinged upon the anode. Thus, the aperture scanned each elementary current of the electron beam, and scanned the electrical image. The electrons impinging upon the target anode constituted the current flowing through the resistance, and the potential drop across the resistance enhanced the output signal, which is proportional at successive instances to the electron or current density of the elementary area of the electron beam being scanned. Thus, Farnsworth's device divided a picture into lines of light and shade, and a quickly changing electromagnetic field scanned the picture line by line. The electrons were collected at the far end of the camera tube and formed a stream of electric pulses that were transmitted to an antenna. In the receiver, the electronic pulses were converted back into a series of lines, and the image was reconstituted on the receiving screen.

At that time, there were other inventors unknown to Philo Farnsworth who were also working on the development of electronic television. Vladimir Zworykin, who had immigrated to the United States from Russia in 1919 and had taken a job with Westinghouse Corporation in Pittsburgh, Pennsylvania, was considered by some to be ahead of Farnsworth in the development of television during the 1920s. Zworykin was highly educated, holding a PhD in electrical engineering from Petrograd Institute of Technology in Russia, where he studied before coming to the United States under scientist Boris Rosing, who was already working on cathode ray tubes for mechanical-scan television. Rosing was attempting to transmit pictures by wire in his physics laboratory in Petrograd. He and Zworykin experimented with a cathode ray tube that had been previously developed by the German Carl Ferdinand Braun. In 1910, Rosing had demonstrated a television system employing a mechanical scanner in the transmitter, and using the electronic Braun tube as the receiver.

In 1923, Zworykin applied for a patent for an approach to television he first encountered while working in Russia with Boris Rosing. The 1923 patent application of Zworykin predated the 1927 patent application filed by Farnsworth for electronic television. More on these patent battles later.

Prior to the mid-1920s, television employed spinning disks and mirrors in attempts to scan, transmit, and reassemble a moving image. Inventors such as Jenkins, Ives, Alexanderson, and Baird, among others, based their work on spiral-perforated spinning disks that were first proposed in the 1880s by the German scientist Paul Nipkow. These concepts did not involve electronic imaging, and today nothing is left of the technology developed by these inventors in the television systems used around the world.

Prior to Farnsworth's developments, other companies such as RCA had created wireless facsimile transmission systems by the end of the 1920s. However, the wireless transmission and reproduction of moving images proved more difficult for those inventors working on electromechanical television systems. Eventually, all-electronic television systems won out worldwide.

Zworykin enrolled as a graduate student at the University of Pittsburgh and received his PhD in 1926. While at Westinghouse, he conducted research on photoelectric vacuum tubes as well as television. Philo Farnsworth began college in Utah, but dropped out of school at the age of 18 when his father passed away and he was required to support his family. In 1925, when Farnsworth was 19 years old, he decided to move forward with his idea for electronic television. He described his idea to two California businessmen, Les Gorrell and George Everson. They agreed to a $6000 investment, allowing Farnsworth to construct a prototype of his television concept. At that time, the two investors were putting up their life's savings. William W. Crocker, President of Crocker National Bank in San Francisco, and Roy Bishop, a respected San Francisco capitalist, also backed Farnsworth's efforts.

With this seed money, Farnsworth and his wife Pem moved to Los Angeles from Salt Lake City and set up a makeshift laboratory in the dining room of their small house in Hollywood. The two investors were also there, winding magnetic coils, putting other components together, and going around town scrounging up materials to help Farnsworth continue his experiments. At that time, Farnsworth could not find existing optical or electrical components, and everything he needed had to be assembled from the beginning. After three months, Farnsworth was ready to test his first electronic television camera tube. With everything in place, Farnsworth pushed the button, and the entire contraption exploded. The power surge from the generator had blown up the total experiment, television tube and all.

After picking themselves up and dusting themselves off, Farnsworth and his investors obtained additional funding from bankers. Farnsworth promised to build a camera tube that would turn an image into a stream of electrons, and a television receiving tube that could convert the string of electrons back into a visual image, in one year. Realizing that he had substantial work to do to overcome his early failure, the circuitry of Farnsworth's devices became more and more complicated. He found it difficult to provide an image in the first prototypes of his camera tubes. Fortunately, each day the particulars of Farnsworth's progress were recorded in his notebooks. These were very important to him when the patent battles began.

At the same time, Zworykin's early efforts to produce electronic television were not received with favor by the Westinghouse research staff. When Zworykin performed his first demonstrations in the 1920s, several of the Westinghouse people who saw the demonstrations were not enthusiastic, and research on the mechanical system of television continued. The mechanical television program moved beyond the research stage in the late 1920s, when the first television drama, "The Queen's Messenger," was broadcast. It is reported that the actors in this performance had no need to fear recognition when they walked in the streets because the images that appeared on the receiving screen were fuzzy.

Also, at the BBC in England, inventor John Logie Baird was successfully using spinning disks in a television system. His devices were shown to the Royal Institution on January 27, 1926, showing two television images in light and shade for the first time. It was an image, although it was barely visible.

Receiving news of the mechanical television systems, Farnsworth's financial backers began to worry. This worry was relayed back to Farnsworth by urging him to progress more rapidly with his all-electronic television development.

On September 7, 1927, Farnsworth successfully demonstrated the principle of his electronic television invention in his San Francisco laboratory at 202 Green Street, where he had moved from Los Angeles. This was the first demonstration of the transmission of an electrical image without mechanical devices. Thus, it is said that Farnsworth replaced the spinning disks and mirrors of the mechanical televisions with the electron, a particle so small and light that it could be deflected back and forth in a vacuum tube tens of thousands of times per second. Farnsworth was the first to form and manipulate an electron beam, which is the quantum leap in knowledge that is used in all televisions and electronic monitors today.

At his demonstration on September 7, 1927, Farnsworth coated a square of glass brick with dark paint, and etched a line in the center of the coated glass. In another room, his brother-in-law, Cliff Gardner, placed the glass between the "Image Dissector," the camera tube that Farnsworth had developed previously that same year, and a very bright carbon arc lamp. Farnsworth, his wife, and one investor, George Everson, saw the straight line image on the receiver, and as Cliff Gardner rotated the image, the viewers saw the receiver image move. Thus, these three people were the first to see an all-electronic television picture. Later that evening, Farnsworth wrote in his laboratory journal: "The received line picture was evident at this time." However, the telegram that George Everson sent to another investor states it more succinctly: "The damned thing works!" The image was only the size of a postage stamp, but it brought Farnsworth a modicum of fleeting fame.

Farnsworth, who was only 22 years old in 1927, wanted to take his fragile prototype to the next step. However, this would require significant additional funding. Farnsworth was concerned that his investors were looking to sell the company, and Farnsworth with it, unless he produced something workable in a short period of time.

An article in the September 3, 1928, *San Francisco Chronicle,* second section, announced Farnsworth's work. It described his invention as follows:

> In any method of transmitting any moving images at a distance, some means must be evolved of breaking the image into pin-points of light. These points are translated into electrical impulses, the electrical impulses are collected at the receiving end and translated back into light, and the image results.

The article went on to state that the television systems then in use employed a revolving disk, two feet in diameter, to break up or "scan" the image. A similar disk was at the receiving end, and the two disks had to revolve at precisely the same instant and the same speed, or blurred vision resulted. Farnsworth's system was reported as using no moving parts. Instead, his system varied electric current that played over the image and thus obtained the necessary scanning.

Farnsworth also created a second major advance, which cut in half the waveband length necessary to prevent television broadcasts from interfering with each other. This was important since television requires approximately four times the waveband length compared to ordinary radio sound broadcasting. The article continued by stating that Farnsworth's system transmitted 20 pictures per second with 8000 elements or pinpoints of light to ensure detail in every picture. The laboratory model Farnsworth built transmitted the image on a screen 1¼ inch square. The article stated that the perfection of Farnsworth's invention was now a matter of engineering.

Meanwhile, David Sarnoff had risen to the top of RCA, which was also part owner of Westinghouse Corporation. At that time, RCA controlled the entire spectrum of radio by owning the transmitters, studios, and the rights to build radios. Sarnoff appeared ready to adapt his vertical integration business techniques to television. Zworykin had demonstrated his invention of the iconoscope in 1923, which was the subject of the patent application he filed that same year. The quality of the iconoscope picture was rather poor, although it was an improvement over the mechanical scanning television devices of the day. Westinghouse withheld funding until Zworykin obtained an audience with David Sarnoff, which meeting took place in 1929. Sarnoff, who himself was a Russian immigrant, when told by Zworykin that it would cost $100,000 to design and build his television invention, approved the beginning of a development program. Ultimately, it turned out that the estimate of $100,000 was off only by an amount of $49,900,000.

Zworykin and other Westinghouse engineers were transferred to the RCA research plant at Camden, New Jersey, and Sarnoff also purchased the Jenkins Television Company in order to obtain their patents on mechanical television systems. Zworykin and Sarnoff realized that they were behind Farnsworth, who had already developed an electronic television camera. In 1929, Zworykin's prototype television could not produce images if the light was too low, and as soon as Sarnoff and Zworykin heard about Farnsworth, they wanted to find out what he was doing, and also figure out how to avoid his patents.

Thus, in the spring of 1930, Zworykin contacted Farnsworth to schedule a meeting at Farnsworth's laboratory in San Francisco to investigate Farnsworth's progress. Farnsworth, it is reported, was pleased to demonstrate his camera to Zworykin, since Farnsworth had depleted his financial resources and was interested in having RCA finance his work. Zworykin visited Farnsworth's laboratory pretending to be a colleague interested in Farnsworth's work. Farnsworth, who was known to be generous with his knowledge and information, showed Zworykin how his image dissector worked. At the meeting, Zworykin looked around closely at all of Farnsworth's equipment, and is reported to have said, "That's a beautiful tube. I wish I had invented it." Then Zworykin advised Farnsworth that he did not think that there was any equipment that he saw that would be useful to RCA's development. However, Zworykin, after going to his hotel room that day, sent a telegram back to RCA describing in detail Farnsworth's image dissector tube.

It is reported that when Zworykin came back east, a prototype of Farnsworth's camera tube had already been built by RCA, and Zworykin set about to see if he could produce a television camera without infringing Farnsworth's patents. It has also been reported that Zworykin was still struggling for a viable solution when he visited Farnsworth's Lab in 1930. He then duplicated Farnsworth's equipment in the Westinghouse laboratory in Pittsburgh, and built his working iconoscope based upon Farnsworth's work. The iconoscope that Zworykin developed after returning to RCA has been characterized as being strikingly similar in function to Farnsworth's image dissector.

On August 26, 1930, Farnsworth's first patent, No. 1,773,980, was issued by the United States Patent Office. Sarnoff was aware of the importance of patents, but he also was firmly against the idea of RCA making royalty payments to anyone. He decided first to buy Farnsworth out by offering him $100,000 for his patents, services, and entire business. However, Farnsworth rejected the idea since he thought of himself as an inventor who should be compensated by receiving a royalty on sales of products embodying his invention.

History then records that upon Farnsworth's rejection of the offer, Sarnoff began a program to promote the idea that Zworykin demonstrated electronic television before Farnsworth, and to defeat Farnsworth by using the patent and legal systems. However, in 1931, Farnsworth obtained a licensee for his television technology, and signed a secret deal in Philadelphia with a company called Philco that was seeking to obtain a jump start in the television field. Part of the agreement between Farnsworth and

Philco was that Farnsworth had to move his laboratories to Philadelphia, the home of Philco. In order to hide his plans from RCA, the entire Philco deal was arranged and carried out in secret. For example, when the Farnsworth employees arrived in Philadelphia they were compelled to eat in the executive dining room. They thought this was a wonderful idea, but they did not realize it was to prevent the employees from talking to anybody else about Farnsworth's deal with Philco.

However, when Philco began test transmissions of television, the signals were picked up by RCA in its nearby Camden, New Jersey plant. Actually, both RCA and Philco were tuning in to each others' experimental television broadcasts, and the pace to develop commercial television advanced exponentially. Sarnoff added financial resources to RCA's commitment to television, and in the early 1930s had a significant team of engineers and patent lawyers ready to go.

Farnsworth ultimately left Philco and set up his own research facility in Philadelphia. More than a year later, in 1934, he made the first successful public demonstration of electronic television at the Franklin Institute in Philadelphia. The demonstration required a viewing screen approximately one foot in diameter, and substantial light since the cameras were not very sensitive at that time.

A year after his public demonstration, Farnsworth won his first patent victory against RCA. But Sarnoff told the newspapers that useful television was still years away, and he instructed his attorneys to appeal the patent decision. In the 1935 appeal decision based upon an April 24, 1934 hearing, the United States Patent Office in Patent Interference No. 64027, "Farnsworth v. Zworykin," decided that priority of invention of electronic television belonged to Farnsworth and not to Zworykin. An interference was a proceeding in the Patent Office to resolve conflicting claims of first inventorship of an invention, since a patent then was awarded to the first inventor. This decision held that the then-pending patent application filed by Zworykin in 1923 did not disclose the concept of an "electrical image" that was specifically stated in the claims and the specification of the Farnsworth patent that had issued in 1930. In other words, the decision held that Zworykin's application did not contain sufficient information to meet the requirement that an "electrical image" could be formed, either demonstrably or inherently, in the structure disclosed in the Zworykin patent application.

Ultimately, the 1923-filed patent application of Zworykin issued (No. 2,141,059) after much modification, and over the objection of the U.S. Patent Office, and not until the Patent Office was overruled by a Court of Appeals. RCA then used the earlier application filing date of 1923 to advertise to the public that Zworykin had invented television before Farnsworth's first successful transmission on September 7, 1927. Sarnoff and RCA appealed the 1934 decision of the United States Patent Office awarding priority of invention to Farnsworth through the courts, but after seven years of litigation, Sarnoff was compelled to admit that he could not defeat the Farnsworth patents. In October 1939, for the first time in RCA's history, RCA began paying royalties to an outside inventor. As the anecdote goes, the RCA lawyer had tears in his eyes upon signing the document agreeing to pay Farnsworth the money for the cross-license agreement.

The question of whether Zworykin's originally disclosed invention in his 1923-filed patent application would work remains open. Some have stated that the idea was on the right track, but the disclosure in that application did not disclose the device that paved the way toward electronic television. For example, the Patent Office decision of 1935 in the interference between Zworykin and Farnsworth concluded that the

Zworykin invention, which was given two different interpretations, did not produce an "electrical image" as was disclosed in the Farnsworth patent application. The Farnsworth application defined the term "electrical image" as follows:

> Light from all portions of the object whose image is to be transmitted is focused at one time upon a light-sensitive plate of a photoelectric cell to develop an electronic discharge from the plate. Each portion of the cross-section of the electronic discharge corresponds in electrical intensity with the intensity of light imposed on that portion of the sensitive plate from which the electrical discharge originated. Such discharge is termed an electrical image.

The Patent Office held that the electric pattern formed by the electron or current density in the electron beam of Farnsworth's device did not describe any form of an electrical pattern that corresponded to an optical image. Thus, the term "electrical image" had a restricted meaning set forth in Farnsworth's application, and the Zworykin device which used photosensitive material in the form of discrete globules, did not fall within the meaning of "electrical image" as set forth in the Farnsworth patent. Therefore, Zworykin could not copy the broad electrical image claim from the Farnsworth patent and insert it into his own patent application.

There is very little evidence that Zworykin ever constructed the system disclosed in his 1923 patent application. The patent interference record is totally void of evidence that the Zworykin 1923 device was successfully constructed and tested. The actual device itself, if it existed, was not introduced in evidence during the taking of testimony in the interference proceedings. Zworykin could not make the count (claim) of the interference because the image in his application was not scanned to produce the television signal. There is one reported story, however, about Zworykin's attempt to demonstrate his 1923 concept to executives of Westinghouse. The report indicates that the demonstration failed, and instead of providing him with further encouragement or funding, Zworykin's managers instructed him to find something "more useful" on which to spend his time.

In 1931 and 1932, Zworykin conducted tests that are disclosed in a December 1933 Institute of Radio Engineers (IRE) paper. This paper indicates that he was still using a mechanical scanning transmitter along with a cathode tube as a picture tube at that time.

Under the Farnsworth system, when an optical image is focused on a photoelectric surface, the light-sensitive chemicals admit an array of electrons—the "electrical image"— which is then scanned to form a fluctuating current. This is the essence of electronic television, and is the subject matter encompassed in claim 15 of Farnsworth's patent. In an attempt to initiate the patent interference, Zworykin attempted to copy Farnsworth's claim 15 into Zworykin's patent application, argue that his application supported that claim, and that he (Zworykin) was the first inventor. The Patent Office disagreed. RCA attempted to show that the 1923 Zworykin application disclosure would have created the same electrical image as disclosed by Farnsworth. The Patent Office ruled in the 1935 interference decision that "Zworykin has no right to make the count because it is not apparent that the device (of Zworykin) would operate to produce a scanned electrical image unless it has discrete globules capable of producing discrete space charges, and the Zworykin application as filed does not disclose such a device."

In the mid-1930s, Farnsworth had also met Englishman John Logie Baird, the inventor of a mechanical television system, with the objective of selling a license to Baird to save Farnsworth's company from bankruptcy because of the patent litigation with RCA. Baird was a Scottish scientist who had been working with cathode ray tubes. By 1926, Baird's machine could produce the discernible image of a face. Farnsworth demonstrated his electronic television system to Baird, and the following day Farnsworth and Baird entered into a contract. Upon his return home, in 1936, Farnsworth launched his own experimental television station in the suburbs of Philadelphia, W3XPF.

However, in the middle and late 1930s, the public was not buying television sets because each manufacturing company was producing incompatible sets. Thus, each brand of television was only able to receive images from its own broadcast station. This led to the introduction of federal broadcast standards that eliminated the problem. These standards, however, were not instituted until after World War II. Farnsworth also purchased a company to start manufacturing television sets, but until his patent dispute with RCA was resolved, he put everything on hold.

This series of events put substantial stress on Farnsworth in the late 1930s, and he was not getting the sleep he needed. He left Philadelphia, and he and his wife bought a home in Maine and left his managers in charge of his television company in Philadelphia. While in Maine, he was hospitalized several times, reportedly because of alcohol-related problems. While Farnsworth was attempting to recover in Maine, David Sarnoff unveiled RCA's television to America at the New York World's Fair in 1939. At that time, Farnsworth's first public demonstration in Philadelphia in 1934 was practically forgotten by the public. Also, when RCA was asked about the invention of television, the spokesperson dwelled upon the work of Sarnoff and Zworykin, but never mentioned Farnsworth.

In 1939, Farnsworth was in an envious position to become very wealthy because of his patent license with RCA. However, fate extended its fickle hand. In 1941, the United States entered the Second World War and created a four-year blackout for commercial television. Television technology was required for defense needs, and although Farnsworth's company contributed to the war effort, the fact that his principal patents would expire in 1947 destroyed any hopes he might have had of making money from royalties on his television invention.

By the war's end, Farnsworth's key patents were close to expiring, RCA quickly increased the production and sales of television sets, and a vigorous public relations campaign promoted both Zworykin and Sarnoff as the fathers of television, while Farnsworth withdrew to his house in Maine. Embodying the concept that no good deed goes unpunished, Farnsworth's Maine house burned to the ground in 1947.

For the remainder of his life, Farnsworth devoted his time to studying nuclear fusion, which to this day has not been brought to practical fruition.

Much credit for refining all the aspects of early television correctly goes to the engineers of RCA. Many, many research engineers and scientists contributed to the further development of electronic television prior to television broadcasting becoming available to the general public in the late 1940s and early 1950s. However, the role of Philo Farnsworth in creating television is now coming to the surface, and he is beginning to receive the recognition he deserves. Statues in his honor have been erected in the Capitol buildings in Utah and in Washington, D.C., and in September 1983, the U.S. Postal Service issued a stamp in commemoration of Farnsworth's achievements.

Farnsworth held the basic television patents covering scanning, focusing, synchronizing contrasts, controls, and power. Farnsworth died on March 11, 1971, but his work lives on as a realization of the spirit and ingenuity of the single inventor.

Why is this story important? Because a large company attempted to convince the public that scientific progress and advancement of the useful arts was the result of the work of corporate institutions, not individuals with the spark of ingenuity. This train of thought would lead each citizen of the general population to place their faith in these corporate institutions, rather than in individual inventors, or even themselves. Invention and creativity are the unique and compelling aspects of the human experience. As stated by Szent-Gyorgi, "Discovery is seeing what everybody has seen, and thinking what nobody else has thought." Farnsworth, rather than one who could see what others were doing and improve upon it, was a true visionary who could see the obvious and think up something entirely different. If the stories of these types of inventors were suppressed, we the public would not be able to understand this important factor of the human character. It is important for all of us to know that a medium such as television was the consequence of individual inventorship and ideas, rather than of corporate engineering. Farnsworth saw how the 19th century visionaries were attempting to send pictures through the air with spinning disks and mirrors. However, he alone had the concept of replacing all the moving parts with invisible electrons, and he kept working until that concept was realized.

In the development of both mechanical and electrical television, the independent inventors are represented by John Logie Baird, Paul Nipkow, C. Francis Jenkins, and Philo Farnsworth, who were compelled to bring their discoveries forward against the power of large corporations. The large corporations are represented by Vladimir Zworykin, David Sarnoff, and Earnst Alexanderson. For more on this, see *Tube: The Invention of Television,* by David E. Fisher and Marshall John Fisher, Washington, DC: Counterpoint, 1996, xvii at 427.

Aug. 26, 1930. P. T. FARNSWORTH 1,773,980

TELEVISION SYSTEM

Filed Jan. 7, 1927 4 Sheets-Sheet 1

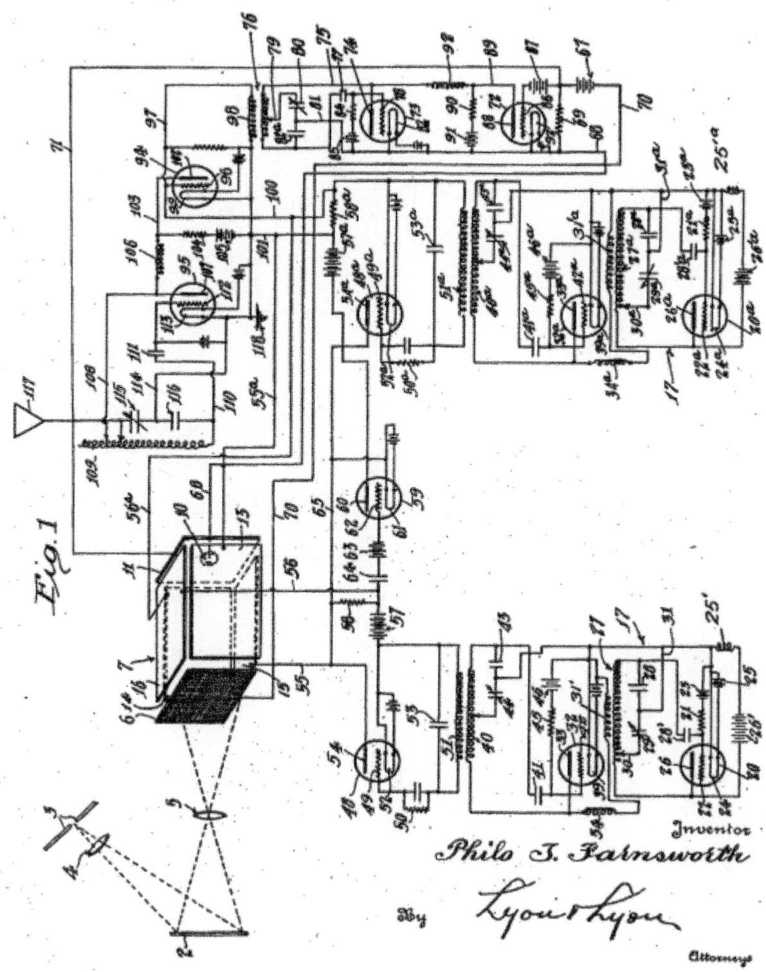

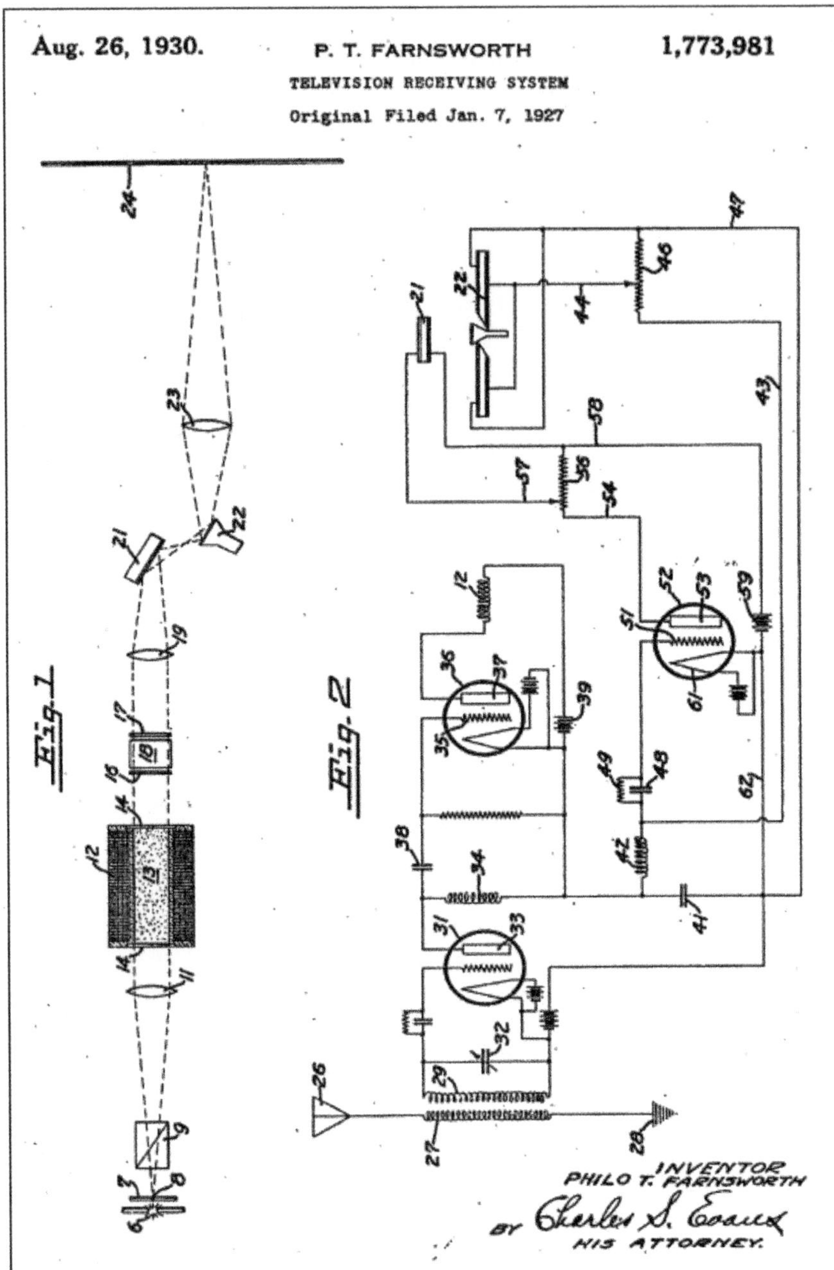
Aug. 26, 1930.
P. T. FARNSWORTH
1,773,981
TELEVISION RECEIVING SYSTEM
Original Filed Jan. 7, 1927
Fig. 1
Fig. 2
INVENTOR
PHILO T. FARNSWORTH
BY
HIS ATTORNEY.

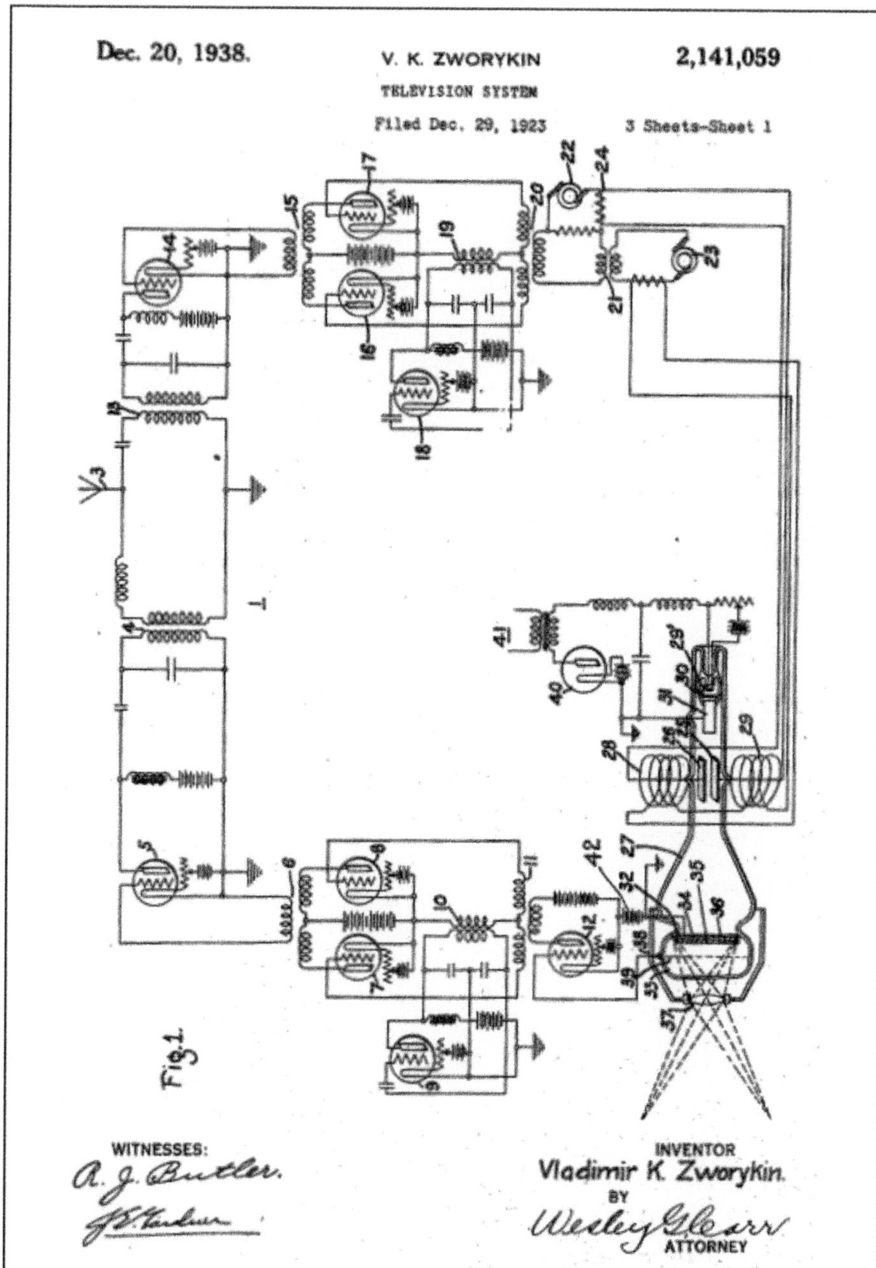
Dec. 20, 1938.
V. K. ZWORYKIN
2,141,059
TELEVISION SYSTEM
Filed Dec. 29, 1923
3 Sheets-Sheet 1
Fig. 1.
WITNESSES:
INVENTOR
Vladimir K. Zworykin.
BY
ATTORNEY

◆ INVENTORS AND INVENTIONS ◆

Robert Adler

ULTRASOUND TELEVISION REMOTE CONTROL

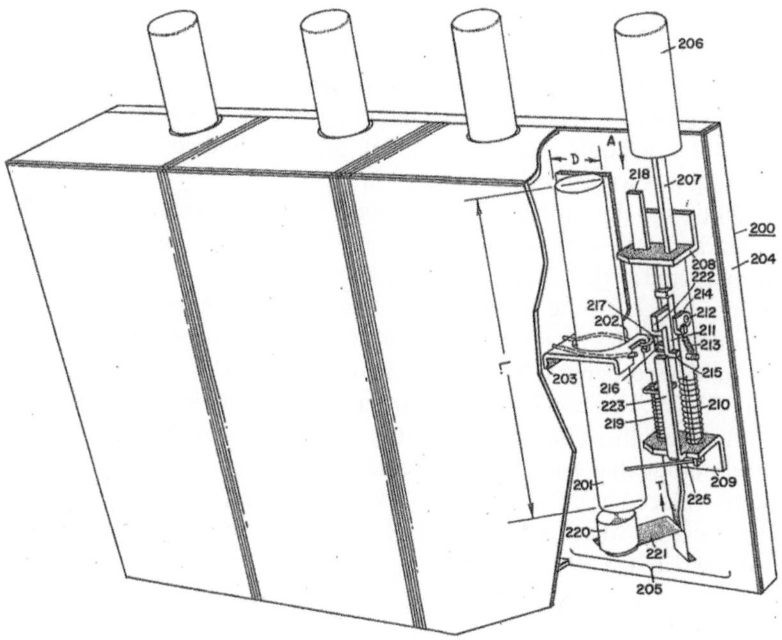

Robert Adler, an Austrian-born American inventor, worked for Zenith Electronics Corporation, and retired as the company's vice president and director of research. He developed early sound-based remote controls for television, which were the standard for operating television sets for 25 years, until replaced by infrared remote controls that could transmit more complex signals.

Adler was born in Vienna in 1913 and earned a PhD in physics at the University of Vienna in 1937. Austria then was annexed by Nazi Germany, and Dr. Adler, who was Jewish, left the country, traveling first to Belgium, then to England, where, upon the advice of friends he immigrated to the United States. He joined Zenith Electronics' U.S. research division in 1941, where he specialized in military communications equipment during World War II. He later focused on television technology, inventing the gated beam vacuum tube, which substantially reduced sound interference. He also led a team that invented a special circuit that improved reception.

Intellectual Property Law for Engineers, Scientists, and Entrepreneurs, Second Edition. Howard B. Rockman.

Published 2020 by John Wiley & Sons, Inc.

The invention Adler is best known for is the wireless, sound-emitting remote control for televisions. His was not the first remote control, but its underlying technology was a significant improvement over other systems available in the 1950s, some of which used cumbersome cords. The first wireless television remote control was invented by Eugene Polley, which replaced the signal-capable remote control devices, which were never a success. The "Flashmatic," earlier developed by Adler, used a directional flashlight in the transmitter device and reception photocells in the television set. One of the shortcomings of this technology was that if the television set was exposed to direct sunlight, one of the remote control functions could be accidentally activated. The company president sent the engineers back to the drawing board to come up with a better solution.

A system based on radio waves was briefly considered, but was rejected because the signals could easily travel through walls, thus inadvertently changing the channel of a neighbor's television. Furthermore, the marketing people at Zenith desired a remote control that did not require batteries, since if the battery died, the customer might think something was wrong with the television set.

Adler's solution to this problem was to generate ultrasound waves beyond the range of human hearing to transmit signals to the television set. The first remote control he developed, marketed as the "Space Command" by Zenith, used aluminum rods similar to tuning forks struck by one of four aluminum rods or hammers toggled by manual movement of the buttons on the remote control device. This produced high-frequency tones that would be recognized by receptors in the television set to control the "channel up," "channel down," "sound off," and "power on/off" functions. Later, in the 1960s, Adler modified his ultrasound wave emitting remote control to one using ultrasonic signals, a technology that was used in television sets manufactured for the subsequent 25 years, until replaced by infrared systems. However, the infrared systems still required batteries to operate. Adler's remote controls were sold with more than nine million television sets before the 1980s.

Dec. 17, 1957 R. ADLER 2,817,025

CONTROL SYSTEM

Original Filed April 16, 1956 5 Sheets-Sheet 1

FIG. 1

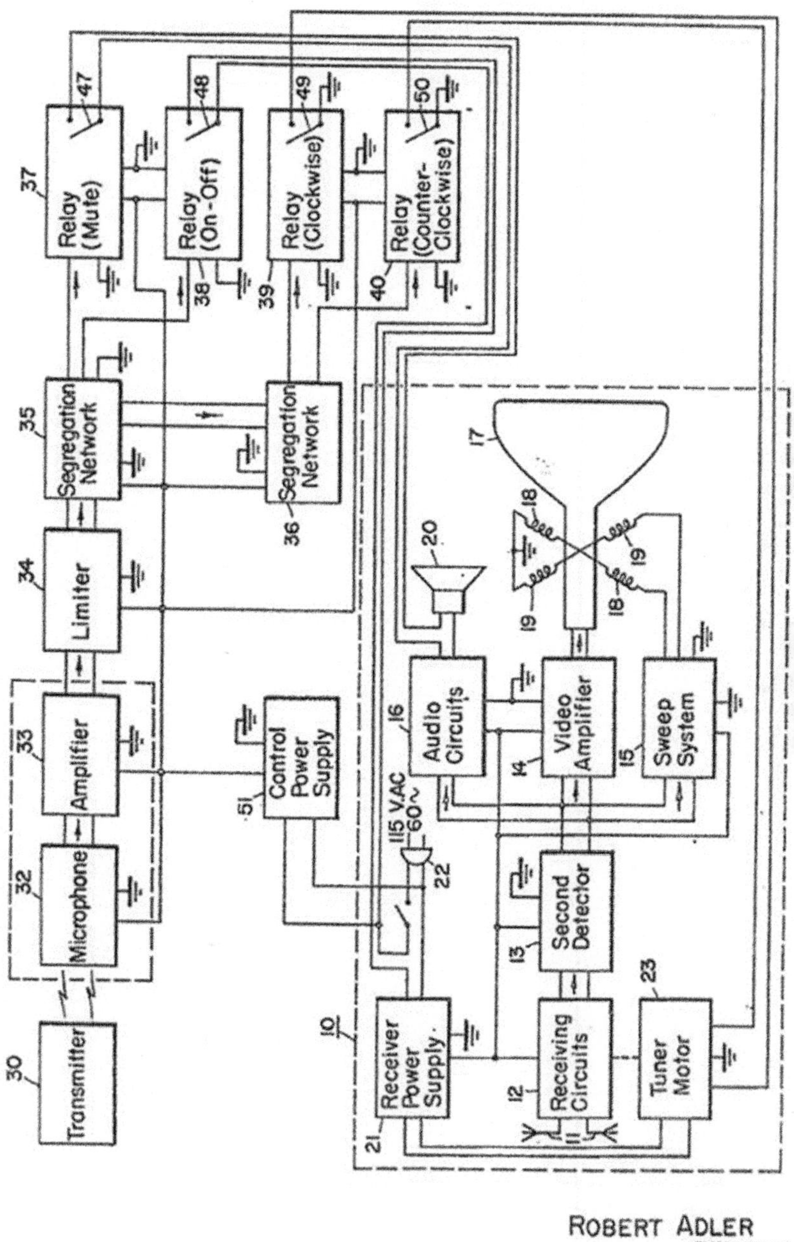

ROBERT ADLER
INVENTOR.

BY John J. Pederson

HIS ATTORNEY.

20 How to Read and Obtain Information from a Modern U.S. Patent

Beginning on the next page is a copy of a U.S. patent that issued on May 31, 2011. The purpose of this chapter is to describe what information is set forth in the pages of that patent, or any modern patent, to enable you to read a patent and gain information about the disclosed and claimed invention with ease of understanding.

20.1 THE INFORMATION PAGE

Referring to the next page, the first page of patents printed today is known as the information page, and at the top left identifies the document as a "United States Patent." The patent number, a seven-digit number, or an eight-digit number, appears in the upper-right-hand corner, No. 7,953,425. Your patent attorney, in correspondence, may refer to a patent by the last three numerals of the patent number, such as "the '425 patent." The last name of the inventor, or first-named inventor, appears on the left side of the page on the second line beneath the identification of the document as a U.S. Patent. This patent was issued to an inventor named Lawrence B. Jordan.

Beneath the patent number at the top left of the information page is the date of issuance of the patent, which also determines the beginning of the enforcement period of the patent. As of June 7, 1995, the term of patent enforcement was changed from 17 years from the date of issue to 20 years from the filing date of the parent non-provisional application from which the patent issued, for patent applications filed subsequent to June 8, 1995. Additional time may be added to the enforceability term due to specified delays occurring in the U.S. Patent & Trademark Office (USPTO), such as the time spent appealing, and reversing, a final rejection of a Patent Examiner.

For patents issuing from patent applications pending on June 8, 1995, or were in force as of that date, the patent enforcement term is the greater of (1) 17 years from the date of issue, or (2) 20 years from the date of filing of the earliest related patent application.

Beneath the above-described identifying nomenclature, the next line on the left side of the information page sets forth the title of the invention, in this case "UNIVERSAL EVENT/DATA RECORDER SYSTEM." The title is required to be placed on the application, and should be descriptive of a structural or result aspect of the invention.

The numbers in brackets throughout the information page are INID Codes, which stands for "Internationally Agreed Numbers for the Identification of Bibliographic

Intellectual Property Law for Engineers, Scientists, and Entrepreneurs, Second Edition. Howard B. Rockman.

Published 2020 by John Wiley & Sons, Inc.

US007953425B2

(12) **United States Patent**
Jordan

(10) **Patent No.:** **US 7,953,425 B2**
(45) **Date of Patent:** **May 31, 2011**

(54) **UNIVERSAL EVENT/DATA RECORDER SYSTEM**

(75) Inventor: **Lawrence B. Jordan**, Bolingbrook, IL (US)

(73) Assignee: **Wi-Tronix, LLC**, Bolingbrook, IL (US)

(*) Notice: Subject to any disclaimer, the term of this patent is extended or adjusted under 35 U.S.C. 154(b) by 415 days.

(21) Appl. No.: **11/464,095**

(22) Filed: **Aug. 11, 2006**

(65) **Prior Publication Data**

US 2007/0076312 A1 Apr. 5, 2007

Related U.S. Application Data

(60) Provisional application No. 60/707,448, filed on Aug. 11, 2005.

(51) **Int. Cl.**
H04B 7/00 (2006.01)
H04B 1/38 (2006.01)
H04W 4/00 (2009.01)

(52) **U.S. Cl.** **455/466**; 455/557; 455/431

(58) **Field of Classification Search** 703/8; 340/681; 455/525, 552.1, 431, 66; 719/2; 701/206, 701/9

See application file for complete search history.

(56) **References Cited**

U.S. PATENT DOCUMENTS

6,148,179 A * 11/2000 Wright et al. 455/66.1
6,324,659 B1 * 11/2001 Pierro 714/48
6,629,183 B1 * 9/2003 Gortz et al. 710/305
2003/0222981 A1 * 12/2003 Kisak et al. 348/148
2004/0093196 A1 5/2004 Hawthorne et al.

OTHER PUBLICATIONS

International Search Report dated Nov. 5, 2007.

* cited by examiner

Primary Examiner — Lester Kincaid
Assistant Examiner — Kuo Woo
(74) *Attorney, Agent, or Firm* — Howard B. Rockman

(57) **ABSTRACT**

A universal event/data recorder system provides a common bridge between various event/data recorders found on mobile assets. The universal event/data recorder system includes an onboard segment that is capable of interfacing with any manufacturer's event/data recorder device. Additionally, the universal event/data recorder system also includes a remote segment for accessing, analyzing and reviewing data collected from any of a plurality of event/data recorders. The universal event/data recorder system may allow accessing data from various event/data recorders using any of a number of communication means including the Internet and a wireless communication network.

23 Claims, 8 Drawing Sheets

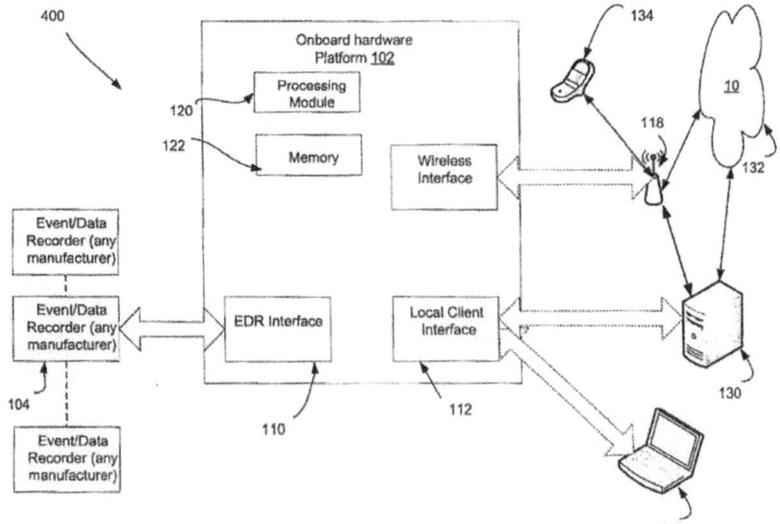

U.S. Patent **May 31, 2011** **Sheet 1 of 8** **US 7,953,425 B2**

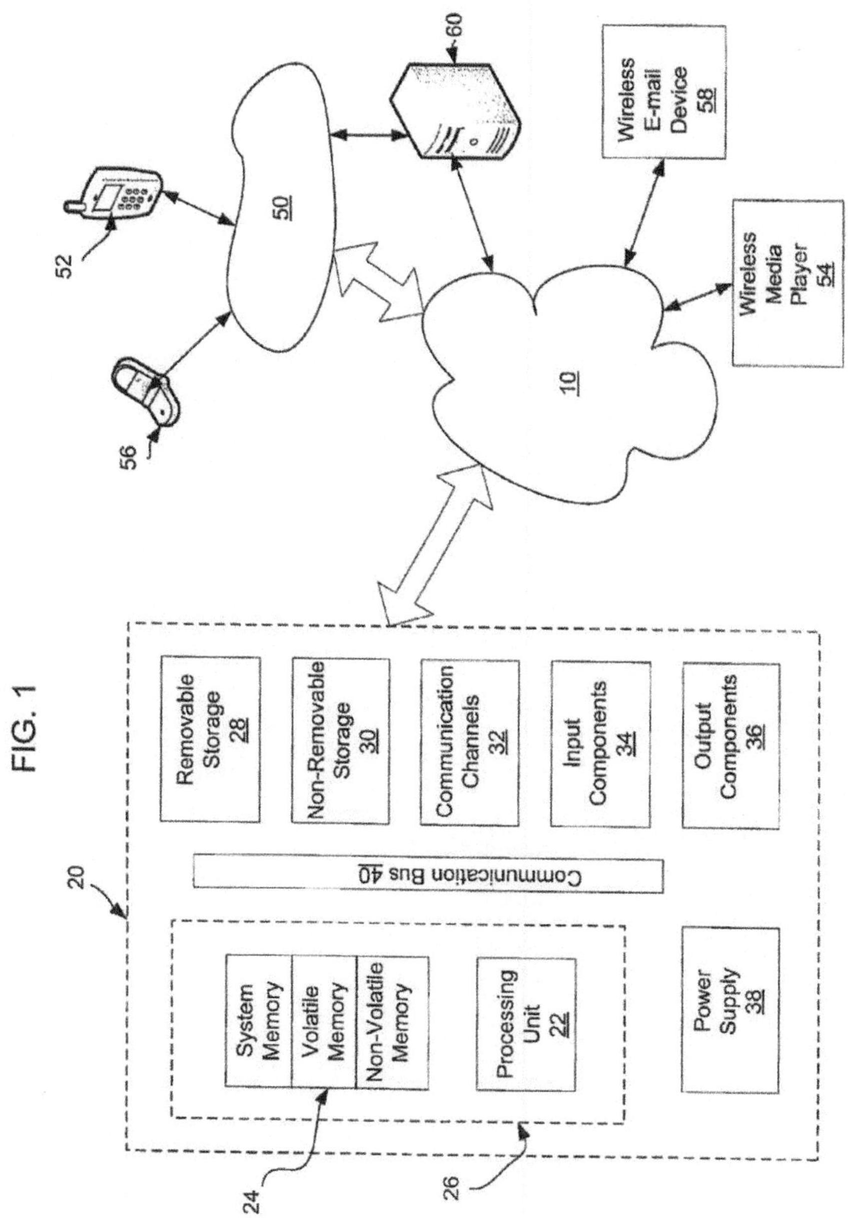

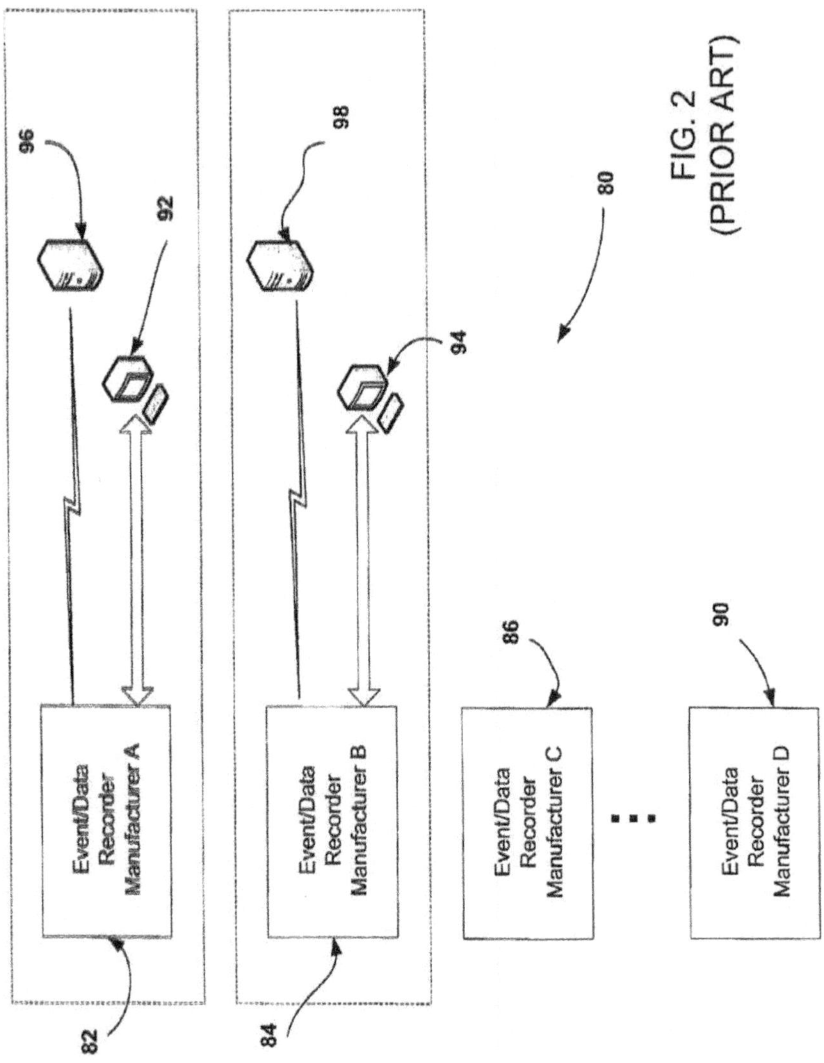

FIG. 2 (PRIOR ART)

U.S. Patent **May 31, 2011** **Sheet 3 of 8** **US 7,953,425 B2**

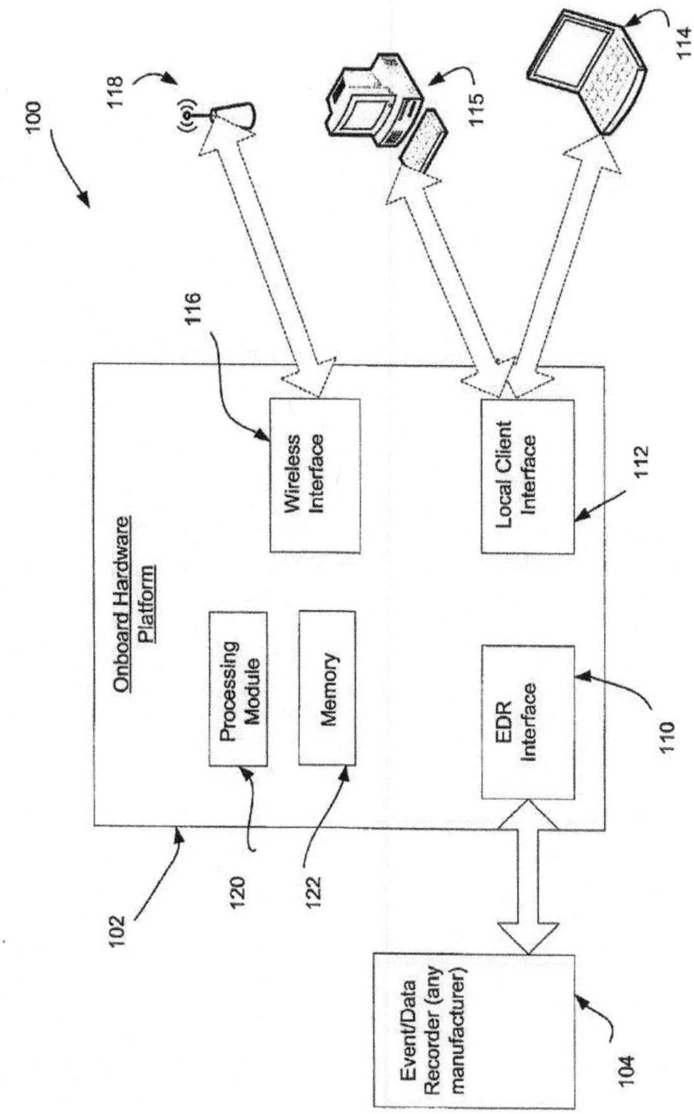

FIG. 3

U.S. Patent May 31, 2011 Sheet 4 of 8 US 7,953,425 B2

FIG. 4

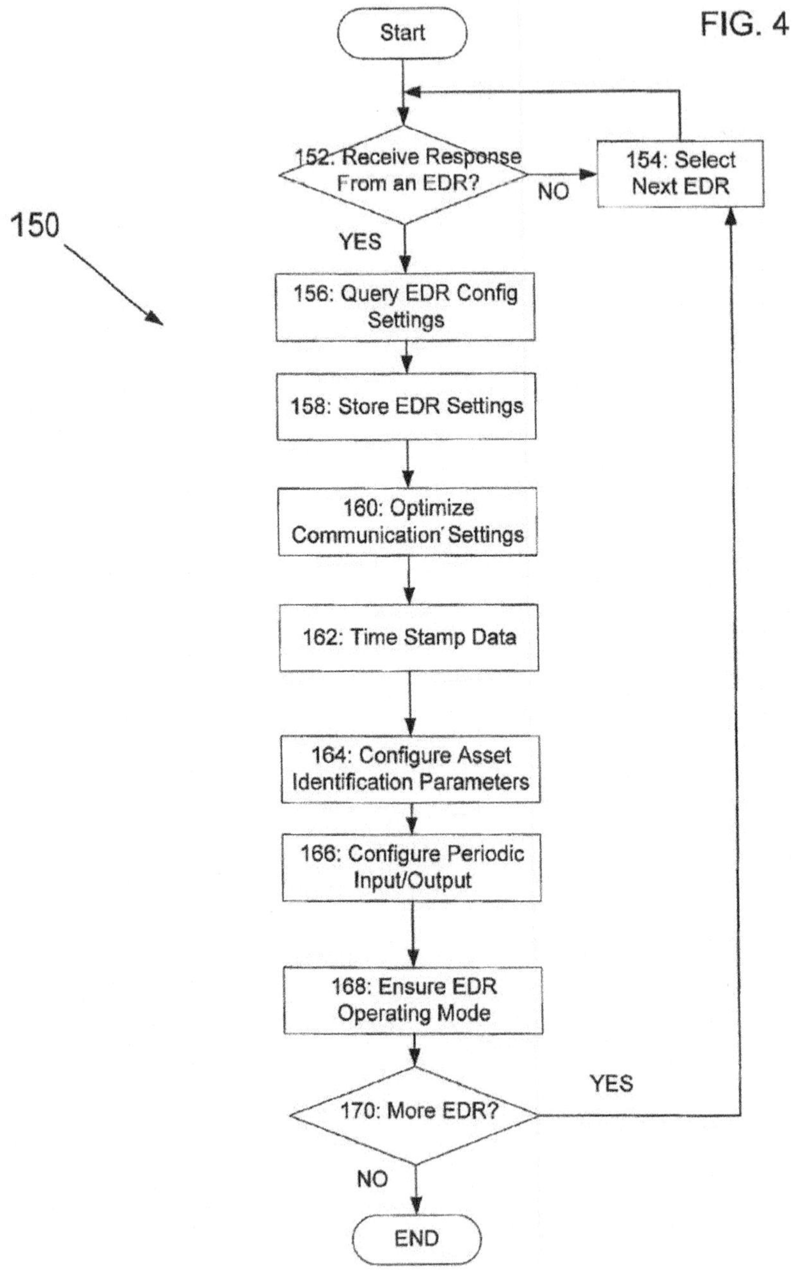

U.S. Patent May 31, 2011 Sheet 5 of 8 US 7,953,425 B2

FIG. 5

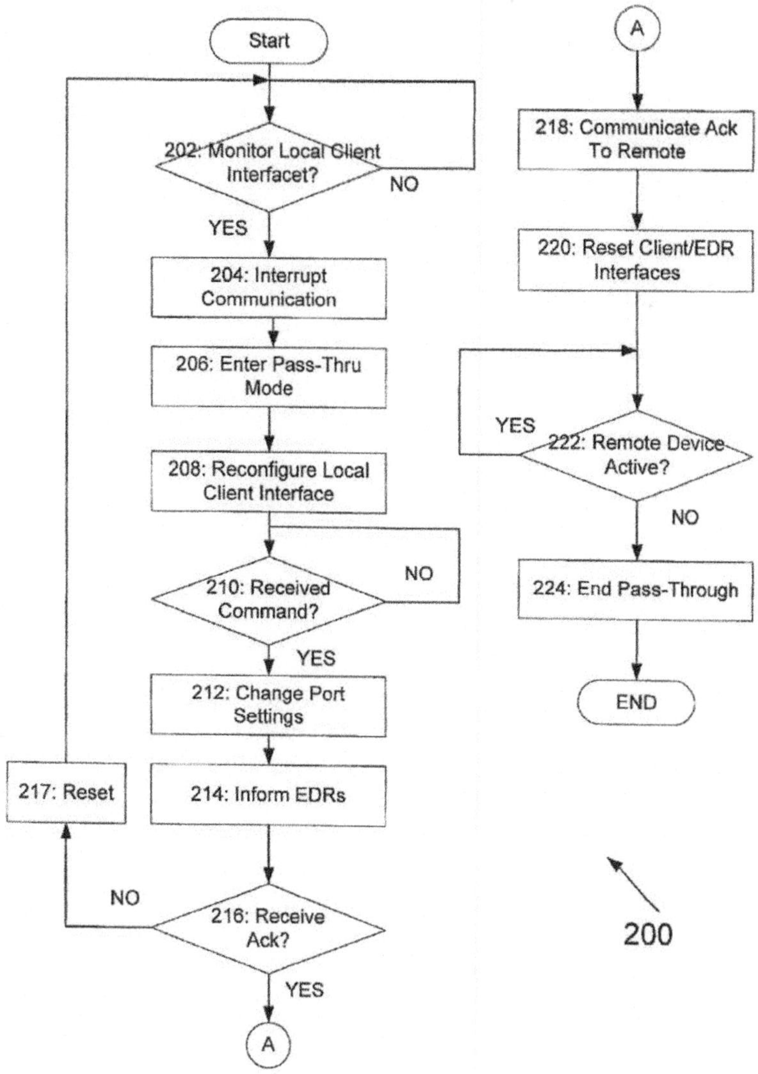

U.S. Patent May 31, 2011 Sheet 6 of 8 US 7,953,425 B2

FIG. 6

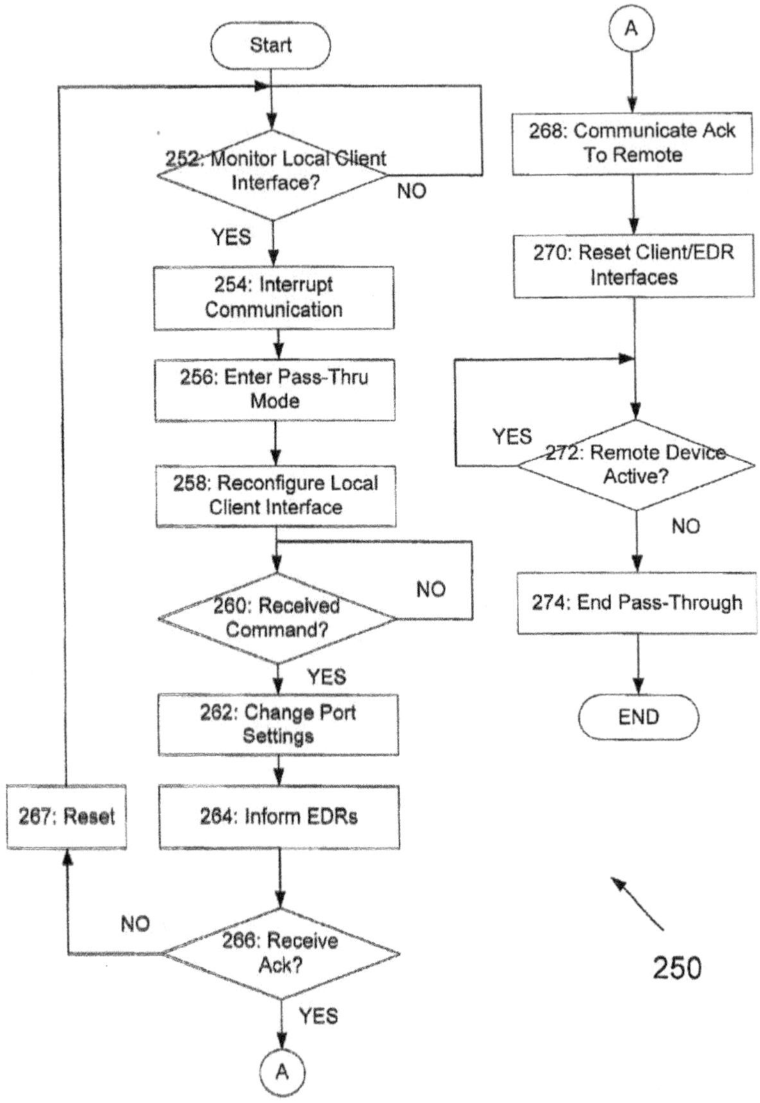

U.S. Patent May 31, 2011 Sheet 7 of 8 US 7,953,425 B2

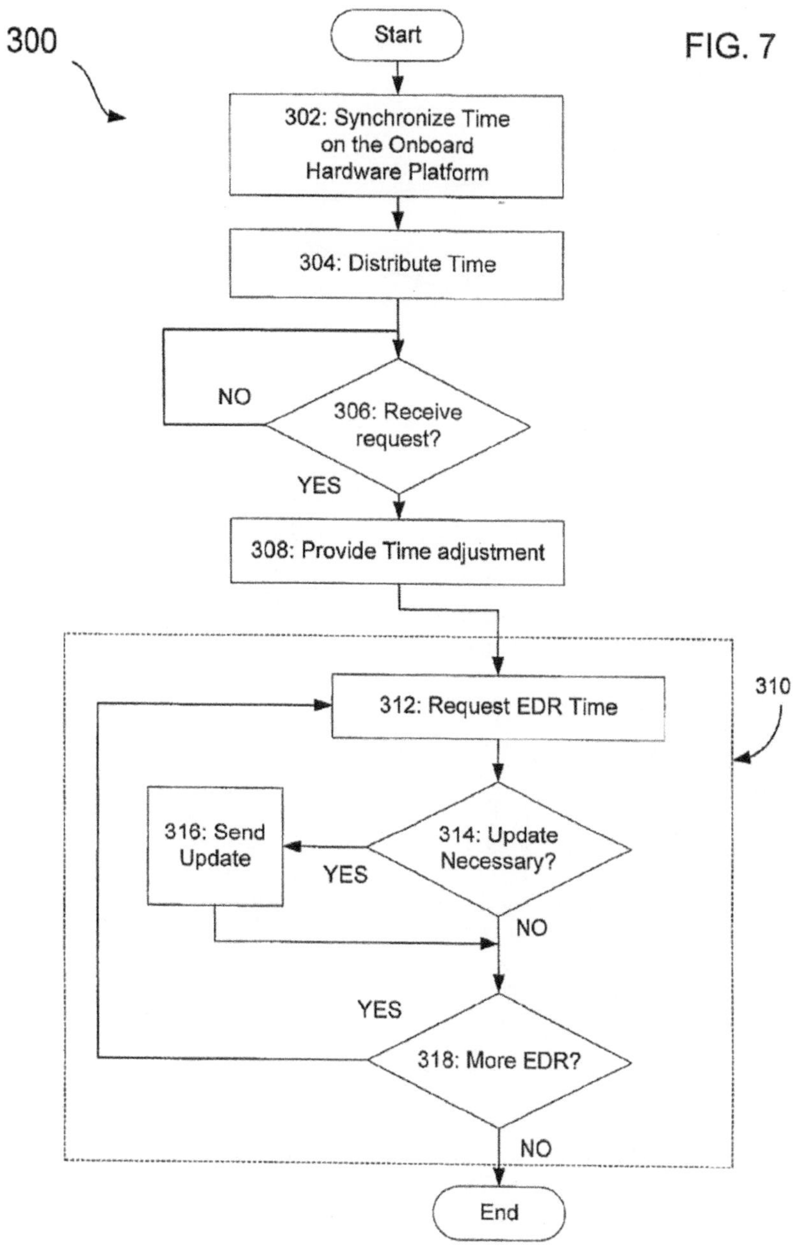

FIG. 7

U.S. Patent May 31, 2011 Sheet 8 of 8 US 7,953,425 B2

FIG. 8

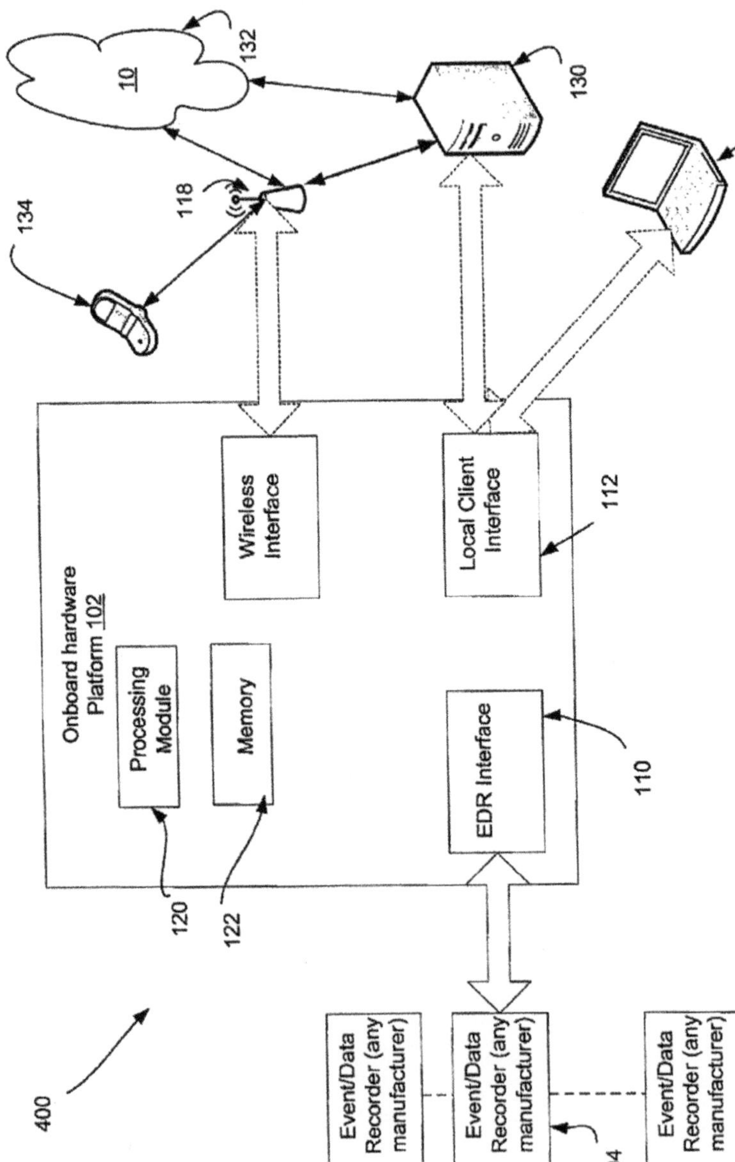

US 7,953,425 B2

1

UNIVERSAL EVENT/DATA RECORDER SYSTEM

CROSS-REFERENCE TO RELATED APPLICATIONS

This application is based on and claims the benefit of U.S. Provisional Application No. 60/707,448, filed on Aug. 11, 2005 and entitled "Universal Event/Data Recorder System," which is incorporated herein by reference in its entirety.

FIELD

This patent generally relates to equipments used in high value assets and particularly, it relates to event/data recorder systems used in high value assets.

BACKGROUND

High value mobile assets such as locomotives, aircrafts, mass transit systems, mining equipment, transportable medical equipment, and marine vessels typically employ onboard event/data recorder "black box" systems. These event/data recorders log a variety of system parameters used for incident investigation, crew performance evaluation, fuel efficiency analysis, maintenance planning, and predictive diagnostics. Recorded data may include such parameters as speed, distance traveled, location, fuel level, engine revolution per minute (RPM), fluid levels, operator controls, pressures, and ambient conditions. In addition to the basic event and operational data, video and audio event/data recording capabilities are also deployed on many of these same mobile assets.

The prevalence of mobile-asset recording, logging, and diagnosing systems has created an environment where an end user may often find multiple event/data recorder manufacturers as well as models across a fleet of mobile assets. In fact, many mobile assets combine one original equipment manufacturer's (OEM's) engine diagnostics with another manufacturer's event/data recorder, another vendor's fuel level monitoring, and yet another manufacturer's video and audio recorder. In such a situation, each of these disparate systems requires use of different data access, data download and data analysis tools (typically PC-based software) to locally download and view data, where such tools are often incompatible with each other. After such data is retrieved, the time offset of each device must be determined for manual data synchronization. As one would appreciate, the task of managing the different data access, data download and data analysis tools, custody and analysis of downloaded data, and archival of the downloaded data from a fleet of thousands of mobile assets is extremely cumbersome.

Moreover, managing the one or more of the data access, data download and data analysis processes using wireless tools further increases complexity of such system because each OEM and event/data recorder supplier may have its own wireless implementation that may require separate wireless hardware both onboard the mobile asset and at fixed stations wirelessly linked to onboard systems.

BRIEF DESCRIPTION OF THE DRAWINGS

While the appended claims set forth the features of the present patent with particularity, the patent, together with its objects and advantages, may be best understood from the following detailed description taken in conjunction with the accompanying drawings, of which:

2

FIG. **1** illustrates an example block diagram of a network that may be used to implement an embodiment of the system and method disclosed herein;

FIG. **2** illustrates prior art implementation of event/data recorder systems;

FIG. **3** illustrates an implementation of event/data recorder system using an onboard hardware platform described herein;

FIG. **4** illustrates a flowchart of a recorder setup program used by the event/data recorder system of FIG. **3**;

FIG. **5** illustrates a flowchart of a remote download program used by the event/data recorder system of FIG. **3**;

FIG. **6** illustrates a flowchart of a wireless download program used by the event/data recorder system of FIG. **3**;

FIG. **7** illustrates a flowchart of a time synchronization program used by the event/data recorder system of FIG. **3**; and

FIG. **8** illustrates a field implementation of the event/data recorder system of FIG. **3**.

DETAILED DESCRIPTION

A universal event/data recorder system disclosed herein provides a common bridge between various event/data recorders found on mobile assets. The universal event/data recorder system includes an onboard segment that is capable of interfacing with any manufacturer's event/data recorder device. Additionally, the universal event/data recorder system also includes a remote segment for accessing, analyzing and reviewing data collected from any of a plurality of event/data recorders. The universal event/data recorder system may allow accessing data from various event/data recorders using any of a number of communication means including the Internet and a wireless communication network.

In the description that follows, various components/implementations of event/data recording systems are described with reference to acts and symbolic representations of operations that are performed by one or more computing devices, unless indicated otherwise. As such, it will be understood that such acts and operations, which are at times referred to as being computer-executed, include the manipulation by the processing unit of the computing device of electrical signals representing data in a structured form. This manipulation transforms the data or maintains them at locations in the memory system of the computing device, which reconfigures or otherwise alters the operation of the computing device in a manner well understood by those skilled in the art. The data structures where data are maintained are physical locations of the memory that have particular properties defined by the format of the data. However, while the patent is being described in the foregoing context, it is not meant to be limiting as those of skill in the art will appreciate that several of the acts and operations described hereinafter may also be implemented in hardware.

Turning to the drawings, wherein like reference numerals refer to like elements, the patent is illustrated as being implemented in a suitable networking environment. The following description is based on illustrated embodiments of the patent and should not be taken as limiting the patent with regard to alternative embodiments that are not explicitly described herein.

Network and Computer

FIG. **1** illustrates a block diagram of a network **10** that may be used to implement the system and method described herein. Each node of the network **10** may reside in a device that may have one of many different computer architectures.

For descriptive purposes, FIG. 1 shows a schematic diagram of an exemplary architecture of a computing device 20 usable at any of the various devices connected to the network 10. The architecture portrayed is only one example of a suitable environment and is not intended to suggest any limitation as to the scope of use or functionality of various embodiments described herein. Neither should the computing devices be interpreted as having any dependency or requirement relating to any one or combination of components illustrated in FIG. 1. Each of the various embodiments described herein is operational with numerous other general-purpose or special-purpose computing or communications environments or configurations. Examples of well known computing systems, environments, and configurations suitable for use with the invention include, but are not limited to, mobile telephones, pocket computers, personal computers, servers, multiprocessor systems, microprocessor-based systems, minicomputers, mainframe computers, and distributed computing environments that include any of the above systems or devices.

In its most basic configuration, the computing device 20 typically includes at least one processing unit 22 and memory 24. The memory 24 may be volatile (such as RAM), non-volatile (such as ROM and flash memory), or some combination of the two. This most basic configuration is illustrated in FIG. 1 by the dashed line 26. The computing device 20 may also contain storage media devices 28 and 30 that may have additional features and functionality. For example, the storage media devices 28 and 30 may include additional storage (removable and non-removable) including, but not limited to, PCMCIA cards, magnetic and optical disks, and magnetic tapes. Such additional storage is illustrated in FIG. 1 by the removable storage 28 and the non-removable storage 30.

Computer-storage media may include volatile and non-volatile, removable and non-removable media implemented in any method or technology for storage of information such as computer-readable instructions, data structures, program modules, or other data. Memory 24, removable storage 28, and non-removable storage 30 are all examples of computer-storage media. Computer-storage media include, but are not limited to, RAM, ROM, EEPROM, flash memory, other memory technology, CD-ROM, digital versatile disks, other optical storage, magnetic cassettes, magnetic tapes, magnetic disk storage, other magnetic storage devices, and any other media that can be used to store the desired information and that can be accessed by the computing device.

The computing device 20 may also contain communication channels 32 that allow it to communicate with other devices. Communication channels 32 are examples of communications media. Communications media typically embody computer-readable instructions, data structures, program modules, or other data in a modulated data signal such as a carrier wave or other transport mechanism and include any information-delivery media. The term computer-readable media as used herein includes both storage media and communications media. The computing device 20 may also have input components 34 such as a keyboard, mouse, pen, a voice-input component, and a touch-input device. Output components 36 include screen displays, speakers, printers, and rendering modules (often called "adapters") for driving them. The computing device 20 has a power supply 38. Various components of the computing device may communicate with each other via an internal communications bus 40. All these components are well known in the art and need not be discussed at length here.

The network 10 may also be communicatively connected to one or more of a plurality of other devices and/or to another network. For example, the network 10 is illustrated to be communicatively connected to another network 50 that may be for example, a virtual private network (VPN), a local area network (LAN), a wireless metropolitan area network MAN), etc. Additionally, the network 10 may also be communicatively connected, directly or via another network 50, to a personal data assistant (PDA) 52, a wireless media player 54, a wireless phone 56, a wireless e-mail device 58, a database server 60, etc.

Event/Data Recording Systems

Event/data recorders when applied to locomotives are defined per U.S. Department of Transportation, Federal Railway Administration Code of Federal Regulations (CFR) 49 §229.5G. However, as it would be obvious to one of ordinary skill in the art, the event/data recording system disclosed herein may be used for any other mobile assets such as airplanes, moving equipments, etc.

Referring to FIG. 2, a typical prior art implementation 80 provides a system for managing, and collecting information from, a number of event/data recorders (EDRs) 82-90. Each of the EDRs 82-90 may be designed by different manufacturers and therefore may operate according to a different protocol than the other EDRs. For example, the EDR 82 may be configured to communicate at 19.2 K baud rate, with eight data bits, no parity, one stop bit and no hardware handshaking. On the other hand, the EDR 84 may be configured to communicate at a 57.6 K baud rate, with sixteen data bits, one parity bit, no stop bit and with hardware handshaking, etc.

In the typical prior art implementation 80, a first local downloading client 92 may be configured to communicate with the EDR 82 according to the communication specifications required by the EDR 82, while a second local downloading client 94 may be configured to communicate with the EDR 84 according to the communication specifications required by the EDR 84, and so on. Similarly, separate remote downloading systems 96, 98, etc., may be used for remote downloading of data from the EDRs 82-90. Moreover, because each of these remote downloading systems operate at different communication and data specification levels, it is difficult to use a common communication medium such as the Internet to facilitate integration of the remote data downloading systems 96, 98, etc.

Compared to the prior art systems, generally speaking, the universal event/data recorder system disclosed herein provides a common bridge between the various EDRs found on mobile assets. Such a universal event/data recorder system may be comprised of two major components, namely an onboard segment and a back office segment, which can be used either separately or as a combined system.

As described further in the following figures, the onboard segment may be comprised of a common hardware and/or software system capable of interfacing with any manufacturer's EDR. The onboard segment provides a common data acquisition interface across an entire fleet of mobile assets regardless of the specific systems installed. This common data acquisition interface provides for wired access, wireless access or a combination of both, and supports downloading data from any onboard EDR regardless of manufacturer, model or data format used by such EDR.

The back office segment of such a universal event/data recorder system is comprised of hardware and/or software to store, archive, retrieve, process and present information retrieved from event/data recorders. Additionally, the back office segment may include hardware and/or software in support of remote connectivity to the onboard segment. Furthermore, such a universal event/data recorder system supports both the standard download and viewing tools provided by each event/data recorder and/or a common back office or Internet-based capability to access, synchronize, analyze, view and/or export the data retrieved from any installed event/data recorder on any mobile asset.

FIG. 3 illustrates an implementation of such an event/data recorder system **100**. The event/data recorder system **100** is shown to include an onboard hardware platform **102** that may be adapted to communicate with an EDR **104**. The onboard hardware platform **102** is designed in a manner so that it may communicate with the EDR **104** irrespective of the manufacturer and/or model of the EDR **104**. The onboard hardware platform **102** may have an EDR interface **110** to communicate with EDRs manufactured by any manufacturers such as the EDR **104**. Additionally, the onboard hardware platform **102** may also have a local client interface **112** to communicate with any local client **114** such as a laptop computer and a wireless interface **116** that may be used to communicate with a remote client **118** such as a wireless access point, remote network access point, etc.

While in the present implementation the local client **114** is illustrated to be communicating with the local client interface **112** by a wired communication method, in an alternate implementation the local client **114** may communicate with the local client interface **112** in a wireless manner. Alternatively, as illustrated in FIG. **3**, the local client interface **112** may be able to communicate with the local client **114** in wired manner and with a remote client **115**, such as a desktop computer, in a wireless manner. Moreover, the remote client **115** may also be able to communicate directly with the remote client **118** in a wireless manner. The remote client **115** may be communicating with the local client interface **112** to download bulk EDR files, to upload software to the onboard hardware platform **102**, to send remote commands, to query status of various EDRs, etc.

The wireless interface **116** may be adapted to communicate with the wireless access point using, but not limited to, any of the following wireless communication technologies: Bluetooth, Wireless LAN (IEEE 802.11a/b/g), Cellular, Satellite and Private or Public data radio networks. The onboard hardware platform **102** is adapted to communicate over any of these communication technologies using data from the EDR (s) **104** in a number of different formats. The wireless access point may also allow the onboard hardware platform **102** to communicate, using the Internet, or any other network, with one or more remote event/data analysis stations. While the onboard hardware platform **102** is illustrated to have one of each of the interfaces **110**, **112** and **116**, in an alternate embodiment two or more of each of such interfaces may also be provided. Yet alternatively, only one of the local client interface **112** and the wireless interface **116** may also be provided.

The onboard hardware platform **102** may also include a local processing module **120** that may be used to functionally manage one or more of the interfaces **110**, **112** and **116**. The onboard hardware platform **102** may also include a memory module **122** that may be used to store one or more instructions from a user, various parameters of the onboard hardware platform **102**, various parameters of the interfaces **110**, **112** and **116**, etc. Moreover, the memory **122** may also be used to store data received from various EDRs and data to be communicated to local clients and/or to remote clients.

The EDR interface **110** is capable of communicating with EDRs or any other onboard system using any of a plurality of communication protocols including, but not limited to, Ethernet, RS232, RS485, RS422, controller area network (CAN) protocol, universal serial bus (USB), etc. Upon initiation, the

EDR interface **110** may perform an initiation sequence to identify a particular protocol used by devices and/or EDRs communicating with the EDR interface **110**. Such initiation sequence is illustrated in further detail in FIG. **4** below. The initiation sequence may allow the EDR interface **110** to receive communication parameters from various EDRs and to store such communication parameters in the memory **122**. Moreover, at any point during its operation, the EDR interface **110** may undertake one of more portions of remote download programs further described in FIGS. **5** and **6** below. The EDR interface **110** is adapted to communicate with EDRs via either wireless or wired communication link. Thus, if an EDR is equipped with a wireless transceiver, such an EDR may be able to communicate with the EDR interface **110** via wireless method.

While the description of the onboard hardware platform **102** is illustrated herein with respect to its communication with only one EDR **104**, it is understood that the onboard hardware platform **102** may operate in a similar manner with any number of EDRs or other similar devices.

The EDR interface **110** functions as a common interface between the local client interface **112** and any EDRs such as the EDR **104** and/or between the wireless interface **116** and any EDRs such as the EDR **104**. The onboard hardware platform **102** may monitor the local client interface **112** and the wireless interface **116** to determine if any download device, such as a computer, etc., is connected to these interfaces and/or if these interfaces have received any request for data downloaded from EDR **104** or any other on-board devices. Upon detecting presence of such a download device, the onboard hardware platform **102** may interrupt any interaction between the EDR interface **110** and the EDR **104**. Subsequently, the onboard hardware platform **102** may enter a pass-through mode in which any commands received from the download device are forwarded to the appropriate EDR. For example, the onboard hardware platform **102** may interrupt any interaction with the EDR **104** upon detecting presence of the local client **114** and enter into a pass-through mode where commands received from the local client **114** are communicated to the EDR **104**, while the data received from the EDR **104** is communicated to the local client **114**.

Furthermore, the onboard hardware platform **102** may support changing the port speed and/or protocols being executed while in the "pass-though" mode based on the port-speed and/or protocols required by the local client **114** or the remote client **118**. Thus, for example, the onboard hardware platform **102** may be communicating with the EDR **104** using a serial communication port that uses the typical 19.2 K baud, 8 data bits, no parity and 1 stop bit with no hardware handshaking. However, the local client **114** may request that the port speed be changed to 57.6 K baud rate using an X-Modem file transfer protocol. In that situation, the onboard hardware platform **102** may listen to the local client **114** while in a pass-through mode for any command being sent from the local client **114** to the EDR **104**. The onboard hardware platform **102** may store such commands in the memory **122** or it may process and interpret such commands using the processing module **120**. Based on the interpretation of the command, the onboard hardware platform **102** may change the port and/or protocol settings of the local client interface **112**.

Subsequently, the command from the local client **114** may be passed through to the EDR **104**, allowing the EDR **104** to internally make any port configuration changes as necessary. The EDR **104** may acknowledge any such changes made by the EDR **104** back to the local client **114** confirming that appropriate port and protocol settings have been made. If the appropriate acknowledgements are not received from the

EDR **104**, the onboard hardware platform **102** may reset the local client interface **112** to its original configuration allowing the local client **114** to reattempt a download from the EDR **104**.

Once the onboard hardware platform **102** has successfully initiated the communication between the local client **114** and the EDR **104**, the local client **114** may continuously download data from the EDR **104** without any interruption from or interaction with the onboard hardware platform **102**. In this situation, the onboard hardware platform **102** may simply monitor the downloading of the data. If the onboard hardware platform **102** notes that there is no downloading activity going on between the local client **114** and the EDR **104**, the onboard hardware platform **102** may resume control of the local client interface **112**, reset any port and protocol configuration changes that may have been made while in the pass-through mode, and reestablish direct communication with the EDR **104** using the EDR interface **110**.

In an alternate embodiment, the download device may be the remote client **118**. In such a situation, the onboard hardware platform **102**, while operating in a pass-through mode, may listen to the wireless interface **116** for any command being sent from the remote client **118** to the EDR **104**. If the onboard hardware platform **102** determines that the remote client **118** is communicating a command to the EDR **104**, the onboard hardware platform **102** may store such commands in the memory **122** or it may process and interpret such commands using the processing module **120**. Based on the interpretation of the command, the onboard hardware platform **102** may change the port and protocol settings of the wireless interface **116**.

Thus, the remote client **118** may download data from the EDR **104** in the same manner as the local client **114** downloads data from the EDR **104** as described above. Note that the remote client **118** may be communicatively connected to wireless devices such as a PDA, a cell-phone, etc., to a network such as the Internet, etc. The wireless interface **116** may provide wireless download capabilities using Bluetooth™ technology (IEEE 802.11a), wireless LAN (IEEE 802.11a/b/g), cellular, satellite, private and public radio networks, etc. Additionally, the onboard hardware platform **102** is designed in a manner so as to support downloading data from the EDR **104** to any of the local client **114**, the remote client **115** and the remote client **118** irrespective of the data format used by the EDR **104**.

Whether the data is downloaded to the local client **114** or to the remote client **118**, the onboard hardware platform **102** ensures that all downloaded data, regardless of the source, format or download methodology, is properly formatted and time synchronized for playback both in its native format of the EDR **104** and in a format to allow Internet based common viewer capability. FIG. **7** below illustrates a flowchart of a program that may be used by the onboard hardware platform **102** to provide synchronized time across all downloaded data from any EDR.

FIG. **4** illustrates a flowchart of an EDR setup program **150** used by the event/data recorder system **100** of FIG. **3**. As illustrated in FIG. **3**, to provide a common event/data recorder interface for local or remote event/data downloads, the onboard hardware platform **102** supports the ability for a single wired or wireless connection EDR interface **110** through which event and data downloads can be retrieved from any connected mobile asset sub-system. Event/data downloads from the EDRs may be triggered automatically based on user configurable parameters or on demand. On demand download commands can originate from either the onboard or back office segments of the event/data recorder system **100**.

The EDR setup program **150** may be stored on the memory **122** in a manner so that it may be implemented using the processing module **120**. At a block **152**, the onboard hardware platform **102** may, using the EDR interface **110**, attempt to communicate with a connected device, such as the EDR **104**, using each of a number of communication protocols/configurations until it gets a response from the EDR **104**. The hardware platform **102** continuously attempts to communicate with potential EDRs using the EDR interface **110** and through any other EDR interfaces if available. If at any point the onboard hardware platform **102** receives a response as a result of using one of the communication protocol/configurations, it stores that configuration as applicable to the EDR **104**. If no EDR responds to any of the communication protocols/configurations, the onboard hardware platform **102** may determine that no EDR, including EDR **104**, is responding at that present moment and store such information in the memory **122**. Subsequently a block **154** may select the next EDR to be setup.

If for any selected EDR, the block **152** determines that the EDR supports at least one of the communication protocols, a block **156** may query the configuration settings of such an operational EDR. For example, the block **156** may query the EDR to determine various information identifying that particular EDR including, but not limited to, EDR manufacturer, EDR model number, EDR serial number, EDR event/data logging capacity, settings of the EDR identification parameters, etc. Subsequently, a block **158** may store the configuration settings of the EDR into the memory **122**.

The onboard hardware platform **102** may have configuration settings, such as communication speeds, communication protocols, etc., related to a number of EDR models/manufacturers stored on the memory **122**. Using such information previously stored on the memory **122**, a block **160** may determine the optimal communication settings, such as the data transmission speed, the communication protocol, etc., used to communicate with that particular EDR. The block **160** may also store the optimized configuration settings of the EDR into the memory **122**.

Subsequently, a block **162** may time stamp the data to be received from the EDR with the date and time of the onboard hardware platform **102**. Time stamping data such date and time parameters of the EDR is important ensure that data received from a number of different EDRs may be analyzed and viewed by an end user in a concurrent and/or proper chronological manner. To ensure proper time stamping of data from each EDR, it may be necessary to synchronize local time of various EDRs. FIG. **7** below illustrates a flowchart of a synchronization program that may be used by the onboard hardware platform **102** to synchronize local time of a plurality of EDRs.

Subsequently, a block **164** may update and configure any asset identification parameters related to the EDR, wherein such parameters may include asset number, asset owner, wheel diameter, wheel sensor type, etc. A block **166** may auto configure any periodic data inputs/outputs required for the EDR. For example, a periodic input to an EDR may be the GPS coordinates of the EDR, while the periodic output from an EDR may be the temperature, pressure level, incremental audio data, etc. Finally, a block **168** may ensure whether the EDR is in its proper operating mode or not. The data and/or information collected by each of the blocks **164**-**168** may be stored on the memory **122** for subsequent use by the onboard hardware platform **102**. Finally, a block **170** may determine if there are any more EDRs to be set-up.

FIG. **5** illustrates a flowchart of a download program **200** used by the event/data recorder system **100** of FIG. **3**, wherein the download program **200** may be used to download data from one or more of a plurality of EDRs to a local or a remote client such as the local client **114**. A block **202** monitors local client interface **112** of the onboard hardware platform **102** for connection of any device, such as any download device capable of downloading data collected from any of the EDRs connected to the onboard hardware platform **102**, a monitoring device, other communication devices, etc.

If the block **202** determines that a sequence of download request commands is received at the local client interface **112** from a remote device connected to the local client interface **112**, a block **204** interrupts communication of the EDR interface **110** with any EDRs.

A block **206** causes the onboard hardware platform **102** to enter into a pass-through mode in which any commands received from a device connected to the local client interface **112** are forwarded to the appropriate EDRs via the EDR interface **110**.

Subsequently, A block **208** causes the onboard hardware platform **102** to change the communication setup of the local client interface **112** so as to support any adaptive changes necessary for the local client interface **112** to function in the pass through mode. For example, during an initial connection of a local client **114** to the local client interface **112**, the local client interface **112** may use a typical 19.2K baud, 8 data bits, no parity and 1 stop bit with no hardware handshaking. However, upon initialization of a download session, the local client **114** may dynamically request that the port speed of the local client interface **112** be changed to 57.6K baud using the Xmodem file transfer mechanism.

Subsequently, while in the pass-through mode a block **210** [diamond] monitors or listens to the local client interface **112** for any commands being sent from any local or remote device to any EDR. If any commands are received, a block **212** interprets these commands and, if required, changes the port settings and protocols for the local client interface **112** as well as for the EDR interface **110**.

A block **214** also generates and sends appropriate commands to any EDR(s) connected to the local client interface **112** in the pass through mode, so that the EDR(s) may also internally make necessary port configuration changes. Subsequently, a block **216** monitors the EDR(s) for acknowledgement of the change in the port configurations. If no acknowledgement is received, a block **217** resets the local client interface **112** to its original setting and sends a message to the local client **114** that its request to change the port speed cannot be granted. As a response, the local client **114** may change its communication settings accordingly. Subsequently the control is transferred back to block **202**.

If an acknowledgement of such port configuration is received from the EDR(s), a block **218** communicates such acknowledgements back to the device requesting the change. However, if no such acknowledgement is received from the EDR(s), a block **220** resets both the local client interface **112** and the EDR interface **110** to their original configurations allowing the local client or the remote client to re-attempt download from the EDR(s).

Finally, a block **222** monitors the local client interface **112** to determine if the local client or the remote client is still active, or that there is any communication received from the local client or the remote client. If no activity is detected, a block **224** resets any port configuration and protocols at the local client interface **112** and at the EDR interface **110** that

may have been made to initiate the pass through communication mode between the remote device and the EDR(s), and relinquishes the control of communication with the EDR(s) back to the processing module **120** of the onboard hardware platform **102**. Subsequently, the onboard hardware platform **102** may directly communicate with the EDR(s) for downloading data from the EDR(s).

The download program **200** provides a user the capability to use a common point of connection from which the user can perform the task of downloading data from any EDR connected to the onboard hardware platform **102**. Any local client or the remote client with any software and hardware can be used to download the data from EDRs as though such remote device were directly connected to the EDRs from which they are retrieving the downloaded data. Note that FIG. **5** illustrates the flowchart for remote download program **200** with respect to the local client **114** and the local client interface **112**, the various steps of the download program **200** may be implemented by substituting the local client interface **112** with the wireless interface **116** and the local client **114** with the remote client **118** to provide a wireless version of the download program **200**.

FIG. **6** illustrates a flowchart of such a wireless download program **250** used by the event/data recorder system **100** of FIG. **3**. Because various functions of the wireless download program **250** are similar to that of the download program **200**, the wireless download program **250** is not described in further detail herein.

FIG. **7** illustrates a flowchart of a time synchronization program **300** used by the event/data recorder system **100** of FIG. **3**. The onboard hardware platform **102** may provide synchronized time across all downloaded data from any EDR sources. To accomplish this, the onboard hardware platform **102** may maintain a common system time synchronized through at least one of: (1) a geographical positioning system (GPS) internal to the onboard hardware platform **102**; (2) a network time source communicatively connected to the onboard hardware platform **102**; and (3) time synchronized from another on-board system. At block **302** may update or synchronize the time on the onboard hardware platform **102** using one of these or other similar sources.

The onboard hardware platform **102** may be set up so as to distribute synchronized time to the EDRs using a predetermined schedule. A block **304** may distribute synchronized time to the EDRs based on such a predetermined schedule. Subsequently, a block **306** determines if there is any request received from any EDRs or from any other onboard hardware platforms to provide the synchronized time, if such a request is received, a block **308** may provide the synchronized time to the requesting source.

Because many EDRs may be designed to generate and keep their internal times, the onboard hardware platform may be used to test the time generated and kept on such EDRs and to update the time if necessary. A module **310** may be implemented to provide such updates to the EDRs' internal times. A block **312** may query an EDR for its internal time. Upon receiving the internal time, a block **314** may compare the received time with the synchronized time stored on the onboard hardware platform **102** to determine if updated time needs to be sent to the EDR.

If the block **314** determines that an update is necessary, a block **316** sends such an update to the EDR, otherwise, block **318** selects the next EDR and control passes back to block **312**. Note that module **310** is not always necessary and it may be operational only in some implementations of the onboard hardware platform **102**.

US 7,953,425 B2

11

As a result of providing synchronized time updates to the EDRs, any files or data received from the EDRs are stamped with correct time stamps. This allows viewing mobile asset downloaded data from multiple onboard EDRs in a synchronized manner using either vendor specific or Internet-based data analysis tools. Thus, operational, video, audio, engine, fuel and diagnostic data from multiple EDRs can be viewed through a single user interface against a common event timeline even when the data was retrieved from multiple onboard systems. A system for viewing and analyzing such data may be provided by the local client, remote client, or at any other node on the network **10** communicatively connected to the event/data recorder system **100**.

As one of ordinary skill in the art would know, the order of one or more blocks of the flowcharts **200-300** may be altered and one or more blocks of the flowcharts **200-300** may also be processed in parallel form. Similarly, additional blocks may be added at any point in these flowcharts and each of the blocks of these flowcharts may be implemented as part of various components of event/data recording system **100**.

FIG. **8** illustrates a field implementation **400** of the event/data recorder system **100** of FIG. **3**. As it can be seen in FIG. **8**, the field implementation **400** includes many components of the event/data recorder system **100** as represented by the like numerals in both systems. The local client interface **112** is further illustrated to be able to communicate simultaneously with multiple computers, such as the local client **114** and a remotely located server **130**. As one of ordinary skill in the art would recognize, the local client interface **112** may be adapted to communicate with number of other nodes as well. Similarly, the wireless access point acting as the remote client **118** may be adapted to communicate with the communication network **10**, the remote server **130**, a wireless phone **134**, etc. Moreover, one or more other onboard hardware platforms located on other mobile assets may also be communicatively connected to the server **130**, via, for example, the communication network **10**. Thus, EDR data from a number of mobile assets may be shared using the implementation of FIG. **8**.

The onboard hardware platform **102** may ensure that all data downloaded from the EDRs, regardless of the source, format or download methodology is properly formatted and time synchronized for playback in any one or all of the following: (1) the native format of the EDRs; (2) a customer specified or customized format; and (3) an Internet-based common viewer capability detailed in a later section of this application.

Therefore, various components and communication capabilities of the event/data recorder system **100** as implemented in FIG. **8** can be used to provide a common Internet based viewer capability for viewing data collected from the EDRs. For example, data downloaded from the EDRs either via the local client interface **112** or via the wireless interface **116** may be downloaded in a database in the server **130**. One or more data analysis program such as SAS®, Excel®, Access®, etc., may be located on the server **130** or on any alternate location to analyze the data and to present the data using Internet based viewing tools. For example, charts, graphs, videos, etc., generated based on the EDR data stored on the server **130** may be viewed using Internet browsers located on various nodes of the communication network **10**. Alternately, the EDR data can also be pushed to various users using really simple syndication (RSS) or other similar technologies. Yet alternatively, alert signals may be generated and communicated to users such as the cellular phone **134**, etc.

Various Internet based EDR data viewer(s) may provide reports including, but not limited to, tabular viewing of all EDR data as per various EDR parameters, graphical viewing of all EDR data as per various EDR parameters, user selected configurations of EDR data for user selected parameters, user selected viewing of data based on variables such as time, distance traveled, speeds of operational exceptions, etc., synchronized Internet based viewing of EDR data at certain event, audio, video, etc.

12

Furthermore, a user may be able to query for specific events or data exceptions using the Internet based or other query tools. Results of such queries, or results of other analysis on the EDR data may be exported to users in formats suitable for common data analysis tools such as spreadsheets and databases. The implementation of the event/data recorder system **100** illustrated in FIG. **8** may allow a user to select for export available data from any EDRs on any of a plurality of mobile assets.

In view of the many possible embodiments to which the principles of this patent may be applied, it should be recognized that the embodiments described herein with respect to the drawing figures are meant to be illustrative only and should not be taken as limiting the scope of patent. For example, for performance reasons one or more components of the method of the present patent may be implemented in hardware, rather than in software. Therefore, the patent as described herein contemplates all such embodiments as may come within the scope of the following claims and equivalents thereof.

What is claimed is:

1. A communication apparatus located on-board a mobile asset, the apparatus comprising:

a plurality of event/data recorders (EDRs), each EDR operating according to a predetermined communication protocol, certain of said communication protocols differing from other said communication protocols;

a memory adapted to store said predetermined communication protocols of each of the plurality of event/data recorders;

a processor adapted to dynamically determine the configuration of an event/data recorder of the plurality of event/data recorders, to select the communication protocol based on the configuration of the event/data recorder, and to configure an EDR interface to communicate with the event/data recorder using the selected communication protocol; and

the EDR interface adapted to communicate with the event/data recorder using the selected communication protocol.

2. The communication apparatus of claim **1**, further comprising a transmitter adapted to transmit data from the event/data recorder to a remote computer.

3. The communication apparatus of claim **2**, wherein the transmitter is a wireless transmitter adapted to transmit data to the remote computer in a wireless manner.

4. The communication apparatus of claim **1**, further comprising a client interface adapted to communicate data from the event/data recorder to a remote computer and to communicate commands from the remote computer to the EDR interface.

5. The communication apparatus of claim **4**, further adapted to:

receive a request from the remote computer at the client interface to communicate with the event/data recorder using a first communication protocol;

interrupt communication between the EDR interface and the event/data recorder;

reconfigure the EDR interface and the client interface to operate in a pass-through mode; and

US 7,953,425 B2

13

operate the client interface and the EDR interface in the pass-through mode.

6. The communication apparatus of claim **5**, further adapted to:

monitor the client interface for any communication from the remote computer; and

discontinue operating the client interface and the EDR interface in the pass-through mode if the remote computer is not active at the client interface.

7. The communication apparatus of claim **6**, wherein the client interface is a wireless interface and the remote computer is a wireless transceiver.

8. The communication apparatus of claim **1**, wherein the memory includes communication protocols used to communicate using at least one of: (1) RS232 protocol; (2) Ethernet protocol; (3) RS485 protocol; (4) RS422 protocol; (5) controller area network (CAN) protocol; and (6) universal serial bus (USB) protocol.

9. The communication apparatus of claim **1**, further adapted to synchronize the time of the communication apparatus to universal time and to communicate the synchronized time to each of the plurality of EDRs.

10. The communication apparatus of claim **1**, further adapted to:

synchronize the time of the communication apparatus to universal time;

request local EDR times from each of the plurality of EDRs;

compare local EDR times with the synchronized time; and

send a command to one or more of the plurality of EDRs to adjust their local EDR times to the synchronized time.

11. The communication apparatus of claim **1**, wherein the memory is further adapted to store a data processing program to process event data received from the plurality of EDR(s), the data processing program comprising:

a first routine to receive data from the EDR in a format generated by the EDR;

a second routine to convert the data received from the EDR into a format presentable via an Internet browser; and

a third routine to communicate the converted data using the client interface.

12. The communication apparatus of claim **11**, wherein the memory is further adapted to store format specifications for data generated by a plurality of EDRs and wherein the second routine uses the format specifications to convert the data received from the EDR.

13. A method of communicating with an event/data recorder (EDR), the method comprising:

determining the configuration of the EDR;

selecting a communication protocol based on the configuration of the EDR;

configuring an EDR interface to communicate with the EDR using the selected communication protocol; and

communicating with the EDR via the EDR interface.

14. The method of claim **13**, wherein the EDR is one of a plurality of EDRs, each of the plurality of EDRs communicating using a different communication protocol.

15. The method of claim **13** further comprising:

receiving EDR data from the EDR;

selecting an EDR data format based on the configuration of the EDR;

14

interpreting the EDR data based on the EDR data format; and

storing the EDR data on a memory of an onboard hardware platform.

16. The method of claim **15**, further comprising:

converting the EDR data into a format readable by an Internet browser software; and

communicating the converted EDR data to a remote computer.

17. The method of claim **16**, wherein communicating the converted data to a remote computer comprises wirelessly communicating the converted data to a remote computer.

18. The method of claim **17**, further comprising:

synchronizing time of the onboard hardware platform with universal time;

receiving the local time on the EDR;

comparing the EDR time with the universal time; and

if the EDR time is different than the universal time, sending a request to the EDR to update its local time.

19. A method of communicating data from an EDR to a remote client using an onboard platform system having an EDR interface communicatively connected to the EDR and a remote client interface communicatively connected to the remote client, the method comprising:

receiving at the remote client interface a request from the remote client for data from the EDR;

dynamically determining the configuration of the EDR and the configuration of the remote client;

selecting a communication protocol based on the configuration of the EDR and the configuration of the remote client;

interrupting any existing communication with the EDR at the EDR interface;

reconfiguring the EDR interface to communicate with the EDR using the selected communication protocol;

reconfiguring the EDR interface and the remote client interface to communicate with each other in a pass-through mode; and

communicating data from the EDR to the remote client using the EDR interface and the remote client interface communicating in the pass-through mode.

20. The method of claim **19**, wherein the remote client communicates with the remote client interface in a wireless manner.

21. The method of claim **19** further comprising providing time adjustment to the EDR to adjust the EDR time to universal time.

22. The method of claim **19**, wherein communicating data from the EDR to the remote client further comprises converting data from the EDR into a format presentable via an Internet browser using at least one of: (1) a data conversion routine stored on the EDR; and (2) a data conversion routine stored on the remote client.

23. The method of claim **19** further comprising:

monitoring the remote client interface for any communication from the remote client; and

discontinuing the pass-through mode when the remote client is not active at the remote client interface.

* * * * *

Data." These code numbers identify the category of information set forth on the issued patent's information page.

Just beneath the title of the invention, the name and resident city and state of the inventor or inventors are listed. Under U.S. Patent Law, the inventor(s) must always be identified, and these must be the inventor or inventors actually responsible for creating the disclosed invention.

Where a patent application was assigned by the individual inventor(s) to a corporation or other entity during the prosecution of the patent, such as the inventor's employer, and that assignment document was submitted to the USPTO for recording, the name and location of the assignee corporation or other entity will appear on the information page below the inventor(s) name and location. The '425 patent was assigned to Wi-Tronix, LLC, of Bolingbrook, Illinois. It is possible, however, that a patent was assigned prior to issuance by an unrecorded assignment document, or by an assignment document executed after the patent issued. In the latter case, if the assignment document is recorded after issue by the USPTO, the assignee's name will not appear on the information page. But, the true owner of the patent may be found through a search of the publicly available assignment records of the USPTO. If an assignee is listed on the information page of a patent, the patent is issued to the owner/assignee.

Beneath the names and addresses of the inventors and the assignee is the date that the patent application was filed with the USPTO, and that is followed by the application Serial Number assigned to the application upon its filing. The application serial number and the issued patent number have no relation to each other. Beneath the filing date and serial number is a statement of related U.S. applications or patent information, or foreign application or patent information, as the case may be. In the present case, the Jordan '425 patent issued on an application that was preceded by an earlier filed provisional patent, application Serial No. 60/707,448, filed August 11, 2005.

Next, the information page sets forth the United States and International search classification in which the technical subject matter of the particular patent is classified, showing the class and subclass of classification in bold. In this particular instance, the patent is classified in U.S. class 455, subclass 466, and is officially cross-referenced in 455/557 and 455/431. Also, the field of search through which the examiner looked during the examination process is indicated beneath the classification information.

Next, in the right column, is a list of all prior art patents and published patent applications either applied and/or cited by the Patent Examiner during the examination of the patent application, which led to the issuance of the Jordan patent, or which were submitted by the applicant's attorney via an Information Disclosure Statement. These patents and patent publications are listed by patent or publication number, issue or publication date, name of first-named inventor, and search class and subclass where copies of these patents are classified and may be found. Since the patents and published applications are identified by number, the references cited can also be obtained from the USPTO's website (www.uspto.gov). Beneath the listing of cited patents and patent publications is a list of "Other Publications" cited by the examiner during examination. In this case, the International Search Report was mentioned, which reports lists patents uncovered by the international search. See Chapter 16, Section 16.3.4.

Next, beneath the prior art listings, is set forth the name of the Primary Patent Examiner, the Assistant Patent Examiner, and the attorney, agent, or law firm that prosecuted the patent application on behalf of the inventor. This is followed by a paragraph constituting the Abstract of the Invention, which is a statement less than 150 words that describes the environment and nature of the invention in concise terms to enable the reader to determine quickly the substance of the invention covered by the patent. Beneath the abstract is a brief statement setting forth the number of claims and drawing figures in the patent.

At the bottom of the information page, one of the figures of the patent drawings, as selected by the applicant, is illustrated. If you look at the eighth page of drawings of the Jordan patent, you will note that the applicant selected Figure 8 to be reprinted on the information page.

20.2 THE DRAWINGS

The next eight pages following the information page of the Jordan '425 patent comprise Figures 1–8, showing various illustrations of the invention covered by the patent. The drawing Figures 1–8 of the Jordan '425 patent contain numerals and lead lines identifying various parts of the invention's structure and elements. These numerals are keyed to the description of the invention found in the specification portion of the issued patent.

The Patent Statute, at 35 U.S.C. §113, requires that drawings of the invention must be submitted "where necessary for the understanding of the subject matter sought to be patented." Where required, the drawings must illustrate each of the elements and features of the claimed invention. The patent drawings are normally a special type of lined mechanical drawing, and are usually prepared by patent draftspersons who are specialists in their field. In patent applications where no drawing is required for explanation of the invention, such as in certain chemical and composition of matter inventions, no drawings are submitted. Since a patent can be obtained based upon drawings or illustrations of the invention, it is not necessary that the inventor actually construct the invention before being granted a patent. The need to submit models of one's invention was abolished long ago.

20.3 THE SPECIFICATION

The seven pages that follow the drawings in the Jordan '425 patent constitute the specification of the patent, ending with the claims that are technically considered part of the specification. The text of the patent specification begins at column 1 with a repetition of the title of the invention, and a statement of the related provisional patent application.

The specification continues with the background of the invention comprising a statement of the field of the invention, i.e., event/data recorder systems used in high-value assets, and a description of the content of the prior art and the problems associated with the prior art.

A brief statement of the drawings appears in columns 1 and 2 on the first page of the specification, followed by a complete description of the illustrative embodiment of the invention. This is the portion of the specification that describes the structure, function, and one cycle of operation of the invention and its embodiments, and keys the numerals and lead lines of the drawings to the description of the invention.

Section 112 of the Patent Statue requires that the specification:

> "... contain a written description of the invention, and the manner and process of making and using it, in such full, clear, concise and exact terms as to enable any person skilled in the art to which it pertains, or with which is most nearly connected, to make and use the same, and shall set forth the best mode contemplated by the inventor of carrying out the invention."

This section of the statute comprises the "written description" requirement, the "enablement" requirement, and the "best mode" requirement. Therefore, when you read a patent, the specification should provide you with a complete description of the invention, and how it operates. The specification description must also enable one skilled in the art to make and use the invention. Lastly, from reading the specification, you can be assured that the best mode of carrying out the invention, as known by the inventor on the patent application filing date, has been disclosed. If these requirements do not come through upon a reading of the patent by one with ordinary skill in the art, the entire patent may be declared by a court to be invalid, except for the best mode requirement, as discussed in Chapter 18, Section 18.3.

20.4 CLAIMS

Beginning at column 12, line 29 of the specification, the claims of the Jordan '425 patent are set forth and continue until the end of the patent at column 14. You will note that this patent has 23 claims, with Claims 1, 13, and 19 being independent and the rest of the claims depending from either Claim 1, Claim 13, or Claim 19, or claims intermediately dependent upon one of these three independent claims. The description of the invention is set forth in the "Detailed Description," while the claims define the scope of protection afforded by this particular patent grant.

20.5 CAVEAT

When reading a patent issued to or owned by someone else, an engineer or scientist alone should *never* arrive at the conclusion that a product you or your employer is making, or is about to introduce to the market, infringes a claim in that patent. Further, the engineer or scientist should *never* put in a memo, letter, e-mail, or voice mail his or her opinion that a product infringes, possibly infringes, or may infringe another's patent. For the reasons stated in the next paragraph, if you do form the impression that the disclosure of a third party patent is of interest to your research and development direction, or to a product you or your company is making, personally and informally bring that patent to the attention of your patent attorney or agent, and orally explain to the attorney or agent why you feel the patent is worth investigating.

There are two primary reasons for rigidly adhering to this policy. The first may sound elitist, and if it is, it is still an important reason. A claim in an issued patent has been written by a trained patent attorney or agent, and has gone through rigid examination, and most likely amendment, as a result of examination by a skilled Patent Examiner. The correct meaning and scope of coverage of that claim cannot be fully understood without (a) a full understanding of the examination history of the patent, and (b) knowledge of the principle of determining literal infringement and the correct application of the Doctrine of Equivalents. This is an evaluation that should be conducted by a trained patent attorney or agent. With all due respect, your "conclusion" of infringement of a patent claim has a good chance of being incorrect.

The second reason is that it is important that no paper, electronic, or voice trail is created with your "concern" that a claim in a patent is or may be infringed by your or your company's product or process. If a patent infringement lawsuit is lodged against your or your company's product or process, during the discovery process in that litigation the opposing lawyer will obtain discovery of every non-privileged document, e-mail, voice mail, notation, etc., that relates to the allegedly infringing product or process. This would include any message of any kind you sent expressing your opinion or conclusion about infringement of the patent asserted against you. Your message could fly in the face of your own attorney's arguments that the patent in question is not infringed.

The problem arises when the lawyer for the patent owner shows your message to the jury, "admitting" that there is infringement. In addition to giving the jury reason to conclude that there is infringement, you or your company may be held liable for willful infringement because you had "prior knowledge" of a possible infringement problem. A finding of willful infringement could lead to a trebling of damages if there is a finding of infringement by the court or jury.

If you have communicated your concern about a potential problem as to a third party patent orally, there is no message trail that can be used against you or your company. In most situations, your conversation bringing the "patent of concern" to the attention of your attorney is a privileged communication. In addition, your patent attorney will later orally give you the results of his or her investigation, while preparing a privileged written or electronic opinion letter to you or your management team with advice on how to avoid any potential infringement problem.

Therefore, it is very important that you not make any discernible record of any conclusion you come to about potential infringement problems when reading a patent issued to another individual or company. Talk to your patent attorney directly, giving him or her the patent number, and asking him or her to investigate the coverage of that patent. Your patent attorney or agent will do the rest.

In addition, when presented with your "patent of interest," your patent attorney or agent will decide whether the patent is material to the examination of any pending patent applications he or she has filed recently, or are about to be filed. If necessary, your patent attorney will furnish the patent to the appropriate Patent Examiner under the duty of full disclosure of known, material prior art.

Remember, read a patent of another party from the standpoint of its relevance as prior art in relation to a research or development project in which you are involved. *Do not* make statements in any tangible medium regarding potential infringement issues. Leave that analysis to the attorneys—that is their job!

SECTION III

Employment Contracts, Ethics and the Engineer or Scientist as an Expert Witness

◆ INVENTORS AND INVENTIONS ◆

Willis Haviland Carrier

AIR-CONDITIONING

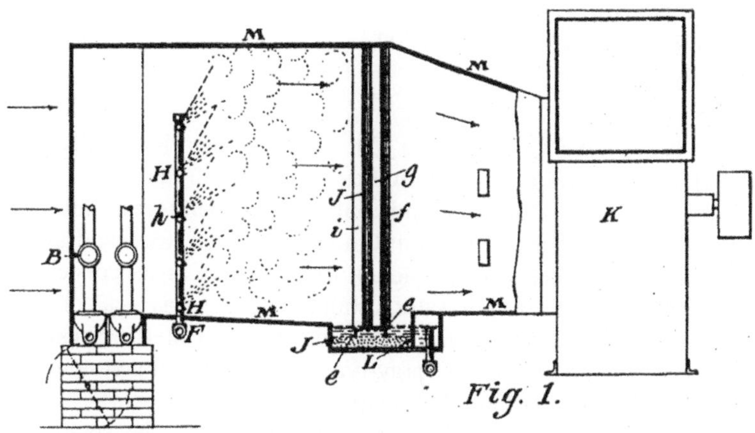

Fig. 1.

Willis Haviland Carrier, an American engineer, is known for inventing modern air-conditioning. He invented the first electrical air-conditioning unit in 1902, and in 1915 he founded Carrier Corporation, which specialized in the manufacture and distribution of heating, ventilating, and air-conditioning (HVAC) systems.

Willis Carrier graduated from Cornell University in 1901 with a B.S. in Engineering. While employed at the Buffalo Forge Company in 1902, he was asked to solve a humidity problem at the Sackett-Wilhems Publishing Company in Brooklyn, New York. The humidity at the printing plant was causing magazine pages to wrinkle, and color printing ink to fail to register properly. Ink was applied one color at a time, and would misalign with the expansion and contraction of the paper due to the high humidity.

Carrier experimented and eventually designed a humidity control system that forced air to flow over cold coils to control room humidity and temperature. His design was submitted as a drawing for what is now considered the world's first modern air-conditioning system. Carrier's system replaced cold water for the steam flowing through heating system coils, balancing the temperature of the coil's surface with the rate of air flow. This lowered the temperature to a desired dew point temperature. The coil system Carrier created was installed in the summer of 1902 at the Sackett-Wilhems

Intellectual Property Law for Engineers, Scientists, and Entrepreneurs, Second Edition. Howard B. Rockman.

Published 2020 by John Wiley & Sons, Inc.

printing plant, along with ducts, heaters, fans, steam pipes with holes for humidification, and temperature controls. Cool water was taken from an artesian well in the summer of 1902, and this cool water source was supplemented by an ammonia compressor in the spring of 1903.

The 1902 installation of Carrier's system had an added humidity control, which is recognized as the birth of air-conditioning, since authorities in the field recognized that air-conditioning has to perform four basic functions:

1. Control temperature.
2. Control humidity.
3. Control air circulation and ventilation.
4. Cleanse the air.

The present Carrier Air Conditioning Co. website states that Willis Carrier was standing on a foggy, cold train platform in Pittsburgh, PA, in the fall of 1902. Carrier recalled thinking: "If I can saturate air and control its temperature at saturation, I can get air with any amount of moisture I want in it. I can do it, too, by drawing the air through a fine spray of water to create actual fog." Thus, Carrier conceived that air could be dried by passing it through water, using the water spray as a condensing surface. This led to the air-conditioning system he installed at the Sackett-Wilhems printing facility in 1902 and 1903, a spray-type air-conditioning system capable of washing and humidifying or dehumidifying air.

Subsequently, Carrier adjusted the humidity by heating the spray water, and controlling the dew point temperature of the air exiting the air-conditioning machine. This resulted in dew point control, which was hailed as "the greatest single factor in modern air conditioning" in a Carrier company brochure.

After several years of field testing, on January 2, 1906, Carrier obtained U.S. Patent No. 808,897, entitled "An Apparatus for Treating Air." This was the world's first spray-type air-conditioning equipment, and was designed to humidify or dehumidify air, heating water for the first function and cooling it for the second.

In 1906, Carrier determined that constant dew point depression provided somewhat constant relative humidity. This later became known among air-conditioning engineers as the "law of constant dew-point depression." Based on this discovery, he proceeded with the design of an automatic control system, for which he was granted U.S. Patent No. 1,085,971, on February 3, 1914.

In 1911, Carrier presented a paper entitled "Rational Psychrometric Formulae" at a meeting of the American Society of Mechanical Engineers. This paper became known as the Magna Carta of psychometrics. In this paper, Carrier joined together the concepts of relative humidity, absolute humidity, and dew point temperature, thus making it possible to design air-conditioning systems to precisely fit the requirements at hand.

With the onset of World War I, seven young engineers who had worked for the Buffalo Forge Company put together their life savings of $32,600 to form the Carrier Engineering Corporation in New York on June 26, 1915. The company eventually moved to Newark, New Jersey.

Despite the development of the centrifugal refrigeration machine and the commercial growth of air-conditioning to cool buildings in the 1920s, the Wall Street crash of October 1929 caused financial difficulties for the Carrier Engineering Corporation. In 1930, Carrier Engineering Corporation merged with Brunswick-Kroeschell Company and York Heating & Ventilating Corporation to form the Carrier Corporation, with Willis Carrier as chairman of the board. The Great Depression slowed residential and commercial use of air-conditioning, and during this time the company spread out over four cities in New Jersey and Pennsylvania, until the company consolidated and moved to Syracuse, New York, in 1937. At that time, the company became one of the largest employers in central New York.

During the post–World War II economic boom beginning in the 1950s, air-conditioning began its tremendous growth and popularity, such that HVAC is used in practically every home and building throughout the world. Ceiling fans and air-conditioning are often used in conjunction with each other. In summer, a ceiling fan allows the thermostat to be set several degrees higher. In winter, a fan can be set to a low speed or reverse direction to bring down stratified heat from the upper volume of a room.

No. 808,897. PATENTED JAN. 2, 1906.

W. H. CARRIER.

APPARATUS FOR TREATING AIR.

APPLICATION FILED SEPT. 16, 1904.

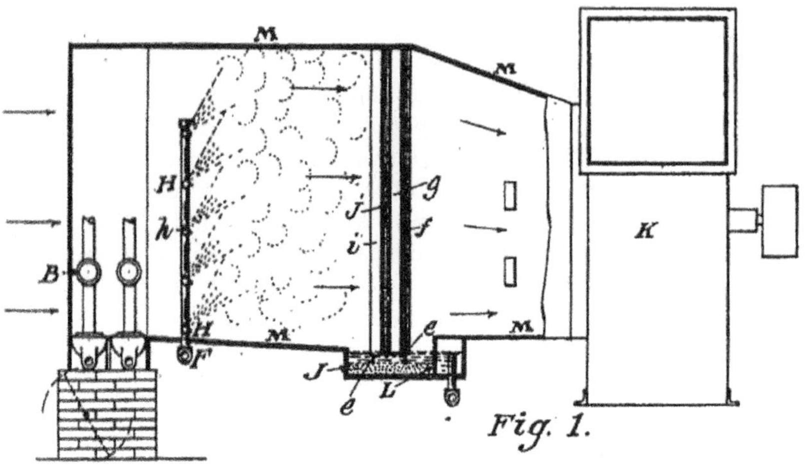

Fig. 1.

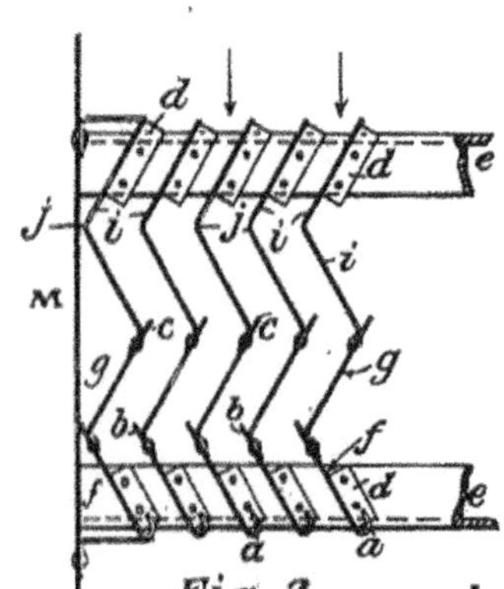

Fig. 2.

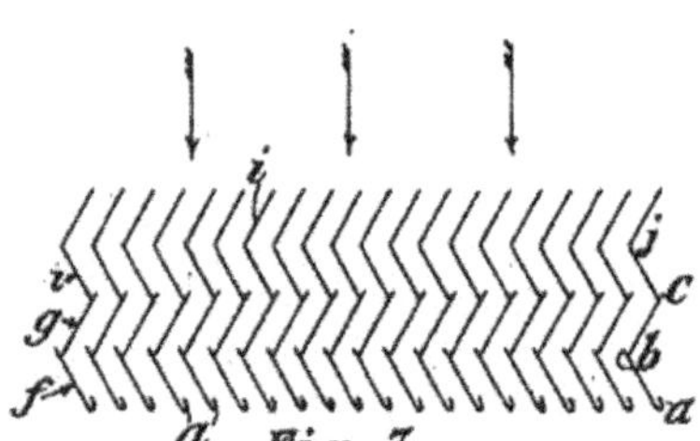

Fig. 3.

Fig. 5.

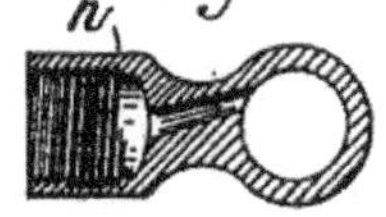

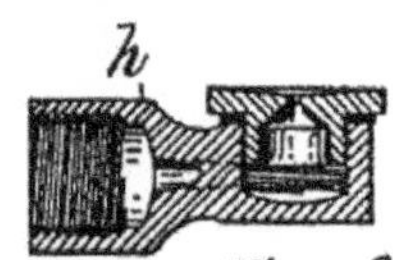

Fig. 6.

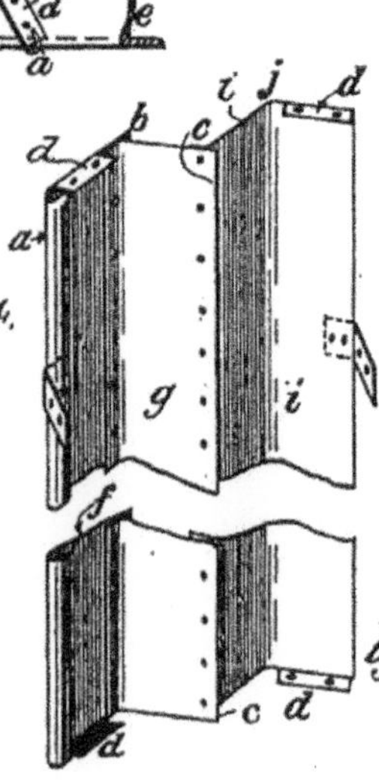

Fig. 4.

Witnesses.

E. A. Volk.

R. W. Ramer.

Inventor.

Willis H. Carrier

by Wilhelm, Parker & Hard

Attorneys

W. H. CARRIER.

METHOD OF HUMIDIFYING AIR AND CONTROLLING THE HUMIDITY AND TEMPERATURE THEREOF.

APPLICATION FILED MAY 17, 1907. RENEWED DEC. 1, 1913.

1,085,971. Patented Feb. 3, 1914.

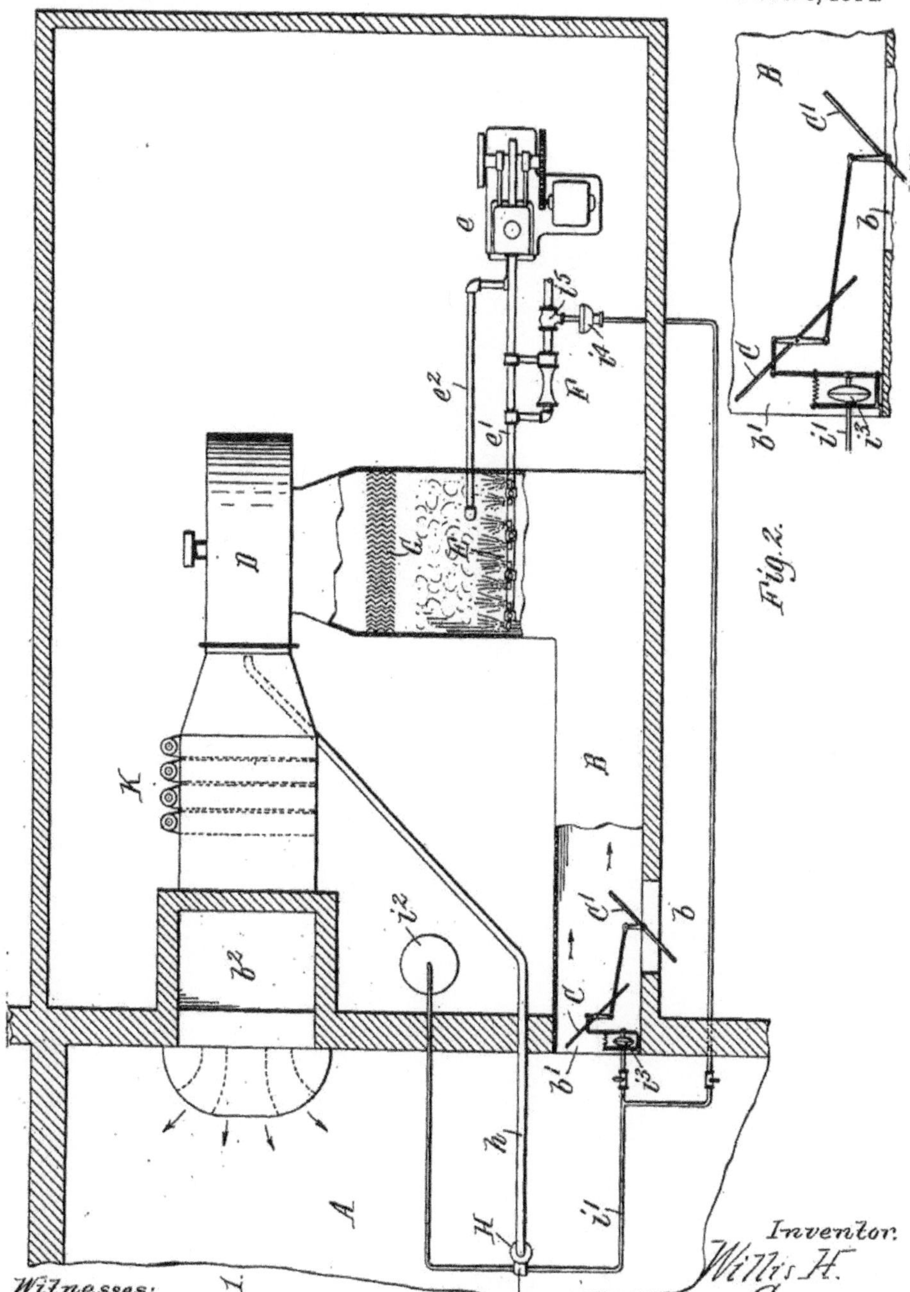

Fig. 1. Fig. 2.

Witnesses:
E. A. Volk.
A. Dimond.

Inventor:
Willis H. Carrier,
By Wilhelm, Parker & Hard Attorneys.

◆ INVENTORS AND INVENTIONS ◆

Ivan A. Getting, Roger L. Easton, Sr. and Bradford Parkinson

GLOBAL POSITIONING SYSTEM (GPS)

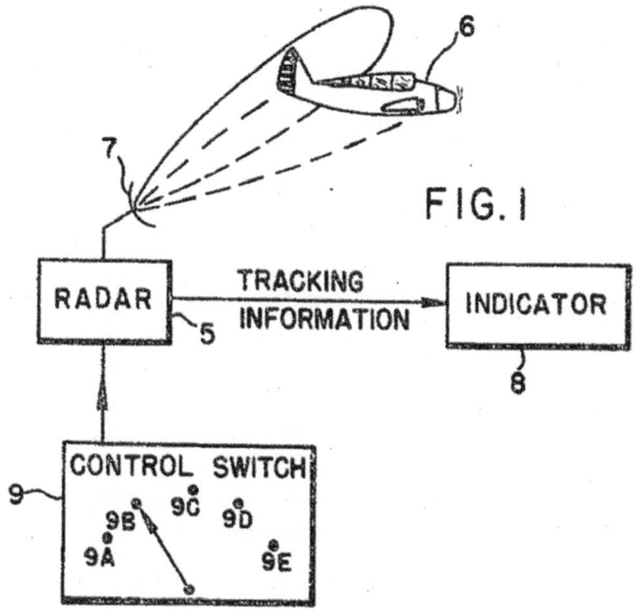

The development of the satellite-based Global Positioning System (GPS) we all use on our mobile devices each day began with the launch of the Russian Sputnik satellite in 1957, when scientists Dr. William Grier and George Weiffenbach at Johns Hopkins University's Applied Physics Laboratory (APL) discovered they were able to pinpoint the satellite's orbital position through shifts in its continuous tone radio signal known as the "Doppler Effect." The signal velocity relative to the ground created a Doppler shift of the signal that was unique. The Director of APL provided them with access to their UNIVAC computer to make the required calculations.

In the spring of 1958, Grier and Weiffenbach were asked by Frank McClure of APL to investigate the reverse problem: Using a known satellite position, could a navigator determine his or her location anywhere in the world after receiving and processing a

Intellectual Property Law for Engineers, Scientists, and Entrepreneurs, Second Edition. Howard B. Rockman.

Published 2020 by John Wiley & Sons, Inc.

satellite radio signal for 15 minutes. This led to the development of the Navy's "Transit" satellite program, also known as the Navy Navigation Satellite System, whose purpose was to provide position information to the U.S. submarine ballistic-missile force then being developed. The Transit system, using five solar-power-operated and gravity-gradient stabilization orbiting satellites was successfully tested in 1960, and became operational in 1964. In 1967, access to Transit was offered to the civilian community.

The Transit program developed a technique necessary for a GPS system: two frequencies were used to calibrate the time delay of the radio signal induced by the ionosphere. Transit also pioneered the accurate prediction of satellite orbits, which is essential for GPS operation.

The development and construction of a navigation system deploying a constellation of navigation satellites were obviously very expensive propositions, and having an accurate navigation system for civilian and military use was not seen by the U.S. Congress as justification for such expenditures of taxpayer dollars. However, during the Cold War, the nuclear threat to the existence of the United States was the single justification Congress needed to warrant the expense. Based on this deterrent effect, the military programs eventually leading to the GPS were funded.

These programs were shrouded in secrecy at the time. The nuclear weapons in the U.S. arsenal consisted of the U.S. Navy's submarine-launched ballistic missiles, and the Air Force's strategic bomber and intercontinental ballistic missiles. Accurate determination of the location of a submarine-launched missile was a vital factor to the U.S.'s nuclear deterrence program.

In the 1960s, both the U.S. Navy and Air Force were working on satellite-based navigation systems that provided the platform from which GPS was eventually born. In addition, in 1964, the U.S. Army orbited a satellite for use in geodetic surveying. This Sequential Collection of Range (SECOR) system comprised three ground-based transmitters from known locations sending signals to an orbiting transponder. A fourth ground-based station, whose position was undetermined, used these signals to fix its location. Ultimately, civilian surveying became one of the first fields to use GPS technology.

In November 1972, Air Force Colonel Bradford Parkinson was engineering director for the Advanced Ballistic Reentry Systems Program, and then was named director of the Air Force's 621B program. Parkinson had a PhD from Stanford in astronautical engineering. On August 7, 1973, Parkinson was invited to a Defense Systems Acquisition Review Council meeting, where the Council voted to drop the 621B program. Dr. Malcolm Curie, the Director of Defense Research and Engineering, immediately after the vote met with Parkinson in Curie's office, and Parkinson was told to develop a proposal for a new system that would combine the best features of all the technical options, and that a joint program involving all the armed services should be included in the program.

Thus, it was finally realized that a satellite navigation system could be developed by combining the best technologies from each of the service programs into a single multi-service program. During the 1973 Labor Day Weekend, about 12 military officers met at the otherwise mostly vacated Pentagon (the "Lonely Hall's meeting") to discuss the creation of a Defense Navigation Satellite System (DNSS), named later that year as NAVSTAR or Navigation System Using Timing and Ranging. Colonel Parkinson was Director of the GPS Joint Program. Ten NAVSTAR "Block I" satellites were launched between 1978 and 1985.

On December 14, 1973, Parkinson's new proposal was approved by the same people who had opposed the 621B program. Col. Parkinson then recruited about 25 Air Force officers with advanced engineering degrees whose backgrounds matched the requirements of the new joint program, particularly in hardware development and inertial guidance system testing. The program also included a select group of Aerospace Corporation technical support engineers and scientists, supported by Ivan Getting, Aerospace's president.

In 1983, Korean Air Lines Flight 007, a Boeing 747 aircraft with 269 people on board, was shot down after accidentally flying over USSR airspace. The President of the United States, Ronald Reagan, directed that GPS would from then on be freely available for civilian use, once developed for such use. The first "Block II" satellite went into orbit on February 14, 1989, and the 24th satellite was launched in 1994. Both GPS systems are owned and operated by the U.S. Government. Today, there are more than a billion GPS receivers in use worldwide, including the one in your pocket or purse. Virtually every mobile phone system relies on GPS for timing.

Certain commentators point out that from its inception, GPS was designed for both military and civilian use. Civilians were to be provided with free access to the signal specification, and to the clear acquisition signal for navigation and additional uses. Col. Parkinson commented on such dual use when he testified before the U.S. Congress on the proposed new GPS system.

Going back in time, on or before 1963, Dr. Ivan Getting, president of Aerospace Corporation, envisioned the need for a new satellite-based navigation system, one that would be available in three dimensions, 24-7. He convinced the U.S. Air Force to create a new satellite navigation program, later named 621B. From 1964 to 1966, Aerospace space-systems engineers James Woodford and Hideyoshi Nakamura conducted a formal system study. Their study was reported at a secret Defense Department briefing in August 1966, which was classified as "secret" until 1979, when the study became publicly available. This study became the foundation of the GPS system.

Key recommendations of the 1966 study called for:

a. Positive ranging from the satellite (which ranging signal to use).
b. Atomic clocks in space, and a technology program to develop space-useful atomic clocks.
c. Additional system studies and experimental demonstrations.

In October 1970, Roger L. Easton, Sr. of the Naval Research Laboratory applied for a patent on a two-satellite, two-dimensional system that required an atomic clock for the user. His Patent No. 3,789,409 issued in 1974.

In 1972, tests of the 621B program satellite system showed that by using a modulated CDMA (spread spectrum) signal, all satellite signals could be received at the same time on the same frequency. The tests also confirmed that ranging to four satellites did away with the need for a highly precise atomic clock, while full, three-dimensional navigation was maintained. Thus, each user of GPS is not required to have a device employing a vastly expensive atomic clock class frequency standard.

In 1964, the U.S. Naval Research Laboratory began a second satellite navigation system development, named Timation, directed by Roger L. Easton, Sr. This program was centered on investigating methods for passive ranging to satellites, and time transfer between several timing centers around the globe. This program launched a small,

85-pound test satellite, producing 6 watts of power, on May 27, 1967. This small satellite encountered two significant problems. First, solar radiation caused shifts in the quartz clock's frequency. Second, the ionospheric group delay created ranging errors.

GPS is a multi-use, space-based radio navigation system owned and operated by the U.S. Government and operated by the U.S. Air Force to meet national defense, homeland security, civil, commercial, and scientific needs. GPS currently provides two levels of service: (1) Standard Positioning Service (SPS), which was the course acquisitions (C/A) code on the L1 frequency, and (2) Precise Positioning Service (PPS), which uses the P(Y) code on both the L1 and L2 frequencies. Access to the PPS is restricted to the U.S. Armed Forces, U.S. Federal agencies, and selected allied armed forces and governments. The SPS is available free to all users on a continuous, worldwide basis, with no direct user charges, governed by the Global Positioning System Performance Standards and Specifications (www.gps.gov/technical/ps/).

GPS helps pinpoint a three-dimensional position to about one meter of accuracy, such as latitude, longitude, and altitude, and provides nanosecond-precise time anywhere on earth. Three different parts comprise GPS:

1. Space Segment: A constellation of at least 24 satellites distributed in six orbital planes inclined 55° from the equator in a medium earth orbit at about 12,550 miles (20,200 kilometers) circling the earth every 12 hours.
2. Control Segment: Land stations on earth, monitoring and maintaining the GPS satellites.
3. User Segment: Receivers that process the navigation signals from the GPS satellite and calculate position and time.

GPS satellites provide geolocation and time information to a GPS receiver on or near the earth where the receiver has an unobstructed line of sight to four or more GPS satellites. There is no need for a user to transmit data, and the system operates independently of any telephonic or Internet reception. GPS became fully operational in 1995, and was opened to civilian use prior to that in the 1980s.

In addition to the GPS system, other systems are in use or under development, mainly because the U.S. Government can selectively deny access to the existing system, as happened to the Indian military in 1999 during the Kargil War, or degrade the service at any time. The Russian Global Navigation Satellite System (GLONASS) was developed contemporaneously with GPS, but suffered from incomplete coverage of the globe until the mid-2000s. GLONASS can be added to GPS devices, making more satellites available and enabling positions to be fixed more quickly and accurately, to within two meters. There are also the European Union Galileo Positioning System, China's BeiDou Navigation Satellite System, India's NAVIC, and Japan's Quasi-Zenith Satellite System.

The design of GPS is partly based on past ground-based radio navigation systems, such as LORAN and the Decca Navigator. The design of the GPS had to consider a factor of general relativity, namely, detecting time slowdown in a strong gravitational field using atomic clocks placed into orbit inside man-made satellites. Special and general relativity both predict that clocks on the GPS satellite would be observed by users on earth to run 38 microseconds faster per day compared to clocks on earth. The position calculated by the GPS would drift into error, amounting to 10 kilometers each day. Using atomic clocks in the GPS system corrected this problem.

May 31, 1955 I. A. GETTING ET AL 2,709,773

REMOTE CONTROL SYSTEM WITH POSITION INDICATING MEANS

Filed Oct. 19, 1945

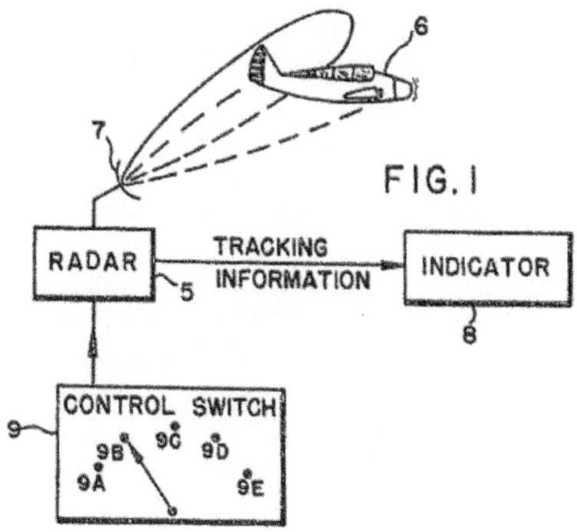

FIG. 1

FIG. 2

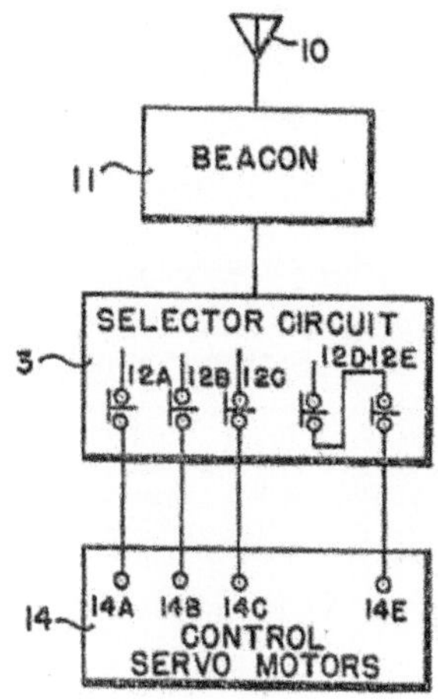

FIG. 3

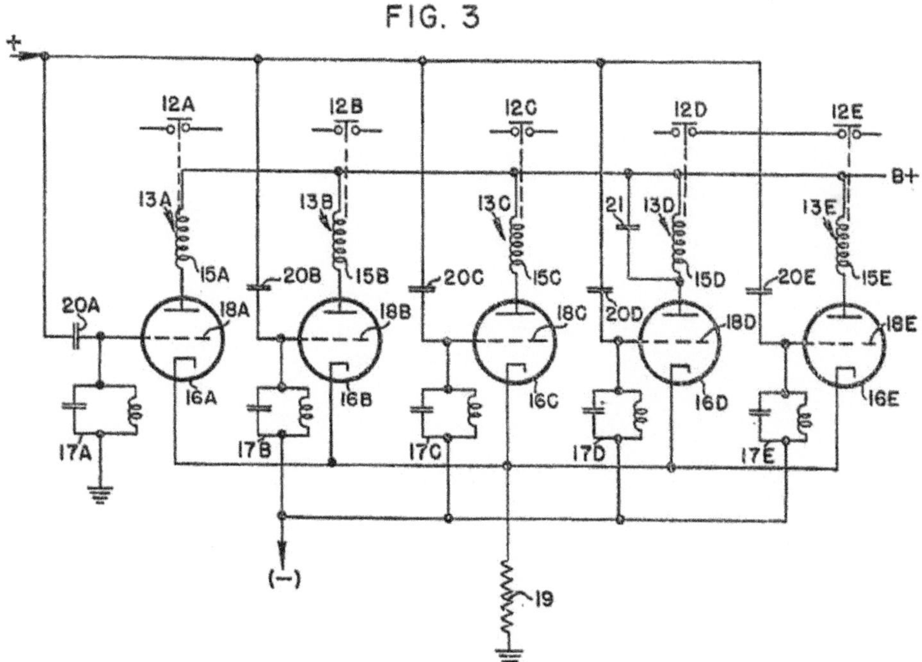

INVENTORS
IVAN A. GETTING
LEE L. DAVENPORT

BY William D. Hall

ATTORNEY

United States Patent [19] [11] **3,789,409**
Easton [45] **Jan. 29, 1974**

[54] **NAVIGATION SYSTEM USING SATELLITES AND PASSIVE RANGING TECHNIQUES**

[76] Inventor: **Roger L. Easton,** 7704 Oxon Hill Rd., Oxon Hill, Md. 20021

[22] Filed: **Oct. 8, 1970**

[21] Appl. No.: **79,307**

[52] **U.S. Cl.**.... **343/112 R,** 343/100 ST, 343/112 D
[51] **Int. Cl.**........................ **G01s 5/14,** G01s 11/00
[58] **Field of Search**....... 343/112 D, 112 R, 100 ST

[56] **References Cited**

UNITED STATES PATENTS

3,643,259	2/1972	Entner	343/112 D X
3,384,891	5/1968	Anderson	343/100 ST UX
2,947,985	8/1960	Cooley	343/112 D UX
3,397,400	8/1968	Maass et al.	343/112 D UX
2,924,820	2/1960	Dishal et al.	343/112 D UX
3,339,202	8/1967	Earp	343/112 D X

Primary Examiner—Richard A. Farley
Assistant Examiner—Richard E. Berger
Attorney, Agent, or Firm—R. S. Sciascia; Arthur L. Branning; J. G. Murray

[57] **ABSTRACT**

A navigation system wherein the navigator's location is obtained by determining the navigator's distance (or range) from one or more satellites of known location. Each satellite transmits multifrequency signals that are derived from a stable oscillator which is phase synchronized with the navigator's equipment that produces similar multifrequency signals. Phase comparison between the signals received from the satellites and the locally produced signals indicates both the distance between the navigator and the satellites and the navigator's location. In determining his location, the presence of the navigator is not revealed since no interrogatory transmission by him is required.

6 Claims, 3 Drawing Figures

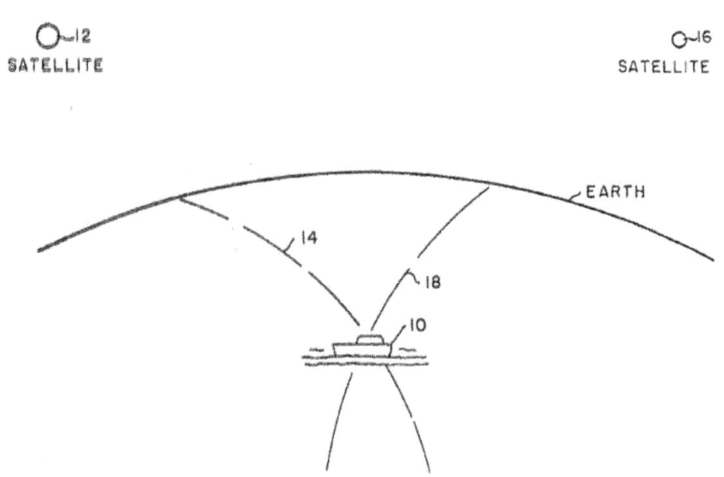

21 Employment Contracts and Non-Compete Restrictions

21.1 EMPLOYMENT CONTRACT PROVISIONS RELATING TO INTELLECTUAL PROPERTY

As a technology professional, your initial contact with intellectual property development and protection may occur while pursuing undergraduate or graduate studies, and most assuredly will be evident when entering the engineering or scientific communities at the end of your studies. In school, one may be working under a foundation, industry, or government grant, and after graduation will normally be working for an established organization, such as a corporation or other entity, engaged in research and development leading to new technology. In any of these situations, a common thread exists. You are being engaged by someone who is relying on your knowledge, skills, and training to develop new technologies for commercial gain. You will be compensated for creative thinking, developing novel ideas, and incorporating those intangible ideas into tangible products, processes, or services for the benefit of your employer, or your own enterprise.

As discussed in Chapters 19 and 24 devoted to Patents and Copyrights, the initial owner of patentable inventions and/or copyrightable works of authorship may be you, the inventor or creator. However, since an employer is compensating you for use of your innovative and technical skills, the employer normally demands assurances that:

a. Any new technology or works of authorship that you develop during your employment that relate to the business of your employer becomes the property of the employer;
b. Any confidential or trade secret information you develop or are made privy to during your employment will be maintained in confidence; and
c. You are restricted from working for a competitor, under reasonable terms and conditions, for a period of time following your employment.

Each of these circumstances is discussed below in more detail. Keep in mind, however, that as an engineer or scientist entering a new employment opportunity, you may be faced with considering and being asked to agree to provisions in an employment contract that you may want to review and possibly amend before signing. For example, before signing the agreement to produce this book, I suggested changes in the agreement regarding the relationship between this copyrightable work and a previous

Intellectual Property Law for Engineers, Scientists, and Entrepreneurs, Second Edition. Howard B. Rockman.

Published 2020 by John Wiley & Sons, Inc.

text I authored for purposes of a law school textbook. The point is that you should carefully review the papers you are signing, and ensure yourself that you have not given away rights to technology developments you may have made in the past.

On the flip side, you may be an employer or the managing director of a technology-driven enterprise that relies on the creative juices of your engineers and scientists to maintain your products and services on the leading edge of technology. Therefore, it is important that all of your employees and consultants have agreed from their first day of engagement to transfer ownership of any business-related invention or creative work of authorship to your company, and that your company's trade secrets will not be divulged to a competitor, and that your employees cannot be easily enticed away to work for a competitor. The following sections are directed to you in the role of either employee or employer.

21.2 OWNERSHIP OF INTELLECTUAL PROPERTY

21.2.1 Inventions

A typical invention rights clause in an employment contract states that in consideration for your present and future employment by the employer, and use of the employer's time, materials, facilities, equipment and funds, including your compensation, (1) any inventions or improvements conceived or developed by the employee during the term of their employment, and possibly for one year thereafter, (2) which pertain to the business of the employer, or to related fields, shall be the property of the employer. The primary consideration is that the employee is being paid to invent, and such inventions belong to the employer. Employment agreements normally include provisions that the employee will sign all formal papers required to assign all rights to intellectual property to the employer. The agreement may also provide that the employee will have opportunities to share in any royalties or other remuneration when the intellectual property developed by the employee is marketed and/or licensed by the employer.

Another typical provision in an employment agreement requires that the employee is under an obligation to disclose to the employer all tangible results of the research that the employee develops, which results relate to the business of the employer, that are conceived, reduced to practice, invented, or otherwise created, either solely or jointly with others, during the course of employment. This provision ensures that the employer has knowledge of and access to any development made by an employee, and the employer is able to decide which technology should be protected. This provides the entire engineering management team with the opportunity to evaluate all projects for their potential importance. The employee also normally agrees to execute all documents necessary to assist the employer, both during and after the term of employment, to obtain and enforce any issued patent covering the intellectual property rights developed by the employee.

The inventor is also normally obligated to maintain records of all research and development work performed during employment, and to document and date such records in an accessible format, such as in lab notebooks, that can be readily evaluated by the employer. The employee is also normally required to turn over such records to the employer when leaving the employment. This latter provision is equally applicable to confidential and trade secret documents and materials in the possession of a departing employee.

If the inventor owns patents of his or her own, or is a named inventor in patents from a previous employer, it is highly recommended that these facts be brought to the attention of the new employer, so that notations can be made in the employment contract indicating that the obligation to assign invention rights does not extend to previous inventions, pending patent applications, or patents.

Note that the above typical provisions pertain to your inventions which relate to the business of the employer. This is an important factor, and an employee should ensure himself or herself that such language does appear in the agreement. I have seen agreements that state that any invention developed by an inventor during the course of employment, whether or not the invention relates to the business of the employer, may become the property of the employer. Only those inventions that relate to the business of the employer should be covered by the agreement. This will enable you to tinker in your kitchen or garage at night and develop a totally unrelated invention that may be worthy of patent protection for your own benefit.

I have also experienced situations where although the inventor developed a new technology that was related to the business of the employer, the employer was not particularly interested in that technology when presented to the employer for evaluation, and the employer granted a waiver to the employee to patent and commercialize the particular invention on his or her own. Thus, keep in mind that even though you have signed an agreement which provides that all inventions you develop during the course of your employment that relate to the business of the employer become the property of the employer, the employer may, if you ask, grant a waiver of that provision, and allow you to develop your invention on your own.

To further protect the intellectual property of the employer, a provision may be included in the employment agreement prohibiting the employee from publishing information about any invention or new technology without the written approval of the employer. For example, if an employee attends a technical conference, and publishes material regarding work the employee is presently conducting relating to product development, such publication may end up being a bar to future patentability. Employees are also normally obligated to devote their best efforts to promote the business and professional interests of the company while in the employ of the company.

21.2.2 Copyrightable Works of Creative Authorship

In addition to compelling the employee to assign all rights to inventions and improvements to the employer, a typical employment agreement usually contains similar provisions relating to works of authorship and copyrightable subject matter, such as software, created by the employee during the term of employment. Again, ownership of any such works of authorship and copyrightable subject matter, in the typical employment agreement, are assigned over to the employer, so long as the subject matter pertains to the business of the employer, or related fields. This clause is particularly important regarding the development of software, and also relates to technical drawings, illustrations, and computer-aided design (CAD) drawings that are developed during the conception and reduction to practice of a computer-related invention.

Normally, all of the above provisions relating to inventions apply to works of authorship and copyrightable subject matter in a typical employment agreement. However, there is one additional clause relating to copyrightable material that should be inserted into the agreement. This clause will state that any work developed by the employee engineer or scientist shall be considered a "work made for hire" pursuant to the agreement, it being recognized between the parties that the work is intended to be owned by and used by the employer during the performance of the employee's duties on behalf of the employer.

Further provisions may indicate that notwithstanding the declaration that the copyrightable work will be a work for hire, in the event that there is any finding by any tribunal or court that the work is not a work for hire, the author agrees to assign to the employer all copyrights in the work worldwide. As you will discover in Chapter 24, Section 24.9, the term "work made for hire" has a particular meaning in the copyright law, and these clauses are usually included in employment contracts to cover the situation where a dispute may arise as to whether or not the work was a "work made for hire" within the meaning of the copyright statute. As a general rule, any work of authorship or other copyrightable subject material created by an employee who is being compensated for such work by his or her employer will automatically be a work for hire, and that work is owned by the employer.

21.3 CONFIDENTIALITY AGREEMENTS OR NONDISCLOSURE AGREEMENTS

During the course of your employment, you will develop and will be provided with information and know-how that has increased value to your employer by the mere fact that this information is not known by others, particularly competitors. This information and know-how are considered as "trade secrets" that are the property of your employer, and that your employment agreement normally includes provisions to protect. Such trade secrets are also normally referred to as "confidential information" or "proprietary information," and the three terms are used interchangeably. Sometimes there is a thin line between a trade secret or confidential information, and the normal skills and knowledge that are known to an engineer or scientist that are learned during employment. If an issue ever rises as to whether trade secrets or confidential information have been misappropriated, the lawyers will assist you in trying to draw this ephemeral line. Trade secret protection is presented in detail in Chapters 27 and 28.

Note also that provisions maintaining the confidentiality of trade secret and proprietary information normally extend beyond the term of employment. Therefore, once you are informed that information is confidential, it would be prudent to make notations of what general categories of information are considered confidential by your present employer, so that if and when upon entering a new employment position, you know not to disclose the details of these general areas of "confidential" technology to your new employer. Also, you will know not to use such confidential information yourself.

In addition to confidential information developed by you as an employee, you will be made familiar with additional trade secret information that has been developed by others during the course of their employment with your employer. The prudent employer will clearly identify such material as confidential, and will make such information available to its employees only on a need-to-know basis. Therefore, you will know what is confidential and what is not, according to the company's policies.

Typical nondisclosure agreements, or nondisclosure clauses of an employment agreement, provide that the employee agrees to keep confidential all trade secrets and proprietary information relating to the employer's business that are developed or received by the employee during the course of employment. In addition, the employee also agrees not to use, publish, or disclose confidential information to anyone outside the company without the written approval of the company. Such proprietary information could include, but is not limited to, technology under development, design practices and procedures, engineering practices and procedures, marketing and business plans, programs, data, formulas, customer and vendor lists, compilations of information, business information such as profit, cost, and other financial data, and any other information that the company deems and identifies as confidential. The employee normally will also agree not to take any confidential materials upon the termination of employment, and will return all such materials to the employer.

There are normally exclusions in the employment confidentiality agreement stating that no information may be considered confidential if (1) the information is in the public domain through no fault of the employee, (2) the information becomes public knowledge during the term of the agreement, (3) the information is not part of the employee's obligation of confidentiality, (4) the information was previously obtained from a third party under lawful circumstances allowing the disclosure and use of such information, or (5) the information was developed by someone else without reference to and totally independent of the employer. The agreement may also provide that confidential information may be disclosed if ordered by a court of law, such as in a patent infringement or breach of confidentiality lawsuit. Such disclosures can be made under a "Protective Order," which maintains the confidentiality of the information during the court proceedings, and after the proceedings end.

Particular care should be taken in working with vendors who are furnishing the employee with information about parts, services, or processes that can be purchased from the vendor. It is important to realize that any confidential information furnished to the vendor during your course of discussions should be covered by a signed confidentiality agreement, where the vendor agrees in writing to not disclose the confidential information to others, and to not use the confidential information for the vendor's own benefit. Also, if you are disclosing a prototype of a new product to a customer or a vendor, marking that particular prototype with the notation "Confidential" or similar language prevents a "public disclosure" bar from arising, as discussed previously in Chapter 5 of this text, as well as identifying the prototype as a "trade secret."

Well-prepared confidentiality agreements should provide that information to be protected will be marked as "Confidential," to distinguish such information from that which is not confidential. Also, typical agreements usually indicate that the confidentiality provision applies to both written and oral disclosures of information, and requires that all oral disclosures of confidential information be followed up in writing, to make such oral transmission tangibly available. It is also prudent to provide that the confidentiality provisions remain in force for a reasonable period beyond termination of employment. It is also recommended that confidentiality agreements clearly advise an employee not to disclose to the employer any proprietary information belonging to any prior employer, or any third party, including trade secrets or confidential information related to the business of the prior employer or third party. The confidentiality agreement should also generally compel the employee not to disclose any ideas, writings, or intellectual property to the new employer, which was owned by the employee and/or a former employer, and were developed while the employee was previously employed. The employment agreement may provide that any invention conceived prior to employment with the new employer is the property of the new employer, even where a patent application has previously been filed, but the invention was reduced to practice during the new employment. Careful consideration has to be given to these situations to avoid possible conflict and avoidable litigation.

21.4 OUTSIDE INFORMATION RECEIVED BY THE EMPLOYEE OR EMPLOYER

In the normal course of conducting one's business, unsolicited ideas from outsiders may be received by the business for consideration. My recommendation is for such business enterprises to initiate a policy that no unsolicited ideas will be considered or reviewed unless the submitter signs a written agreement that the submitter will never bring an action against the company for misappropriating the submitted idea, and will only enforce any rights the submitter may have under the appropriate patent or copyright laws. The submitter will also agree that they are not submitting the information in confidence, but reserve their rights only under the patent and copyright laws.

The reason behind this recommendation is that a majority of unsolicited ideas received by a company are reviewed, rejected, and returned to the submitter with an indication that the company is not interested in that particular idea at that time. Assume, however, that subsequently an employee of the company independently comes up with the same idea, totally on his or her own, having forgotten about or never being made aware of the earlier submittal. The company at that later time becomes interested in the idea and proceeds to produce a product embodying that idea. In my hypothetical scenario, the previous submitter of the unsolicited idea then files a lawsuit accusing the company of stealing the submitter's trade secrets. At this later point in time, without adequate records, it would be difficult for the company to prove that its employees did not use the ideas that were submitted years previously.

Therefore, to insulate a company from a possible legal action by the submitter, the unsolicited idea is initially taken by the company only on a non-confidential basis, which eliminates a theft of trade secret lawsuit from being filed several years later. However, the submitter is also allowed to protect the idea under the patent or copyright laws, and pursue an action against the company if such laws are violated in the future. It also has been my experience that if the developer of an unsolicited idea has patent or copyright protection, that makes the idea more sellable to the company, since not only is the idea being offered, but the intellectual property protection on the idea also forms part of the proposal.

When an unsolicited idea is properly submitted, before review of the idea is embarked upon by the recipient company, a due diligence should be conducted inside the company to determine whether similar development work is already in progress within your own R&D or other departments. If your R&D department is working on the same or a similar idea, it may be desirable to return the unsolicited submittal without a technical review to avoid even the appearance of adoption of the unsolicited idea. It is also prudent to keep documented records showing that the company was working on the idea prior to receiving the unsolicited submission.

Also, while working with vendors, ensure that no confidential material is given to them without protecting the secrecy of the information. It is prudent to have a broad confidentiality agreement in place with all of your regular vendors to prevent them from divulging any confidential information within the vendor's organization, or to other customers of the vendor. It is also prudent to add to the confidentiality contracts with vendors, that any work of authorship that they develop during the course of your mutual dealings is a "work made for hire," and therefore any copyrights belong to your company.

In addition to confidentiality agreements that obligate one party to not disclose confidential information to another, there are many forms of mutual disclosure agreements and provisions that allow two companies or entities to exchange confidential technology or other information, without being in a position later of defending oneself against an accusation of theft of trade secrets. Such mutual confidentiality agreements normally contain the same provisions as above, but are equally applicable to both parties.

As previously noted, the provisions signed by an employee regarding maintaining the confidentiality of trade secrets and confidential material that comes into the employee's purview during employment may extend beyond the term of employment. Therefore, when the engineer or scientist enters into a new employment relationship, it is important to disclose to the new employer that you have signed confidentiality agreements with your previous employer, and define in broad and general terms the field of technology that you were engaged in at your prior position. This is important in allowing the new employer to place you in a position in the company where you will not be tempted to disclose or use trade secret information learned from a prior employer. Of course, you are free to use the skills, knowledge, and training you learned at your prior position.

21.5 NON-COMPETE PROVISIONS

A brief comment is in order regarding typical non-compete clauses in employment contracts. My first suggestion is that before signing any non-compete clause, any engineer or scientist should first obtain advice, possibly from a qualified employment law specialist, to determine what the state laws are regarding the scope and enforceability of non-compete clauses in the jurisdiction where the employment agreement is effective. Non-compete provisions usually require the employee to agree that for a certain period of time following the termination of his or her employment, the employee will not seek or enter into employment with a competitor of the business of the employer. However, since the legal system looks harshly at provisions that would deprive a skilled professional of the ability to earn a living, non-compete restrictive clauses must be reasonable in time, scope, and geographical extent before they are deemed enforceable. For example, certain states limit the effectiveness of non-compete clauses to a term of just one year. Thus, if a non-compete clause in your employment contract states that you cannot be employed by a competitor for three years following termination, if the applicable state law indicates that three years is unreasonable, either that provision will be held invalid altogether, or a court may interpret that provision as just being applicable for one year, and no more.

Also, non-compete provisions may prevent you from being employed by a competitor in the same line of business as your current employer, and within a certain geographical area. Again, the individual state laws must be reviewed to determine the applicability of these provisions and the extent to which they are enforceable.

Additionally, note that if a new employee is placed in a position where it is inevitable that he or she will disclose or use trade secrets of a former employer, a court may enjoin that employee from working in that new position.

Several comments have recently appeared suggesting that non-compete provisions in employment agreements should be outlawed altogether. Today, there is more movement among employees from one employment to another, particularly in the high-tech industry, where talent is in short supply, and employers seem to be constantly seeking to hire highly trained and experienced employees. The writers of these comments advance the idea that there should be no restrictions on an employee's ability to achieve upward mobility, even if that means being lured away to work for a direct competitor of one's present employer. These writers, of course, rely on the assumption that such new hires would carefully segregate the trade secrets of their prior employer from the general knowledge, skills, and training they obtained at their prior employment, and would be very careful not to disclose or use any such trade secrets in their new employment.

However, when one leaves an employment position, it is an easy task to clean out one's desk and hard drive. However, it is not as easy to clean out one's mind of the knowledge they have of their prior employer's business. In my judgment, the present non-compete agreements will be around for a while, if and until courts or legislatures adopt the position that freedom of movement of employees outweighs the desire of employers to prevent their skilled employees from leaving their employ and working for a direct competitor.

21.6 ENFORCEABILITY OF A NON-COMPETE AGREEMENT

Generally speaking, the legitimacy of a non-compete or restrictive covenant in various jurisdictions depends upon (1) whether the terms of the agreement are reasonable and necessary as to time, territory, and activities, and (2) are the restrictions necessary to protect a legitimate business interest of the employer. What is "reasonable" necessarily turns on the facts and circumstances of each case. Most courts in the United States will generally enforce one- and two-year restrictive employment agreements. Some courts, in my experience, have held that three years was reasonable under the circumstances, but I suggest that restrictive agreements beyond three years have a poor chance of being upheld. Courts are generally against enforcing restrictive employment agreements that are overly broad in geographic scope. However, as with time restrictions, each situation is decided on its own facts. Courts generally look to see if the geographic area of exclusion is co-extensive with the territory in which the employer is conducting its business. For example, where the employer was doing business nationwide, a restrictive covenant having no geographical limitation was upheld.

Restrictions against a former employee that are merely an attempt by the employer to prevent competition are per se unenforceable. For example, a restriction that prohibited the employee from contacting any potential customers of the employer was stricken as being unenforceable. Likewise unenforceable was a restrictive covenant that forbade the employee from associating with any company that engaged in the same type of activity as the employer. However, a court is likely to uphold a restrictive employment agreement that is reasonable as to time and territory, where the employer provided valuable training to its employees and/or substantial time and resources in cultivating its clients. Also, a restrictive covenant was found to be valid where the purpose of the restriction was to protect the employer from losing customers to a former employee who, by virtue of his employment for the employer, gained special knowledge and familiarity with the customer's product lines and requirements.

The Illinois courts, for example, have recognized two situations in which an employer has a legitimate business interest to justify enforcement of a covenant not to compete: (1) where the customer relationships are near permanent and but for the employee's association with the employer, the employee would not have had contact with the customers; and (2) where the former employee acquired trade secrets or other confidential or proprietary information through his employment and subsequently tried to use such information for his or her own benefit, or divulged such information to third parties.

Several factors are considered in determining whether the relationship between an employer and its customer is "near permanent" for purposes of analyzing the reasonableness of a restrictive employment agreement. These factors include:

a. The time, cost, and difficulty in developing and maintaining the customer relationship;
b. The intention of the employer and customer to remain affiliated for a long period of time; and
c. The continuity and duration of the relationship.

The nature of the business itself is also considered. Professional relationships such as doctors, veterinarians, and the like are mostly treated as near-permanent relationships. Courts will also look at the source of the customer relationship. For example, was the customer a company or institutional customer, or was the customer developed by the employee? It is clear from a review of the court decisions on the enforceability of restrictive employment contracts that in the case of businesses which do not create customer loyalty with a unique product or specialized personal service, or where businesses are one of several suppliers to a customer for a given product or service, the customer-business relationship is unlikely to meet the "near-permanency" test.

Courts are more likely to find information a "trade secret" or "confidential" if the information has been developed by the employer over a given span of time, at considerable expense, maintained under tight security, and is not generally known to the public. In situations involving former employees charged with usurping the trade secrets of their former employer, information that is readily available to all employees or others in the trade, or can be found online, in phone books or trade directories, or where customers can be identified by others outside of the company, will not be found to be confidential.

For a restrictive covenant to be reasonable, it must not be greater than necessary to protect the employer, must not be oppressive to the employee, and must not be injurious to the general public. For example, generally speaking, a contractual obligation in an employment agreement to maintain the secrecy of proprietary information will not be considered to be void or unenforceable solely for lack of geographical limitation.

Where the services to be performed under an employment contract are unique and special, such as those of an entertainer, athlete, or the like, you usually find terms that state that the personal services are irreplaceable, and such contracts may be enforced to compel the employee to perform.

If a non-compete clause does not set forth territorial and time limit restrictions, a court, when asked to enforce an agreement, may insert such provisions. Also, it is generally deemed unreasonable to expect the parties to intend that a non-compete restriction goes on forever, or that the non-compete provision would cover geographical territories in which the employer does not do business. Certain courts have indicated that the absence of limitations as to time and geographic scope in a non-compete agreement will result in invalidation of the provision. In other cases, covenants containing no geographic limitation have been upheld as reasonable when the purpose of the restriction was to protect the employer from losing customers to a former employee who, by virtue of his employment, gained special knowledge and familiarity with the customer's requirements. In this case, the employee was only restrained from contacting former customers, and a geographic limitation would not serve any purpose.

Courts are hesitant to enforce non-competition agreements that prohibit employees from soliciting customers they never solicited or had no contact with while employed. The courts usually uphold only those non-competition agreements that protect the employer's legitimate business interests, and not those agreements whose effect is to prevent competition per se. Thus, an activity restraint, such as a covenant not to solicit other customers which lacks both a geographic limitation and any qualifying language concerning the particular customers to which it applies, generally will be struck down as unreasonable.

As an example of the wide range of state laws regarding restrictive covenants, note that with certain limited exceptions, California presently renders non-competition clauses void, while Maryland law permits them so long as they are reasonable in scope and duration. The California law invalidates employment contracts that prohibit an employee from working for a competitor when the employment has terminated, unless necessary to protect the employer's trade secrets.

Under Illinois law, for example, it is generally recognized that upon the termination of employment, an employee may not take with him or her confidential, particularized plans or processes developed by his or her employer and disclosed to him or her during the employer/employee relationship. This applies to trade secrets that are unknown to others in the industry and that give the employer an advantage over its competitors. On the other hand, an employee is free to take with him or her general skills and knowledge acquired during employment with the former employer. The courts have emphasized that the right of an individual to follow and pursue the particular occupation for which he or she is best trained is a most fundamental right of our extremely mobile and competition-based free economy. One who has worked in a particular field cannot be compelled to erase from his or her mind all of the general skills, knowledge, and expertise acquired through experience while employed. These skills are valuable to the employee in the marketplace for his or her services. Restraints cannot be lightly placed upon the right of the employee to compete in the area of his or her greatest worth. In the case of *Colson Co. v. Wittell,* 210 Ill. App. 1030, 1039, 569 N.E.2d 1082, 1087; appl denied, 141 Ill. 2d. 537, 580 N.E.2d 110 (1991), the court said:

> . . . any other rule would force a departing employee to perform a prefrontal lobotomy on himself or herself. It would disserve the free market goal of maximizing available resources to foster competition . . . it would not strike a proper balance between the purposes of trade secret law and the strong policy in favor of fair and vigorous business competition.

21.7 INEVITABLE DISCLOSURE

If you embark upon a new employment that will "inevitably" lead you to rely on a former employer's trade secrets, your former employer may take legal action in an effort to stop you from taking that position. In such cases, the former employer has the burden of proving that in your new employment, you could not perform your new duties or meet your new responsibilities without using the former employer's trade secrets.

21.8 FORM AGREEMENTS

At the end of this chapter are sample employee intellectual property agreements and sample mutual and individual confidentiality agreements. However, the inclusion of these sample agreements in this text does not indicate that these forms of agreement should be used without the consultation and advice of a qualified employment and/or intellectual property attorney. There are no two employment situations that are alike, and each agreement should be tailored to meet the specific needs of both the employer and the employee for their mutual benefit. Thus, these are merely suggestions, and not the end point of any agreement that may be applicable to your situation.

Certain employers may have a written intellectual property, confidentiality, and non-compete policy statement that the employee must read, and which terms are incorporated by reference into the terms of the employment agreement.

21.9 CONSULTANTS

When dealing with consultants, it is extremely important that the consultant contract include a provision compelling the consultant to assign all inventions and other intellectual property developed in the course of performance under the consultant's contract, and/or performance under a sponsored research project of the employer to the employer, in consideration for the consultant's compensation. All such agreements should be in writing, and cover contributions to patentable inventions, trade secret generation, and copyrightable subject matter created by the consultant relating to work performed pursuant to the consulting agreement.

If a proper consulting agreement is not in place, there is no way to obtain an assignment of patent rights to you from the consultant in a situation where the consultant is one of, or the sole, contributor to the intellectual property development. As a result, the consultant may be the legitimate owner, or part owner of rights to the technology you employed the consultant to assist you with. Take my word for it—this has caused problems for some of my clients several times over the course of my practice, but only where these clients have consulted with me after they made an oral or improper written agreement with the consultant.

SAMPLE EMPLOYEE INTELLECTUAL PROPERTY AGREEMENT

I, the below named EMPLOYEE, in consideration of my employment by [Employer], an ________ corporation, or if such employment has already commenced, in consideration of my continued employment with [Employer], which I acknowledge would be terminated but for my execution of this Agreement and my willingness to be bound by the terms of this Agreement, and in further consideration of subsequent salaries and wages which are to be paid to me, agree as follows:

1. All inventions, improvements, works of authorship, and copyrightable subject matter authored, conceived or developed by me during the term of my employment by [Employer], and for one year thereafter, which pertain to the business of [Employer], or to related fields, shall be disclosed promptly by me to [Employer], are hereby presently assigned by me to [Employer]. I agree to execute, upon request, such formal papers as may be required to assign and transfer my entire right, title and interest in and to such inventions, improvements and copyrights, including applications for and/or letters patent of the United States and all other countries, and copyrights to [Employer], and at [Employer's] expense, to do all things necessary to perfect [Employer's] ownership therein, except those inventions, improvements, works of authorship, and copyrightable subject matter which [Employer] has agreed in writing are to be owned by me.

2. To keep secret and confidential any confidential or proprietary information or any other information relating to [Employer's] business, not generally known to the trade or to the public, received by me from [Employer], or developed by me on [Employer's] behalf, and I agree that no such information shall be published or disclosed to others without the written authority of [Employer]. Such information shall include, but not be limited to, design practices and procedures, engineering practices and procedures, marketing plans and programs, trade secrets, data, formulas, compilations of information, business and financial information, customer lists and any other information of [Employer], or its customers, or vendors, whether or not authored, invented, developed or discovered by me during the course of my employment with [Employer]. I further agree not to disclose to [Employer] any information which is confidential or proprietary to others. These obligations shall apply to any information which is considered confidential or to otherwise be trade secrets of either [Employer] or its customers or vendors.

3. To devote my best efforts to the interests of [Employer].

4. Upon termination of my employment by [Employer], for any reason, I will promptly deliver to [Employer] all files, sketches, drawings, blueprints, manuals, letters, notebooks, reports and all other materials which relate to [Employer] or its customer's or vendor's businesses that are in my possession or control.

5. I represent and warrant that there are no agreements between myself and others that would in any way impede my full performance under this Agreement and I agree not to enter into any agreement which would conflict with this Agreement. I further represent and warrant that I am not now actively pursuing, prosecuting, developing or licensing any intellectual property owned by me or a business owned or controlled by me. [Note: If this is not true, discuss with your employer.]

6. If I am transferred to, or perform work for any successor, division, subsidiary or affiliated concern of [Employer], this Agreement shall remain in force and effect and shall define my relationship to [Employer] and its successor, division, subsidiary or affiliated concern.

7. [Employer's] remedy in the form or monetary damages for any breach by me of any provision of this Agreement is likely to be inadequate to adequately compensate [Employer] for such breach, and, in addition to any such remedy for breach, [Employer] shall be entitled to institute and maintain any appropriate proceeding or proceedings, including suit for specific performance and/or injunction against me and any company which employs me in violation of the terms of this Agreement.

8. This Agreement shall be binding upon my heirs, executors, administrators, legal representatives, nominees and assigns and shall inure to the benefit of the successors of [Employer]. Should any part of this Agreement be held to be void or voidable or unenforceable in whole or in part by any court, the remainder of this Agreement shall remain in full force and effect. This Agreement shall be deemed to be made in the State of _____, and all of its provisions shall be governed by the laws of the State of _____ and enforceable in the courts of _____.

EMPLOYER	EMPLOYEE
Date:	Date:
Name: ______________________	Name: ______________________
Title: ______________________	

SAMPLE MUTUAL CONFIDENTIALITY AND NONDISCLOSURE AGREEMENT

This Agreement is made this _____ day of _____ by and between ABC Co. and XYZ Co.

WHEREAS, the undersigned parties recognize that each others business involves specialized and proprietary knowledge, information, methods, processes, techniques and skills peculiar to their security and growth;

WHEREAS, the parties acknowledge that any disclosure of such knowledge, information, methods, processes, techniques and skills or other confidential or proprietary information would substantially injure the parties' businesses, impair the parties' investments and goodwill and jeopardize the parties' relationship with the parties' clients and customers,

WHEREAS, the parties presently desire to mutually discuss and pursue certain potential business opportunities;

WHEREAS, in the course of such mutual discussions and pursuit of such business opportunities, the parties anticipate disclosing to each other certain information of a novel, proprietary or confidential nature and desire that such information be subject to all the terms and conditions set forth below.

NOW THEREFORE, in consideration of the obligations herein contained and for other good and valuable consideration, the receipt and sufficiency of which is acknowledged, the parties agree as follows:

1. Definition. Confidential, proprietary or novel information ("Information") shall mean and include, but not be limited to, any written or electronic Information in the form of financial and statistical data, sales data, client information, trade secrets, inventions, copyrights, methods, techniques, prototypes, drawings, technical data, know-how and business plans pertaining to the above parties' businesses that is identified in writing as confidential at the time of disclosure and marked "Confidential" or "Proprietary." Information which is orally or visually disclosed to the recipient shall not be deemed confidential unless at the time of oral disclosure, the disclosing party indicates the Information is confidential or proprietary and such party then reduces the Information to a writing or electronic version within five days of the initial disclosure. The Information shall not include material which the recipient party can by reasonable proof:
   - (a) show that such Information, in its disclosed combinations, is in the public domain through no fault of recipient;
   - (b) show that such Information becomes public knowledge during the term of this Agreement without breach of this Agreement;
   - (c) show that such Information is contained in a written record in the recipient's files without an obligation of confidentiality prior to the date of its receipt from the proprietor.
   - (d) show that the recipient had at any time lawfully obtained said Information from a third party under circumstances permitting its disclosure and use.
   - (e) show that such Information was developed by the receiving party without reference to, and totally independent from, the information.
2. Dissemination of Information. Neither party shall use the Information of the other party in any manner which may be detrimental to that other party. The

parties agree that they will not publish, disclose, communicate or reveal any Information to any person, corporation or third party or to any of their own employees who do not need to know the information in the performance of their duties. Proprietary information or data marked with a restrictive notice shall be delivered only to the following individuals authorized to receive such data.

ABC Co. 123 Fourth Street Any City, USA	XYZ Co. 567 8th Blvd. Anyplace, Worldwide

3. Protection of Information. The standard of care for protecting Information, imposed on the party receiving the Information, will be that degree of care the receiving party uses to prevent disclosure, publication, or dissemination of its own proprietary or confidential information, but in no event less than reasonable care.

4. Ownership of Information, The parties agree that any Information revealed to the other by them remains the exclusive property of the disclosing proprietor. The parties agree that, upon the termination of their relationship and upon written request, they will either surrender to each other any Information transmitted to them by the other party or certify that such Information has been destroyed.

5. Term. This Agreement shall remain in effect for one year from the date set forth above, except for the obligations of the receiving party with respect to Information received prior to the termination of this Agreement, which shall survive such termination for (3) years after the date of disclosure.

6. Termination. Either party hereto, upon written notice to the other, may terminate this Agreement. Such termination shall be effective thirty (30) days after receipt of such notice to the address specified in Paragraph 2 above. All obligations arising under this Agreement shall survive any termination of this Agreement for three (3) years after the date of disclosure.

7. Severability of Provisions. Should any part of this Agreement be declared invalid by a court of law, such decision shall not affect the validity of any remaining portion which shall remain in full force and effect as if the invalid portion was never a part of this Agreement when it was executed. As it is the parties' intent that this Agreement be enforced to the fullest extent permitted by law, such invalidated section shall be deemed amended so as to avoid the reasons for its invalidity.

   Should the severance or amendment of any such part of this Agreement materially affect any other rights and obligations of the parties, the parties will negotiate in good faith to amend this Agreement in a manner satisfactory to the parties.

8. Non-Assignability. Neither party hereto shall, directly or indirectly, assign or purport to assign this Agreement or any of its rights and obligations in whole or part to any third party without the prior written consent of the other party.

9. Amendment. This Agreement shall not be amended, modified or altered, except as set out in Paragraph 7 above, except in writing, duly accepted and executed by both parties.

10. Governing Law. This Agreement shall be governed by, and construed in accordance with the laws of the State of _____, without regard to its conflict of law provisions.

11. Entire Agreement. This Agreement constitutes the entire, agreement and understanding of the parties hereto, and no representations or promises have been made that are not fully set forth herein.

IN WITNESS WHEREOF the parties hereto have caused this Agreement to be executed by a duly authorized officer.

By:	By:
Title:	Title:
Date:	Date:

SAMPLE CONFIDENTIAL DISCLOSURE AND NON-USE AGREEMENT (LONG FORM)

____________ (hereinafter "DISCLOSER") is the owner of certain confidential information, for a ____________ as described on the product description, a copy of which is attached hereto (hereinafter "INFORMATION").

____________ (hereinafter "RECIPIENT") currently makes and offers numerous ____________ products and has been requested to review the INFORMATION for possible use in developing RECIPIENT'S own products for ____________. For their mutual benefit, RECIPIENT accepts and DISCLOSER is willing to furnish such INFORMATION to RECIPIENT upon the following terms and conditions:

The parties agree that:

1. The precise INFORMATION disclosed to RECIPIENT under this Agreement and marked as CONFIDENTIAL will be received and held in confidence by RECIPIENT, and RECIPIENT will take such steps as may be reasonably necessary to prevent disclosure of said information to others, and will not disclose the same to others without the prior consent of DISCLOSER, said standard not requiring greater security steps than RECIPIENT uses for its own information.
2. RECIPIENT will not use or allow others to use said INFORMATION, except for _____ without the written consent of DISCLOSER.
3. The commitments set forth in the preceding paragraphs shall not extend to any portion of the disclosed INFORMATION which:
   (a) is in the public domain at the time of receipt by RECIPIENT;
   (b) was known to RECIPIENT prior to the receipt of same from DISCLOSER;
   (c) is now or hereafter through no fault on the part of RECIPIENT becomes generally available to the public:
   (d) is an application of commonly known principles of _____ manufacturing;
   (e) which is published or furnished to RECIPIENT by any third party not under a duty of nondisclosure;
   (f) is discovered by independent development;
   (g) is discovered starting with a known product and working backward to find the method by which it was developed (reverse engineering);
   (h) observation of the item in public use or on public display; or
   (i) obtaining the INFORMATION from published literature.
4. This Agreement shall remain in effect for one year from the date hereof.
5. This Agreement shall be governed by the laws of the State of _____ and any enforcement action must be brought in Federal court for the _____, or a state court in _____.

(RECIPIENT)	(DISCLOSER)
____________________	____________________
By: ____________________	By: ____________________
Title: ____________________	Title: ____________________

SAMPLE CONFIDENTIAL DISCLOSURE AND NON-USE AGREEMENT (SHORT FORM)

_____ (hereinafter Discloser) owns confidential information, trade secrets and inventions for a _____ (hereinafter "Confidential Information");

_____ (hereinafter Recipient) has expressed a desire to learn certain aspects of said Confidential information for evaluation. For their mutual benefit, Recipient accepts and Discloser is willing to furnish such Confidential Information to Recipient upon the terms and conditions set forth below. The parties recognize that the Confidential Information has or may have commercial value;

Recipient agrees that: (1) all Confidential Information disclosed to Recipient under this Agreement will be received and held in confidence by Recipient, and Recipient will take such steps as may be reasonably necessary to prevent disclosure of said information to others and will not disclose the same to others without the prior written consent of Discloser; and (2) Recipient will not use said information, except for said evaluation without the written consent of Discloser.

The commitments set forth in the preceding paragraphs shall not extend to any portion of the disclosed Confidential Information which: (1) was known to the Recipient prior to the receipt thereof from Discloser; or (2) is now or hereafter through no act on the part of the Recipient becomes generally available to the public; or (3) which is furnished to Recipients by any third party having a bona fide right to do so.

This Agreement shall be governed by the laws of the State of _____.

ACCEPTED:

______________________	______________________
By: ______________________	By: ______________________
Title: ______________________	Title: ______________________
Date: ______________________	Date: ______________________

◆ INVENTORS AND INVENTIONS ◆

Grace Hopper

COBOL COMPUTER LANGUAGE

"If it's a good idea, go ahead and do it. It is much easier to apologize than it is to get permission." Grace Hopper

Grace Hopper was a mathematician, computer scientist, U.S. Navy Rear Admiral, and a pioneer in the field of computer programming. She is best known as one of the developers of a compiler that was a predecessor to the COBOL computer language. She also made significant contributions in creating industry-wide standards for evaluating computer systems and components compatibility with each other.

Grace Brewster Murray was born on December 9, 1906, in New York City. She was a very inquisitive child, who often disassembled alarm clocks in a quest to discover how they functioned. She disassembled seven alarm clocks before her parents discovered the results of her curiosity. She was then given only one clock. She attended Vassar College, earning bachelor's degrees in mathematics and physics in 1928. Hopper went on to earn a master's degree from Yale University in 1930. In 1934, she became one of the first women to receive a PhD in mathematics from Yale. Grace Brewster Murray married Vincent Foster Hopper in 1930. They divorced in 1945, but she kept his surname.

Hopper began her career teaching mathematics at Vassar, and decided to join the military shortly after Japan's attack on Pearl Harbor in 1941. She was initially denied enlistment in the Navy for being too old (at 34), too short, and too thin. A further explanation was that her job as a mathematics professor at Vassar was too important to the war effort for Hopper to leave the school. Finally, in 1943, Hopper was granted a leave of absence from Vassar, and was able to join the U.S. Navy Reserves.

Her initial duty as a Navy lieutenant was an assignment with the Bureau of Ships Computation Project at Harvard University. Hopper's first significant project involved the Mark 1 Automatic Sequence Controlled Calculator and calculating Naval gunnery tables to improve the accuracy of guns through analysis of wind speed, weight, and air density. The Mark 1 performed work in one day that beforehand had taken a month. The Mark 1 ran continuously, and Hopper and her colleagues were frequently required to sleep alongside the computer to offer immediate service if something went awry.

At the end of Word War II, Hopper was offered a full professorship at Vassar. She turned it down to continue working for the Navy. In 1949, Hopper decided to move on, and accepted a job as a Senior Mathematician at the Eckert-Mauchly Computer Corporation. Her first order of business was to help create the UNIVAC I (Universal Automated Computer). While working on the UNIVAC I, she asked programmers to collect and share their common program segments. These early compilations of code

Intellectual Property Law for Engineers, Scientists, and Entrepreneurs, Second Edition. Howard B. Rockman.

Published 2020 by John Wiley & Sons, Inc.

were required to be copied by hand, but the compilation effort lessened boredom, reduced mistakes, and avoided duplication of effort. She developed her first compiler, the A-O while at Eckert-Mauchly. The A-O compilers she developed translated symbolic mathematical code into machine code, permitting specification of call numbers assigned to the program routines stored on the magnetic media. The computer would then locate the call numbers on the media, and then perform the mathematical calculations. NASA later used this technology to communicate with astronauts.

As Hopper's work continued, she envisioned a wider use of computers in the business world. She aimed to create a system in which lay individuals could program computers. Until this point, computers required commands to be written in machine code. Hopper set out to create a way to convert English words into computer code. Her idea was initially rejected, and she was told that her concept was not workable because computers did not understand English.

In 1952, Hopper developed a link-loader, called a compiler at the time. Her compiler translated mathematical expressions into machine code, which was fine for one versed in mathematics, but not so much for a data processor, who did not understand symbol manipulation. If one were a symbol manipulator at the time, they went on to become mathematicians, not data processors. But it is much easier for someone to write a statement in English than to use symbols. Hopper decided data processors should write their programs in English, and the computer would do the translation into machine-understandable code. This eventually resulted in COBOL (Common Business-Oriented Language).

In 1954, Grace Hopper was appointed as the first director of automatic programming. The division she led developed FLOW-MATIC AND MATH-MATIC, some of the first compiler-based programming languages. FLOW-MATIC applications were readily understood in English, and were developed for use in business to calculate payroll and produce electronic billing. It also allowed mainstream use of computer programs in the business world. She was able to make coding languages practical and readily available by devising technology that converted source mathematical code into English.

In 1959, computer scientists gathered for CODASYL, the Conference on Data Systems Languages. Grace Hopper attended as a technical consultant. During a committee meeting, COBOL was defined. The novel language expanded as FLOW-MATIC, and included input from IBM's COMTRAN. Hopper was passionate about persuading business executives of the need for COBOL and the utility of English language compilers. Hopper's fervor brought her back to the Navy, where she was able to convince the entire Navy it needed to adopt COBOL. Hopper also created technical manuals and materials for understanding the use of COBOL. COBOL became the leading computer language for use in business throughout the 20th century.

In the late 1960s, it became apparent that various businesses were using different versions of COBOL. This directly contradicted Hopper's vision for COBOL, which was to create a common network. To combat these issues, Hopper developed a set of "industry wide standards." She created a certifier, which is a computer program that is able to confirm if a version of COBOL is compatible with all computers. For all of these accomplishments, Grace Hopper was the first person to receive the Computer Science Man-of-the-Year award.

Grace Hopper received many awards and accolades during her life. Despite all of her achievements, Grace Hopper said, "The most important thing I've accomplished, other than building the compiler, is training young people.'" She died on January 1, 1992, at the age of 85. In 2016, President Obama honored her posthumously with the Presidential Medal of Freedom.

◆ INVENTORS AND INVENTIONS ◆

THE HUBBLE SPACE TELESCOPE

Since 1990, the orbiting Hubble Space Telescope has been transmitting spectacular images of deep space back to Earth. The Hubble is considered one of the most technologically advanced instruments that the United States has put into orbit. It has helped scientists make important discoveries of our universe, the planets, the stars, the galaxies, and all of cosmology. The Hubble has also provided astronomers insight into the fate and history of our universe. While the Hubble telescope is named after Edwin P. Hubble, a notable astronomer who conducted extensive research into stars and galaxies, and was the first to prove that the universe is expanding, the actual Hubble telescope was invented by a committee of astronomers, scientists, researchers, and technicians. There is no one single inventor that can be credited with the development of the Hubble telescope. The Hubble was the work of many.

Intellectual Property Law for Engineers, Scientists, and Entrepreneurs, Second Edition. Howard B. Rockman.

Published 2020 by John Wiley & Sons, Inc.

The origins of the Hubble telescope date back to German rocket scientist Herman Oberth, who suggested in 1923 that a space-bound telescope would avoid frustrating problems, such as cloudy and misty observing nights, the twinkling of stars on clear nights, and absorption of the ultraviolet and infrared parts of the spectrum. It has been explained that the Earth's atmosphere blurs and distorts light coming from the stars. Even the most precise and advanced ground-based telescopes cannot avoid this phenomenon. However, a telescope in orbit can. In addition, the Earth's atmosphere blocks X-rays emitted from high-temperature phenomena in stars and other space objects that cannot be detected by instruments on the Earth's surface. A space telescope, it was determined, would also allow scientists to accurately measure these emissions as well.

The first serious concept of a space-based optical observatory began just after World War II. In 1946, Lyman Spitzer, a Yale University professor and researcher, posited that a space telescope would offer significant advantages over a ground-based observatory. While teaching at Princeton University, Spitzer was asked to head a National Academy of Science ad hoc committee on a large space telescope. At the first meeting in 1966, this committee performed comprehensive studies on possible uses for a large space-based telescope, and in 1969, the committee published "Scientific Uses of Large Space Telescope," wherein the National Academy of Science urged the construction of a space telescope that would allow scientists to study the stars, measure distances to galaxies, and investigate the physics behind the existence of our universe.

To move the concept forward, the telescope needed support from NASA, the National Aeronautics and Space Administration of the United States. NASA was considered to be the only agency with the capability of executing the National Academy's recommendations. Wernher Von Braun, who came to the United States from Germany after World War II, had previously examined the challenges of a space telescope with his team at the Marshall Space Flight Center in the 1960s.

In the mid-1960s, NASA and its outside contractors conducted studies into the feasibility of a large space telescope. Although there was initial dissent by some within NASA over whether the agency should work its way up to a large-scale observatory, or just take one giant leap to the final product, the decision to develop the space shuttle program improved the flexibility NASA had in designing the space telescope and maintaining the operability of the telescope while in space by sending astronauts on periodic service missions to the telescope. In 1971, George Low, NASA's acting administrator, gave approval to the Large Space Telescope Science Steering Group to move forward.

With NASA on board, the next step was to obtain funding for the project from the U.S. Congress. The telescope's initial estimated cost was between $400 and $500 million dollars, making it a tough sell to Congress. In point of fact, the original funding request was denied by the U.S. House Appropriations Committee in 1975, but this resulted in a massive lobbying effort by NASA, including leading astronomers led by Spitzer and John Bahcall, another Princeton astronomer. The European Space Research Organization, later to become the European Space Agency, was also invited to participate in the project by producing inexpensive solar panels and taking part in observations and research. NASA's ploy here was to take advantage of international cooperation to reduce the overall cost of the program to U.S. taxpayers, which made it more likely to receive Congressional support. The European organization accepted this invitation in 1975. A mirror reduction from 3 to 2.4 meters also helped bring the project estimated cost down to about $200 million dollars, which proposal was ultimately accepted by Congress in 1977.

In 1978, contracts were awarded to the Perkin-Elmer Corporation to construct the mirror and optical assembly, and to the Lockheed Missile and Space Company to construct the spacecraft and its support systems. The Europeans were then mainly responsible for the solar array that would power the Hubble while in orbit. One of the major technological advances used in the telescope's construction was the computer-based laser grinding system used by Perkin-Elmer to craft the observatory's primary mirror.

NASA originally planned to launch the Hubble in 1983, but the program experienced a rather large delay. The Perkin-Elmer mirror was completed in 1981, but the entire optical assembly was not put together until 1984. After that, final assembly of the space craft did not take place until 1985. Turning back to 1983, that year marked the founding of the Space Telescope Science Institute at Johns Hopkins University. A part of the Association of Universities for Research in Astronomy, the institute would be in charge of Hubble's scientific program.

The Hubble telescope was finally launched into an orbit 360 miles above the Earth aboard the Discovery shuttle on April 24, 1990. The telescope's original equipment package included the Wide Field Planetary Camera, Goddard High Resolution Spectrograph, Faint Object Camera, Faint Object Spectrograph, and High-Speed Photometer.

A few weeks after operations started aboard the Hubble, the scientists noticed that images being sent back were slightly blurred, and not the razor-sharp images that NASA advertised. This resulted in less than spectacular images, and some of the original mission could not be fulfilled. The Hubble telescope's primary mirror was expected to receive 70% of a star's light to a focal point, but instead only 15% or less was achieved. Analysis found that the shape of the concave mirror, moving radially outward, was shallow by the width of one fifth of a human hair.

How to fix the problem became a matter of intense study. First, slight changes were made to the shape of the primary mirror using actuators on the rear of the mirror that were operated upon command from the Earth scientists. This fix failed because the parabola of the mirror was wrong. The problem was the existence of a spherical aberration, ultimately found to have resulted from a small 3-mm-wide washer inserted into a null corrector used to monitor the mirror's configuration during its manufacture several years earlier. Apparently, the primary mirror had been perfectly ground, but to the wrong shape.

As a result of this spherical aberration, the faint object and high-resolution light-splitting spectrographs in the Hubble telescope were only about 50% efficient. Also, the European Space Agency's Faint Object Camera was adversely affected. The Wide Field Planetary Camera (WFPC) was the biggest victim of the flaw, and this was the system expected to produce dazzling images of the cosmos the public would appreciate seeing, not to mention the high value of these images to astronomers.

The key to fixing the Hubble's flawed mirror problem lay in the fortuitous fact that a backup duplicate Wide Field Planetary Camera 2 (WFPC2) had been constructed seven years earlier. The WFPC2 could be reground in a way that countered the spherical aberration in WFPC1, and perfect focus could be expected. With this solution in mind, it was still not clear what could be done about the other instrumentation aboard the Hubble. However, one senior engineer came up with the idea of placing the

High Speed Photometer in a box having several handles that would position small mirrors to refocus the light from the telescope mirror into the two spectrographs and the Faint Object Camera.

In late 1993, the shuttle Endeavor was launched to the Hubble telescope with WFPC2, the box with the new High Speed Photometer with small moveable mirrors, a new set of solar arrays, and other components. The first servicing mission went just as planned. Following intensive training on the use of new tools that had never been used before in space, two teams of astronauts completed repairs during a record five back-to-back spacewalks. The corrective optics space telescope axial replacement was installed, and the wide field/planetary camera was replaced with a second version of the same camera, which was designed to compensate for the mirror problem. The astronauts also performed basic maintenance, installed new solar arrays, and replaced several of Hubble's gyroscopes. On December 18, 1993, the first clear images of stars were received by NASA from the Hubble. The new results were revealed to the public at a January 13, 1994, press conference, and from that date, NASA's reputation has continued to soar. The public was treated to breathtaking photos of star, galaxies, nebulae, and other stunning outer space objects.

Additional shuttle service missions accomplished periodic repair and parts replacement aboard the Hubble. In February 1997, astronauts installed a near-infrared camera, a multi-object spectrometer, and the space telescope imaging spectrograph to detect infrared light from deep space objects, and to take detailed photos of celestial objects. In December 1999, all six of the telescope's aging gyroscopes were replaced. These were the gyroscopes that aimed the Hubble at its target. The astronauts also at that time replaced one of the telescope's three fine guidance centers and installed a new computer. In March 2002, members of the crew of the Columbia space shuttle installed a new advanced camera for surveys with a sharper vision, a wider field of view, and quicker data gathering capabilities than WFPC2. The astronauts on this mission also replaced Hubble's solar panels with a more efficient array and conducted repairs on other parts of the spacecraft. In 2009, astronauts upgraded Hubble's scientific capabilities again, installing a new main camera and an instrument designed to help answer profound questions about the large-scale structure and origins of the cosmos.

At present, the Hubble telescope's future is being analyzed as new space-bound telescopes are being developed.

22 The Engineer and Scientist as Expert Witness

22.1 THE ROLE OF AN EXPERT WITNESS

At a trial where complex scientific or technical matters are raised, and are in dispute, the court will allow one side, and usually both sides, to offer testimony from an expert in the relevant field of science or technology. These expert witnesses are permitted to testify as to their expert qualifications, to lay a foundation for their testimony by establishing the experiments, tests, analysis, or research they conducted that is pertinent to their testimony, and then state their opinion based upon the investigative work they conducted.

Opinion testimony from ordinary non-expert witnesses in a trial is inadmissible. Opinion testimony is predicated upon the conjecture, deduction, or supposition of the witness, based upon the analysis by the expert. Such conjecture is not a pure fact, and can be termed an "indeterminate conclusion," which the law courts look upon with disfavor in the case of ordinary fact testimony. However, in many, if not most legal situations, making a close as possible determination of these "indeterminate conclusions" will assist the judge or jury to understand the cause of the problem, and fault that led to the lawsuit.

For example, a factory worker is injured when a machine he or she was operating malfunctioned. The operator may not have the technical skills to know what went wrong, but an expert, or experts, in the design, function, and operation of the specific machine can analyze the machine after the accident, and can usually pinpoint what caused the problem and where the fault lies. If the expert witness convinces the judge or jury that there is a design, manufacturing, or failure to warn defect in the production or sale of the machine, the manufacturer of the machine may be liable for the operator's injury. However, if the expert testimony shows that the machine was in perfect operating condition, and that the accident most likely occurred due to the operator failing to heed warnings or instructions, the operator may be found to be the cause of his or her own injury.

In similar fashion, the design and manufacturing criteria of a structural member that failed would be the proper subject of expert testimony. Also, the "similarity" between a copyrighted work and an allegedly "pirated" work would be the subject of a literary or music expert. In patent cases, testimony about the comparisons between the prior art and the patent claims, and the comparisons between the patent claims and

Intellectual Property Law for Engineers, Scientists, and Entrepreneurs, Second Edition. Howard B. Rockman.

Published 2020 by John Wiley & Sons, Inc.

the allegedly infringing product or method, are presented by technical expert testimony. An expert witness also normally presents estimates of damages incurred by an injured party in a court of law.

Those of you who have witnessed films of the Galloping Gertie Bridge failure at Takoma Narrows can understand and appreciate that testimony regarding the design stages of a span to be constructed across a windy chasm, after the span has collapsed, can be developed through opinion testimony of bridge and harmonic experts who have studied the situation. Usually the studies take place after the accident has occurred, where the experts also look at the adequacy of the studies made during the design and construction phases.

22.1.1 Need for Experts

Lawyers are not qualified to testify in courts of law about facts, nor give opinions as to facts, since they do not have the requisite personal, first-hand knowledge of the facts. They are just guiding the testimony of the fact witnesses for the benefit of the court. There is also a presumption that the court and the jury are incapable of drawing intelligent conclusions based on complicated scientific or technical questions. For such purposes, a technical expert witness, such as an engineer or scientist, is needed. An "expert" is one who has specific skill, knowledge, or experience in a given technology or other field that an ordinary person would not have. The expert must be qualified in the given technology or field through education, on-the-job experience, training, or observation.

Before an expert witness testifies, that witness presents evidence to the court setting forth his or her qualifications to provide opinion testimony in a specified area. The expert qualifies himself or herself as a credible witness by testifying about his or her education, experience in related projects in which he or she has been involved, specialized training, whether he or she is registered, and other similar attributes. Upon cross-examination, normally the opposing counsel challenges the witness' qualifications, and the witness must be so well qualified, and prepared as to withstand any such challenge. Based on this type of presentation, the court and jury then determines whether the witness is qualified or not to present expert testimony on the qualifying subject.

Consider also that both sides will present experts to provide their opinions on a certain factual matter, each expert coming to a different conclusion, based sometimes on the same set of facts. Therefore, which expert is to be believed sometimes depends on the quality of the qualifications of the particular expert. Obviously, the more detailed the examination, testing, analysis, and research conducted by the expert witness prior to testifying, and the clarity of the presentation based on that examination, the more that witness's testimony is likely to be believed over the conflicting testimony of the opposition's expert witnesses.

Remember, just because you offer expert testimony, there is no guarantee that a judge or jury will ultimately believe that testimony, whether it is the best opinion or not.

22.1.2 The Standard for Admissibility of Expert Testimony—The *Daubert* Decision

Prior to the U.S. Supreme Court's decision in *Daubert et al. v. Merrell Dow Pharmaceuticals, Inc.*, 509 U.S. 579 (1993), the courts allowed expert testimony based on a scientific technique to be presented to a judge or jury if the technique was "generally accepted" as reliable in the relevant scientific community. Prior to the *Daubert* decision, there was concern among those in the legal profession that "junk science" was being admitted into evidence in certain cases. Rule 702 of the Federal Rules of Civil Procedure was interpreted by the Supreme Court in *Daubert* to place limits on the admissibility of scientific evidence by making the trial judge a "gatekeeper," responsible for ensuring that an expert's testimony both rests on a reliable foundation, and is relevant to the issues in the lawsuit. The "reliability" standard requires that an expert's testimony pertains to "scientific knowledge," where the adjective "scientific" implies a grounding in recognized scientific methods and procedures. The term "knowledge" connotes a body of known facts or of ideas inferred from such facts or accepted as true on good grounds. The expert testimony must help the trier of fact (jury or judge) to understand the evidence or to determine a fact in issue. To meet the relevance requirement, the expert testimony must display a valid scientific connection to the issue at hand as a precondition to being admitted.

Under Rule 702, the trial judge must make a preliminary assessment, before the actual trial, to be sure that the proposed expert testimony's underlying reasoning and methodology are scientifically valid, and can be properly applied to the facts in the lawsuit. The Court defined "scientific methodology" as the process of formulating hypotheses, and then conducting experiments to prove or falsify the hypothesis facts in the lawsuit. *Daubert* held that there are many considerations that will influence the determination of the quality and validity of the proposed expert testimony, among those being:

1. Whether the theory or technique in question can be (and has been) tested;
2. Whether it has been subjected to peer review and publication;
3. Its known or potential error rate;
4. The existence and maintenance of standards controlling its operation; and/or
5. Whether it has attracted widespread acceptance within a relevant scientific community.

The court may rely on only one, or possibly several of these tests in deciding to admit the subject expert testimony into evidence. In *Daubert*, the Court held that the inquiry into the reliability and relevance of proposed expert testimony is a flexible one, focusing solely on the scientific principles and methodology, and not on the conclusions they generate. In practice, the party opposing the introduction of expert testimony may present a pre-trial notice, after reading the expert witness' report and deposing the expert witness, seeking to exclude the expert testimony as not meeting any of the five *Daubert* factors enumerated above. In making his or her decision, the trial judge must determine whether it is more likely than not that the expert's methods are reliable and have been reliably applied to the facts at hand.

22.1.3 Expert Assistance by Engineers and Scientists in Complex Litigation

There are three ways that you may be engaged to provide expert assistance in a legal matter. You may be engaged to participate in one, two, or all three of these capacities. You may be asked to provide consulting advice, where you assist the lawyers in the preparation of the presentation of the technical issues in the case. You may also be asked to assist at the counsel's table at trial, and be present during the examination and cross-examination of the opposing expert witnesses in the area of your scientific or technical expertise. You may also be asked to present expert testimony at the trial, and to prepare yourself for rigorous cross-examination.

22.1.3.1 Advice and Consultation

As in most matters in life, it is often necessary for a person such as an engineer or a scientist who is thoroughly familiar with a technical or scientific concept to explain that concept to ordinary people, such as a lawyer preparing for trial, or ultimately a judge and/or jury. A jury is composed of a sampling of a given community, and is not a panel of experts on some particular scientific or technical viewpoint. Therefore, part of an engineer's or scientist's function when providing advice and consultation in preparation for trial is to present to their attorney the technical facts in the case such that an ordinary person can understand the complexities inherent in the facts. In patent litigation, at least one of the lawyers usually has an engineering or science degree or background, for this is a requirement of becoming a licensed patent attorney. However, most patent attorneys are involved in many technical disciplines, and are the master of no particular technology. Thus, the engineer expert advisor must not only have technical proficiency, but also have the ability to effectively express his or her knowledge. Even the patent attorney must be able to understand the expert's expression of the relevant facts, and how opinions were developed from those facts.

In preparation for acting effectively as an advising consultant or as an expert testifying witness, you must be so thoroughly familiar with the facts of the case that no opposition attack will come as a surprise. Drawings, sketches, or specifications may have to be thoroughly reviewed, substances and materials thoroughly tested, building codes or other laws fully examined, and/or prior art technical material may have to be analyzed. As an expert, you will then be asked to advise the attorney on your side of the case about every step you took in conducting your research, analysis, testing, and examination. Also, assistance in the preparation of a legal brief requires that your technical analysis be complete and strong enough to repel the opposing side's attack from its own expert.

An engineer providing assistance to an attorney in the preparation of a trial, or at the trial of a case, must have an open and objective approach to the technical facts. The engineer must present to the lawyer facts to support a client's claim, as well as, importantly, all opposing facts known to the engineer that may rebut or go against the client's position. There are two sides to any legal issue, and the engineer as an expert consultant must be willing to show the attorney and the client both sides of important issues bearing on the factual and legal questions in the case. This enables the attorney to prepare an effective rebuttal to expected adverse testimony from the opposing expert(s).

22.1.3.2 Trial Assistance

The engineer expert acting as a trial assistant prepares questions that the attorney should ask the opposing expert witnesses, and the opposing fact witnesses on cross-examination, to convince the jury that your presentation of the testimony is the correct one. Some of these questions arise unplanned as the trial progresses.

For example, your parties' attorney might not catch a mistake in the technical argument by an opposition expert witness, but it probably would not escape your notice as a technical expert. The expert witness giving trial assistance will be able to prepare the attorney to ask the appropriate questions on cross-examination that may show that the opposing expert did not do his or her homework properly. Also, such assistance may be used to prepare questions to be presented to your own testifying expert when placed on the stand to counter the opposition's expert testimony.

22.1.3.3 Opinion Testimony

Again, expert technological and scientific testimony must be presented in a court of law in a simple way that can be readily understood by individuals with no technical background, such as the judge and members of the jury. This is accomplished by the expert witness providing a basic, easily understood foundation for his or her testimony, and then relating all of the more complex facts and opinions to that basic foundation. It usually takes the cooperation of the expert and the attorney to get the expert's testimony to this point of a lay person's comprehension.

The expert witness is usually called upon to testify regarding technical or scientific principles and comparing them to events that happen every day, or with science principles the average judge or juror may recall from high school or college. Charts, pictures, electronic presentations, models, and drawings can be used by the expert witness to establish a clear meaning of the technology. The expert usually dedicates several hours to preparing such demonstrative evidence, and cannot rely upon the work of others, with the exception of "learned treatises." Also, each part of the evidence must be presented with such accuracy and clarity that it is incapable of successfully being adversely rebutted by opposing counsel.

The testifying expert must be completely honest in presenting his or her testimony, even if it means making a statement that does not fully support the client's allegations. The opposing attorney will look for any point you make on the witness stand that is not fully truthful in an effort to destroy your credibility. Any small gap in the fabric of truth of the evidence can destroy the total effect of the testimony. Thus, the truth and presenting honest opinions are imperatives.

In presenting expert testimony, if an engineer witness does not know the answer to a particular question on cross-examination by opposing counsel, a perfectly proper answer is "I don't know." If the question relates to testimony you gave previously, such as on direct examination, you as an expert witness may request the reading of the previous testimony before responding to the question. If a question requires mathematical analysis or other calculations, or a consultation with other witnesses or your attorney, time for such calculation or consultation may be requested from the court, and may or may not be granted.

One of the most important facets of giving expert testimony is the presence, attitude, and demeanor of the expert on the witness stand. He or she must come across to the judge and jury as inspiring confidence in the truth and honesty of his or her abilities and testimony. If you equivocate, the judge and jury may not accept anything you say. The expert witness' conduct and attitude throughout the entire proceeding must be favorably received by those who are evaluating the credibility of the technical or scientific testimony. During cross-examination, opposing counsel will attempt to discredit you, or demean you, or pick apart testimony damaging to your opponent's case.

The more damaging your expert testimony is to the opposing attorney's case, the more the opposing attorney will try to destroy your credibility and weaken the effect of your expert testimony. If this fails, the opposing attorney may attempt to harass the expert witness and have the witness become angry on the stand. Attorneys commonly use this tactic in an attempt to transfer the witness' anger among the jurors, who will then direct their anger to the witness. Therefore, it is most important for the witness to remain calm and provide thought-out responses. Courtesy, assuredness in your answers, and self-control must be exercised at all times. A simple "yes sir," "no sir," "yes ma'am," or "no ma'am" in your cross-examination responses is greatly appreciated by your attorney.

Your expert opinion testimony may include reference to texts, materials, and writings by acknowledged authorities in technical fields relating to your testimony. Sometimes a quotation from a "learned treatise" or textbook is more meaningful than oral testimony by the author of the text.

22.1.4 Expert Report and Deposition

If you are designated by the trial counsel who retained you to appear and present expert testimony at the trial of a technically complex case, after you have prepared your testimony and prepared a written "expert report," and prior to trial, you will be presented for a discovery deposition to be taken by the opposing counsel, who may examine you as to the experimentations, tests, examinations, and/or analysis you have made, and the conclusions drawn from your work relating to the issues in the lawsuit as described in your expert report. You will also be required to bring with you all of the documents and other materials you relied upon in preparing your testimony. The deposition affords opposing counsel the ability to know what your testimony is going to be before you testify. This is part of the American judicial system, and not only your expert testimony but the testimony of all witnesses on both sides will be known prior to trial through the use of discovery depositions taken by counsel for both parties.

22.1.5 Deciding Whether You Can Provide the Requisite Expert Assistance

It is very important that scientists and engineers who are requested to testify or work as expert witnesses, either as a testifying or consultant expert, first come to the conclusion that they truly believe they can honestly testify for the prospective client's position. You must firmly believe in the case of your client, and in the testimony you are to give, or else you should decline to act as an expert witness. First, you should not be compelled or even asked to testify as to matters that you yourself do not believe are accurate or soundly founded in fact. Second, if you testify with anything less than full conviction in the substance of your testimony, your lack of conviction will be apparent in the manner in which you will be testifying before the court and jury, and your testimony will not be worth very much when subjected to vigorous cross-examination.

22.1.6 Expert Witness Fees

All expert witnesses in litigation are paid for their services, unless they choose not to accept fees. Engineers and scientists testifying as expert witnesses in highly complex matters are thus paid fees for the presentation of their testimony.

Your expert witness fee must not be contingent on the outcome or result of the case. Normally, at deposition and during trial, the expert witness will be asked if he or she is being paid for their testimony, and will also be asked how much. These are legitimate questions, and you should not hesitate to answer truthfully and positively. If you are being paid only on the contingency that your client wins the case, then the jury can conclude that your testimony is biased. However, if you are getting paid on a straight time or on a flat fee basis for your testimony, the jury can assume that you were just paid for your services, and that your testimony is credible.

By way of example, many years ago I was representing a chemical formulation company in a case my client brought against two former employees of the company, alleging that the two former employees had stolen trade secret formulas of my client, which the defendants then used to start a competing business. We engaged the services of a chemist who owned a competing chemical formulation company to provide expert testimony comparing the defendants' formulas to our client's original formulas. The expert witness did not request a fee, and received none for his testimony. During cross-examination of our expert witness by the defendants' attorney, the expert was asked if he was receiving a fee for his testimony, which is a legitimate and regularly asked question of expert witnesses on cross-examination. Our witness replied "No." At this point, a good lawyer knows not to ask a question on cross-examination where he or she does not know the answer. However, the defendants' lawyer than asked "Why?" Our witness stated, "Because the scum that you represent have to be eradicated from our industry."

INVENTORS AND INVENTIONS

John Bardeen, Walter Brattain, and William Shockley

THE TRANSISTOR

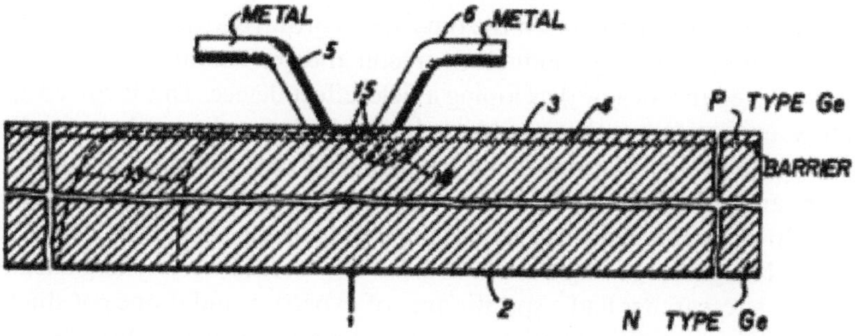

In November–December 1947, John Bardeen and Walter Brattain invented the transistor while working at Bell Labs in Murray Hill, New Jersey. The transistor was a major breakthrough in the field of solid-state electronics, which dates back to the invention of the solid-state rectifier in 1874 by Ferdinand Braun. Braun's rectifier used a point contact based on lead sulfide, which resulted in a rather unstable device. Later in the 1800s, the vacuum tube was invented, which rapidly made the Braun solid-state point contact rectifier obsolete. Subsequently, scientists working at very high frequencies found that vacuum tubes would not work at the desired frequencies, and the idea of a point contact rectifier was rethought. In the 1920s, the theoretical development of quantum mechanics became an important driving force in solid-state electronics, and a comprehensive understanding of solid materials and their conductivity was developed.

In 1936, Mervin Kelly, President of Bell Labs, the research arm of AT&T, decided to start a solid-state device group. He employed people such as Bill Shockley, Russell Ohl, Jack Scaff, and others to commence work in the new group. Kelly felt that vacuum tubes were reaching the limits of their potential as voice signal amplifiers, and were not going to be the ultimate answer in electronics, particularly in telephone systems and for military use. The objective of Bell Labs' solid-state physics group was to provide a new, sturdy, and more efficient amplifier to replace the vacuum tube in AT&T's telephone system.

Intellectual Property Law for Engineers, Scientists, and Entrepreneurs, Second Edition. Howard B. Rockman.

Published 2020 by John Wiley & Sons, Inc.

By 1940, the members of the solid-state team at Bell Labs had completed a great deal of work in understanding silicon crystals. For example, they learned that depending upon how single crystals of silicon were prepared, either N- or P-type silicon resulted. In those days, this indicated whether the rectifier was positive or negative. Russell Ohl made a sample in which the top part was a P-type region and the bottom was N-type; when light struck the device, a voltage developed. The Bell Labs management gave Ohl's sample to Walter Brattain for re-measurement and verification. Brattain was able to confirm Ohl's effect.

The solid-state group of engineers and physicists at Bell Labs was disbanded during the Second World War. When the war ended, Kelly restarted the group for the purpose of continuing their work in solid-state electronics. In 1946, Kelly appointed Bill Shockley and Stanley Morgan as heads of the team, which included Walter Brattain, John Bardeen, and several others. At the outset, this group decided that it would begin work with the simplest of semiconductors, silicon and germanium.

Shockley revived the idea of developing a field-effect device. This involved applying a voltage to a semiconductor that would result in a change in the conductivity. Bardeen found through simple calculations that a relatively low concentration of surface states would screen any voltage from the interior of the semiconductor. Bardeen suggested that they might clean the surface to reduce the effects of the surface states and make a useful device. The group of engineers and scientists worked very synergistically with each other. Each researcher had a specific area of expertise, and if one got stuck on an experiment, there was always another person to turn to for help. Their research was based on the quantum mechanics theories about semiconductors that had been developed during the 1930s.

On November 17, 1947, Walter Brattain dumped an entire experiment into a thermos of water. The silicon device he was experimenting with was designed to help him analyze how electrons behaved on the surface of a semiconductor, and why these electrons were behaving such that it was impossible to build an amplifier. In his previous experiments, condensation kept forming on the silicon and ruined each experiment. Brattain conducted this whole experiment under water, which was effective in getting rid of the condensation. He was surprised to find that the wet device created the most significant amplification he had achieved to date. He and one of the other scientists, Robert Gibney, found that by turning up a positive voltage, the effect was increased even more. Turning the voltage to negative would get rid of the effect completely. Apparently, whatever the electrons were doing on the semiconductor surface to block amplification was somehow cancelled out by the water. Thus, the obstacle to building an amplifier had been overcome.

Walter Brattain then told John Bardeen of his results, and Bardeen suggested pushing a metal point into the silicon, surrounded by distilled water. His thought was that the water would eliminate the electron problem just under the point as it had in Walter Brattain's thermos of water. The contact point could not touch the water; it could only touch the silicon. Ultimately, Walter Brattain built the proposed amplifier and it worked, producing only a tiny bit of amplification. However, it did work.

The engineers and scientists at Bell Labs had obtained a small amount of amplification using a tiny drop of water, but Bardeen and Brattain deduced that by using different materials, setups, and electrolytes in place of the water, even larger increases in current could be obtained. On December 8, 1947, Bardeen suggested that the silicon be replaced with germanium, which resulted in a current jump or amplification of 330 times. However, the jump was in the exact opposite direction they expected. Instead of moving the electrons (the negatively charged elements in the silicon), the electrolyte was moving the holes (the positively charged elements in the silicon).

It was determined that the increase in amplification worked only for certain types of current, ones with very low frequencies. This was unacceptable for use in a phone line that handled the complex frequencies of a person's voice. So the work continued to try to obtain amplification at various frequencies.

Bardeen and Brattain replaced the liquid with germanium oxide, which is equivalent to a little bit of germanium rust. On December 12, Brattain inserted the point contacts, but nothing happened. As Brattain repeatedly poked the gold contacts into the germanium, he realized there was no oxide layer on the germanium. It had been washed off by accident. Brattain continued to manipulate the point contact, and to his surprise, voltage amplification was produced at all frequencies, but at a low level. The gold contact made holes in the germanium, and these positively charged holes cancelled out the effect of the negatively charged electrons at the surface in the same manner that the water had done previously. This was considered an improvement because the device was now increasing the current at all frequencies.

Therefore, at this juncture, Bardeen and Brattain were obtaining large amplification at some frequencies, and small amplification for all frequencies. The objective now was to combine the two to produce a workable device. The key components of their experiment at that time were a piece of germanium and two gold point contacts, just fractions of a millimeter apart. Walter Brattain then placed a ribbon of gold foil around a plastic triangle, and sliced through the gold at the tip of the triangle with a razor blade, resulting in two gold contacts approximately 0.002 inches apart. The entire triangle was then held over a crystal of germanium using a spring, and the contacts lightly touched the surface of the germanium. The germanium sat on a metal plate attached to a voltage source. By placing the point of the triangle on the germanium, a signal came in through one gold contact and increased as it raced out the other. This small amount of gold, germanium, and plastic resulted in the first working solid-state amplifier.

This first transistor was gigantic in dimension, being approximately half an inch high. Consider that, by today's standards, seven million transistors fit on a single computer chip. The reason the transistor worked was that germanium is a semiconductor and, if properly treated, allows a significant amount of current through it, or none at all. The germanium had an excess of electrons, but when an electric signal traveled in through the gold foil, it injected holes into the surface. This created a thin layer along the top of the germanium with too few electrons.

N-type semiconductors are those with too many electrons. P-type semiconductors are those with too few electrons. The boundary between these two kinds of semiconductors is known as a P–N junction. At this junction, current flows from one side to the other, and in Brattain's first transistor, current flowed toward the second gold contact. Thus, a small current passing through one contact changed the nature of the semiconductor, resulting in a separate current flowing across the germanium and out the second contact. As a result, a small current flow could alter the flow of a much larger one, thus amplifying the current. When the input signal creates additional holes in the germanium, the way current flows across the crystal is altered, and the output current becomes larger and smaller, duplicating the input.

Germanium is a grayish-white element with brilliant metallic luster and a crystalline structure having a diamond pattern. A semiconductor is a crystalline solid material having electrical properties that may be varied over wide ranges by the addition of small quantities of other elements. Electrons having a negative charge, and that are within the semiconductor materials, carry the electric current. Current is also carried by the positively charged holes. The reason germanium was used as a semiconductor material in the early experiments of Bardeen and Brattain was that shortly after World War II, methods of purifying germanium to the requisite degree had already been developed. The electrical properties of semiconductors are sensitive to traces of other elements, such that only one part per billion of other elements can be tolerated in material to be used for making semiconductor devices. During the late 1950s, the purification of silicon succeeded, and this new material was used for semiconductor devices, as it is today.

A transistor (short for "transfer resistance") is basically a switch or an electronic gate that opens and closes to allow the passage of current. They are solid-state and based on semiconductor materials such as silicon. Crystals of these elements have properties that are between those of conductors and insulators, hence the name "semiconductors." A semiconductor crystal can be produced to act as a conductor for electrical current passing through the material in one direction by adding impurities, such as small amounts of boron or phosphors.

In the first transistor, the bottom electrode was the base of a germanium crystal. The other two leads were formed on the tip of a block above the germanium crystal. The tip had a first coat of metal, then a wax layer over the top, and another metal layer. The bottom was sheared off, leaving essentially an inside metal layer, a layer of insulating wax, and a layer of metal. This assembly was pressed onto the germanium surface, the inside metal became the collector, and the outside metal became the emitter. In the initial experiment, the outside metal made contact with an electrolyte. Thus, the first time gain was realized, the device was conducting current through the electrolyte, and the gain configuration was such that the emitter-to-collector current was modulated by the base current.

In those days, a point contact device was the only configuration under study. However, Brattain rapidly realized that painting two metal stripes close together on the surface of the germanium produced a much better device. This improved device was built and presented to the management of Bell Labs on Christmas Eve, 1947.

Public announcement of the discovery of the first transistor was delayed for several months until June 1948 to allow the inventors time to obtain an understanding of the device, and to prepare their patent position. The public reaction to the announcement appeared to be "oh well." It has been stated that it was very difficult in 1948 to understand the full implication of something such as the transistor invention, unless you were a scientist or an engineer. Because Bell Labs was operating under various consent decrees in those days, it had no choice but to license the invention. Thus, the transistor was offered to all responsible parties at an advance license fee of $25,000, which was applied against royalties.

William Shockley had been away in Europe on a short sabbatical during late 1947 and early 1948, and was aware when he returned that he was not part of the invention of the transistor. However, Shockley subsequently made very important contributions to the further development of the transistor. At that time, Bardeen felt that the conductivity on the surface layer of the transistor was being changed, and the change in conductivity was causing the amplification. Shockley had a different opinion. He felt that the bulk of the crystal was somehow involved in the amplification. During the next two months, in the beginning of 1948, Shockley proceeded to expand on his theory of the bipolar junction transistor, which theory depended on the introduction of minority carriers. Thus, Shockley was the first person to both clearly see and discuss minority carrier injection into the semiconductor. However, Shockley kept this idea secret for some time. In February of 1948, John Shive conducted an experiment that verified Shockley's idea that minority carrier injection was indeed involved in the amplification of the transistor.

Although transistors today are at the heart of computer science and technology, they were actually used before the digital explosion, and were the basis of important improvements in existing analog systems, such as radios and stereo music amplifiers. Solid-state technology has allowed the mass production of transistors by the millions on a sliver of a silicon semiconductor chip. In 1956, Bardeen, Brattain, and Shockley were awarded the Nobel Prize in Physics for their invention of the transistor.

The first computer, the ENIAC, built in 1946 at the University of Pennsylvania, comprised more than 1800 vacuum tubes, weighed 30 tons, filled an entire room, and consumed 150 kilowatts of electricity per hour. This computer must be compared with the laptops of today, which weigh about 5 kilograms, are driven by batteries, and run 100,000 times faster than the ENIAC.

By the 1960s, computers were being developed that employed hundreds of thousands of transistors. This, coupled with the need for lightweight electronic missile guidance systems, resulted in the invention of the integrated circuit independently by Jack Kilby of Texas Instruments in 1958, and by Jean Hoerni and Robert Noyce of Fairchild Semiconductor in 1959. Kilby is credited with developing the concept of integrating device and circuit elements into a single silicon chip, whereas Noyce conceived the method for integrating the separate elements. Thus, the integrated circuit was a further development begun by the invention of the transistor. In late 1970, the first microprocessor was introduced, which contained the arithmetic, logic, and control circuitry necessary to perform the functions of a computer's central processing unit. This type of large-scale integrated circuit was developed by a team at Intel Corporation.

April 4, 1950

W. SHOCKLEY

SEMICONDUCTOR AMPLIFIER

Filed Sept. 24, 1948

2,502,488

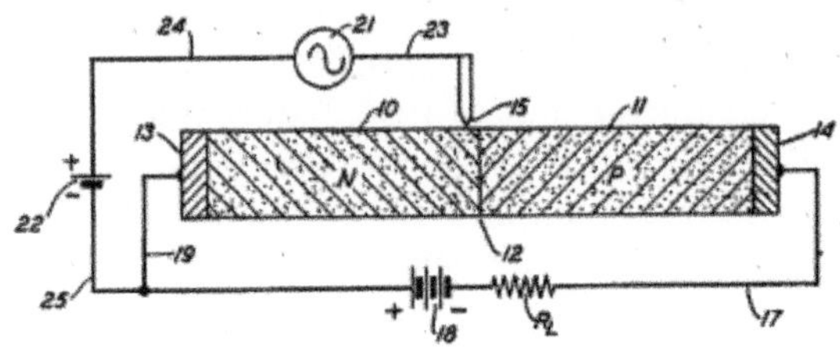

INVENTOR
W. SHOCKLEY

BY

ATTORNEY

Oct. 3, 1950 J. BARDEEN ET AL **2,524,035**

THREE-ELECTRODE CIRCUIT ELEMENT UTILIZING SEMICONDUCTIVE MATERIALS

Filed June 17, 1948 3 Sheets-Sheet 1

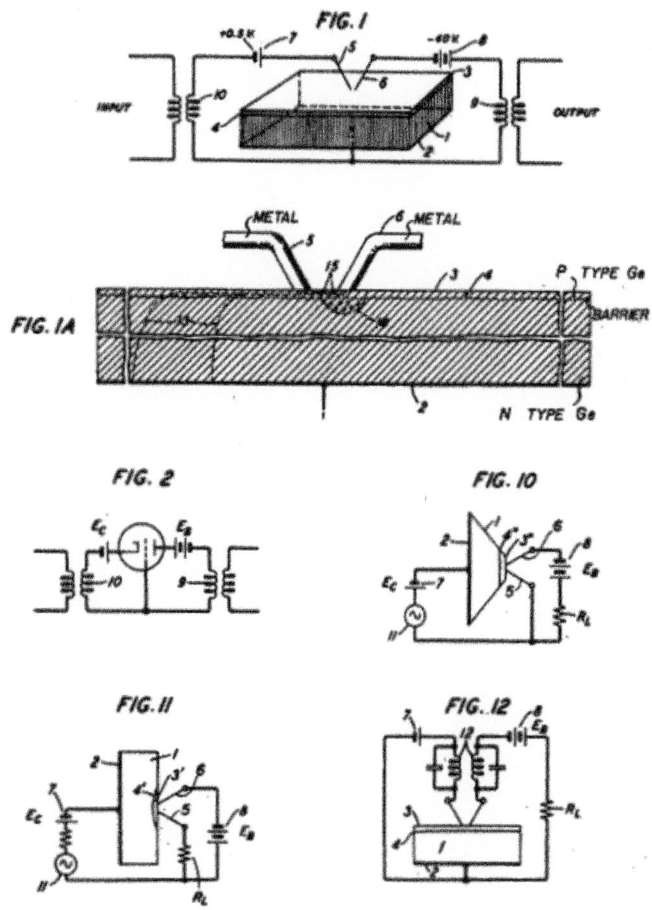

INVENTORS: J. BARDEEN
W. H. BRATTAIN

BY Harry C. Hart

ATTORNEY

23 Ethics

23.1 THE PROFESSIONS

Over the past hundred years, the science and engineering disciplines have reached the level of professionalism often accorded the fields of medicine, law, and theology. While engineering as a technology-oriented discipline has existed for nearly two centuries, only in recent times has it been considered a profession. Also, with the advance of technology, many new and different areas of interest inside the professions of engineering and science have been created. The current technology explosion is causing new scientific and engineering areas to be created regularly.

The dictionary meaning of the term "profession" is "a vocation or occupation requiring advanced training in some liberal art or science, and usually involving mental rather than manual work." It is an endeavor where the labor and skill involved is predominantly mental or intellectual, as compared to physical or manual, per *Black's Law Dictionary.* For example, the United States Labor Management Relations Act defines the term "professional employee" as follows:

> An employee engaged in work predominantly intellectual and varied in character as opposed to routine mental, manual, mechanical or physical work, or involving consistent exercise of discretion and judgment in his performance.

To some extent, the states have varying requirements for members of a profession. For example, doctors, lawyers, and certain engineers are obligated to obtain a state registration or license before they can practice their profession in that state. Professionals are normally organized into professional societies, which provide substantial peer self-regulation of the profession's members and conduct. The professions are normally those vocations that have a large component of public interest and public service built into their way of earning a living, and whose conduct is guided by a Professional Code of Ethics or a Code of Professional Responsibility.

Today, in the profession of engineering, civil engineers and public works engineers, among others, are required to register with the state in which they work. Under normal circumstances, engineers working for corporations or as consultants are usually exempt from registration requirements. Many states require professional engineers to be registered before they are allowed to practice, and many states have reciprocal agreements allowing an engineer registered in one state to work in another state.

Intellectual Property Law for Engineers, Scientists, and Entrepreneurs, Second Edition. Howard B. Rockman.

Published 2020 by John Wiley & Sons, Inc.

The purpose of the registration laws is to protect the public from unacceptable and improper engineering work products. To become registered, an engineer must establish to the satisfaction of the Board of Examiners that he or she possesses the requisite abilities established by state standards. Registration normally involves a review of the candidate's past engineering work experience, training, and an examination must be successfully completed. It is also quite true that the acceptance of an occupation as a profession requires continuing education efforts to maintain high standards of service to the public.

23.2 PROFESSIONAL SOCIETIES

Many of today's established engineering disciplines have at least one society of its members such as IEEE, ASME, AIChE, and others. Likewise, societies of scientists abound, each one dedicated to providing professional stature to their members, and serving as a conduit for the exchange and validation of new ideas. The Accreditation Board of Engineering and Technology (ABET), among other functions, examines accredited engineering and technology curriculum in schools of higher education at least once every six years.

The American Association of Engineering Societies was formed in 1979 to advance the development and practice of the public interest in engineering. The association also acts as an information exchange agency for its member's interests and activities.

The National Society of Professional Engineers (NSPE), formed in 1934, is largely responsible for the passage of engineering registration laws in the various states, and in promoting public recognition of engineering as a profession.

23.3 CODES OF ETHICS

"Ethics" is defined as "a system or code of morals of a particular group, profession, etc." Ethics are the rules and regulations we each impose on ourselves to govern our day-to-day conduct, in accordance with what we individually believe is right or wrong. Our desire is to have others trust in our abilities, and we engage in our professions so as to earn and receive this trust from others. Honesty and integrity are two important ingredients making up one's character that are visible to others, and which result in loyalty from those whom you desire to engage in a business/professional relationship. For example, no Constitution, federal, or state law requires an engineer or scientist to provide a totally honest, unbiased report of the results of his or her analyses. However, engineers and scientists are guided on the straight track of truth and honesty by two important factors of conscience. One is the moral code guiding that person in practicing his or her profession, and in expressing the results of his or her work. The other is the peer review that will test the integrity of their work when made public. One's life experiences, observations, and teachers contribute to the make-up of an individual's moral platform. These are layered over the engineering and science experiences one gains during development as a professional, which evolves into the moral standards one applies to oneself at any given time.

A Code of Ethics does not stand as a body of rigid, unchangeable regulations or standards. Ethics exist as a guiding light to direct an engineer's or scientist's own moral standards, and to assist in altering the engineer's conduct to satisfy those standards. Any standard of ethics has great value to an individual in his or her communications and conduct with others, and indicates the path toward professionalism in the work of the engineer and scientist.

23.4 BRIEF COMMENTS REGARDING THE NSPE CODE OF ETHICS FOR ENGINEERS

This code requires that engineers exhibit the highest standards of honesty and integrity, that the services provided by engineers be performed impartially, fairly, and equitably, and must be directed toward the protection of public health, safety, and welfare. This latter provision is of utmost importance, since the average person who observes or uses the work of an engineer cannot tell what degree of expertise or quality went into that work, but just assumes that the bridge they are crossing or the television they are turning on is safe for their use.

Some of the fundamental cannons of the NSPE Code of Ethics are:

- Holding high the health, safety, and welfare of the public.
- Performing only in one's areas of competence, experience, and education.
- Being objective and truthful in issuing public statements.
- Providing services for each employer or client as faithful agents or trustees.
- Avoiding deceptive acts.
- Conducting oneself honorably, responsibly, ethically, and lawfully to enhance the honor, reputation and usefulness of the engineering profession.

The NSPE Code also provides guidelines to assist an engineer in exercising his or her own judgment, for example, where his or her judgment may be overruled under circumstances that could endanger life or property. Under such circumstances, the engineer is ethically required to advise an employer, client, or such other authority as may be appropriate of their opinion or conclusions. Also, engineers shall not permit the use of their names in endeavors which they have reason to believe involve fraudulent and dishonest enterprises. Further, if engineers have knowledge of any violation of the code of ethics by others, they are morally obligated to report such violation of another to an appropriate professional body, and when deemed relevant, to public authorities.

Engineers are also obligated under the NSPE Code of Ethics to disclose all or known potential conflicts of interest that could influence, or appear to influence, their judgment or the quality of their services. Also, if an engineer is compelled by a client or employer to conduct him or herself in an unprofessional or illegal manner, the engineer is obligated under the Code to notify the proper authorities, and withdraw from further service on the project.

The Code also includes a very important provision restricting engineers from disclosing, without consent, confidential information or trade secrets concerning the business affairs or technical processes of any present or former client, employer, or public body on which they serve. Such disclosure could result in a trade secret misappropriation legal action against both the new employer and the engineer, which becomes costly and could interfere with the engineer's new position. A further provision regarding confidentially provides that engineers should not participate in or represent an adversary interest in connection with a project in which the engineer has gained particular specialized confidential knowledge on behalf of a former client. This provision requires an engineer, upon taking a new position, to fully disclose to the new employer all previous positions and generally describe projects he or she has worked on, to avoid the appearance of a conflict of interest. Also, any previous non-compete agreements that the engineer has signed should be made fully available to the new employer.

Under the Code, engineers are also obligated to give credit and attribution for engineering work to those to whom credit is due, and to recognize the proprietary interests of others. This requires engineers to honestly name the person or persons who may be individually responsible for designs, inventions, writings, and other accomplishments. For example, the true inventors of an invention must be named in a U.S. patent application filing, or the patent ultimately issued may be held invalid and unenforceable. Therefore, there is no advantage in naming uninvolved individuals as inventors in patent applications. Also, my experience has shown that acknowledging the fine work of others can create a high level of morale in an organization or project team. Everyone wants to be told that the work they are doing is valued.

Engineers using designs supplied by a client must recognize that the designs are the property of the client and remain so, and may not be used or duplicated by the engineer for other projects without express permission of the client for whom the designs were first made.

The Code also provides that before undertaking work for others in connection with which the engineer may make improvements to existing works, plans, designs, inventions, or other works that may justify copyrights or patents, the engineer should enter into a written agreement regarding ownership of such improvements, etc. In most situations, if the engineer is being paid to develop such improvements or inventions, ownership will vest in the person making payment to the engineer.

An engineer's designs, data, records, and notes referring exclusively to an employer's work are the employer's property, and cannot be taken with the engineer once employment is terminated. The employer also should indemnify the engineer for use of the information for any purpose other than the original purpose.

23.5 COMPARING THE LAW AND ETHICS

An unethical action is not necessarily "illegal." Thus, neither the examining boards nor the courts regulate or are involved in the ethical practices of engineers. Negligence of engineers is another story, and the courts become directly involved with negligence in engineering design and manufacturing practices. The redress for moral misconduct of an engineer comes from engineering societies. For example, the American Medical Association and the local state bar associations have the ability to deprive a doctor or lawyer of the right to practice his or her profession in a given state. However, there is no such society with equivalent powers in the engineering profession. It is quite possible that procedures for holding hearings on unethical engineering practices may be developed at some future date. Today, if an engineer is guilty of performing an unethical practice, that engineer may be removed from membership in an engineering society. Other penalties would include the loss of a job or project. Public knowledge of such censure is a severe factor curtailing the offender's ability to earn a living.

The various codes of professional ethics that are in existence lead to the conclusion that those who are honest and loyal and adhere to a standard of moral and professional ethics in dealing with others often find that, as a result, others are honest and loyal in reciprocal dealings with them.

To maintain the impartiality and integrity of engineers and scientists, many corporations and governmental agencies that employ engineers have adopted policies restricting or eliminating receipt of gifts by engineers from vendors, where the engineer is in a position to specify the purchase of products from among a plurality of vendors. Those in the engineering profession correctly understand that an engineer's integrity cannot and should not be purchased by those whom the engineer deals with on the employer's behalf.

23.6 ETHICAL DILEMMAS

The market for qualified engineering and science professionals ebbs and flows. In years of rapidly advancing technology in a viable economy, qualified engineers and scientists have been in short supply. Industry sources have reported that this can lead to odd, and even objectionable, recruiting activities. In an economy where there is a shortage of engineers, one company will usually contact another company's engineers in an effort to lure them away. This is considered by some to be unethical; however, it is a common practice. Of course, if the engineer makes the first move to seek a new position, the resulting job change usually is considered to be proper.

Sometimes, a company that loses its engineers to a competitor has only itself to blame. For example, the management of a company may have a policy of ignoring contributions made by their engineers, such as where an engineer's design change results in substantial savings to the employer. Engineers and scientists normally feel that good work should result in recognition, for example, in the way of monetary or other reward for saving the company money. The company, on the other hand, may take the position that engineers are paid both for periods in which their contributions are outstanding and for other periods in which their achievements are quite lackluster. Because of these conflicting points of view, engineers may become disillusioned, and they begin to seek out offers of new employment. Therefore, one important way to maintain the integrity of your workforce is to give praise where praise is due for outstanding jobs.

An engineer's ethics will be tested many times on the job. For example, consider the hypothetical situation where an engineer knows of a design problem with the speaker system of a new cellular phone regarding radiation emissions. The engineer is told that management has decided that the \$0.75 per unit required for repair of the design is too huge of a cost factor. What should the engineer do? Send an e-mail questioning the decision? Discuss the matter with a supervisor, mentioning that the old design could be a health hazard? Advise the press of the potential health hazard? Send a memorandum questioning the decision and emphasizing that lives may be at risk? Provide the press with information about the chosen design and the cost of alternatives? The ultimate decision becomes: when has the engineer done enough to satisfy his or her ethical obligation? This has to be decided by each engineer on a case-by-case basis, and brings into play the engineer's own moral convictions.

An example of an engineer's ethical dilemma can be found in classic literature. Suppose an engineer becomes aware of a discharge of a carcinogenic chemical into a river used as a source for drinking water. Does the engineer have a duty to report the discharge? If so, to whom: the engineer's supervisor, the Environmental Protection Agency, the local authorities using the river for drinking water, or the press? No clear answers exist; hence, the engineer must base such decisions on personal ethics and values. Over a hundred years ago, the Danish author, Henrik Ibsen, wrote a play titled *Enemy of the People,* in which an engineer for a city's waterworks did exactly this—he tried to shut down the water supply of a city known for its warming spas and healthful waters because of an unacceptable high level of bacteria in the water. Everyone ultimately chastised him for his work. Thus, the title of the play: *Enemy of the People.* Under today's standards, the "hero" of Mr. Ibsen's play would be praised and not condemned.

SECTION IV

Copyrights

◆ INVENTORS AND INVENTIONS ◆

Jack Kilby and Robert Noyce

MINIATURIZED INTEGRATED CIRCUITS

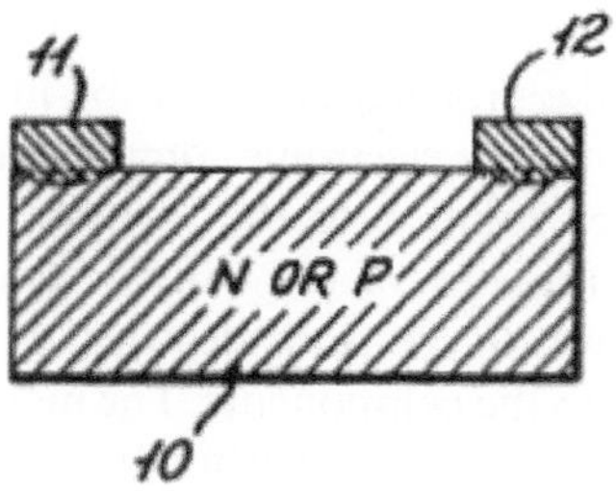

Jack Kilby and Robert Noyce are credited with the invention and development of the semiconductor integrated circuit, and the interconnection techniques used to make the circuits (ICs) practical. Semiconductor integrated circuits are also known as monolithic integrated circuits, or microchips. An integrated circuit combines transistors, resistors, and capacitors on a single semiconductor chip, which is a monolithic IC. The work of these two gentlemen furnished the conceptual and technical basis for the field of modern microelectronics, providing the breakthrough that resulted in the sophisticated high-speed computers and large-capacity semiconductor memories used today. The development of the microchip transformed yesterday's house-size computers into today's array of minicomputers, personal computers, and mainframes that are available to everyone.

Jack St. Clair Kilby was born on November 8, 1923, in Jefferson City, Missouri, and obtained a BS degree in electrical engineering from the University of Illinois in 1947 and his MS degree in electrical engineering from the University of Wisconsin in 1950. From 1947 to 1958, he was employed by Centralab Division of Globe Union, Inc., where he was engaged in the design and development of semiconductor devices with ceramic-based, silk-screened circuits. In June 1958, Kilby began working for Texas Instruments, Inc. (TI) at TI's semiconductor lab in Texas. However, to complete the story of Jack Kilby and Robert Noyce's work, the proper historical perspective must first be laid.

The thinking that led Kilby to eventually develop the integrated circuit began in the way most inventors begin their projects: he attempted to find the solution to a specific problem. The specific problem was called the "the tyranny of numbers." For practically the first 50 years of the 20th century, the electronics industry used vacuum tube technology. These vacuum tubes, for those of us who can remember them, were fragile, unreliable devices that used lots of power and produced a considerable amount of heat.

Intellectual Property Law for Engineers, Scientists, and Entrepreneurs, Second Edition. Howard B. Rockman.

Published 2020 by John Wiley & Sons, Inc.

In 1947, the invention of the transistor by Bell Telephone Laboratories developed technology that replaced vacuum tubes. Transistors were much smaller compared to vacuum tubes, had a high degree of reliability, produced less heat, used less power, and lasted much longer. With the advent of the transistor in 1947, engineers began to design and create more complex electronic circuits and equipment that contained hundreds or even thousands of small components such as transistors, diodes, rectifiers, resistors, and capacitors. This led to another problem: all of these components had to be connected to each other to form electrical circuits. The hand-soldering technique that had to be used in the beginning to connect thousands of components to thousands of bits of wire was expensive and time-consuming, and was also unreliable. Those of you who have constructed your own electronic circuits realize that every soldered joint was a source of potential problems. Thus, the problem facing Kilby in 1958 was to find low-cost, efficient, and reliable ways to produce electronic components and interconnect them.

Prior to 1958, an attempted solution to the "tyranny of numbers" problem was known as the Micro-Module Program of the United States Army Signal Corps. The impetus behind this program was to create all electrical components in a uniform size and shape, with wiring built into the components. The modules could then be snapped together to make circuits, which eliminated wiring the connections together.

When Kilby began working at TI in 1958, TI was already working on the Micro-Module Program. Kilby began working in the semiconductor building of TI, and quickly concluded that the Micro-Module was not the answer to the problem, since it did not address the situation caused by large quantities of components in complex electronic circuits. He decided that the only thing a semiconductor house such as TI could make cost-effectively was a semiconductor. As Kilby wrote in a 1976 article titled "Invention of the IC," he concluded in 1958 that semiconductors were all that were really required. Resistors and capacitors (passive devices), could be made from the same material as the active devices (transistors). He also realized that since all the components could be made of a single material, they could also be made in place and interconnected to form a complete circuit.

In July 1958, Kilby began to work on his ideas, and recorded and illustrated his thoughts as his development project progressed. During the summer of 1958, most TI employees had left for the traditional two-week vacation period, except Kilby. As a new employee with no vacation time earned, he had to stay to man the shop. Kilby worked with borrowed and improvised equipment to conceive and construct the first electronic circuit in which all of the components, both active and passive, were fabricated in a single piece of semiconductor material half the size of a paper clip. By September 1958, he was ready to demonstrate his working integrated circuit, which he constructed on a piece of semiconductor material. This demonstration took place on September 12, 1958, in front of several executives of Texas Instruments. Kilby showed them a slice of germanium with protruding wires, and a transistor and other components glued to a glass slide. It was an extremely crude device, but when Kilby turned on the current, an unending sine curve undulated across an oscilloscope screen. Kilby's invention, on a 7/16 inch by 1/16 inch substrate, was called an integrated circuit, and marked the beginning of the revolution in the electronics industry that is still going on today.

The United States Air Force showed interest in Kilby's integrated circuit, but skepticism defined industry's reaction. However, the integrated circuit gained acceptance when the Air Force adopted the silicon chips for its first computers in 1961, and for the Minute Man missile in 1962. At that time, the chairman of TI, Patrick E. Haggerty, wanted Kilby to come up with a "demonstration product" that would show the wide uses that the integrated circuit chip could be put to. Haggerty challenged Kilby to design a calculator that would be as powerful as the large electro-mechanical desktop calculators used at that time, but small enough to fit into a coat pocket. Kilby met the challenge, produced a small electronic hand-held calculator that is credited with the beginning of the successful commercialization of the integrated circuit.

Kilby's work was the breakthrough that made possible the sophisticated high-speed computers and large-capacity semiconductor memories of today's information age. He later was also a coinventor of the thermal printer that is used in portable data terminals. From 1978 to 1984, he held the position of distinguished professor of electrical engineering at Texas A & M University.

In 2000, Jack Kilby was awarded the Nobel Prize in Physics for his part in the invention and development of the integrated circuit. He passed away on June 20, 2005.

The second inventor in the integrated circuit equation is Robert N. Noyce, who was born in Burlington, Iowa, on December 12, 1927. Noyce received a BA degree, and gained Phi Beta Kappa, at Grinnell (Iowa) College in 1949. He then obtained a PhD degree in physical electronics at MIT in 1953. Upon completion of his schooling, he was employed by the research division of Philco Corporation, working in developing high-performance germanium surface-barrier transistors. He later joined the Shockley Semiconductor Laboratory of Beckmann Instruments in Palo Alto, California, shortly after its formation in 1956. There he worked on diffused silicon devices.

Shortly thereafter, in 1957, Noyce was one of the founders of Fairchild Semiconductor Company, where he was Director of Research. He was responsible for the commercial realization of the double-diffused mesa and planar silicon transistors. During this period of time, he contributed heavily to the practical integrated circuit.

Soon after Fairchild Semiconductor was formed, Noyce began constructing silicon transistors, which were wired together by hand after manufacture. Fairchild's principals soon came to the realization that if they were to be successful, an improved production method had to be found. Noyce and Fairchild cofounder Gordon Moore began studying methods of joining transistors that would do away with after-production wiring. They developed the theory that transistors could be combined in a solid block of silicon. Noyce began making notes in his lab notebook, totally unaware that a somewhat similar theory had been developed the summer before in the Texas Instruments semiconductor laboratories by Jack Kilby.

After Kilby announced his discovery of the integrated circuit on September 12, 1958, development work at Fairchild Semiconductor accelerated; the Fairchild research and development engineers were focused on making the connections between the small transistors and the other components an integral part of the manufacturing process itself. Jean Hoerni, another of Fairchild's original founders, developed the "planar" process, using oxidation and heat diffusion to create a smooth insulating layer on the surface of a silicon chip. This allowed the embedding of insulated layers of transistors and other electronic components in silicon. The planar process provided insulation between layers, so that each layer could be isolated electrically, thus eliminating the requirement to cut apart the layers and wire them back together again.

On July 30, 1959, Fairchild Semiconductor filed for a patent covering a semiconductor integrated circuit based on the planar process. This began a ten-year-long legal battle between Texas Instruments and Fairchild. TI had previously filed a similar patent based on Kilby's technology. Years later, the U.S. Court of Customs and Patent

Appeals decided that Noyce's claims on interconnection techniques had priority, but Kilby and Texas Instruments were given credit for constructing the first working integrated circuit. Thus, without knowing each other, through two independent paths, both Kilby and Noyce invented, almost at the same time, the integrated circuit, which today is commonly known as "the chip."

In July 1968, Robert Noyce continued his entrepreneurial bent when he and Gordon Moore cofounded Intel Corporation. Noyce was president of Intel until 1975, and Chairman of the Board of Intel from 1975 to 1979. Robert Noyce passed away on June 3, 1990.

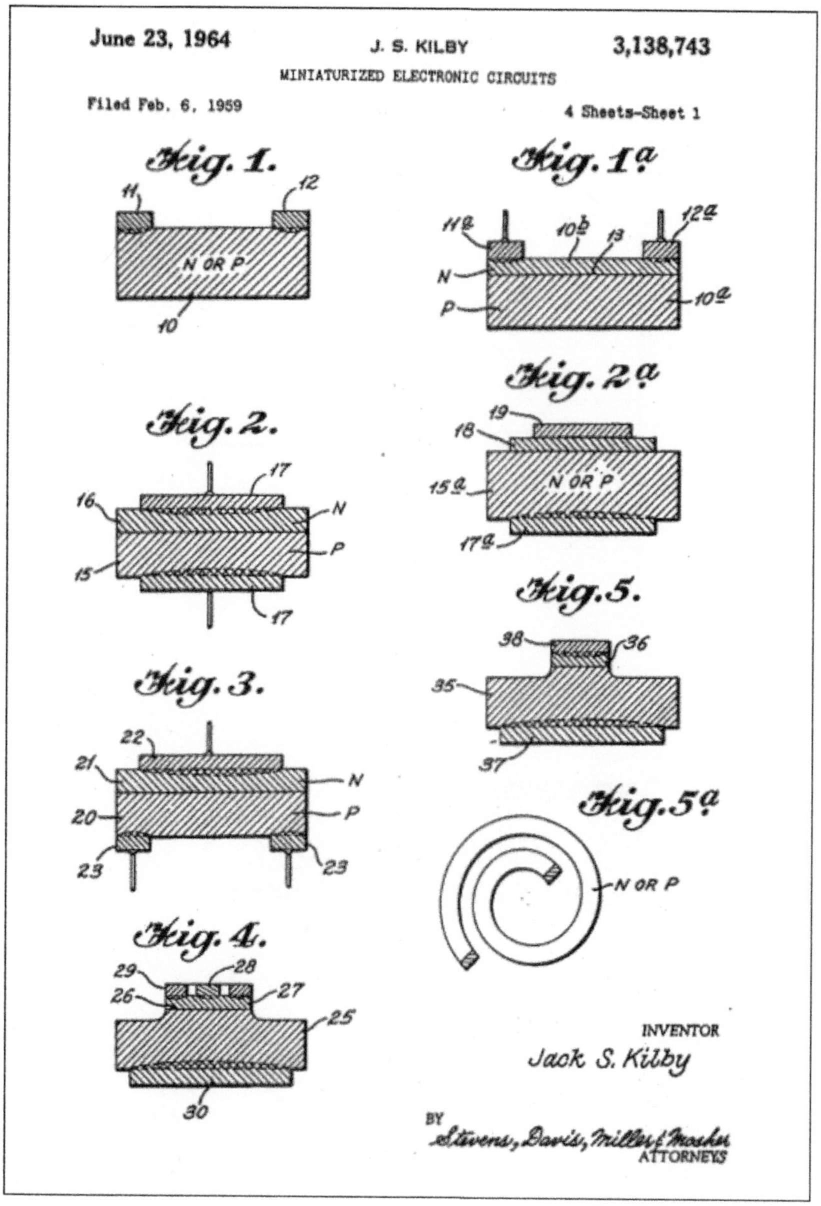
June 23, 1964
J. S. KILBY
3,138,743
MINIATURIZED ELECTRONIC CIRCUITS
Filed Feb. 6, 1959
4 Sheets-Sheet 1
Fig. 1.
N OR P
Fig. 1a
Fig. 2a
N OR P
Fig. 2.
Fig. 5.
Fig. 3.
Fig. 5a
N OR P
Fig. 4.
INVENTOR
Jack S. Kilby
BY
Stevens, Davis, Miller & Mosher
ATTORNEYS

April 25, 1961 R. N. NOYCE **2,981,877**

SEMICONDUCTOR DEVICE-AND-LEAD STRUCTURE

Filed July 30, 1959 3 Sheets-Sheet 1

FIG-1

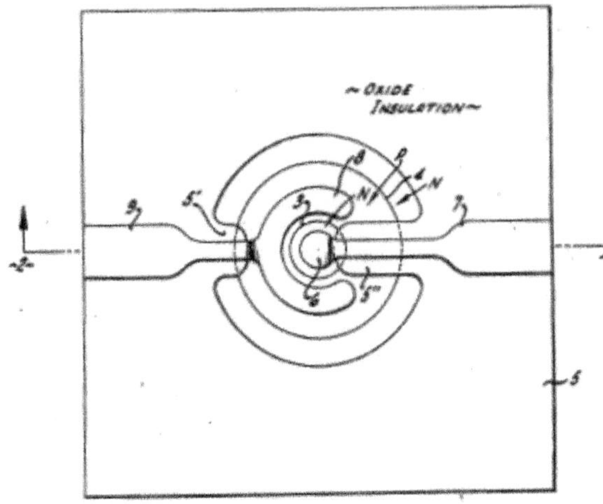

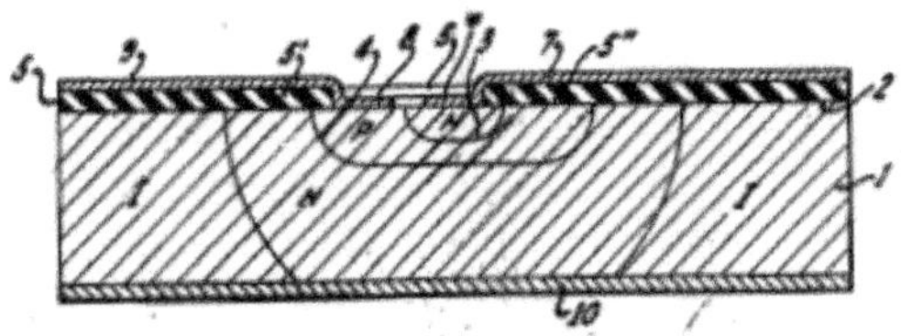

FIG-2

INVENTOR.
ROBERT N. NOYCE
BY Lippincott & Ralls
ATTORNEYS

24 Copyrights as a Vehicle for Technology Protection

24.1 A BRIEF HISTORY OF COPYRIGHT LAW

24.1.1 Pre-U.S. Constitution English Law

As the name of this aspect of intellectual property law implies, we are now dealing with the effect of "copying" the original, creative expression of the work of another. At this point, I'd like to pose a rhetorical question: When, in the scheme of civilized history, did the need for a copyright law arise? You each have a few moments to ponder this question. Now that the few moments are up, if you were thinking about the "copy" window on your computer, a DVR, or the use of xerographic copying machines, or an audio tape deck having two decks in tandem, or photography, your answers would have been close, but not quite on the mark. The answer is: The invention of the printing press with moveable type that could produce and reproduce massive amounts of printed material, by German inventor Johannes Gutenberg about the year 1454. This single invention is credited with the beginning of the dissemination of learning throughout the world, and the need for copyright laws.

Imagine that prior to the invention of the printing press, if you caught someone copying your secret, unpublished work, and tried to imprison them, the court would probably be faced with the problem of imprisoning a monk who was part of a religious order, and was copying your manuscript by hand. Also, prior to the invention of the printing press, how many duplicates of your manuscript could that monk make? Gutenberg's printing press, a hallmark invention in the progress of civilization and information technology, made works available to be copied and furnished to a wide audience. Copying on the new Gutenberg press could also be done relatively inexpensively, therefore providing a profit to whoever performed the copying. Consider also that under the common law in England prior to 1709, the author's rights in his/her manuscript were depleted once the manuscript was published, and there was no legal way to prevent the mass production of the work after it had been initially published and disseminated.

In 1556, the English Crown under Mary I placed all printing in the realm under its control. A group of publishers known as the Stationers' Company, formed as a guild in 1403, was granted exclusive rights under a royal charter to conduct printing. Those desiring to publish a work were necessarily required to approach the Stationers' Company, and no one else, who then granted the right to exclusively publish that work forever.

Intellectual Property Law for Engineers, Scientists, and Entrepreneurs, Second Edition. Howard B. Rockman.

Published 2020 by John Wiley & Sons, Inc.

However, these restrictions in England on printing ended at the end of the 17th century, and the members of the Stationers' Company found that this had cost them their exclusive publication rights. In response, they sought legislation from Parliament, and in 1709 Parliament enacted the Statute of Anne, 8 Anne c.19, "An act for the encouragement of learning by vesting the copies of printed books in the authors or purchasers of such copies, during the times therein mentioned." The purpose of the Act was to control the printing, reprinting and publishing of books and other writings with the consent of their authors or their owners, rather than the publisher, and to encourage learned men to compose and write useful books.

The Statute of Anne provided writers of new works the exclusive right to publish their works for 14 years, measured from the date of first publication. A second 14-year term would also vest in the author, if alive. Before enforcing these rights, the work was required to be registered and copies deposited at official libraries. Penalties were imposed upon those who unlawfully printed covered works without the authors' permission, and fines were assessed and books were destroyed. Research shows that no one was beheaded. At the advent of the American Revolution, the state of copyright law in England was as described above. As mentioned previously, the framers of the American Constitution adopted a provision to protect inventors and authors, which is the foundation for American Intellectual Property Law covering both copyrights and patents.

24.1.2 U.S. Constitution and Statutes

U.S. copyright law stems from the portion of the U.S. Constitutional provision relating to authors and their writings. Article I, Section 8. In Federalist Paper 43, James Madison described the aims of this particular clause of the Constitution as follows:

> "The utility of this power will scarcely be questioned. The copyright of authors has been solemnly judged in Great Britain, to be a right of common law. The right to useful invention seems with equal reason to belong to inventors. The public good fully coincides in both cases with the claims of individuals. The States cannot separately make effectual provision for either of these cases, and most of them have anticipated the decision of this point, by laws passed at the instance of Congress."

In 1790, the Congress of the United States passed the first Federal Copyright Statute. That statute granted protection to charts, books and maps for a term of 14 years. The term was non-renewable. As the industrial revolution steamed forward, and new technology was continually being brought to the forefront, Congress over a period of time extended the effective life of a copyright, and also brought additional subject matter under the jurisdiction of copyright protection. For example, new covered subject matter included prints (1802); musical compositions (1831); dramatic works (1856); photography works (1865); and the fine arts (1870).

In 1909, a comprehensive new U.S. copyright statute was enacted, and this statute remained in effect until 1976. The 1909 statute covered "all the writings of an author," in an effort to encompass any material that can be considered the work product of one who is an "author." However, since the law was enacted in 1909, and technology moved rapidly after that time with the advent of radio, television, computers, VCRs, CDs, DVDs, and other electronic devices, it became apparent that the 1909 act had to be revised.

Between the years 1955 to 1976, twenty-one years, the U.S. Congress wrestled with creating a new copyright act, which eventually became effective in 1976. It is interesting to note that in the year following enactment of that statute, VCRs hit the United States market, enabling anybody to tape a signal off of their television transmission, which was not directly covered in the 1976 law. It is also important to note that the Copyright Act of 1976 resulted from compromises between many diverse groups who lobbied their positions between the authors, publishers, and the users of copyrighted works. For example, should a doctor who is treating a rare disease be compelled to buy one or more volumes of books that relate to that disease, or merely call the National Institutes of Health Library in Bethesda, Maryland, and have NIH copy only the relevant pages of these texts? The Copyright Act established compromises for that type of duplication, as well as compromises relating to the use of copyrighted works in classroom study material and many other situations.

Moving backwards in time for a moment, following the American Revolution in 1776, many of the newly constituted states enacted copyright statutes, most resembling the English Statute of Anne. Some of the state statutes based the grant of exclusive rights to authors under their statutory power, while other states saw copyright as a "natural right" of the creator or author of the work. There was a lack of uniformity in these laws, and works that were disseminated across state lines at that time were not easily protected. This dilemma was solved when the Constitution placed copyright enactment and enforcement provisions exclusively in the hands of the newly formed Federal Government, to eliminate the diversity among the state laws.

As the copyright law evolved from 1790 in the United States, subsequent enactments have expanded the scope and protection of the copyright law by broadening the type of subject matter included under the law, and this usually came about in response to technological advancement. Subsequent legislation has also lengthened the term of copyright protection, which was under attack as I shall explain ahead, as well as broadening the array of exclusive rights that the copyright law encompasses.

Most importantly, the copyright law progression has reduced the formalities and other barriers to protection that were involved in earlier copyright laws, and today the adherence by the U.S. to the Berne Convention for the Protection of Literary and Artistic Works (the "Berne Convention") provides a truly internationalization of copyright protection. Whereas patent and trademark protection must be obtained in each of the countries in which you desire protection, your copyright is now created automatically upon fixation of the work in a tangible medium of expression, and your copyright is enforceable in all of the countries signatory to the Berne Convention. My prediction is that following the lead of the Berne Convention, ultimately there may be an international patent and trademark. However, as previously noted, that is still a work in process.

The adherence of the United States to the Berne Convention began on March 1, 1989, and congress made significant changes in the U.S. Copyright Act. The most significant of these changes was the elimination of the requirement that a notice be placed on all copyrighted works to secure copyright. Therefore, prior to 1989, everyone was accustomed to seeing the copyright notice with a familiar © in a circle and the year, and sometimes the word "Copyright," or the words "All Rights Reserved." However, such notice is no longer required under United States law. The 1976 Copyright Act also eliminated the renewal term in favor of a single term for copyrights measured then in the life of the author plus 50 years for works created by individuals.

In 1980, Congress also amended the definition of "literary works" to ensure that the copyright law included computer programs, to address the problem of copying of software. In 1990 Congress protected the commercial rental of computer software. In 1992, Congress clarified that audio taping strictly for home use was legal, while a royalty had to be imposed on the sale of digital recording media and devices. Congress also required such devices to embody controls against copying to prevent serial copying of digital works. In 1995, Congress enacted a public performance right for a limited purpose for sound recordings played by digital subscription services. In 1989, Congress passed the Digital Millennium Copyright Act, discussed in Chapter 25. Congress has also enacted other changes to the copyright laws, which are rather extensive and complicated, and I will leave it to other professional resources to furnish you with information about such changes as the need arises in your careers.

24.2 THE NATURE OF COPYRIGHTS

24.2.1 What a Copyright Is, and Is Not

Understanding what a copyright is, and is not, is a difficult concept to grasp. However, we will move forward and I will try to enlighten you on this very arcane subject. Of all the intellectual property rights, however, copyright is the one that is more "in your face" than any of the other laws. Every time you pick up a book, read a newspaper, see a billboard, listen to music, watch television or a movie, VHS tape, or DVD, or download content to your electronic device, you are involved in the vast scheme of copyright law protection.

In its most simplistic of terms, the copyright is the right of an author to control the reproduction of the expression embodied in his or her intellectual creation. Intellectual creations can take many forms, as I will discuss shortly. It is quite apparent that whenever a work of an author is disclosed to the public, it then becomes possible for the public to reproduce that work. Every one of you know how easy it is to duplicate content from a software disc or an online app. Copying machines have been around for approximately 70 years that enable you to copy almost any document. The copyright law is a legal device granting the author or creator of the work the right to control reproduction of his/her work after the work has been fixed in a tangible medium of expression.

An important precept to remember is that copyright does not preclude others from using the information or ideas that are embodied in the author's work. Copyright protection pertains only to the form in which the author expresses the creative and intellectual concepts. Thus, the copyright law is designed to prevent the public from copying the author's expression, while anyone is free to evolve their own expression of the same concepts, or to use the expressions of the author, so long as there are no copies made. For example, if I wanted to write a story about an obsessive sea captain chasing a great white whale, I could do so, so long as I did not copy any or all of the passages from Herman Melville's classic *Moby Dick*, presuming copyright protection for the book had not expired.

24.2.2 Intangible Rights in a Work Embodied in a Tangible Medium of Expression

Copyright, as the patent right, is a unique type of intangible right. Thus, to be effectively protected, the author's intellectual and creative work must be embodied in a tangible medium of expression, such as a manuscript, a book, a painting or sculpture, a record, a film or even a digital disc or tape. These tangible articles containing and embodying the work may ultimately be distributed to many persons other than the copyright owner, and these persons may use the work for their own enjoyment. However, the copyright law restrains the one in possession of that work from reproducing that work without the owner's consent.

To provide you with a better understanding of this concept of the nature of copyrights, visualize if you would the original physical tangible copy of an authors work, such as a written work, software, music, painting, sculpture, words to a song, a dance or any other material that fits within the realm of covered copyrightable works. Imagine also, hovering over that tangible work are several intangible rights of copyright provided by the Federal Copyright system. The mere act of creation of a completed copyrightable work in a tangible medium of expression instantly creates these intangible rights of copyright that are owned by the author of the work. As I will discuss, the "author" could be the creator him or herself, or could be the employer of the creator.

As soon as the work is fixed in a tangible medium of expression, the copyright laws automatically come into play. For example, fixing an electronic program on a CD, disc or hard drive is considered as fixing that program in a tangible medium of expression. Thus, once the work is reduced to writing or recorded on a tape or canvas or block of granite or film or a phonograph or on a CD or a hard drive, the Federal Copyright Act automatically applies and the intangible rights of copyright are created in the author.

24.2.3 Moral Rights

A quick word on "moral rights." In the United States, the legal commentators generally agree that the U.S. Copyright Act is founded on property rights. However, in some European countries, commentators have characterized the copyright as the personal right of the author, or even as a combination of personal and property rights. An author's intellectual creation, such commentators say, has the stamp of his or her personality and is identified with that author. But these rights also can be assigned to other persons and survive after the author's death. Thus, they are a unique kind of personal rights, since personal rights usually expire as the author expires.

You usually find in the copyright laws of European and other countries provisions for protecting the "moral rights" of authors. These are intended to protect the author against certain acts that may injure their personal identity or reputation. In some countries, the author has the right under the moral right provisions to have his or her name appear on all copies of the work, to prevent the attribution of him or her to another persons work, and to prevent reproduction of his work in a distorted or degrading form. In some countries the moral rights survive the authors' death and may be enforced by his/her heirs.

In the United States, the moral rights of authors have never been treated as an attribute of copyright. However, authors in this country have been given much the same protection of their personal rights under general principles of the common law, such as those relating to unfair competition, misrepresentation and defamation. California has a specific statute that prevents one from using the name of a deceased movie star for profitable uses without permission from the decedent's estate.

24.2.4 Protecting the Balance Between the Public and the Author

It must be kept in mind that one of the primary purposes of the copyright law is to engender the creation and dissemination of intellectual works for the public welfare. The opposing balancing factor in the copyright law is to provide authors the reward due to them for their contributions to society, and to encourage authors to create more works of benefit to society. Authors, like all of us, could not devote themselves to their creative efforts without knowing that they may be remunerated for such efforts. By providing authors with a vehicle for securing the economic reward afforded by the marketplace, the copyright law stimulates the creation and dissemination of intellectual works. Also, copyright protection allows publishers and other distributors to invest their resources in making the works of the creators available to the public.

One of the important aspects of copyright law is to allow certain material to remain in the public domain, such as ideas, facts and generic forms of expression that may be required for authors in the future to create their own new and intelligent works. Thus, new authors must be able to rely upon pre-existing forms of expression in creating their new works. When developing a new work, an author usually refers to certain works that preceded his/her new work to incorporate, and to some extent, the ideas and facts set forth in the pre-existing work. For example, the writer of a play may base their characters on characters drawn from real human beings, or on other playwrights' characters, as the controversy several years ago over the *Gone With the Wind* characters appearing in a subsequent book proved. Authors of novels usually draw their information from their own experiences, or from plots and facts within other materials. Also, software authors use the logic in programming in previous software programs. This is not considered piracy today; this is considered creatorship. Thus, the copyright law as enacted by Congress must draw a balance between providing incentives to create from material already in the public domain and provide the widest access to such material, and on the other hand provide a system that will reward authors so they may extend their efforts towards creating new copyrightable works to advance knowledge.

You may often hear the argument that the copyright law may intrude into the exercise of free speech and free press under the Constitution. However, the copyright law does not stop one from copying or making use of another's ideas, it merely prohibits the unauthorized copying of the expression of those ideas by the first author. Additionally, fair use defenses (covered below) set forth in the copyright law, and other specific exemptions to liability, give the public wide latitude to use an author's expression when the First Amendment may be in conflict.

24.2.5 Requirements of Copyrightable Subject Matter

To be copyrightable, the law requires that the subject matter be original, and that it be fixed in a tangible medium of expression. These standards for copyrightability are much lower than the standards for obtaining a patent. Also, note that to obtain a patent, you must file a patent application with the United States Patent and Trademark Office, and that application goes through vigorous examination. However, under the U.S. Copyright Act, your copyright is effective automatically, as a matter of law, as soon as your work of authorship is fixed in a tangible medium of expression, such as a book manuscript, a canvas for a painting, or a digital disc containing a program, movie, sound or other material. Your copyright exists whether or not you have applied for a copyright registration. However, in the United States you must have been granted a copyright registration before you can enforce your copyright in court. In those situations in the United States where you do apply for a copyright registration, the application is examined for compliance with registration requirements, but the work referenced in the application is not compared to other works to verify originality.

Also, the protection afforded by copyright is lower than that afforded by a patent. As the first four letters of the word copyright indicate, your copyright only protects against copying. If someone else independently creates your same work, there is no infringement. In other words, the copyright law prevents someone else from copying your particular method of expression of your ideas or facts, while giving no protection to the ideas or facts themselves.

The requirement of "originality" is met by most works, so long as they embody some creative effort, and are not merely copies or plagiarism. There are some instances where works that are created by an author or creator fail to meet the originality requirement, especially if the work consists of factual, historical information or previously published material. However, compilations of factual or historical information, even the telephone directory, are susceptible to copyright protection as new "compilations" of material.

The "originality" requirement is exemplified in one of my own personal life experiences. Many years ago I conceived of printing coffee mugs with a tart quotation from the immortal bard, William Shakespeare. The quote: "The first thing we do, let's kill all the lawyers!" from the play *2 Henry VI,* Act IV, Scene II. The expression appeared in a conversation relating to two characters' plot to overthrow the Crown, and they expressed their feeling that lawyers could interfere with their evil plot. Thus, the expression is a compliment to the lawyers of Shakespeare's time.

I filed an application to register my coffee mug/expression combination for copyright protection. The application was refused since the expression was not original to me, and neither were my coffee mugs. I continued to sell the mugs, however, without protection.

Ownership and transfer of the original physical copy of a copyrightable work are covered by state concepts of contract law. However, the federal Copyright Act governs the ownership, transfer and protection of the intangible rights of copyright that flow from the creation and fixation of the original work in a tangible medium of expression. For example, the federal Copyright Act controls who may inherit rights of renewal in certain copyrightable works created prior to 1976. When music previously written by a deceased person is subject to copyright renewal, arguments arise as to who has the right of renewal. I have personally been through such matters, and they are extremely complex.

24.3 EXCLUSIVE RIGHTS OF COPYRIGHT

When someone purchases an original physical copy of an authors work, such as an original painting, or a lithograph, or a book, the purchaser will have the right to look at, privately display, and enjoy the painting or lithograph, or to read the book. If the work is a piece of music, the purchaser will be able to play and listen to the music for his or her own enjoyment. However, unless the purchaser also purchased the intangible rights of copyright in that work, the purchaser does not have the right to make copies of the work, to reproduce the work or to use the work to prepare derivative works, or to distribute copies of the work to the public. The purchaser does not even have the right to publicly display the work except under certain conditions, such as at home.

The rights obtained under copyright are exclusionary in nature; they allow the copyright owner certain exclusive rights with respect to the work and the right to prevent others from engaging in those activities. The Federal Copyright Act, at Section 106, gives the owner of the copyright five intangible exclusive rights:

1. The exclusive right to copy or reproduce the work;
2. The exclusive right to prepare derivative works based upon the original work;
3. The exclusive right to distribute copies of the work to the public by sale or other transfer of ownership, or by rent, lease, lending or license;
4. The exclusive right to perform the work publicly if the work is a literary, musical, dramatic, choreographic, audio visual work, a pantomime or motion picture; and
5. The exclusive right to display the work publicly.

This bundle of rights can be licensed to others in one fell swoop, or can be broken up and each right can be sold or licensed independently of the others. For example, the owner of the copyright in a literary work, such as a novel, can license a publishing house to publish the book, and then issue a second license to a movie studio to make the movie. A third license can be granted to present the book in segments over the Internet, and a fourth to create a stage drama or musical adaptation of the novel.

Once the copyright owner has sold a copy of a work, unless specifically provided otherwise in the contract of sale, there is no limitation on certain of the buyer's rights to "use" the work. For example, when a copyrighted novel or software is sold to a buyer, the buyer can use the work by reading it as many times as he or she wishes, or the buyer can sell, lease or rent that specific copy of the work to another, or the owner may even mutilate and destroy the work. However, the user cannot copy the work. The same is true of copyrighted drawings, manuals, or the product literature of a company which is sold to third parties without any specific limitations on how the third parties may use the works. A competitor of a company producing product literature cannot copy the product literature of another in advertising its own products.

24.4 FAIR USE

There is one important limitation or carve-out on the exclusive rights granted to the copyright owner. This is known as the doctrine of "fair use," which are acts of copying that are not considered an infringement of the copyright of the creator or copyright owner. The "fair use" moniker is somewhat confusing since the doctrine allows fair "copying." One who legally obtains a copyrighted work can "use" that work in any legitimate way, but can make copies only if such copying is "fair."

The "fair use" doctrine was long a part of court-developed law, and was codified by Congress in Section 107 of the Copyright Act of 1976 (17 U.S.C. §107). The Copyright Act sets forth certain examples of copying that can take place without constituting an infringing act. These examples can be extrapolated by courts to other equivalent situations in determining fair use copying on a case-by-case basis.

Section 107 of the Copyright Act states that making a copy of a protected work for purposes such as criticism, comment, news reporting, teaching (including multiple copies for classroom use), scholarship or research does not constitute an infringement of the copyright. The law also sets out certain factors to be considered when the fair use doctrine is applied. The factors given by way of example in the statute are as follows:

1. Consideration of the purpose and character of the use, such as whether the use is commercial, or is it for a non-profit educational purpose;
2. The nature of the copyrighted work;
3. The amount and substantially of the portion used in relation to the copyrighted work as a whole; and
4. The effect of the use upon the potential market for, or value of, the copyrighted work.

Note that these factors are only examples. For instance, making one copy of a video tape of a movie for your home use is considered fair use. If you try to sell that copy or other copies you made from the original work or from your copy, that would constitute an infringement of the copyright.

In one famous case, the U.S. Supreme Court noted that the question of when, where and how a work was to be initially published were important decisions reserved to the author of a protected work. As a result, the court held that the publication of excepts of President Gerald Ford's memoirs in the *Nation* magazine, prior to their scheduled publication in *Time* magazine, constituted copyright infringement, and was not a fair use.

The determination of what constitutes fair use varies from case to case. The most important factor is the effect of the use of the work on the commercial market for the original work. Since the purpose of the Copyright Law is to provide incentives for authors to create, usages which adversely impact the commercial market for the author's work are viewed as frustrating the intent of the Copyright Law and are not considered fair use. Thus the parameters of fair use are narrowed when the use of a copyrighted work is commercial.

For the application of principles akin to fair use, see Chapter 25 covering the Digital Millennium Copyright Act of 1998.

24.5 INFRINGEMENT OF A COPYRIGHT

It is often difficult to prove the act of copying, since the copying by the alleged infringer may have taken place in a darkened room with no one else around but the copier. However, circumstantial or non-direct evidence can be relied upon to prove the act of copying. Under present court decisions, the circumstantial evidence required to support a finding of infringement is: a) that the alleged infringer had access to the copyrighted work, and b) the infringing work is substantially similar to the copyrighted work. Normally, detailed expert testimony is presented to establish the substantial similarity of works involved in a copyright infringement lawsuit.

24.6 NOTICE

For many, many years up until March 1, 1989, the U.S. Copyright Act required the placement of a statutory notice, such as the letter © in a circle, and the date of first publication on all publicly distributed protected works to advise the public of the existence of the copyright owner's rights. Normally you would also see "All Rights Reserved" on a work to satisfy the requirements of a treaty known as the Buenos Aires Convention, which is a treaty to which the United States and several Latin American countries belong. However, most countries, such as the European countries and other English speaking countries belonged to other treaty arrangements, which did not require this additional phrase or any copyright notice at all. One such treaty is the Berne Convention to which the United States became an adherent in 1989. The Berne Convention dates back to 1886, and includes approximately 80 countries within its bounds. To conform to the Berne Convention, the U.S. Congress passed a law that as of March 1, 1989, the long-standing U.S. requirement of the copyright notice for works published after March 1, 1989 was abolished. The act defines the term "publication" as the distribution of copies of the work to the public by sale, rental, lease, lending or license. However, there are many, many copyrighted works that presently exist that were published before March 1, 1989, and the prior laws regarding notice as to works published before that date are still in effect.

This author recommends that applying a notice to your copyrightable work is still a good idea. Sections 401–406 of the U.S. Copyright Act provide that authors who place a notice of copyright on their works obtain advantages when enforcing their copyrights. For example, if the defendant in a copyright infringement lawsuit had access to your work with notice applied, no weight is given to a defense of innocent infringement in mitigation of actual or statutory damages, except in limited non-profit and public broadcast "fair use" instances.

24.7 COPYRIGHT REGISTRATION AND ITS IMPORTANCE

The U.S. Copyright Act provides that at any time during the existence of a copyright, the owner of the copyright in the work may obtain a federal registration of its copyright claim by applying to the Copyright Office, paying the requisite fee, and making the required deposit of the work to be protected along with the application. No legal action in the courts for infringement of a work created in the United States can be taken until the owner of the copyright has obtained copyright registration. However, as to works originated outside of the United States, no registration is required to bring an action for infringement of the copyright in that work in the U.S. courts.

The U.S. Copyright Act provides "statutory damages" for infringement. This is applied where actual damages are minimal; statutory damages usually are sufficient to prevent an infringer from getting away with a minor slap on the wrist. The Copyright Act also provides that an infringer is liable for either the copyright owner's actual damages and any additional profits of the infringer, or statutory damages. Thus, the copyright laws are strict, in that an infringer could pay the copyright owner's actual damages and, in addition to that, the actual profits of the infringer. Statutory damages are defined as not less than $500 or more than $20,000 as the court considers just for each infringing work. If the court finds that the infringement was willful or purposeful, the court may increase the award of statutory damages to the sum of not more than $100,000 for each infringing work.

It is important that registration under the federal Copyright Act be sought within three months after first publication of the work, since no award of statutory damages or of attorney's fees may be made for infringement of copyrighted works commenced after the first publication date and before the effective date of the registration, unless the registration is made within three months of the first publication.

24.8 THE DURATION OF INTANGIBLE RIGHTS OF COPYRIGHT

Since copyrights cannot be granted in perpetuity, the Copyright Act grants rights which expire after a certain time period. On October 27, 1998, the Sonny Bono Copyright Term Extension Act was signed into law in the U.S. effectively extending the life of copyright rights for an additional 20 years compared to the terms established in the previous 1976 act. Specific provisions are:

1. For works created after January 1, 1978, copyright protection endures for the life of the author plus an additional 70 years. For a joint work, the term is 70 years after the last survivor's death. For anonymous and pseudonymous works, and works for hire such as where the owner of a copyright is a corporation or entity other than a natural person, the term is 95 years from the year of first publication or 120 years from the year of creation, whichever expires first.
2. For works created but not published or registered before January 1, 1978, the term is the life of the author plus 70 years, but in no case will such copyright expire earlier than December 31, 2002. If the work is published before December 31, 2002, the term of copyright will not expire before December 31, 2047.
3. For works created prior to 1978 which are still in their original or renewal term of copyright, the total term is extended to 95 years from the date that copyright was originally obtained.

Take, for example, the first "publication" of the Mickey Mouse character in the cartoon film *Steamboat Willie* in 1928, which was an adaptation of an earlier Buster Keaton movie *Steamboat Bill, Jr.* Without copyright extension as enacted in 1998, Mickey's copyright would have entered the public domain in 2004. However, he is now protected until 2024.

The 1998 copyright term extension law was originally opposed by public domain advocates, such as internet publishers and certain academics, and resulted in a lawsuit challenging the authority of Congress to grant "limited" rights in copyright that now extend for generations in some circumstances. However, on January 15, 2003, the U.S. Supreme Court, in the case of *Eldred v. Ashcroft,* No. 01-618, held in a 7-2 decision that Congress had not exceeded its authority under the patent/copyright clause of the U.S. Constitution. The Court held that it was not deciding whether extending copyrights for so long a time was or was not a good idea when balancing the rights of authors and creators against the public's unfettered right to eventually use such writings and creations. The Court instead decided the case on the grounds that the wisdom of Congress' action was not within the province of the Supreme Court to second guess, and that: "It is Congress that has been assigned the task [under the Constitution] of defining the scope of the limited monopoly that should be granted to authors to give the public appropriate access to their work product."

Additional provisions in the Sonny Bono law cover specific situations, such as sound recordings made prior to February 15, 1972, presumption of an author's death, and the like. Note however, that this law does not restore copyright protection to any works that have previously fallen into the public domain, except certain foreign created works.

After the copyright expires, anyone can slavishly copy the work. For example, if one could lawfully obtain access to an original Rembrandt painting in the museum, since the rights of copyright have expired, one could photograph the painting, creating a derivative work, and then sell the photographic copies. For this reason, many museums are very careful to whom they loan their paintings, and may prohibit their patrons from photographing the works.

24.9 WORKS MADE FOR HIRE

The individual who creates a work is deemed to be the "author" of the work and is the initial owner of all copyrights. There are two situations where another entity is the author of the work, both exceptions being referred to as "works made for hire."

The first exception is where the work was created in the course and scope of employment of the creator. In that situation, the employer is deemed to be "the author" of the work and is the owner of all rights of copyright. Note however, that the various federal courts have reached somewhat different results recently as to when certain persons are to be considered an "employee" for purposes of the copyright laws. For example, if the author has an independent contractual relationship with the person who commissioned the work, that may affect the outcome of copyright ownership.

The second exception occurs when the individual who creates the work was commissioned to create the work on an independent contractor basis for one of nine specified purposes, *and* a written contract is signed by the independent contractor stating that the work is made for hire. The nine specified purposes are:

1. A contribution to a collective work;
2. A part of a motion picture or other audio/visual work;
3. A translation;
4. A supplementary work;
5. A compilation;
6. An instructional text;
7. A test;
8. Answer material for a test; and
9. An atlas.

The present version of the Copyright Act provides that the sale or transfer of the physical object upon which copyrights are based does not in and of itself transfer any of the intangible rights of copyright. The only way to effect a valid transfer of the copyright is by a written document signed by the owner of the rights conveyed, or his or her duly authorized agent.

By way of example, if an individual employed by a company creates a copyrightable work during employment, the company is deemed to be the author of the work and is the owner of the physical work as well as the exclusive rights of copyright in that work. Thus, the company would have the right to prepare derivative works, to make copies of the work, to distribute those copies and otherwise license the work. The employee retains none of those rights. However, where the employee creates a work outside the scope and course of his or her employment, the employee is deemed to be the author and the initial owner of all the exclusive rights of copyright. If the individual used the company's time, facilities and/or materials to create his or her unrelated copyrightable work, the company has a right to use the ideas embodied in the work. However, the company will not have the right to reproduce or market the form of expression embodied in the copyrighted work owned by the employee.

A common situation occurs where a corporation commissions or hires a professional photographer to photograph the corporation's goods for use in a catalog. The photographer provides the corporation with the negatives. If the contract included the magic words "work made for hire," the company would own all rights in the negatives and the photographs. However, if those magic words or their equivalent were not utilized in the contract, and the photographs did not fall within any of the nine specified uses provided in the Copyright Act under the work made for hire definition, since the photographer is not an employee of the corporation, and the photographer is deemed to be the "author" of the works, the corporation will not have the right to reproduce the works or use the negatives to create additional works without the approval of the photographer. Believe it or not, this happens over and over again in the trade. During my career as a practicing attorney, I have run into this situation several times. This problem can be solved by placing language in the agreement with the photographer that all works he creates during his engagement are "works made for hire" or a similar provision.

24.10 COPYRIGHT REGISTRATION FOR COMPUTER PROGRAMS

The U.S. Copyright Act defines a computer program as a set of statements or instructions to be used directly or indirectly in a computer to bring about a certain result. Copyright protection extends to all of the original copyrightable expression embodied in a computer program. However, keep in mind that your protection extends to all copyrightable expression embodied in a tangible form in the computer program, but does not cover the ideas, program logic, algorithms, systems, methods, concepts or layouts in the program.

The author of a computer program is the one who creates the computer program itself, the entire text of the program, the entire program code, the text of the user's manual, etc. If your computer program contains a substantial amount of previously published, registered or public domain material, such as sub-routines, modules, text or images, or if the work was developed using an underlying computer program or authorized tool, your work is known in copyright parlance as a "derivative work" or a "compilation." Derivative works and compilations are copyrightable under the U.S. Copyright Act to the author who prepared the derivative work. When obtaining registration of a derivative work, pre-existing work is identified in the application for registration.

To obtain the full benefits of registration, each individually published version of a computer program must be separately registered, provided each contains a sufficient amount of new or revised authorship to sustain a claim to copyright. If the deposit material accompanying the application for the computer program does not provide a printed title and/or version indicator, the title and any indicia that appropriately identifies the particular program must be added.

24.10.1 Protecting Computer Programs That Do Not Contain Trade Secrets

If the computer program you are attempting to protect under a copyright registration does not contain any trade secret material, the copyright application filed with the Copyright Office will be accompanied by transmitting a "deposit" of one copy of identifying portions of the program. This is accomplished by furnishing the first 25 and last 25 pages of the source code, reproduced in a form visually perceptible without the aid of a machine or device, either on paper or in microform, together with the page or equivalent unit containing the copyright notice, if a copyright notice has been applied. For programs less than 50 pages in length, the application must be accompanied by a visually perceptible copy of the entire source code. If the program is so structured that it has no identifiable beginning or end, the copyright applicant makes a determination as to which pages of the source code reasonably represent the first 25 and last 25 pages.

By now, several of you may have undergone a case of apoplexy when I mentioned that the source code had to be furnished to the Copyright Office, because materials furnished to the Copyright Office become publicly available, and many, if not all programmers have no desire to reveal their source code. Therefore, the Copyright Office provides that where an applicant for registration is unable or unwilling to deposit the source code, the object code may be furnished instead. However, the applicant must state in writing that the work as deposited in object code contains copyrightable authorship. The Copyright Office will then send a letter to the applicant stating that registration has been made under its rule of doubt, and warning that the existence of copyrightable authorship has not been determined.

If a published user's manual or other printed documentation accompanies a computer program copyright application, one copy of the user's manual is also deposited with the copyright application, along with one copy of the identifying material for the program, which comprises either the requisite pages of the source code or the object code.

For programs written in HyperCard® and other scripted languages, the script is considered the equivalent of source code. Thus, the same number of pages of script would be required as are required when submitting a source code. Note that reproductions of onscreen text, buttons and commands are not an appropriate substitute for the source code deposit.

24.10.2 Computer Programs Containing Trade Secrets

The Copyright Office has also provided for the registration and deposit of copyrightable material in software programs that contain trade secret material which the applicant desires to maintain in secret. Thus, where a computer program contains trade secret material, the copyright applicant is instructed to include a cover letter with the application stating that the copyrightable work contains trade secrets, along with the page containing the copyright notice if any, plus one of the following:

24.10.2.1 Entirely New Computer Programs

Submit the first 25 and last 25 pages of source code with portions containing trade secrets blocked out, or the first 10 and last 10 pages of the source code alone with no blocked-out portions, or the first 25 and last 25 pages of object code plus any 10 or more consecutive pages of source code, with no blocked out portions. For programs 50 pages or less in length, the entire source code with trade secret portions blocked out must be submitted.

24.10.2.2 Revised Computer Programs

If revisions to a revised computer program are present in the first 25 and last 25 pages, any one of the four options above is appropriate for the deposit requirement with the copyright application. If the revisions are not present in the first 25 and the last 25 pages, the applicant must submit either 20 pages of source code containing the revisions with no blocked-out portions, or any 50 pages of source code containing the revisions with portions blocked out.

The Copyright Office requires that when filing such applications, the blocked out portions must be proportionally less than the material remaining, and the visible portion must represent an appreciable amount of original computer code.

24.10.3 Screen Displays

The Copyright Office has consistently held a position that a single registration is sufficient to protect the copyright in a computer program and the related screen displays, including video games, without a separate registration for the screen displays or a specific reference to them in the application to register the computer program. By defining the description of the nature of authorship in the application as an "entire work," or as a "computer program," such description will cover any copyrightable authorship contained in the computer program and screen displays, regardless of whether identifying material for the screen is deposited. A specific copyright claim in the screen displays may be asserted in the application, and in such case, identifying materials for the screens must then be deposited with the application.

However, a copyright registration covering a two-dimensional technical drawing created by a computer aided design (CAD) program does not protect the CAD file itself. A separate registration must be obtained directed to the CAD file.

In certain cases, the "look and feel" of the screen display or audio/visual images created by the computer program can be covered by copyright, such as the audio/visual works produced by video games. In addition, the copyrightability of the screens and the flow of screens through a program has been upheld.

24.10.4 Special Rules for Copyrighting Software

There are a few special rules for copyright in software. For example, someone who owns a copy of a computer program can make another copy or adaptation of the program if the new copy is created as an essential step in utilization of the computer program in connection with a machine, and is used in no other manner. This happens, for example, when a program on a CD-ROM is loaded into a computer. A copy can also be made if the new copy is for archival (back-up) purposes only, provided all archival copies are destroyed if continued possession of the computer program is no longer authorized. The archival copies do not have to be destroyed if they are leased, sold or otherwise transferred along with the copy from which the archival copies were prepared, as part of the transaction. However, adaptions so prepared may only be transferred with the authorization of the copyright owner.

It is also legal to make a copy of a computer program if the copy is made solely by virtue of the activation of a machine that contains an authorized copy of the program, for purposes only of maintenance or repair of that machine. However, the new copy cannot be used in any other manner and must be destroyed immediately after the maintenance or repair is completed. If any part of the computer program is not necessary for the machine to be activated, that part cannot be accessed or used other than to make the new copy by virtue of the activation of the machine.

Another unusual aspect of the Copyright Act is that someone who owns a lawful copy of a computer program cannot rent, lease or lend the program without permission of the copyright owner, although the software can be sold outright. There are exceptions to this rule, though. For example, a nonprofit library or nonprofit educational institution can rent, lease or lend copies of software to its faculty, staff and students. However, nonprofit libraries can only lend computer programs for nonprofit purposes by placing a warning on each copy of the computer program that is lent. This rule does not apply to computer programs embedded in a machine or product which cannot be copied during the ordinary operation or use of the machine or product. It also does not apply to computer programs embodied in or used in conjunction with a limited purpose computer designed for playing video games. This allows video games to be purchased by a retailer and then rented to the retailer's customers.

24.10.5 Patent, Copyright, and Trade Secret Protection of Computer Software

As gleaned from the material in this text, both patents and copyright registrations are available to protect the unlawful duplication and copying of computer software. Although patents usually provide stronger intellectual property rights, patents are normally more costly and possibly more difficult to obtain than copyright registrations. The Patent Law requires a full disclosure of the best mode of carrying out the steps in the computer program invention as they were contemplated by the inventor. In contrast, as stated above, copyright registration is available for software where the owner prefers aspects of the software to remain secret.

Keep in mind that unlike patents, copyrights only provide protection from copying, and not independent creation of a same or similar work. Also, in most countries throughout the world, copyright protection is automatically available whenever a work is created in a tangible form. This contrasts with the Patent Law, where protection does not arise until the examination process in the U.S. or foreign Patent and Trademark Office has been completed and the patent has been issued by a governmental body. Also, copyright registration must take place within three months after the first publication of the work to provide the full range of remedies under the U.S. Copyright Act. By using the methods described above where trade secret material is blocked out, the owner of a computer program can obtain meaningful copyright protection without revealing any trade secrets that are embedded in the program.

Deposit material is sent to the Copyright Office as a means of subsequently identifying the work covered by the copyright certificate if the copyright registration is being enforced in litigation. When you obtain a certificate of registration from the Copyright Office, the work that was deposited with the Copyright Office does not accompany that registration, and certain deposits of works are ultimately destroyed. Therefore, the registration certificate must contain sufficient information to allow the proper identification of the work covered by the certificate.

24.10.6 Contracts and "Shrink-Wrap" and "Click" Licenses

Software copying can also be prevented through the use of an arm's length agreement entered into between the producer and purchaser of software. The agreement can clearly state the limits on use and prohibitions against disclosure and reverse engineering of the software by the purchaser, that making copies except for backup is prohibited, and proscribe the penalties, monetary and injunctive, if the terms of the agreement are breached. This type of arrangement is particularly useful for the sale of custom software for use on sizable computer networks.

In the case of mass-marketed software, a written signed agreement between producer and buyer is not practical. Many software publishers sell or license their software through a so-called "shrink-wrap" license. A typical shrink-wrap license provides that by opening the cellophane packaging surrounding the program and removing the contents, the customer accepts the terms of the software provider written on or in the package. Typical shrink-wrap licenses specify that uses otherwise permissible under copyright law, or at least considered a "fair use," are not allowed by the purchaser under the contract, such as using the same software on a second computer owned by the same purchaser.

Several state courts have held shrink-wrap licenses enforceable. In similar fashion, on-screen agreements are normally embedded in software programs that are displayed during installation. The user must click to "accept" these terms in order to proceed with the installation. This is sometimes referred to as a "click" license. Legend has it that no one bothers to read these terms when they appear, however, if you are a frequent user of new software programs, and you occasionally "manipulate" a program or two, it may be wise to stop and read the agreement terms the next time one pops into view. I have no doubt that you will be held to these terms if an issue of misuse arises, even though you may not have bothered to read the terms.

24.11 COPYRIGHT REGISTRATION FOR AUTOMATED DATABASES

The Copyright Office defines an automated database as a body of facts, data, or other information assembled into an organized format suitable for use in a computer and comprising one or more files. The Copyright Act does not specifically enumerate databases as copyrightable subject matter, however the Copyright Office has determined that the legislative history of the Copyright Act indicates that Congress considered computer databases and compilations of data as "literary works" that were subject to copyright protection. Thus, databases may be considered copyrightable as a form of compilation, which is a work formed by the collection and assembling of pre-existing materials or of data that is selected, coordinated, or arranged in such a way that the resulting work as a whole constitutes an original work of authorship. Thus, a compilation of pre-existing data is eligible for copyright protection, where the compilation represents original authorship.

The Copyright Act distinguishes between "published" and "unpublished" works. Here is one of those situations where the Copyright Act and its definitions may be outdone by the very nature of cyberspace. The Copyright Act defines publication as "the distribution of copies or phonorecords of a work to the public by sale or other transfer of ownership, or by rental, lease or lending." Also, the offering to distribute copies of a work to a group of persons for purposes of further distribution, public performance or public display constitutes publication. The Copyright Office has made a positive determination that it is "unclear" whether online availability, with or without printers for the user, constitutes publication of a work. Thus it is left up to the copyright owner to determine whether their particular database is "published" or not.

Registration for copyright protection covering an automated database is accomplished using a single copyright application, making a deposit with the Copyright Office, and paying the appropriate filing fee. Automated databases may be registered in either one of two ways:

1. As a single basic registration covering the database as published on a given date, or if unpublished, as created on a given date; or
2. As a group registration for a database with its updates or revisions (or for only its updates/revisions) added over a period of time, whether or not they are published, but only if certain conditions are met. These conditions are available from the Copyright Office, or a copyright professional.

24.12 COPYRIGHT REGISTRATION FOR ONLINE WORKS

Online works made available over a communications network such as the Internet are subject to copyright protection. This also applies to works accessed via a network, such as World Wide Web sites and home pages, FTP sites and Gopher sites, and files and documents transmitted and/or downloaded by a network. For works transmitted online, the copyrightable authorship may consist of text, artwork, music, audio-visual material (including any sounds), sound recordings, etc. Note that copyright does not protect ideas, procedures, systems, or methods of operation of online works.

For all online works other than computer programs and databases, the copyright registration extends only to the copyrightable content of the work as received in the Copyright Office and identified as the subject of the claim for copyright protection. For published works, the registration will be limited to the content of the work asserted to be published on the date set forth in the copyright application.

24.12.1 Revisions and Updates

Many works transmitted online are revised or updated frequently. For individual works, however, there is no blanket registration available to cover revisions published on multiple dates. A revised version for each periodic revision may be registered separately, provided the revisions constitute copyrightable authorship. Thus, a separate application, and the filing fee would be required for each separately published update.

24.12.2 Databases

In some cases, a frequently updated online work may constitute an automated database. A group of updates to a database, published or unpublished, covering up to a three-month period within the same calendar year may be combined in a single copyright registration.

24.12.3 Serials and Newsletters

Group registration (a single registration covering multiple issues published on different dates) is available for serials (published weekly or less often) and daily newsletters (published more often than weekly), including those published online.

To obtain copyright registration for works transmitted online, there are two types of deposit requirements that define the material to be submitted with the application to identify the work to the Copyright Office. The first option is submitting a computer disc, clearly labeled with the title and the author's name, containing the entire work, and in addition, representative portions of the authorship being registered in a format that could be examined by the Copyright Office, such as a printout, and audio cassette or a video tape. The second option is a reproduction of the entire work, regardless of length. If the second option is used, no computer disc is required to accompany the application.

24.13 ARCHITECTURAL WORKS

24.13.1 The AWCPA

Congress passed the Architectural Works Copyright Protection Act in 1990 (AWCPA), which provides copyright protection to original architectural designs in practically any form. Prior to that time, the Copyright Act protected architectural blueprints, models and plans as "pictorial, graphic and sculptural works" under the 1976 Copyright Act. However, this protection did not extend to the design features of the building itself when the building was constructed. When the United States decided to become signatory to the Berne Convention in 1989, the U.S. was required to protect architectural works, including the constructed building itself, as well as the architectural plans and the drawings, creating a new category of copyright protectable works.

Section 101 of the Copyright Act now defines an architectural work as:

> "... the design of a building as embodied in any tangible medium of expression, including a building, architectural plans, or drawings. The work includes the overall form as well as the arrangement and composition of spaces and elements in the design, but does not include individual standard features."

According to the U.S. Copyright Office, gazebos and garden pavilions are included as "buildings," along with structures that are habitable by humans and intended to be permanent and stationary structures designed for human occupancy.

The AWCPA covers architectural designs created on or after December 1, 1990, and unpublished plans or drawings but not constructed as of December 1, 1990, but were constructed before January 1, 2003. Structures other than buildings, such as bridges, cloverleafs, dams, walkways, tents, recreational vehicles, mobile homes and boats, are not covered under the AWCPA.

To enforce an architectural copyright in the U.S., registration must first be obtained. If the plans or building is a "work made for hire," copyright protection lasts for 95 years from the date of publication of the work (i.e., made available to the public. Construction of the building does not constitute publication), or 120 years from the date of creation of the work, whichever term is less. If the copyright registration is in the name of the original designer as the author of the work, protection extends for the life of the author plus 70 years.

A copyright registration directed to architectural drawings of the design of the work does not cover the building itself. A separate registration must be obtained for the building.

Prior to joining the Berne Convention, copying architectural plans or blueprints were acts of copyright infringement, but the use of the plans to construct a building without the architect's approval was not an infringement of the copyright in the plans, because the plans were not "copied." The building per se could be considered a "useful article," and only the artistic features of the building, separate from the utilitarian features, could be covered by copyright prior to the AWCPA.

Of course, sometimes it is difficult to determine what constitutes the design or overall form of a building, excluding individual standard features which, of course, are not protected by copyright.

Under AWCPA, a second building may infringe another's building whether or not the plans or blueprints were copied. In determining whether one building infringes the copyright in a prior building, a court will determine whether the second building is "substantially similar" to the protected work, applying one of two tests. First, the "total look and feel" test examines whether ordinary observers would conclude that the buildings are substantially similar. Under this test, small changes made in the design of the second building that do not alter the overall "look and feel" of the first building will not avoid infringement.

Under the second test, the court "removes" the non-original and standard features from its consideration of the protected building, such as windows, doors, standard configurations of spaces, methods of construction, skylights, atriums, or other commonly used or functional features before determining whether the second building is "substantially similar" to the first. Protection extends to the overall form of the building, as well as the arrangement and composition of spaces and elements in the design. However, any functional element whose design or placement is dictated solely by utilitarian concerns is deleted from consideration. Note also that the owner of the copyright in an architectural work does not have to establish that the alleged infringer had an "intent to copy." As in other copyright infringement litigation, the owner of the protected work can establish infringement by showing that the alleged infringer had access to the protected work, and that the two works are substantially similar. Intent is not a factor in proving infringement.

The owner of a copyright in an architectural work has the exclusive right to make and distribute copies and to prepare derivative works. However, these rights are subject to "fair use" by others. Congress also adopted new laws specifying that the making, distributing or displaying of pictures, paintings or photographs of a building that has been constructed to be visible from a public place is not an infringement of the copyright in the design of that building. For similar practical reasons, Congress also adopted a provision to allow the owner of a building to make or authorize alterations, or even the demolition of the building.

24.13.2 Avoiding Infringement of Architectural Copyrights

Many owners of buildings who have contracted with architects to design the buildings have the mistaken conception that they own the architectural plans and the building design, because they paid for the plans and for the construction, and that they have paid for the right to reproduce or share the plans and the building. This is wrong in many cases.

Where the owner of the building to be built contracts with an architect to design the building, if the written contract does not provide that the resulting copyrights are transferred from the architect to the owner, such as by a "work made for hire" clause or the like, the architect retains ownership of all copyright rights, regardless of the fact that the architect has been paid by the owner for the design services rendered. In effect, the owner obtains a non-exclusive license to have the plans used for that particular construction project, with no right conveyed to use the plans for any other project. The owner does not even have the right to stop the architect from offering or selling the plans to other site owners.

A savvy builder will demand that the contract with the architect provides that all copyrights and other intellectual property rights in the design plans and constructed building are assigned to the owner within the body of the written contract. Quite possibly the architect may seek additional payment for this assignment. Further, an owner should obtain the written authority of the architect before using previously purchased architectural designs or plans on additional building projects.

The sharing of architectural plans and designs among competitive bidders also raises potential copyright infringement issues. This is fine, if the contract between the original designer and the builder, or the request for bid document, clearly states that designs from the original designer may be shared with other bidders. If such is not the case, a subsequent designer who refines or changes the original designer's plans, or constructs a building that is "substantially similar" to the original design, has infringed the copyright in the original design. Therefore, a subsequent architect or designer who receives the plans of an original designer should carefully investigate to be sure that copying, modifying and/or using the original design plans will not result in a charge of copyright infringement.

Another prudent practice for one who is receiving or sharing the architectural or design plans created by an original designer for copying, use and/or modification is to ask the providing party to indemnify the receiving party from copyright infringement liability, and to defend at their expense any lawsuit brought by the original designer. As a general rule, comprehensive liability insurance policies do not normally provide coverage for copyright infringement liability.

◆ INVENTORS AND INVENTIONS ◆

Federico Faggin, Marcian Hoff, and Stanley Mazor

SINGLE-CHIP CPU

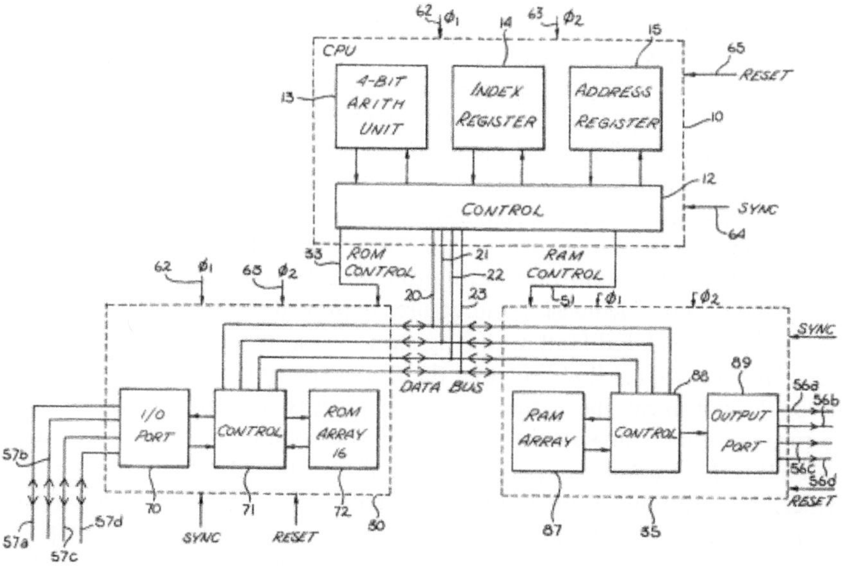

Dr. Federico Faggin was born in Vicenza, Italy, in December 1941. He graduated from the Institute Industriale at Vicenza in 1960, and obtained his doctorate in physics from the University of Padua in 1965. He was employed by Fairchild Semiconductor Corp., where he developed the original silicon gate technology. In 1970, he joined the 4004 Project at Intel Corp. He has produced new chip designs for the personal computer industry since 1974, and has founded several technology companies.

Dr. Marcian Edward (Ted) Hoff, Jr. was born in Rochester, New York, in October 1937. He earned his BEE degree in 1958 from Rensselaer Polytechnic Institute in Troy, New York. He attended Stanford as a National Science Foundation Fellow, and received his MS (1959) and PhD (1962), both in electrical engineering. He joined Intel as a Fellow, the highest technical position in the company. He has also worked for Atari and Teklicon, Inc.

Intellectual Property Law for Engineers, Scientists, and Entrepreneurs, Second Edition. Howard B. Rockman.

Published 2020 by John Wiley & Sons, Inc.

Stanley Mazor was born in Chicago, Illinois, in October 1941, and went on to study mathematics and computer programming at San Francisco State University. He eventually joined Fairchild Semiconductor in 1964 as a programmer, and then worked as a computer designer in the digital research department. In 1969, he joined Intel. He began his teaching career in Intel's technical training group, and later taught at Stanford, the University of Santa Clara, KTH in Stockholm, and Stellenbosch, S.A. In 1984, he worked at Silicon Compiler Systems. He coauthored a book on chip design language while at Synopsis from 1988 to 1994. He presented "The History of the Micro Computer" at the 1995 IEEE proceeding, and in 2008 was the training director at BEA Systems.

In the late 1960s, there was much discussion in the computer industry about the possibility of a computer embedded on a semiconductor chip. A semiconductor is a material that conducts electricity better than insulators, such as a ceramic or glass, but does not provide the conductivity of well-known electrical conductors such as copper, iron, and the like. However, it was the consensus of the industry that integrated circuit technology was not quite ready for on-chip computers. In the late 1960s, Federico Faggin had invented a MOS (metal-on-silicon) process called silicon gate technology, that became the dominant semiconductor process for advanced integrated circuits. Eventually, it was recognized that silicon-gated MOS technology might evolve into a single-chip computer if a sufficiently simple chip architecture could be developed. Ted Hoff developed such an architecture with just over 2000 transistors.

In 1969, a Japanese calculator manufacturer requested Intel to design and produce a new set of chips, and Ted Hoff was assigned to work with the Japanese company's engineers. Hoff realized at that time that the 12-chip design used by the Japanese calculator could not meet the project's cost objectives. He proposed an alternate architecture in which a single-chip general-purpose computer central processor unit (CPU) could be programmed to perform most of the calculator functions.

Further modifications in the architecture and logic design were made by Stanley Mazor and Federico Faggin. Faggin was the one who brought the silicon chip to fruition. The first working CPU was delivered to the Japanese customer in February 1971. The single chip had as much computer power as the first electronic computer, the 1946 ENIAC, which used vacuum tubes and filled an entire room at the University of Pennsylvania.

Hoff, Mazor, and Faggin eventually convinced Intel to sell single-chip CPUs to the entire industry. The Intel 4004 CPU was formally introduced in November 1971. Since the 4004 was designed under contract for the Japanese customer, the Japanese company owned the rights to it. However, Intel bought back the rights to the 4004 by returning the $60,000 development costs, and agreed to produce the chip at a lower cost for the Japanese customer. This was followed by the modern computer revolution, and it now appears that the $60,000 paid back to the Japanese customer was the best investment Intel ever made.

Hoff, Mazor, and Faggin were also involved in developing Intel's second- and third-generation CPUs, the 8008 and the 8080.

The chip is now commonly known as a microprocessor.

United States Patent [19]
Hoff, Jr. et al.

[11] **3,821,715**
[45] **June 28, 1974**

[54] **MEMORY SYSTEM FOR A MULTI-CHIP DIGITAL COMPUTER**

[75] Inventors: **Marcian Edward Hoff, Jr.**, Santa Clara; **Stanley Mazor**, Sunnyvale; **Federico Faggin**, Cupertino, all of Calif.

[73] Assignee: **Intel Corporation**, Santa Clara, Calif.

[22] Filed: **Jan. 22, 1973**

[21] Appl. No.: **325,511**

[52] **U.S. Cl.** .... **340/172.5**, 340/173 R, 340/173 SP, 307/238

[51] **Int. Cl.** **G06f 13/00**, G11c 11/44

[58] **Field of Search** .... 340/172.5, 173 SP, 173 R; 307/238, 279

[56] **References Cited**

UNITED STATES PATENTS

3,460,094	8/1969	Pryor	340/172.5
3,641,511	2/1972	Cricchi et al.	307/238 X
3,680,061	7/1972	Arbab et al.	340/173 R
3,681,763	8/1972	Meade et al.	340/173 R
3,685,020	8/1972	Meade	340/172.5
3,702,988	11/1972	Haney et al.	340/172.5
3,719,932	3/1973	Cappon	340/173 R
3,731,285	5/1973	Bell	340/172.5
3,735,368	5/1973	Beausoleil	340/173 R
3,737,866	6/1953	Gruner	340/172.5
3,740,723	6/1973	Beausoleil et al.	340/172.5

OTHER PUBLICATIONS

Schuenemann, "Computer Control" in IBM Technical Disclosure Bulletin, Vol. 14, No. 12, May 1972; pp. 3794–3795.

Primary Examiner—Paul J. Henon
Assistant Examiner—Melvin B. Chapnick
Attorney, Agent, or Firm—Spensley, Horn & Lubitz

[57] **ABSTRACT**

A general purpose digital computer which comprises a plurality of metal-oxide-semiconductor (MOS) chips. Random-access-memories (RAM) and read-only-memories (ROM) used as part of the computer are coupled to common bi-directional data buses to a central processing unit (CPU) with each memory including decoding circuitry to determine which of the plurality of memory chips is being addressed by the CPU. The computer is fabricated using chips mounted on standard 16 pin dual in-line packages allowing additional memory chips to be added to the computer.

17 Claims, 5 Drawing Figures

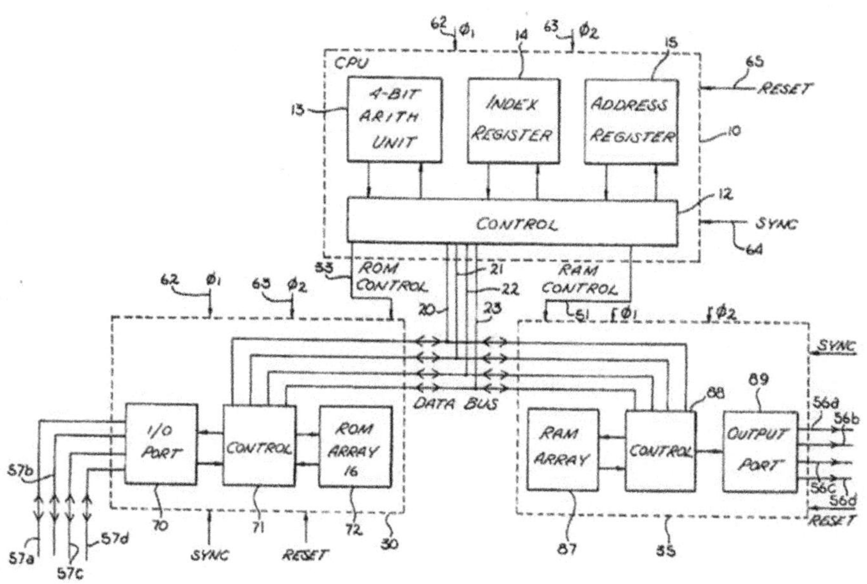

◆ INVENTORS AND INVENTIONS ◆

Josephine Cochrane

AUTOMATIC DISHWASHER

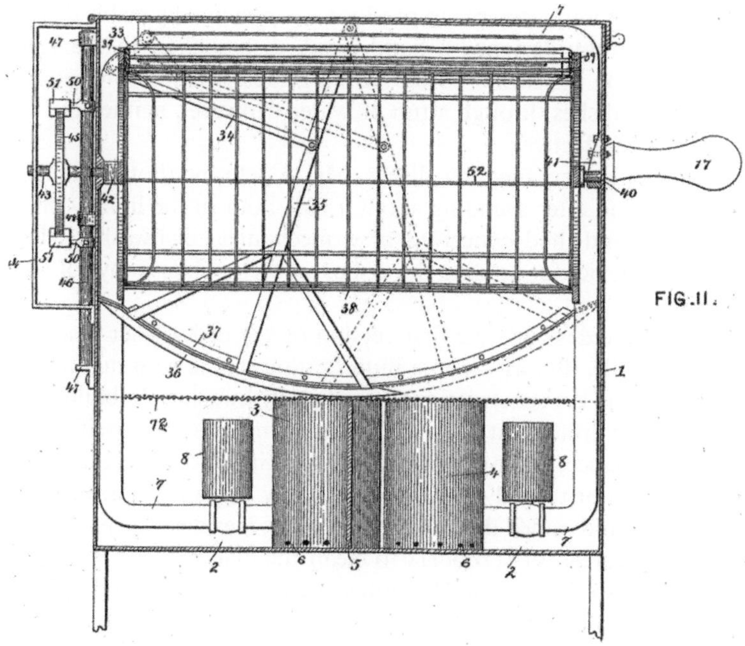

FIG. 11.

Josephine Garis Cochrane of Chicago, Illinois, was the inventor of the first commercially successful automatic dishwasher, which she constructed together with a mechanic named George Butters. She was born in 1839, and married William Cochran in 1858, who went on to become a prosperous dry good merchant and Democratic Party politician in Illinois. Josephine asserted her self-confidence by adopting her new husband's family name but spelling it with an "e" at the end, a point not well appreciated by her spouse's family.

In 1870, the Cochrane's moved into a mansion, and during one of their dinner parties where heirloom china allegedly dating from the 1600s was used, the servants,

Intellectual Property Law for Engineers, Scientists, and Entrepreneurs, Second Edition. Howard B. Rockman.

Published 2020 by John Wiley & Sons, Inc.

while washing the dishes, carelessly chipped some of them, causing Mrs. Cochrane to search for a safer alternative to handling dishware. She did not let the servants handle her expensive dishes after that, and performed the dishwashing chores herself, wondering why, in the industrial age of the late 19th Century, someone had not already invented a machine to automate the chore of dishwashing. She also had the aim of relieving tired housewives of the time from the chores of washing dishes after a meal. Rumor has it that at one time she ran through the street screaming with blood in her eyes, "If nobody else is going to invent a dishwashing machine, I'll do it myself."

Mrs. Cochrane's husband died in 1883 when she was 45 years old, leaving her with debts that significantly motivated her to start developing her dishwasher.

There had been previous attempts to produce a commercially viable dishwasher. In 1850, one Joel Houghton designed a hand crank dish soaker. In the 1860s, L. A. Alexander improved on the earlier device with a geared mechanism that allowed the user to spin racks of dishes through a tub of water. However, neither of these inventions was particularly effective.

One morning, while scrubbing her dishes, Mrs. Cochrane thought of designing a dishwasher herself, and after spending about a half hour in the library of her home, with a cup in her hand, had conceived of a mechanical dishwasher. Her concept involved a rack-like device for holding the dishes securely, while sprays of soapy water cleaned the dishes.

Josephine Cochrane designed the first version of her dishwasher in a shed behind her house in Shelbyville, Illinois. George Butters, a mechanic with the Illinois Central Railroad, assisted her in the construction of the first dishwasher. To build her machine, she first measured the dishes and built wire compartments, each specifically designed to fit plates, cups, or saucers. The compartments were inside a wheel that lay flat inside a copper boiler. A motor turned the wheel and soapy hot water sprayed up from the bottom of the boiler and rained down over the dishes. Her dishwasher was the first to use water pressure, instead of scrubbers to clean the dishes inside the machine. She received U.S. Patent No. 355,139 on December 28, 1886, covering her invention.

Notably, her name on her issued patent eliminates the "e" she had added to her husband's family name. My research was unable to determine the reason for this distinction.

Cochrane disclosed her design to a few men for their comments as to initial interest, which led to the men failing to agree with her concepts. It was after this experience that she obtained the services of mechanic George Butters to help construct her machine. The first machine was installed in Josephine's kitchen and except for being operated by a hand crank, used the same operating concepts as today's electric dishwashers. Soapy water was sprayed onto dishes secured on wire racks inside a water-tight metal container. To rinse the dishes, the user poured water over the soap-clad dishes. Later, a steam engine powered the dishwasher, and an internal rinse cycle was added.

Since Cochrane decided that housewives would not spend money on her invention, she decided to market her dishwasher to hotels. Her first sale was to the Palmer House hotel in Chicago. Then she made a call on the Sherman House hotel, also in Chicago, which purchased $800 worth of dishwashers from her.

Her invention was shown in Machinery Hall at the 1893 World's Columbian Exposition in Chicago, and won the highest prize for best mechanical construction, durability, and adaptation to its line of work. She also had convinced nine restaurants and pavilions at the Exposition to use her dishwasher. Her success in 1893 led her to open her own factory in an abandoned schoolhouse. She sold her machines to more hotels, and to hospitals and colleges, the latter appreciating the sanitizing resulting from the hot water rinse after the soaping and spraying process. Eventually, households began purchasing her automatic dishwashers.

In 1897, Josephine Cochrane established the Garis-Cochrane Dishwashing Machine Company to produce her invention. In 1912, at age 73, she was still actively selling her machines. She died in 1913, and in 1916 her company was purchased by Hobart Manufacturing Company, and Hobart introduced dishwashers for home use in 1949 under the KitchenAid brand, which is presently owned by Whirlpool.

It was not until the 1950s that dishwashers became a common household item after suburban homes were built with the plumbing needed to handle the extra hot water.

(No Model.) 8 Sheets—Sheet 1.

J. G. COCHRAN.

DISH WASHING MACHINE.

No. 355,139. Patented Dec. 28, 1886.

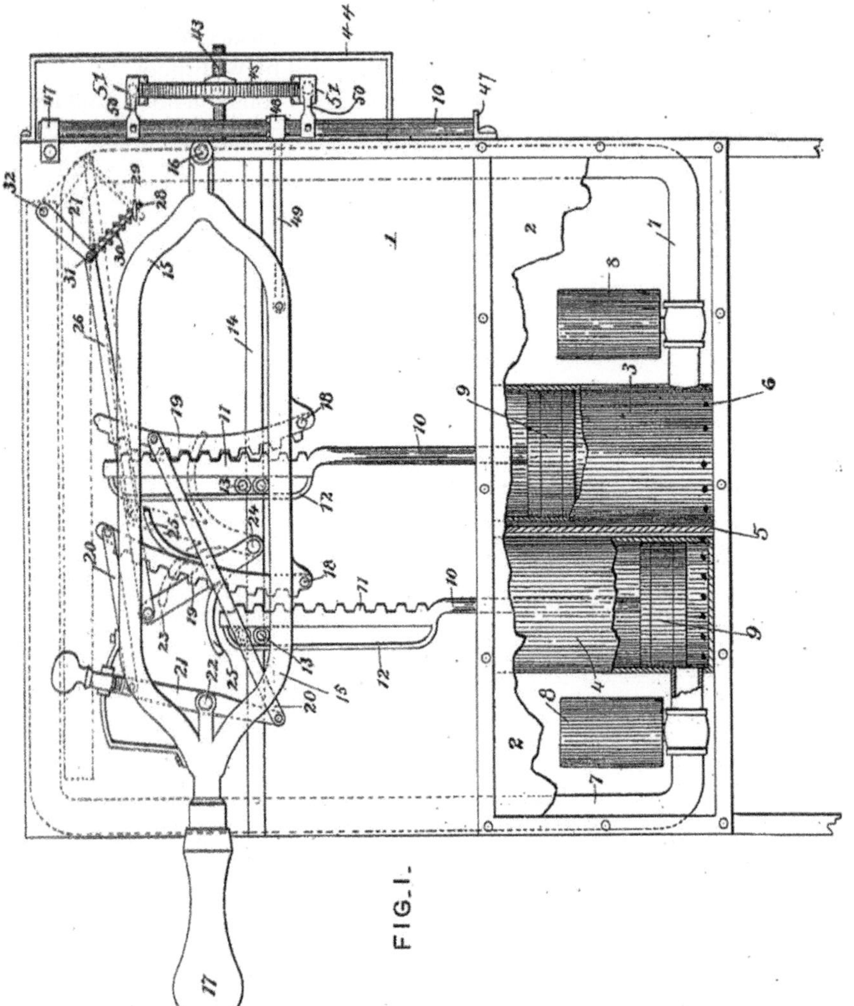

FIG. I.

Attest
Geo. T. Smallwood.
F. A. Hopkins

Inventor:
Josephine G. Cochran.
By Knight Bros
Att'ys

N. PETERS, Photo-Lithographer, Washington, D.C.

25 The Digital Millennium Copyright Act of 1998 (DMCA)—An Overview

25.1 PURPOSE OF THE DMCA

The course of history has shown that as technology advances, at whatever speed, new laws of intellectual property protection are enacted or old laws are given a new interpretation to keep pace. In 1980, the U.S. Supreme Court held that new and non-obvious living creatures (human-made, genetically engineered bacterium) were patentable in *Diamond v. Chakrabarty,* 447 U.S. 303 (1980), providing a significant boost to the biotechnology industry. In 1998, the Court of Appeals for the Federal Circuit held that new and non-obvious methods of doing business that produce a useful, concrete, and tangible result fell within the definition of "patentable subject matter" (35 U.S.C. §101). See *State Street Bank & Trust Co. v. Signature Financial Group, Inc.,* 149 F.3rd 1368 (Fed. Cir. 1998). The U.S. Patent and Trademark Office (USPTO) has since 1996 repeatedly published updated guidelines to assist Patent Examiners (and inventors) in reviewing computer software patent applications, which a few years earlier were considered as covering non-patentable subject matter. These guidelines are accessible on the USPTO website, www.uspto.gov, and discussed in Chapter 13.

Since the 1980s, the transmission and use of data on digital-based platforms and interconnecting systems has transformed how information is stored, delivered, and made available worldwide to anyone with access to a computer or smartphone. Along with the "digital revolution" has come readily available means to copy almost anything that can be digitally transmitted, including works of authorship that are protected against copying by national copyright laws, and international treaties that bind the national copyright laws together, such as the Berne Convention (see Chapter 24). This ease of copying, including textual material, music, and video works has caused concern among copyright owners, particularly those in the entertainment industry, who began to use digital encryption codes in their products that prevented duplication. However, others began to develop technology that would avoid or nullify the encryption codes, thus enabling the duplication of the encrypted and protected works. Copyright owners responded by seeking ways to prevent others from breaking their encryption and disseminating unlawful copies of their works.

In 1996, the World Intellectual Property Organization (WIPO) developed two treaties: the WIPO Copyright Treaty and the WIPO Performances and Phonograms Treaty. These treaties compelled signatory member nations to enact

Intellectual Property Law for Engineers, Scientists, and Entrepreneurs, Second Edition. Howard B. Rockman.

Published 2020 by John Wiley & Sons, Inc.

laws that prohibited the circumvention of technology embedded in works for the purpose of inhibiting access to copyrighted works. The treaties also required members to provide legal measures to prohibit tampering with copyright management information (CMI) encoded into copyrighted works. The U.S. Congress followed by enacting legislation that implemented these two WIPO treaties into U.S. law, and also several additional provisions not in the WIPO treaties, to strengthen the ability of an owner of a digital work to prevent unlawful duplication. For example, the U.S. law prohibits the dissemination of devices and products that enable one to circumvent encoded anti-copying measures, and includes criminal penalties for those who violate the law. The legislation, when still before the U.S. Congress, was commented upon by those who felt the new law would impede legitimate academic research into, and development of, encryption techniques. Several exemptions were written into the original law, which are discussed ahead in Section 25.3.2.1. Provisions were included to allow the Librarian of Congress to issue additional exemptions from the prohibition against circumvention of access control technology. On October 28, 1998, President Clinton signed the Digital Millennium Copyright Act (DMCA) into law as part of the U.S. Copyright Law, 17 U.S.C. §1, *et seq*.

What follows is a brief overview of the DMCA, which taken as a whole is a complex piece of legislation that has undergone multiple court interpretations and administrative changes, and further amendments by Congress, to deal with the competing interests that were considered during the pre-enactment discussion before Congressional committees, such as claims that the DMCA would stop reverse engineering in the development of software, and put a damper on the dissemination of education and research.

As technology advances and new digital techniques are developed to transmit and access digital works, the use of legal remedies to protect copyright owners may have to be repeatedly examined and modified.

25.2 THE GENERAL PROVISIONS OF THE DMCA

Here in a nutshell are the topics covered by the DMCA:

1. Title I provides copyright-protection technology anti-circumvention provisions, including specific actions that are illegal, some both civil and criminal, and specific exemptions to the anti-circumvention provisions.
2. Title II provides a "safe harbor," relieving qualifying online service providers (OSPs) from copyright infringement liability resulting from infringing material being posted by a user of the OSP's platform.
3. Title III allows those repairing computers to make temporary, limited copies of protected materials while repairing a computer. This provision specifically reversed a 1993 Federal Court of Appeals decision that held the opposite.
4. Title IV of the DMCA includes several provisions that:
   a. Added to and clarified the responsibility of the U.S. Copyright Office regarding administration of the DMCA, such as the promulgation of new exemptions to the anti-circumvention provisions of the DMCA, where warranted.

   b. Added provisions to facilitate online education.
   c. Assisted libraries in making legitimate copies of protected works for interlibrary transfer.
   d. Provided for the transfer of motion picture rights and collective bargaining rights.

5. Title V added provisions for the protection of boat hull designs, which were not previously protected under the Copyright Law, since boats were considered as useful, functional articles, where the shape of the hull could not be separated from the function of the hull.

Only the anti-circumvention measures and the notice-and-takedown provisions of the DMCA are discussed in this text, as being the most important provisions for engineers, scientists, and technology owners who use the Internet and other websites. Information on the remaining DMCA topics, and additional information regarding the rapid ebb and flow of enforcement of all provisions of the DMCA can be obtained by contacting your intellectual property professional.

25.3 CIRCUMVENTION OF TECHNOLOGICAL PROTECTION MEASURES

25.3.1 General Approach

Pursuant to each of the WIPO treaties, each member state of the WIPO, which includes the United States, was obligated to enact laws that (1) prevent circumvention of technological measures that are adopted by a copyright owner to protect copyrighted works, and (2) prevent tampering with the integrity of the CMI embedded in a copyrighted work, such as the identity of the owner of the copyright, the author, and other licensing information. Under the treaties, these are considered as technological adjuncts to the exclusive rights granted by Copyright Law.

In the words of the WIPO treaty, contracting parties are obligated to provide effective legal remedies "against the circumvention of effective technological measures that are used by authors in connection with the exercise of their rights ..." to protect their copyrightable works. Section 1201 of the U.S. Copyright Law, Title 17 of the U.S. Code, divides technological measures into two categories. The first are those that prevent unauthorized access to a copyrighted work, and the second are measures that prevent unauthorized copying of a copyrighted work. The production or selling of devices or services that are used to circumvent either category of technological measures is prohibited in certain circumstances. The prohibition against acts of circumvention took effect two years after the effective date of the DMCA; however, the prohibition on the manufacture and distribution of circumvention devices took effect on October 28, 1998.

The law prohibits one from circumventing measures used to prevent access to a copyrighted work, but does not prohibit the circumvention of measures that prohibit copying of the work. This distinction was employed in the act to ensure that the public has the continued ability to make "fair use" of copyrighted works, under circumstances previously discussed in this text. However, since the doctrine of fair use is not a defense to the act of gaining unauthorized access to a work, the act of circumventing a technological measure to gain access is prohibited in its entirety.

Section 1201 of the DMCA clarifies that the prohibition on circumvention devices does not obligate manufactures of consumer electronics, computer equipment, or telecommunications devices to design their products to respond to any particular technological measure. Despite this general "no mandate" rule, the law does mandate one affirmative response. The DMCA requires that all analog video recorder makers build in support for a specific type of copy protection encryption technology created by Macrovision (now Rovi Corporation) to prevent analog video-recording copying via analog cables. When a DVD is played via an analog video cable, and recorded via VCR, this technology distorts the copy. This technology was in use when the DMCA was being considered, and some critics of the DMCA argue that this provision compels makers of analog video equipment to support the proprietary technology of one commercial company. Other critics claim that this anti-circumvention system has caused some VCRs to misread the copy-prevention encryption, resulting in a distortion of the video image on both the original and the copy. As discussed below, others complained that the anti-circumvention technology violated the user's fair use rights, and blocked the use of educational use recording.

The provision of the DMCA prohibiting the production or selling of products or services used to defeat technological measures controlling access to copyrighted works includes those "black boxes" that are created for the purpose of circumventing protection measures, and which have no other commercial value. These black boxes normally are marketed solely for the purpose of circumventing digital encoding measures, and are therefore unlawful.

25.3.2 Exceptions to the Prohibitions

25.3.2.1 The Original Exemptions

In an effort to meet the requirements of the competing interests that lobbied against the enactment of stringent provisions of the DMCA, §1201 of Title 17 of the U.S. Code includes several exemptions to the operation of the anti-circumvention provisions of the law.

The broadest exemptions in the statute establish an ongoing administrative rule-making proceeding within the Library of Congress, with the recommendations of the Register of Copyrights, to evaluate the impact of the prohibition against the act of circumventing access control measures. This prohibition did not take effect until the year 2000, and once in effect, the prohibition against circumventing has been subject to an exemption for users of a work that is in a particular class of works if the user is, or is likely to be, adversely affected by virtue of the prohibition against making non-infringing uses.

The Library of Congress makes periodic rules to ensure that one has access to encrypted works, specifically for the purpose of non-infringing uses. The Library of Congress, and the Register of Copyrights were compelled to consider various factors during the two-year transition period that ended on October 28, 2000, and for succeeding three-year periods, in determining who would be adversely affected by the prohibition against their ability to make non-infringing uses of a class of works. Various factors to be considered are the use of a work for non-profit, archival preservation, and educational purposes; any impact that the law has on criticism, news reporting, comment, scholarship, teaching, or research; and any effect the law may have on the marketability or value of copyrighted works.

The exemptions written into the original law are as follows:

1. Law enforcement, intelligence, and other governmental activity uses.
2. Non-profit libraries, archives, and educational institutions are permitted to circumvent encrypted digital works solely for the purpose of making a good faith determination as to whether they desire to obtain authorized access to the work.
3. To allow reverse engineering of a copyrighted digital work, an exemption permits circumvention, and the development of technological means for such circumvention, by a person who has lawfully obtained a right to use a copy of the computer program, for the sole purpose of identifying and analyzing elements of the program necessary to achieve interoperability with other programs.
4. The law also contains an exemption for encryption research that permits circumvention of access control measures, and the development of technological means to do so, for the purpose of identifying flaws and vulnerabilities of encryption technologies.
5. The protection of minors exemption allows a court, applying the prohibition to a component or part, to consider the necessity for its incorporation in technology that prevents access of minors to material on the Internet.
6. The personal privacy exemption permits circumvention when the technological measure, or the work it protects, is capable of collecting or disseminating personally identifying information about the online activities of a natural person.
7. The security testing exemption permits circumvention of access control measures and the development of technological means for such circumvention for the purpose of testing the security of a computer, computer system, or computer network with the authorization of its owner or operator.

Each of the above exemptions has its own applicability provisions that are set forth in the statute.

25.3.2.2 The Triennial Exemptions to the Circumvention Prohibitions

The circumvention prohibition exemption rules are revised every three years based on proposals submitted by the public to the Register of Copyrights. Final rules are issued by the Librarian of Congress after hearings on the public comments. All exemptions issued by the Librarian of Congress expire after three years, but may be resubmitted by interested and affected parties for the next rulemaking cycle.

Exemptions are normally granted when an interested or affected party establishes that a certain technology devised to control or limit access to copyrighted works has had a significant adverse effect on allowing one to reproduce non-infringing copies of a copyright-protected work. As of the writing of this text, the most recent exemptions were issued by the Copyright Office on October 26, 2018, and can be found in U.S. Federal Register, Vol. 83, No. 208, pg. 54010-54031, under the title "Library of Congress, U.S. Copyright Office, 37 CFR Part 201, Exemption to Prohibition on Circumvention of Copyright Protection Systems for Access Control Technologies." These recent exemption rules are rather extensive and quite detailed, and are not reprinted here. Also, a revised set of exemption rules will be published again in 2021. For the most recent version of the exemption rules, see https://www.govinfo.gov/content/pkg/FR-2018-10-26/pdf/2018-23241.pdf.

One of the 2018 exemptions is worthy of mention. On or about October 28, 2016, the Librarian of Congress authorized security researchers who are acting in good faith to conduct controlled research on computer programs that operate on lawfully acquired devices or machines to circumvent copyright prohibiting measures, so long as the research does not violate other laws such as the Computer Fraud and Abuse Act. This rule greatly assists security researchers and consumers who will benefit from the increased security testing of the products they purchase and use.

Without this exemption, researchers would be unable to investigate and uncover security vulnerabilities in consumer products, if doing so requires reverse engineering or circumventing anti-copying controls, such as hidden code. During research, the device and computer program should operate solely for the purpose of good faith security research, which must be conducted in a controlled setting designed to avoid harm to individuals or the public.

This exemption defines good faith security research as accessing a computer program solely for purposes of good faith testing, investigation, and/or correction of a security flaw or vulnerability where such activity is carried out in a controlled environment designed to avoid any harm to individuals or the public, and where the information derived from the activity is used primarily to promote the security or safety of the class of devices or machines on which the computer program operates, or those who use such devices or machines, and is not used or maintained in a manner that facilitates copyright infringement. Responsible disclosure is considered a factor in establishing good faith security testing. This would indicate that disclosing vulnerabilities to companies manufacturing certain devices would be a positive factor in establishing good faith.

This exemption covers all devices and machines primarily designed for use by individual consumers, such as electric toothbrushes, home thermostats, connective appliances, automobiles, and smart TVs. The exemption also covers medical devices as long as the devices are not connected to humans during research.

25.3.2.3 Fair Use, Non-Infringing Uses, and Anti-Circumvention

Many, if not all, of the exemptions to the anti-circumvention provisions of the DMCA are the result of public comments directed to possible adverse effects on the "fair use" of copyrighted materials and other non-infringing uses, which the law was specifically not intended to stifle. Fair use could include circumvention for reverse engineering, security testing, privacy protection, encryption research, educational purposes, and other legitimate research projects.

For example, Section 108 of the DMCA permits archive facilities and libraries to reproduce and distribute one copy of a work, such as book portions, journal articles, and the like, and send this single copy to another library through inter-library loan procedures. Libraries may also make copies of protected material for preservation purposes.

Fair use is a broad concept with no exact parameters that is determined case by case. A purchaser of a DVD or software can normally make one copy of the material for backup or preservation purposes under the fair use rule. However, a line is crossed when that copy is used on a second computer of the same purchaser. Also, critics of DMCA argued prior to 2015 that under the law, researchers who were engaged in good faith efforts to test security measures in industrial and consumer products expressed concern that they would face potential criminal liability and jail if they circumvented technological protective measures in analyzing the protection measures for flaws that could result in hacking. The 2018 exemptions issued by the Librarian of Congress made good faith security and cryptography research and study lawful.

In 2014, the Unlocking Consumer Choice and Wireless Competition Act was passed by the U.S. Congress, granting an exemption from the DMCA allowing cell phones to be unlocked, enabling a cell phone user to switch telecommunications carriers and keep their same phone and phone number.

Prior to this law, once a consumer signed up for exclusive use with a carrier, the phone was often locked to prevent the phone from working with another carrier. The DMCA made it illegal to use software technology to circumvent the copyrighted locking system in the phone. In 2010, the Copyright Office granted an exemption to the anti-circumvention provisions to allow unlocking, but when that exemption expired in October 2012, the Copyright Office did not renew the cellphone unlocking exemption.

In March 2013, the FCC and the Obama administration felt that consumers should be able to keep their same phone and number when changing service carriers. The law passed in 2014 reestablishes the previous Copyright Office exemption again permitting the use of computer programs that enable used wireless telephone handsets to connect to a wireless telecommunication network, when circumvention is initiated by the owner of the copy of such computer program solely to connect to the desired network, and the new network service authorizes such access.

25.4 LIMITATIONS ON COPYRIGHT INFRINGEMENT LIABILITY FOR ONLINE SERVICE PROVIDERS

25.4.1 Background

When the DMCA was being considered by the U.S. Congress, OSPs such as ISPs, hosting services, and interactive services were asked for their support for the anti-circumvention provisions in the pending legislation. Apparently, in exchange for their support, OSPs wanted protection from copyright infringement liability resulting from the content of a posting or transmission by a user of the provider's or carrier's network, or the use of information location tools and hyperlinks. The DMCA, as passed, included such a provision, provided the OSP immediately disables access to or takes down infringing material described in a formal takedown notice submitted by the copyright owner to the OSP. One issue this title is aimed at addressing is the posting of a picture or pictures of your products taken from your official website by one, possibly in a foreign country, offering to sell knock-offs of your products through the "pirate's" website. I have encountered this several times in my practice.

A party seeking the benefits of these "safe harbor" provisions must first qualify as a "service provider," defined in the statute as "an entity offering the transmission, routing or providing of connections for digital online communications, between or among points specified by the user, of material of the user's choosing, without modification to the content of the material as sent or received." If qualified OSPs follow the remaining requirements of the DMCA discussed below, they will be limited in their copyright infringement liability resulting from transitory communications, systems caching, storage of information on systems or networks at the direction of users, and information location tools.

25.4.2 The Notice and Takedown Procedures

Prudent OSPs have established copyright infringement notification policies as a means of ensuring they avoid liability for copyright infringement, and have posted these policies on their website for public access. If you are posting or transmitting data via an OSP, it is highly recommended that you carefully read your OSP's posted infringement policy to prevent your website or transmissions from being taken down.

If you post or transmit content that is protected under the Copyright Law, there is a high likelihood that the owner of the copyright in the protected work will send a "DMCA Copyright Infringement Notice" to the OSP (not to you), establishing a violation of the owner's copyright identifying where the allegedly infringing work is located on the OSP's site, such as by URL, and requesting that the OSP delete, or "take down" the allegedly infringing material. The notice expresses a good faith belief that the copyright owner did not authorize the alleged infringing copy, and a statement under penalty of perjury that the information in the notice is correct. The copyright owner sending the notice can be liable for damages incurred by the user of the OSP system if the owner purposefully misrepresents that the posted or transmitted work is an infringement. The OSP will notify the user of the takedown after the content has been removed, but not before removal, if the OSP complies with the notice.

The DMCA requires that OSPs receiving a DMCA Notice of Copyright Infringement immediately take down the allegedly infringing work, even before examining the infringement allegation for accuracy or reasonableness, or determining if the fair use doctrine is applicable to the posting or transmission. If the OSP hesitates and does not act quickly on the notice, they may lose their own immunity for copyright infringement liability.

25.4.3 Counter DMCA Notification Procedures

A user whose content has been removed from its OSP website can have the content restored if the user certifies that its use is not a copyright infringement in a written counter-notification, and where the copyright owner does not file a lawsuit against the user within 14 days.

A counter-notice must be in writing, and sent to the OSP, stating under penalty of perjury that the user's material has been improperly and wrongfully removed. The OSP then notifies the copyright owner of the user's objection to the takedown. Upon receiving the counter-notice information, the copyright owner must file a copyright infringement lawsuit in a U.S. Federal District Court within 14 days. If a lawsuit is filed, it is highly likely that both parties will request immediate injunctive relief, the copyright owner seeking to keep the content off the OSP's system, and the user asking the court to restore the content to the OSP's system immediately.

If the user can prove that the owner of the copyright knowingly made false material statements in its takedown notice, the copyright owner may be found liable for damages to the user resulting from the unlawful takedown, including possible costs and attorney's fees.

OSPs are also obligated under the DMCA to terminate accounts of repeat copyright infringers, which policy must also be given to the OSP's users. OSPs must also register with the U.S. Copyright Office, and provide the office with and post on their website the contact information of a designated agent authorized to receive DMCA Copyright Infringement Notices.

25.5 COPYRIGHT MANAGEMENT INFORMATION

The DMCA also comprises §1202 of the Copyright Act to protect the integrity of CMI. The statute defines CMI as identifying information about the work, the author, the copyright owner, and in certain cases, the performer, writer, or director of the work, as well as the terms and conditions for use of the work such as licensing and other information that the Register of Copyrights may prescribe by regulation. The purpose of embedding this information in a digital work is to allow ease of finding the copyright owner so that a license agreement can be reached for use of the protected work. The DMCA prohibits the knowing provision or distribution of false CMI, if accomplished with the intent to induce, enable, facilitate, or conceal infringement. The statute also bars the intentional removal or alternation of CMI without authority, as well as the dissemination of CMI or copies of works, knowing that the CMI has been removed or altered without authority. Liability under the act requires that such conduct be done with knowledge, or with respect to civil remedies, with reasonable grounds to know that such conduct will induce, enable, facilitate, or conceal an infringement.

The DMCA also includes limitations on the liability of broadcast stations and cable systems for removal or alteration of CMI in certain circumstances where there is no intent to induce, enable, facilitate, or conceal infringement.

25.6 REMEDIES FOR DMCA VIOLATIONS

The DMCA is quite stringent, and includes both criminal and civil liability for violation of the act. For example, a willful violation of either §§1201 or 1202 of the act, and for purposes of commercial advantage or private financial gain, is a criminal act. Penalties for criminal violations range up to $500,000 fines or up to five years imprisonment for a first offense, and up to a one million dollar fine or up to ten years in prison for subsequent offenses. However, non-profit libraries, archives, and educational institutions are entirely exempt from criminal liability.

Any copyright owner injured by a violation of §§1201 or 1202 may bring a civil action in a federal court, and the courts are given the power to grant a range of equitable and monetary remedies similar to those under the Copyright Act, including statutory damages. Special protection is given to non-profit libraries, archives, and educational institutions, which are entitled to a complete remission of damages in circumstances where they can prove that they were not aware, and had no reason to believe, that their acts constituted a violation of the DMCA.

25.7 EXAMPLE OF POTENTIAL CONFLICT

Consider the following true facts. On September 6, 2000, the Secured Digital Music Initiative Foundation (SDMI), a consortium of almost 200 companies in the recording, consumer electronics, information technology, security technology, and Internet service provider industries, invited the public to attack then present digital security measures and other technologies that protect copyrighted digital materials, for the purpose of allowing SDMI to determine which security system it should recommend for adoption by its members. The challenge invited the public to defeat the security measures, by altering or removing such measures, but not adversely affecting the quality of a digital music performance. Also, the digital performance must be available to be downloaded. Those challengers who were successful could either receive monetary compensation and assign their patent and copyright rights to SDMI, or they could retain ownership rights to the circumventing intellectual property with encouragement to submit the results of their successful challenges to SDMI. The entrants to the challenge were only authorized to attack the encoded digital music samples and files, where SDMI and their copyright owners retained all their rights, and the challengers were prohibited from reproducing, modifying, performing, distributing, or making any use of the samples derived during the challenge.

One team of challengers successfully attacked five of the six technologies offered by SDMI. This team wrote a technical paper setting forth the research and successful attacks, and desired to submit this paper to a peer review scientific conference for subsequent publication. The paper was originally accepted for publication, and communications began between the challengers and one of the companies that produced one of the technologies used in the challenge. This company expressed concern about dissemination of the detailed information provided in the paper describing the challenger's research. The challenger then received a letter from the Recording Industry Association of America (RIAA), stating that the company's security measures were being used commercially, and the publication of the challenger's research paper could seriously jeopardize such security technology. The RIAA letter also indicated that if the research were published, the DMCA would subject the research team to liability.

On June 6, 2001, the head of the challenging research team filed a lawsuit against RIAA, stating in its complaint that the DMCA goes against the Constitution of the United States by restricting freedom of speech and of the press, as well as academic freedom. The research team leader was asking the court to declare that full and open access to research in areas potentially covered by the DMCA was required, because otherwise scientists and programmers working on digital works could not exchange ideas and fully develop their own research. The allegation was made that the DMCA would thus harm the advance of science. In this particular litigation, the court ultimately dismissed the complaint of the challenge research team's leader, on the basis that the leader and other team members did not have standing to pursue their claim.

In this case, the research team was allowed under the DMCA to conduct its research to circumvent the security measures embedded in the digital work; however, they were not allowed to disseminate the results of that research in published form. The question for debate is whether or not the encryption defeating research would be distributed in a manner that advances the state of knowledge, or in a way that allows ease of future infringement. The research team was seeking the right to advance the right to publish information obtained through individual research, a practice common throughout the entire engineering and scientific community. Thus, although the research that was conducted fell under the protection of an exemption of the DMCA, subsequent publication of that research may be considered a violation of the law if such distribution is interpreted as allowing copyright infringement to be facilitated.

This case illustrates the conflicting rights between the interests of the copyright holders to ensure protection for their copyright holders' rights, and the technological, engineering, and scientific communities' need to advance technology through the use of publication, peer review, and commentary, and to openly discuss weaknesses in encryption technology. This type of independent security research into malfunctions, security flaws, or vulnerabilities in computer programs appears to now be lawful by the 2018 security research exemption discussed in Section 25.3.2.2.

◆ INVENTORS AND INVENTIONS ◆

Stephen Wozniak

PERSONAL COMPUTERS

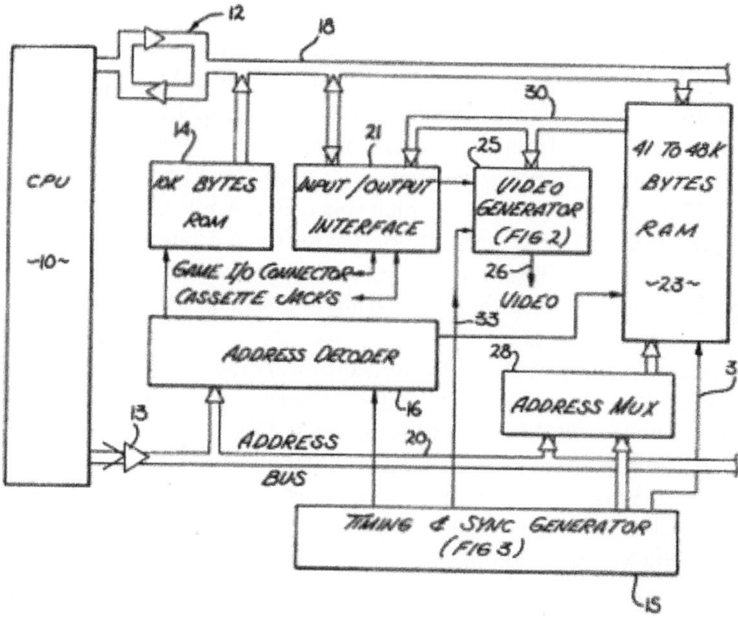

Stephen Wozniak developed the Apple II computer, which was one of the first personal computers to be used by medium- to large-size businesses and, ultimately, by home users. Wozniak, along with Steve Jobs, created Apple Computers, Inc., the first in the market with personal computers. They are credited with beginning the computer industry, which is still on an exponential rise.

Stephen G. Wozniak was born in 1950, and as a child was extremely interested in mathematics and computers. He was the son of a Lockheed engineer, who first incubated his technology interests. Wozniak's father assisted him in science fair projects devoted to electronic themes. By fifth grade, Wozniak was building large computer-like science fair projects, and in sixth grade he built a computer that played tic-tac-toe. He also built his own amateur radio station and received his ham radio license in the sixth grade. He designed complete computers and constructed them all through high school and college. He built his first computer at age 13, and was president of the Electronics Club in high school. This drive led him on a path to becoming an engineer;

Intellectual Property Law for Engineers, Scientists, and Entrepreneurs, Second Edition. Howard B. Rockman.

Published 2020 by John Wiley & Sons, Inc.

however, in the mid-1970s, Wozniak decided to drop out of his engineering studies at the University of California at Berkeley. He went to work for Hewlett-Packard designing calculator chips, and there he met a fellow worker, John Draper, who was working in his spare time on a "blue box," an illegal phone attachment permitting users to make free long-distance telephone calls. Wozniak also met a summer employee, Steve Jobs, and Jobs soon was helping Wozniak sell the blue boxes.

While still working at Hewlett-Packard, Wozniak joined and then became the "spiritual" leader of a group of computer "wonks" in Palo Alto, California, known as the Home Brew Computer Club. In 1975, Steve Jobs also began attending meetings of the club. Working in Steve Jobs' bedroom, Wozniak and Jobs designed what would later become the Apple I computer. The prototype was constructed in Job's garage. Jobs then convinced a local electronic retailer to order 25 Apple I computers. To obtain the capital necessary to manufacture these 25 machines, Jobs sold his Volkswagen Microbus, and Wozniak sold his HP scientific calculator, enabling them to raise $1300. They also obtained credit from local electronic suppliers, and began producing the Apple I. Wozniak later resigned from Hewlett-Packard and became Vice President in charge of R&D of this new company, which was called Apple Computers.

Urban legend holds that the name "Apple" came from a summer job that Jobs had picking apples in Oregon. The company logo, an Apple with a bite missing from it, is a reference to the computer term "byte," which is defined as a sequence of binary digits acted upon by a computer.

Steve Wozniak is credited with single-handedly designing and constructing the Apple I computer, which initially sold for $666 and was the first single-circuit-board computer with read-only memory (ROM). The ROM instructed the computer how to load additional programs from external sources. The computer also had a built-in video interface. During the time of Wozniak's development, the prices of microprocessors and memory chips had dropped so low that he could afford, from his Hewlett-Packard salary, enough to design and build his own computer. Wozniak owned a TV set and a typewriter, and that got him to thinking that a computer should be designed as a typewriter with a video screen. His high school electronics courses taught him enough about circuitry to understand how to drive a TV monitor and to get it to draw shapes of characters and other things. With the Apple I, Wozniak had constructed a computer that could place words on a screen using a keyboard, and operate a programming language for playing games. He was proud of the fact that he did this all himself. After he had developed his Apple I, he brought it to work at Hewlett-Packard and solved some engineering and design problems he was working on for HP. He also assisted others to construct their own computers by passing out schematics and going over to friend's houses and soldering wires together. Then Steve Jobs saw what Wozniak was doing and suggested that they make a PC board that could be sold for $40 and would cost only $20 to make. This was the beginning of Apple Computer. Neither of them gave up their daytime jobs. Steve Jobs lived at home with his parents, and Wozniak continued working for Hewlett-Packard. Six hundred Apple I computers were sold by Apple, generating revenues of $775,000.

Among Wozniak's early achievements was the development of a computer in which the disc drive, which had up to then been built with 50 chips, was built with five chips. This resulted from his successful effort to build a small circuit that could output a signal on a disc or tape, and somehow, when it was played back, figure out what it is. The development of these new chips also assisted Wozniak in the development of his computers.

Wozniak then set out to design and introduce the Apple II computer, which he also single-handedly designed. The Apple II began when Wozniak designed, in hardware form, the game "Breakout" for Atari. Wozniak desired to create "Breakout" in software for

Apple II, which he found easy to do since he had written the Basic program that translated instructions to machine language. After obtaining a ball bouncing around on the screen, he added sound by adding speakers. Then he developed a minimum-slip paddle circuit to provide paddles to move the ball. In collaboration with Randy Wigginton, Wozniak developed a disc operating system that would load files from fixed locations on the discs in response to one-letter commands. However, this Basic control program did not provide the flexibility for efficient use of the disc drive.

Further effort was required to create a disc operating system (DOS), because one side of the RAM memory in the Apple II comprised the floppy disc and the disc drive hardware. These components are adapted to accept a program to be loaded and executed on the other side of an electronic chasm constituting the interface card and the connecting cable. The control program that Wozniak wrote has been compared to a rope bridge crossing a chasm. Wozniak's development became a foundation for the operating system, and after further development, Apple came out with DOS 3.1. The Apple II circuitry allowed the computer to operate directly with a color video monitor.

The Apple II first appeared at the West Coast Computer Faire in 1977, and included a central processing unit (CPU), a keyboard, and a floppy disc drive. To promote use of the Apple II, Jobs challenged programmers to develop applications for the machine, which resulted in the generation of several programs, including VisiCalc, which was a budget analyzer, and myriads of games. In a span of three years, the Apple II created earnings of approximately $140 million, and was the best-selling computer for five years straight, with a growth rate of 700 percent. Wozniak and Jobs came to represent the free-spirited, open-minded "nerd" ingenuity that could succeed when applied to commercial enterprises. The later-developed Apple II Plus and Apple III did not reach the same sales popularity as the Apple II, and the Apple III was recalled in 1981 due to design flaws. At the same time, IBM developed and introduced its new PC, garnering a major share of the office computer business from Apple.

In February 1981, Wozniak was involved in a private plane crash, and received a concussion that temporarily prevented him from remembering things. For example, he could not recall that he was in an accident, he could not recall playing games with his computer, and he could not recall who visited him earlier in the day. When he recovered from the concussion, he took a sabbatical from Apple, married, returned to college at Berkeley, and, in 1982, received his degrees in electrical engineering and computer science. He participated in other companies involving computer technology until June 1983, when he decided to return to Apple and provide his assistance to the company once again. Steve Wozniak helped Apple develop the Macintosh computer upon his return. In 1985, both Steve Wozniak and Steve Jobs received the National Technology Medal from President Regan at the White House. Wozniak decided then it was time to leave Apple (again), and Steve Jobs left shortly thereafter.

It is undisputed that Steve Wozniak was one of the major players in creating the computer industry that today touches the lives of almost everyone in the world in one way or another. Steve Wozniak has credited his high school electronics teacher as greatly encouraging his development work. He recalled that his high school teacher wrote his own courses and assignments. Today, Wozniak is teaching computer classes using the same technique.

Steve Wozniak is presently involved in various philanthropic and business ventures. He created an initiative in 1990 to place computers in schools in the former Soviet Union. He has also donated computers and even entire computer labs to schools, and has worked on providing servers and Internet access to students, providing laptops for students and computer training for teachers and students.

United States Patent [19]

Wozniak

[11] **4,136,359**

[45] **Jan. 23, 1979**

[54] **MICROCOMPUTER FOR USE WITH VIDEO DISPLAY**

[75] Inventor: **Stephen G. Wozniak**, Cupertino, Calif.

[73] Assignee: **Apple Computer, Inc.**, Cupertino, Calif.

[21] Appl. No.: **786,197**

[22] Filed: **Apr. 11, 1977**

[51] **Int. Cl.**[2] **H04N 9/44**
[52] **U.S. Cl.** **358/17**
[58] **Field of Search** 358/17, 148, 150

[56] **References Cited**

U.S. PATENT DOCUMENTS

3,581,011 5/1971 Ward et al. 358/17

Primary Examiner—Richard Murray

Attorney, Agent, or Firm—Blakely, Sokoloff, Taylor & Zafman

[57] **ABSTRACT**

A microcomputer including a video generator and timing means which provides color and high resolution graphics on a standard, raster scanned, cathode ray tube is disclosed. A horizontal synchronization counter is synchronized at an odd-submultiple of the color subcarrier reference frequency. A "delayed" count is employed in the horizontal synchronization counter to compensate for color subcarrier phase reversals between lines for the non-interlaced fields. This permits vertically aligned color graphics without substantially altering the standard horizontal synchronization frequency. Video color signals are generated directly from digital signals by employing a recirculating shift register.

8 Claims, 4 Drawing Figures

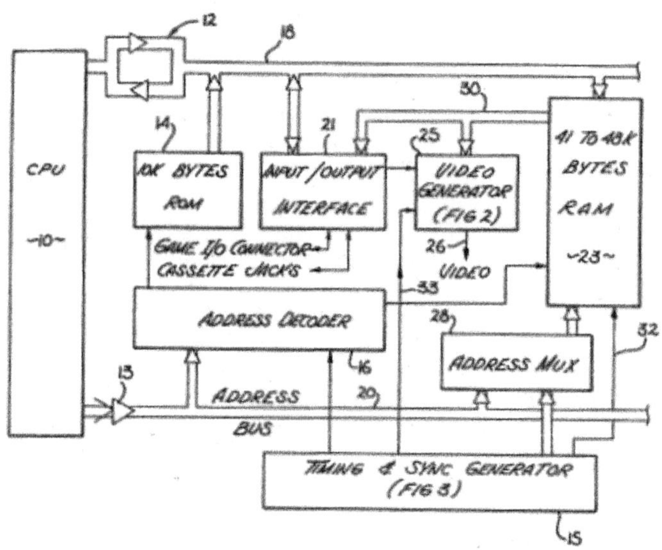

◆ INVENTORS AND INVENTIONS ◆

Jaap Haartsen and Sven Mattisson

BLUETOOTH®-SHORT DISTANCE WIRELESS COMMUNICATION SYSTEMS

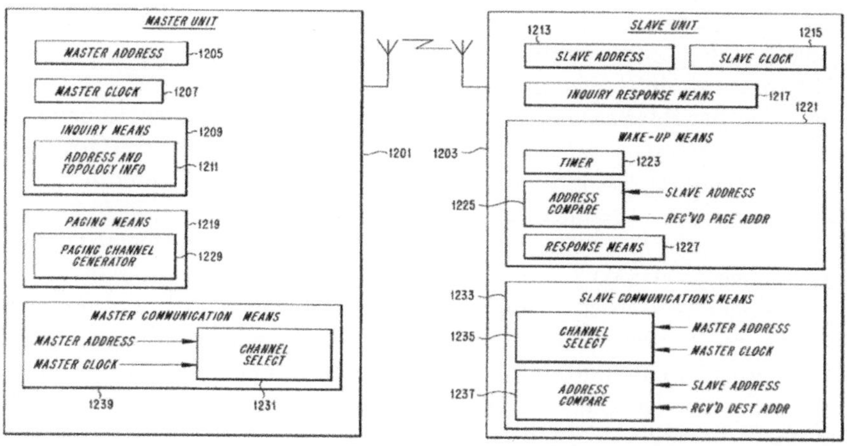

In 1984, sales of cellular phones and handsets were rapidly increasing, and executives at Ericsson, the Swedish handset manufacturer, were seeking ways to differentiate its phones from those in the crowded market. This search led to the creation of Bluetooth technology, which, ironically enough, was so quickly adapted by all other cell phone manufacturers that the technology was never thought to differentiate Ericson's cell phones from others.

In 1989, Nils Rydbeck, chief technology officer at Ericsson Mobile in Sweden, and Johan Ullman, gave Tord Wingren, Jaap Haartsen, and Sven Mattisson the task of developing wireless headsets according to two inventions previously developed by Johan Ullman. Haartsen and Mattisson were instructed to produce an optimal "short link" radio technology standard for transmitting signals between personal and hand-held computers to wireless headsets that Ericsson was planning to bring to the market. The specification ultimately developed, known as Bluetooth, is based on frequency hopping spread spectrum technology, described previously in this text.

Jaap Haartsen's directive included developing technology to send and receive data to cell phone accessories over handsets. Existing technology used for wireless handsets in 1989 was not capable of transmitting data, so something more powerful was needed

Intellectual Property Law for Engineers, Scientists, and Entrepreneurs, Second Edition. Howard B. Rockman.

Published 2020 by John Wiley & Sons, Inc.

that would not compromise the cell phone's battery life. From the beginning, Bluetooth was meant to be a wireless low-power, short-range radio technology connecting handsets to handhelds, laptop systems, and personal computers.

Using frequency hopping over 32 frequencies, Haartsen was able to overcome the need for the device to always be "on," always listening for another device that wanted to connect. Bluetooth units, he stated, are just floating, they are not in stand-by, and they are always open. Bluetooth's frequency hopping allows the receiving unit to be asleep, waking up every two seconds and listening for a signal on one specific frequency. If no device is sending data, the receiver goes back to sleep and reawakens two seconds later listening on the next frequency. The device will repeat this process as it hops through all 32 frequencies. At the other end, the sender stays awake for 10 minutes solving the "time frequency uncertainty" as Haartsen mentioned, by sending the message to all 32 frequencies simultaneously.

Six months after Haartsen began his project to develop the wireless technology, he was joined by an interface expert, Sven Mattisson, and the two worked together on what was called Project MC Link, which later became known as Bluetooth.

Bluetooth operates at frequencies between 2402 and 2408 MHz, including guard bands 2 MHz, then 3.5 MHz. This is in the globally unlicensed but regulated industrial scientific and medical (ISM) 2.4 GHz short-range radio frequency band. By using frequency hopping spread spectrum technology, Bluetooth divides the transmitted data into packets, and transmits each packet on 1 of 79 designated Bluetooth channels. Each channel has a bandwidth of 1 MHz and performs 800 hops per second with Adaptive Frequency Hopping (AFH) enabled. Bluetooth Low Energy uses 2 MHz spacing, accommodating 40 channels.

Bluetooth technology allows several devices to be paired together via short-range radio signals that form a network, with each device functioning as a component of a larger system. Bluetooth technology is not tied to any product, but is implemented by the Bluetooth Special Interest Group (SIG), described below. Bluetooth makes use of short-range, low-power radio technology to connect devices to one another, and the technology does not require line-of-sight connection to other devices. The Bluetooth device consists of a radio unit, a link control unit, and a support unit, the latter being where the link management occurs. The SIG oversees development of the specifications for the Bluetooth systems, manages the qualification program, and protects the trademarks. A manufacturer needs to meet Bluetooth SIG standards to market their product as a Bluetooth-capable device.

Bluetooth SIG was founded originally by five companies to develop the Bluetooth concept as a possible wireless technology standard: Ericsson, Intel, IBM, Toshiba, and Nokia. Other companies such as Microsoft, Lucent, 3Com, and Motorola later joined the Bluetooth SIG, and today there are approximately 2400 companies that have joined this group. SIG develops specifications and promotes the use of Bluetooth technology.

Jaap Haartsen is named as the sole inventor on the patent that is basic to protecting the Bluetooth communications systems. In the United States, the patent number is 6,590,928. The patent discloses a wireless network with a master unit and a slave unit, the master unit capable of communicating with the slave unit through a virtual frequency hopping channel. Voice and data transmissions are enabled by self-organization techniques to efficiently use the limited available radio spectrum. The first Bluetooth-enabled mobile phone, the Ericsson T36, was introduced to the market in

2000. The following year the first Bluetooth-enabled printers, laptop computers, and hands-free automobile kits were introduced. At the end of 2014, the 2400 members in Bluetooth SIG were connected to 90% of the mobile phone market.

So where did the name Bluetooth come from? Well, during the 10th century, there was a Danish king named Harald Blatand, who was also known as Harald Bluetooth. One of Harald Bluetooth's major accomplishments was the expansion of the Danish kingdom into parts of present-day Norway, and uniting many Danish tribes into a single country.

US006590928B1

(12) **United States Patent**
Haartsen

(10) **Patent No.: US 6,590,928 B1**
(45) **Date of Patent: *Jul. 8, 2003**

(54) **FREQUENCY HOPPING PICONETS IN AN UNCOORDINATED WIRELESS MULTI-USER SYSTEM**

(75) Inventor: **Jacobus Cornelis Haartsen**, Borne (NL)

(73) Assignee: **Telefonaktiebolaget LM Ericsson (publ)**, Stockholm (SE)

(*) Notice: This patent issued on a continued prosecution application filed under 37 CFR 1.53(d), and is subject to the twenty year patent term provisions of 35 U.S.C. 154(a)(2).

Subject to any disclaimer, the term of this patent is extended or adjusted under 35 U.S.C. 154(b) by 332 days.

(21) Appl. No.: **08/932,911**

(22) Filed: **Sep. 17, 1997**

(51) **Int. Cl.**^{7} **H04L 27/30**
(52) **U.S. Cl.** **375/134**; 375/137
(58) **Field of Search** 375/200, 202, 375/134, 132, 133, 135, 136, 137; 380/34

(56) **References Cited**

U.S. PATENT DOCUMENTS

4,466,060 A	8/1984	Riddle	
5,274,666 A	* 12/1993	Dowdell et al.	375/1
5,287,384 A	2/1994	Avery et al.	
5,412,654 A	5/1995	Perkins	
5,414,731 A	5/1995	Antunes et al.	
5,515,509 A	5/1996	Rom	
5,574,979 A	11/1996	West	
5,729,680 A	* 3/1998	Belanger et al.	395/200.1
5,896,375 A	4/1999	Dent et al.	
5,940,431 A	8/1999	Haartsen et al.	

FOREIGN PATENT DOCUMENTS

EP	0465090 A1	1/1992
EP	0695059 A1	1/1996

OTHER PUBLICATIONS

Matthijs A. Visser, et al., "Voice and Data Transmission over an 802.11 Wireless Network", Proc. of PIMRC '95, Toronto, Sep. 1995, pp. 648–652.
Adriaan Kamerman, "Spread-Spectrum Techniques Drive WLAN Performance", Microwaves & RF, Sep. 1996, pp. 109–114.

(List continued on next page.)

Primary Examiner—William Luther
(74) *Attorney, Agent, or Firm*—Burns, Doane, Swecker & Mathis, L.L.P.

(57) **ABSTRACT**

A wireless network includes master and slave units. The master sends a master address and clock to the slaves. Communication is by means of a virtual frequency hopping channel whose hopping sequence is a function of the master address, and whose phase is a function of the master clock. Transmitted inquiry messages solicit slave address and topology information from the slaves, which may be used to generate a configuration tree for determining a route for a connection between the master and slave units. Slave address and topology information may include an own address from each of the slave units and only first order address lists from each of the slave units. Generating the configuration tree involves generating a hierarchy of connectivity rings from the first order address lists. Each connectivity ring may be generated in accordance with a rule that a higher-numbered connectivity ring cannot include nodes representing units that are already represented by a node in a lower-numbered connectivity ring. Alternatively, each connectivity ring may be generated by considering a present numbered connectivity ring having parent nodes, and including in a next higher-numbered connectivity ring those nodes representing all children of the parent nodes such that no descendant of a parent can represent the same unit as the parent; no descendant of a parent's child can represent the same unit as any of the parent's children; and no child of any parent can have the same name as any other child of said any parent.

28 Claims, 9 Drawing Sheets

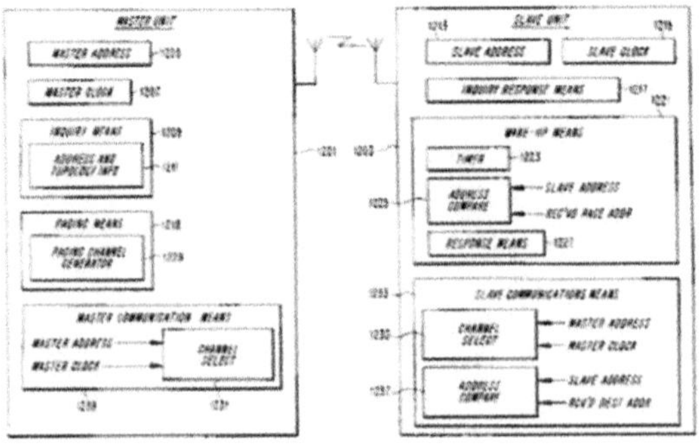

26 Mask Work Protection

26.1 INTRODUCTION

This chapter is directed to a discussion of the protection afforded to semiconductor chips under the U.S. Copyright Law, in an amendment enacted in 1984 to provide protection against piracy of chip topography. The subject law is discussed, as well as the definition of "mask works" subject to the law's protection, the rights acquired by the creator of a mask work; the ownership, transfer, and licensing of mask works; and the limitations on the exclusive rights obtained by the creator of a mask work.

Caveat: It is the consensus today of a segment of the semiconductor chip industry that market advancements, technological enhancements, and improved industry and technology practices have had more influence on protecting chip manufacturers than the enactment of this law. However, the law is discussed in this treatise in the event that a reader may have a reason to use the law, or to discuss the law with his or her intellectual property professional.

26.2 THE SEMICONDUCTOR CHIP PROTECTION ACT OF 1984

In 1984, the United States Congress passed the Semiconductor Chip Protection Act of 1984, 17 U.S.C. §902 *et seq.* (the "Chip Act"). Although the Chip Act is part of the Copyright Law and is administered by the Copyright Office, the law embodies both copyright and patent law concepts to provide protection for the physical "chips" upon which computer technology depends. Because of the nature of the covered technology, the Chip Act protects computer code as circuitry, including code fixed in ROM chips. Before the enactment of the Chip Act in 1984, this type of code was not universally protected under Copyright Law.

Mask works protected under the Chip Act are defined as follows:

> A series of related images, however fixed or encoded (1) having or representing the predetermined three dimensional pattern of metallic, insulating or semiconductor material present or removed from the layers of a semiconductor chip product; and (2) in which series the relation of the images to one another is that each image has the pattern of the surface of one form of the semiconductor chip product.

Intellectual Property Law for Engineers, Scientists, and Entrepreneurs, Second Edition. Howard B. Rockman.

Published 2020 by John Wiley & Sons, Inc.

The integrated circuits, better known as "semiconductor chips," are defined in the Chip Act as:

> The final or intermediate form of any product (1) having two or more layers of metallic, insulating, or semiconductor material, deposited or otherwise placed on or etched away or otherwise removed from a piece of semiconductor material in accordance with a predetermined pattern; and (2) intended to perform electronic circuitry functions."

Protection under the Chip Act extends to the three-dimensional images or patterns formed on or in the layers of metallic insulating or semiconductor material, and fixed in a semiconductor chip product. This is also defined as the "topography" of the chip. These patterns are purely functional, and normally would not be covered under the standard Copyright Law. However, under the Chip Act, they are protected, provided that the mask work configuration is not dictated by a particular electronic function, and is not one of only a few available design choices that will implement that function. Protection of a mask work is initiated upon registration according to the law, or commercial exploitation, whichever occurs first. Commercial exploitation consists of distributing a semiconductor chip comprising the mask work to the public for commercial purposes, or a written offer to sell a chip that is already in existence. The Chip Act also requires that the mask work be original, and mere ideas are not protected, which is in keeping with the overall provisions of the Copyright Law.

Prior to enactment of the Chip Act, semiconductor computer chip designs were not considered as copyrightable subject matter, as being "useful articles" under the Copyright Law. The Chip Act is based on Congress' powers under the Constitution to protect "writings" under the intellectual property clause found in Article I, Section 8 of the Constitution. Also, as in the case of patents or copyright infringement, the federal court system has exclusive jurisdiction over infringement actions relating to mask work protection.

26.3 MASK WORKS GENERALLY

As mentioned previously, the Chip Act defines semiconductors and the mask works used to create them. The law also defines what constitutes fixing of a mask work on a chip product. The owner of a protectable right under the Chip Act is the creator, or the one to whom the rights in the mask work have been transferred. If the mask work is made by an employee, the employer is automatically considered the owner of rights in the mask work.

The owner of the mask work can register a claim of protection under Section 908 of the Copyright Act with the U.S. Copyright Office of the Library of Congress to protect the mask work. The application must be filed within two years of the first commercial exploitation of the work anywhere in the world, and identifying material for the mask work must be submitted with the application. Protection is effective from the application filing date, when the identifying material and filing fee have been submitted with the application. If a registration certificate is refused by the Copyright Office, this refusal can be appealed to a United States District Court.

26.4 SUBJECT MATTER OF MASK WORK PROTECTION

The law protects a mask work fixed in a semiconductor chip product. There is no protection if the mask work is not original. Also, there is no protection if the mask work consists of designs that are staple, commonplace, or familiar in the semiconductor industry, or variations combined whereby when considered as a whole, the combination is not original. In no case does protection for mask works extend to any idea, procedure, process, system, method of operation, concept, principle, or discovery regardless of the form in which it is described, explained, illustrated, or embodied in such work. This follows the general theme of the Copyright Law that only expressions of ideas fixed in a tangible medium are protectable, not the ideas themselves.

The placement of logic groupings in a mask work is not to be considered an abstract concept, unworthy of protection. The logic groupings are embedded in the chip, and affect the chip's performance and efficiency, as well as the chip's timing.

26.5 OWNERSHIP, TRANSFER, AND LICENSING OF THE MASK WORK

The exclusive rights in the mask work belong to its owner, who may transfer or license those exclusive rights, or a subset of those rights, by a written document. Also, these rights may be bequeathed by will and be passed as personal property upon the death of the owner. Documents relating to the ownership or transfer of a mask work may be recorded in the Copyright Office to establish and prove transfer and ownership at a later date. The recordation provides all persons with constructive notice of the facts stated in the document regarding the transfer.

Mask works prepared by an officer or employee of the U.S. Government are not subject to protection under the Copyright Law, but the Government may receive and hold exclusive rights in mask works transferred to it.

26.6 DURATION OF PROTECTION

Protection begins on the date a mask work is registered, or on the date the mask work is first commercially exploited anywhere in the world, whichever occurs first. Mask work protection lasts for ten years from the date upon which the protection commences, and the term of protection runs until the end of the calendar year in which the registration would otherwise expire.

26.7 RIGHTS OF OWNERSHIP IN A MASK WORK

The owner of a mask work has the exclusive right to do, or to authorize others to do, the following:

1. To reproduce the mask work by optical, electronic, or any other means.
2. To import or distribute a semiconductor chip product in which the mask work is embodied.
3. To induce or knowingly to cause another person to do any of the first two acts.

26.8 LIMITATIONS ON EXCLUSIVE RIGHTS, REVERSE ENGINEERING, AND FIRST SALE

The exclusive rights of the owner of a mask work are not infringed where one reproduces the mask work solely for the purpose of teaching, analyzing, or evaluating the concepts or techniques embodied in the mask work, or in the circuitry, logic flow, or organization of components used in the mask work. Also, there is no infringement where a person performs analyzes or evaluations by reverse engineering to incorporate the results in a new original mask work that is made to be distributed. Further, the purchaser of a semiconductor chip product made by the owner of the mask work or one authorized by the owner may import, distribute, or otherwise dispose of or use, but not reproduce, that particular semiconductor chip product without the authority of the owner of the mask work.

An innocent purchaser of an infringing semiconductor chip product bears no liability for infringement prior to the time the innocent purchaser has notice of the protection, and is liable for a reasonable royalty only after having notice of such protection.

26.9 MASK WORK NOTICE

There is no absolute notice requirement; however, the owner of mask work protection may affix a notice to the mask work and to the semiconductor chip products embodying the mask work to provide reasonable public notice of such protection. As stated above, this provision is not obligatory. Placing notice of protection on the product is not a condition of protection under the Chip Act, but does constitute prima facie evidence of the fact that you have given notice to others of your protection. If you do apply the notice, it shall consist of the word "Mask Work," the symbol "M" or the symbol "M" in a circle, followed by the name of the owner or owners of the mask work, or an abbreviation by which the owner can be recognized or identified.

26.10 INFRINGEMENT OF MASK WORK PROTECTION RIGHTS

Actions may be brought in the U.S. federal courts to enforce mask work protection rights. Exclusionary orders for infringing imported products may be issued pursuant to provisions of the Secretary of Treasury and the U.S. Postal Service, and the infringing chips will not be allowed into the country.

In an infringement action, one found liable for violating another's mask work protection rights may be compelled to pay the owner of those rights the infringer's profits, plus the amount of damages caused to the owner of those rights. The law also provides for the impounding of semiconductor chips subject to a lawsuit under the Chip Act.

26.11 GENERAL COMMENTS ABOUT MASK WORK PROTECTION

The Chip Act provides the owner of mask work protection the exclusive right to reproduce the mask work by any method, as well as to import and distribute a semiconductor chip that embodies the protected mask work. Remember, however, that it is not infringement to “reverse engineer” the mask work for most purposes. You may also incorporate the results of your reverse engineering analysis into a new mask work, so long as the new mask work meets the originality requirement. Under the law, if you sell a chip embodying a mask work, the right to copy that mask work is not conveyed with the sale. This is the same as the Copyright Law that provides that you do not purchase the right to copy a book when you purchase the book. You may only read the book or use it in other legitimate ways.

SECTION V

Trade Secrets

Stephanie Kwolek

KEVLAR®

Fig. I.

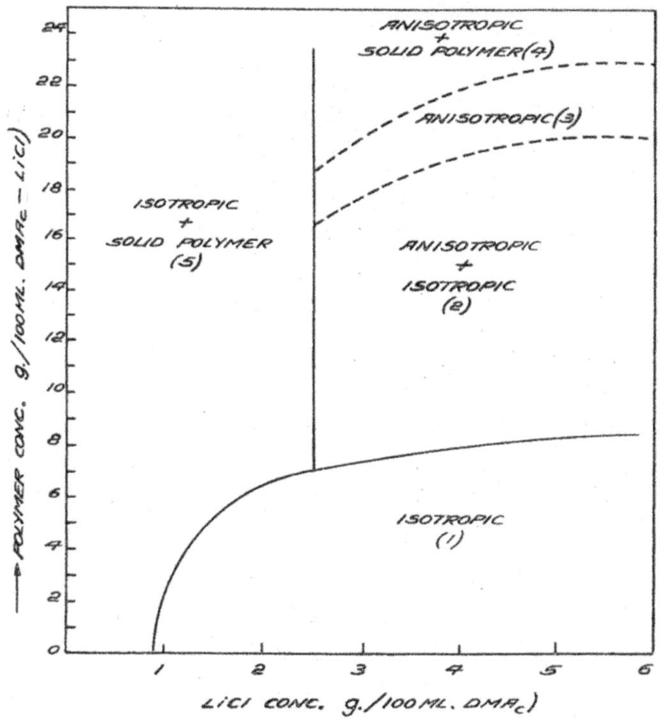

Stephanie Louise Kwolek, an American chemist whose career at DuPont Company spanned over 40 years, is best known for inventing the first family of para-aramid synthetic fibers of exceptional strength and stiffness: poly-paraphenylene terephthalamide, better known as Kevlar. Kwolek was the fourth woman to be admitted to the National Inventor's Hall of Fame.

Kwolek, the daughter of Polish immigrant parents, was born in the Pittsburgh suburb of New Kensington, Pennsylvania, in 1923. Before her father passed away

Intellectual Property Law for Engineers, Scientists, and Entrepreneurs, Second Edition. Howard B. Rockman.

Published 2020 by John Wiley & Sons, Inc.

when she was 10 years old, Stephanie gained an interest in science as a result of her father's interest in exploring the natural world.

In 1946, Kwolek was offered a position at DuPont after obtaining a chemistry degree from Margaret Morrison Carnegie College of Carnegie Mellon University. This opportunity became available to her as a woman because of the number of men then oversees due to World War II. Initially, Kwolek was interested in pursuing a medical career, and only intended to work for DuPont on a temporary basis. However, she found the work she was doing interesting because it combined her interest in science and textiles, and she decided to stay at DuPont rather than pursuing a medical career. She moved to Wilmington, Delaware, in 1950, where she continued to work for DuPont. In 1959, she won a publication award from the American Chemical Society for her paper entitled "The Nylon Rope Trick," which demonstrated a way of reducing nylon in a beaker at room temperature, which is still used today as the basis of a classroom experiment.

In 1964, anticipating a gasoline shortage, Kwolek and her group at DuPont began searching for a lightweight, strong fiber to be used in tires. The polymers she had been working with at that time, poly-p-phenylene terephthalate and polybenzamide, formed liquid crystals in solution that at the time had to be melt-spun at over 392°F. This process produced weaker and less stiff fibers. The objective of the unique technique used in her new projects, and the melt-condensation polymerization process, was to reduce these temperatures to between 32 and 104°F. She later explained in a 1993 speech that the solution she proposed was unusually (low viscosity) turbid, *stir-opalescent*, buttermilk-like in appearance, and thin. Conventional polymer solutions were usually clear or translucent and had the viscosity of molasses, more or less. The solution that she prepared at the time, as she stated, appeared as a dispersion that was totally filterable through a fine porous filter. This was a liquid crystalline solution, but she did not know this at the time, she said. This sort of cloudy solution was usually thrown away; however, Kwolek persuaded the technician, Charles Smullen, who ran the *spinneret* to test her solution. They were amazed to find that the resulting new fiber would not break at the point where nylon was typically severed. Her strand was stronger than nylon and ultimately proved to be five times stronger than steel by weight. As a result of her accidental discovery, a new field of polymer chemistry quickly arose. Her discovery of liquid crystalline polyamides led to the Kevlar aramid fibers. Kwolek learned that the fibers could be made even stronger by heat treating. The polymer molecules shaped like rods from matchsticks, are highly oriented, which gives Kevlar its extraordinary strength. In 1971, modern Kevlar was introduced. Kevlar is also extremely lightweight, and does not corrode or rust.

Kwolek was not involved in subsequent development of practical applications for Kevlar. Once the DuPont managers were informed of her discovery, they assigned the whole group to work on different aspects and also, as is typical in major corporations in the United States, she had signed over the Kevlar patent rights to DuPont. Kevlar today is used in more than 200 applications, including tennis rackets, airplanes, ropes and cables, tires, and most notably bullet-proof vests. Also included are hockey sticks, hockey goalie masks, and armored cars, as well as protective building materials such as bomb-proof materials and bridge reinforcements. Note also that Motorola's Droid Razr cellphone has a Kevlar unibody.

Kevlar is best known for its use in multi-ply body armor vests, where a handgun bullet is caught in a web of very strong fibers. The fibers absorb and disperse the energy of the impact throughout the vest, causing deformation or "mushrooming" of the bullet. Additional energy from the impact is absorbed by each successive layer of vest material until movement of the bullet stops. The fibers work with each other in the individual layer, and with other material layers in the vest, and a large area of the vest becomes involved in stopping the bullet before reaching the wearer of the vest. As a result, forces that can cause non-penetrating trauma to internal organs are dissipated.

In the United Kingdom, the Royal Society of Chemistry grants a biannual Stephanie L. Kwolek award, recognizing the exceptional contributions to the area of material chemistry and science from a scientist working outside the United Kingdom.

After Kwolek retired, she became heavily involved in introducing young children, particularly girls, to scientific fields.

United States Patent [19]

Kwoleck

CERT OF CORR ON LAST PAGE

[11] **3,819,587**

[45] **June 25, 1974**

[54] **WHOLLY AROMATIC CARBOCYCLIC POLYCARBONAMIDE FIBER HAVING ORIENTATION ANGLE OF LESS THAN ABOUT 45°**

[75] Inventor: **Stephanie Louise Kwoleck,** Wilmington, Del.

[73] Assignee: **E. I. du Pont de Nemours and Company,** Wilmington, Del.

[22] Filed: **Sept. 7, 1971**

[21] Appl. No.: **178,184**

Related U.S. Application Data

[63] Continuation-in-part of Ser. No. 827,345, May 23, 1969, Pat. No. 3,671,542, which is a continuation-in-part of Ser. No. 736,410, June 12, 1968, abandoned, which is a continuation-in-part of Ser. No. 644,851, June 9, 1967, abandoned, which is a continuation-in-part of Ser. No. 556,934, June 13, 1966, abandoned.

[52] **U.S. Cl.** .... **260/78 R,** 57/140 R, 161/227, 260/30.2, 250/30.6 R, 260/30.8 R, 260/32.6 N, 260/37 N, 260/78 A, 260/78 S, 264/210 F, 264/235

[51] **Int. Cl.** **C08g 20/20,** C08g 20/38

[58] **Field of Search** ... 260/78 R, 78 A, 78 S, 47 CZ

[56] **References Cited**

UNITED STATES PATENTS

3,079,219	2/1963	King	260/78 S
3,094,511	6/1963	Hill et al.	260/78 R
3,228,902	1/1966	Beste	260/78 S
3,287,324	11/1966	Sweeny	260/78 R
3,354,127	11/1967	Hill et al.	260/78 R
3,554,971	1/1971	Jones et al.	260/78 R

Primary Examiner—Harold D. Anderson

[57] **ABSTRACT**

Fibers of unique internal structure (evidenced by low orientation angle and/or high sonic velocity) and exceptionally high tensile properties (e.g., initial modulus) are prepared from spinning dopes of selected carbocyclic aromatic polyamides in suitable liquid media.

16 Claims, 9 Drawing Figures

◆ INVENTORS AND INVENTIONS ◆

Percy Julian

THE SYNTHESIS OF CORTISONE

Percy Lavon Julian, a prominent chemist, was born in Montgomery, Alabama, on April 11, 1899, the oldest of six children born to James Julian, a railroad mail clerk, and his wife, who was a school teacher. Julian's parents both emphasized the importance of education. Percy Julian spent his life in chemical research, often making use of soybean products, which led to inventions and discoveries in the manufacture of inexpensive drugs, hormones, vitamins, amino acids, and paint and paper products. Julian's research resulted in over 100 patents being awarded in his name, as well as many honors being bestowed upon him by professional and community organizations.

Percy Julian attended high school at the State Normal School for Negroes in Montgomery, Alabama, and, in 1916, he entered by DePauw University in Green Castle, Indiana. He began as a "subfreshman" student, and was compelled to take upper-level high school courses along with his freshman and sophomore class load. He earned his way through undergraduate school at DePauw by digging ditches and waiting on fraternity house tables. As a result of his innate brightness, he became a member of Sigma Xi honorary society, as well as Phi Beta Kappa. He was the class valedictorian at his graduation from DePauw in 1920. However, he was discouraged from applying to graduate school at that time because of the possibility of adverse racial sentiment. Instead, he became a chemistry teacher at Fisk University, an African-American college in Nashville, Tennessee.

Two years later, Julian earned the Austin Fellowship in Chemistry at Fisk, and then attended Harvard University in Cambridge, Massachusetts, where he finally had the opportunity to engage in graduate-level studies, in which he excelled. Julian finished at the top of his Harvard class, and received a master's degree in chemistry in 1923. However, because of his race, he was unable to obtain a position at a major university as a teaching assistant, reportedly due to the perception that white students would refuse to learn under an African-American instructor. Therefore, Julian took a position at the West Virginia State College for Negroes, and after that became associate professor of chemistry at Howard University in Washington, D.C., for two years.

In 1929, Julian received a fellowship from the General Education Board, and in 1931 he obtained a PhD degree in chemistry in Vienna, Austria. It was in Vienna that he developed an interest in soybeans, and he focused on organic chemistry.

Upon returning to the United States, Julian served at Howard University as the head of the chemistry department, but he soon left Howard and moved back to DePauw, where he was appointed as an instructor in organic chemistry. While at

Intellectual Property Law for Engineers, Scientists, and Entrepreneurs, Second Edition. Howard B. Rockman.

Published 2020 by John Wiley & Sons, Inc.

DePauw, he and an associate from Vienna, Dr. Josef Pikl, developed the synthesis of physostigmine, a pharmaceutical product used to treat glaucoma by reducing the pressure inside the eyeball. This work brought Julian international acclaim, and he *almost* became the chair of the chemistry department at DePauw. However, the Dean of the university was compelled to change his mind by others in the department, reportedly due to concerns over Julian's race.

Upon returning to DePauw, Julian became interested in drug synthesis, including investigating traditional medicinal plants, such as the African calabar bean, from which physostigmine was first synthesized. On December 24, 1935, Julian married Anna Johnson.

During the 1935–1936 period, Julian learned that chemists in Germany were discovering that the steroid stigmasterol, which Julian had recovered as a by-product of the physostigmine synthesis process but knew was also obtainable from soybeans, could be used in the preparation of sex hormones. Julian followed up this lead, and in 1936 wrote to the Glidden Company in Chicago, requesting sample soybean oil. Glidden's vice president, W. J. O'Brien, heard about Julian's accomplishments, and offered him a position as Director of Research of the Glidden Soya Products Division. The Glidden Company was a leading manufacturer of vanishes and paints, and wanted Julian to research and develop compounds from soy-based products for use in paints and other products. Julian accepted the job, and remained at Glidden until 1954, at which time he founded his own company, Julian Laboratories.

While at Glidden, Julian noticed one day in 1939 that a water leak in a tank of purified soybean oil produced a unique by-product: the soy sterol created by this leak could be used to manufacture female and male hormones, progesterone and testosterone, respectively. Progesterone later proved efficient in treating cancer and problem pregnancies. He synthesized the hormones progesterone and testosterone from soybean oil, and also obtained a patent on an early liquid crystal. Julian also developed many commercial processes, including the isolation and preparation of soybean protein, which is used to coat and size paper, create cold-water paints, and size textiles.

During the Second World War, Percy Julian created a foam product, Aero-Foam, from soy protein that was useful in smothering oil and gas fires. This fire-extinguishing material was rapidly adopted by the military, and it is reported that countless sailors' lives were saved during the war by Julian's Aero-Foam product.

The Mayo Clinic, in 1948, discovered cortisone, a compound that was effective in relieving rheumatoid arthritis. However, natural cortisone was very difficult and expensive to obtain, since it had to be extracted from the adrenal glands of oxen, and cost hundreds of dollars per drop. However, Percy Julian attacked the problem, and in October 1949, his team had completed the process of synthesizing a cortisone substitute that cost only pennies per ounce, rather than hundreds of dollars per drop for the natural substance. Julian located a wild sweet potato in Guatemala, and discovered how to synthesize cortisone from it for just pennies a gram. As a result of his work on cortisone, the City of Chicago in 1950 named Julian Chicagoan of the Year.

In 1949, Julian published a paper directed to a synthesis for Reichstein's substance, which is also present in the adrenal cortex, and differs from cortisone by lacking a single oxygen atom at a specific molecular position. Hydrocortisone is today produced from the substance. It enables those suffering from rheumatoid arthritis to regain the use of their limbs.

In 1950, Julian, his wife, and his two children moved to the Chicago suburb of Oak Park, famous for its Frank Lloyd Wright homes. Soon after purchasing his home, an arsonist set fire to their house on Thanksgiving Day of 1950. A year later, dynamite was thrown at the house from a passing car, exploding beneath the bedroom window of Julian's children. As a result of these atrocities, a community group in Oak Park rose to the defense of the Julian's rights as the first African-Americans to live in Oak Park, and the community offered support to the family. Julian remained in Oak Park and became a lifelong resident of the community, as well as a symbol for racial integration in the village. In 1985, Hawthorne School in Oak Park was renamed to honor Percy Julian. Today, Julian's birthday is celebrated as a holiday in Oak Park.

Julian left the Glidden Company in 1954, and established his own company, Julian Laboratories, producing his synthetic cortisone. Upon discovering that the yams in Mexico could be used to produce synthetic cortisone and some of his other products, he opened Laboratorios Julian de Mexico, which farmed the yams and sent them back to Oak Park for synthesis. In 1961, he sold his Oak Park and Mexico plants to Smith, Kline and French, a pharmaceutical company, for the sum of 2.3 million dollars. He also sold another chemical plant in Guatemala to Upjohn Company in 1961.

During his lifetime of research, Julian received numerous awards and honors, including the prestigious Spingarn Medal from the NAACP, 19 honorary doctorate degrees, 9 schools and buildings named by universities in his honor, induction into the National Inventors Hall of Fame, and election to the National Academy of Sciences. Percy Julian also assisted in founding the Legal Defense and Educational Fund of Chicago, an organization whose purpose is to enhance the living conditions of African-Americans. In 1956, he was the first African-American and first layman to lead the Counsel for Social Action of the Congregational Christian Churches. An additional school on the south side of Chicago was also named after Percy Julian.

Percy Julian succumbed to liver cancer in 1975, leaving behind a life and a career that stands as a beacon both in the world of chemistry, and for future generations of African-American scientists.

United States Patent Office 2,752,339 Patented June 26, 1956

1

2,752,339

PREPARATION OF CORTISONE

Percy L. Julian, Maywood, John Wayne Cole, Oak Park, and Edwin W. Meyer and William J. Karpel, Chicago, Ill., assignors to The Glidden Company, Cleveland, Ohio, a corporation of Ohio

No Drawing. Application September 9, 1950, Serial No. 184,124

29 Claims. (Cl. 260—239.55)

The present invention relates to the preparation of 4-pregnene-17α,21-diol-3,11,20-trione and its 21-monoacetate, generally known as cortisone and cortisone acetate, respectively.

The name "cortisone" has been given to the compound previously known as "Kendall's Compound E," which is 4-pregnene-17α,21-diol-3,11,20-trione. The discovery by Kendall and his coworkers that cortisone is beneficial in the relief of the symptoms of rheumatoid arthritis greatly stimulated research on the partial synthesis of this material from other steroid raw materials. These partial syntheses involve degradation of the side chain of sterols, bile acids and steroid saponins to an acetyl group, introduction of a 17α-hydroxy group, introduction of a 21-hydroxy or acyloxy group, introduction of an 11-keto group, conversion of a 3-hydroxy group to a keto group, and formation of a 4,5 double bond where this is not already present. Processes are known whereby each of these results may be achieved. However, there is a multiplicity of steps involved, the overall yield is, of course, low, and in all cases consideration must be given to the particular reactions being carried out in the light of the various functional groups present.

The present invention is not concerned with the introduction of the 11-keto group, nor with the formation of the acetyl group in the 17-position of the molecule, but is concerned with the other conversions and reactions mentioned.

It is accordingly an object of the present invention to provide a novel process for the manufacture of cortisone.

Another object of the invention is to provide a process for producing cortisone from 10,13-dimethyl-3-hydroxy-11,20 - diketocyclopentanopolyhydrophenanthrene compounds of the C-21 series.

A further object of the invention is to provide a series of reactions useful in the production of cortisone.

An additional object of the invention is to produce new compounds useful for producing cortisone.

Other objects will be apparent to those skilled in the art from the following description:

A fundamental aspect of the invention is the use of 16,17-oxido-pregnan-3α-ol-11,20-dione for the manufacture of cortisone. This oxido compound may conveniently be made by treatment of 16-pregnen-3α-ol-11,20-dione with a suitable epoxidizing agent such as perbenzoic acid, or more conveniently with alkaline hydrogen peroxide.

The conversion of the 16,17-oxido-pregnan-3α-ol-11,20-dione into cortisone involves the following reactions: (1) the conversion of the 16,17-oxido group to a 17α-hydroxy group by treatment with HBr, followed by removal of the 16-bromo group thus introduced by treatment with Raney nickel; (2) introduction of a 21-acyloxy group by first brominating to introduce a 21-bromo group, followed by treatment with a metal salt of a carboxylic acid, such as sodium or potassium acetate, formate, benzoate, etc., to replace the 21-bromo

2

group with an acyloxy group; (3) oxidation of the 3α-hydroxy group to a keto group; and (4) introduction of a 4,5-double bond by first brominating a 3-keto compound at the 4-position, followed by removal of HBr. It is not essential that the various reactions or steps be carried out in the order recited, but in some cases certain of the reactions must take place subsequent to others. Thus considerable flexibility is inherent in the overall procedure, as is shown by the flow sheet and as will be more fully explained.

PREPARATION OF 17α-HYDROXY COMPOUNDS

The 16,17-oxidopregnan-3α-ol-11,20-dione may be prepared from 16-pregnen-3α-ol-11,20-dione, which may in turn be prepared as described in co-pending application Serial No. 152,752, filed March 29, 1950, by treatment of the pregnene with epoxidizing agents such as perbenzoic acid, or, preferably, by treatment with alkaline hydrogen peroxide, as is more fully disclosed in co-pending application Serial No. 165,120, filed May 9, 1950.

The first step in the conversion of the oxido group is the treatment of the oxido compound with HBr, which results in the production of a 16-bromo-17α-hydroxybromhydrin. The treatment with HBr may take place at any stage of the process at which the oxido group is present. The oxido group is restored when the α-bromhydrin structure is subjected to an alkaline treatment. Thus, treatment of the 21-bromo compound with the metal salt to introduce the 21-acyloxy group will inherently restore the oxido group where the bromhydrin grouping is also present. Also in some instances it may be desirable to deliberately restore the oxido group by a mild alkaline treatment, since the oxido compounds are generally high-melting materials and readily crystallized. Also, since the presence of a 17α-hydroxy group is preferred for introduction of the 21-bromo group, as will more fully appear, it will be apparent that the opening up of the oxido group and its restoration may in some cases be advantageous. Of course, ultimately the conversion of the oxide to the bromhydrin and removal of the 16-bromo group must be brought about.

The 16-bromo group may be removed at any stage in the process up to and including the last step in the formation of the cortisone acetate. The treatment with Raney nickel, however, would remove a 21-bromo group, if present, and as no useful purpose would be served by such removal, the treatment with Raney nickel of a 21-bromo compound is ordinarily to be avoided.

INTRODUCTION OF THE 21-ACYLOXY GROUP

The first step in the introduction of the 21-acyloxy group is the treatment with bromine. The presence of the 17α-hydroxy group is essential to the introduction of the 21-bromo group. If an oxido compound is treated with bromine, some HBr will be formed which will open up the oxide ring, and introduction of a 21-bromo group will follow. However, such a procedure leads to difficultly separable mixtures and low yields and is to be avoided for best practice.

The bromination may be carried out in a variety of solvents. When a solvent such as acetic acid, or other acylating mixture, is used, the 3-OH group will, of course, be acylated, and when the use of such a solvent is contemplated for the bromination, it is preferred to first acylate the 3-OH group before brominating. However, non-acylating solvents such as carbon tetrachloride, chloroform, and the like, may be employed.

The replacement of the 21-bromo group by an acyloxy group is effected by treatment with a metallic salt of a carboxylic acid, such as potassium or sodium acetate,

27 Trade Secrets Protection

27.1 THE DEVELOPMENT OF TRADE SECRET LAW

The next aspect of intellectual property protection, apart from the patent, trademark, and copyright laws, is the law governing the protection of trade secrets. Trade secret law developed from the common law, and not from statutory or legislative origins. This area of the law encompasses two broad policies: to provide an enforceable standard of commercial ethics, and to encourage innovation by providing protection that is supplemental to that offered by the Federal Patent and Copyright Laws. Also, unlike a patent or a copyright, a trade secret has no limited life, and may last forever under certain conditions, since trade secret law does not derive from the Constitutional provision mentioned previously. Moreover, trade secret protection extends to practically all types of information, and protection is acquired without any need to file any applications for registration or without any other formalities, except that efforts must be made to maintain the confidentiality and secrecy of the information. Once the information legally becomes public knowledge, the secrecy is lost, and protection is also lost. Further, trade secrets can also be licensed to others.

Since 1939, and up to May 2016, trade secret law has been governed solely by state law, and is substantially influenced by Sections 259, 757, and 758 of the First Restatement of Torts. The Restatement, published by the American Law Institute, is a compilation of laws by legal scholars, in an attempt to summarize the existing court-developed common law on several important subjects. Since the misappropriation of one's trade secret is considered a tort, the Restatement of Torts, at the sections mentioned, set forth the law as it has been known and has evolved, governing many of the court decisions on trade secret law.

Section 757 of the First Restatement of Torts states as follows:

"One who discloses or uses another's trade secret, without a privilege to do so, is liable to the other if:

1. He discovered the secret by improper means, or
2. His disclosure or use constitutes a breach of confidence reposed in him by the other in disclosing the secret to him, or

Intellectual Property Law for Engineers, Scientists, and Entrepreneurs, Second Edition. Howard B. Rockman.

Published 2020 by John Wiley & Sons, Inc.

3. He learned the secret from a third person with notice of the fact that it was a secret and that the third person discovered the secret by improper means or that the third person's disclosure of the secret was otherwise a breach of his duty to the other, or
4. He learned the secret with notice of the fact that it was a secret and that its disclosure was made to him by mistake."

Restatement Section 758 provides:

"One who learns another's trade secret from a third person without notice that it is a secret and that the third person's disclosure is a breach of his duty to the other, or who learns the secret through a mistake without notice of the secrecy and the mistake,

1. is not liable to the other for disclosure or use of the secret prior to receipt of such notice, and
2. is liable to the other for a disclosure or use of the secret after the receipt of such notice, unless prior thereto he has in good faith paid value for the secret or has so changed his position that to subject him to liability would be inequitable.[1]"

In 1979, the National Conference of Commissioners on Uniform State Laws published the Uniform Trade Secrets Act. This Act was not a national or state law, but was promulgated to encourage state legislators to adopt the law. As of the present, most of the states of the Union have adopted the 1979 version, or a revised version that was promulgated in 1985. The Uniform Trade Secrets Act and the Restatement of Torts are quite similar in many respects, and the Restatement provisions continue to be influential in interpretations of the various state Uniform Trade Secrets Acts.

In May 2016, the U.S. Congress enacted the Federal Defend Trade Secrets Act of 2016, providing for the first time a federal cause of action in Federal Court for the misappropriation of trade secrets. The provisions of the new federal trade secret act are discussed in Chapter 28.

27.2 THE NATURE OF A TRADE SECRET

When analyzing trade secret misappropriation claims, two basic questions are analyzed. First, does the information or idea at issue qualify as a trade secret? And second, if it is a trade secret, is the defendant's acquisition, disclosure, or use of the trade secret prohibited under one or more of the concepts set forth in either the Restatement of Torts or the Uniform Trade Secrets Act if that Act is in effect in the state where the misappropriation took place. It must be kept in mind that state trade secret law prohibits the disclosure of confidential industrial technology developed by its owner, even though that technology is not patented or even patentable. Thus, trade secret law addresses different, non-inventive subject matter, where the focus is directed on the unlawful conduct utilized to obtain the secret information, as compared to technology

---

[1] Copyright 1939 by American Law Institute. All rights reserved. Reprinted with permission.

that was independently developed by the one acquiring the information, such as by reverse engineering.

Trade secret laws of the United States and the states and the federal Patent Law co-exist. Thus, the concept of trade secret misappropriation up to the enactment of the Federal Law in 2016 was handled primarily at the state court level, and under state laws, either statutory or common law, while the Federal Doctrine of Preemption applies to the patent and copyright laws. Under the Doctrine of Preemption, the copyright law and the patent law are entirely federal jurisdictional matters. In contrast, trade secret law is within the purview of the states and now under the new Federal Law also.

Trade secret protection is obtained without publicly disclosing the secret, which is in contrast to a patent, which provides the inventor a definite period of exclusive rights in exchange for the inventor's disclosure of the invention. Under the new Federal Law, the Uniform Trade Secrets Act, and under the common law affecting trade secrets, one who discloses or uses another's trade secret is generally liable if he or she discovered or obtained the secret by improper means, or if the disclosure or use constitutes a breach of confidence between the one who is charged with liability and the owner of the trade secret.

27.3 THE DEFINITION OF A "TRADE SECRET"

The applicable law normally defines a trade secret as consisting of any formula, pattern, device, or compilation of information that gives the owner an opportunity to obtain an advantage over competitors or other persons who do not know or use the particular secret, which competitors or other persons can obtain economic value from the disclosure or use of the trade secret information. The definition includes chemical formulas, programs, manufacturing processes, machine patterns, customer and vendor lists, pricing and financial information, future business plans, personnel data, and the like. A trade secret is normally considered a process or device for continuous use in the operation of a business, and not merely a secret bit of information that just has usefulness for a very short time period or instantaneously. To identify a trade secret in your organization, look for operations of high efficiency that provide a competitive advantage.

By way of example, the Illinois Trade Secrets Act, found at Illinois Revised Statutes 1991, Chapter 140, Paragraph 352, Section 2(d), defines a trade secret as follows:

> "Trade secret" means information, including but not limited to, technical or non-technical data, a formula, pattern, compilation, program, device, method, technique, drawing, process, financial data, or list of actual or potential customers or suppliers that:
>
> 1. is sufficiently secret to derive economic value, actual or potential, from not being generally known to other persons who can obtain economic value from its disclosure or use; and
> 2. is the subject of efforts that are reasonable under the circumstances to maintain its secrecy or confidentiality.

The above provision of the Illinois Trade Secret Statute, court decisions defining common law rights in the owner of a trade secret, the new Federal Trade Secrets Law, and other state statutes normally define the existence of the trade secret in quite the same way. Thus, the above definitions to some extent are generally universal, and include any information that has long-term usefulness for a corporation or other entity where the information is maintained in secrecy, and that gives the owner of the trade secret information a competitive advantage.

27.4 THE CREATION OF AN ENFORCEABLE TRADE SECRET RIGHT

Trade secrets drive the competitive advantage in shareholder value of many of today's global and national companies. Since the existence and value of trade secrets depend to a large degree on the legal protections provided to these assets, the value of one's trade secrets can be increased by appropriate trade secret management policies and practices, and can be totally destroyed by improper trade secret policies and practice. The success of business ventures that rely heavily on trade secrets in their business depends on how well they identify, acquire or develop, manage, and take steps to protect their trade secrets. Once a trade secret is publicly disclosed, it cannot be retrieved. You cannot reconstruct a burst bubble.

To establish an enforceable trade secret right, the owner of the alleged trade secret must show that positive concrete steps were taken to maintain the secrecy of the information. Thus, if the information sought to be protected as a trade secret is obvious and totally apparent upon viewing an object or device embodying the secret, or if the information is merely a base of experimental knowledge that is readily available to others in the same industry, it is highly unlikely that a court would protect the information as a trade secret. However—and this is important—the availability of information through publicly accessible sources is irrelevant, and a violation of one's trade secret rights can be proven, if the information is shown to have been maintained in a secret status by the owner, and the one accused of misappropriating and using or disseminating the secret information acquired the secret information through a breach of a confidential relationship, or through the use of other unlawful and improper means.

Several factors are considered in determining whether or not a certain body of information is confidential enough to support a claim of trade secrecy:

1. Is the information known outside of the trade secret owner's business?
2. How extensive is the information made known to employees and others involved in the business of the owner of the alleged trade secret?
3. What specific steps have been taken by the owner of the trade secret to control and guard the secrecy of the information, and to restrict its access to others, including employees not involved in use of the secret information?
4. What is the value of the alleged secret information to the trade secret owner and to his competition?
5. How much in terms of resources and effort has the owner of the alleged trade secret spent in protecting the confidentiality of the secret information?
6. How easy is it for the information to be properly acquired, duplicated, or reverse engineered by others, such as competitors?

If the information attempted to be maintained as a trade secret can be obtained through reverse engineering of a product embodying the trade secret, such as using chemical analysis equipment, and the alleged thief of the trade secret has used such reverse engineering to obtain knowledge of the trade secret, the alleged thief faces no liability, for they have done nothing wrong. However, the essence of trade secret law is that if one used improper means, such as theft of the trade secret formula, or a bribe to an employee of the owner of the trade secret to unlawfully divulge the secret information, this constitutes the tort of theft of a trade secret, and the one perpetrating the theft will be held liable to the owner for misappropriation of the trade secret.

Note that even though the trade secret may be able to become public knowledge through legal reverse engineering, if the alleged thief did not resort to such lawful means as reverse engineering, but instead unlawfully misappropriated the trade secret through unlawful or underhanded measures, the tort of misappropriation of the trade secret can be established. In every trade secret litigation in which I have been involved, the defendant who has had his hand caught in the cookie jar always comes into court arguing that the alleged secret information is available to the public, and therefore is not a trade secret. We consistently rebut this argument by establishing the steps taken to maintain the confidentiality of the information by the trade secret owner, and proving to the court that the actions taken by the defendant were not the lawful route, but rather the unlawful route. Thus, the availability of information through public sources is not an adequate defense in a trade secret misappropriation case, unless the accused thief can show that he or she actually used the particular public source to acquire the information.

It is apparent that only certain information can be maintained in secret. If the information is available to anyone once a machine or process is used in public, that information obviously cannot be maintained as a secret. Certain items, such as chemical formulas, compositions of materials, chip architecture and operation, and the like can be maintained in secret, so long as the actual use or sale of the product does not inherently divulge the secret information.

Since the heart of trade secret misappropriation is the use of unlawful steps to obtain the secret information from its owner, independent development by another of the same information is a proper way of acquiring the information, even though the trade secret owner maintained the secrecy of the information. Courts have held that one who obtains knowledge of a process or secret without spending the time, money, and effort to discover the information independently has improperly obtained such information, unless the holder of the secret voluntarily discloses the information, or if the holder of the secret information fails to take reasonable precautions to ensure the secrecy of the information. As stated in the opening sentences of this chapter, the rationale behind this body of law is to establish and maintain standards of commercial morality. For those of you who doubt that there is such a thing as commercial morality, I suggest that you revisit the Enron scenario of several years ago to see what happens when the ethics of commercial morality are disregarded.

The requirement that confidential information be kept secret by its owner is not an absolute requirement. For example, if others know of the same information through independent sources, but are also keeping the information secret, the first owner of the same information has a trade secret that can be protected. The standard of secrecy requires that a sufficient element of secrecy must exist so that except by the use of improper means, it would be difficult, if not impossible, to acquire the information from its owner.

Computer programs are initially created in a source code, which is a mathematical and word language that those trained in the art can understand. Upon completion, a source code is converted to an object code to guide and deliver the electrical impulses that operate the computer. Normally, the object code cannot be read, and it is this object code that is embedded on the chips, discs, or other medium distributed to the user of the program. What would happen if a software company mass produced and distributed CDs containing its program to the public, but kept the source code in confidence, and maintained it in secrecy? Would the program be deemed sufficiently secret to merit trade secret protection? In the case of *Q-Co. Industries, Inc. v. Hoffman*, 625 F. Supp. 608; 228 USPQ 554 (SDNY 1985), the court held that the program was still sufficiently secret to support trade secret protection.

Obviously, if one creates a trade secret in the course of their business, others connected with the business must be able to access and use the secret information in order to manufacture the goods or provide the services that the company produces to generate income. Thus, it is quite common that secret information is disclosed to a select group of the owner's employees, licensees, distributors, vendors, and others working in close relationship. This practice is permissible without destroying the trade secret status of the information, as long as the information is restricted to those who actually have the need to use the information, and the owner takes reasonable precautions, such as confidentiality agreements, to ensure that the information is kept confidential among the small group that uses the information.

27.5 EVEN THREATENED TRADE SECRET THEFT CAN BE STOPPED

Once a trade secret is out, it cannot be returned to its secret status—you cannot unpop a balloon. As a result, threatened or sometimes inevitable misappropriation of a trade secret may be stopped by a court before it happens. Suppose, for example, an employee has taken a new position working for a direct competitor, and that employee had knowledge of your company's trade secrets. In the new position, the employee will be placed in a job with identical or similar tasks compared to his former employment for your company. In this situation, even though no secrets have been shown to have been misappropriated, a court may prevent the employee from entering into employment with your competitor for a reasonable time period after leaving your employ. One court, in such a situation, stated that unless an employee possesses an uncanny ability to compartmentalize information in his or her head, he or she of necessity will be using and relying upon the former employer's trade secrets. The rationale for this "inevitable" potential use of the former employer's trade secrets was stated as follows: "When an employee is placed in a position where he is called upon to solve problems similar to or the same as those solved for his past employer, the employee, consciously or unconsciously, will inevitably draw upon the knowledge, including trade secret information, obtained while working for his past employer." See *C&F Packing Co. v. IBP, Inc.*, 1998 U.S. Dist. Lexis 3221 (N.D. Ill. 1998), slip opinion at 23, 25; aff'd. 224 F. 3d 1296, 1303 (Fed. Cir 2000); *PepsiCo, Inc. v. Redmond,* 54 F. 3d 1262, 1268 (7th Cir. 1995). The "inevitable disclosure" rule is not applied in all cases. For example, the wood and building products business was considered comparatively "low-tech," and a former employee's tasks for his former employer were considered to be driven by general expertise he learned on the job, rather than by highly technical, proprietary, or secret information. Thus, the employee was allowed to accept his new job. See: *International Paper Co. v. Suwyn,* 996 F. Supp. 246 (S.D.N.Y. 1997).

This theory has been adopted by some courts, and rejected by others. The recently enacted Federal Defend Trade Secrets Act of 2016, discussed in Chapter 28, apparently rejects the "inevitable disclosure doctrine" by preventing the granting of injunctions to prevailing trade secret owners that would prevent a person from entering an employment relationship. See Chapter 28, Section 28.3.1.

The concept of protecting trade secrets from unlawful disclosure is also an important consideration in crafting confidentiality and non-competition agreements between employees and their employers. As stated previously in this text, an employee leaving one position to begin working for a competitor of the former employer is allowed to use the normal skills, expertise, and knowledge that were learned during the prior employment at his or her new employment. However, a line is drawn in the sand preventing the employee from using or disclosing trade secret, proprietary, or confidential information (they all mean the same thing) that was made known to, or developed by, the employee at the former position. I therefore recommend that whether you are an employee about to embark on a new employment, or if you are the manager or owner of a business that has a portfolio of trade secret information, be sure that you enter into trade secret agreements with full knowledge of what is expected of you if and when your employment picture changes. Your skilled intellectual property and/or employment legal professional can assist you.

27.6 CREATING A VIABLE TRADE SECRET PROTECTION PROGRAM

As you continue along your careers, it will be important for you to identify the protectable trade secrets and confidential business information you use on a regular, ongoing basis. You will probably be asked to establish, or may be working with, a trade secret protection protocol that is designed to protect such information. The identification and protection of trade secret information is a continuing dynamic process, and does not remain static. Your, and your company's, portfolio of trade secrets will constantly change, as certain information becomes obsolete and is no longer commercially valuable, and new information is created that may be extremely valuable, and must be properly protected.

A recommended starting point for the development of a trade secret protection program is an audit of relevant intellectual property to identify the company's protectable trade secrets. This audit should be conducted in conjunction with your intellectual property attorney, so that the results of the audit can be protected from discovery if litigation involving the trade secrets arises. The audit should be conducted often enough to establish a viable trade secret program, possibly once every year or every other year.

The first facet of the audit is to identify each element of confidential, proprietary information used in your organization that may concern research and development, production or production processes, and/or quality control procedures. The audit should also identify proprietary business information relating to sales, marketing, customers, vendors, financial information, business plans, and administrative information intended to be kept secret. After this categorization is completed, and if practical, identify the steps or levels of security necessary to maintain secrecy of the information. The more confidential the information, the higher the number of steps of secrecy that should be maintained, for obvious reasons. However, keep in mind that any information that you ultimately desire to hold as confidential must be subject to some degree of security.

To organize the trade secrets within an organization, it is first recommended that employees be given training on how to distinguish trade secret technology and business developments from other, non-confidential information. Second, the trade secret information developed by employees, and additional trade secret information of others, such as clients or customers, that your organization is using is collected and organized, with the elimination of redundancies. The next steps are to create internal procedures and policies to protect the trade secrets from theft by both those inside and outside the organization.

The following are examples of suggested steps that can be taken to protect trade secrets. Not all are required to establish an effective program; however, those that are practical to implement should be adopted:

1. Most importantly, each internal and external recipient of your trade secrets must be notified, preferably in writing, that the transmitted information is confidential and/or proprietary, and that the information is not to be disclosed to others, or used by the recipient for the recipient's benefit, without the express written approval of the owner of the trade secret. This is usually accomplished by placing a confidentiality notice on all proprietary drawings, documents, and media that are submitted to the recipient of the trade secrets, as well as the word "Confidential" placed on each page or item. The recipient should also sign a confidentiality or non-disclosure agreement, which can be a short document that merely states that the recipient shall not disclose the confidential information to others, nor use the information for the recipient's own benefit without the written authorization of the trade secret owner.
2. Confidentiality and non-disclosure agreements should be signed by each employee of your company on the day they are hired, including management.
3. Create a written or electronic confidential and trade secret maintenance policy that sets forth procedures to be used inside the company to maintain the confidentiality of your proprietary information. This policy statement should be given to each employee, and each employee should sign a document acknowledging receipt and understanding of the confidentiality policy.
4. The trade secret policy information given to employees should include procedures preventing the inadvertent disclosure of trade secrets in written publications, speaking engagements, at trade shows or other situations where trade secrets may be divulged while one is trying to sell the company's products. This procedure should be particularly applicable to your sales force.
5. Access to your plant or research and development facility should be made available only to your employees upon identification, and to all others who sign in at a front desk or loading dock. Also, your facility should have doors that can be locked when the facility is not in use, as well as alarm systems on the doors and windows, and, if necessary, after-hours security personnel. A

physical security system can be created based upon the specific needs of your company, and the specific nature of its proprietary information.

6. The trade secret documents inside your facility should only be disseminated to those on a "need to know" basis. These employees should sign a log indicating when they have the proprietary information in their possession, and when they have returned the information, preferably to a vault or other secure vessel.
7. If possible, you should apply codes, preferably secret, to identify data or ingredients in your proprietary information.
8. Where possible or practical, the components of a trade secret can be segregated among the different departments or company personnel so that each has only a "piece of the puzzle." This is particularly applicable in the development of software.
9. Keep all confidential drawings and documents in locked drawers or areas.
10. Enter agreements with each of your vendors regarding their obligation to maintain your confidential information secret. It is also wise to enter into agreements with your vendors that if they are part of a group that develops patentable or proprietary subject matter while working on your projects, that you and your company become the owner of such new technology.
11. Erect physical barriers inside your facility to prevent the unauthorized viewing of proprietary process technology. Install "Keep Out" or "Authorized Personnel Only" signage at the entrance points to sensitive areas of the facility, and have a written policy regarding who may enter the authorized areas.
12. Ensure that each of your employees knows that they are prohibited from remaining in the plant after hours without express permission from authorized personnel, and inform your security staff to rigidly enforce such rules and regulations.
13. Make sure your employees know which areas they are allowed to access freely, and which areas require special access permits.
14. Require employees to wear identification badges or carry identification cards. This is something that is more and more common these days, and your employees should not object to such identification criteria.
15. Reproduce only a limited number of sensitive documents and maintain procedures for retrieving and collecting all copies used by your employees. This includes a written procedure for ensuring that all copies that were disseminated have been returned after use.
16. Use authorized access codes or passwords for copying machines, scanners, fax machines, and computers. Also, use key and encrypted computer data access to control theft of secret computer-stored information. Do not electronically transmit sensitive materials through unsecured electronic paths.
17. Have written and established policies and procedures controlling the destruction of sensitive documents when they are no longer viable.
18. Establish a program to regularly advise the company's employees regarding the maintenance of trade secrets and confidential business information.
19. Hold "exit interviews" to obtain the return of all confidential company documents and to remind ex-employees of their obligation not to use or disclose confidential information of the company to others, or to use such confidential information for their own benefit or the benefit of their new employer.

I realize fully that it will be impractical for you or your company to incorporate all of the above suggestions into a confidentiality program. However, to maintain the secrecy of your confidential information, those measures that are reasonable under the circumstances to maintain secrecy should be implemented. Remember, that if you are compelled to charge a former employee with theft of trade secrets, you must first establish to the satisfaction of the court and/or jury that you took reasonable precautions to ensure that your confidential information was adequately protected. Note that unduly expensive or extreme procedures are not required by the courts to be implemented to protect trade secrets.

27.7 DAMAGES AND INJUNCTIONS

Where the trade secret owner has taken action against one who has misappropriated their trade secrets, the Uniform Trade Secrets Act provides for injunctive relief, monetary damages, and under certain circumstances the recovery of attorney's fees. Appropriate injunctive relief prohibits the defendant from further use or dissemination of the secret information and from further use or sale of any product or process that incorporates the secret information. It is also possible for the owner of a trade secret to obtain relief against a threatened misappropriation of trade secrets, as well as actual misappropriation. Monetary damages could include both the actual loss in terms of dollars caused by the misappropriation, and the value of the unjust enrichment caused by the misappropriation that is not taken into account in computing actual loss. If neither of these factors can be proved by a preponderance of the evidence, it is possible for the court or jury to award damages measured in terms of a reasonable royalty for the misappropriator's unauthorized disclosure or use of the trade secret. Keep in mind that if willful and malicious misappropriation exists, the court may award reasonable attorney's fees to the prevailing party. In my experience, it has always been that the one who misappropriates another's trade secrets does it willfully and with malicious intent. It seems very difficult to steal one's trade secrets without fully intending to do so.

27.8 CONFIDENCE

A breach of one's trade secret rights may arise from a breach of confidence or confidentiality, such as a situation arising from a fiduciary relationship. Examples are the attorney–client relationship, partner and partner relationship, and those relationships arising informally, from moral, social, domestic, or purely personal interactions. For example, several courts have found that confidential relationships exist when the parties' relationship is that of partners, joint venturers, licensor and licensee, and employer and employee. Generally, not all employment relationships involve a degree of confidentiality. However, where an employee acquires an intimate knowledge of the employer's business, and the nature of that business is to maintain its knowledge and technology in secret, the relationship can be deemed a confidential one. In such situations, the law implies as a part of the employment relationship an agreement not to use or disclose confidential information that an employee receives incident to the employment, when the employee knows or should have known that the employer desires such information to be kept secret. Any unauthorized use or disclosure of trade secret information learned through a confidential relationship constitutes misappropriation of that trade secret. This confidentiality extends even beyond the term of employment.

The courts have developed a rule that a former employee is free to use the general knowledge, skills, and experience gained during prior employment. This is true even when the employee has increased his or her skills or has received complex training during the former employment. However, the employee, in his or her next employment, is absolutely forbidden from using information that constitutes the trade secrets or confidential information of the former employer. Therefore, as you move from one position to another during your career, you must remember that any information that was given to you in confidence by a prior employer cannot be used for your benefit or for the benefit of your new employer.

27.9 CAN TRADE SECRETS, AFTER USE, BE PATENTED?

In 1946, the Second Circuit Court of Appeals handed down its judgment in the case of *Metalizing Engineering Company v. Kenyan Bearing and Auto Parts Company,* 153 F.2d 516, 520 (2nd Cir. 1946) prohibiting the patenting of a trade secret process used in making a commercial product that had been sold over a long period of time. However, recent commentary suggests that the change to 35 U.S.C. §102(a) by the AIA may have reversed this decision, thus enabling an inventor who kept his or her invention a trade secret for a good many years to now be able to obtain a patent on that secret invention.

The AIA at Section 102(a) reads in part:

> A person shall be entitled to a patent unless the claimed invention was patented, described in a printed publication, or in public use, on sale, or otherwise available to the public before the effective filing date of the claimed invention.

The term "or otherwise available to the public" is new, and was not in the previous patent statute. The legislative history of the AIA appears to indicate that Congress intended that an inventor's own secret prior art, including products that are made commercial using a secret process to manufacture the products, will be eliminated as prior art. The commentators have noticed that there is an ambiguity in this particular language, as to whether the term "or otherwise available to the public" modifies the term "public use" or whether it is a separate category of prior art. Legislative history indicates to certain commentators that the purpose in the law was to overrule the *Metalizing Engineering* case, allowing an inventor to use a secret process, for example, for manufacturing a product sold commercially for many years, and then seek patent protection for that process. Patent protection, of course, would last for another 20 years. The interpretation is that the secret use of an invention that is not discernible by the public upon purchasing a product embodying the invention or made by the invention shall not be considered as prior art, therefore allowing the patent to be obtained later on for that secret invention.

As of the preparation of this text, there have been no decisions on this point. This writer anticipates that many people will attempt to obtain patents on secret processes, arguing the legislative history of the AIA allows such patenting. As soon as the Supreme Court weighs in on this topic, this commentary will be updated. As of now, this is one of the "definite maybes" embodied in the Patent Law.

◆ INVENTORS AND INVENTIONS ◆

Chester F. Carlson

ELECTROPHOTOGRAPHY

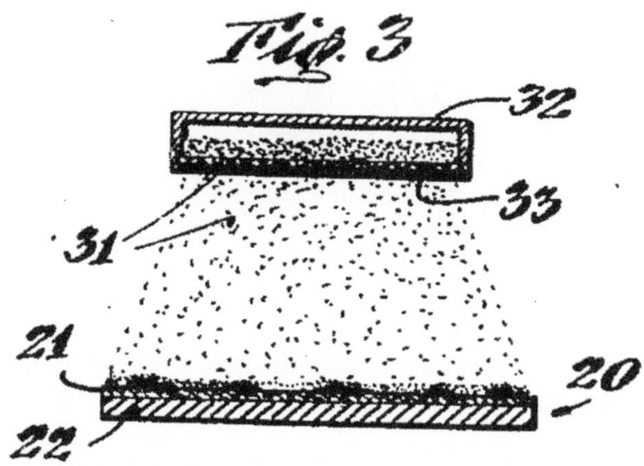

This essay is dedicated to today's inventors and entrepreneurs who are seeking instant rewards and gratification based on the new technology they developed. Normally, the speed at which some expect to reach a high plateau does not happen. In my opinion, Chester Carlson is the "poster child" of all inventors who have employed perseverance and doggedness in the face of numerous rejections to eventually develop what later became one of the most important inventions of the modern world. Please read on.

Chester Carlson was an American physicist, inventor, and patent attorney, best known for having invented the process of electrophotography, which produced a dry copy of an image, rather than a wet copy as was produced by the mimeograph or other processes preceding his inventions. Carlson's process was subsequently renamed "xerography," a term literally meaning "dry writing."

In the early 1930s, Chester Carlson began working for Bell Telephone Laboratories in New York as a research engineer. After a year, he transferred to the patent department as an assistant to one of the company's patent attorneys.

He kept coming back to his love of printing, especially since his job in the patent department gave him impetus to find a better way to make copies of documents. In the course of his patent work, he frequently needed copies of patent specifications and drawings and there was no convenient way to get them. The patent department at Bell Labs primarily made copies by having typists retype the patent application in its

Intellectual Property Law for Engineers, Scientists, and Entrepreneurs, Second Edition. Howard B. Rockman.

Published 2020 by John Wiley & Sons, Inc.

entirety using carbon paper to make multiple copies at once. Other methods such as mimeographs and Photostats were available, but were more expensive than carbon paper, and had other limitations that made them impractical. Carlson aimed to invent a copy machine that could take an existing document and copy it onto one new piece of paper without any intermediate steps.

In 1936, Carlson began studying law at night at the New York Law School, and received an LLB degree in 1939. He studied at the New York Public Library, copying long hand from the library's law books because he was not able to buy them. The pains in his hands from this laborious copying hardened his resolve to find a way to build a true copying machine, and he began supplementing his law studies with visits to the public library's science and technology department. He located an article written by Hungarian physicist Pál Selényi in an obscure German scientific journal. He began experimenting in his apartment kitchen; the experiments were smoky, smelly, and occasionally explosive. In one set of experiments, he was melting pure crystalline sulfur, which is a photoconductor, onto a plate of zinc by moving the sulfur over the flame of his kitchen stove. This often resulted in a sulfur fire, causing the building to smell of rotten eggs. In another experiment, the chemicals he was working with caught fire, and he and his wife extinguished the flames.

Also, during this period of time he developed arthritis of the spine. However, he kept working on his experiments in addition to his law school studies and his regular job. Having learned about the value of patents in his early career as a patent clerk and attorney, Carlson patented each new development, filing his first patent application on October 18, 1937.

In 1938, Carlson's wife persuaded him that his experiments had to be conducted somewhere else, and he rented a room on the second floor of a house in Queens. He then hired Otto Kornei, an Austrian physicist, to assist him.

Carlson was aware that several major corporations were simultaneously looking into devices and processes for copying images onto paper. The Haloid Company had the Photostat, which it licensed to Eastman Kodak. However, these companies did their research along photographic lines and their systems required special chemicals and special papers. The Photostat system, for example was essentially a photograph of the document that was being copied.

Selényi's article described a way of transmitting and printing facsimiles of printed images using a beam of directive ions placed onto a rotating drum with insulating material. The ions would create an electrostatic charge on the drum and a fine powder could then be dusted on the drum. The powder would stick to the parts of the drum that had been charged much as a balloon would stick to a static-charged stocking.

Up to this point, Carlson's apartment kitchen experiments in constructing a copying machine had involved trying to generate an electric current in the original piece of paper using light. Selényi's article convinced Carlson to do the opposite: use light to remove the static charge from a uniformly-ionized photoconductor. As no light would reflect from the black marks on the paper, those areas would remain charged on the photoconductor and would therefore retain the fine powder. The powder could then be transferred to a fresh blank sheet of paper resulting in a duplicate of the original. This approach provided his invention with an advantage over the Photostat, the latter which created only a photographic negative of the original.

A breakthrough occurred on October 22, 1938. The words "ten-twenty two-thirty eight" and the word "Astoria" were written on a glass microscope slide. Kornei prepared a zinc plate with a sulfur coating, darkened the room, rubbed the sulfur surface with a cotton handkerchief to which was applied an electrostatic charge, and then placed the slide on the plate and exposed it to a bright, incandescent light. They removed the slide, sprinkled lycopodium powder onto the sulfur surface, blew the excess powder away and transferred the image to a sheet of waxed paper. They then heated the waxed paper, softening the wax so that the lycopodium powder would adhere to the waxed paper, and had the world's first xerographic copy. They repeated the experiment to make sure it worked. It worked, and then Carlson and Kornei celebrated with a modest lunch.

The process of electrophotography is based on two natural phenomena. First, materials of opposite electrical charges attract each other, and second, some materials become better conductors of electricity when exposed to light. The process used by Carlson to transfer an image from one surface to another, using these phenomena, comprises providing a positive electrical charge to a photoconductor surface. The photoconductor surface is then exposed to an image on a document. Because the illuminated sections (the non-image areas) become more conductive, the charge dissipates in the exposed areas. Negatively charged powder is spread over the surface and adheres through electrostatic attraction to the positively charged image areas. A sheet of paper is then placed over the powder image and given a positive charge. The negatively charged powder is attracted to the paper as it is separated from the photoconductor. Finally, heat fuses the powder image to the paper, producing a copy of the original image.

Carlson's road to success, and the success of xerography along with him, was not an easy one. His requests for funding were rejected by more than twenty companies between 1939 and 1944. He tried, for example, at one time to sell the invention to IBM, but no one at the company saw merit in the concept. His next-to-last attempt to obtain the interest and funding required to commercialize the invention was a meeting with the Department of the Navy. The Navy had a specific interest in the production of dry copies, but they did not see what Carlson saw, and this approach went nowhere.

On October 6, 1942, the U.S. Patent Office issued Carlson's patent on Electrophotography, No. 2,297,691. Carlson was about to give up trying to have his invention commercialized when in 1944, Russell W. Dayton, an engineer from Battelle Memorial Institute in Columbus, Ohio, visited the patent department at Mallory, where Carlson was then working. Dayton had been brought in as an expert witness in a patent appeal case by Mallory, and he thought that Carlson might be the type of individual who was interested in new ideas, as Dayton was. Although, Battelle had not previously developed ideas that had been generated outside their own institution, Dayton was fascinated by Carlson's ideas, and invited Carlson to Columbus to demonstrate his invention.

Battelle eventually decided to take a risk on Carlson's invention. A scientist at Battelle thought that electrophotography had practically no foundation in previous scientific work, but that Carlson had put together a combination of separate natural phenomena, each of which was obscure in itself, and none of which had previously been put together in anyone's thinking. The result was what became the biggest invention in imaging since photography itself. Additionally, Carlson had got to this point entirely without the help of a favorable scientific climate.

In the fall of 1945, Battelle became Carlson's agent for his patents, paid for further research, and developed his ideas. Battelle approached major printing and photography companies such as Eastman Kodak and Harris-Seybold in an effort to license the invention, but without success. The commercial breakthrough did come, however, when John Dessauer, the head of research at the Haloid Company, became aware of Carlson's invention. Haloid was looking for a way out of the shadow of its Rochester, New York, neighbor, Eastman Kodak. By previous acquisitions, Haloid was then in the duplicating machine business, and decided that electrophotography would allow Haloid to expand into a new commercial field that Kodak did not dominate.

In December 1946, over nine years since Carlson filed his first patent application, Battelle, Carlson, and Haloid entered into the first agreement to license electrophotography for a commercial product. This contract granted Haloid a non-exclusive license to produce electrophotography-based copy machines limited to make no more than 20 copies of an original. Battelle was concerned by Haloid's somewhat small size, and Haloid had concerns about electrophotography's potential success. This is the nail-biting phase of the commercialization of any invention.

Battelle conducted most of the basic research into electrophotography, while Haloid concentrated on trying to produce a commercial product based on the research. In 1948, Haloid's CEO Joseph Wilson convinced the U.S. Army Signal Corp to make a $100,000 investment in the technology. The Signal Corp was concerned about nuclear war, and the traditional photographic techniques then in use for reconnaissance would not function properly when exposed to radiation from a nuclear attack. The film would fog in the same way that consumer photographic film can be fogged by an airport x-ray machine. The Signal Corp considered that electrophotography might be developed into a product that would be immune to such radiation. Through the 1950s, over half the money Battelle spent developing electrophotography came from government contracts.

In 1947, Chester Carlson was concerned that Battelle was not developing his processes fast enough, particularly since his patent would expire in ten more years. Carlson then accepted an offer to become a consultant to Haloid, and he moved to the Rochester area. Battelle spent several years trying to interest additional licensees in electrophotography, but to no avail, so Battelle eventually agreed to renegotiate with Haloid, making Haloid the exclusive licensee for Carlson's invention, except for a few minor uses that Battelle retained for itself.

By 1948, Haloid realized that it would have to make a public announcement about electrophotography to retain its claim to the technology. However, the term electrophotography was not easy for Haloid to swallow. For one thing, its inclusion of the term "photography" invited unwelcome comparisons with traditional duplicating technologies. Haloid considered several options and adopted the term suggested by a classics professor at Ohio State University: "xerography," which is a combination of the Greek words *xeros*, which means dry, and *graphia*, which means writing.

Haloid's CEO, Joe Wilson, and Haloid's Board of Directors voted to adopt the name "xerography." On October 22, 1948, Haloid made the first public announcement on xerography. In 1949, it shipped its first photocopier, the Xerox Model A copier. The Model A was admittedly difficult to use, requiring 39 mostly manual steps to make a single copy. The product could have been a failure except that it turned out to be an excellent way to make paper masters for offset printing presses. Sales of the Model A to the printing departments of companies like Ford Motor Company kept the product alive.

Before the Model A, to make a paper lithographic master for a lithographic press such as the Multigraph 1250, one had two choices: either type a new master using wax-coated carbon paper on a special master sheet, or use a metal plate coated with a modified silver halide photographic emulsion. If it was not feasible to retype the document, the photographic method could be used, but it was slow and expensive. Because the Model A's toner repelled water but attracted oil-based inks, a lithographic master could be made by simply making a copy of the document with the Model A onto a blank paper master. This reduced the cost of creating a lithographic master from an existing document from approximately $3.00 to less than $.40. Ford is reported to have saved so much money by using the Model A copier that the savings were specifically mentioned in a Ford annual report.

Following the Model A, Haloid released a number of xerographic copiers to the market, but none of them were easy to use. At the same time, competitors such as Kodak and 3-M brought out their own copying devices using other technologies. Kodak's Verifax, for example, was able to sit on one side of a desk and sold for $100.00. Haloid's competing machines were substantially larger and more expensive.

In 1955, Haloid entered into a new agreement with Battelle, giving Haloid full title to Carlson's xerography patents with Battelle receiving 50,000 shares of Haloid stock. Carlson received forty percent of the cash and stock from that deal due to his agreement with Battelle. The same year, Rank Organization, a British Motion Picture Company, was looking for a product to sit alongside the small business it had making camera lenses. Thomas A. Law, who was the head of this subsidiary business, was reading a scientific magazine that he picked up by chance, which described an invention that could produce copies of documents as good as the original. Mr. Law contacted Haloid. To commercialize those patents in Europe, Haloid partnered with the Rank Organization in a joint venture called Rank Xerox. As photocopying advanced around the world, so did Rank's profits. According to the managing director, it was "a stroke of luck that turned out to be a touch of genius. If Tom Law had not seen that magazine we would not have known about xerography, or at least not before it was too late."

Haloid's existing offices in Rochester were old and scattered, but Haloid needed to grow. In 1955, Haloid purchased land in the Rochester suburb of Webster, New York, which eventually became the company's main research campus. Haloid CEO, Joseph Wilson, decided that the company needed a new name as early as 1954. After years of debate within the company, the Board of Directors in 1958 approved a name change to Haloid Xerox. This change reflected the fact that xerography was now the company's main line of business.

The first modern copier was the Xerox 914, which was large and crude by today's standards. However, it allowed an operator to place an original document on a sheet of glass, press a button and receive a copy on plain paper. The Xerox 914 was introduced to the market in New York City on September 16, 1959. Of the two demonstration units at the hotel, one caught fire and the other worked fine. Following this demonstration, the Xerox 914 became rather successful. Between 1959 and 1961, Haloid Xerox's revenues nearly doubled. The 914 was relatively easy to use, its design carried no risk of damage to the original, and its low operating costs compared to the other machines that required a special paper led to its success. Further, Haloid Xerox made the decision to rent the 914 at a cost of $25 per month plus the cost of copies at four cents each with a minimum of $49 per month. This made the 914 more affordable than a similar competing copier. In 1961, based on the success of the Xerox 914, the company changed its name again to Xerox Corporation.

Recall that it was in 1937 when Chester Carlson filed his first patent applications regarding the xerography process, and it was not until 1961 that the company he was instrumental in founding became successful. For Carlson, the commercial success of the Xerox 914 was the highlight of his life's work. He had invented a device that could quickly and inexpensively make an exact copy of an existing document. After the 914, Carlson decreased his involvement with the company and began pursuing philanthropic interests.

Oct. 6, 1942. C. F. CARLSON 2,297,691

ELECTROPHOTOGRAPHY

Filed April 4, 1939

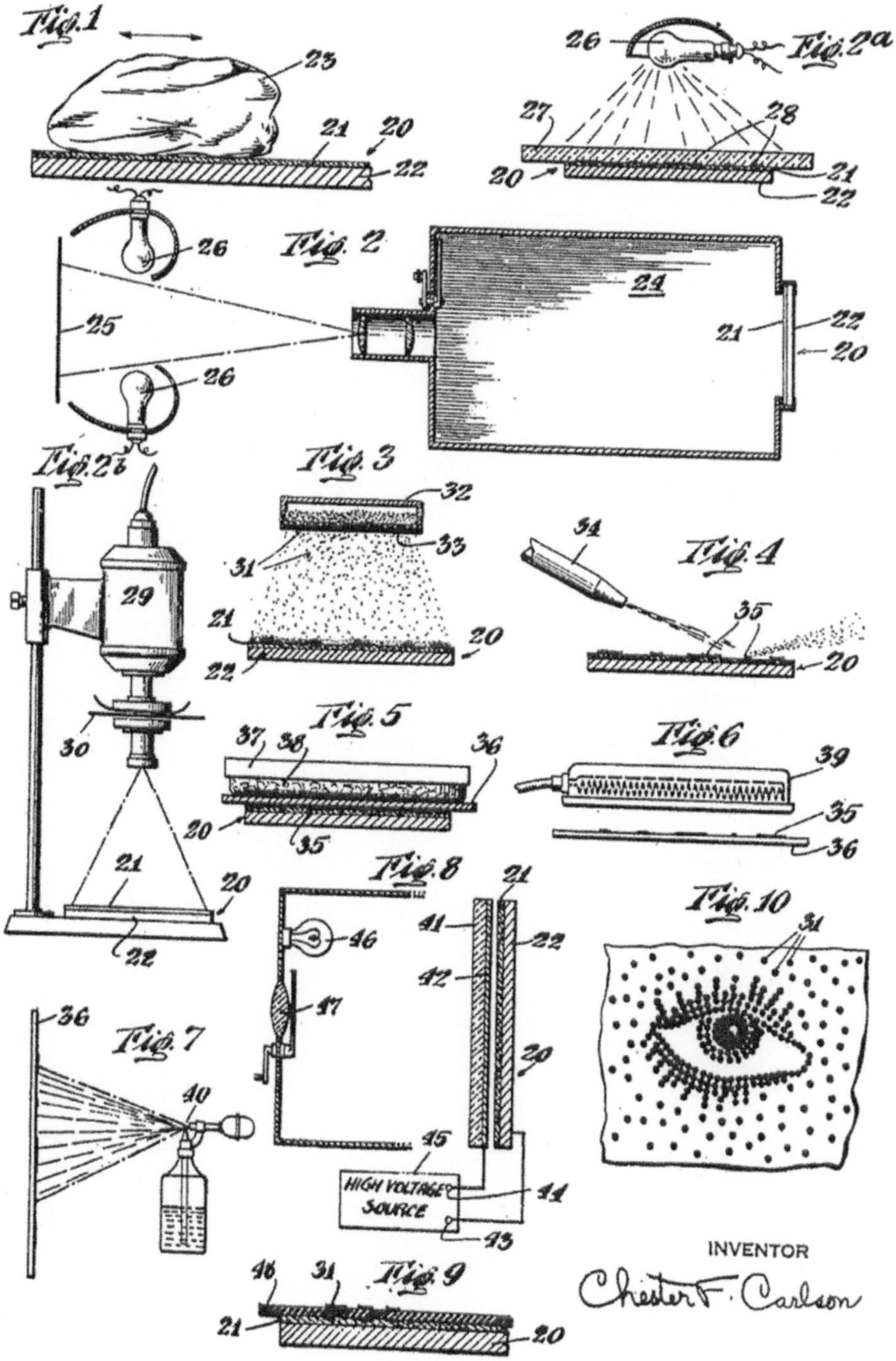

INVENTOR

Chester F. Carlson

28 The Federal Defend Trade Secrets Act of 2016

28.1 INTRODUCTION

Prior to 2016, one who alleged that someone misappropriated, or stole, their trade secrets was compelled to take legal action in the state courts under most circumstances. There was no U.S. federal trade secret law the injured party could rely upon to enjoin the misuse of the trade secret, and seek damages.

That has changed. On May 11, 2016, the U.S. Federal Defend Trade Secrets Act of 2016 (DTSA) was enacted by the U.S. Congress, and is now in force. The new law has many similarities with the Uniform Trade Secrets Act (UTSA) adopted by most states, and with the common law protecting trade secrets in Massachusetts and New York, two states that have not adopted the UTSA. The new law also has many unique and significant features that are not found in the state laws.

One feature of the new federal trade secrets law is a provision that is common in most federal legislation—the owner of a misappropriated trade secret can bring an action in a federal court under the law only "if the trade secret is related to a product or service *used in, or intended for use in, interstate or foreign commerce*" (emphasis added). If there is no intended or actual use by the defendant of the trade secret across state lines, or internationally, the owner of the trade secret can only apply to the state courts for relief, such as enjoining the defendant from using or disclosing the trade secret. The following discussion is directed to the new features of the Federal Defend Trade Secrets Act of 2016, in somewhat the same order as set forth in the Act.

28.2 CIVIL SEIZURE

The federal DTSA differs from the UTSA in one notable aspect. The DTSA allows for an ex parte seizure order where a plaintiff/trade secret owner, fearful that their trade secrets may be exposed to the public by the person misappropriating the trade secrets, is allowed to take steps to have the government seize the trade secrets prior to giving any notice of the lawsuit to the prospective defendant. These seizures, however, are limited in that they may only be instituted in "extraordinary circumstances," and rather strict rules must be followed to obtain a civil seizure of the alleged misappropriated goods. New ex parte seizure provisions allow trade secret owners to approach

Intellectual Property Law for Engineers, Scientists, and Entrepreneurs, Second Edition. Howard B. Rockman.

Published 2020 by John Wiley & Sons, Inc.

courts to obtain an order for the seizure of the property "necessary to prevent the propagation or dissemination of the trade secret." The ex parte seizure application may be brought before a court without any notice to the potential defendant.

28.2.1 Requirements for Obtaining an Ex Parte Order for Civil Seizure.

There are several strict requirements that must be met by a plaintiff seeking an order to have the misappropriated trade secret material seized by the courts. The first of these is that the plaintiff must make a showing that obtaining a normal injunction order from a court for equitable relief would be inadequate to achieve the purpose of restraining use and dissemination of the trade secret because the party against whom the order would be issued will evade, avoid, or otherwise not comply with the order. The second requirement is a showing that an immediate and irreparable injury would occur if the seizure is not ordered. Third, it must be shown that the harm to the applicant of denying the application outweighs any potential harm to the legitimate interests of the person against whom seizure would be ordered, and that issuing the order would substantially outweigh the harm to any third party who may be affected by such seizure.

Fourth, the trade secret owner must show that the information is actually a trade secret, and that the person against whom seizure would be ordered misappropriated the trade secrets of the applicant by improper means, or that the potential defendant conspired to use improper means to misappropriate the trade secrets of the plaintiff.

Fifth, it must be established that the person against whom seizure would be ordered has actual possession of the trade secret and any property to be seized. Sixth, the plaintiff must describe with reasonable particularity the items to be seized, and to the extent reasonable under the circumstances, identify the location where the items are to be seized.

Seventh, the person against whom seizure would be ordered, or persons acting in concert with such person, would destroy, move, hide, or otherwise make such items inaccessible to the court if the applicant were to proceed on notice to such person. Eighth, it must be shown that the applicant has not publicized the requested seizure.

28.2.2 Elements of the Seizure Order

If the court issues a seizure order, the order shall:

1. Set forth findings of fact and conclusions of law required to support the order.
2. Provide for the narrowest seizure of property necessary to achieve the purpose of the application, and direct that the seizure be conducted in a manner that minimizes any interruption of the business operations of third parties, and to the extent possible does not interrupt the legitimate business operations of the person accused of misappropriating the trade secret.
3. The order must also be accompanied by a provision protecting the seized property from disclosure by prohibiting access to the trade secret by the applicant or the person against whom the order is directed, and prohibiting any copying in whole or in part of the seized property to prevent undue damage to the party against whom the order has been issued or others until such parties have had an

opportunity to be heard in court. If access is granted by the court to the applicant or person against whom the order is directed, the access shall be consistent with provisions in the law directing how materials in the custody of the court will be handled.

4. The order must provide guidance to the involved law enforcement officials that clearly delineates the scope of authority of the officials in executing the seizure order, including the hours during which the seizure may be executed and whether force may be used to access locked areas.
5. The order must set a date for a court hearing described in the law at the earliest possible time and not later than seven days after the order has issued, unless the party against whom the order is directed consents to another date for the hearing, except that a party against whom the order has issued or any person harmed by the order may move the court to dissolve or modify the order after giving notice to the applicant.
6. The order must require the person obtaining the order to provide security determined adequate by the court for the payment of damages as a result of a wrongful or excessive seizure, or wrongful or excessive attempted seizure.

28.2.3 Protection from Publicity

The court must take necessary actions to protect the person against whom the order is directed from publicity about the seizure by or at the behest of the person obtaining the order.

28.2.4 Materials in Court Custody

The law provides that any materials seized shall be taken into the custody of the court. If the materials include a storage medium, such as a CD-ROM or the like, the court will prohibit the medium from being connected to a network or the Internet without the consent of both parties until the hearing required by the law takes place. The court also must take appropriate measures to protect the confidentiality of the seized materials that are unrelated to the trade secret information, unless the person against whom the order is entered consents to the disclosure of the non-confidential material.

The court may also appoint a Special Master to locate and isolate all misappropriated trade secret information and to facilitate the return of unrelated property and data to the persons from whom the property was seized.

28.2.5 Service of the Order

Service of a copy of the order granted by the court is to be made by a federal law enforcement officer who, upon making service, shall carry out the seizure under the order. State or local law enforcement officials may participate if the court so orders, but the order may not permit the applicant or any agent of the applicant to participate in the seizure. Further, at the request of law enforcement officials, the court may allow a technical expert who is unaffiliated with the applicant and who is bound by a court-approved non-disclosure agreement to participate in the seizure, if the court determines that the participation of the expert will aid the efficient execution of, and minimize the burden of, the seizure.

28.2.6 Seizure Hearing

The seizure order will specify a date upon which a hearing on the seizure order shall be held. At the hearing, the party who obtained the order shall have the burden to prove the facts supporting the findings of fact and conclusions of law necessary to support the order. If that burden is not met, the seizure order will be dissolved or modified appropriately. The court may also issue orders modifying the time limits for discovery under the Federal Rules of Civil Procedure if deemed necessary to prevent the frustration of the purposes of the hearing under the order.

28.2.7 Action for Damages Caused by a Wrongful Seizure

Anyone who suffers due to a wrongful or excessive seizure has a cause of action against the applicant or plaintiff who obtained the order under which such seizure was made, and shall be entitled to the same relief provided under the Trademark Act, 15 U.S.C. §1116(d)(11), which provides that the one damaged by the improper seizure can be awarded its lost profits, cost of materials, loss of good will, punitive damages, and its attorney's fees. Any security posted with the court shall not limit recovery by a defendant or third parties for damages the defendant or third party incurred due to a wrongful seizure.

28.2.8 Motion for Encryption

The law provides that anyone who claims to have an interest in the seized subject matter may make a motion which can be heard only by that party in front of the court (ex parte) to encrypt any material seized or to be seized that is stored on a storage medium. The order shall include, when possible, the desired encryption method.

28.3 REMEDIES

28.3.1 Injunctions

Once a plaintiff has established its case under the DTSA, the plaintiff may be awarded an injunction to prevent any actual or threatened misappropriation, provided the order does not prevent a person from entering into an employment relationship, and that conditions placed on such employment shall be based on evidence of threatened misappropriation and not merely on the information the person knows, or otherwise conflicts with an applicable state law prohibiting restraints on the practice of a lawful profession, trade, or business. If the court deems it appropriate, it can order that affirmative actions be taken to protect the trade secrets. In exceptional circumstances that render an injunction inequitable to protect the trade secret, the court may condition future use of the trade secret upon payment of a reasonable royalty for no longer than the period of time for which such use could have been prohibited.

28.3.2 Award of Damages

A successful plaintiff may also obtain damages for actual loss caused by the misappropriated trade secret, and damages for any unjust enrichment caused by the misappropriation that is not addressed in computing damages for actual loss. In lieu of damages measured by any other methods, the court may award damages caused by the misappropriation measured by imposition of liability for reasonable royalties for the misappropriator's unauthorized disclosure or use of the trade secrets. The law also contains a provision that damages may be the greater of five million dollars or three times the value of the stolen trade secrets to the organization, including expenses for research and design and other costs of reproducing the trade secrets that the organization has avoided by misappropriation.

28.3.3 Willful and Malicious Appropriation

The new law provides that if the trade secret is willfully and maliciously misappropriated, exemplary damages of no more than two times the amount of the damages awarded may be assessed against the defendant.

28.3.4 Claim of Misappropriation Made in Bad Faith by Plaintiff

The law specifically states that if a misappropriation claim by the plaintiff is asserted in bad faith, which may be established by circumstantial evidence, or a motion to terminate an injunction is made or opposed in bad faith, or the trade secret was willfully and maliciously misappropriated, the court may award reasonable attorney's fees to the prevailing party. The award of attorney's fees is discretionary with the court, and is not automatic.

28.3.5 Period of Limitations

An action for misappropriation of a trade secret under the DTSA must be brought no later than three years after the misappropriation has been discovered by the plaintiff, or should have been discovered through the use of reasonable diligence by the plaintiff. The statute also applies to any act that occurs on or after the date of enactment of the law, which was May 11, 2016. Interestingly, the DTSA also has a provision that this law shall not be construed to be defined as a law pertaining to intellectual property for purposes of any other act of Congress.

28.4 RIGHTS OF TRADE SECRET OWNERS

The new DTSA also contains provisions to protect the rights of trade secret owners. One such provision states that the court may not authorize or direct the disclosure of any information the owner of the trade secret asserts to be a trade secret, unless the court allows the owner the opportunity to file a submission under seal that describes the interest of the owner in keeping the information confidential. The prosecution by the federal government for theft of trade secrets, or the providing of information relating to a trade secret to the U.S. Government or to the courts in connection with a criminal prosecution shall not constitute a waiver of trade secret protection, and the disclosure of information relating to a trade secret in connection with such prosecution shall not constitute a waiver of trade secret protection unless the trade secret owner expressly consents to such waiver.

Importantly, the DTSA does not preempt the use of state causes of action for theft of trade secrets. Therefore, if there is an interstate component to a theft of trade secret cause of action, the plaintiff has the option of taking the lawsuit to either the state court or the federal court.

28.5 WHISTLE-BLOWER PROVISIONS

The DTSA includes protections for whistle-blowers who disclose trade secrets to law enforcement in confidence for the purpose of reporting or investigating a suspected violation of law, and for the confidential disclosure of a trade secret in a lawsuit including an anti-retaliation proceeding.

The law provides that an individual should not be held criminally or civilly liable under any federal or state trade secret law for the disclosure of a trade secret that is made (1) in confidence to a federal, state, or local government official either directly or indirectly or to an attorney, and (2) solely for the purpose of reporting or investigating a suspected violation of law, or (3) is made in a complaint or other document filed in the lawsuit or other proceeding, if such filing is made under seal.

28.5.1 Use of Trade Secret Information in an Anti-Retaliation Lawsuit

The DTSA provides that any individual who files a lawsuit for retaliation by an employer for reporting a suspected violation of law may disclose the trade secret to the attorney of the individual and use the trade secret information in the court proceeding, if (1) the individual files a document containing the trade secret information under seal, and (2) does not disclose the trade secret, except under a court order.

28.5.2 Notice of Immunity

An important provision of the DTSA provides that an employer must provide notice of the immunity discussed previously in any contract or an agreement with an employee that governs the use of trade secrets or other confidential information. Compliance with this notice provision can be made if the employer provides a cross-reference to a policy document provided to the employee that sets forth the employer's reporting policy for a suspected violation of law. If an employer does not comply with this notice requirement, the employer may not be awarded exemplary damages or attorney's fees under the provisions of this law in an action against an employee to whom notice was not provided for theft of trade secrets. This provision shall apply to contracts and agreements that are entered into or updated after the date of enactment of the law. Additionally, for the purposes of this provision of the trade secrets law, the term "employee" includes any individual performing work as a contractor or consultant for an employer, as well as regular employees. Therefore, if you are the management of a company that is involved in trade secrets, it is imperative that you submit a notice of this whistle-blower provision to your employees. I suggest you contact your intellectual property attorney for the appropriate wording of a notice under this provision of the law, if your company is involved in maintaining the secrecy of confidential information.

SECTION VI

Trademarks, Service Marks and Cybersquatting

◆ INVENTORS AND INVENTIONS ◆

Samuel E. Blum, Rangaswamy Srinivasan, and James Wynne

EXCIMER LASER SURGERY (LASIK)

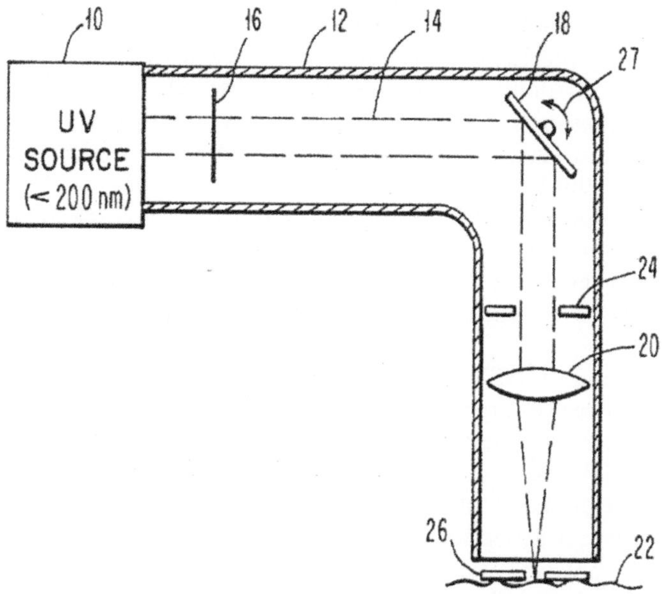

In 1981, Samuel Blum, materials scientist, James Wynne, physicist, and Rangaswamy Srinivasan, physical chemist, were working at IBM's T.J. Watson Research Center when they observed that an ultraviolet excimer laser could be utilized to etch designs into polymers. An excimer laser uses reactive gases, for example, chlorine and fluorine, combined with inert gases, such as argon, krypton, and xenon. When electrically charged, the gas medley discharges energetic pulses of ultraviolet light. These UV light pulses can create very precise, slight changes to irradiated materials, like polymers. Until this point, these lasers were used to drill polymers to produce computer circuit boards and ink jet printer nozzles. The research team had the notion that it may be possible to etch living biological tissue using the excimer laser. To test this idea, on November 27, 1981, Srinivasan brought his family's leftover Thanksgiving turkey into the lab for experimentation.

Intellectual Property Law for Engineers, Scientists, and Entrepreneurs, Second Edition. Howard B. Rockman.

Published 2020 by John Wiley & Sons, Inc.

The research team discovered that it was possible to create precisely etched patterns in deceased animal tissue. Their research established that an ultraviolet excimer laser, pulsed at 193 nm, etched living tissue precisely, without causing thermal damage to surrounding tissue. The team believed that the laser could be used to make clean, precise cuts in surgeries involving delicate tissue. Srinivasan called this procedure ablative photodecomposition (ADP). The research team used this new technology to develop the laser technology that became the foundation of LASIK (laser-assisted in situ keratomileusis) eye surgery. LASIK allows precise and accurate adjustments to be made for near-sightedness, far-sightedness, and astigmatism.

In 1983, an ophthalmic surgeon named Stephen Trokel learned of the IBM procedure, and approached Srinivasan regarding the possibility of using the ADP for surgery on the cornea of the eye to correct vision. Up to this time, "cold steel" or scalpel surgery was the only permanent solution to correct vision problems. These surgeries were not very precise, often resulted in a weakened cornea and led to a long recovery time. Trokel, along with Srinivasan, and researcher Bodil Braren, explored through experimentation the idea of using the excimer laser to permanently alter the shape of the cornea to correct vision. For several more years, doctors and scientists explored the use of this laser technology to correct vision issues.

Several patents were issued for the procedures related to the development of LASIK surgery. Blum, Wynne, and Srinivasan were issued U.S. Patent No. 4,784,135 on the ultraviolet excimer laser for use on organic tissue in 1988. This patent was thought to be the foundation for the subsequent several patents that led to the development of LASIK surgery.

During the period of 1987–1988, Dr. Trokel and a colleague performed the first laser-based refractive eye surgery on a woman diagnosed with malignant melanoma. In 1991, Dr. Stephen Slade and scientist Dr. Stephen Brint were the first ophthalmologists to perform LASIK surgery in the United States.

In 1995, the U.S. Food and Drug Administration approved the commercial procedure for laser refractive surgery. The initial clinical trials for LASIK began in 1996. The LASIK procedure was approved in the United States in 1999.

In 1992, Stephen Trokel filed a patent application for the LASIK surgical procedure, asserting that it was his sole invention. In 2000, the application was declared invalid by the International Trade Commission, citing that Srinivasan should have been included on the application as a co-inventor.

LASIK is currently the most popular vision corrective surgery performed around the world due to its ability to greatly improve or eliminate vision problems with very minimal downtime for the patient.

An interesting factoid is that the autonomous rendezvous and docking technology to assist NASA's Space Shuttle in servicing satellites resulted in an eye-tracking device for LASIK vision correction surgery. Called LADARTracker, this technology measures eye movements at a rate of 4000 times per second, four times the established safety margin, to ensure the safety and effectiveness of LASIK surgery. The technology is manufactured by Alcon Laboratories of Fort Worth, Texas, and is used in conjunction with the company's systems for LASIK surgery, employed by eye surgeons across the country.

United States Patent [19]
Blum et al.

[11] **Patent Number: 4,784,135**
[45] **Date of Patent: Nov. 15, 1988**

[54] **FAR ULTRAVIOLET SURGICAL AND DENTAL PROCEDURES**

[75] Inventors: **Samuel E. Blum**, White Plains; **Rangaswamy Srinivasan**, Ossining; **James J. Wynne**, Mt. Kisco, all of N.Y.

[73] Assignee: **International Business Machines Corporation**, Armonk, N.Y.

[21] Appl. No.: **894,520**

[22] Filed: **Aug. 11, 1986**

Related U.S. Application Data

[63] Continuation of Ser. No. 448,123, Dec. 9, 1982, abandoned.

[51] **Int. Cl.**[4] **A61B 17/36**
[52] **U.S. Cl.** **128/303.1**; 128/395
[58] **Field of Search** .... 128/4-8, 128/132 D, 303.1, 395-398, 633; 604/20, 22; 250/459.1, 461.1, 504 R; 362/32, 84, 259

[56] **References Cited**

U.S. PATENT DOCUMENTS

2,249,610	7/1941	James et al.	128/396
3,769,963	11/1973	Goldman et al.	128/665
3,769,983	11/1973	Merav	128/351
3,821,510	6/1974	Muncheryan	128/395
3,956,048	5/1976	Nordgren	128/132 D
4,049,987	9/1977	Helms	250/504
4,273,110	6/1981	Groux	128/6
4,273,535	1/1981	Yamamoto et al.	128/303.1
4,316,467	2/1982	Muckerheide	128/303.1
4,388,924	6/1983	Weissman et al.	128/303.1

OTHER PUBLICATIONS

J. Taboada et al., *Health Physics*, 40, pp. 677-683, 1981, "Response of the Corneal Epithelium to KrF Excimer Laser Pulses".

J. Taboada et al., "An Extreme Sensitivity in the Corneal Epithelium . . . , "Aerospace Medical Assoc. 1981, Meeting, San Antonio, TX.

"Ablative Photodecomposition: Action of Far-Ultraviolet (193 nm) Laser Radiation on Poly(Ethylene Teraphthilade) Films", Srinivasan and Leigh Dec. 1, 1982 *J. Am. Chem. Soc.* 1982, 104, 6784-6785.

Primary Examiner—Max Hindenburg
Attorney, Agent, or Firm—Jackson E. Stanland

[57] **ABSTRACT**

A method and apparatus are described for photoetching organic biological matter without requiring heat as the dominant etching mechanism. Far-ultraviolet radiation of wavelengths less than 200 nm are used to selectively remove organic biological material, where the radiation has an energy fluence sufficiently great to cause ablative photodecomposition. Either continuous wave or pulse radiation can be used, a suitable ultraviolet light source being an ArF excimer laser having an output at 193 nm. The exposed biological material is ablatively photodecomposed without heating or damage to the rest of the organic material. Medical and dental applications include the removal of damaged or unhealthy tissue from bone, removal of skin lesions, cutting or sectioning healthy tissue, and the treatment of decayed teeth.

21 Claims, 1 Drawing Sheet

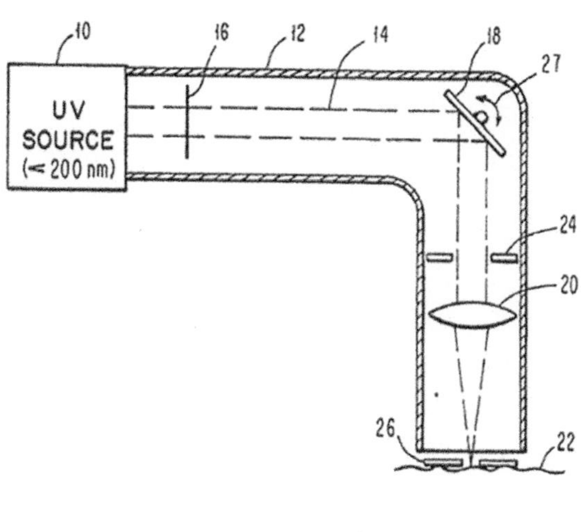

29 Trademarks and Service Marks

29.1 ORIGINS OF THE PROTECTION OF TRADEMARKS AND SERVICE MARKS

The area of trademark and service mark law has developed over many centuries to protect the goodwill and reputation of a manufacturer or distributor as a source of a product, or the source of a service, from being unlawfully usurped by a competitor or others in an attempt to confuse the public into believing that the quality of the competing producer's products or services are somehow the same as the first user's products or services. This goodwill is primarily embodied in the brand names, logos, or product configuration designs used by manufacturers and service providers in association with their products, or in the delivery of their services to the consuming public. You can think of many brand names, such as Coca-Cola, Ford, Xerox, Google, and IBM, where it can be argued that the most valuable corporate asset of the owner of the mark is the trademark or service mark itself. Thus, a major purpose underlying the trademark laws is to protect the public so that a consumer may be confident that when purchasing a product bearing a particular trademark, logo, or configuration with which the consumer is familiar, and is favorably inclined toward, the consumer will receive the product and the quality that it asks for and wants to obtain.

"Trademark" is the term used with reference to identifying the source of a product, whereas the term "Service Mark" is a source identifier of a service. Throughout this chapter, the term "Trademark" will be used generically to refer to both trademarks and service marks.

A second purpose of the trademark laws applies where the owner of a trademark has spent energy, time, and resources in advertising its product to the public. The manufacturer's investment is protected from misappropriation by "tyrants and cheats." Thus, trademark laws were designed to protect not only the consumer but the manufacturer or service provider as well.

Most writers today on the subject of trademarks attribute the origins of trademark laws to the medieval era, when skilled craftspersons and artisans formed guilds. The symbols of those guilds and/or of the individual craftspersons were applied to products to indicate the source or identity of the makers of those products. The time reference of this history is undergoing some revision as of late, since archeologists are uncovering artifacts from times predating the medieval years showing the use of symbols on products to identify their makers.

Intellectual Property Law for Engineers, Scientists, and Entrepreneurs, Second Edition. Howard B. Rockman.

Published 2020 by John Wiley & Sons, Inc.

The English common law, which predated the establishment of the United States, protected trademarks through actions for deceit. At about the beginning of the 19th century, English and American common law advanced the tort of fraud and deceit into an action called "passing off" or "palming off." This unlawful act was committed when a producer passed off or palmed off his goods as the goods of another.

Trademark rights, and their enforcement, still exist in the common law today, primarily in those countries that base their legal systems on the English common law system. However, the U.S. Congress has periodically taken steps toward federalizing the protection of trademarks, and the U.S. law today exists in parallel with the state common law systems, while not replacing the state systems. Congress enacted the first federal trademark statute in 1870, which law was ultimately held unconstitutional by the U.S. Supreme Court on the grounds that Congress did not have the authority to enact such a law. Remember that Article 1, Section 8 of the Constitution provides a Constitutional framework for the establishment of patent and copyright laws. However, the entire Constitution is silent as to trademark protection.

To overcome this rebuke by the Supreme Court, Congress reenacted new trademark legislation and based its foundation on the Commerce Clause of the Constitution by indicating that the federal protection of trademarks would apply only to those trademarks that are used in interstate commerce, or in foreign trade. This is still the law today. If your trademark is used on goods or services that pass only within the borders of your state, the mark cannot be protected under the federal trademark law, but can be protected by your state trademark laws. For example, the name of a single restaurant is considered an interstate use, since patrons from other states may eat at the restaurant. Each state has its own trademark law that adequately protects the users of purely intrastate marks. The current version of Federal Trademark Law is the Lanham Act, enacted in 1946 and updated many times since then. The Lanham Act today acts in parallel with the state common laws and state trademark statutes to provide extensive protection for trademark owners.

One of the features of the federal trademark statute is that by applying for and obtaining a federal registration for your trademark after examination by the U.S. Patent and Trademark Office (USPTO), you have established that you have a *prima facie* exclusive right to use the mark on the products or services listed in your registration. Thus, if you deem it necessary to file a lawsuit against an infringer of your mark, you do not have to spend time or effort in court proving that you have used the mark extensively, how much you have spent in advertising the mark, and what your total sales have been to establish that you have an exclusive right to use your mark. The federal registration provides notice to the world that you are the owner of that trademark registration, and that you have the exclusive ownership right to use that mark in commerce on the goods or services recited in your registration. The burden then shifts to the alleged infringer to attempt to invalidate that trademark registration on one of several grounds, or to prove that the accused mark is not the same as or confusingly similar to your registered mark.

An equally important reason for the trademark registration system is that upon filing an application to register a trademark, that trademark, along with information describing the goods or services with which the mark is used or intended to be used, is listed in the federal trademark search database. Thus, you can easily conduct a search to determine whether a trademark that you propose to adopt and use would be the same as or confusingly similar to someone else's mark. The search will indicate to you, before you adopt your mark, whether or not it would be prudent to move forward and use that particular trademark. If someone else is using the same or similar mark for similar or related goods or services, you can avoid very expensive litigation by changing to another non-infringing mark. One of the major legal services that I have been furnishing to clients over the years provides clearance of their proposed trademarks or service marks before they begin to use them, to avoid problems in the future.

When a trademark applied to a product or a service mark is used in conjunction with a service, the mark's primary purpose is to identify the "origin" or "source" of the product or services. A trademark or service mark serves its function even though it may differ from the name of the company that offers the product. For example, many people know of Scotch tape, but not necessarily that the product is made by the 3M Company.

29.2 TRADEMARK SELECTION AND ADOPTION PROCESS

Earlier chapters in this text have been directed toward your inventive and creative efforts in producing new or improved products or process, or expressions of ideas and concepts that can be protected under the patent and/or copyright laws. Once these products or processes are introduced to the market, they usually bear a trademark or service mark by which each product or service is identified as having originated with you or your company. The field of trademark law is dedicated toward protecting your rights in that trademark by preventing someone else from adopting and using your mark, or a confusingly similar mark, that might confuse purchasers into buying another's products when they think they are buying yours. An equally important premise in trademark law is the protection against the consumer being deceived into purchasing a product or service that bears a confusingly similar trademark or service mark compared to a well-advertised or well-known brand. Therefore, when a producer or service provider selects a mark, a mark should be chosen that is not confusingly similar to someone else's mark and is not likely to cause consumer confusion. Also, a mark should be selected that is not too descriptive of goods or services, as it may not be registrable.

Over the years, trademarks have empirically been divided into four types: (1) arbitrary, (2) suggestive, (3) descriptive, and (4) generic. Arbitrary and suggestive marks are registrable and usable without further proof that the marks are distinctive; that is, they distinguish your goods from those of a competitor. This, of course, presumes that the mark does not conflict with another earlier mark. An arbitrary mark is one that is made up and has no meaning in the relevant market, such as KODAK, which has no defined meaning in any language. A suggestive mark is one that would require an observer of the mark to go through several mental steps before associating the mark with its related goods or services. EVEREADY for a reliable flashlight battery comes to mind, for example.

A descriptive mark, however, is one that describes a quality, characteristic, or other feature of the product or service with which the mark is associated. These are usually weak marks, but they can be registered with proof of eventual distinctiveness or "secondary meaning" after years of use. The term "secondary meaning" in trademark law is equivalent to "distinctiveness." This means that a term used as a trademark distinguishes the products or services of the mark's user from those of its competitors, and the mark has been accepted by the public as a source identifier. Such "secondary meaning" as a source identifier can be shown for a descriptive mark by extensive advertising of a mark, and sales of the product associated with the mark, over a long period of time, whereby consumers begin to recognize the mark as having two meanings: (1) recognizing you as a source of products or services associated with the mark, and (2) the normal everyday meaning of the same mark. I mention the mark BEST BUY for your consideration.

Generic terms are the accepted common meaning of goods and/or services, and can never be registered as trademarks, since once a trademark is registered, that word is removed from the public domain and cannot be used by others in association with the listed products or services. It is against public policy in the United States and most every other jurisdiction to remove a generic term from the realm of the public and deprive competitors of the right to use the same generic term to describe and offer their goods. For example, the terms "escalator," "aspirin," and "cellophane" are former trademarks that became generic of their respective products to the extent that competitors could not sell their products without using these terms to define or describe their competing products. Eventually, the registrations for these trademarks were cancelled. Within recent memory, the mark "thermos" also lost its registrability and became available for competitors to use as a generic term. In case you are wondering, the generic name for a thermos bottle, without using the name thermos, would be "vacuum bottle." How many people go into a store and order a "vacuum bottle?" Thus, the competitors of King Sealy, the former owner of the "thermos" trademark, argued that they could not sell their competing products unless they were also permitted to call them "thermos bottles" because of the public's generic use of that term.

Keep in mind that a trademark never stands by itself. It is always used as an adjective followed by the descriptive term or generic term for the goods or services with which the mark is associated. Thus, Scotch is followed by the word "tape." Xerox is followed by the term "copying machine."

29.2.1 Creating a Trademark

The creation of a trademark normally begins in a brainstorming session of a business entity where the technical and marketing people have defined the "point of difference" between your new product (or service) and that of a competitor, and have decided where they want to position the new product in the marketplace *vis à vis* competing products already being offered. Next, prospective trademarks, symbols, logos, or other source identifying devices are tossed onto the table in an effort to find a brand name that will highlight the "point of difference" of the product, yet not be generic or descriptive of the different qualities or capabilities of the product. For example, consider the number of brands incorporating the prefix or suffix "max" to imply the "maximum" strength, ability, or value of a product compared to the competition. Normally, at these sessions, several prospective marks or brands are initially chosen, to hedge against the possibility that one or more of the marks may not be available for use.

Care must also be taken when creating a mark or brand to avoid foreign translations that may have a negative slant when applied to your product. For example, "Nova," a mark once used for a car, in Spanish means "no go." Also, the mark must not be misleading, such as "Metl-Wax" for a polishing product that contains no wax.

The marks that you propose should be capable of becoming strongly identified with your product, while at the same time not be descriptive of a component, quality, or characteristic of the product.

29.2.2 Screening or Narrowing Step

Once a list of prospective trademarks has been created, the next step is to narrow the list to four or five good candidates. First, those marks that may be descriptive or may be negatively viewed in other countries should be eliminated. Next, a preliminary computer database search is conducted to identify, and avoid, those prospective marks that may be the same as, or similar to, marks already used by others for similar or related products. This “screening” search can be conducted inexpensively using the database of U.S. federal trademark registrations and applications (www.uspto.gov), and other databases of state and international registrations and applications. Note that these preliminary screening searches are inadequate to be used for a final determination whether a mark you adopt may conflict with a prior mark. The full clearance process, described in the next section, is mandatory before making a final decision on adopting a mark or brand name for your product.

29.2.3 Clearance Process for Determining the Availability of a Trademark for Your Use

The list of trademarks surviving the preliminary screening process are furnished to your marketing people or trademark attorney for a comprehensive search to determine the availability of the selected trademarks. The person conducting the analysis is furnished with two things: first the trademark or service mark that you propose to adopt, and second, the goods and/or services with which the mark is intended to be used, including the relevant channels of commerce through which the goods will pass or services will be provided.

The above information is then furnished to the person responsible for conducting the search. A full search is conducted on a database comprising corporate names, trade directory or journal information, website domain names, telephone directories, and other sources of information about products and services. There are several electronic databases that can furnish this information. The typical intellectual property law office usually includes one or several individuals who are trained in conducting such trademark searches. The search develops a list of trademarks that both the computer program and the individual conducting the search deem relevant for your perusal to determine whether or not there exist any potentially conflicting marks. The primary function of this search is to determine (a) whether any marks identical or confusingly similar to your proposed marks for similar or related goods have been uncovered, and (b) whether or not a likelihood of confusion will arise between any of the trademarks or service marks uncovered by the search, which are in use, and the mark that you are interested in adopting.

Factors used in comparing your mark to existing marks to determine if a likelihood of confusion between source or origin may occur are the degree of similarity of the trademarks in appearance, pronunciation, and suggested meaning; the relationship between the goods or services themselves; the respective channels of distribution and/or marketing of the goods or services in question; and the possible expansion of the first user of a relevant mark into your line of products. There are other factors to be considered; however, your trademark professional can discuss these factors with you when the time comes for you to conduct the trademark search.

It is apparent that certain marks taken directly from the English language can be used by a variety of business concerns in selling their products or services, so long as there is no conflict. A prime example is the trademark "United" which identifies an airline, a national moving company, and a soccer team, among others. These entities can all use the same marks because their goods or services do not travel in the same channels of commerce, and no confusion as to source or origin is likely to occur.

If a potentially conflicting mark is found from the comprehensive search, an additional investigation is conducted to determine if the conflicting mark is still being used by its indicated owner. If the mark has not been used by its owner for several years, the registration for that mark may be considered invalid, and thus not a bar to your adoption and use of the same or similar mark. Consider, for example, Packard and Hudson for automobiles.

If the search results indicate that your mark does not conflict with any other mark, you may begin to use the mark immediately, and apply for federal registration, which has a high degree of certainty of ultimately being granted. However, if your prospective trademark is deemed to be confusingly similar to someone else's mark on goods or services that pass in the same or similar channels of commerce, conventional wisdom dictates that you would be wise to choose another mark, and not adopt your first mark. If you are the second user of a confusingly similar trademark, most certainly the first user of that trademark will threaten you with a lawsuit and an immediate injunction unless you stop using the mark. Your trademark attorney may advise you that you do not stand a very good chance of winning such a lawsuit, which would be expensive to fight, and the wise path would be to choose another mark. Thus, the primary function of the search is to provide you with information that you can use to avoid walking into expensive litigation.

Another reason for conducting a trademark search is that the USPTO will examine the application for registration of your trademark by comparing it for similarity to other registered and pending marks. If a previously registered mark is found to be the same as, or confusingly similar, to yours, and the goods or services are related, the trademark examiner will refuse registration. Therefore, there appears to be no good reason to adopt a mark that is found to be potentially problematic as a result of the search.

The USPTO uses the International Trademark Classification system to categorize the different types of goods or services for which marks are registered. If a registered mark is found during your search in the same class as that in which your proposed mark is likely to fall under, there is a high probability that if the marks are confusingly similar, the goods are also traded in the same channels of commerce. It is also possible that the search skipped over a relevant mark in a totally different class, which could cause confusion if the goods are still related. For example, you may be searching the availability a mark for tires and find that the same or a similar mark is being used for automobiles. This could cause confusion, due to the relationship between automobiles and tires. By way of contradicting myself, note that the Jeep Wrangler vehicle and Wrangler tires are made by two different companies; however, Wrangler tires are sometimes used on Jeep Wrangler vehicles. I am sure that this is through agreement between the two companies that manufacture the respective products. However, this indicates that trademark decisions are made with many, many factors in mind.

It also must be remembered that because the basis of trademark law in the United States is the common law system, and the same is true in many other English-speaking countries around the world, enforceable trademark rights can be gained by merely using a trademark in a certain trading channel for a period of time, without bothering to obtain a state or federal registration of that mark. Under the common law, you may secure exclusive rights in your trademark through prior use that would defeat a second users' right to use the mark, even if the second user obtained registration. However, to establish your right to enforce the mark, it is easier and less expensive to obtain a registration for your mark.

29.3 FILING FOR REGISTRATION OF YOUR TRADEMARK

A trademark application covering your finally selected and properly cleared mark is then filed with the USPTO. Your trademark professional will assist you in properly completing the application, which identifies the mark to be registered, the owner of the mark (which can be a corporation, partnership, individual, organization, or any other entity), the identification of the goods or services associated with the mark, the classification of the goods or services, and the dates of first use anywhere and first use in interstate commerce, if use of the mark has commenced at the time of filing the application. This application, along with a specimen of how the mark is being used on the product or service, such as a label, nameplate, hangtag, advertisement in the case of a service mark, etc., is filed with the appropriate fee with the USPTO.

Under today's U.S. trademark laws, you may also file an application to register a trademark without having started actual use of the mark on your products or with your services. An application may be filed based upon your "bona fide intent" to use the mark in the near future. Your intent-to-use application will be examined, and possibly approved. However, before your trademark will be registered in the United States, evidence of the commencement of actual use of the mark must be submitted to the U.S. trademark examining attorney.

Upon filing a trademark application, an examining attorney researches the proposed mark to determine whether any other identical or confusingly similar marks have been previously registered or applied for or are in use in commerce. The application is also examined to ensure that the goods associated with the work are properly identified. If no conflicting marks for similar or related goods are discovered, your application is approved for publication in the *Official Gazette* of the USPTO, a public document. Anyone who believes they or their business will be adversely affected by registration of your mark can file an opposition, and present evidence to the USPTO showing why your mark should not be registered. You then respond stating why your mark should be registered, and a tribunal in the USPTO (the Trademark Trial & Appeal Board) then decides whether your mark should be registered in view of the opposition.

If no opposition is filed, or if you successfully rebuff the opposing party, your trademark application will proceed to registration. Upon receipt of registration, and not before, you are entitled to apply the familiar registration symbol ® next to your mark each time it is used, both on the product, and in advertising the product. Prior to obtaining registration, it is customary to use the symbols TM (trademark) or SM (service mark) adjacent the mark to alert the public that you consider the mark as identifying your company as the source or origin of your products or services.

If your trademark application encounters delay during examination, it may be advantageous to obtain several state trademark registrations for your mark. This will provide trademark protection while you are establishing the distinctiveness of your mark through sales and advertising. Each state has its own trademark registration system, which is primarily used for those products and services that do not enter into interstate commerce, such as a local plumbing or roofing business. State trademark registrations are usually easier and quicker to obtain than federal registrations.

29.4 PROTECTING AND MAINTAINING YOUR TRADEMARK REGISTRATION

To adequately protect your trademark rights, vigilance is required to uncover the use by another of the same or confusingly similar mark on or in association with similar or related goods or services, hypothetically such as FJORD for a Norwegian brand of automobile. Trademark "watch" services are available to monitor trademarks entering the market that may infringe upon, or dilute the uniqueness of, your registered mark. In addition, your sales force is a good source of uncovering competing products with confusingly similar brand names.

Each week, the *Official Gazette* of the USPTO publishes a list of approved marks, with their goods and services, which may identify potentially conflicting new marks. Also, trade and industry journals provide fertile grounds for discovering what new brand names your competitors have begun to use, or are planning to use.

Protection of your mark also involves furnishing your employees with instructions and guidelines on proper use of your company's trademarks, such as always placing the generic product identification after the trademark each time the mark is used, whether on the products themselves, or in advertising and promotions for the product. For example, "XEROX copying machine" is proper. A "XEROX" is totally improper. Failure to adequately protect trademarks caused aspirin, cellophane, escalator, and thermos to become generic names and enter the public domain. The purpose of protecting your mark is to ensure that it maintains its unique and distinctive status as identifying you as the source of your product in the eye and mind of the consumer.

Maintenance of your trademark registration is also an ongoing concern. Between the fifth and sixth year following U.S. registration of your trademark, an affidavit or declaration must be filed with the USPTO, attesting to continual use of the trademark, or setting forth a good reason why use of the mark has stopped, and also stating that you intend to resume use of the mark in the foreseeable future. If this declaration or affidavit is not properly filed, the registration will be cancelled and purged from the Trademark Register. Also, trademark registrations in the United States must be renewed every ten years.

29.5 TRADEMARK PROTECTION OUTSIDE THE UNITED STATES

If you are a U.S. producer, it is more than likely that any product you introduce to the market will ultimately be sold in countries outside the United States. To protect your trademark in other countries, several approaches are available. One way is to file an application and obtain registration of that mark in each selected country.

In many nations throughout the world, particularly those that are based on the civil code legal system rather than the common law of the English-origin countries, the trademark rights that you obtain in those countries are strictly granted by the government, and rights are not obtained by use of the mark. Therefore, in a foreign country, someone can register a trademark without ever having used it. Also, in many foreign countries, when your trademark application is filed, it is not examined for confusing similarity with someone else's registered trademark. Therefore, two exact trademarks can be issued by the trademark offices in certain countries covering the same or similar goods. The foreign trademark office takes the position that if there is a conflict between two trademarks, let the parties fight it out in court, rather than have the government spend money to determine any likelihood of confusion. As you can see from my previous comments, the situation in the United States is just the opposite.

Because of the fact that trademarks can be registered in many foreign countries by someone who has not actually used those trademarks, the problems that have arisen are probably quite evident to you. For example, if a trade journal announces that your company is introducing a new product line under a new brand name, individuals in foreign countries can read that trade journal, and then spend a few hundred dollars to register that trademark for the same goods in their home country. Later, when your product is successful and you proceed to introduce your product in foreign countries, someone knocks on your door and advises you that you are infringing their trademark rights. Their object is to sell the trademark back to you at a handsome price. This practice is much more prevalent throughout the world than you would think. For one of my clients, I was involved in a transaction where the client was compelled to pay U.S. $100 000.00 to buy its primary trademark back from a "pirate" in Argentina. I have anecdotal information that Holiday Inn paid a substantial amount to buy their trademark back from someone who had hung a sign on several hotels in Mexico with the same mark before Holiday Inn started doing business in Mexico. Thus, if you ever get to the point where your products are going to be marketed internationally, and you want to use your U.S. trademark in those foreign countries, talk to your trademark attorney early on, and be sure that you have taken adequate steps to protect your mark and prevent piracy.

Another foreign trademark system was created by the European Union, which established a single trademark registration designated the Community Trademark or CTM, which covers 28 member European states with one trademark application and registration. Elsewhere throughout the world, registrations presently must be obtained individually in each country to obtain trademark protection. However, in 2003, the United States and several other countries joined the Madrid Protocol, which provides trademark and service mark protection in many countries by filing a single trademark application in your home country and designating those member countries in which you desire to obtain registration of your mark.

There are several other aspects of trademark law that are quite complicated. For example, the resolution of many trademark issues center around attempting to predict the impression on consumers made by the use of one or a few words, symbols, or logos. I cannot overemphasize the importance of seeking the advice of a trademark law professional before beginning to adopt and use a new mark, to adequately ensure that you protect yourself, and that you do not interfere with the trademark rights of others.

29.6 THE MADRID PROTOCOL—THE "INTERNATIONAL" TRADEMARK—AN OVERVIEW

At the end of 2003, the United States implemented the Protocol Relating to the Madrid Agreement Concerning the International Registration of Marks. The Madrid Protocol, as the treaty is commonly called, is an international treaty originally dating back to 1891, that allows individual, corporate, or other owners of trademark registrations or applications in their home country to obtain enforceable trademark rights in other member countries. For a current list of contracting countries, refer to http://www.wipo.org/treaties/registration/madrid/index.html.

In accordance with the Madrid Protocol, one who is using or intends to use a trademark files an application to register that mark in his or her home country. The application can be filed in the English or French language. It is not necessary to obtain the services of a trademark "agent" in other countries. Fees are paid in a single currency, such as dollars for U.S. applicants. Using the Madrid Protocol makes it about fifty percent less expensive to extend your trademark rights to six or eight countries compared to filing individual applications in each country, which is still an option.

To extend trademark rights to additional countries based on the home application, steps are taken to obtain registration of the mark in the register of the International Bureau of the World Intellectual Property Organization (WIPO) by filing an international application with the home country trademark registration office.

The national trademark registration office checks the international application for conformity to the rules, and then forwards the application to a WIPO examiner. The WIPO examiner reviews the application for formalities (fees, goods, proper class), and the mark is published in "Marques," the WIPO official listing of applied-for marks. Notice of the application is then forwarded to each of the trademark registration offices of those countries the applicant designates for protection. The application is then examined within 18 months by each national trademark registration office receiving a copy of the application from WIPO. If the application passes examination, the mark is published for opposition by others. Upon issue, each national registration is valid for 10 years from the date of filing of the international application. Each registration may be renewed for additional ten-year periods upon the payment of a fee.

The Madrid Protocol provides trademark owners with a relatively inexpensive procedure to obtain trademark protection in many countries, through the filing of a single application in one language. Search and clearance procedures for international marks may be conducted through competent search engines, enabling marks filed with WIPO from any member country to be properly searched. The Madrid Protocol provides that the International Bureau may undertake searches for anticipation (likelihood of confusion) among marks that are the subject of international registrations.

◆ INVENTORS AND INVENTIONS ◆

John Mauchly and John Presper Eckert

THE ENIAC COMPUTER

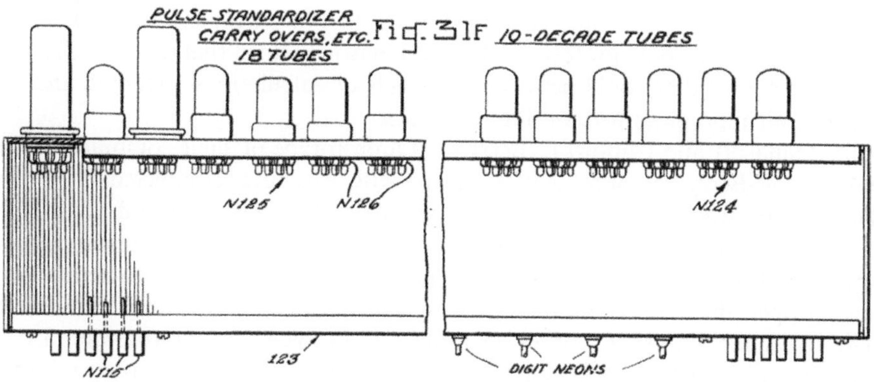

John W. Mauchly and John Presper Eckert, Jr. are widely credited with developing the first electronic general-purpose digital computer, the ENIAC.

In the summer of 1941, John W. Mauchly attended a defense training course for electronics at the University of Pennsylvania Moore School of Electrical Engineering in Philadelphia, where he met the lab instructor, J. Presper Eckert. They then formed a long-standing working relationship. After the course was over, Mauchly was hired as an instructor of electrical engineering at the Moore School, and in 1943 was promoted to assistant professor of electrical engineering. At the outbreak of World War II, the United States Army Ordinance Ballistic Research Laboratory contracted the Moore School to build an electronic computer, which, as proposed by Mauchly and Eckert, would accelerate recomputation of artillery firing tables for new artillery the Army was developing for the war effort.

In 1942, Mauchly circulated a memo in the Moore School proposing the design of a general-purpose electronic computer. The significance of his memo and the project was not immediately recognized. Mauchly's proposal emphasized that enormous speed advantages could be gained by using digital electronics with no moving parts. Lieutenant Herman Goldstine, who was appointed the liaison between the Army and the Moore School, was intrigued by the idea and requested Mauchly to prepare a formal proposal. In April 1943, the Army contracted with the Moore School to build an "Electronic Numerical Integrator and Computer" (ENIAC). Mauchly led the

Intellectual Property Law for Engineers, Scientists, and Entrepreneurs, Second Edition. Howard B. Rockman.

Published 2020 by John Wiley & Sons, Inc.

conceptual design of the ENIAC, while Eckert led the hardware engineering. As you might expect, many other talented engineers also contributed to the project. The ENIAC through its programming could perform sequences and loops of addition, subtraction, multiplication, division, square root, input/output functions, and conditional branches. Programming was initially accomplished with patch cords and switches, and reprogramming took days. In 1948, the ENIAC was redesigned to allow the use of stored programs with some loss in speed.

The idea of huge computing machines had previously been thought of at that time. In 1939, Harvard professor Howard Aiken was building the Mark 1, which was a large calculator. At Bletchley Park in England, cryptographers were constructing a special purpose code-breaking machine called Colossus. In 1941, Mauchly had discussions with Iowa State University professor John V. Atanasoff, who at that time was planning to build a machine that could perform thousands of calculations a second, and that could be easily reprogrammed for different tasks.

John Atanasoff and Clifford E. Berry built a prototype of their computer in 1939 (the Atanasoff-Berry computer, ABC), but the ABC was never completed.

The ENIAC when completed operated approximately one thousand times faster than an electro-mechanical calculating machine. In addition, the general-purpose programmability of the ENIAC computer made it interesting to both scientists and businesspeople alike. Its combination of speed and programmability allowed the ENIAC to make thousands of calculations for problems in short order. In the beginning, the ENIAC calculated trajectories in 30 seconds that took a human 20 hours to accomplish.

The ENIAC design and construction was financed by the United States Army, and the total cost was approximately $487,000, which would be equivalent to close to $6,740,000 today. The construction contract was signed on June 5, 1943, and design work on the computer began in secret at the Moore School the following month. The design team leadership comprised John Mauchly and J. Presper Eckert, both of the University of Pennsylvania, and their team of several other design engineers assisting in the development. The ENIAC was a modular computer composed of individual panels performing different functions. For example, 20 modules were accumulators, which could not only add and subtract, but could hold a ten-digit decimal number in memory. Numbers were passed between these modular units across several general-purpose buses (or trays, as they were called at that time). To achieve high speeds, the panels needed to be able to send and receive numbers, compute, save the answer, and trigger the next operation, all without any moving parts. The only moving parts in the ENIAC were the electrons passing through the system. Important to the versatility of the ENIAC was its ability to branch-trigger different operations, depending upon the sign of a computed result.

In 1944, the ENIAC design was frozen to allow construction of the computer to begin. Eckert and Mauchly were already aware of the limitations of the machine, and began plans for a second computer, eventually called the EDVAC. By January 1945, they had obtained a contract to construct the EDVAC, which was a stored-program computer. Eckert proposed a mercury delay line memory to store both program and data. Later that same year, mathematician John von Neumann became aware of the EDVAC project, and joined in some of the engineering discussions. He later produced an internal document describing the EDVAC, entitled "The First Draft of a Report of the EDVAC" dated June 30, 1945, which was an early written account of a general-purpose stored-program computing machine. Goldstine, in a move that later became controversial, removed any reference to Eckert or Mauchly, and distributed the document to a number of Neumann's associates across the country. The first draft document was also later cited as one of the causes for the 1973 invalidation of the ENIAC patent, discussed a few paragraphs later in this essay.

At the time the ENIAC construction was completed, it contained 20,000 vacuum tubes, 7,200 crystal diodes, 1,500 relays, 70,000 resistors, 10,000 capacitors, and approximately 5,000,000 hand-soldered joints. Its weight was over 27 tons, and the machine was roughly 2.4 meters × 0.9 meters × 30 meters in size. It occupied an area of 167 square meters and consumed 150 kilowatts of electricity. Conventional wisdom, which was probably just a rumor, was that whenever the computer was turned on, the lights in Philadelphia dimmed.

Input to the ENIAC was from an IBM card reader, and an IBM card punch was used for the output. While the ENIAC initially did not have a system to store memory, punched cards were used for external memory storage. In 1953, a 100-word magnetic core memory built by Burroughs Corporation was added to the ENIAC.

The ENIAC comprised 10-position ring counters to store digits; each digit required 36 vacuum tubes, 10 of which were the dual triodes making up the flip-flops of the ring counter. The arithmetic was performed by "counting" pulses with the ring counters and generating carry pulses if the counter "wrapped around," the idea being to electronically emulate the operation of the digit wheels of a mechanical adding machine.

The ENIAC was distinguished from subsequent computers in the way instructions were set up. The process was similar to plugboards of small punched card machines, but ENIAC had about 40 plugboards. Seven wires were plugged in for each instruction for a problem, amounting to thousands of steps each time a problem was started. This took several days and many more days to verify. When that was completed, the problem was run as long as there was input data. Changeovers to new problems occurred only once every few weeks.

It was possible to wire the carry of one accumulator into another accumulator to perform double precision arithmetic, but the accumulator carry circuit timing prevented wiring for higher precision. ENIAC used four of the accumulators controlled by a special multiplier unit to perform up to 385 multiplication operations per second. Five of the accumulators were controlled by a special divider/square-rooter unit to perform up to 40 division operations per second or 3 square root operations per second. The other nine units of the ENIAC originally were the initiating unit that started and stopped the machine, the cycling unit used for synchronizing the other units, the master programmer that controlled loop sequencing, the reader that controlled an IBM punch card reader, the printer that controlled an IBM card punch, the constant transmitter, and three function tables. The basic machine cycle for the ENIAC was 200 microseconds, or 5,000 cycles per second for operations on the 10-digit numbers.

The ENIAC used common octal-based radio tubes that were available at that time. During operation, several tubes burned out practically every day, leaving the ENIAC somewhat non-functional about half of its time. In 1948, high-reliability tubes became available. The earlier failures occurred during the warm-up and cool-down periods when the tube heaters and cathodes were under the most thermal stress. Engineers reduced the ENIAC's tube failure to the more acceptable rate of one tube every two days.

The ENIAC could be programmed to perform complex sequences of operations including loops, branches, and subroutines. As differentiated from the stored-program computers of today, ENIAC was a large collection of arithmetic machines that had programs hard-coded into the machines, with function tables each containing 1200 ten-way switches. Taking a problem and mapping onto the machine was complex and took weeks. Due to the complexity of mapping programs onto the machine, programs were only changed after huge numbers of tests of the program. After the program was figured out on paper, the process of getting the program into the ENIAC by manipulating its switches and cables took several more days followed by periods of verification and debugging.

The ENIAC had six primary women programmers: Kay McNulty, Betty Jennings, Betty Snyder, Marlyn Wescoff, Fran Bilas, and Ruth Lichterman. They determined how to input ENIAC programs and also developed an understanding of ENIAC's inner workings such that they could debug a problem by crawling inside the structure of the ENIAC to find bad joints and bad tubes.

The ENIAC engineers had little or no time to prepare teaching manuals or classes to help the women programmers, so all of the women became self-taught. They learned ENIAC's operation from the logic and electrical block diagrams used to construct and operate the machines, and figured out how to program the device based on their own analyses. The women created their own flowcharts and programming formats, then wrote the programs and loaded them onto the ENIAC using a not-so-easy physical interface, comprising a multitude of wires and 3,000 switches.

The six women who programmed the initial ENIAC were not widely recognized for over 50 years. As a matter of fact, 50 years after the invention of the ENIAC, most of the female programmers were not invited to the 50th anniversary event. These early women programmers were selected from a group of about 200 female "computers" who studied at the Moore School of Electrical Engineering. One of the few technical job categories available to women in the 1940s was computing the results of mathematical formulas for science and engineering, usually with a mechanical calculator and a differential analyzer. Betty Holberton (originally Betty Snyder) became the inventor of the first sorting algorithm, and helped design the first commercial electronic computers (the UNIVAC and BINAC) alongside Jean Jennings. Under the direction of Herman and Adele Goldstine, these early programmers studied ENIAC's blueprints and physical structure to determine how to manipulate its switches and cables, rather than learning a programming language. Since that time, many woman computers have been recognized for their contributions to the early days of computing.

The Ballistic Research Laboratory of the United States Army was the original sponsor of the ENIAC. As narrated earlier, one year into the project, John von Neumann, a mathematician working on a hydrogen bomb at Los Alamos National Laboratory, became aware of the ENIAC computer, and eventually the Los Alamos Lab became so involved with the ENIAC that the first test problem run on the ENIAC consisted of computations for the hydrogen bomb, not artillery tables. The input/output for this particular test comprised one million punch cards.

The ENIAC was formally accepted by the U.S. Army Ordinance Corp. in July of 1946. In 1947, the ENIAC was transferred to the Aberdeen Proving Grounds in Maryland. On July 29, 1947, it was turned on in Maryland and was in continuous operation until 11:45 p.m., October 2, 1955.

ENIAC was a one-of-a-kind design that was never repeated. The design was frozen in 1943 to allow construction of the ENIAC to begin, and at the time the design of the computer lacked certain innovations that later became well developed, particularly the ability to store a program. Eckert and Mauchly started work on the EDVAC, which was simpler and more powerful to operate. Following 1948, however, a number of improvements were made to the ENIAC. Among others, these included a primitive read-only stored programming mechanism using the function tables as program ROM, an idea included in the ENIAC patent.

ENIAC was able to run an arbitrary sequence of mathematical operations, but did not read them from a tape. Like the Colossus, the ENIAC was programed by plugboards and switches. The ENIAC combined complete programmability with electronic speed. The Atanasoff-Berry ABC computer design, the ENIAC, and the British Colossus all used vacuum tubes. ENIAC's registers performed decimal arithmetic rather than binary arithmetic as did other computers. ENIAC required rewiring to reprogram until September 1948. Three months earlier, in June 1948, the Manchester Small Scale Experimental Machine (SSEM) operated its first program and earned the distinction as the first stored-program computer. The idea of a stored-program computer with combined memory for program and data was conceived during the development of the ENIAC, but was not initially implemented in ENIAC due to World War II priorities that required the machine to be completed quickly, and ENIAC's 20 storage locations would be too small to hold data and programs. The Z_3, a German computer, and Colossus were developed independently of each other, and independently of ABC and ENIAC during World War II. The Z_3 was destroyed by Allied bombing raids in Berlin in 1943. The ten Colossus machines were part of the United Kingdom's war effort, and their existence only became generally known in the 1970s, although the U.K. staff and invited American observers knew about their capabilities. Work on the ABC of Iowa State University was stopped in 1942 after John Atanasoff went to Washington as a physics researcher for the U.S. Navy, and the ABC was subsequently dismantled. ENIAC, however, was operated for the press in 1946 and captured the world's imagination. The Colossus was used to decrypt Russian messages up until the 1960s and was kept confidential for almost 40 years. It did not become public knowledge until the late 1960s.

For a variety of reasons, one of which included Mauchly's June 1941 examination of the ABC, prototyped in 1939, U.S. Patent No. 3,120,606 for the ENIAC, which was applied for in 1947 and not issued until 1964, was held invalid in a 1973 court decision in the landmark Federal Circuit Court Case of *Honeywell v. Sperry Rand*, discussed ahead, putting the invention of the electronic digital computer in the public domain, and providing, among some, legal recognition to Atanasoff as the inventor of the first electronic digital computer.

By the time the ENIAC was completed the war was over. The computer did not boot up until November 1945 in a basement room at the Moore School of Engineering. Two 20 hp blowers provided cool air so the ENIAC would not melt down.

The ENIAC was the first computer to take advantage of electronic processing speeds and to "think" for itself using conditional branching and nested subroutines. It was entirely electronic. Similar to Charles Babbage's Analytical Engine from the early 1800s, and the British World War II Colossus computer, the ENIAC's conditional branching allowed the it to execute different instructions or to alter the order of execution of instructions based on the value of certain data. For example, if Y>8, go to line 17. This feature gave ENIAC the ability to solve a broad range of problems. The ENIAC was first made public on Friday, February 15, 1946, and was described in an article in the *New York Times* on that date.

The entire project of building the ENIAC took 30 months. The ENIAC performed its operations by generating very accurately timed electrical impulses at a speed of 100,000 per second, and could perform one operation every 20th pulse, thus performing addition, for example, at the rate of 5,000 per second. In operation, the ENIAC obtained its original input numbers from a series of cards in which holes were punched to indicate the initial and boundary conditions of the problem. When the problem was punched into the cards, they were dropped into a slot in the "reader." A master programmer oversaw the computation to ensure it was carried out. At one point, the ENIAC was asked to multiply to 97,367 by itself 5,000 times. The operation took place in less than a blink of an eye. After a problem was resolved to its essentials, and punched on a card and run through an IBM reader, the reader translated the mathematical language to that of the ENIAC, and numerical values covering a wide range of scientific constants were interjected as and when required. This was accomplished by one of the four varied types of memory in the ENIAC.

In March 1946, after the public announcement of the ENIAC, the Moore School and the University of Pennsylvania changed their patent policy to allow the school to gain commercial rights on past and future computer developments at the school. Eckert and Mauchly did not accept this change of policy, and resigned from the Moore School of Engineering. However, they had previously been contracted by the school to prepare and give a series of lectures on computer design. They presented the lectures entitled "The Theory and Techniques for Design of Digital Computers," which was presented from July 8 to August 31, 1946. "The Moore School Lectures," as they became known, were attended by representatives from the Army, Navy, MIT, National Bureau of Standards, the Institute for Advanced Study, IBM, Bell Labs, Eastman Kodak, General Electric, National Cash Register, and others. A number of those attending the lectures later made important developments in computer design and construction.

In 1947, Eckert and Mauchly formed the first computer company, the Eckert-Mauchly Computer Corporation, with Mauchly as president. They obtained a contract from the National Bureau of Standards to build an EDVAC II, later named UNIVAC. UNIVAC was the first computer designed for business applications and had several technical advantages over the ENIAC, such as magnetic tape for mass data storage. After forming the Eckert-Mauchly Computer Corporation, Mauchly decided that they needed to provide new users with software necessary to obtain the user's objectives with the computer. He knew it would be difficult to sell computers without application materials, and without training on how to use the systems. So in early 1947, his company assembled mathematicians interested in coding. Mauchly's experience with programming the ENIAC and machines that followed the ENIAC led him to eventually create Short Code. This was the first programming language actually used on a computer and was a pseudo-code interpreter for mathematical problems proposed in 1949 and run on the UNIVAC 1 and 2. The Eckert-Mauchly company, however, was in poor financial condition, and was sold to Remington Rand in 1950, where it became the UNIVAC Division of Remington Rand.

Referring to the eventual patent controversy, Mauchly and Eckert filed a patent application directed to the ENIAC in 1947, and Patent No. 3,120,606 issued in 1964,

17 years later. The patent was later invalidated by a U.S. Federal Court Judge in October 1973 for several reasons. Some of these reasons were based on the more than one year between publication of the first draft document in 1945 by Neumann and the patent filing date of 1947. The Federal Judge also ruled that the subject matter of the patent was derived from the earlier ABC design. On the basis of an examination of the materials related to the ENIAC and the origination of computers, many people do not agree with the Judge's conclusion. These critics point out that at a component level, there is nothing common between the ABC and the ENIAC. The ABC for example was binary; the ENIAC was decimal. The ABC used regenerative memory; the ENIAC used electronic decade counters. The ABC used tubes to implement the binary serial adder; while the ENIAC used tubes to implement a complete set of decimal operations. The ENIAC's general-purpose instruction set, together with the ability to automatically sequence instructions to them, made it a general-purpose computer. One of the bases for the court's decision was also that Mauchly had complete access to Atanasoff's prototype and the documents describing it before the ENIAC was completed and before the ENIAC patent was filed. Letters that Mauchly wrote to Atanasoff show that Mauchly was at one time at least considering employing Atanasoff's approach. Meanwhile, Mauchly maintained that the use of high-speed electronic flip-flops in cosmic ray counting devices at Swarthmore College gave him the idea for computing and for electronic speeds.

The delay in issuing the ENIAC patent resulted from technical disputes of several kinds, chiefly between Sperry Rand, which had taken over the ENIAC patent rights from Remington Rand, and Bell Labs, which contended that the ENIAC patent interfered with several of its own patents. The disputes were eventually settled by the Board of Patent Interferences of the U.S. Patent Office, and the patent was ultimately granted. Sperry then began notifying computer companies that they were in violation of the ENIAC patent, and Sperry offered its competitors patent licenses at a fee of 1.5% of the selling price of their computers. IBM was excluded since it had previously reached a 10 million dollar royalty agreement with Sperry in 1956. For the remaining computer makers, millions of dollars were at stake; no other competitors accepted Sperry's offer of a license, and the controversy ended up in the courts.

In May 1967, Sperry filed a federal lawsuit against Honeywell and Control Data Corporation alleging infringement of the ENIAC patent. Honeywell countersued accusing Sperry of unlawfully enforcing a fraudulently obtained patent. The Honeywell-Sperry lawsuits were consolidated, and assigned to the Federal District Court in Minneapolis, Honeywell's home city. The Sperry-Control Data lawsuit proceeded to a Federal Court in Baltimore. In the Control Data case, Sperry was seeking to enforce a 1954 patent that covered Eckert's and Mauchly's mercury delay line memory. This patent covered the idea of regenerative memory, which involves retaining stored information by periodically reenergizing the memory. In the Honeywell case, Sperry was seeking to uphold the ENIAC No. 3,120,606 patent. However, the Judge decided to rule on the regenerative memory patent as well.

As history relates, in 1967, a Control Data lawyer read about John Atanasoff, who had retired after serving as vice president of the Aero Jet General Corporation. The literature appeared to indicate that several of Eckert and Mauchly's patent claims were derived from Atanasoff's work, and Atanasoff agreed to help Honeywell and Control Data in their effort to overturn Sperry's patents. The Honeywell/Sperry trial began on June 1, 1971, and ended on March 13, 1972, after 77 witnesses and

32,654 exhibits were entered into evidence. A working model of part of Atanasoff's machine was demonstrated in court, and Sperry's attorneys glossed over the experiments Mauchly had performed in analog and digital electronics before he met Atanasoff. Some commentators have said that this shortcoming was because Sperry's attorneys may have underestimated the seriousness of Atanasoff's legal threat and because the evidence surrounding Mauchly's early work seemed too insubstantial to stand up in court.

On October 19, 1973, Judge Earl Larsen of the Minneapolis court decided the case, and Sperry lost on every count. Judge Larsen invalidated the ENIAC patent on four grounds, each one of which would have been sufficient alone to strike down Eckert and Mauchly's ENIAC patent claims. The Judge held first that the patent had been filed more than a year after the machine had been put into public use in February 1946. Second, the Judge decided that von Neumann's "First Draft of a Report on the EDVAC" constituted a prior publication that invalidated the ENIAC patent. Third, the Judge decided that Eckert and Mauchly's attorneys had engaged in misconduct by deliberately delaying the patenting process, hoping to delay the day that the patent issued, and thus increasing its financial value to Sperry Rand. And fourth, and most consequential to those historians of the computer age, Judge Larsen found that Eckert and Mauchly did not themselves first invent the automatic electronic digital computer, but instead derived that subject matter "from one Dr. John Vincent Atanasoff." The Judge also invalidated the regenerative memory patent on the grounds that it too had been derived from Atanasoff.

Subsequently, commentators tend to agree that Atanasoff's machine did embody many technical innovations that ended up in the ENIAC, and also that it appears that Mauchly was directly influenced by Atanasoff's work. Critics, however, hold that there are some contradictory aspects in the Judge's decision. For example, Atanasoff was credited by the Judge with having invented an "automatic electronic digital computer," but there was nothing automatic about Atanasoff's machine. ENIAC was a much better example of an automatic electronic digital computer, and the critics wonder what the Judge had in mind by the term "automatic." Sperry, which had spent about $1,000,000 on the litigation with Honeywell decided not to appeal, and the Honeywell and Control Data cases stopped there.

The Judge's decision was rendered seven months following the end of trial testimony, and the 248-page decision was published on October 19, 1973. The publication of the *Honeywell v. Sperry Rand* decision coincided with the so-called Saturday Night Massacre, one of the many gripping events in the then ongoing Watergate scandal during Richard Nixon's presidency. The media did not focus on Judge Larsen's decision because of the press' preoccupation with the Watergate controversy.

Judge Larson's decision offers two learning points that I deem of high importance to developers of patentable inventions. First, the ENIAC patent was invalidated due to the amount of time the inventors permitted to elapse following ENIAC's public disclosure on February 15, 1946, before filing the patent application. The public use date was prior to the "critical date" of June 26, 1946, which is the date one year before the patent application's filing. As indicated previously in this text, any public disclosure of an invention prior to the critical date rendered a corresponding U.S. patent invalid. The Judge also found that December 1, 1945, was the date the ENIAC was given to the Army Ordinance Corps, and beyond that date no further modifications could be considered as "experimental."

Second, the ENIAC patent was invalidated due to the time interval between when the inventors filed the patent application and its placement on sale. The construction contract for the ENIAC placed the intended delivery date at December 31, 1945, and the first working parts of the ENIAC consisting of two accumulators were shown to be operational in July 1944. These components, the Judge held, were in themselves an automatic electronic digital computer, thus moving the date before which Eckert and Mauchly should have applied for the patent to July 1945.

For more information as to the development of the ENIAC, and the patent controversy that followed, this author suggests reference to the material listed in the bibliography related to this essay.

Feb. 4, 1964 J. P. ECKERT, JR., ETAL 3,120,606

ELECTRONIC NUMERICAL INTEGRATOR AND COMPUTER

Filed June 26, 1947 91 Sheets-Sheet 1

FLOOR PLAN

Fig.1.

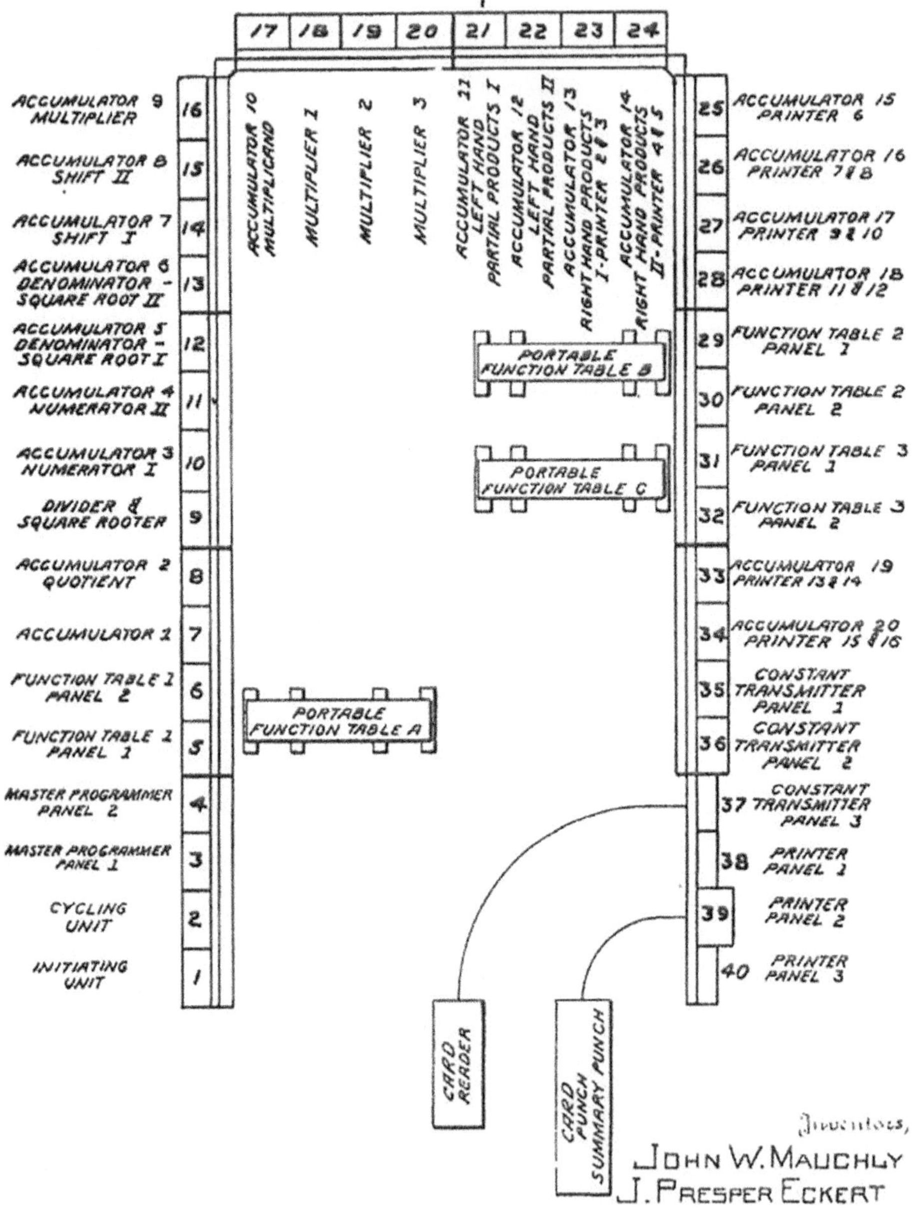

Inventors,
JOHN W. MAUCHLY
J. PRESPER ECKERT

By
J. H. Church, W. E. Thibodeau + M. L. Libman
Attorneys

Feb. 4, 1964 J. P. ECKERT, JR., ET AL 3,120,606

ELECTRONIC NUMERICAL INTEGRATOR AND COMPUTER

Filed June 26, 1947 91 Sheets-Sheet 24

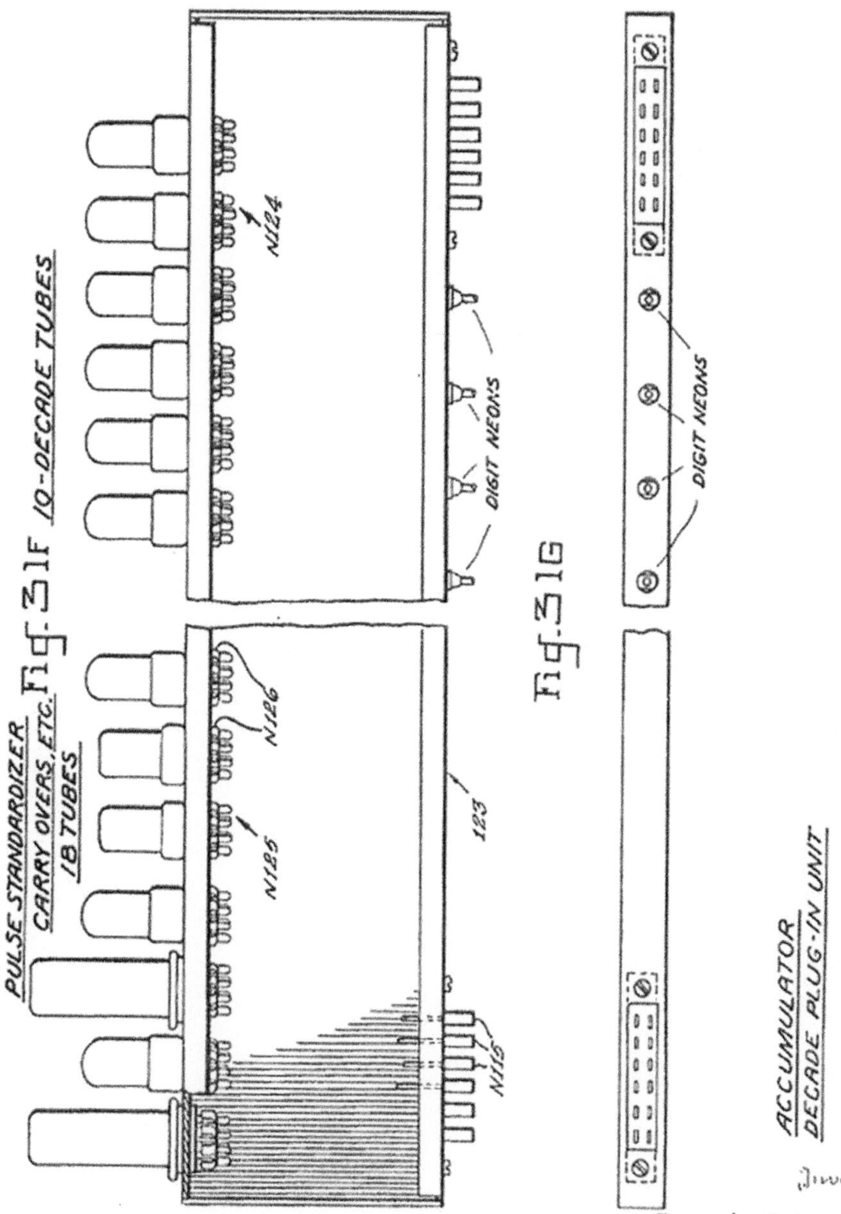

Inventors
JOHN W MAUCHLY
J. PRESPER ECKERT
By
J. H. Church, W. E. Thibodeau & M. L. Libman
Attorneys

30 Cybersquatting

Before going further in this chapter, some knowledge is assumed. First, it is assumed that the reader knows the basics of what a trademark is (registered or otherwise). Second, the reader should have a basic understanding of the Internet and what domain names, webpages, and the like are. Third, this chapter will be limited to U.S. law. While certain of the points made will apply to marks registered and established outside of the United States, the chapter will not explore non-U.S. trademark law, or its impact on the topics covered in this chapter.

30.1 WHAT IS CYBERSQUATTING?

Cybersquatting is simply an Internet-related way to infringe a trademark. However, since each different domain name can only resolve to one webpage, someone else using your trademark for their website effectively shuts you out of the market (at least for that top-level domain such as .com). Further, using a domain name that is similar to (in sound, spelling, or punctuation) as a domain name can also be considered cybersquatting. A famous example of the benefits one can reap from "cybersquatting" type behavior was the domain name "whitehouse.com." While the executive branch of the United States government operates "whitehouse.gov," another person registered "whitehouse.com." Middle and high school students and others looking for information about the executive branch, but mistakenly typing in ".com" instead of ".gov" were taken not to the official site of the executive branch of government, but rather to a site offering pornography.

A related form of cybersquatting is to use a common misspelling of a trademark (or changing an "o" to a zero, reversing the order of letters such as an "i" and an "e," adding "www" without a dot to the beginning of a trademark, or other common misspellings of trademarks such as "Google" spelled as Gooogle (with an extra "o")) to steal traffic. This type of cybersquatting is sometimes referred to as "typosquatting." Typosquatting actually began well before the Internet when Holiday Inn had a 1-800 number that was 1-800-HOLIDAY (465-4329). An "enterprising" person obtained 1-800-405-4329, exchanging the "o" in Holiday for a zero and presumably obtaining some phone calls meant for Holiday Inn.

Intellectual Property Law for Engineers, Scientists, and Entrepreneurs, Second Edition. Howard B. Rockman.

Published 2020 by John Wiley & Sons, Inc.

As cybersquatting activity increased, trademark holders began besieging domain name registrars to fix the problem. In effect, this made the registrars (private, non-governmental entities) arbiters of trademark rights, something that they had no experience in and no desire to do (especially with the attendant legal risks of being wrong). Further, trademark holders wanted a way to obtain damages for such infringement. This situation resulted in the creation of two different procedures that can be used to combat cybersquatting.

First, the Internet Corporation for Assigned Names and Numbers (ICANN), which oversees Internet domain name processes and registrars, created the Uniform Domain-Name Dispute-Resolution Policy (UDRP). The UDRP created a procedure by which domain name holders could obtain cancellation or re-registration to themselves of domain names that were identical to or confusingly similar to their trademarks. This is discussed in Section 30.2.2.

Second, the U.S. Federal government enacted the Anticybersquatting Consumer Protection Act (ACPA). The ACPA provides a forum in the federal court under the Lanham (Trademark) Act for a private lawsuit by the trademark holder against the alleged cybersquatter. The ACPA provides for both injunctive as well as monetary relief. This is discussed in Section 30.3 below.

30.2 THE UDRP

ICANN adopted the UDRP in 1999 after a lengthy process. As the body overseeing all domain name registrars, ICANN required all registrars to comply with the UDRP. It is worth noting that the UDRP does not cover all trademark-related disputes involving domain names and websites. Rather, it applies only to cybersquatting and other abusive registrations of domain names. A UDRP proceeding is an expedited process that is determined on the basis of paper submissions through a service provider approved by ICANN. The concept is to create an efficient way to deal with a specific (yet commonly occurring) type of dispute between trademark holders and domain registrants. The remedies under the UDRP are likewise limited to cancellation or transfer of the concerned domain name(s). Monetary damages are not awarded. There is also no direct appeal right under the UDRP.

30.2.1 Administration of the UDRP

A UDRP proceeding is an arbitration-like proceeding that is determined on paper submissions. For purposes of the UDRP, ICANN has authorized only certain providers to handle these types of disputes. Currently, ICANN has approved five providers:

- Asian Domain Name Dispute Resolution Centre.
- National Arbitration Forum (NAF).
- World Intellectual Property Organization (WIPO).
- Czech Arbitration Court Arbitration Center for Internet Disputes.
- Arab Center for Domain Name Dispute Resolution (ACDR).

A trademark holder intending to bring a UDRP complaint, however, should check the ICANN website (https://www.icann.org/resources/pages/providers-6d-2012-02-25-en) to confirm which providers are approved, as ICANN, at times, has removed providers (e.g., CPR (International Institute for Conflict Prevention and Resolution and eResolution) was, but no longer is, an approved provider).

As an aid to trademark holders and attorneys, decisions from prior proceedings before approved providers can be accessed online as research, to seek support for a claim, and to determine if a registrant is a serial cybersquatter.

30.2.2 Process for A UDRP Claim

A trademark holder—termed a Complainant under the UDRP—can bring a UDRP claim by filing a Complaint with its chosen approved provider. Providers usually supply sample or form Complaints that help organize the information that is required for logistical purposes (such as parties, domain name at issue, etc.) as well as the information required to support one's claim (covered in more detail below). The Complainant will also select whether to have the dispute determined by one arbitrator or a three-member panel. The Complainant is also required to provide a signed statement (a) releasing the provider, panelist(s), the registrar, ICANN, and related parties from all claims and (b) certifying that the information provided in the Complaint is accurate and submitted in good faith. Additionally, the Complainant can provide documentary evidence to support his or her claim. A Complainant may also cite prior panel decisions as support that his or her evidence and allegations meet all required elements of a cybersquatting claim.

Once the Complaint is filed, the dispute resolution provider will review the Complaint to determine if it complies with the applicable rules and the UDRP. If the Complaint is "deficient," the provider will give the Complainant five days to correct all problems, or the action will be deemed withdrawn (subject to being refiled). If the provider finds the Complaint is compliant, the provider will send the Complaint and notice of the proceeding to the Respondent. The date that the provider determines the Complaint is compliant with the relevant rules and policy, and sends the Complaint to the Respondent is the official "commencement" of the UDRP proceeding.

The UDRP also provides the Respondent an opportunity to respond. Within 20 days of the commencement date, the Respondent can submit its written response. The response provides various logistical information about the Respondent, but also must specifically respond to the allegations of the Complaint and provide the reasons that the Respondent should be allowed to keep the registration of the domain name at issue. The Respondent can also provide its own documentary evidence. In its response, the Respondent can change the arbitration to a three-member panel, if the Complainant selected a single member. The Respondent must also identify any other legal proceedings involving the domain name at issue. Along with sending the response, and any documentary evidence supporting its position, to the provider, the Respondent must also send such items to the Complainant.

After the Respondent submits its response, the panel (single-member or three-member panel depending on the applicable choice made) is appointed according to procedure. After the panel is appointed, the provider will notify the parties of who the panelist(s) is/are and the date by which, absent extraordinary circumstances, the panel will make a decision (which, by the rules, will be in writing with reasoning). As part of its process, the panel can request further statements or documents from the Complainant, Respondent, or both prior to making a decision.

If separate legal proceedings are brought regarding the domain name at issue before or during the UDRP proceeding, the panel has the discretion to suspend or terminate the proceeding, or to continue it.

Because the UDRP is done solely on (usually) two paper submissions, there is no motion practice, no discovery, and no trial; it is usually less costly than normal litigation, and can be completed in a much shorter time frame.

30.2.3 UDRP Requirements

In order to prevail in an action under the UDRP, the Complainant must prove that (a) the domain name at issue is "identical or confusingly similar" to the Complainant's trademark or servicemark, (b) that the Respondent has no rights or "legitimate interest" in the domain name, and (c) that the domain name was registered and is being used in "bad faith." A failure of proof of any one of these elements results in a denial of the claim. Each of these elements is discussed below.

30.2.3.1 Identical or Confusingly Similar to a Trademark

There are two parts to this element. First, the Complainant must show that he or she has rights in the trademark. Second, the Complainant must show that the domain name is identical, or confusingly similar, to that trademark.

The easiest way to prove rights in a mark is through a federal trademark registration. Panels generally accept that such registrations are proof of ownership. This is different from a state trademark registration, as those, in many cases, are not "examined" prior to registration as are federal marks. Thus, simple state registration does not prove your right in the mark, but rather only that you registered it with a particular state as your mark. However, you may also have acquired common law rights in an unregistered mark if it is distinctive or has acquired secondary meaning through use (see Chapter 29 on trademarks).

Whether the domain name is identical or confusingly similar involves a simple comparison of the claimed mark and the domain name. It is not the same as the test under U.S. trademark law for "likelihood of confusion," which is more in depth and depends on a number of factors. Notably, the removal of spaces and the addition of a top-level domain (such as .com) and the use of "www." are not relevant for this determination. Additionally, panels have stated that the addition of a geographic term, slight misspellings, prefixes, the addition of a pejorative term, and other small changes on their own do not make a domain name not confusingly similar. While these items may be probative for other requirements, the confusingly similar requirement focuses only on a simple comparison of the visual or phonetic overall similarity between the mark and the domain name at issue.

30.2.3.2 No Legitimate Interest

The UDRP lists three instances when a domain holder will have a legitimate interest in a domain name, even if it is confusingly similar to a mark. (See https://www.icann.org/resources/pages/policy-2012-02-25-en#4b.) While the Complainant has the burden on this element (as with all elements of the claim), panels have noted the difficulty in proving a negative and have only required the Complainant to make a *prima facie* showing of a lack of legitimate interest and then shift the burden to the

Respondent to prove a legitimate interest exists. However, that burden may not be too great, as some panels have noted that all a Respondent need show is "a plausible, non-infringing explanation for selecting the disputed domain name." (See http://www.wipo.int/amc/en/domains/decisions/html/2000/d2000-1512.html.)

First, a legitimate interest will be found if the panel determines that the Respondent used, or had made demonstrable preparations to use the domain name in connection with a "bona fide" offering of goods or services prior to notice of the dispute. Using a confusingly similar domain name to sell competing goods, obtain click-through advertising revenue, or knowingly using a famous mark to sell goods and services have been found not to be "bona fide" uses. On the other hand, using trademarked words also found in the dictionary and used in a descriptive sense and selling goods or services so described has been found to be a bona fide use. Finally, the issue of the use of a trademark in a domain name by resellers of trademarked goods has met mixed results, with the specific facts of each case being relevant, including whether such use may have been authorized by the mark holder. It is also worth noting that evidence that the mark was "famous" or that the Respondent knew (or must have known) about the mark will weigh against finding a legitimate interest under this factor.

Second, the UDRP indicates that if the Respondent is commonly known by the domain name (even without accompanying trademark rights), then that qualifies as a legitimate interest in the domain name. The analysis for this element is usually fact intensive. Panels will look not only at the website at issue, but also outside evidence such as affidavits, proof of corporate existence and registration (to show that the registrant exists using the name at issue), and similar factors. Outside evidence and public records (customer statements, advertising, phone book evidence, official company filings, etc.) are more probative and given more weight than self-serving affidavits from owners and employees. However, panels are well aware that this showing may be easily asserted, and have cautioned against a lax acceptance of a Respondent's claim that they are commonly known by a name. As one panel pointed out:

> Since a 'legitimate interest' is sufficient in order to defeat a Complaint under the Policy, a Panel must be careful when considering whether or not a claim by the Respondent that he or she has 'been commonly known' by the domain name is legitimate. It is not sufficient for the Respondent to merely assert that he or she has been commonly known by the domain name in order to show a legitimate interest. The Respondent must produce evidence in order to show that he or she has been 'commonly known' by the domain name. See, e.g. *Red Bull GmbH v. Harold Gutch*, WIPO Case No. D2000-0766, where the Panel rejected the claim that Respondent was known by nickname 'Red Bull' since childhood because Respondent did not provide any evidence to support contention. See also, e.g. *DIMC Inc, & The Sherwin-Williams Company v. Quang Phan*, WIPO Case No. D2000-1519, where the Panel rejected claim that Respondent was known by nickname 'Krylon' due to absence of evidence when the alleged nickname was adopted and how it was used.

World Natural Bodybuilding Federation, Inc. v. Daniel Jones TheDotCafe, WIPO Case No. D2008-0642, *quoting Banco Espirito Santo S.A. v. Bancovic*; WIPO Case No. D2004-0890.

Finally, a legitimate, noncommercial or fair use of the domain name, with no intent for commercial gain or to divert customers or tarnish the trademark, qualifies as a legitimate interest. One of the key issues under this factor is the "noncommercial" use of the website. Thus, selling goods on the website, selling advertising space for revenue, and offering services can be found to be commercial and preclude a finding of a legitimate interest under this factor. Even where the website itself was not commercial but provided a link to a Respondent's other page where related goods were sold, the panel refused to find a noncommercial use. (See http://www.wipo.int/amc/en/domains/decisions/html/2004/d2004-0498.html.) This category will usually consider "____ sucks," gripe and similar criticism sites, so long as they are actually commentary sites and not something else, as a situation where the Respondent has a legitimate interest. Indeed, an information-only site (for example, to provide information about a business and its services), without criticism, has been considered a fair use and noncommercial under this factor. (See http://www.wipo.int/amc/en/domains/decisions/html/2000/d2000-1647.html.) The elements of no intent to divert customers or tarnish the trademark are also important. For example, making a noncommercial use by posting family pictures, but using a famous trademark as your domain name, forcing customers searching for the trademark holder to view your beautiful family will not pass muster.

30.2.3.3 Bad Faith

The UDRP provides a non-exhaustive list of actions that will constitute bad faith. These examples are:

i. circumstances indicating that you have registered or you have acquired the domain name primarily for the purpose of selling, renting, or otherwise transferring the domain name registration to the complainant who is the owner of the trademark or service mark or to a competitor of that complainant, for valuable consideration in excess of your documented out-of-pocket costs directly related to the domain name; or
ii. you have registered the domain name in order to prevent the owner of the trademark or service mark from reflecting the mark in a corresponding domain name, provided that you have engaged in a pattern of such conduct; or
iii. you have registered the domain name primarily for the purpose of disrupting the business of a competitor; or
iv. by using the domain name, you have intentionally attempted to attract, for commercial gain, Internet users to your web site or other on-line location, by creating a likelihood of confusion with the complainant's mark as to the source, sponsorship, affiliation, or endorsement of your web site or location or of a product or service on your web site or location.

(UDRP at Paragraph 4(b), https://www.icann.org/resources/pages/policy-2012-02-25-en.) The bad faith analysis can also be very fact intensive, getting into not only the timing of registration and outward actions, but also the intent of the Respondent.

30.2.4 Remedies

The UDRP provides for only two remedies if a Complainant prevails in a proceeding. When the action is filed, the Complainant is required to elect at that time which remedy they will want if they prevail. The first remedy is transfer of the domain name at issue. If a Complainant selecting this remedy prevails, the panel will enter an order directing the registrar to transfer ownership of the domain name to the Complainant. At that time, there are usually some simple logistical issues to work out, but the transfer is fairly smooth. The second remedy is cancellation of the domain name. Under this remedy, the Respondent's registration for the domain name at issue is cancelled, and the Respondent no longer "owns" the domain name and putting the address in a browser will not resolve to the Respondent's website. The UDRP does not offer any monetary damages.

30.3 THE ANTICYBERSQUATTING CONSUMER PROTECT ACT (ACPA)

The ACPA was enacted into federal law in 1999 and became part of the Lanham (Trademark) Act. 15 U.S.C. §1125(d). The ACPA creates a cause of action for trademark holders against a person that:

i. has a bad faith intent to profit from that mark, including a personal name which is protected as a mark under this section; and
ii. registers, traffics in, or uses a domain name that –
    I. in the case of a mark that is distinctive at the time of registration of the domain name, is identical or confusingly similar to that mark;
    II. in the case of a famous mark that is famous at the time of registration of the domain name, is identical or confusingly similar to or dilutive of that mark; or
    III. is a trademark, word, or name protected by reason of section 706 of Title 18 or section 220506 of Title 36.

15 U.S.C.A. §1125(d). The ACPA, as part of the federal trademark act, provides for a federal forum for cybersquatting claims, and the process follows the normal course of federal litigation. Similarly, the cost of an ACPA claim can be higher (sometimes exponentially higher) than a UDRP claim as federal litigation involves motion practice, discovery, and trial. Further, unlike the UDRP, in addition to transfer orders, a federal court can also award damages under the ACPA.

30.3.1 Elements of an ACPA Claim

In order to establish a claim under the ACPA, the statute lays out three basic requirements. First, that the defendant register, traffic in, or use a domain name. Second, that the domain name at issue be identical or confusingly similar to the trademark. Third, that the defendant have a bad faith intent to profit from the use of the infringing domain name.

Establishing the first element is fairly easy. Registering and using a domain name are obvious concepts. Trafficking under the ACPA refers to "transactions that include, but are not limited to, sales, purchases, loans, pledges, licenses, exchanges of currency, and any other transfer for consideration or receipt in exchange for consideration." 15 U.S.C. §1125(d)(1)(E).

The second element requires that the domain name be identical or confusingly similar to the mark at issue. Courts generally note that the test for "confusingly similar" is different from the "likelihood of confusion" test for trademark infringement.

Generally, courts look at the mark and the domain name and see if there is enough identity or overlap to be considered identical or confusingly similar. Thus, it is a straightforward comparison of the mark and domain name that is similar to that performed under the UDRP.

Finally, the ACPA requires the plaintiff to prove a bad faith intent by the defendant. The ACPA provides a non-exhaustive list of factors the court can consider in making a determination of the existence or not of bad faith intent. These are:

I. the trademark or other intellectual property rights of the person, if any, in the domain name;
II. the extent to which the domain name consists of the legal name of the person or a name that is otherwise commonly used to identify that person;
III. the person's prior use, if any, of the domain name in connection with the bona fide offering of any goods or services;
IV. the person's bona fide noncommercial or fair use of the mark in a site accessible under the domain name;
V. the person's intent to divert consumers from the mark owner's online location to a site accessible under the domain name that could harm the goodwill represented by the mark, either for commercial gain or with the intent to tarnish or disparage the mark, by creating a likelihood of confusion as to the source, sponsorship, affiliation, or endorsement of the site;
VI. the person's offer to transfer, sell, or otherwise assign the domain name to the mark owner or any third party for financial gain without having used, or having an intent to use, the domain name in the bona fide offering of any goods or services, or the person's prior conduct indicating a pattern of such conduct;
VII. the person's provision of material and misleading false contact information when applying for the registration of the domain name, the person's intentional failure to maintain accurate contact information, or the person's prior conduct indicating a pattern of such conduct;
VIII. the person's registration or acquisition of multiple domain names which the person knows are identical or confusingly similar to marks of others that are distinctive at the time of registration of such domain names, or dilutive of famous marks of others that are famous at the time of registration of such domain names, without regard to the goods or services of the parties; and
IX. the extent to which the mark incorporated in the person's domain name registration is or is not distinctive and famous within the meaning of subsection (c). 15 U.S.C. §1125(d)(1)(B)(i).

Notably, the ACPA also provides a safe harbor precluding a finding of bad faith if the defendant reasonably believed that the use of the domain name was fair use or not illegal:

> (ii) Bad faith intent described under subparagraph (A) shall not be found in any case in which the court determines that the person believed and had reasonable grounds to believe that the use of the domain name was a fair use or otherwise lawful.

15 U.S.C. §1125(d)(1)(B)(ii).

30.3.2 Remedies

Under the ACPA, like the UDRP, a court can order that the domain name at issue be transferred to the trademark holder, or that the domain name be forfeited or cancelled (see 15 U.S.C. §1125(d)(1)(C)). Additionally, however, the court can also award monetary damages. These damages can be the same measures of damages as allowed for other trademark infringement type claims (see 15 U.S.C. §1114 and 1117). However, the ACPA provides for a special election option where the trademark holder can elect, instead of actual damages and profits, to have the court make a statutory award of between $1000 and $100,000 per domain name at issue (see 15 U.S.C. §1117(d)). The court has discretion in this award and can look at a number of factors. One court noted that these factors include "'the egregiousness or willfulness of the defendant's cybersquatting, the defendant's use of false contact information to conceal its infringing activities, the defendant's status as a 'serial' cybersquatter … and other behavior by the defendant evidencing an attitude of contempt towards the court of the proceedings'" (see *Wecosign, Inc. v. IFG Holdings, Inc.*, 845 F. Supp. 2d 1072, 1086 (C.D. Cal. 2012).

In addition, under the Lanham Act, a court can also award attorneys' fees in "exceptional" cases.

SECTION VII

The Commercialization and Management of Intellectual Property

◆ INVENTORS AND INVENTIONS ◆

George de Mestral

HOOK-AND-LOOP FASTENER (VELCRO®)

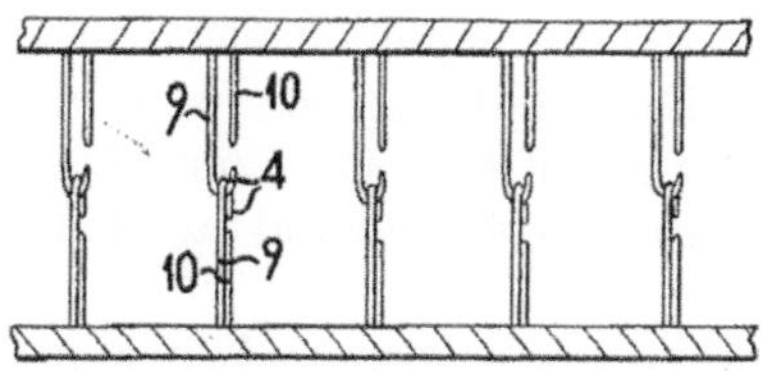

George de Mestral was a Swiss citizen who attended the Polytechnique of Lausanne, where he graduated with an electrical engineering degree in 1930. One day in 1941, he went for a hike while on a skiing trip, and when he came back he discovered that his dog and his coat were covered in burdock burrs or seeds that had attached themselves to his and his dog's coat and fur. He examined the burrs under a microscope, finding there were hundreds of hooks on the burrs that caught on anything with a loop, such as animal fur, hair, clothing, etc. He conceived of the possibility of making two materials reversible in similar fashion, if he could figure out how to manufacture the hooks and loops.

At first, he and his ideas were not taken seriously. However, he took his idea to Lyon, France, a weaving center, where he managed to obtain the help of a weaver who made two cotton strips that worked. Unfortunately, the cotton wore out quickly, so de Mestral turned to synthetic fibers such as nylon and polyester. Through trial and error, he determined that nylon was the best synthetic to use. Eventually he determined that nylon-formed hooks were optimal for the hook side of the fastener when sewn under a hot infrared light, since nylon did not wear with use. However, two things still stood in his way: he had yet to determine how to mechanize the manufacturing process, and how to make the loop side. He found, however, that nylon thread when woven into loops and then heat treated retains its shape and is resilient. However, the loops had to be cut in just the right spot, so they could be repeatedly fastened and unfastened many times. Eventually, he bought a pair of shears and trimmed the tops off the loops, creating hooks that would match up with mating loops.

De Mestral's fasteners consisted of two components. First, a lineal fabric strip with tiny hooks that could mate with a second fabric strip with smaller loops, attaching temporarily until pulled apart.

Intellectual Property Law for Engineers, Scientists, and Entrepreneurs, Second Edition. Howard B. Rockman.

Published 2020 by John Wiley & Sons, Inc.

As you might imagine, mechanizing a process of weaving 300 loops and hooks per square inch onto cloth tape took eight more years, plus another year to create the loom that trimmed the loops after weaving. All in all it took ten years to create a workable mechanized process. In 1951, he filed for a patent in Switzerland on his idea, and the patent was granted in 1955. De Mestral adopted the name Velcro for his invention, which is a mixture of the French words *velours*, which means velvet, and *crochet*, which means hook. He also gave the name to his company.

The adoption of hook-and-loop fasteners by the textile industry took some time, primarily because of appearance. High-end designers did not like its look, since in the 1960s, hook-and-loop fasteners looked like they had been made from leftover bits of cheap fabric, which certainly did not impress manufacturers of stylish clothing. The first notable use of hook-and-loop fasteners was in the aerospace industry, where it helped astronauts get into and out of their space suits. Later, skiers noted the similar advantage of a suit that was easy to get into and out of. The scuba and marine gear industries followed.

In the early 1960s, Apollo astronauts also used hook-and-loop fasteners to secure pens and other objects and equipment they did not want floating away in their gravityless space capsules. Hospitals eventually affixed hook-and-loop fasteners to everything from blood pressure gauges to patient gowns. Notably, at a fashion show in 1959 at the Waldorf Astoria Hotel in New York City, manufacturers showed hook-and-loop fasteners on everything from diapers to golf jackets, and showed them to the stylish society matrons of New York City. However, at that time, even with a colored hook-and-loop fastener, it was still unattractive, and for a long time the fasteners were relegated to athletic equipment. In 1968, Puma became the first major shoe company to offer sneakers with hook-and-loop fasteners. By the 1980s, it appeared that every child in the United States owned at least one pair of hook-and-loop fastener clasped sneakers. However, by then the Velcro Company's original patent had expired, and companies in Europe, Mexico and Asia were manufacturing copied versions.

De Mestral eventually started a company to manufacture Velcro, which he later sold along with the worldwide patent rights to the present Velcro Company SA, a Swiss company, now known as Velcro International.

In an interesting event, in 1984 David Letterman, host of a late-night U.S. television show, was interviewing Velcro Corporation U.S.A.'s director of industrial sales, and Letterman was wearing a hook-and-loop suit. When the interview was over, Letterman used a trampoline to cast himself onto a hook-and-loop-covered wall, and he got stuck. A few years later, a New Zealand tavern owner provided patrons with Velcro wall jumping equipment and held "human fly" contests. By 1992, Velcro jumping had spread to the United States; however, the game never gained national momentum, but even today every once in a while the game shows up at carnivals and fairs. In 1991, toy companies conceived of a toy in which a furry tennis ball is thrown and caught with a paddle shaped hook-and-loop-fastener-equipped mitt. This was 50 years after Velcro's invention. Also, techies have determined that they could apply an adhesive on the back of their mobile phones and turned them into desk, wall, and car mounts using a hook-and-loop fastener system.

Not all uses of Velcro became valuable. In 2004, the U.S. Army came up with a combat uniform with hook-and-loop fasteners. However, the soldier's name tags fell off, and the loops got dirty due to the dust in the Middle East and would not fasten. Significantly, the loud sound produced by opening pockets made by hook-and-loop fasteners made it hard for soldiers to hide in the bushes from the enemy. Eventually, the U.S. Army did away with the hook-and-loop fasteners, and came up with an alternate solution to this problem: buttons.

As a result of the military experience, keep in mind that the tearing noise of the Velcro fasteners on pockets is also a useful weapon against pickpockets. It is our understanding that research continues to find a silent Velcro.

Today, Velcro International is making every effort to ensure that the trademark Velcro does not fall into the public domain as a generic term for any hook-and-loop fastener. The company wants everyone to know that Velcro is the name of their company and is a registered trademark for its products. The generic name of its products is a hook-and-loop fastener, or touch fastener.

Sept. 13, 1955 G. DE MESTRAL 2,717,437

VELVET TYPE FABRIC AND METHOD OF PRODUCING SAME

Filed Oct. 15, 1952

Fig. 1

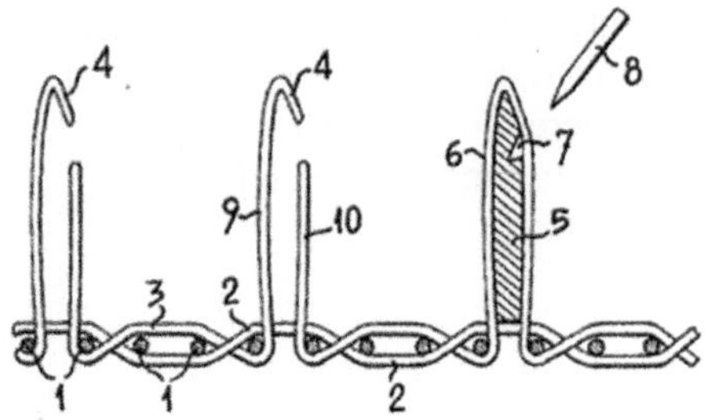

Fig. 2

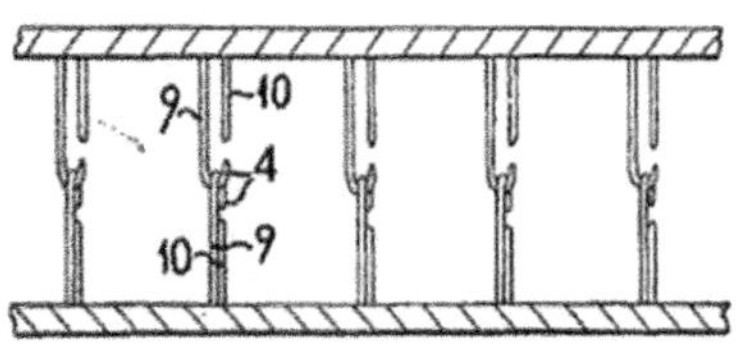

INVENTOR

George de Mestral.

BY [signature]

ATTORNEY

◆ INVENTORS AND INVENTIONS ◆

John A. Roebling

SUSPENSION BRIDGES

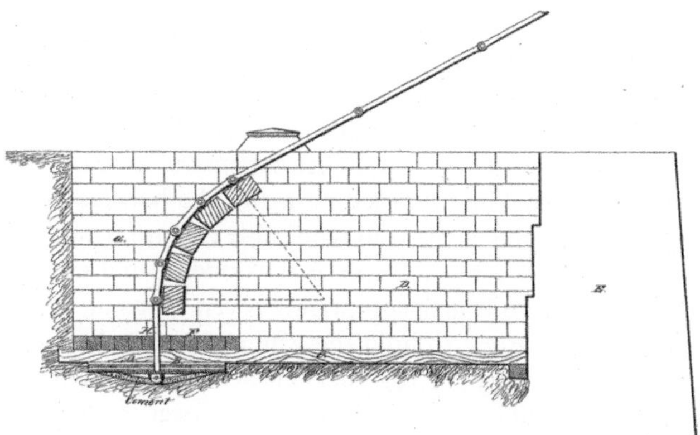

John A. Roebling was an American civil engineer of German birth, who designed and built wire rope suspension bridges, and most notably designed the Brooklyn Bridge in New York. While still in Germany, Roebling worked at Arnsberg, Westphalia, on military road construction for four years, and during this period he made several sketches regarding suspension bridge designs.

In May of 1831, Roebling emigrated from Prussia with his brother Carl and a friend John Adolphus Etzler, along with a group of others, all whom believed that there was a technological utopia in America. They left Prussia also since engineers had economic difficulties in Prussian society as a result of the Napoleonic wars, which lasted until 1815, during which time investment in infrastructure had been all but eliminated. It was also during this time that Prussia was undergoing political unrest as authoritarian governments took the place of democratic states. Etzler had ideas about creating a haven for the engineers in the United States, but en route to the United States the group of three broke up. In 1831, John and Carl Roebling purchased 1582 acres of land in Pennsylvania, intending to establish a German settlement. Other settlers on the trip remained with Etzler.

At the time the Roeblings and the others arrived in the United States, transportation between the Eastern industrial hubs of the country and the farming markets to the West had become a matter of national and popular pride and commercial interest. Many

Intellectual Property Law for Engineers, Scientists, and Entrepreneurs, Second Edition. Howard B. Rockman.

Published 2020 by John Wiley & Sons, Inc.

railroad and transportation hubs were established near where Roebling chose for his colony, but instead of continuing in the engineering profession, Roebling took up farming.

However, Roebling ultimately found toiling in the ground unsatisfying, and the colony he tried to establish in Pennsylvania attracted very few settlers. In 1837, after his brother Carl passed away, Roebling returned to engineering, working on projects to improve river navigation and constructing canals. He spent several years conducting surveys for railroads across the Allegheny Mountains between Harrisburg and Pittsburgh for the state of Pennsylvania. In 1840, he wrote to suspension bridge designer, Charles Ellet, Jr., offering to help design a bridge close to Philadelphia. His writings of the time expressed an interest in designing suspension bridges.

While in Pennsylvania, in 1841 Roebling began producing wire rope. At that time, canal boats from Philadelphia were transported over the Allegheny Mountains on railroad cars and deposited in the waterways on the other side of the mountains. The railroad cars were hauled up the inclines in the mountains by long loops of thick hemp rope approximately 7 cm thick. These ropes were expensive, wore out rapidly, and had to be replaced frequently. Roebling recalled an article he had read previously about wire ropes and began developing a 7 strand wire cable on his farm.

In 1844, Roebling received a bid to replace a wooden canal aqueduct across the Allegheny River. He designed a bridge comprising seven spans of 163 feet each. Each span consisted of a wooden truck to hold the water, supported by continuous cable made of many parallel wires wrapped together on each side of the truck. He followed this innovation in 1845 by building a suspension bridge over the Monongahela River. In 1848, Roebling designed and constructed several suspension aqueducts on the east coast, mainly in Delaware and New Jersey. In Trenton, New Jersey, Roebling also built a large industrial complex to manufacture wire cable.

In 1851, Roebling entered into a four-year project involving construction of a bridge with a span of 1825 feet over the Niagara River. This bridge had two levels: one for vehicles and one for rail traffic. The American Civil War brought a temporary halt to Roebling's bridge construction; however, in 1863, building resumed on a bridge over the Ohio River at Cincinnati, which had been started in 1856, but was halted due to lack of financing. This bridge was completed in 1867, and at the time it was finished was the world's longest suspension bridge. It spans the Ohio River to this day.

Roebling devised an equilibrium strength approach to his suspension bridge designs in which equilibrium is always satisfied, but compatibility of deformations is not enforced. This was essentially an approximation method where Roebling first computed the dead and live loads, then divided the load between the cables and the space. Roebling added an increased safety factor to the divided loads, then solved for the forces. This approach gave a sufficiently accurate analysis of the space structure, given the assumption that the structure was sufficiently ductile to handle the resulting deformation.

In 1867, Roebling began designing what is now known as the Brooklyn Bridge across the East River in New York. On June 28, 1869, at Colton Ferry, he was standing at the edge of a dock setting the location where the bridge would be built. His foot was crushed by an arriving ferry and his injured toes were ultimately amputated. He refused additional medical treatment and tried treating his injured foot by the continuous pouring of water over his wound. His condition deteriorated and he died on July 22, 1869, of tetanus at the home of his son on Hicks Street in Brooklyn Heights.

Subsequent to Roebling's death, his son Washington Roebling, and Washington's wife, Emily Warren Roebling, continued the work on the Brooklyn Bridge, while another son, Ferdinand, continued and expanded the Roebling wire rope business. A third son, Charles Roebling, designed and invented an 80 ton wire rope machine and founded the town of Roebling, New Jersey.

The Brooklyn Bridge is a hybrid cable-stayed/suspension bridge. It was begun in 1869 and completed in 1883, fourteen years later. The bridge has a main span of 1595 feet and was the world's first dual wire suspension bridge. The towers of the bridge were constructed of limestone, granite, and Rosendale cement. The bridge had many passageways and compartments in its anchorages, and the city of New York rented out the large vaults under the Manhattan anchorage to raise money to construct the bridge. Opening in 1876, these vaults were used to store wine since the vaults were at a steady temperature of 60°F. Thus, while the city of New York could not sell you the Brooklyn Bridge, it could rent you space in the anchorages of the bridge.

The Brooklyn Bridge's two towers were constructed by floating two caissons, which are giant upside-down boxes made of southern pine, in the span of the East River, and then building stone towers over the caissons, causing the caissons to sink to the bottom of the river. Compressed air was then pumped into the caissons, and workers entered the space to remove the sediment until the caissons sank to bedrock. The entire weight of the Brooklyn Bridge to this day sits upon a 15 foot thickness of Southern Yellow Pine wood under the sediment.

Washington Roebling suffered a paralyzing injury as a result of "caisson disease" shortly after ground was broken for the Brooklyn Bridge tower foundation in 1870. His condition left him unable to supervise the construction on site. As a result, Washington, as chief engineer, supervised the entire construction project from his apartment from which he viewed the work, designing caissons and other equipment. He was assisted by his wife, Emily Warren Roebling, who provided the critical link between her husband and the engineers on the job site. Under her husband's guidance, Emily studied higher mathematics, the calculation of catenary curves, strength of materials, bridge specifications, and other intricate construction matters. She spent the next 11 years assisting Washington Roebling supervise the Brooklyn Bridge's construction.

When probes underneath the caissons for the Manhattan tower found the bedrock to be deeper than first thought, Washington Roebling halted construction due to the increased risk of depression sickness that could be suffered by the workers in the caissons. He subsequently determined that the sandy subsoil overlaying the bedrock 30 feet below to be firm enough to support the tower base, and construction continued.

The architectural style of the towers is neo-gothic with characteristic pointed arches above the passageway through the stone towers. Roebling designed the bridge and truss system six times stronger than it needed to be. As a result, the Brooklyn Bridge is still standing while many contemporary bridges have disappeared or have been replaced. This is also true in spite of the substitution of inferior quality wiring in the cabling supplied by the contractor, and by the time it was discovered it was too late to replace the cabling that had already been used for construction. Roebling determined that the inferior wire would leave the bridge four, rather than six times as strong as necessary, so it was eventually allowed to stand, with the addition of 250 cables.

If you are interested in more information about the construction of the Brooklyn Bridge, this author recommends the book *The Great Bridge* by David McCullough, written in 1962. In addition, the first PBS documentary film by Ken Burns is entitled *The Brooklyn Bridge* and debuted in 1981.

J. A. Roebling.
Suspension Bridge.
No. 4,710. Patented Aug. 26, 1846.

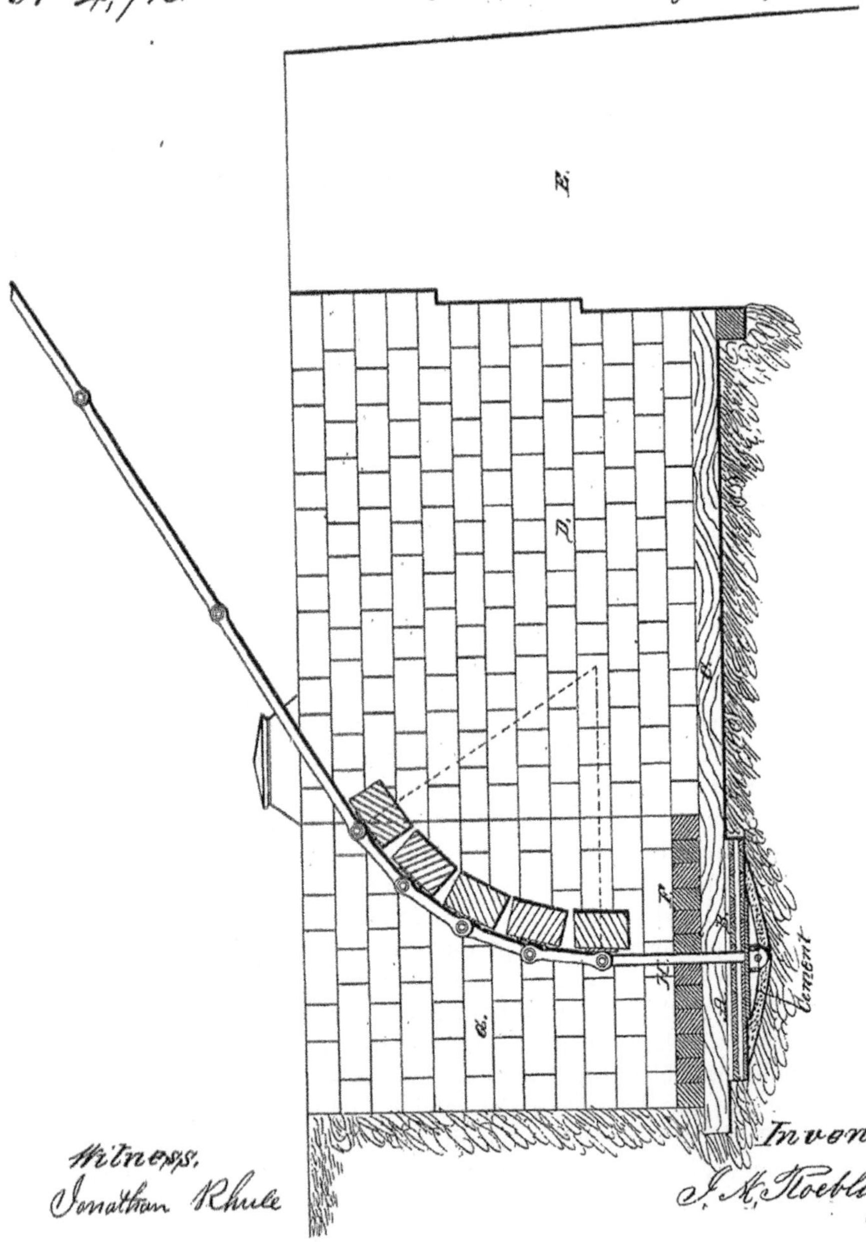

Witness.
Jonathan Rhule

Inventor.
J. A. Roebling.

H. PETERS, PHOTO-LITHOGRAPHER, WASHINGTON, D. C.

31 Engineering Management and Commercialization of Intellectual Property

31.1 INTRODUCTION

31.1.1 The Rapidity of Technological Change

Advances in technology and science over the past century have been the most rapid in history. While we live today with a plethora of scientific wonders that were not available, or even thought of a generation or two ago, the changes that occur day by day in our time seem to make things obsolete before you can pronounce the names of the systems that embody the new technology. For example, 4G wireless communication networks were introduced to replace the 3G network, with the near-simultaneous announcement that the 4G networks would be replaced in the next several years. As of this writing, 5G networks are nearly here. For someone who went through engineering college with a slide rule attached to his belt as I did (along with the ubiquitous pocket protector), keeping up with the rapid changes in technology and its effects on our daily life is at the same time intimidating and fascinating.

Think for a moment of a graph, plotting on the Y-axis the fastest speed a human being could travel from place to place. The X-axis plots time, beginning with the year 2000 BCE and extending to the present. For all the years prior to circa 1840 CE, the graph would reflect a horizontal line at about 35 mph, which is the approximate speed of a horse. Then, your curve takes a slight upward trajectory, reflecting the advent of steam engines introduced by the railroads, and then automobiles, and then air travel. Then, beginning in the late 1950s through the 1960s and up to today, your curve leaps upward almost in a vertical trajectory, off the chart reflecting the speed of about 23,000 mph, the speed of the astronauts who are lodged in the International Space Station as these words are written. This graph, as I see it, is a rhetorical depiction of the rapidity of technology advances and changes taking place today, and that will continue into the foreseeable future, and beyond.

A further indication of where we are today is the Hubble Telescope, and my vision of a future version of that wondrous bit of science. We have all marveled at the images of galaxies, nebulae, and universes captured by the Hubble and posted on NASA's website and in journals of all varieties. The most amazing thing to me, however, is the fact that the light entering the Hubble's "lenses" took millions and sometimes billions of years to reach those lenses. We, therefore, are viewing an image of a celestial body, or bodies, as they existed millions or billions of years ago, not as they exist today. As a result, we are actually looking back in time, our own "Back to the Future."

Intellectual Property Law for Engineers, Scientists, and Entrepreneurs, Second Edition. Howard B. Rockman.

Published 2020 by John Wiley & Sons, Inc.

Here is where that technology may someday take us. A scientific theory today postulates that nothing can travel faster than the speed of light. So far, this is true. However, it is possible that someday scientists, with particle accelerators, may be able to accelerate matter to a speed beyond the speed of light. Expanding on this concept, it is my prediction that someday, man-made objects such as a Hubble-type telescope may be capable of traveling at speeds beyond the speed of light.

Carrying my hypothesis one step further, I envision launching a Hubble-type telescope into space at a speed exceeding that of light. When the telescope reaches a predetermined position above the Earth, in geosynchronous orbit, its lenses are focused toward the Earth to capture light rays that left the Earth, thousands of years ago. By electronically transforming these light rays into images, many of the historical events about our planet that are still grounds for speculation may be discovered. What were the origins of our planet? When and how did man/woman evolve? What did happen to the dinosaurs? What did those humans of our pre-history, and early recorded history, look like and do? This scenario is only hypothetical, lodged in the far reaches of my imagination, scoffed at by many I have spoken to, and purely speculative today. But so was landing a man on the moon a hypothesis pre-1969. I propose that technology advancement may not be limited by the imagination. The technology of the future may exceed our imaginations.

31.1.2 People and Technology Development

Several changes in the world's political and demographic makeup beginning in the 1990s and continuing today are having, and will continue to have, an accelerating effect on the rapidity with which technology is advancing, and new innovations are introduced for the benefit of us all. The one thought that interests me is the groundswell of new minds that entered the worldwide technology genre in the past fifty or so years via China, India, Brazil, several Middle-Eastern countries, and other nations. Start with China and India, where one out of every three people on our planet live. India, since it decided to enter the global economy in the latter years of the last century by allowing outside investment, created several India Institutes of Technology (IITs) that have graduated many thousands of computer scientists and engineers over the past several years. Since these technology graduates presently work at wages lower than the salary of a comparable worker in the United States or Europe, the Indian technology sector has been able to attract large swaths of outsourced technology development jobs from the industrialized nations.

China has also entered the global economy, and today is providing technology and engineering educations to thousands of young people. In addition to its manufacturing sector, China, through its education system, has increased its ability to conduct research and development in fields leading to new innovations.

Brazil, the most populous nation in Latin America, has developed automotive engines that operate on a sugar-cane-based ethanol fuel. In the Brazilian State of Amapa that embraces the mouth of the Amazon River, the state government has established the State University of Amapa, with courses on sustainable development for the Amazon region.

In the United Arab Emirates, there are presently several technological universities of higher education. In Thuwal, Saudi Arabia, the King Abdullah University of Science and Technology was established on the Red Sea in 2009, using English as the official language of instruction.

Many other countries around the world are discovering, as the industrialized nations determined long ago, that the success of a nation, and its population, and indeed of the world, depends on developing, and then mining the intellect of its human assets, which increase with population growth. Those nations that historically mined only the natural resources under their feet, and neglected the intellect of their human assets, have seen a progressive decline in their ability to maintain a stable, prosperous, gainfully employed, and happy populace.

As a result of the developing nations of the globe moving today toward a "Knowledge Economy," think about how many new engines of thought, i.e., our individual and collective human minds, have moved from "off" to "on" to solve human and other problems through innovation and technology advancements. With China and India alone adding to the global technology pool from which they were absent a generation or two ago, the world's number of human minds, or human "assets," involved in technology development, creativity, and innovation has increased by approximately one-third. When the other countries, such as Brazil and the Middle-East countries are added to the mix, I expect that the number of scientists and engineers in the world addressing new technology will increase by at least fifty percent in the near future.

With all of these additional technologically engaged minds working on advancing science, developing new products and processes, and directly developing solutions to the worlds' problems, both large and small, the number of new and useful innovations that change and improve our lives will increase exponentially. As a direct result, the number of inventions that need intellectual property protection will also increase at an expanding rate. As many more entities such as corporations, research institutions, individuals, and universities throughout the world produce innovations in science and technology, competition between these entities will increase, and intellectual property protection for their novel developments will be sought. To engage in this enlarged global competitive technology arena, each entity must carefully manage a tenable innovation development program, and consequently its intellectual property management skills to (1) secure its market position to prevent having its important technology misappropriated by competitors, and (2) avoid infringing on the rights of other intellectual property rights holders, for example, when the entity introduces a new product to the market.

This chapter recommends steps and considers strategies to properly manage, develop, and protect the output of your human intellectual assets, which are lodged in the minds of your innovators. The output of these human assets leads to the creation of intellectual property rights established by the laws of almost every nation in the world. This chapter presents many suggestions for managing your intellectual assets and intellectual property that may or may not be appropriate for your organization's size or field of technology. It is my intention to offer you advice to assist you in managing your intellectual property rights, and lead you to adopt tested measures that satisfy your particular needs.

31.1.3 Intellectual Property Strategy

There is no "right way" or "one size fits all" when it comes to developing and implementing a plan to maximize the use and commercialization of your intellectual property assets. In some organizations, intellectual property asset management plans are repeatedly changed until an optimum plan is formulated. The most efficient use of the intellectual property assets of a business organization derives from a strategy that guides managers in making and implementing day-to-day tactics and decisions. Properly, the intellectual property strategy is congruent with the innovation strategy and overall business strategy of the organization. With all of these stars in alignment, the merger of the intellectual property strategy plan with the business plan will expand the total value of the organization, and give the organization the ability to improve and maintain its competitive edge at higher levels.

Innovation strategies, as well as business strategies, take many forms. Each organization has its own business model. The most rewarding innovation strategies are those that work hand in glove with the organization's business strategy.

Those organizations that already have a business strategy and an innovation strategy that dovetails with the business strategy should also have an intellectual property strategy that is aligned with both the business strategy and the innovation strategy. Proper execution of the intellectual property strategy will increase the value of the business and improve its competitive position. Many organizations find it appropriate to change their strategy on a regular basis until they find one that actually gives them the desired results. Optimally, the intellectual property strategy may also have to change as the conditions of competition continue to change and technology changes accordingly.

Many organizations today do not realize that the output of the intellectual innovations and creativity of their employees forms the intellectual property of their business. While innovation itself increases value, the intellectual property provides the means for extraction of greater value from the innovation. An intellectual property strategy dovetailing with the business strategy provides the framework for acquiring, protecting, leveraging, managing, and profiting from intellectual property.

An organization's intellectual property strategy that focuses merely on obtaining patents, and possibly licensing some of those patents for additional revenue, falls short of "monetizing" intellectual property. In many organizations, the patenting and licensing model is divorced from the business and innovation strategy of the organization. This places short-term profits ahead of the long-term strategic goals of the company, and may risk the future viability of the organization itself. However, when aligned with the business strategy, a properly executed innovation, development, patenting, and licensing strategic model can produce significant additional revenues.

Intellectual property protection has been around since the city-state of Venice developed a procedure for rewarding its creators and those who brought new technology into the city-state in the 1460s.

Several commentators have indicated that today intellectual property has replaced manufacturing as a means for extracting value in a business organization. In April 2007, Congressman Robert Wexler estimated the value of intellectual property at 17% of the GDP. Congressman Wexler also indicated that intellectual property is the only sector in the United States that runs a trade surplus with every nation in the world, which is still true.

Under this new thinking, all organizations, whether high-tech or not, should consider developing intellectual property as providing a means of maximizing revenues for the organization. Further, these organizations must conduct an inventory to determine what results of their innovative endeavors actually involve intellectual property, which is more than just patents. Small companies, for example, have value in their copyrights, trademarks, trade secrets, know-how, source code for computers, business processes, customer, supplier and vendor lists, licenses, contracts, etc. Thought should be given to each of these to determine whether leverage, and additional revenue, can be developed through commercializing these different forms of intellectual property assets.

Intellectual property strategies vary from organization to organization. Using a broad definition of intellectual property, there are four functional strategies that should be used by an organization attempting to commercialize its intellectual property to increase its revenues as well as enhance its competitive position. The four functional strategies are: (1) the acquisition of intellectual property, (2) the protection of the organization's core business, (3) leveraging the intellectual property, (4) and management of the intellectual property. These functional strategies should properly be integrated within a company, and in such a way that the intellectual property strategy merges with the business strategy and the innovation strategy of the organization. The purpose of this chapter is to advise intellectual property managers and those involved in the development of intellectual property how to develop an effective strategy that will enhance the value of the business organization and extract maximum value from the innovations that support the intellectual property assets.

31.1.4 Motivations Supporting Innovation

31.1.4.1 Individual and Organizational Motivations

Individual humans are normally motivated by curiosity, realization, and recognition. Business entities such as corporations are motivated to innovate primarily to drive asset value and to increase profits. Many large corporations and even smaller organizations thrive on a culture of innovation. However, the continuance of this culture is not self-sustaining. It requires support from the management level of the organization as well as adherence to the program by the employees involved in the innovation process. Some organizations are compelled to change the culture of innovation on a day-to-day, week-to-week, or month-to-month basis. These companies achieve this goal by understanding the different perspectives of innovation as viewed by the organization, and as viewed by the individual employees. Both these aspects of innovation must be taken into consideration to implement a successful innovation program. Thus, your business organization is most likely motivated by the need for a competitive advantage, the desire to gain general or industry-specific knowledge, pursuing increased market share, providing more efficient service to its existing market, improving product quality, expansion of its product range, among others.

Individuals, however, are not corporations or enterprises. At their basic level, individuals have physiological needs that in turn yield to safety needs. Once these basic needs are covered, individuals then seek their own societal needs and the acknowledgment and respect of others, which reinforces their own self-esteem.

An organization is made up of individuals. Within this organization, an individual's decisions are made with the aim of advancing the goals of the organization, including the relationship between the individual and the organization. When an organization or corporation offers inducements for innovations, they are designed to form, strengthen, and maintain this identification between the organization and the individuals the organization employs.

There are many factors in the working environment, some that motivate individuals to think and to innovate, and some that do just the opposite. For example, working conditions, job security, corporate policies, and sometimes even salary structure are elements that are needed to motivate a worker to think and innovate. An enhancement in these factors, however, has not been shown to increase employee motivation. Rather, positive factors that have been seen to be motivational include a sense of achievement, peer acceptance, and an opportunity for personal professional growth and development. These, along with recognition by peers and management, give individuals the self-esteem they need, and drive them to achieve even more.

31.1.4.2 Intrinsic and Extrinsic Motivations

Extrinsic innovative motivation factors are neither inherent in the behavior of individuals nor representative of the goals established by them. An external force, such as the corporation, controls the setting of goals for individuals and the setting of rewards for achieving them. Management normally creates these external motivations, including performance planning and review processes, monetary policies, and job descriptions. Believe it or not, fear is also an external motivator.

Since external motivations are normally within the control of the organization, the wise organization will tailor these motivations to elicit desired individual behavior, which then inherently would support the innovation goals of the organization.

Intrinsic motivation comes from within the individual self. The reward is often the act itself, and in the case of innovation, the act of innovating may be the reward in and of itself. Intrinsic motivations may also include a personal interest or simply fun. Innovation itself may motivate individuals to innovate again. Success breeds success. Intrinsic motivations may depend on the experience levels of the individual and perhaps the management levels of the various individuals. Also, the level of education, the socioeconomic background of the individual, and the personal values of the individual are factors in the motivational qualities of each of us. Obviously, the organization cannot exercise control over intrinsic motivation. That is solely up to the individual.

31.1.4.3 Economic Motivation

Pure economic motives are also present in the innovation process. Small organizations innovate primarily to sell their innovations to the highest bidder, or to license their innovations as a means of gaining profit. It has been determined that with economic motivation, the innovator is not necessarily the owner of any one particular outcome, but is willing to try anything within an acceptable risk level to achieve the goal. These innovators are willing to fail fast to cut potential losses and move on to the next opportunity.

31.1.4.4 Socio-Political Motivation

A social-political motivation in an individual will lead that individual to innovate in order to enhance the living standards of the general population or segments of the population. This altruistic goal will drive many people toward an innovative level.

31.1.4.5 Possible Conflict Between Organizational and Individual Motivations

Normally, a business organization's strategy is to create value and to earn profit from that value. Employees, on the other hand, may not be motivated by the same goals, and if this is the case, the likelihood of successful innovation programs in an organization decreases.

The motivations of the organization and the motivations of the individuals should work synergistically together, and this takes planning by the organization and cooperation and buy-in by the individual. When individual motivations are properly managed by the organization, the motivations of both sides align to achieve the expected goals.

31.1.4.6 Developing Successful Motivations

In a well-constructed technology organization, the result of proper innovation is not only successful commercial products, but also the development of intellectual property assets. The intellectual property, of course, adds value to the efforts of both the individuals and the organization. Successful corporations have, among other things, created training programs with the aim of emphasizing the benefits of considering innovation and intellectual property within the framework of the business strategy. In several situations, this policy includes an incentive award program in which innovators are rewarded for disclosing inventions. It is quite apparent that the disclosure of inventions from the individuals upward through management is one of the prime goals of technology-driven companies throughout the world. In this way, a prosperous culture of innovation will be developed within the organization.

A successful company will innovate across the company each day to accelerate the development and delivery of new products and services. The company should also maintain a keen focus on the needs of its customers, actively participate in standards bodies, and keep abreast of relevant industry trends. Combining all these factors will continually increase the innovation output.

The successful organization will, as stated above, clearly recognize the difference between the motivational attributes of individuals and those of the organization. Successful companies have shown that it is important that individuals be trained in intellectual property awareness and innovation to create a culture whereby innovation is encouraged and rewarded by the company. By encouraging the employees to innovate in their day-to-day activities, a tangible benefit is provided in terms of recognition as part of performance appraisals. This motivation for innovation will create value and benefit the organization. New products, services, and information assets are continually being developed and marketed, both in the way of new and improved products, services, and the licensing of intellectual property. As a result, in successful companies, market share increases as customer satisfaction rises.

The successful organization constantly ensures that its innovation policies are linked with a congruent intellectual property strategy. An appropriate innovation program for a large corporation would involve both basic research, and additional research linked to developing products that fit within the business strategy of the enterprise. The successful company will show a direct correlation between profits, research, and development spending.

31.2 INTRODUCTION TO INTELLECTUAL PROPERTY BUSINESS STRATEGIES

In today's and tomorrow's "technology-driven" economy, the proper development of intellectual property assets is seen as crucial to business survival and advancement. Lately, many organizations have included intellectual property strategies in their business plans early on, rather than merely wait for a new development to emerge from their R&D department, and then try to figure out how to best use and protect that new development. Also, in the past several years, different types of inventions have been added to the list of patentable subject matter that were not so considered before. These include computer software, methods of doing business, and biotechnology innovations, as discussed previously in this book. Along with the increase in patentable subject matter, many businesses have developed creative thinking in strategizing the development and use of their intellectual property. Today, intellectual property is on the radar scope of upper management, where patents, copyrights, trademarks, trade secrets, know-how, etc., are now part of strategic thinking, planning, and implementation involving all levels of the organization.

Without the intellectual property systems for granting limited exclusive rights in innovation described in the previous chapters, technology would be submerged by their creators and kept from public use. Therefore, the intellectual property systems throughout the world serve the purpose of providing full public access and use of innovative ideas (which promotes innovation), and providing a foundation for economic wealth for the innovator during the period of exclusivity.

Although each country has its own procedures for obtaining intellectual property protection, the substance of the requirements for protectable subject matter are somewhat universal on this planet. To obtain a patent, for example, practically every country requires that an invention be useful in a real-world environment, be novel or new (not previously publicly known), and be non-obvious, or comprise an inventive step, over the relevant preceding "prior art." The trademark laws of each country normally require that a mark you use in commerce cannot be overly descriptive, and does not confusingly conflict with a mark used on similar goods or services by another. Copyrights are broader in scope of enforceability, where the owner of a copyright in one country can normally enforce that copyright in another country, and copyrights are enforceable in most countries (except the United States) without seeking or obtaining government registration of the copyright.

31.3 OBJECTIVES OF INTELLECTUAL PROPERTY MANAGEMENT

This discussion is dedicated to the economic and business factors involved in the generation and effective use of your entire intellectual property portfolio to maximum commercial advantage. These principles apply not only to the management of an established business, but also to the entrepreneur who is using the strength of one or several patents or other intellectual property vehicles to launch a new venture by creating an organization that will continue to develop new ideas and technology based upon an initial innovative concept. Many entrepreneurs recognize that a patent or a copyright may be the primary vehicle for intellectual property protection, which is the lifeblood of high-tech start-ups and other small companies created upon research, innovation, and creativity. Patents and other intellectual property also attract capital to these new technology-based ventures. Several primary objectives of a business strategy crafted to achieve optimum development, use, and protection of intellectual property are:

1. To create procedures within the organization that will encourage early and full disclosure of all potentially patentable and otherwise protectable technology from your research and development teams (i.e., bringing the ideas to the surface).

2. To establish criteria for evaluating invention and other innovation disclosures, and determining which new technology warrants consideration for patenting or copyright protection (i.e., what do we want to protect).
3. To establish additional criteria for deciding in which countries patent and/or trademark protection should be obtained, as contrasted to where patent or trademark protection may not be cost beneficial, or where patents and trademarks may not be readily enforceable (i.e., where do we want protection).
4. To create an awareness among all of the organization's technical personnel of patent, trademark, and copyright infringement avoidance, and from whom to seek guidance in avoiding infringement of another's intellectual property rights.
5. To create a patent and intellectual property portfolio that has both offensive and defensive capabilities vis-à-vis your competitors and potential competitors, and which portfolio increases the value of your and your company's intangible assets.
6. If your company is primarily driven by technology, it is highly recommended that an Intellectual Property Audit be conducted, and periodically updated. This audit is for the purpose of providing an inventory of your company's intellectual property assets so that information is readily available when it becomes necessary to enforce, license or sell any of those assets. A proper audit, in broad terms:
   a. identifies all intellectual property in your portfolio, including patents, trademarks, copyrights, trade secrets, know-how, license agreements, technology transfer agreements, and anything else your company considers as intellectual property;
   b. analyzes the categories of subject matter your company desires to protect, and includes a plan for identifying the categories of technology you desire to protect in the future; and
   c. includes a policy statement or manual setting forth internal procedures for the protection of your company's intellectual property, and for maintaining the confidentiality of your company's proprietary and trade secret information.

In today's large business environment, many companies with extensive patent and intellectual property assets have no idea what the totality of these assets are. Therefore, it is wise to create a searchable database with important information on all intellectual property assets. The database should, for example, record all important data from your patents, and a scanned image of the patent drawings. This helps you and the other engineers to readily identify the innovation that pertains to the database information. This database will also allow you to identify obsolete technology that can be dropped rather than expending money on patent maintenance fees.

31.4 THE SOLE INVENTOR IN AN ALIEN FIELD

Many inventors and creators are those who have developed an idea or concept into a workable embodiment, which idea or concept falls into a technology arena totally alien to the field of their everyday work or activities. I am referring to the homemaker who conceives of a new childproof safety lock for a food jar, or the insurance salesman who jots down on paper a new lubricating system for the two-cycle engine on his lawnmower, by way of examples. These are the inventors and creators who can easily obtain exclusive protection for their novel and creative ideas through copyrights, patents, trade secret agreements, and the like. However, during my practice, I have noted that many, if not most, of these sole inventors encounter great difficulty in overcoming the inherent hurdles in bringing their idea to the marketplace.

The primary reason for tripping over the hurdles is that many of these inventors and creators desire to start their own businesses to develop, produce, market, and sell the products or services incorporating their ideas. This requires financing, and in most cases much more than our homemaker or insurance salesman can come up with. For example, if the novel product can be injection-molded out of plastic, an initial expenditure of $40,000–$60,000 (at the time of writing this text) may be required to design and manufacture a mold that will produce the first prototype. Then, the costs of finalizing and testing the design, manufacturing production versions, marketing the product, and creating a sales distribution network for the product can require financing of a million dollars or more. This is before a single dollar in income has been produced by the new product. A few of my clients have attempted to profit on their ideas in this way, but found it difficult, if not impossible to obtain the necessary financing for a new, but yet unknown, marketable product. As a result, I have seen several potentially good ideas literally die on the vine.

To those of you who fall into the category of innovators who are unable to fully fund the development, marketing, and sales of your new product, my advice is to explore the licensing path with the assistance of your patent professional. By granting an exclusive (or non-exclusive) license to a company or other entity that is already in the marketplace selling products which are similar to, but not as good as, yours, you will achieve the goals of:

1. Successfully having your new product produced and into the hands of consumers.
2. Receiving royalty income from the sale of products embodying your idea without lifting a finger.
3. Avoiding the agony of raising funds, or using your own limited resources, to launch your new product into the marketplace.

I have recommended to many individual inventor and creator clients that they pursue the licensing route rather than start their own business, as the least expensive, quickest, least frustrating, and most profitable way to commercialize their novel idea or concept. For information on patent licensing, see Chapter 19, Section 19.2 of this text. Also, I strongly recommend that the sole entrepreneurs who are reading this seek advice from both a patent professional and a financial advisor to assist you in deciding how best to bring your idea to consumers, and how to make money at the same time without risking your own resources beyond your reasonable capability.

If you have no desire to license your invention or creation, venture capital can be sought after you have begun the pursuit of your intellectual property rights. Your banker should be able to connect you with a venture capital group that may seek investors for a business founded upon the intellectual property rights in your new invention or creation. In such cases, the investors may demand a controlling interest in your business venture in exchange for their providing the finances to get you started.

Besides licensing your invention, you also have the right to sell all of your rights in your invention or creation to a company that is already marketing a similar product. You will then "assign" your intellectual property rights to that company, and receive a lump sum payment for the assignment, or be compensated on a percentage of sales of products or services comprising your invention or creation. Assignments of patent rights are discussed in Chapter 19, Section 19.1 of this text.

31.5 STRATEGIC DEVELOPMENT OF INTELLECTUAL PROPERTY

It is important when conducting a successful business that a sound intellectual property development and protection strategy be developed covering the entire business. I recommend that at least the following steps be taken:

- First, the marketing focus of the company's products is identified, including the needs of potential customers and how competitive products or services presently fail to adequately meet those needs.
- Second, the new technology and efforts to develop the technology required to meet the demands of customers is determined. This includes identifying current technologies and products and services having strategic importance over the next three to five years, and identifying emerging technologies of your company, universities, and other companies that are likely to be used by you or by competitors to meet your customer's future needs.
- Third, research and development resources and personnel are allocated to create the new technology.
- Fourth, a strategy is put in place to identify those innovations that should and can be protected with the appropriate intellectual property vehicles (i.e., patents, trade secrets, copyrights, etc.), and how unpatented technology such as know-how can also be protected.
- Fifth, patents and other filings are put in place before any public disclosure of the technology.
- Sixth, continual monitoring of the technology development process takes place to ensure that adequate protection is obtained in a timely manner on all improvements to, and new uses of, the basic technology.

This strategy is better achieved at a high management level and on a company-wide basis. Combining all, or most, of these strategies should lead to achieving a competitive advantage through new technology.

Thus, consideration should be given to generating an entire program of innovation protection from the start, rather than just filing for patents or other intellectual property protection on new technology without considering how that technology fits into your overall business opportunities. The goal is to achieve a higher value for the entire new technology area. For example, when reviewing the claims of a patent application on your invention to ensure that the claims adequately cover your invention, extend your thoughts "outside the box" and think how a competitor might use alternate devices, materials, steps, etc., to achieve the same result as your invention. Also, think how your invention can be used in other, non-competing products or processes that are not within the scope of your company's business sphere. In each of these cases, suggest to your patent professional how the patent claims can be broadened to encompass your thoughts "outside the box."

If broad patent protection is not possible due to close prior art, strategic efforts can be directed to obtaining several limited, but sound, patents that can be just as efficient as having one broad patent. These several patents should be crafted to close all possible avenues open to competitors aiming to encroach upon your technology. This strategy could be combined with securing maximum market position through coordinated advertising and using your established, well-known trademarks for your products.

One possibility for managing your business' intellectual property is to establish a unit with specific responsibility for carrying out this mission. This unit should report directly to management to function properly. If a licensing program is established by this unit, the unit could become its own profit center. Most importantly, the members of this unit should be in direct and frequent contact with product managers to ensure that all potential intellectual property developments are brought to the attention of management.

31.6 DISGORGING PATENTABLE INVENTIONS

Based on my experience, waiting for scientists and engineers to bring their innovations to the intellectual property department is a bad idea. Instead, I recommend that the intellectual property department include an engineering team that swoops down on the R&D and product development people, for the purpose of inquiring (or pestering), identifying, and documenting patentable and otherwise protectable technology. This process should be accomplished early and often, and on a regular basis. The sooner new technology is ferreted out and protection is sought, the better.

Your technology development personnel should be aware of the benefits to them and to the company in submitting invention and new technology disclosures for possible patenting or other protection. These personnel should understand that they are part of the innovation process, and what the intellectual property program is. This will let each innovator know the value of intellectual property to himself/herself and to the company, and will encourage the disclosure of quality inventions and other innovations. To provide this awareness to the engineering and scientific personnel, it is recommended that guidelines be established and disseminated identifying the primary and secondary product lines or services of the business unit, and identifying how the business unit plans to utilize its patent and other technology assets to maximum advantage.

After new technology has been placed in an understandable format or embodiment, such as a prototype or drawings, a disclosure of the invention should be furnished to the intellectual property department. Also, the developer of the technology should be asked to define those additional technology areas (both inside and outside the company's core business) in which the innovation may be used. The developer should also provide information on ways that someone else could "design around" the innovation, since it would be wise to cover such design around in a subsequently filed patent application.

A proven way to insure that innovative technology bubbles to the surface is to create an invention or innovation incentive or reward program. This involves recognizing the submittal of patentable technology through monetary or non-monetary incentives. Here are some ideas that may be adopted:

- The innovator shares in a percentage of the profits or sales of the product or service embodying the new technology.
- The innovator is paid a monetary "reward" upon the filing and/or patenting of an invention. If the reward is paid upon filing only, the inventor may not be motivated to assist during prosecution of the patent, and may be less inclined to remain employed during the patent prosecution cycle. I recommend that the monetary reward be given upon both the filing and issuance of the patent. This program nullifies the two disadvantages mentioned above by providing the inventor with an incentive to help in obtaining issuance of the patent, and to stay with the company. The monetary reward could consist of cash or stock. On the negative side, the potential inventors must be forewarned that not all of their invention disclosures will be accepted for patenting, and they should not be dissuaded from submitting additional new technology disclosures after a previous disclosure has been turned down or consideration has been deferred.
- The innovator may be recognized with a non-monetary gesture, such as a plaque, luncheon or dinner, extra vacation time, or payment of tuition for advanced education courses.

No matter which system above is adopted or if no reward system is adopted, the key thing to remember is that promotions and advancements within the company, as well as compensation, are normally a direct result of the innovations brought to the attention of management by the R&D, engineering, scientific, and other technology personnel.

31.7 DETERMINING WHAT AND WHAT NOT TO PATENT

Since most new engineering and scientific technology developments are protectable through patents, rather than copyrights and trademarks, this section presents the factors for considering what should and should not be patented in a typical technology business environment. Also covered are several suggestions for implementing intellectual property protection strategies into an overall business plan. Your intellectual property can be used in several basic ways:

- Defensively, to protect and enhance your market position in the protected product or service by preventing competitors from copying your new products. This could include developing protectable technology that would build a wall around other patents or technology your company owns, or to build a fence around your competitor's technology.
- The generation of income revenues through the strategic licensing, or possible sale, of intellectual property assets.
- As an effective wedge in entering a new product market or geographic area, and gaining market share from a competitor.

- Assisting you in making trade-offs to acquire needed technology from a competitor.
- Convincing a competitor to establish a strategic business partnership with you to complete a business deal that you could not accomplish on your own.
- The merger with or acquisition of a competitor.

The discussion of what to patent and, in fact, any other intellectual property matters, should include personnel involved in R&D, engineering, product development, marketing and sales, licensing, intellectual property development and enforcement, and of equal importance, finance. This group should be embedded with managements' policies and goals to guide the decision-making process.

31.7.1 Patentability Search Results

The results of the patentability search directed toward your invention, described in detail in Chapter 8, Section 8.1, will allow you to determine whether broad or more limited patent protection is available. If your invention is truly unique, and broad patent protection is available, the patent you obtain on your invention should allow you to market your new product without serious competition during the introductory offering period, until and if a competitor figures out how to design around your patent, or develops an improvement on your patented technology.

However, your patentability search results may disclose that something less than broad claims, or possibly quite limited claims, may be all that are available to cover your invention. With these results, it is possible that a competitor may be able to readily design around your patent claims soon after your new product introduction, thus reducing the ability of the patent protection you obtain to insulate you from effective competition. In such cases, where only limited patent protection appears to be available, it may not be worth the expense to pursue patents. Also, consider whether the required disclosure of your invention to the public is worth obtaining only limited patent claim coverage.

By "limited patent protection," we refer to those situations where the search results show that you may obtain patent protection covering, for example, only a small, new element forming part of the overall invention, or covering only a slight improvement over the prior art that may not be significant in marketing your new product. In the latter case, competitors may be able to keep your market share low by selling their present products at a cheaper price without your improvement. For example, does everyone need a car equipped with a heater and air-conditioner system that responds to the sound of your voice?

Thus, where the search results suggest that only limited patent protection may be available for your invention, further business considerations of a practical rather than emotional nature come into the equation. The cost of obtaining a patent or patents in the various markets where the invention has value must be weighed against the degree and nature of exclusivity a limited patent will provide. If a cost–benefit analysis shows that competitors will probably not be kept at bay by a limited patent, the decision may be to avoid the cost of patenting a particular invention, and to proceed with an aggressive advertising, marketing, and sales campaign to launch and promote your new product.

31.7.2 Business Factors Determining Whether to Obtain Patent Protection

A proper intellectual property evaluation system should:

- Determine those individuals, and where they are in your company or organization, who are responsible for, or are likely to, develop or create innovations related to new products or existing products.
- Establish a procedure where those individuals periodically advise management of all innovations they are working toward and/or have developed.
- Create a protocol for review of each innovation to determine whether intellectual property protection should be sought, based on the criteria set forth in the sections below.

In determining whether patent protection should be sought covering an invention, the criteria listed in the sections below are considered, usually by a team made up of design/technical, new product marketing, management—and all important—financial personnel from your organization. Also, a patent attorney or patent agent may sit in on such discussions to offer guidance, when needed, when patenting procedure issues arise.

31.7.2.1 Importance of the Technology

If the technology embodied in the invention under consideration relates to one or more of the important product lines of your company, or to an important new product, strong consideration should be given to obtaining patent protection covering the invention. If the technology relates only to a small portion of the company's business, and the marketing people indicate that the potential for gaining new market share based on this invention is minor or non-existent, the importance factor may be minimal, leaning toward a decision not to obtain patent protection.

In determining the value of an invention or new technology, consideration should be given to the following:

- To what use will you or your company put the invention or technology?
- Would a patent be effective in preventing a competitor from copying or using the invention or technology? Or would a competitor or another be interested in obtaining a license to practice the invention or technology?
- Is the invention or technology capable of effective protection through trade secret and/or confidentiality processes and, if so, is this preferable to patenting?
- How much time and money will it take to develop the invention or technology into a profitable product? Does the company have the personnel and equipment required to develop and produce products incorporating the invention or technology?
- Would the development of this technology interfere with the intellectual property rights of a competitor, or of a non-competitor, whose rights may be purchased or licensed?
- Could the subject invention be submitted as a new industry standard?

After the invention has been discussed with those having the authority to make decisions on whether patents should be filed or not, an analysis should be made of the importance of the invention to the company's product lines prior to making the decision of whether or not a patent should be obtained. This analysis should be presented to the decision makers so that they have all the facts in front of them when making their determination.

31.7.2.2 Competitive Advantage

Another factor in determining whether or not patent protection should be sought is the competitive advantage to be gained by obtaining patent protection on the subject invention, which will give your company the right to exclude others from making, using, selling, or importing products containing similar technology. For example, determine which technology will provide an advantage over competitors, and what competitors' features make their products marketable.

The marketing experts should compare the product embodying the invention to other products in the market, and make a determination as to whether the invention will provide the product, or product line, with a distinct advantage in gaining consumer acceptance and desire for the product.

Also, if the state of the prior art indicates that only limited patent protection may be available, the marketing department may determine, such as through focus groups, that the competitive advantage to be gained by patent protection is minimal. The ability of competitors to design around the patent and avoid its claims, if the claims are limited, must also be given consideration in determining whether or not to obtain patent protection for a particular invention. Also, keep in mind that if your competitors are increasingly obtaining patents on their innovations, you should have a policy of building your intellectual property portfolio to avoid being left behind in the possession of enforceable innovation protection rights.

31.7.2.3 Enforceability

On the basis of the above factors, you may have determined that patent protection should be sought. The next question to consider is whether or not the patent that you obtain will be readily enforceable. For example, if your patent is directed to a process that is used internally in a manufacturing facility, or in a chemical processing plant, a question arises as to whether or not you will be able to determine whether your competitor is using the particular patented process or not. Your competitor will probably be producing products similar to yours, and then it becomes necessary for you to investigate whether or not the competitor is using the patented process to produce such products, which may or may not be evident from an examination of the final product.

In certain cases where significant sales and profits are involved, companies have actually resorted to industrial espionage to obtain valuable trade secret information from their competitors, including information regarding the processes used to manufacture the competitor's products. Of course, such industrial espionage is illegal if one gets caught. However, it is my experience and understanding that such espionage continues even today.

If it becomes necessary to resort to underhanded tactics to police your patent rights, it may not be worthwhile to file for a patent in the first place. However, if your process patent is such that the final product will indicate whether or not the patented process has been used, then obtaining patent protection may be valuable since the enforceability of the patent will not involve extra expense or underhanded practices. The enforceability of the patent will also be a factor in determining in what countries the patent application should be filed, which subject is discussed in Section 31.10.

31.7.2.4 Commercial Value

An additional factor to be considered in determining whether or not patent protection should be sought is the commercial or cost–benefit value of the invention, and of the product in which the invention is embodied. If the invention itself will be costly to implement in the new product, but at the same time the product is in such a market that you will not be able to increase its price to cover the cost of implementing the new technology, then patent protection may not be worth the expenditure of resources. Also, if the project in which the invention is used is one that has a terminal date, that is, when the product will be taken off the market to be replaced by new products that are also in development, again the patent may not be worth the anticipated cost.

On the other hand, if your new technology can be readily incorporated into the product without much additional cost, and even though you cannot increase the price of the product to your customers, but you determine that sales of the product will be greatly enhanced by implementation of the new invention, the filing of a patent application is quite worthwhile. Also, if the new technology will lengthen the sales life of the product in which the invention is used, again this will be a factor supporting the filing the patent application.

An intangible commercial value of obtaining patents is the creation of a positive image for your company, both inside and outside the organization. A visible patent program shows the employees that innovation is the expected norm, and will be rewarded. In this regard, many large companies provide financial incentives to their employees upon the filing of patent applications and/or issuance of patents. The existence of a patent program also advises outsiders, such as competitors, investors, and the general public, of the technology advances your company has made, and will be expected to make in the future, thus providing intangible value to your enterprise.

31.7.2.5 Licensing Value

The licensing value of the subject invention, and the establishment of a licensing program for your company, are important considerations in determining whether to file a patent application. The new technology may have value to someone who is not a competitor, and who may be willing to obtain a license covering your technology. Eventually, if you or your company develops a significant patent portfolio, you may be able to establish a profitable licensing program involving many of your patents. By way of anecdotal information, several years ago a major technology-driven company earned $500 million from licensing its patents in one year.

If you or your company establishes a licensing program, it is important to keep the patent professionals who are preparing your intellectual property documents aware of your program. For example, if you desire to license your patented technology outside the area of your core business, it is necessary that your patent application include claims, and supporting descriptive material to support a license of products and processes outside of your primary business. For example, if you produce steam irons, and your R&D department has developed the combination of a new iron with a new switch that automatically turns the iron off when the iron is moved to a vertical orientation, make sure your patent application includes claims directed to both the combination of the iron plus switch, and claims directed to just the new switch alone. This will enable you to offer licenses to others to produce the switch alone on non-competing products, and provide you with income from their sales of these non-competing products.

After your company has established a patent portfolio, a program can be established to offer licenses to those non-competing companies that may find value in the technology embodied in your patents. Since those entities are not directly competing with the core business of your company, they can freely use your inventions in a way that will not affect your market position.

Another strategy involves offering licenses under your technology to those who are competitors of your primary business. Factors that may make it feasible to offer such licenses include:

Would your market position be harmed, or even helped, if alternate sources for your new product were available, such as in geographical areas where you do not have a strong marketing position?

Does technology in your industry become obsolete so rapidly that you will have "newer" technology developed by the time a competitor can come on line with your "new" technology?

In comparison to your profit margin, would it be advantageous to have a competitor sell your new technology to the market, and you get a share in the profits of those sales?

Is there an advantageous possibility that you may have to partner with a competitor or an emerging company to bid on a large project that could benefit from your new technology?

After you have developed a patent portfolio, your licensing program should begin by seeking out potential licensees for the technology not only covered by your patents, but also embodied in confidential proprietary information and know-how that has not been subject to patent protection. As such, a licensing program can be administered by marketing personnel, or by a licensing coordinator if your company is of sufficient size. Potential purchasers of licenses under your technology are identified on a case-by-case basis after an investigation and analysis of companies that may be interested in your technology. An aggressive patent licensing program can generate substantial additional revenues for you and/or your company from the technology covered by your patents, and other proprietary technology in the possession of your company.

31.7.2.6 Foreign Markets

It is quite possible that the technology embodied in your latest invention may not have an impact on the U.S. market, but for other reasons may have a significant impact in foreign markets where your company operates. In such cases, in order to obtain patents in the foreign countries, it is required that you first file a patent application in the United States, or your home country, and then file corresponding patents in those foreign countries of interest. Therefore, all of the above factors must also be applied to each foreign country in which your company is marketing its products. This analysis, when the above considerations are applied to a foreign market, may lead to a different conclusion than that arrived at when analyzing your home country market position.

31.7.2.7 Defensive Patenting

By defensive patenting, consider the situation where you or your company, once you develop and market your new products, may be accused of infringing someone else's patent or patents. Let us assume that when such accusations are made, you have a large portfolio of patents that cover the technology you developed over the last 20 or so years. Thus, immediately upon receiving a charge of infringement, usually in the form of a letter from a competitor's attorney, you search your patent portfolio and compare the claims of those patents to the products sold by the competitor who is charging you with infringement. In many instances, it is possible to find certain patents that you own which are, or may be, infringed by your competitor. If this is the case, you write to your competitor indicating that you are counter-charging them with infringement of your patents, and possibly the whole situation can be resolved by both parties retreating back to their own baselines, and continuing to market each party's own products without expensive patent litigation.

This reminds me of the bumper sticker I once saw that said "My lawyer can beat up your lawyer." If you have a meaningful and substantial patent portfolio, you can withstand the charges of infringement lodged by your competitors by throwing your legal department and your patents in the direction of the competitor.

31.7.2.8 Timing of Public Disclosure of the Invention

A further consideration that determines whether or not to obtain patent protection is the timing of the public disclosure of the subject invention and the possibility that competitors will become aware of the invention and may incorporate your technology into their own development projects. One way of warning competitors to keep away from your technology is to use the statement "Patent Pending" on your products, or advertising or packaging, when introducing your product. You cannot legally use the term "Patent Pending" unless you actually have a patent application on file and pending in the U.S. Patent & Trademark Office (USPTO). To do otherwise will give your competitor cause to file a false advertising claim against you. Therefore, if your new technology is such that you believe your competitors will immediately incorporate your technology once they see your new product in the market, filing a patent application and using "Patent Pending" in your advertising and product literature will give such competitors second thoughts when attempting to utilize your technology for their own use.

I have previously gone through such an analysis where a client sent me a competitor's product bearing the statement "Patent Pending." I conducted an analysis to determine whether or not our client could make a similar product even though I could not determine what patents the other party had on their product, since the patents we did uncover did not bear any relation to the competitor's product, and we did not uncover pending patent applications. However, I did determine that the device my client wanted to make could be produced from technology existing in the prior art, and I concluded that the competitor could not obtain a patent on its product broad enough to cover the product that my client was manufacturing due to the volume of related prior art, for example, expired patents.

In addition to those factors discussed in the previous section, consider also the development of several related inventions in a particular technology or product area, that when combined, provide a major potential for a new and profitable business foundation. In this scenario, several patents will be developed, each fitting with the other like the teeth on a group of mating gears. This strategy protects the technology by developing patents that cover alternate devices or processes for accomplishing the same objectives as your technology. Also, as research on this new technology moves forward, this business strategy calls for obtaining additional "improvement" patents to maintain the exclusive market position of the technology for an extended period of time.

This strategy also includes considering how your business should be extended into related areas based on your successful technology patenting program, and protecting extended product lines with patents covering specific new products incorporating your technology. For example, envision the development of heat-resistant ceramics for aircraft and space vehicles, and how that technology was adapted to cookware. This strategy calls for the coordination of imaginative efforts between the technology team, the marketing and business development team, and the intellectual property team.

Therefore, consider the relative market positions of your organization and that of your competitors, and whether or not the initial launch of your product will cause your competitors to incorporate your technology into their development efforts. The designation "Patent Pending" may be a decided marketing advantage.

31.8 DETERMINING WHO WOULD BE AN APPROPRIATE LICENSEE FOR YOUR INVENTION

We previously discussed the possibility of establishing a program to license your patented technology, as well as your unpatented trade secrets, know-how, and other proprietary information, to non-competitors. Consider also that it may be beneficial to license a portion of your technology to your competitors, under carefully devised conditions where the competitors will not gain an advantage over you and your products in the marketplace.

The first way of determining who might be approached with an offer of a license under your technology is to compile a list of all the competitors in the industry related to your products. Your marketing staff could readily come up with such a list. Also, your marketing people can identify non-competitor companies that may be interested in using the technology embodied in your patent applications and your patents. It is my understanding that certain databases exist that can identify entities and companies that are involved in specified technological areas. It would then be incumbent upon you or someone under your direction to review the list of companies, and their products, to determine which of these companies could be approached for consideration of a license arrangement.

The above licensing factors are particularly relevant in the field of software, where your software can be used by different competitors and non-competitors to operate certain programs that analyze different data or produce different results that are not competitive with or do not damage your business.

Another way to determine who would be a potential licensee for your technology is to review the patents developed by the patentability searches directed toward your inventions that were conducted by your patent attorney, and look at the names of the owners of the patents that were uncovered by the searches. As discussed previously, the searches should have uncovered those patents that are most closely related to your technology. By definition, the owners of these patents are involved in the development of the same technology as your company, and therefore would most likely be good prospects for a potential license, if competitive factors do not prohibit such an arrangement. Also, it may be advantageous to review the prior art patents that are cited in the patent applications and patents in your portfolio that relate to the same or similar technology. These patents will reveal the names of owners of similar technology, who may also be considered as potential licensees.

Another recommended procedure to obtain potential licensees is through the trade associations of which you are members.

31.9 DRAFTING STRATEGIC PATENT CLAIMS

After your or your company's strategic goals for intellectual property have been established, guidelines should be created to direct the patent professional in the preparation of patent application claims that dovetail with these goals. The claims of your patents should be able to encompass the products and/or processes of a broad range of infringing conduct by present and future competitors at the manufacturing, distribution and user levels. This is most important in the electronic and computer hardware and software industries. You should discuss the scope of the claims in all patent applications with your patent professional before the patent application is filed, to ensure that the guidelines have been satisfied. By way of example, in a computer-related patent application, different types of claim structures should be included, where applicable. This may include system claims, method claims, computer-readable medium claims, and data structure claims where applicable. These types of patent claims are discussed in more detail in Chapter 13 of this text.

31.10 DETERMINING WHERE TO OBTAIN PATENTS

If your product will be or is being offered in the global market, your technology should be protected in those countries where (1) your products are being sold, (2) the company reasonably expects to be marketing its products, and (3) your competitors can be expected to begin manufacturing competing and potentially infringing products. The process of determining where corresponding foreign patents should be filed should begin six months after your U.S. or home country patent application has been filed, since the foreign patent treaties and conventions require that action be taken within one year of the filing of the U.S. or home country application to protect your ability to file corresponding foreign patent applications in the countries you selected.

Careful consideration must be given to the question of international patent filings, primarily due to the cost factors involved. Filing, prosecution, and maintenance (annuity) costs could, if not thought out, far outweigh the benefits of having a patent position in a particular foreign country.

My recommendation is that the following criteria be used to determine if and where foreign counterpart patent applications should be filed. In specific industries, other more tailored considerations will also be important:

- In which foreign countries will your technology be manufactured and marketed, or reasonably expected to be marketed by you and your company?

- What is the possibility and probability of enforcement of the patent in the respective foreign countries? As you have undoubtedly read in the press, there are certain countries in the world today where intellectual property piracy is rampant, and the enforceability of intellectual property under the laws in those countries seems very difficult if not impossible to obtain. Consider, however, that most countries are currently expressing a desire to be members of the World Trade Organization (WTO), which requires a member country to establish a system for the enforcement of intellectual property rights, including patents. Therefore, if you determine that a country today does not have a strong system for enforcing intellectual property rights, consider what may change in the near future.
- Where can your competitors be expected to manufacture and/or import or export competing and potentially infringing products? Those countries should definitely be included in your list of foreign patent filings.
- What is the cost benefit of the expenses anticipated to be incurred in filing and prosecuting foreign counterpart patent applications versus the commercial value of that technology to the company? If your company generates only small sales in one particular country, and does not foresee those sales increasing, the advantage of obtaining patent protection in that country may not be worth the expense.
- Consider also that there may be secondary or smaller foreign markets in which patent protection should be obtained. These could be countries where you currently may not have a marketing position; however, your foreign sales personnel are now discussing potential marketing or manufacturing arrangements with potential licensees or distributors in those countries.
- Are there countries where you or your company can potentially license your technology to a manufacturer, distributor, competitor, or to an entity in a totally different industry? If such possibilities exist, it may be in you and your company's best interests to obtain patent protection in those countries.

31.11 DETERMINING OTHER INDUSTRIES THAT MAY BENEFIT FROM A LICENSE

This requires a determination of those other industries and related technologies that can find value in the technology you are now considering for patent protection. If, for example, you developed a new heating element for use in the engine block of your company's tractors, can that heating element also be used by the automotive industry, in oil well drilling equipment in cold environments, and other equipment used in colder weather such as air compressors, etc.? Once you have selected other products that can benefit from your technology, your marketing people should be able to furnish you with the names of potential licensees in those particular industries. You should then approach these companies with the prospect of a license.

31.12 ENSURING YOUR PRODUCT OR PROCESS DOES NOT VIOLATE THE PATENT RIGHTS OF OTHERS

It is important that before you introduce your new product or process to the market, a patent infringement, or freedom-to-use search and analysis be conducted to uncover any potential unexpired patents that may be infringed by the marketing of your new product. Recall also that your product can infringe the patent of another even though your product is covered by its own patent. This infringement analysis should be conducted just before your new product is released for introduction to the marketplace. If you discover that your product may have potential infringement problems, it may be wise to either redesign the product, or have your patent attorney determine whether or not the potentially infringed patent can be invalidated.

However, I do want to emphasize that it is quite important that your new patented product does not violate the patent rights of others upon its market introduction. Patent infringement can lead to unnecessary and costly patent litigation, and can ultimately result in your product being removed from the market. One glaring example, mentioned briefly before, is the expense that Kodak went to several years ago to introduce its instant imaging photography to the market, only to have Polaroid attack them in patent litigation, and force Kodak to make the decision to exit the market. Thus, the importance of this type of infringement analysis cannot be overstated.

31.13 POLICING THE MARKET FOR POTENTIAL INFRINGEMENTS OF YOUR PATENTS

Your sales force periodically should be made aware of the protection afforded your products by the issued patents and pending patent applications that comprise your patent portfolio. Then, when your salespeople go into a customer's facility, if they determine that the customer has been approached by one of your competitors to sell a similar product, and usually at a lower price, your salesperson can report back to you the existence of those competing products, and you can then initiate an analysis to determine whether or not those competing products are covered by any of the patents or pending patent applications in your portfolio. Today, in industries that use computer chips to operate their equipment, for example, it may not be easy for the salesperson to determine that a competing product is infringing, and competing product literature and website information may have to be reviewed.

The market should also be surveyed for potential infringing importations. Today, a vast amount of products are manufactured overseas, and then brought into this or another country by importers, where the importers never bothered to determine whether or not a patent may be infringed by the imported product. Therefore, it is up to you to police the importation and introduction of these foreign-made products into the marketplace to determine whether or not any of the patents in your portfolio may be infringed.

31.14 THE ENFORCEMENT OF PROCESS PATENT CLAIMS AGAINST AN IMPORTER OF A FOREIGN-MADE PRODUCT

The U.S. Process Patent Act of 1988 introduced a new element into the enforcement of U.S. process or method patents. Under that act, if a foreign manufacturer uses a process outside the United States, which process is covered and claimed in a U.S. process patent, the importation into the United States of the product made by that patented process constitutes an infringement of the U.S. process patent. This is relatively new in our law, since prior to 1988 if an infringing process were used overseas, that process did not infringe a U.S. patent, and the product manufactured by that process could be freely imported into the United States. However, this 1988 act of the U.S. Congress now provides that such importation is an infringement of the U.S. process patent. This is one reason why it is important to include method claims in your patent applications where feasible. The 1988 act covers the importation of products that may or may not be covered by a U.S. article patent, but where the product is manufactured overseas by a process that violates a U.S. method patent, the importation of that product into the United States may be halted.

31.15 TRIMMING THE INTELLECTUAL PROPERTY TREE

As with anything else, the costs of developing and maintaining an effective intellectual property portfolio must be kept under control. One way to accomplish this is to periodically trim the fat (unnecessary patents and technology) from your program. This will prevent the unnecessary payment of maintenance (U.S.) and annuity (elsewhere) fees on patents covering obsolete technology, for example. Therefore, at regular intervals, the individual technology elements making up your intellectual property portfolio should be reviewed for:

- You or your company's present and future interest in the technology.
- Any current business requirement involving the technology.
- The technical importance of the technology to competitors or others.
- The intended or future use, if any, by you or your company of the technology.

31.16 ESSAY ON INNOVATION MANAGEMENT

I once attended a lecture on Innovation Management, where the speaker said: "Each technology push needs a market pull." I interpret this to mean that the need for new and better products in the marketplace is the pull that provides the push behind innovations in technology. If a need or desire exists, technologists will provide the means to satisfy that need or desire.

The speaker also defined "innovation" as the successful implementation of a new idea. Thus, the acts of technology implementation track the ideas that are born in an effort to solve problems. If you are able to recognize the existence of a problem, you will be led to the solution of that problem through imagination, innovation and creativity.

The beginning of problem solving may be the work of a single thought process, or more likely the result of a "brainstorming" or information gathering session among the members of a research or development team. In the latter situation, you have a broad skill base from which to generate ideas, and no idea is considered a bad idea. In a good brainstorming session, everyone must speak, and everything mentioned is written down for later analysis. In these sessions, the newer members of the team gain the benefit of the knowledge of the more experienced engineers and scientists, each member gets to know the other members and their knowledge, and each participant gains an awareness of the analytical approach to problem solving used by other team members.

The implementation of a new idea begins with the work of the inventor or inventors. Management can construct a framework for this process by advising inventors how to find a patentable invention or otherwise unique feature in their work. The patent attorney can assist management in this educational aspect of the invention process. The patent attorney can also use the problem solving process to define a search profile of each technology project, and then conduct a search to determine if unexpired patents exist that stand in the way of the current direction of your research.

Once an innovative idea has been reduced to feasibility of implementation, the idea must be sold to the decision makers, usually management. Remember, since the idea is unique, it must be sold to those who may be skeptical about changing the current technology. Therefore, the innovative idea must be presented with all the technical benefits of making the change, along with marketing, sales, and financial (e.g., cost, profit, time saving) benefits. Hopefully, your presentation will be made to a listener who will leave the presentation with a full understanding of the innovative technology, and who is now encouraged by the prospect of adopting the new technology as a result of his or her recognition of the economic opportunity in the innovation.

The purpose of this presentation is to convince management that they should buy into the innovative idea. Expect that management will initially respond with questions, and you should be prepared to promptly respond to those questions. Some of those questions may require comparisons of your recommended new approach to other ideas that were brainstormed and discarded. It is helpful if the R&D organization maintains a systemized store of ideas that can easily be retrieved. This allows the innovation team to provide important assistance in the decision-making process.

◆ INVENTORS AND INVENTIONS ◆

Les Paul

SOLID BODY ELECTRIC GUITAR

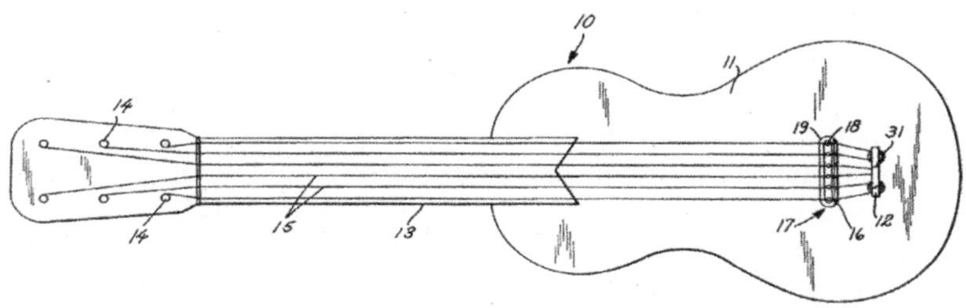

Les Paul, born Lester William Polsfuss, in 1915 in Waukesha, Wisconsin, was an American jazz, country, and blues guitarist and pioneer in the invention of the solid body electric guitar. Those of you who are my age may remember that he recorded with his then wife, Mary Ford, in the 1950s, selling millions of records. He is the only member of both the Rock and Roll Hall of Fame and the National Inventor's Hall of Fame.

At the age of 8, Les Paul began playing the harmonica, and then after trying to learn the piano he switched to the guitar. He played in drive-ins and roadhouses in Waukesha and nearby when he was a teenager, but desired to make himself heard by more people in attendance at the local venues to earn more tips. To accomplish this, he first stuck the mouthpiece from his mother's telephone into a wooden broom handle, and ran it through his mother's radio speaker to amplify his voice. Someone in the back of the room hollered: "Red, your voice and harmonica are fine but your guitar's not loud enough." This led Paul to try many different ways to electrify his guitar. He finally inserted the needle from the arm of his father's radio phono player into the guitar's bridge, and then played through the amplified speaker. Thus, teenager Lester Paul had invented a primitive electric guitar. Eventually, in 1938, Paul moved to New York City.

While in New York, Paul was dissatisfied with the acoustic electric guitars available in the 1930s, and started experimenting at his apartment in Queens, New York. He created designs for a solid body electric guitar, coming up with the first version and then later versions of "the Log," which was a length of common four by four lumber with a bridge, neck, strings, and pick-up taken from a normal guitar. For the sake of

Intellectual Property Law for Engineers, Scientists, and Entrepreneurs, Second Edition. Howard B. Rockman.

Published 2020 by John Wiley & Sons, Inc.

appearances, he attached the body of an Epiphone hollow body guitar sawn lengthwise with the Log in the middle. This structure solved two problems. First, feedback, since there was no acoustic body that could resonate with the amplified sound. Second, sustained sound, since the energy of the strings was not dissipated by generating sound through the guitar body. Over the years, Paul constantly improved and modified this guitar.

Paul's innovative guitar, the Log, built on his own time during weekends at the Epiphone Guitar Factory in 1940, was a 4″ × 4″ chunk of pine with strings, a pick-up, bridge and neck, and was one of the first solid body electric guitars. Although the Log was criticized for its looks, it produced the sound Les Paul was looking for.

Solid body electric guitars had appeared previously, but they were not workable. To produce his first guitar, Paul sawed the body, wings, and neck of the guitar from a full-depth Epiphone archtop and attached them to a pine four by four that formed the center of the guitar. The instrument was equipped with a pair of home-wound pick-ups and a vibrato tailpiece of his own making. The result did not look very good, but Paul used his contraption on several professional recording and performance dates throughout the 1940s and early 1950s.

Leo Fender also independently created a single pick-up solid body model, the Fender "Esquire" in 1948. When Paul had originally approached the Gibson Guitar Company in 1941 with his idea of a solid body guitar, Gibson showed no interest. However, when Fender began marketing its Esquire, which later added a second pick-up, Gibson's interest was aroused and Gibson began talking again with Les Paul.

Gibson was selling Les Paul's guitar until 1961, when reduced sales encouraged Gibson to alter the design without Paul's knowledge, creating a thinner, lighter, more aggressive-looking guitar. Paul outspokenly expressed his dislike for this guitar, because of problems with the strength of the body and the neck. Even after Gibson adopted the principles embodied in the Log, Paul was rarely entirely satisfied with the results and never quite lived with the standard version of Les Paul's guitar that Gibson produced and sold throughout the years. Paul was famously irate that a semi-trapeze tailpiece of his own design was used with too flat a neck angle on the very first gold top Les Paul models of 1952 and early 1953. This design forced a far less playable setup, involving wrapping the strings under the bridge bar rather than over those as intended. Les Paul returned to Gibson as an endorsee in the late 1960s. The company saw this as an important opportunity to bring the original carved top single cutaway design back into production. In 1968, the Les Paul model and the Les Paul deluxe and custom models came to the market.

Also, at that time, Les Paul was going through a divorce with Mary Ford, and in 1961 he ended his endorsement and use of his name on Gibson guitars until 1966. His guitar was named the "Gibson SG," which stands for Solid Guitar. The original Gibson Les Paul design regained its popularity when Eric Clapton began playing the instrument a few years later. Paul resumed his relationship with Gibson in 1966 and endorsed the original Gibson Les Paul guitar from that point onward. Paul himself always used his self-wound pick-ups and customized methods of switching between pick-ups and his guitars. To this day, several models of the Gibson Les Paul guitar are in use throughout the world by both beginner and professional guitarists. Musicians such as Keith Richards and Paul McCartney, in addition to Eric Clapton, all use Les Paul guitars.

Jan. 30, 1962 L. PAUL **3,018,680**

ELECTRICAL MUSICAL INSTRUMENT

Filed Dec. 3, 1959 2 Sheets-Sheet 1

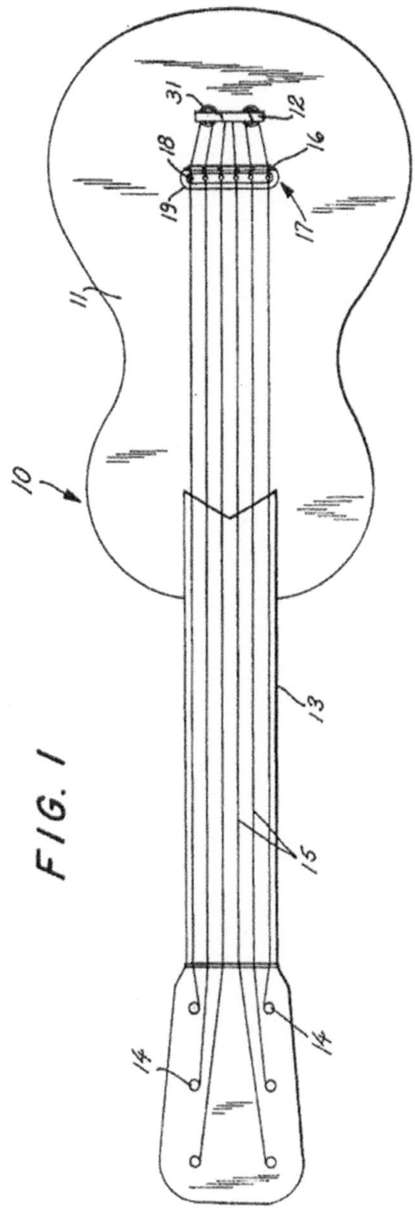

FIG. 1

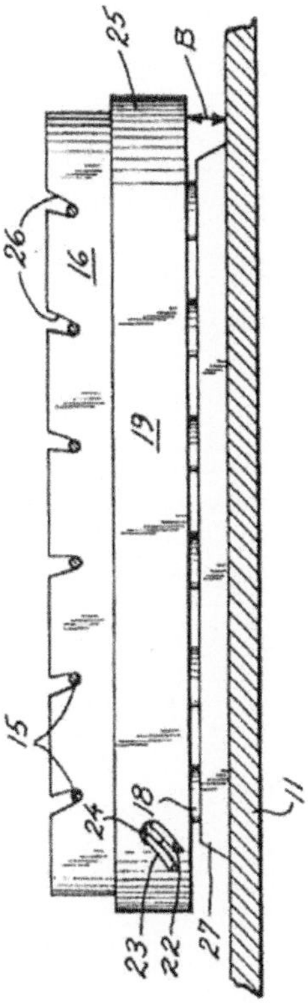

FIG. 3

INVENTOR.
LES PAUL
BY Myron Amer
ATTORNEY

32 "Sue the Bastards"—Business Factors Controlling Intellectual Property Litigation Strategies

32.1 INTRODUCTION TO INTELLECTUAL PROPERTY LITIGATION STRATEGIES AND TACTICS

All of the laws creating exclusive intellectual property rights (IP rights) in an invention, creative work, trade secret, or source-identifying mark allow the owner of such IP right or rights to use one or more of the legal systems in the United States and other countries to take action to stop (enjoin) injurious infringing conduct of another, and to collect damages from the infringer where such damages are proven. Enforcement of an IP right against an infringer is initiated by the owner of the IP right filing a lawsuit against the alleged infringer. This chapter explores the many factors a business entity should consider, and steps to be taken, well prior to making the decision to initiate a lawsuit. Also discussed are the alternatives to litigation, such as entering into a negotiated license or other contractual relationship with the alleged infringer, and mediation and arbitration of IP disputes. Factors and considerations that relate to all aspects of IP rights litigation are presented, with importance placed on the consideration and steps taken before deciding to institute litigation.

Also discussed are the steps an entity can take to mitigate the risk that the entity's new products and new technology will violate the IP rights of another, and how to respond to a cease and desist letter or lawsuit that accuses you of IP rights infringement. Also, we will advise one who has been charged with IP rights infringement of the several defenses that are available to repulse the infringement charge.

32.2 THE DAWN OF AN IP RIGHTS INFRINGEMENT LAWSUIT

32.2.1 Got IP?

Before accusing someone of infringing your IP rights, it is necessary that you first have obtained, still own, and have properly maintained the IP rights you find it necessary to enforce. Previous chapters have discussed the steps necessary to secure your IP rights under the relevant laws, so we will begin this discussion with the presumption that you have obtained, or are in the process of obtaining, valid patents covering your novel and non-obvious useful products and/or processes. We also presume that you have taken the appropriate steps to establish an appropriate trade secret shield around your

Intellectual Property Law for Engineers, Scientists, and Entrepreneurs, Second Edition. Howard B. Rockman.

Published 2020 by John Wiley & Sons, Inc.

businesses' proprietary information and data, have identified those materials developed by and used in your business that are subject to automatic copyright protection upon being embedded in a tangible medium of expression, and have taken the necessary steps to register your valuable trademark and/or service mark rights.

Litigation through the legal system of any country is not for the timid. A brief high-level summary of the enforcement of IP rights, and as a matter of fact, the enforcement of any legal right in a court of law is discussed here. First, the party contemplating taking legal action (the Plaintiff) against someone else (the Defendant) must first establish that the Plaintiff has a "right" created under the law. In an accident case, you have a right to be free of someone else's negligence. With IP rights, the Plaintiff must establish that it possesses the exclusivity embedded in a valid patent, trade secret, copyright, or trademark/service mark right that appears to have been infringed by the Defendant.

Second, it must be shown that the alleged infringer has violated the exclusive right you possess. In an accident case, one driving his car into yours has violated your right to be free from another's negligence. In the IP genre, the violation is caused by the Defendant-infringer's conduct that unlawfully adopts the exclusive rights you have in your IP.

Third, the infringer's conduct has injured your business by violating your exclusive rights, and fourth, that injury has caused you damage, such as a loss of sales and/or market share, the right to keep your trade secrets for your exclusive use, the right to control the copying and distribution of the creative works that are important to your business; or in trademark matters, the Defendant-infringer's activities may cause you to lose control over your own business reputation.

32.2.2 A Potential Infringement of Your IP Rights Bubbles to the Surface

During the course of your normal business activities, one or several events may happen that provide a clue that an infringement of your IP rights may be occurring. You may notice the advertisements of your competitors offering a product or process quite similar to yours, at a significantly lower price. This is evidence that the competitor did not bear substantial research and development costs and merely copied your product or process. In addition, your customers may have told you, or your salespeople, that they can obtain similar products or services from your competitor at a lower price. You may also hear reports from your salespeople that they are having an increasingly hard time closing deals for your products or services due to competition, despite the IP you obtained. You may also notice incremental, or rapid, decreases in your market share beginning when your competitor entered your supposedly protected field.

Other situations, including returns of products to you for refunds that were made by a competitor and not you, and your credit position being changed because an entity is selling a product with a name or logo similar to yours, provide clues that someone else has intentionally or inadvertently invaded your IP space. It is at this point that serious investigation begins to determine your ability to stop the infringing activities, the costs of doing so, and the business considerations that determine whether to seek enforcement of your IP rights or not. Keep in mind that in general, three options exist. First, you take legal action against the IP infringer and pursue the lawsuit to conclusion or to a settlement. Second, you advise the infringer of your intent to take action, and then negotiate an out-of-court settlement with the infringer on terms that mitigate or eliminate the infringer's intrusion into your market. Note that these settlement negotiations may, and in many cases do, take place after an infringement lawsuit is filed. Third, you may decide to do nothing to enforce your IP rights. The factors in play upon which these business decisions are based are discussed below. Keep in mind that there is no one-size-fits-all yardstick when litigation decisions must be made.

32.2.3 Conducting an Audit of Your IP

Quite naturally, once a potential infringer of your IP rights surfaces, one of the first steps is to determine what IP rights you have in your arsenal that may have been infringed. After an initial brief analysis has been made of the infringing product or service, your IP portfolio is reviewed to determine which of your IP rights can be asserted against the infringer. The identified IP is then provided to an IP professional, e.g., a patent, trademark, copyright, trade secret attorney, who then initiates the analysis to determine, at first glance, which of your IP rights should be further investigated to establish that a case of infringement could be successfully supported in a court of law. The elements of this pre-suit analysis are described in the next section.

Once the initial brief analysis has identified those IP rights that appear to have been infringed, the status of each of those IP rights must be determined to ensure that none of the IP rights you intend to enforce have lapsed, which would place your IP in the public domain and deprive you of the ability to exert an exclusive right against a competitor.

For example, if a U.S. apparatus or method patent is to be asserted against the infringer, have all of the maintenance fees been paid? If not, the patent rights have lapsed, and even through you can revive your patent rights after the failure to pay maintenance fees, damages cannot be obtained for infringing activity that took place during the lapse period. Also, were the appropriate large entity versus small entity fees paid during the prosecution of the patent application? For example, a sole inventor or small company may initially file for patent protection, claiming small entity status resulting in lower USPTO fees. However, if the patent application, or issued patent, is licensed or sold to a large entity (presently over 500 employees), all government fees, including maintenance fees, must be paid at the large entity rate, which is double the small entity rate. These fees may be paid late, with certain restrictions, but if the appropriate large entity fees are not paid, you patent will be unenforceable.

If you are contemplating enforcing a registered trademark or service mark, has the required Sections 8 and 15 Declaration or Affidavit been filed with the USPTO during the fifth and sixth years of registration? Has the registration been renewed within the 10-year first or subsequent registration period? Have you stopped using, and thus abandoned, the mark you intend to enforce against products or services similar to those marketed by the potential infringer? These and other questions must be answered, since an invalid trademark or service mark cannot be enforced.

Prior to filing a lawsuit in the United States for copyright infringement, the copyright owner (individual or business entity) must first obtain a valid registration of that copyright from the U.S. Copyright Office. Prior to asserting the copyright registration against an infringer, it must be established that the registration was properly filed and obtained, and can withstand a Defendant's attack asserting the copyright registration is invalid and unenforceable. For example, does the identification of the work to be protected by the registration correspond correctly with the work that was deposited in support of the registration? The file of your copyright registration must be reviewed to establish that there were no irregularities in the facts and/or statements presented to Copyright Office while your application was being considered for registration. In some instances, mistakes in an original copyright registration may be corrected by filing a Supplementary Registration Application.

If you plan to enforce a trade secret right, your audit must ensure that during the course of your normal business activities, procedures were in place, and enforced, to ensure that all of your confidential business information was maintained in secret, and was not available or accessible to outsiders. For example, was all confidential information prominently labeled as "CONFIDENTIAL?" Were all employees compelled to sign a confidential non-disclosure agreement upon the initiation of employment? Was all confidential material locked up at night, and were visitors to the business facility required to sign in when entering and kept away from "Restricted" areas? These, and other factors, are considered by a court of law in determining whether your business had in place sufficient procedures to restrict access to its confidential data, and that employees, vendors, and visitors were made aware of these procedures.

Once you have assured yourself of the validity and enforceability of the IP rights you are considering asserting against a purported infringer, the next step is to have your IP professional compare the alleged infringing product or service with your IP rights.

32.3 LITIGATION CONSIDERATIONS IN IP RIGHTS ENFORCEMENT

32.3.1 The Pre-Filing Investigation

32.3.1.1 Patent Enforcement

32.3.1.1.1 Infringement Analysis

If you are considering asserting your patent rights against a perceived infringer, the most important step is to provide a copy of the patent or patents you believe have been violated, along with the examination history of the patent(s) before the USPTO and information about the potentially infringing product or process, to your patent professional for a pre-filing infringement analysis. The patent professional will then review the subject patent or patents, including the examination history of the patent(s), the prior art applied by the Patent Examiner during examination, and the comments of the attorney/agent responsive to the examiner's position(s), to determine the scope of the claim coverage and possible interpretations of the claims that may, or may not, cover the potentially infringing device or process. Next, your patent professional will make a comparison of the claims of your patent(s) with the allegedly infringing product or process.

It is important to keep in mind that where significant products and processes are concerned, the patent professional representing the supposed infringer has probably read your patent(s), and advised his or /her client of design steps to take toward avoiding the coverage of your patent claims. Alleged infringing products and processes are rarely precise duplicates of the products or processes covered by your patent claims. Thus, your patent claims may have to be "interpreted" to define a scope of claim coverage that encompasses the allegedly infringing device or process.

Under the patent laws practically worldwide, an accused infringing device or process may "literally" fall within the scope of a patent claim or claims, where each element of the patent claim is found in the infringing product or process. This makes proving infringement easy. However, in most situations, one or more of the elements of your patent claim are not found in the alleged infringing product or process, and another element or several have been substituted.

However, if the substituted element performs substantially the same function in substantially the same way to achieve substantially the same result as the element in your patent claim, and there are "insubstantial differences" between the claimed element and the substituted element, patent infringement can be established under the Doctrine of Equivalents.

The prosecution history of the patent claims in question must be analyzed to determine if, in obtaining issuance of the patent, the patent attorney/agent amended the claims to specifically avoid reading on a prior art patent disclosure that showed the substituted element as part of the prior art. Application of the Doctrine of Equivalents is a complicated legal/technical analysis, and it should be left to the patent professional to determine whether a strong case for patent infringement under the Doctrine of Equivalents can be supported. In other words, do not try this at home!

Putting the shoe on the other foot for a moment, if one of your products or processes has been accused of infringing another's patent, the first thing to do is to have your patent professional determine whether any claim (or claims) of the asserted patent covers your accused product or process, either literally or under the Doctrine of Equivalents. If either of these results is a reasonable possibility, have your patent professional analyze how your product or process may be altered, or "designed around," to avoid coverage of the patent claim(s) in question, without increasing the cost of the product or process. The patent professional will also determine whether there is any relevant and material prior art that was not considered by the Patent Examiner during the examination procedure regarding the patent being analyzed. If such "new" prior art is available, it may support a defense that the asserted claim is invalid and never should have issued in the first place. More on this subject appears at the end of this chapter. There are many other defenses to a charge of patent infringement that are available to a potential defendant. Facts supporting many of these defenses may not be known until after a lawsuit has been started, and the discovery of relevant information and documents proceeds.

32.3.1.1.2 Validity and Enforcement Analysis

An important part of due diligence in conducting the pre-filing investigation is to ensure that the owner of the subject patent, and the inventors, have not taken steps that may negatively impact the validity or enforceability of the patent.

32.3.1.1.2.1 The Statutory Bars The U.S. Patent Laws state that once an inventor or the entity asserting ownership of the patent rights *publicly* discloses the claimed invention by selling, offering to sell, using, or publishing information about the invention, a patent application must be filed in the USPTO within one year of such public disclosure. In most industrialized foreign countries, there is no such one-year grace period. In those countries, a patent application must be on file in your home country Patent Office prior to such public disclosure, or patent rights in that country are lost. Under international treaties, filing a patent application in the USPTO or your home

Patent Office before any public disclosure of your invention will preserve your right to obtain foreign patent protection. A public disclosure of an experimental version of your technology is not deemed a public disclosure of the claimed invention.

As part of the pre-filing investigation, the patent professional must determine whether there were any activities of the inventor, or owner of the patent rights, more than a year prior to the patent application filing date, that would be considered by a court or jury as a "public disclosure" of your invention. If public disclosure activities are found to have existed, was the public disclosure of an experimental prototype, or of the complete invention? Since all such pre-filing information will be made known to the alleged infringer's lawyer through the discovery process provided under the Federal Rules of Civil Procedure (FRCP) governing the procedure in lawsuits in the U.S. Federal Courts, it is important for your patent professional to determine before filing suit whether any potentially patent invalidating or disqualifying activities took place more than a year before the patent application filing date.

32.3.1.1.2.2 Disclosure of Known Prior Art During Prosecution of the Patent Application Another area of potential concern is establishing that all prior art known to the inventor or to his or her patent professional, both before and during the entire examination process, that could potentially be material to the examiner's decision to allow or deny issuance of the patent was disclosed to the Patent Examiner. Failure to comply with this rule makes it highly probable that the issued patent will be held unenforceable on the grounds of "inequitable conduct" before the USPTO.

32.3.1.1.2.3 True Inventorship and Correct Ownership The pre-filing investigation should also ensure that the actual inventors are named in the subject patent you intend to assert, and that, for example, a division manager who had nothing to do with conceiving the invention or reducing the invention to practice is not erroneously named as an inventor merely because he or she wanted to enhance his or her standing in the corporate hierarchy. In addition, it should be established that the patent rights have properly been assigned or licensed to the entity contemplating bringing the lawsuit. Your patent professional can readily look into these issues.

32.3.1.1.2.4 Updating the Prior Art Search In most cases, a search of the prior art related to the invention disclosed and claimed in the patent(s) you are now considering enforcing was conducted before the patent application was filed, and during examination by the USPTO additional prior art was most likely applied by the Patent Examiner. It is now prudent to have your patent professional request an updated and possibly more intensive search to determine if additional prior art exists that was overlooked by your original search, or by the Patent Examiner. Such additional prior art could possibly be relied upon by the alleged infringer to attack the validity of your patent. Remember that prior art previously considered by the Patent Examiner cannot be used (in practically all cases) by a defendant in support of a patent invalidity defense. Also, any new additional prior art uncovered must be more material to your claimed invention than the prior art considered by the Patent Examiner during the examination process.

32.3.1.1.3 Injunction and Damages Analysis

The objective of any lawsuit is to obtain an award from the court of all the relief you are seeking. In patent infringement cases, this normally would be (1) an injunction against the infringer preventing further infringement of your patent rights, (2) an award of monetary damages for past infringement, based on your lost profits or a reasonable royalty, (3) enhanced damages (up to three times the actual damages) where the defendant was fully aware of your patent rights, but even with this knowledge willfully continued the infringing conduct, and (4) in rare cases, an award of your attorneys' fees and costs to be paid by the defendant. If you and the infringer are the only producers of the patented product, you have the possibility of being awarded lost profits. If equivalent, non-infringing products are on the market, you may only be awarded a reasonable royalty if you prevail in your lawsuit.

Thus, prior to initiating the lawsuit, the importance of an injunction on your future market share, profits, and position in the industry must be carefully thought out, and if possible, given a monetary value. Also, using available data, try to determine the amount of sales of infringing products that have been made by the prospective defendant, and what your profits would have been had you made those sales, and what amount of damages could be based on a reasonable royalty applied to those sales. These values are then compared to the overall cost of litigation, a subject that will be delved into in detail in a subsequent portion of this chapter.

Under a Supreme Court decision of a few years ago, obtaining an injunction against a patent infringer is no longer automatic upon winning the lawsuit. To obtain the injunction, during the lawsuit your IP litigation counsel will have to establish that you have a better than even chance of prevailing on the merits, you will suffer irreparable harm if the injunction is not ordered, the balance of hardships upon you and the infringer favors you if the defendant must cease future infringing activities, and that granting the injunction would not be against the public interest. During the discussions with your patent professional/litigation attorney (who may be one and the same) prior to initiating the lawsuit, the specific injunction aspects peculiar to your case will be discussed in more detail.

32.3.1.2 Trademark/Service Mark Enforcement

These lawsuits are brought when a second user, usually a competitor, is using a trademark, brand name, logo, distinctive product shape, etc., for a product or service, and the trademark, brand name, logo, etc., is similar enough to yours to be likely to cause a consumer or one in the trade to be confused as to the source of the products or services of you and your competitor. When such likelihood of confusion arises, you, as the first user, promoter, and advertiser of the mark, face a potential loss of sales revenues due to the infringement. But also, and probably most important, the trademark or service mark infringement will cause you to lose control of the reputation and goodwill of your business that you have worked hard to build over a long period of time. In this chapter, when the term "trademark" is used, service marks are also included within the definition. A trademark is a mark used on a product, container of a product, or tag attached to a product to identify the brand or source of the product. A service mark is used to identify the source of services, such as a retail food store, insurance sales, a sports team, or the like.

In the United States, you have exclusive rights to a mark that you have used to identify your business as the source of your products or services, and these exclusive rights are protected under Federal Law (The Lanham Act, 1946), State Trademark Laws, and the common law upon which about half of the U.S. legal system is based. Under each of these legal systems, your continued use of a mark as a source identifier provides you with the ability to stop a second user from offering its products or services to your market bearing a mark or brand that is "confusingly similar" to yours.

32.3.1.2.1 The Three Legal Avenues For Protection Of Trademarks

32.3.1.2.1.1 The Federal Lanham Act Where your U.S. trademark is used on a product that is shipped across state lines, or in conjunction with a service that is offered and delivered across state lines, your mark is eligible for registration with the U.S. Patent and Trademark Office (USPTO) on either the Principal Trademark Register or the Supplemental Trademark Register. The former is for the listing of "distinctive" marks, and the latter is for the listing of marks the USPTO has deemed "descriptive." Once a mark on the Supplemental Register has been used continuously for a period of years, say five years, and the mark has, through this use, acquired a "secondary meaning" as identifying you as the source of the goods or services so marked, the law provides a procedure for applying to list your mark on the Principal Register. Listing on the Principal Register provides additional benefits, such as establishing your *prima facie* right to exclusive use of the mark as an identification of source, and limiting the defenses an infringer can assert against you in an infringement lawsuit.

There are two primary functions of the Principal and Supplemental Trademark Registers, and the Federal Lanham Act. First, the two Registers provide a publicly available listing of marks others have registered and may still be using for the associated products or services, and marks that others have applied to have registered, and marks that others intend to use. Therefore, one seeking to use a new mark in their business can conduct a search of the Principal and Supplemental Registers before adopting the mark to determine if the adoption and use of the subject mark will cause a likelihood of confusion with another mark listed on one of the Registers. Where the second user moves forward and adopts a confusingly similar mark, the Lanham Act provides the first user of the mark, or a similar mark, the ability to file a lawsuit in a Federal District Court to stop such infringing use, and to be awarded damages for the monetary injury the first user suffered. The Federal Lanham Act also includes an unfair competition provision that allows a user of a mark in interstate commerce to file a lawsuit for infringement of that mark even though the mark has not been registered in the USPTO. In such cases, additional evidence has to be presented in court to establish that the first user indeed has trademark rights that have been infringed. Another provision also protects "famous" marks.

32.3.1.2.1.2 The State Trademark Laws Each of the states of the United States has also enacted a trademark registration and enforcement system. These state laws are useful for registering and enforcing marks where the associated goods and services do not pass across state lines, such as a dentist office, local florist, local plumbing service, and the like. These state laws provide the same ability to search for the freedom to use a mark in the state before adoption, and to stop an infringer from using a confusingly similar mark by filing a lawsuit in the relevant state court system.

Additionally, several states have Unfair Competition and Fair Business Practices statutes that provide jurisdiction for bringing a trademark infringement action in the state court system. A usual lawsuit finds the plaintiff/first user of the trademark seeking relief under all of the laws that may apply to the particular situation, such as the Federal Lanham Act, the State Unfair Competition and Fair Business Practices Act, and the common law of the state, which is discussed next.

32.3.1.2.1.3 The Common Law The United States, at its founding, adopted the Common Law system of England, which provides remedies in a court for damage caused by the injurious conduct of others, even in the absence of a specific law or statute regarding such action. The common law resides in the decisions of judges who, over the years, have tried factually similar cases, and rendered decisions that are warranted under the proven circumstances. These decisions make up the body of U.S. Law known as the common law.

In the United States, the common law of each state provides the first user of a trademark the right to stop a second user of a confusingly similar mark from continuing to use the mark with related goods or services, and to collect monetary damages when such damages can be proven. Therefore, if you have been using a mark long enough to establish that a significant portion of the consuming public and/or the trade recognizes the mark as identifying you as the source of your products or services, you may seek relief from infringement of your mark in the state court system, even through you have not registered your mark under either the federal or state trademark laws. However, you will be more secure in your trademark rights if you do take steps to register your marks under the appropriate federal or state law.

32.3.1.2.1.4 Injunctive Relief In instances of trademark infringement, and other acts of unfair competition, it has long been held that such continued infringement could produce irreparable harm to the business and the valuable reputation of the first user of the mark. As a result, most trademark litigation is resolved at the preliminary injunction stage. Without going into all of the details, this involves the first user of the mark discovering the second user of the mark, and asking legal counsel to file a lawsuit to stop the infringement immediately. Once the attorney conducts the pre-filing due diligence, discussed next, and determines there is a provable infringement of your trademark rights, a complaint for trademark infringement is quickly prepared and filed in the appropriate federal or state court. At the same time the complaint is filed, a Motion for a Temporary Restraining Order and Preliminary Injunction is filed with the court, along with a verified statement, or statements, of fact and a legal memorandum (in certain cases) showing the court that you are entitled to, and require, the granting of an immediate injunction halting the infringing use of your trademark, or a confusingly similar trademark, by the infringer. An immediate restraining order may or may not be granted. Restraining orders are sometimes issued where the second user has expressed the intent to use the infringing mark, but has not actually begun using the mark.

An evidentiary hearing will take place on your Motion for Preliminary Injunction in ten days or so, whether an immediate restraining order had previously been issued or not. This evidentiary hearing takes place without too much time for the attorneys to take full discovery, or interview many witnesses. But the lawyers move at warp speed to put together the plaintiff's and defendant's cases at the evidentiary hearing. At the conclusion of the hearing, the judge will decide whether or not the first user has established that he or she most likely will prevail on the merits, that he or she will be irreparably harmed if the infringement is not halted immediately, that the balance of hardships favors the first user, and that the public interest is served by enjoining the infringing actions of the second user. If so, an injunction is granted.

In many trademark infringement lawsuits, the case is ended after the preliminary injunction is either granted or denied. If a preliminary injunction is granted, the second user is compelled to immediately use a different mark if the products or services are to be further offered and marketed. If no preliminary injunction is granted, the parties may find a way to compromise and settle their differences rather than go through the expense of full litigation.

One important fact must be understood by the first user in contemplating bringing a lawsuit for trademark infringement. A positive result by the first user will prevent the competitor from continuing to use the confusingly similar mark. However, forcing the competition to change the mark does not prevent the competitor from marketing and selling the competing products or services under a different mark. That type of relief is only available if the competitor is also infringing your patent, trade secret, or copyright rights of exclusivity in marketing the goods or services.

32.3.1.2.2 Ensuring You Have Enforceable Trademark Rights Prior to Filing a Lawsuit Against an Infringer

Once you determine that a second user, usually a competitor, has initiated use or has stated that he or she will start use of a trademark that is the same as or is confusingly similar to yours, in association with the same or related goods or services, you will probably elect to take legal action to stop such infringing use before real damage is caused to your business goodwill and/or reputation. As in other IP litigation scenarios, a pre-filing investigation must be conducted to (1) ensure that your trademark rights are sufficiently strong to be enforced against an alleged infringer, and (2) that a likelihood of confusion among consumers and/or the trade can be established before a court or jury. Since most trademark lawsuits are resolved at the preliminary injunction stage, a judge makes the decision, and not a jury.

The first step of your due diligence is to determine whether your mark could be attacked as descriptive of the goods and services with which your mark is used, and therefore not enforceable as a valid trademark. If your mark has been used for five years or more, is federally registered, and an Affidavit of Continued Use was filed with the USPTO between the fifth and sixth year of use of your mark, the defense of descriptiveness is not available to be raised by the second user. If you have used your mark for less than five years, and the mark bears some relationship to the definition, quality, or intended consumers of your product or service, your IP professional will advise you of the evidence you will need to support proof of the distinctiveness of your mark. These may be the length of time of use of the mark in the marketplace; the unit and dollar sales of products or services associated with the mark, and advertising dollars spent; placement of your ads; impressions and expenditures related to the mark; and public relations pieces extolling your product and using your mark when discussing your product.

Once you have established the strength and enforceability of your mark, the next step is to assess your ability to prove to a court that the competitor's or second user's mark is sufficiently similar to yours to cause a likelihood of confusion among consumers or the trade, which is the definition of trademark infringement.

32.3.1.2.3 The Likelihood of Confusion

The second due diligence step is to evaluate the facts necessary to establish that you can prevail on the merits in establishing a likelihood of confusion among consumers and/or the relevant trade when your mark and the second user's mark are compared. There are three general ways to establish a likelihood of confusion:

1. Survey evidence.
2. Evidence of incidents of actual confusion.
3. Arguments based on a clear inference arising from a comparison of the conflicting marks and the environment of their use.

32.3.1.2.3.1 Survey Evidence In cases where the expense can be justified, a marketing survey is conducted by a professional organization in a venue such as a shopping mall to determine the degree of likely confusion between your branded product and the second user's product or process. The survey results are then analyzed to determine if they support a likelihood of confusion. If so, your case against the second user can move forward.

Preparing a survey that is admissible in court is complicated, and should be conducted by an organization that has experience and a track record of success in testifying in trademark infringement cases. Your IP professional can help you select a suitable survey organization.

32.3.1.2.3.2 Actual Confusion The best evidence of a likelihood of confusion is evidence of actual confusion caused by the second user's mark. Incidents of actual confusion are defective products of the second user being returned to you with complaints; misdirected phone calls, mail, and e-mail; lowering of your credit standing because the second user failed to pay a vendor, and the like. Therefore, records and notes of such incidents of confusion and the persons being confused should be kept as they occur to support your lawsuit.

32.3.1.2.3.3 Arguments Establishing a Likelihood of Confusion When attempting to establish by argument that a likelihood of confusion exists based on a clear inference arising from a comparison of the conflicting marks, certain tests are applied: (1) the degree of similarity of the marks in (a) appearance, (b) pronunciation, (c) verbal translation of images conveyed by the mark, and (d) suggestion; (2) the intent of the junior user when adopting the mark; (3) the relationship between the goods or services themselves, their channels of distribution and/or marketing of the goods in question; (4) the degree of care to be exercised by a purchaser of the goods; i.e., is the purchase by impulse, or is it a studied purchase; (5) evidence of actual confusion, which is usually considered the strongest evidence of a likelihood of confusion; (6) normal areas of product expansion by either of the trademark users; and (7) the existence of other somewhat similar marks in the marketplace for similar or related goods that coexist side by side without causing confusion.

When considering the phonetic similarity between two marks, each one of the marks in their entirety is pronounced in their normal vernacular. Consider these examples: (1) Arrow v. Air-O; (2) ESSO v. S.O.

The similarity of appearance between two potentially conflicting marks is determined by merely making an "eyeball" test. This test usually pertains to logos or design trademarks. It is also applied to foreign word marks having no meaning to Americans. Thus, if two trademarks look somewhat similar, this is one factor against the second user.

In determining the similarity of meaning between two allegedly conflicting trademarks, determine the mental impact on the consumer regarding the meaning between the two terms. If the two marks convey the same or a similar idea, stimulate the same or similar mental reaction in the consumer, or have the same or similar meaning, these factors support a likelihood of confusion between the marks.

The meanings of words are determined from standard dictionaries, For example, the terms "Cyclone" and "Tornado" were held to have the same meaning for use in association with wire fences, while the term "EZ" was held not similar to "CZ" since, at that time, one term had a meaning and the other did not. Thus, the term EZ conjures a mental image of easy, while the letters CZ give no mental image. Note that this case was decided before the term CZ was used descriptively to define a form of imitation diamonds. Also, the terms "Playboy" and "Playmen" were considered to have similar meaning.

Another strong factor in establishing a likelihood of confusion when comparing two marks is the intent of the second user. There are many instances where it appears evident that the second user has made an attempt to "ride the coattails" of the first user's advertising campaign, such as where not only are the brand names similar, the second user may have adopted similar color combinations and statements in its advertising in an obvious attempt to confuse consumers. Such intent can usually be proven by deposition testimony of the second user once the lawsuit has commenced.

Also, if the goods or services of the first and second user of the marks are the same or similar, or enter the same channels of distribution and marketing, such evidence goes toward establishing a likelihood of confusion between the marks. Of course, the opposite is also true. For example, the mark UNITED in the United States identifies an airline company, a van line company, a soccer team, and probably many other sources of goods or services. However, since each product or service is in a different market area, there is no likelihood of consumer confusion.

If a purchaser spends substantial time and gives a lot of thought to making a purchasing decision, this would mitigate against a likelihood of confusion if the two marks are not identical. Think of the studied purchase of a car or large home appliance. You will be sure you know the source of the product or service before putting your money on the line. On the other hand, if the goods or services are subject to an "impulse" purchase decision, such as detergent, small toys, beverages, etc., the likelihood of confusion between two conflicting marks is greater.

If your salespeople or customers have provided you with instances of actual confusion as to the source of goods between you and your competitor, and if you have had consumers return your competitor's goods to you seeking a refund, these actual instances of confusion provide strong evidence that you will prevail in a court of law in establishing a likelihood of confusion. These are only a few examples of such evidence. However, the author recommends that as soon as you uncover the first of any instance of actual confusion, contact your IP attorney immediately to determine whether a preliminary injunction should be sought to stop such trademark infringement at its inception.

If a second user has adopted a mark similar to yours for goods or services that may not presently be in the same marketing channels, consider whether the goods or services of the second user are in a normal area of product expansion for your business. If so, the second user's mark, if not challenged, may ultimately prevent you from using your brand to expand your product line.

Also, if the marketplace consists of several other somewhat similar marks for similar or related goods or services, this mitigates against being able to establish trademark or service mark infringement. For example, how many sinus disorder treatment products are out there where the first part of the brand includes the term "SINE."

The following are several points to be considered in comparing marks, and in analyzing the differences and similarities between two marks under consideration:

1. The trademarks must be compared in their entireties, and not dissected into their component parts and analyzed piece by piece. The test of proving likelihood of confusion is the impression of the mark as a whole on the purchaser.
2. Similarities and differences between the marks must be weighed against each other.
3. A house mark prefixed to a second portion of a mark may sometimes be used in an effort to eliminate the likelihood of confusion between marks. However, adding on the second user's name or trademark will not necessarily avoid a likelihood of confusion when the first user has been using one portion of the mark.
4. Composite trademarks may have a dominant portion. If the dominant portions of the two marks being analyzed are the same, the likelihood of confusion is heightened. An example is found in a comparison of the marks "Listerine" versus "Listogen." The term "List," of course, was considered important due to the suggestive relationship with Lord Lister and his medical work.
5. A portion of a trademark may also be weak if it is a descriptive term, or is a term in common use by other sellers in the marketplace.
6. If a portion of one of the trademarks under consideration is a generic term, this lessens the likelihood of confusion. For example, how many trademarks include the word "cola"?

In conducting an analysis of whether a likelihood of confusion exists between two trademarks, it is quite possible, and often the case, that two trademark attorneys will arrive at different and opposite conclusions. This is what leads to costly litigation. Remember, if your analysis takes place at the point in time when your competitor has only just begun using the mark, it is possible that your threats and persuasive abilities directed to your competitor can be used to dissuade the competitor from using that particular mark if to do so will lead to unnecessary and costly litigation.

32.3.1.3 Copyright Litigation

The pre-filing investigation that precedes the filing of a copyright infringement lawsuit takes into consideration two top-level factors:

a. Is the second work similar to yours?
b. Did the supposed infringer have access to your copyrighted work?

Unlike patents, infringement of a copyright involves establishing actual copying of your protected work. Independent creation of a similar work by the proposed defendant does not amount to copyright infringement. Also, keep in mind that no copier ever admits they copied your work.

So, the legal system says that if you can establish circumstantial evidence that the alleged infringing work is similar to yours, and that the alleged infringer had access to your work (since your work had been previously published, for instance), you have established a *prima facie* case of copyright infringement, and the burden of proving that no copying took place falls on the alleged infringer.

Before filing a copyright infringement lawsuit, several housekeeping steps must be taken to establish that you have a valid and enforceable copyright in the first place. In the United States, unlike most other countries, you must obtain a valid copyright registration from the U.S. Copyright Office before you have "standing" to file your lawsuit. After filing suit, the supposed infringer may defend by attacking the validity of your copyright registration. You can file for and obtain the copyright registration, if you have not previously, subsequent to uncovering the possible acts of copyright infringement.

The filing of an application for copyright registration in the United States includes submitting an original, or *bona fide* copy, of the work for which you are seeking exclusive rights, along with the application itself that names the author(s), which is your company if the work was authored by an employee, or was a "work for hire" pursuant to a written contract between you and the author(s), and the date the subject work was first published. This information provides positive identification of the work subject to registration, as distinguished, for example, from a later version of the same work. If you advise the Copyright Office that you need to expedite the registration due to an act of infringement, and of course pay an additional fee, your registration will issue in a very short time if the application and deposit are in proper order. You should be sure that the application names the appropriate author, date of first publication, the identification of any preexisting material, etc., to ensure that upon filing suit, the validity of your registration cannot be successfully attacked by the alleged infringer.

Also, before filing suit, have your IP attorney conduct an analysis to confirm that your work and the second work are similar enough to support a case of copying, and that the work was accessible to the alleged infringer. With this circumstantial evidence in hand, plus your knowledge that you have a valid copyright registration, you are ready to commence your lawsuit, after you have considered the costs versus the benefits, and the other considerations generic to all IP litigation that are discussed in this chapter.

32.3.1.4 *Trade Secret Enforcement*

32.3.1.4.1 Establishing the Existence of a Trade Secret Right

A lawsuit alleging theft, or misappropriation, of your trade secrets is normally filed and litigated in the state courts, since up to 2016 there was no federal trade secrets law, but the theft is considered a tort in every state, for which relief, particularly injunctive relief, may be obtained. Also, as stated previously in this text, many states have enacted the Uniform Trade Secrets Act, which provides a statutory basis for filing a lawsuit to stop one from further use of unlawfully obtained trade secrets.

The pre-filing investigation that precedes filing of a theft of trade secrets lawsuit focuses first on your ability to establish that necessary procedures were and are in place to prove that the stolen information or device was subject to a confidentiality system specifically designed and implemented to ensure that no theft of the confidential and proprietary information or device could take place. Some of the policies and steps you should have in place to establish trade secret rights are:

1. Have each employee, from top to bottom, sign a confidential non-disclosure agreement upon commencing employment, agreeing not to disclose the employer's proprietary information to anyone outside the company. Also, provide each

employee with a written copy of your company's confidentiality policy and rules, and have each employee sign a document confirming they have read and understood the policy and rules.

2. Clearly mark all proprietary information as "CONFIDENTIAL" on all pages of such documents, and in a prominent location on all proprietary physical devices. If oral confidential information is discussed, the comment should be made that the information discussed was confidential, followed by a memo confirming with whom and when confidential information was discussed.
3. When disclosing confidential information outside your business organization, have a policy in place, and enforced, that no proprietary information is disclosed until a proper non-disclosure or non-use agreement (NDA) is signed by the recipient of the information prior to disclosure.
4. Ensure that you have an oversight policy and procedures requiring prior submittal, review, and approval of all material to be discussed in publications, seminars, speaking engagements, and trade shows by employees. This will prevent the inadvertent disclosure of your trade secrets.
5. Install plant security measures, such as fencing the perimeter of your facility where trade secret information is kept, having a limited number of entrances and exits, having all visitors sign in and out of the facility, using "Authorized Personnel Only" signs on entrances to internal areas as appropriate, using alarms and self-locking doors in sensitive areas, hiring after-hours security personnel, having trash deposited in a secure location each day and having the trash hauled to a secure location, and other measures that may be appropriate for your specific business needs.
6. Disseminate confidential information to employees on a "need to know" basis only.
7. Secretly encode documents, ingredients, data, prototype devices, etc.
8. Keep proprietary documents and items locked when not used.
9. Have vendors sign confidentiality agreements.
10. Restrict employee movement into restricted areas they need not be in to perform their normal duties.
11. Have a policy forbidding the unnecessary duplication or electronic display of sensitive information. Require access codes to operate copying and scanning machines.
12. Have a document destruction and shredding policy.
13. Conduct exit interviews to obtain the return of company property, and to reinforce in the mind of the departing employee of their continuing obligation not to disclose or use your proprietary information in their subsequent employment.

There may be additional policies and procedures in place to protect your trade secrets, and you need not implement all of the above suggested steps. In trade secret litigation, where the plaintiff has the burden of establishing that the purloined information and/or materials were indeed maintained in secret, proving "absolute" secrecy is not required. However, you must establish that the security measures you did take were reasonable under the circumstances to maintain the secrecy or confidentiality of your proprietary information. Extreme or unduly expensive secrecy procedures need not be taken. For example, I was able to establish in a lawsuit that my client took reasonable steps to classify his formulations as "secret," where each employee had knowledge of the confidential nature of the formulae, but the employees had not been requested to sign confidentiality agreements with the company.

32.3.1.4.2 Proving Acts of Misappropriation

Once it has been established that you have sufficient policies and procedures in place to consider your confidential data as "trade secrets," your pre-filing investigation should determine what evidence you have that tends to establish that the potential defendant had access to the stolen materials, and used or disclosed your secret data to your detriment, causing injury and damages. You cannot expect the potential defendant(s) to admit that your proprietary information was taken, so the strength of circumstantial evidence is examined:

a. Did the suspected defendant have access to your confidential data? Was he or she a former or present employee, vendor, or the like?
b. Did your sales to existing customers drop after the supposed thief began competing with you? Did you begin to lose long-standing customers?
c. Do your competitor's products bear names or model numbers that are the same as or similar to yours?
d. Is it apparent that the products offered by the suspected thief embody your trade secrets, and that it is highly unlikely that the competing products could have been as similar to yours through just "reverse engineering."

Of course, other pieces of circumstantial evidence may also exist to support the filing of a complaint alleging misappropriation of trade secrets. Before signing off on filing a complaint and starting down the litigation highway, we strongly suggest that you have your IP attorney or legal adviser advise you regarding the strengths and possible weakness of relying upon your circumstantial evidence to win in court.

32.3.2 The Benefits Of Litigation v. The Costs

One of the absolutisms in our legal system, which system is particularly low on guarantees and absolutes, is that IP litigation is expensive. No IP professional will deny this. Before authorizing filing of an IP lawsuit, you must convince yourself that the benefits of achieving your goals in litigation outweigh the anticipated litigation costs and other disruptions to your normal business operations. This portion of the chapter provides you with guidelines to (1) determine the benefits of prospective IP litigation, (2) come up with an estimated cost of the litigation, and (3) determine the potential monetary damages you may be awarded upon the successful conclusion of the litigation.

32.3.2.1 Value of Potential Benefits of Litigation

Filing a lawsuit to enforce your IP rights should take place only after you have firmly identified the objectives you intend to reach at the end of the day, and confirm that those potential benefits outweigh the costs and risks inherent in IP litigation. Also, to the extent practical, a value should be applied to each potential benefit of litigation for your business. A consideration of the benefits of litigation, and how to place a monetary value on these benefits, follows.

32.3.2.1.1 An Injunction and the Potential Value

One of the usual awards granted to a successful IP owner in an IP lawsuit is the granting of an injunction against further infringing activities. Injunctive relief is not automatically granted to the IP owner. In such cases, the owner of the IP must establish before the court that injunctive relief should be awarded. Your IP counsel will explain what needs to be proven to obtain an injunction, such as the strength of your case, a balance of hardships, and what is in the best public interest. If you have proven that the defendant has infringed your IP rights, if no injunction is awarded, you may have to settle with a royalty-bearing license that allows the defendant to continue as before, but being required to pay you for that privilege.

For the purposes of this discussion, one of your objectives is to stop further acts of infringement by the potential competitor, who may be a direct competitor. Since you will ultimately have to weigh the benefits of filing a successful lawsuit against the costs and risks, it is prudent to conduct an analysis of the potential value of an injunction, i.e. (1) how much in lost sales and lost profits will you incur if the infringement is allowed to continue? (2) will you be able to regain customers lost to the infringer, who is most likely undercutting your price points? (3) will you be able to regain your market share in the product or service covered by your IP, and recover your company's stock value? and (4) how will your ability to offer new improved products in the future as your customer's needs change be affected if the infringer also develops improved, follow-up products based on your protected technology or innovations? Other factors specific to your industry and market should also be considered. Your finance, sales, and marketing people can crunch the numbers and provide you with approximate monetary values of allowing the infringement to go unchallenged. These values are then weighed against the projected costs of litigation and other litigation risks, discussed below.

One other factor must be mentioned here. If you have noticed that activities infringing your IP rights are taking place, you cannot elect to do nothing now, wait until later when you realize that the infringer is having a major impact on your sales and market share, and then file a lawsuit. The law has an established general doctrine called "laches" that prevents one who sees their IP rights or other rights infringed from sitting on those rights, allowing the infringer to establish a foothold in the market, and then pouncing on the infringer with a lawsuit. The amount of time you can wait after notice of infringement before taking legal action is a variable time period that is decided case by case.

For example, the U.S. Patent Law allows a successful patent holder to collect damages for infringing conduct occurring going back only six years prior to the date the lawsuit is filed. Thus, for many years, courts allowed patent holders to wait six years after becoming aware of the infringing conduct before filing a patent infringement lawsuit. However, more recent court decisions have taken into account the rapidity with which things change and become obsolete in the 21st century, and have held that a patent owner is barred from bringing a patent infringement lawsuit for a lesser period of time following receipt of notice of infringement, such as two to three years in certain cases. The reasoning behind the "laches" doctrine is that if an infringer observes that the IP owner has not taken legal action in a reasonable period of time after becoming aware of the infringement, the IP owner has given tacit permission to the infringer to continue investing in the infringing activity.

Therefore, keep in mind during the evaluation of whether or not to file a lawsuit against an infringer of your IP rights, that if you decide to wait until the infringer has had a marked impact on your market share, your waiting may bar you from asserting your IP rights at the later date.

After you have analyzed the monetized and/or business value of obtaining an injunction against an alleged infringer of your IP rights, the next possible benefit to pursue is the potential for recovering the monetary value of the infringement by way of damages against the infringer.

32.3.2.1.2 Potential Infringement Damages

The injunctive relief discussed in the section above may, in some instances, be obtained in the early stages of the litigation, upon successfully filing a Motion for Preliminary Injunction, whose purpose is to halt the infringing activity during the pendency of the lawsuit. Where such motions are granted, you have successfully prevented the infringer from causing you losses in sales, profits, customers, and market share. At the same time, you have prevented the infringer from building up sales and revenues upon which recovery of a substantial damage award could be based. Thus, one of the pre-filing considerations to be discussed with your IP litigation attorney is whether the chances of obtaining a preliminary injunction are favorable. If so, and you select that route, the damages award once infringement has been proven may be severely limited. But that is the trade-off for taking action to immediately prevent erosion of your market position and your business.

If infringing activities have taken place for a significant amount of time before you had notice of the infringement, a successful infringement lawsuit could lead to a substantial award of money damages. The award of money damages would act as deterrent against the defendant, and others, from future infringement of your IP rights, and would naturally offset the costs of the litigation.

When awarded in an IP infringement lawsuit, damages are usually based on one of two standards. The first is damages awarded as a reasonable royalty the plaintiff would have received were the defendant granted a license rather than sued. The royalty rate is selected by the court among varying rates offered by the plaintiff and defendant during the trial. These rates may be based on what is usual and normal in the industry, what the plaintiff and/or defendant receive in royalties based on other IP licenses in which they are a party, whether the plaintiff and defendant had unsuccessfully negotiated a royalty-bearing license before or during the lawsuit, and a myriad of other factors. In deciding, prior to initiating a lawsuit against an infringer, how much you stand to possibly receive as an award of damages, you should calculate the high and low end ranges of potential recovery on the basis of varying royalty rates, and a good faith estimate of sales of infringing products by the prospective defendant. The latter estimates can be gleaned from public statements, investment offerings, and government filings by the prospective defendant in describing the state of its business.

In cases where the court finds it warranted, the measure of damages may be the IP holder's loss of profits during the period of infringement. In some instances, damages comprising a reasonable royalty and lost profits may be awarded as damages. Your IP litigation counsel will advise you on this possibility on the basis of the statute or case law upon which your IP infringement action is based.

In patent infringement actions, an award of lost profits, which is normally greater than an award based on a reasonable royalty, is granted where the IP holder can establish that it was the only available source of the protected product in the subject market until the infringer came along, and that no other feasible competing product is available. In other words, but for the infringement, the IP holder would have made the sales, and profits, achieved by the infringer. This argument involves defining whether there are suitable non-infringing products on the market, where the IP holder would not have necessarily made the infringer's sales. For example, if the IP covered an improvement to an electric razor, would straight-bladed razors be a competitive product? In trademark and copyright litigation, recovery of the defendant's profits resulting from the acts of infringement is allowed by the federal statutes.

We suggest that in your analysis prior to deciding to commence patent litigation, have your marketing gurus determine whether a reasonable argument can be made that in a definable market segment, only your product and the infringing product or process exist. If your IP attorney agrees that this argument is reasonably supported, and believable, you should aim to factor the potential for recouping lost profits as an objective of the litigation.

32.3.2.1.3 Your Reputation for Aggressive Enforcement of Your IP Rights

For obvious reasons, if you have established a reputation in your industry and among your competition for aggressively enforcing your IP rights, others will think twice before entering your markets with products or processes that infringe, or may infringe, your IP rights. Most prudent businesses shy away from litigation immediately after introducing a new product to the market. If the potential competitor's IP counsel advises that the new product "could" infringe another's intellectual property, the competitor may choose to redesign the product or process to further move away from your intellectual property rights, if the competitor realizes you have a proven track record of vigorously enforcing all of your IP rights.

By way of example, before adopting and using a new trademark for your products, it is normal and prudent to have a search conducted among the various databases to be certain that your use of the new mark will not cause a likelihood of confusion with (i.e., infringe) an existing mark used on the same, similar, or related goods of another. The search produces a number of marks used and/or registered by others, along with information as to actions brought by the existing mark's owner against previous potential infringers. On many occasions, I have counseled clients against adopting a selected mark that "could be" considered close to another mark, after noting from the search that the owner of the prior used mark aggressively took legal action in the past against those who attempted to adopt similar marks.

Thus, in deciding whether to enforce your IP against an alleged infringer, one of the factors to be considered is the market advantage you gain from building a reputation for IP enforcement. On the basis of my long experience in the IP industry, the "fear factor" does have value.

32.3.2.1.4 The Possibility of a Licensing Outcome from Litigation

While giving consideration to initiating litigation against a potential infringer of your IP rights, be aware that a large majority of lawsuits are settled between the parties before a full trial. And in IP lawsuits, the resulting settlement could result in a license being granted to the alleged infringer. So, in viewing all of the positives and negatives of going forward with an IP lawsuit, think about your market share, pricing, etc., if the infringer is ultimately granted a license under you IP rights. One of the major points is that if such a license is granted, the royalty rate must be sufficiently high to prevent the licensee from undercutting your price points. Additional reasonable restrictions on the licensee's activities can also be included in an eventual license agreement to protect your market position and revenue level. However, prior to deciding to move forward with litigation, thought should be given to "what if" your prospective competitor becomes a licensee under your IP rights.

Also, prior to filing a lawsuit against the alleged infringer, and after considering that you might be able to live with the infringer in the market with a suitable royalty rate and other restrictions in a license agreement, it may be prudent to contact the alleged infringer and see if they are interested in a license arrangement that would forestall litigation. Keep in mind that by so notifying the potential infringer of your IP rights, the infringer may, if they so desire, file a declaratory judgment action against you in their home court, seeking a court declaration that your IP rights are invalid and/or not infringed. A tactic often used to prevent having to litigate in the infringer's home court is to file an IP infringement lawsuit against the infringer in your home court, but do not serve the complaint on the infringer. You have 90 days to serve your opponent with the lawsuit, during which time you try to negotiate a license with the defendant. Your IP litigation counsel will advise you of your options when considering litigation or discussing a license with the potential infringer. The license option is primarily a business decision, involving your marketing, finance, and management personnel.

32.3.2.2 Litigation Costs

IP litigation, particularly patent litigation, is expensive. There are several reasons for this. The time span of relevant fact gathering to establish your case and rebut the other party's positions normally covers a period of several years beginning with the date research and development began that led to the issuance of the asserted patent, and moving forward from that date. Many events relevant to the validity of your patent, and relevant to proving infringement, occurred during this multi-year span, and it takes an attorney time to investigate, develop, and analyze the relevance of these facts to the lawsuit. Compare this to an accident lawsuit, where most of the relevant facts happened over a span of a few moments.

Since IP cases are among the "complicated" genre of litigation matters, it may be necessary to retain one or several expert witnesses to explain technical, marketing, or artistic concepts and analyses to the judge or jury. In trademark infringement cases, your IP counsel may recommend that a survey be conducted to establish a likelihood of confusion as to source between the two brands or marks at the heart of the litigation. The cost of conducting the survey, and the cost of the expert to testify about the results, can be expected to be significant.

The cost of litigation is also directly affected by the degree of vigor with which the other side fights back. In certain lawsuits, even the smallest of your maneuvers may be met with an aggressive challenge, just because the opposing lawyer wants to show his or her client that the lawyer is a real leg-biter. The actions of the judge, for example, in requiring the submittal of briefs on every contested issue in the lawsuit, also have a direct effect on the cost of the lawsuit. The list goes on.

The best suggestion I can make here is to recommend that, as part of your pre-litigation considerations, you have your IP litigation counsel prepare a proposed estimated anticipated budget of expected litigation tasks and expenses. Certain litigation tasks are normal in legal proceedings, and a range of cost estimates for these tasks can be anticipated within a fairly predictable range. These tasks, among others, include the pre-filing investigation and initial fact gathering process, preparation of the complaint, possibly answering a counterclaim, complying with the court requirements for the initial exchange of information and documents with the opposing party, preparation of and responding to interrogatories and document requests (known as "discovery"), preparation for and taking the depositions of the other side's fact and expert witnesses and defending the deposition of your fact and expert witnesses, reviewing and preparing all of the deposition and document information obtained through discovery and formulating the fact story you want to present to the court, preparing compliance with a Pre-Trial Order, the preparation for the trial of the case, and the trial itself. Your calculations may also include the possible expense of an appeal. In patent cases, add the cost of preparing for, briefing, and arguing your position regarding the construction of your patent's asserted claims (the "Markman Hearing"). The cost of possible Motions to Dismiss and Motions for Summary Judgment should also be taken into consideration.

There are many other tasks conducted by your IP litigation counsel that are required to advance the lawsuit to a successful conclusion, not the least of which is keeping you and your officers informed of important litigation matters each step of the way. To account for the entire estimated costs of an IP lawsuit, it is common to estimate the costs of the "known" tasks mentioned in the above paragraph, and double those costs to arrive at a final working estimate. This working estimate is then used to balance against the potential litigation benefits mentioned above.

32.3.2.3 The Disruption to Employees and Normal Business Activities

This section is not suggested as a deterrent where litigation is otherwise justified. The following discussion is offered more as a statement of expectations as to officer and employee involvement before and during an IP lawsuit above and beyond their normal work responsibilities.

A lawsuit involves the discovery and presentation of facts to the court to establish those facts upon which a proper legal decision is based. All of the relevant facts and documents, electronic, paper, oral, etc., must therefore be marshaled, investigated, and analyzed, and your employees are the ones in possession of such knowledge and documents. Thus, the impact on your employee's time and productivity—and the associated expense—of the lawsuit should be part of your considerations.

32.3.2.3.1 The Pre-Filing Investigation

This is the time period when your IP litigation counsel team will first advise you not to delete or destroy any documents, e-mails, or materials that may have some relevance to the lawsuit you are contemplating filing. This includes items that may work against you, such as failures upon testing a patented product during the development stage, lack of security issues with your trade secrets, and similar bumps on the road. This information will be made available to the opposing lawyers as they seek to establish facts to support their defenses pursuant to the open and liberal discovery process in U.S. litigation under the FRCP.

The same material is used by your IP litigation counsel to prepare a rebuttal or minimization of any negative data lurking in your files. This happens in practically every IP lawsuit, so let your lawyer deal with these matters. Just do not destroy any material information. That would be more harmful to your lawsuit than allowing negative evidence to be introduced.

During the pre-filing investigation period, you, your employees, and your data storage systems will be questioned by members of your IP litigation team in their effort to reconstruct all relevant information about your IP, its conception, research, development, testing, quality control, licensing, marketing, advertising, sales, and profits of related products. Your employees will be asked to search files, electronic and otherwise, dating back to the generation of your IP, and even before that in technology cases to determine what problem the inventor/innovator was attempting to solve when the IP was created, your knowledge of how others tried to solve the same problem, and in patent cases, what prior art existed before and during the development of your patented invention. This normally requires employee time in searching through old data systems, files, and storage areas. And if something deemed important by your IP counsel is not found during the first search, your employees may be asked to dig deeper. For example, if an e-mail refers to an attached document or an earlier e-mail, you will probably be asked to search again for the earlier e-mail or missing attachment.

These efforts are necessary to allow your IP litigation team to locate all of the relevant evidence they need to build a strong case against the potential infringer, and you and your employees are expected to offer their full support to the litigation team. It is suggested that a brief calculation be made of the expected personnel time the search for information may require, and determine if it would be cost-effective to hire temporary help to assist the IP litigation team with the more time-consuming and routine tasks, such as database searching.

32.3.2.3.2 Marshaling Information to Furnish to Your Opponent Under the Discovery Rules

The U.S. legal systems, both federal and state, provide that once a lawsuit is filed, each party has the right to request the production of relevant non-privileged documents, e-mails, materials and other information from the other party within reasonable limits. To this extent, upon filing a lawsuit, you tacitly agree to open a portion of your business's doors to the court and to the opposing party. Do not worry; your IP litigation team is fully aware of the limits placed on so-called "fishing expeditions" for information sought by the opposing party, and is also aware of the necessary steps to protect your more sensitive confidential, proprietary, and trade secret data against exposure to your opponent or to the public by entering a Protective Order into the record of the court proceedings. The court rules even allow information to be submitted "in camera," or away from the eyes and ears of your opponent, where necessary.

Recently enacted rules of procedure in many courts require each party to disclose to the other party information that the disclosing party expects to rely upon in establishing its case at trial, even before such information is requested by the opposition. This may include, among others, the names of all persons who may have information relating to the infringement and/or validity of your IP, the identity or copies of documents you will rely upon to establish you have IP rights to begin with, and other information set forth by the rules. This information most likely has been accumulated by your IP litigation team during the pre-filing investigation, so a smaller amount of your employees' time and effort may be required to comply with this aspect of the court rules. However, it is best to appoint a point person the litigation team can contact to ensure that the additional information is promptly located and produced.

32.3.2.3.3 Responding to the Opposition's Discovery Requests

Early in the litigation process, your IP litigation counsel will receive discovery requests for all relevant documents, e-mails, and materials that relate in any way to (1) the IP rights asserted in the lawsuit, (2) the issue of alleged infringement, and (3) support for possible defenses the alleged infringer is exploring. Your counsel will also receive a list of questions, called "Interrogatories," relevant to the lawsuit, such as the identity of all persons that have knowledge of the facts set forth in your complaint. Your counsel may also receive a statement of facts from the opposition that you and your counsel must admit or deny. Upon receipt of document requests, interrogatories, or requests for admission, your side of the lawsuit is obligated under court rules to respond to this discovery process by furnishing the requested information and/or materials, objecting to certain requests for one or more reasons allowed by the rules (i.e., irrelevance, burdensome, not understood, etc.), or stating that you do not have the requested materials or information in your custody, possession, or control. This is a reciprocal process, and your IP counsel will submit discovery requests to the opposing party.

All parties to the litigation have subjected themselves to the authority of the court, and must abide by the rules governing court procedures. Failure to comply with discovery requests could result in sanctions against the recalcitrant party, such as fines, and in rare cases, jail time. In addition, if certain information and materials are requested from you by the other side, and are not produced to the other side, your IP litigation counsel will not be allowed to enter such evidence at the trial of the case. The protection of confidential trade secret information will be discussed in Section 32.3.2.4.

It is clear that once the above-mentioned discovery requests are received from the opposing party, you will be required to have one or several employees search for the information and materials requested, which normally is in addition to and more detailed than the information and materials you searched for during the pre-filing investigation discussed previously. Depending on the scope of the relevant time period covered by the lawsuit, the quest for items requested through discovery could consume the time and energy of several employees who must be shifted from their normal duties to work with IP litigation counsel and obtain the requested data. I recommend that after the pre-filing investigation for documents and materials is complete, an employee among the group working on the project be assigned as a point person whom IP litigation counsel can interface down the road when the discovery requests are received from the other side.

32.3.2.3.4 Preparation for and Taking Depositions from You and Your Employees

Another distraction from the normal affairs of your business occurs when you and your employees are notified that opposing counsel has scheduled their depositions. In most litigation processes, after one party has obtained the documents, e-mails, and other materials from the earlier phases of discovery, those individuals who are identified as potential witnesses, or are known to have relevant information about the facts of the case, are notified or subpoenaed, and advised that their depositions will be taken. This results in the designated deponent sitting before a court reporter where the witness is compelled to give honest answers to questions propounded by the opposing lawyer. The deponent will be represented, or "defended," by either your IP litigation counsel, or counsel of the witness's choice. The defending counsel will raise objections to questions he or she perceives as improper. A transcript of the entire deposition is prepared and furnished to both parties.

In most, if not all, IP litigation matters, you and/or some of your employees will be notified that their depositions will be taken by the opposing counsel on a specified date, which can be changed to accommodate the convenience of all concerned. Once your counsel has received a notice of the deposition, or depositions, each person designated will meet with your IP litigation counsel to prepare the person(s) to give their deposition. Counsel and the deposition witness will review all of the documents, e-mails, and materials of which the witness has, or should have, knowledge, so that the witness can provide background and more in-depth testimony regarding the events described in the documentary evidence. The preparation of the witness also includes preparing the witness to answer questions from opposing counsel that are not most favorable to your side of the case, and how to recognize questions that should be subject to objection at the deposition session. You and the witness can expect that it may take one or more days to prepare you or one of your employees to testify at a deposition session in a complex lawsuit. This is in addition to the time, up to seven hours, for the witness's attendance at the deposition session itself.

Your IP counsel will instruct each of the deposition witnesses on your side of the case to be sure they understand each question before they offer an answer, to answer each proper question honestly and truthfully, and just answer the question asked and not to volunteer information not specifically asked for. In some instances, you or your employee's depositions may be videotaped, which increases the stress the deposition witness must deal with. Your IP litigation counsel will advise you and the other witnesses on how to deal with the emotional side of the deposition process.

It is apparent, however, that the choice of moving forward with IP litigation includes committing the time of certain of your employees in assisting IP litigation counsel in the preparation of, and sitting for, depositions. This expected time away from normal business activities should be thought about at the time the question of filing an IP infringement lawsuit is under discussion, so that work schedules can be altered to avoid interfering with normal business duties, or so that additional employees can fill in the breach while deposition witnesses prepare for deposition and then are deposed in the litigation.

32.3.2.3.5 Preparation for and Testifying at Trial

An additional and potentially greater stage of employee work disruption happens when your IP litigation team must prepare you and your other employee-witnesses for trial of the lawsuit. Depositions, mentioned above, take place outside of the courtroom, but the "big show" takes place in the courtroom before judge and/or jury. The preparation of witnesses for trial is rather time consuming, as each witness must be prepared to answer broad-based questions that do not lead the witness to give, or suggest, the correct answer to the question. Thus, you and your employee-witnesses must be prepared by counsel to know the relevant facts of the case, how to respond to non-leading questions by your counsel on direct examination, and how to respond to leading, direct, and usually hostile questioning by opposing counsel on cross-examination. This process is reminiscent of rehearsing for, and then presenting, a dramatic theatrical performance. There are many similarities between a courtroom proceeding and theater.

Again, the preparation for and trial of the lawsuit will consume many hours of your employees' time, and your time too. This is over and above the stress of testifying correctly and honestly, and withstanding hostile cross-examination. As during the deposition phase, care must be given to scheduling additional personnel to take up the slack left by those employees off assisting IP litigation counsel during the trial of the lawsuit.

32.3.2.4 Preventing the Disclosure of Trade Secret, Proprietary, and Confidential Information to Your Competitor or to the Public During Litigation.

32.3.2.4.1 Protective Orders and Court Rules

In most IP litigation matters, you are facing a competitor or potential competitor who wants to enter your market without bearing the expanse of research and development of the innovation underlying the establishment of your IP rights. A competitor such as this could benefit greatly by having access to your trade secret, proprietary, and confidential information, regarding not only your technology, but your business information such as customers, suppliers, cost data, future plans, etc. In litigation, you may be requested or compelled during the discovery process to produce confidential information that you desire to keep from your competitor. You may need to rely on some of your confidential information at trial to prove your amount of damages, for example, but you do not want to disclose your sales, revenue, cost, or profit data to your competitor or to the public in an open courtroom.

Not to worry! The court rules provide for the exchange of confidential information in a way that allows the confidential information and material to be considered by the court, and also be kept away from the eyes and ears of your competitor.

The FRCP, and the state court rules as well, provide that the parties to a lawsuit can enter into a stipulated "Protective Order" that allows each party to mark its proprietary information as "CONFIDENTIAL." In the Protective Orders that I have agreed to over the years, a first tier of CONFIDENTIAL material can be viewed by the opposing party and their attorney, but neither the opposing party nor its attorney may disclose the CONFIDENTIAL marked material to anyone else.

A second tier of confidentiality is applied to those sensitive, highly confidential documents and materials you need to present to the court to establish your case, but which you want to keep away from the defendant, who may be a competitor. Such documents, data, and materials are marked with the designation "HIGHLY CONFIDENTIAL–ATTORNEY'S EYES ONLY." Materials so marked will be given to the opposing attorneys and their staff, who are prevented under the Protective Order from disclosing such materials to his or her client. How do you know that the attorney will not allow the client to see the ATTORNEY'S EYES ONLY material? Simple. The Protective Order is signed by all attorneys in the case, and signed by the judge. We attorneys are all licensed in the state or states in which we practice. If it ever becomes known that ATTORNEY'S EYES ONLY materials were leaked to an unauthorized person, such as your learning later that the defendant is using the protected information in his or her publicly offered products or services, the attorney would rather quickly lose his or her license to practice law and face contempt of court sanctions. Since we all earn our living under the auspice of our licenses, I for one have concluded that the pressure of one client asking me to divulge ATTORNEY'S EYES ONLY materials is not enough to overcome my desire to continue earning a living in the practice of law. In other words, you may feel highly confident that the opposing lawyer will not divulge ATTORNEY'S EYES ONLY materials to his or her client, or to anyone else. Also, if the conduct of the opposing attorney is particularly grievous, the attorney may be sentenced to jail under the court's contempt powers.

32.3.2.4.2 Depositions

When a deposition is taken during the discovery phase of a lawsuit, each of the parties to the lawsuit is allowed to attend the deposition session. During the deposition, the person being deposed may be asked about sensitive highly confidential information or materials that fall within the ATTORNEY'S EYES ONLY protective umbrella. When such topics arise, the opposing party must leave the deposition room and may not return until testimony about the highly confidential material has been completed. This procedure may be repeated several times during a single deposition session, each time questions about highly confidential subjects arise.

At the close of the deposition session, transcripts of the confidential and highly confidential portions are prepared separately, and related documents and materials are separated from the non-confidential material. The confidential and highly confidential transcripts are then kept by the attorney or his or her client in a space that is kept secure from unauthorized persons. Deposition transcripts are not submitted to the court during discovery, but portions of transcripts may be used to support or respond to a motion filed by a party, such as a Motion for Summary Judgment. If a confidential portion of a transcript is used, that material is kept from the eyes of the party whom the responding attorney represents.

32.3.2.4.3 Use of Confidential and Highly Confidential Data During Trial

The Protective Order and court rules govern the use of confidential and highly confidential information during the trial of an IP lawsuit that takes place in an open public courtroom. The court may receive evidence "in camera" that has been seen only by the opposing attorney and client, or only the opposing attorney. The judge will be careful to ensure that the confidential and highly confidential material is kept secure by the courtroom deputies who come in contact with such sensitive materials. The court's decision may also have a portion that is withheld from the public, and the opposing party, when necessary.

So when considering whether or not to initiate IP litigation against an identified infringer, be aware that it may be necessary to divulge some of your highly confidential and sensitive material. But you should also be reassured that the Protective Order, the court rules, and the opposing lawyer's fear of losing his or her ability to earn a living provide adequate protection for your sensitive information. At the end of the lawsuit, all confidential and highly confidential materials are returned to the proper party.

32.3.2.5 Short Notes on Other Litigation Factors

The previous segments of this chapter have explained in detail many of the important factors that should be considered and discussed with your IP litigation counsel prior to deciding to "sue the bastards." I want to conclude with a few brief comments about other items that should be discussed with those responsible for operating your business, as well as your IP litigation counsel.

32.3.2.5.1 Start-Up Business Litigation Concerns

It is a cardinal rule of business that all activities have to be properly financed. This is particularly true if you are in the process of starting a new company or venture fortified by your IP. If an infringer of your IP appears during the initial phase of getting your business off the ground, the resources necessary to protect your business against the infringer will most likely be beyond your financial capability, unless you have thought ahead and taken prior steps to respond to a potential infringement situation. When an infringer appears during the initial stage of your business, you have two options. One, do nothing because you cannot afford an IP infringement lawsuit, and let the infringer erode your potential market share by introducing an infringing product or process at a price point lower than the price points in your business plan, thus possibly causing your business to face failure before it even stands on its own two feet.

The second option is to challenge the infringer with a lawsuit, after finding the resources to support the litigation. This is where my comment above about thinking ahead comes in. Most technology based start-ups and new ventures go through initial phases of raising capital by presenting a business plan to prospective investors. The business plan normally establishes the amounts of investor revenue needed to be contributed before revenue streams result from the sale of the venture's products or services. I strongly recommend that the section of the business plan that sets forth the investment needed to get the venture started include an amount in the range of one half to one million dollars in reserve to be used only to take legal action, if necessary, to enforce your IP rights in the event an infringer appears in the market you intend to enter. If no such legal action is necessary, the reserve fund could be returned to the investors, or by agreement used to further the goals of the business operation.

As an alternative, if an infringer enters the stage, you may find an attorney who will represent you on a contingency fee basis, taking his or her fee from any damages award, or settlement amount resulting from the lawsuit. Partial contingency arrangements may also be workable between you and an IP litigation counsel.

32.3.2.5.2 Licensing as a Litigation Strategy

When you notice someone, such as a competitor, possibly infringing your IP rights, your team may decide that it would be more beneficial to let them become a second source for your IP-based products or services and pay you a royalty rather than go through the risk and expense of a lawsuit. For example, the increase in the cost of adding new production capability to meet the expected demand for your new IP-based technology, plus the cost of litigation, may be greater than the profit you can gain from being the sole source of the subject product or service. So, you decide that offering a royalty-bearing license is to your advantage.

But the competition in this case may not believe it has to have a license and to pay you a reasonable royalty, and declines your offer. A possible follow-up strategy on your behalf is to threaten to file a lawsuit or actually file a lawsuit, with the strategic goal of convincing the competitor that a settlement with the competitor accepting a royalty-bearing license is much more beneficial than the uncertainty of the cost and outcome of an IP lawsuit. One tactic in this strategic plan is to file the lawsuit, and after the answer is filed, seek a mediation of the controversy. In a mediation, an experienced mediator works with both parties, usually using shuttle diplomacy, to assist the parties to work out an agreement they can both live with, and gain the certainty that a settlement brings.

In some courts, the judges or magistrate judges act as mediators if both parties agree to a mediation. In other situations, a private, qualified, and experienced mediator is hired, with both parties sharing the fee for the mediator's time.

The mediator cannot force either party to agree to something they do not want to. The mediator's only function is to listen to what each party wants from the mediation, and then convince or cajole the parties to make concessions and reach a settlement where the parties have an agreement they can both live with.

Since your initial strategic goal was to have the other party accept a license under your IP rights going into the mediation session, you should have already decided what concessions you are willing to make, and those you cannot make in the mediation. Keep in mind, however, that bottom lines and lines in the sand can shift during a serious mediation. You may have arrived at a minimum royalty rate you can accept to allow the competitor to compete with you at price points that cannot be below what you charge your customers. If the mediated royalty rate starts going below that line, you may want to shift to other tactics, such as geographically limiting the competitor's sales to those territories where your sales are traditionally weak, and keeping the competitor away from your stronger geographic markets. The concept of mediation includes give and take, but mediation is a great process if your ultimate goal is to grant a license to your competitor, and avoid the (1) uncertainty and (2) cost of asking a judge or jury to decide your dispute.

An arbitration is not the same as a mediation. If you agree to a mediation, the mediator cannot force you to agree to a deal you do not want. If you agree to an arbitration, however, the arbitration panel hears both sides, and makes a decision that is binding on all parties.

32.3.2.5.3 Settlement Analysis

At any point after a lawsuit has been filed, the matter in controversy can be resolved by agreement of the parties. Many courts compel the parties and their litigation attorneys to take part in settlement discussions in the first few months after the lawsuit has been initiated before the judge, magistrate judge, or private mediator to see if the court's time and resources can be saved. As a result, before the lawsuit reaches critical mass, you may have to think about how you and your competitor/infringer can come to an agreement to avoid litigation. I recommend that when considering all of the factors that go into a decision regarding whether or not to file a lawsuit, you also prepare a settlement strategy to be used before or during the expected mediation session. These pre-filing strategy points should include the minimum royalty rate you could accept in a license agreement and protect your price points and market share at the same time, those strong markets of yours that you want you competitor/licensee to keep out of, and restrictions on the use of your IP-protected technology by the licensee to develop improved products, unless you gain the ownership of such improvements by grant back clauses. Prior to filing an IP lawsuit, your IP litigation counsel and your marketing department can advise you of those reasonable and business-sensible terms you should aim to reach during settlement discussions directly with your competitor or at mediation sessions. Also, remember that some of your "bottom lines" may have to shift during settlement discussions or mediation.

32.3.2.5.4 Avoiding IP Litigation—Brief Comments

Before bringing your new product or service to the market, there are several steps to be taken to reduce or eliminate the risk that your product or service will infringe the IP rights of another. It must be remembered that even if you have patent, trademark, or other IP protection granted or pending, that same product, service, or brand may be accused of and found to infringe the IP rights of someone else.

32.3.2.5.4.1 Patent Infringement Avoidance After your product or service has reached its final sign-off phase and you have selected a brand name, a search of active patents and pending patent applications, and a full trademark search should be conducted. We presume at this point that no one copied from a protected source or misappropriated anyone else's trade secrets during the process of designing and producing your product or service, so that possible copyright or trade secret problems are not on the radar screen.

The patent freedom-to-use search provides your IP counsel with those relevant issued patents that are still within the enforceable time period beginning with the effective filing date of the patent application, and factoring in additional days of enforcement granted by the USPTO in some cases. The search should also include relevant pending, non-issued published patent applications that include claims that may have a bearing on your product or process. Given today's examination backlog, most pending applications, which are published 18 months after their priority filing date (which could be a provisional application filing date), have not reached a first examination by their date of publication, and the claims of the published application are not in their final form. In reviewing these pending applications, your IP professional should provide you with an opinion as to how the claims in the pending applications may be read upon issue, based on the state of the prior art. This opinion should advise you whether any claims of active issued patents or of pending applications could be infringed literally or under the Doctrine of Equivalents.

If the opinion uncovers some potentially problematic patents or pending applications, several steps can be taken to avoid being sued for patent infringement. The first step is to determine if a reasonable cost-effective and non-debilitating design-around is possible. Here, your R&D team and the IP professional work together to come up with a change that avoids the patent claim or claims of another patent or pending application, and hopefully the change can be implemented.

The second step, if a design-around is not feasible, is to conduct a validity, or knock-out search of the problematic patent or application to determine whether the patent or application could be found to be invalid based on prior art not previously considered by the Patent Examiner. Here, you are trying to establish a strong defense against the validity of the patent were it to be asserted against your product or process after market introduction.

The third step, if the first and second steps are not feasible or practical, is to seek a license from the owner of the patent or application that allows you to move forward with your business strategy. Obviously, this last option is the least desirable since moving forward with your product or process depends on the whim of someone else, possibly a direct competitor.

A further precautionary measure to minimize the threat or accusation of patent infringement upon the market introduction of your product or process is to conduct a freedom-to-use patent search once the design and development direction of your product or process has been established internally, and not wait until sign-off of the final design. This search will identify patents and published applications that may cause infringement problems in the future. The prosecution history of any relevant issued patents, and those published applications in an advanced stage of examination, can be reviewed by your IP professional to possibly offer guidance to your R&D personnel as to any changes in the design and development direction that would be helpful in avoiding subsequent patent infringement problems.

This writer highly recommends that your IP professional be brought into the picture at the stage when the design and development direction has been established to offer advice, rather than waiting for the entire product or process to be finalized, when changes to avoid infringement will certainly face increased resistance.

32.3.2.5.4.2 Trademark/Service Mark Infringement Avoidance Prior to adopting and using a brand name for your new product or service, a search should be conducted of existing marks that are either registered on the federal or state registers, or are applied for, or are in use without any registration or application. Recall from an earlier chapter of this text that exclusive trademark and service mark rights can exist merely from one using the mark in their business, without having obtained a registration covering that mark. These searches in the United States are normally conducted among the federal and all state trademark/service mark databases, and a privately available database that attempts to catalog all uses of marks by analyzing corporate name directories, phone listings, trade product name directories and journals, Internet uses, and other sources where a prior used brand name may be found. Once this search is concluded, your IP professional will provide you with an opinion as to whether there may be a prior user of a confusingly similar (not necessarily the exact same) mark who may be prompted to file a lawsuit, or send a cease and desist letter, challenging your right to use your mark of choice. On the basis of the results of this search, you have the opportunity to change the brand name to avoid possible litigation.

Keep in mind that having to change a brand name to avoid even the possibility of having to defend yourself against a lawsuit filed by the owner of a previously used mark does not mean you have to change anything regarding your product or process. So, if necessary, change your brand, even though you, your marketing department, and your spouse think the brand name is a terrific choice.

32.4 CONCLUSION

The above comments are intended to provide you with thinking points when going through the stressful decision-making process regarding filing a lawsuit for IP infringement, or taking steps to prevent someone else from accusing you of IP infringement. By no means are these comments exhaustive. The considerations, steps, and defensive actions I recommend should all be discussed thoroughly with your IP litigation counsel prior to taking definitive action. There are most likely many other factors peculiar and relevant to your industry, or your company, that should be factored into the litigation or defensive posture equation.

◆ INVENTORS AND INVENTIONS ◆

Igor Sikorsky

HELICOPTER

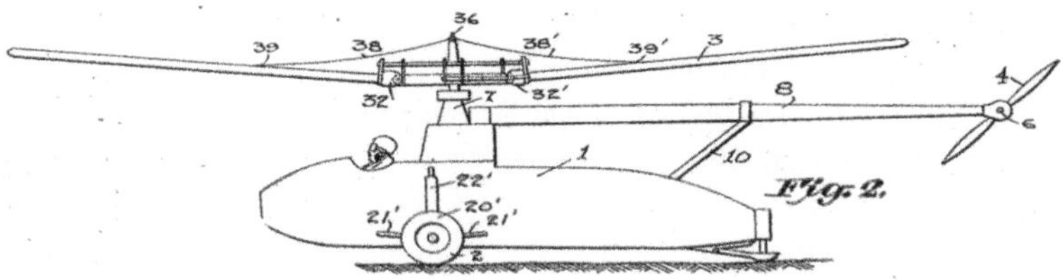

Earlier references to vertical flight originated in China. Since about the year 400 BCE, children in China played with bamboo flying tops consisting of a stick inserted into a hole in a rotor with opposite angled blades on either side of the hole. The stick is rotated by the child's hands, and the rotating rotor then lifts off the stick and flies upward. In the 1480s, Leonardo da Vinci drew a design of a flying machine that looked like an "aerial screw," but there is no recorded evidence of da Vinci building or flying his concept.

In the 1920s, Argentinian Raúl Pateras-Pescara de Castelluccio, working in Europe at the time, successfully demonstrated one of the first applications of cyclic pitch, where two coaxial, contra-rotating horizontal biplane rotors could be warped to cyclically increase and decrease the lift produced. Also, the rotor hub could be tilted forward slightly, allowing the aircraft to move forward without a separate propeller to push or pull the aircraft. Patents were granted in Britain in 1927 to Albert Gillis von Baumhauer covering cyclic and collective pitch rotor controls.

Early rotor blade flight was hindered by the unbalanced rolling movement created when attempting takeoff, resulting from the asymmetry of lift between the advancing and retreating blade portions, one portion moving into the wind and the other portion moving with the wind. In 1923, Juan de la Cierva of Spain corrected this problem with a flopping hinge used in his first successful four-blade rotor autogyro. This craft, however, also had short wings and a front-mounted propeller, and relied on conventional fixed-wing aircraft controls for pitch, roll, and yaw.

A major problem with the autogyro was connecting the rotor to the engine before takeoff. To do so would cause counter-rotation of the entire aircraft in the direction opposite to the rotation of the rotor. After trying several solutions, the problem was solved with a direct drive from the engine to the rotor, and the rotor could be accelerated to top speed. The rotor clutch was then disengaged to disconnect the rotor from

Intellectual Property Law for Engineers, Scientists, and Entrepreneurs, Second Edition. Howard B. Rockman.

Published 2020 by John Wiley & Sons, Inc.

the engine prior to takeoff. The front propeller then drove the aircraft forward for liftoff, with the rotor spinning freely and developing lift, keeping the craft aloft.

During World War II, Germany used a small number of helicopters for observation, transport, and medical evacuation. Repeated bombing by Allied forces stopped Germany from the mass production of helicopters during the war.

Igor Sikorsky is considered the father of vertical takeoff and landing aircraft—helicopters—not because he was the first to invent rotary aircraft, but because he invented the first successful helicopter rotor design upon which subsequent designs were based.

He was born in Kiev, then Russia, now Ukraine, on May 25, 1889. An afficionado of Da Vinci and Jules Verne, at 12 years old he made a small rubber-band-powered helicopter that actually lifted into the air.

In 1905, he entered the Petrograd Naval Academy, but left in 1906 to study engineering in Paris for one year and then studied in St. Petersburg. He ultimately completed his degree at the Mechanical Engineering College of the Polytechnic Institute in Kiev. While there, he conceived of his first helicopter, which he built and tested beginning in 1909. However, he abandoned this effort because although satisfying all control and dynamic requirements of flight, the two craft he designed and constructed would not lift from the ground because the weight of the 25-horsepower engine necessary to drive the rotor was greater than the lift forces developed by the rotor. He recorded and kept his data, and moved on to fixed-winged aircraft design primarily for financial reasons. In 1908, he visited Germany with his father, where he learned of the work of the Wright Brothers, and of Ferdinand von Zeppelin's dirigible, which trip convinced him to devote his life to aviation.

While in Russia, with financial assistance from his sister Olga, Sikorsky began designing and building fixed-wing aircraft. His S-1 biplane was tested in 1910. The S-1 engine was too small, so he redesigned and tested the S-2, S-3, S-4, and S-5 versions, each improved over the other, which he personally flew successfully. His S-8 version was supplied to the Russian military.

In May 1913, while employed by the Russian Baltic Railroad Car Factory, Sikorsky constructed and piloted the "Le Grand," the world's first four-engine aircraft, weighing 4500 pounds with a 92-foot wingspan and four 100-horsepower engines. The Le Grand also included an outside platform or balcony where four of the passengers could stroll outside of the aircraft. For obvious reasons, the speed of today's aircraft has made this feature obsolete, but at 1913 speeds, I suppose this was a desirable passenger feature.

When the Bolshevik revolution began, Sikorsky moved to France. When World War I ended, he left for the United States, arriving in New York on March 30, 1919. Sikorsky survived his early days in the United States by teaching mathematics, astronomy, and aviation to other newly arrived Russian immigrants in New York City, which introduced him to others who shared his interest in aviation. In 1923, his sisters arrived in New York, along with his six-year-old daughter Tania from an earlier short-lived marriage in Russia. In 1927, Sikorsky married a fellow immigrant, and they had four sons.

On March 5, 1923, after Sikorsky's friends persuaded him to start his own aircraft company, the Sikorsky Aero Engineering Company was formed in a barn on a Long Island chicken farm near Roosevelt Field. The first product manufactured by the new company was the S-29-A, a fixed-wing passenger airplane which was moderately successful. In 1928, Sikorsky became a U.S. citizen. In 1929, the company became part of

United Aircraft and Transport Corporation, now United Technologies Corporation, occupying a large plant in Bridgeport, Connecticut.

In the late 1930s, Sikorsky returned to his earlier interest in helicopter design and production, particularly in developing aircraft that could take off and land in difficult areas performing rescue and medical emergency tasks. Sikorsky's final fixed-wing aircraft design was the S-44, built in 1937. All of his subsequent craft were helicopters. Consider that when Sikorsky revisited his love of helicopters, there was little reliable technical information available, and no one with helicopter piloting experience. However, by the 1930s, aircraft construction engineering and aerodynamic theory and concepts had made significant advances compared what was available in 1910.

In early 1939, with a talented engineering team behind him, Sikorsky began construction of the Vought-Sikorsky VS-300 helicopter, which successfully lifted from the ground in a tethered, short flight on September 14, 1939, in Stratford, Connecticut, with Sikorsky piloting the craft. The helicopter was the first to employ a single three-blade main rotor and tail rotor design. The first free flight was on May 13, 1940. Sikorsky received U.S. Patent No. 1,994,488, on March 19, 1934, directed to a vertical-lift aircraft, which disclosed all of the important features of the VS-300.

In 1941, in an improved version, an international endurance record of 1 hour 32.4 seconds was established. The VS-300 was the precursor of the helicopter rotor configuration used by most present helicopters. In 1941, the Sikorsky R-4 became the world's first mass-produced helicopter. Sikorsky's last VS-300 rotor configuration, with a single primary rotor and a single anti-torque tail rotor, is also used in most modern helicopters manufactured today. The R-4 received a contract from the U.S. Army Air Corps in 1941 and was the only model used in World War II. It was deployed on life-saving missions to rescue people trapped in locations inaccessible to fixed-wing airplanes.

Unlike his predecessors, who designed vertical-lift aircraft with multiple rotors, Sikorsky concentrated on a single main rotor aircraft. A more difficult problem was the design, number, and arrangement of the vertically rotating tail rotor that prevented the aircraft from spinning horizontally out of control due to the connection between the engine and the rotor drive shaft. Eventually, Sikorsky found that a single rotor mounted vertically on the tail of the aircraft produced the optimum desired results.

Substantially high-power engines are required to drive rotating helicopter blades, explaining the delay in helicopter development after the Wright brothers' invention of the fixed-wing powered aircraft. The turboshaft engine, invented in the 1940s, matched the rotary wing power demands.

In a helicopter, as the rotor creates lift, torque is also created in the helicopter body attached to the rotor shaft. This torque will spin the aircraft body in the direction opposite to the rotary movement if left uncontrolled. A small vertical propeller at the rear of the helicopter body, gear-connected to the main rotor, counteracts the torque force to keep the helicopter stable. The rear propeller is designed to overcompensate for torque, which causes the machine to drift. Controlling the rear vertical propeller to compensate for the drift is one of the operator's tasks.

A helicopter's direction of movement is controlled by tilting the spinning rotor blades, the machine banking and rolling, moving in the direction of right or left tilt, and climbing or descending in the direction of an up-or-down tilt. Leveling the blades keeps the direction of movement to vertical only, and power adjustment maintains a hovering or still position. Left or right turning is accomplished by altering the angle of the tail propeller, which then acts as a rudder. The unique ability of a helicopter to fly backward is also controlled by the tilt of the rotor blades.

The aim in flying a helicopter is to keep the power, controlled by the throttle, matched to the requirements for directional movement of the aircraft, and avoiding engine stalling. Each change of main rotor pitch calls for matching power to the rotors to keep the system stable.

For horizontal, level flying, the pilot must add foot movement to the hand movement already occupied with tilt and throttle. A pair of foot pedals operate the tail propeller pitch (or angle), turning the craft to the left or right and at the same time compensating for torque and drift.

March 19, 1935. I. I. SIKORSKY 1,994,488

DIRECT LIFT AIRCRAFT

Filed June 27, 1931 9 Sheets-Sheet 1

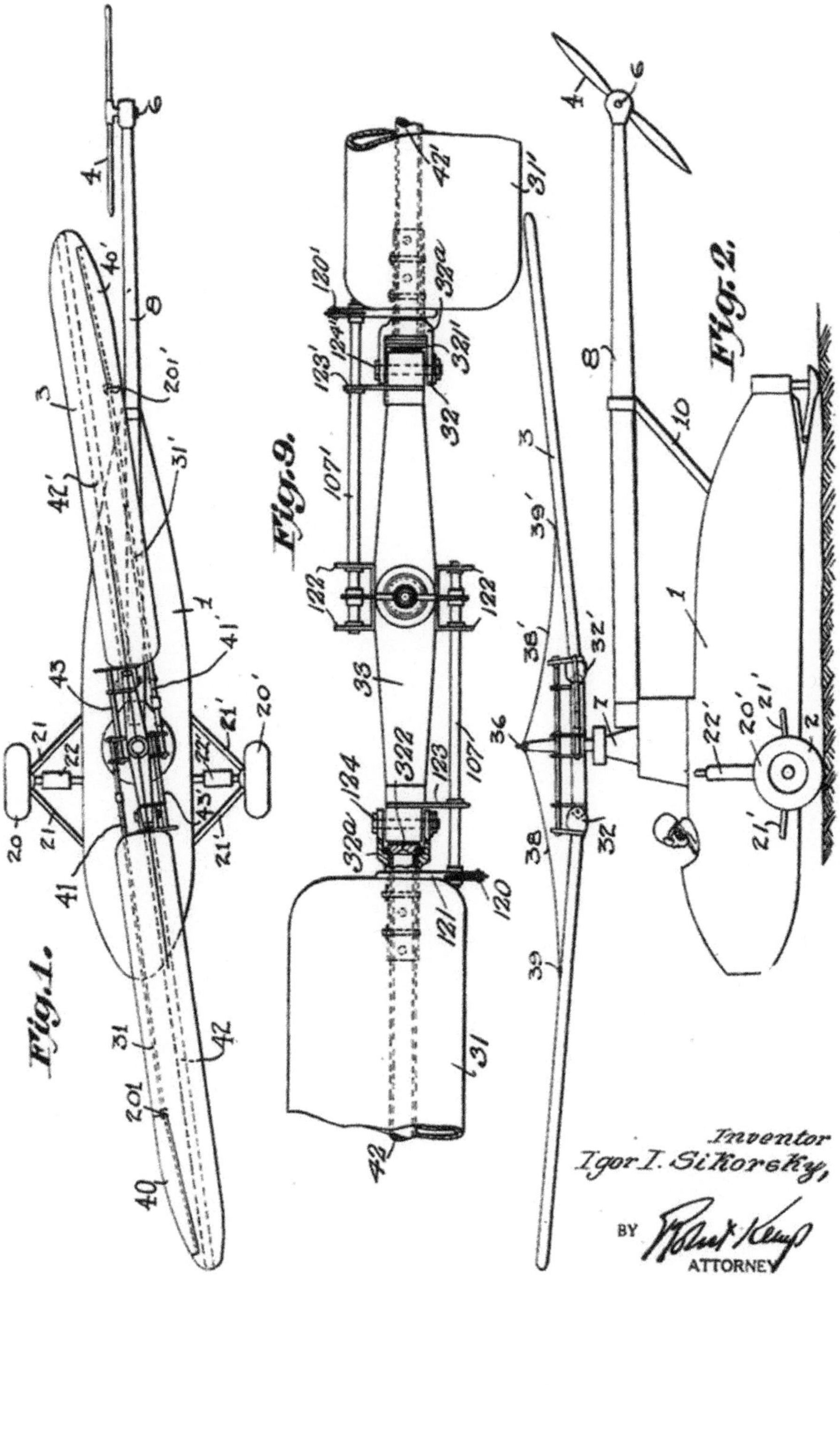

◆ INVENTORS AND INVENTIONS ◆

Frank Zamboni

ICE RESURFACER

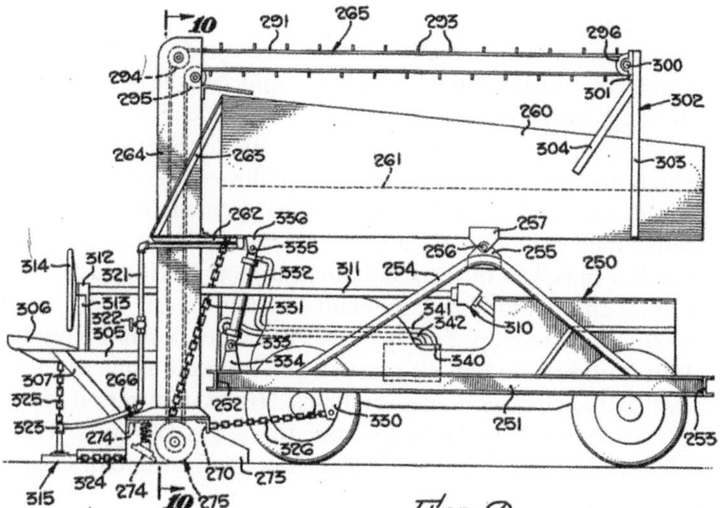

FIG. 9.

Beginning in the 1920s, brothers Frank and Lorenzo Zamboni were producing block ice for the food industry. However, electrically operated refrigeration came into being and was constantly being improved, and the block ice market disappeared. Ice skating was sky rocketing in popularity in the late 1930s, so the Zamboni brothers and a cousin built the Iceland Skating Rink in Paramount, California, about 30 miles southeast of Los Angeles in 1940. They found that maintaining a quality ice surface was nearly impossible. Resurfacing the ice was expensive and time consuming, requiring several workers to shave the ice, haul the scrapings away, squeegee the surface, and then spray water and wait for it to freeze. The skaters either moved through sludge on bad ice or waited a long time to get back to skating. The entire resurfacing process at that time took about 90 minutes.

In 1942, Frank Zamboni began experimenting with several ice resurfacing systems with water, heat, chassis, storage, and engines. In 1949, he developed what became the Model A, which was built on a jeep platform. In the original Model A, Zamboni modified the vehicle upon which his machine was constructed, adding a blade that shaved the ice smooth, a device that swept up the shavings into a tank, and an apparatus that

Intellectual Property Law for Engineers, Scientists, and Entrepreneurs, Second Edition. Howard B. Rockman.

Published 2020 by John Wiley & Sons, Inc.

rinsed the ice and left a very thin top layer of water that would freeze within a minute. A wooden box held the ice shavings, and water dripped from a tank to wash the ice and was pumped back into a bucket. Then another layer of water was laid down for a fresh, clean surface. The vehicle was not much to look at, but it worked, resurfacing the rink with a clean sheet of ice in 15 minutes.

The initial Zamboni machine included a hydraulic cylinder from an A-20 attack plane, a chassis from an oil derrick, a jeep engine, a wooden bin to catch the shavings, and a series of pulleys. The machine shaved ice off the surface, collected the shavings, washed the ice, and spread a thin coat of fresh water onto the surface. It took Frank Zamboni nine years to develop this particular machine. He also set up the Frank J. Zamboni and Company organization to build and sell the machines.

The second Zamboni machine, the Model B, was created in 1950 at the request of figure skater and former Olympian, Sonja Henie, who saw the Model A and wanted one for herself. Sonja Henie toured the world with her ice show, taking a Zamboni machine with her wherever she performed. The NHL's Boston Bruins bought a Zamboni machine and put it to work in 1954, followed by many other National Hockey League teams. The Model B was awarded a patent in 1953 based upon a patent application filed in 1949. A Zamboni ice resurfacer was used in the 1960 Olympics for the first time. Use of the Zamboni resurfacer has increased since then, as many municipalities and schools began to build ice rinks.

In the 1970s, Zamboni developed and patented machines to remove water from outdoor artificial turf surfaces, to remove paint stripes from the same surfaces, and roll out and lay down artificial ice in domed stadiums. His final invention in 1983 was an automatic edger to remove ice build-up from the edges of rinks. The Zamboni Company is still owned and operated by the Zamboni family. All told, Frank Zamboni obtained 15 U.S. patents.

The Iceland ice rink built by the Zamboni brothers and their cousin in Paramount, California, is still in operation today, several blocks from the Zamboni factory. It is quite usual in Paramount to see Zamboni ice resurfacers being driven on the neighborhood streets on their way to be tested at the Iceland rink.

June 23, 1953 F. J. ZAMBONI 2,642,679

ICE RINK RESURFACING MACHINE

Filed May 16, 1949 4 Sheets-Sheet 1

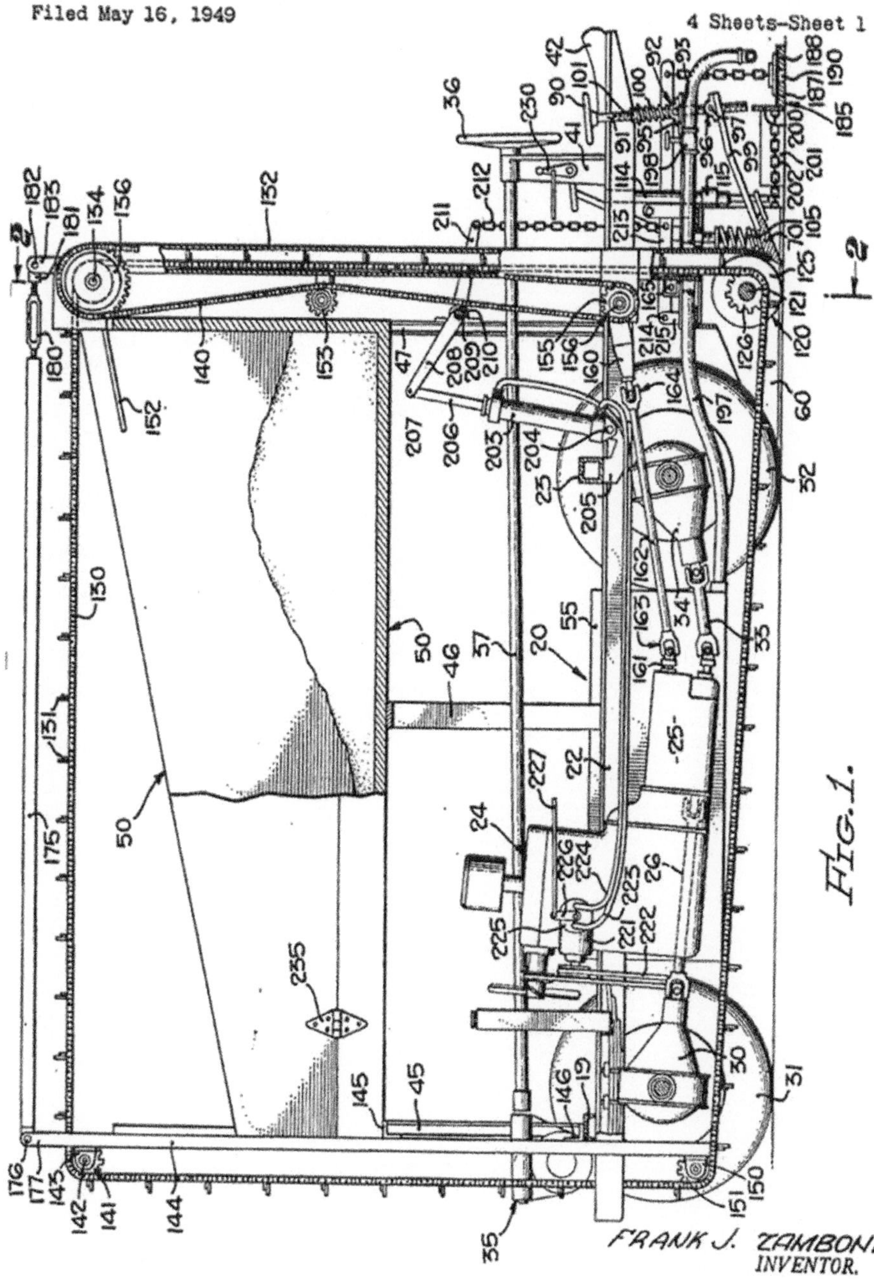

FIG. 1.

FRANK J. ZAMBONI,
INVENTOR.

BY Forrest J. Lilly
ATTORNEY

33 Technology Transfer—Universities, Hospitals, and Research Centers

33.1 INTRODUCTION

Up to here, a good portion of this text has addressed intellectual property subjects of interest to individual inventors, companies, and other entities that commercially market products that incorporate, or will incorporate, their inventions or copyrightable materials. However, given my long-time association with academia, it is clear to me that significant creations of useful processes, products, and works of authorship have evolved, and will continue to evolve, from the research conducted at universities, hospitals, and other research centers, which are not directly involved in marketing the beneficial results of their research.

Many of these universities, hospitals, and research center institutions have developed programs that allow the results of their internal academic research to follow a unique path from initial concept to commercialization, thus benefiting the general public, the faculty, and the institution. These systems and programs are generically referred to as "technology transfer" or "technology management" programs, and are found in most major universities, hospitals, and other research centers, and in some cases earn an income each year in the hundreds of millions of dollars for their respective institutions. These technology transfer programs encourage the disclosure of inventions and copyrightable material from the employees of the institution, which includes students who may not technically be classified as employees.

The technology transfer systems also conduct searches (1) to determine if the inventions or copyrightable material are protectable under one or more of the intellectual property laws, and (2) to identify potential licensees who are interested in further development and commercialization of the newly developed product, process, or copyrightable work. In many situations, the institution's internal Office of Technology Management (OTM) files patent applications on those developments deemed worthy of commercialization, and which developments may ultimately provide financial resources to help support additional innovation.

The institution may also be able to provide funding at different stages in the commercialization process. Such resources can be furnished by the university or institution itself, or in partnership with external programs, such as non-profit or commercial organizations. For example, a professor and a cohort of students who have developed a new product, process, or copyrightable work as part of their research project for

Intellectual Property Law for Engineers, Scientists, and Entrepreneurs, Second Edition. Howard B. Rockman.

Published 2020 by John Wiley & Sons, Inc.

credit may receive funding and other assistance from their university to create a start-up entity to bring the innovation to the market. In some of these instances, the university receives a royalty-based income from the successful commercialization of the product or process, or the university may even take an equity or ownership share in the new start-up entity. The income derived by the university is then used to support additional research projects, and to help fund future start-up ventures.

This chapter is directed to those universities, hospitals, and research centers that have a small or no technology transfer program in place, and desire to benefit from the research and development projects conducted at the institution that result in innovations each semester or quarter.

33.2 OWNERSHIP OF INSTITUTION-DEVELOPED INNOVATIONS

The establishment of a workable technology transfer program at an institution where research is conducted first requires that the institution itself promulgate a set of rules defining under what conditions the institution owns the intellectual property rights to innovations developed by the students or employees, what rights it retains and what rights may be released to the inventors/creators, and to what extent revenues received by the institution may be shared with the inventors/creators.

It is important that each employee/student of the research institution be fully advised of the institution's intellectual property ownership provisions. In the best of all possible worlds, each employee, including master's degree and PhD students who receive a stipend from the university, sign an agreement on the first day of their employment that assigns all intellectual property they take part in developing to the institution. This avoids needless arguments over who owns what when a professor and his or her student team develop a product or process that has significant commercialization potential.

In certain instances, where the institution concludes that the development and related intellectual property have no or slight commercialization potential, but the professor and the student development team think differently, many institutions have a waiver policy where the institution releases the innovators from their obligation to assign the intellectual property rights to the institution, which provides the innovator team with the right to commercialize the innovation on their own, and for their own future benefit.

33.2.1 Typical University Ownership Policies and Provisions

Each institution, be it university, hospital, or other research center, has its own rules and policies as to ownership of intellectual property rights regarding developments by employees/students at the institution. Each institution also has its own rules regarding the sharing of revenues received from the commercialization of the innovation. To explain how these aspects of technology transfer work, I am using as an example the system currently in place and implemented by the OTM of the University of Illinois at Chicago (UIC) where I teach courses in Engineering Law and Intellectual Property Law for Engineers as a member of the adjunct faculty. The information that follows is used with the permission of the authorities of the University of Illinois, as stated in the Acknowledgements portion at the beginning of this text. Other institutions, of course, may have different technology transfer rules and policies, and if you are starting or enhancing a technology transfer program at your institution, I suggest you adopt procedures and policies that fit your particular institution's needs. Remember that such rules and policies will have to be approved at the highest level of the institution's administration before being implemented.

Prior to initiating or enhancing a technology transfer program at your institution, you can find a vast amount of information on the topic from the Association of University Technology Managers (AUTM), whose contact and other information is available online at www.autm.net.

33.2.1.1 What Is Owned by the University

In a university landscape, undergraduate students who pay tuition to attend are not considered "employees" of the university. Graduate students, who normally are paid by the university for their research and/or teaching, plus the faculty and other staff members are employees of the university. A typical ownership provision, and the one currently in place at UIC, states that intellectual property shall belong to the university if made (1) by a university employee as a result of the employee's duties, or (2) through the use by any person, including a university employee or student, of university resources such as facilities, equipment, resources, or funds under the control of or administered by the university, except if otherwise specified by the university in writing. This applies to any individual or group of individuals who make, conceive, reduce to practice, author, or otherwise make a substantive intellectual contribution to the creation of intellectual property. This covers both the definition of an "inventor" under U.S. Patent Law, and the definition of "author" under U.S. Copyright Law.

33.2.1.2 Copyrights and the Academic Exception

Works authored independently by a student and at the student's own initiative for traditional academic purposes are owned by the student, but the university retains certain rights to use such works. These include class notes, reports, papers, and works prepared as part of degree requirements, such as a thesis or dissertation. The student owns the copyright in the expression, but the student may not own the underlying invention or development described in the work created by the student.

For example, if a thesis describes research performed in a university laboratory, the university owns the underlying intellectual property such as laboratory notebooks, original research records, and the resulting inventions or software.

It is occasionally necessary to delay publication of a student thesis for a limited period of time for the purposes of (a) protecting potentially patentable inventions, and (b) complying with the terms of sponsored research agreements (such as prepublication review). The intellectual property terms of sponsored research contracts and grants, both government and private, usually require diligent disclosure and protection of inventions, both U.S. and worldwide. In addition, private contracts often contain prepublication review provisions, deferring publication of a thesis or paper for a period of time for the purposes of protecting intellectual property. Recall from earlier chapters that the public disclosure of an invention before a patent application is filed can destroy the ability to obtain patent rights in a significant number of countries other than the United States.

A student's degree requirements can still be fulfilled even though publication of the thesis is delayed. The optimal way to protect intellectual property and adhere to sponsor agreement requirements is the formal submission to OTM of a request to withhold a thesis for patent considerations and compliance with contractual terms. This must be done prior to or concurrent with thesis deposit in the Graduate College, and this step delays publishing of the thesis. This mechanism provides an absolute "blackout" of information contained in the thesis. The author, title, and abstract are not accessible in any way.

33.2.1.3 Ownership of Intellectual Property Created by University Students

As mentioned above, the university owns all intellectual property developed by a university employee, or by anyone, including students, using university facilities, equipment, or funds. Since the university also has a policy of encouraging student innovation and entrepreneurship, the university usually grants exceptions to the rules regarding ownership of student inventions when certain criteria are met. An exception will not be granted if the innovation incorporates, depends upon, or is derived directly from university-owned background intellectual property, which includes any university property, and the legal rights to such property, that was or is created, developed, or reduced to practice outside the scope of the student activity or class project.

One situation that should be covered in these rules is where a professor (employee) is working with several undergraduate students (non-employees) on a research project that results in a commercially viable product or process. The group, including the professor, may desire to create a start-up to commercialize the innovation. The university rules should include examples of how intellectual property ownership rights are managed in these situations, or at least set forth criteria as to how these situations shall be managed when they arise. Typically, the intellectual property rights would be jointly owned by the students and the university.

Many engineering and science universities have established campus initiatives for supporting student-created start-up activities. These include providing limited funding, space, equipment, and other resources, and assistance in obtaining intellectual property protection, such as patent filings. The university will usually allow the students to retain ownership of the intellectual property resulting from these efforts, even though university facilities and resources may have been used. It may be necessary to obtain a written exception to the university rules from the university administration to transfer the intellectual property rights to the students. Of course, if a graduate student and/or a professor were also part of the intellectual property development team along with the students, a procedure for making case-by-case decisions on such situations may be a part of the OTM and the university administration procedures.

Certain undergraduate courses, such as industrial arts design or engineering senior design, may result in inventions developed as part of the course. A general exception can be made in the university rules that allows the students to own the inventions and intellectual property developed as part of the course. At UIC, this exemption applies when the only university resources used were those routinely made available by the college/department to all students enrolled in the course. This exception should be memorialized in writing prepared by the course instructor in conjunction with OTM before the course begins.

Such project-oriented courses often engage sponsors to provide funding, and/or specific projects for the students to work on. If the sponsor desires to claim ownership of any resulting inventions or innovations, the student working on the project must agree in writing at the beginning of the course of their obligation to transfer ownership of any innovations to the sponsor. A student who does not so agree may not work on the project. If the course is a degree requirement, the student must be given an option to work on other projects that allow the student to retain intellectual property rights. If at the end of the course, neither the sponsor nor the university is interested in the innovation, the students in the course are free to own their own inventions, and to enter into agreements involving their inventions with others.

If university-owned background intellectual property is required for work on a course project, the university usually owns any resulting intellectual property rights. When a student sees that such university-owned intellectual property is necessary to conduct the course work, he or she is obligated to inform the course faculty member and obtain permission before using such background resources in the classroom.

The intellectual property ownership situations discussed above are only some of those that predictably may occur in the university or teaching hospital environment. However, never discount the human ability to create research and development processes that defy predictability when it comes to deciphering who owns the intellectual property rights for a new and promising innovation arising from the university–faculty member–student combination, with a possible sponsor thrown in for good measure. My advice is that the faculty member leading such research courses should discuss the following with OTM prior to the start of the course: how the course is to be conducted, what intellectual property may be developed in the course, and what pre-existing background intellectual property can be expected to be used during the course. The OTM experts will be able to provide the faculty member with guidance based on OTM's experience with applying the rules to similar situations in the past. The problem to avoid is attempting to solve various claims of intellectual property ownership after the course is long over, and the results of the course research have been wildly successful in the market. The vision of dollar signs by those involved in the product or process development in the university course may cloud the sense of reason, and each member of the development team will "lawyer up" to seek significant sums of money. Prior ownership analysis of possible outcomes goes a long way toward preventing future aggravation.

33.3 A TYPICAL UNIVERSITY TECHNOLOGY TRANSFER PROGRAM

33.3.1 Purpose of the OTM

Technology transfer is the transfer of knowledge, ideas, inventions, discoveries, innovations, and creations to the public, with the ultimate goal of benefiting the general public. An institution's technology transfer function includes the evaluation of such developments for usefulness to the public, and steps of protection, marketing, and licensing of intellectual property developed at the institution to start-ups and to existing companies or organizations. While technology transfer management may seek licensees on a global basis, licensees located in the community of the institution are particularly sought out to economically benefit the area of the institution.

The OTM of an institution typically evaluates innovation disclosures for potential commercial value, files for and obtains patents or copyright registrations for those that pass the first hurdle, and then seeks licensees for the subject intellectual property. The institution may also establish a separate entity, such as a limited liability company (LLC) to provide consultation services, potential funding, and business development support for early-stage technology research companies, such as start-ups based on institution-developed intellectual property.

In addition, the institution may help create and associate itself with research parks and technology incubators that offer technical and other resources to nurture the growth of early-stage development projects. These research parks and incubators enhance research and development collaboration between the institution and partners in industry and government. Also, established companies that may benefit from a close working and synergistic relationship with a university's faculty, staff, and physical resources may be attracted to such research parks and incubators and become a licensee of institution-developed innovations.

A successful technology transfer system in a university also assists in recruiting and retaining top-level faculty, staff, and students, while building long-term relationships between the university, its faculty, students and alumni, industry, and public agencies. The benefits to the university, the private sector, and government technology structure is, in my judgment, incalculable.

33.3.2 The Bayh–Dole Act

Enacted by the U.S. Congress in 1980, the Bayh–Dole Act allows small businesses and non-profit organizations, including non-profit universities, to own inventions made under federally funded research programs. Universities are:

- Responsible for the management of inventions in compliance with the Bayh–Dole Act.
- Expected to file patent applications on inventions they elect to own.
- Encouraged to collaborate with commercial concerns via licensing the selected inventions, to promote the utilization of inventions developed under federally funded projects.
- Expected to give licensing preferences to small businesses that demonstrate sufficient capability.
- Submit progress reports to the funding agency.
- Share resulting royalties with the inventors.

The U.S. Small Business Administration (SBA) establishes the definition of a "small business," which varies and is subject to several criteria. To determine if your business qualifies as "small," I suggest you contact the SBA, or have a lawyer knowledgeable in small business matters determine if your business is eligible to benefit from the licensing preference provisions of Bayh–Dole.

Under Bayh–Dole, the federal government retains certain rights to the subject inventions and corresponding intellectual property. These include requiring use of the licensed invention to prevent the licensee from withholding or sequestering an invention from the public, requiring U.S. manufacture for exclusive licenses, and retaining non-exclusive rights for government use of the invention.

33.3.3 Sponsored Research

The university or other institution commonly enters into research agreements involving government and corporate sponsors. External sponsorship agreements define the role of the sponsor in the commercialization process of the intellectual property developed by the university. Material transfer agreements are entered into covering the materials being transferred by the external sponsor into the university for use in the university research programs. Mutual non-disclosure agreements involving the university research and the company or sponsor are also entered into. Importantly, provisions must also be included in such agreements as to the ownership of the intellectual property that is jointly developed during the research project by the university and the external sponsor. In certain situations, the external sponsor obtains the rights to commercialize the results of the joint research program with the university or other institution sharing in the revenues created by such commercialization. These agreements also cover the role of visiting scientists to the university and university facilities. Other agreements may involve material transfer agreements of an outbound nature covering university materials transferred to colleagues and others outside the university.

33.3.4 Patent Filing Decisions

Decisions to file patent applications are made by the OTM. These are business decisions based upon market considerations, the necessity of protection, the probability of success in licensing and recovering expenses, and potential market impact. There is an expectation that all patents filed are potentially commercially valuable enough to recoup at least the expenses of patenting. Periodically, the OTM reviews the patent portfolio, and in cases where the patent is not licensed, the OTM assesses whether to continue the prosecution or maintenance of applications and patents that have been filed previously.

University technology developments usually occur at a very early stage and well in advance of a product or process being ready for the market. The OTM process removes technologies that are not patentable, those that cannot provide an exclusionary position, those that are in a technology area that has been unsuccessfully pursued before, or are in the market area where investment cannot be justified.

International patent considerations involve escalating expenses, and as a consequence, OTMs are much more selective and conservative regarding filing international patent applications than they are in filing U.S. applications. As a general matter, the OTMs pursue the Patent Cooperation Treaty (PCT) and foreign patent applications when the technology has been licensed and the licensee pays such expenses, or in cases where there are significant foreign markets.

Converting a PCT application into a national foreign country or regional application has much greater cost implications than the decision to file in the United States. This is primarily because of the combination of the country-by-country amplification effect, and necessity for translations and the employment of additional attorneys or agents in foreign countries. Furthermore, the laws in foreign countries vary as to the value of patent protection afforded the owner, such that the value of foreign patent protection may be less than the corresponding value in the United States.

33.3.5 Intellectual Property Disclosures/Reports of Research Progress

A typical OTM actively reaches out to faculty and research students to encourage the disclosure of new innovations. A disclosure comprises a written statement outlining a new innovation and documenting the circumstances of its development. A disclosure also identifies potential applications of the technology and what companies might be interested in licensing and commercializing the intellectual property, if that information is known.

Disclosure forms help the OTM begin the process of evaluating the technology transfer and potential for the intellectual property development, and if the disclosure also complies with the obligations of Bayh–Dole. An OTM technology manager is usually assigned to guide a disclosure through the technology transfer process.

Submitting a disclosure form to your OTM does not by itself protect the intellectual property. Only a patent or copyright can accomplish that. Also, disclosure of the technology to your OTM is confidential and is not considered a public disclosure under the Patent Law. However, a disclosure to someone outside the university is a public disclosure unless you have a confidential non-disclosure agreement in place.

It is recommended that inventors submit a disclosure to the OTM between eight and twelve weeks before publication of any information regarding the innovation so that necessary actions can be taken to protect both U.S. and foreign intellectual property rights. Once publicly disclosed, the invention may not be patentable in many important foreign countries. It is wise to inform the OTM of any imminent or prior presentations that include the intellectual property during this eight- to twelve-week period.

Inventors typically meet with OTM staff to discuss their inventions and clarify aspects of the disclosure. Once a decision is made on whether to pursue patenting, the inventor will be contacted to discuss the outcome.

Inventors and OTM professionals communicate with the patent attorney during the patenting process. Also, inventors will need to review drafts of documents, and sign assignments and other legal documentation involving the patentability process. The inventors are usually guided through this signing obligation by the OTM.

33.3.6 Screening, Evaluation, and Assessment

The screening review process leads to a decision to pursue or abandon commercialization efforts for the submitted technology. Within six to eight weeks of receiving the invention disclosure, the OTM staff normally completes a business case analysis, also called a screening evaluation, and recommends a course of action on commercialization. The results of the screening evaluation, which includes patent searches, marketplace analysis, and identification of possible licensees, are then shared with the inventors.

For technologies the OTM decides to patent, an initial patent strategy is identified. In most cases, an independent patent law firm is hired to prepare and prosecute the patent application.

33.3.7 Market Assessment

Detailed analyses, sometimes through the engagement of outside consultants who connect with industry experts, add to the OTM's understanding of the potential market for the technology and help determine further patenting and marketing actions. The inventors themselves often help in identifying interested licensees because the inventors normally have developed many contacts through their own research, and via the alumni of the university.

33.3.8 Release by License or Assignment to Inventor

If the OTM decides not to pursue or to discontinue pursuit of commercialization efforts of an innovation, they will normally release the invention and may assign the university's ownership rights to the inventors if the inventors are interested in independently pursuing a patent and commercialization for the innovation. For any federally funded invention, the federal agency must approve the assignment, which may take weeks or months to finalize.

33.3.9 Marketing or Seeking Partners

The OTM staff engages in a variety of marketing activities to advocate for university research and intellectual property. Time and resources are devoted to understanding market needs and contacting potential partners, either to license existing technologies or to cultivate new relationships such as sponsored research that may lead to licenses. The tools to market a technology vary from industry to industry. Therefore, each OTM engages in activities depending on the situation and technologies.

Such activities may include:

- Showcasing university technologies to venture capitalists, investors, and corporate representatives through OTM-hosted events on campus and around the country.
- Attending trade shows and professional meetings.
- Making calls and sending collateral materials, including brochures and sell sheets.
- Maintaining websites, sending press releases, and using social media to cultivate contacts.
- Creating campaigns to promote portfolios of technologies and hosting events so that inventors can get to know the OTM's services.

Locating interested partners usually takes time since many university innovations are on the cutting edge and well in advance of the needs of the existing marketplace. The OTMs work with inventors to determine the best time to begin to market a technology. Inventors are often quite involved in the early stages of recruiting commercial partners and licensees because the inventors' expertise is often critically important to interface with these potential licensees. Inventors are normally involved in creating the details of pre-licensing agreements. The inventor's role in licensing is a logical extension of their role in marketing since their expertise is often important to transferring the technology and related know-how to the licensee.

If your technology is licensed, you can still continue research using a licensed invention even if it is exclusively licensed. Normal practice allows the university the right to use licensed inventions in further academic research and teaching.

33.3.10 Marketing and Related Agreements or Pre-Licensing

Once the OTM identifies a potential corporate partner or start-up for a technology, non-disclosure agreements are used to protect the confidentiality of any non-public information. Material transfer agreements and evaluation agreements may also be used to provide the outside companies with certain rights to use the technology for short-term evaluation purposes only.

Option agreements reserve the right of a company to negotiate a commercial license. Options may be stand-alone agreements negotiated directly through OTM or may be clauses contained in other agreements, such as sponsored research agreements or a pre-license agreement.

If intellectual property is developed by more than one institution, an inter-institutional agreement is often negotiated to set out the terms under which the two or more universities will cooperate to assess, protect, market, license, and share revenues from the jointly owned property.

33.3.11 Licensing

The goal of the OTM and the inventors is to obtain a license to commercialize the invention. The license is the technology transfer agreement that grants some of the university's rights as the owner of the intellectual property to a company or other organization that has agreed to certain obligations and responsibilities to commercialize the intellectual property. The university licenses its varied technologies through patents, software, databases, and copyrights to companies and organizations that demonstrate the capability and commitment to develop the early-stage innovations into commercial products. Sometimes both the inventors and university agree that the best entity to bring a technology to market is a start-up company.

Whether the licensee is an existing company or a start-up company, licensees also demonstrate such commitment by providing a written technology development plan to the university. This plan includes, but should not be limited to, a description of the technologies to be licensed, the resulting product, a market analysis, a product development timeline, and the company resources committed to development. The terms of the license are also negotiated to reflect the licensee's plan.

33.3.12 License Compliance

After a technology is licensed, the OTM manages the license to be sure that all terms and conditions are adhered to by the licensee and that the technology reaches its fullest potential. If the licensee does not comply, steps are taken to terminate the license, in which case the technology would again be available for licensing to another company.

Other common ways of transferring university intellectual property include academic and research use licenses, creative commons licenses, and open source licenses. Academic and research use licenses permit research institutions or individual researchers to use a program or material free of charge or at a research use rate, but do not permit those institutions to transfer the software or materials to third parties or make commercial use of the technology. Such research use licenses also leave open the possibility of future traditional revenue generating commercial licensing.

Creative commons licenses are a matrix of licenses allowing free use and sharing or redistribution of a copyrighted work with proper attribution. The options include whether modifications to the work can be made, whether the work can be used for commercial purposes, and whether further sharing of the work must carry the same options for redistribution.

Open source licenses allow free and less restricted distribution of software including commercial use, and promote testing and further development and adoption of the software in a collaborative environment. Most federally funded research directed to software development requires open source dissemination. However, open source licenses may limit future proprietary commercial licensing potential.

In the software community, open source is a form where multiple unaffiliated parties have access to the source code of a software program for the purpose of collaborative development. Those who participate in the open source system believe that more scrutiny brings greater reliability, and that the software is an evolving entity that can achieve its fullest potential without the restrictions of commercial sale. As with decisions for publication, the faculty or head of the research program makes the recommendation for open source dissemination or not. Often the decision to release code is made early in the software development process either as a condition for funding, a requirement for participation in the software community, or as a consequence of incorporating third party code that requires placement in the open source. An open source license through the OTM places minimal restrictions on use, thereby maximizing flexibility of use and dissemination of the software program.

Academic and research use licenses are often used for software, biological materials, and data sets, and allow use by other institutions for academic purposes only. Creative commons licenses are often used for literary and artistic works, providing a matrix of options for both academic and commercial uses. Open source licenses are often used for software with the object of making source code available for commercial and non-commercial uses under certain conditions.

All of the three licenses retain copyright for the creator and stipulate proper attribution to the creator when used. Even though such transfers and disseminations do not generate revenue for the university, they promote visibility and public use of the university research, and potentially aid in the university's mission for the public good.

◆ INVENTORS AND INVENTIONS ◆

Ferdinand von Zeppelin

RIGID AIRSHIPS

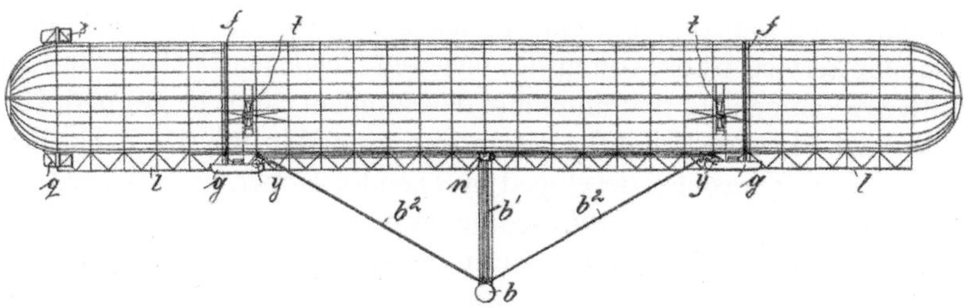

Ferdinand Adolph Heinrich August Graf von Zeppelin was a general in the Prussian Army, and later an aircraft manufacturer who founded the Zeppelin Airship Company. In 1863, Zeppelin took leave of the Prussian Army to act as an observer for the Union Armies of the Potomac in the American Civil War in Virginia. Zeppelin had obtained a pass signed by President Abraham Lincoln that enabled him to travel with the Union army. He traveled to the upper Midwest with a group that probably included two Russians, and was led by Native American guides. The entourage canoed and portaged from the western end of Lake Superior up the St. Louis River and across to Crow Wing, Minnesota. Upon reaching St. Paul, Zeppelin encountered a German-born itinerant balloonist named John Steiner. Steiner invited Zeppelin to make a tethered balloon aerial ascent from a site near the International Hotel in St. Paul. This was Zeppelin's first aerial ascent, and many years later, Zeppelin attributed the beginning of his interest in dirigible lighter-than-air craft to this balloon experience in the United States.

Zeppelin's ideas for large airships was first expressed in a diary entry dated March 25, 1874, in which he outlined the basic principle of a craft including a large, rigid framed outer envelope enclosing several separate gas cells. In 1887, two others in France had successfully constructed an airship, which prompted Zeppelin to send a letter to the King of Württemberg regarding the military necessity for dirigibles, and commenting on the lack of German development in this field.

After his resignation from the Prussian Army in 1891, Zeppelin devoted his full attention to airships, hiring Theodore Gross, an engineer to test materials and to study

Intellectual Property Law for Engineers, Scientists, and Entrepreneurs, Second Edition. Howard B. Rockman.

Published 2020 by John Wiley & Sons, Inc.

available engines for both fuel efficiency and power-to-weight ratio. They also tested propellers, and began to source high-purity hydrogen gas from suppliers.

Zeppelin initially underestimated air resistance, but solved the problem by sourcing light but powerful engines. Zeppelin urged one of his supporters to press Daimler Motoren Gesellschaft to design and build more efficient engines. He wanted to catch up with the French.

Zeppelin's organization constructed a rigid aluminum framework covered in a fabric envelope. Also, multiple separate internal gas cells were installed, each being allowed to expand and contract, thus obviating the need for ballonets. His structure also included a modular frame allowing the addition of sections and gas cells, with controls, engines, and the gondola rigidly attached. Zeppelin submitted his idea to the Prussian Airship Service, whose committee reviewed the idea in 1894, and in June 1895 the committee recommended that minimum development funds be granted. However, this offer was later rescinded, and the design was rejected in July 1895. The design of this particular aircraft was also developed by Theodor Kober, who assisted Zeppelin in the design. In August 1895, Zeppelin's company received a patent for Kober's design, which described the device as an airship-train or a steerable airship-train with several carrier structures arranged one behind another. The patent describes the airship as having three rigid sections, where the front 385-foot-long section is intended to contain the crew and the engines and had a gas capacity of 336,000 cubic feet. The middle section was 52 feet long with a load of 1321 pounds. The rear section was 131 feet long with an intended load of 4400 pounds.

In 1896, Zeppelin presented a lecture on steerable airship designs to the Association of German Engineers (VDI) that impressed the association to initiate a public appeal for financial support for Zeppelin's ideas. This led to a contact with Carl Berg, who supplied aluminum alloys that Zeppelin had tested, and in May 1898, Berg, Zeppelin, Philipp Holzmann, Daimler, Max von Eyth, Carl von Lindee, and Friedrich Voith formed a joint stock company with Zeppelin supplying over half of the total capital.

On July 2, 1900, Zeppelin made the first flight with the LZ1, in southern Germany. The airship rose from the ground and remained in the air for 20 minutes, but was damaged upon landing. The airship was repaired, and two further flights were made in October 1900. However, the government did not see reason to make any further investment in the project. The experiments had exhausted Zeppelin's funds, and he was forced to suspend his work.

However, Zeppelin was still supported by the King of Württemberg, who initiated a state lottery, along with 50,000 marks received from the Prussian government. Zeppelin raised the remainder of the necessary funds by mortgaging his wife's estate. He then constructed his second airship, the LZ2, which was completed by November 1905. A ground handling mishap caused the bow to be pulled into the water, damaging the forward control circuits. Repairs were completed in 1906, and the LZ2 made its only flight. Excessive ballast was jettisoned on takeoff, and the airship rose to an altitude of 1401 feet. A stiff breeze was encountered, and the failure of the forward engine due to cooling problems followed by the failure of the other engine due to a broken clutch spring left the airship at the mercy of the wind. The LZ2 was finally brought down in the nearby mountains, with damage caused by the stern contacting trees during mooring. The airship was severely damaged by high winds the next night, and was dismantled.

In May 1906, Zeppelin began work on a third airship, the LZ3, which had a greater gas capacity than the LZ2. This airship made two successful flights at a ground speed of 30 mph, and obtained a speed of 36 mph in 1907. The success of the LZ3 changed the official attitude toward his work, and the German Reichstag then awarded Zeppelin 500,000 marks to continue his work. The purchase by the government of an airship, however, was conditioned on the successful completion of a 24-hour trial flight. This was beyond the capabilities of the LZ3, and work was started on a larger airship, the LZ4, which first flew on June 20, 1908. A final financial breakthrough came only after the LZ4 was destroyed by fire after breaking free of its moorings during a storm. However, the earlier flights of the airship had initiated such public interest in airships that a subsequent collection campaign raised over 6,000,000 German marks. Following repairs of damage to the LZ3, which occurred when a floating hanger broke free of its moorings during a storm, the airship was lengthened by 8 meters. The LZ3 was re-inflated in October 1908, and a series of test flights lasting 5 hours and 55 minutes took place with the Kaiser's brother onboard. On November 7, 1908, with Crown Prince William as a passenger, the Zeppelin airship flew 50 miles to where the Kaiser was then staying. The flight succeeded, and two days later the LZ3 was officially accepted by the government. On November 10, 1908, Zeppelin received an official visit by the Kaiser. After a short demonstration flight over Lake Konstantz, Zeppelin was awarded the Order of the Black Eagle.

Zeppelin's relationship with the German Army later deteriorated, and one of his company's business directors decided to capitalize on the public enthusiasm for Zeppelin's airship by establishing a civilian passenger transport business in 1910. Up until 1914, the German Aviation Association, which was the company they formed, transported 37,250 people on more than 1600 flights without an incident.

Ferdinand Zeppelin died in 1917, before the end of World War I, and did not live to see the provisional shut down of the Zeppelin project due to the Treaty of Versailles, or the second resurgence of Zeppelin under his successor, Hugo Eckener. Two rigid airships, the world- circling LZ127 Graf Zeppelin, and LZ130 Graf Zeppelin II, twin to the Hindenburg, were named after him.

Zeppelin piloted and commanded most of the early airships he built himself. As a military man, Zeppelin saw his invention primarily in military terms, to be adopted by the Army and Navy, and his early efforts were dedicated to winning their support and convincing the armed forces to purchase and operate his airships. Perhaps as a result of his background as a German aristocrat, he may have seen the idea of carrying paying passengers to generate revenue as unworthy of his ships. Zeppelin ultimately had a very uneasy relationship with the leaders of the German Army and Navy, and the latter did not share the public's enthusiasm for his creations. However, more than 100 Zeppelins were used for military operations in World War I.

The destruction of the Hindenburg in 1937 and the upcoming construction of heavier-than-air aircraft, led to the easing out of lighter-than-air aircraft throughout the world.

As an incidental note, the official website of the rock music group Led Zeppelin dated February 28, 1970, indicates that the name of the British rock group was derived from the Zeppelin airship. Count Zeppelin's granddaughter, Countess Eva von Zeppelin, the website says, once threatened to sue the rock group for illegal use of their family name while the group was performing in Copenhagen.

No. 621,195. Patented Mar. 14, 1899.

FERDINAND GRAF ZEPPELIN.

NAVIGABLE BALLOON.

(Application filed Dec. 29, 1897.)

(No Model.) 4 Sheets—Sheet 1.

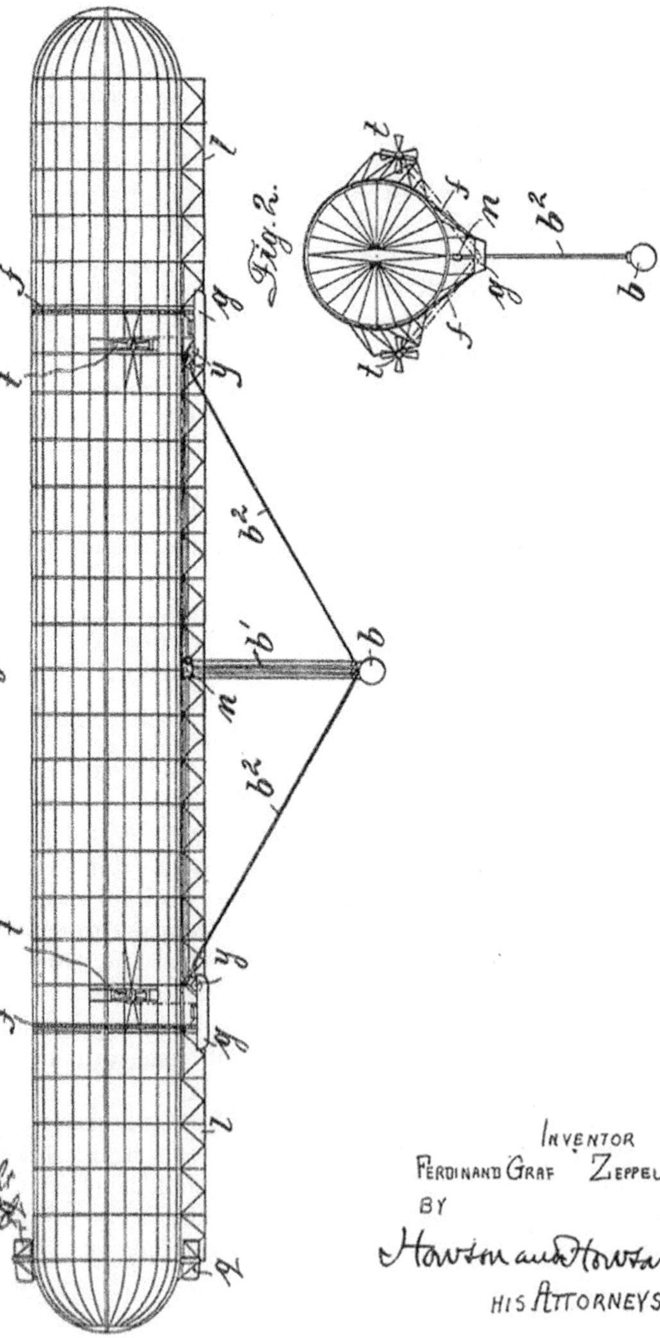

Witnesses:
F. W. Wright
H. L. Abbott

Inventor
Ferdinand Graf Zeppelin
By
Howson and Howson
His Attorneys.

◆ INVENTORS AND INVENTIONS ◆

Bernard Silver and Norman Joseph Woodland

OPTICALLY SCANNED BAR CODE

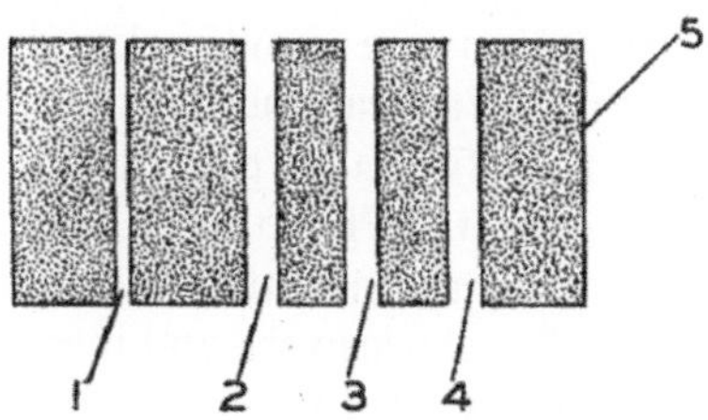

Bernard Silver and Norman Joseph Woodland developed the format that became the Universal Product Code (UPC) which is commonly seen today on product labeling and checkout counters.

In 1948, Bernard Silver and Norman Joseph Woodland collaborated to develop an automated way to read product data. At the time, they were both Drexel Institute of Technology graduate students. Development began when a small food vendor realized the tediousness of keeping track of inventory and prices in their supermarket. The vendor contacted Drexel to seek help in solving this problem. At that time, Drexel showed no interest; however, Bernard Silver overheard the conversation, accepted the challenge, and began investigating the problem. He started by trying to find an automatic solution to keeping a record of the items sold, and soon Silver and some of his students realized that the answer was in ultraviolet rays, scanner, and ink. Silver mentioned the problem to Woodland, and after pondering some preliminary ideas, Woodland was persuaded that they could work together to create a product. The president of the food sales company was particularly looking for a way to automate the checkout process.

Some sources say that Woodland cashed in some stock market earnings, quit his teaching job, and moved to his grandfather's Florida apartment. He was at the beach and was considering the problem posed to him by Silver, and recalled from his Boy Scout days how Morse code dots and dashes were used to send messages electronically. These sources say he drew dots and dashes in the sand similar to the shapes used in the Morse code. He then pulled the dots and dashes downward with this finger, producing thin lines resulting from the dots and thick lines from the dashes. This gave him the

Intellectual Property Law for Engineers, Scientists, and Entrepreneurs, Second Edition. Howard B. Rockman.

Published 2020 by John Wiley & Sons, Inc.

concept of a two-dimensional linear Morse code. After sharing this idea with Silver, and adapting optical film technology, they applied for a patent in October 1949, which patent issued as U.S. Patent No. 2,612,994 on October 7, 1952, covering both linear bar codes and circular bulls-eye printing designs.

Silver and Woodland's initial thought was to use the Morse code extended vertically, producing the narrow and wide bars. Later, however, they changed to using a bulls-eye-type bar code with concentric circular stripes. They also created a prototype using ultraviolet sensitive ink; however, it turned out to be too expensive and unstable for printing patterns.

Silver and Woodland constructed a bar code reader that could read their code electronically. The bar code reader was constructed by Woodland, an IBM employee at the time, and Silver in 1952. This prototype included a 500 watt lightbulb and a photomultiplier vacuum tube made by RCA for movie soundtracks, which were printed optically on film. This prototype was not very practical since the output went to an oscilloscope, and the 500 watt light bulb nearly set fire to the paper containing the first sample bar code. In 1962, the two sold their patent to Philco for $15,000.00, which is all they ever made from their invention. Eventually the invention of the laser in 1960 permitted bar code readers to be manufactured less expensively, and integrated circuit development made decoding of the bar code practical. In 1952, Philco sold the patent to RCA, which attempted to develop a commercial application through the 1960s until the patent expired in 1969, about five years before bar codes were used in grocery stores.

A bar code is a machine readable representation of information in a visual format applied to a surface. Original bar codes stored data in the width and spacings of printed parallel lines, but today readable codes also use patterns of dots, concentric circles, and hidden images. Bar codes today can be read by optical scanners called bar code readers, or scanned from an image by special software.

The initial code symbology developed by Silver and Woodland comprised a dark background with four white lines. The first of the lines was a datum line, with the other lines fixed according to the first line. Information was coded and decoded as the absence and presence of lines; thus, seven different article classifications were permitted using this procedure. It was noted by the inventors that if additional lines were included, more classifications would be possible such that with approximately 10 lines, 1023 classifications were possible.

In 1969, RCA obtained interest from the National Association of Food Chains in bar code technology. RCA and the association then formed the U.S. Supermarket Ad Hoc Committee on the Uniform Grocery Product Code. IBM became involved in 1971 when they discovered Woodland's work and transferred Woodland to their North Carolina facility. Here, Woodland was key in developing the most important version of the technology, the UPC, which eventually prevailed over the RCA system in a competition.

In 1972, a Kroger grocery store in Cincinnati, Ohio, experimented using a bulls-eye bar code reader with assistance from RCA. However, the bulls-eye bar codes were easy to smudge during printing, and were not successful. These bulls-eye codes were not pre-printed on the goods, but applied by the store's employees. This system developed problems, and the stores kept looking for a code where consistency was maintained. Meanwhile, Woodland at IBM was developing the linear bar code that was adopted on April 3, 1973, as the UPC.

On June 26, 1974, the first retail product, which was a 10 pack of Wrigley's Juicy Fruit gum was sold to a customer using a bar code reader. This occurred at Marsch's

Supermarket in Troy, Ohio. From a historical standpoint, it is important to know that this pack of gum is presently displayed in the Smithsonian National Museum of American History in Washington D.C.

Bar codes and other machine readable items such as RFID are employed wherever physical objects are required to be tagged with information to be processed by computers. The operator only has to display the code to the bar code reader. These processes also work well in fully automated environments such as baggage routing at airports. In the simplest case, an identification number is used as an index in a database where the complete information is kept.

In other situations, the bar code itself holds the complete information, without the need for an external database. This procedure eventually evolved into the development of bar code symbologies, which can express more characters. These symbologies range from encoding only the uppercase alphabet, to coding the complete ASCII character set and beyond. The ambition to encode even more information in combination with the space requirements of simple bar codes led to the development of matrix codes, which are 2D bar codes comprising a grid of square cells. Stacked bar codes are a compromise between true 2D bar codes and linear codes. These are formed by taking a traditional linear symbology and applying it to an envelope that allows multiple rows.

Consider this: there are approximately 7.6 billion people in the world today, and it is estimated that 5 billion scans of the UPC take place worldwide every day.

Oct. 7, 1952 N. J. WOODLAND ET AL 2,612,994

CLASSIFYING APPARATUS AND METHOD

Filed Oct. 20, 1949 3 Sheets-Sheet 1

FIG. 1

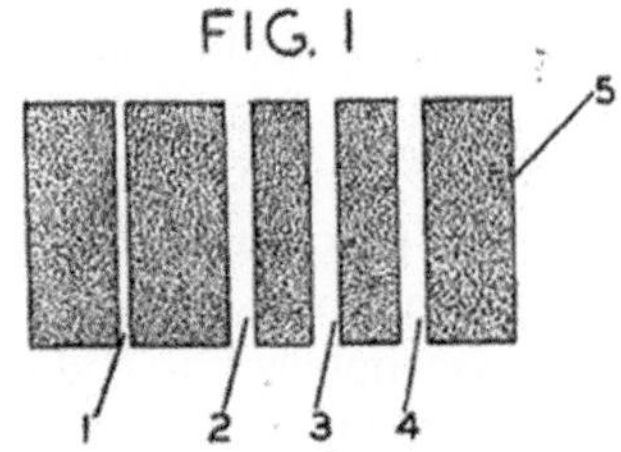

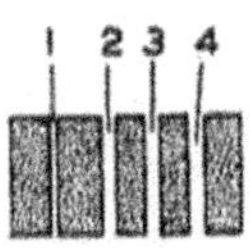

FIG. 2

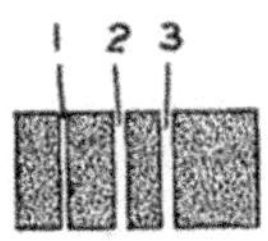

FIG. 3

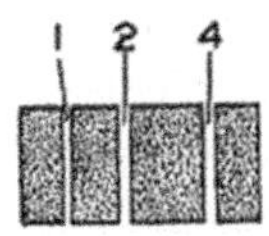

FIG. 4

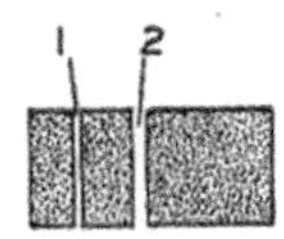

FIG. 5

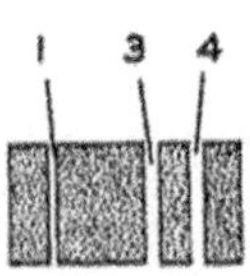

FIG. 6

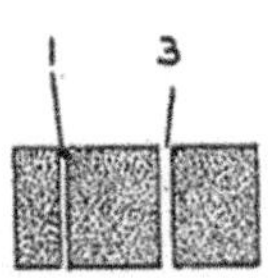

FIG. 7

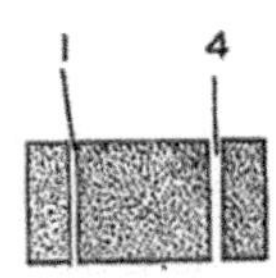

FIG. 8

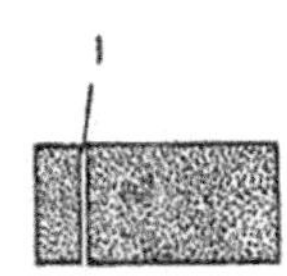

FIG. 9

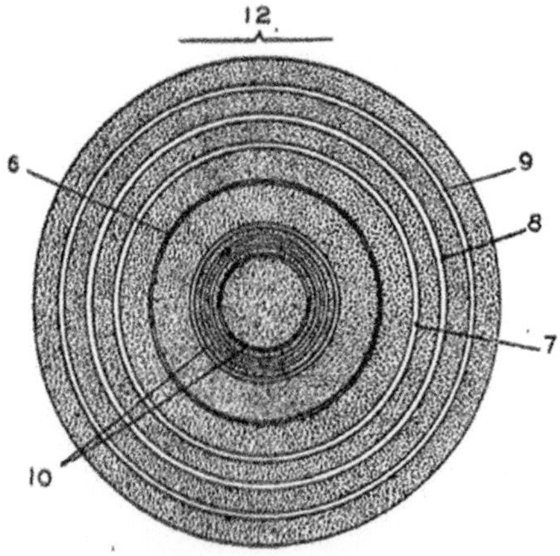

FIG. 10

NOTE: LINES 6, 7, 8, AND 9 ARE LESS REFLECTIVE THAN LINES 10.

INVENTORS:
NORMAN J. WOODLAND
BERNARD SILVER
BY THEIR ATTORNEYS
Howson & Howson

34 International Intellectual Property Creation, Protection, and Enforcement Strategies

34.1 INTRODUCTION

In developing international marketing and distribution for your new product or process incorporating your new innovation, consideration should be given to (1) targeting international intellectual property (IP) protection, including where you are projecting international commercialization, (2) the availability of IP protection and obtaining it in international settings, and (3) IP sharing. The IP laws of every country govern the use and enforcement of IP in that country. There is, with the exception of the European Union and other regional IP consortiums, no true international IP law. Foreign laws govern the use of IP in each foreign country. If a company or a person fails to gain IP protection in a country where that IP is being used, the IP will typically be freely usable by others with no limitations. It must be borne in mind that because many countries' laws must be considered and their respective procedures must be followed to gain IP protection in the various countries, it is often quite expensive to gain protection for an invention across the world in all of the countries in which IP might be important. Therefore, the range of countries where protection is sought is typically given careful thought and is limited by costs.

Technical IP will often need to be protected in many countries. For example, an electrical engineering advance developed in Belgium might be patented there for convenience by the research and development staff responsible for the advance. However, if that advance had commercial significance, another dimension of protection would be to protect the development through IP, where related products would be produced so that parties that were working with the technology in production facilities would be limited in how they could handle and reuse the IP in those countries. Furthermore if there are commercially significant products that are being produced that include the new IP, there would be a need to gain protection in the countries where the products are being or will be substantially marketed.

Another consideration in international IP protection is that foreign IP originators are given the same treatment as citizens of each country under the IP laws of each country, such that citizens and non-citizens of a given country are equal both with respect to rights and ownership of IP. Thus, when a party from the United States goes overseas, they are accorded IP ownership and IP rights similar to those accorded to citizens of those countries. Also, foreign IP originators will have the same rights in the United States as IP originators here. So, this principle of neutrality of equal treatment

Intellectual Property Law for Engineers, Scientists, and Entrepreneurs, Second Edition. Howard B. Rockman.

Published 2020 by John Wiley & Sons, Inc.

in international IP law, sometimes referred to as national treatment, is very important, because it means that foreign parties receive the same treatment as nationals or citizens of a given country.

Although there are generally no international IP rights per se, there are several important processes that somewhat streamline the country-by-country filings to obtain IP rights. In the patent area, the process is often referred to under the treaty that set it up, the Patent Cooperation Treaty (PCT) discussed at Chapter 16. Similarly, and more recently, the U.S. Trademark Law has adopted the Madrid Protocol, which allows for assistance in multi-country trademark filings to obtain trademark rights in multiple countries discussed in Chapter 29. The Berne Convention, discussed in Chapter 24, provides worldwide enforcement of copyrights.

It is often important for parties who are considering originating or using IP to make decisions about IP creation, protection, and use well in advance of carrying out the commercialization effort, to ensure both an efficient process of obtaining full international IP rights, and also to ensure that proper steps are taken to gain all available IP rights in an effective manner. A delay in seeking IP rights may preclude those rights from being obtained, particularly with respect to patentable inventions.

34.2 IP CREATION STRATEGIES TO MAXIMIZE GLOBAL IP PROTECTION

General issues should be addressed by a party considering how to create IP and gain the maximum IP rights to implement a program of protected international commercialization of a newly developed product or process. There are decisions to be made not only about IP protection, although these are a central consideration, but also considerations about where to produce the product implementing the new IP and where to provide funding that will support the production of IP. Considerations include (1) where investment sources and methods will be most effective, (2) where the technology development program will be most effective, (3) where IP protections are needed and can be obtained in an effective manner, (4) where subsequent product production process may be carried out, and (5) where product marketing processes may be effective.

34.2.1 Investment Sources

Investment sources are often a key feature of the production of new IP, such as in what countries investments are sought, and where a company may establish its facilities and its investment generation activities. The choices of investment sources depend typically on the location of the investors themselves, the efficiency and integrity of the related securities markets and the laws that govern those markets, and limitations on foreign investments. If the new product is to be made in a given country where foreign investment is difficult, that country may have to be ruled out as a new IP development target. The ability to move funds into the technical development location will also affect how easy it is to bring investment from a foreign setting to a given country, and therefore how easy it is to develop IP with funds that come from a foreign source. The ability to move profits out of that country may also affect the choice as well. It would not be advantageous to have a profitable entity subsequently find that the monies generated cannot be brought back to the investors because of limitations on movement of profits out of the country in which the profits were generated. And finally, if key development partners are physically located in a given country, that may favor that country as a source of investment for a new technical enterprise.

34.2.2 Technology Development Location Choices

The technology development program location choices depend on where effective technical expertise and supporting resources can be found. If there is a community of experts with the relevant technical expertise in a country, then that country will become a possible technology development target. Conversely, if there is very little expertise in a given country, that would probably be an important negative factor. Supporting resources that certain lines of production or types of production require are also considerations in locating an IP production effort in a given country. The strength of private physical and process protections for technologies, and the degree to which either physical security and supported resources promoting physical security are available in a given country may be factors in making the country an attractive target for IP development. The strength of legal protections for newly developed technology is also often very important as the new technology is being developed. If anyone abuses that IP in the early stages, it is helpful to have strong IP protections in place to ensure not only remedies, but also established deterrents against that kind of abuse.

Finally, the availability of local IP professionals to take the steps necessary to gain IP protection, such as patent or trademark filings and prosecution, will be critically important because typically the IP will be protected in the country where it was first originated as a first step toward a broader international protection plan. The availability of IP protection in the various countries that are possible production choices will also affect the location choices for the development of new IP. The country laws mentioned earlier will often be a substantial factor in determining what can be and cannot be protected by the IP laws of those countries. If the particular technology is a type that is not eligible for protection under the IP laws of the particular country, or the scope of the protections or the type of material that is intended to be developed are weak in a given country, that may rule the country out for selection as an IP origin source.

In addition to the substantive scope of the IP laws, the difficulties in gaining protection, particularly the nature of the procedures that a party filing for IP protection needs to go through, would be a consideration as well. It is one thing to say that the IP law "can" cover a certain type of IP, but if it is very difficult to gain the needed IP protection, the country is not a favorable IP protection location.

A question would be whether it is practically convenient as a matter of administrative ease to go to a second country for the first round of foreign IP protection. The scope of protection that would be available under the IP laws of the different countries determines the scope of protection one gets as a patent holder or copyright holder under those laws, and what kinds of remedies for infringement are readily available. Obviously, this has some bearing on the strength of the IP protections and the importance in seeking those protections as a first foreign IP protection vehicle. If the subsequent product production plans include the country of IP origination, that would be a second reason to choose that country because there now are two different reasons to gain IP protection there: one, the original protection of the early-stage IP, and two, the protection during the production phase. Similarly, if that foreign country is on the list for product marketing, there is a further reason to select it for IP development because there would be dual reasons to gain IP protection, protecting both the development process and the marketing process.

34.2.3 Product Production Location Choices

Once IP is already in existence, there would be further choices to make regarding where to produce the products based on that new IP, such as choices of where to produce the product and also possible new needs for IP protection. The factors affecting the location choice regarding product production include labor and other production costs in the various countries in which the product might be produced, the availability of component inputs needed for production, other materials needed to produce the new product, and the availability of potential subcontractors who could furnish some of the work needed to produce the product. It may make little sense to take new IP into a country with extremely weak IP protection for production purposes, since that will increase the number of persons familiar with the IP and therefore increase the risks of IP misuse and infringement.

Another consideration is the size of the in-country market for the products being produced. It is often very convenient to both produce and market the products in a single country, and if there is a large market to be served in that country, it would make sense to have production activities there as well. The size of a nearby country's markets is also important, applying the similar logic that it is easy to ship products across country boundaries to nearby markets. This also enhances the desirability of the country where the product is being produced. As a related matter, the cost of transportation to those nearby markets is a factor because if the transportation costs overshadow the merit of the size of the nearby markets, that would undercut the availability of nearby large markets as a desirable factor in choosing a country for production purposes.

Some additional factors also affect the choice of where to produce products. These include patterns of product counterfeiting in particular countries. Countries known for having a track record involving counterfeiting of similar products would be less desirable as a production site because similar counterfeiting would be expected to be a significant risk for the new product. Similarly, the follow-up and strength of follow-up of IP law enforcement in that country, including how seriously public officials take IP and will pursue significant IP misuse with public sanctions such as criminal penalties, will be factors in how that country would be perceived as a production target.

Also consider the strength of product quality laws in those countries, particularly where those quality laws might be used to prevent counterfeits from being marketed and thereby protect the originator of the real product. These are the factors that could combat counterfeits and complement IP protections as a means of combating counterfeiting efforts.

Unfair competition laws can also be used to combat IP misuse in many countries. Factors such as trade secret theft are handled as a matter of unfair competition, and therefore the strength of those laws has a bearing on preventing improper use of IP in one of those countries. The strength of private processes for identifying counterfeits is also important because if the counterfeits pass unnoticed along with the legitimate goods, then the various legal processes that might be triggered by counterfeited efforts will never be initiated and the counterfeits will have a substantial negative impact on the commercialization of the products based on the new IP. Finally, cultural attitudes to the propriety of copying vary in different countries: if copying is viewed as a normal day-to-day matter, it is unlikely there will be any resistance to copying, or that parties who are beneficiaries of copying will see anything wrong in utilizing the fruits of a counterfeiting effort.

34.2.4 Marketing Considerations

Factors that may affect the choice of marketing processes may include the size of the potential customer base in particular countries; the probable prices the market will bear in those countries; how the new product will compete against other products that satisfy similar consumer needs; the ability to distribute, market, and establish retail settings related to the products based on new IP; and the linkages to existing products and marketing. Also, will the new product based on new IP aid in the marketing of your products that are already being presented in particular countries and thereby aid in the commercial benefits to the company in an overall marketing sense? The scope of IP protections afforded to products and marketing programs entails not only protections against misuse of the IP in the products themselves, but also protections of legitimate marketing efforts against false advertising or other misuse of the marketing processes that would hinder the ability to successfully present the new products to the targeted markets. Finally, there is the ability to market to multicultural regions of countries and thereby establish marketing that actually covers multiple areas of countries in an efficient manner.

The separate enforcement against marketers beyond the producers of counterfeit goods is an important factor in considering the marketing process where the counterfeit items are made outside the country where the marketing occurs. The key question for enforcement of IP laws or other laws is whether the infringing marketers, retailers, and/or distributors can be curtailed by the national laws, thus bringing their activities to a halt; because combating the actual counterfeit production activities may be infeasible because they are outside the country where the unlawful marketing is occurring. Finally, the enforcement of IP laws against infringers, that is, the parties that buy the counterfeit goods and use them, may also be an effective means of working against counterfeit sales. Can actions be brought against these users effectively under the IP laws of the country where the marketing is being considered?

34.3 LEGAL CONSIDERATIONS REGARDING WHERE TO OBTAIN IP PROTECTION

34.3.1 Legal Concerns

There are particular legal issues that may affect where to seek protection for new IP. What are the substantive legal issues that determine in which countries, other than the country of invention, to file international patent applications, as a party goes forward with new IP? For discussion purposes, let us think of this as IP that was created in the United States, and for which U.S. IP protections have already been applied for. What other countries would the originator of that IP want to seek protection in?

In determining where else to seek protection, some of the substantive legal issues that will determine that answer include particularly the scope of protectable obtainable subject matter, as mentioned before. If the subject matter of the IP that has been produced or is intended to be produced is unprotectable in certain jurisdictions, those will be unwise jurisdictions for further IP-related production activities or IP-related marketing activities. There simply will be no legal recourse against the use of IP in those countries by others.

Beyond the basic question of whether the type of subject matter can be protected, the standards that govern particular issues, especially the standards governing patent availability, including the standards under which the newness or novelty of the invention will be measured under those laws of the country being considered will be important. Some countries look to whether a given invention has ever been produced anywhere in the world and will consider it not novel and not available for patenting if it is available in public records anywhere in the world prior to your first IP filing date. Other countries have additional more narrow views of novelty and will measure novelty based on whether the invention appears in records of public documents or usage in the country in which patenting is being sought. So, the scope of standards for measuring an invention's novelty can often determine whether protection will be available in a given country.

Another consideration governing patent availability in many countries is the degree of IP description and disclosure that is needed to gain protection in that country. It may be that detailed disclosures are required, and that a company does not want to disclose the full range of trade secrets that will be needed to obtain a patent in a given country. The company may therefore consider that country an undesirable target for patent protection. Further considerations include the ability of a patent holder to limit the use of the patented item if the rights that would be obtained from gaining a patent in a given country would not be significant, and would not allow significant limitations to be imposed on parties that misuse the patented item without permission.

Then it might not be favorable to go through the patenting process in that country since the rights that come out of that process would not be worth the time and resources. And then finally the lack of an enforcement impact of the patents in that country may make obtaining protection there unwise. If the degree of commercial activity that is contemplated in the country involved is going to be small, then there is no substantial reason to pursue the cost of obtaining a patent in that country.

34.3.2 Procedural Concerns

Beyond the substantive legal issues mentioned previously, there are procedural considerations that will determine in which countries, other than the country of invention, parties may wish to file patent applications. These procedural issues typically are related to the costs of seeking further protection by pursuing procedures for obtaining a patent in a second or third country after the initial country process goes forward.

The procedural issues to be considered as parties examine in which additional countries to pursue patent protection include questions of filing fees to gain an additional patent application in that country, the availability of local consult and associations in that country to work with the patent laws of the target country, and to assess both how a patent application should be different in content and different in procedural handling because of the peculiarities of the laws of the additionally targeted countries. The nature of the application document needed to be filed and the differences in those documents from the prior applications are important considerations. If the disclosures and document contents are about the same as for the first round of protection, it will be easy to produce a second set of country filings. On the other hand, if the disclosures needed in the second or subsequent country are significantly different from the disclosures made in the first country of protection, the costs in making a second subsequent filing will typically be larger.

Another consideration is, how long will the application examination process take? This is particularly important since in many countries, including the United States, the duration of protection depends on the particular period from the date of filing the patent application, such that a long period of application processing works against the rights holder by shortening the effective period of rights availability for enforcement.

A very important feature that varies substantially from country to country involves the amounts of maintenance fees that need to be paid if a patent is obtained and is desired to be kept enforceable. Maintenance fees are essentially fees needed to be paid to keep the patent alive, to keep it enforceable, and in many countries they can be high. These fees need to be paid over the life of the patent so it is often the case that an initial period of protection can be obtained at modest expense with higher maintenance fees to be paid later in the patent term. But the overall scope of these fees and when they need to be paid is an important consideration in seeking patent protection in additional countries.

34.4 MARKETING AND BUSINESS CONCERNS

Important considerations about where to file for IP protection beyond the initial country relate to business issues stemming from the potential size of the markets in those countries.

34.4.1 Potential Market Size

One business consideration that determines which countries other than the original country of IP protection should be targets of additional IP protection include, first of all, market location. Is the second targeted country one in which a marketing effort will have possible regional implications and therefore be particularly important? As spillover affects the marketing in broader settings, it would be a logical target of IP protections. Typically for patent purposes, the market should be at least five million U.S. dollars in size (varying by product and industry) to justify consideration as a target of further patent protection related to marketing. Anything less than this amount suggests that the profits related to marketing in that additional country would be eaten up by the costs of obtaining that protection, and by the costs of establishing a new marketing effort there.

However, a market that is currently below this five million dollar threshold might still be targeted because it is an emerging market and the company involved wants to establish a strong marketing effort with strong IP protections to be ready for market growth that will increase its sales more substantially. In addition, the market might be important because it will be served by the production in the first country of IP production. For example, if a new product based on IP is going to be produced under patent protection in the United States, it might make substantial sense to protect markets that will be served by exports from that U.S. production. Certainly that would entail markets such as Canada, Mexico, and perhaps Europe.

But in whatever country there are expected to be follow-on marketing activities based on production in the original country of protection, those markets should be targets of additional IP protections as well. Also, markets in which "cargoed" products are important may be targets for IP protection of a base product. For example, a copier that has substantial patented components might be sold in a given market. The total profits available to the patent holder in that market would not only be those from the patented copier equipment itself but from other products such as ink or toner cartridges that are conveniently bought by consumers when they buy the patented product and are carried along as cargo, meaning additional sales of unpatented items in the sales of the patented item undertaken in the same jurisdiction. If these additional cargoed products are substantial in number, the profits from those can significantly expand the importance of a given market for the patented item.

34.4.2 Product Life Cycle and Other Factors

Another factor that might make a country a desirable target for additional patent protection includes the life cycle of the product that would be protected by a patent in that country. If the life cycle of the product will be brief, the merit of the patent protection in that country may be equally brief, and so obtaining a patent might not be cost-effective. This may occur if the product is likely to be superseded by other products that do not include the patented feature.

Another consideration would be: is a given target country both a marketing target and a production target? If a country is expected to be the site of a significant manufacturing plant, then that will expand the reasons to obtain IP protection there, even if the marketing activity in that country is anticipated to be rather small.

Another significant advantage of additional patent protection in further countries may be that those additional patents will serve as defensive patents that can fend off patent suits from competitors in those interested countries. If competitors in the additional countries already have a large number of patents in those countries, they may be very aggressive in enforcing them against new market entries. If the company presenting a new technology obtains defensive patents, then these defensive patents can be used either in counter-suits or as a deterrent against the initiation of suits by those already established competitors.

34.4.3 Taxes

Taxes may have a bearing on whether production activities in a remote country are desirable. In some situations, there are significant tax advantages to producing goods in a remote setting and bringing them for marketing purposes into a different country. Those tax advantages may make a country desirable as a production source, which in turn means that IP protection for that production source will become more important.

34.5 NON-PARIS CONVENTION AND NON-PCT COUNTRY PATENT PROTECTION

There are a few countries that are not part of the Paris Union Convention (see Chapter 16), and some that are not members of the PCT. If patent protection is sought in any of these countries, corresponding patent applications must be filed in these countries immediately after a foreign filing license has been obtained, if the initial patent application is filed in the United States, and before any public disclosure of the invention anywhere in the world. If necessary, the United States Patent and Trademark Office (USPTO) may be requested to expedite the issuance of the foreign filing license. Consult with your patent professional to sort out those countries where immediate patent application filings have to be made, and those others in which you have one year to file a corresponding patent application.

34.6 FILING A PCT PATENT APPLICATION FIRST

A special strategy where a company sees commercial potential in a new IP-based product is available in only a specific smaller number of countries. In this setting, instead of filing an initial application in the United States or the company's home country, the company might file a PCT application at the outset that designates the United States (or the home country) and names additional countries of interest as the designated recipients of the follow-on country-by-country applications. In addition, any non-Paris Convention and non-PCT countries should be the target of immediate filings as well. The advantage of this approach over the ones discussed previously is there is essentially only one initial filing through the PCT process that covers all of the countries that may be of interest. This would be the efficient route in lieu of pursuing both initial U.S. or home country filing, and a separate PCT filing at a later point. It would also gain priority rights in the countries initially designated. However, this strategy does have the downside that the parties need to decide which countries they are going to seek protection in through the PCT process at the outset so that the ability to delay consideration for the longer PCT application will not be one of the benefits gained.

34.7 JOINT VENTURE RELATIONSHIPS

34.7.1 Why Create a Joint Venture

Established IP, particularly patent rights, can be a vehicle for constructing commercial joint venture relationships. The potential roles of IP rights in a joint venture include establishing the value of the contributions of the joint venture partners, increasing the willingness of new partners who have not had previous relationships to engage in trust with their copartners, establishing terms and limitations of the activities of the joint venture, and defining the nature of monitoring and enforcement strategies regarding parties outside the joint venture who might be competitors or abusers of the IP upon which the joint venture is based.

There are a number of reasons that parties might enter into a joint venture based on sharing of IP. These include the fact that the partners in the joint venture have complementary technology expertise. One party may have strong expertise in a portion of the product design, and the other may have strong expertise in another portion, such as marketing. Together they can produce and sell better products than either could alone.

Another reason to create a joint venture based on IP sharing is that the parties have complementary technology and design expertise. One party may have expertise in the raw technology, and another party might have expertise in how to design follow-along products, so together they can produce better products than either could separately.

Another version of a joint venture based on IP sharing is one in which the operational expertise of one of the parties is combined with the technological expertise of the second party to create a setting where the product production or product marketing expertise is added to the raw technological knowledge of the additional party.

Another version of the joint venture that is often very productive is where one of the parties to the joint venture has unused manufacturing capacity and can, by joining with a party that needs a product that can be produced with that capacity, produce a particularly effective joint venture that makes efficient use of the manufacturing capacity overall.

Yet another version of a joint venture based on IP sharing would be one in which one of the parties has a service expertise that can be combined with the IP holder's manufacturing capability such that the joint venture can not only sell but also service the items being produced and marketed by the joint venture.

34.7.2 Drawing Investment to the Joint Venture

34.7.2.1 The Strength of IP Assets

A joint venture based on sharing of IP can achieve significant advantages in drawing investment through the use of IP rights. IP rights can define assets that are brought to the joint venture to be combined with cash investments by investors in the same joint venture, and the IP rights and the potential for profits that stem from those rights become an asset that can be compared with the cash investments of the other participants who are coming forward as pure investors. In addition, those IP rights may reassure the parties who are bringing forward dollar investments about the potential for the business activity they are becoming involved with. IP rights establish exclusive marketing opportunities and potential profits that arise from those exclusive opportunities, and those will be the sources of return on investment that will attract many new investors to a joint venture based on commercialization of new IP.

The IP rights may also define and facilitate later product marketing and commercialization. They will establish the frameworks in which product distribution and commercialization will occur, and finally, these rights will be a key feature of preparing the company for a possible buyout and exit strategy.

IP rights define assets for bargaining with investors in particularly useful ways. At business founding, they can establish that an inventor or a technology specialist who has experience in a particular technology has something to contribute of immediate value to the business at the time of business founding, such that other parties that are bringing forward cash contributions feel that they are being joined by other important assets at business founding. In this setting, the early-stage co-owners will see a desirable bargain in their contribution of cash assets and the contribution, typically via assignment of patents involved, of the technology specialist as they form a new joint venture or other new business entity. As the business entity is formed and then operates, and produces new IP, that new IP can form the basis for additional funding. Advantages of using additionally generated IP as the basis for seeking new funding is that typically the additional IP will have an extended duration beyond whatever IP was initially brought to the company, particularly whatever patents were brought to the company at the outset. And so newly generated IP can establish new levels of business potential in the future, as well as, perhaps new technologies of business control that can be the basis for seeking additional funding as the business grows and goes forward.

34.7.2.2 Reassuring Investors

IP rights can reassure investors in a new joint venture in several ways. The most important is they provide long-term reassurance against free riders, the notion that but for IP limitations on the use of new technologies or new product designs based on new IP, other companies could utilize those designs, make profits out of them, and act as free riders not paying for any of the product technology development costs. In that regard, patents in particular are often fundamental business tools to give assurance that parties making investments in new technology and new product developments will be the primary partners to receive the return from that investment.

IP rights may also be important in informing investors or potential investors about the likely scope for later IP policing efforts by the company. The IP rights define under what circumstances uses of the company's IP by others will be deemed improper or unlawful, and therefore provide the company the ability to limit the activities of a competitor, as well as to seek monetary remedies from a competitor. So, in essence the IP rights establish a certain range of plans for the company regarding IP policing and IP monitoring efforts in the future.

34.7.2.3 Technology Licensing

Finally, with respect to the possibilities of returns on investments, IP rights can establish the bases for technology transfers in addition to the company's primary business strategy. What this typically means is that IP rights give the company an opportunity for technology licensing efforts that can make the company's technology available, at a substantial profit through the licensing process, to businesses that are not engaged in the same business or primary business category. This whole licensing process, however, is possible because the earlier-obtained IP rights impose limitations on the use of the technology by other parties, except when a party obtains a license from the originating company.

34.7.2.4 IP as a Foundation of Marketing Strategies

IP rights can be important in helping to draw investment to a joint venture by establishing the viability of later product marketing and commercialization steps in several ways. For example, IP rights can induce a party with significant product development abilities to be involved in a project as the exclusive licensee of a given technology. Or a party can be involved as the exclusive marketer of a patented product, thereby establishing a market strategy that turns on the IP rights involved. The scope of IP rights in particular markets can define the profit potential for those markets as well as the desire for marketing channels to fully realize those profits. The scope of IP rights themselves will help the company define the markets it will pursue in the future and the types of marketing it will undertake to maximize profits from those markets, and thereby inform investors of where the company will be going in those key business areas. In addition, as the company carries out marketing-related efforts, such as distribution, the ability to assure a distributor or retailer that they will be exclusive parties able to market a given patented product will help to establish those relationships and reassure those additional business partners of their opportunities as they come forward to be distributors and retailers.

34.7.2.5 *IP and Buyout Strategies*

One last step in which IP rights will be important, both in the future of a company that is commercializing a new technology, and also to investors as they think about investing money into such a company during the early stages of activity, is that IP rights help define the buyout and exit strategies of a company that has continued to develop new technology. It is frequently the case for a small company that has a new technology under development to be contemplating an end of a process in which that technology has been proven to be a viable commercial vehicle, and the company itself therefore becomes a buyout target for acquisition by a much larger entity. The IP rights would be part of the bundle of company assets that would be sold with the company in that buyout process. At the end of the early stages of company activities where the company is a buyout target, the company ideally will have proven the viability of the product designs based on its new technology, the ability to manufacture related follow-on products, and the ability to market the related products to at least a limited extent. This will enable the company to show to a larger company considering a buyout, that the technology and the related products are successful commercial vehicles worthy of being brought to a broader set of marketing and production levels by the large company. In this setting, IP rights are an important part of the package because if the company considering the corporate purchase can be reassured they will be the only ones marketing the patented item after the corporate buyout, they will be interested in spending the substantial amounts required to acquire the technology. Thus, IP rights that define the future commercial opportunities that will come with the corporate buyout also deter the acquiring company from simply using the technology without executing the buyout. These are key parts of establishing that a rising company is worthy of a corporate buyout.

This has implications earlier in the company's life for investors such as venture capital specialists who are contemplating investment in a company with the expectation that the company will be successful and will be a buyout candidate down the road. If the venture capitalists cannot be reassured of at least some early-stage enforceable IP rights and that the company will be a buyout candidate with IP rights at a later point, then the venture capitalists will not be interested in the company at the earlier stage either. Thus, developing IP rights at an early stage with the idea of making them part of the bundle of assets available for buyout at a later point is a key piece of the strategy establishing the buyout and exit strategy for the company in a buyout process.

34.8 FORMING A JOINT VENTURE BASED ON IP

The key in bringing together joint venture parties based on sharing IP where the parties have not previously engaged with each other in projects is the establishment of a careful management follow-up process to the sharing of IP, particularly where sharing of IP is part of this new effort together. It is typically important for the parties to work together on a more formal basis until they establish a trust between them that will allow for more informal activities and interactions down the road. The key question is often what kinds of formal steps should new IP-sharing partners be thinking about as they share IP, including when IP is shared across national boundaries.

Questions of IP management, and particularly IP management in international settings, are extremely complex and vary company to company and industry to industry. Some of the major considerations in these initial formal IP management techniques are that first the IP management system in this setting should aim at reasonable diligence to ensure that the commercial potential of the IP is fully realized and that the IP involved is not abused or infringed in ways that will harm the success of the joint venture or the IP owner. Reasonable diligence suggests that not every opportunity will be realized and not every mistake will be prevented, but that reasonable cost-effective efforts will be taken toward achieving these goals. The risks of either missing an IP opportunity or allowing IP misuse should be constantly under consideration as features of the joint venture are plotted out and executed. Risk assessment in this regard should be the basis of designing the enterprise; implementing steps to carry forward the commercialization effort; evaluating how IP is being handled, administered, and updated along the way; and periodically redesigning the process of IP sharing and IP commercialization. The entire management system here is one of cycles in which risk assessment is made, reacted to, and then reassessed and re-reacted to over time as the enterprise goes forward.

Components of the management system, with respect to IP usage, would include the same types of management components as any corporate management process of importance to the entity. And these would include, with respect to IP, setting standards about how IP of significant commercial importance should be handled, should be addressed and constantly updated, and should be considered in both production and marketing decisions. Training in IP administration by those that will have access to IP, taking into account that in some settings IP has not been a major feature of the business to this point and that key individuals may not be experienced with handling sensitive IP in the past, requires training about the important considerations and important handling techniques of IP.

Monitoring of the administration of IP actually entails two different types of assessments. One is to consider whether the IP of interest is being used to maximum advantage, which is essentially a business analysis and opportunity assessment, and the second is to determine whether the IP that the company thinks is being protected is in fact being carried forward with protection. Both legal interests are needed to protect the business interests of the company and provide additional IP protection by limiting physical access to the IP.

◆ INVENTORS AND INVENTIONS ◆

Godfrey Hounsfield and Allan Cormack

CAT SCANNER

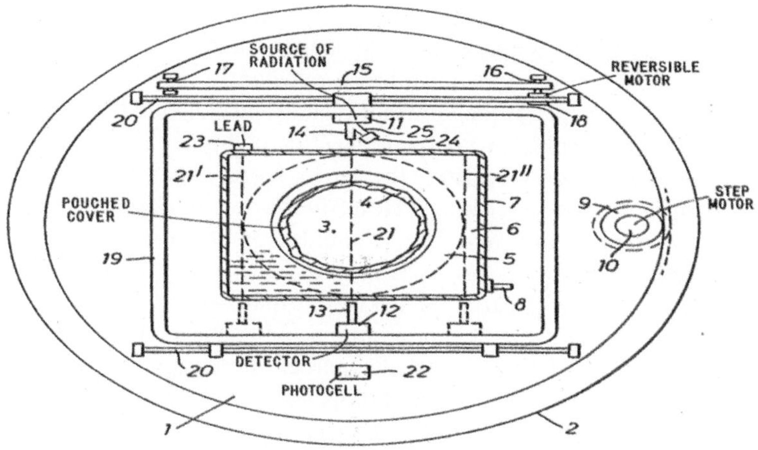

Godfrey Hounsfield and Allan Cormack shared the 1979 Nobel Prize for physiology/medicine for developing the diagnostic technique of X-ray computed tomography, known as CT, or computerized axial tomography (CAT) scanning. This scanning technology allows doctors to visualize the soft tissues inside the body, unlike conventional X-ray, which produces only the outlines of bones and organs. CT scanning uses a computer to produce detailed cross-sectional images or slices of the body such that doctors can examine the body in one narrow slice at a time to pinpoint specific areas of medical concern.

The CT scan was invented in 1972 by two scientists working independently. One was British engineer Godfrey Hounsfield of EMI Laboratories, who invented the CT scan in England, and South-African-born physicist Allan Cormack of Tufts University, who invented it in the United States. The first CT scanners were installed between 1974 and 1976 and originally designed to scan only the head. Whole-body systems became available in 1976.

Godfrey Hounsfield was an English electrical engineer who initially was fascinated by the electrical gadgets and machines found at his parents' farm. In 1949, Hounsfield joined EMI Limited in England, where he researched guided weapons systems and radar. At EMI, he also became interested in computers, and in 1958, helped design the first commercially available, all-transistor computer made in Great Britain.

Intellectual Property Law for Engineers, Scientists, and Entrepreneurs, Second Edition. Howard B. Rockman.

Published 2020 by John Wiley & Sons, Inc.

While on an outing in the English countryside, Hounsfield thought of an idea that could enable one to determine what was inside a box by taking several X-ray readings around the box. He then constructed a computer that could take the input from X-rays at several angles to create an image of the object inside the box in slices. Applying this idea to the medical field, he eventually envisaged what is known today as computer tomography. At that time, Hounsfield was not aware of the work that Cormack had done on the theoretical mathematics for such a device.

In 1969, Dr. James Ambrose, a neuroradiologist at a hospital in London, received a call from an engineer named Godfrey Hounsfield of EMI. Hounsfield had contacted Dr. Ambrose to introduce him to his work on reconstructing a 3-D image of an item in a box by considering the image as a series of slices. Hounsfield had previously been dismissed as a crank by many renowned radiologists, and Ambrose likewise initially dismissed Hounsfield's ideas. Later, Ambrose reluctantly met with Hounsfield to discuss Hounsfield's concept. At the time that Hounsfield contacted Ambrose in 1969, Hounsfield had already built a prototype of his first computer tomography scanner. The word *tomography* is derived from the Greek word *tomos* meaning "slice" or "section." *Graphica* means "describing." Hounsfield's device took multiple thin photographic slices of objects that were later combined on the computer to create 3-D composite images.

In the late 1960s, using a research budget of less than $40,000, Hounsfield and his team of three (an electronics expert, a programmer, and a mechanic) built a prototype CT scanner on the bed of a lathe. Hounsfield's earlier photographs of the prototype in use were those of pig bodies and human brains obtained from a museum. The first scanner took nine days to capture a full 3-D image, and operated by rotating the scan mechanism around an object one degree at a time for 160 traverses, using gamma rays as its light source. Hounsfield later switched the energy source to X-rays, reducing the scanning time to nine hours.

It was Ambrose who sent Hounsfield the human brain from a local museum to test. Five weeks later, Ambrose received the first brain images produced by a CT scan, and immediately he decided that the field of medical imaging could benefit from this invention. Hounsfield and Ambrose then worked together to construct a CT prototype for clinical use. Their collaboration was almost terminated several times due to money issues. However, a doctor at the British Department of Health placed an early order for a machine, injecting sufficient capital to allow the project to continue.

In 1971, with four newly built scanners, Hounsfield and Ambrose photographed the brain of a patient in a London hospital having a frontal lobe tumor. After surgery, the surgeon remarked that the tumor in the body looked exactly like the CT picture.

Hounsfield's technique initially divided the object to be scanned into axial slices, and the X-ray beam was collimated to a narrow pencil width beam of X-rays. This beam width typically specifies the slice thickness to be imaged as the narrow X-ray beam sweeps through the slice. Measurements of X-ray transmission through the subject were made by the detector at many locations. The set of measurements made during the translation and their associated rays is known as a "view." Hounsfield's first scanner measured the transmission of 160 rays per view. After completion of the translation, the tube-detector assembly was rotated around the subject by one degree, and the translation was repeated to collect a second view. The first scanner repeated this process in one-degree increments to collect 180 views over 180 degrees of rotation. Data collection was accomplished by a single narrow beam and a single sodium iodide

(NAI) scintillation detector. The initial scanner used by Hounsfield actually used two adjacent detectors with 26-millimeter-wide X-ray beams aimed in the sliced thickness direction to simultaneously collect data for two slices. At the end of the scan, he had 28 800 measurements (180 views × 160 rays) for each slice taken at many angles and positions. An image was then generated on the computer using this data.

Alan McLeod Cormack, originally from South Africa, obtained a BSc degree in physics in 1944, and an MSc degree in crystallography in 1945, both from the University of Cape Town. In 1957, he and his wife moved to the United States, where he became a professor at Tufts University, Medford, Massachusetts. He pursued an interest in CAT scanning off and on as time permitted, and in 1963 and 1964 he published the results of his work in the *Journal of Applied Physics*, but received practically no medical or scientific response. His articles were directed to the idea that X-rays of human body elements, including the brain, could be taken from several different angles, keeping in mind the varying results when taking X-rays of soft tissue compared to dense, thicker tissue. A computer would then program the resulting images into three-dimensional displays. His two published papers are regarded as the theoretical basis of CAT scanning, where the details of a flat section of soft tissues could be calculated from measurements of the attenuation of X-rays taken from several various angles. Cormack, however, had no access to a computer that could process information from a scan.

In 1970–1972, Cormack became aware of Hounsfield's work of building the first actual CAT scanner, and Cormack then devoted much of his time to CAT developments. Hounsfield and Cormack had never worked together, but jointly received the Nobel Prize for Medicine/Physiology in 1979. The first time they met each other was at the Nobel Prize presentation in Stockholm. Some in the medical genre consider CAT scanning to be the most important advance in radiology since Wilhelm Conrad Rontgen discovered X-rays in 1895, by allowing accurate and early diagnoses and exact detection of tumors.

United States Patent [19] [11] **3,965,357**
Hounsfield [45] **June 22, 1976**

[54] **APPARATUS FOR EXAMINING A BODY BY MEANS OF PENETRATING RADIATION**

[75] Inventor: **Godfrey Newbold Hounsfield,** Newark, England

[73] Assignee: **EMI Patents Limited,** Hayes, England

[22] Filed: **Mar. 1, 1974**

[21] Appl. No.: **447,381**

[52] **U.S. Cl.**................................ **250/360;** 250/312; 250/445 T; 250/460; 250/510

[51] **Int. Cl.**[2].. **G01M 23/00**

[58] **Field of Search**................ 250/510, 445 T, 358, 250/360, 460, 312

[56] **References Cited**

UNITED STATES PATENTS

2,870,336	1/1959	Fountain et al.	250/360
3,509,341	4/1970	Hindel et al.	250/510
3,518,431	1/1970	Rowe	250/360
3,670,163	6/1972	Lajus	250/320
3,715,587	2/1973	Burkhalter	250/510
3,715,588	2/1973	Rose	250/510

Primary Examiner—Harold A. Dixon
Attorney, Agent, or Firm—Fleit & Jacobson

[57] **ABSTRACT**

The invention relates to apparatus for examining a body by means of penetrating radiation in which a source of radiation produces a beam of radiation which passes through the body, and a detector receives the radiation emerging from the body. The source and the detector are mounted on a scanning structure which can undergo successive lateral scans at a succession of orbital positions so that a plane section of the body is traversed by a set of parallel beams at each of the orbital positions. A reference attenuator provides a known attenuation of the beam at the beginning of each lateral scan, and means are provided for modifying the output signals during each lateral scan in response to the signal obtained when the beam is passing through the reference attenuator. In this way compensation is effected for rapid changes in the sensitivity of the detector.

9 Claims, 3 Drawing Figures

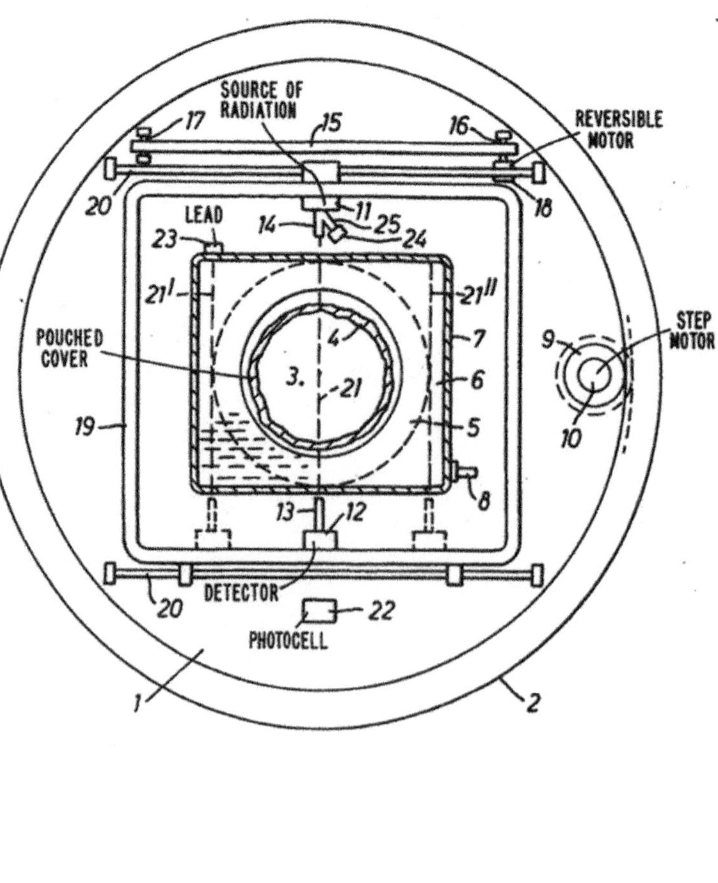

◆ INVENTORS AND INVENTIONS ◆

Paul Lauterbur and Peter Mansfield

MAGNETIC RESONANCE IMAGING

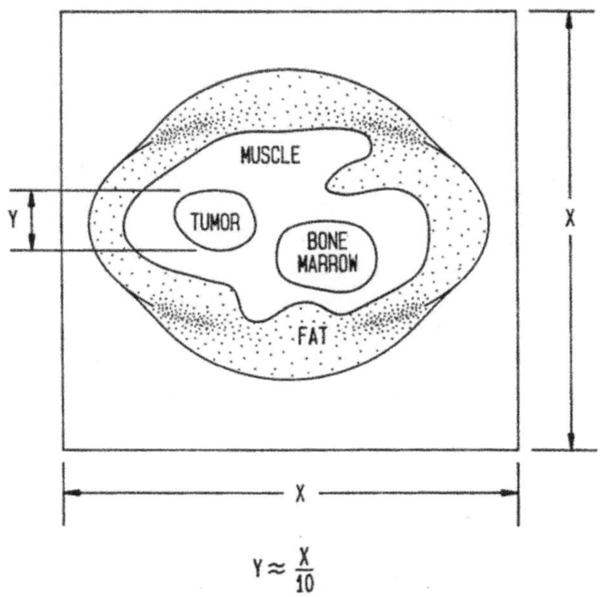

American chemist Peter Lauterbur and English physicist Peter Mansfield worked together to develop magnetic resonance imaging (MRI), which provides detailed pictures of the inside of the human body. In 2003, Lauterbur and Mansfield received the Nobel Prize in Physiology and Medicine for their discoveries that led to the invention of the MRI; however, there is controversy surrounding this prestigious award. Raymond Damadian, medical doctor and research scientist, declares that he is the true inventor of the MRI. He believes that Lauterbur and Mansfield merely made improvements to his discovery.

The path to the invention of MRI spanned over more than 50 years, and included input from chemists, engineers, mathematicians, computer scientists, physicists, and medical doctors. Beginning in the early 1950s, Felix Bloch and Edward Purcell shared the Nobel Prize for discovering a technique for measuring the phenomenon that supports MRI, namely nuclear magnetic resonance (NMR). In NMR, magnetic fields

Intellectual Property Law for Engineers, Scientists, and Entrepreneurs, Second Edition. Howard B. Rockman.

Published 2020 by John Wiley & Sons, Inc.

and radio waves are used to prompt atoms to emit minute radio signals. Currently, NMR is utilized to ascertain the molecular composition of chemical compounds.

In the late 1960s–early 1970s, Damadian considered using NMR to scan the human body as a tool for medical diagnosis. He discovered that distinct types of tissues, for example, cancerous versus non-cancerous tissues, emit different response signals. He published these findings in the 1971 *Journal of Science*. In 1974, Damadian was granted a patent for an "apparatus and method for detecting cancer in tissue." This patent was globally the first to be granted in the field, which would later come to be to known as MRI. Damadian continued his research, and in 1977 introduced the first apparatus capable of scanning the entire human body. He called his method of scanning the human body, point by point, as Field Focusing Nuclear Magnetic Resonance (FONAR). Damadian had thought the scan would provide only data at first use. However, the scan produced an image of a living man's chest cavity. He named this machine the "Indomitable."

Simultaneous to Damadian, in the early 1970s, Lauterbur and Mansfield worked separately on developing NMR technology for use in producing images of the human body. Arguably continuing to improve on Damadian's discoveries, Lauterbur developed the gradient field concept that is now central to the operation of MRI scanners. His theory was to superimpose gradients into the fixed magnetic field generally utilized in NMR. Although Damadian's research was never referenced or acknowledged, in 1973, Lauterbur published his findings in *Nature*. Meanwhile, in the United Kingdom, Peter Mansfield, building on Lauterbur's theory, developed a mathematical method to enhance the speed of the imaging procedure, and invented the "slice section" that was used for MRI. These discoveries paved the way for the construction of the first functional MRI.

Lauterbur tried to file patents related to his discoveries in order to profit from his work. The State University in New York, where Lauterbur's research was performed, decided not to pursue the patents. However, the University of Nottingham, where Mansfield made his discoveries, did file patents.

By the 1980s, more advanced and refined MRI machines were being developed. Technology companies such as IBM, General Electric, Phillips, Johnson & Johnson, and others competed to perfect the technology. Damadian was determined to succeed, and founded FONAR in 1978 to rival these industry giants. After all, he held the 1974 patent for an "Apparatus and method for detecting cancer in tissue." In 1997, after a lengthy legal battle against General Electric, Damadian's resolve was rewarded by the U.S. Supreme Court. GE was required to pay about $130,000,000 to Damadian for patent infringement. Damadian also collected smaller sums from other companies.

Damadian finally felt he had received the recognition he deserved, and that his accomplishments were rewarded. He was awarded America's National Medal of Technology, among other accolades. Despite all of these successes, Damadian reportedly felt dejected when Lauterbur and Mansfield received the Nobel Prize in 2003. He felt that he deserved at least to share the honor with Lauterbur and Mansfield. Damadian's attempts to persuade the Nobel committee were not successful.

The argument against Damadian's position is that the "gradient field" theory founded by Lauterbur, and further enhanced by Mansfield's research, was the vital invention factor that led to the MRI in use today.

US005081992A

United States Patent [19]

Levin et al.

[11] **Patent Number: 5,081,992**

[45] **Date of Patent: Jan. 21, 1992**

[54] **METHOD FOR CALCULATING LOCALIZED MAGNETIC RESONANCE SPECTRA FROM A SMALL NUMBER OF SPATIALLY-ENCODED SPECTROSCOPIC SIGNALS**

[75] Inventors: **David N. Levin; Xiaoping Hu**, both of Chicago; **Paul C. Lauterbur**, Urbana, all of Ill.; **Thomas Spraggins**, Charlottesville, Va.

[73] Assignee: **Siemens Medical Systems**, Iselin, N.J.

[21] Appl. No.: **622,204**

[22] Filed: **Nov. 30, 1990**

Related U.S. Application Data

[63] Continuation of Ser. No. 494,867, Mar. 14, 1990, abandoned, which is a continuation of Ser. No. 172,107, Mar. 23, 1988, abandoned.

[51] **Int. Cl.**[5] **A61B 5/055**

[52] **U.S. Cl.** **128/653.2**; 324/307; 324/309

[58] **Field of Search** .... 128/653 A, 653.2; 324/300, 307, 309, 312, 316; 436/173

[56] **References Cited**

U.S. PATENT DOCUMENTS

4,585,992	4/1986	Maudsley et al.	324/309
4,697,149	9/1987	Moran	324/309
4,736,160	4/1988	Sano et al.	324/312
4,761,612	8/1988	Holland et al.	324/307
4,803,624	2/1989	Pilbrow et al.	324/316
4,812,760	3/1989	Bottomley et al.	324/309

Primary Examiner—Lee S. Cohen
Assistant Examiner—Krista M. Pfaffle
Attorney, Agent, or Firm—Mark H. Jay

[57] **ABSTRACT**

An MR imaging study precedes an MR spectroscopic study. Structural information from the imaging study is combined with MR spectra from the spectroscopic study to produce localized MR spectra.

8 Claims, 1 Drawing Sheet

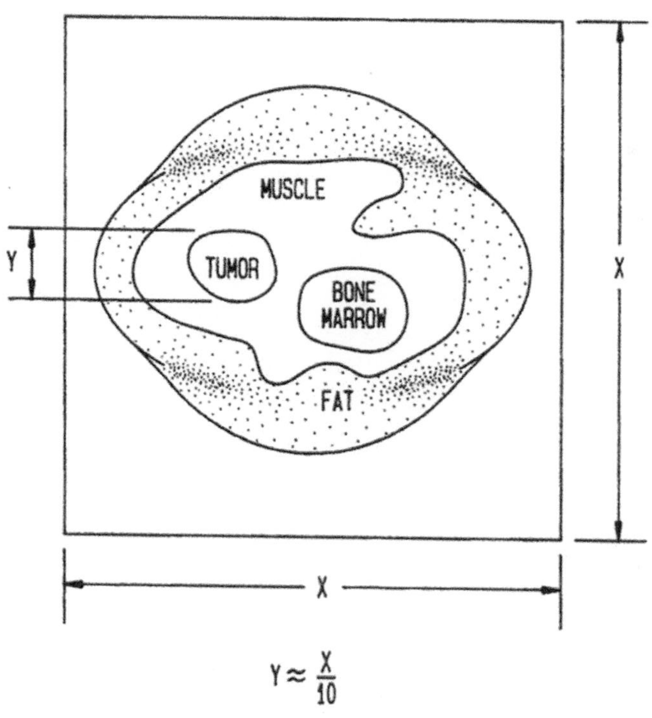

35 The Future

35.1 RATIONAL THOUGHT APPLIED TO PROBLEM SOLVING

The existence of problems and the search for their solutions are a certainty of life. Even nature, as espoused by Darwin, solves problems by evolution. The human brain has advanced, giving us the ability to solve problems faster than the natural process, and these brains have also created tools such as computers, sub-atomic research capabilities, and the ability to work in space, which have accelerated the human ability to solve problems.

The world, and the 7.6 billion people in it as of 2019, will continue to face problems, some of which arise when we solve a previous problem. Cases in point: nuclear energy can supply the world's need for energy, but what do we do with the spent fuel rods? Combustion of fossil fuels provides energy, but at what cost to the ozone layer? Even in the non-technology "dismal science" of economics, in the last 200 years the number of humans living a "middle income" life above a feudal level of poverty has increased thanks to the application of advances in technology, and in mathematical and other disciplines. But the economic problems of humanity persist, with new solutions being proposed, tried, succeeding, failing, followed by several additional solutions being offered as each problem arises. Problem solving regarding the environment in which we all live is another example of creative and inventive solutions to potentially life-endangering existential problems.

One thing is clear: the human mind's desire and ability to seek and find creative and innovative solutions to problems will continue as long as the individual and collective human brain is capable of rational thought about steps that have not yet been tried. And it also appears that a greater percentage of the world's population will be working on solutions to big and small problems as humanity advances. The establishment and then the increase in the number of technology institutes of higher learning in countries that fifty or so years ago showed no interest in technology, modernization, or a global economy testifies to the importance of, and need for, technology solutions to problems the world faces from this day forward. Examples abound: the proliferation of the Indian Institutes of Technology, the technology institutes in China, the more than a dozen technology colleges in the United Arab Emirates, and the King Abdullah University of Science and Technology in Saudi Arabia. Imagine the increase in the past 70 years of the number of human brains that are being educated to solve, and are

Intellectual Property Law for Engineers, Scientists, and Entrepreneurs, Second Edition. Howard B. Rockman.

Published 2020 by John Wiley & Sons, Inc.

working toward solving, problems using technology, science, engineering, mathematics, and other areas of rational thinking.

It is fair to postulate that the number of creative and innovative solutions to problems will continue to increase, linearly in some fields, and exponentially in others. And it is important that these creations and innovations are made available for the benefit of *all* members of the global population. This requires the encouragement of, and providing incentives for, the study, research, and trial-and-error experimentation that form the backbone of all technology and science advancement. Human nature being what it is, altruism alone is not sufficient to encourage beneficial innovation and creation. The pat on the back just will not do it anymore. But the exchange of exclusivity for a limited period of time in return for the disclosure of one's creation, innovation, or invention to the public, known as the protection of intellectual property rights, has been for over 500 years an effective way to encourage thinkers to apply their skills toward the development of solutions to problems, and to provide the public with the ability to benefit from those solutions. The various global systems for the protection of intellectual property rights should, and will continue to grow, and encompass more and more thinkers, creators, and innovators as time moves forward. The continued increase in the number of patent applications filed in the United States Patent and Trademark Office (USPTO) each year over the past two decades provides evidence of the present scale of advances in innovative thought.

So if and until a better system evolves of rewarding innovators for public disclosure of their solutions to problems of every sort, the existing laws regarding the generation and protection of intellectual property rights, with regular tweaks here and there, will remain the main engine behind innovative and creative discourse for the benefit of all.

35.2 WHAT INVESTORS WILL LOOK FOR IN THE FUTURE RELATIVE TO INTELLECTUAL PROPERTY

Investors today are looking at a corporation, LLC, start-up, or other business organization's patent policies and portfolios when determining whether to invest in the organization, and some writers opine that knowledgeable managers and organizations that fully understand the dynamics of patents as the building blocks of business will be in short supply in the future. Once such thinker is Ian Harvey, who contributed an essay entitled "Creating Tomorrow – IP and the Future of Business," that appeared in the anthology *From Ideas to Assets – Investing Wisely in Intellectual Property*, edited by Bruce Berman, published by John Wiley & Sons, Inc. (2002) ISBN 0-471-40068-8. Mr. Harvey, the CEO of BTG, a company that finds, develops, and commercializes technologies, believes that technology managers in the future will be required to understand the differences between patentability and freedom to use an invention, which could be called "patent literacy." The information in this text has aimed to put you on the right track by providing you with the skills needed to use intellectual property effectively in your management of technology corporations, universities, start-ups, and other technology-based entities. Investors will be asking about the knowledge of the corporate executives regarding intellectual property, whether intellectual property is part of the corporation's strategy, and does the combined intellectual property and corporate strategy merge to unlock the value of the knowledge within the company and therefore drive the company's profits. Many people who predict the future of intellectual property have stated that those directly working in the technology sectors will have to become patent literate, and not just the attorneys or patent agents.

There is no question that technology is moving forward at an exponential pace, or even faster. Along with it, the consequential granting and enforcement of intellectual property rights associated with the development of technology are also moving as fast as the technology. It is also clear that technology, and intellectual property along with it, are important to the economic growth of all countries throughout the world. As evidenced by the World Trade Organization (WTO), most governments now believe that intellectual property protection should be awarded to inventors, creators, and innovators, and to the employers of those innovators and creators, to encourage investment in developing inventions and creations, eventually evolving into products that will work for the benefit of their populations. Over the last 50 years, governments of the world have continued to strengthen their intellectual property laws, including the United States, which in 2011 introduced a new amendment to the existing patent law, the major portion of which turns the United States into a first-to-file country, rather than a first-to-invent country. Even India, which opposed intellectual property 40 or so years ago, has come into the intellectual property fold through the WTO. Also, about 50 years ago, China enacted the patent law that it is using today. It is our understanding that enforcement of the patent laws and other intellectual property laws in China today is on the increase.

Certain issues regarding intellectual property will probably continue to be problematic in the future. One of these foreseeable problems is the "access to medicines" problem in developing countries that have seen epidemics of diseases such as malaria and AIDS on such a scale that the government cannot fund the treatment required to save lives. These same governments also know that the intellectual property laws are very important to create technology and to commercialize the inventions protected by the intellectual property in their countries, and these governments try to create a balance between the health of their people and encouraging innovation in the life sciences. The importance of intellectual property is one of many factors that are more widely recognized as drivers of economic growth, rather than the opposite. This is increasingly so as international treaties continue to break down the restrictions on world trade. The old paradigm of being able to compete solely based on brand, and by being the first one to enter the market with a product, is being replaced by the new importance of intellectual property. The new paradigm is that with strong patents, the producer of innovative products can stop other people from manufacturing and selling the products covered by the patents for a given time period, sufficient to make the cost of developing and producing such products worthwhile.

To attract investment in the new development, it is important that technology companies today and in the future incorporate intellectual property policies into their overall business strategies. These policies will begin with the research and development focus of the company, and its search for new products that its customers will need today, and five and ten years from today. Intellectual property must be included in this strategic mix. This mix will include combinations of copyright, patent and trade secret rights, and in many cases brand and trademark rights.

One of the purposes of this text is to impart knowledge about intellectual property to those of you who are in the technology field, or are about to enter the technology field, from which innovations and technology in the future will be generated. We patent and intellectual property professionals generally conclude that there is an unhealthy lack of interest, and sometimes knowledge, among the technology leaders of today's businesses about intellectual property rights. Obviously, one purpose of this text is to bridge this shortfall of knowledge. For example, many business entities will publish the research and development they are working on before filing at least a provisional patent application, which disclosure completely destroys major important foreign patent rights. In my opinion, this premature disclosure should be avoided.

Although it is my belief that technology companies need to pay more attention to their intellectual property, it is only over the last several years that some corporations have begun to think about elevating intellectual property as a major factor in their strategic business plans. This change is due to the fact that investors in these companies, particularly start-ups, put questions about intellectual property strategy at the top of the list of inquiries made before they commit their investment resources. Therefore, the more that technology company managers understand and incorporate intellectual property into their business strategy, the easier it will be to attract investors into their business. As Mr. Harvey stated, "The ability of intellectual property to sustain a commercial advantage is one of the few lifelines that companies can look to for regaining competitive advantage." He also predicts that companies that fail to think very hard and seriously about intellectual property as an important part of their overall business strategy are much less likely to succeed.

The business strategy that intellectual property should become a part of will also include a manufacturing, marketing, and sales strategy along with a research strategy, with all parts dovetailing to make a unitary whole. It is also important that managers of technology organizations take prudent steps to enhance and protect their intellectual property assets to retain value in their corporation.

Given the large number of people in the world who are engaged today in innovation, creation, and invention of new ideas and products, there are relatively few who can be designated as "patent or intellectual property astute," those who have the knowledge to efficiently and properly manage a business entity's intellectual property assets. One of the considerations is that the patent laws are universally substantively the same. However, the procedures for operating under the patent laws vary from country to country. For example, there is yet no international patent. You must generally protect your inventions on a country-by-country basis. In addition, obtaining patent protection in the significant countries in which your company markets its products may involve a substantial expense, and that expense should be calculated on a country-by-country basis as to whether or not the expenditures to obtain patent protection should be made. As commented upon previously in this text, it is also possible for a business entity to use its patents effectively as a stand-alone profit center. It is important that technology company executives understand this possible use of intellectual property.

Before even drafting patent applications, a technology company should consider what its patent portfolio can do for the company, and how the company intends to use the patent portfolio. A patent on a single invention can be written in several different ways, depending upon the use to which it will be put and the existence of other "prior art" patents. The person preparing the patent application should be fully informed as to the context in which the corporation desires to use the patented subject matter. For example, the claiming portion of the patent application should include protections not only for the compound or product itself, but for the methods of using the particular compound or product. Thus, the individual creating the patent document should know beforehand how that patent document will fit into the overall corporate strategy of the business.

It is apparent that in the future, the demand for innovators, creators, and inventors in the technology sectors will continue to increase, and it is anticipated that the engineering and technical universities can train and furnish the minds to create the intellectual assets that will be in demand. Also, as the technology sector expands, and more of these minds are involved in creative endeavors, more and more people with an understanding of patents and intellectual property and their value to a business's overall strategy will also be in demand.

Investors now possess a sophisticated knowledge of how patents provide a company with an enforceable advantage regarding its business, thereby further providing them with an increased return on their original capital investment. One purpose of this text is to provide valuable information to technology managers who will fully understand the connections between technology, intellectual property, and the marketplace. More and more, business schools throughout the world are including courses on intellectual property directed to future business managers, including those of technology-based companies.

Mr. Harvey, in the aforementioned article, presents the thought that in the future, single companies, and the research and development departments of those single companies, will not be able, alone, to perform the research and development necessary to come up with the products that will be demanded by future consumers. He states that any business must be connected to a network of other sources of research to identify key technology changes early and then capitalize on these changes. I agree. Historical anecdotal information shows that breakthrough technologies tend to come from interconnections among research and development teams or among individuals. For example, the electronics industry will probably rely more on the nanotechnology industry in the future to build more powerful but smaller machines. Mr. Harvey concludes that any technology company desiring to capitalize on future innovations must be able to draw on a wide network of researchers in different fields, and to find ways of having the different disciplines it needs mate with each other and make ideas happen. Thus, the networks of research people working in the various companies will probably come together for research endeavors more and more in the future. This includes the small research corporations and the start-ups that will most likely fit into this research and development network. The result will be the creation of strategic alliances between organizations that are involved in separate parts of the process of creating a new product or process and bringing it to market. A well-thought-out intellectual property strategy is an important factor in holding such alliances together.

The future will see more and more governments of countries taking steps to encourage new ideas. Even today, some are better at this than others. It is equally important that the country support an education system that encourages innovation and creativity, and does not solely encourage conformity and rote learning. The former is one of the hallmarks of the U.S. education system and is one of the reasons why people from the world over come to the United States for an education.

We need education systems throughout the world that encourage people to think, to ask questions, and to challenge the ordinary way that things are done. These are very important ingredients for the innovation and creation process. Even government support for failing companies is a positive factor because, as Mr. Harvey puts it, innovation is unlikely to thrive if there is no incentive to solve problems or to face up to the consequence of failure. Recall that Thomas Edison and his group of 20 researchers took two years to come up with a light bulb filament that would work and last for a usable period of time, after previously announcing to the public and the press that the inventive process would take only six months. Thus, in the research and development process, failure *is* an option. Students in the technology disciplines must be taught to challenge accepted wisdom and not to blindly accept the status quo, since these are negative indicators of future creativity. Experiments may fail, and then you move on with another approach.

Another factor is that entrenched businesses do not like to deal with shifts in technology because it disrupts their existing business models and product lines. Therefore, if a start-up company or university develops a new product or process, the licensee of that technology may often be a small company or another start-up. This is why new products are often very important for the start-up industry. If a technology is likely to provide the basis for several different products in different areas, a start-up company is probably the best licensee to take the development to the point where a number of other companies can start to create their own particular products. Also, if your research and development functions are networked through several organizations, you will probably have an easier time creating a strategy that is particularly tailored to each new innovation project and is supported by patents and other intellectual property. An example that Mr. Harvey provides in his essay is that JVC, the owner of VHS patents, licensed other companies around the world to use that format. Their competitor using Betamax technology kept it solely for its own products. As a result, the VHS format for a while became the industry standard because everyone started using it. Betamax dropped by the wayside. Mr. Harvey also points to a glassmaker who developed the flat glass process, and decided to license his competitors that earned the glassmaker $750 million in royalties. The company then used the proceeds to purchase many of their licensees and ultimately became the world's largest manufacturer of flat glass.

As stated above, it may be wise to license corporations with which you also compete. This would be the JVC example. JVC ended up collecting royalty payments from the entire industry. Mr. Harvey also states, and I strongly agree, that many breakthrough innovations are derived from small research groups, universities, and biotech firms. Therefore, the pattern of future business appears to be headed toward networks of partnerships of all types and sizes, built around strong intellectual property.

When companies today in the technology sector perform an accounting to determine the market value of a company, increasingly the value of the intellectual property is becoming a larger and larger factor in their valuation. Certain factors that may determine this value will be whether or not the company has patents covering the strategic areas in which they intend to market their products in the future. If they are involved in patenting processes, have they adequately covered the processes they are using in the manufacturing or delivery of their services? Do the managers of the company have the necessary expertise regarding intellectual property, and is there an understanding of what patents are and how they can be capitalized upon by management? This intellectual-property-based value of a company is derived from the fact that intellectual property is increasingly going to determine the future success of a product or process. This bottom line determination based upon intellectual property protection feeds back to the valuation of the company itself. Even service companies these days are obtaining patents for the novel and non-obvious features of the way they conduct their business. An example that Mr. Harvey gives is of British Airways, which patented the design of their seats involving sleeper beds in the first class section of their aircraft, and a clever seating layout providing privacy and greater space utilization. Their patent protection justified the heavy investment needed to develop the new seats which competitors could not duplicate. This will create revenue for British Airways, and another way to create such revenue is to license other airlines to use the same seating design and patterns.

An important consideration is that there is a present worldwide trend to harmonize the patent laws of the various countries. The one-year grace period between disclosure of an invention and the filing of a patent application that is allowed in the United States is in conflict with the "absolute novelty" rule of many other countries. Therefore, if a U.S.-based technology organization decides to publish or make available its innovations before filing U.S. patent applications on the applicable technology, much of the foreign patent rights will be absolutely destroyed. It can be expected in the future that either U.S. or foreign law will be modified to prevent a developer of technology from making a choice that would destroy intellectual property rights in most of the industrialized world.

The patenting of business methods in Europe and other jurisdictions around the world is constantly the subject of commentary, particularly as business methods, specifically those driven by computers, begin to obtain value on their own and support the developer's business. Those countries and jurisdictions that do not allow the patenting of computer programs and computer-related inventions may also be compelled in the future to change their practices because of the real value generated through computer-based inventions.

One aspect of patents that is continually coming under criticism is whether or not the patent term, i.e., the enforceable life of the patent, is long enough to do the job properly, or is too long and restricts necessary access to important innovations, particularly in the life sciences area. There are many genres of technology innovation where the research time is long and expensive. Therefore, it takes more time to recoup the research costs for what could be a minor but important technical innovation. If a drug were to be developed to solve the Alzheimer's disease problem, and it took years to develop that product, should the patent period be longer? Investors ask this question because they do not want to make large investments over long periods of time for a product that while making modern life easier for people who are stricken with diseases, will have a very short earning period under remaining patent protection. Certain steps have been taken in the United States to lengthen the period of a patent grant depending upon the government regulatory procedures necessary to approve the product.

The United States also enacted legislation that went into effect in 2013 that created bodies within the USPTO that have jurisdiction to resolve conflicts as to the validity of patents and other patent-related matters. The value of patents, therefore, can be judged by a government agency rather than the courts in the United States. Only time can tell how this particular innovation in the U.S. patent system will either harm or energize the patent system. The patent enforcement term argument will continue to be debated because some people think that the period is too long and some think it is too short, and some think it is satisfactory the way it is.

With pharmaceutical products, it takes a long time to determine whether the drugs work after clinical analysis. Computer and electronics industry people may have fewer concerns about the life of a patent, since those in that industry consider the patent system too slow to be effective in an industry that moves along as rapidly as the electronics industry. This brings to mind why there are no design patents on articles of clothing, because by the time the patent issues, the clothing will be out of style.

Mr. Harvey also comments that the patent and intellectual property laws throughout the world are created by governments, and governments enact these laws based upon debates and input from industry in an attempt to create a compromise between opposing interests who have a stake in the outcome. He emphatically states that the intellectual property professionals in the United States and the rest of the world should take part in the debates that are raging today and will rage in the future regarding the scope and content of the intellectual property laws. He also encourages these same intellectual property professionals to reverse the perceived ignorance of most people about the basic principles of intellectual property and its growing importance. He quotes a comment from a European Union Trade Commissioner as saying, "Patents are a restraint on free trade." This to me reflects an educational gap on the part of that individual.

Since governments have a relatively lackluster track record in investing in technology, the private sector must be the leader in such investment. Mr. Harvey concludes that it is necessary to have patents and other intellectual property protections available to create the platform for this investment, and that it is the patent professionals who must reach the technology public's ear to deliver this message. Hopefully, this text will help achieve this goal.

Mr. Harvey predicts that the United States and European patent law will eventually move closer together. My personal prediction is that the rest of the world will follow if the U.S. and European patent laws are brought into joinder. It is also clear that intellectual property strategy in the future is going to be the heart of any successful technology business strategy. Intellectual property portfolios, intellectual property strategy, and the external perceptions of intellectual property will underpin the value of technology companies in the future. You members of the technology sector are part of the new cadre of technology professionals who have become "patent literate," the type that investors look for in a new technology business.

35.3 DEVELOPING COUNTRIES

Developing countries are being encouraged to increase their capabilities to manage intellectual property as a way of meeting their own needs and of bolstering their economies. Innovation is a complex process of which intellectual property is only one component. Today it is difficult to document the impact of innovation of the worldwide World Trade Organization (WTO) and the Agreement on Trade-Related Aspects of Intellectual Property Rights (TRIPS) (1995) regulations on innovation. The conventional wisdom is that any impact on the increase in innovation throughout the world will be the result of a combination of factors, of which intellectual property will be an important one, but not the only factor.

The WTO sets forth rules regarding intellectual property that countries must adopt to become members. There is a body of opinion that each country, particularly developing countries, should have a degree of freedom to adopt and implement intellectual property laws and regulations that fit its own needs, particularly in the medical, pharmaceutical, and public health areas. The countries with high instances of AIDS epidemics, for example, should be able to opt out of requiring treatment drugs to be part of an intellectual property system. Therefore, the conventional wisdom also states that intellectual property management capabilities in developing countries need to be rapidly improved to ensure that intellectual property is used to improve health and not to hold back treatments. National governments should support product development efforts, which include the rewards and benefits of an intellectual property system, as well as at the same time encourage innovation for public welfare.

The world is slowly moving (sometimes in fits and starts) to a dominant political/social framework of capitalistic markets, with these systems giving high priority to the protection of intellectual property. It is presumed that this framework will be with us for the foreseeable future, and the public sector needs to find ways to achieve its goals within this framework. Intellectual property is important to the private sector since it helps investors achieve high return on their investments.

However, intellectual property should also be of importance to the public sector because the public sector can mobilize the resources necessary to take a product through the process of research and development, particularly to prove a product's safety and efficacy. Innovation can also help those in the lower economic strata. For example, creative license practices can help ensure global access and affordability to life-saving and life-enhancing products. To achieve these goals, intellectual property management capabilities have to be improved throughout the world, particularly in developing countries, so that intellectual property can be managed for the benefit of all levels of humanity, and at the same time encourage investment in research and development.

The components of innovation and creation include:

1. Intellectual property.
2. Public and private sector support for research and development.
3. Developing national product programs that sustain domestic markets, including distribution systems, in both the public and private sectors, particularly in developing countries.
4. The programs must be conducive to facilitating trade in technology, health, and agriculture.
5. In the agricultural field, as an example, government policies should support high-quality manufacturing of pharmaceuticals and vaccines, balanced with encouraging investments in high-quality seed production and other agricultural inputs that will increase the food supply necessary to sustain humans on this planet.
6. Governments need to adopt effective regulation systems to protect the health, safety and well being of their populations. In the future, this will apply to the food, feed, fiber, and seed industries throughout the world, which will become more and more important as the world population advances from the present 7.6 billion people, and food production capabilities reach their peak.

Each country should take advantage of the freedoms granted by the WTO and TRIPS regulations to formulate and implement policies and practices that best meet its own needs. This includes collaborative efforts between the public and private sectors, and cross-border collaborative efforts where beneficial. Countries benefit substantially from developing their internal intellectual property management capabilities, strengthening their intellectual property enforcement and court systems and patent offices, and according priority to meet the needs of all of their constituents to avoid widespread poverty. Success in these categories will require knowledge, capacity, and active engagement between all sectors of society, and among those, a knowledge of the best practices in intellectual property management will be critical.

35.4 UNIVERSITY TECHNOLOGY TRANSFER

In the United States, the Bayh–Dole Act allows universities and public research institutions to patent inventions based on publicly funded research, and then license them to the private sector. The purpose is to advance government-sponsored inventions from the university laboratory onto store shelves by attracting the private investment necessary for commercialization. Today, most of the countries of the world have copied the Bayh–Dole model. The European Union, Japan, China, India, and other countries hope to tap into their own cutting-edge university research to develop new products and technologies, and make these innovations available to their constituents. This has led to a rising tide of global innovation that has the capacity to improve the quality of life for people in both developed and developing nations.

Data reported by universities reveals that academic technology commercialization continues to thrive even through the global financial crisis that began in 2008, providing a steady stimulus to the world's economy. The majority of start-ups formed through university technology transfer are located in the licensing institution's home state, demonstrating that the Bayh–Dole Act continues to have a major impact on local economies across the United States. In addition to enabling academic institutions and businesses to retain titles to inventions made under federally funded research programs, the Bayh–Dole Act created a uniform intellectual property management program for the federal agencies that fund research. In 2016, 800 new university-generated commercial products were introduced, 7575 total licenses and options were executed, 1024 new companies based on academic inventions were formed, and there were 8208 federally funded invention disclosures from academic research. Further, $66.9 billion was spent in total sponsored research, there were 25 825 invention disclosures, and almost $3.0 billion total licensing income (see AUTM U.S. 2016 Licensing Survey, FY 2016, www.autm.net).

Each of these licenses reflects a one-to-one relationship between a U.S. academic institution and a company or start-up focused on a product development project. This is part of what has become known as "the knowledge economy." As technology transfer expands inside developed and developing countries and their academic institutions, creative mechanisms will continually emerge to further the impact of the resulting new technologies and bring them to bear on global beneficial outcomes.

Rather than asking existing companies to develop university-based products, universities and their faculties are increasingly turning to a new mechanism: the spinout company. This would be a new company typically created to produce and market intellectual property developed at a university by one of its employees, such as a professor.

These types of new creative developments are raising the world's expectations and allowing companies and academics to pursue hopes that seemed unattainable before technology transfer released the power of human imagination at the academic level. Universities, by definition, have always been the site of visionary imagination, and it is fitting that a new age of potentially greater global equity has been envisioned in the classrooms and laboratories of universities. The success of academic technology transfer measures has broadened beyond economics to include the number of lives saved, reduction in disease burden, improvements in the quality of life, and increases in productivity.

Because of the altruism embedded in the mindset of university personnel, some university technology transfer offices today are modifying their licensing practices regarding patents relevant to healthcare in developing countries. Rather than universities deciding to stop patenting medically related inventions and put everything in the public domain, these universities have decided that patents have been shown to be a powerful tool for directing investment into the development of technologies that would otherwise lie fallow. University inventions are normally at an early stage, such that investment and development requires substantial risk, since neither the technical practicality nor the market acceptability of the invention is proven at that time. Many inventions fail to reach the market, particularly in the medical field. However, patents have been seen as an essential way for companies and investors to manage their risk.

It is true that universities and research institutions aim for a degree of financial return from their patents. However, university royalty rates are normally lower than those extant in the private sector. For example, universities receive licensing royalties equivalent to only two to four percent of their research budgets. From available studies, it appears that most universities believe that the primary purpose of their technology transfer activities is either (1) to induce investment in the developing technologies to bring products to the public; (2) to aid local economic development through spinout companies based on licenses of their technology; or (3) both. Given this commitment to encouraging the development of new technologies via patenting, universities require sophisticated policies, procedures, and education in patenting policies and licensing to ensure that the entire public spectrum will have access to health-related and other beneficial inventions based on the university's technology. According to one optimistic thought, the access policies developed by universities may, if practical and properly implemented and publicized, become norms that will more widely be adopted by the private sector.

35.5 MASTER OF ENGINEERING MANAGEMENT DEGREES AT U.S. UNIVERSITIES

The Master of Engineering Management degree offered at several universities today is popular among engineers who want to integrate technical know-how with business and law knowledge, especially those who desire to manage cutting-edge technologies, or manage start-ups. Students taking these courses are those that aim to be a chief technology officer rather than a chief operating or chief executive officer of a business. These courses are directed to the preparation of engineering managers, with the purpose of creating technology team leaders with knowledge of how their technology expertise fits within their organization's overall business strategy. These managers, in addition to their engineering capabilities, also require a thorough understanding of their organization's operation and goals. Students in these courses take a mix of advanced engineering classes along with core business courses in marketing, finance, management, and accounting. Of course, I contend that business use of intellectual property should be a core component of all of these engineering management courses.

35.6 CONCLUSION

Nations of the world in the 21st century are realizing that they have to tap into the intellectual assets of their constituents, and that they have to support innovation and creativity. There are several motivations: to raise the standard of living of its citizens, to create well-paying jobs and full employment, and to develop products to sell on the world market, to name just a few. Globally speaking, innovation in one country helps all countries by reducing poverty and increasing the purchasing power of its own citizens, creating more efficiency in the production and distribution of products and services, and opening up world markets for technology products.

However, innovation must be stimulated initially in the minds of those individuals or groups of individuals whose task it is to think, create, and innovate. National policies must be directed to stimulate thought, particularly in technology. Such steps include policies for creating efficient communications systems for the exchange of ideas; building a solid technology infrastructure; encouraging capital investment in start-ups, entrepreneurship, and innovation through effective intellectual property creation and enforcement policies; and making education available and affordable to create a well-educated, high-tech, business-savvy work force. In education, ways must be found to encourage more students to stay involved in the science, technology, engineering, and mathematics (STEM) disciplines, where they learn what innovation is, and a culture conducive to thinking and creativity is cultivated.

Engineers, scientists, and others in the STEM disciplines create jobs because they create ideas, invent new products and processes, and grow the business enterprises they work for, or start anew. The necessary raw material for innovation is the human brain, and its ability to think about solving problems. Encouraging and unlocking the power and ability of the human brain to think, innovate, and create is one of the most important factors in improving life on this planet. To this end, it is important that the technology business community, universities and feeder schools, and professional technology societies work together to share knowledge at a pace that will sustain the rapid changes in technology, culture, and the political makeup of the globe that are taking place all around us, every day.

Innovation requires an environment that can tolerate risks, and expects occasional failures. During the process of innovating, you do not know what will work or not. This must be explained to those who are asked to invest their resources in new ideas. Therefore, the management and transparency of risk is an important factor in keeping innovation alive. Think of Edison's two years to create a workable incandescent bulb, after he announced that the bulb would be available in six months. To paraphrase Eleanor Roosevelt, you must teach your investors to light a candle rather than curse the darkness of occasional failures. Successful intellectual property policies by governments and universities, and efficient intellectual property management by businesses are important factors in risk management and support for investment.

Innovation begins with an idea toward solving a problem, developing that idea into a workable and practical concept, and then developing a product or process from that concept. However, until the research results are commercialized and made available for the public's benefit, it is not really innovation. Intellectual property rights are an important, but not the only, part of the equation for successful commercialization of innovation. The intellectual property rights resulting from research and development efforts, as discussed in the previous chapters of this text, allow the entrepreneur, start-up, or business organization to gain an exclusive position in the market for the new product or process for a specific number of years, that will hopefully more than repay the time, effort, and expenditure of resources spent in innovating, creating, and bringing the new product or process to market. Creating and enforcing intellectual property rights are vital links in the advancement of technology. The efficient and most advantageous use of intellectual property rights requires coordination between those in a business enterprise responsible for the management of engineering, technology, innovation strategy, and the allocation of resources. Hopefully, the information you gained from this text has provided you with tools for thought in successfully guiding the intellectual property strategy of your organization in a forward direction.

May the future of technology be with you.

◆ INVENTORS AND INVENTIONS ◆

Harry Coover

SUPER GLUE®

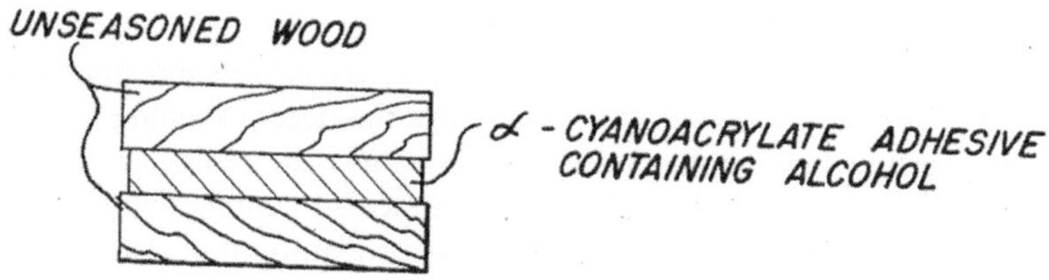

Harry Coover obtained an MS and a PhD in chemistry from Cornell University. He was employed as a chemist for Eastman Kodak from 1944 to 1973, and then became vice president of the company from 1973 to 1984.

In 1942, while working for Kodak, Coover was researching materials from which to produce clear plastic gun sights for use by the military in the Second World War. One of the group of materials he examined was cyanoacrylates, but this material was rejected as being too sticky for the purpose, since it stuck to everything. The compound he had developed did not work well for gun sights, but it worked well as an extremely quick bonding adhesive. Coover abandoned that formulation since it was not suitable for his then current project.

Eight or nine years later, in 1951 Coover was in charge of Kodak chemists who were looking at heat-resistant polymers for jet plane canopies, when cyanoacrylates were once again tested. However, they again proved too sticky. But this time, Coover saw that he had discovered a unique adhesive that eventually turned into the adhesive marketed by Kodak as Super Glue in 1958.

Much attention was given to the glue's capacity to bond solid materials. However, Coover was the first to recognize and patent cyanoacrylates as a tissue adhesive, first used in the Vietnam War to patch the internal organs of injured soldiers until they could be transferred to a surgery location. Today, these tissue adhesives are used worldwide for a variety of sutureless surgical procedures.

Back in 1951, while Coover and Fred Joyner were working on the same Kodak research team on cockpit canopies, they had tested hundreds of compounds looking for a temperature-resistant coating for the canopies. Joyner eventually spread the 910th compound they tried between two lens prisms on a refractometer to take a reading on the velocity of light through the meter. However, he discovered that he was unable to separate the lenses, and his initial reaction was panic because of the loss of the expensive equipment he had ruined with his experiment. Fred Joyner was

Intellectual Property Law for Engineers, Scientists, and Entrepreneurs, Second Edition. Howard B. Rockman.

Published 2020 by John Wiley & Sons, Inc.

embarrassed for ruining the test equipment, and he apologized to Dr. Coover. But Dr. Coover did not get angry and saw entirely new possibilities for the compounds. He realized the potential of a product that would quickly bond to a variety of materials, only needing a little water to be activated. The water is generally available in the air or in the materials to be bonded together. Coover continued to refine the material until it was introduced to the public in 1958 under the name Eastman 910.

Cyanoacrylate is an acrylic resin that rapidly polymerizes in the presence of water, specifically the hydroxide ions. This reaction forms long, strong chains adhering the bonded surfaces together. Exposure to moisture in the air can cause a tube of glue to become unstable. To prevent an open container of glue from setting before use, the Super Glue must be stored in an airtight jar or bottle with a package of silica gel. Another convenient way is to attach a hypodermic needle into the opening of the glue container. After applying, residual glue soon clogs the needle keeping moisture out. The clog is removed by heating the needle such as by a cigarette lighter before use.

Super Glue adheres almost instantly when it comes into contact with the hydroxyl ions in water. Since most materials have at least a trace amount of water at their surface, adding water to objects is not necessary, though it can help in creating a stronger bond. The anionic polymerization that the glue undergoes as it bonds causes heat to be generated. Therefore, if enough Super Glue is applied to your finger, you can actually burn yourself.

The principle ingredient in Super Glue is methyl cyanoacrylate. Cyanoacrylate glues comprise polymer chains made of thousands of units called monomers. Cyanoacrylates change from a liquid to a solid when they interact with weak bases.

Eastman Kodak later renamed the product Super Glue, and Eastman 910 was then licensed to a company called Loctite, which then sold it as Loctite Quick Set 404. Loctite later developed its own version, calling it Super Bonder.

At one point in time, a radio station found out about Super Glue, and decided to test the product at a local junkyard. The test was to lift an automobile with a crane using only Eastman's No. 910 Super Glue. The car was lifted successfully by the crane without the bond breaking.

Not long after Super Glue hit the market, Dr. Coover appeared on the television show "I've Got a Secret," which was hosted by Garry Moore. Dr. Coover's secret was that he had invented Super Glue, and then he was asked to demonstrate how the product worked. To conduct the demonstration, a crossbar was connected on each side to a metal cylinder sealed only with a single drop of Eastman 910 Super Glue hung above the stage. Dr. Coover grabbed the crossbar and was lifted well above the stage floor on the strength of his glue. He and the bar did not fall, and the audience cheered this demonstration. Then, Dr. Coover was lowered back to the stage. Suddenly, Garry Moore himself decided maybe the glue could hold two people, and he called for the stage hands to hoist himself and Dr. Coover up together. The glue held them both, and this was in front of a national television audience, which caused product sales to skyrocket.

As mentioned above, it was ultimately found that Super Glue had uses in medical situations. In 1966, cyanoacrylates were tested on site during the Vietnam War by a specially trained surgical team. The compound could stop bleeding, and Dr. Coover developed disposable cyanoacrylate sprays for use on the battlefield. One of the battlefield problems was to stop bleeding so that the patient could be transported to a hospital area. As a point of irony, the U.S. Food and Drug Administration (FDA) had not given approval for the medical use of the compound at that time; however, the military used the substance anyway. Today, a form of cyanoacrylate is often used in medical situations in place of or along with traditional sutures. The advantages of using this form of Super Glue in medical situations are that its use reduces the chances of infection. It is also quicker to apply to seal a wound and reduces adverse cosmetic side effects.

Despite the fact that cyanoacrylate glues were found to be useful on the battlefield, the FDA was reluctant to approve the medical use of the product for civilians. This was due to a tendency of earlier compounds made from "methyl-2-cyanoacrylate" to irritate the skin. Since the glue reacted with water and cured in the skin, cyanoacetate and formaldehyde were released. Ultimately, an improved cyanoacrylate glue was developed for medical applications. This medical revision of the product was 2-octyl-cyanoacrylate, which had improved flexibility and strength and resulted in less skin irritation. In 1998, the FDA approved the latter compound for use in closing wounds and surgical incisions. In 2001, the product was approved for use as a barrier against common bacterial microbes including certain staphylococci, pseudomonads, and *Escherichia coli*. This product is also available for home use, and is sold under the name Band-Aid Brand Liquid Bandage. Thus, for medical applications of Super Glue, please be sure you are using the medically approved glue and not the ordinary kind.

Kodak did not ultimately capitalize commercially on Dr. Coover's discovery of Super Glue, and sold the business to National Starch in 1980. Further, Super Glue did not become a commercial success until the patents on the product had expired.

If there is a moral to the story of Dr. Coover's development of Super Glue, it is this: As a creative person, do not quickly discard any of your ideas, no matter what they are. As Dr. Coover demonstrated, if a product does not seem to have any applicable use now, that does not mean it will not prove highly successful sometime in the future.

Oct. 23, 1956 H. W. COOVER, JR **2,768,109**

ALCOHOL-CATALYZED α-CYANOACRYLATE ADHESIVE COMPOSITIONS

Filed June 2, 1954

Fig. 1

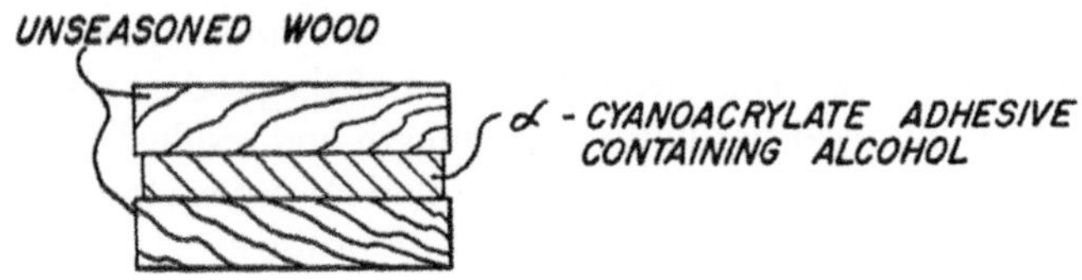

Fig. 2

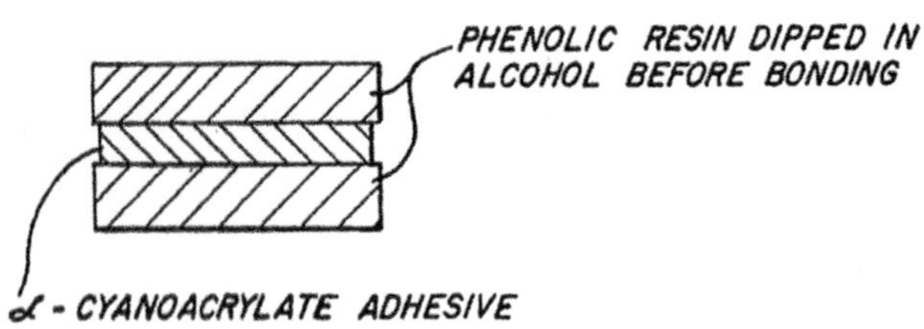

HARRY W. COOVER JR
INVENTOR.

BY Daniel I. Mayne,
George W. Peterson
ATTORNEYS

◆ INVENTORS AND INVENTIONS ◆

Spencer Silver

POST-IT® NOTES

Spencer Silver is an American chemist who earned his doctorate in organic chemistry from the University of Colorado in Boulder in 1966. He then took a position as a senior chemist in 3M's central research laboratory.

Silver's most significant invention was not an immediate success. In 1968, he developed a high-quality, low tack adhesive. He based his invention on a patented formula from Shiro Takemoto, and the result was an adhesive whose grip was strong enough to hold papers together, but at the same time was weak enough to permit the papers to be pulled apart again without being torn, and more importantly, the adhesive could be reused again and again. Silver desired to sell the adhesive as a spray or as a surface for bulletin boards from which temporary notices could be posted and then removed. For five years he attempted to interest his colleagues at 3M to market the product. However, a marketable form of the product remained elusive.

The adhesive that Silver had developed was based on acrylate copolymer microspheres, which comprise tiny bubbles that prevented glue from bonding firmly. Silver obtained U.S. Patent No. 3,691,140 directed to his microspheres on September 12, 1972. This was an odd and rather useless invention at the time because 3M was looking for a stronger adhesive, not a weaker one. Silver was working on a project to create super-strong adhesives for use in the aerospace industry for building airplanes. Instead of a super-strong adhesive, he accidently created an incredibly weak pressure-sensitive adhesive using his microspheres. 3M management considered this adhesive too weak to be useful, although it did have two interesting features. First, when stuck to a surface, the item being adhered could be peeled away without any remaining residue. Specifically, the acrylic spheres only stuck well to surfaces where they are tangent to the surface, thus allowing weak adhesion for easy peeling. Silver's idea of coating bulletin boards with his new adhesive, however, was not well received due to low sales of bulletin boards.

The second interesting feature was that the adhesive was reusable, because microspheres are incredibly strong and resist breaking, dissolving, or melting. However, despite these features, no one, not even Silver himself, could conceive of a good marketable product that used this weak adhesive. Even with Silver promoting it for five years to various 3M employees, the adhesive was more or less shelved.

One day in about 1973, Arthur Fry, another 3M employee, attended one of Silver's seminars. The important factor is that Fry was a singer in his church choir and was continually frustrated with the paper bookmarks he was using to mark the songs in his

Intellectual Property Law for Engineers, Scientists, and Entrepreneurs, Second Edition. Howard B. Rockman.

Published 2020 by John Wiley & Sons, Inc.

hymnal during rehearsal, because the bookmarks would not stay in the book on Sundays. The problem that Fry continually had was accidently losing his paper song page markers in his hymnal while singing. He then had what many consider a stroke of genius while attending Silver's seminar: use Silver's adhesive to help keep the bookmarks in the hymnal.

Fry then suggested to other 3M management that they were thinking of using the adhesive backward. Instead of sticking the adhesive to a bulletin board, they should place the adhesive on a piece of paper and then stick the paper to anything. In 1973, Fry obtained samples of the adhesive and began experimenting, coating only one edge of the paper so that the portion extending from his hymnal would not be sticky. He also used some of his experiments to write notes to his boss.

During the years after Fry first had the idea of using Silver's adhesive to prevent markers from falling out of his hymnal, Silver and Fry made removable bookmarks for use in their own offices as a note on a work file, for example. Other 3M workers began to stop by asking for bookmarks they could also use, before Silver and Fry were able to convince executives at 3M to try using them in 1977. During the development of Silver's adhesive, early prototypes resulted in adhesive detaching from the paper and adhering to the object to which the paper was supposed to be stuck to, or leaving some of the adhesive behind. Two other 3M employees, Roger Merrill and Henry Courtney, were tasked with developing a coating that can be placed on the paper to make the adhesive remain bonded to the paper, and not be left behind when the paper was removed. They eventually successfully developed such a coating. In 1977, 3M began test marketing "Press N Peel" pads in four U.S. cities; however, the results were disappointing. A year later, in 1978, 3M issued free samples to consumers in Boise, Idaho, and 94 percent of those who tried them said they would buy the product. The product was sold as Post-Its in 1979–1980 when the product rollout began.

Post-It Notes did not come to fruition until the 1980s both due to technical problems with production and management's doubts about the product's sales potential. It also took Silver five years to develop machinery to manufacture Post-It Notes. However, Post-It Notes were introduced to the national market in 1979–1980, and in 1981 3M itself named Post-It Notes its outstanding new product. On March 16, 1993, Arthur Fry obtained Patent No. 5,194,299 on a method of making repositionable pressure-sensitive adhesive sheet material.

The original note's distinctive yellow color remained a registered 3M trademark, with terms such as "reposition notes" used for similar products manufactured by competitors. The original Post-It Notes' yellow color was chosen strictly by accident since the laboratory next to the Post-It team only had yellow scrap paper to use.

Today, the same adhesive that is used in Post-It Notes has been applied to other products ranging from medical bandages to interior decorating kits. According to the conditions of Silver's employment at 3M, the patents that he filed covering the Post-It Notes belonged to 3M, and Silver did not receive any royalties. He retired from 3M in 1996.

As a postscript regarding intellectual property, Alan Amron made claims in 1974 to be the inventor who in 1973 disclosed the technology used in Post-It Notes to 3M. His 1997 lawsuit against 3M was settled, and 3M paid Amron. As part of the settlement, Amron undertook not to make any future legal claims against the company unless there was a breach of the settlement agreement. However, in 2016, Amron filed another lawsuit asserting that 3M was wrongly claiming to be the inventors and seeking $400 million in damages. The Court held a preliminary hearing, and a federal judge ordered the parties to undergo mediation. The lawsuit was subsequently dismissed, declaring the previous 1998 settlement agreement to be upheld.

In 2003, 3M began marketing Post-It brand super sticky notes with a stronger glue that adheres better to vertical and non-smooth surfaces. From the above story, you can determine that it took 12 years, from 1968 when the technology behind Post-It Notes was first developed until 1980 when the finished product was finally introduced to the market.

United States Patent

Silver

[15] **3,691,140**

[45] **Sept. 12, 1972**

[54] **ACRYLATE COPOLYMER MICROSPHERES**

[72] Inventor: **Spencer Ferguson Silver,** 3 M Center, St. Paul, Minn. 55101

[22] Filed: **March 9, 1970**

[21] Appl. No.: **17,880**

[52] **U.S. Cl.** ....**260/78.5,** 117/155, 117/161, 260/29.6, 260/30.4, 260/31.2, 260/32.8, 260/33.4, 260/33.6, 260/79.3, 260/80.73, 260/80.8, 260/80.81, 260/86.1 R, 260/86.1 N

[51] **Int. Cl.**..**C08f 15/26**

[58] **Field of Search**....260/86.1 N, 79.3, 78.5, 80.73, 260/80.8, 80.81

[56] **References Cited**

UNITED STATES PATENTS

2,892,822	6/1959	Gray et al.	260/86.1 N
3,257,478	6/1966	Jubilee et al.	260/86..1 N
3,385,839	5/1968	Honig et al.	260/86.1 N
3,428,617	2/1969	Sobolev	260/86.1 N
3,485,806	12/1969	Bloomquist et al.	260/86.1 N
3,527,802	9/1970	Slagel	260/86.1 N

Primary Examiner—Harry Wong, Jr.
Attorney—Kinney, Alexander, Sell, Steldt & Delahunt

[57] **ABSTRACT**

Infusible, solvent-dispersible, solvent-insoluble, inherently tacky, elastomeric copolymer microspheres consist essentially of about 90 percent to about 99.5 percent by weight of at least one alkyl acrylate ester and about 10 to about 0.5 percent by weight of at least one monomer selected from the group consisting of substantially oil-insoluble, water-soluble, ionic monomers and maleic anhydride. The microspheres are prepared by aqueous suspension polymerization utilizing emulsifier in an amount greater than the critical micelle concentration in the absence of externally added protective colloids or the like.

19 Claims, No Drawings

US005194299A

United States Patent [19]

Fry

[11] **Patent Number: 5,194,299**

[45] **Date of Patent: Mar. 16, 1993**

[54] **REPOSITIONABLE PRESSURE-SENSITIVE ADHESIVE SHEET MATERIAL**

[75] Inventor: **Arthur L. Fry**, Saint Paul, Minn.

[73] Assignee: **Minnesota Mining and Manufacturing Company**, St. Paul, Minn.

[21] Appl. No.: **948,095**

[22] Filed: **Dec. 31, 1986**

Related U.S. Application Data

[60] Division of Ser. No. 662,605, Oct. 19, 1984, abandoned, which is a continuation-in-part of Ser. No. 662,605, Oct. 19, 1984, abandoned.

[51] **Int. Cl.^{5}** **B32B 31/00**

[52] **U.S. Cl.** **427/208.6**; 427/421; 427/284; 427/285; 428/194; 428/198; 428/201; 428/202; 428/211; 428/343

[58] **Field of Search** 428/194, 198, 211, 343, 428/40, 202, 201; 427/208.6, 421, 284, 285

[56] **References Cited**

U.S. PATENT DOCUMENTS

1,944,834	1/1934	Bennett, Jr.	154/43
2,000,475	5/1935	O'Donnell	154/43
2,116,289	5/1938	Shepherd	91/50
2,264,629	12/1941	Engert et al.	40/2
2,349,709	5/1944	Evans	117/44
2,386,731	10/1945	Wenzelberger	91/50
2,515,4:3	7/1950	Ptasnik	117/44
2,721,810	10/1955	Schram	117/45
2,729,193	1/1956	Scholl	118/202
2,750,942	6/1956	Robson	128/156
2,940,868	6/1960	Patchell	117/38
3,033,702	5/1962	Fenselau	117/38
3,174,888	3/1965	Morgan	156/230
3,671,284	6/1972	Uhrig	117/21
3,691,140	9/1972	Silver	260/78.5
3,741,786	6/1973	Torrey	117/3.1
3,808,088	4/1974	Knechiges et al.	161/148
3,811,438	5/1974	Economou	128/156
3,857,731	12/1974	Merrill, Jr. et al.	117/122
3,900,642	8/1975	Michel	428/40
3,967,624	7/1976	Milnamow	128/287
4,004,049	1/1977	Horwat et al.	427/208.6
4,063,559	12/1977	Tritsch	128/287
4,166,152	8/1979	Baker et al.	428/522
4,460,634	7/1984	Hasegawa	428/124

FOREIGN PATENT DOCUMENTS

1541311 2/1979 United Kingdom .

Primary Examiner—Alexander S. Thomas

Attorney, Agent, or Firm—Gary L. Griswold; Walter N. Kirn; Thomas J. Odar

[57] **ABSTRACT**

Pressure-sensitive adhesive sheet material having the ability to be applied to paper and removed therefrom without lifting fibers or delaminating the paper. The otherwise conventional pressure-sensitive adhesive is applied to the backing by spraying, resulting in a non-repetitive pattern of adhesive islands.

5 Claims, 1 Drawing Sheet

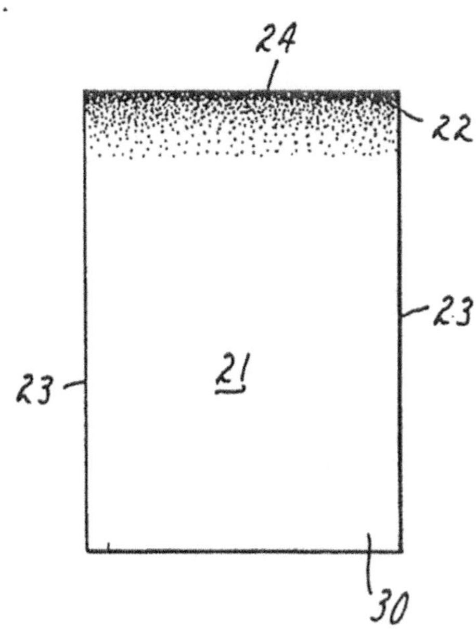

36 Entrepreneurship Law

36.1 INTRODUCTION

It is safe to presume that some of you reading this text, or possibly all of you, have thought, or will think, of starting your own successful business enterprise someday—thus becoming an "entrepreneur"—either alone or with some of your friends or acquaintances. With the pervasive publicity about our present entrepreneur class of billionaires visible through every media outlet, it is natural to think: "Why not me? I have great ideas." Indeed, I have the utmost confidence that some of you will someday take steps, or may already have taken steps to create your own enterprise, possibly based on a technological advance for an existing product, developing a totally new product, or using the Internet as a springboard for your new business.

Today's entrepreneur, in general terms, is one who starts with an idea of a product, process, or service that has a high probability of public acceptance, or in capitalistic terms, commercialization. The entrepreneur then forms and organizes a business entity, assembling the necessary financing, intellectual property protection, and skilled personnel necessary to start the venture. After the new business has been organized, the entrepreneur manages the venture to develop a customer base, attract a flow of new customers, and has the ability to deliver and service its products or services. To get this far, the entrepreneur also assumes a great majority of the risk of success or failure, primarily by investing his or her own resources to jump-start the venture, usually at risk to his or her own business reputation, and giving up an otherwise steady, somewhat guaranteed income stream. The entrepreneur hopes to balance these risks against the possibility of gains in income in great multiples of the initial investment.

As you may have deduced by now, each step taken in arranging, financing, and managing a new enterprise requires knowledge of, and adherence to, a myriad of laws, regulations, and customs of the trade. As one small example, the law limits how many potential investors you may approach to obtain the initial financing for your enterprise before you are required to submit documentation, usually at significant expense, to the federal Securities and Exchange Commission (SEC). The purpose of this chapter is to provide you with an overview of some of the legal issues you will encounter in moving forward with your new enterprise to ensure you do not run afoul of the law, which could possibly stop your business venture in its tracks before it leaves the station, and to ensure that you incur only necessary and acceptable legal risks in your venture, and do not get involved in unnecessary and avoidable legal expenses.

Intellectual Property Law for Engineers, Scientists, and Entrepreneurs, Second Edition. Howard B. Rockman.

Published 2020 by John Wiley & Sons, Inc.

36.2 TRANSITION FROM EMPLOYEE TO EMPLOYER

36.2.1 Restrictions Emanating from Your Current Employment

36.2.1.1 During and after Employment

Several clients of mine over the years have conceived of and took the initial steps to start a new business while still an employee of another company or entity. This raises two primary sets of issues that must be considered. The first issue involves duties and obligations of an employee under state laws, even if there is no employment contract. The second set of issues requires a review of any employment or other contract the employee signed upon the start of his or her present employment. Under either situation, certain obligations of the entrepreneur will cease to exist when employment stops, while other important obligations to the present employer will continue even beyond employment. The three primary areas of concern involve (1) the fiduciary duties owed to an employer by an employee, (2) ensuring that the rules against "unfair competition" are not violated, and (3) the maintenance of trade secret obligations by the departing employee. These areas of legal responsibility are created under the common law, and in most instances regardless of contractual terms.

36.2.1.2 Fiduciary Duties

A fiduciary relationship is defined as one in which the parties place trust and confidence in each other. This is the relationship that the parties are expected to follow as they conduct business with each other. Fiduciary duties usually extend along a line downward in a business organization. For example, an employee who is characterized as a key employee or skilled employee will owe certain duties of loyalty and honesty and care similar to the duties owed by a director of the same organization.

The analysis of fiduciary duties arises when the current employee decides to leave their present employer to start a new business. It must be determined whether or not the employee is of the type that owes a duty of loyalty or fiduciary duty to the employer, assuming that a key employee such as a high-ranking vice president, executive, or a skilled employee such as an engineer will likely owe such a duty. However, a rank-and-file employee (such as a draftsman) will likely not owe such a fiduciary duty to his or her former employer. In other words, the higher up you are in the hierarchy of your company, the greater the fiduciary duty that is owed to your company.

In deciding to leave your present employment, it must be determined whether or not you have taken any actions that would violate the fiduciary duty you owe your present or former employer. A prime example is directly competing with your employer while still an employee, which is characterized as disloyalty. Directly competing after termination of the employment, which terminates the fiduciary relationship, is permissible since no duty of loyalty is owed after the termination of the employment relationship. However, this would not apply if you had signed a non-compete agreement with your employer.

In the normal course of events, taking initial steps to create a new business that will compete with the present employer is not in and of itself disloyal when conducted while the employment relationship exists. For example, you could work on a business plan for a competing business or explore renting office space while still employed by your employer, provided that such efforts do not interfere with or take the time of your present job responsibilities.

36.2.1.3 Trade Secrets

We have discussed trade secret law previously in this text in Chapters 27 and 28. Most states, and now the federal legal system, have trade secret statutes that apply to workers who have access to their employer's confidential information. The trade secret information of your employer is, of course, information that provides your company with a competitive advantage over its competitors where the company has taken steps to keep this information confidential. If the entrepreneur takes confidential information such as password-protected customer lists, codes, secret formulas, chemical compositions, any internal business strategy, private marketing data, or confidential technology from the former employer and uses any of this information for a new venture, the entrepreneur has violated the state and federal trade secret law and is subject to a lawsuit resulting in damages and an injunction against the use of such confidential information. The entrepreneur who is leaving the employment of the employer must be careful not to take with them any sensitive information of the current employer.

36.2.1.4 Unfair Competition

The state common law tort of unfair competition is directed to preventing economic harm resulting from unfair business practices. This is a broad definition, and an employee can commit the tort of unfair competition rather easily by violating a fiduciary duty of loyalty to his or her employer, or also by misappropriating confidential information. Basically, anything that an employee does that is dishonest or unjust in order to form their entrepreneurial venture when they leave their employment could result in a possible claim under unfair competition law. Therefore, the entrepreneur while still employed by the employer must avoid anything dubious.

36.2.2 Restrictions Arising from an Employment Contract

Most employment starts with an employment contract between the employer and employee, which normally establishes several restrictions on the employee's conduct. The non-contractual issues enumerated in Section 36.2.1.1 above also apply whether or not the employee has a contract with the employer. Three general types of provisions in normal employment contracts may restrain the entrepreneur from starting a new business while still employed. If you are currently employed, I strongly suggest you obtain a copy of your employment agreement, and see what it says regarding the activities discussed below.

36.2.2.1 Moonlighting Provisions

Most employment contracts contain provisions restraining the employee from working on any outside businesses, which would also include businesses that do not compete with the employer, and also those that relate in any way to the employer's products or services. These restrictions are enforceable by the courts and also present a significant challenge to entrepreneurs who may have signed such contracts and who desire to form a new company while still working for their present employer. Basically, if the entrepreneur agrees not to work for any outside businesses, the entrepreneur is contractually prohibited from diverting any time, on the job or off, toward launching a new business. Therefore, the entrepreneur should be careful to read the employment contract he or she signs.

36.2.2.2 Non-Competition and Non-Solicitation Restrictive Covenants

The rules on non-competition implied by the duty of loyalty to your employer terminate at the end of employment. Therefore, many employment contracts contain clauses restricting the employee from taking a new position in competition with the former employer for some reasonable time period after the end of the employment. Although covenants not to compete fly in the face of policies that permit or encourage free competition and policies that discourage restraints on trade, employers have claimed that they have legitimate business interests that can be seriously harmed when employees leave to compete with them by forming a competing business or go to work with a competing employer. Normally, covenants not to compete are enforceable in most jurisdictions if they are reasonable in geographic scope and time duration, and if they protect a legitimate business interest of the prior employer. In litigation, each of these points must be proven by the employer who is trying to restrict the employee from forming their new business, or going to work for another employer.

A lawyer representing an entrepreneur must advise their client on two matters. First, is the covenant not to compete in fact enforceable, within the parameters of being reasonable? Second, is the former employer likely to sue the entrepreneur or the new venture, thereby causing financial harm regardless of whether the covenant is enforceable or not? In addition, non-solicitation covenants in employment agreements prohibit the employee, once they form their new business or go into business with someone else, from soliciting customers or employees of the previous employer after the worker ceases working for the former employer.

36.2.2.3 Protection of Intellectual Property and Confidential Information of the Employer

Most, if not all, workers in the technology sector are required to sign confidentiality provisions in their employment agreements, agreeing to maintain the confidentiality of an employer's confidential information, and this provision could be enforceable forever. These types of agreements are generally enforceable. Workers may also agree, and most do, to assign to the employer all intellectual property, such as patentable and copyrightable subject matter they create or invent while engaged by the employer, usually limited to inventions or creative works that relate to the business of the employer.

These employment provisions must be carefully reviewed by the entrepreneur, because sometimes they cover inventions or copyrightable works that the entrepreneur might have created on their own time and using their own resources, who is then upset to find that these are still the property of their previous employer. Entrepreneurs are usually surprised at how little of their creative efforts used during their prior employment are actually owned by them. It is important when starting a new business that the entrepreneur correctly determine whether their current or former employers have ownership claims on the intellectual property that the entrepreneur intends to use for its new venture. This must be carefully worked out before the new business is started, to avoid crippling lawsuits. Therefore, it is extremely important for new entrepreneurs to have their present and past employment contracts reviewed by a lawyer to determine what they can and cannot do.

Keep in mind also that if any such provisions do exist, it may be possible for the entrepreneur or the entrepreneur's lawyer to negotiate a waiver with the former employer giving the entrepreneur permission to start the new business. This may even involve an assignment of the intellectual property from the previous employer to the entrepreneur. If the entrepreneur has a good relationship with the former employer even though the entrepreneur is leaving the employment situation, this may help in transition negotiations between the entrepreneur and the previous employer.

36.3 ORGANIZING THE NEW BUSINESS

36.3.1 Overview

There are several business entity formations the new venture can take. A primary reason for forming the new entity is to shield the entrepreneur from personal liability that may arise from the debts or adverse action of the business. Another important aspect of the new business is the necessity of a written agreement between all of the co-founders. So, what business entity formats are available, and what advantages do they provide? The prudent entrepreneur will seek the advice of an attorney knowledgeable in this area of the law. The following is only a top-level look at business entity formation. The expert will fill in the details when needed.

36.3.1.1 Sole Proprietorship

Many people conduct business without any formal structure. These are known as sole proprietorships and are usually not incorporated. Under the law, a sole proprietorship is considered as an extension of the entrepreneur himself or herself. Any liability or risk associated with the business rests with and falls on the entrepreneur individually, and all assets of the business are really just assets of the individual. The individual is responsible for paying taxes on the income of the business since the business income is really just the entrepreneur's income. The sole proprietorship can be sold like any other element of personal property owned by the entrepreneur, and if the entrepreneur dies, the sole proprietorship dies with him or her. Under most state laws, people operating under sole proprietorships must register the name of their company with the Secretary of State of that particular state. Other than that, there normally are no special filings associated with operating as a sole proprietorship.

36.3.1.2 General Partnership

Partnership structures for businesses are controlled by state statutes. Normally, a partnership is formed when two or more individuals come together as co-owners to conduct a business for profit. Several people working under a shared profit and shared controlled business environment usually have established something called a co-ownership partnership. Normally, no formal partnership agreement is required. However, it is suggested that if you intend to operate your entrepreneurship business under a partnership, a formal partnership agreement between the parties be created.

If there is no such agreement, state law dictates that each partner will share the control and profits of the new venture equally regardless of how much initial capital each has invested in the business. It is highly recommended that a written partnership agreement be created early on in the beginning of the business. In a general partnership, all partners are personally liable for any debts or activities of the partnership business. Also, each partner owes a fiduciary duty of care and loyalty to the partnership itself, and also to the other partners. The duty of loyalty cannot be eliminated.

36.3.1.3 Limited Partnership

A limited partnership is not created automatically. It is created by filing with the secretary of state a document establishing the limited partnership. Limited partnerships have two types of partners: the general partner, who is the one who controls the business and has unlimited personal liability for the debts of the partnership, and limited partners, who are typically outside investors who have no control over the business and have no liability for the partnership's debts. Limited partnerships are usually controlled by state law and also require a limited partnership agreement to govern the matters of profits, losses, and the authority of the general partner. Taxes of the limited partnership are the responsibility of the partners in proportion to their share of the partnership income.

36.3.1.4 Limited Liability Partnership

A limited liability partnership (LLP) is created by filing documents with the Secretary of State and is governed by state statute. Many states limit LLPs to certain service-providing professions such as attorneys or accountants who are also formed as professional corporations in some states. LLPs are taxed as general partnerships with each partner paying taxes on his or her share of the partnership's income. However, the liability of the partners is quite different from a general partnership. The various state laws on this matter are different, but a common approach is that each partner is individually liable for his own malpractice or other bad acts, but not for the misconduct or negligence of his or her partners. In addition, each partner may be liable for all the general business debts that are not related to any individual partner's provision of services.

36.3.1.5 Corporation

A corporation is formed by filing Articles of Incorporation with the Secretary of State, and a corporation then becomes a separate legal entity distinct from its owners. Corporations are primarily formed to insulate their owners and investors from individual liability. Units of ownership in the corporation are called shares, and the owners are shareholders. The shareholders then elect a board of directors who are responsible and have fiduciary duties of care and loyalty to the corporation. The directors in turn elect the officers of the corporation, such as president, secretary, and treasurer, who run the corporation on a day-to-day basis. Therefore, the corporation management now has three levels of individuals: the shareholders, the board of directors, and the officers.

As mentioned earlier, in any corporation the shareholders are insulated from liability for the debts of the business. However, if the conduct of a shareholder or officer leads to certain negative circumstances, the law provides a provision called "piercing the corporate veil," which makes the individual personally liable for their unlawful or improper activities. For example, piercing the corporate veil is justified if a shareholder does not treat the corporation as a separate legal entity, but treats the corporation as an extension of himself or herself.

Income from businesses organized as corporations are taxed in two different ways. A traditional "C" corporation is taxed as a separate legal entity on the income tax form of the corporation. A dividend declared by the corporation is taxable to the individual shareholders.

The entrepreneurship also has the option to form a corporation under Chapter S of the Internal Revenue Code, known as an S corporation. S corporations are taxed as partnerships where the shareholders each pay tax on their share of the corporation's income.

36.3.1.6 Limited Liability Company

A limited liability company (LLC) is a more recent business structure formed by filing articles of organization with the Secretary of State. An LLC, as these companies are commonly called, is a separate legal entity, distinct from its owners. The owners are called members, and are shielded from liability in a manner similar to shareholders of a corporation. Members also owe fiduciary duties to the entity and also to each of the other members, but these duties can be cut back significantly in a written document governing the LLC, which is called an operating agreement or an LLC agreement.

State statutes typically provide significant opportunity for flexible customization of the LLC governance in the operating agreement. LLCs are often categorized as member-managed organizations, meaning the entity is run directly by its owners, such as a general partnership. Also, an LLC can be manager-managed, meaning that the entity is run by a manager or group of managers elected by the members. The flexibility of the LLC extends beyond management style and includes the ability to structure different kinds of equity ownership. From a tax perspective, LLCs can be taxed on a flow-through basis as a partnership, or can elect to be taxed as a C corporation and be subject to double taxation. It is highly recommended that when forming an entrepreneurship under an LLC structure, an attorney and an accountant be consulted to ensure that you are not being taken advantage of by the tax laws.

36.3.2 Brief Comments on Choosing an Advantageous Business Entity Structure

If the start-up is formed as a sole proprietorship, or as a partnership, the founders bear the liability for the debts or malfeasance of the organization. That is why these types of organizations are not usually selected by the founders. Entity selection these days usually becomes a choice between an LLC and a corporation. S Corporations, which are state law corporations to which the Internal Revenue Service gives flow-through tax treatments, are sometimes used for initial start-ups. Therefore, the choice for a new venture moving forward is generally between a C corporation and an LLC. The differences between corporations and LLCs fall into two categories: (1) financial and economic aspects and (2) management and governance aspects. On the financial side, the key difference is that a C corporation is subject to double taxation, and LLCs benefit from flow-through taxation.

On the governance side, corporations have formal governance structures put in place by state statute. LLCs are also significantly more flexible than corporations. For example, LLCs can mimic the corporate governance structure with members electing a board that selects officers, or an LLC can operate more like a partnership with members directly running the business, or an LLC can be something in between with members electing a manager who runs the business. This is clearly more flexible than the corporate structure defined by law. Also, for members of an LLC, the duties are more akin to the duties a partner has toward the partnership and the other partners, but can be modified significantly in the operating agreement to more closely match the duties of a corporation.

There are many nuances and considerations in forming an appropriate business entity. It is at this point, among others, that the entrepreneur should contact a lawyer who is well versed in the corporate law of the jurisdiction where the business intends to operate.

36.4 INTELLECTUAL PROPERTY ASSETS

You have previously been exposed to the precepts of "Intellectual Property Law" in the preceding chapters of this this text. Here, then, briefly mentioned are the important precepts of the development and protection of the intellectual property that forms the core of the new venture. Two key matters of concern to the entrepreneur are (1) protecting the intellectual property developments of the new business and (2) taking steps to ensure that the new business does not infringe on the intellectual property rights of another individual or entity. In certain start-up situations, the most important assets of the new venture are the intellectual property rights created in the innovative technology and branding developed through entrepreneurship.

The previous materials in this text relating to patents, trademarks, copyrights, and trade secrets need not be repeated here. You already know the importance of the exclusivity your intellectual property rights provide, and how that exclusivity can be successfully utilized to protect the niche market position of your new business against initial competition, allowing you to gain a secure foothold in the marketplace.

36.5 FINANCING

36.5.1 Introduction and Overview

Ask any entrepreneur and they will tell you that it is practically impossible to start a new business venture without adequate financing. There are many initial steps that require payment before a product is manufactured and introduced to the market or a service offered to the public by the new entity. As one example, it is necessary to initiate protection of the intellectual property upon which a new venture will be based before starting the venture. Costs are involved in protecting the intellectual property, and the financing for this initial aspect of a business operation must be covered. The formation of the entity itself will also require an initial outlay of funds.

There are two primary ways entrepreneurs receive the cash needed to begin their business. They can either sell an ownership interest in the business, or the business itself could borrow the necessary funds. Under the first approach, called Equity Financing, the business sells shares if it is a corporation, or membership interests if it is an LLC, or partnership interests if the venture is a partnership. These interests are sold to the founder or founders, or to third parties who are known as equity investors.

The founders share the gains with all the equity investors when the venture is successful, but they all also share the risk of loss if the venture fails.

Under the second arrangement, called debt financing, the business borrows money from the founder or a third party such as a bank, securing the loan by collateral that a lender can foreclose upon if the loan is not repaid. Many factors go into determining the most advisable way for the entrepreneur to obtain the initial capital to start the business. Throughout its active life, a business will typically have both investors and debt.

When entrepreneurs initially conceive their business and need funding to begin their operation, they often look to their own personal assets, known as "bootstrapping." Sometimes entrepreneurs will use their own savings and credit cards, or mortgage their homes to obtain the initial capital. The benefits of obtaining cash by bootstrapping are the immediate availability of money without going through third parties, not having the social pressure and anxiety of potentially losing your friends' and family's money, and not owing fiduciary duties to anyone else other than yourself as the founder. Additionally, it is quite possible that future investors may be more interested in putting their funds into a business in which the founders have invested their own money, as this demonstrates both the confidence and commitment of the founders.

As expected, the entrepreneur beginning a business by bootstrapping also faces significant risks. You may have already quit your job to start the new venture and, therefore, you do not have a regular paycheck. You may not have health insurance or retirement benefits or any other financial security. Risking additional savings may put the entrepreneur in a precarious financial position, causing undue stress on the individual as well as tension in family relationships, neither of which is good for business during the start-up phase, and may also affect the entrepreneur's ability to have a clear and focused head to make wise business decisions. Also, businesses that are funded by founders miss out on having the expertise and contacts that outside investors bring to the organization. Entrepreneurs who are limited to their own financial sources may preclude quick growth of the business.

As a generalization, entrepreneurs tend to invest in their own businesses initially, then quickly look to friends and family to help, move on to angel investors, and then if the stars are aligned and the business has established a certain level of success, they identify an appropriate venture capital firm. Simultaneously, the founders may look to a bank or a third party for a loan. Keep in mind that most, if not all, banks today will not loan money to a business unless it or its owners have sufficient assets to secure the amount of the loan. Thus, if you have a new venture that does not have much capitalization or many assets, bank loans are often not an option until the business has grown sufficiently and acquired a tangible value to support repayment of the loan. For example, the primary assets of a start-up are the intellectual property assets, which are very difficult to collateralize or value at the initial stages of the venture's operations.

Often, the founders together with family and friends become the only investors in the initial seed round of obtaining financing. An additional round of financing may be obtained from "angels." These are typically successful businesspeople with a high net worth who invest in and often advise start-up companies. The amount of money you may obtain from an angel varies widely based upon the amount of money the angel feels safe in investing and the limits to which the angel can invest in the first place.

Following these early stages of financing, entrepreneurs may then approach venture capitalists to fund the company's growth. Venture capital involves a substantial equity investment in a non-public enterprise that does not involve active control of the firm. Experience and maturity of the management team of an entrepreneurial company, however, is necessary to attract a venture capitalist to invest money into the new business.

Venture capital organizations differ from angels in that venture capitalists typically invest other investors' capital in promising young start-ups. Keep in mind that if you are a founder of a start-up, you may have to relinquish and give up an increasing ownership interest as venture capitalists re-value the start-up, and want to obtain a larger interest in it in exchange for their investment. Also, consider that most venture capitalists, and even you yourself as the founder of the start-up, may be aiming to someday build the company's value to a point where the company can be sold.

36.5.2 Equity Financing

Sophisticated investors usually prefer to own large percentages of the new business, rather than divide the ownership into fractional percentages among many people. Having fractional ownership usually results in administrative and management headaches because multiple individuals are involved in making decisions.

One way to encourage the creation of a good organization at an early stage of operation is to have the entrepreneur purchase their ownership share of the business by making a cash deposit in the new business's bank account and signing a simple document assigning their intellectual property to the new entity. In exchange for the cash and intellectual property, the business will issue equity securities to the founder. In other words, the founder's contribution to the company is the intellectual property and initial cash. It is important that when a company is formed, a formal separation is made between the founders and the new venture itself.

A friends-and-family financing route is normally the way small businesses get started. Your friends and family usually do little negotiation and often would be willing to take non-voting equity in small percentages, having faith in the fact that they know you, or may be related to you.

Angel investors typically have more cash available to invest than your friends and family, and they also negotiate for better advantages in the form of a larger percentage of the ownership of the business or preferred returns on their investment. They also may want to get involved in the management of the company and be sure they have a vote when certain important activities are embarked upon by the company. One advantage of the angel-type investment system is that the angel contributes much more than cash to the company. For example, mentorship guidance, personal contacts, and industry experience can be more valuable and instrumental than money in allowing the company to reach successful goals.

If you are dealing with a venture capitalist, the process is normally started by a terms sheet used by the businesspeople to negotiate the key terms of the transaction. The terms sheet does not cover every legal contingency and nicety that is covered in a so-called formal agreement. The terms sheet is designed to highlight the key terms and present them in a practical format that is subsequently workable into a negotiated contract. In the process of forming your company, your lawyer will provide you the information you need regarding what goes into a terms sheet, and how you should consider the factors that go into the making of a terms sheet.

The lawyer will also provide you with advice as to whether or not securities regulations and registrations are necessary to make your capital-raising activities legal under the securities laws of the United States and some states. The securities laws that the entrepreneur will have to deal with are rather complicated, and sound legal advice should be sought in the field of securities during the creation of the start-up.

36.5.3 Bank Financing

At some point, your business will need to seek a bank loan, either a term loan or a revolving loan. A term loan is used to finance the working capital requirements of a business for a specific period of time. Under a revolving line of credit, the loan amount will fluctuate depending on the borrower's everyday cash needs. A borrower may re-borrow amounts it has repaid under a revolving loan up to a specified limit. Also, term loans can be made for specific business purposes, such as purchasing equipment. Term loans are generally made in lump sums or installments and may be re-borrowed as amounts borrowed under the term loan are repaid.

Keep in mind that bank lenders generally require that business loans be secured by collateral owned by the borrower. There is a law called the Uniform Commercial Code that has been adopted by all the states and provides the mechanics and regulations for enforcing a security interest by a bank, for example, in the physical property and fixtures of an organization, and/or in the intellectual property of the organization.

To secure a bank loan, it will probably be necessary for the founders or members to sign a personal guarantee in favor of the lender. Normally, if the owners themselves do not personally secure the loan, the bank will not provide the necessary financial resources. It is quite apparent that a bank, instead of relying on the corporation, which is short of assets for collateral, will obviously rely on the personal guarantees of the owners of the business. When a personal guarantee is signed, the entrepreneur is normally protected by virtue of the limited liability of corporations against most of the corporate creditors, except the bank. When taking out the loan, care should be taken since the personal guarantee could expose an individual to significant personal liability to the bank. However, this form of financing is commonplace in the business world since it is usually necessary to get a new corporation or new business venture off the ground.

36.6 EMPLOYMENT LAW

36.6.1 Employee or Independent Contractor?

The decision of whom to hire is a very important decision by the start-up company. A great deal of thought must be given to hiring a management team as well as other employees and workers for the company. However, from the first time an entrepreneur hires an employee or deals with a contractor, he or she faces several legal considerations both on the state and federal levels, including regulations and common law rules. The entrepreneur must determine the worker's correct classification as an employee or otherwise, such as an independent contractor, because such classification determines the legal protections afforded the worker as well as benefits, management expectations, and liability issues. For example, there are laws that prohibit discrimination among employees and also provide workplace benefits to employees. On top of the federal regulations, some states impose additional and sometimes harsher restrictions on employers by providing employees with broad rights and protections in the workplace.

Many of the federal laws only apply to workers who fall within the category of "employees." Workers hired as "independent contractors" are usually not subject to these laws. Thus, there is a legal distinction between employees and independent contractors, and the classification between these two is not something that the worker and the company can agree to on their own. The United States legal system, the courts, and even the Internal Revenue Service apply various factors to determine if a worker in a certain situation was properly classified as an employee or as an independent contractor.

When a worker is engaged as an independent contractor as opposed to an employee, the company is not required to withhold income taxes, pay Social Security and Medicare, or provide worker's compensation insurance and many other benefits. Also, the company is not subject to many employment laws that apply to employees and not to independent contractors. However, it is crucial to properly classify workers as either independent contractors or employees due to the penalties that may accrue for misclassification. In addition, in the absence of a written agreement defining the employee or independent contractor status of a worker, the ownership of intellectual property work products created by a worker could be in dispute, such as inventions and copyrightable works created by the worker. This concept was discussed previously in Chapter 24 of the text regarding works for hire. Sometimes, a small start-up company can conduct its business in a more informal way than an established business might do, which may lead to problems regarding whether a worker is classified as an employee or independent contractor. The entrepreneur should check with their lawyer to determine that they have all of the employment pegs in the right holes.

36.6.2 Employment Statutes

The federal government over the course of many years, and many states, have enacted several employment laws that are applicable to every business. The following is a list and brief description of only some of the more important laws.

36.6.2.1 The Fair Labor Standards Act

This federal act establishes a national minimum wage, guarantees overtime pay in certain jobs, and restricts child labor. Certain employees are exempt from the law, who generally are those who are higher-paid employees and who work with less supervision.

36.6.2.2 Worker's Compensation Laws

Worker's Compensation statutes require employers to provide a form of insurance that covers income replacement and medical benefits for employees who are injured in the course of employment. The workers receive these benefits regardless of the level of care the employer took to prevent such accidents, something akin to strict liability under tort law. The damages available to injured employees are usually capped and are lower than a typical lawsuit result.

36.6.2.3 Occupational Safety and Health Act (OSHA)

OSHA requires workplaces to be free from recognized hazards that could cause serious injury or death to a worker. The Act also created the Occupational Safety and Health Administration that sets up rules regarding the health of safety of workers in workplaces.

36.6.2.4 Title VII of the Civil Rights Act

Title VII of the Civil Rights Act of 1964 prohibits discrimination in employment based on race, color, religion, sex, or national origin. The Act was later amended to cover sex discrimination and discrimination based on pregnancy, childbirth, and related medical conditions, and marriage status, for women. All businesses with 15 or more employees are subject to this legislation. This is the law that covers sexual harassment, which still causes many problems in the workplace where someone is denied promotions or benefits upon refusal to submit to sexual advances by a supervisor. Harassment can also be shown by establishing that a hostile work environment existed. There are certain defenses under Title VII that an employer may have. For example, an employer can make an employment decision based on religion, sex, or national origin if one of those classes is a bona fide occupational qualification reasonably necessary for the normal operation of that particular business. For example, if someone's religion requires that they wear a hat during work, but the hat is a definite safety hazard to the employee when working, someone with that particular religious background may not be hired for a certain job.

36.6.2.5 The Americans with Disabilities Act

This act prohibits discrimination on the basis of a disability and requires an employer to make reasonable accommodations so that employees with disabilities may perform job responsibilities. It does not require employers to make accommodations that would constitute an undue hardship on the employer, and this particular law covers employers with 15 or more employees who work at least 20 or more weeks a year.

36.6.2.6 Age Discrimination in Employment Act

This act prohibits discrimination on the basis of age and covers workers of age 40 and older, and applies to all companies and organizations that have at least 20 employees.

36.6.3 Employment Agreements

It is important when establishing a new business to enter into written agreements with all employees, even all of management. These agreements should include specific definitions of the duties to be performed by the worker, a work schedule, compensation, termination provisions, and severance provisions. The agreement would also define specifically whether the worker is being hired as an employee or as an independent contractor.

As discussed previously in this text, the written agreement should also include a confidentiality clause, a provision for the assignment of intellectual property created during the course of employment that relates to the employer's business, a non-compete clause, and a non-solicitation of employees clause. In some instances, it is appropriate to furnish the prospective employee with an offer letter that offers at-will employment at a particular starting salary. This particular letter would not be used to guarantee any term of employment or severance, but can be used as a good recruitment tool.

36.6.4 Compensation with Equity in the New Venture

New ventures find themselves short on cash at the same time they need to build a strong management and work team to get their business moving. The strength of the management team is one of the most important ingredients of the successful venture. To attract and retain top talent while preserving as much cash as possible to build and grow the business is an important business decision that has to be made by the founders. One method of attracting good talent is to offer equity compensation to supplement the initial lower salaries of the workers. Compensating with equity in addition to a smaller salary closely aligns the incentives of the employees with those of the founders and investors.

Many equity packages come in the form of stock options to the employee. This provides a right to purchase shares of stock of a company in the future at today's price, which is hopefully lower. As the price of the stock increases, the worker can pay a lower price for something that is worth much more. Stock options are usually granted to the worker but cannot be exercised immediately. Instead they vest over time and can be sold after the company reaches certain financial goals. This encourages the more desirable employees to remain with the company for longer times, and to perform better to meet the goal of having their stock options vested at increased values.

Again, stock options are rather a complicated way of compensating workers of your start-up company, and the stock plan should be carefully vetted by the venture's attorney and accountant.

36.7 FINANCIAL STATEMENTS

Much has been said about the "bottom line" of an entrepreneurial organization. It is the financial statements created by accountants that provide the information necessary to measure a venture's success, whether you are a manager or investor. Briefly discussed below are the balance sheet, the income statement, and the cash flow statement.

36.7.1 The Purpose of Financial Statements

Financial statements are important for firm management and also for providing information to outsiders who interact with the entrepreneurial venture. Financial statements are used quite often to make decisions about a business's future by relying on the accounting figures that show past successes and growth of the organization. In addition, financial statements can pinpoint certain failures in the organization's growth that can be addressed and rectified.

Managers may sometimes prepare pro forma financial statements based on assumptions about future events and showing how these future events will have an effect on the company's bottom line. Also, entrepreneurs and investors rely on pro forma filing of financial statements to make decisions as to how the company should move forward.

Financial statements also supply information to those outside the company who deal with the new venture. These include investors, creditors, customers, suppliers, potential employees, and regulators. Investors, of course, use the information in the pro forma financial statement to determine whether or not they have made a wise decision investing in the new venture.

One consideration that the entrepreneur must look at is that the collection and assembly of useful financial information can be a major expense for any business, particularly a start-up. An experienced accountant must be hired to put this information together. Therefore, in the initial business plan for the company, funds should be allocated for proper accounting measures. Consider also that financial statements are a valuable trade secret of the company and, therefore, must be protected in accordance with the company's trade secret policies.

36.7.2 Basic Accounting Concepts

Businesses usually prepare financial statements and tax returns based on their fiscal year, which is a 12-month period that can follow the calendar year or any other 12-month period the company decides is appropriate.

In preparing financial records, there are two primary ways to account for income and expenses. The basic form is called cash basis accounting, where transactions are recorded in the accounting books at the same time as the company actually receives money from selling a product, or pays money to an outsider, such as a vendor or supplier. The second method is called accrual accounting, where revenues and expenses are recorded when they are incurred, not when money is actually received or paid out. Accrual accounting income is counted when the sale is made, not when the cash is received from the customer. Expenses are counted when the order is made and goods received, not when the company has actually paid the bill. Accrual accounting is the method required for a company's financial statements, and thus any audited financial statements must be prepared on an accrual accounting basis.

36.7.3 The Types of Financial Statements

36.7.3.1 The Balance Sheet

The balance sheet provides an instant view of the company's financial position at any particular moment. It lists the venture's assets and liabilities as of a certain date, with the difference representing the so-called owner's equity. The balance sheet also describes the sources of the company's assets. The balance sheet always balances out according to the formula "assets equal liabilities plus owner's equity." This means that the amount by which a company's assets exceed its liabilities is a statement of the net worth of the company that is held by its owners, and the value of a business is sometimes measured by the extent to which its assets exceed the amount it owes.

An asset is anything that was acquired at a cost, was obtained or controlled by the company, is expected to produce future economic benefits, and arises from a past transaction or event. Assets therefore are valuable items that are owned by the venture. A liability is anything that is a probable future sacrifice of economic resources by the entity, is estimated with reasonable certainty, will be transferred to another entity, and is a present obligation arising from a past transaction or event. Liabilities, therefore, are valuable things that are currently in possession of the venture, but are owed to others.

Owner's equity is the difference between the value of the venture's assets and the value of its liabilities. This represents the money that is available to the business.

36.7.3.2 *The Income Statement*

The income statement, which is also known as the profit and loss statement, shows the financial performance of the venture over a period of time rather than at one specific moment. Income statements report the amount of revenues and expenses of the organization. Net income is calculated by subtracting expenses from revenue. Net income for the period is included on the balance sheet as an addition to the retained earnings entry.

Income statements include only information pertaining to the particular accounting period covered by the statement. The top of the income statement shows the revenue for the period followed by a deduction for returned items for the period. After deriving the net sales, the costs of products or services sold during the period are deducted, and the remainder is known as the gross profit. Operating expenses such as research and development, sales expenses, payment of utilities, rent, and so forth, are deducted from gross profits to reveal the entity's net profit before taxes. Finally, to derive the net income, taxes are subtracted from the profit that is calculated before taxes.

36.7.3.3 *The Cash Flow Statement*

A cash flow statement shows the change in the organization's cash balance over a specified period of time. It shows how the changes in the balance sheet and income statement affect the cash held by the enterprise. The cash flow statement is used to forecast needs and also for assessing the liability of the enterprise in terms of meeting its immediate obligations.

Profit is a financial calculation not necessarily tied to the cash levels on a company's balance sheet. For example, if sales have been made on credit cards, or by another use of credit, the cash flow statement would show that the firm needs cash rather than accounts receivable to pay debts as they become due.

A cash flow statement is organized into sections showing (1) cash from operations, (2) cash from investing activities, and (3) cash from financing activities. Cash from operations shows transactions that relate to the operations of the enterprise. This could be both cash inflow and cash outflow.

Cash from investing activities shows the cash flow from the purchase and sale of long-term assets including the sale or purchase of property and equipment, patents and other intellectual property, investments, and long-term securities.

Cash from financing activities may include cash from borrowing from or repaying a bank, issuing and redeeming debt and equity, treasury stock, payments of dividends, and proceeds from the repayment of loans.

36.8 RECOMMENDATION AND ACKNOWLEDGMENT

As you can gather from this chapter, launching an entrepreneurial venture involves an astute understanding of, and compliance with, many laws, regulations, and even moral and ethical restrictions. In my judgment, it is important that the entrepreneur, at the outset, seek the advice of a competent attorney and accountant for expert guidance through the legal and financial thickets described above. Seeking and complying with such professional advice can prevent many potential headaches and unnecessary expenses in the future.

If you are interested in obtaining additional information regarding legal considerations in starting and operating an entrepreneurship, I suggest the following text: *Entrepreneurship Law, Cases and Materials*, Stephen F. Reed and Esther S. Barron; Wolters Kluwer Law and Business, Publisher, 2013.

37 Current Events

37.1 AC VERSUS DC

One of the most bizarre battles between competing technologies, and U.S. corporate moguls, took place in the late 1800s, and as a result practically every electric power system in the world today uses alternating current (AC) rather than direct current (DC). The story of this intense struggle includes tales of lighting the "White City" at the Chicago Colombian Exposition in 1893, animals purposely sacrificed for electrocution, and the invention of the electric chair.

As chronicled earlier in this work, after Thomas A. Edison successfully developed a practical incandescent light bulb in 1880 that could safely illuminate the indoors with electricity, he also had his research and development team create complete systems for generating electricity, including networks for transmitting and distributing the current to the homes and buildings that were customers for his light bulbs. Edison concluded (mistakenly) that only DC at 110 volts could be used to power his bulbs. As we shall see, he stubbornly held to this idea for over 20 years, which led him and his cohorts to engage in a battle that cost animal and human lives before he was convinced that AC could also light his bulbs. However, let us not get ahead of our story.

Nikola Tesla, in 1887, formed the Tesla Electric Company in New York City, a few short blocks from Edison's work facilities. A. K. Brown, the manager of Western Union Telegraph Company, gave Tesla the financial help he needed to use this new company to develop an AC system for providing and using electricity. Tesla started immediately to develop, engineer, and file patents for his complete AC polyphase systems for single-phase, two-phase, and three-phase AC. For each system, he created dynamos, transformers, and controls.

At this point in time, AC, DC, and gas were already in use for various forms of electrical power and illumination. High-voltage electric carbon-arc illumination was used in street lighting, with wires carrying approximately 1000 volts strung precariously on poles along and above city streets; each light produced about 4000 candlepower. Since the carbon arc light could not be subdivided (broken down into smaller units that would not blind people), this form of lighting was not suitable for indoor use. Gas lights and lamps were still the light source of choice for homes and buildings, the gas being supplied through a network of gas mains meandering beneath the city streets.

Intellectual Property Law for Engineers, Scientists, and Entrepreneurs, Second Edition. Howard B. Rockman.

Published 2020 by John Wiley & Sons, Inc.

Prior to 1887, and following Edison's introduction of his DC illumination system anchored at Pearl Street in New York City, many central stations producing and delivering AC had been established in America, using many different circuits and equipment. Thomson-Houston had installed a small transformer and alternators in 1886 to light its factory. William Stanley, chief engineer for Westinghouse Electric Company, had designed a transformer system in 1886, based on the U.S. Gauland-Gibbs patent rights acquired by Westinghouse. Transformers were required to decrease and increase voltages in power transmission over short and long distances. By 1887, Westinghouse was operating over 30 AC power-generating plants.

When Tesla began developing his AC systems in 1887, there was no workable AC motor in existence. Six months after starting his new business, Tesla had constructed, tested, and filed patent applications for the commutator-less AC induction motor he had sketched in the dust in Budapest several years earlier, which had practically no moving parts to wear out. Between 1887 and 1891, Tesla obtained 40 patents covering his AC motor and systems. Tesla received wide acclaim for his new motor, and lectured about his systems before the American Institute of Electrical Engineers on May 16, 1888. Using Tesla's AC systems, higher voltages could be transmitted over greater distances compared to DC, and Edison's light bulb could be lit using AC or DC. Also, AC generating systems did not require a substation every several miles.

George Westinghouse decided that Tesla's AC patents were the missing link in Westinghouse's AC systems and, in 1888, after making a personal inspection of the new, quiet AC motors humming in Tesla's shop, he convinced Tesla to sell Westinghouse the patents Tesla had been accumulating. The agreement between Tesla and Westinghouse dated July 7, 1888, granted Tesla $60,000, comprising $5000 in cash and 150 shares in Westinghouse Electric Company. Of more importance, however, Tesla was also to receive $2.50 for each horsepower of electrical power sold by Westinghouse using Tesla's systems. Tesla was obliged to share this income with A. K. Brown and his other investors, so although Tesla became comfortable (for a while) and socially acceptable in New York, he never became one of the ultra-rich.

Tesla decided that the ideal AC cycle for his induction motor was 60 cycles per second. Westinghouse's engineers had previously developed a 133-cycle system, and it took many months of expensive experiments and arguments before Tesla convinced the other engineers that he was right. Ever since then, 60 cycles has been the standard upon which AC is generated and used.

When Edison found out about the Westinghouse–Tesla agreement, and since he was stubbornly committed to his DC system, he decided to launch a public relations battle to establish the superiority of DC over AC. This battle eventually made today's political fights seem like child's play by comparison. Previously, Edison was involved in a campaign to prove the desirability of his electric incandescent lamps compared to gas lamps, with tactics that today might be called into question. Edison, upon publicly announcing his light bulb, was met with extra-strength resistance from the gas monopolies of the day. Edison responded by reporting and publishing commentary exposing, with joy, the extreme hazards of gas main explosions, incidents in which employees in gas-lit plants and buildings experienced health problems due to gas, and damage to vision caused by gas lights. With this background and experience, Edison launched his response to the incursion of Westinghouse and Tesla's AC into his DC domain. Edison's propagandists began barraging the public and industry in an alarming fashion about the dangers of AC. Not only did Edison take advantage of AC electrical accidents that did occur, several additional "accidents" were created just for the purpose of Edison's campaign bent on proving that AC would ruin the entire electric light and power industry.

Edison's West Orange, New Jersey R&D laboratory became the epicenter for "scientific" information used in a vitriolic press battle, with Edison's point being the dangers of AC. In 1887, several "experiments" were carried out, such as the electrocution of stray cats and dogs, before the press and "guests," by placing the animals on a tin sheet and passing 1000 volts AC through the tin and animal. In one such display, one of Edison's key assistants, Charles Batchelor, was badly throttled when he received an electric shock himself while holding a puppy on the plate. Batchelor recovered in a few days; not the dog, however.

Soon, the neighbors around Edison's West Orange facility became fearful of losing their pets when Harold Brown, a self-appointed crusader for Edison's anti-AC holy war, began paying a reward of 25 cents for each canine and feline brought in for electrocution by local children. These "experiments" were augmented in February 1888 with press releases by Edison's forces, warning the public of electrical fatalities in factories, theaters, and along high-voltage arc-light power lines, and to be wary of Westinghouse and others who were attempting to plug AC into their very homes. Westinghouse replied by issuing statements that Edison was wrong; that Stanley's transformers were located outside of the buildings, stepping down the high-tension voltage and delivering AC current to the building at a low voltage, comparable to that of the DC system.

Harold Brown was a former Edison laboratory assistant in West Orange, and by that time an engineering and electrical consultant. He launched his campaign against AC after a 15-year-old New York peddler boy and new immigrant was electrocuted when he grabbed a fallen live telegraph wire, which wire had been dangling free in the street for months following a severe blizzard and ice storm that hit New York on March 12, 1888, dumping 22 inches of snow in its wake. Brown wrote a letter to the June 5, 1888 edition of the *New York Evening Post,* in which part of his comments were directed to branding AC and its potential dangers as "damnable," and subjecting the public to "constant danger from sudden death." His letter demanded passing a law to prohibit AC transmission above 300 volts, which would make AC useless. Note that the *Evening Post* was published by an Edison investor, Henry Villard, who later became president of Edison's company. Brown himself apparently had no direct ties to the Edison camp, and no one knows why he carried out his campaign against AC. However, he became a man of action in support of DC, and carried Edison's written and oral slings against AC to a higher, or perhaps lower, latitude.

In July 1888, Westinghouse's pro-AC forces began to fight back. On June 8, 1888, Brown had proposed new safety rules for electricity to the New York City Board of Electrical Control, insisting that his published letter to the newspaper be made of record. His comments were sent to several electric companies, including Westinghouse, for a response. Westinghouse responded by pointing to fires that had caused three DC central electrical generating stations to be destroyed, including the Boston station, and the destruction by fire of a large theater in Philadelphia supplied with DC, as well as many other fires caused by DC.

Harold Brown allegedly was supported by Edison and his DC forces, and he decided to create and deliver the "scientific" evidence his critics were demanding on the all-important safety issue. On July 30, 1888, Brown conducted a "demonstration" at the School of Mines of Columbia College (now Columbia University) attended by over 70 invitees, including reporters. Brown's combativeness was already a given, and the room was filled with expectation. Brown began by extolling DC over AC, stating that his prior testing had shown that animals could withstand electrical shocks from continuous DC better than AC. Brown then proceeded to place a 76 pound black retriever dog into a cage, the dog's legs attached to wires. He applied first 300 volts DC, than 400, 700, and 1000 volts DC to the wires. Those in the audience watched the dog struggle, cry, and thrash in the cage. Many left, others yelled to Brown to cease the torturous exhibition. Brown stopped at 1000 volts DC, then attached an alternator to the wires, applied 330 volts AC, and the dog died. Both a reporter for the *New York World* and a representative of the American Society for the Prevention of Cruelty to Animals (ASPCA) approached Brown and demanded that he not electrocute any more dogs. Observing the hostile audience in front of him, Brown agreed.

Many in the audience felt that Brown had not presented scientific evidence of the dangers of AC, since they concluded that the DC jolts had sufficiently weakened the dog to the point where 330 volts AC would prove fatal. Brown retaliated by announcing to the spectators as they left the hall that he had previously experimented on a sufficient amount of dogs to assure them of AC's dangers to the entire mammal kingdom.

Undaunted, four days later Brown returned to Columbia College, where, before a smaller crowd of reporters, health administrators for the city, and his helpers, he electrocuted a 61-pound dog using less than 300 volts AC, a 91-pound Newfoundland in 8 seconds, and a 53-pound Setter–Newfoundland mixed breed in 4 painful minutes, all with AC current. The warm and humid heat of the night wafted the aroma of the dissection of one of the deceased animals over those in the audience, leaving them with a vivid and lasting impression of the events of the evening. Brown felt he had proved his point: any current that could kill a healthy dog would do the same to a human. He used the term "Westinghoused" to refer to the electrocution processes he applied to the dogs.

After returning from a brief rest in the mountains, Brown began an even more horrendous episode in the AC–DC war. The New York State assembly in the fall of 1888 passed a law substituting electrocution instead of hanging as the means of carrying out capital punishment in the state, as a result of lobbying efforts by both the AC and DC camps. The lawmakers were convinced that electrocutions would be fast, humane, and painless, leaving no marks on the body. A state committee was formed to obtain advice from the Medical-Legal Society of New York on the best use of electricity to kill humans. The committee chairman, Dr. Peterson, happened to be Harold Brown's aide in the two dog electrocution "shows" at Columbia College. Brown, although a DC advocate, was obsessed with having the rival AC used as the preferred form of electrocution. This, apparently, would help in his campaign to expound on the dangers of AC to human life.

Brown and Dr. Peterson conducted heinous experiments in Edison's West Orange laboratory on how to efficiently kill mammals larger than dogs using electricity. On December 5, 1888, before a group of reporters and others at the West Orange laboratory, and also graced by the presence of Thomas Alva Edison himself, who up to then was content to stay in the background, more experiments took place. First, 700 volts AC were applied to a 124-pound calf. The calf was dispatched in about 30 seconds. A second 145-pound calf was electrocuted in 5 seconds. Then, a 1230-pound healthy horse was killed using 700 volts AC. The Medical-Legal Society adopted a resolution recommending to the state that the official means of criminal electrocution be by AC, on a table or sitting in a chair.

George Westinghouse responded in published newspaper articles describing the number of people who had survived 1000 volt AC jolts and lived to tell about it, and that his companies were illuminating approximately 12 times the number of lights as Edison's companies. He claimed that his company would not have had such success if AC were unsafe.

Edison's DC forces had, at this time, successfully framed the AC versus DC debate on the issue of safety, pushing aside the need for thicker copper wires, the higher expense of DC, and the fact that DC was only suitable for use in crowded cities. Brown was also chosen to design the apparatus for electrocution to be used by New York. His aim was to have Westinghouse AC electricity permanently associated with human mortality.

The first man scheduled to be electrocuted in New York's electric chair was one William Kemmler of Buffalo, who had axed Tillie Ziegler, his female partner in March 1889. Harold Brown had been referring to AC as "the executioner's current," and this was his chance to prove it. Brown, who was seeking Edison's help in purchasing a Westinghouse AC dynamo to perform the electrocution at Auburn prison, was initially unsuccessful in doing so. Then, Charles Coffin, J. P. Morgan's man running Thomson-Houston Company, stepped up. At that time, Thomson-Houston and Edison Electric Co. were on the verge of a merger, and Coffin aided Brown in obtaining used Westinghouse Electric AC generators for Auburn and two other prisons. Thus, Westinghouse's AC dynamos were poised to kill humans, one of Brown's marketing goals. In August, 1889, someone broke into Brown's office and took over 40 pieces of correspondence showing that he had been advised and paid by the Edison Electric Company, and by Thomson-Houston, both Westinghouse competitors. The *New York Sun* obtained the letters, and ran the story under the headline "FOR SHAME, BROWN!"

Prior to Kemmler's execution, a Western Union Telegraph lineman, while working 40 feet over the street near New York City's City Hall, was electrocuted while cutting a wire he thought was inert. He was burned, sparks were flying, and he actually seemed to be on fire. He fell across several other wires that kept him suspended 40 feet over the street, his corpse held in mid-air for 45 minutes as crowds gathered and watched to their horror. It was not until the current was turned off that he was brought to the ground.

Public outcries compelled the New York electric companies to cease operating their high-voltage electric arc street lights, and to upgrade the maze of wires suspended above the streets. After this event, Edison himself came to the forefront of the War of the Currents, personally calling for the demise of high-voltage AC entirely. He continually urged politicians and the public that only low-voltage DC moving along buried cables was safe. His campaign was predicated upon instilling a fear of AC among the citizens, and William Kemmler was slated to become the "poster boy" for the DC forces.

After Kemmler had run the appeal process to its end, the "experimental" execution was scheduled for August 6, 1890, at Auburn prison. Executives of Edison's company were ready to convince the public that Mr. Kemmler had been "Westinghoused," since Westinghouse's dynamos were to be used to carry out the electrocution.

The AC dynamos at Auburn prison were located several hundred yards from the electric chair, and bells were used to communicate between the operators and the electrocutioner. As Kemmler was strapped into and "connected to" the chair, the Buffalo District Attorney left the room of 24 official witnesses, went into the corridor, and reportedly fainted.

The switch in the room with the AC generators was thrown at approximately 6:40 a.m. Kemmler's face went white as ash, and the prison physician pronounced Kemmler dead. The switch was turned off less than 20 seconds after the first jolt. But blood was coming from a small cut on Kemmler's finger, signifying that his heart was still beating. His chest was still throbbing, and he appeared to be trying to breathe. The scalp electrode was reattached, and the switch was thrown a second time. Kemmler became rigid, his skin and hair notably burned. His clothes were on fire, and the odor was awful. The current remained turned on for several minutes, after which the doctors present declared him dead again. For the witnesses, it was not a pleasant sight.

Kemmler's autopsy showed that his body had been rigidly formed into a sitting position by rigor mortis, and scorch marks identified where metal pieces had contacted his body. Some concluded that Kemmler may have been cooked to death in a rather inhumane way. Indeed, the newspaper reports described the execution in every morbid detail. The public's first impression of electrocution was not a favorable one, although the problems were ultimately solved, and the electric chair has been widely used to inflict capital punishment for many years, replaced of late by injections of lethal chemicals.

For unknown reasons, Harold Brown made no comment after the botched Kemmler electrocution. In point of fact, Harold Brown was never heard from publicly again.

* * * *

One footnote to this story is worthy of mention. Westinghouse, in 1890, saw his AC electric business increase, despite the Kemmler execution. But all of the large electric power-generating companies were on slippery financial footing due to the capital investment required. The debt of both Edison Electric and Westinghouse Electric grew, and financiers such as J. P. Morgan gained increasingly more power over the electric companies. On February 17, 1892, it was announced that the Edison Electric Company had merged with the Thomson-Houston Company, under the presidency of Charles Coffin, who worked for the House of Morgan. From that day to the present, the merged company would be known as General Electric Company.

Rumors also circulated that Westinghouse Electric would soon be absorbed into General Electric. If this latter takeover took place, Morgan would be able to control the future of electrifying America, both AC and DC. To make this monopoly a reality, Morgan would need control over the Tesla AC patents, owned by Westinghouse. But Westinghouse was obsessed with proving that his AC system was superior and should replace DC systems. Westinghouse refused to play Morgan's game, and Morgan started rumors of mismanagement at Westinghouse, driving Westinghouse stock downward. Westinghouse fought back by merging with smaller companies, such as Consolidated Electric Light Company and U.S. Electric Company.

The patent royalties owed to Tesla by Westinghouse, due to the success of AC power generation, were enormous. While no records were kept, Tesla was on the brink of becoming one of the world's richest men. Westinghouse's investors insisted that the Tesla royalty contract be terminated. George Westinghouse resisted, but the banks insisted. An embarrassed George Westinghouse met with Tesla and told him that if the AC system royalty contract were not modified in some way, Westinghouse Electric would cease to be under his control. Westinghouse also told Tesla that if Tesla agreed to forgo royalties, he would continue to move forward with plans to electrify America with AC systems and current.

Tesla, not being an astute businessman or financial wizard, but trusting in George Westinghouse's judgment, tore up the royalty contract and reportedly accepted the total sum of $216,600 for the full assignment of his AC patent rights to Westinghouse, forgoing the receipt of any future royalties.

Westinghouse remained true to his promise to Tesla, and worked to bring AC electrification to the dominant position it enjoys worldwide today. In 1892–1893, Westinghouse successfully outbid General Electric Company for the right to provide the electric incandescent light system for Chicago's Columbian Exposition. George Westinghouse and Nikola Tesla appeared at the Exposition, showing off the wonders of AC electricity in what became known as the "White City." The Westinghouse Electric and Manufacturing Company grew and prospered. Tesla never wavered in his admiration for George Westinghouse.

When Tesla gave up his claim to past and future royalties from his AC patents, he probably did himself, and the world, a great disservice. He managed to live comfortably for another 10 years or so, working on additional inventions. However, Tesla ultimately encountered a shortage of money for additional research and development lasting over the remainder of his life. Therefore, the question must be asked: how many potential future beneficial inventions and discoveries were denied to the populace due to the financial stifling of Tesla's immense capacity for creativity?

In this essay, I have only scratched the surface of the lives and accomplishments of those inventors and industrialists who brought electricity out of the fictional arms of the mythical god Thor, and developed the machinery and processes that deliver it in useful abundance to every corner of the globe. For additional information about the extraordinary, and many times ordinary, lives of these creative individuals, I highly recommend further reading of the fine books and other sources of biographical material in the Bibliography.

Tesla, not being an astute businessman or financial wizard, but trusting in George Westinghouse's judgment, tore up the royalty contract and accepted [illegible] the total sum of $216,000 for the full assignment of his AC patent rights to Westinghouse, forgoing the receipt of any future royalties.

With a [illegible] from [illegible] the [illegible] and worked [illegible] [illegible] [illegible] 1893 [illegible] [illegible] the right to provide the [illegible] of light [illegible] for Chicago's Columbian Exposition. [illegible] Westinghouse and Tesla [illegible] at the Exposition, showing off the wonders of AC [illegible] known as the "[illegible]" The [illegible] Chicago and [illegible] [illegible] and [illegible] [illegible] in [illegible] [illegible] Tesla [illegible]

[illegible] AC [illegible] [illegible]

Bibliography

ELI WHITNEY

History.com Staff, *Cotton Gin and Eli Whitney*, History.com, A&E Network (2010), www.history.com/topics/inventions/cotton-gin-and-eli-whitney, accessed 8/17/18.

National Park Service, U.S. Department of the Interior, *Eli Whitney*, https://www.nps.gov/people/eli-whitney.htm, accessed 8/17/18.

Eli Whitney Museum and Workshop: The Cotton Gin (2018), https://eliwhitney.org/7/museum/eli-whitney/cotton gin, accessed 8/8/18.

Brodsky, Joan, *Eli Whitney's Patent for the Cotton Gin*, U.S. National Archives & Records Administration, Washington, D.C. (2016), http://www.archives.gov/digital-classroom/lessons/cotton-gin-patent/cotton-gin-patent.html, accessed 9/18/18.

Wilson, Mitchell, *American Science and Inventions: A Pictorial History*, Simon & Schuster, N.Y. (1954), pp. 78–83.

Eli Whitney Museum, *The Inventor*, http://www.eliwhitney.org/7/museum/about-eli-whitney/inventor, accessed 9/18/18.

CHARLES BABBAGE

Swade, Doron, *The Difference Engine, Charles Babbage and the Quest to Build the First Computer*, Viking Penguin, a member of Penguin Putnam, Inc. (2001).

Computer History Museum, *Ada Lovelace*, http://www.computerhistory.org/babbage/adalovelace/, accessed 5/26/18.

Charles Babbage (1791–1871), BBC (2014), http://www.bbc.co.uk/history/historic_figures/babbage_charles.shtml, accessed 1/14/18.

O'Connor, J.J., Robertson, E.F., *Charles Babbage*, School of Mathematics and Statistics, Univ. of St. Andrews, Scotland (1998), http://www-history.mcs.st-andrews.ac.uk/mathematicians/Babbage.html, accessed 1/14/18.

Isaacson, Walter, *The Innovators*, Simon & Schuster (2014), Ada, Countess of Lovelace, pp. 7–33.

CHAPTER 1

United States Constitution, Article 1, Section 8, Clause 8 (1787).

United States Patent Statutes, 35 U.S.C. § 1–376.

United States Patent No. 4,736,866 (April 12, 1988).

United States Patent No. 4,259,444 (March 31, 1981).

Diamond v. Chakrabarty, 477 U.S. 303, 306 USPQ 193 (Supreme Court 1980).

Intellectual Property Law for Engineers, Scientists, and Entrepreneurs, Second Edition. Howard B. Rockman.

Published 2020 by John Wiley & Sons, Inc.

State Street Bank & Trust Co. v. Signature Financial Group, Inc. 149 F. 3d 1368 (Fed. Cir. 1988), *cert denied*, 525 U.S. 1093 (Supreme Court 1999).

United States Trademark Act, 15 U.S.C. §§ 1051–1129.

United States Copyright Act, 17 U.S.C. §§ 101–1332.

Uniform Trade Secrets Act, 1985 revised form, National Conference of Commissioners on Uniform State Laws (1985).

The Semiconductor Chip Protection Act of 1984, 17 U.S.C. §§ 901–914.

FRANK J. SPRAGUE

Target Study, *Electric Streetcar*, https://targetstudy.com/knowledge/invention/90/electric-streetcar.html, accessed 3/11/18.

Editors of Encyclopaedia Britannica, *Streetcar*, https://www.britannica.com/technology/streetcar, accessed 3/11/18.

The Electronic Encyclopedia of Chicago, *Street Railways*, https://www.encyclopedia. chicago-history.org/pages/1207.html, accessed 3/11/18.

Frank J. Sprague Biography, http://www.browsebiography.com/bio-frank_j_sprague.html, accessed 3/11/18.

Frank J. Sprague (2016), https://ethw.org/Frank_J._Sprague, accessed 3/11/18.

Wikipedia, *Frank J. Sprague* (2017), https://en.wikipedia.org/wiki/Frank_J._Sprague, accessed 11/24/17.

Wikipedia, *Streetcars in North America* (2018), https://en.wikipedia.org/wiki/Streetcars_in_North_America, accessed 3/11/18.

Brooklyn Historic Railway Association, *The Great Transportation Conspiracy* (2012), http://www.brooklynrail.net/NationalCityLinesCompany.html, accessed 3/11/18.

United States v. National City Lines, Inc., et al., 186 F. 2d 562 (7th Cir. 1951).

MARY ANDERSON

Engle, KeriLynn, *Mary Anderson, Inventor*, Amazing Women in History (2012), http://www.amazingwomeninhistory.com/mary-anderson-inventor/, accessed 12/27/17.

History.com Staff, *November 10, 1903: Mary Anderson Patents Windshield Wiper*, A&E Television Networks, LLC (2017), http://www.history.com/this-day-in-history/mary-anderson-patents, accessed 12/27/17.

Mary Anderson, Inventor of Windshield Wipers, Famous Women Inventors (2017), http://www.women-inventors.com/Mary-Anderson.asp, accessed 12/27/17.

CHAPTER 2

History.com Editors, *Code of Hammurabi*, History, A&E Television Networks (2009, 2018), https://www.history.com/topics/ancient-history/hammurabi, accessed 10/8/18.

The Ten Commandments, Bible, Old Testament, Exodus 20:1–17, Deuteronomy 5:4–21.

Kent, James, *Commentaries on American Law*, Published by O. Halstead, New York (1826).

The Laws of the Twelve Tables, Roman Commissions (circa 450 BC).

Lobban, Dr. Michael, *The Common Law Mind in the Age of Sir Edward Coke*, Amicus Curiae, Issue 33, pp. 18–21 (2001), https://sas-space.sas.ac.uk/3766/1/1348-1484-1-SM.pdf, accessed 10/8/18.

Constitution of the United States, Article III; Amendments 6 and 7.

CHARLES GOODYEAR

The World Book Encyclopedia, *Goodyear*, vol. 8, *Charles*, World Book, Inc., Chicago (1994), vol. 8, p. 270.

Goodyear Corporate, *The Strange Story of Rubber*, reprinted from *Readers Digest*, Jan. 1958 ed. (2018), http://www.goodyear.com/en_US/about/history/charlesgoodyear-story.html, accessed 9/29/18.

Goodyear, Charles, *Gale Encylcopedia of U.S. Economic History*, Encyclopedia.com (2018), http://www.encyclopedia.com/history/encyclopedia-almanacs-transcripts-and-maps/goodyear-charles, accessed 9/29/18.

JOHN BOYD DUNLOP

History of the Passenger Tire, Continental Tire (2018), http://www.continentaltire.com/content/history-passenger-tire, accessed 1/28/18.

Ament, Phil, *Pneumatic Tire*, Great Idea Finder (2007), http://www.ideafinder.com/history/inventions/pneumatictire.htm, accessed 1/28/18.

Boyd, Andy, *No. 3045: The Pneumatic Tire*, The Engines of Our Ingenuity, University of Houston (2016), https://www.uk.edu/engines/epi3045.htm, accessed 1/28/18.

CHAPTER 3

Rockman, H.B., *The Practice of Intellectual Property Law*, Law Bulletin Publishing Company, Chicago (1998), pp. 7–8.

Walterscheid, E.C., *To Promote the Progress of the Useful Arts*, Fred B. Rothman & Co., Littleton, CO. (1998), pp. 23–80.

Constitution of the United States, Article 1, Section 8 (1787).

The United State Patent Statutes, 35 U.S.C. §§ 1 et seq.

U.S. Code of Federal Regulations, 37 C.F.R., Chapter I, Subchapter A, Part 1, Rules of Practice in Patent Cases (2017, 2018).

GEORGE WESTINGHOUSE

Jonnes, Jill, *Empires of Light*, Random House, New York (2003), pp. 118–119, 121–122.

Larson, Erik, *The Devil in the White City*, Crown Publishers, New York (2003), pp. 5, 131, 141.

Cheney, Margaret, *Tesla, Man Out of Time*, Dorset Press, New York (1989).

Pennsylvania Biographies, George Westinghouse (2003), www.geocities.com/heartland/4547/westinghouse, accessed 9/27/18.

Freeberg, Ernest, *The Age of Edison*, Penguin Press, New York (2013).

Moore, Graham, *The Last Days of Night-A Novel*, Random House, New York (2016).

Abrams, Michael, *George Westinghouse*, American Society of Mechanical Engineers (ASME) (2012), https://www.asme.org/engineering-topics/articles/energy/george-westinghouse, accessed 9/27/18.

Allerhand, Adam, *A Contrarian History of Early Electric Power Distribution*, Proceedings of the IEEE, vol, 105, no. 5, pp. 768–778 (2017), https://reexplore.ieee.org/stamp/stamp.jsp?arnumber=7885139, accessed 9/27/18.

Engineering and Technology History Wiki, Archives: Papers of George Westinghouse (2014), https://ethw.org/Archives:Papers_of_George_Westinghouse, accessed 9/27/18.

Levine, I.E., *Inventive Wizard – George Westinghouse*, Julian Messner, Inc. New York (1961), p. 136.

GIDEON SUNDBACK

Shandrow, Kim Lachance, *The Fasten-ating History of the Humble Zipper*, Entrepreneur Media, Inc. (2017), https://www.entrepreneur.com/article/251975, accessed 12/17/17.

Bellis, Mary, *The History of the Zipper*, About, Inc. (2006), http://theinventors.org/library/weekly/aa082497.htm, accessed 12/17/17.

Wikipedia, *Gideon Sundback* (2017), https://en.wikipedia.org/wiki/Gideon_Sundback, accessed 11/24/17.

CHAPTER 4

United States Patent Statutes, 35 U.S.C. §§ 101, 102, 103.

Diamond v. Chakrabarty, 477 U.S. 303, 306 USPQ 193 (Supreme Court 1980).

State Street Bank & Trust Co. v. Signature Financial Group, Inc. 149 F. 3d 1368 (Fed. Cir. 1988), *cert denied*, 525 U.S. 1093 (Supreme Court 1999).

United States Constitution, Article I, Section 8, Clause 8 (1787).

JOHN DEERE

Dahlstrom, Neil and Jeremy, *The John Deere Story: A Biography of Plowmakers John and Charles Deere*, Northern Illinois University Press (2005).

Past Leaders – John Deere, Deere & Company (2018), https://www.deere.com/en/our-company/about-john-deere/past-leaders/john-deere, accessed 9/29/18.

Biography.com Editors, *John Deere Biography*, Biography.com (2017), https://www.biograph.com/people/john-deere-9269591, accessed 9/29/18.

ERASTUS BRIGHAM BIGELOW

December 6, 1879, Erastus Bigelow Dies, Mass Moments, Mass Humanities (2017), https://www.massmoments.org/moment-details/erastus-bigelow-dies.html, accessed 12/13/17.

1838 Bigelow's Patent Model of a Loom, Smithsonian Museum of American History-Kenneth E. Behring Center, http://americanhistory.si.edu/collections/search/object/mmah_1070864, accessed 12/13/17.

Bishop, J.L., Freedley, E.T., Young, E., *Erastus Brigham Bigelow A History of American Manufacturers from 1608 to 1860 (1866)*, vol. 2 (2017), Today in Science History, https://todayinsci.com/B/Bigelow_Erastus/BigelowErastus.htm, accessed 12/13/17.

*Erastus Brigham Bigelow Biography (*1814–1879*)*, Advameg, Inc. (2017) http://madehow.com/inventorbios/35/Erastus-Brigham-Bigelow.html, accessed 12/13/17.

CHAPTER 5

Rockman, H.B., *The Practice of Intellectual Property Law*, Law Bulletin Publishing Company, Chicago (1998), pp. 27–36.

United States Patent Statutes, 35 U.S.C. §§ 102, 351–376.

United States Patent and Trademark Office (USPTO), *General Information Concerning Patents – Novelty and Non-Obviousness, Conditions for Obtaining a Patent*, https://www.uspto.gov/patents-getting-started/general-information-concerning-patents#heading-5, accessed 9/28/17.

ALFRED NOBEL

Arreseigor, Juan Jose Sanchez, *The Explosive Origins of the Nobel Prizes*, History Magazine, National Geographic Society (2017), https://www.nationalgeographic.com/archaeology-and-history/magazine, accessed 9/27/18.

Ringertz, Nils, *Alfred Nobel – His Life and Work*, NobelPrize.org, Nobel Media AB (2018), https://www.nobelprize.org/alfred-nobel/alfred-nobel-his-life-and-work/, accessed 9/29/18.

Alfred Nobel, Science History Institute (2017), https://www.sciencehistory.org/historical-profile/alfred-nobel, accessed 9/29/18.

Alfred Nobel's Will, NobelPrize.org, Nobel Media AB (2018) https://www.nobelprize.org/alfred-nobel/alfred-nobels-will-2/, accessed 9/29/18.

The Curious History of the Nobel Peace Prize, The Conversation (2016), theconversation.com/the-curious-history-of-the-nobel-peace-prize-66609, accessed 9/29/18.

CHAPTER 6

United States Patent Statutes, 35 U.S.C. §103 (1952, 2011).

Hotchkiss v. Greenwood, 42 U.S. (11 HOW.) 248 (1850).

Atlantic Works v. Brady, 107 U.S. 192 (1882).

Goodyear Rubber and Tire Company v. Ray-O-Vac Company, 321 U.S. 275 (1944).

Cuno Engineering Corp. v. Automatic Devices Corp., 314 U.S. 84 (1941).

The Great Atlantic & Pacific Tea Company v. Supermarket Equipment Corporation, 340 U.S. 147 (1950).

Graham v. John Deere Company, 383, U.S. 1 (1966).

KSR Intl. Co. v. Teleflex, Inc., 550 U.S. 398 (2007).

Rockman, Howard, *Obviousness in the Wake of KSR – What Has and Has Not Changed*, Patent Resources Group, Inc. (2009).

LOUIS PASTEUR

Biography.com Editors, *Louis Pasteur Biography*, Biography.com (2014), https://www.biography.com/people/louis-pasteur-9434402, accessed 9/20/18.

Ullmann, Agnes, *Louis Pasteur, French Chemist and Microbiologist*, Encyclopaedia Britannica (2018), https://www.britannica.com/biography/Louis-Pasteur, accessed 9/25/18.

Louis Pasteur, *Famous Scientists*. famousscientists.org (2018), www.famousscientists.org/louis-pasteur/, accessed 9/20/18.

Cohn, D.V., *The Life and Times of Louis Pasteur*, Lecture, February 11 (1996), www.pasteurbrewing.com/the-life-and-times-of-louis-pasteur/, accessed 9/20/18.

ELISHA OTIS

Quirk, Vanessa, *A Brief, Interesting History of the Otis Elevator Company*, ArchDaily (2013), https://www.archdaily.com/354494/a-brief-interesting-history-of-the-otis-elevator-company, accessed 1/28/18.

Amet, Phil, *Elevator*, The Great Idea Finder (2007), http://www.ideafinder.com/history/inventions/elevator.htm, accessed 1/28/18.

The Editors of Encyclopaedia Britannica, *Elisha Otis, American Inventor*, Encyclopaedia Britannica (2018), https://www.britannica.com/biography/Elisha-Otis, accessed 1/28/18.

Crawford, Mark, *Elisha Graves Otis,* American Society of Mechanical Engineers (2012), https://www.asme.org/engineering-topics/articles/elevators/elisha-graves-otis, accessed 1/28/18.

Upton, Emily, *Who Invented the Elevator?* Gizmodo (2014), https://gizmodo.com/who-invented-the-elevator-1570745196, accessed 1/28/18.

CHAPTER 7

United States Patent Statutes, 35 U.S.C. §§ 100, 101, 102(a), (b), (c) and (d), 103, 111, 112, 115, 116, 119, 135, 151, 152, 261, 262, and 282 (b)(3)(A).

United States Code of Federal Regulations, 37 C.F.R. §1.56 (2018).

ALEXANDER GRAHAM BELL

Bruce, R.V., *Bell: Alexander Graham Bell and the Conquest of Solitude*, Little, Brown and Company, Boston (1973), pp. 157–187, 258–280.

United States v. The American Bell Telephone Company, 128 U.S. 315 (Supreme Court 1888).

Brittain, J.E., *Electrical Engineering Hall of Fame,* ieeexplore, Institute of Electrical and Electronic Engineers, Proceedings of the IEEE, vol. 93, no. 2 (2005), https://ieeexplore.ieee.org/document/1386663/authors#authors, accessed 9/20/18.

History.com Editors, *Alexander Graham Bell*, History (2018), https://www.history.com/topics/inventions/alexander-graham-bell, accessed 9/20/18.

The World Book Encyclopedia, *Bell, Alexander Graham*, vol. 2, World Book, Inc., Chicago (1994), pp. 240–241.

Gorman, M.E., University of Virginia, *Alexander Graham Bell's Path to the Telephone and references cited therein* (1994, 2015), www2.iath.virginia-edu/albell/homepage.html, accessed 9/27/18.

U.S. House of Representatives, *Text of House Resolution 269 Honoring the Achievements of Antonio Meucci*, June 11, 2002, (2003), www.alexcell.org/HR269, accessed 9/27/18.

Fosella, Congressman V.J., *Representative Fossella's Resolution Honoring True Inventor of Telephone to Pass House Tonight*, June 11, 2002, (2003), www.house.gov/fossella/pr020611, accessed 9/27/18.

Grosvenor, Edwin S., *News Flash: U.S. House of Representatives Says Alexander Graham Bell Did Not Invent the Telephone*, September 17, 2002, (2003), http://hnn.us.comments/2642.html.

Meucci and Bell: The Facts, www.alecbell.org/BellvGlobe, accessed 9/27/18.

Complete Text of the Ruling in the Antonio Meucci Case, American Bell Telephone Co. v Globe Telephone Co., and Others, 31 Fed. 728 (S.D.N.Y. 1887), www.alexbell.org/BellvGlobe, accessed 9/27/18.

Zanuck, Darryl F., *The Story of Alexander Graham Bell*, 20th Century Fox Film Corporation, released 1939 with Don Ameche and Loretta Young, 20th Century Fox Studio Classic.

CHAPTER 8

United States Patent Statutes, 35 U.S.C. §§ 102, 302–318, www.govinfo.gov/content/pkg/USCODE-2017-title35.pdf.

Rockman, H.B., *The Practice of Intellectual Property Law*, Law Bulletin Publishing Company, Chicago (1998), pp. 27–31.

U.S. Patent and Trademark Office, Manual of Classification, available at www.uspto.gov/web/offices/ac/ida/oeip/taf/mor/jobjects/search.htm (2018).

THOMAS EDISON

Jonnes, Jill, *Empires of Light*, Random House, New York (2003), pp. 55–71.

Josephson, M., *Edison – A Biography*, Francis Parkman Prize Edition, History Book Club, New York (1959, reprinted 2003), pp. 175–279.

Larson, Erik, *The Devil in the White City*, Crown Publishers, New York (2003), pp. 5, 131, 155, 247, 285.

Cheney, M., *Tesla – Man Out of Time*, Dorset Press, New York (1981), pp. 28, 33.

Friedel, R., *New Light on Edison's Light*, Great Inventions that Changed the World, American Heritage Division of Forbes, Inc. Des Moines, IA (1994), pp. 26–31.

U.S. National Park Service, *Edison Biography* (2015), https://www.nps.gov/edis/learn/historyculture/edison-biography.htm, accessed 9/10/18.

United States Library of Congress, *American Memory, The Life of Thomas Alva Edison*, https://www.loc.gov/collections/edison-company-motion-pictures-and-sound-recordings/articles-and-essays/biography/life-of-thomas-alva-edison, accessed 9/10/18.

Freeberg, Ernest, *The Age of Edison*, Penguin Press, New York (2013).

Moore, Graham, *The Last Days of Night, A Novel*, Random House, New York (2016).

Paul B. Israel, Director and General Editor, Rutgers School of Arts and Sciences, *Thomas A. Edison Papers,* Rutgers University (2018), Edison.rutgers.edu, accessed 9/10/18.

CHAPTER 9

Understanding Provisional Patent Applications, Thoughts to Paper (2015), http://www.thoughtstopaper.com/blog/understanding-provisional-patent-applications, accessed 2/9/17.

35 U.S.C. §111(b) (1995).

Office of the Deputy Commissioner for Patent Examination Policy, *Provisional Application for Patent* (2015), USPTO, https://www.uspto.gov/patents-getting-started/patent-basics/types-patent-applications/provisional-application-patent, accessed 8/24/18.

Quinn, Gene, *The Benefits of a Provisional Patent Application*, ipwatchdog (2017), www.ipwatchdog.com/2017/05/13/benefits-provisional-patent-application/id=83161, accessed 8/24/18.

Hodge, Rob, *The Provisional Patent Application: Is it for Me?* Inventor's Edge, USPTO (2017), https://uspto.gov/learning-and-resources/newsletter/inventors-eye/provisional-patent-application-it-me, accessed 8/24/18.

United States Patent & Trademark Office, MPEP, Chapter 600, Sections 601, 608.01(a) to (h) (2018), www.uspto.gov/web/offices/pac/mpep/s601.html.

Rockman, H.B., *The Practice of Intellectual Property Law*, Law Bulletin Publishing Company, Chicago (1998), pp. 8–11, 83–98.

GEORGE EASTMAN

George Eastman, Eastman Kodak Co. (2018), https://www.kodak.com/US/en/corp/aboutus/heritage/georgeeastman/default.htm, accessed 8/20/18.

George Eastman – Easy-to-Use-Camera, PBS, www.pbs.org/wghb/theymadeamerica/whomade/eastman_hi.html, accessed 8/20/18.

Smil, Vaclav, *September 1888: George Eastman Patents His Kodak Camera*, IEEE Spectrum Magazine (2018).

Ament, Phil, *George Eastman, The Great Idea Finder* (2006), www.ideafinder.com/history/inventors/eastman.htm, accessed 8/20/18.

The World Book Encyclopedia, *Eastman, George*, vol. 6, World Book, Inc., Chicago, IL (1994), p. 47.

EMILE BERLINER

The Gramophone-Early Sound Recording Devices, U.S. Library of Congress, https://www.loc.gov/collections/emile-berliner/articles-and-essays/gramophone/, accessed 2/11/18.

Bell-Tainter Graphophone Type K-1895, http://www.edisoninfoil.com/bell.htm, accessed 2/18/18.

Bellis, Mary, *Emile Berliner and the History of the Gramophone*, Thought Co. (2018), https://www.thoughtco.com/emile-berliner-history-of-the-gramophone-1991854, accessed 2/11/18.

CHAPTER 10

United States Patent & Trademark Office, MPEP, Chapter 600, Sections 608.01(a) to (n) (2017), uspto.gov.

Rockman, H.B., *The Practice of Intellectual Property Law*, Law Bulletin Publishing Company, Chicago (1998), pp. 10, 11, 45–82.

OTTMAR MERGENTHALER

The World Book Encyclopedia, *Mergenthaler, Ottmar*, World Book, Inc., Chicago (1994), vol. 13, p. 418.

Kahan B., *Ottmar Mergenthaler – The Man and His Machine*, Oak Knoll Press, New Castle, Del. (1999).

Butterman, Eric, *Ottmar Merganthaler*, American Society of Mechanical Engineers (2012), https://www.asme.org/topics-resources/content/ottmar-merganthala accessed 10/5/18.

Iles, George, *Leading American Inventors*, Henry Hold & Co, New York, NY (1912), pp. 393–434.

THEODORE MAIMAN & GORDON GOULD

Townes, Charles H., *The First Laser*, A Century of Nature, University of Chicago Press (2003), http://www.press.uchicago.edu/Misc/Chicago/284158_townes.html, accessed 3/30/18.

Miller, Katie, *A Story of Invention: the Laser*, Intellectual Ventures Laboratory (2013), http://www.intellectualventureslab.com/invent/a-story-of-invention-the-laser, accessed 3/30/18.

Hintze, Christine, *Gordon Gould: The Long Battle for the Laser Patent*, Electronic Design (2006), http://www.electronicdesign.com/print/51591, accessed 4/7/18.

Pyatt, Rudolph A., Jr., *Laser Patent Holder Here Wins Battle*, The Washington Post (1982), https://www.washingtonpost.com/archive/business/1982/03/02/laser, accessed 4/7/18.

Hall, Carla, *Inventor Beams Over Laser Patents: After 30 Years, Gordon Gould Gets Credit He Deserves*, The Washington Post (1987), http://articles.latimes.com/print/1987-12-17/news/vw-29544_1_patents/, accessed 4/7/18.

Rose, Melinda, *A History of the Laser: A Trip Through the Light Fantastic*, Photonics Media (2010), https://www.photonics.com/Articles/A_History_of_the_Laser_A_Trip_Through_the_Light/a42299, accessed 3/30/18.

Woodford, Chris, *Lasers*, Explain This Stuff (2017), http://www.explainthatstuff.com/lasers.html, accessed 3/30/18.

Who Invented the Laser, American Institute of Physics (2018), https://history.aip.org/exhibits/laser/sections/whoinvented.html, accessed 3/30/18.

The Race to Build a Laser, American Institute of Physics (2018), https://history.aip.org/exhibits/laser/sections/therace.html, accessed 3/30/18.

CHAPTER 11

United States Patent & Trademark Office, MPEP, Chapter 700, Sections 701–724.06, 1300, 1401 et seq. 2200 (2015, 2018).

Rockman, H.B., *The Practice of Intellectual Property Law*, Law Bulletin Publishing Company, Chicago (1998), pp. 99–138.

NIKOLAUS OTTO AND RUDOLF DIESEL

Bellis, Mary, *Biography of Nicolaus Otto and the Modern Engine*, ThoughtCo (2018), thoughtco.com/Nicolaus-otto-engine-design-4072867, accessed 10/5/18.

Nikolaus Otto, YourDictionary, n.d. Web (2018), http://biograph7.yourdictionary.com/nikolaus-otto, accessed 10/6/18.

Daimler, *The Development of the Gasoline Engine*, Daimler A.G. (2018), https://media.daimler.com/marsMediaSite/en/instance/kv/The-development-of-the-gasoline-engine.xhtml?oid=9361448, accessed 10/5/18.

Bellis, Mary, *The History of the Automobile*, Inventors.org (2006), theinventors.org/library/weekly/aacarsgasa.htm, accessed 10/6/18.

Famous Scientists, Rudolf Christian Karl Diesel, FamousScientists.org (2018), https://www.famousscientists.org/rudolph-christian-karl-diesel/, accessed 10/4/18.

Harford, Tim, *How Rudolf Diesel's Engine Changed the World*, British Broadcasting Company (2018), https://www.bbc.com/news/business-38302874, accessed 10/5/18.

Diesel Engines, Deutsches Museum, Munich (2018), www.deutsches-museum.de/en/collections/machines/power-engines/combustion-engines/, accessed 10/4/18.

Jaaskelainen, Hannu, *Early History of the Diesel Engine*, DieselNet Technology Guide (2013), https://www.dieselnet.com/tech/diesel_history.php#diesel, accessed 10/5/18.

CHAPTER 12

Akhbari, Kourosh, *Design Patent Laws* (2017), http://www.legalmatch.com/law-library/article/design-patent-laws.html, accessed 6/29/17.

Gene Quinn, *Design Patents: The Under Utilized and Overlooked Patent* (2016), the IP Watchdog, https://www.ipwatchdog.com/2016/09/10 design-patents/id=72714/, accessed 6/29/17.

Ngo, Sylvia, *Egyptian Goddess v. Swisa. Patently Obvious Reconciling the Ordinary Observer and Point of Novelty Tests*, Houston Business and Tax Journal, vol. 10, pp. 111–138 (2010).

U.S. Patent Statutes, 35 U.S.C. §§171–173.

U.S. Copyright Statutes, 17 U.S.C. §§102(a).

World Intellectual Property Organization (WIPO), *Industrial Designs* (2017), http://www.wipo.int/designs/en/, accessed 6/29/17.

Wikipedia, *Hague Agreement Concerning the International Deposit of Industrial Designs*, https://en.wikipedia.org/wiki/Hague_Agreement_Concerning_the_Inter...of Industrial Designs, accessed 7/1/17.

USPTO, *Hague Agreement Concerning the International Registration of Industrial Designs* (2019), https://www.uspto.gov/patent/initiatives/hague-agreement-concerning-international-registration-industrial-designs, accessed 8/25/19.

Samsung *Electronics co., Ltd. et al. v. Apple, Inc.*, U.S. Supreme Court No. 15–777, decided December 6, 2016, slip opinion, ____U.S.___; 137 S. Ct. 429 (2016).

Crouch, Dennis, *Samsung v. Apple: Design Patent Damages May Be Limited to Components*, PatentlyO (2016), https://patentlyo.com/patent/2016/12/samsung-limited-components.html, accessed 7/2/17.

Reichman, Courtland and Sokhansanj, *Samsung. v. Apple: Impacts Beyond Damages*, Law 360.com, Portfolio Media, Inc. (2016), https://www.law360.com/articles/866580/samsung-v-apple-impacts-beyond-damages, accessed 7/2/17.

Allyson Wallace v. Ideavillage Products Corp., Case No. 2015-1077, U.S. Court of Appeals for the Federal Circuit, decided March 3, 2016.

NIKOLA TESLA

Popvic, V., Horat, R., and Nikolic, N., *Nikola Tesla, Lectures, Patents, Articles, Nikola Tesla Museum*, Belgrade, Yugoslavia (1956).

Cheney, M., *Tesla – Man Out of Time*, Dorset Press, New York (1981), pp. 1–41, 62–75, 176–184.

Marconi Wireless Telegraph Company of America v. United States, 320 U.S. 1, 87 L. Ed. 1731 (Supreme Court 1943).

Anderson, Leland, *Priority in the Invention of Radio – Tesla v. Marconi*, Antique Wireless Association, MONOGRAPH (New Series) No. 4, March (1980), pp. 1–9.

Gunderman, Richard, *The Extraordinary Life of Nikola Tesla*, Smithsonian Magazine (2018), https://www.smithsonianmag.com/innovation/extraordinary-life-nikola-tesla-180967758/, accessed 10/4/18.

Palace, Steve, *FBI Releases Long Held Nikola Tesla Documents*, The Vintage News (2018), https://www.thevintagenews.com/2018/06/27/nikola-tesla-fbi/, accessed 10/6/18.

Cawthorne, Nigel, *Tesla – The Life and Times of an Electric Messiah*, Chartwell Books, New York, NY (2014).

CLARENCE BIRDSEYE

Clarence Birdseye, Encyclopedia Britannica, Inc. (2018), http://www.britanica.com/biography/Clarence-Birdseye, accessed 9/12/18.

Clarence Birdseye, Famous Scientists (2018), http://www.famousscientists.org/clarence-birdseye/, accessed 9/12/18.

Clarence Birdseye, NNDB (2014), http://www.nndb.com/people/590/000162104/, accessed 9/12/18.

Rosen, Jake. *9 Chilly Facts About Frozen Food Pioneer: Clarence Birdseye*, Mental Floss (2017), http://mentalfloss.com/article/502640/9-chi8lly-facts-about-frozen-food-pioneer-clarence-birdseye, accessed 9/12/18.

CHAPTER 13

Patent Eligible Subject Matter: Report on Views and Recommendations from the Public, USPTO (2017), https://www.uspto.gov/sites/default/files/documents/101-Report_FINAL.pdf, accessed 8/24/18.

Subject Matter Eligibility, USPTO (2018), https://www.uspto.gov/patent/laws-and-regulations/examination-policy/subject-matter-eligibility, accessed 8/24/18.

§2016.04(a) Abstract Ideas, Manual of Patent Examination Procedure, USPTO (2018), https://www.uspto.gov/web/offices/pac/mpep/s2106.html, accessed 8/24/18.

Wilmer Cutler Pickering Hale and Dorr LLP, *The Origin of Click-Wrap: Software Shrink-Wrap Agreements* (2000), Publication and News, https://www.wilmerhale.com/pages/publicationsandnewsdetail.aspx, accessed 2/10/17.

Alice *Corporation Pty. Ltd. v. CLS Bank Int. et al.*, 573 U.S. ___, 134 S.Ct. 2347 (2014).

Davis, Ryan and Penton, Kevin, *Fed. Cir. Gives Apple, Others Alice Win on Menu Patents*, Law360.com, Portfolio Media, Inc. (2016), http://www.law360.com/articles/866825/, accessed 11/30/16.

USPTO, Manual of Patent Examining Procedure (MPEP) Section 2106, *Patent Subject Matter Eligibility*, https://www.uspto.gov/web/offices/pac/mpep/s2106.html, accessed 7/4/17.

Guidelines for Examination – Part F – The European Patent Application – Chapter IV – Claims – 3. Kinds of Claims – 3.9 Claims Directed to Computer-Implemented Inventions, European Patent Office (EPO) (2017), https://www.epo.org/law-practice/legal-texts/html/guidelines/e/f_iv_3_9.htm, accessed 12/2/17.

Patentability of Software and Business Method Inventions in Europe, Mewburn Ellis LLP (2017), www.mewburn.com, accessed 8/9/17.

Patents *for Software-European Law and Practice*, European Patent Office (EPO) (2013), www.epo.org, accessed 8/9/17.

Brunner, John, Small, Gary, and O'Kane, Sean, *Software and Business Method Patents in Europe and the U.K.*, Carpmaels and Ramsford (2017), https://www.carpmaels.com/software-and-business-method-patents-in-europe-and-the-uk/, accessed 8/8/17.

Campbell, Anne, and Wraige, David, *Software and Business Methods – Patentable Subject – Matter in Europe*, Mintz Levin (2013), https://www.mintz.com/newsletter/2013/Advisories/3465-1013-NAT-IP/index.html, accessed 8/8/17.

HEDY LAMARR

Rhodes, Richard, *Hedy's Folly – The Life and Breakthrough Inventions of Hedy Lamarr, the Most Beautiful Woman in the World*, Doubleday Division of Random House, Inc., New York (2011), pp. 133–153.

Photograph obtained with permission from http://silverscreensirens.com/galleries/hedy.28.htm.

Hedy Lamarr, *Biography, Engineering and Technology History Wiki*, IEEE (2018), https://ethw.org/Hedy_Lamarr, accessed 10/5/18.

Bisset, Jennifer, *Bombshell Shatters Myth Around Wi-Fi Inventor Hedy Lamarr*, CNET (2018), https://www.cnet.com/.../bombshell-shatters-myth-of-wi-fi-bluetooth-inventor-hedy-lamarr, accessed 10/6/18.

Hedy Lamarr: *Inventor of Frequency Hopping*, Electronics Notes (2018), https://www.electronics-notes.com/articles/.../hedy-lamarr-biography-invention.php., accessed 10/6/18.

King, Gilbert, *Team Hollywood's Secret Weapons System*, Smithsonian.com (2012), https://smithsonianmag.com/...team-hollywood-secret-weapons-system-1036199, accessed 10/6/18.

HERMAN HOLLERITH

da Cruz, Frank, *Herman Hollerith*, Columbia University Computing History (2018), www.columbia.edu/cu/computinghistory/hollerith.html, accessed 10/4/18.

Census History Staff, *History – Herman Hollerith*, U.S. Census Bureau (2018), https://www.census.gov/history/www/census-then-now/notable_alumni/herman_hollerith.html, accessed 10/4/18.

Giges, Nancy, *Herman Hollerith – Biography*, American Society of Mechanical Engineers (ASME) (2012), https://www.asme.org/engineering-topics/articles/mechanisms-systems-devices/herman-hollerith, accessed 10/4/18.

Aul, William R., *Herman Hollerith: Data Processing Pioneer,* Think, IBM employee publication, pp. 22–24 (1972), https://www-03.ibm.com/ibm/history/exhbitis/builders/builders_hollerith.html, accessed 10/5/18.

CHAPTER 14

1930 Plant Protection Act, 35 U.S.C. §§ 161–164.

1970 Plant Variety Protection Act, 7 U.S.C. §§ 2321–2331, 2351–2357, 2371–2372, 2401–2404, 2421–2427, 2441–2443, 2461–2463, 2481–2486, 2501–2504, 2531–2532, 2541–2545, 2561–2570, 2581–2583.

35 U.S.C. §§ 101, 287(c)(1996).

UN Convention on Biological Diversity (1993), Article 2, https://www.cbd.int/convention/articles/default.shtml?a=cbd-02, accessed 8/31/17.

International Service for the Acquisition of Agri-Biotech Applications (2018), www.isaaa.org/resources/publications/briefs/54/exectivesummary/default.asp, accessed 8/26/19.

U.S. Office of Energy Efficiency & Renewable Energy (2017), https://www.energy.gov/eere/office-energy-efficiency-renewable-energy, accessed 8/31/17.

Hatch-Waxman Act, Public Law 98-417 (1984), 21 U.S.C Ch. 9 §§301, 355 and 360, https://www.govinfo.gov/content/pkg/STATUTE-98/pdf/STATUTE.

FDA Electronic Orange Book, https://www.fda.gov/drugs/resourcesforyou/healthprofessionals/ucm388798.htm, accessed 8/31/17.

Biologics Price Competition and Innovation Act of 2009 (BPCIA), 42 U.S.C §§ 262(k)(l) et al. (2009), https://www.fda.gov/downloads/drugs/.../UCM216146.pdf, accessed 9/1/17.

General Agreement on Tariffs and Trade (GATT), *Trade-Related Aspects of Intellectual Property* (TRIPPS), Article 27(3)(a), Uruguay Round Agreements Act, 108 Stat. 4809, 4973-4900 (1994); See also: www.wto.org/english/docs_e/legal_e/27-trips.pdf, accessed 9/1/17.

ROSALIND FRANKLIN, JAMES WATSON, FRANCIS CRICK, & MAURICE WILKINS

Maddox, B., *Rosalind Franklin, The Dark Lady of DNA*, Harper Collins, New York (2002).

Watson, James D. and Berry, A., *DNA, The Secret of Life*, Alfred A. Knopf, New York (2003), pp. 35–61.

Strak, M., *Race to the Double Helix Took Many Twists, Turns*, The Sunday Sun Newspaper, Baltimore, MD, February 23 (2003), pp. 1A, 14A.

Nelson, B., *Watson On: the Discovery, The Controversy, The Legacy*, Newsday.com (2003), http://www.newsday.com/james-watson-on-the-discovery-the-controversy-the-legacy-1.427315, accessed 10/9/18.

Public Broadcasting System, *A Science Odyssey, People and Discoveries, Rosalind Franklin, 1920–1958* (1998), http://www.pbs.org/wgbh/aso/databank/entries/bofran.html.

Lau, Ken Ph.D., *Women in Science: Rosalind Franklin and the Double Helix*, Biolegend, Inc. (2018), https://biolegend.com/newsdetail/1515/, accessed 10/8/18.

Goddard, Jolyon, Editor, *A Concise History of Science & Inventions*, National Geographic (2010), pp. 282–283.

HERBERT W. BOYER & STANLEY N. COHEN

United States Patent Nos. 4,237,224; 4,468,464; 4,740,470

Feldman, M.P., Colaianni, A, Liu, C.K., *Lessons from the Commercialization of the Cohen-Boyer Patents: The Stanford University Licensing Program* (2007), Handbook of Best Practices, pp. 1797–1807, http://www.iphandbook.org/handbook/chPDFs/ch17/ipHandbook-Ch%2017%2022%20Feldman-Colaianni0Liu%20Cohen-Boyer%20Patents%20and%20Licenses.pdf.

Genome News Network, 1973 (2004), J. Craig Venter Institute, http://www.genomenewsnetwork.org/resources/timeline/1973_Boyer, accessed 11/14/17.

Wikipedia, *Stanley Norman Cohen* (2018), https://en.wikipedia.org/wiki/Stanley_Norman_Cohen, accessed 11/14/17.

Herbert W. Boyer and Stanley N. Cohen (2017), Science History Institute, https://www.sciencehistory.org/historical-profile/herbert-w-boyer-and-stanley-n-cohen, accessed 11/14/17.

Wikipedia, *Herbert Boyer* (2018), https://en.wikipedia.org/wiki/Herbert_Boyer, accessed 11/14/17.

CHAPTER 15

Griffin, Kelcee, *Fed. Cir. Clarifies Scope of AIA Business Method Review*, Law 360, Portfolio Media, Inc. (2017), https://www.law360.com/articles/894077, accessed 2/22/17.

Quinn, Gene, *Patenting Business Methods and Software Still Requires Concrete and Tangible Descriptions*, IPwatchdog (2015), http://www.ipwatchdog.com/2015/08/29/patenting-business-methods-and-software/id=54576/, accessed 9/2/17.

Hollerith, Herman, U.S. Patent Nos. 395,781; 395,782 and 395,783 (January 8, 1889).

State Street Bank & Trust Co. v. Signature Financial Group, Inc., 149 F.3d 1368, 1375-7 (Fed. Cir. 1998).

United States Patent Statutes, 35 U.S.C. §§ 101, 273.

European Patent Convention, Rule 52(2), https://www.epo.org/law-practice/legal-texts/html/epc/2016/e/ar52.html, accessed 10/8/18.

Love, J.J. and Coggins, W.W., *Successfully Preparing and Prosecuting a Business Method Patent Application*, Speech presented at American Intellectual Property Law Association meeting (Spring 2001), http://www.uspto.gov/web/menu/pbmethod/aiplapaper.rtf, accessed 10/8/18.

United States Patent and Trademark Office, White Paper, *Automated Financial or Management Data Processing Methods (Business Methods)* (2009, 2011), http://www.uspto.gov/patents-getting-started/patent-basics/types-patent-application/utility-patent/business-methods-20, accessed 10/8/18.

Manual of Patent Examining Procedure, USPTO, MPEP §§ 2106.04(a)(2), Parts I-IV (2014).

United States Patent and Trademark Office, *Subject Matter Eligibility*, Examples 37–42 (2019), https://www.uspto.gov/patents/laws-and-regulations/examination-policy/subject-matter-eligibility, accessed 8/26/19.

Crouch, Dennis and Merges, Robert P., *Operating Efficiently Post-Bilski by Ordering Patent Doctrine Decision-Making*, 25 Berkley Tech. L.J. 1673 (2010).

YVONNE BRILL

Childs, Martin, *Yvonne Brill: Rocket Scientist Who Developed a System to Keep Satellites In Their Orbits*, The Independent (2013), https://www.independent.co.uk/news/obituaries/yvonne-brill-rocket-scientist-who-developed-a-system-to-keep-satellites-in-their-orbits-8673644.html, accessed 12/24/17.

Douglas, Martin, *Yvonne Brill, a Pioneering Rocket Scientist, Dies at 88*, The New York Times (2013), https://www.nytimes.com/2013/03/31/science/space/yvonne-brill-rocket-scientist-dies-at-88.html, accessed 12/24/17.

Wikipedia, *Yvonne Brill* (2017), https://en.wikipedia.org/wiki/Yvonne_Brill, accessed 11/24/17.

LUTHER BURBANK

United States Plant Patent No. 15, April 5, 1932.

Barker, D., *The Forgotten Story of Luther Burbank*, Freethought Today, August (1993). http://www.ffrf.org/fttoday/back/burbankbio.html, accessed 10/9/18.

Janick, Jules, Editor, *Luther Burbank, Plant Breeder, Horticulturist, American Hero*, Purdue University, Department of Horticulture and Landscape Architecture (2015), https://hort.purdue.edu/newcrop/pdfs/burbank-workshop.pdf, accessed 10/9/18.

Luther Burbank, Biography, Facts and Pictures, Famous Scientists.org (2018), https://www.famousscientists.org/luther-burbank/, accessed 10/9/18.

Weiseler, Wayne, *Biography: Luther Burbank, 1849–1926*, Two Spirit Group (2017), http://www.wschsgrf.org/articles/biographylutherburbank1849-1926, accessed 10/9/18.

CHAPTER 16

1801, Basic Patent Cooperation Treaty (PCT) Principles, Manual of Patent Examining Procedure, USPTO, 2018, https://www.uspto.gov/web/offices/pac/mpep/s/1801.html, accessed 8/26/19.

PCT Information Service, *PCT FAQs*, World Intellectual Property Organization (WIPO) (2015), www.wipo.int/pct/en/, accessed 8/9/17.

Hocking, Adrian, *The Unitary Patent System and How it Affects You*, Morningside IP (2017), info@morningsideip.com, accessed 8/9/17.

Mewburn Ellis LLP, *Patentability of Software and Business Method Inventions in Europe* (2017), www.mewburn.com, accessed 8/9/17.

WILBUR AND ORVILLE WRIGHT

Crouch, T., *The Bishop's Boys – A Life of Wilbur and Orville Wright,* W.W. Norton, New York (1989).

The Published Writings of Wilbur and Orville Wright, edited by Jakabar, P.L. and Young, R., Smithsonian Institution Press, Washington D.C. (2000).

Young. R.C., *Controversy at Kitty Hawk – Who Were the Real Fathers of Powered Flight?* Unpublished Paper, Blue Island IL (2003).

Smithsonian National Air and Space Museum Core Exhibition Team, *The Wright Brothers – The Invention of the Aerial Age* (2018), https://airandspace.si.edu/exhibitions/wright-brothers/online/index.cfm, accessed 10/8/18.

McCullough, David, *The Wright Brothers*, Simon & Schuster, New York (2016).

CHAPTER 17

United States Patent Statutes, 35 U.S.C. §§271–273, 281–297.

Rockman, H.B., *The Practice of Intellectual Property Law*, Law Bulletin Publishing Company, Chicago (1998), pp. 29–30, 139–148.

United States Patent and Trademark Office, *Official Gazette*, published on Tuesday of every week throughout the year.

Stobbs, G.A., *Software Patents*, 2nd edn., Aspen Publishers, Inc. (2000), pp. 648–662.

ROBERT GODDARD

Garner, Rob, Editor, *Dr. Robert H. Goddard, American Rocketry Pioneer*, NASA Goddard Space Flight Center (2017), https://www.nasa.gov/centers/goddard/about/history/dr_goddard.html, accessed 10/11/18.

Robert H. Goddard: American Rocket Pioneer, Smithsonian Institution Archives (2018), https://siarchives.si.edu/history/featured-topics/stories/robert-h-goddard, accessed 10/11/18.

Robert Goddard – Biography, Facts and Pictures, Famous Scientists.org (2018), https://www.famousscientists.org/robert-goddard/, accessed 10/11/18.

Dr. Robert H. Goddard Collection, Clark University Archives and Special Collections (2018), https://www2.clarku.edu/research/archives/goddard/about.cfm, accessed 10/9/18.

C. DONALD BATEMAN

Dunn, Sydni, *C. Donald Bateman*, National Science and Technology Medals Foundation (2010), http://www.nationalmedals.org/laureate/c-donald-bateman, accessed 9/12/18.

C. Donald Bateman, Wiki Visually (2018), http://wikivisually.com/wiki/C_Donald_Bateman, accessed 9/12/18.

CHAPTER 18

Manzo, Edward D., *Patent Reform 2011*, Thomson Reuters West Publisher U.S. (2011).

Leahy-Smith America Invents Act, Public Law 112-29-112th Congress, September 16, 2011, 125 STAT 284 et seq. (2011), https://www.uspto.gov/sites/default/files/aia_implementation/20110916-pub-l112-29.pdf, accessed 10/13/18.

Tramposch. Albert, *The Global Impact of the America Invents Act*, WIPO Magazine (2011), www.wipo.int/wipo_magazine/en/2011/06/article_0002.html, accessed 10/13/18.

Stim, Richard, *Summary of Leahy-Smith America Invents Act*, Congressional Research Service (2011, 2018), https://www.nolo.com/legal-encyclopedia/summary-leahy-smith-america-invents-act.html, accessed 10/13/18.

CHARLES KETTERING

The World Book Encyclopedia, *Kettering, Charles Franklin,* World Book, Inc., Chicago, (1994), vol. 11, p. 307.

Parssinen, Carol and Hammer, Bo, Special Project Team Directors, *Case Files: Charles F. Kettering*, Center for Innovation in Science Learning, The Franklin Institute (2018), https://www.fi.edu/case-files/charles-f-kettering, accessed 10/1/18.

Bernstein, Mark, *Charles F. Kettering – The Self-Starter Who Gave Us the Self-Starter*, Dayton Innovation Legacy; Smithsonian Magazine (1998), http://www.daytoninnovationlegacy.org/kettering.html, accessed 10/1/18.

CALVIN SOUTHER FULLER, GERALD PEARSON AND DARYL CHAPIN

Perlin, John, *The Invention of the Solar Cell*, Popular Science (2014), https://www.popsci.com/article/science/invention-solar-cell, accessed 1/13/18.

Storing Solar Energy: How Solar Batteries Work, Energy Sage (2016), https://www.energysage.com/solar/solar-energy-storage/how-do-solar-batteries-work/, accessed 1/13/18.

Bellis, Mary, *History of Definition of a Solar Cell*, Thought Co. (2017), https://www.thoughtco.com/history-of-solar-cells-1992435, accessed 1/13/18.

Gruen, Abby, *Solar Panels Invented in N.J. 55 Years Ago*, The Star-Ledger (2010), https://www.nj.com/business/index.ssf/2010/10/solar_panels.html, accessed 1/13/18.

Wikipedia, *Calvin Souther Fuller* (2017), https://en.wikipedia.org/wiki/Calvin_Souther_Fuller, accessed 11/24/17.

CHAPTER 19

United States Patent Statutes, 35 U.S.C. §§ 101, 102, 115, 116, 151, 152, 261 and 262.

Arrow, K.A., *Managing IP Financial Assets – Principles from the Securities Markets, From Ideas to Assets*, edited by Berman, B., John Wiley & Sons, Inc., New York (2002), pp. 111–116.

Stobbs, G.A., *Software Patents, The Beta Testing License Agreement*, Aspen Publishers, Inc., New York (2000), pp. 628–230.

Licensing of Intellectual Property Rights, a Vital Component of the Business Strategy of Your SME (Small and Medium Sized Enterprise), WIPO (2018), www.wipo.int/sme/en/ip_business/licensing/licensing.htm. accessed 10/14/18.

PHILO T. FARNSWORTH

National Inventor's Hall of Fame, *Inventor Profile, Philo Taylor Farnsworth – Television System, Cathode-Ray Tube* (2016), http://www.invent.org/hall_of_fame/56.html.

Abramson, Albert, *Pioneers of Television – Philo Taylor Farnsworth*, IEEE, SMPTE Journal (1992), https://ieeexplore.org/document/7236331, accessed 9/30/18.

United States Patent and Trademark Office, Decision of Board of Patent Interferences, Patent Interference No. 64027, *Farnsworth v. Zworykin*, Decision date: July 22, 1934; Final hearing: April 24, 1934, obtained by author from Paul Schatzkin, who advised that he obtained the copy from Mrs. Philo T. Farnsworth.

The American Experience, WGBH Boston, *Big Dream – Small Screen – The Story of the Invention of Television*, WGBH Educational Foundation (2011), blogdogit.com/article.php?story20110408112644399, accessed 10/11/18.

Eschner, Kat, *The Farmboy Who Invented Television*, Smithsonian Institution and U.S. Patent & Trademark Office (2017), https://www.smithsonianmag.com/smart-news/farmboy-who-invented, accessed 10/1/18.

Brigham Young High School Alumni, *Philo T. Farnsworth, Mathematician, Inventor, Father of Electronic Television*, Brigham Young Academy and Brigham Young High School Alumni Association (2018), http://www.byhigh.org/History/Farnsworth/PhiloT1924.html, accessed 10/1/18.

Gregersen, Erik, *Philo Farnsworth – American Inventor*, Encyclopaedia Britannica (2018), https://www.britannica.com/biography/Philo-Farnsworth, accessed 10/1/18.

Farnsworth, Elma G., *Distant Vision: Romance and Discovery of the Invisible Frontier* (Philo T. Farnsworth, Inventor of Television) Pemberly Kent Pub. (1990).

Schatzkin, Paul, *The Boy Who Invented Television*, TeamCom Books, Silver Spring, MD (2002).

Farnsworth, Philo Taylor, Philo T. and Elma G. Farnsworth Papers (1924–1992), Archives West, Orbis Cascade Alliance (1993), archiveswest.orbiscascade.org/ark:80444/xv98312, accessed 10/1/18.

ROBERT ADLER

Gartner, Jon, *A Clicker Is Born*, The New York Times Magazine (2007), https://www.nytimes.com/2007/12/30/magazine/30Adler-t.html, accessed 9/12/18.

Robert Adler, Britannica Online Encyclopedia (2018, http://www.britannica.com/biography/Robert-Adler, accessed 9/12/18.

Robert Adler, NNDB (2014), http://www.nndb.com/people/744/000165249/, accessed 9/12/18.

Sullivan, Patricia, Robert *Adler, 93; Engineer, Co-Inventor of TV Remote Control*, Washington Post (2007), http://www.washingtonpost.com/wp-dyn/content/article/2007/02/16/AR2007021602039_pdf.html.

CHAPTER 20

United States Patent Statues, 35 U.S.C. §§ 112, 154.

United States Patent and Trademark Office, Manual of Patent Examining Procedure ("MPEP"), Edition 9 (2018), Chapter 0600.

Rockman, H.B., *The Practice of Intellectual Property Law*, Law Bulletin Publishing Company, Chicago (1998), pp. 8–11.

WILLIS CARRIER

Willis Carrier: The Inventor of Modern Air Conditioning, Carrier Corporation (2018), http://www.carrier.com/carrier/en/us/about-carrier/wilis-carrier/, accessed 9/9/18.

The Invention That Changed the World, Carrier Corporation (2018), http://www.williscarrier.com/1876-1902.php, accessed 9/9/18.

Willis Carrier – Air Conditioning, Who Made America? Public Broadcasting Corp., https://www.pbs.org/wgbh/theymadeamerica/whomade/carrier_hi.html, accessed 9/9/18.

Wikipedia, *Willis Carrier*, https://en.wikipedia.org/wiki/Willis_Carrier, accessed 11/20/17.

IVAN A GETTING, ROGER L. EASTON AND BRADFORD W. PARKINSON

Mai, Thuy, *Global Positioning System*, U.S. National Aeronautical and Space Administration (NASA) (2017), https://www.nasa.gov/directorates/heo/scan/communications/policy/GPS_History.html, accessed 1/15/18.

Mai, Thuy, *Global Positioning System History*, NASA (2017), https://www.nasa.gov/directorates/heo/scan/communications/policy/GPS_History.html, accessed 1/15/18.

Mai, Thuy, *NASA's Utilization of Global Positioning System* (GPS), NASA (2017), https://www.nasa.gov/directorates/heo/scan/communications/policy/GPS_Utilization.html, accessed 8/19/18.

Bradford W. Parkinson and Stephen T. Power, and GPS World Staff, *Part 1: The Origins of GPS, and the Pioneers Who Launched the System*, GPS World (2010), http://gpsworld.com/origins-gps-part-1/, accessed 1/15/18.

Bradford W. Parkinson and Stephen T. Power, and GPS World Staff, *Part 2: The Origins of GPS, Fighting to Survive*, GPS World (2010), http://gpsworld.com/origins-gps-part-2-fighting-survive/, accessed 1/15/18.

Wikipedia, *Ivan A. Getting*, (2017), https://en.wikipedia.org/wiki/Ivan_A_Getting, accessed 11/24/17.

Wikipedia, *Roger L. Easton*, (2017), https://en.wikipedia.org/wiki/Roger_L_Easton, accessed 11/24/17.

Wikipedia, *Bradford Parkinson*, (2017) https://en/wikipedia.org/wiki/Bradford_Parkinson, accessed 11/24/17.

CHAPTER 21

Gayton, Cynthia M., *Legal Aspects of Engineering, Design and Innovation*, 10th edn, Kendall Hunt Publishing Company, Dubuque, Iowa (2017), pp. 177–178.

Ball, F.R., Silverman, M. and Daley, P., *Seminar, Protect Your Client: Non-Competition Agreement Enforcement*, National Business Institute, Duane Morris Law Firm, Chicago (2003).

Kenyon, R., *Intellectual Property Provisions in Employment Contracts and Policies*, The European Legal Alliance, Paper, Field Fisher Waterhouse (2002).

GRACE HOPPER

Grace Hopper, Famous Scientist (2018), https://www.famousscientists.org/grace-murray-hopper/, accessed 6/13/18.

Howe, Elizabeth, *Grace Hopper: 'First Lady of Software,'* Space.com (2016), https://www.space.com/34885-grace-hopper-biography.html, accessed 6/13/18.

Grace Murray Hopper, Grace Hopper Celebration of Women in Computing 1994 Conference (1994), http://www.cs.yale.edu/homes/tap/files/hopper-story.html, accessed 6/13/18.

Grace Hopper Biography, The Biography.com (2018), https://www.biography.com/people/grace-hopper.21406809, accessed 6/13/18.

Wikipedia, *Grace Hopper* (2018), https://en.wikipedia.org/wiki/Grace_Hopper, accessed 6/13/18.

Isaacson, Walter, *The Innovators*, Simon & Schuster (2014), pp. 88–95, Grace Hopper.

HUBBLE TELESCOPE

U.S. National Aeronautics and Space Administration, *Hubble Space Telescope, Hubble Servicing Mission Overview* (2019), https://www.nasa.gov/mission_pages/huble/servicing/index.html, accessed 9/1/19.

Harwood, William, *How NASA Fixed Hubble's Flawed Vision – and Reputation*, CBS News, http://www.cbsnews.com/news/an-ingenius-fix-for-hubbles-formerly-flawwed-vision/, 4/22/15, accessed 9/1/19.

Okalaski, Gabriel, National Aeronautics and Space Administration, *A Brief History of the Hubble Space Telescope*, https://history.nasa.gov/hubble, accessed 9/11/18.

History: *How Hubble Came About*, http://www.spacetelescope.org/about/history, accessed 7/11/18.

CHAPTER 22

Daubert et al. v. Merrell Dow Pharmaceuticals, Inc., 509 U.S. 379 (Supreme Court 1993).

Gayton, Cynthia M., *Legal Aspects of Engineering, Design, and Innovation*, 10th edn, Kendall Hunt Pub. Co. Dubuque IA (2017), pp. 50–52.

Federal Rules of Civil Procedure, as amended to 2018, Rules 26(a)(2)(B); 26(b)(4); 43.

Federal Rules of Evidence, as amended to 2018, Rules 701–705.

JOHN BARDEEN, WALTER BRATTAIN AND WILLIAM SHOCKLEY

Brinkman, W.F., Haggan, D.E. and Troutman, W.W., *A History of the Invention of the Transistor and Where It Will Lead Us*, IEEE Journal of Solid State Circuits, December (1997), vol. 32, no. 12, pp. 1858–1865.

American Institute of Physics and ScienCentral, Inc., *Solid State Science Takes Root at Bell*, Public Broadcasting System (1999), http://www.pbs.org/transistor/background/events/ssgroup.html, accessed 10/11/18.

National Inventors Hall of Fame, *Inventor Profile – John Bardeen* (2016), http://www.invent.org/hall_of_fame/8/html.

National Inventors Hall of Fame, *Inventor Profile – Walter H. Brattain* (2016), http://www.invent.org/hall_of_fame/19.html.

National Inventors Hall of Fame, *Inventor Profile – William Bradford Shockley* (2016), http://invent.org/hall_of_fame/134.html

Macaulay, D., *The Way Things Work*, Houghton Mifflin Company, Boston (1988), pp. 342–343.

Trefil, J., *Encyclopedia of Science and Technology*, Routledge, New York – London (2001), pp. 484–485.

John Bardeen – Facts, NobelPrize.org. Nobel Media AB (2018), https://www.nobelprize.org/prizes/physics/1956/bardeen/biographical/, accessed 10/11/18.

William B. Shockley – Facts, NobelPrize.org. Nobel Media AB (2018), https://www.nobelprize.org/prizes/physics/1956/shockley/facts/, accessed 10/11/18.

Walter Houser Brattain – Facts, NobelPrize.org. Nobel Media AB (2018), https://nobelprize.org/prizes/physics/1956/brattain/facts/, accessed 10/11/18.

University of Illinois at Urbana Champaign, *John Bardeen*, Illinois Physics, College of Engineering (2018), https://www.physics.illinois.edu/people/memorial/bardeen, accessed 10/11/18.

Shockley, Brattain and Bardeen – Clashing Egos to the End, ScienCentral, Inc. and the American Institute of Physics (1999), https://www.pbs.org/transistor/album1/add1bios/egos.html, accessed 10/11/18.

Watkins, Thayer, *The History of the Transistor*, San Jose State University (2018), http://www.sjsu.edu/faculty/watkins/transist.htm, accessed 10/11/18.

Transistorized, ScienCentral and the American Institute of Physics (1999), http://www.pbs.org/transistor/album1/, accessed 10/11/18.

CHAPTER 23

Ibsen, Henrik, *Enemy of the People*, Penguin, New York, NY (1882, 1977).

National Society of Professional Engineers (NSPE), *Code of Ethics for Engineers*, as revised 2018, Publication #1102. nspe.org., accessed 8/17/18.

Gayton, Cynthia M., *Legal Aspects of Engineering, Design and Innovation*, 10th edn, Kendall Hunt Pub. Co., Dubuque, IA (2017), pp. 14–16.

Institute of Electrical and Electronic Engineers, *IEEE Code of Ethics (1963 to present)*, https://www.ieee.org/about/compliance.html#code-of-ethics, accessed 8/18/18.

JACK KILBY AND ROBERT NOYCE

Jack Kilby (1923–2005) Inventor of the Integrated Circuit, IEEE Signal Processing Magazine (2005), https://ieeexplore.ieee.org/stamp/stamp.jsp?arnumber=1511813, accessed 10/12/18.

Smil, Vaclav, *July 1958, Kilby Conceives the Integrated Circuit*, IEEE Spectrum Magazine (2018), https://spectrum.ieee.org/semiconductors/devices/july-1958-kilby-conceiver-the-integratedcircuit, accessed 10/12/18.

The Chip that Jack Built, Texas Instruments Co. (2018), www.ti.com/corp/docs/kilbyctr/jackbuilt.shtml, accessed 10/13/18.

Schroeder, H.R., *The Man Behind the Microchip: Robert Noyce and the Invention of Silicon Valley*, IEEE Technology and Society Magazine (2006), https://ieeexplore.ieee.org/document/1700022/authors#authors, accessed 10/13/18.

Jack S. Kilby, Biographical, NobelPrize.org. Nobel Media AB (2000), https://www.nobelprize.org/prizes/physics/2000/kilby/auto-biography/, accessed 10/13/18.

The Integrated Circuit of Jack Kilby and Robert Noyce, History of Computers and Computing, Birth of the Modern Computer (2018), http://history-computer.com/ModernComputer/Basis/IC.html, accessed 10/13/18.

Wood, Daniel B., *Why Robert Noyce Should Have Won Two Nobel Prizes, But Didn't*, The Christian Science Monitor (2011), https://www.csmonitor.com/USA/2011/1212/Why-Robert-Noyce-should-have-won-two-Nobel-Prizes-but-didn-t, accessed 10/13/18.

Biography of Robert Noyce, History of Computers and Computing, People, Robert Noyce (2018), http://history-computer.com/People/Noycebio.html, accessed 10/13/18.

CHAPTER 24

United States Copyright Statute, 17 U.S.C.:

Architectural Works – §§ 101, 102(a)(8), 120.

Copyrightable Works – §§ 102, 103, 104.

Enforcement – §§ 501, 505, 507(b), 508, 511, 512, 513.

Exclusive Rights – §§ 106, 107.

Fair Use – §§ 107.

Fixed in a Tangible Medium – § 102.

Literary Works – § 101.

Notice – §§ 401–406.

Registration – §§ 408–412.

Term of Copyright – §§ 301–305.

Works for Hire – §§ 101, 201(b).

Library of Congress, Copyright Office, *Copyright Registration for Computer Programs*, Circular 61 (2017), https://www.copyright.gov/circs/circ61.pdf, accessed 3/10/17.

Library of Congress, Copyright Office, Copyright Registration for Online Works Circular 66 (2017), https://www.copyright.gov/circs/circ66.pdf.

English Statute of Anne, *An Act for the Encouragement of Learning by Vesting the Copies of Printed Books in the Authors or Purchasers of Such Copies, During the Times Therein Mentioned, 8 Anne* c. 19 (1709).

Constitution of the United States, Article I, Section 8, Clause 8 (1787).

Convention for the Protection of Literary and Artistic Works, (Berne Convention) signed at Berne, Switzerland, September 9, 1886, accession by United States March 1, 1989, Treaty Document 99-27, 828 U.N.T.S. 221 (Paris rev. 1971).

Harper & Row Publishers, Inc. v. Nation Enterprises, 471 U.S. 539 (U.S. Supreme Court 1985) (The Gerald Ford Autobiography case).

World Intellectual Property Organization (WIPO), *Summary of the Berne Convention for the Protection of Literary and Artistic Works* (1886), http://www.wipo.int/treaties/en/ip/berne/summary-berne.html, accessed 3/10/17.

Wilmer Cutler Pickering Hale and Door LLP, The *Origin of Click-Wrap: Software Shrink-Wrap Agreements* (2000), Publication and News, https://www.wilmerhale.com/en/insights/publications/the-origin-of-click-wrap-software-shrink-wrap-agreements-march-22-2000, accessed 2/18/17.

Quirk, Vanessa, *The 10 Things You Must Know About Architectural Copyrights*, ArchDaily (2013), http://www.archdaily.com/328870/the-10-thing-you-must-know-about-architectural-copyrights/, accessed 9/3/17.

Shipley, David E., *The Architectural Works Copyright Protection Act at Twenty: Has Full Protection Made a Difference*, University of Georgia School of Law, Journal of Intellectual Property Law, vol. 18, no. 1 (2018), pp. 1–60.

U.S. Copyright Office Circular 41, *Copyright Claims in Architectural Works* (2012).

Drozd, Vaughn, *The Building Blocks of Copyright Protection for Architectural Works: Roadblock or Masterpiece?* The John Marshall Law School, Review of Intellectual Property Law (2015), vol. 14, pp. 607–627.

FEDERICO FAGGIN, MARCIAN HOFF, AND STANLEY MAZOR

Dufresne, Steven, *Federico Faggin: The Real Silicon Man*, Hackaday.com (2018), https://hackaday.com/2018/06/19/federico-faggin-the-real-silicon-man/, accessed 10/6/18.

Federico Faggin, European Inventor of the Year, European Patent Office (EPO) (2015), https://www.epo.org/learning-events/european-inventor/finalist/20, accessed 10/6/18.

Bellis, Mary, *Inventors of the Modern Computer*, Thought Co. (2018), https://www.thoughtco.com/inventors-of-the-modern-computer-19, accessed 10/6/18.

The Microprocessor, History of Computers and Computing, Birth of the Modern Computer (2018), http://history-computer.com/ModernComputer/Basis/microprocessor, accessed 10/6/18.

National Inventors Hall of Fame, *Federico Faggin* (2016), www.invent.org/honor/inductees/inductee-detail/?11D=55, accessed 10/6/18.

National Inventors Hall of Fame, *Marcian "Ted" Hoff* (2016), www.invent.org/honor/inductees/inductee-detail/?11D=79, accessed 10/6/18.

National Inventors Hall of Fame, *Stanley Mazor* (2016), www.invent.org/honor/inductees/inductee-detail/?11D=100, accessed 10/6/18.

The Great Idea Finder, *Invention of the Microprocessor*, Ideafinder (2005), http://www.ideafinder.com/history/inventions/microprocessor.htm.

The Great Idea Finder, *M.E. "Ted" Hoff*, Ideafinder (2005), http://www.ideafinder.com/history/inventors/hoff.htm.

Davidson, M.W., *Molecular Expressions: The Silicon Zoo-Federico Faggin*, University of Florida, 1995–2003, (2004), http://micro.magnet.fsu.edu/creatures.pages/faggin.html.

JOSEPHINE COCHRANE

Foulkes, Debbie, *Josephine Cochrane (1839–1913) Invented the Dishwasher*, Forgotten Newsmakers (2010), https://forgottennewsmakers.com/2010/04/20/josephine-cochrane-1839-1913-invented-the dishwasher/, accessed 8/18/18.

Josephine Cochrane Biography (2011), Browse Biography (2011), http://www.browsebiography.com/bio-josephine_cochrane.html, accessed 8/18/18.

Josephine Cochrane, Inventor of the Automatic Dishwashing Machine (2018), The Robinson Library (2018), http://www.robinsonlibrary.com/technology/mechanical/biography/cochrane.htm, accessed 8/18/18.

CHAPTER 25

U.S. Copyright Office Summary, *The Digital Millennium Copyright Act of 1998*, Pub. L. No. 105-304, 112 Stat. 2860 (Oct. 28, 1998), https://www.copyright.gov/legislation/dmca.pdf, accessed 4/14/18.

United States Copyright Statutes, 17 U.S.C. §§ 117, 1201, 1202.

Convention for the Protection of Literary and Artistic Works (Berne Convention), signed at Berne, Switzerland, September 8, 1886, accession by United States March 1, 1898, Treaty Document 99-27, 828 U.N.T.S. 221 (Paris rev. 1971).

WIPO (World Intellectual Property Organization) Copyright Treaty, Adopted by the Diplomatic Conference on December 20, 1996.

WIPO Performance and Phonograms Treaty, Adopted by the Diplomatic Conference on December 20, 1996.

The Digital Millennium Copyright Act of 1998, Public Law No. 105-304, 111 Stat. 2860 (1998).

Goldstein, P., *Copyright, Patent, Trademark and Related State Doctrines*, 5th edn, Foundation Press, New York (2002), pp. 732–735.

United States Copyright Office, *Rulemaking on Exemptions from Prohibition on Circumvention of Technological Measures that Control Access to Copyrighted Works* (2018), http://www.copyright.gov1201/, accessed 9/2/19.

DMCA: The Digital Millennium Copyright Act, American Library Association (2017), http://www.ala.org/advocacy/copyright/dmca, accessed 9/3/17.

Kravets, David, *10 Years Later, Misunderstood DMCA is the Law that Saved the Web*, Wired (2008), https://www.wired.com/2008/10/ten-years-later/, accessed 9/3/17.

DMCA is the Cornerstone of Our Antipiracy Service, MUSO (2017), https://www.muso.com/magazine/story/dmca-explained/, accessed 9/3/17.

Harr, You-Jin, *The Basics of the Digital Millennium Copyright Act*, Reporters Committee for Freedom of the Press (2012), https://www.rcfp.org/browse-media-law-resources/news-media-law/news-media-and-law-winter-2012/basics-digital-millennium-c, accessed 9/3/17.

STEVE WOZNIAK

Lapsley, Phil, *The Definitive Story of Steve Wozniak, Steve Jobs, and Phone Phreaking*, Exploding the Phone, Grove/Atlantic, Inc. (2013), https://www.theatlantic.com/technology/archive/2013/02/the-definitive, accessed 9/20/18.

Sattel, Sam, *Steve Wozniak & the Computer Industry*, Autodesk EAGLE (2017), https://www.autodesk.com/products/eagle/blog/steve-wozniak-com, accessed 9/20/18.

Isaacson, Walter, *Steve Jobs*, Simon & Schuster (2011).

Schawbel, Dan, *Steve Wozniak: His Career Challenges, Steve Jobs, Tech Trends and Advice*, Forbes (2012), https://www.forbes.com/sites/danschawbel/2012/11/26/steve-wozniak, accessed 9/20/18.

HAARTSEN – BLUE TOOTH

Schwartz, Ephraim, *2003 InfoWorld Innovator: Jaap DFC. Haartsen*, InfoWorld (2003), https://www.infoworld.com/article/2681786/networking/2005-infoworld-inventor-jaap-c--hartsen.html, accessed 11/24/17.

Touner, Dominic, *The Bluetooth Blues*, Information Age (2001), http://information-age.com/2001/may/the_bluetooth_blues, accessed 11/24/17.

Nguyen, Tuan, *Who Invented Bluetooth*, Thought Co. (2017), https://www.thoughtco.com/who-invented-bluetooth-4038864?print, accessed 1/13/18.

Invention of Bluetooth Technology, Blogspot (2010), http://bluetoothtech-invention.blogspot.com/, accessed 1/13/18.

Brachmann, Steve, *Evolution of Technology: Bluetooth, the Once and Future King*, IPWatchdog (2015), https://stg.ipwatchdog.com/2015/05/10/evolution-of-technology-bluetooth-the-once-and-future-king/id=57473/, accessed 1/13/18.

CHAPTER 26

Semiconductor Chip Protection Act of 1984, 17 U.S.C. §§ 902–914.

United States Copyright Office, *Federal Statutory Protection for Mask Works*, Circular 100, 2012, https://www.copyright.gov/circs/circ100.pdf.

United States Copyright Office, *Part 211 – Mask Work Protection* (2003), a257.g.akamaitech.net/7/257/2422/14mar20010800/edocket.access.gpo.gov/cfr_2002/julqtr/pdf/37cfr211.2.pdf.

Cornell University, Legal Information Institute, U.S. Code Collection, 17 U.S. Code Chapter 9, Protection of Semiconductor Chip Products (2018), https://www.law.cornell.edu/uscode/text/17/chapter-9, accessed 10/13/18.

Tysver, Daniel A., *Mask Works and Copyright*, Bitlaw (2015), https://www.bitlaw.com/copyright/maskwork.html, accessed 9/12/17.

Crouch, Dennis, *Ninth Circuit Upholds Semiconductor Chip Act Claim Asserting Protection for Logic Groupings*, Patently O (2005), https://patentlyo.com/patent/2005/09/ninth-circuit_u.html, accessed 9/12/17.

STEPHANIE KWOLEK – KEVLAR

Bellis, Mary, *The Story of Kevlar – Stephanie Kwolek*, Thought Co (2017), https://www.thoughtco.com/history-of-kelvar-stephanie-kwolek-4076518?print, accessed 1/14/18.

Fascinating Facts About the Invention of Kevlar by Stephanie Kwolek in 1985, Idea Finder, https://www.ideafinder.com/history/inventions/kevlar.htm, accessed 1/14/18.

Engel, KeriLynn, *Stephanie Kwolek, Inventor of Kevlar*, Amazing Women in History (2011), http://www.amazingwomeninhistory.com/stephanie-kwolek-inventor-kevlar/, accessed 1/14/18.

Aramid Fiber, Fibermax Composites, http://www.aramid.eu/history.html, accessed 1/14/18.

PERCY JULIAN

A Steroid Chemist and an Entrepreneur, Science History Institute (2017), https://www.sciencehistory.org/historica-profile/percy-lavon-julian, accessed 9/27/18.

Depauw University, Greencastle, Indiana, *Synthesis of Physostigmine*, National Historic Chemical Landmarks Program, American Chemical Society (1999), https://www.aca.org/content/acs/en/education/whatischemistry/lan, accessed 9/27/18.

Wilkop, Bernhard, *Percy Lavon Julian, 1899–1975*, National Academy Press, Washington D.C., Biographical Memoirs, vol. 52 (1980).

Chamberlain, Gaius, *Percy Julian*, the Black Inventor Online Museum (2012), http://blackinventor.com/percy-julian/, accessed 9/27/18.

Percy Lavon Julian, Famous Scientists (2018), http://www.famousscientists.org/percy-lavon-julian/, accessed 9/27/18.

Who Was Percy Julian, NOVA, PBS (2007), www.pbs.org/wgbh/nova/julian/lrk-whowasjulian-exp.html, accessed 9/28/18.

Hometown Legends – Percy Julian, Oak Park River Forest Museum (2018), oprfmuseum.org/people/percy-julian, accessed 9/17/18.

CHAPTER 27

American Law Institute, First Restatement of Torts, Sections 757, 758, Copyright 1939, Reprinted with the permission of the American Law Institute.

National Conference of Commissioners on Uniform State Laws, Uniform Trade Secrets Act, Chicago, 1979, rev. 1986.

U.S. Defend Trade Secrets Act of 2016, Public Law 114-153 – May 11, 2016, 130 STAT. 376.

Gabriel, Allan, *Defend Trade Secrets Act: What Does it Mean in the Real World – and What do Lawyers do Now?* Inside Counsel Magazine (2016), http://www.insidecounsel.com/2016/06/23/

defend-trade-secrets-act-what-does-it-mean-in-the? slreturn=1483224058, accessed 12/31/16.

Kaplan, Sebastian and Premo, Patrick, *The Defend Trade Secrets Act of 2016 Creates Federal Jurisdiction for Trade Secret Litigation*, IPWatchdog (2016), http://ipwatchdog.com/2016/05/23/defend-trade-secrets-act-2016-creates-federal-jurisdiction-trade-secret-litigation/id=69245/, accessed 12/31/16.

Esmond, Robert W. et al., *A Best Kept Secret: AIA Allows Patenting of Trade Secrets*, Bloomberg BNA, Patent, Trademark & Copyright Journal (2016).

Quinn, Gene, *AIA Oddities: Trade Secrets, Repatenting and Best Mode*, IPWatchdog (2013), http://ipwatchdog.com/2013/09/18/aia-oddities-trade-secrets-re-patenting-and-best-mode/id=45108/, accessed 3/11/17.

CHESTER F. CARLSON

Dinsdale, A. *Chester F. Carlson, Inventor of Xerography – A Biography*, The Journal of Photographic Science and Engineering (1963), https://www.library.rochester.edu/carlson/chester/biography, accessed 11/21/17.

Dickerson, Kelly, *This Is the First Xerox Copy Ever Made*, Business Insider (2013), https://www.businessinsider.com/chester-carlson-and-the-first-xerox-copy-2013-10, accessed 11/21/17.

Chester Carlson and Xerography, Xerox Corporation (2017), https://www.xerox.com/en-us/innovation/chester-carlson-xerography, accessed 11/21/17.

Wikipedia, *Chester Carlson*, (2017) https://en.wikipedia.org/wiki/Chester_Carlson, accessed 11/20/17.

The Story of Xerography, Xerox Corporation (1999), https://www.xerox.com/downloads/usa/en/s/Storyofxerography.pdf, accessed 9/3/18.

CHAPTER 28

Public Law 114-153, 114th Congress May 11, 2016 – Defend Trade Secrets Act of 2016, U.S. Government Printing Office, 130 Stat. 376 (2016), https://congress.gov/114/plaws/publi53/PLAW-114publ15.pdf.

Trading Secrets-Latest Updates on Federal Trade Secrets Legislation, Seyfarth Shaw (2016), http://www.tradesecretslaw.com/latest-updates-on-federal-trade-secret-legislation/, accessed 12/31/16.

Lee, P., Dharnidharka, R. and Cheung, K., *Obama Signs Federal Trade Secret Bill Into Law*, DLA Piper (2016), https://www.dlapiper.com/en/us/insights/publications/2016/05/obama-signs-federal-tradesecret-bill-into-law/, accessed 12/31/16.

Gabriel, Allan, *Defend Trade Secrets Act: What Does It Mean in the Real World-and What Do Lawyers Do Now*, Inside Counsel Magazine (2016), https://www.law.com/insidecounsel/alm ID/576b116f150ba037029ddf31, accessed 12/31/16.

Esmond, Robert W. et al., *A Best Kept Secret: AIA Allows Patenting of Trade Secrets*, Bloomberg BNA Patent, Trademark & Copyright Journal (2016), 91 PTCJ 1064.

Quinn, Gene, *AIA Oddities: Trade Secrets, Repatenting and Best Mode*, IPwatchdog (2013), http://www.ipwatchdog.com/2013/09/18/aia-oddities-trade-secrets-re-patenting-and-bestmode/id45108, accessed 12/31/16.

Elkind, Stephen, *Secrets, Secrets Are No Fun: Balancing Patent Law and Trade Secret Law Under the American Invents Act*, The Federal Circuit Bar Journal, George Washington University Law School (2013), pp. 443–457.

SAMUEL BLUM, JAMES WYNNE AND RANGASWAMY SRINIVASAN

NASA Spinoff, NASA Technology Transfer Program, *The Right Track for Vision Correction*, NASA (2003), https://spinoff.nasa.gov/spinoff2003/hm_1.html, accessed 5/30/18.

NASA Spinoff, NASA Technology Transfer Program, *Space Shuttle Spinoffs*, NASA (2011), https://spinoff.nasa.gov/Spinoff2011/shuttle_spinoffs.html, accessed 5/10/18.

Gornall, Jonathan, *Night Vision and Laser Surgery Trace Their Roots to Shuttle*, The National (Abu Dhabi) (2018), https://www.thenational.ae/uae/night-vision-and-laser-surgery-trace-their-roots-to-shuttle-1.414160?videoId=5766484581001, accessed 5/10/18.

Excimer Laser Surgery, IBM100, http://www-03.ibm.com/ibm/history/ibm100/us/en/icons/excimer/, accessed 1/27/18.

History of Refractive Surgery, Eye Doctor Network, http://www.eyedoctornetwork.org/history-of-refractive-surgery.htm, accessed 1/27/18.

Wikipedia, *LASIK*, (2018), https://en.wikipedia.org/wiki/LASIK#History, accessed 2/11/18.

CHAPTER 29

United States Constitution, Article 1, Section 8, Clause 8 (1787).

The Lanham Act Trademark Statute, 15 U.S.C. §§1051–1129 (1946):

Applications for Registration, Use Based and Intent to Use §§1051, 1057–1072.

Cancellation Proceedings §1064.

Declaration of Continued Use §1065.

Descriptive Marks §1052(e).

Distinctiveness; Secondary Meaning §1052(f).

Federal Search Database §1112.

Generic Marks §1052(e).

Infringement §1114.

Searching; The International Classification System §1112.

Opposition Proceedings §1063.

Publication of Marks §1062.

Registration Symbol ® §1111.

Renewal of Registration §1059

Rights Obtained by Registration; Exclusive Rights §1115.

Supplemental Register §1091.

Rockman, H.B., *The Practice of Intellectual Property Law*, Law Bulletin Publishing Company, Chicago (1998), pp. 157–180.

Cotrone, C., *The United States and The Madrid Protocol: A Time to Decline, A Time to Accede*, Marquette Intellectual Property Law Review, 4 Marq. Intell. Prop. L. Rev. 75 (2000), accessed 10/13/18.

World Intellectual Property Organization (WIPO), *Protocol Relating to the Madrid Agreement Concerning the International Registration of Marks* (as signed at Madrid on June 27, 1989), WIPO Publication No. 204(E) (2003), https://www.ipo.int/edocs/pubdocs/en/wipo_pub_204_2017_2.pdf, accessed 10/13/18.

Wilner, Peter, *The Madrid Protocol: A Voluntary Model for the Internationalization of Trademark Law*, DePaul Journal of Art, Technology & Intellectual Property Law (2003), https://via.library.depaul.edu/jatip/vol13/iss1/3/, accessed 10/13/18.

JOHN MAUCHLY AND JOHN PRESPER ECKERT

Levy, Steven, *The Brief History of the ENIAC Computer* (2013), Smithsonian Magazine, https://www.smithsonianmag.com/history/the-brief-history-of-the-eniac-computer-3889120/, accessed 12/23/17.

Wink, Christopher, *ENIAC: 10 Things You Should Know About the Original Super Computer 65 Years Later* (2011), Techical.ly Philly, https://technical.ly/philly/2011/02/15/eniac-10-things-you-should-know-about-the-original-modern-super-computer-65-years-later/, accessed 12/23/17.

da Cruz, Frank, *Programming the ENIAC* (2017), Columbia University Computing History, http://www.columbia.edu/cu/computinghistory/eniac.html, accessed 12/23/17.

Swaine, Michael R. and Freibeyer, Paul A., *ENIAC Computer*, (2017), Encyclopedia Britannica, https://www.britannica.com/technology/ENIAC, accessed 12/13/17.

Wikipedia, *ENIAC*, (2017) https://en.wikipedia.org/wiki/ENIAC, accessed 12/23/17.

Bit by Bit, *7.8 The Honeywell Sperry Case* (2017), Quaker and Special Collections, Haverford College, Haverford, PA, http://ds-wordpress.haverford.edu/bitbybit/bit-by-bit-contents/chapter-seven/7-8-the-honeywell-sperry-case/, accessed 12/23/17.

JVA Imitative Committee and Iowa State University, *John Vincent Atanasoff and the Birth of Electronic Digital Computing – Patent/Court Case – Honeywell vs Sperry Rand* (2017), Iowa State University Department of Computer Science, http://jva.cs.iastate.edu/courtcase.phys, accessed 12/23/17.

Isaacson, Walter, *The Innovators*, Simon & Schuster (2014), pp. 35–85, The Computer.

CHAPTER 30

The Anticybersquatting Consumer Protection Act (ACPA), 15 U.S.C. §1125(d) (1999).

Internet Corporation for Assigned Names and Numbers (ICANN), https://www.icann.org/, accessed 1/15/18.

ICANN Uniform Domain-Name Dispute-Resolution Policy (1998), https://www.icann.org/resources/pages/help/dndr/udrp-en, accessed 1/15/18.

GEORGE DE MESTRAL

Eschner, Kat, *Before Velcro's Patent Expired, It Was a Niche Product Most People Hadn't Heard Of*, Smithsonian Magazine (2017), https://www.smithsonianmag.com/smart-news/velcros-patent-expired-it-was-niche-product-most-people-hadnt-heard-180962701/, accessed 12/23/17.

Suddath, Claire, *A Brief History of Velcro*, Time Magazine (2010), http://content.time.com/time/nation/article/0,8599,1996883,00.html, accessed 12/23/17.

Stephens, Thomas, *How a Swiss Invention Hooked the World*, SWI SwissInfo (2007), https://www.swissinfo.ch/eng/how-a-swiss-invention-hooked-the-world/5653568, accessed 12/24/17.

Wikipedia, *George de Mestral* (2017), https://en.wikipedia.org/wiki/George_de_Mestral, accessed 11/20/17.

JOHN A. ROEBLING

The John A. Roebling Suspension Bridge (Cincinnati), Roebling Suspension Bridge Committee (2018), https://roeblingbridge.org, accessed 8/25/18.

Wikipedia, *John A. Roebling* (2018), https://en.wikipedia.org/wiki/John_A_Roebling, accessed 6/10/18.

CHAPTER 31

Byers, Thomas H., Dorf, Richard C. and Nelson Andrew J., *Technology Ventures – From Idea to Enterprise*, 4th edn, McGraw Hill Education, New York, NY (2015).

Berman, Bruce, Editor, *From Ideas to Assets*, John Wiley & Sons, Inc., New York, NY (2002).

Shearer, Robert, *Business Power – Creating New Wealth from IP Assets*, John Wiley & Sons, Inc., Hoboken, New Jersey (2007).

Govindarajau, Vijay, and Trimble, Chris, *Beyond the Idea – How to Execute Innovation in Any Organization*, St. Martin's Press, New York, NY (2013), pp. 25–28.

Grant, Adam, *Motivating Creativity At Work: The Necessity of Others Is the Mother of Invention*, Psychological Sciences Agenda, American Psychological Association (2011), https://www.apa.org/science/about/psa/2011/07/motivating-creativity, accessed 10/19/18.

Invention and Innovation: An Introduction, The Open University (2018), http://open.edu/open/learn/science-maths-technology/engineering, accessed 10/19/18.

A. Stahlbrost & B. Bergvall-Kareborn, "Exploring Users Motivation in Innovation Communities," *International Journal of Entrepreneurship and Innovation Management 14(4):298–314*, Inderscience Enterprises, Ltd. (2011).

G. Llopis, "5 Ways Leaders Enable Innovation In Their teams," Forbes, https://www.forbes.com/sites/glennllopis/2014/04/07/5-ways-leaders... (2014), accessed 5/10/18.

M. Antikainen, M. Makipaa & M. Ahonen, "Motivating and Supporting Collaboration in Open Innovation," European Journal of Innovation Management *13*(1):100–119, Emerald Group Publishing (2010).

LES PAUL

King, Steve and Putman, Johnnie, "A Little More Les," Steve and Johnnie Media, LLC (2015) ISBN 978-0-9850673-7-3.

Quarto Explores, *Les Paul: The Man Behind the Electric Guitar*, Quarto Knows (2016), https://www.quartoknows.com/blog/quartoexplores/les-paul-the-man-behind-the-electric-guitar, accessed 12/16/17.

Biography.com Editors, *Les Paul, Guitarist, Inventor* (1915–2009), A&E Television Network (2017), https://www.biography.com/people/les-paul-9435046, accessed 12/16/17.

The Man Behind the Guitar, The Les Paul Guide (2011), http://lespaulguide.com/the-man-behind-the-les-paul/, accessed 12/16/17.

Baker, Sue, *Les Paul's Inventions – Part II*, Les Paul Foundation Blog (2014).

CHAPTER 32

Federal Rules of Civil Procedure – 2018 Edition, National Court Rules Committee (2018), https://www.federalrulesofcivilprocedure.org, accessed 4/18/18.

Federal Rules of Evidence – 2018 Edition, National Court Rules Committee (2018), https://www.rulesofevidence.org, accessed 4/18/18.

IGOR SIKORSKY

Parssimon, Carol, Hammer, Bo et al., *Case Files: Igor Sikorsky*, The Franklin Institute (2018), https://www.fi.edu/case-files/igor-sikorsky, accessed 3/11/18.

Johnston, S. Paul, *Igor Sikorsky*, Britannica Online Encyclopedia (2018), https://www.britannica.com/print/article/543984, accessed 3/11/18.

Igor Sikorsky, Sikorsky Archives (2012), https://www.sikorskyarchives.com/Igor_Sikorsky.php, accessed 3/11/18.

Bellis, Mary, *History of the Helicopter*, ThoughtCo. (2018), https://www.thoughtco.com/history-of-the-helicopter-1991899, accessed 3/11/18.

World's First Helicopter – Today in History: September 14, CT Humanities, https://connecticuthistory.org/worlds-first-helicopter-today-in-history/, accessed 3/11/18.

Giges, Nancy S., *Igor Sikorsky: Aviation Pioneer*, ASME, https://www.asme.org/engineering-topics/articles/aerospace-defense/igor-sikorsky-aviation-pioneer, accessed 3/11/18.

History of the Helicopter from Concept to Modern Day, Prime Industries (2015), https://primeindustriesusa.com/history-of-the-helicopter/, accessed 3/11/18.

FRANK ZAMBONI

Murphy, Cait, *This is How the First Zamboni Machine Was Invented*, A History of American Sports in 100 Objects (2016), http://time.com/4508517/zamboni-history/, accessed 12/17/17.

Bellis, May, *The History of Zamboni*, ThoughtCo. (2017), https://www.thoughtco.com/the-history-of-zamboni-1992696, accessed 12/17/17.

The Zamboni Story, Frank J. Zamboni & Co. (2017), https://zamboni.com/about/zamboni-archives/the-zamboni-story/, accessed 12/17/17.

Wikipedia, *Frank Zamboni*, (2017), https://en.wikipedia.org/wiki/Frank_Zamboni, accessed 12/17/17.

CHAPTER 33

Feldman, M.P., Colaianni, A., and Lin, C.K., *Lessons from the Commercialization of the Cohen-Boyer Patents: The Stanford University Licensing Program, Handbook of Best Practices* (2007), pp. 1787–1807; http://www.iphandbook,org/handbook/chPDFs/ch17/ipHandbook-Ch%2017%2022%20Feldman-Colaianni0Liu%20Cohen-Boyer%20Patents%20and%20Licenses.pdf, accessed 12/3/17.

AUTM, Association of University Technology Managers, 2019, https://www.autm.net.

What is Technology Transfer? University of Rochester, UR Ventures (2017), http://www.rochester.edu/ventures/about/what-is-technology-transfer/, accessed 10/16/17.

Inventor's Guide, Stanford University Office of Technology Licensing (2017), https://otl.stanford.edu/sites/default/files/otl_inventor_guide_2017.pdf, accessed 12/31/17.

A Handbook for Inventors and Innovators, Offices of Technology Management, University of Illinois (2013), https://otm.illinois.edu/sites/default/files/2013_InventorsHandbook%20for%20web.pdf, accessed 12/31/17.

The Start-Up Handbook, Offices of Technology Management, University of Illinois (2014), https://otm.illinois.edu/sites/default/files/Start-Up%20Handbook%20for%20web.pdf, accessed 12/31/17.

FERDINAND VON ZEPPELIN

Count Ferdinand von Zeppelin, Airships.net (2017), http://www.airships.net/airship-people/count-ferdinand-von-zeppelin/, accessed 1/7/18.

The Editors of Encyclopedia Britannica, *Ferdinand, Graf von Zeppelin*, Encyclopedia Britannica (2017), https://www.britannica.com/biography/Ferdinand-Graf-von-Zeppelin, accessed 1/7/18.

Wikipedia, *Ferdinand von Zeppelin*, (2017), https://en.wikipedia.org/wiki/Ferdinand_von_Zeppelin, accessed 11/24/17.

BERNARD SILVER AND NORMAN WOODLAND

Inventors Hall of Fame Inducts Father of Barcode, The Barcode News (2017), https://barcode.com/20110307497/inventors-hall-of-fame-inducts-fathers-of-barcode.html, accessed 1/15/18.

Verma, Samidha, *Invention Story of Barcode*, Engineer Garage (2016), https://www.engineersgarage.com/invention-stories/barcodes-history, accessed 1/15/18.

Bar Code Laser Engraver – Epilog Laser System, Edinformatics (1999), https://www.edinformatics.com/inventions _Inventors/bar_code.htm, accessed 1/15/18.

Wikipedia, *Bernard Silver* (2017), https://en.wikipedia.org/wiki/Bernard_Silver, accessed 1/24/17.

Wikipedia, *Norman Joseph Woodland* (2017), https://en.wikipedia.org/wiki/Norman_Joseph_Woodland, accessed 1/24/17.

CHAPTER 34

Yin, Ronald and Cunningham, Sean, *Filing and Defending Patents in Different Jurisdictions*, Krattinger A., Mohoney, R.T., Nelsen, L., Thomson, J.A., Bennett, A.B., Satyanarayana, K., Graff, G.D., Fernandez, C., and Kowalski, S.P. (editors), *Intellectual Property Management in Health and Agricultural Innovation: A Handbook of Best Practices 953* (2007) (available in two volumes at www. iphandbook.org).

National Science Board, *Industry, Technology, and the Global Marketplace*, Science and Engineering Indicators (2018), https://nsf.gov/statistics/2018/nsb20181/report/sections/industry-technology-and-the-global-marketplace/patterns-and-trends-of-knowledge, accessed 8/31/18.

John Fraser, *IP Management and Deal Making for Global Health Outcomes: The New Return of Imagination* (ROI), Krattinger A., Mohoney, R.T., Nelsen, L., Thomson, J.A., Bennett, A.B., Satyanarayana, K., Graff, G.D., Fernandez, C., and Kowalski, S.P. (editors), *Intellectual Property Management in Health and Agricultural Innovation: A Handbook of Best Practices 953* (2007) (available in two volumes at www. iphandbook.org).

Eiss, Robert, Hanna, Kathi E., and Mahoney, Richard T., *Ensuring Global Access Through Effective IP Management: Strategies of Product-Development Partnerships*, Krattinger A., Mohoney, R.T., Nelsen, L., Thomson, J.A., Bennett, A.B., Satyanarayana, K., Graff, G.D., Fernandez, C., and Kowalski, S.P. (editors), *Intellectual Property Management in Health and Agricultural Innovation: A Handbook of Best Practices 953* (2007) (available in two volumes at www. iphandbook.org).

GODFREY HOUNSFELD & ALLAN CORMACK

Asiado, Tel, *CT Scan: Computed Axial Tomography (CAT) Scan*, Decoded Everything (2011), https://www.decodedscience.org/ct-scan-computed-axial-tomography-cat-scan/772, accessed 1/13/18.

Brief History of CT, The Women's Health & Wellness Resource Network, http://www.imaginis.com/ct-scan/brief-history-of-ct, accessed 1/13/18.

Grunnell, Dustin, *When Hounsfield Met Ambrose, The Invention of Computed Tomography*, Eureka (2012), http://eureka.criver.com/the-invention-of-computed-tomography/, accessed 1/13/18.

CT Scan and MRI Introduced, A Science Odyssey, PBS (1998), http://www.pbs.org/wgbh/aso/databank/entries/dh72ct.html, accessed 1/13/18.

Yearwood, Courtney, *The History of Evolution of CAT Scans*, Prezi (2014), https://prezi.com/qd7wtneothur/the-history-and-evolution-of-cat-scans/, accessed 1/13/18.

Goldman, Lee W., *Principles of CT and CT Technology*, Journal of Nuclear Medicine Technology (2007), http://tech.snmjournals.org/content/35/3/115, accessed 1/13/18.

Cormack, Allan M., *Allan M. Cormack – Biographical*, The Nobel Prizes (1979), https://www.nobelprize.org/prizes/medicine/1979/cormack/auto-biography/, accessed 2/3/18.

The Editor of the Encyclopedia Britannica, *Allan MacLeod Cormack – American Physicist*, Encyclopedia Britannica, https://www.britannica.com/biography/Allan-MacLeod-Cormack, accessed 2/3/18.

Allan M. Cormack, NNBD, http://www.nndb.com/people/498/000131105/, accessed 2/3/18.

PAUL LAUTERBUR & PETER MANSFIELD

Belllis, May, *Magnetic Resonance Imaging MRI*, ThoughtCo (2017), https://www.thoughtco.com/magnetic-resonance-imaging-mri-1992133?print, accessed 1/13/18.

MRI's Inside Story, The Economist (2003), https://www.economist.com/node/2246166#print, accessed 1/13/18.

Wikipedia, *Paul Lauterbur* (2017), https://en.wikipedia.org/wiki/Paul_Lauterbur, accessed 11/24/17.

Wikipedia, *Peter Mansfield* (2017), https://en.wikipedia.org/wiki/Peter_Mansfield, accessed 1/24/17.

CHAPTER 35

Berman, Bruce, Editor, *Ideas to Assets-Investing Wisely in Intellectual Property*, John Wiley & Sons, Inc. (2002), pp. 541–558.

The America Invents Act, Public Law 112-29,125 Stat. 284, (2011), Section 7.

Bayh-Dole Patent and Trademark Act Amendments of 1980, Public Law 96-517, 94 Stat. 3015, 35 U.S.C. §§ 200–212, 37 C.F.R. § 401 (1980).

Agreement Between the World Intellectual Property Organization and the World Trade Organization (WTO) (1995) – Agreement on Trade-Related Aspects of Intellectual Property Rights (TRIPPS Agreement) (1994), WIPO Publication No. 223(E), www.wipo.int/edocs/pubdocs/en/wipo_pub_223.pdf, accessed 1/17/18.

AUTM, *Technology Transfer Infographic*, Association of University Technology Managers (2018), https://autm.net/AUTM/media/Survey_ReportsPDF/AUTM_2017_Infographic.pdf, accessed 1/17/18.

HARRY COOVER

Hickey, Daven, *Super Glue Was Invented by Accident, Twice*, Today I Found Out (2011), http://www.todayifoundout.com/index.php/2011/08/super-glue-was-invented-by-accident-twice/, accessed 3/10/18.

The Invention of Super Glue, Bartleby Writing (2018), https://www.bartleby.com/essay/The-Invention-of-Super-Glue-P3XZFJPFBZ6PS, accessed 3/10/18.

Harris, Elizabeth A., *Harry Coover, Super Glue's Inventor, Dies at 94*, The New York Times, March 27, 2011.

Kazan, Dick, *Today: How Harry Coover Invented Super Glue by Accident*, Kazan Today (2011), http://www.kazantoday.com/WeeklyArticles/harry-coover.html, accessed 3/10/18.

Una, *Was Super Glue Invented to Seal Battle Wounds in Vietnam?* The Straight Dope (2004), https://www.straightdope.com/columns/read/2187/was-super-glue-invented-to-seal-battle-wounds-in-vietnam/, accessed 3/10/18.

SPENCER SILVER

Spencer Silver, Soylent Communications (2014), http://www.nndb.com/people/758/000173239/, accessed 11/24/17.

History Timeline: Post-It® Notes, 3M (2017), https://www.post-it.com/3M/en_US/post-it/contact-us/about-us/, accessed 11/24/17.

Glass, Nick and Hume, Tim, *The 'Hallelujah Moment' Behind the Invention of the Post-It Notes*, CNN (2013), https://edition.cnn.com/2013/04/04/tech/post-it-note-history/index.html, accessed 1/15/18.

The Editions of Publications International, Ltd., *9 Things Invented or Discovered by Accident*, How Stuff Works, (2007), https://science.howstuffworks.com/innovation/scientific-experiments/9-things-invented-or-discovered-by-accident.htm, accessed 1/15/18.

Hickey, Daven, *Post-It Notes Were Invented by Accident*, Today I Found Out (2011), http://www.todayifoundout.com/index.php/2011/11/post-it-notes-were-invented-by-accident/, accessed 1/15/18.

Bellis, May, *Post-It Note – Arthur Fry, Invented the Post-It Note, But Spencer Silver Invented the Glue*, ThoughtCo. (2017), https://www.thoughtco.com/history-of-post-it-note-1992326, accessed 1/15/18.

CHAPTER 36

Reed, Stephen F. and Barron, Esther S., *Entrepreneurship Law, Cases and Materials.*, Wolters Kluver Law and Business (2013).

Johnson, Anthony, *3 Areas of Law Every Entrepreneur Should Know*, Entrepreneur Media, Inc. (2018), https://www.entrepreneur.com/article/253041, accessed 10/20/18.

Welcome to Entrepreneurship Law! EshipLaw (2018), http://www.eshiplaw.org/, accessed 10/20/18.

Tyra, Neil, *Where Law & Entreprneurship Meet*, The Law Entrepreneur (2015), http://thelawentrepreneur.com/ accessed 10/20/18.

CURRENT EVENTS

Josephson, Matthew, *Edison – A Biography*, History Book Club, New York (1959, 2003), pp. 343–350.

Jonnes, Jill, *Empires of Light*, Random House, New York (2003), pp. 141–229, 247–275.

Larson, Erik, *The Devil in the White City*, Crown Publishers, New York (2003), pp. 131, 247, 373.

Cheney, M., *Tesla – Man Out of Time*, Dorset Press, New York (1981), pp. 38–50, 70, 88.

Tesla, Nikola, *On Electricity*, Speech, The Ellicott Club, Buffalo, New York, January 12, 1897, Nikola Tesla, Lectures, Patents Articles, Nikola Tesla Museum, Belgrade (1956), pp. A-101–A-108.

Index

Intellectual Property Law for Engineers, Scientists, and Entrepreneurs, Second Edition. Howard B. Rockman.

Published 2020 by John Wiley & Sons, Inc.

Printed and bound by CPI Group (UK) Ltd, Croydon, CR0 4YY
17/09/2026
14964323-0001